Java Language Features

With Modules, Streams, Threads, I/O, and Lambda Expressions

Second Edition

Kishori Sharan

Apress®

Java Language Features: With Modules, Streams, Threads, I/O, and Lambda Expressions

Kishori Sharan
Montgomery, Alabama, USA

ISBN-13 (pbk): 978-1-4842-3347-4   ISBN-13 (electronic): 978-1-4842-3348-1
https://doi.org/10.1007/978-1-4842-3348-1

Library of Congress Control Number: 2018932349

Managing Director, Apress Media LLC: Welmoed Spahr
Acquisitions Editor: Steve Anglin
Development Editor: Matthew Moodie
Coordinating Editor: Mark Powers

Cover designed by eStudioCalamar

Cover image designed by Freepik (www.freepik.com)

Distributed to the book trade worldwide by Springer Science+Business Media New York, 233 Spring Street, 6th Floor, New York, NY 10013. Phone 1-800-SPRINGER, fax (201) 348-4505, e-mail orders-ny@springer-sbm.com, or visit www.springeronline.com. Apress Media, LLC is a California LLC and the sole member (owner) is Springer Science + Business Media Finance Inc (SSBM Finance Inc). SSBM Finance Inc is a **Delaware** corporation.

For information on translations, please e-mail rights@apress.com, or visit http://www.apress.com/rights-permissions.

Apress titles may be purchased in bulk for academic, corporate, or promotional use. eBook versions and licenses are also available for most titles. For more information, reference our Print and eBook Bulk Sales web page at http://www.apress.com/bulk-sales.

Any source code or other supplementary material referenced by the author in this book is available to readers on GitHub via the book's product page, located at www.apress.com/9781484233474. For more detailed information, please visit http://www.apress.com/source-code.

Printed on acid-free paper

Contents

About the Author xix

About the Technical Reviewers xxi

Acknowledgments xxiii

Introduction xxv

Chapter 1: Annotations 1

What Are Annotations? 1

Declaring an Annotation Type 4

Restrictions on Annotation Types 7

Restriction #1 7

Restriction #2 8

Restriction #3 8

Restriction #4 9

Restriction #5 9

Restriction #6 9

Default Value of an Annotation Element 9

Annotation Type and Its Instances 10

Using Annotations 11

Primitive Types 12

String Types 12

Class Types 13

Enum Type 14

Annotation Type 16

Array Type Annotation Element 16

No Null Value in an Annotation 17
Shorthand Annotation Syntax 17
Marker Annotation Types 19
Meta-Annotation Types 19
The Target Annotation Type 20
The Retention Annotation Type 23
The Inherited Annotation Type 24
The Documented Annotation Type 24
The Repeatable Annotation Type 25
Commonly Used Standard Annotations 26
Deprecating APIs 27
Suppressing Named Compile-Time Warnings 38
Overriding Methods 39
Declaring Functional Interfaces 40
Annotating Packages 41
Annotating Modules 41
Accessing Annotations at Runtime 42
Evolving Annotation Types 47
Annotation Processing at Source Code Level 47
Summary 53
Chapter 2: Inner Classes 57
What Is an Inner Class? 57
Advantages of Using Inner Classes 59
Types of Inner Classes 59
Member Inner Class 59
Local Inner Class 61
Anonymous Inner Class 65
A static Member Class Is Not an Inner Class 68
Creating Objects of Inner Classes 70

Accessing Enclosing Class Members 73
Restrictions on Accessing Local Variables 80
Inner Class and Inheritance 81
No static Members in an Inner Class 83
Generated Class Files for Inner Classes 84
Inner Classes and the Compiler Magic 85
Closures and Callbacks 89
Defining Inner Classes in static Contexts 91
Summary 91
Chapter 3: Reflection 97
What Is Reflection? 97
Reflection in Java 98
Loading a Class 99
Using Class Literals 99
Using the Object::getClass() Method 100
Using the Class::forName() Method 100
Class Loaders 103
Class Loaders in JDK8 103
Class Loaders in JDK9 104
Reflecting on Classes 107
Reflecting on Fields 112
Reflecting on Executables 114
Reflecting on Methods 116
Reflecting on Constructors 118
Creating Objects 120
Invoking Methods 121
Accessing Fields 122

Deep Reflection ... 124
Deep Reflection Within a Module ... 125
Deep Reflection Across Modules ... 129
Deep Reflection and Unnamed Modules ... 134
Deep Reflection on JDK Modules ... 134
Reflecting on Arrays ... 136
Expanding an Array ... 138
Who Should Use Reflection? ... 140
Summary ... 140
Chapter 4: Generics ... 143
What Are Generics? ... 143
Supertype-Subtype Relationship ... 147
Raw Types ... 148
Unbounded Wildcards ... 149
Upper-Bounded Wildcards ... 152
Lower-Bounded Wildcards ... 153
Generic Methods and Constructors ... 155
Type Inference in Generic Object Creation ... 157
No Generic Exception Classes ... 160
No Generic Anonymous Classes ... 160
Generics and Arrays ... 160
Runtime Class Type of Generic Objects ... 161
Heap Pollution ... 162
Varargs Methods and Heap Pollution Warnings ... 163
Summary ... 165
Chapter 5: Lambda Expressions ... 169
What Is a Lambda Expression? ... 169
Why Do We Need Lambda Expressions? ... 171

Syntax for Lambda Expressions 173
Omitting Parameter Types 174
Declaring a Single Parameter 175
Declaring No Parameters 175
Parameters with Modifiers 175
Declaring Body of Lambda Expressions 176
Target Typing 176
Functional Interfaces 184
Using the @FunctionalInterface Annotation 184
Generic Functional Interface 185
Intersection Type and Lambda Expressions 187
Commonly Used Functional Interfaces 188
Using the Function<T,R> Interface 188
Using the Predicate<T> Interface 190
Using Functional Interfaces 191
Method References 196
static Method References 197
Instance Method References 200
Supertype Instance Method References 203
Constructor References 205
Generic Method References 208
Lexical Scoping 209
Variable Capture 211
Jumps and Exits 214
Recursive Lambda Expressions 215
Comparing Objects 216
Summary 218
Chapter 6: Threads 223
What Is a Thread? 223
Creating Threads in Java 226

Specifying Your Code for a Thread 228
Inheriting Your Class from the Thread Class 229
Implementing the Runnable Interface 229
Using a Method Reference 230
A Quick Example 230
Using Multiple Threads in a Program 231
Issues in Using Multiple Threads 232
Java Memory Model 235
Atomicity 236
Visibility 236
Ordering 236
Object's Monitor and Threads Synchronization 237
Rule #1 244
Rule #2 245
The Producer/Consumer Synchronization Problem 250
Which Thread Is Executing? 254
Letting a Thread Sleep 255
I Will Join You in Heaven 256
Be Considerate to Others and Yield 259
Lifecycle of a Thread 259
Priority of a Thread 263
Is It a Demon or a Daemon? 264
Am I Interrupted? 266
Threads Work in a Group 270
Volatile Variables 271
Stopping, Suspending, and Resuming Threads 273
Spin-Wait Hints 277
Handling an Uncaught Exception in a Thread 278
Thread Concurrency Packages 280

Atomic Variables 280
Scalar Atomic Variable Classes 281
Atomic Arrays Classes 281
Atomic Field Updater Classes 282
Atomic Compound Variable Classes 282
Explicit Locks 283
Synchronizers 288
Semaphores 289
Barriers 292
Phasers 295
Latches 304
Exchangers 306
The Executor Framework 310
Result-Bearing Tasks 315
Scheduling a Task 318
Handling Uncaught Exceptions in a Task Execution 321
Executor's Completion Service 322
The Fork/Join Framework 325
Steps in Using the Fork/Join Framework 326
A Fork/Join Example 328
Thread-Local Variables 330
Setting Stack Size of a Thread 333
Summary 334
Chapter 7: Input/Output 337
What Is Input/Output? 337
Working with Files 338
Creating a File Object 338
Knowing the Current Working Directory 339
Checking for a File's Existence 340
Which Path Do You Want to Go? 340

Creating, Deleting, and Renaming Files 342
Working with File Attributes 346
Copying a File 346
Knowing the Size of a File 346
Listing Directories and Files 347
The Decorator Pattern 350
Input/Output Streams 358
Reading from a File Using an Input Stream 359
Writing Data to a File Using an Output Stream 363
Input Stream Meets the Decorator Pattern 366
BufferedInputStream 369
PushbackInputStream 370
Output Stream Meets the Decorator Pattern 371
PrintStream 373
Using Pipes 375
Reading and Writing Primitive Data Types 378
Object Serialization 380
Serializing Objects 381
Deserializing Objects 383
Externalizable Object Serialization 385
Serializing transient Fields 389
Advanced Object Serialization 389
Writing an Object Multiple Times to a Stream 389
Class Evolution and Object Serialization 393
Stopping Serialization 394
Readers and Writers 395
Custom Input/Output Streams 399
Random Access Files 402
Copying the Contents of a File 404
Standard Input/Output/Error Streams 405

Console and Scanner Classes 410
StringTokenizer and StreamTokenizer 412
Summary 415
Chapter 8: Working with Archive Files 419
What Is an Archive File? 419
Data Compression 419
Checksum 420
Compressing Byte Arrays 422
Working with ZIP File Format 427
Creating ZIP Files 427
Reading the Contents of ZIP Files 431
Working with the GZIP File Format 434
Working with the JAR File Format 435
Creating a JAR File 437
Updating a JAR File 438
Indexing a JAR File 438
Extracting an Entry from a JAR File 439
Listing the Contents of a JAR File 439
The Manifest File 439
Sealing a Package in a JAR File 441
Using the JAR API 442
Accessing Resources from a JAR File 446
Summary 447
Chapter 9: New Input/Output 449
What Is NIO? 449
Buffers 450
Reading from and Writing to a Buffer 453
Read-Only Buffers 460
Different Views of a Buffer 461

Character Set ... 462
Channels ... 471
Reading/Writing Files ... 473
Memory-Mapped File I/O ... 477
File Locking ... 478
Copying the Contents of a File ... 480
Knowing the Byte Order of a Machine ... 481
Byte Buffer and Its Byte Order ... 482
Summary ... 483
Chapter 10: New Input/Output 2 ... 487
What Is New Input/Output 2? ... 487
Working with a File System ... 488
Working with Paths ... 490
Creating a Path Object ... 491
Accessing Components of a Path ... 491
Comparing Paths ... 493
Normalizing, Resolving, and Relativizing Paths ... 495
Symbolic Links ... 497
Different Forms of a Path ... 497
Performing File Operations on a Path ... 499
Creating New Files ... 499
Deleting Files ... 500
Checking for Existence of a File ... 501
Copying and Moving Files ... 501
Commonly Used File Attributes ... 503
Probing the Content Type of a File ... 504
Reading the Contents of a File ... 504
Writing to a File ... 507
Random Access to a File ... 508

Traversing a File Tree 511
Matching Paths 516
Managing File Attributes 517
Checking for a File Attribute View Support 518
Reading and Updating File Attributes 520
Managing the Owner of a File 524
Managing ACL File Permissions 526
Managing POSIX File Permissions 529
Watching a Directory for Modifications 532
Creating a Watch Service 533
Registering the Directory with the Watch Service 533
Retrieving a WatchKey from the Watch Service Queue 533
Processing the Events 534
Resetting the WatchKey after Processing Events 534
Closing the Watch Service 534
Asynchronous File I/O 536
Summary 546
Chapter 11: Garbage Collection 549
What Is Garbage Collection? 549
Memory Allocation in Java 551
Garbage Collection in Java 552
Invoking the Garbage Collector 553
Object Finalization 555
Finally or Finalize? 557
Object Resurrection 559
State of an Object 561
Weak References 562
Accessing and Clearing a Referent's Reference 566

Using the SoftReference Class 569
Using the ReferenceQueue Class 573
Using the WeakReference Class 574
Using the PhantomReference Class 578
Using the Cleaner Class 581
Summary 585
Chapter 12: Collections 587
What Is a Collection? 587
Need for a Collection Framework 589
Architecture of the Collection Framework 590
The Collection<E> Interface 591
Methods for Basic Operations 591
Methods for Bulk Operations 592
Methods for Aggregate Operations 592
Methods for Array Operations 593
Methods for Comparison Operations 593
A Quick Example 593
Traversing Elements in Collections 594
Using an Iterator 595
Using a for-each Loop 598
Using the forEach() Method 599
Using Different Types of Collections 600
Working with Sets 600
Working with Lists 613
Working with Queues 618
Working with Maps 641
Applying Algorithms to Collections 655
Sorting a List 655
Searching a List 656
Shuffling, Reversing, Swapping, and Rotating a List 657

Creating Different Views of a Collection 659
Read-Only Views of Collections 659
Synchronized View of a Collection 660
Checked Collections 661
Creating Empty Collections 662
Creating Singleton Collections 662
Understanding Hash-Based Collections 663
Summary 668
Chapter 13: Streams 675
What Are Streams? 675
Streams Have No Storage 676
Infinite Streams 676
Internal Iteration vs. External Iteration 676
Imperative vs. Functional 678
Stream Operations 678
Ordered Streams 680
Streams Are Not Reusable 680
Architecture of the Streams API 680
A Quick Example 682
Creating Streams 686
Streams from Values 686
Empty Streams 689
Streams from Functions 689
Streams from Arrays 694
Streams from Collections 695
Streams from Files 695
Streams from Other Sources 697
Representing an Optional Value 698
Applying Operations to Streams 703
Debugging a Stream Pipeline 704
Applying the ForEach Operation 705

Applying the Map Operation 706
Flattening Streams 708
Applying the Filter Operation 710
Applying the Reduce Operation 713
Collecting Data Using Collectors 721
Collecting Summary Statistics 725
Collecting Data in Maps 727
Joining Strings Using Collectors 729
Grouping Data 730
Partitioning Data 734
Adapting the Collector Results 735
Finding and Matching in Streams 739
Parallel Streams 740
Summary 742
Chapter 14: Implementing Services 747
What Is a Service? 747
Discovering Services 749
Providing Service Implementations 750
Defining the Service Interface 752
Obtaining Service Provider Instances 752
Defining the Service 756
Defining Service Providers 758
Defining a Default Prime Service Provider 758
Defining a Faster Prime Service Provider 760
Defining a Probable Prime Service Provider 761
Testing the Prime Service 763
Testing Prime Service in Legacy Mode 767
Summary 769

Chapter 15: The Module API 771

What Is the Module API? 771

Representing Modules 773

Describing Modules 773

Representing Module Statements 774

Representing a Module Version 776

Other Properties of Modules 777

Knowing Module Basic Info 778

Querying Modules 781

Updating Modules 783

Accessing Module Resources 786

Accessing Resources Before JDK9 786

Accessing Resources in JDK9 790

Annotation on Modules 803

Working with Module Layers 805

Finding Modules 807

Reading Module Contents 809

Creating Configurations 811

Creating Module Layers 813

Summary 821

Chapter 16: Breaking Module Encapsulation 825

What Is Breaking Module Encapsulation? 825

Command-Line Options 826

The --add-exports Option 826

The --add-opens Option 827

The --add-reads Option 827

The --illegal-access Option 828

An Example 829

Using Manifest Attributes of a JAR 837

Summary 841

Chapter 17: Reactive Streams 843
What Is a Stream? 843
What Are Reactive Streams? 844
The Reactive Streams API in JDK9 846
Publisher-Subscriber Interactions 846
Creating Publishers 847
Publishing Items 848
A Quick Example 849
Creating Subscribers 851
Using Processors 856
Summary 859
Chapter 18: Stack Walking 861
What Is a Stack? 861
What Is Stack Walking? 862
Stack Walking in JDK8 862
Drawbacks in Stack Walking 865
Stack Walking in JDK9 866
Specifying Stack-Walking Options 866
Representing a Stack Frame 866
Obtaining a StackWalker Class 868
Walking the Stack 869
Knowing the Caller's Class 874
Stack-Walking Permissions 877
Summary 878
Index 881

About the Author

Kishori Sharan works as a senior software engineer lead at IndraSoft, Inc. He earned a master's of science degree in computer information systems from Troy State University, Alabama. He is a Sun-certified Java 2 programmer and has over 20 years of experience in developing enterprise applications and providing training to professional developers using the Java platform.

About the Technical Reviewers

Manuel Jordan Elera is an autodidact developer and researcher who enjoys learning new technologies for his own experiments and creating new integrations.

Manuel won the 2010 Springy Award - Community Champion and Spring Champion 2013. In his little free time, he reads the Bible and composes music on his guitar. Manuel is known as dr_pompeii. He has tech reviewed numerous books for Apress, including *Pro Spring Messaging* (2017), *Pro Spring, 4th Edition* (2014), *Practical Spring LDAP* (2013), *Pro JPA 2, Second Edition* (2013), and *Pro Spring Security* (2013).

Read his 13 detailed tutorials about many Spring technologies, contact him through his blog at `http://www.manueljordanelera.blogspot.com`, and follow him on his Twitter account at `@dr_pompeii`.

Jeff Friesen is a freelance teacher and software developer with an emphasis on Java. In addition to authoring *Java I/O, NIO, and NIO.2* (Apress) and *Java Threads and the Concurrency Utilities* (Apress), Jeff has written numerous articles on Java and other technologies (such as Android) for JavaWorld (`JavaWorld.com`), informIT (`InformIT.com`), Java.net, SitePoint (`SitePoint.com`), and other websites. Jeff can be contacted via his website at `JavaJeff.ca` or via his LinkedIn profile (`www.linkedin.com/in/javajeff`).

Acknowledgments

I would like to thank my family members and friends for their encouragement and support: my mom Pratima Devi, my elder brothers, Janki Sharan and Dr. Sita Sharan, my nephews, Gaurav and Saurav; my sister Ratna; my friends Karthikeya Venkatesan, Rahul Nagpal, Ravi Datla, Mahbub Choudhury, Richard Castillo, and many more friends not mentioned here.

My wife, Ellen, was always patient when I spent long hours at my computer working on this book. I want to thank her for all of her support in writing this book.

Special thanks to my friend Preethi Vasudev, for offering her valuable time and providing solutions to the exercises in this book. She likes programming challenges, particularly with Google Code Jam. I bet she enjoyed solving the exercises in this book.

My sincere thanks are due to the wonderful team at Apress for their support during the publication of this book. Thanks to Mark Powers, the Editorial Operations Manager, for providing excellent support. Thanks to the technical reviewers Manuel Jordan Elera and Jeff Friesen, for their technical insights and feedback during the review process. They were instrumental in weeding out several technical errors. Last but not least, my sincere thanks to Steve Anglin, the Lead Editor at Apress, for taking the initiative to publish this book.

Introduction

How This Book Came About

My first encounter with the Java programming language was during a one-week Java training session in 1997. I did not get a chance to use Java in a project until 1999. I read two Java books and took a Java 2 programmer certification examination. I did very well on the test, scoring 95 percent. The three questions that I missed on the test made me realize that the books that I had read did not adequately cover details of all the topics. I made up my mind to write a book on the Java programming language. So, I formulated a plan to cover most of the topics that a Java developer needs to use Java effectively in a project, as well as to become certified. I initially planned to cover all essential topics in Java in 700 to 800 pages.

As I progressed, I realized that a book covering most of the Java topics in detail could not be written in 700 to 800 pages. One chapter alone that covered data types, operators, and statements spanned 90 pages. I was then faced with the question, "Should I shorten the content of the book or include all the details that I think a Java developer needs?" I opted for including all the details in the book, rather than shortening its content to maintain the original number of pages. It has never been my intent to make lots of money from this book. I was never in a hurry to finish this book because that rush could have compromised the quality and coverage. In short, I wrote this book to help the Java community understand and use the Java programming language effectively, without having to read many books on the same subject. I wrote this book with the plan that it would be a comprehensive one-stop reference for everyone who wants to learn and grasp the intricacies of the Java programming language.

One of my high school teachers used to tell us that if one wanted to understand a building, one must first understand the bricks, steel, and mortar that make up the building. The same logic applies to most of the things that we want to understand in our lives. It certainly applies to an understanding of the Java programming language. If you want to master the Java programming language, you must start by understanding its basic building blocks. I have used this approach throughout this book, endeavoring to build upon each topic by describing the basics first. In the book, you will rarely find a topic described without first learning about its background. Wherever possible, I tried to correlate the programming practices with activities in daily life. Most of the books about the Java programming language available in the market either do not include any pictures at all or have only a few. I believe in the adage, "A picture is worth a thousand words." To a reader, a picture makes a topic easier to understand and remember. I have included plenty of illustrations in the book to aid readers in understanding and visualizing the concepts. Developers who have little or no programming experience have difficulty in putting things together to make it a complete program. Keeping them in mind, the book contains over 390 complete Java programs that are ready to be compiled and run.

I spent countless hours doing research when writing this book. My main sources were the Java Language Specification, whitepapers, and articles on Java topics, and Java Specification Requests (JSRs). I also spent quite a bit of time reading the Java source code to learn more about some of the Java topics. Sometimes, it took a few months of researching a topic before I could write the first sentence on it. Finally, it was always fun to play with Java programs, sometimes for hours, to add them to the book.

Introduction to the Second Edition

I am pleased to present the second edition of the *Java Language Features* book. It is the second book in the three-volume *Beginning Java 9* series. It was not possible to include all JDK9 changes in the one volume. I have included JDK9-specific changes at appropriate places in the three volumes, including this one. If you are interested in learning only JDK9-specific topics, I suggest you read my *Java 9 Revealed* book (ISBN 978-1484225912), which contains only JDK9-specific topics. There are several changes in this edition, as follows:

- I added the following five chapters to this edition: Implementing Services (Chapter 14), The Module API (Chapter 15), Breaking Module Encapsulation (Chapter 16), Reactive Streams (Chapter 17), and Stack Walking (Chapter 18).
- Implementing services in Java is not new to JDK9. I felt this book was missing a chapter on this topic. Chapter 14 covers in detail how to define services and service interfaces, and how to implement service interfaces using JDK9-specific and pre-JDK9 constructs. This chapter shows you how to use the `uses` and `provides` statements in a module declaration.
- Chapter 15 covers the Module API in detail, which gives you programmatic access to modules. This chapter also touches on some of the advanced topics, such as module layers. The first volume of this series covered basics on modules, such as how to declare modules and module dependence.
- Chapter 16 covers how to break module encapsulation using command-line options. When you migrate to JDK9, there will be cases requiring you to read the module's internal APIs or export non-exported packages. You can achieve these tasks using command-line options covered in this chapter.
- Reactive Streams is an initiative for providing a standard for asynchronous stream processing with non-blocking backpressure. It is aimed at solving the problems processing a stream of items, including how to pass a stream of items from a publisher to a subscriber without requiring the publisher to block or the subscriber to have an unbounded buffer. Chapter 17 covers the Reactive Streams API, which was added in JDK9.
- Chapter 18 covers the Stacking-Walking API, which was added in JDK9. This API lets you inspect the stack frames of threads and get the class reference of the caller class of a method. Inspecting a thread's stack and getting the caller's class name were possible before JDK9, which I covered in Chapter 13 of the first volume. The new Stack-Walking API lets you achieve this easily and efficiently.
- I received several e-mails from the readers about the fact that the books in this series do not include questions and exercises, which are needed mainly for students and beginners. Students use this series in their Java classes and many beginners use it to learn Java. Due to this popular demand, I spent over 60 hours preparing questions and exercises at the end of each chapter. My friend Preethi offered her help and provided the solutions.

Apart from these additions, I updated all the chapters that were part of the first edition. I edited the contents to make them flow better, changed or added new examples, and updated the contents to include JDK9-specific features.

It is my sincere hope that this edition will help you learn Java better.

Structure of the Book

This is the second book in the three-book *Beginning Java* series. This book contains 18 chapters. The chapters contain language-level topics of Java such as annotations, generics, lambda expressions, threads, I/O, collections, streams, etc. Chapters introduce Java topics in increasing order of complexity. The new features of Java 9 are included wherever they fit in these chapters. The Module API, Reactive Streams, and Stack-Walking API, which were added in Java 9, are covered in depth in their own chapters.

After finishing this book, you can take your Java knowledge to the next level by learning the Java APIs and modules, which are covered in the final book in the series, *Java APIs, Extensions and Libraries*.

Audience

This book is designed to be useful to anyone who wants to learn the Java programming language. If you are a beginner, with little or no programming background in Java, you are advised to read the companion book, *Beginning Java 9 Fundamentals,* before reading this book. This book contains topics of various degrees of complexity. As a beginner, if you find yourself overwhelmed while reading a section in a chapter, you can skip to the next section or the next chapter, and revisit it later when you gain more experience.

If you are a Java developer with an intermediate or advanced level of experience, you can jump to a chapter or to a section in a chapter directly. If a section covers an unfamiliar topic, you need to visit that topic before continuing the current one.

If you are reading this book to get a certification in the Java programming language, you need to read almost all of the chapters, paying attention to all of the detailed descriptions and rules. Most of the certification programs test your fundamental knowledge of the language, not the advanced knowledge. You need to read only those topics that are part of your certification test. Compiling and running over 390 complete Java programs will help you prepare for your certification.

If you are a student who is attending a class in the Java programming language, you should read the chapters of this book selectively. Some topics—such as lambda expressions, collections, and streams—are used extensively in developing Java applications, whereas other topics—such as threads and archive files—are infrequently used. You need to read only those chapters that are covered in your class syllabus. I am sure that you, as a Java student, do not need to read the entire book page by page.

How to Use This Book

This book is the beginning, not the end, of learning the Java programming language. If you are reading this book, it means you are heading in the right direction to learn the Java programming language, which will enable you to excel in your academic and professional career. However, there is always a higher goal for you to achieve and you must constantly work hard to achieve it. The following quotations from some great thinkers may help you understand the importance of working hard and constantly looking for knowledge with both your eyes and mind open.

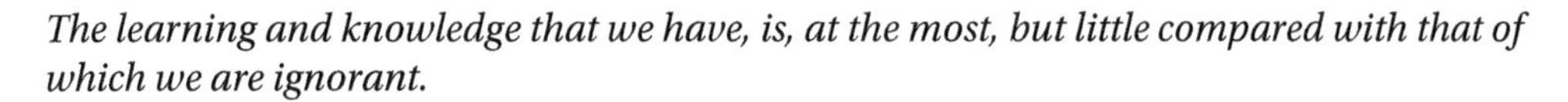

> *The learning and knowledge that we have, is, at the most, but little compared with that of which we are ignorant.*
>
> —Plato

> *True knowledge exists in knowing that you know nothing. And in knowing that you know nothing, that makes you the smartest of all.*
>
> —Socrates

Readers are advised to use the API documentation for the Java programming language as much as possible while reading this book. The Java API documentation includes a complete list of everything available in the Java class library. You can download (or view) the Java API documentation from the official website of Oracle Corporation at `www.oracle.com`. While you read this book, you need to practice writing Java programs. You can also practice by tweaking the programs provided in the book. It does not help much in your learning process if you just read this book and do not practice writing your own programs. Remember that "practice makes perfect," which is also true in learning how to program in Java.

Source Code and Errata

Source code for this book can be accessed by clicking the Download Source Code button located at `www.apress.com/9781484233474`.

Note At the time of going to print, Java 10 had just been announced. To provide you with useful information on some of its features and the new Java versioning scheme, I have written three appendices that you can download for free via the **Download Source Code** button referenced above. These appendices will give you a head-start on the most important features of Java 10.

Questions and Comments

Please direct all your questions and comments for the author to `ksharan@jdojo.com`.

CHAPTER 1

Annotations

In this chapter, you will learn:

- What annotations are
- How to declare annotations
- How to use annotations
- What meta-annotations are and how to use them
- Commonly used annotations that are used to deprecate APIs, to suppress named compile-time warnings, override methods, and declare functional interfaces
- How to access annotations at runtime
- How to process annotations in source code

All example programs in this chapter are a member of a `jdojo.annotation` module, as declared in Listing 1-1.

Listing 1-1. The Declaration of a jdojo.annotation Module

```
// module-info.java
module jdojo.annotation {
    exports com.jdojo.annotation;
}
```

What Are Annotations?

Before I define annotations and discuss their importance in programming, let's look at a simple example. Suppose you have an `Employee` class, which has a method called `setSalary()` that sets the salary of an employee. The method accepts a parameter of the type `double`. The following snippet of code shows a trivial implementation for the `Employee` class:

```
public class Employee {
    public void setSalary(double salary) {
        System.out.println("Employee.setSalary():" + salary);
    }
}
```

Electronic supplementary material The online version of this chapter (https://doi.org/10.1007/978-1-4842-3348-1_1) contains supplementary material, which is available to authorized users.

K. Sharan, *Java Language Features*, https://doi.org/10.1007/978-1-4842-3348-1_1

A Manager class inherits from the Employee class. You want to set the salary for managers differently. You decide to override the setSalary() method in the Manager class. The code for the Manager class is as follows:

```
public class Manager extends Employee {
    // Override setSalary() in the Employee class
    public void setSalary(int salary) {
        System.out.println("Manager.setSalary():" + salary);
    }
}
```

There is a mistake in the Manager class, when you attempt to override the setSalary() method. You'll correct the mistake shortly. You have used the int data type as the parameter type for the incorrectly overridden method. It is time to set the salary for a manager. The following code is used to accomplish this:

```
Employee ken = new Manager();
int salary = 200;
ken.setSalary(salary);
```

```
Employee.setSalary():200.0
```

This snippet of code was expected to call the setSalary() method of the Manager class but the output does not show the expected result.

What went wrong in your code? The intention of defining the setSalary() method in the Manager class was to override the setSalary() method of the Employee class, not to overload it. You made a mistake. You used the type int as the parameter type in the setSalary() method, instead of the type double in the Manager class. You put comments indicating your intention to override the method in the Manager class. However, comments do not stop you from making logical mistakes. You might spend, as every programmer does, hours and hours debugging errors resulting from this kind of logical mistake. Who can help you in such situations? Annotations might help you in a few situations like this.

Let's rewrite your Manager class using an annotation. You do not need to know anything about annotations at this point. All you are going to do is add one word to your program. The following code is the modified version of the Manager class:

```
public class Manager extends Employee {
    @Override
    public void setSalary(int salary) {
        System.out.println("Manager.setSalary():" + salary);
    }
}
```

All you have added is a @Override annotation to the Manager class and removed the "dumb" comments. Trying to compile the revised Manager class results in a compile-time error that points to the use of the @Override annotation for the setSalary() method of the Manager class:

```
Manager.java:2: error: method does not override or implement a method from a supertype
        @Override
        ^
1 error
```

The use of the @Override annotation did the trick. The @Override annotation is used with a non-static method to indicate the programmer's intention to override the method in the superclass. At source code level, it serves the purpose of documentation. When the compiler comes across the @Override annotation, it makes sure that the method really overrides the method in the superclass. If the method annotated does not override a method in the superclass, the compiler generates an error. In your case, the setSalary(int salary) method in the Manager class does not override any method in the superclass Employee. This is the reason that you got the error. You may realize that using an annotation is as simple as documenting the source code. However, they have compiler support. You can use them to instruct the compiler to enforce some rules. Annotations provide benefits much more than you have seen in this example. Let's go back to the compile-time error. You can fix the error by doing one of the following two things:

- You can remove the @Override annotation from the setSalary(int salary) method in the Manager class. It will make the method an overloaded method, not a method that overrides its superclass method.
- You can change the method signature from setSalary(int salary) to setSalary(double salary).

Since you want to override the setSalary() method in the Manager class, use the second option and modify the Manager class as follows:

```
public class Manager extends Employee {
    @Override
    public void setSalary(double salary) {
        System.out.println("Manager.setSalary():" + salary);
    }
}
```

Now the following code will work as expected:

```
Employee ken = new Manager();
int salary = 200;
ken.setSalary(salary);
```

```
Manager.setSalary():200.0
```

Note that the @Override annotation in the setSalary() method of the Manager class saves you debugging time. Suppose you change the method signature in the Employee class. If the changes in the Employee class make this method no longer overridden in the Manager class, you will get the same error when you compile the Manager class again. Are you starting to understand the power of annotations? With this background in mind, let's start digging deep into annotations.

According to the Merriam Webster dictionary, the meaning of annotation is

"A note added by way of comment or explanation".

This is exactly what an annotation is in Java. It lets you associate (or annotate) metadata (or notes) to the program elements in a Java program. The program elements may be a module, a package, a class, an interface, a field of a class, a local variable, a method, a parameter of a method, an enum, an annotation, a type parameter in a generic type/method declaration, a type use, etc. In other words, you can annotate any declaration or type use in a Java program. An annotation is used as a "modifier" in a declaration of a program element like any other modifiers (public, private, final, static, etc.). Unlike a modifier, an annotation does not modify the meaning of the program elements. It acts like a decoration or a note for the program element that it annotates.

An annotation differs from regular documentation in many ways. A regular documentation is only for humans to read and it is "dumb." It has no intelligence associated with it. If you misspell a word, or state something in the documentation and do just the opposite in the code, you are on your own. It is very difficult and impractical to read the elements of documentation programmatically at runtime. Java lets you generate Javadocs from your documentation and that's it for regular documentation. This does not mean that you do not need to document your programs. You do need regular documentation. At the same time, you need a way to enforce your intent using a documentation-like mechanism. Your documentation should be available to the compiler and the runtime. An annotation serves this purpose. It is human readable, which serves as documentation. It is compiler readable, which lets the compiler verify the intention of the programmer; for example, the compiler makes sure that the programmer has really overridden the method if it comes across an @Override annotation for a method. Annotations are also available at runtime so that a program can read and use it for any purpose it wants. For example, a tool can read annotations and generate boilerplate code. If you have worked with Enterprise JavaBeans (EJB), you know the pain of keeping all the interfaces and classes in sync and adding entries to XML configuration files. EJB 3.0 uses annotations to generate the boilerplate code, which makes EJB development painless for programmers. Another example of an annotation being used in a framework/tool is JUnit version 4.0. JUnit is a unit test framework for Java programs. It uses annotations to mark methods that are test cases. Before that, you had to follow a naming convention for the test case methods. Annotations have a variety of uses, which are documentation, verification, and enforcement by the compiler, the runtime validation, code generation by frameworks/tools, etc.

To make an annotation available to the compiler and the runtime, an annotation has to follow rules. In fact, an annotation is another type like a class and an interface. As you have to declare a class type or an interface type before you can use it, you must also declare an annotation type.

An annotation does not change the semantics (or meaning) of the program element that it annotates. In that sense, an annotation is like a comment, which does not affect the way the annotated program element works. For example, the @Override annotation for the setSalary() method did not change the way the method works. You (or a tool/framework) can change the behavior of a program based on an annotation. In such cases, you use the annotation rather than the annotation doing anything on its own. The point is that an annotation by itself is always passive.

Declaring an Annotation Type

Declaring an annotation type is similar to declaring an interface type, except for some restrictions. According to Java specification, an annotation type declaration is a special kind of interface type declaration. You use the interface keyword, which is preceded by the @ sign (at sign) to declare an annotation type. The following is the general syntax for declaring an annotation type:

```
[modifiers] @ interface <annotation-type-name> {
    // Annotation type body goes here
}
```

[modifiers] for an annotation declaration is the same as for an interface declaration. For example, you can declare an annotation type at the public or package level. The @ sign and the interface keyword may be separated by whitespace or they can be placed together. By convention, they are placed together as @interface. The interface keyword is followed by an annotation type name. It should be a valid Java identifier. The annotation type body is placed within braces.

Suppose you want to annotate your program elements with the version information, so you can prepare a report about new program elements added in a specific release of your product. To use a custom annotation type (as opposed to a built-in annotation, such as @Override), you must declare it first. You want to include the major and the minor versions of the release in the version information. Listing 1-2 contains the complete code for your first annotation declaration.

Listing 1-2. The Declaration of an Annotation Type Named Version

```
// Version.java
package com.jdojo.annotation;

public @interface Version {
    int major();
    int minor();
}
```

Compare the declaration of the `Version` annotation with the declaration of an interface. It differs from an interface definition only in one aspect: it uses the @ sign before its name. You have declared two abstract methods in the `Version` annotation type: `major()` and `minor()`. Abstract methods in an annotation type are known as its *elements*. You can think about it in another way: an annotation can declare zero or more elements, and they are declared as abstract methods. The abstract method names are the names of the elements of the annotation type. You have declared two elements, `major` and `minor`, for the `Version` annotation type. The data types of both elements are `int`.

■ **Tip** Although you can declare static and default methods in interface types, they are not allowed in annotation types. static and default methods are meant to contain some logic. Annotations are meant to represent just the values for elements in the annotation type. This is the reason that static and default methods are not allowed in annotation types.

You need to compile the annotation type. When `Version.java` file is compiled, it will produce a `Version.class` file. The simple name of your annotation type is `Version` and its fully qualified name is `com.jdojo.annotation.Version`. Using the simple name of an annotation type follows the rules of any other types (e.g., classes, interfaces, etc.). You will need to import an annotation type the same way you import any other types.

How do you use an annotation type? You might be thinking that you will declare a new class that will implement the `Version` annotation type, and you will create an object of that class. You might be relieved to know that you do not need to take any additional steps to use the `Version` annotation type. An annotation type is ready to be used as soon as it is declared and compiled. To create an instance of an annotation type and use it to annotate a program element, you need to use the following syntax:

```
@annotationType(name1=value1, name2=value2, name3=value3...)
```

The annotation type is preceded by an @ sign. It is followed by a list of comma-separated `name=value` pairs enclosed in parentheses. The name in a `name=value` pair is the name of the element declared in the annotation type and the value is the user-supplied value for that element. The `name=value` pairs do not have to appear in the same order as they are declared in the annotation type, although by convention `name=value` pairs are used in the same order as the declaration of the elements in the annotation type.

Let's use an instance of the `Version` type, which has the `major` element value as `1` and the `minor` element value as `0`. The following is an instance of your `Version` annotation type:

```
@Version(major=1, minor=0)
```

You can rewrite this annotation as `@Version(minor=0, major=1)` without changing its meaning. You can also use the annotation type's fully qualified name as

```
@com.jdojo.annotation.Version(major=0, minor=1)
```

You use as many instances of the Version annotation type in your program as you want. For example, you have a VersionTest class, which has been in your application since release 1.0. You have added some methods and instance variables in release 1.1. You can use your Version annotation to document additions to the VersionTest class in different releases. You can annotate your class declaration as

```
@Version(major=1, minor=0)
public class VersionTest {
    // Code goes here
}
```

An annotation is added in the same way you add a modifier for a program element. You can mix the annotation for a program element with its other modifiers. You can place annotations in the same line as other modifiers or in a separate line. It is a personal choice whether you use a separate line to place the annotations or you mix them with other modifiers. By convention, annotations for a program element are placed before all other modifiers. Let's follow this convention and place the annotation in a separate line by itself, as shown. Both of the following declarations are technically the same:

```
// Style #1
@Version(major=1, minor=0) public class VersionTest {
    // Code goes here
}

// Style #2
public @Version(major=1, minor=0) class VersionTest {
    // Code goes here
}
```

Listing 1-3 shows the sample code for the VersionTest class.

Listing 1-3. A VersionTest Class with Annotated Elements

```
// VersionTest.java
package com.jdojo.annotation;

// Annotation for class VersionTest
@Version(major=1, minor=0)
public class VersionTest {
    // Annotation for instance variable xyz
    @Version(major=1, minor=1)
    private int xyz = 110;

    // Annotation for constructor VersionTest()
    @Version(major=1, minor=0)
    public VersionTest() {
    }

    // Annotation for constructor VersionTest(int xyz)
    @Version(major=1, minor=1)
    public VersionTest(int xyz) {
        this.xyz = xyz;
    }
```

```
    // Annotation for the printData() method
    @Version(major=1, minor=0)
    public void printData() {
    }

    // Annotation for the setXyz() method
    @Version(major=1, minor=1)
    public void setXyz(int xyz) {
        // Annotation for local variable newValue
        @Version(major=1, minor=2)
        int newValue = xyz;

        this.xyz = xyz;
    }
}
```

In Listing 1-3, you use @Version annotation to annotate the class declaration, class field, local variables, constructors, and methods. There is nothing extraordinary in the code for the VersionTest class. You just added the @Version annotation to various elements of the class. The VersionTest class would work the same, even if you remove all @Version annotations. It is to be emphasized that using annotations in your program does not change the behavior of the program at all. The real benefit of annotations comes from reading it at compile-time and runtime.

What do you do next with the Version annotation type? You have declared it as a type. You have used it in your VersionTest class. Your next step is to read it at runtime. Let's defer this step for now; I cover it in detail in a later section. I discuss more on annotation type declarations first.

Restrictions on Annotation Types

An annotation type is a special type of interface with some restrictions. I cover some of the restrictions in the sections to follow.

Restriction #1

An annotation type cannot inherit from another annotation type. That is, you cannot use the extends clause in an annotation type declaration. The following declaration will not compile because you have used the extends clause to declare the WrongVersion annotation type:

```
// Won't compile
public @interface WrongVersion extends BasicVersion {
    int extended();
}
```

Every annotation type implicitly inherits from the java.lang.annotation.Annotation interface, which is declared as follows:

```
package java.lang.annotation;

public interface Annotation {
    boolean equals(Object obj);
    int hashCode();
```

```
    String toString();
    Class<? extends Annotation> annotationType();
}
```

This implies that all of the four methods declared in the Annotation interface are available in all annotation types. A word of caution needs to be mentioned here. You declare elements for an annotation type using abstract method declarations. The methods declared in the Annotation interface do not declare elements in an annotation type. Your Version annotation type has only two elements, major and minor, which are declared in the Version type itself. You cannot use the annotation type Version as @Version(major=1, minor=2, toString="Hello"). The Version annotation type does not declare toString as an element. It inherits the toString() method from the Annotation interface.

The first three methods in the Annotation interface are the methods from the Object class. The annotationType() method returns the class reference of the annotation type to which the annotation instance belongs. The Java creates a proxy class dynamically at runtime, which implements the annotation type. When you obtain an instance of an annotation type, that instance class is the dynamically generated proxy class, whose reference you can get using the getClass() method on the annotation instance. If you get an instance of the Version annotation type at runtime, its getClass() method will return the class reference of the dynamically generated proxy class, whereas its annotationType() method will return the class reference of the com.jdojo.annotation.Version annotation type.

Restriction #2

Method declarations in an annotation type cannot specify any parameters. A method declares an element for the annotation type. An element in an annotation type lets you associate a data value to an annotation's instance. A method declaration in an annotation is not called to perform any kind of processing. Think of an element as an instance variable in a class having two methods, a setter and a getter, for that instance variable. For an annotation, the Java runtime creates a proxy class that implements the annotation type (which is an interface). Each annotation instance is an object of that proxy class. The method you declare in your annotation type becomes the getter method for the value of that element you specify in the annotation. The Java runtime will take care of setting the specified value for the annotation elements. Since the goal of declaring a method in an annotation type is to work with a data element, you do not need to (and are not allowed to) specify any parameters in a method declaration. The following declaration of an annotation type would not compile because it declares a concatenate() method, which accepts two parameters:

```
// Won't compile
public @interface WrongVersion {
    // Cannot have parameters
    String concatenate(int major, int minor);
}
```

Restriction #3

Method declarations in an annotation type cannot have a throws clause. A method in an annotation type is defined to represent a data element. Throwing an exception to represent a data value does not make sense. The following declaration of an annotation type would not compile because the major() method has a throws clause:

```
// Won't compile
public @interface WrongVersion {
    int major() throws Exception; // Cannot have a throws clause
    int minor(); // OK
}
```

Restriction #4

The return type of a method declared in an annotation type must be one of the following types:

- Any primitive type: `byte`, `short`, `int`, `long`, `float`, `double`, `boolean`, and `char`
- `java.lang.String`
- `java.lang.Class`
- An enum type
- An annotation type
- An array of any of the previously mentioned types, for example, `String[]`, `int[]`, etc. The return type cannot be a nested array. For example, you cannot have a return type of `String[][]` or `int[][]`.

■ **Tip** The reason behind these data type restrictions is that all values for allowed data types must be represented in the source code, which the compiler should be able to represent for compile-time analysis.

The return type of `Class` needs a little explanation. Instead of the `Class` type, you can use a generic return type that will return a user-defined class type. Suppose you have a `Test` class and you want to declare the return type of a method in an annotation type of type `Test`. You can declare the annotation method as shown:

```
public @interface GoodOne {
    Class element1();                  // Any Class type
    Class<Test> element2();            // Only Test class type
    Class<? extends Test> element3(); // Test or its subclass type
}
```

Restriction #5

An annotation type cannot declare a method, which would be equivalent to overriding a method in the `Object` class or the `Annotation` interface.

Restriction #6

An annotation type cannot be generic.

Default Value of an Annotation Element

The syntax for an annotation type declaration lets you specify a default value for its elements. You are not required to, but you can, specify a value for an annotation element that has a default value specified in its declaration. The default value for an element can be specified using the following general syntax:

```
[modifiers] @interface <annotation-type-name> {
    <data-type> <element-name>() default <default-value>;
}
```

The keyword `default` is used to specify the default value. The default value of the type must be compatible with the data type for the element.

Suppose you have a product that is not frequently released, so it is less likely that it will have a minor version other than zero. You can simplify your `Version` annotation type by specifying a default value for its `minor` element as zero, as shown:

```
public @interface Version {
    int major();
    int minor() default 0; // Set zero as default value for minor
}
```

Once you set the default value for an element, you do not have to pass its value when you use an annotation of this type. Java will use the default value for the missing element.

```
@Version(major=1)          // minor is zero, which is its default value
@Version(major=2)          // minor is zero, which is its default value
@Version(major=2, minor=1) // minor is 1, which is the specified value
```

All default values must be compile-time constants. How do you specify the default value for an array type? You need to use the array initializer syntax. The following snippet of code shows how to specify default values for an array and other data types:

```
// Shows how to assign default values to elements of different types
public @interface DefaultTest {
    double d() default 12.89;
    int num() default 12;
    int[] x() default {1, 2};
    String s() default "Hello";
    String[] s2() default {"abc", "xyz"};
    Class c() default Exception.class;
    Class[] c2() default {Exception.class, java.io.IOException.class};
}
```

The *default value* for an element is not compiled with the annotation. It is read from the annotation type definition when a program attempts to read the value of an element at runtime. For example, when you use `@Version(major=2)`, this annotation instance is compiled as is. It does not add the `minor` element with its default value as zero. In other words, this annotation is not modified to `@Version(major=2, minor=0)` at the time of compilation. However, when you read the value of the `minor` element for this annotation at runtime, Java will detect that the value for the `minor` element was not specified. It will consult the `Version` annotation type definition for its default value. The implication of this mechanism is that if you change the default value of an element, the changed default value will be read whenever a program attempts to read it, even if the annotated program was compiled before you changed the default value.

Annotation Type and Its Instances

I use the terms "annotation type" and "annotation" frequently. *Annotation type* is a type like an interface. Theoretically, you can use annotation type wherever you can use an interface type. Practically, we limit its use only to annotate program elements. You can declare a variable of an annotation type as shown:

```
Version v = null; // Here, Version is an annotation type
```

Like an interface, you can also implement an annotation type in a class. However, you are never supposed to do that, as it will defeat the purpose of having an annotation type as a new construct. You should always implement an interface in a class, not an annotation type. Technically, the code in Listing 1-4 for the DoNotUseIt class is valid. This is just for the purposes of demonstration. Do not implement an annotation in a class even if it works.

Listing 1-4. A Class Implementing an Annotation Type

```
// DoNotUseIt.java
package com.jdojo.annotation;

import java.lang.annotation.Annotation;

public class DoNotUseIt implements Version {
    // Implemented method from the Version annotation type
    @Override
    public int major() {
        return 0;
    }

    // Implemented method from the Version annotation type
    @Override
    public int minor() {
        return 0;
    }

    // Implemented method from the Annotation annotation type,
    // which is the supertype of the Version annotation type
    @Override
    public Class<? extends Annotation> annotationType() {
        return null;
    }
}
```

The Java runtime implements the annotation type to a proxy class. It provides you with an object of a class that implements your annotation type for each annotation you use in your program. You must distinguish between an annotation type and instances (or objects) of that annotation type. In your example, Version is an annotation type. Whenever you use it as @Version(major=2, minor=4), you are creating an instance of the Version annotation type. An instance of an annotation type is simply referred to as an *annotation*. For example, we say that @Version(major=2, minor=4) is an annotation or an instance of the Version annotation type. An annotation should be easy to use in a program. The syntax @Version(...) is shorthand for creating a class, creating an object of that class, and setting the values for its elements. I cover how to get to the object of an annotation type at runtime later in this chapter.

Using Annotations

In this section, I discuss the details of using different types of elements while declaring annotation types. Keep in mind that the supplied value for elements of an annotation must be a compile-time constant expression and you cannot use null as the value for any type of elements in an annotation.

Primitive Types

The data type of an element in an annotation type could be any of the primitive data types: byte, short, int, long, float, double, boolean, and char. The Version annotation type declares two elements, major and minor, and both are of int data type. The following code snippet declares an annotation type called PrimitiveAnnTest:

```
public @interface PrimitiveAnnTest {
    byte a();
    short b();
    int c();
    long d();
    float e();
    double f();
    boolean g();
    char h();
}
```

You can use an instance of the PrimitiveAnnTest type as

```
@PrimitiveAnnTest(a=1, b=2, c=3, d=4, e=12.34F, f=1.89, g=true, h='Y')
```

You can use a compile-time constant expression to specify the value for an element of an annotation. The following two instances of the Version annotation are valid and have the same values for their elements:

```
@Version(major=2+1, minor=(int)13.2)
@Version(major=3, minor=13)
```

String Types

You can use an element of the String type in an annotation type. Listing 1-5 contains the code for an annotation type called Name. It has two elements, first and last, which are of the String type.

Listing 1-5. Name Annotation Type, Which Has Two Elements, first and last, of the String Type

```
// Name.java
package com.jdojo.annotation;

public @interface Name {
    String first();
    String last();
}
```

The following snippet of code shows how to use the Name annotation type in a program:

```
@Name(first="John", last="Jacobs")
public class NameTest {
    @Name(first="Wally", last="Inman")
    public void aMethod() {
        // More code goes here...
    }
}
```

It is valid to use the string concatenation operator (+) in the value expression for an element of a `String` type. The following two annotations are equivalent:

```
@Name(first="Jo" + "hn", last="Ja" + "cobs")
@Name(first="John", last="Jacobs")
```

Typically, you will use string concatenation in an annotation when you want to use compile-time constant such as a final class variable as part of the value for an annotation element. In the following annotation, `Test` is a class that defines a compile-time constant `String` class variable named `UNKNOWN`:

```
@Name(first="Mr. " + Test.UNKNWON, last=Test.UNKNOWN)
```

The following use of the `@Name` annotation is not valid because the expression `new String("John")` is not a compile-time constant expression:

```
@Name(first=new String("John"), last="Jacobs")
```

Class Types

The benefits of using the `Class` type as an element in an annotation type are not obvious. Typically, it is used where a tool/framework reads the annotations with elements of a class type and performs some specialized processing on the element's value or generates code. Let's go through a simple example of using a class type element. Suppose you are writing a test runner tool for running test cases for a Java program. Your annotation will be used in writing test cases. If your test case must throw an exception when it is invoked by the test runner, you need to use an annotation to indicate that. Let's create a `DefaultException` class, as shown in Listing 1-6.

Listing 1-6. A DefaultException Class That Is Inherited from the Throwable Exception Class

```
// DefaultException.java
package com.jdojo.annotation;

public class DefaultException extends java.lang.Throwable {
    public DefaultException() {
    }

    public DefaultException(String msg) {
        super(msg);
    }
}
```

Listing 1-7 shows the code for a `TestCase` annotation type.

Listing 1-7. A TestCase Annotation Type Whose Instances Are Used to Annotate Test Case Methods

```
// TestCase.java
package com.jdojo.annotation;

import java.lang.annotation.ElementType;
import java.lang.annotation.Retention;
import java.lang.annotation.RetentionPolicy;
import java.lang.annotation.Target;
```

```
@Retention(RetentionPolicy.RUNTIME)
@Target(ElementType.METHOD)
public @interface TestCase {
    Class<? extends Throwable> willThrow() default DefaultException.class;
}
```

The return type of the willThrow element is defined as the wildcard of the Throwable class, so that the user will specify only the Throwable class or its subclasses as the element's value. You could have used the Class<?> type as the type of your willThrow element. However, that would have allowed the users of this annotation type to pass any class type as its value. Note that you have used two annotations, @Retention and @Target, for the TestCase annotation type. The @Retention annotation type specified that the @TestCase annotation would be available at runtime. It is necessary to use the retention policy of RUNTIME for your TestCase annotation type because it is meant for the test runner tool to read it at runtime. The @Target annotation states that the TestCase annotation can be used only to annotate methods. I cover the @Retention and @Target annotation types in detail in later sections when I discuss meta-annotations. Listing 1-8 shows the use of your TestCase annotation type.

Listing 1-8. A Test Case That Uses the TestCase Annotations

```
// PolicyTestCases.java
package com.jdojo.annotation;

import java.io.IOException;

public class PolicyTestCases {
    // Must throw IOException
    @TestCase(willThrow=IOException.class)
    public static void testCase1(){
        // Code goes here
    }

    // We are not expecting any exception
    @TestCase()
    public static void testCase2(){
        // Code goes here
    }
}
```

The testCase1() method specifies, using the @TestCase annotation, that it will throw an IOException. The test runner tool will make sure that when it invokes this method, the method does throw an IOException. Otherwise, it will fail the test case. The testCase2() method does not specify that it will throw an exception. If it throws an exception when the test is run, the tool should fail this test case.

Enum Type

An annotation can have elements of an enum type. Suppose you want to declare an annotation type called Review that can describe the code review status of a program element. Let's assume that it has a status element and it can have one of the four values: PENDING, FAILED, PASSED, and PASSEDWITHCHANGES. You can declare an enum as an annotation type member. Listing 1-9 shows the code for a Review annotation type.

Listing 1-9. An Annotation Type That Uses an enum Type Element

```
// Review.java
package com.jdojo.annotation;

public @interface Review {
    ReviewStatus status() default ReviewStatus.PENDING;
    String comments() default "";

    // ReviewStatus enum is a member of the Review annotation type
    public enum ReviewStatus {PENDING, FAILED, PASSED, PASSEDWITHCHANGES};
}
```

■ **Tip** The enum type used as the type of an annotation element need not be declared as a nested enum type of the annotation type, as you did in this example. The enum type can also be declared outside the annotation type.

The `Review` annotation type declares a `ReviewStatus` enum type and the four review statuses are the elements of the enum. It has two elements, `status` and `comments`. The type of the `status` element is the enum type `ReviewStatus`. The default value for the `status` element is `ReviewStatus.PENDING`. You have an empty string as the default value for the `comments` element.

Here are some of the instances of the `Review` annotation type. You will need to import the `com.jdojo.annotation.Review.ReviewStatus` enum in your program to use the simple name of the `ReviewStatus` enum type.

```
// Have default for status and comments. Maybe the code is new.
@Review()

// Leave status as Pending, but add some comments
@Review(comments="Have scheduled code review on December 1, 2017")

// Fail the review with comments
@Review(status=ReviewStatus.FAILED, comments="Need to handle errors")

// Pass the review without comments
@Review(status=ReviewStatus.PASSED)
```

Here is the sample code that annotates a `Test` class indicating that it passed the code review:

```
import com.jdojo.annotation.Review.ReviewStatus;
import com.jdojo.annotation.Review;

@Review(status=ReviewStatus.PASSED)
public class Test {
    // Code goes here
}
```

Annotation Type

An annotation type can be used anywhere a type can be used in a Java program. For example, you can use an annotation type as the return type for a method. You can also use an annotation type as the type of an element inside another annotation type's declaration. Suppose you want to have a new annotation type called `Description`, which will include the name of the author, version, and comments for a program element. You can reuse your `Name` and `Version` annotation types as its `name` and `version` elements type. Listing 1-10 shows the code for the `Description` annotation type.

Listing 1-10. An Annotation Type Using Other Annotation Types as Its Elements

```
// Description.java
package com.jdojo.annotation;

public @interface Description {
    Name name();
    Version version();
    String comments() default "";
}
```

To provide a value for an element of an annotation type, you need to use the syntax that creates an annotation type instance. For example, `@Version(major=1, minor=2)` creates an instance of the `Version` annotation. Note the nesting of an annotation inside another annotation in the following snippet of code:

```
@Description(name=@Name(first="John", last="Jacobs"),
             version=@Version(major=1, minor=2),
             comments="Just a test class")
public class Test {
    // Code goes here
}
```

Array Type Annotation Element

An annotation can have elements of an array type. The array type could be one of the following types:

- A primitive type
- `java.lang.String` type
- `java.lang.Class` type
- An enum type
- An annotation type

You need to specify the value for an array element inside braces. Elements of the array are separated by a comma. Suppose you want to annotate your program elements with a short description of a list of things that you need to work on. Listing 1-11 creates a `ToDo` annotation type for this purpose.

Listing 1-11. ToDo Annotation Type with String[] as Its Sole Element

```
// ToDo.java
package com.jdojo.annotation;
```

```
public @interface ToDo {
    String[] items();
}
```

The following snippet of code shows how to use a @ToDo annotation:

```
@ToDo(items={"Add readFile method", "Add error handling"})
public class Test {
    // Code goes here
}
```

If you have only one element in the array, you can omit the braces. The following two annotation instances of the ToDo annotation type are equivalent:

```
@ToDo(items={"Add error handling"})
@ToDo(items="Add error handling")
```

■ **Tip** If you do not have valid values to pass to an element of an array type, you can use an empty array. For example, @ToDo(items={}) is a valid annotation where the items element has been assigned an empty array.

No Null Value in an Annotation

You cannot use a null reference as a value for an element in an annotation. Note that it is allowed to use an empty string for the String type element and an empty array for an array type element. Using the following annotations will result in compile-time errors:

```
@ToDo(items=null)
@Name(first=null, last="Jacobs")
```

Shorthand Annotation Syntax

The shorthand annotation syntax is little easier to use in a few circumstances. Suppose you have an annotation type Enabled with an element having a default value, as shown:

```
public @interface Enabled {
    boolean status() default true;
}
```

If you want to annotate a program element with the Enabled annotation type using the default value for its element, you can use the @Enabled() syntax. You do not need to specify the values for the status element because it has a default value. You can use shorthand in this situation, which allows you to omit the parentheses. You can just use @Enabled instead of using @Enabled(). The Enabled annotation can be used in either of the following two forms:

```
@Enabled
public class Test {
    // Code goes here
}
```

```
@Enabled()
public class Test {
    // Code goes here
}
```

An annotation type with only one element also has a shorthand syntax. You can use this shorthand if you adhere to a naming rule for the sole element in the annotation type. The name of the element must be `value`. If an annotation type has only one element that is named `value`, you can omit the name from `name=value` pair from your annotation. The following snippet of code declares a `Company` annotation type, which has only one element named `value`:

```
public @interface Company {
    String value(); // the element name is value
}
```

You can omit the name from `name=value` pair when you use the `Company` annotation, as shown here. If you want to use the element name with the `Company` annotation, you can always do so as `@Company(value="Abc Inc.")`.

```
@Company("Abc Inc.")
public class Test {
    // Code goes here
}
```

You can use this shorthand of omitting the name of the element from annotations, even if the element data type is an array. Consider the following annotation type called `Reviewers`:

```
public @interface Reviewers {
    String[] value(); // the element name is value
}
```

Since the `Reviewers` annotation type has only one element, which is named `value`, you can omit the element name when you are using it.

```
// No need to specify name of the element
@Reviewers({"John Jacobs", "Wally Inman"})
public class Test {
    // Code goes here
}
```

You can also omit the braces if you specify only one element in the array for the value element of the `Reviewers` annotation type.

```
@Reviewers("John Jacobs")
public class Test {
    // Code goes here
}
```

You just saw several examples using the name of the element as `value`. Here is the general rule of omitting the name of the element in an annotation: if you supply only one value when using an annotation, the name of the element is assumed `value`. This means that you are not required to have only one element in the annotation type, which is named `value`, to omit its name in the annotations. If you have an annotation type, which has an element named value (with or without a default value) and all other elements have default values, you can still omit the name of the element in annotation instances of this type. Here are some examples to illustrate this rule:

```
public @interface A {
    String value();
    int id() default 10;
}

// Same as @A(value="Hello", id=10)
@A("Hello")
public class Test {
    // Code goes here
}

// Won't compile. Must use only one value to omit the element name
@A("Hello", id=16)
public class WontCompile {
    // Code goes here
}

// OK. Must use name=value pair when passing more than one value
@A(value="Hello", id=16)
public class Test {
    // Code goes here
}
```

Marker Annotation Types

A marker annotation type does not declare any elements, not even one with a default value. Typically, a marker annotation is used by the annotation processing tools, which generate boilerplate code based on the marker annotation type.

```
public @interface Marker {
    // No element declarations
}

@Marker
public class Test {
    // Code goes here
}
```

Meta-Annotation Types

Meta-annotation types are used to annotate other annotation type declarations. The following are meta-annotation types:

- Target
- Retention

- `Inherited`
- `Documented`
- `Repeatable`

Meta-annotation types are part of the Java class library. They are declared in the `java.lang.annotation` package. I discuss meta-annotation types in detail in subsequent sections.

■ **Tip** The `java.lang.annotation` package contains a `Native` annotation type, which is not a meta-annotation. It is used to annotate fields indicating that the field may be referenced from native code. It is a marker annotation. Typically, it is used by tools that generate some code based on this annotation.

The Target Annotation Type

The `Target` annotation type is used to specify the context in which an annotation type can be used. It has only one element named `value`, which is an array of the `java.lang.annotation.ElementType` enum type. Table 1-1 lists all constants in the `ElementType` enum.

Table 1-1. *List of Constants in the java.lang.annotation.ElementType enum*

Constant Name	Description
`ANNOTATION_TYPE`	Used to annotate another annotation type declaration. This makes the annotation type a meta-annotation.
`CONSTRUCTOR`	Used to annotate constructors.
`FIELD`	Used to annotate fields and enum constants.
`LOCAL_VARIABLE`	Used to annotate local variables.
`METHOD`	Used to annotate methods.
`MODULE`	Used to annotate modules. It was added in Java 9.
`PACKAGE`	Used to annotate package declarations.
`PARAMETER`	Used to annotate parameters.
`TYPE`	Used to annotate class, interface (including annotation type), or enum declarations.
`TYPE_PARAMETER`	Used to annotate type parameters in generic classes, interfaces, methods, etc. It was added in Java 8.
`TYPE_USE`	Used to annotate all uses of types. It was added in Java 8. The annotation can also be used where an annotation with `ElementType.TYPE` and `ElementType.TYPE_PARAMETER` can be used. It can also be used before constructors, in which case it represents the objects created by the constructor.

The following declaration of the `Version` annotation type annotates the annotation type declaration with the `Target` meta-annotation, which specifies that the `Version` annotation type can be used with program elements of only three types: any type (class, interface, enum, and annotation types), constructors, and method.

```
// Version.java
package com.jdojo.annotation;

import java.lang.annotation.Target;
import java.lang.annotation.ElementType;

@Target({ElementType.TYPE, ElementType.CONSTRUCTOR, ElementType.METHOD})
public @interface Version {
    int major();
    int minor();
}
```

The Version annotation type cannot be used on any program elements other than the three types specified in its Target annotation. Its following use is incorrect because it is being used on an instance variable (a field):

```
public class WontCompile {
    // A compile-time error. Version annotation cannot be used on a field.
    @Version(major = 1, minor = 1)
    int id = 110;
}
```

The following uses of the Version annotation are valid:

```
// OK. A class type declaration
@Version(major = 1, minor = 0)
public class VersionTest {
    // OK. A constructor declaration
    @Version(major = 1, minor = 0)
    public VersionTest() {
        // Code goes here
    }

    // OK. A method declaration
    @Version(major = 1, minor = 1)
    public void doSomething() {
        // Code goes here
    }
}
```

Prior to Java 8, annotations were allowed on formal parameters of methods and declarations of packages, classes, methods, fields, and local variables. Java 8 added support for using annotations on any use of a type and on type parameter declarations. The phrase "any use of a type" needs little explanation. A type is used in many contexts, for example, after the extends clause as a supertype, in an object creation expression after the new operator, in a cast, in a throws clause, etc. From Java 8, annotations may appear before the simple name of the types wherever a type is used. Note that the simple name of the type may be used only as a name, not as a type, for example, in an import statement. Consider the declarations of the Fatal and NonZero annotation types shown in Listing 1-12 and Listing 1-13.

Listing 1-12. A Fatal Annotation Type That Can Be Used with Any Type Use

```
// Fatal.java
package com.jdojo.annotation;

import java.lang.annotation.ElementType;
import java.lang.annotation.Target;

@Target({ElementType.TYPE_USE})
public @interface Fatal {
}
```

Listing 1-13. A NonZero Annotation Type That Can Be Used with Any Type Use

```
// NonZero.java
package com.jdojo.annotation;

import java.lang.annotation.ElementType;
import java.lang.annotation.Target;

@Target({ElementType.TYPE_USE})
public @interface NonZero {
}
```

The `Fatal` and `NonZero` annotation types can be used wherever a type is used. Their uses in the following contexts are valid:

```
public class Test {
    public void processData() throws @Fatal Exception {
        double value = getValue();
        int roundedValue = (@NonZero int) value;

        Test t = new @Fatal Test();

        // More code goes here
    }

    public double getValue() {
        double value = 189.98;

        // More code goes here

        return value;
    }
}
```

■ **Tip** If you do not annotate an annotation type with the `Target` annotation type, the annotation type can be used everywhere, except in a type parameter declaration.

The Retention Annotation Type

You can use annotations for different purposes. You may want to use them solely for documentation purposes, to be processed by the compiler, and/or to use them at runtime. An annotation can be retained at three levels.

- Source code only
- Class file only (the default)
- Class file and the runtime

The `Retention` meta-annotation type is used to specify how an annotation instance of an annotation type should be retained by Java. This is also known as the *retention policy* of an annotation type. If an annotation type has a "source code only" retention policy, instances of its type are removed when compiled into a class file. If the retention policy is "class file only," annotation instances are retained in the class file, but they cannot be read at runtime. If the retention policy is "class file and runtime" (simply known as runtime), the annotation instances are retained in the class file and they are available for reading at runtime.

The `Retention` meta-annotation type declares one element, named `value`, which is of the `java.lang.annotation.RetentionPolicy` enum type. The `RetentionPolicy` enum has three constants, `SOURCE`, `CLASS`, and `RUNTIME`, which are used to specify the retention policy of source only, class only, and class-and-runtime, respectively. The following code uses the `Retention` meta-annotation on the `Version` annotation type. It specifies that the `Version` annotations should be available at runtime. Note the use of two meta-annotations on the `Version` annotation type: `Target` and `Retention`.

```
// Version.java
package com.jdojo.annotation;

import java.lang.annotation.Target;
import java.lang.annotation.ElementType;
import java.lang.annotation.Retention;
import java.lang.annotation.RetentionPolicy;

@Target({ElementType.TYPE, ElementType.CONSTRUCTOR,
         ElementType.METHOD})
@Retention(RetentionPolicy.RUNTIME)
public @interface Version {
    int major();
    int minor();
}
```

■ **Tip** If you do not use the `Retention` meta-annotation on an annotation type, its retention policy defaults to class file only. This implies that you will not be able to read those annotations at runtime. You will make this common mistake in the beginning. You would try to read annotations and the runtime will not return any values. Make sure that your annotation type has been annotated with the `Retention` meta-annotation with the retention policy of `RetentionPolicy.RUNTIME` before you attempt to read them at runtime. An annotation on a local variable declaration is never available in the class file or at runtime irrespective of the retention policy of the annotation type. The reason for this restriction is that the Java runtime does not let you access the local variables using reflection at runtime; unless you have access to the local variables at runtime, you cannot read annotations for them.

The Inherited Annotation Type

The Inherited annotation type is a marker meta-annotation type. If an annotation type is annotated with an Inherited meta-annotation, its instances are inherited by a subclass declaration. It has no effect if an annotation type is used to annotate any program elements other than a class declaration. Let's consider two annotation type declarations: Ann2 and Ann3. Note that Ann2 is not annotated with an Inherited meta-annotation, whereas Ann3 is.

```
public @interface Ann2 {
    int id();
}

@Inherited
public @interface Ann3 {
    int id();
}
```

Let's declare two classes, A and B, as follows. Note that class B inherits class A.

```
@Ann2(id=505)
@Ann3(id=707)
public class A {
    // Code for class A goes here
}

// Class B inherits Ann3(id=707) annotation from the class A
public class B extends A {
    // Code for class B goes here
}
```

In this snippet of code, class B inherits the @Ann3(id=707) annotation from class A because the Ann3 annotation type has been annotated with an Inherited meta-annotation. Class B does not inherit the @Ann2(id=505) annotation because the Ann2 annotation type is not annotated with an Inherited meta-annotation.

The Documented Annotation Type

The Documented annotation type is a marker meta-annotation type. If an annotation type is annotated with a Documented annotation, the Javadoc tool will generate documentation for all of its instances. Listing 1-14 has the code for the final version of the Version annotation type, which has been annotated with a Documented meta-annotation.

Listing 1-14. The Final Version of the Version Annotation Type

```
// Version.java
package com.jdojo.annotation;

import java.lang.annotation.Documented;
import java.lang.annotation.Target;
import java.lang.annotation.ElementType;
import java.lang.annotation.Retention;
import java.lang.annotation.RetentionPolicy;
```

```
@Target({ElementType.TYPE, ElementType.CONSTRUCTOR, ElementType.METHOD, ElementType.MODULE,
         ElementType.PACKAGE, ElementType.LOCAL_VARIABLE, ElementType.TYPE_USE})
@Retention(RetentionPolicy.RUNTIME)
@Documented
public @interface Version {
    int major();
    int minor();
}
```

Suppose you annotate a Test class with your Version annotation type as follows:

```
package com.jdojo.annotation;

@Version(major=1, minor=0)
public class Test {
    // Code for Test class goes here
}
```

When you generate documentation for the Test class using the Javadoc tool, the Version annotation on the Test class declaration is also generated as part of the documentation. If you remove the Documented annotation from the Version annotation type declaration, the Test class documentation would not contain information about its Version annotation.

The Repeatable Annotation Type

Prior to Java 8, you could not repeat an annotation in the same context. For example, the following repeated use of the Version annotation would generate a compile-time error in Java 7:

```
@Version(major=1, minor=1)
@Version(major=1, minor=2)
public class Test {
    // Code goes here
}
```

Java 8 added a Repeatable meta-annotation type. An annotation type declaration must be annotated with a @Repeatable annotation if its repeated use is to be allowed. The Repeatable annotation type has only one element named value whose type is a class type of another annotation type. Creating a repeatable annotation type is a two-step process:

- Declare an annotation type (say T) and annotate it with the Repeatable meta-annotation. Specify the value for the annotation as another annotation that is known as containing an annotation for the repeatable annotation type being declared.
- Declare the containing annotation type with one element that is an array of the repeatable annotation.

Listing 1-15 and Listing 1-16 contain declarations for the ChangeLog and ChangeLogs annotation types. ChangeLog is annotated with the @Repeatable(ChangeLogs.class) annotation, which means that it is a repeatable annotation type and its containing annotation type is ChangeLogs.

Listing 1-15. A Repeatable Annotation Type That Uses the ChangeLogs as the Containing Annotation Type

```
// ChangeLog.java
package com.jdojo.annotation;

import java.lang.annotation.Repeatable;
import java.lang.annotation.Retention;
import java.lang.annotation.RetentionPolicy;

@Retention(RetentionPolicy.RUNTIME)
@Repeatable(ChangeLogs.class)
public @interface ChangeLog {
    String date();
    String comments();
}
```

Listing 1-16. A Containing Annotation Type for the ChangeLog Repeatable Annotation Type

```
// ChangeLogs.java
package com.jdojo.annotation;

import java.lang.annotation.Retention;
import java.lang.annotation.RetentionPolicy;

@Retention(RetentionPolicy.RUNTIME)
public @interface ChangeLogs {
    ChangeLog[] value();
}
```

You can use the `ChangeLog` annotation to log change history for the `Test` class, as shown:

```
@ChangeLog(date="08/28/2017", comments="Declared the class")
@ChangeLog(date="09/21/2017", comments="Added the process() method")
public class Test {
    public static void process() {
        // Code goes here
    }
}
```

Commonly Used Standard Annotations

Java API defines many standard annotation types. This section discusses four of the most commonly used standard annotations. They are defined in the `java.lang` package. They are

- `Deprecated`
- `Override`
- `SuppressWarnings`
- `FunctionalInterface`

Deprecating APIs

Deprecating APIs in Java is a way to provide information about the lifecycle of the APIs. You can deprecate modules, packages, types, constructors, methods, fields, parameters, and local variables. When you deprecate an API, you are telling its users:

- Not to use the API because it is dangerous.
- To migrate away from the API because a better replacement for the API exists.
- To migrate away from the API because the API will be removed in a future release.

How to Deprecate an API

The JDK contains two constructs that are used to deprecate APIs:

- The `@deprecated` Javadoc tag
- The `java.lang.Deprecated` annotation type

The `@deprecated` Javadoc tag was added in JDK 1.1 and it lets you specify the details about the deprecation with a rich set of text formatting features of HTML. The `java.lang.Deprecated` annotation type was added to JDK 5.0 and it can be used on the API elements, which are deprecated. Before JDK9, the `Deprecated` annotation type did not contain any elements. It is retained at runtime.

The `@deprecated` tag and the `@Deprecated` annotation are supposed to be used together. Both should be present or both absent. The `@Deprecation` annotation does not let you specify a description of the deprecation, so you must use the `@deprecated` tag to provide the description.

■ **Tip** Using a `@deprecated` tag, but not a `@Deprecated` annotation, on an API element generates a compiler warning. Prior to JDK9, you needed to use the `-Xlint:dep-ann` compiler flag to see such warnings.

Listing 1-17 contains the declaration for a class named `FileCopier`. Suppose this class is shipped as part of a library.

Listing 1-17. A FileCopier Utility Class

```
// FileCopier.java
package com.jdojo.deprecation;

import java.io.File;

/**
 * The class consists of static methods that can be used to
 * copy files and directories.
 *
 * @deprecated Deprecated since 1.4. Not safe to use. Use the
 * <code>java.nio.file.Files</code> class instead. This class
 * will be removed in a future release of this library.
 *
 * @since 1.2
 */
```

```
@Deprecated
public class FileCopier {
    // No direct instantiation supported
    private FileCopier() {
    }

    /**
     * Copies the contents of src to dst.
     * @param src The source file
     * @param dst The destination file
     * @return true if the copy is successfully, false otherwise.
     */
    public static boolean copy(File src, File dst) {
        // More code goes here
        return true;
    }

    // More code goes here
}
```

The `FileCopier` class is deprecated using the `@Deprecated` annotation. Its Javadoc uses the `@deprecated` tag to give the deprecation details such as when it was deprecated, its replacement, and its removal notice. Before JDK9, the `@Deprecated` annotation type did not contain any elements, so you had to provide all details about the deprecation using the `@deprecated` tag in the Javadoc for the deprecated API. Note that the `@since` tag used in the Javadoc indicates that the `FileCopier` class has existed since version 1.2 of this library, whereas the `@deprecated` tag indicates that the class has been deprecated since version 1.4 of the library.

The Javadoc tool moves the contents of the `@deprecated` tag to the top in the generated Javadoc to draw the reader's attention. The compiler generates a warning when non-deprecated code *uses* a deprecated API. Annotating an API with `@Deprecated` does not generate a warning; however, using an API that has been annotated with a `@Deprecated` annotation does. If you used the `FileCopier` class outside the class itself, you will receive a compile-time warning about using the deprecated class.

Enhancements to the Deprecated Annotation in JDK9

Suppose you compiled your code and deployed it to production. If you upgraded the JDK version or libraries/frameworks that contain new, deprecated APIs that your old application uses, you do not receive any warnings and you would miss a chance to migrate away from the deprecated APIs. You must recompile your code to receive warnings. There was no tool to scan and analyze the compiled code (e.g., JAR files) and report the use of deprecated APIs. Even worse is the case when a deprecated API is removed from the newer version and your old, compiled code receives unexpected runtime errors. Developers were also confused when they looked at a deprecated element Javadoc—there was no way to express when the API was deprecated and whether the deprecated API will be removed in a future release. All you could do was specify these pieces of information in text as part of the `@deprecated` tag. JDK9 attempted to solve these issues by enhancing the `@Deprecated` annotation. The annotation received two new elements in JDK9: `since` and `forRemoval`. They are declared as follows:

- `String since() default "";`
- `boolean forRemoval() default false;`

Both new elements have default values specified, so the existing uses of the annotation do not break. The `since` element specifies the version in which the annotated API element became deprecated. It is a string and you are expected to follow the same version naming convention as the JDK version scheme, for example "9" for JDK9. It defaults to the empty string. Note that JDK9 did not add an element to the `@Deprecated` annotation type to specify a description of the deprecation. This was done for two reasons:

- The annotation is retained at runtime. Adding descriptive text to the annotation would add to the runtime memory.
- The descriptive text cannot be just plain text. For example, it needs to provide a link to the replacement of the deprecated API. The existing `@deprecated` Javadoc tag already provides this feature.

The `forRemoval` element indicates that the annotated API element is subject to removal in a future release and you should migrate away from the API. It defaults to `false`.

■ **Tip** The `@since` Javadoc tag on an element indicates when the API element was added, whereas the `since` element of the `@Deprecated` annotation indicates when the API element was deprecated. In JDK9, reasonable efforts have been made to backfill these two elements' values in most, if not all, use-sites of the `@Deprecated` annotations in the Java SE APIs.

Before JDK9, the deprecation warnings were issued based on the use of the `@Deprecated` annotation on the API element and its use-site, as shown in Table 1-2. The warnings were issued when a deprecated API element was used at a non-deprecated use-site. If both the declaration and its use-site were deprecated, no warnings were issued. You were able to suppress deprecation warnings by annotating the use-sites with a `@SuppressWarnings("deprecation")` annotation.

Table 1-2. *Matrix of Deprecation Warnings Issued Before JDK9*

API Use-Site	API Declaration Site	
	Not Deprecated	Deprecated
Not Deprecated	N	W
Deprecated	N	N
N = No warning, W = Warning		

Addition of the `forRemoval` element in the `@Deprecation` annotation type has added five more use-cases. When an API is deprecated with `forRemoval` set to `false`, such a deprecation is known as *ordinary deprecation* and the warnings issued in such cases are called *ordinary deprecation warnings*. When an API is deprecated with `forRemoval` set to `true`, such a deprecation is known as *terminal deprecation* and the warnings issued in such cases are called *terminal deprecation warnings* or *removal warnings*. Table 1-3 shows the matrix of deprecation warnings issued in JDK9.

Table 1-3. *Matrix of Deprecation Warnings Issued in JDK9*

API Use-Site	API Declaration Site		
	Not Deprecated	Ordinarily Deprecated	Terminally Deprecated
Not Deprecated	N	OW	RW
Ordinarily Deprecated	N	N	RW
Terminally Deprecated	N	N	RW

N = No warning, OW = Ordinary deprecation warning, RW = Removal deprecation warning

For backward compatibility, four upper-left uses cases in Table 1-3 are the same as in Table 1-2. That is, if your code generated a deprecation warning in JDK8, it will continue to generate an ordinary deprecation warning in JDK9. If the API has been terminally deprecated, its use-sites will generate removal warnings irrespective of the deprecated status of the use-site.

In JDK9, the warning issued in one case, where both the API and its use-site are terminally deprecated, needs a little explanation. Both API and the code that uses it have been deprecated and both will be removed in the future, so what is the point of getting a warning in such a case? This is done to cover cases where the terminally deprecated API and its use-site are in two different codebases and are maintained independently. If the use-site codebase outlives the API codebase, the use-site will get an unexpected runtime error because the API it uses no longer exists. Issuing a warning at the use-site will give its maintainers a chance to plan for alternatives in case the terminally deprecated API goes away before the code at use-sites.

Suppressing Deprecation Warnings

Introduction of removal warnings in JDK9 has added a new use-case for suppressing deprecation warnings. Before JDK9, you could suppress all deprecation warnings by annotating the use-site with a `@SuppressWarnings ("deprecation")` annotation. Consider a scenario:

- In JDK8, an API is deprecated and the use-site suppresses the deprecation warning.
- In JDK9, the API's deprecation changes from ordinary deprecation to terminal deprecation.
- The use-site compiles fine in JDK9 because it has suppressed deprecation warnings in JDK8.
- The API is removed and the use-site receives an unexpected runtime error without receiving any removal warning earlier.

To cover such scenarios, JDK9 does not suppress removal warnings when you use `@SuppressWarnings ("deprecation")`. It suppresses only ordinary deprecation warnings. To suppress removal warnings, you need to use `@SuppressWarnings("removal")`. If you want to suppress both ordinary and removal deprecation warnings, you need to use `@SuppressWarnings({"deprecation", "removal"})`.

An Example

In this section, I show you all use-cases of deprecating APIs, using the deprecated API with and without suppressing warnings with a simple example. In the example, I deprecate only methods and use them to generate compile-time warnings. You are, however, not limited to deprecating only methods. Comments on the methods should help you understand the expected behavior. Listing 1-18 contains the code for a class named `Box`. The class contains three methods—one in each category of deprecation—not deprecated, ordinarily deprecated, and terminally deprecated. I have kept the class simple, so you can focus on the deprecation being used. Compiling the Box class will not generate any deprecation warnings because the class does not use any deprecated API, rather it contains the deprecated APIs.

Listing 1-18. A Box Class with Three Types of Methods: Not Deprecated, Ordinarily Deprecated, and Terminally Deprecated

```
// Box.java
package com.jdojo.annotation;

/**
 * This class is used to demonstrate how to deprecate APIs.
 */
public class Box {
    /**
     * Not deprecated
     */
    public static void notDeprecated() {
        System.out.println("notDeprecated...");
    }

    /**
     * Deprecated ordinarily.
     * @deprecated  Do not use it.
     */
    @Deprecated(since="2")
    public static void deprecatedOrdinarily() {
        System.out.println("deprecatedOrdinarily...");
    }

    /**
     * Deprecated terminally.
     * @deprecated  It will be removed in a future release. Migrate your code now.
     */
    @Deprecated(since="2", forRemoval=true)
    public static void deprecatedTerminally() {
        System.out.println("deprecatedTerminally...");
    }
}
```

Listing 1-19 contains the code for a BoxTest class. The class uses all methods of the Box class. A few methods in the BoxTest class have been deprecated ordinarily and terminally. The first nine methods correspond to nine use-cases in Table 1-3, which will generate four deprecation warnings—one ordinary warning and three terminal warnings. Methods named like m4X(), where X is a digit, show you how to suppress ordinary and terminal deprecation warnings.

Listing 1-19. A BoxTest Class That Uses Deprecated APIs and Suppresses Deprecation Warnings

```
// BoxTest.java
package com.jdojo.annotation;
```

```
public class BoxTest {
    /**
     * API: Not deprecated
     * Use-site: Not deprecated
     * Deprecation warning: No warning
     */
    public static void m11() {
        Box.notDeprecated();
    }

    /**
    * API: Ordinarily deprecated
    * Use-site: Not deprecated
    * Deprecation warning: No warning
    */
    public static void m12() {
        Box.deprecatedOrdinarily();
    }

    /**
     * API: Terminally deprecated
     * Use-site: Not deprecated
     * Deprecation warning: Removal warning
     */
    public static void m13() {
        Box.deprecatedTerminally();
    }

    /**
     * API: Not deprecated
     * Use-site: Ordinarily deprecated
     * Deprecation warning: No warning
     * @deprecated Dangerous to use.
     */
    @Deprecated(since="1.1")
    public static void m21() {
        Box.notDeprecated();
    }

    /**
    * API: Ordinarily deprecated
    * Use-site: Ordinarily deprecated
    * Deprecation warning: No warning
    * @deprecated Dangerous to use.
    */
    @Deprecated(since="1.1")
    public static void m22() {
        Box.deprecatedOrdinarily();
    }
```

```
/**
 * API: Terminally deprecated
 * Use-site: Ordinarily deprecated
 * Deprecation warning: Removal warning
 * @deprecated Dangerous to use.
*/
@Deprecated(since="1.1")
public static void m23() {
    Box.deprecatedTerminally();
}

/**
 * API: Not deprecated
 * Use-site: Terminally deprecated
 * Deprecation warning: No warning
 * @deprecated Going away.
 */
@Deprecated(since="1.1", forRemoval=true)
public static void m31() {
    Box.notDeprecated();
}

/**
* API: Ordinarily deprecated
* Use-site: Terminally deprecated
* Deprecation warning: No warning
* @deprecated Going away.
*/
@Deprecated(since="1.1", forRemoval=true)
public static void m32() {
    Box.deprecatedOrdinarily();
}

/**
 * API: Terminally deprecated
 * Use-site: Terminally deprecated
 * Deprecation warning: Removal warning
 * @deprecated Going away.
*/
@Deprecated(since="1.1", forRemoval=true)
public static void m33() {
    Box.deprecatedTerminally();
}

/**
 * API: Ordinarily and Terminally deprecated
 * Use-site: Not deprecated
 * Deprecation warning: Ordinary and removal warnings
*/
public static void m41() {
    Box.deprecatedOrdinarily();
    Box.deprecatedTerminally();
}
```

```
    /**
     * API: Ordinarily and Terminally deprecated
     * Use-site: Not deprecated
     * Deprecation warning: Ordinary warnings
    */
    @SuppressWarnings("deprecation")
    public static void m42() {
        Box.deprecatedOrdinarily();
        Box.deprecatedTerminally();
    }

    /**
     * API: Ordinarily and Terminally deprecated
     * Use-site: Not deprecated
     * Deprecation warning: Removal warnings
    */
    @SuppressWarnings("removal")
    public static void m43() {
        Box.deprecatedOrdinarily();
        Box.deprecatedTerminally();
    }

    /**
     * API: Ordinarily and Terminally deprecated
     * Use-site: Not deprecated
     * Deprecation warning: Removal warnings
    */
    @SuppressWarnings({"deprecation", "removal"})
    public static void m44() {
        Box.deprecatedOrdinarily();
        Box.deprecatedTerminally();
    }
}
```

You need to compile the BoxTest class using the -Xlint:deprecation compiler flag, so the compiler emits deprecation warnings. Note that the following command is entered on one line, not two lines.

```
C:\Java9LanguageFeatures>javac -Xlint:deprecation -d build\modules\jdojo.annotation
src\jdojo.annotation\classes\com\jdojo\annotation\BoxTest.java
```

```
src\jdojo.annotation\classes\com\jdojo\annotation\BoxTest.java:20: warning: [deprecation]
deprecatedOrdinarily() in Box has been deprecated
        Box.deprecatedOrdinarily();
           ^
src\jdojo.annotation\classes\com\jdojo\annotation\BoxTest.java:29: warning: [removal]
deprecatedTerminally() in Box has been deprecated and marked for removal
        Box.deprecatedTerminally();
           ^
src\jdojo.annotation\classes\com\jdojo\annotation\BoxTest.java:62: warning: [removal]
deprecatedTerminally() in Box has been deprecated and marked for removal
        Box.deprecatedTerminally();
```

```
             ^
src\jdojo.annotation\classes\com\jdojo\annotation\BoxTest.java:95: warning: [removal]
deprecatedTerminally() in Box has been deprecated and marked for removal
        Box.deprecatedTerminally();
           ^
src\jdojo.annotation\classes\com\jdojo\annotation\BoxTest.java:104: warning: [deprecation]
deprecatedOrdinarily() in Box has been deprecated
        Box.deprecatedOrdinarily();
           ^
src\jdojo.annotation\classes\com\jdojo\annotation\BoxTest.java:105: warning: [removal]
deprecatedTerminally() in Box has been deprecated and marked for removal
        Box.deprecatedTerminally();
           ^
src\jdojo.annotation\classes\com\jdojo\annotation\BoxTest.java:116: warning: [removal]
deprecatedTerminally() in Box has been deprecated and marked for removal
        Box.deprecatedTerminally();
           ^
src\jdojo.annotation\classes\com\jdojo\annotation\BoxTest.java:126: warning: [deprecation]
deprecatedOrdinarily() in Box has been deprecated
        Box.deprecatedOrdinarily();
           ^
8 warnings
```

static Analysis of Deprecated APIs

Recall that deprecation warnings are compile-time warnings. You will not get any warnings if compiled code for your deployed application starts using an ordinarily deprecated API or generates a runtime error because an API that was once valid had been terminally deprecated and removed. Before JDK9, you had to recompile your source code to see deprecation warnings when you upgraded your JDK or other libraries/frameworks. JDK9 improves this situation by providing a *static* analysis tool called `jdeprscan` that scans compiled code to give you the list of deprecated APIs being used. Currently, the tool reports the use of only deprecated JDK APIs. If your compiled code uses deprecated APIs from other libraries, say, Spring or Hibernate, or your own libraries, this tool will not report those uses.

The `jdeprscan` tool is in the `JDK_HOME\bin` directory. The general syntax to use the tool is as follows:

```
jdeprscan [options] {dir|jar|class}
```

Here, `[options]` is a list of zero or more options. You can specify a list of space-separated directories, JARs, fully qualified class names, or class file paths as arguments to scan. The available options are as follows:

- `-l, --list`
- `--class-path <CLASSPATH>`
- `--for-removal`
- `--release <6|7|8|9>`
- `-v, --verbose`
- `--version`
- `--full-version`
- `-h, --help`

The --list option lists the set of deprecated APIs in Java SE. No arguments specifying the location of compiled classes should be specified when this option is used.

The --class-path specifies the class path to be used to find dependent classes during the scan.

The --for-removal option restricts the scan or list to only those APIs that have been deprecated for removal. It can be used only with a release value of 9 or later because the @Deprecated annotation type did not contain the forRemoval element before JDK9.

The --release option specifies Java SE release that provides the set of deprecated APIs during scanning. For example, to list all deprecated APIs in JDK 6, you will the tool as follows:

```
jdeprscan --list --release 6
```

The --verbose option prints additional messages during the scanning process.

The --version and --full-version options print the abbreviated and full versions of the jdeprscan tool, respectively.

The --help option prints a detailed help message about the jdeprscan tool.

Listing 1-20 contains the code for a JDeprScanTest class. The code is trivial. It is intended to just compile, not run. Running it will not produce any interesting output. It creates two threads. One thread is stopped using the stop() method of the Thread class and another thread is destroyed using the destroy() method of the Thread class. The stop() and destroy() methods have been ordinarily deprecated since JDK 1.2 and JDK 1.5, respectively. JDK9 has terminally deprecated the destroy() method, whereas it continued to keep the stop() method ordinarily deprecated. I use this class in the following examples.

Listing 1-20. A JDeprScanTest Class That Uses The Ordinarily Deprecated Method stop() and the Terminally Deprecated Method destroy() of the Thread Class

```
// JDeprScanTest.java
package com.jdojo.annotation;

public class JDeprScanTest {
    public static void main(String[] args) {
        Thread t = new Thread(() -> System.out.println("Test"));
        t.start();
        t.stop();
        Thread t2 = new Thread(() -> System.out.println("Test"));
        t2.start();
        t2.destroy();
    }
}
```

The following command prints the list of all deprecated APIs in JDK9. It will print a long list. The command takes a few seconds to start printing the results because it scans the entire JDK.

```
C:\Java9LanguageFeatures>jdeprscan --list
```

```
@Deprecated java.lang.ClassLoader
javax.tools.ToolProvider.getSystemToolClassLoader()
...
```

The following command prints all terminally deprecated APIs in JDK9. That is, it prints all deprecated APIs that have been marked for removal in a future release:

```
C:\Java9LanguageFeatures>jdeprscan --list --for-removal
```

```
@Deprecated(since="9", forRemoval=true) class java.lang.Compiler
...
```

The following command prints the list of all APIs deprecated in JDK8:

```
C:\ Java9LanguageFeatures >jdeprscan --list --release 8
```

```
@Deprecated class javax.swing.text.TableView.TableCell
...
```

The following command prints the list of deprecated APIs used by the `java.lang.Thread` class.

```
C:\Java9LanguageFeatures>jdeprscan java.lang.Thread
```

```
 class java/lang/Thread uses deprecated method java/lang/Thread::resume()V
```

Note that the previous command does not print the list of deprecated APIs in the `Thread` class. Rather, it prints the list of APIs in the `Thread` class that *uses* those deprecated APIs.

The following command lists all uses of deprecated JDK APIs in this chapter's compiled code. The `Java9LanguageFeatures/build/modules/jdojo.annotation` directory in the downloadable code for this book contains the compiled code for this chapter.

```
C:\Java9LanguageFeatures>jdeprscan build/modules/jdojo.annotation
```

```
Directory build/modules/jdojo.annotation:
class com/jdojo/annotation/ImportDeprecationWarning uses deprecated class java/io/
StringBufferInputStream
class com/jdojo/annotation/JDeprScanTest uses deprecated method java/lang/Thread::stop()V
class com/jdojo/annotation/JDeprScanTest uses deprecated method java/lang/
Thread::destroy()V (forRemoval=true)
```

```
C:\Java9LanguageFeatures>jdeprscan --for-removal build/modules/jdojo.annotation
```

```
Directory build/modules/jdojo.annotation:
class com/jdojo/annotation/JDeprScanTest uses deprecated method java/lang/
Thread::destroy()V (forRemoval=true)
```

Dynamic Analysis of Deprecated APIs

The jdeprscan tool is a static analysis tool, so it will skip dynamic uses of deprecated APIs. For example, you can call a deprecated method using reflection, which this tool will miss during scanning. You can also call deprecated methods in providers loaded by a ServiceLoader, which will be missed by this tool.

In a future release, the JDK may provide a dynamic analysis tool named jdeprdetect that will track the uses of deprecated APIs at runtime. The tool will be useful to find dead code referencing deprecated APIs that are reported by the static analysis tool jdeprscan.

No Deprecation Warnings on Imports

Until JDK9, the compiler generated a warning if you imported deprecated constructs using import statements, even if you used a @SuppressWarnings annotation on all use-sites of the deprecated imported constructs. This was an annoyance if you were trying to get rid of all deprecation warnings in your code. You just could not get rid of them because you cannot annotate import statements. JDK9 improved on this by *omitting* the deprecation warnings on import statements.

Suppressing Named Compile-Time Warnings

The SuppressWarnings annotation type is used to suppress named compile-time warnings. It declares one element named value whose data type is an array of String. Let's consider the code for the SuppressWarningsTest class, which uses the raw type for the ArrayList<T> in the test() method. The compiler generates an unchecked named warning when you use a raw type.

Listing 1-21. A Class That Will Generate Warnings When Compiled

```
// SuppressWarningsTest.java
package com.jdojo.annotation;

import java.util.ArrayList;

public class SuppressWarningsTest {
    public void test() {
        ArrayList list = new ArrayList();
        list.add("Hello"); // The compiler issues an unchecked warning
    }
}
```

Compile the SuppressWarningsTest class with an option to generate an unchecked warning using the command

```
javac -Xlint:unchecked SuppressWarningsTest.java
```

```
com\jdojo\annotation\SuppressWarningsTest.java:10: warning: [unchecked] unchecked call to
add(E) as a member of the raw type ArrayList
                list.add("Hello"); // The compiler issues an unchecked warning
                        ^
  where E is a type-variable
    E extends Object declared in class ArrayList
1 warning
```

As a developer, sometimes you are aware of such compiler warnings and you want to suppress them when your code is compiled. You can do so by using a `@SuppressWarnings` annotation on your program element by supplying a list of the names of the warnings to be suppressed. For example, if you use it on a class declaration, all specified warnings will be suppressed from all methods inside that class declaration. It is recommended that you use this annotation on the innermost program element on which you want to suppress the warnings.

Listing 1-22 uses a `@SuppressWarnings` annotation on the `test()` method. It specifies two named warnings: `"unchecked"` and `"deprecation"`. The `test()` method does not contain code that will generate a `"deprecated"` warning. It was included here to show you that you could suppress multiple named warnings using a `SuppressWarnings` annotation. If you recompile the `SuppressWarningsTest` class with the same options shown previously, it will not generate any compiler warnings.

Listing 1-22. The Modified Version of the SuppressWarningsTest Class

```
// SuppressWarningsTest.java
package com.jdojo.annotation;

import java.util.ArrayList;

public class SuppressWarningsTest {
    @SuppressWarnings({"unchecked", "deprecation"})
    public void test() {
        ArrayList list = new ArrayList();
        list.add("Hello"); // The compiler does not issue an unchecked warning
    }
}
```

Overriding Methods

The `java.lang.Override` annotation type is a marker annotation type. It can only be used on methods. It indicates that a method annotated with this annotation overrides a method declared in its supertype. This is very helpful for developers to avoid typos that lead to logical errors in the program. If you mean to override a method in a supertype, it is recommended to annotate the overridden method with a `@Override` annotation. The compiler will make sure that the annotated method really overrides a method in the supertype. If the annotated method does not override a method in the supertype, the compiler will generate an error.

Consider two classes, `A` and `B`. Class `B` inherits from class `A`. The `m1()` method in the class `B` overrides the `m1()` method in its superclass `A`. The annotation `@Override` on the `m1()` method in class `B` just makes a statement about this intention. The compiler verifies this statement and finds it to be true in this case.

```
public class A {
    public void m1() {
    }
}

public class B extends A {
    @Override
    public void m1() {
    }
}
```

Let's consider class C.

```
// Won't compile because m2() does not override any method
public class C extends A {
    @Override
    public void m2() {
    }
}
```

The method m2() in class C has a @Override annotation. However, there is no m2() method in its superclass A. The method m2() is a new method in class C. The compiler finds out that method m2() in class C does not override any superclass method, even though its developer has indicated so. The compiler generates an error in this case.

Declaring Functional Interfaces

An interface with one abstract method declaration is known as a functional interface. Previously, a functional interface was known as a SAM (Single Abstract Method) type. The compiler verifies that all interfaces annotated with a @FunctionalInterface really contain one and only one abstract method. A compile-time error is generated if the interfaces annotated with this annotation are not functional. It is also a compile-time error to use this annotation on classes, annotation types, and enums. The FunctionalInterface annotation type is a marker annotation.

The following declaration of the Runner interface uses a @FunctionalInterface annotation. The interface declaration will compile fine.

```
@FunctionalInterface
public interface Runner {
    void run();
}
```

The following declaration of the Job interface uses a @FunctionalInterface annotation, which will generate a compile-time error because the Job interface declares two abstract methods, and therefore it is not a functional interface.

```
@FunctionalInterface
public interface Job {
    void run();
    void abort();
}
```

The following declaration of the Test class uses a @FunctionalInterface annotation, which will generate a compile-time error because a @FunctionalInterface annotation can only be used on interfaces.

```
@FunctionalInterface
public class Test {
    public void test() {
        // Code goes here
    }
}
```

■ **Tip** An interface with only one abstract method is always a functional interface whether it is annotated with a `@FunctionalInterface` annotation or not. Use of the annotation instructs the compiler to verify the fact that the interface is really a functional interface.

Annotating Packages

Annotating program elements such as classes and fields are intuitive, as you annotate them when they are declared. How do you annotate a package? A package declaration appears in a compilation unit as part of top-level type declarations. Further, the same package declaration occurs multiple times in different compilation units. The question arises: how and where do you annotate a package declaration?

You need to create a file, which should be named `package-info.java`, and place the annotated package declaration in it. Listing 1-23 shows the contents of the `package-info.java` file. When you compile the `package-info.java` file, a class file will be created.

Listing 1-23. Contents of a package-info.java File

```
// package-info.java
@Version(major=1, minor=0)
package com.jdojo.annotation;
```

You may need some `import` statements to import annotation types or you can use the fully qualified names of the annotation types in the `package-info.java` file. Even though the `import` statements appear after the package declaration, it should be okay to use the imported types. You can have contents like the following in a `package-info.java` file:

```
// package-info.java
@com.jdojo.myannotations.Author("John Jacobs")
@Reviewer("Wally Inman")
package com.jdojo.annotation;

import com.jdojo.myannotations.Reviewer;
```

Annotating Modules

You can use annotations on module declarations. In JDK9, the `java.lang.annotation.ElementType` enum has a new value called `MODULE`. If you use `MODULE` as a target type on an annotation declaration, it allows the annotation type to be used on modules. In JDK9, two annotations—`java.lang.Deprecated` and `java.lang.SuppressWarnings`—have been updated to be used on module declarations. They can be used as follows:

```
@Deprecated(since="1.2", forRemoval=true)
@SuppressWarnings("unchecked")
module com.jdojo.myModule {
    // Module statements go here
}
```

When a module is deprecated, the use of that module in `requires`, but not in `exports` or `opens` statements, causes a warning to be issued. This rule is based on the fact that if module `M` is deprecated, a "`requires M`" statement will be used by the module's users who need to get the deprecation warnings. Other statements such as `exports` and `opens` are within the module that is deprecated. A deprecated module does not cause warnings to be issued for uses of types within the module. Similarly, if a warning is suppressed in a module declaration, the suppression applies to elements within the module declaration and not to types contained in that module.

■ **Tip** You cannot annotate individual module statements. For example, you cannot annotate an `exports` statement with a `@Deprecated` annotation indicating that the exported package will be removed in a future release. During the early design phase, it was considered and rejected on the ground that this feature will take a considerable amount of time that is not needed at this time. This could be added in the future, if needed.

Accessing Annotations at Runtime

Accessing annotations on a program element is easy. Annotations on a program element are Java objects. All you need to know is how to get the reference of objects of an annotation type at runtime. Program elements that let you access their annotations implement the `java.lang.reflect.AnnotatedElement` interface. There are several methods in the `AnnotatedElement` interface that let you access annotations of a program element. The methods in this interface let you retrieve all annotations on a program element, all declared annotations on a program element, and annotations of a specified type on a program element. I show some examples of using those methods shortly. The following classes implement the `AnnotatedElement` interface:

- `java.lang.Class`
- `java.lang.reflect.Executable`
- `java.lang.reflect.Constructor`
- `java.lang.reflect.Field`
- `java.lang.reflect.Method`
- `java.lang.reflect.Module`
- `java.lang.reflect.Parameter`
- `java.lang.Package`
- `java.lang.reflect.AccessibleObject`

Methods of the `AnnotatedElement` interface are used to access annotations on these types of objects.

■ **Caution** It is very important to note that an annotation type must be annotated with the `Retention` meta-annotation with the retention policy of runtime to access it at runtime. If a program element has multiple annotations, you would be able to access only annotations, which have runtime as their retention policy.

Suppose you have a Test class and you want to print all its annotations. The following snippet of code will print all annotations on the class declaration of the Test class:

```
// Get the class object reference
Class<Test> cls = Test.class;

// Get all annotations on the class declaration
Annotation[] allAnns = cls.getAnnotations();
System.out.println("Annotation count: " + allAnns.length);

// Print all annotations
for (Annotation ann : allAnns) {
    System.out.println(ann.toString());
}
```

The toString() method of the Annotation interface returns the string representation of an annotation. Suppose you want to print the Version annotation on the Test class. You can do so as follows:

```
Class<Test> cls = Test.class;

// Get the instance of the Version annotation of Test class
Version v = cls.getAnnotation(Version.class);
if (v == null) {
    System.out.println("Version annotation is not present.");
} else {
    int major = v.major();
    int minor = v.minor();
    System.out.println("Version: major=" + major + ", minor=" + minor);
}
```

This snippet of code shows that you can use the major() and minor() methods to read the value of the major and minor elements of the Version annotation. It also shows that you can declare a variable of an annotation type (e.g., Version v), which can refer to an instance of that annotation type. The instances of an annotation type are created by the Java runtime. You never create an instance of an annotation type using the new operator.

You will use the Version and Deprecated annotation types to annotate your program elements and access those annotations at runtime. You will also annotate a package declaration and a method declaration. You will use the code for the Version annotation type, as listed in Listing 1-24. Note that it uses the @Retention(RetentionPolicy.RUNTIME) annotation, which is needed to read its instances at runtime.

Listing 1-24. A Version Annotation Type

```
// Version.java
package com.jdojo.annotation;

import java.lang.annotation.Documented;
import java.lang.annotation.Target;
import java.lang.annotation.ElementType;
import java.lang.annotation.Retention;
import java.lang.annotation.RetentionPolicy;
```

```
@Target({ElementType.TYPE, ElementType.CONSTRUCTOR, ElementType.METHOD, ElementType.MODULE,
ElementType.PACKAGE})
@Retention(RetentionPolicy.RUNTIME)
@Documented
public @interface Version {
    int major();
    int minor();
}
```

Listing 1-25 shows the code that you need to save in a `package-info.java` file and compile it along with other programs. It annotates the `com.jdojo.annotation` package. Listing 1-26 contains the code for a class for demonstration purposes that has some annotations.

Listing 1-25. Contents of package-info.java File

```
// package-info.java
@Version(major=1, minor=0)
package com.jdojo.annotation;
```

Listing 1-26. AccessAnnotation Class Has Some Annotations, Which Will Be Accessed at Runtime

```
// AccessAnnotation.java
package com.jdojo.annotation;

@Version(major=1, minor=0)
public class AccessAnnotation {
    @Version(major=1, minor=1)
    public void testMethod1() {
        // Code goes here
    }

    @Version(major=1, minor=2)
    @Deprecated
    public void testMethod2() {
        // Code goes here
    }
}
```

Listing 1-27 is the program that demonstrates how to access annotations at runtime. Its output shows that you are able to read all annotations used in the `AccessAnnotation` class successfully. The `printAnnotations()` method accesses the annotations. It accepts a parameter of the `AnnotatedElement` type and prints all annotations of its parameter. If the annotation is of the `Version` annotation type, it prints the values for its major and minor versions.

Listing 1-27. Using the AccessAnnotationTest Class to Access Annotations

```
// AccessAnnotationTest.java
package com.jdojo.annotation;

import java.lang.annotation.Annotation;
import java.lang.reflect.AnnotatedElement;
import java.lang.reflect.Method;
```

```
public class AccessAnnotationTest {
    public static void main(String[] args) {
        // Read annotations on the class declaration
        Class<AccessAnnotation> cls = AccessAnnotation.class;
        System.out.println("Annotations for class: " + cls.getName());
        printAnnotations(cls);

        // Read annotations on the package declaration
        Package p = cls.getPackage();
        System.out.println("Annotations for package: " + p.getName());
        printAnnotations(p);

        // Read annotations on the methods declarations
        System.out.println("Method annotations:");
        Method[] methodList = cls.getDeclaredMethods();
        for (Method m : methodList) {
            System.out.println("Annotations for method: " + m.getName());
            printAnnotations(m);
        }
    }

    public static void printAnnotations(AnnotatedElement programElement) {
        Annotation[] annList = programElement.getAnnotations();
        for (Annotation ann : annList) {
            System.out.println(ann);
            if (ann instanceof Version) {
                Version v = (Version) ann;
                int major = v.major();
                int minor = v.minor();
                System.out.println("Found Version annotation: "
                        + "major=" + major + ", minor=" + minor);
            }
        }

        System.out.println();
    }
}
```

```
Annotations for class: com.jdojo.annotation.AccessAnnotation
@com.jdojo.annotation.Version(major=1, minor=0)
Found Version annotation: major=1, minor=0

Annotations for package: com.jdojo.annotation
@com.jdojo.annotation.Version(major=1, minor=0)
Found Version annotation: major=1, minor=0

Method annotations:
Annotations for method: testMethod1
@com.jdojo.annotation.Version(major=1, minor=1)
Found Version annotation: major=1, minor=1
```

```
Annotations for method: testMethod2
@com.jdojo.annotation.Version(major=1, minor=2)
Found Version annotation: major=1, minor=2
@java.lang.Deprecated(forRemoval=false, since="")
```

Accessing instances of a repeatable annotation is a little different. Recall that a repeatable annotation has a companion *containing* annotation type. For example, you declared a `ChangeLogs` annotation type that is a containing annotation type for the `ChangeLog` repeatable annotation type. You can access repeated annotations using either the annotation type or the containing annotation type. Use the `getAnnotationsByType()` method, passing it the class reference of the repeatable annotation type to get the instances of the repeatable annotation in an array. Use the `getAnnotation()` method, passing it the class reference of the containing annotation type to get the instances of the repeatable annotation as an instance of its containing annotation type.

Listing 1-28 contains the code for a `RepeatableAnnTest` class. The class declaration has been annotated with the `ChangeLog` annotation twice. The `main()` method accesses the repeated annotations on the class declaration using both of these methods.

Listing 1-28. Accessing Instances of Repeatable Annotations at Runtime

```
// RepeatableAnnTest.java
package com.jdojo.annotation;

@ChangeLog(date = "09/18/2017", comments = "Declared the class")
@ChangeLog(date = "10/22/2017", comments = "Added the main() method")
public class RepeatableAnnTest {
    public static void main(String[] args) {
        Class<RepeatableAnnTest> mainClass = RepeatableAnnTest.class;
        Class<ChangeLog> annClass = ChangeLog.class;

        // Access annotations using the ChangeLog type
        System.out.println("Using the ChangeLog type...");
        ChangeLog[] annList = mainClass.getAnnotationsByType(ChangeLog.class);
        for (ChangeLog log : annList) {
            System.out.println("Date=" + log.date() + ", Comments=" + log.comments());
        }

        // Access annotations using the ChangeLogs containing annotation type
        System.out.println("\nUsing the ChangeLogs type...");

        Class<ChangeLogs> containingAnnClass = ChangeLogs.class;
        ChangeLogs logs = mainClass.getAnnotation(containingAnnClass);
        for (ChangeLog log : logs.value()) {
            System.out.println("Date=" + log.date() + ", Comments=" + log.comments());
        }
    }
}
```

```
Using the ChangeLog type...
Date=09/18/2017, Comments=Declared the class
Date=10/22/2017, Comments=Added the main() method
```

```
Using the ChangeLogs type...
Date=09/18/2017, Comments=Declared the class
Date=10/22/2017, Comments=Added the main() method
```

Evolving Annotation Types

An annotation type can evolve without breaking the existing code that uses it. If you add a new element to an annotation type, you need to supply its default value. All existing instances of the annotation will use the default value for the new elements. If you add a new element to an existing annotation type without specifying a default value for the element, the code that uses the annotation will break.

Annotation Processing at Source Code Level

This section is for experienced programmers. You may skip this section if you are learning Java for the first time.

This section discusses in detail how to develop annotation processors to process annotation at the source code level when you compile Java programs. The University of Washington developed a Checker Framework that contains a lot of annotations to be used in programs. It also ships with many annotation processors. You can download the Checker Framework from `http://types.cs.washington.edu/checker-framework`. It contains a tutorial for using different types of processors and a tutorial on how to create your own processor.

Java lets you process annotations at runtime as well as at compile time. You have already seen how to process annotations at runtime. Now, I discuss, in brief, how to process annotations at compile time (or at the source code level).

Why would you want to process annotations at compile time? Processing annotations at compile time opens up a wide variety of possibilities that can help Java programmers during development of applications. It also helps developers of Java tools immensely. For example, boilerplate code and configuration files can be generated based on annotations in the source code; custom annotation-based rules can be validated at compile time, etc.

Annotation processing at compile time is a two-step process. First, you need to write a custom annotation processor. Second, you need to use the `javac` command line utility tool. You need to specify the module path for your custom annotation processor to the `javac` compiler using the `--processor-module-path` option. The following command compiles the Java source file, `MySourceFile.java`:

```
javac --processor-module-path <path> MySourceFile.java
```

Using `-proc` option, the `javac` command lets you specify if you want to process annotation and/or compile the source files. You can use the `-proc` option as `-proc:none` or `-proc:only`. The `-proc:none` option does not perform annotation processing. It only compiles source files. The `-proc:only` option performs only annotation processing and skips the source files compilation. If the `-proc:none` and the `-processor` options are specified in the same command, the `-processor` option is ignored. The following command processes annotations in the source file `MySourceFile.java` using custom processors: `MyProcessor1` and `MyProcessor2`. It does not compile the source code in the `MySourceFile.java` file.

```
javac -proc:only --processor-module-path <path> MySourceFile.java
```

To see the compile-time annotation processing in action, you must write an annotation processor using the classes in the `javax.annotation.processing` package, which is in the `java.compiler` module.

While writing a custom annotation processor, you often need to access the elements from the source code, for example, the name of a class and its modifiers, the name of a method and its return type, etc. You need to use classes in the `javax.lang.model` package and its subpackages to work with the elements of the source code. In your example, you will write an annotation processor for your @Version annotation. It will validate all @Version annotations that are used in the source code to make sure the major and minor values for a Version are always zero or greater than zero. For example, if @Version(major=-1, minor=0) is used in source code, your annotation processor will print an error message because the major value for the version is negative.

An annotation processor is an object of a class, which implements the Processor interface. The AbstractProcessor class is an abstract annotation processor, which provides a default implementation for all methods of the Processor interface, except an implementation for the process() method. The default implementation is fine in most circumstances. To create your own processor, you need to inherit your processor class from the AbstractProcessor class and provide an implementation for the process() method. If the AbstractProcessor class does not suit your need, you can create your own processor class, which implements the Processor interface. Let's call your processor class VersionProcessor, which inherits the AbstractProcessor class, as shown:

```
public class VersionProcessor extends AbstractProcessor {
    // Code goes here
}
```

The annotation processor object is instantiated by the compiler using a no-args constructor. You must have a no-args constructor for your processor class, so that the compiler can instantiate it. The default constructor for your VersionProcessor class will meet this requirement.

The next step is to add two pieces of information to the processor class. The first one is about what kind of annotations processing are supported by this processor. You can specify the supported annotation type using @SupportedAnnotationTypes annotation at the class level. The following snippet of code shows that the VersionProcessor supports processing of com.jdojo.annotation.Version annotation type:

```
@SupportedAnnotationTypes({"com.jdojo.annotation.Version"})
public class VersionProcessor extends AbstractProcessor {
    // Code goes here
}
```

You can use an asterisk (*) by itself or as part of the annotation name of the supported annotation types. The asterisk works as a wildcard. For example, "com.jdojo.*" means any annotation types whose names start with "com.jdojo.". An asterisk only ("*") means all annotation types. Note that when an asterisk is used as part of the name, the name must be of the form PartialName.*. For example, "com*" and "com.*jdojo" are invalid uses of an asterisk in the supported annotation types. You can pass multiple supported annotation types using the SupportedAnnotationTypes annotation. The following snippet of code shows that the processor supports processing for the com.jdojo.Ann1 annotation and any annotations whose name begins with com.jdojo.annotation:

```
@SupportedAnnotationTypes({"com.jdojo.Ann1", "com.jdojo.annotation.*"})
```

You need to specify the latest source code version that is supported by your processor using a @SupportedSourceVersion annotation. The following snippet of code specifies the source code version 9 as the supported source code version for the VersionProcessor class:

```
@SupportedAnnotationTypes({"com.jdojo.annotation.Version"})
@SupportedSourceVersion(SourceVersion.RELEASE_9)
public class VersionProcessor extends AbstractProcessor {
    // Code goes here
}
```

The next step is to provide the implementation for the process() method in the processor class. Annotation processing is performed in rounds. An instance of the RoundEnvironment interface represents a round. The javac compiler calls the process() method of your processor by passing all annotations that the processor declares to support and a RoundEnvironment object. The return type of the process() method is boolean. If it returns true, the annotations passed to it are considered to be claimed by the processor. The claimed annotations are not passed to other processors. If it returns false, the annotations passed to it are considered as not claimed and other processor will be asked to process them. The following snippet of code shows the skeleton of the process() method:

```
public boolean process(Set<? extends TypeElement> annotations, RoundEnvironment roundEnv) {
    // The processor code goes here
}
```

The code you write inside the process() method depends on your requirements. In your case, you want to look at the major and minor values for each @Version annotation in the source code. If either of them is less than zero, you want to print an error message. To process each Version annotation, you will iterate through all Version annotation instances passed to the process() method as follows:

```
for (TypeElement currentAnnotation : annotations) {
    // Code to validate each Version annotation goes here
}
```

You can get the fully qualified name of an annotation using the getQualifiedName() method of the TypeElement interface.

```
Name qualifiedName = currentAnnotation.getQualifiedName();

// Check if it is a Version annotation
if (qualifiedName.contentEquals("com.jdojo.annotation.Version")) {
    // Get Version annotation values to validate
}
```

Once you are sure that you have a Version annotation, you need to get all its instances from the source code. To get information from the source code, you need to use the RoundEnvironment object. The following snippet of code will get all elements of the source code (e.g., classes, methods, constructors, etc.) that are annotated with a Version annotation:

```
Set<? extends Element> annotatedElements = roundEnv.getElementsAnnotatedWith(currentAnnotation);
```

At this point, you need to iterate through all elements that are annotated with a Version annotation; get the instance of the Version annotation present on them; and validate the values of the major and minor elements. You can perform this logic as follows:

```
for (Element element : annotatedElements) {
    Version v = element.getAnnotation(Version.class);
    int major = v.major();
    int minor = v.minor();
    if (major < 0 || minor < 0) {
        // Print the error message here
    }
}
```

You can print the error message using the printMessage() method of the Messager. The processingEnv is an instance variable defined in the AbstractProcessor class that you can use inside your processor to get the Messager object reference, as shown next. If you pass the source code element's reference to the printMessage() method, your message will be formatted to include the source code file name and the line number in the source code for that element. The first argument to the printMessage() method indicates the type of the message. You can use Kind.NOTE and Kind.WARNING as the first argument to print a note and warning, respectively.

```
String errorMsg = "Version cannot be negative. major=" + major + " minor=" + minor;
Messager messager = this.processingEnv.getMessager();
messager.printMessage(Kind.ERROR, errorMsg, element);
```

Finally, you need to return true or false from the process() method. If a processor returns true, it means it claimed all the annotations that were passed to it. Otherwise, those annotations are considered unclaimed and they will be passed to other processors. Typically, your annotation processors should be packaged in a separate module. Listing 1-29 contains the declaration for a jdojo.annotation.processor module, which contains the annotation processor named VersionProcessor for the Version annotation type, as shown in Listing 1-30.

Listing 1-29. The Declaration for a jdojo.annotation.processor Module

```
// module-info.java
module jdojo.annotation.processor {
    exports com.jdojo.annotation.processor;
    requires jdojo.annotation;
    requires java.compiler;
    provides javax.annotation.processing.Processor
        with com.jdojo.annotation.processor.VersionProcessor;
}
```

The module reads the jdojo.annotation module because it uses the Version annotation type in the VersionProcessor class. It reads the java.compiler module to use annotation processor related types. Notice the use of the provides statement in the module's declaration. JDK9 will load all annotation processors on the processor module path mentioned in the with clause of the provides statement. The statement specifies that the VersionProcessor class provides an implementation for the Processor service interface. Refer to Chapter 14 for more details on the provides statement and implementing services.

Listing 1-30. An Annotation Processor to Process Version Annotations

```
// VersionProcessor.java
package com.jdojo.annotation.processor;

import java.util.Set;
import javax.annotation.processing.AbstractProcessor;
import javax.annotation.processing.Messager;
import javax.annotation.processing.RoundEnvironment;
import javax.annotation.processing.SupportedAnnotationTypes;
import javax.annotation.processing.SupportedSourceVersion;
import javax.lang.model.SourceVersion;
import javax.lang.model.element.Element;
import javax.lang.model.element.Name;
import javax.lang.model.element.TypeElement;
import javax.tools.Diagnostic.Kind;
```

```
@SupportedAnnotationTypes({"com.jdojo.annotation.Version"})
@SupportedSourceVersion(SourceVersion.RELEASE_9)
public class VersionProcessor extends AbstractProcessor {
    // A no-args constructor is required for an annotation processor
    public VersionProcessor() {
    }

    @Override
    public boolean process(Set<? extends TypeElement> annotations, RoundEnvironment
    roundEnv) {
        // Process all annotations
        for (TypeElement currentAnnotation: annotations) {
            Name qualifiedName = currentAnnotation.getQualifiedName();

            // check if it is a Version annotation
            if (qualifiedName.contentEquals("com.jdojo.annotation.Version" )) {
                // Look at all elements that have Version annotations
                Set<? extends Element> annotatedElements;
                annotatedElements = roundEnv.getElementsAnnotatedWith(currentAnnotation);
                for (Element element: annotatedElements) {
                    Version v = element.getAnnotation(Version.class);
                    int major = v.major();
                    int minor = v.minor();
                    if (major < 0 || minor < 0) {
                        // Print the error message
                        String errorMsg = "Version cannot be negative." +
                                    " major=" + major +
                                    " minor=" + minor;

                        Messager messager = this.processingEnv.getMessager();

                        messager.printMessage(Kind.ERROR, errorMsg, element);
                    }
                }
            }
        }

        return true;
    }
}
```

Now you have an annotation processor. It is time to see it in action. You need to have a source code that uses invalid values for the major and minor elements in the `Version` annotation. You will place the source code in a module named `jdojo.annotation.test`, as shown in Listing 1-31. The `VersionProcessorTest` class in Listing 1-32 uses the `Version` annotation three times. It uses negative values for major and `minor` elements for the class itself and for the method `m2()`. The processor should catch these two errors when you compile the source code for the `VersionProcessorTest` class.

Listing 1-31. The Declaration of a jdojo.annotation.test Module

```
// module-info.java
module jdojo.annotation.test {
    exports com.jdojo.annotation.test;
    requires jdojo.annotation;
}
```

Listing 1-32. A Test Class to Test VersionProcessor

```
// VersionProcessorTest.java
package com.jdojo.annotation.test;

@Version(major = -1, minor = 2)
public class VersionProcessorTest {
    @Version(major = 1, minor = 1)
    public void m1() {
    }

    @Version(major = -2, minor = 1)
    public void m2() {
    }
}
```

To see the processor in action, you need to run the following command. You need to specify the path for the `VersionProcessor` class' module using the `--processor-module-path` option. The modules that the annotation processor depends on should also be specified in the processor module path. When the command is run, the compiler will automatically discover the `VersionProcessor` as an annotation processor and it will pass all `@Version` instances to this processor. The output displays two errors with the source file name and the line number at which errors were found in the source file.

```
C:\Java9LanguageFeatures>javac --module-path dist\jdojo.annotation.jar
--processor-module-path dist\jdojo.annotation.processor.jar;dist\jdojo.annotation.jar
-d build\modules\jdojo.annotation.test
src\jdojo.annotation.test\classes\module-info.java
src\jdojo.annotation.test\classes\com\jdojo\annotation\test\VersionProcessorTest.java
```

```
src\jdojo.annotation.test\classes\com\jdojo\annotation\test\VersionProcessorTest.java:7:
error: Version cannot be negative. major=-1 minor=2
public class VersionProcessorTest {
       ^
src\jdojo.annotation.test\classes\com\jdojo\annotation\test\VersionProcessorTest.java:13:
error: Version cannot be negative. major=-2 minor=1
    public void m2() {
                ^
2 errors
```

Summary

Annotations are types in Java. They are used to associate information to the declarations of program elements or type uses in a Java program. Using annotations does not change the semantics of the program.

Annotations can be available in the source code only, in the class files, or at runtime. Their availability is controlled by the retention policy that is specified when the annotation types are declared.

There are two types of annotations: regular annotation or simply annotations, and meta-annotations. Annotations are used to annotate program elements, whereas meta-annotations are used to annotate other annotations. When you declare an annotation, you can specify its targets that are the types of program elements that it can annotate. Prior to Java 8, annotations were not allowed to be repeated on the same element. Java 8 lets you create repeatable annotations.

Java library contains many annotation types that you can use in your Java programs—`Deprecated`, `Override`, `SuppressWarnings`, `FunctionalInterface`, etc. are a few of the commonly used annotation types. They have compiler support, which means that the compiler generates errors if the program elements annotated with these annotations do not adhere to specific rules.

Java lets you write annotation processors that can be plugged into the Java compiler to process annotations when Java programs are compiled. You can write processors to enforce custom rules based on annotations.

Deprecation in Java is a way to provide information about the lifecycle of the API. Deprecating an API tells its users to migrate away because the API is dangerous to use, a better replacement exists, or it will be removed in a future release. Using deprecated APIs generates compile-time deprecation warnings. The `@deprecated` Javadoc tag and the `@Deprecated` annotation are used together to deprecate API elements such as modules, packages, types, constructors, methods, fields, parameters, and local variables. Before JDK9, the annotation did not contain any elements. It is retained at runtime.

JDK9 has added two elements to the `Deprecated` annotation type: `since` and `forRemoval`. The `since` element defaults to an empty string. Its value denotes the version of the API in which the API element was deprecated. The `forRemoval` element's type is `boolean` and it defaults to `false`. Its value of `true` denotes that the API element will be removed in a future release.

The JDK9 compiler generates two types of deprecation warnings depending on the value of the `forRemoval` element of the `@Deprecated` annotation: *ordinary deprecation warnings* when `forRemoval=false` and *removal warnings* for `forRemoval=true`.

Before JDK9, you could suppress the deprecation warnings by annotating the use-sites of the deprecated APIs with a `@SuppressWarnings("deprecation")` annotation. In JDK9, you need to use `@SuppressWarnings("deprecation")` to suppress ordinary warnings, `@SuppressWarnings("removal")` to suppress removal warnings, and `@SuppressWarnings({"deprecation", "removal"})` to suppress both types of warnings. Before JDK9, importing a deprecated construct using an `import` statement generated a compile-time deprecation warning. JDK9 omits such warnings.

QUESTIONS AND EXERCISES

1. What are annotations? How do you declare them?
2. What are meta-annotations?
3. What is the difference between an annotation type and annotation instances?
4. Can you inherit an annotation type from another annotation type?
5. What are marker annotations? Describe their use. Name two marker annotations available in Java SE API.

6. Name the annotation type whose instances are used to annotate an overridden method. What is the fully qualified name of this annotation type?

7. What are the allowed return types for methods in an annotation type declaration?

8. Declare an annotation type named `Table`. It contains one `String` element named `name`. The sole element does not have any default value. This annotation must be used only on classes. Its instances should be available at runtime.

9. What is wrong with the following annotation type declaration?

```
public @interface Version extends BasicVersion {
    int extended();
}
```

10. What is wrong with the following annotation type declaration?

```
public @interface Author {
    void name(String firstName, String lastName);
}
```

11. Briefly describe the use of the following built-in meta-annotations: `Target`, `Retention`, `Inherited`, `Documented`, `Repeatable`, and `Native`.

12. Declare an annotation type named `ModuleOwner`, which contains one element `name`, which is of the `String` type. The instances of the `ModuleOwner` type should be retained only in the source code and they should be used only on module declarations.

13. Declare a repeatable annotation type named `Author`. It contains two elements of `String` type: `firstName` and `lastName`. This annotation can be used on types, methods, and constructors. Its instances should be available at runtime. Name the containing annotation type for the `Author` annotation type as `Authors`.

14. What annotation type do you use to deprecate your APIs? Describe all the elements of such an annotation type.

15. What annotation type do you use to annotate a functional interface?

16. How do you annotate a package?

17. Create an annotation type named `Owner`. It should have one element, `name`, of the `String` type. Its instances should be retained at runtime. It should be repeatable. It should be used only on types, methods, constructors, and modules. Create a module named `jdojo.annotation.test` and create a class named `Test` in the `com.jdojo.annotation.exercises` package. Add a constructor and a method to the class. Annotate the class, its module, constructor, and method with the `Owner` annotation type. Add a `main()` method to the `Test` class and write code to access and print the details of these instances of the `Owner` annotation.

18. Consider the following declaration of an annotation type named `Status`:

```
public @interface Status {
    boolean approved() default false;
    String approvedBy();
}
```

Later you need to add another element to the `Status` annotation type. Modify the declaration of the annotation to include a new element named `approvedOn`, which is of the `String` type. The new element will contain a date in ISO format whose default value may be set to `"1900-01-01"`.

19. Consider the declaration of the following annotation type named `LuckyNumber`:

```
public @interface LuckyNumber {
    int[] value() default {19};
}
```

Which of the following uses of the `LuckyNumber` annotation type is/are invalid? Explain your answer.

a) `@LuckyNumber`
b) `@LuckyNumber({})`
c) `@LuckyNumber(10)`
d) `@LuckyNumber({8, 10, 19, 28, 29, 26})`
e) `@LuckyNumber(value={8, 10, 19, 28, 29, 26})`
f) `@LuckyNumber(null)`

20. Given a `LuckyNumber` annotation type, is the following variable declaration valid?

```
LuckNumber myLuckNumber = null;
```

21. Consider the following declaration for a `jdojo.annotation.exercises` module:

```
module jdojo.annotation.exercises {
    exports com.jdojo.annotation.exercises;
}
```

The module exists since version 1.0. The module has been deprecated and will be removed in the next version. Annotate the module declaration to reflect these pieces of information.

CHAPTER 2

Inner Classes

In this chapter, you will learn:

- What inner classes are
- How to declare inner classes
- How to declare member, local, and anonymous inner classes
- How to create objects of inner classes

All example programs in this chapter are a member of a `jdojo.innerclasses` module, as declared in Listing 2-1.

Listing 2-1. The Declaration of a jdojo.innerclasses Module

```
// module-info.java
module jdojo.innerclasses {
    exports com.jdojo.innerclasses;
}
```

What Is an Inner Class?

You have worked with classes that are members of a package. A class, which is a member of a package, is known as a top-level class. For example, Listing 2-2. shows a top-level class named `TopLevel`.

Listing 2-2. An Example of a Top-Level Class

```
// TopLevel.java
package com.jdojo.innerclasses;

public class TopLevel {
    private int value = 101;

    public int getValue() {
        return value;
    }

    public void setValue (int value) {
        this.value = value;
    }
}
```


K. Sharan, *Java Language Features*, https://doi.org/10.1007/978-1-4842-3348-1_2

The TopLevel class is a member of the com.jdojo.innerclasses package. The class has three members:

- One instance variable: value
- Two methods: getValue() and setValue()

A class can also be declared within another class. This type of class is called an *inner* class. If the class declared within another class is explicitly or implicitly declared static, it is called a nested class, not an inner class. The class that contains the inner class is called an *enclosing* class or an *outer* class. Consider the following declaration of the Outer and Inner classes:

```
// Outer.java
package com.jdojo.innerclasses;

public class Outer {
    public class Inner {
        // Members of the Inner class go here
    }

    // Other members of the Outer class go here
}
```

The Outer class is a top-level class. It is a member of the com.jdojo.innerclasses package. The Inner class is an inner class. It is a member of the Outer class. The Outer class is the enclosing (or outer) class for the Inner class. An inner class can be the enclosing class for another inner class. There are no limits on the levels of nesting of inner classes.

An instance of an inner class can only exist within an instance of its enclosing class. That is, you must have an instance of the enclosing class before you can create an instance of an inner class. This is useful in enforcing the rule that one object cannot exist without the other. For example, a computer must exist before a processor can exist; an organization must exist before a president for that organization exists. In such cases, Processor and President can be defined as inner classes whereas Computer and Organization are their enclosing classes, respectively. An inner class has full access to all the members, including private members, of its enclosing class.

Java 1.0 did not support inner classes. They were added to Java 1.1 without any changes to the way the JVM used to handle the class files. How was it possible to add a new construct like an inner class without affecting the JVM? Inner classes have been implemented fully with the help of the compiler. The compiler generates a separate class file for each inner class in the compilation unit. The class files for inner classes have the same format as the class files for the top-level classes. Therefore, the JVM treats the class files for inner and top-level classes the same. However, the compiler has to do a lot of behind-the-scenes work to implement inner classes. I discuss some of the work done by the compiler to implement inner classes later in this chapter.

You may ask whether it is possible to achieve everything in Java that is facilitated by inner classes without using them. To some extent, the answer is yes. You can implement most of the functionalities, if not all, provided by inner classes without using inner classes. The compiler generates additional code for an inner class. Instead of using inner class constructs and letting the compiler generate the additional code for you, you can write the same code yourself. This idea sounds easy. However, who wants to reinvent the wheel?

Advantages of Using Inner Classes

The following are some of the advantages of inner classes. Subsequent sections in this chapter explain all of the advantages of inner classes with examples.

- They let you define classes near other classes that will use them. For example, a computer will use a processor, so it is better to define a `Processor` class as an inner class of the `Computer` class.
- They provide an additional namespace to manage class structures. For example, before the introduction of inner classes, a class can only be a member of a package. With the introduction of inner classes, top-level classes, which can contain inner classes, provide an additional namespace.
- Some design patterns are easier to implement using inner classes. For example, the adaptor pattern, enumeration pattern, and state pattern can be easily implemented using inner classes.
- Implementing a callback mechanism is elegant and convenient using inner classes. Lambda expressions in Java 8 offer a better and more concise way of implementing callbacks in Java. I discuss lambda expressions in Chapter 5.
- It helps implement closures in Java.
- You can have a flavor of multiple inheritance of classes using inner classes. An inner class can inherit another class. Thus, the inner class has access to its enclosing class members as well as members of its superclass. Note that accessing members of two or more classes is one of the aims of multiple inheritance, which can be achieved using inner classes. However, just having access to members of two classes is not multiple inheritance in a true sense.

Types of Inner Classes

You can define an inner class anywhere inside a class where you can write a Java statement. There are three types of inner classes. The type of an inner class depends on the location of its declaration and the way it is declared.

- Member inner class
- Local inner class
- Anonymous inner class

Member Inner Class

A member inner class is declared inside a class the same way a member field or a member method for the class is declared. It can be declared as `public`, `private`, `protected`, or package-level. The instance of a member inner class may exist only within the instance of its enclosing class. Consider the example of a member inner class shown in Listing 2-3.

Listing 2-3. Tire Is a Member Inner Class of the Car Class

```
// Car.java
package com.jdojo.innerclasses;

public class Car {
    // A member variable for the Car class
    private final int year;

    // A member inner class named Tire
    public class Tire {
        // A member variable for the Tire class
        private final double radius;

        // A constructor for the Tire class
        public Tire(double radius) {
            this.radius = radius;
        }

        // A member method for the Tire class
        public double getRadius() {
            return radius;
        }
    } // The member inner class declaration ends here

    // A constructor for the Car class
    public Car(int year) {
        this.year = year;
    }

    // A member method for the Car class
    public int getYear() {
        return year;
    }
}
```

In Listing 2-3, Car is a top-level class and Tire is a member inner class of the Car class. The fully qualified name for the Car class is com.jdojo.innerclasses.Car. The fully qualified name of the Tire class is com.jdojo.innerclasses.Car.Tire. The Tire inner class has been declared public. That is, its name can be used outside the Car class. For example, you can declare a variable of Car.Tire type outside the Car class as follows:

```
Car.Tire t;
```

The constructor for the Tire class is also declared public. This means you can create an object of the Tire class outside the Car class. Since Tire is a member inner class of the Car class, you must have an object of the Car class before you can create an object of the Tire class. The new operator is used differently to create an object of a member inner class. The "Creating Objects of Inner Classes" section in this chapter explains how to create objects of an inner member class.

Local Inner Class

A local inner class is declared inside a block. Its scope is limited to the block in which it is declared. Since its scope is always limited to its enclosing block, its declaration cannot use any access modifiers such as `public`, `private`, or `protected`. Typically, a local inner class is defined inside a method. However, it can also be defined inside static initializers, non-static initializers, and constructors. You would use a local inner class when you need to use the class only inside a block. Listing 2-4 shows an example of a local inner class.

Listing 2-4. An Example of a Local Inner Class

```
// TitleList.java
package com.jdojo.innerclasses;

import java.util.ArrayList;
import java.util.Iterator;

public class TitleList {
    private ArrayList<String> titleList = new ArrayList<>();

    public void addTitle (String title) {
        titleList.add(title);
    }

    public void removeTitle(String title) {
        titleList.remove(title);
    }

    public Iterator<String> titleIterator() {
        // A local inner class - TitleIterator
        class TitleIterator implements Iterator<String> {
            int count = 0;

            @Override
            public boolean hasNext() {
                return (count < titleList.size());
            }

            @Override
            public String next() {
                return titleList.get(count++);
            }
        } // Local Inner Class TitleIterator ends here

        // Create an object of the local inner class and return the reference
        TitleIterator titleIterator = new TitleIterator();
        return titleIterator;
    }
}
```

A TitleList object can hold a list of book titles. The addTitle() method adds a title to the list. The removeTitle() method removes a title from the list. The titleIterator() method returns an iterator for the title list. The titleIterator() method defines a local inner class called TitleIterator, which implements the Iterator interface. Note that the TitleIterator class uses the private instance variable titleList of its enclosing class. At the end, the titleIterator() method creates an object of the TitleIterator class and returns the object's reference. Listing 2-5 shows how to use the titleIterator() method of the TitleList class.

Listing 2-5. Using a Local Inner Class

```
// TitleListTest.java
package com.jdojo.innerclasses;

import java.util.Iterator;

public class TitleListTest {
    public static void main(String[] args) {
        TitleList tl = new TitleList();

        // Add three titles
        tl.addTitle("Java 9 Revealed");
        tl.addTitle("Beginning Java 9");
        tl.addTitle("Learn JavaFX 9");

        // Get the iterator
        Iterator<String> iterator = tl.titleIterator();

        // Print all titles using the iterator
        while (iterator.hasNext()) {
            System.out.println(iterator.next());
        }
    }
}
```

```
Java 9 Revealed
Beginning Java 9
Learn JavaFX 9
```

The fact that the scope of a local inner class is limited to its enclosing block has some implications on how to declare a local inner class. Consider the following class declaration:

```
package com.jdojo.innerclasses;

public class SomeTopLevelClass {
    public void someMethod() {
        class SomeLocalInnerClass {
            // Code for SomeLocalInnerClass goes here
        }

        // SomeLocalInnerClass can only be used here
    }
}
```

SomeTopLevelClass is a top-level class. The someMethod() method of SomeTopLevelClass declares the SomeLocalInnerClass local inner class. Note that the name of the local inner class, SomeLocalInnerClass, can only be used inside the someMethod() method. This implies that objects of the SomeLocalInnerClass can only be created and used inside the someMethod() method. This limits the use of a local inner class to only being used inside its enclosing block—in your case the someMethod() method. At this point, it may seem that a local inner class is not very useful. However, Listing 2-5 demonstrated that the code for the local inner class TitleIterator can be called from another class, TitleListTest. This was possible because the local inner class TitleIterator implemented the Iterator interface.

To use a local inner class outside its enclosing block, the local inner class must do one or both of the following:

- Implement a public interface
- Inherit from another public class and override some of its superclass methods

The name of the interface or another class must be available outside the enclosing block that defines the local inner class. Listing 2-4 and Listing 2-5 illustrate the first case where a local inner class implements an interface. Listing 2-6 and Listing 2-7 illustrate the second case, where a local inner class inherits from another public class. Listing 2-8 provides a test class to test a local inner class. The example is trivial. However, it illustrates the concept of how to use a local inner class by inheriting it from another class. Note that you may get a different output when you run the program in Listing 2-8.

Listing 2-6. Declaring a Top-Level Class, Which Is Used as the Superclass for a Local Class

```
// RandomInteger.java
package com.jdojo.innerclasses;

import java.util.Random;

public class RandomInteger {
    protected Random rand = new Random();

    public int getValue() {
        return rand.nextInt();
    }
}
```

Listing 2-7. A Local Inner Class That Inherits from Another Class

```
// RandomLocal.java
package com.jdojo.innerclasses;

public class RandomLocal {
    public RandomInteger getRandomInteger() {
        // A local inner class that inherits from the RandomInteger class
        class RandomIntegerLocal extends RandomInteger {
            @Override
            public int getValue() {
                // Get two random integers and return the average ignoring the fraction part
                long n1 = rand.nextInt();
                long n2 = rand.nextInt();
```

```
                int value = (int) ((n1 + n2)/2);
                return value;
            }
        }

        return new RandomIntegerLocal();
    } // End of the getRandomInteger() method
}
```

Listing 2-8. Testing a Local Inner Class

```
// LocalInnerTest.java
package com.jdojo.innerclasses;

public class LocalInnerTest {
    public static void main(String[] args) {
        // Generate random integers using the RandomInteger class
        RandomInteger rTop = new RandomInteger();
        System.out.println("Random integers using a top-level class:");
        System.out.println(rTop.getValue());
        System.out.println(rTop.getValue());
        System.out.println(rTop.getValue());

        // Generate random integers using the RandomIntegerLocal class
        RandomLocal local = new RandomLocal();
        RandomInteger rLocal = local.getRandomInteger();

        System.out.println("\nRandom integers using a local inner class:");
        System.out.println(rLocal.getValue());
        System.out.println(rLocal.getValue());
        System.out.println(rLocal.getValue());
    }
}
```

```
Random integers using a top-level class:
-947391317
-678893674
-826257063

Random integers using a local inner class:
-120430809
2074796197
-293854159
```

The RandomInteger class contains a getValue() method. The only purpose of the RandomInteger class is to get a random integer using this method. The RandomLocal class is another class, which has a getRandomInteger() method, which declares a local inner class called RandomIntegerLocal, which inherits from the RandomInteger class. The RandomIntegerLocal class overrides its parent's getValue() method. The overridden version of the getValue() method generates two random integers. It returns the average of the two integers. The LocalInnerTest class illustrates the use of the two classes. The name RandomIntegerLocal is not available outside the method in which it is declared because it is a local inner class. Two things are worth noting.

- The getRandomInteger() method of the RandomLocal class declares that it returns an object of the RandomInteger class, not the RandomIntegerLocal class. Inside the method, it is allowed to return an object of the RandomIntegerLocal class because the RandomIntegerLocal local inner class inherits from the RandomInteger class.
- In the LocalInnerTest class, you declared the rLocal reference variable of the RandomInteger type.

  ```
  // Generate random integers using the RandomIntegerLocal class
  RandomLocal local = new RandomLocal();
  RandomInteger rLocal = local.getRandomInteger();
  ```

  However, at runtime, rLocal will receive a reference of the RandomIntegerLocal class. Since getValue() method is overridden in the local inner class, the rLocal object will generate random integers differently.

Anonymous Inner Class

An anonymous inner class is the same as a local inner class with one difference: it does not have a name. Since it does not have a name, it cannot have a constructor. Recall that a constructor name is the same as the class name. You may wonder how you can create objects of an anonymous class if it does not have a constructor. An anonymous class is a one-time class. You define an anonymous class and create its object at the same time. You cannot create more than one object of an anonymous class. Since anonymous class declaration and its object creation are interlaced, an anonymous class is always created using the new operator as part of an expression. The general syntax for creating an anonymous class and its object is as follows:

```
new <interface-name or class-name> (<argument-list>) {
    // The body of the anonymous class goes here
}
```

The new operator is used to create an instance of the anonymous class. It is followed by either an existing interface name or an existing class name. Note that the interface name or class name is not the name for the newly created anonymous class. Rather, it is an existing interface/class name. If an interface name is used, the anonymous class implements that interface. If a class name is used, the anonymous class inherits from that class.

The <argument-list> is used only if the new operator is followed by a class name. It is left empty if the new operator is followed by an interface name. If <argument-list> is present, it contains the actual parameter list for a constructor of the existing class to be invoked. The anonymous class body is written, as usual, inside braces. The previous syntax can be broken into two for simplicity: the first syntax is used when the anonymous class implements an interface and the second one is used when it inherits a class.

```
new Interface() {
    // The body of the anonymous class goes here
}
```

and

```
new Superclass(<argument-list-for-a-superclass-constructor>) {
    // The body of the anonymous class goes here
}
```

Anonymous classes are very powerful. However, the syntax is not easy to read and is somewhat unintuitive. The anonymous class body should be short for better readability. Let's start with a simple example of an anonymous class. You will inherit your anonymous class from the `Object` class, as shown:

```
new Object() {
    // The body of the anonymous class goes here
}
```

This is the simplest anonymous class you can have in Java. It is created and it dies anonymously without making any noise!

Now you want to print a message when an object of an anonymous class is created. An anonymous class does not have a constructor. Where do you place the code to print the message? Recall that all instance initializers of a class are invoked when an object of the class is created. Therefore, you can use an instance initializer to print the message in your case. The following snippet of code shows your anonymous class with an instance initializer:

```
new Object() {
    // An instance initializer
    {
        System.out.println ("Hello from an anonymous class.");
    }
}
```

Listing 2-9 contains the complete code for a simple anonymous class, which prints a message on the standard output.

Listing 2-9. An Anonymous Class Example

```
// HelloAnonymous.java
package com.jdojo.innerclasses;

public class HelloAnonymous {
    public static void main(String[] args) {
        new Object() {
            // An instance initializer
            {
                System.out.println ("Hello from an anonymous class.");
            }
        }; // A semicolon is necessary to end the statement
    }
}
```

```
Hello from an anonymous class.
```

Since an anonymous inner class is the same as a local class without a class name, you can also implement the examples in Listing 2-4 and Listing 2-5 by replacing the local inner classes with anonymous inner classes. Listing 2-10 rewrites the code for the `TitleList` class to use an anonymous class. You will notice the difference in the syntax inside the `titleIterator()` method shown in Listing 2-4 and Listing 2-10. When using an anonymous class, it is important to indent the code properly for better readability. You can test the `TitleListWithInnerClass` by replacing `TitleList` with `TitleListWithInnerClass` in Listing 2-5 and you will get the same output.

Listing 2-10. The TitleList Class Rewritten Using an Anonymous Class as TitleListWithInnerClass

```
// TitleListWithInnerClass.java
package com.jdojo.innerclasses;

import java.util.ArrayList;
import java.util.Iterator;

public class TitleListWithInnerClass {
    private final ArrayList<String> titleList = new ArrayList<>();

    public void addTitle(String title) {
        titleList.add(title);
    }

    public void removeTitle(String title) {
        titleList.remove(title);
    }

    public Iterator<String> titleIterator() {
        // An anonymous class
        Iterator<String> iterator  = new Iterator<String>() {
            int count = 0;

            @Override
            public boolean hasNext() {
                return (count < titleList.size());
            }

            @Override
            public String next() {
                return titleList.get(count++);
            }
        }; // The anonymous inner class ends here

        return iterator;
    }
}
```

The titleIterator() method of TitleListWithInnerClass has two statements. The first statement creates an object of an anonymous class and stores the object's reference in the iterator variable. The second statement returns the object reference stored in the iterator variable. In such cases, you can combine the two statements into one statement. The getRandomInteger() method shown in Listing 2-7 can be rewritten using an anonymous class as follows:

```
public RandomInteger getRandomInteger() {
    // Anonymous inner class that inherits from the RandomInteger class
    return new RandomInteger() {
        public int getValue() {
            // Get two random integers and return the average ignoring the fraction part
            long n1 = rand.nextInt();
            long n2 = rand.nextInt();

            int value = (int)((n1 + n2)/2);
            return value;
        }
    };
}
```

A static Member Class Is Not an Inner Class

A member class defined within the body of another class may be declared static. The following snippet of code declares a top-level class A and a static member class B:

```
package com.jdojo.innerclasses;

public class A {
    // A static member class
    public static class B {
        // The body of class B goes here
    }
}
```

A static member class is not an inner class. It is considered a top-level class. It is also called a nested top-level class. Since it is a top-level class, you do not need an instance of its enclosing class to create its object. An instance of class A and an instance of class B can exist independently because both are top-level classes. A static member class can be declared public, protected, package-level, or private to restrict its accessibility outside its enclosing class.

What is the use of a static member class if it is nothing but another top-level class? There are two advantages of using a static member class:

- A static member class can access the static members of its enclosing class, including the private static members. In your example, if class A has any static members, those static members can be accessed inside class B. However, class B cannot access any instance members of class A because an instance of class B can exist without an instance of class A.

- A package acts like a container for top-level classes by providing a namespace. Within a namespace, all entities must have unique names. Top-level classes having static member classes provide an additional layer of namespaces. A static member class is the direct member of its enclosing top-level class, not a member of the package in which it is declared. In your example, class A is a member of the package `com.jdojo.innerclasses`, whereas class B is a member of class A. The fully qualified name of class A is `com.jdojo.innerclasses.A`. The fully qualified name of class B is `com.jdojo.innerclasses.A.B`. This way, a top-level class can be used to group together related classes defined as its static member classes.

An object of a static member class is created the same way you create an object of a top-level class using the new operator. To create an object of class B, you write

```
A.B bReference = new A.B();
```

Since the simple name of class B is in the scope inside class A, you can use its simple name to create its object inside class A as

```
// This statement appears inside the code for class A
B bReference2 = new B();
```

You can also use the simple name B outside class A by importing the `com.jdojo.innerclasses.A.B` class. However, using the simple name B outside class A is not intuitive. It gives an impression to the reader that class B is a top-level class, not a nested top-level class. You should use A.B for class B outside class A for better readability. Listing 2-11 declares two static member classes, Monitor and Keyboard, which have ComputerAccessory as their enclosing class. Listing 2-12 shows how to create objects of these static member classes.

Listing 2-11. An Example of Declaring static Member Classes

```
// ComputerAccessory.java
package com.jdojo.innerclasses;

public class ComputerAccessory {
    // A static member class - Monitor
    public static class Monitor {
        private final int size;

        public Monitor(int size) {
            this.size = size;
        }

        public String toString() {
            return "Monitor - Size:" + this.size + " inch";
        }
    }

    // A static member class - Keyboard
    public static class Keyboard {
        private final int keys;
```

```
        public Keyboard(int keys) {
            this.keys = keys;
        }

        public String toString() {
            return "Keyboard - Keys:" + this.keys;
        }
    }
}
```

Listing 2-12. An Example of Using static Member Classes

```
// ComputerAccessoryTest.java
package com.jdojo.innerclasses;

public class ComputerAccessoryTest {
    public static void main(String[] args) {
        // Create two monitors
        ComputerAccessory.Monitor m17 = new ComputerAccessory.Monitor(17);
        ComputerAccessory.Monitor m19 = new ComputerAccessory.Monitor(19);

        // Create two Keyboards
        ComputerAccessory.Keyboard k122 = new ComputerAccessory.Keyboard(122);
        ComputerAccessory.Keyboard k142 = new ComputerAccessory.Keyboard(142);

        System.out.println(m17);
        System.out.println(m19);
        System.out.println(k122);
        System.out.println(k142);
    }
}
```

```
Monitor - Size:17 inch
Monitor - Size:19 inch
Keyboard - Keys:122
Keyboard - Keys:142
```

Creating Objects of Inner Classes

Creating objects of a local inner class, an anonymous class, and a static member class is straightforward. Objects of a local inner class are created using the new operator inside the block, which declares the class. An object of an anonymous class is created at the same time the class is declared. A static member class is another type of top-level class. You create objects of a static member class the same way you create objects of a top-level class.

Note that to have an object of a member inner class, a local inner class, and an anonymous class, you must have an object of the enclosing class. In the previous examples of local inner classes and anonymous inner classes, you placed these classes inside instance methods. You had an instance of the enclosing class on which you called those instance methods. Therefore, instances of those local inner classes and anonymous inner classes had the instance of their enclosing classes on which those methods were called. For example, in Listing 2-5, first you created an instance of `TitleList` class and you stored its reference in `t1` as shown:

```
TitleList tl = new TitleList();
```

To get the iterator of `t1`, you called the `titleIterator()` method:

```
Iterator iterator = tl.titleIterator();
```

The method call `t1.titleIterator()` creates an instance of the `TitleIterator` local inner class inside the `titleIterator()` method as

```
TitleIterator titleIterator = new TitleIterator();
```

Here, `titleIterator` is an instance of the local inner class and it exists within `t1`, which is an instance of its enclosing class. This relationship exists for all inner classes, as depicted in Figure 2-1.

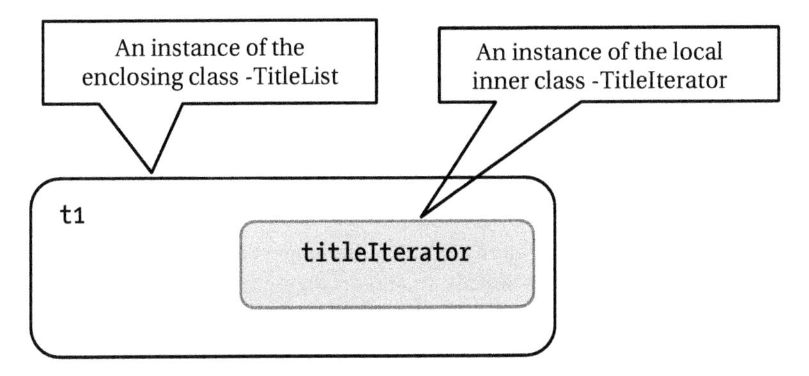

Figure 2-1. *The relationship between an instance of an inner class and an instance of its enclosing class*

■ **Note** There are situations where an instance of the enclosing class is not required for the existence of an instance of a local inner class or an anonymous inner class. This happens when local inner classes or anonymous inner classes are defined inside a static-context, for example, inside a static method or a static initializer. I discuss these cases later in this chapter.

An instance of a member inner class always exists within an instance of its enclosing class. The `new` operator is used to create the instance of the member inner class with a slightly different syntax. The general syntax to create an instance of a member inner class is as follows:

```
outerClassReference.new MemberInnerClassConstructor()
```

Here, outerClassReference is the reference of the enclosing class followed by a dot, which is followed by the new operator. The member inner class's constructor call follows the new operator. Let's revisit the first example of the member inner class, which is as follows:

```
package com.jdojo.innerclasses;

public class Outer {
    public class Inner {
    }
}
```

To create an instance of the Inner member inner class, you must first create an instance of its enclosing class Outer:

```
Outer out = new Outer();
```

Now, you need to use the new operator on the out reference variable to create an object of the Inner class.

```
out.new Inner();
```

To store the reference of the instance of the Inner member inner class in a reference variable, you can write the following statement:

```
Outer.Inner in = out.new Inner();
```

After the new operator, you always use the constructor name, which is the same as the simple class name for the member inner class. Since the new operator is already qualified with the enclosing instance reference (as in out.new), the Java compiler figures out the fully qualified name of the enclosing class name automatically. It is a compile-time error to qualify the inner class constructor with its outer class name while creating an instance of an inner class. The following statement will result in a compile-time error:

```
Outer.Inner in = out.new Outer.Inner(); // A compile-time error
```

Consider the following class declaration with inner classes nested at multiple levels:

```
package com.jdojo.innerclasses;

public class OuterA {
    public class InnerA {
        public class InnerAA {
            public class InnerAAA {
            }
        }
    }
}
```

To create an instance of InnerAAA, you must have an instance of InnerAA. To create an instance of InnerAA, you must have an instance of InnerA. To create an instance of InnerA, you must have an instance of OuterA. Therefore, to create an instance of InnerAAA, you must start by creating an instance of OuterA.

The important point is that to create an instance of a member inner class, you must have an instance of its immediate enclosing class. The following snippet of code illustrates how to create an instance of InnerAAA:

```
OuterA outa = new OuterA();
OuterA.InnerA ina = outa.new InnerA();
OuterA.InnerA.InnerAA inaa = ina.new InnerAA();
OuterA.InnerA.InnerAA.InnerAAA inaaa = inaa.new InnerAAA();
```

Listing 2-13 uses the member inner class called Car.Tire from Listing 2-3 to illustrate the steps needed to create an instance of a member inner class.

Listing 2-13. Creating Objects of a Member Inner Class

```
// CarTest.java
package com.jdojo.innerclasses;

public class CarTest {
    public static void main(String[] args) {
        // Create an instance of Car with year as 2018
        Car c = new Car(2018);

        // Create a Tire for that car of 9.0 inch radius
        Car.Tire t = c.new Tire(9.0);

        System.out.println("Car's year: " + c.getYear());
        System.out.println("Car's tire radius: " + t.getRadius());
    }
}
```

```
Car's year: 2018
Car's tire radius: 9.0
```

Accessing Enclosing Class Members

An inner class has access to all instance members, instance fields, and instance methods of its enclosing class. Listing 2-14 declares a class called Outer and a member inner class called Inner.

Listing 2-14. Accessing Instance Members of the Enclosing Class from an Inner Class

```
// Outer.java
package com.jdojo.innerclasses;

public class Outer {
    private int value = 1116;

    // The Inner class starts here
    public class Inner {
        public void printValue() {
            System.out.println("Inner: value = " + value);
        }
    } // The Inner class ends here
```

```
    // An instance method for the Outer class
    public void printValue() {
        System.out.println("Outer: value = " + value);
    }

    // Another instance method for the Outer class
    public void setValue(int newValue) {
        this.value = newValue;
    }
}
```

The Outer class has a private instance variable called value, which is initialized to 1116. It also defines two instance methods: printValue() and setValue(). The Inner class also defines an instance method called printValue(), which prints the value of the value instance variable of its enclosing class Outer.

Listing 2-15 creates an instance of the Inner class and invokes its printValue() method. The output shows that the inner class instance can access the instance variable value of its enclosing instance out.

Listing 2-15. Testing an Inner Class That Accesses the Instance Members of its Enclosing Class

```
// OuterTest.java
package com.jdojo.innerclasses;

public class OuterTest {
    public static void main(String[] args) {
        Outer out = new Outer();
        Outer.Inner in = out.new Inner();

        // Print the value
        out.printValue();
        in.printValue();

        // Set a new value
        out.setValue(828);

        // Print the value
        out.printValue();
        in.printValue();
    }
}
```

```
Outer: value = 1116
Inner: value = 1116
Outer: value = 828
Inner: value = 828
```

Let's make things a little complex by adding an instance variable named value to the inner class. Let's call the classes Outer2 and Inner2, as shown in Listing 2-16. Note that the instance variables for the Outer2 and Inner2 classes have the same name as value.

Listing 2-16. A Member Inner Class Having the Same Instance Variable Name as Its Enclosing Class

```
// Outer2.java
package com.jdojo.innerclasses;

public class Outer2 {
    // An instance variable for the Outer2 class
    private int value = 1116;

    // The Inner2 class starts here
    public class Inner2 {
        // An instance variable for Inner2 class
        private int value = 1720;

        public void printValue() {
            System.out.println("Inner2: value = " + value);
        }
    } // The Inner2 class ends here

    // An instance method for the Outer2 class
    public void printValue() {
        System.out.println("Outer2: value = " + value);
    }

    // Another instance method for the Outer2 class
    public void setValue(int newValue) {
        this.value = newValue;
    }
}
```

If you run the Outer2Test class as shown in Listing 2-17, the output is different from the output when you ran the OuterTest class in Listing 2-15.

Listing 2-17. Testing an Inner Class That Accesses the Instance Members of Its Enclosing Class

```
// Outer2Test.java
package com.jdojo.innerclasses;

public class Outer2Test {
    public static void main(String[] args) {
        Outer2 out = new Outer2();
        Outer2.Inner2 in = out.new Inner2();

        // Print the value
        out.printValue();
        in.printValue();

        // Set a new value
        out.setValue(828);
```

```
        // Print the value
        out.printValue();
        in.printValue();
    }
}
```

```
Outer2: value = 1116
Inner2: value = 1720
Outer2: value = 828
Inner2: value = 1720
```

Note that the output has changed. When printing the value for the first time, the Outer2 class's instance prints 1116, whereas the Inner2 class's instance prints 1720. After you set the new value using out.setValue(828), the Outer2 class's instance prints the new value of 828, whereas Inner2 class's instance still prints 1720. Why does the output differ?

To fully understand this output, you need to understand the concept of the current instance and the keyword this. So far, you understand that the keyword this refers to the current instance of the class. For example, inside the setValue() instance method of the Outer2 class, this.value refers to the value field of the current instance of the Outer class.

You need to revise the meaning of the keyword this with respect to the instance of a class. The meaning of the keyword this that it refers to the current instance is sufficient as long as you deal with only instances of top-level classes. In dealing with only top-level classes, there is only one current instance in context when a piece of code is executed. In such cases, you can use the keyword this to qualify the instance member names to refer to the instance members of the class. You can also qualify the keyword this with the class name to refer to the instance of the class in context. For example, inside the setValue() method of the Outer2 class, instead of writing this.value, you can also write Outer2.this.value. If the name of a variable used inside a class in a non-static context is an instance variable name, the use of the keyword this is implicit. That is, the use of the simple name of a variable inside a class in a non-static context refers to the instance variable of that class unless that variable hides the name of an instance variable with the same name in its superclass. The use of the keyword this alone and its use qualified with class name is illustrated in Listing 2-18. The program in Listing 2-19 tests the uses of the keyword this concept.

Listing 2-18. Use of the Keyword this Qualified with the Class Name

```
// QualifiedThis.java
package com.jdojo.innerclasses;

public class QualifiedThis {
    // Instance variable - value
    private int value = 828;

    public void printValue() {
        // Print value using simple name of instance variable
        System.out.println("value = " + value);

        // Print value using keyword this
        System.out.println("this.value = " + this.value);

        // Print value using keyword this qualified with the class name
        System.out.println("QualifiedThis.this.value = " + QualifiedThis.this.value);
    }
```

```
    public void printHiddenValue() {
        // Declare a local variable named value, which hides the value instance variable
        int value = 131;

        // Print value using simple name, which refers to the local variable - 131
        System.out.println("value = " + value);

        // Print value using keyword this, which refers to the instance
        // variable value with value 828
        System.out.println("this.value = " + this.value);

        // Print value using keyword this qualified with the class name,
        // which refers to instance variable value as 828
        System.out.println("QualifiedThis.this.value = " + QualifiedThis.this.value);
    }
}
```

Listing 2-19. Testing the Use of the Keyword this Qualified with the Class Name

```
// QualifiedThisTest.java
package com.jdojo.innerclasses;

public class QualifiedThisTest {
    public static void main(String[] args) {
        QualifiedThis qt = new QualifiedThis();
        System.out.println("printValue():");
        qt.printValue();

        System.out.println("\nprintHiddenValue():");
        qt.printHiddenValue();
    }
}
```

```
printValue():
value = 828
this.value = 828
QualifiedThis.this.value = 828

printHiddenValue():
value = 131
this.value = 828
QualifiedThis.this.value = 828
```

You can refer to an instance variable in any of the following three ways, if its name is not hidden:

- Using the simple name, such as value
- Using the simple name qualified with the keyword this, such as this.value
- Using the simple name qualified with the class name and the keyword this, such as QualifiedThis.this.value

If the instance variable name is hidden, you must qualify its name with the keyword this or the class name as well as the keyword this. The code inside an inner class always executes in the context of more than one current instance. The number of current instances depends on the level of nesting of the inner class. Consider the following class declaration:

```
public class TopLevelOuter {
    private int v1 = 100;

    // Here, only v1 is in scope

    public class InnerLevelOne {
        private int v2 = 200;

        // Here, only v1 and v2 are in scope

        public class InnerLevelTwo {
            private int v3 = 300;

            // Here, only v1, v2, and v3 are in scope

            public class InnerLevelThree {
                private int v4 = 400;

                // Here, all v1, v2, v3, and v4 are in scope

            }
        }
    }
}
```

When the code for the InnerLevelThree class is executed, there are four current instances: one for the InnerLevelThree class and one for each of its three enclosing classes. When the code for the InnerLevelTwo class is executed, there are three current instances: one for the InnerLevelTwo class and one for each of its two enclosing classes. When the code for the InnerLevelOne class is executed, there are two current instances: one for the InnerLevelOne class and one for its enclosing class. When the code for the TopLevelOuter class is executed, there is only one current instance because it is a top-level class. When the code for an inner class is executed, all instance members, instance variables, and methods of all current instances are in scope unless hidden by local variable declarations.

The previous example has comments indicating which instance variables are in scope in an inner class. When an instance member is hidden inside an inner class, you can always refer to the hidden member by using the keyword this qualified with the class name. Listing 2-20 is the modified version of Listing 2-16. It illustrates the use of the class name with the keyword this to refer to the instance member of the enclosing class of an inner class. Listing 2-21 contains the code to test the ModifiedOuter2 class.

Listing 2-20. Using the Keyword this Qualified with the Class Name

```
// ModifiedOuter2.java
package com.jdojo.innerclasses;

public class ModifiedOuter2 {
    // An instance variable for the ModifiedOuter2 class
    private int value = 1116;
```

```
    // The Inner class starts here
    public class Inner {
        // An instance variable for the Inner class
        private int value = 1720;

        public void printValue() {
            System.out.println("\nInner - printValue()...");
            System.out.println("Inner: value = " + value);
            System.out.println("Outer: value = " + ModifiedOuter2.this.value);
        }
    } // The Inner class ends here

    // An instance method for the ModifiedOuter2 class
    public void printValue() {
        System.out.println("\nOuter - printValue()...");
        System.out.println("Outer: value = " + value);
    }

    // Another instance method for the ModifiedOuter2 class
    public void setValue(int newValue) {
        System.out.println("\nSetting Outer's value to " + newValue);
        this.value = newValue;
    }
}
```

Listing 2-21. Testing the ModifiedOuter2 Class

```
// ModifiedOuter2Test.java
package com.jdojo.innerclasses;

public class ModifiedOuter2Test {
    public static void main(String[] args) {
        ModifiedOuter2 out = new ModifiedOuter2();
        ModifiedOuter2.Inner in = out.new Inner();

        // Print the value
        out.printValue();
        in.printValue();

        // Set a new value
        out.setValue(828);

        // Print the value
        out.printValue();
        in.printValue();
    }
}
```

```
Outer - printValue()...
Outer: value = 1116

Inner - printValue()...
Inner: value = 1720
Outer: value = 1116

Setting Outer's value to 828

Outer - printValue()...
Outer: value = 828

Inner - printValue()...
Inner: value = 1720
Outer: value = 828
```

■ **Note** Java restricts you from naming the inner class the same as its enclosing class. This is needed for the inner classes to access the hidden members of their enclosing classes using the enclosing class name with the keyword `this`.

Restrictions on Accessing Local Variables

A local inner class is declared inside a block—typically inside a method of a class. A local inner class can access the instance variables of its enclosing class as well as the local variables, which are in scope. The instance of an inner class exists within an instance of its enclosing class. Therefore, accessing the instance variables of the enclosing class inside a local inner class is not a problem because they exist throughout the lifecycle of the instance of the local inner class. However, the local variables in a method exist only during the execution of that method. All local variables become inaccessible when method execution is over. Java makes a copy of the local variables that are used inside a local inner class and stores that copy along with the inner class object. However, to guarantee that the values of the local variables can be reproduced when accessed inside the local inner class code after the method call is over, Java puts a restriction that the local variables must be *effectively final*. An effectively final variable is a variable whose value does not change after it is initialized. One way to have an effectively final variable is to declare the variable `final`. Another way is not to change its value after it is initialized. Therefore, a local variable or an argument to a method must be effectively final if it is used inside a local inner class. This restriction also applies to an anonymous inner class declared inside a method.

■ **Tip** Prior to Java 8, a local variable must be declared `final` if it is accessed inside a local inner class or an anonymous class. Java 8 changed this rule: the local variable need not be declared `final`, but it should be effectively final.

The program in Listing 2-22 demonstrates the rules for accessing local variables inside a local inner class. The main() method declares two local variables called x and y. Both variables are effectively final. The variable x is never changed after it is initialized and the variable y cannot be changed because it is declared as final.

Listing 2-22. Accessing Local Variables Inside Local Classes

```
// AccessingLocalVariables.java
package com.jdojo.innerclasses;

public class AccessingLocalVariables {
    public static void main(String... args) {
        int x = 100;
        final int y = 200;

        class LocalInner {
            void print() {
                // Accessing the local variable x is fine as it is effectively final.
                System.out.println("x = " + x);

                // The local variable y is effectively final as it has been declared final.
                System.out.println("y = " + y);
            }
        }

        /* Uncommenting the following statement will make the variable x no longer
           an effectively final variable and the LocalInner class will not compile.
         */
        // x = 100;
        LocalInner li = new LocalInner();
        li.print();
    }
}
```

```
x = 100
y = 200
```

Inner Class and Inheritance

An inner class can inherit from another inner class, a top-level class, or its enclosing class. For example, in the following snippet of code, inner class C inherits from inner class B; inner class D inherits from its enclosing top-level class A, and inner class F inherits from inner class A.B:

```
public class A {
    public class B {
    }

    public class C extends B {
    }
```

```
    public class D extends A {
    }
}

public class E extends A {
    public class F extends B {
    }
}
```

The situation becomes trickier when you want to inherit a top-level class from an inner class:

```
public class G extends A.B {
    // This code won't compile
}
```

Before I discuss why this code will not compile, recall that you must have an instance of the enclosing class before you can create an instance of an inner class. In this case, if you want to create an instance of class G (using new G()), you must also create (indirectly though) an instance of A.B, because A.B is its parent class. Here, A.B is an inner class. Therefore, in order to create an instance of the inner class A.B, you must have an instance of its enclosing class A. Therefore, you must create an instance of class A before you can create an instance of class G. You must also make the instance of class A available to class G so that it can be used as the enclosing instance when A.B instance is created while creating an instance of its subclass G. The Java compiler enforces this rule. In this case, you must declare a constructor for class G, which accepts an instance of class A and calls the parent's constructor on that instance. The previous class declaration for class G must be changed to the following:

```
public class G extends A.B {
    public G(A a) {
        a.super(); // Must be the first statement
    }
}
```

To create an instance of class G, you should follow two steps:

```
// Create an instance of class A first
A a = new A();

// Pass class A's instance to G's constructor
G g = new G(a);
```

You can combine these two statements into one:

```
G g = new G(new A());
```

Note that inside G's constructor you have added one statement: a.super(). The compiler requires this to be the first statement. At the time of compilation, the compiler modifies a.super() to super(a). Here, super(a) means call the constructor of its parent, which is class B, passing the reference of class A. In other words, with the coding rule, the Java compiler ensures that the constructor of class B gets a reference to its enclosing class A when the instance of class B is created.

Let's change the declaration of the class E in the example to the following:

```
// The following code won't compile
public class E {
    public class F extends A.B {
    }
}
```

This code will not compile. To create an instance of the inner class F, you need an instance of A.B, which in turn requires an instance of class A. In the earlier case, E was inherited from A. Therefore, it was guaranteed that an instance of A exists when an instance of E is created. An instance of F can only be created when you have an instance of its ancestor's A.B's enclosing class A. When E inherited from A, it was guaranteed, when an instance of E was created, you always had an instance of class A. To make this code work, you need to apply the same logic as you did for class G. You need to declare a constructor for class F that takes an instance of class A as its parameter, like so:

```
// The following code will compile
public class E {
    public class F extends A.B {
        public F(A a) {
            a.super(); // Must be the first statement
        }
    }
}
```

No static Members in an Inner Class

The keyword static in Java makes a construct a top-level construct. Therefore, you cannot declare any static members (fields, methods, or initializers) for an inner class. The following code will not compile because inner class B declares a static field DAYS_IN_A_WEEK:

```
public class A {
    public class B {
        // Cannot have the following declaration
        public static int DAYS_IN_A_WEEK = 7; // A compile-time error
    }
}
```

However, it is allowed to have static fields in an inner class that are compile-time constants.

```
public class A {
    public class B {
        // Can have a compile-time static constant field
        public final static int DAYS_IN_A_WEEK = 7; // OK

        // Cannot have the following declaration, because it is not
        // a compile-time constant, even though it is final
        public final static String str = new String("Hello");
    }
}
```

■ **Tip** A member interface and a member enum are implicitly static and, therefore, they cannot be declared inside an inner class.

Generated Class Files for Inner Classes

Each inner class is compiled into a separate class file. The names of the generated class files follow a naming convention. The class file name format for a member inner class and a nested class is as follows:

```
<outer-class-name>$<member-or-nested-class-name>
```

The format for the class file name for a local inner class is as follows:

```
<outer-class-name>$<a-number><local-inner-class-name>
```

The format for the class file name for an anonymous class is as follows:

```
<outer-class-name>$<a-number>
```

`<a-number>` in a class file name is a number that is generated sequentially starting from 1 to avoid any name conflicts. The following nine class files, one for the top-level and eight for inner classes, are generated when you compile the source code in Listing 2-23:

- `InnerClassFile.class`
- `InnerClassFile$MemberInnerClass.class`
- `InnerClassFile$NestedClass.class`
- `InnerClassFile$1$LocalInnerClass.class`
- `InnerClassFile$1$LocalInnerClass$LocalInnerClass2.class`
- `InnerClassFile$1$AnotherLocalInnerClass.class`
- `InnerClassFile$1.class`
- `InnerClassFile$2$AnotherLocalInnerClass.class`
- `InnerClassFile$1$TestLocalClass.class`

Listing 2-23. An Example for Generating File Names for Inner Classes

```
// InnerClassFile.java
package com.jdojo.innerclasses;

public class InnerClassFile {
    public class MemberInnerClass {
    }

    public static class NestedClass {
    }
```

```
    public void testMethod1() {
        // A local class
        class LocalInnerClass {
            // A local class
            class LocalInnerClass2 {
            }
        }

        // A local class
        class AnotherLocalInnerClass {
        }

        // Anonymous Inner class
        new Object() {
        };
    }

    public void testMethod2() {
        // A local class. Its name is the same as a local class in testMethod1() method
        class AnotherLocalInnerClass {
        }

        // Another local class
        class TestLocalClass {
        }
    }
}
```

Inner Classes and the Compiler Magic

Inner classes are implemented with the help of the compiler. The compiler does all the magic behind the scenes for the features provided by inner classes by altering your code and adding new code. Here is the simplest example of an inner class:

```
public class Outer {
    public class Inner {
    }
}
```

When the `Outer` class is compiled, two class files are generated: `Outer.class` and `Outer$Inner.class`. If you decompile these two class files, you get the following output. You can use any available decompilers for class files. Some Java class file decompilers are available free on the Internet. You can also use the `javap` tool, which ships with the JDK, to decompile class files. The `javap` utility is located on your machine in the `JAVA_HOME\bin` folder, where `JAVA_HOME` is the JDK installation folder.

```
// Decompiled code from Outer.class file
public class Outer {
    public Outer() {
    }
}
```

```
// Decompiled code from Outer$Inner.class file
public class Outer$Inner {
    final Outer this$0;
    public Outer$Inner(Outer outer) {
        this$0 = outer;
        super();
    }
}
```

The following points may be observed in the decompiled code:

- As usual, the compiler provided a default constructor for the `Outer` class because you did not provide one in your source code.
- The `Inner` class definition is removed entirely from the body of the `Outer` class. Therefore, the `Inner` class becomes a class that stands by itself in its compiled form. Its class name is changed to `Outer$Inner` per the rules discussed earlier in this chapter. By just looking at the definition of only the `Outer$Inner` class, no one can notice that `Outer$Inner` is an inner class.
- In the `Inner` class definition (the `Outer$Inner` class in the decompiled code), the compiler added an instance variable named `this$0`, which is of its enclosing class type `Outer` (see the declaration "`final Outer this$0;`" in the decompiled code).

Since you did not include any constructors for the `Inner` class, you were expecting that the compiler would add a default constructor. However, that is not the case. In the case of an inner class, if you do not provide a constructor, the compiler includes a constructor, which has one argument. The argument type is the same as its enclosing class. If you include a constructor for an inner class, the compiler adds one argument to all the constructors you have included. The argument is added in the beginning of the constructor's arguments list. The argument type is the same as the enclosing class type. Consider the following declaration of the `Inner` class:

```
public class Outer {
    public class Inner {
        public Inner(int a) {
        }
    }
}
```

Now the compiler will add an extra argument to its constructor, as shown:

```
public class Outer$Inner {
    final Outer this$0;
    public Outer$Inner(Outer outer, int i) {
       this$0 = outer;
       super();
   }
}
```

The constructor's body for the compiled `Inner` class is as follows:

```
this$0 = outer;
super();
```

The first statement assigns the constructor's argument, which is the reference to its enclosed class instance, to the instance variable. The second statement calls the default constructor of the parent of the Inner class, which is the Object class in this case. Recall that if there is a call to the parent's constructor inside a constructor of a class, it must be the first statement inside the constructor. However, it is the second statement for the synthesized inner class, as shown previously. Can you think of a reason why the call to the ancestor's constructor is placed as the second statement as opposed to the first statement?

Let's add an instance variable to the outer class and access that instance variable inside the inner class. To keep the example simple, you have added a new getValue() method to the Inner class in order to access the Outer class's instance variable called dummy. The modified code is as follows:

```
public class Outer {
    int dummy = 101;

    public class Inner {
        public int getValue() {
            // Access Outer's class dummy field
            int x = dummy + 200;
            return x;
        }
    }
}
```

The decompiled code for the Outer.class and Outer$Inner.class files are as follows:

```
// Decompiled code from the Outer.class file
public class Outer {
    int dummy = 0;

    public Outer() {
        dummy = 101;
    }
}

// The decompiled code from the Outer$Inner.class file
public class Outer$Inner {
    final Outer this$0;

    public Outer$Inner(Outer outer) {
        this$0 = outer;
        super();
    }

    public int getValue() {
        int x = this$0.dummy + 200;
        return x;
    }
}
```

Note the use of this$0.dummy to access the instance variable of the Outer class inside the getValue() method of the Inner class. The dummy instance variable in the Outer class has a package-level access. Since an inner class is always part of the same package as its enclosing class, this method of referring to the instance variable of the Outer class from outside works fine. However, if the instance variable dummy is declared private, the Outer$Inner class code cannot refer to it directly as it did in the previous example. The compiler uses a different way to access the private instance variable of the outer class from an inner class. The following is the modified code and the corresponding decompiled code for the Outer and Inner classes:

```
// Modified Outer class code with dummy as private instance variable
public class Outer {
    private int dummy = 101; // Declare dummy as private

    public class Inner {
        public int getValue() {
            int x = dummy + 200; // Access Outer's dummy field
            return x;
        }
    }
}

// Decompiled code from the Outer.class file
public class Outer {
    private int dummy = 0;

    public Outer() {
        dummy = 101;
    }

    // A method added by the compiler to access the dummy private field
    static int access$000(Outer outer) {
        return outer.dummy;
    }
}

// Decompiled code from the Outer$Inner.class file
public class Outer$Inner {
    final Outer this$0;
    public Outer$Inner(Outer outer) {
        this$0 = outer;
        super();
    }

    public int getValue() {
        int x = Outer.access$000(this$0) + 200;
        return x;
    }
}
```

Note that the compiler added a new static method to the Outer class, which is declared as

```
static int access$000(Outer outer)
```

The compiler adds a new method to the enclosing class for each of its private instance variables accessed inside the inner class. The method, `access$000()`, is known as a synthetic method because it is synthesized by the compiler. The compiler sets a flag for each synthetic method in order to prevent direct access to these methods from the source code. Another difference for you to note is that inside the `getValue()` method of the `Inner` class the compiler has used the synthetic method `Outer.access$000(this$0)` to access the `Outer` class's `dummy` instance variable.

The compiler does many things to implement inner classes. To learn more about the implementation details of inner classes, you can write inner classes; compile the code to generate class files; and then, decompile the generated class files to see the work done by the compiler.

Closures and Callbacks

In functional programming, a higher order function is an anonymous function that can be treated as a data object. That is, it can be stored in a variable and passed around from one context to another. It might be invoked in a context that did not necessarily define it. Note that a higher order function is an anonymous function, so the invoking context does not have to know its name. A closure is a higher order function packaged with its defining environment. A closure carries with it the variables in scope when it was defined, and it can access those variables even when it is invoked in a context other than the context in which it was defined.

In object-oriented programming, a function is called a method and it is always part of a class. An anonymous class in Java allows a method to be packaged in an object that can be treated much as a higher order function. The object can be stored in a variable and passed around from one method to another. The method defined in an anonymous class can be invoked in a context other than the one in which it was defined. However, one important difference between a higher order function and a method defined in an anonymous class is that a higher order function is anonymous, whereas a method in an anonymous class is named. The invoker of the anonymous class method must know the method name. An anonymous class carries with it its environment. An anonymous class can use the local variables and the parameters of a method inside which it is defined. However, Java places a restriction that local variables and parameters to the method must be effectively final if they are accessed inside an anonymous class.

The callback mechanism can be implemented using anonymous classes and interfaces. In the simplest form, you register an object, which implements an interface. A particular method is called (back) on the registered object later. Let's define an interface named `Callable` with one method named `call()`, as shown in Listing 2-24.

Listing 2-24. A Callable Interface to Implement a Callback Mechanism

```
// Callable.java
package com.jdojo.innerclasses;

public interface Callable {
    void call();
}
```

The `CallbackTest` class in Listing 2-25 illustrates the implementation details of the callback mechanism. The `main()` method creates three `Callable` objects using anonymous inner classes and registers them to be called later. The `register()` method registers a `Callable` object and stores the object's reference in an `ArrayList` so that these object's `call()` method can be executed later. The `callback()` method calls back all registered objects by invoking their `call()` methods.

Listing 2-25. Implementing the Callback Mechanism Using Anonymous Classes

```
// CallbackTest.java
package com.jdojo.innerclasses;

import java.util.ArrayList;

public class CallbackTest {
    // To hold all registered Callable objects
    private final ArrayList<Callable> callableList = new ArrayList<>();

    public static void main(String[] args) {
        CallbackTest cbt = new CallbackTest();

        // Create three Callable objects and register them
        cbt.register(new Callable() {
            @Override
            public void call() {
                System.out.println("Called #1");
            }
        });

        cbt.register(new Callable() {
            @Override
            public void call() {
                System.out.println("Called #2");
            }
        });

        cbt.register(new Callable() {
            @Override
            public void call() {
                System.out.println("Called #3");
            }
        });

        // Callback all the registered Callable objects
        cbt.callback();
    }

    private void callback() {
        // Callback all the registered Callable objects
        for (Callable c: callableList) {
            c.call();
        }
    }

    public void register(Callable c) {
        this.callableList.add(c);
    }
}
```

```
Called #1
Called #2
Called #3
```

The callback mechanism described in this section is used extensively in Java when working with GUI applications developed using Swing and JavaFX.

■ **Note** Java 8 introduced lambda expressions that make working with callbacks more concise. I discuss lambda expressions in Chapter 5.

Defining Inner Classes in static Contexts

You can also define an inner class in a static context such as inside a static method or a static initializer. There is no current instance of the outer class present in a static context, and therefore such an inner class cannot access instance fields of the outer class. However, all static field members are accessible to such an inner class.

```
public class Outer {
    static int k = 1001;
    int m = 9008;

    public static void staticMethod() {
        // Class Inner is defined in a static context
        class Inner {
            int j = k; // OK. Referencing static field k
            int n = m; // An error. Referencing non-static field m
        }
    }
}
```

Summary

Classes declared inside the body of another class are called inner classes. The class within which the inner class is declared is known as the enclosing class. Inner classes have direct access to all members of their enclosing class. Instances of inner classes exist only within an instance of the enclosing class, except when they are declared in a static context, for example, inside a static method.

There are three types of inner classes: member inner class, local inner class, and anonymous inner class. Inner classes are declared in non-static contexts. A member inner class is declared inside a class the same way a member field or a member method for the class is declared. It can be declared as `public`, `private`, `protected`, or package-level. A local inner class is declared inside a block. Its scope is limited to the block in which it is declared. An anonymous inner class is the same as a local inner class with one difference: it does not have a name. An anonymous class is a one-shot class; it is declared and an object of the class is created at the same time.

A class declared inside another class as a static member is simply called a nested class. A nested class has access to the static members of the enclosing class.

Inside an inner class, the keyword this refers to the current instance of the inner class. To refer to the current instance of the enclosing class, you need to qualify the keyword this with the class name of the enclosing class.

You cannot declare a static member for inner classes. This implies that interfaces and enums cannot be declared as members for inner classes.

QUESTIONS AND EXERCISES

1. What is an inner class? Differentiate between member, local, and anonymous inner classes.

2. What is the fully qualified name of the inner class B, which is declared as follows?

```
// A.java
package com.jdojo.innerclasses.exercises;

public class A {
   public class B {
   }
}
```

3. Consider the following declaration for top-level class named Cup and a member inner class named Handle:

```
// Cup.java
package com.jdojo.innerclasses.exercises;

public class Cup {
   public class Handle {
       public Handle() {
          System.out.println("Created a handle for the cup");
       }
   }

   public Cup() {
       System.out.println("Created a cup");
   }
}
```

Complete the code in the main() method of the following CupTest class that will create an instance of the Cup.Handle inner class:

```
// CupTest.java
package com.jdojo.innerclasses.exercises;
```

```
public class CupTest {
   public static void main(String[] args) {
       // Create a Cup
       Cup c = new Cup();

       // Create a Handle
       Cup.Handle h = /* Your code goes here */ ;
   }
}
```

4. What will be the output when the following `Outer` class is run?

```
// Outer.java
package com.jdojo.innerclasses.exercises;

public class Outer {
    private final int value = 19680112;

    public class Inner {
        private final int value = 19690919;
            public void print() {
            System.out.println("Inner: value = " + value);
            System.out.println("Inner: this.value = " + this.value);
            System.out.println("Inner: Inner.this.value = " +
                                Inner.this.value);
            System.out.println("Inner: Outer.this.value = " +
                                Outer.this.value);
        }
    }

    public void print() {
        System.out.println("Outer: value = " + value);
        System.out.println("Outer: this.value = " + this.value);
        System.out.println("Outer: Outer.this.value = " +
                           Outer.this.value);
    }

    public static void main(String[] args) {
        Outer out = new Outer();
        Inner in = out.new Inner();
        out.print();
        in.print();
    }
}
```

5. The following declaration of an `AnonymousTest` class does not compile. Describe the reasons and steps you might take to fix the error.

```
// AnonymousTest.java
package com.jdojo.innerclasses.exercises;

public class AnonymousTest {
   public static void main(String[] args) {
       int x = 100;

       Object obj = new Object() {
           {
               System.out.println("Inside. x = " + x);
           }
       };

       x = 300;
       System.out.println("Outside. x = " + x);
   }
}
```

6. Consider the following declaration for a top-level class `A` and a member inner class `B`:

```
// A.java
package com.jdojo.innerclasses.exercises;

public class A {
    public class B {
        public B() {
            System.out.println("B is created.");
        }
    }

    public A() {
        System.out.println("A is created.");
    }
}
```

Consider the following incomplete declaration of class `C`, which inherits from the inner class `A.B`:

```
// C.java
package com.jdojo.innerclasses.exercises;

public class C extends A.B {
```

```
    /* Define a constructor for class C here */

    public static void main(String[] args) {
        C c = /* Your code goes here */;
    }
}
```

Add an appropriate constructor for class C and complete the statement in the main() method. When class C is run, it should print the following to the standard output:

```
A is created.
B is created.
C is created.
```

7. Which of the following is true about an anonymous inner class?

   a. It can inherit from one class and implement one interface.

   b. It can inherit from one class and implement multiple interfaces.

   c. It can inherit from one class or implement one interface.

   d. It can implement multiple interfaces, but inherits from only one class.

8. How many class files will be generated when the following declaration of the Computer class is compiled? List the names of all generated class files.

```
// Computer.java
package com.jdojo.innerclasses.exercises;

public class Computer {
    public class Mouse {
        public class Button {
        }
    }

    public static void main(String[] args) {
        Object obj = new Object() {
        };

        System.out.println(obj.hashCode());
    }
}
```

9. The following declaration of class H does not compile. Point out the problem and suggest a solution.

```
// H.java
package com.jdojo.innerclasses.exercises;

public class H {
   private int x = 100;

   public static class J {
       private int y = x * 2;
   }
}
```

10. Consider the following declaration of a top-level class P and a nested static class Q:

```
// P.java
package com.jdojo.innerclasses.exercises;

public class P {
   public static class Q {
       {
            System.out.println("Hello from Q.");
       }
   }
}
```

Complete the `main()` method of the following `PTest` class that will create an object of the nested static class Q. When class `PTest` is run, it should print a message `"Hello from Q."` to the standard output.

```
// PTest.java
package com.jdojo.innerclasses.exercises;

public class PTest {
   public static void main(String[] args) {
       P.Q q = /* Your code goes here */;
   }
}
```

CHAPTER 3

Reflection

In this chapter, you will learn:

- What reflection is
- What a class loader is and about the built-in class loaders
- How to use reflection to get information about classes, constructors, methods, etc. at runtime
- How to access fields of an object and a class using reflection
- How to create objects of a class using reflection
- How to invoke methods of a class using reflection
- How to create arrays using reflection

Most example programs in this chapter are a member of a `jdojo.reflection` module, as declared in Listing 3-1. I use more modules in this chapter, which I show later.

Listing 3-1. The Declaration of a jdojo.reflection Module

```
// module-info.java
module jdojo.reflection {
    exports com.jdojo.reflection;
}
```

What Is Reflection?

Reflection is the ability of a program to query and modify its state "as data" during the execution of the program. The ability of a program to query or obtain information about itself is known as *introspection*. The ability of a program to modify its execution state, modify its own interpretation or its meaning, or add new behaviors to the program as it is executing is called *intercession*. Reflection is further divided into two categories:

- Structural reflection
- Behavioral reflection

The ability of a program to query about the implementation of its data and code is called structural introspection, whereas its ability to modify or create new data structure and code is called structural intercession.

K. Sharan, *Java Language Features*, https://doi.org/10.1007/978-1-4842-3348-1_3

The ability of a program to obtain information about its runtime environment is called behavioral introspection, whereas its ability to modify the runtime environment is called behavioral intercession.

Providing the ability to a program to query or modify its state requires a mechanism for encoding the execution state as data. In other words, the program should be able to represent its execution state as data elements (as objects in objected-oriented languages such as Java) so that it can be queried and modified. The process of encoding the execution state into data is called *reification*. A programming language is called reflective if it provides the programs with reflection capability.

Reflection in Java

The support for reflection in Java is mostly limited to introspection. It supports intercession in a very limited form. The introspection features provided by Java let you obtain class information about an object at runtime. Java also lets you obtain information about the fields, methods, modifiers, and the superclass of a class at runtime.

The intercession features provided by Java let you create an instance of a class whose name is not known until runtime, invoke methods on such instances, and get/set its fields. However, Java does not allow you to change the data structure at runtime. For example, you cannot add a new field or a method to an object at runtime. All fields of an object are always determined at compile-time. Examples of behavioral intercession are the ability to change the method execution at runtime or add a new method to a class at runtime. Java does not provide any of these intercession features. That is, you cannot change a class's method code at runtime to change its execution behavior; neither can you add a new method to a class at runtime.

Java provides reification by providing an object representation for a class and its methods, constructors, fields, etc. at runtime. In most cases, Java does not support reification for generic types. Java 5 added support for generic types. Refer to Chapter 4 for more details on generic types. A program can work on the reified objects in order to get information about the runtime execution. For example, you have been using the object of `java.lang.Class` class to get the information about the class of an object. A `Class` object is the reification of the bytecode for the class of an object. When you want to gather information about the class of an object, you do not have to worry about the bytecode of the class from which the object was instantiated. Rather, Java provides the reification of the bytecode as an object of the `Class` class.

The reflection facility in Java is provided through the reflection API. Most of the reflection API classes and interfaces are in the `java.lang.reflect` package. The `Class` class, which is central to the reflection in Java, is in the `java.lang` package. Some of the frequently used classes in reflection are listed in Table 3-1.

Table 3-1. *Commonly Used Classes in Reflection*

Class Name	Description
`Class`	An object of this class represents a single class loaded by a class loader in the JVM.
`Field`	An object of this class represents a single field of a class or an interface. The field represented by this object may be a static field or an instance field.
`Constructor`	An object of this class represents a single constructor of a class.
`Method`	An object of this class represents a method of a class or an interface. The method represented by this object may be a class method or an instance method.
`Modifier`	This class has static methods that are used to decode the access modifiers for a class and its members.
`Parameter`	An object of this class represents a method's parameter.
`Array`	This class provides static methods that are used to create arrays at runtime.

Some of the things you can do using the reflection features in Java are as follows:

- If you have an object reference, you can determine the class name of the object.
- If you have a class name, you can know its full description, for example, its package name, its access modifiers, etc.
- If you have a class name, you can determine the methods defined in the class, their return type, access modifiers, parameters type, parameter names, etc. The support for parameter names was added in Java 8.
- If you have a class name, you can determine all field descriptions of the class.
- If you have a class name, you can determine all constructors defined in the class.
- If you have a class name, you can create an object of the class using one of its constructors.
- If you have an object reference, you can invoke its method knowing just the method's name and method's parameter types.
- You can get or set the state of an object at runtime.
- You can create an array of a type dynamically at runtime and manipulate its elements.

Loading a Class

The `Class<T>` class is central to reflection in Java. The `Class<T>` class is a generic class. It takes a type parameter, which is the type of the class represented by the `Class` object. For example, `Class<String>` represents the class object for the `String` class. `Class<?>` represents a class type whose class is unknown.

The `Class` class lets you discover everything about a class at runtime. An object of the `Class` class represents a class in a program at runtime. When you create an object in your program, Java loads the class's byte code and creates an object of the `Class` class to represent the byte code. Java uses that `Class` object to create any object of that class. No matter how many objects of a class you create in your program, Java creates only one `Class` object for each class loaded by a class loader in a JVM from one module. Each class from a module is also loaded only once by a particular class loader. In a JVM, a class is uniquely identified by its fully qualified name, its class loader, and its module. If two different class loaders load the same class, the two loaded classes are considered two different classes and their objects are not compatible with each other.

You can get the reference to the `Class` object of a class in one of the followings ways:

- Using class literal
- Using the `getClass()` method of the `Object` class
- Using the `forName()` static method of the `Class` class

Using Class Literals

A class literal is the class name or interface name followed by a dot and the word "class." For example, if you have a class `Test`, its class literal is `Test.class` and you can write

```
Class<Test> testClass = Test.class;
```

Note that the class literal is always used with a class name, not with an object reference. The following statement to get the class reference is invalid:

```
Test t = new Test();
Class<Test> testClass = t.class; // A compile-time error. Must use Test.class
```

You can also get the class object for primitive data types and the keyword `void` using class literals as `boolean.class`, `byte.class`, `char.class`, `short.class`, `int.class`, `long.class`, `float.class`, `double.class`, and `void.class`. Each wrapper class for these primitive data types has a static field named `TYPE`, which has the reference to the class object of the primitive data type it represents. Therefore, `int.class` and `Integer.TYPE` refer to the same class object and the expression `int.class == Integer.TYPE` evaluates to `true`. Table 3-2 shows the class literals for all primitive data types and the `void` keyword.

Table 3-2. *Class Literals for Primitive Data Types and the void Keyword*

Data Type	Primitive Class Literal	Wrapper Class static Field
boolean	boolean.class	Boolean.TYPE
byte	byte.class	Byte.TYPE
char	char.class	Character.TYPE
short	short.class	Short.TYPE
int	int.class	Integer.TYPE
long	long.class	Long.TYPE
float	float.class	Float.TYPE
double	double.class	Double.TYPE
void	void.class	Void.TYPE

Using the Object::getClass() Method

The `Object` class contains a `getClass()` method, , which returns the reference to the `Class` object of the class of the object. This method is available in every class in Java because every class in Java, explicitly or implicitly, inherits the `Object` class. The method is declared final, so no descendant class can override it. For example, if you have `testRef` as a reference to an object of class `Test`, you can get the reference to the `Class` object of the `Test` class as follows:

```
Test testRef = new Test();
Class<Test> testClass = testRef.getClass();
```

Using the Class::forName() Method

The `Class` class has a `forName()` static method, which loads a class and returns the reference to its `Class` object. It is an overloaded method. Its declarations are as follows:

- `Class<?> forName(String className) throws ClassNotFoundException`
- `Class<?> forName(String className, boolean initialize, ClassLoader loader) throws ClassNotFoundException`
- `Class<?> forName(Module module, String className)`

The forName(String className) method takes the fully qualified name of the class to be loaded. It loads the class, initializes it, and returns the reference to its Class object. If the class is already loaded, it simply returns the reference to the Class object of that class.

The forName(String className, boolean initialize, ClassLoader loader) method gives you options to initialize or not to initialize the class when it is loaded, and which class loader should load the class. The first two versions of the method throw a ClassNotFoundException if the class could not be loaded.

The forName(Module module, String className) method loads the class with the specified className in the specified module without initializing the loaded class. If the class is not found, the method returns null. This method was added to the Class class in JDK9.

To load a class named pkg1.Test, you would write:

```
Class testClass = Class.forName("pkg1.Test");
```

To get a Class object reference using the forName() method, you do not have to know the name of the class until runtime. The forName(String className) method initializes the class if it is not already initialized, whereas the use of a class literal does not initialize the class. When a class is initialized, all its static initializers are executed and all static fields are initialized. Listing 3-2 lists a Bulb class with only one static initializer, which prints a message on the console. Listing 3-3 uses various methods to load and initialize the Bulb class.

Listing 3-2. A Bulb Class to Demonstrate Initialization of a Class

```
// Bulb.java
package com.jdojo.reflection;

public class Bulb {
    static {
        // This will execute when this class is loaded and initialized
        System.out.println("Loading class Bulb...");
    }
}
```

Listing 3-3. Testing Class Loading and Initialization

```
// BulbTest.java
package com.jdojo.reflection;

public class BulbTest {
    public static void main(String[] args) {
        /* Uncomment only one of the following statements at a time.
           Observe the output to see the difference in the way the Bulb
           class is loaded and initialized.
         */

        BulbTest.createObject();
        // BulbTest.forNameVersion1();
        // BulbTest.forNameVersion2();
        // BulbTest.forNameVersion3();
        // BulbTest.classLiteral();
    }
```

```
    public static void classLiteral() {
        // Will load the class, but won't initialize it.
        Class<Bulb> c = Bulb.class;
    }

    public static void forNameVersion1() {
        try {
            String className = "com.jdojo.reflection.Bulb";

            // Will load and initialize the class
            Class c = Class.forName(className);
        } catch (ClassNotFoundException e) {
            System.out.println(e.getMessage());
        }
    }

    public static void forNameVersion2() {
        try {
            String className = "com.jdojo.reflection.Bulb";
            boolean initialize = false;

            // Get the classloader for the current class
            ClassLoader cLoader = BulbTest.class.getClassLoader();

            // Will load, but not initialize the class, because we have
            // set the initialize variable to false
            Class c = Class.forName(className, initialize, cLoader);
        } catch (ClassNotFoundException e) {
            System.out.println(e.getMessage());
        }
    }

    public static void forNameVersion3() {
        String className = "com.jdojo.reflection.Bulb";

        // Get the module reference for the current class
        Module m = BulbTest.class.getModule();

        // Will load, but not initialize, the class
        Class c = Class.forName(m, className);

        if(c == null) {
            System.out.println("The bulb class was not loaded.");
        } else {
            System.out.println("The bulb class was loaded.");
        }

    }
```

```
    public static void createObject() {
        // Will load and initialize the Bulb class
        new Bulb();
    }
}
```

```
Loading class Bulb...
```

Class Loaders

At runtime, every type is loaded by a class loader, which is represented by an instance of the `java.lang.ClassLoader` class. You can get the reference of the class loader of a type by using the `getClassLoader()` method of the `Class` class. The following snippet of code shows how to get the class loader of the `Bulb` class:

```
Class<Bulb> cls = Bulb.class;
ClassLoader loader = cls.getClassLoader();
```

Class loaders have changed a bit in JDK9. However, the code behavior of class loading and class loaders remains the same in JDK9. The following sections describe the class loaders in JDK8 and JDK9.

Class Loaders in JDK8

Prior to JDK9, the runtime used three class loaders to load classes as shown in Figure 3-1. The direction of the arrows indicates the delegation direction. These class loaders load classes from different locations and of different types. You can add more class loaders, which would be a subclass of the `ClassLoader` class. Using custom class loaders, you can load classes from custom locations, partition user code, and unload classes. For simple applications, the built-in class loaders are sufficient.

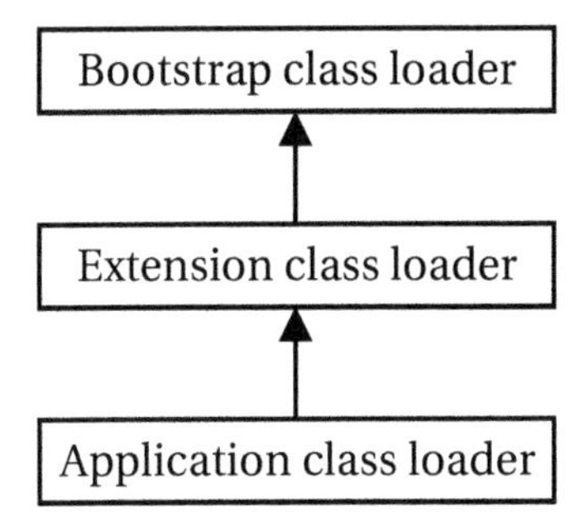

Figure 3-1. *Class loaders hierarchy in the JDK prior to version 9*

Class loaders work in a hierarchical fashion—the bootstrap class loader being at the top of the hierarchy. A class loader delegates a request to load a class to the one above it. For example, if the application class loader is requested to load a class, it delegates the request to the extension class loader, which in turn delegates the request to the bootstrap class loader. If the bootstrap class loader cannot load the class, the extension class loader attempts to load it. If the extension class loader cannot load the class, the application class loader attempts to load it. If the application class loader cannot load it, a `ClassNotFoundException` is thrown.

The bootstrap class loader is the parent of the extension class loader. The extension class loader is the parent of the application class loader. The bootstrap class loader has no parent. By default, the application class loader will be the parent of additional class loaders you create.

■ **Tip** You can get the reference of the parent of a class loader by using the `getParent()` method of the `ClassLoader` class.

The bootstrap class loader loads bootstrap classes that consist of the Java platform, including the classes in the `JAVA_HOME\lib\rt.jar` and several other runtime JARs. It is entirely implemented in the virtual machine. You can use the `-Xbootclasspath/p` and `-Xbootclasspath/a` command-line options to prepend and append additional bootstrap directories. You can specify a bootstrap class path using the `-Xbootclasspath` option, which will replace the default bootstrap class path. At runtime, the `sun.boot.class.path` system property contains the read-only value of the boot class path. The bootstrap class loader is represented by `null`. That is, you cannot get its reference. For example, the `Object` class is loaded by the bootstrap class loader and the expression `Object.class.getClassLoader()` returns `null`.

The extension class loader is used to load classes available through the extension mechanism located in JARs in the directories specified by the `java.ext.dirs` system property. To get the reference of the extension class loader, you need to get the reference of the application class loader (see the next paragraph) and use the `getParent()` method on that reference.

The application class loader loads classes from the application class path that is specified by the `CLASSPATH` environment variable or command-line option `-cp` or `-classpath`. The application class loader is also known as the *system class loader*, which is a kind of misnomer that gives a false impression that it loads system classes. You can get a reference of the application class loader using the static method named `getSystemClassLoader()` of the `ClassLoader` class.

Class Loaders in JDK9

JDK9 keeps the three-level hierarchical class loader architecture for backward compatibility. However, there are a few changes to the way they load classes from the module system. Figure 3-2 shows the JDK9 class loader hierarchy.

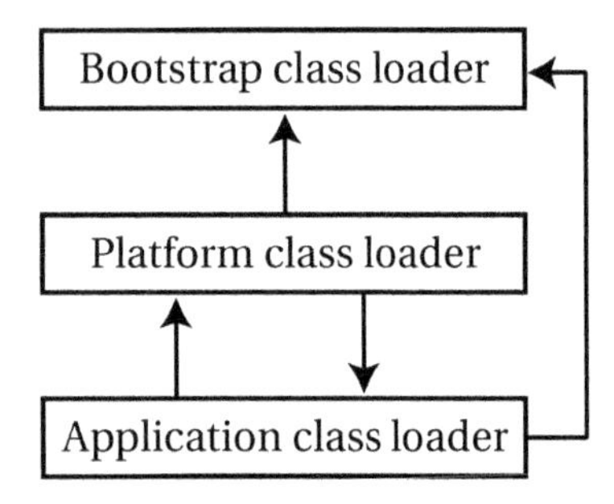

Figure 3-2. *Class loaders hierarchy in JDK9*

Notice that in JDK9, the application class loader can delegate to the platform class loader as well as the bootstrap class loader; the platform class loader can delegate to the application class loader.

In JDK9, the bootstrap class loader is implemented in the library code and in the virtual machine. For backward compatibility, it is still represented by `null` in a program. For example, `Object.class.getClassLoader()` still returns `null`. Not all Java SE Platform and JDK modules are loaded by the bootstrap class loader. To name a few, modules loaded by the bootstrap class loader are `java.base`, `java.logging`, `java.prefs`, and `java.desktop`. Other Java SE Platform and JDK modules are loaded by the platform class loader and the application class loader, which are described next. Options to specify the boot class path, `-Xbootclasspath`, and `-Xbootclasspath/p`, and the system property, `sun.boot.class.path`, are no longer supported in JDK9. The `-Xbootclasspath/a` option is still supported and its value is stored in the system property `jdk.boot.class.path.append`.

JDK9 no longer supports the extension mechanism. However, it retains the extension class loader under a new name called *platform class loader*. The `ClassLoader` class contains a new static method named `getPlatformClassLoader()`, which returns the reference of the platform class loader. Table 3-3 lists the modules loaded by the platform class loader.

Table 3-3. *The JDK Modules Loaded by the Platform Class Loader in JDK9*

java.activation	java.transaction	jdk.deploy
java.compiler	java.xml.bind	jdk.dynalink
java.corba	java.xml.crypto	jdk.localedata
java.scripting	java.xml.ws	jdk.naming.dns
java.se	java.xml.ws.annotation	jdk.scripting.nashorn
java.se.ee	jdk.accessibility	jdk.security.auth
java.security.jgss	jdk.charsets	jdk.security.jgss
java.smartcardio	jdk.crypto.cryptoki	jdk.zipfs
java.sql	jdk.crypto.ec	
java.sql.rowset	jdk.crypto.mscapi	

The platform class loader serves another purpose. Classes loaded by the bootstrap class loader are granted all permissions by default. However, several classes did not need all permissions. Such classes have been de-privileged in JDK9 and they are loaded by the platform class loader.

The application class loader loads the application modules found on the module path and a few JDK modules that provide tools or export tool APIs, as listed in Table 3-4. In JDK9, you can still use the static method named `getSystemClassLoader()` of the `ClassLoader` class to get the reference of the application class loader.

Table 3-4. *The JDK Modules Loaded by the Application Class Loader in JDK9*

jdk.attach	jdk.internal.le	jdk.jdi
jdk.compiler	jdk.internal.opt	jdk.jdwp.agent
jdk.editpad	jdk.jartool	jdk.jlink
jdk.internal.ed	jdk.javadoc	jdk.jshell
jdk.internal.jvmstat	jdk.jdeps	jdk.jstatd

Tip Before JDK9, the extension class loader and the application class loader were an instance of the `java.net.URLClassLoader` class. In JDK9, the platform class loader (the erstwhile extension class loader) and the application class loader are an instance of an internal JDK class. If your code relied on the methods specific to the `URLClassLoader` class, your code may break in JDK9.

The JDK modules not listed in Table 3-3 and Table 3-4 are loaded by the bootstrap class loader. Listing 3-4 shows you how to print module names and their class loader names. A partial output is shown. The output depends on the modules resolved by the runtime. To print all JDK modules and their class loaders, you should add a "`requires java.se.ee`" in your module declaration before running this class. I discuss module layers in Chapter 15.

Listing 3-4. Listing the Names of Loaded Modules by Class Loader

```
// ModulesByClassLoader.java
package com.jdojo.reflection;

public class ModulesByClassLoader {
    public static void main(String[] args) {
        // Get the boot layer
        ModuleLayer layer = ModuleLayer.boot();

        // Print all module's names and their class loader names in the boot layer
        for (Module m : layer.modules()) {
            ClassLoader loader = m.getClassLoader();
            String moduleName = m.getName();
            String loaderName = loader == null ? "bootstrap" : loader.getName();
            System.out.printf("%s: %s%n", loaderName, moduleName);
        }
    }
}
```

```
platform: java.xml.ws
app: jdk.compiler
platform: java.transaction
platform: jdk.naming.dns
bootstrap: java.datatransfer
bootstrap: jdk.jfr
app: jdk.jlink
...
```

The class loading mechanism in JDK9 has changed a bit. The three built-in class loaders work in tandem to load classes. When the application class loader needs to load a class, it searches modules defined to all class loaders. If a suitable module is defined to one of these class loaders, that class loader loads the class, implying that the application class loader can now delegate to the bootstrap class loader and the platform class loader. If a class is not found in a named module defined to these class loaders, the application class loader delegates to its parent, which is the platform class loader. If class is still not loaded, the application class loader searches the class path. If it finds the class on the class path, it loads the class as a member of its unnamed module. If it does not find the class on the class path, a `ClassNotFoundException` is thrown.

When the platform class loader needs to load a class, it searches modules defined to all class loaders. If a suitable module is defined to one of these class loaders, that class loader loads the class, implying that the platform class loader can delegate to the bootstrap class loader as well as the application class loader. If a class is not found in a named module defined to these class loaders, the platform class loader delegates to its parent, which is the bootstrap class loader.

When the bootstrap class loader needs to load a class, it searches its own list of named modules. If a class is not found, it searches the list of files and directories specified through the command-line option `-Xbootclasspath/a`. If it finds a class on the bootstrap class path, it loads the class as a member of its unnamed module. If a class is still not found, a `ClassNotFoundException` is thrown.

Reflecting on Classes

This section demonstrates the features of Java reflection that enable you to get the description of a class, such as its package name, access modifiers, etc. You will use a `Person` class, as listed in Listing 3-5, to demonstrate the reflection features. It is a simple class with two instance fields, two constructors, and some methods. It implements two interfaces.

Listing 3-5. A Person Class Used to Demonstrate Reflection

```
// Person.java
package com.jdojo.reflection;

import java.io.Serializable;

public class Person implements Cloneable, Serializable {
    private int id = -1;
    private String name = "Unknown";

    public Person() {
    }

    public Person(int id, String name) {
        this.id = id;
        this.name = name;
    }

    public int getId() {
        return id;
    }

    public String getName() {
        return name;
    }

    public void setName(String name) {
        this.name = name;
    }
```

```
    @Override
    public Person clone() {
        try {
            return (Person) super.clone();
        } catch (CloneNotSupportedException e) {
            throw new RuntimeException(e.getMessage());
        }
    }

    @Override
    public String toString() {
        return "Person: id=" + this.id + ", name=" + this.name;
    }
}
```

Listing 3-6 illustrates how to get the description of a class. It lists the class access modifiers, the class name, its superclass name, and all interfaces implemented by the class.

Listing 3-6. Reflecting on a Class

```
// ClassReflection.java
package com.jdojo.reflection;

import java.lang.reflect.Modifier;
import java.lang.reflect.TypeVariable;

public class ClassReflection {
    public static void main(String[] args) {
        // Print the declaration of the Person class
        String clsDecl = getClassDescription(Person.class);
        System.out.println(clsDecl);

        // Print the declaration of the Class class
        clsDecl = getClassDescription(Class.class);
        System.out.println(clsDecl);

        // Print the declaration of the Runnable interface
        clsDecl = getClassDescription(Runnable.class);
        System.out.println(clsDecl);

        // Print the declaration of the class representing the int data type
        clsDecl = getClassDescription(int.class);
        System.out.println(clsDecl);
    }

    public static String getClassDescription(Class<?> cls) {
        StringBuilder classDesc = new StringBuilder();

        // Prepare the modifiers and construct keyword (class, enum, interface etc.)
        int modifierBits = 0;
        String keyword = "";
```

```
// Add keyword @interface, interface or class
if (cls.isPrimitive()) {
    // We do not want to add anything
} else if (cls.isInterface()) {
    modifierBits = cls.getModifiers() & Modifier.interfaceModifiers();

    // An annotation is an interface
    if (cls.isAnnotation()) {
        keyword = "@interface";
    } else {
        keyword = "interface";
    }
} else if (cls.isEnum()) {
    modifierBits = cls.getModifiers() & Modifier.classModifiers();
    keyword = "enum";
} else {
    modifierBits = cls.getModifiers() & Modifier.classModifiers();
    keyword = "class";
}

// Convert modifiers to their string representation
String modifiers = Modifier.toString(modifierBits);

// Append modifiers
classDesc.append(modifiers);

// Append the construct keyword
classDesc.append(" ");
classDesc.append(keyword);

// Append simple name
String simpleName = cls.getSimpleName();
classDesc.append(" ");
classDesc.append(simpleName);

// Append generic parameters
String genericParms = getGenericTypeParams(cls);
classDesc.append(genericParms);

// Append super class
Class superClass = cls.getSuperclass();
if (superClass != null) {
    String superClassSimpleName = superClass.getSimpleName();
    classDesc.append(" extends ");
    classDesc.append(superClassSimpleName);
}

// Append Interfaces
String interfaces = ClassReflection.getClassInterfaces(cls);
if (interfaces != null) {
```

```
            classDesc.append(" implements ");
            classDesc.append(interfaces);
        }

        return classDesc.toString().trim();
    }

    public static String getClassInterfaces(Class<?> cls) {
        // Get a comma-separated list of interfaces implemented by the class
        Class<?>[] interfaces = cls.getInterfaces();
        if (interfaces.length == 0) {
            return null;
        }

        String[] names = new String[interfaces.length];
        for (int i = 0; i < interfaces.length; i++) {
            names[i] = interfaces[i].getSimpleName();
        }

        String interfacesList = String.join(", ", names);
        return interfacesList;
    }

    public static String getGenericTypeParams(Class<?> cls) {
        StringBuilder sb = new StringBuilder();
        TypeVariable<?>[] typeParms = cls.getTypeParameters();

        if (typeParms.length == 0) {
            return "";
        }

        String[] paramNames = new String[typeParms.length];
        for (int i = 0; i < typeParms.length; i++) {
            paramNames[i] = typeParms[i].getTypeName();
        }

        sb.append('<');
        String parmsList = String.join(",", paramNames);
        sb.append(parmsList);
        sb.append('>');

        return sb.toString();
    }
}
```

```
public class Person extends Object implements Cloneable, Serializable
public final class Class<T> extends Object implements Serializable, GenericDeclaration,
Type, AnnotatedElement
public abstract interface Runnable
int
```

The getName() method of the Class class returns the fully qualified name of the class. To get the simple class name, use the getSimpleName() method of the Class class, like so:

```
String simpleName = c.getSimpleName();
```

The modifiers of a class are the keywords that appear before the keyword class in the class declaration. In the following example, public and abstract are the modifiers for the MyClass class:

```
public abstract class MyClass {
    // Code goes here
}
```

The getModifiers() method of the Class class returns all modifiers for the class. Note that the getModifiers() method returns an integer. To get the textual form of the modifiers, you need to call the toString(int modifiers) static method of the Modifier class, passing the modifiers value in an integer form. Assuming cls is the reference of a Class object, you get the modifiers of the class as shown:

```
// You need to AND the returned value from the getModifiers() method with
// appropriate value returned from xxxModifiers() method of the Modifiers class
int mod = cls.getModifiers() & Modifier.classModifiers();
String modStr = Modifier.toString(mod);
```

It is straightforward to get the name of the superclass of a class. Use the getSuperclass() method of the Class class to get the reference of the superclass. Note that every class in Java has a superclass except the Object class. If the getSuperclass() method is invoked on the Object class, it returns null.

```
Class superClass = cls.getSuperclass();
if (superClass != null) {
    String superClassName = superClass.getSimpleName();
}
```

Tip The getSuperclass() method of the Class class returns null when it represents the Object class, a class for an interface such as List.class, and a class for a primitive type such as int.class, void.class, etc.

To get the names of all interfaces implemented by a class, you use the getInterfaces() method of the Class class. It returns an array of Class object. Each element in the array represents an interface implemented by the class.

```
// Get all interfaces implemented by cls
Class<?>[] interfaces = cls.getInterfaces();
```

The getClassDescription() method of the ClassReflection class puts all parts of a class declaration into a string and returns that string. The main() method of this class demonstrates how to use this class.

■ **Note** Java 8 added a method called `toGenericString()` to the `Class` class that returns a string describing the class. The string contains the modifiers and type parameters for the class. The call `Person.class.toGenericString()` will return `public class com.jdojo.reflection.Person`.

Reflecting on Fields

A field of a class is represented by an object of the `java.lang.reflect.Field` class. The following four methods in the `Class` class can be used to get information about the fields of a class:

- `Field[] getFields()`
- `Field[] getDeclaredFields()`
- `Field getField(String name)`
- `Field getDeclaredField(String name)`

The `getFields()` method returns all the accessible public fields of the class or interface. The accessible public fields include public fields declared in the class or inherited from its superclass. The `getDeclaredFields()` method returns all the fields that appear in the declaration of the class. It does not include inherited fields. The other two methods, `getField()` and `getDeclaredField()`, are used to get the `Field` object if you know the name of the field. Let's consider the following declarations of classes `A` and `B`, and an interface `IConstants`:

```
interface IConstants {
    int DAYS_IN_WEEK = 7;
}

class A implements IConstants {
    private int aPrivate;
    public int aPublic;
    protected int aProtected;
}

class B extends A {
    private int bPrivate;
    public int bPublic;
    protected int bProtected;
}
```

If `bClass` is the reference of the `Class` object for class `B`, the expression `bClass.getFields()` will return the following three fields that are accessible and `public`:

- `public int B.bPublic`
- `public int A.aPublic`
- `public static final int IConstants.DAYS_IN_WEEK`

The bClass.getDeclaredFields() method will return the three fields that are declared in class B:

- private int B.bPrivate
- public int B.bPublic
- protected int B.bProtected

To get all the fields of a class and its superclass, you must get the reference of the superclass using the getSuperclass() method and use the combinations of these methods. Listing 3-7 illustrates how to get the information about the fields of a class. Note that you do not get anything when you call the getFields() method on the Class object of the Person class because the Person class does not contain any public fields.

Listing 3-7. Reflecting on Fields of a Class

```
// FieldReflection.java
package com.jdojo.reflection;

import java.lang.reflect.Field;
import java.lang.reflect.Modifier;
import java.util.ArrayList;

public class FieldReflection {
    public static void main(String[] args) {
        Class<Person> cls = Person.class;

        // Print declared fields
        ArrayList<String> fieldsDescription = getDeclaredFieldsList(cls);

        System.out.println("Declared Fields for " + cls.getName());
        for (String desc : fieldsDescription) {
            System.out.println(desc);
        }

        // Get the accessible public fields
        fieldsDescription = getFieldsList(cls);

        System.out.println("\nAccessible Fields for " + cls.getName());
        for (String desc : fieldsDescription) {
            System.out.println(desc);
        }

    }

    public static ArrayList<String> getFieldsList(Class c) {
        Field[] fields = c.getFields();
        ArrayList<String> fieldsList = getFieldsDescription(fields);
        return fieldsList;
    }

    public static ArrayList<String> getDeclaredFieldsList(Class c) {
        Field[] fields = c.getDeclaredFields();
        ArrayList<String> fieldsList = getFieldsDescription(fields);
        return fieldsList;
    }
```

```
    public static ArrayList<String> getFieldsDescription(Field[] fields) {
        ArrayList<String> fieldList = new ArrayList<>();

        for (Field f : fields) {
            // Get the modifiers for the field
            int mod = f.getModifiers() & Modifier.fieldModifiers();
            String modifiers = Modifier.toString(mod);

            // Get the simple name of the field type
            Class<?> type = f.getType();
            String typeName = type.getSimpleName();

            // Get the name of the field
            String fieldName = f.getName();

            fieldList.add(modifiers + " " + typeName + " " + fieldName);
        }

        return fieldList;
    }
}
```

```
Declared Fields for com.jdojo.reflection.Person
private int id
private String name

Accessible Fields for com.jdojo.reflection.Person
```

■ **Tip** You cannot use this technique to describe the `length` field of an array object. Each array type has a corresponding class. When you try to get the fields of an array class using the `getFields()` method, you get an array of `Field` objects of zero length. The array length is not part of the array's class definition. Rather, it is stored as part of the array object in the object header. For more information on array's `length` field, refer to Chapter 11.

Reflecting on Executables

An instance of the `Method` class represents a method. An instance of the `Constructor` class represents a constructor. Structurally, methods and constructors have a few things in common. Both use modifiers, parameters, and throws clause. Both can be executed. Java 8 refactored these classes to inherit them from a common abstract superclass, `Executable`. Methods to retrieve information common to both have been added/moved to the `Executable` class.

A parameter in an `Executable` is represented by an object of the `Parameter` class, which was added in Java 8. The `getParameters()` method in the `Executable` class returns all parameters of an `Executable`

Parameter[]. By default, the formal parameter names are not stored in the class files to keep the file size smaller. The getName() method of the Parameter class returns synthesized parameter names like arg0, arg1, etc. unless the actual parameter names are retained. If you want to retain the actual parameter names in class files, you need to compile the source code using the -parameters option with the javac compiler.

The getExceptionTypes() method of the Executable class returns an array of Class objects, which describes the exceptions thrown by the Executable. If no exceptions are listed in the throws clause, it returns an array of length zero.

The getModifiers() method of the Executable class returns the modifiers as an int.

The getTypeParameters() method of the Executable class returns an array of TypeVariable that represents the type parameters for generic methods/constructors. The examples in this chapter do not include the generic type variable declarations in method/constructors.

Listing 3-8 contains a utility class that consists of static methods to get information about an Executable such as the list of modifiers, parameters, and exceptions. I use this class when I discuss methods and constructors in the subsequent sections.

Listing 3-8. A Utility Class to Get Information for an Executable

```
// ExecutableUtil.java
package com.jdojo.reflection;

import java.lang.reflect.Constructor;
import java.lang.reflect.Executable;
import java.lang.reflect.Method;
import java.lang.reflect.Modifier;
import java.lang.reflect.Parameter;
import java.util.ArrayList;

public class ExecutableUtil {
    public static ArrayList<String> getParameters(Executable exec) {
        Parameter[] parms = exec.getParameters();
        ArrayList<String> parmList = new ArrayList<>();
        for (int i = 0; i < parms.length; i++) {
            // Get modifiers, type, and name of the parameter
            int mod = parms[i].getModifiers() & Modifier.parameterModifiers();
            String modifiers = Modifier.toString(mod);
            String parmType = parms[i].getType().getSimpleName();
            String parmName = parms[i].getName();
            String temp = modifiers + " " + parmType + " " + parmName;

            // Trim it as it may have leading spaces when modifiers are absent
            parmList.add(temp.trim());
        }

        return parmList;
    }

    public static ArrayList<String> getExceptionList(Executable exec) {
        ArrayList<String> exceptionList = new ArrayList<>();
        for (Class<?> c : exec.getExceptionTypes()) {
            exceptionList.add(c.getSimpleName());
        }
```

```
        return exceptionList;
    }

    public static String getThrowsClause(Executable exec) {
        ArrayList<String> exceptionList = getExceptionList(exec);
        String exceptions = ExecutableUtil.arrayListToString(exceptionList, ",");
        String throwsClause = "";

        if (exceptionList.size() > 0) {
            throwsClause = "throws " + exceptions;
        }

        return throwsClause;
    }

    public static String getModifiers(Executable exec) {
        // Get the modifiers for the class
        int mod = exec.getModifiers();

        if (exec instanceof Method) {
            mod = mod & Modifier.methodModifiers();
        } else if (exec instanceof Constructor) {
            mod = mod & Modifier.constructorModifiers();
        }

        return Modifier.toString(mod);
    }

    public static String arrayListToString(ArrayList<String> list, String saparator) {
        String[] tempArray = new String[list.size()];
        tempArray = list.toArray(tempArray);
        String str = String.join(saparator, tempArray);
        return str;
    }
}
```

Reflecting on Methods

The following four methods in the `Class` class can be used to get information about the methods of a class:

- `Method[] getMethods()`
- `Method[] getDeclaredMethods()`
- `Method getMethod(String name, Class... parameterTypes)`
- `Method getDeclaredMethod(String name, Class... parameterTypes)`

The `getMethods()` method returns all the accessible public methods of the class. The accessible public methods include any public method declared in the class or inherited from the superclass. The `getDeclaredMethods()` method returns all the methods declared only in the class. It does not return any methods that are inherited from the superclass. The other two methods, `getMethod()` and getDeclaredMethod(), are used to get the Method object if you know the name of the method and its parameter types.

The getReturnType() method of the Method class returns the Class object, which contains information about the return type of the method.

Listing 3-9 illustrates how to get information about the methods of a class. You can uncomment the code in the main() method to print all methods in the Person class—declared in the Person class and inherited from the Object class.

Listing 3-9. Reflecting on Methods of a Class

```
// MethodReflection.java
package com.jdojo.reflection;

import java.lang.reflect.Method;
import java.util.ArrayList;

public class MethodReflection {
    public static void main(String[] args) {
        Class<Person> cls = Person.class;

        // Get the declared methods
        ArrayList<String> methodsDescription = getDeclaredMethodsList(cls);
        System.out.println("Declared Methods for " + cls.getName());
        for (String desc : methodsDescription) {
            System.out.println(desc);
        }

        /* Uncomment the following code to print all methods in the Person class
        // Get the accessible public methods
        methodsDescription = getMethodsList(c);
        System.out.println("\nMethods for " + c.getName());
        for (String desc : methodsDescription) {
            System.out.println(desc);
        }
         */
    }

    public static ArrayList<String> getMethodsList(Class c) {
        Method[] methods = c.getMethods();
        ArrayList<String> methodsList = getMethodsDescription(methods);
        return methodsList;
    }

    public static ArrayList<String> getDeclaredMethodsList(Class c) {
        Method[] methods = c.getDeclaredMethods();
        ArrayList<String> methodsList = getMethodsDescription(methods);
        return methodsList;
    }

    public static ArrayList<String> getMethodsDescription(Method[] methods) {
        ArrayList<String> methodList = new ArrayList<>();
```

```
        for (Method m : methods) {
            String modifiers = ExecutableUtil.getModifiers(m);

            // Get the method return type
            Class returnType = m.getReturnType();
            String returnTypeName = returnType.getSimpleName();

            // Get the name of the method
            String methodName = m.getName();

            // Get the parameters of the method
            ArrayList<String> paramsList = ExecutableUtil.getParameters(m);
            String params = ExecutableUtil.arrayListToString(paramsList, ",");

            // Get the Exceptions thrown by method
            String throwsClause = ExecutableUtil.getThrowsClause(m);

            methodList.add(modifiers + " " + returnTypeName + " "
                    + methodName + "(" + params + ") " + throwsClause);
        }

        return methodList;
    }
}
```

```
Declared Methods for com.jdojo.reflection.Person
public String toString()
public Object clone()
public String getName()
public int getId()
public void setName(String arg0)
```

Reflecting on Constructors

Getting information about constructors of a class is similar to getting information about methods of a class. The following four methods in the `Class` class are used to get information about the constructors represented by a `Class` object:

- `Constructor[] getConstructors()`
- `Constructor[] getDeclaredConstructors()`
- `Constructor<T> getConstructor(Class... parameterTypes)`
- `Constructor<T> getDeclaredConstructor(Class... parameterTypes)`

The `getConstructors()` method returns all public constructors. The `getDeclaredConstructors()` method returns all declared constructors. The other two methods, `getConstructor()` and `getDeclaredConstructor()`, are used to get the `Constructor` object if you know the parameter types of the constructor. Listing 3-10 illustrates how to get information for the constructors represented by a `Class` object.

Listing 3-10. Reflecting on Constructors of a Class

```
// ConstructorReflection.java
package com.jdojo.reflection;

import java.lang.reflect.Constructor;
import java.util.ArrayList;

public class ConstructorReflection {
    public static void main(String[] args) {
        Class<Person> cls = Person.class;

        // Get the declared constructors
        System.out.println("Constructors for " + cls.getName());
        Constructor[] constructors = cls.getConstructors();
        ArrayList<String> constructDescList = getConstructorsDescription(constructors);
        for (String desc : constructDescList) {
            System.out.println(desc);
        }
    }

    public static ArrayList<String> getConstructorsDescription(Constructor[] constructors) {
        ArrayList<String> constructorList = new ArrayList<>();
        for (Constructor constructor : constructors) {
            String modifiers = ExecutableUtil.getModifiers(constructor);

            // Get the name of the constructor
            String constructorName = constructor.getName();

            // Get the parameters of the constructor
            ArrayList<String> paramsList
                    = ExecutableUtil.getParameters(constructor);
            String params = ExecutableUtil.arrayListToString(paramsList, ",");

            // Get the Exceptions thrown by the constructor
            String throwsClause = ExecutableUtil.getThrowsClause(constructor);

            constructorList.add(modifiers + " " + constructorName
                    + "(" + params + ") " + throwsClause);
        }

        return constructorList;
    }
}
```

```
Constructors for com.jdojo.reflection.Person
public com.jdojo.reflection.Person()
public com.jdojo.reflection.Person(int arg0,String arg1)
```

Creating Objects

Java lets you use reflection to create objects of a class. The class name need not be known until runtime. You can create the object by invoking one of the constructors of the class using reflection. You can also access the values of fields of objects, set their values, and invoke their methods. If you know the class name and have access to the class code at compile-time, do not use reflection to create its object; rather use the new operator in your code to create objects of the class. Typically, frameworks and libraries use reflection to create objects.

You can create an object of a class using reflection. You need to get the reference of the constructor before you can create an object. The previous section showed you how to get the reference of a specific constructor of a class. Use the `newInstance()` method of the `Constructor` class to create an object. You can pass the actual parameter to the constructor to the `newInstance()` method, which is declared as follows:

```
public T newInstance(Object... initargs) throws InstantiationException,
IllegalAccessException, IllegalArgumentException, InvocationTargetException
```

Here, `initargs` are the actual parameters for the constructor. You will not pass any parameters for the no-args constructor.

Tip The `newInstance()` method of the `Class` class creates a new object of the class using its no-args constructor. The method has been deprecated since JDK9 because it does not propagate the exceptions thrown by the no-args constructor properly. Use the `newInstance()` method of the `Constructor` class to create an object of a class using its no-args and all other constructors.

The following snippet of code gets the reference of the no-args constructor of the `Person` class and invokes it. I have omitted the exception handling for brevity:

```
Class<Person> cls = Person.class;

// Get the reference of the Person() constructor
Constructor<Person> noArgsCons = cls.getConstructor();
Person p = noArgsCons.newInstance();
```

Listing 3-11 contains the complete code to illustrate how to use the `Person(int, String)` constructor of the `Person` class to create a `Person` object using reflection. Note that the `Constructor<T>` class is a generic type. Its type parameter is the class type that declares the constructor, for example, the `Constructor<Person>` type represents a constructor for the `Person` class.

Listing 3-11. Using a Specific Constructor to Create a New Object

```
// InvokeConstructorTest.java
package com.jdojo.reflection;

import java.lang.reflect.Constructor;
import java.lang.reflect.InvocationTargetException;

public class InvokeConstructorTest {
    public static void main(String[] args) {
        Class<Person> personClass = Person.class;
```

```
        try {
            // Get the constructor "Person(int, String)"
            Constructor<Person> cons = personClass.getConstructor(int.class, String.class);

            // Invoke the constructor with values for id and name
            Person chris = cons.newInstance(1994, "Chris");
            System.out.println(chris);
        } catch (NoSuchMethodException | SecurityException
                | InstantiationException | IllegalAccessException
                | IllegalArgumentException | InvocationTargetException e) {
            System.out.println(e.getMessage());
        }
    }
}
```

```
Person: id=1994, name=Chris
```

Invoking Methods

You can invoke methods of an object using reflection. You need to get the reference to the method that you want to invoke. Suppose you want to invoke the `setName()` method of the `Person` class. You can get the reference to the `setName()` method as follows:

```
Class<Person> personClass = Person.class;
Method setName = personClass.getMethod("setName", String.class);
```

To invoke this method, call the `invoke()` method on the method's reference, which is declared as follows:

```
public Object invoke(Object obj, Object... args) throws IllegalAccessException,
IllegalArgumentException, InvocationTargetException
```

The first parameter of the `invoke()` method is the object on which you want to invoke the method. If the `Method` object represents a static method, the first argument is ignored or it may be `null`. The second parameter is a varargs parameter in which you pass all the actual parameters in the same order as declared in the method's declaration.

Since the `setName()` method of the `Person` class takes a `String` argument, you need to pass a `String` object as the second argument to the `invoke()` method. Listing 3-12 illustrates how to invoke a method on a `Person` object using reflection.

Listing 3-12. Invoking a Method on an Object Reference Using Reflection

```
// InvokeMethodTest.java
package com.jdojo.reflection;

import java.lang.reflect.InvocationTargetException;
import java.lang.reflect.Method;
```

```
public class InvokeMethodTest {
    public static void main(String[] args) {
        Class<Person> personClass = Person.class;

        try {
            // Create an object of Person class
            Person p = personClass.newInstance();

            // Print the details of the Person object
            System.out.println(p);

            // Get the reference of the setName() method
            Method setName = personClass.getMethod("setName", String.class);

            // Invoke the setName() method on p passing passing "Ann"
            // as the actual parameter
            setName.invoke(p, "Ann");

            // Print the details of the Person object
            System.out.println(p);
        } catch (InstantiationException | IllegalAccessException
                | NoSuchMethodException | SecurityException
                | IllegalArgumentException | InvocationTargetException e) {
            System.out.println(e.getMessage());
        }
    }
}
```

```
Person: id=-1, name=Unknown
Person: id=-1, name=Ann
```

Accessing Fields

You can read or set the value of a field of an object using reflection. First, you need get the reference of the field you want to work with. To read the field's value, you need to call the getXxx() method on the field, where Xxx is the data type of the field. For example, to read a boolean field value, you would call the getBoolean() method, and to read an int field you would call the getInt() method. To set the value of a field, you call the corresponding setXxx() method. The following are the declarations of the getInt() and setInt() methods where the first argument, obj, is the object's reference whose field is being read or written:

- int getInt(Object obj) throws IllegalArgumentException, IllegalAccessException
- void setInt(Object obj, int newValue) throws IllegalArgumentException, IllegalAccessException

---

■ **Tip** static and instance fields are accessed the same way. In case of static fields, the first argument to the `get()` and `set()` methods is the reference of the class/interface.

Note that you can access fields only that have been declared as accessible, such as a public field. In the `Person` class, all fields are declared private. Therefore, you cannot access any of these fields using normal Java programming language rules. To access a field that is not normally accessible, for example, if it is declared `private`, refer to the "Deep Reflection" section later in this chapter. You will use the `PublicPerson` class listed in Listing 3-13 to learn the technique to access the fields.

Listing 3-13. A PublicPerson Class with a Public Name Field

```
// PublicPerson.java
package com.jdojo.reflection;

public class PublicPerson {
    private int id = -1;
    public String name = "Unknown";

    public PublicPerson() {
    }

    @Override
    public String toString() {
        return "Person: id=" + this.id + ", name=" + this.name;
    }
}
```

Listing 3-14 demonstrates how to get the reference of a field of an object and how to read and set its value.

Listing 3-14. Accessing Fields Using Reflection

```
// FieldAccessTest.java
package com.jdojo.reflection;

import java.lang.reflect.Field;

public class FieldAccessTest {
    public static void main(String[] args) {
        Class<PublicPerson> ppClass = PublicPerson.class;

        try {
            // Create an object of the PublicPerson class
            PublicPerson p = ppClass.newInstance();

            // Get the reference of the name field
            Field name = ppClass.getField("name");

            // Get and print the current value of the name field
            String nameValue = (String) name.get(p);
            System.out.println("Current name is " + nameValue);
```

```
            // Set the value of name to Ann
            name.set(p, "Ann");

            // Get and print the new value of name field
            nameValue = (String) name.get(p);
            System.out.println("New name is " + nameValue);
        } catch (InstantiationException | IllegalAccessException
                | NoSuchFieldException | SecurityException
                | IllegalArgumentException e) {
            System.out.println(e.getMessage());
        }
    }
}
```

```
Current name is Unknown
New name is Ann
```

Deep Reflection

There are two things you can do using reflection:

- Describe an entity
- Access the members of an entity

Describing an entity means knowing the entity's details. For example, describing a class means knowing its name, modifiers, packages, modules, fields, methods, and constructors. Accessing the members of an entity means reading and writing fields and invoking methods and constructors. Describing an entity does not pose any issues of access control. If you have access to a class file, you should be able to know the details of the entity represented in that class file. However, accessing members of an entity is controlled by the Java language access control. For example, if you declare a field of a class as private, the field should be accessible only within the class. Code outside the class should not be able to access the private field of the class. However, this is half-true. The Java language access control rules are applied when you access members statically. The access control rules can be suppressed when you access members using reflection. The following snippet of code accesses the private name field of the Person class. This code will compile only within the Person class:

```
Person john = new Person();
String name = john.name; // Accessing the private field name statically
```

Java has been allowing access to rather inaccessible members such as a private field of a class outside the class using reflection. This is called *deep reflection*. Reflective access to inaccessible members made it possible to have many great frameworks in Java such as Hibernate and Spring. These frameworks perform most of their work using deep reflection. You can access the private name field of the Person class outside the Person class using deep reflection.

So far in this chapter, I kept the examples simple and stayed away from violating the Java language access control. I accessed only public fields, methods, and constructors; the accessed members and the accessing code were in the same module. Before JDK9, accessing inaccessible members was easy. All you had to do was call the `setAccessible(true)` method on the inaccessible `Field`, `Method`, and `Constructor` objects before accessing them. Introduction of the module system in JDK9 has made deep reflection a bit complicated. In this section and its sub-sections, I walk you through rules and examples for deep reflection in JDK9.

■ **Tip** If a security manager is present, the code performing deep reflection must have a `ReflectPermission("suppressAccessChecks")` permission.

To perform deep reflection, you need to get the reference of the desired field, method, and constructor using the `getDeclaredXxx()` method of the `Class` object, where `Xxx` can be `Field`, `Method`, or `Constructor`... Note that using the `getXxx()` method to get the reference of an inaccessible field, method, or constructor will throw an `IllegalAccessException`. The `Field`, `Method`, and `Constructor` classes have the `AccessibleObject` class as their superclass. The `AccessibleObject` class contains the following methods to let you work with the `accessible` flag:

- `void setAccessible(boolean flag)`
- `static void setAccessible(AccessibleObject[] array, boolean flag)`
- `boolean trySetAccessible()`
- `boolean canAccess(Object obj)`

The `setAccessible(boolean flag)` method sets the `accessible` flag for a member (`Field`, `Method`, and `Constructor`) to `true` or `false`. If you are trying to access an inaccessible member, you need to call `setAccessible(true)` on the member object before accessing the member. The method throws an `InaccessibleObjectException` if the `accessible` flag cannot be set. The static `setAccessible (AccessibleObject[] array, boolean flag)` is a convenience method to set the accessible flag for all `AccessibleObject` in the specified array.

JDK9 added the `trySetAccessible()` method that attempts to set the `accessible` flag to `true` on the object on which it is called. It returns `true` if the `accessible` flag was set to `true` and `false` otherwise. Compare this method with the `setAccessible(true)` method. This method does not throw a runtime exception on failure, whereas the `setAccessible(true)` does.

JDK9 added the `canAccess(Object obj)` method, which returns `true` if the caller can access the member for the specified `obj` object. Otherwise, it returns `false`. If the member is a static member or a constructor, the `obj` must be `null`.

I discuss accessing rather inaccessible members within a module, across modules, in unnamed modules, and of JDK modules in the next sections.

Deep Reflection Within a Module

Let's start with an example. You want to access the private `name` field of a `Person` object. First, you get the reference of the `name` field in a `Field` object and try reading its current value. Listing 3-15 contains the code for the `IllegalAccess1` class.

Listing 3-15. Accessing the Private Name Field of the Person Class

```
// IllegalAccess1.java
package com.jdojo.reflection;

import java.lang.reflect.Constructor;
import java.lang.reflect.Field;
```

```
public class IllegalAccess1 {
    public static void main(String[] args) throws Exception {
        // Get the class reference for the Person class
        String className = "com.jdojo.reflection.Person";
        Class<?> cls = Class.forName(className);

        // Create a Person object
        Constructor<?> cons = cls.getConstructor();
        Object person = cons.newInstance();

        // Get the reference of the name field
        Field nameField = cls.getDeclaredField("name");

        // Try accessing the name field by reading its value
        String name = (String) nameField.get(person);

        // Print the person and its name separately
        System.out.println(person);
        System.out.println("name=" + name);
    }
}
```

```
Exception in thread "main" java.lang.IllegalAccessException: class com.jdojo.reflection.
IllegalAccess1 (in module jdojo.reflection) cannot access a member of class com.jdojo.
reflection.Person (in module jdojo.reflection) with modifiers "private"
        at java.base/jdk.internal.reflect.Reflection.newIllegalAccessException(Reflection.
        java:361)
        at java.base/java.lang.reflect.AccessibleObject.checkAccess(AccessibleObject.
        java:589)
        at java.base/java.lang.reflect.Field.checkAccess(Field.java:1075)
        at java.base/java.lang.reflect.Field.get(Field.java:416)
        at jdojo.reflection/com.jdojo.reflection.IllegalAccess1.main(IllegalAccess1.
        java:21)
```

In Listing 3-15, I added the Exception class in the throws clause of the main() method to keep the logic simple inside the method. I keep doing this for all examples in this section, so you can focus on the illegal access rules rather than on exception handling. The IllegalAccess1 and the Person class are in the same jdojo.reflection module. You were able to create a Person object successfully because you used the public no-args constructor of the Person class. The name field in the Person class is declared as private and accessing it from another class failed. Fixing this error is simple—you set the accessible flag to the Field object using the setAccessible(true) or the trySetAccessible() method. Listing 3-16 contains the complete code.

Listing 3-16. Accessing the Private Name Field of the Person Class After Making It Accessible

```
// IllegalAccess1.java
package com.jdojo.reflection;

import java.lang.reflect.Constructor;
import java.lang.reflect.Field;
```

```
public class IllegalAccess2 {
    public static void main(String[] args) throws Exception {
        // Get the class reference for the Person class
        String className = "com.jdojo.reflection.Person";
        Class<?> cls = Class.forName(className);

        // Create a Person object
        Constructor<?> cons = cls.getConstructor();
        Object person = cons.newInstance();

        // Get the reference of the name field
        Field nameField = cls.getDeclaredField("name");

        // Try making the name field accessible before accessing it
        boolean accessEnabled = nameField.trySetAccessible();

        if (accessEnabled) {
            // Try accessing the name field by reading its value
            String name = (String) nameField.get(person);

            // Print the person and its name separately
            System.out.println(person);
            System.out.println("name=" + name);
        } else {
            System.out.println("The Person.name field is not accessible.");
        }
    }
}
```

```
Person: id=-1, name=Unknown
name=Unknown
```

So far, everything looks fine. You might think that if you cannot access the private member of a class, you can always use reflection to access them. However, this is not always true. Access to otherwise inaccessible members of a class is handled through the Java security manager. By default, when you run your application on your computer, the security manager is not installed for your application. The absence of the security manager for your application lets you access all fields, methods, and constructors of a class in the same module after you set the accessible flag to `true` as you did in the previous example. However, if a security manager is installed for your application, whether you can access an inaccessible class member depends on the permission granted to your application to access such members. You can check if the security manager is installed for your application or not by using the following piece of code:

```
SecurityManager smgr = System.getSecurityManager();
if (smgr == null) {
    System.out.println("Security manager is not installed.");
}
```

You can install a default security manager by passing the -Djava.security.manager option on the command line when you run the Java application. The security manager uses a Java security policy file to enforce the rules specified in that policy file. The Java security policy file is specified using the -Djava.security.policy command-line option. If you want to run the IllegalAccess2 class with a Java security manager with the Java policy file stored in the C:\Java9LanguageFetaures\conf\myjava.policy file, you would use the following command:

```
C:\Java9LanguageFeatures>java -Djava.security.manager
-Djava.security.policy=conf\myjava.policy --module-path build\modules\jdojo.reflection
--module jdojo.reflection/com.jdojo.reflection.IllegalAccess2
```

```
Exception in thread "main" java.security.AccessControlException: access denied
("java.lang.reflect.ReflectPermission" "suppressAccessChecks")
        at java.base/java.security.AccessControlContext.checkPermission
        (AccessControlContext.java:472)
        at java.base/java.security.AccessController.checkPermission
        (AccessController.java:895)
        at java.base/java.lang.SecurityManager.checkPermission(SecurityManager.java:558)
        at java.base/java.lang.reflect.AccessibleObject.checkPermission
        (AccessibleObject.java:85)
        at java.base/java.lang.reflect.AccessibleObject.trySetAccessible
        (AccessibleObject.java:245)
        at jdojo.reflection/com.jdojo.reflection.IllegalAccess2.main
        (IllegalAccess2.java:26)
```

The myjava.policy file is empty when this command was run, which means that the application did not have permission to suppress the Java language access control.

If you want to allow your program to access an inaccessible field of a class using reflection, the contents of the myjava.policy file would look as shown in Listing 3-17.

Listing 3-17. Contents of the conf\myjava.policy File

```
grant {
    // Grant permission to all programs to access inaccessible members
    permission java.lang.reflect.ReflectPermission "suppressAccessChecks";
};
```

Let's re-run the IllegalAccess2 class with a security manager and the Java policy as shown in Listing 3-17:

```
C:\Java9LanguageFeatures>java -Djava.security.manager
-Djava.security.policy=conf\myjava.policy
--module-path build\modules\jdojo.reflection
--module jdojo.reflection/com.jdojo.reflection.IllegalAccess2
```

```
Person: id=-1, name=Unknown
name=Unknown
```

This time, you were able to access the private name field of the Person class when you granted the appropriate security permission. The rules for accessing the inaccessible members have just begun. You saw the rules for deep reflection within a module, when the code gaining illegal access and the code being illegally accessed were in the same module. The next section describes the illegal access behavior across modules.

Deep Reflection Across Modules

Let's set up a new module named jdojo.reflection.model, as shown in Listing 3-18, and a simple class in it called Phone, as shown in Listing 3-19. The module declaration contains no module statements. The Phone class contains a number instance variable, two constructors, and a getter and a setter for the number instance variable. The toString() method returns the phone number.

Listing 3-18. The Declaration of a jdojo.reflection.model Module

```
// module-info.java
module jdojo.reflection.model {
    // No module statements at this time
}
```

Listing 3-19. A Phone Class

```
// Phone.java
package com.jdojo.reflection.model;

public class Phone {
    private String number = "9999999999";

    public Phone() {
    }

    public Phone(String number) {
        this.number = number;
    }

    public String getNumber() {
        return number;
    }

    public void setNumber(String number) {
        this.number = number;
    }

    @Override
    public String toString() {
        return this.number;
    }
}
```

Let's create a class called IllegalAccess3 in the jdojo.reflection module. The class will try to create an object of the Phone class in the jdojo.reflection.model module and read the object's private field, number. The IllegalAccess3 class in Listing 3-20 contains the complete code. It is very similar to the IllegalAccess2 class. The only difference is that you are accessing the Phone class and its private instance variable across the module's boundary.

Listing 3-20. Accessing the Private Number Field of the Phone Class

```
// IllegalAccess1.java
package com.jdojo.reflection;

import java.lang.reflect.Constructor;
import java.lang.reflect.Field;

public class IllegalAccess3 {
    public static void main(String[] args) throws Exception {
        // Get the class reference for the Phone class
        String className = "com.jdojo.reflection.model.Phone";
        Class<?> cls = Class.forName(className);

        // Create a Phone object
        Constructor<?> cons = cls.getConstructor();
        Object phone = cons.newInstance();

        // Get the reference of the number field
        Field numberField = cls.getDeclaredField("number");

        // try making the number field accessible before accessing it
        boolean accessEnabled = numberField.trySetAccessible();

        if (accessEnabled) {
            // Try accessing the number field by reading its value
            String number = (String) numberField.get(phone);

            // Print the phone number
            System.out.println("number=" + number);
        } else {
            System.out.println("The Phone.number field is not accessible.");
        }
    }
}
```

Let's run the IllegalAccess3 class using the following command:

```
C:\Java9LanguageFeatures>java
--module-path build\modules\jdojo.reflection;build\modules\jdojo.reflection.model
--module jdojo.reflection/com.jdojo.reflection.IllegalAccess3
```

```
Exception in thread "main" java.lang.ClassNotFoundException: com.jdojo.reflection.model.Phone
        at java.base/jdk.internal.loader.BuiltinClassLoader.loadClass(BuiltinClassLoader.
        java:582)
        at java.base/jdk.internal.loader.ClassLoaders$AppClassLoader.loadClass(ClassLoaders.
        java:185)
        at java.base/java.lang.ClassLoader.loadClass(ClassLoader.java:496)
        at java.base/java.lang.Class.forName0(Native Method)
        at java.base/java.lang.Class.forName(Class.java:292)
        at jdoj9o.reflection/com.jdojo.reflection.IllegalAccess3.main(IllegalAccess3.java:11)
```

Can you guess what is wrong with the command? The error is indicating that the runtime did not find the Phone class. You were able to compile the IllegalAccess3 class because the class does not use the Phone class reference in the source code. It attempts to use the Phone class using reflection at runtime. You have included the jdojo.reflection.model module in the module path. However, including a module in the module path does not resolve the module. The jdojo.reflection module does not read the jdojo.reflection.model module, so running the IllegalAccess3 did not resolve the jdojo.reflection.model module and this is why the runtime did not find the Phone class. You need to resolve the module manually by using the --add-modules command-line option:

```
C:\Java9LanguageFeatures>java
--module-path build\modules\jdojo.reflection;build\modules\jdojo.reflection.model
--add-modules jdojo.reflection.model
--module jdojo.reflection/com.jdojo.reflection.IllegalAccess3
```

```
Exception in thread "main" java.lang.IllegalAccessException: class com.jdojo.reflection.
IllegalAccess3 (in module jdojo.reflection) cannot access class com.jdojo.reflection.
model.Phone (in module jdojo.reflection.model) because module jdojo.reflection.model does
not export com.jdojo.reflection.model to module jdojo.reflection
        at java.base/jdk.internal.reflect.Reflection.newIllegalAccessException
        (Reflection.java:361)
        at java.base/java.lang.reflect.AccessibleObject.checkAccess
        (AccessibleObject.java:589)
        at java.base/java.lang.reflect.Constructor.newInstance(Constructor.java:479)
        at jdojo.reflection/com.jdojo.reflection.IllegalAccess3.main(IllegalAccess3.java:15)
```

This time, the runtime was able to find the Phone class, but it complained about accessing the Phone class in the jdojo.reflection.model module from another module, jdojo.reflection. The error is stating that the jdojo.reflection.model module does not export the com.jdojo.reflection.model package, so the Phone class is in the com.jdojo.reflection.model package and is not accessible outside the jdojo.reflection.model module. Listing 3-21 contains the modified version of the jdojo.reflection.model module. Now it exports the com.jdojo.reflection.model package.

Listing 3-21. The Modified Declaration of a jdojo.reflection.model Module

```
// module-info.java
module jdojo.reflection.model {
    exports com.jdojo.reflection.model;
}
```

Let's re-run the IllegalAccess3 class using the previous command:

```
C:\Java9LanguageFeatures>java
--module-path build\modules\jdojo.reflection;build\modules\jdojo.reflection.model
--add-modules jdojo.reflection.model
--module jdojo.reflection/com.jdojo.reflection.IllegalAccess3
```

```
The Phone.number field is not accessible.
```

This time, you were able to instantiate the Phone class, but you would not access its private number field. Notice that the jdojo.reflection module does not read the jdojo.reflection.model module. Still the IllegalClass3 class is able to access the Phone class and instantiate it using reflection. If you write the following snippet of code in the IllegalAccess3 class, it would not compile:

```
Phone phone = new Phone();
```

When module M accesses the types in module N using reflection, a read from module M to module N is granted implicitly. Such a read must be specified explicitly using a requires statement when such access is needed statically (without reflection). This is what the previous command did when creating an object of the Phone class.

If you used the setAccessible(true) in the IllegalAccess3 class to make the number field accessible, the previous command would have produced an error message similar to the following:

```
Exception in thread "main" java.lang.reflect.InaccessibleObjectException: Unable to make
field private java.lang.String com.jdojo.reflection.model.Phone.number accessible: module
jdojo.reflection.model does not "opens com.jdojo.reflection.model" to module jdojo.
reflection
...
```

This error message is loud and clear. It is stating that the runtime could not make the private number field accessible because the jdojo.reflection.model module does not open the com.jdojo.reflection.model package to the jdojo.reflection module. Here comes the concept of opening a module's package and opening an entire module.

Exporting a package of a module grants access to the public types in the package and the accessible public members of those types to another module. Exporting a package grants the access at compile-time and at runtime. You can use reflection to access the same accessible public members that you can access without reflection. That is, Java language access control is always enforced for exported packages of a module.

If you want to allow deep reflection on types of a package in a module by code in other modules at runtime, you need to *open the package* of the module using the opens statement. The syntax for the opens statement is as follows:

```
opens <package-name> [to <module-name>,<module-name>...];
```

The syntax allows you to open a package to all other modules or a set of specific modules. In the following declaration, module M opens its package p to modules S and T:

```
module M {
    opens p to S, T;
}
```

In the following declaration, module N opens its package q to all other modules:

```
module N {
    opens q;
}
```

It is possible that a module exports and opens the same package. It is needed if other modules need to access the types in the package statically at compile-time and runtime, and using deep reflection at runtime. The following module declaration exports and opens the same package p to all other modules:

```
module J {
    exports p;
    opens p;
}
```

An opens statement in a module declaration allows you open one package to all other modules or selective modules. If you want to open *all packages* of a module to all other modules, you can declare the module itself as an *open module*. You can declare an open module by using the open modifier in the module declaration. The following declares an open module named K:

```
open module K {
    // Other module statements go here
}
```

An open module cannot contain an opens statement. This is because an open module means it has opened all its packages to all other modules for deep reflection. The following declaration of module L is invalid because it declares the module as open and, at the same time, contains an opens statement:

```
open module L {
    opens p; // A compile-time error

    // Other module statements go here
}
```

It is fine to export package in an open module. The following declaration of module D is valid:

```
open module D {
    exports p;

    // Other module statements go here
}
```

So, now you know what to do with the jdojo.reflection.model module for the jdojo.reflection module to perform deep reflection on the Phone class. You need to do either of the following:

- Open the com.jdojo.reflection.model package of the jdojo.reflection.model module to all other modules or at least to the jdojo.reflection module.
- Declare the jdojo.reflection.model module as an open module.

Listing 3-22 and Listing 3-23 contain the modified module declaration of the jdojo.reflection.model module. You will need to use one of them, not both. For this example, you do not need to export the package in the module's declaration because you are not accessing the Phone class at compile-time in the jdojo.reflection module.

Listing 3-22. The Modified Declaration of a jdojo.reflection.model Module, Which Opens the com.jdojo.reflection.model Package to All Other Modules

```
// module-info.java
module jdojo.reflection.model {
    exports com.jdojo.reflection.model;
    opens com.jdojo.reflection.model;
}
```

Listing 3-23. The Modified Declaration of a jdojo.reflection.model Module, Which Declares it as an open Module

```
// module-info.java
open module jdojo.reflection.model {
    exports com.jdojo.reflection.model;
}
```

Let's re-run the `IllegalAccess3` class using the previous command with the `com.jdojo.reflection.model` package open. This time, you will received the desired output.

```
C:\Java9LanguageFeatures>java
--module-path build\modules\jdojo.reflection;build\modules\jdojo.reflection.model
--add-modules jdojo.reflection.model
--module jdojo.reflection/com.jdojo.reflection.IllegalAccess3
```

```
number=9999999999
```

Deep Reflection and Unnamed Modules

All packages in an unnamed module are open to all other modules. Therefore, you can always perform deep reflection on types in unnamed modules.

Deep Reflection on JDK Modules

Prior to JDK9, deep reflection was allowed on members of all types—JDK internals and your types. One of the main goals of JDK9 is strong encapsulation and you should not be able to access rather inaccessible members of an object using deep reflection. However, enforcing strong encapsulation for JDK types would have broken many existing applications or required them to be changed before migrating to JDK9. This meant that either those applications will be migrated to JDK9 slowly or they will never be migrated to JDK9 at all. Java designers try their best to keep the new JDK backward compatible. To deliver on the backward compatibility, JDK9 allows deep reflection on members of JDK internal types from the code in unnamed modules. Upon the first such illegal access, the runtime issues a warning. Such illegal access to JDK internal types will be disallowed in a future version. This means that applications using deep reflection on JDK types in JDK8 will continue to work in JDK9 if they are deployed on the class path. Recall that all types loaded from the class path are part of unnamed modules. If such applications are modularized in JDK9, the code using illegal reflective access to JDK internals in such applications needs to be fixed. Refer to Chapter 16 for more on this topic.

Let's walk through an example of this. The java.lang.Long class is immutable. It contains a private field named value to hold the long value that this object represents. Listing 3-24 shows you how to access and modify the private value field of the Long class using deep reflection, which is not possible using the Long class statically.

Listing 3-24. Accessing and Modifying the Private Value Field of the java.lang.Long Class Using Deep Reflection

```
// IllegalAccess1.java
package com.jdojo.reflection;

import java.lang.reflect.Field;

public class IllegalAccessJDKType {
    public static void main(String[] args) throws Exception {
        // Create a Long object
        Long num = 1969L;
        System.out.println("#1: num = " + num);

        // Get the class reference for the Long class
        String className = "java.lang.Long";
        Class<?> cls = Class.forName(className);

        // Get the value field reference
        Field valueField = cls.getDeclaredField("value");

        // try making the value field accessible before accessing it
        boolean accessEnabled = valueField.trySetAccessible();

        if (accessEnabled) {
            // Get and print the current value of the Long.value private field of the
            // num object that you created in the beginning of this method
            Long value = (Long) valueField.get(num);

            System.out.println("#2: num = " + value);

            // Change the value of the Long.value field
            valueField.set(num, 1968L);
            value = (Long) valueField.get(num);

            System.out.println("#3: num = " + value);
        } else {
            System.out.println("The Long.value field is not accessible.");
        }
    }
}
```

In the beginning of the main() method, you create a Long object, called num, and set its value to 1969L.

```
Long num = 1969L;
System.out.println("#1: num = " + num);
```

Later, you get the reference of the Class object for the Long class and get the reference of the private value field and try to make it accessible. If you were able to make the field accessible, you read its current value, which would be 1969L. Now you change its value to 1968L and read it back in your program.

The IllegalAccessJDKType class is a member of the jdojo.reflection module. Let's run it using the following command:

```
C:\Java9LanguageFeatures>java --module-path build\modules\jdojo.reflection
--module jdojo.reflection/com.jdojo.reflection.IllegalAccessJDKType
```

```
#1: num = 1969
The Long.value field is not accessible.
```

You were not able to make the private value field of the Long class accessible because the IllegalAccessJDKType class is part of a named module and code in named modules is not allowed to have illegal access to the members of the JDK internal types. The following command re-runs the class from the class path and you get the desired output. Notice the one-time warnings even though you have accessed the private field three times.

```
C:\Java9LanguageFeatures>java --class-path build\modules\jdojo.reflection com.jdojo.
reflection.IllegalAccessJDKType
```

```
#1: num = 1969
WARNING: An illegal reflective access operation has occurred
WARNING: Illegal reflective access by com.jdojo.reflection.IllegalAccessJDKType
(file:/C:/Java9LanguageFeatures/build/modules/jdojo.reflection/) to field java.lang.Long.value
WARNING: Please consider reporting this to the maintainers of com.jdojo.reflection.
IllegalAccessJDKType
WARNING: Use --illegal-access=warn to enable warnings of further illegal reflective access
operations
WARNING: All illegal access operations will be denied in a future release
#2: num = 1969
#3: num = 1968
```

Reflecting on Arrays

Java provides special APIs to work with arrays. The Class class lets you find out if a Class reference represents an array by using its isArray() method. You can also create an array and read and modify its element's values using reflection. The java.lang.reflect.Array class is used to dynamically create an array and manipulate its elements. As stated before, you cannot reflect on the length field of an array using a normal reflection procedure. However, the Array class provides the getLength() method to get the length value of an array. Note that all methods in the Array class are static and most of them have the first argument as the array object's reference on which they operate.

To create an array, use the newInstance() static method of the Array class. The method is overloaded and has two versions.

- Object newInstance(Class<?> componentType, int arrayLength)
- Object newInstance(Class<?> componentType, int... dimensions)

One version of the method creates an array of the specified component type and the array length. The other version creates an array of the specified component type and dimensions. Note that the return type of the `newInstance()` method is `Object`. You need to use an appropriate cast to convert it to the actual array type.

If you want to create an array of `int` of length 5, you would write

```
int[] ids = (int[]) Array.newInstance(int.class, 5);
```

This statement has the same effect as the following statement:

```
int[] ids = new int[5];
```

If you want to create an array of `int` of dimension 5x8, you would write:

```
int[][] matrix = (int[][]) Array.newInstance(int.class, 5, 8);
```

Listing 3-25 illustrates how to create an array dynamically and manipulate its elements.

Listing 3-25. Reflecting on Arrays

```
// ArrayReflection.java
package com.jdojo.reflection;

import java.lang.reflect.Array;

public class ArrayReflection {
    public static void main(String[] args) {
        try {
            // Create the array of int of length 2
            Object arrayObject = Array.newInstance(int.class, 2);

            // Print the values in array element. Default values will be zero
            int n1 = Array.getInt(arrayObject, 0);
            int n2 = Array.getInt(arrayObject, 1);
            System.out.println("n1 = " + n1 + ", n2 = " + n2);

            // Set the values to both elements
            Array.set(arrayObject, 0, 101);
            Array.set(arrayObject, 1, 102);

            // Print the values in array element again
            n1 = Array.getInt(arrayObject, 0);
            n2 = Array.getInt(arrayObject, 1);
            System.out.println("n1 = " + n1 + ", n2 = " + n2);
        } catch (NegativeArraySizeException | IllegalArgumentException
                | ArrayIndexOutOfBoundsException e) {
            System.out.println(e.getMessage());
        }
    }
}
```

```
n1 = 0, n2 = 0
n1 = 101, n2 = 102
```

Java does not support a truly multi-dimensional array. Rather, it supports an array of arrays. The Class class contains a method called getComponentType(), which returns the Class object for an array's element type. Listing 3-26 illustrates how to get the dimension of an array.

Listing 3-26. Getting the Dimension of an Array

```
// ArrayDimension.java
package com.jdojo.reflection;

public class ArrayDimension {
    public static void main(String[] args) {
        int[][][] intArray = new int[6][3][4];
        System.out.println("int[][][] dimension is " + getArrayDimension(intArray));
    }

    public static int getArrayDimension(Object array) {
        int dimension = 0;
        Class c = array.getClass();

        // Perform a check that the object is really an array
        if (!c.isArray()) {
            throw new IllegalArgumentException("Object is not an array.");
        }

        while (c.isArray()) {
            dimension++;
            c = c.getComponentType();
        }

        return dimension;
    }
}
```

```
int[][][] dimension is 3
```

Expanding an Array

After you create an array, you cannot change its length. You can create an array of a bigger size and copy the old array elements to the new one at runtime. The Java collection classes such as ArrayList apply this technique to let you add elements to the collection without worrying about its length. You can use the combination of the getComponentType() method of the Class class and the newInstance() method of the Array class to create a new array of a given type. You can use the arraycopy() static method of the System class to copy the old array elements to the new array. Listing 3-27 illustrates how to create an array of a particular type using reflection. All runtime checks have been left out for clarity.

Listing 3-27. Expanding an Array Using Reflection

```
// ExpandingArray.java
package com.jdojo.reflection;

import java.lang.reflect.Array;
import java.util.Arrays;

public class ExpandingArray {
    public static void main(String[] args) {
        // Create an array of length 2
        int[] ids = {101, 102};

        System.out.println("Old array length: " + ids.length);
        System.out.println("Old array elements: " + Arrays.toString(ids));

        // Expand the array by 1
        ids = (int[]) expandBy(ids, 1);

        // Set the third element to 103
        ids[2] = 103; // This is newly added element
        System.out.println("New array length: " + ids.length);
        System.out.println("New array elements: " + Arrays.toString(ids));
    }

    public static Object expandBy(Object oldArray, int increment) {
        // Get the length of old array using reflection
        int oldLength = Array.getLength(oldArray);
        int newLength = oldLength + increment;

        // Get the class of the old array
        Class<?> cls = oldArray.getClass();

        // Create a new array of the new length
        Object newArray = Array.newInstance(cls.getComponentType(), newLength);

        // Copy the old array elements to new array
        System.arraycopy(oldArray, 0, newArray, 0, oldLength);

        return newArray;
    }
}
```

```
Old array length: 2
Old array elements: [101, 102]
New array length: 3
New array elements: [101, 102, 103]
```

Who Should Use Reflection?

If you have used any integrated development environment (IDE) to develop a GUI application using drag-and-drop features, you have already used an application that uses reflection in one form or another. All GUI tools that let you set the properties of a control, say a button, at design time use reflection to get the list of the properties for that control. Other tools such as class browsers and debuggers also use reflection. As an application programmer, you will not use reflection much unless you are developing advanced applications that use dynamism provided by the reflection API. It should be noted that using too much reflection slows down the performance of your application.

Summary

Reflection is the ability of a program to query and modify its state "as data" during the execution of the program. Java represents the byte code of a class as an object of the `Class` class to facilitate reflection. The class fields, constructors, and methods can be accessed as an object of the `Field`, `Constructor`, and `Method` classes, respectively. Using a `Field` object, you can access and change the value of the field. Using a `Method` object, you can invoke the method. Using a `Constructor` object, you can invoke a given constructor of a class. Using the `Array` class, you can also create arrays of a specified type and dimension using reflection and manipulate the elements of the arrays.

Java has been allowing access to rather inaccessible members such as a private field of a class outside the class using reflection. This is called *deep reflection*. Before you can access the inaccessible member, you need to call the `setAccessible(true)` on that member, which could be a `Field`, a `Method` or a `Constructor`. The `setAccessible()` method throws a runtime exception if the accessibility cannot be enabled. JDK9 added a `trySetAccessible()` method for the same purpose, which does not throw a runtime exception. Rather it returns `true` if accessibility is enabled and `false` otherwise.

Deep reflection in JDK9 across modules is prohibited by default. If a module wants to allow deep reflection on types in a given package, the module must open that package to at least the module that will use deep reflection. You can open a package using the `opens` statement in a module declaration. You can declare a module as an open module, which opens all packages in the module for deep reflection. If a named module `M` uses reflection to access types in another module `N`, the module `M` implicitly reads module `N`. All packages in an unnamed module open for deep reflection.

JDK9 allows deep reflection on JDK internal types by code on the class path. JDK9 issues a warning on the first such illegal access to the member of JDK internal types. The illegal reflective-access to JDK internal types will be removed in a future release.

QUESTIONS AND EXERCISES

1. What is reflection?
2. Name two Java packages that contain the reflection related classes and interfaces.
3. What does an instance of the `Class` class represent?
4. List three ways to get the reference of an instance of the `Class` class.
5. When do you use the `forName()` method of the `Class` class to get an instance of the `Class` class?
6. Name three built-in class loaders. How do you get references of these class loaders?

7. If you get a reference of the `Class` class, how do you know if this reference represents an interface?

8. What do instances of the `Field`, `Constructor`, and `Method` classes represent?

9. What is the difference between using the `getFields()` and `getDeclaredFields()` methods of the `Class` class?

10. You need to use `setAccessible(true)` or `trySetAccessible()` method of the `AccessibleObject` class to make a `Field`, `Constructor`, and `Method` object accessible even if they are inaccessible (e.g., they are declared private). What is the difference between these two methods?

11. Assume that you have two modules named `R` and `S`. Module `R` contains a public `p.Test` class with a public method `m()`. The code in module `S` needs to use the class `p.Test` to declare variables and create its objects. Module `S` also needs to use reflection to access the public method `m()` of the `p.Test` class in module `R`. What is the minimum you need to do while declaring module `R`, so module `S` can perform these tasks?

12. What is opening a package in a module? What is an open module?

13. What is the difference between exporting and opening a package of a module? Give an example when you will need to export and open the same package of a module.

14. Consider the declarations of a module named `jdojo.reflection.exercise.model` and a `MagicNumber` class in that module as follows:

```
// module-info.java
module jdojo.reflection.exercises.model {
    /* Add your module statements here */
}

// MagicNumber.java
package com.jdojo.reflection.exercises.model;

public class MagicNumber {
    private int number;

    public int getNumber() {
        return number;
    }

    public void setNumber(int number) {
        this.number = number;
    }
}
```

Modify the module declaration so that code in other modules can perform deep reflection on the objects of the `MagicNumber` class. Create a class named `MagicNumberTest` in a module named `jdojo.reflection.exercises`. The code in the `MagicNumberTest` class should use reflection to create an object of the `MagicNumber` class, set its private `number` field directly, and read the current value of the number field using the `getNumber()` method.

15. Can you access private members of JDK classes in Java 9? If your answer is yes, describe the rules and restrictions for such access.

16. Assume there are two modules, `P` and `Q`. Module `P` is an open module. Module `Q` wants to perform deep reflection on types in module `P`. Is module `Q` required to read module `P` in its module's declaration?

17. Assume there are two modules, `M` and `N`. Module `M` does not open any of its packages to any modules, but it exports a `com.jdojo.m` to all other modules. Can module `N` use reflection to access publically accessible members of the `com.jdojo.m` package of module `M`?

CHAPTER 4

Generics

In this chapter, you will learn:

- What generics are
- How to define generic types, methods, and constructors
- How to define bounds for type parameters
- How to use wildcards as the actual type parameters
- How the compiler infers the actual type parameters for generic type uses
- Generics and their limitations in array creations
- How the incorrect use of generics may lead to heap pollution

All example programs in this chapter are a member of a `jdojo.generics` module, as declared in Listing 4-1.

Listing 4-1. The Declaration of a jdojo.generics Module

```
// module-info.java
module jdojo.generics {
    exports com.jdojo.generics;
}
```

What Are Generics?

Generics let you write true polymorphic code that works with any type. Refer to Chapter 1 of the first volume of this *Beginning Java 9* series for more information on polymorphism and writing polymorphic code.

Let's discuss a simple example before I define what generics are and what they do for you. Suppose you want to create a new class whose sole job is to store a reference to any type, where "any type" means any reference type. Let's call this class `ObjectWrapper`, as shown in Listing 4-2.

Listing 4-2. A Wrapper Class to Store a Reference of Any Type

```
// ObjectWrapper.java
package com.jdojo.generics;

public class ObjectWrapper {
    private Object ref;
```


K. Sharan, *Java Language Features*, https://doi.org/10.1007/978-1-4842-3348-1_4

```
    public ObjectWrapper(Object ref) {
        this.ref = ref;
    }

    public Object get() {
        return ref;
    }

    public void set(Object ref) {
        this.ref = ref;
    }
}
```

As a Java developer, you would agree that you write this kind of code when you do not know the type of the objects that you have to deal with. The `ObjectWrapper` class can store a reference of any type in Java, such as `String`, `Integer`, `Person`, etc. How do you use the `ObjectWrapper` class? The following is one of the ways to use it to work with the `String` type:

```
ObjectWrapper stringWrapper = new ObjectWrapper("Hello");
stringWrapper.set("Another string");
String myString = (String) stringWrapper.get();
```

There's one problem in this snippet of code. Even though you knew that you stored (and wanted to) a `String` in the `stringWrapper` object, you had to cast the return value of the `get()` method to a `String` type in `(String) stringWrapper.get()`. Consider writing the following snippet of code:

```
ObjectWrapper stringWrapper = new ObjectWrapper("Hello");
stringWrapper.set(new Integer(101));
String myString =(String) stringWrapper.get();
```

This snippet of code compiles fine. However, the third statement throws a `ClassCastException` at runtime because you stored an `Integer` in the second statement and attempted to cast an `Integer` to a `String` in the third statement. First, it allowed you to store an `Integer` in `stringWrapper`. Second, it did not complain about the code in the third statement because it had no knowledge of your intent that you only wanted to use a `String` with `stringWrapper`.

Java has made some progress with the way it helps developers write type-safe programs. Wouldn't it be nice if the `ObjectWrapper` class allowed you to specify that you want to use this class only for a specific type, say, `String` this time and `Integer` the next? Your wish is fulfilled by generics in Java. They let you specify a *type parameter* with a type (class or interface). Such a type is called a *generic type* (more specifically generic class or generic interface). The *type parameter value* could be specified when you declare a variable of the generic type and create an object of your generic type. You have seen specifying parameters for method. This time, I am talking about specifying parameters for types such as classes or interfaces.

■ **Tip** A type with type parameters in its declaration is called a generic type.

Let's rewrite the ObjectWrapper class to use generics naming the new class simply Wrapper. The formal parameters of a generic type are specified in the generic type's declaration. Parameter names are valid Java identifiers and are specified in angle brackets (< >) after the name of the parameterized type. You will use T as the type parameter name for the Wrapper class:

```
public class Wrapper<T> {
}
```

It is an unwritten convention that type parameter names are one character, and to use T to indicate that the parameter is a type, E to indicate that the parameter is an element, K to indicate that the parameter is a key, N to indicate the parameter is a number, and V to indicate that the parameter is a value. In the previous example, you could have used any name for the type parameter, like so:

```
public class Wrapper<Hello> {
}

public class Wrapper<MyType> {
}
```

Multiple type parameters are separated by a comma. The following declaration for MyClass takes four type parameters named T, U, V, and W:

```
public class MyClass<T, U, V, W> {
}
```

You will be using your type parameter named T inside the class code in instance variable declarations, constructors, the get() method, and the set() method. Right now, T means any type for you, which will be known when you use this class. Listing 4-3 contains the complete code for the Wrapper class.

Listing 4-3. Using a Type Parameter to Define a Generic Class

```
// Wrapper.java
package com.jdojo.generics;

public class Wrapper<T> {
    private T ref;

    public Wrapper(T ref) {
        this.ref = ref;
    }

    public T get() {
        return ref;
    }

    public void set(T ref) {
        this.ref = ref;
    }
}
```

Are you confused about using T in Listing 4-3? Here, T means any class type or interface type. It could be String, Object, com.jdojo.generics.Person, etc. If you replace T with Object everywhere in this program and remove <T> from the class name, it is the same code that you had for the ObjectWrapper class.

How do you use the Wrapper class? Since its class name is not just Wrapper, rather it is Wrapper<T>, you may specify (but do not have to) the value for T. To store a String reference in the Wrapper object, you create it as follows:

```
Wrapper<String> greetingWrapper = new Wrapper<String>("Hello");
```

How do you use the set() and get() methods of the Wrapper class? Since you have specified the type parameter for class Wrapper<T> to be String, the set() and get() method will work only with String types. This is because you used T as an argument type in the set() method and T as the return type in the get() method declarations. Imagine replacing T in the class definition with String and you should have no problem understanding the following code:

```
greetingWrapper.set("Hi");                 // OK to pass a String
String greeting = greetingWrapper.get(); // No need to cast
```

This time, you did not have to cast the return value of the get() method. The compiler knows that greetingWrapper has been declared of type Wrapper<String>, so its get() method returns a String. Let's try to store an Integer object in greetingWrapper.

```
// A compile-time error. You can use greetingWrapper only to store a String.
greetingWrapper.set(new Integer(101));
```

The statement will generate the following compile-time error:

```
error: incompatible types: Integer cannot be converted to String
        greetingWrapper.set(new Integer(101));
```

You cannot pass an Integer to the set() method. The compiler will generate an error. If you want to use the Wrapper class to store an Integer, your code will be as follows:

```
Wrapper<Integer> idWrapper = new Wrapper<Integer>(new Integer(101));
idWrapper.set(new Integer(897)); // OK to pass an Integer
Integer id = idWrapper.get();

// A compile-time error. You can use idWrapper only with an Integer.
idWrapper.set("hello");
```

Assuming that a Person class exists that contains a constructor with two parameters, you store a Person object in Wrapper as follows:

```
Wrapper<Person> personWrapper = new Wrapper<Person>(new Person(1, "Chris"));
personWrapper.set(new Person(2, "Laynie"));
Person laynie = personWrapper.get();
```

The parameter that is specified in the type declaration is called a *formal type parameter*; for example, T is a formal type parameter in the Wrapper<T> class declaration. When you replace the formal type parameter with the actual type (e.g., in Wrapper<String> you replace the formal type parameter T with String), it is called a *parameterized type*. A reference type in Java, which accepts one or more type parameters, is called a generic type. A generic type is mostly implemented in the compiler. The JVM has no knowledge of generic types. All actual type parameters are erased at compile time using a process known as *erasure*. Compile-time type-safety is the benefit that you get when you use a parameterized generic type in your code without the need to use casts.

Polymorphism is about writing code in terms of a type that also works with many other types. In the first volume of this *Beginning Java 9* series, you learned how to write polymorphic code using inheritance and interfaces. Inheritance in Java offers inclusion polymorphism where you write code in terms of the base type and the code also works with all subtypes of that base type. In this case, you are forced to have all other types fall under a single inheritance hierarchy. That is, all types for which the polymorphic code works must inherit from the single base type. Interfaces in Java lifts this restriction and lets you write code in terms of an interface. The code works with all types that implement the interface. This time, all types for which the code works do not have to fall under one type hierarchy. Still, you had one constraint that all those types must implement the same interface. Generics in Java takes you a step closer to writing "true" polymorphic code. The code written using generics works for any type. Generics in Java do have some restrictions as to what you can do with the generic type in your code. Showing you what you can do with generics in Java and elaborating on the restrictions are the topics of discussion in this chapter.

Supertype-Subtype Relationship

Let's play a trick. The following code creates two parameterized instances of the `Wrapper<T>` class, one for the `String` type and one for the `Object` type:

```
Wrapper<String> stringWrapper = new Wrapper<String>("Hello");
stringWrapper.set("a string");

Wrapper<Object> objectWrapper = new Wrapper<Object>(new Object());
objectWrapper.set(new Object());

// Use a String object with objectWrapper
objectWrapper.set("a string"); // OK
```

It is fine to store a `String` object in `objectWrapper`. After all, if you intended to store an `Object` in `objectWrapper`, a `String` is also an `Object`. Is the following assignment allowed?

```
objectWrapper = stringWrapper;
```

No, this assignment is not allowed. That is, a `Wrapper<String>` is not assignment compatible to a `Wrapper<Object>`. To understand why this assignment is not allowed, let's assume for a moment that it was allowed and you could write code like the following:

```
// Now objectWrapper points to stringWrapper
objectWrapper = stringWrapper;

// We could store an Object in stringWrapper using objectWrapper
objectWrapper.set(new Object());

// The following statement will throw a runtime ClassCastException
String s = stringWrapper.get();
```

Do you see the danger of allowing an assignment like `objectWrapper = stringWrapper`? The compiler cannot make sure that `stringWrapper` will store only a reference of `String` type if this assignment was allowed.

Remember that a `String` is an `Object` because `String` is a subclass of `Object`. However, a `Wrapper<String>` is not a `Wrapper<Object>`. The normal supertype/subtype rules do not apply to parameterized types. Don't worry about memorizing this rule if you do not understand it. If you attempt such assignments, the compiler will tell you that you can't.

Raw Types

Implementation of generic types in Java is backward compatible. If an existing non-generic class is rewritten to take advantage of generics, the existing code that uses the non-generic version of the class should keep working. The code may use (though it is not recommended) a non-generic version of a generic class by just omitting references to the generic type parameters. The non-generic version of a generic type is called a *raw type*. Using raw types is discouraged. If you use raw types in your code, the compiler will generate unchecked warnings, as shown in the following snippet of code:

```
// Use the Wrapper<T> generic type as a raw type Wrapper
Wrapper rawType = new Wrapper("Hello"); // An unchecked warning

// Using the Wrapper<T> generic type as a parameterized type Wrapper<String>
Wrapper<String> genericType = new Wrapper<String>("Hello");

// Assigning the raw type to the parameterized type
genericType = rawType; // An unchecked warning

// Assigning the parameterized type to the raw type
rawType = genericType;
```

The compiler generates the following warnings when this snippet of code is compiled:

```
warning: [unchecked] unchecked call to Wrapper(T) as a member of the raw type Wrapper
        Wrapper rawType = new Wrapper("Hello"); // An unchecked warning
                          ^
  where T is a type-variable:
    T extends Object declared in class Wrapper

warning: [unchecked] unchecked conversion
        genericType = rawType; // An unchecked warning
                      ^
  required: Wrapper<String>
  found:    Wrapper
2 warnings
```

Unbounded Wildcards

Let's start with an example. It will help you understand the need for as well as the use of wildcards in generic types. Let's build a utility class for the Wrapper class and call it WrapperUtil. Add a static utility method called printDetails() to this class, which will take an object of the Wrapper<T> class. How should you define the argument of this method? The following is the first attempt:

```
public class WrapperUtil {
    public static void printDetails(Wrapper<Object> wrapper){
        // More code goes here
    }
}
```

Since your printDetails() method is supposed to print details about a Wrapper<T> of any type, Object as the type parameter seems to be more suitable. Let's use your new printDetails() method, as shown:

```
Wrapper<Object> objectWrapper = new Wrapper<Object>(new Object());
WrapperUtil.printDetails(objectWrapper); // OK

Wrapper<String> stringWrapper = new Wrapper<String>("Hello");
WrapperUtil.printDetails(stringWrapper); // A compile-time error
```

The compile-time error is as follows:

```
error: method printDetails in class WrapperUtil cannot be applied to given types;
        WrapperUtil.printDetails(stringWrapper); // A compile-time error
                   ^
  required: Wrapper<Object>
  found: Wrapper<String>
  reason: argument mismatch; Wrapper<String> cannot be converted to Wrapper<Object>
1 error
```

You are able to call the printDetails() method with the Wrapper<Object> type, but not with the Wrapper<String> type because they are not assignment compatible, which is contradictory to what your intuition tells you. To understand it fully, you need to know about the *wildcard type* in generics. A wildcard type is denoted by a question mark, as in <?>. For a generic type, a wildcard type is what an Object type is for a raw type. You can assign a generic of known type to a generic of wildcard type. Here is the sample code:

```
// Wrapper of String type
Wrapper<String> stringWrapper = new Wrapper<String>("Hi");

// You can assign a Wrapper<String> to Wrapper<?> type
Wrapper<?> wildCardWrapper = stringWrapper;
```

The question mark in a wildcard generic type (e.g., <?>) denotes an *unknown* type. When you declare a parameterized type using a wildcard (means unknown) as a parameter type, it means that it does not know about its type.

```
// wildCardWrapper has unknown type
Wrapper<?> wildCardWrapper;
```

```
// Better to name it as an unknownWrapper
Wrapper<?> unknownWrapper;
```

Can you create a Wrapper<T> object of an unknown type? Let's assume that John cooks something for you. He packs the food in a packet and hands it over to you. You hand over the packet to Donna. Donna asks you what is inside the packet. Your answer is that you do not know. Can John answer the same way you did? No. He must know what he cooked because he was the person who cooked the food. Even if you did not know what was inside the packet, you had no problem in carrying it and giving it to Donna. What would be your answer if Donna asked you to give her the vegetables from the packet? You would say that you do not know if vegetables are inside the packet.

Here are the rules for using a wildcard (unknown) generic type. Since it does not know its type, you cannot use it to create an object of its unknown type. The following code is illegal:

```
// Cannot use <?> with new operator. It is a compile-time error.
new Wrapper<?>("");
```

```
error: unexpected type
        new Wrapper<?>("");
                   ^
  required: class or interface without bounds
  found:    ?
1 error
```

As you were holding the packet of unknown food type (John knew the type of food when he cooked it), a wildcard generic type can refer to a known generic type object, as shown:

```
Wrapper<?> unknownWrapper = new Wrapper<String>("Hello");
```

There is a complicated list of rules as to what a wildcard generic type reference can do with the object. However, there is a simple rule of thumb to remember. The purpose of using generics is to have compile-time type-safety. As long as the compiler is satisfied that the operation will not produce any surprising results at runtime, it allows the operation on the wildcard generic type reference.

Let's apply the rule of thumb to your unknownWrapper reference variable. One thing that this unknownWrapper variable is sure about is that it refers to an object of the Wrapper<T> class of a known type. However, it does not know what that known type is. Can you use the following get() method? The following statement generates a compile-time error:

```
String str = unknownWrapper.get(); // A compile-time error
```

```
error: incompatible types: CAP#1 cannot be converted to String
        String str = unknownWrapper.get(); // A compile -time error
                                       ^
  where CAP#1 is a fresh type-variable:
    CAP#1 extends Object from capture of ?
1 error
```

The compiler knows that the get() method of the Wrapper<T> class returns an object of type T. However, for the unknownWrapper variable, type T is unknown. Therefore, the compiler cannot ensure that the method call, unknownWrapper.get(), will return a String and its assignment to str variable is fine at runtime. All you have to do is convince the compiler that the assignment will not throw a ClassCastException at runtime. Will the following line of code compile?

```
Object obj = unknownWrapper.get(); // OK
```

This code will compile because the compiler is convinced that this statement will not throw a ClassCastException at runtime. It knows that the get() method returns an object of a type, which is not known to the unknownWrapper variable. No matter what type of object the get() method returns, it will always be assignment-compatible with the Object type. After all, all reference types in Java are subtypes of the Object type. Will the following snippet of code compile?

```
unknownWrapper.set("Hello");         // A compile-time error
unknownWrapper.set(new Integer());   // A compile-time error
unknownWrapper.set(new Object());    // A compile-time error
unknownWrapper.set(null);            // OK
```

Were you surprised by errors in this snippet of code? You will find out that it is not as surprising as it seems. The set(T a) method accepts the generic type argument. This type, T, is not known to unknownWrapper, and therefore the compiler cannot make sure that the unknown type is a String type, an Integer type, or an Object type. This is why the first three calls to set() are rejected by the compiler. Why is the fourth call to the set() method correct? A null is assignment-compatible to any reference type in Java. The compiler thought that no matter what type T would be in the set(T a) method for the object to which unknownWrapper reference variable is pointing to, a null can always be safe to use. The following is your printDetails() method's code. If you pass a null Wrapper object to this method, it will throw a NullPointerException.

```
public class WrapperUtil {
    public static void printDetails(Wrapper<?> wrapper) {
        // Can assign get() return value to an Object
        Object value = wrapper.get();
        String className = null;

        if (value != null) {
            className = value.getClass().getName();
        }

        System.out.println("Class: " + className);
        System.out.println("Value: " + value);
    }
}
```

■ **Tip** Using only a question mark as a parameter type (<?>) is known as an *unbounded wildcard*. It places no bounds as to what type it can refer. You can also place an upper bound or a lower bound with a wildcard. I discuss bounded wildcards in the next two sections.

Upper-Bounded Wildcards

Suppose you want to add a method to your WrapperUtil class. The method should accept two numbers that are wrapped in your Wrapper objects and it will return their sum. The wrapped objects may be an Integer, Long, Byte, Short, Double, or Float. Your first attempt is to write the sum() method as shown:

```
public static double sum(Wrapper<?> n1, Wrapper<?> n2) {
    //Code goes here
}
```

There are some obvious problems with this method signature. The parameters n1 and n2 could be of any parameterized type of Wrapper<T> class. For example, the following call would be a valid call for the sum() method:

```
// Try adding an Integer and a String
sum(new Wrapper<Integer>(new Integer(125)), new Wrapper<String>("Hello"));
```

Computing the sum of an Integer and a String does not make sense. However, the code will compile and you should be ready to get some runtime exceptions depending on the implementation of the sum() method. You must restrict this kind of code from compiling. It should accept two Wrapper objects of type Number or its subclasses, not just anything. Therefore, you know the upper bound of the type of the actual parameter that the Wrapper object should have. The upper bound is the Number type. If you pass any other type, which is a subclass of the Number type, it is fine. However, anything that is not a Number type or its subclass type should be rejected at compile-time. You express the upper bound of a wildcard as

```
<? extends T>
```

Here, T is a type. <? extends T> means anything that is of type T or its subclass is acceptable. Using your upper bound as Number, you can define your method as

```
public static double sum(Wrapper<? extends Number> n1, Wrapper<? extends Number> n2) {
    Number num1 = n1.get();
    Number num2 = n2.get();
    double sum = num1.doubleValue() + num2.doubleValue();
    return sum;
}
```

The following snippet of code inside the method compiles fine:

```
Number num1 = n1.get();
Number num2 = n2.get();
```

No matter what you pass for n1 and n2, they will always be assignment-compatible with Number because the compiler will make sure that the parameters passed to the sum() method follow the rules specified in its declaration of <? extends Number>. The attempt to compute the sum of an Integer and a String will be rejected by the compiler. Consider the following snippet of code:

```
Wrapper<Integer> intWrapper = new Wrapper<Integer>(new Integer(10));
Wrapper<? extends Number> numberWrapper = intWrapper; // OK
numberWrapper.set(new Integer(1220)); // A compile-time error
numberWrapper.set(new Double(12.20)); // A compile-time error
```

Can you figure out the problem with this snippet of code? The type of numberWrapper is <? extends Number>, which means it can refer to (or it is assignment-compatible with) anything that is a subtype of the Number class. Since Integer is a subclass of Number, the assignment of intWrapper to numberWrapper is allowed. When you try to use the set() method on numberWrapper, the compiler starts complaining because it cannot make sure at compile-time that numberWrapper is a type of Integer or Double, which are subtypes of a Number. Be careful with this kind of compile-time error when working with generics. On the surface, it might look obvious to you and you would think that code should compile and run fine. Unless the compiler ensures that the operation is type-safe, it will not allow you to proceed. After all, compile-time and runtime type-safety is the primary goal of generics!

Lower-Bounded Wildcards

Specifying a lower-bound wildcard is the opposite of specifying an upper-bound wildcard. The syntax for using a lower-bound wildcard is <? super T>, which means "anything that is a supertype of T". Let's add another method to the WrapperUtil class. You will call the new method copy() and it will copy the value from a source wrapper object to a destination wrapper object. Here is the first attempt. The <T> is the formal type parameter for the copy() method. It specifies that the source and dest parameters must be of the same type. I explain generic methods in detail in the next section.

```
public class WrapperUtil {
    public static <T> void copy(Wrapper<T> source, Wrapper<T> dest) {
        T value = source.get();
        dest.set(value);
    }
}
```

Copying the content of a Wrapper<String> to a Wrapper<Object> using your copy() method will not work.

```
Wrapper<Object> objectWrapper = new Wrapper<Object>(new Object());
Wrapper<String> stringWrapper = new Wrapper<String>("Hello");
WrapperUtil.copy(stringWrapper, objectWrapper); // A compile-time error
```

This code will generate a compile-time error because the copy() method requires the source and the dest arguments be of the same type. However, for all practical purposes a String is always an Object. Here, you need to use a lower-bounded wildcard, as shown:

```
public class WrapperUtil {
    // New definition of the copy() method
    public static <T> void copy(Wrapper<T> source, Wrapper<? super T> dest){
        T value = source.get();
        dest.set(value);
    }
}
```

Now you are saying that the dest argument of the copy() method could be either T, same as source, or any of its supertype. You can use the copy() method to copy the contents of a Wrapper<String> to a Wrapper<Object> as follows:

```
Wrapper<Object> objectWrapper = new Wrapper<Object>(new Object());
Wrapper<String> stringWrapper = new Wrapper<String>("Hello");
WrapperUtil.copy(stringWrapper, objectWrapper); // OK with the new copy() method
```

Since Object is the supertype of String, the new copy() method will work. However, you cannot use it to copy from an Object type wrapper to a String type wrapper, because “an Object is a String is not always true. Listing 4-4 shows the complete code for the WrapperUtil class.

Listing 4-4. A WrapperUtil Utility Class That Works with Wrapper Objects

```
// WrapperUtil.java
package com.jdojo.generics;

public class WrapperUtil {
    public static void printDetails(Wrapper<?> wrapper) {
        // Can assign get() return value to Object
        Object value = wrapper.get();
        String className = null;

        if (value != null) {
            className = value.getClass().getName();
        }

        System.out.println("Class: " + className);
        System.out.println("Value: " + value);
    }

    public static double sum(Wrapper<? extends Number> n1, Wrapper<? extends Number> n2) {
        Number num1 = n1.get();
        Number num2 = n2.get();
        double sum = num1.doubleValue() + num2.doubleValue();
        return sum;
    }

    public static <T> void copy(Wrapper<T> source, Wrapper<? super T> dest) {
        T value = source.get();
        dest.set(value);
    }
}
```

Listing 4-5 shows you how to use the Wrapper and WrapperUtil classes.

Listing 4-5. Using the WrapperUtil Class

```
// WrapperUtilTest.java
package com.jdojo.generics;
```

```
public class WrapperUtilTest {
    public static void main(String[] args) {
        Wrapper<Integer> n1 = new Wrapper<>(10);
        Wrapper<Double> n2 = new Wrapper<>(15.75);

        // Print the details
        WrapperUtil.printDetails(n1);
        WrapperUtil.printDetails(n2);

        // Add numeric values in two WrapperUtil
        double sum = WrapperUtil.sum(n1, n2);
        System.out.println("sum: " + sum);

        // Copy the value of a Wrapper<Double> to a Wrapper<Number>
        Wrapper<Number> holder = new Wrapper<>(45);
        System.out.println("Original holder: " + holder.get());
        WrapperUtil.copy(n2, holder);
        System.out.println("After copy holder: " + holder.get());
    }
}
```

```
Class: java.lang.Integer
Value: 10
Class: java.lang.Double
Value: 15.75
sum: 25.75
Original holder: 45
After copy holder: 15.75
```

Generic Methods and Constructors

You can define type parameters in a method declaration. They are specified in angle brackets before the return type of the method. The type that contains the generic method declaration does not have to be a generic type, so you can have generic methods in a non-generic type. It is also possible for a type and its methods to define different type parameters.

■ **Tip** Type parameters defined for a generic type are not available in static methods of that type. Therefore, if a static method needs to be generic, it must define its own type parameters. If a method needs to be generic, define just that method as generic rather than defining the entire type as generic.

The following snippet of code defines a generic type `Test` with its type parameter named as `T`. It also defines a generic instance method `m1()` that defines its own generic type parameter named `V`. The method also uses the type parameter `T`, which is defined by its class. Note the use of `<V>` before the return type void of the `m1()` method. It defines a new generic type named `V` for the method.

```
public class Test<T> {
    public <V> void m1(Wrapper<V> a, Wrapper<V> b, T c) {
        // Do something
    }
}
```

Can you think of the implication of defining and using the generic type parameter V for the m1() method? Look at its use in defining the first and second parameters of the method as Wrapper<V>. It forces the first and the second parameters to be of the same type. The third argument must be of the same type T, which is the type of the class instantiation.

How do you specify the generic type for a method when you want to call the method? Usually, you do not need to specify the actual type parameter when you call the method. The compiler figures it out for you using the value you pass to the method. However, if you ever need to pass the actual type parameter for the method's formal type parameter, you must specify it in angle brackets (< >) between the dot and the method name in the method call, as shown:

```
Test<String> t = new Test<String>();
Wrapper<Integer> iw1 = new Wrapper<Integer>(new Integer(201));
Wrapper<Integer> iw2 = new Wrapper<Integer>(new Integer(202));

// Specify that Integer is the actual type for the type parameter for m1()
t.<Integer>m1(iw1, iw2, "hello");

// Let the compiler figure out the actual type parameters using types for iw1 and iw2
t.m1(iw1, iw2, "hello"); // OK
```

Listing 4-4 demonstrated how to declare a generic static method. You cannot refer to the type parameters of the containing class inside the static method. A static method can refer only to its own declared type parameters.

Here is the copy of your copy() static method from the WrapperUtil class. It defines a type parameter T, which is used to constrain the type of arguments source and dest.

```
public static <T> void copy(Wrapper<T> source, Wrapper<? super T> dest) {
    T value = source.get();
    dest.set(value);
}
```

The compiler will figure out the actual type parameter for a method whether the method is non-static or static. However, if you want to specify the actual type parameter for a static method call, you can do so as follows:

```
WrapperUtil.<Integer>copy(iw1, iw2);
```

You can also define type parameters for constructors the same way as you do for methods. The following snippet of code defines a type parameter U for the constructor of class Test. It places a constraint that the constructor's type parameter U must be the same or a subtype of the actual type of its class type parameter T.

```
public class Test<T> {
    public <U extends T> Test(U k) {
        // Do something
    }
}
```

The compiler will figure out the actual type parameter passed to a constructor by examining the arguments you pass to the constructor. If you want to specify the actual type parameter value for the constructor, you can specify it in angle brackets between the new operator and the name of the constructor, as shown in the following snippet of code:

```
// Specify the actual type parameter for the constructor as Double
Test<Number> t1 = new <Double>Test<Number>(new Double(12.89));

// Let the compiler figure out that we are using Integer as the actual type parameter
// for the constructor
Test<Number> t2 = new Test<Number>(new Integer(123));
```

Type Inference in Generic Object Creation

In many cases, the compiler can infer the value for the type parameter in an object-creation expression when you create an object of a generic type. Note that the type inference support in the object-creation expression is limited to the situations where the type is obvious. Consider the following statement:

```
List<String> list = new ArrayList<String>();
```

With the declaration of `list` as `List<String>`, it is obvious that you want to create an `ArrayList` with type parameter as `<String>`. In this case, you can specify empty angle brackets, `<>` (known as the diamond operator or simply the diamond), as the type parameter for `ArrayList`. You can rewrite this statement as shown:

```
List<String> list = new ArrayList<>();
```

Note that if you do not specify a type parameter for a generic type in an object-creation expression, the type is the raw type and the compiler generates unchecked warnings. For example, the following statement will compile with an unchecked warning:

```
// Using ArrayList as a raw type, not a generic type
List<String> list = new ArrayList(); // Generates an unchecked warning
```

```
warning: [unchecked] unchecked conversion
        List<String> list = new ArrayList(); // Generates an unchecked warning
                            ^
  required: List<String>
  found:    ArrayList
1 warning
```

Sometimes the compiler cannot correctly infer the parameter type of a type in an object-creation expression. In those cases, you need to specify the parameter type instead of using the diamond operator (`<>`). Otherwise, the compiler will infer a wrong type, which will generate an error.

When the diamond operator is used in an object creation expression, the compiler uses a four-step process to infer the parameter type for the parameterized type. Let's consider a typical object-creation expression:

```
T1<T2> var = new T3<>(constructor-arguments);
```

1. First, it tries to infer the type parameter from the static type of the constructor-arguments. Note that constructor-arguments may be empty, for example, `new ArrayList<>()`. If the type parameter is inferred in this step, the process continues to the next step.
2. It uses the left side of the assignment operator to infer the type. In the previous statement, it will infer `T2` as the type if the constructor-arguments are empty. Note that an object-creation expression may not be part of an assignment statement. In such cases, it will use the next step.
3. If the object-creation expression is used as an actual parameter for a method call, the compiler tries to infer the type by looking at the type of the formal parameter for the method being called.
4. If all else fails and it cannot infer the type using these steps, it infers `Object` as the type parameter.

Let's discuss a few examples that involve all steps in the type inference process. Create the two lists, `list1` of `List<String>` type and `list2` of `List<Integer>` type:

```
import java.util.Arrays;
import java.util.List;

// More code goes here...

List<String> list1 = Arrays.asList("A", "B");
List<Integer> list2 = Arrays.asList(9, 19, 1969);
```

Consider the following statement that uses the diamond operator:

```
List<String> list3 = new ArrayList<>(list1); // Inferred type is String
```

The compiler used the constructor argument `list1` to infer the type. The static type of `list1` is `List<String>`, so the type `String` was inferred by the compiler. The previous statement compiles fine. The compiler did not use the left side of the assignment operator, `List<String> list3`, during the inference process. You may not trust this argument. Consider the following statement to prove this:

```
List<String> list4 = new ArrayList<>(list2); // A compile-time error
```

```
required: List<String>
found:    ArrayList<Integer>
1 error
```

Do you believe it now? The constructor argument is list2 whose static type is List<Integer>. The compiler inferred the type as Integer and replaced ArrayList<> with ArrayList<Integer>. The type of list4 is List<String>, which is not assignment-compatible with the ArrayList<Integer>, which resulted in the compile-time error.

Consider the following statement:

```
List<String> list5 = new ArrayList<>(); // Inferred type is String
```

This time, there is no constructor argument. The compiler uses the second step to look at the left side of the assignment operator to infer the type. On the left side, it finds List<String> and it correctly infers the type as String. Consider a process() method that is declared as follows:

```
public static void process(List<String> list) {
    // Code goes here
}
```

The following statement makes a call to the process() method and the inferred type parameter is String:

```
// The inferred type is String
process(new ArrayList<>());
```

The compiler looks at the type of the formal parameter of the process() method, finds List<String>, and infers the type as String.

■ **Tip** Using the diamond operator saves some typing. Use it when the type inference is obvious. However, it is better, for readability, to specify the type, instead of the diamond operator, in a complex object-creation expression. Always choose readability over brevity.

JDK9 added support for the diamond operator in anonymous classes if the inferred types are denotable. You cannot use the diamond operator with anonymous classes—even in JDK9—if the inferred types are non-denotable. The Java compiler uses types that cannot be written in Java programs. Types that can be written in Java programs are known as *denotable* types. Types that the compiler knows but cannot be written in Java programs are known as *non-denotable* types. For example, String is a denotable type because you can use it in programs to denote a type; however, Serializable & CharSequence is not a denotable-type, even though it is a valid type for the compiler. It is an intersection type that represents a type that implements both interfaces, Serializable and CharSequence. Intersection types are allowed in generic type definitions, but you cannot declare a variable using this intersection type:

```
// Not allowed in Java code. Cannot declare a variable of an intersection type.
Serializable & CharSequence var;

// Allowed in Java code
class Magic<T extends Serializable & CharSequence> {
    // More code goes here
}
```

Java contains a generic Callable<V> interface in the java.util.concurrent package. It is declared as follows:

```
public interface Callable<V> {
    V call() throws Exception;
}
```

In JDK9, the compiler will infer the type parameter for the anonymous class as Integer in the following snippet of code. Prior to JDK9, you had to write "new Callable<Integer>()".

```
// A compile-time error in JDK8, but allowed in JDK9.
Callable<Integer> c = new Callable<>() {
    @Override
    public Integer call() {
        return 100;
    }
};
```

No Generic Exception Classes

Exceptions are thrown at runtime. The compiler cannot ensure the type-safety of exceptions at runtime if you use a generic exception class in a catch clause, because the erasure process erases the mention of any type parameter during compilation. This is the reason that it is a compile-time error to attempt to define a generic class, which is a direct or indirect subclass of java.lang.Throwable.

No Generic Anonymous Classes

An anonymous class is a one-time class. You need a class name to specify the actual type parameter. An anonymous class does not have a name. Therefore, you cannot have a generic anonymous class. However, you can have generic methods inside an anonymous class. Your anonymous class can inherit a generic class. An anonymous class can implement generic interfaces. Any class, except an exception type, enums, and anonymous inner classes, can have type parameters.

Generics and Arrays

Let's look at the following code for a class called GenericArrayTest:

```
public class GenericArrayTest<T> {
    private T[] elements;

    public GenericArrayTest(int howMany) {
        elements = new T[howMany]; // A compile-time error
    }

    // More code goes here
}
```

The GenericArrayTest class declares a type parameter T. In the constructor, it attempts to create an array of the generic type. You cannot compile the previous code. The compiler will complain about the following statement:

```
elements = new T[howMany]; // A compile-time error
```

Recall that all references to the generic type parameter are erased from the code when a generic class or code using it is compiled. An array needs to know its type when it is created, so that it can perform a check at runtime when an element is stored in it to make sure that the element is assignment-compatible with the array type. An array's type information will not be available at runtime if you use a type parameter to create the array. This is the reason that the statement is not allowed.

You cannot create an array of generic type because the compiler cannot ensure the type-safety of the assignment to the array element. You cannot write the following code:

```
Wrapper<String>[] gsArray = null;

// Cannot create an array of generic type
gsArray = new Wrapper<String>[10]; // A compile-time error
```

It is allowed to create an array of unbounded wildcard generic types, as shown:

```
Wrapper<?>[] anotherArray = new Wrapper<?>[10]; // Ok
```

Suppose you want to use an array of a generic type. You can do so by using the newInstance() method of the java.lang.reflect.Array class as follows. You will have to deal with the unchecked warnings at compile-time because of the cast used in the array creation statement. The following snippet of code shows that you can still bypass the compile-time type-safety check when you try to sneak in an Object into an array of Wrapper<String>. However, this is the consequence you have to live with when using generics, which does not carry its type information at runtime. Java generics are as skin deep as you can imagine.

```
Wrapper<String>[] a = (Wrapper<String>[]) Array.newInstance(Wrapper.class, 10);

Object[] objArray = (Object[]) a;
objArray[0] = new Object();  // Will throw a java.lang.ArrayStoreExceptionxception
a[0] = new Wrapper<String>("Hello"); // OK. Checked by compiler
```

Runtime Class Type of Generic Objects

What is the class type of the object for a parameterized type? Consider the program in Listing 4-6.

Listing 4-6. All Objects of a Parameterized Type Share the Same Class at Runtime

```
// GenericsRuntimeClassTest.java
package com.jdojo.generics;

public class GenericsRuntimeClassTest {
    public static void main(String[] args) {
        Wrapper<String> a = new Wrapper<String>("Hello");
        Wrapper<Integer> b = new Wrapper<Integer>(new Integer(123));
```

```
        Class aClass = a.getClass();
        Class bClass = b.getClass();

        System.out.println("Class for a: " + aClass.getName());
        System.out.println("Class for b: " + bClass.getName());
        System.out.println("aClass == bClass: " + (aClass == bClass));
    }
}
```

```
Class for a: com.jdojo.generics.Wrapper
Class for b: com.jdojo.generics.Wrapper
aClass == bClass: true
```

The program creates objects of the `Wrapper<String>` and `Wrapper<Integer>`. It prints the class names for both objects and they are the same. The output shows that all parameterized objects of the same generic type share the same class object at runtime. As mentioned earlier, the type information you supply to the generic type is removed from the code during compilation. The compiler changes the `Wrapper<String> a;` statement to `Wrapper a;`. For the JVM, it's business as usual (before pre-generics)!

Heap Pollution

Representing a type at runtime is called *reification*. A type that can be represented at runtime is called a *reifiable type*. A type that is not completely represented at runtime is called a *non-reifiable type*. Most generic types are non-reifiable because generics are implemented using erasure, which removes the type's parameters information at compile time. For example, when you write `Wrapper<String>`, the compiler removes the type parameter `<String>` and the runtime sees only `Wrapper` instead of `Wrapper<String>`.

Heap pollution is a situation that occurs when a variable of a parameterized type refers to an object not of the same parameterized type. The compiler issues an unchecked warning if it detects possible heap pollution. If your program compiles without any unchecked warnings, heap pollution will not occur. Consider the following snippet of code:

```
Wrapper nWrapper = new Wrapper<Integer>(101);     // #1

// Unchecked warning at compile-time and heap pollution at runtime
Wrapper<String> sWrapper = nWrapper; // #2
String str = sWrapper.get();         // #3 - ClassCastException
```

The first statement (labeled #1) compiles fine. The second statement (labeled #2) generates an unchecked warning because the compiler cannot determine if `nWrapper` is of the type `Wrapper<String>`. Since parameter type information is erased at compile-time, the runtime has no way of detecting this type mismatch. The heap pollution in the second statement makes it possible to get a `ClassCastException` in the third statement (labeled #3) at runtime. If the second statement was not allowed, the third statement will not cause a `ClassCastException`.

Heap pollution may also occur because of an unchecked cast operation. Consider the following snippet of code:

```
Wrapper<? extends Number> nW = new Wrapper<Long>(1L); // #1

// Unchecked cast and unchecked warning occurs when the
// following statement #2 is compiled. Heap pollution occurs,
// when it is executed.
Wrapper<Short> sw = (Wrapper<Short>) nW; // #2
short s = sw.get();                      // #3 - ClassCastException
```

The statement labeled #2 uses an unchecked cast. The compiler issues an unchecked warning. At runtime, it leads to heap pollution. As a result, the statement labeled #3 generates a runtime `ClassCastException`.

Varargs Methods and Heap Pollution Warnings

Java implements the varargs parameter of a varargs method by converting the varargs parameter into an array. If a varargs method uses a generic type varargs parameter, Java cannot guarantee the type-safety. A non-reifiable generic type varargs parameter may possibly lead to heap pollution.

Consider the following snippet of code that declares a `process()` method with a parameterized type parameter. The comments in the method's body indicate the heap pollution and other types of problems.

```
public static void process(Wrapper<Long>...nums) {
    Object[] obj = nums;                 // Heap pollution
    obj[0] = new Wrapper<>("Hello");    // An array corruption
    Long lv = nums[0].get();            // A ClassCastException
    // Other code goes here
}
```

■ **Tip** You need to use the `-Xlint:unchecked,varargs` option with the `javac` compiler to see the unchecked and varargs warnings.

When the `process()` method is compiled, the compiler removes the type information `<Long>` from its parameterized type parameter and changes its signature to `process(Wrapper[] nums)`. When you compile the declaration of the `process()` method, you get the following unchecked warning:

```
warning: [unchecked] Possible heap pollution from parameterized vararg type Wrapper<Long>
        public static void process(Wrapper<Long>...nums) {
                                                       ^
1 warning
```

Consider the following snippet of code that calls the `process()` method:

```
Wrapper<Long> v1 = new Wrapper<>(10L);
Wrapper<Long> v2 = new Wrapper<>(11L);
process(v1, v2); // An unchecked warning
```

When this snippet of code is compiled, it generates the following compiler unchecked warning:

```
warning: [unchecked] unchecked generic array creation for varargs parameter of type
Wrapper<Long>[]
                process(v1, v2);
                       ^
1 warning
```

Warnings are generated at the method declaration as well as at the location of the method call. If you create such a method, it is your responsibility to ensure that heap pollution does not occur inside your method's body.

If you create a varargs method with a non-reifiable type parameter, you can suppress the unchecked warnings at the location of the method's declaration as well as the method's call by using `@SafeVarargs` annotation. By using `@SafeVarargs`, you are asserting that your varargs method with non-reifiable type parameter is safe to use. The following snippet of code uses the `@SafeVarargs` annotation with the `process()` method:

```
@SafeVarargs
public static void process(Wrapper<Long>...nums) {
    Object[] obj = nums;                   // Heap pollution
    obj[0] = new Wrapper<String>("Hello"); // An array corruption
    Long lv = nums[0].get();               // A ClassCastException
    // Other code goes here
}
```

When you compile this declaration of the `process()` method, you do not get an *unchecked* warning. However, you get the following *varargs* warning because the compiler sees possible heap pollution when the varargs parameter `nums` is assigned to the `Object` array `obj`:

```
warning: [varargs] Varargs method could cause heap pollution from non-reifiable varargs
parameter nums
                Object[] obj = nums; // Heap pollution
                               ^
1 warning
```

You can suppress the *unchecked* and *varargs* warnings for a varargs method with a non-reifiable type parameter by using the `@SuppressWarnings` annotation as follows:

```
@SuppressWarnings({"unchecked", "varargs"})
public static void process(Wrapper<Long>...nums) {
    // Code goes here
}
```

Note that when you use the `@SuppressWarnings` annotation with a varargs method, it suppresses warnings only at the location of the method's declaration, not at the locations where the method is called.

Summary

Generics are the Java language features that allow you to declare types (classes and interfaces) that use type parameters. Type parameters are specified when the generic type is used. The type when used with the actual type parameter is known as a parameterized type. When a generic type is used without specifying its type parameters, it is called a raw type. For example, if Wrapper<T> is a generic class, Wrapper<String> is a parameterized type with String as the actual type parameter and Wrapper as the raw type. Type parameters can also be specified for constructors and methods. Generics allow you to write true polymorphic code in Java—code using a type parameter that works for all types.

By default, a type parameter is unbounded, meaning that you can specify any type for the type parameter. For example, if a class is declared with a type parameter <T>, you can specify any type available in Java, such as <String>, <Object>, <Person>, <Employee>, <Integer>, etc., as the actual type for T. Type parameters in a type declaration can also be specified as having upper bounds or lower bounds. The declaration Wrapper<U extends Person> is an example of specifying an upper bound for the type parameter U that specifies that U can be of a type that is Person or a subtype of Person. The declaration Wrapper<? super Person> is an example of specifying a lower bound; it specifies that the type parameter is the type Person or a supertype of Person.

Java also lets you specify the wildcard, which is a question mark, as the actual type parameter. A wildcard as the actual parameter means the actual type parameter is unknown; for example, Wrapper<?> means that the type parameter T for the generic type Wrapper<T> is unknown.

The compiler attempts to infer the type of an expression using generics, depending on the context in which the expression is used. If the compiler cannot infer the type, it generates a compile-time error and you will need to specify the type explicitly.

The supertype-subtype relationship does not exist with parameterized types. For example, Wrapper<Long> is not a subtype of Wrapper<Number>.

The generic type parameters are erased by the compiler using a process called *type erasure*. Therefore, the generic type parameters are not available at runtime. For example, the runtime type of Wrapper<Long> and Wrapper<String> are the same, which is Wrapper.

EXERCISES

1. What are generics (or generic types), parameterized types, and raw types? Give an example of a generic type and its parameterized type.

2. The Number class is the superclass of the Long class. The following snippet of code does not compile. Explain.

```
List<Number> list1= new ArrayList<>();
List<Long> list2= new ArrayList<>();
list1 = list2;  // A compile-time error
```

3. Write the output when the following ClassNamePrinter class is run. Rewrite the code for the print() method of this class after the compiler erases the type parameter T during compilation .

```
// ClassNamePrinter.java
package com.jdojo.generics.exercises;

public class ClassNamePrinter {
    public static void main(String[] args) {
        ClassNamePrinter.print(10);
        ClassNamePrinter.print(10L);
        ClassNamePrinter.print(10.2);
    }

    public static <T extends Number> void print(T obj) {
        String className = obj.getClass().getSimpleName();
       System.out.println(className);
    }
}
```

4. What are unbounded wildcards? Why does the following snippet of code not compile?

```
List<?> list = new ArrayList<>();
list.add("Hello"); // A compile-time error
```

5. Consider the following incomplete declaration of the `Util` class:

```
// Util.java
package com.jdojo.generics.exercises;

import java.lang.reflect.Array;
import java.util.ArrayList;
import java.util.Arrays;
import java.util.List;

public class Util {
    public static void main(String[] args) {
        Integer[] n1 = {1, 2};
        Integer[] n2 = {3, 4};
        Integer[] m = merge(n1, n2);
        System.out.println(Arrays.toString(m));

        String[] s1 = {"one", "two"};
        String[] s2 = {"three", "four"};
        String[] t = merge(s1, s2);
        System.out.println(Arrays.toString(t));

        List<Number> list = new ArrayList<>();
        add(list, 10, 20, 30L, 40.5F, 50.9);
        System.out.println(list);
    }
```

```
    public static <T> T[] merge(T[] a, T[] b) {

    }

    public static /* Add type parameters here */ void add(List<T> list,
U... elems) {

        /* Your code to add elems to list goes here */
    }
}
```

Complete the body of the `merge()` method, so it can concatenate the two arrays passed in as its parameters and return the concatenated array.

Complete the `add()` method by specifying its type parameters and adding the code in its body. The first parameter to the method is a parameterized `List<T>` and the second parameter is a varargs parameter of the type `T` or its descendant. That is, the second parameter type is any type whose objects can be added to the `List<T>`.

Running the `Util` class should produce the following output:

```
[1, 2, 3, 4]
[one, two, three, four]
[10, 20, 30, 40.5, 50.9]
```

6. Create a generic `Stack<E>` class. Its objects represent a stack that can store elements of its type parameter `E`. The following is a template for the class. You need to provide implementation for all its methods. Write test code to test all methods. Method names are standard method names for a stack. Any illegal access to the stack should throw a runtime exception.

```
// Stack.java
package com.jdojo.generics.exercises;

import java.util.LinkedList;
import java.util.List;

public class Stack<E> {
    // Use LinkedList instead of ArrayList
    private final List<E> stack = new LinkedList<>();

    public void push(E e) {}
    public E pop() { }
    public E peek() { }
    public boolean isEmpty() { }
    public int size() { }
}
```

7. What is heap pollution? What types of warnings does the compiler generate when it detects a possibility of heap pollution? How do you print such warnings during compilation? How do you suppress such warnings?

8. Describe the reasons that the following declaration of the `Test` class does not compile.

```
public class Test {
   public <T> void test(T t) {
      // More code goes here
   }

   public <U> void test(U u) {
      // More code goes here
   }
}
```

CHAPTER 5

Lambda Expressions

In this chapter, you will learn:

- What lambda expressions are
- Why we need lambda expressions
- The syntax for defining lambda expressions
- Target typing for lambda expressions
- Commonly used built-in functional interfaces
- Method and constructor references
- Lexical scoping of lambda expressions

All example programs in this chapter are a member of a `jdojo.lambda` module, as declared in Listing 5-1.

Listing 5-1. The Declaration of a jdojo.lambda Module

```
// module-info.java
module jdojo.lambda {
    exports com.jdojo.lambda;
}
```

What Is a Lambda Expression?

A lambda expression is an unnamed block of code (or an unnamed function) with a list of formal parameters and a body. Sometimes a lambda expression is simply called a *lambda*. The body of a lambda expression can be a block statement or an expression. An arrow (`->`) is used to separate the list of parameters and the body. The term "lambda" has its origin in Lambda calculus that uses the Greek letter lambda (λ) to denote a function abstraction. The following are some examples of lambda expressions in Java:

```
// Takes an int parameter and returns the parameter value incremented by 1
(int x) -> x + 1

// Takes two int parameters and returns their sum
(int x, int y) -> x + y

// Takes two int parameters and returns the maximum of the two
(int x, int y) -> { int max = x > y ? x : y;
                    return max;
                  }
```


K. Sharan, *Java Language Features*, https://doi.org/10.1007/978-1-4842-3348-1_5

```
// Takes no parameters and returns void
() -> { }

// Takes no parameters and returns a string "OK"
() -> "OK"

// Takes a String parameter and prints it on the standard output
(String msg) -> { System.out.println(msg); }

// Takes a parameter and prints it on the standard output
msg -> System.out.println(msg)

// Takes a String parameter and returns its length
(String str) -> str.length()
```

At this point, you will not be able to understand the syntax of lambda expressions completely. I cover the syntax in detail shortly. For now, just get the feel of it, keeping in mind that the syntax for lambda expressions is similar to the syntax for declaring methods.

■ **Tip** A lambda expression is not a method, although its declaration looks similar to a method. As the name suggests, a lambda expression is an expression that represents an instance of a functional interface.

Every expression in Java has a type, and so does a lambda expression. The type of a lambda expression is a functional interface type. When the abstract method of the functional interface is called, the body of the lambda expression is executed. Consider the lambda expression that takes a `String` parameter and returns its length:

```
(String str) -> str.length()
```

What is the type of this lambda expression? The answer is that we do not know. By looking at the lambda expression, all you can say is that it takes a `String` parameter and returns an `int`, which is the length of the `String` parameter. Its type can be any functional interface type with an abstract method that takes a `String` as a parameter and returns an `int`. The following is an example of such a functional interface:

```
@FunctionalInterface
interface StringToIntMapper {
    int map(String str);
}
```

The lambda expression represents an instance of the `StringToIntMapper` functional interface when it appears in the assignment statement, like so:

```
StringToIntMapper mapper = (String str) -> str.length();
```

In this statement, the compiler finds that the right side of the assignment operator is a lambda expression. To infer its type, it looks at the left side of the assignment operator that expects an instance of the `StringToIntMapper` interface; it verifies that the lambda expression conforms to the declaration of the `map()` method in the `StringToIntMapper` interface; finally, it infers that the type of the lambda expression is the `StringToIntMapper` interface type. When you call the `map()` method on the `mapper` variable passing a `String`, the body of the lambda expression is executed as shown in the following snippet of code:

```
StringToIntMapper mapper = (String str) -> str.length();
String name = "Kristy";
int mappedValue = mapper.map(name);
System.out.println("name=" + name + ", mapped value=" + mappedValue);
```

```
name=Kristy, mapped value=6
```

So far, you have not seen anything that you could not do in Java without using lambda expressions. The following snippet of code uses an anonymous class to achieve the same result as the lambda expression used in the previous example:

```
StringToIntMapper mapper = new StringToIntMapper() {
    @Override
    public int map(String str) {
        return str.length();
    }
};

String name = "Kristy";
int mappedValue = mapper.map(name);
System.out.println("name=" + name + ", mapped value=" + mappedValue);
```

```
name=Kristy, mapped value=6
```

At this point, a lambda expression may seem to be a concise way of writing an anonymous class, which is true as far as the syntax goes. There are some subtle differences in semantics between the two. I discuss those differences when I discuss more details later.

■ **Tip** Java is a strongly-typed language, which means that the compiler must know the type of all expressions used in a Java program. A lambda expression by itself does not have a type, and therefore, it cannot be used as a standalone expression. The type of a lambda expression is always inferred by the compiler by the context in which it is used.

Why Do We Need Lambda Expressions?

Java has supported object-oriented programming since the beginning. In object-oriented programming, the program logic is based on mutable objects. Methods of classes contain the logic. Methods are invoked on objects, which typically modify objects' states. In object-oriented programming, the order of method invocation matters as each method invocation may potentially modify the state of the object, thus producing side effects. static analysis of the program logic is difficult as the program state depends on the order in which the code will be executed. Programming with mutating objects also poses a challenge in concurrent programming in which multiple parts of the program may attempt to modify the state of the same object concurrently.

As the processing power of computers has increased in recent years, so has the amount of data to be processed. Nowadays, it is common to process data as big as terabytes in size, requiring the need for parallel programming. Now it is common for computers to have a multi-core processor that give users the opportunity to run software programs faster; at the same time, this poses a challenge to programmers to write more parallel programs, taking advantage of all the available cores in the processor. Java has supported concurrent programming since the beginning. It added support for parallel programming in Java 7 through the fork/join framework, which was not easy to use.

Functional programming, which is based on Lambda calculus, existed long before object-oriented programming. It is based on the concept of functions, a block of code that accepts values, known as parameters, and the block of code is executed to compute a result. A function represents a functionality or operation. Functions do not modify data, including its input, thus producing no side-effects; for this reason, the order of the execution of functions does not matter in functional programming. In functional programming, a higher order function is an anonymous function that can be treated as a data object. That is, it can be stored in a variable and passed around from one context to another. It might be invoked in a context that did not necessarily define it. Note that a higher order function is an anonymous function, so the invoking context does not have to know its name. A closure is a higher order function packaged with its defining environment. A closure carries with it the variables in scope when it was defined, and it can access those variables even when it is invoked in a context other than the context in which those variables were defined.

In recent years, functional programming has become popular because of its suitability in concurrent, parallel, and event-driven programming. Modern programming languages such as C#, Groovy, Python, and Scala support functional programming. Java did not want to be left behind, and hence, it introduced lambda expressions to support functional programming, which can be mixed with its already popular object-oriented features to develop robust, concurrent, parallel programs. Java adopted the syntax for lambda expressions that is very similar to the syntax used in other programming languages, such as C# and Scala.

In object-oriented programming, a function is called a method and it is always part of a class. If you wanted to pass functionality around in Java, you needed to create a class, add a method to the class to represent the functionality, create an object of the class, and pass the object around. A lambda expression in Java is like a higher-order function in functional programming, which is an unnamed block of code representing a functionality that can be passed around like data. A lambda expression may capture the variables in its defining scope and it may access those variables later in a context that did not define the captured variable. This features let you use lambda expressions to implement closures in Java.

Java 8 introduced lambda expressions that represent an instance of a functional interface. You were able to do everything prior to Java 8 using anonymous classes that you can do with lambda expressions. Functional interfaces are not new to Java 8; they have existed since the beginning.

So why and where do we need lambda expressions? Anonymous classes use a bulky syntax. Lambda expressions use a very concise syntax to achieve the same result. Lambda expressions are not a complete replacement for anonymous classes. You will still need to use anonymous classes in a few situations. Just to appreciate the conciseness of the lambda expressions, compare the following two statements from the previous section that create an instance of the `StringToIntMapper` interface; one uses an anonymous class, taking six lines of code, and another uses a lambda expression, taking just one line of code:

```
// Using an anonymous class
StringToIntMapper mapper = new StringToIntMapper() {
    @Override
    public int map(String str) {
        return str.length();
    }
};

// Using a lambda expression
StringToIntMapper mapper = (String str) -> str.length();
```

Syntax for Lambda Expressions

A lambda expression describes an anonymous function. The general syntax for using lambda expressions is very similar to declaring a method. The general syntax is

```
(<LambdaParametersList>) -> { <LambdaBody> }
```

A lambda expression consists of a list of parameters and a body separated by an arrow (`->`). The list of parameters is declared the same way as the list of parameters for methods. The list of parameters is enclosed in parentheses, as is done for methods. The body of a lambda expression is a block of code enclosed in braces. Like a method's body, the body of a lambda expression may declare local variables; use statements including `break`, `continue`, and `return`; throw exceptions, etc. Unlike a method, a lambda expression does not have the following four parts:

- A lambda expression does not have a name.
- A lambda expression does not have a return type. It is inferred by the compiler from the context of its use and from its body.
- A lambda expression does not have a `throws` clause. It is inferred from the context of its use and its body.
- A lambda expression cannot declare type parameters. That is, a lambda expression cannot be generic.

Table 5-1 contains some examples of lambda expressions and equivalent methods. I have given a suitable name to methods as you cannot have a method without a name in Java. The compiler infers the return type of lambda expressions.

Table 5-1. *Examples of Lambda Expressions and Equivalent Methods*

Lambda Expression	Equivalent Method

`(int x, int y) -> {`
`    return x + y;`
`}`
	`int sum(int x, int y) {`
	`    return x + y;`
	`}`

`(Object x) -> {`
`    return x;`
`}`
	`Object identity(Object x) {`
	`    return x;`
	`}`

`(int x, int y) -> {`
`    if (x > y) {`
`        return x;`
`    } else {`
`        return y;`
`    }`
`}`
	`int getMax(int x, int y) {`
	`    if (x > y) {`
	`        return x;`
	`    } else {`
	`        return y;`
	`    }`
	`}`

(*continued*)

Table 5-1. (*continued*)

Lambda Expression	Equivalent Method

`(String msg) -> {`
`    System.out.println(msg);`
`}`
	`void print(String msg) {`
	`    System.out.println(msg);`
	`}`

`() -> {`
`    System.out.println(LocalDate.now());`
`}`
	`void printCurrentDate() {`
	`    System.out.println(LocalDate.now());`
	`}`

`() -> {`
`    // No code goes here`
`}`
	`void doNothing() {`
	`    // No code goes here`
	`}`

One of the goals of lambda expressions is to keep its syntax concise and let the compiler infer the details. The following sections discuss the shorthand syntax for declaring lambda expressions.

Omitting Parameter Types

You can omit the declared type of the parameters. The compiler will infer the types of parameters from the context in which the lambda expression is used.

```
// Types of parameters are declared
(int x, int y) -> { return x + y; }

// Types of parameters are omitted
(x, y) -> { return x + y; }
```

If you omit the types of parameters, you must omit it for all parameters or for none. You cannot omit for some and not for others. The following lambda expression will not compile because it declares the type of one parameter and omits for the other:

```
// A compile-time error
(int x, y) -> { return x + y; }
```

■ **Tip** A lambda expression that does not declare the types of its parameters is known as an implicit lambda expression or an implicitly-typed lambda expression. A lambda expression that declares the types of its parameters is known as an explicit lambda expression or an explicitly-typed lambda expression.

Declaring a Single Parameter

Sometimes a lambda expression takes only one parameter. You can omit the parameter type for a single parameter lambda expression as you can do for a lambda expression with multiple parameters. You can also omit the parentheses if you omit the parameter type in a single parameter lambda expression. The following are three ways to declare a lambda expression with a single parameter:

```
// Declares the parameter type
(String msg) -> { System.out.println(msg); }

// Omits the parameter type
(msg) -> { System.out.println(msg); }

// Omits the parameter type and parentheses
msg -> { System.out.println(msg); }
```

The parentheses can be omitted only if the single parameter also omits its type. The following lambda expression will not compile:

```
// Omits parentheses, but not the parameter type, which is not allowed.
String msg -> { System.out.println(msg); }
```

Declaring No Parameters

If a lambda expression does not take any parameters, you need to use empty parentheses.

```
// Takes no parameters
() -> { System.out.println("Hello"); }
```

It is not allowed to omit the parentheses when the lambda expression takes no parameter. The following declaration will not compile:

```
-> { System.out.println("Hello"); }
```

Parameters with Modifiers

You can use modifiers, such as `final`, in the parameter declaration for explicit lambda expressions. The following two lambda expressions are valid:

```
(final int x, final int y) -> { return x + y; }

(int x, final int y) -> { return x + y; }
```

The following lambda expression will not compile because it uses the `final` modifier in parameter declarations, but omits the parameter type:

```
(final x, final y) -> { return x + y; }
```

Declaring Body of Lambda Expressions

The body of a lambda expression can be a block statement or a single expression. A block statement is enclosed in braces; a single expression is not enclosed in braces.

The body of a lambda expression is executed the same way as a method's body. A `return` statement or the end of the body returns the control to the caller of the lambda expression.

When an expression is used as the body, it is evaluated and returned to the caller. If the expression evaluates to `void`, nothing is returned to the caller. The following two lambda expressions are the same; one uses a block statement and the other an expression:

```
// Uses a block statement. Takes two int parameters and returns their sum.
(int x, int y) -> { return x + y; }

// Uses an expression. Takes two int parameters and returns their sum.
(int x, int y) -> x + y
```

The following two lambda expressions are the same; one uses a block statement as the body and the other an expression that evaluates to `void`:

```
// Uses a block statement
(String msg) -> { System.out.println(msg); }

// Uses an expression
(String msg) -> System.out.println(msg)
```

Target Typing

Every lambda expression has a type, which is a functional interface type. In other words, a lambda expression represents an instance of a functional interface. Consider the following lambda expression:

```
(x, y) -> x + y
```

What is the type of this lambda expression? In other words, an instance of which functional interface does this lambda expression represent? We do not know the type of this lambda expression at this point. All we can say about this lambda expression with confidence is that it takes two parameters named `x` and `y`. We cannot tell its return type as the expression `x + y`, depending on the type of `x` and `y`, may evaluate to a number (`int`, `long`, `float`, or `double`) or a `String`. This is an implicit lambda expression, and therefore, the compiler has to infer the types of two parameters using the context in which the expression is used. This lambda expression may be of different functional interface types depending on the context in which it is used.

There are two types of expressions in Java:

- Standalone expressions
- Poly expressions

A standalone expression is an expression whose type can be determined without knowing the context of its use. The following are examples of standalone expressions:

```
// The type of expression is String
new String("Hello")

// The type of expression is String (a String literal is also an expression)
"Hello"
```

```
// The type of expression is ArrayList<String>
new ArrayList<String>()
```

A poly expression is an expression that has different types in different contexts. The compiler determines the type. The contexts that allow the use of poly expressions are known as *poly contexts*. All lambda expressions in Java are poly expressions. You must use it in a context to know its type. Poly expressions existed in Java prior to Java 8 and lambda expressions. For example, the expression `new ArrayList<>()` is a poly expression. You cannot tell its type unless you provide the context of its use. This expression is used in the following two contexts to represent two different types:

```
// The type of new ArrayList<>() is ArrayList<Long>
ArrayList<Long> idList = new ArrayList<>();

// The type of new ArrayList<>() is ArrayList<String>
ArrayList<String> nameList = new ArrayList<>();
```

The compiler infers the type of a lambda expression. The context in which a lambda expression is used expects a type, which is called the *target type*. The process of inferring the type of a lambda expression from the context is known as *target typing*. Consider the following pseudocode for an assignment statement, where a variable of type `T` is assigned a lambda expression:

```
T t = <LambdaExpression>;
```

The target type of the lambda expression in this context is `T`. The compiler uses the following rules to determine whether the `<LambdaExpression>` is assignment compatible with its target type `T`:

- `T` must be a functional interface type.
- The lambda expression has the same number and type of parameters as the abstract method of `T`. For an implicit lambda expression, the compiler will infer the types of parameters from the abstract method of `T`.
- The type of the returned value from the body of the lambda expression is assignment compatible to the return type of the abstract method of `T`.
- If the body of the lambda expression throws any checked exceptions, those exceptions must be compatible with the declared `throws` clause of the abstract method of `T`. It is a compile-time error to throw checked exceptions from the body of a lambda expression, if its target type's method does not contain a `throws` clause.

Let's look at a few examples of target typing. Consider two functional interfaces, `Adder` and `Joiner`, as shown in Listing 5-2 and Listing 5-3, respectively.

Listing 5-2. A Functional Interface Named Adder

```
// Adder.java
package com.jdojo.lambda;

@FunctionalInterface
public interface Adder {
    double add(double n1, double n2);
}
```

Listing 5-3. A Functional Interface Named Joiner

```
// Joiner.java
package com.jdojo.lambda;

@FunctionalInterface
public interface Joiner {
    String join(String s1, String s2);
}
```

The `add()` method of the `Adder` interface adds two numbers. The `join()` method of the `Joiner` interface concatenates two strings. Both interfaces are used for trivial purposes; however, they will serve the purpose of demonstrating the target typing for lambda expressions very well. Consider the following assignment statement:

```
Adder adder = (x, y) -> x + y;
```

The type of the `adder` variable is `Adder`. The lambda expression is assigned to the variable `adder`, and therefore, the target type of the lambda expression is `Adder`. The compiler verifies that `Adder` is a functional interface. The lambda expression is an implicit lambda expression. The compiler finds that the `Adder` interface contains a `double add(double, double)` abstract method. It infers the types for `x` and `y` parameters as `double` and `double`, respectively. At this point, the compiler treats this statement as shown:

```
Adder adder = (double x, double y) -> x + y;
```

The compiler now verifies the compatibility of the returned value from the lambda expression and the return type of the `add()` method. The return type of the `add()` method is `double`. The lambda expression returns `x + y`, which would be of a `double` as the compiler already knows that the types of `x` and `y` are `double`. The lambda expression does not throw any checked exceptions. Therefore, the compiler does not have to verify anything for that. At this point, the compiler infers that the type of the lambda expression is the type `Adder`.

Apply the rules of target typing for the following assignment statement:

```
Joiner joiner = (x, y) -> x + y;
```

This time, the compiler infers the type for the lambda expression as `Joiner`. Do you see an example of a poly expression where the same lambda expression `(x, y) -> x + y` is of the type `Adder` in one context and of the type `Joiner` in another?

Listing 5-4 shows how to use these lambda expressions in a program. Note that it's business as usual after you use a lambda expression to create an instance of a functional interface. That is, after you create an instance of a functional interface, you use the instance as you used before Java 8. The lambda expression does not change the way the instance of a functional interface is used to invoke its method.

Listing 5-4. Examples of Using Lambda Expressions

```
// TargetTypeTest.java
package com.jdojo.lambda;

public class TargetTypeTest {
    public static void main(String[] args) {
        // Creates an Adder using a lambda expression
        Adder adder = (x, y) -> x + y;
```

```
        // Creates a Joiner using a lambda expression
        Joiner joiner = (x, y) -> x + y;

        // Adds two doubles
        double sum1 = adder.add(10.34, 89.11);

        // Adds two ints
        double sum2 = adder.add(10, 89);

        // Joins two strings
        String str = joiner.join("Hello", " lambda");

        System.out.println("sum1 = " + sum1);
        System.out.println("sum2 = " + sum2);
        System.out.println("str = " + str);
    }
}
```

```
sum1 = 99.45
sum2 = 99.0
str = Hello lambda
```

I now discuss the target typing in the context of method calls. You can pass lambda expressions as arguments to methods. Consider the code for the `LambdaUtil` class shown in Listing 5-5.

Listing 5-5. A LambdaUtil Class That Uses Functional Interfaces as an Argument in Methods

```
// LambdaUtil.java
package com.jdojo.lambda;

public class LambdaUtil {
    public void testAdder(Adder adder) {
        double x = 190.90;
        double y = 8.50;
        double sum = adder.add(x, y);
        System.out.print("Using an Adder:");
        System.out.println(x + " + " + y + " = " + sum);
    }

    public void testJoiner(Joiner joiner) {
        String s1 = "Hello";
        String s2 = "World";
        String s3 = joiner.join(s1,s2);
        System.out.print("Using a Joiner:");
        System.out.println("\"" + s1 + "\" + \"" + s2 + "\" = \"" + s3 + "\"");
    }
}
```

The LambdaUtil class contains two methods: testAdder() and testJoiner(). One method takes an Adder as an argument and another a Joiner as an argument. Both methods have simple implementations. Consider the following snippet of code:

```
LambdaUtil util = new LambdaUtil();
util.testAdder((x, y) -> x + y);
```

The first statement creates an object of the LambdaUtil class. The second statement calls the testAdder() method on the object, passing a lambda expression of (x, y) -> x + y. The compiler must infer the type of the lambda expression. The target type of the lambda expression is the type Adder because the argument type of the testAdder(Adder adder) is Adder. The rest of the target typing process is the same as you saw in the assignment statement before. Finally, the compiler infers that the type of the lambda expression is Adder.

The program in Listing 5-6 creates an object of the LambdaUtil class and calls the testAdder() and testJoiner() methods.

Listing 5-6. Using Lambda Expressions as Method Arguments

```
// LambdaUtilTest.java
package com.jdojo.lambda;

public class LambdaUtilTest {
    public static void main(String[] args)  {
        LambdaUtil util = new LambdaUtil();

        // Call the testAdder() method
        util.testAdder((x, y) -> x + y);

        // Call the testJoiner() method
        util.testJoiner((x, y) -> x + y);

        // Call the testJoiner() method. The Joiner will add a space between the two strings
        util.testJoiner((x, y) -> x + " " + y);

        // Call the testJoiner() method. The Joiner will reverse the strings and join resulting
        // strings in reverse order adding a comma in between
        util.testJoiner((x, y) -> {
            StringBuilder sbx = new StringBuilder(x);
            StringBuilder sby = new StringBuilder(y);

            sby.reverse().append(",").append(sbx.reverse());

            return sby.toString();
        });
    }
}
```

```
Using an Adder:190.9 + 8.5 = 199.4
Using a Joiner:"Hello" + "World" = "HelloWorld"
Using a Joiner:"Hello" + "World" = "Hello World"
Using a Joiner:"Hello" + "World" = "dlroW,olleH"
```

Notice the output of the LambdaUtilTest class. The testJoiner() method was called three times, and every time it printed a different result of joining the two strings "Hello" and "World". This is possible because different lambda expressions were passed to this method. At this point, you can say that you have parameterized the behavior of the testJoiner() method. That is, how the testJoiner() method behaves depends on its parameter. Changing the behavior of a method through its parameters is known as *behavior parameterization*. This is also known as passing code as data because you pass code (logic, functionality, or behavior) encapsulated in lambda expressions to methods as if it were data.

It is not always possible for the compiler to infer the type of a lambda expression. In some contexts, there is no way the compiler can infer the type of a lambda expression; those contexts do not allow the use of lambda expressions. Some contexts may allow using lambda expressions, but the use itself may be ambiguous to the compiler; one such case is passing lambda expressions to overloaded methods.

Consider the code for the LambdaUtil2 class shown in Listing 5-7. The code for this class is the same as for the LambdaUtil class in Listing 5-5, except that this class changed the names of the two methods to the same name, test(), making it an overloaded method.

Listing 5-7. A LambdaUtil2 Class That Uses Functional Interfaces as an Argument in Methods

```
// LambdaUtil2.java
package com.jdojo.lambda;

public class LambdaUtil2 {
    public void test(Adder adder) {
        double x = 190.90;
        double y = 8.50;
        double sum = adder.add(x, y);
        System.out.print("Using an Adder:");
        System.out.println(x + " + " + y + " = " + sum);
    }

    public void test(Joiner joiner) {
        String s1 = "Hello";
        String s2 = "World";
        String s3 = joiner.join(s1,s2);
        System.out.print("Using a Joiner:");
        System.out.println("\"" + s1 + "\" + \"" + s2 + "\" = \"" + s3 + "\"");
    }
}
```

Consider the following snippet of code:

```
LambdaUtil2 util = new LambdaUtil2();
util.test((x, y) -> x + y); // A compile-time error
```

The second statement results in the following compile-time error:

```
Reference to test is ambiguous. Both method test(Adder) in LambdaUtil2 and method
test(Joiner) in LambdaUtil2 match.
```

The call to the test() method fails because the lambda expression is implicit and it matches both versions of the test() method. The compiler does not know which method to use: test(Adder adder) or test(Joiner joiner). In such circumstances, you need to help the compiler by providing some more information. The following are the some of the ways to help the compiler resolve the ambiguity:

- If the lambda expression is implicit, make it explicit by specifying the type of the parameters.
- Use a cast.
- Do not use the lambda expression directly as the method argument. First, assign it to a variable of the desired type, and then pass the variable to the method.

Let's discuss all three ways to resolve the compile-time error. The following snippet of code changes the lambda expression to an explicit lambda expression:

```
LambdaUtil2 util = new LambdaUtil2();
util.test((double x, double y) -> x + y); // OK. Will call test(Adder adder)
```

Specifying the type of parameters in the lambda expression resolved the issue. The compiler has two candidate methods: test(Adder adder) and test(Joiner joiner). With the (double x, double y) parameter information, only the test(Adder adder) method matches.

The following snippet of code uses a cast to cast the lambda expression to the type Adder:

```
LambdaUtil2 util = new LambdaUtil2();
util.test((Adder)(x, y) -> x + y); // OK. Will call test(Adder adder)
```

Using a cast tells the compiler that the type of the lambda expression is Adder, and therefore, helps it choose the test(Adder adder) method.

Consider the following snippet of code that breaks down the method call into two statements:

```
LambdaUtil2 util = new LambdaUtil2();
Adder adder = (x, y) -> x + y;
util.test(adder); // OK. Will call test(Adder adder)
```

The lambda expression is assigned to a variable of type Adder and the variable is passed to the test() method. Again, it helps the compiler choose the test(Adder adder) method based on the compile-time type of the adder variable.

The program in Listing 5-8 is similar to the one shown in Listing 5-6, except that it uses the LambdaUtil2 class. It uses explicit lambda expressions and a cast to resolve the ambiguous matches for lambda expressions.

Listing 5-8. Resolving Ambiguity During Target Typing

```
// LambdaUtil2Test.java
package com.jdojo.lambda;

public class LambdaUtil2Test {
    public static void main(String[] args) {
        LambdaUtil2 util = new LambdaUtil2();

        // Calls the testAdder() method
        util.test((double x, double y) -> x + y);
```

```
        // Calls the testJoiner() method
        util.test((String x, String y) -> x + y);

        // Calls the testJoiner() method. The Joiner will add a space between the two strings
        util.test((Joiner) (x, y) -> x + " " + y);

        // Calls the testJoiner() method. The Joiner will reverse the strings and join
        // resulting strings in reverse order adding a comma in between
        util.test((Joiner) (x, y) -> {
            StringBuilder sbx = new StringBuilder(x);
            StringBuilder sby = new StringBuilder(y);

            sby.reverse().append(",").append(sbx.reverse());

            return sby.toString();
        });
    }
}
```

```
Using an Adder:190.9 + 8.5 = 199.4
Using a Joiner:"Hello" + "World" = "HelloWorld"
Using a Joiner:"Hello" + "World" = "Hello World"
Using a Joiner:"Hello" + "World" = "dlroW,olleH"
```

Lambda expressions can be used only in the following contexts:

- *Assignment context*: A lambda expression may appear to the right side of the assignment operator in an assignment statement. For example

  ```
  ReferenceType variable1 = LambdaExpression;
  ```

- *Method invocation context*: A lambda expression may appear as an argument to a method or constructor call. For example

  ```
  util.testJoiner(LambdaExpression);
  ```

- *Return context*: A lambda expression may appear in a `return` statement inside a method, as its target type is the declared return type of the method. For example

  ```
  return LambdaExpression;
  ```

- *Cast context*: A lambda expression may be used if it is preceded by a cast. The type specified in the cast is its target type. For example

  ```
  (Joiner) LambdaExpression;
  ```

Functional Interfaces

A functional interface is simply an interface that has exactly one abstract method. The following types of methods in an interface do not count for defining a functional interface:

- Default methods
- static methods
- Public methods inherited from the Object class

Note that an interface may have more than one abstract method, and can still be a functional interface if all but one of them is a redeclaration of the methods in the Object class. Consider the declaration of the Comparator class that is in the java.util package, as shown:

```
package java.util;

@FunctionalInterface
public interface Comparator<T> {
    // An abstract method declared in the interface
    int compare(T o1, T o2);

    // Re-declaration of the equals() method in the Object class
    boolean equals(Object obj);

    // Many more static and default methods that are not shown here.
}
```

The Comparator interface contains two abstract methods: compare() and equals(). The equals() method in the Comparator interface is a re-declaration of the equals() method of the Object class, and therefore it does not count against the one abstract method requirement for it to be a functional interface. The Comparator interface contains several default and static methods that are not shown here.

A lambda expression is used to represent an unnamed function as used in functional programming. A functional interface represents one type of functionality/operation in terms of its lone abstract method. This commonality is the reason why the target type of a lambda expression is always a functional interface.

Using the @FunctionalInterface Annotation

The declaration of a functional interface may optionally be annotated with the annotation @FunctionalInterface, which is in the java.lang package. So far, all functional interfaces declared in this chapter, such as Adder and Joiner, have been annotated with @FunctionalInterface. The presence of this annotation tells the compiler to make sure that the declared type is a functional interface. If the annotation @FunctionalInterface is used on a non-functional interface or other types such as classes, a compile-time error occurs. If you do not use the annotation @FunctionalInterface on an interface with one abstract method, the interface is still a functional interface and it can be the target type for lambda expressions. Using this annotation gives you an additional assurance from the compiler. The presence of the annotation also protects you from inadvertently changing a functional interface into a non-functional interface, as the compiler will catch it.

The following declaration for an Operations interface will not compile, as the interface declaration uses the @FunctionalInterface annotation and it is not a functional interface (defines two abstract methods):

```
@FunctionalInterface
public interface Operations {
    double add(double n1, double n2);
    double subtract(double n1, double n2);
}
```

To compile the Operations interface, either remove one of the two abstract methods or remove the @FunctionalInterface annotation. The following declaration for a Test class will not compile, as @FunctionalInterface cannot be used on a type other than a functional interface:

```
@FunctionalInterface
public class Test {
    // Code goes here
}
```

Generic Functional Interface

A functional interface can have type parameters. That is, a functional interface can be generic. An example of a generic functional parameter is the Comparator interface with one type parameter T.

```
@FunctionalInterface
public interface Comparator<T> {
    int compare(T o1, T o2);
}
```

A functional interface may have a generic abstract method. That is, the abstract method may declare type parameters. The following is an example of a non-generic functional interface called Processor whose abstract method process() is generic:

```
@FunctionalInterface
public interface Processor {
    <T> void process(T[] list);
}
```

A lambda expression cannot declare type parameters, and therefore, it cannot have a target type whose abstract method is generic. For example, you cannot represent the Processor interface using a lambda expression. In such cases, you need to use a method reference, which I discuss in the next section, or an anonymous class.

Let's look at a short example of a generic functional interface and instantiate it using lambda expressions. Listing 5-9 shows the code for a functional interface named Mapper.

Listing 5-9. A Mapper Functional Interface

```
// Mapper.java
package com.jdojo.lambda;

@FunctionalInterface
public interface Mapper<T> {
```

```
    // An abstract method
    int map(T source);

    // A generic static method
    public static <U> int[] mapToInt(U[] list, Mapper<? super U> mapper) {
        int[] mappedValues = new int[list.length];

        for (int i = 0; i < list.length; i++) {
            // Map the object to an int
            mappedValues[i] = mapper.map(list[i]);
        }

        return mappedValues;
    }
}
```

Mapper is a generic functional interface with a type parameter T. Its abstract method map() takes an object of type T as a parameter and returns an int. The mapToInt() method is a generic static method that accepts an array of type U and a Mapper of a type that is U itself or a supertype of U. The method returns an int array whose elements contain the mapped value for the corresponding elements passed as an array.

The program in Listing 5-10 shows how to use lambda expressions to instantiate the Mapper<T> interface. The program maps a String array and an Integer array to int arrays.

Listing 5-10. Using the Mapper Functional Interface

```
// MapperTest.java
package com.jdojo.lambda;

public class MapperTest {
    public static void main(String[] args) {
        // Map names using their length
        System.out.println("Mapping names to their lengths:");
        String[] names = {"David", "Li", "Doug"};
        int[] lengthMapping = Mapper.mapToInt(names, (String name) -> name.length());
        printMapping(names, lengthMapping);

        System.out.println("\nMapping integers to their squares:");
        Integer[] numbers = {7, 3, 67};
        int[] countMapping = Mapper.mapToInt(numbers, (Integer n) -> n * n);
        printMapping(numbers, countMapping);
    }

    public static void printMapping(Object[] from, int[] to) {
        for (int i = 0; i < from.length; i++) {
            System.out.println(from[i] + " mapped to " + to[i]);
        }
    }
}
```

```
Mapping names to their lengths:
David mapped to 5
Li mapped to 2
Doug mapped to 4

Mapping integers to their squares:
7 mapped to 49
3 mapped to 9
67 mapped to 4489
```

Intersection Type and Lambda Expressions

Java 8 introduced a new type called an *intersection type* that is an intersection (or subtype) of multiple types. An intersection type may appear as the target type in a cast. An ampersand (&) is used between two types, such as (Type1 & Type2 & Type3), and it represents a new type that is an intersection of Type1, Type2, and Type3. Consider a marker interface called Sensitive, shown in Listing 5-11.

Listing 5-11. A Marker Interface Named Sensitive

```
// Sensitive.java
package com.jdojo.lambda;

public interface Sensitive {
    // It is a marker interface. So, no methods exist.
}
```

Suppose you have a lambda expression assigned to a variable of the Sensitive type.

```
Sensitive sen = (x, y) -> x + y; // A compile-time error
```

This statement does not compile. The target type of a lambda expression must be a functional interface; Sensitive is not a functional interface. However, you should be able to make such an assignment, as a marker interface does not contain any methods. In such cases, you need to use a cast with an intersection type that creates a new synthetic type that is a subtype of all types. The following statement will compile:

```
Sensitive sen = (Sensitive & Adder) (x, y) -> x + y; // OK
```

The intersection type Sensitive & Adder is still a functional interface, and therefore, the target type of the lambda expression is a functional interface with one method from the Adder interface.

In Java, you can convert an object to a stream of bytes and restore the object back later. This is called *serialization*. A class must implement the java.io.Serializable marker interface for its objects to be serialized. If you want a lambda expression to be serialized, you will need to use a cast with an intersection type. The following statement assigns a lambda expression to a variable of the Serializable interface:

```
Serializable ser = (Serializable & Adder) (x, y) -> x + y;
```

■ **Tip** I cover the Serializable interface and the serialization of objects in Chapter 7.

Commonly Used Functional Interfaces

Java 8 has added many frequently used functional interfaces in the java.util.function package . They are listed in Table 5-2.

Table 5-2. *Functional Interfaces Declared in the java.util.function Package*

Interface Name	Method	Description
Function<T,R>	R apply(T t)	Represents a function that takes an argument of type T and returns a result of type R.
BiFunction<T,U,R>	R apply(T t, U u)	Represents a function that takes two arguments of types T and U and returns a result of type R.
Predicate<T>	boolean test(T t)	In mathematics, a predicate is a boolean-valued function that takes an argument and returns true or false. The function represents a condition that returns true or false for the specified argument.
BiPredicate<T,U>	boolean test(T t, U u)	Represents a predicate with two arguments.
Consumer<T>	void accept(T t)	Represents an operation that takes an argument, operates on it to produce some side effects, and returns no result.
BiConsumer<T,U>	void accept(T t, U u)	Represents an operation that takes two arguments, operates on them to produce some side effects, and returns no result.
Supplier<T>	T get()	Represents a supplier that returns a value.
UnaryOperator<T>	T apply(T t)	Inherits from Function<T,T>. Represents a function that takes an argument and returns a result of the same type.
BinaryOperator<T>	T apply(T t1, T t2)	Inherits from BiFunction<T,T,T>. Represents a function that takes two arguments of the same type and returns a result of the same.

shows only the generic versions of the functional interfaces. Several specialized versions of these interfaces exist. They have been specialized for frequently used primitive data types; for example, IntConsumer is a specialized version of Consumer<T>. Some interfaces in the table contain convenience default and static methods. The table lists only the abstract method, not the default and static methods.

Using the Function<T,R> Interface

Six specializations of the Function<T,R> interface exist:

- IntFunction<R>
- LongFunction<R>
- DoubleFunction<R>
- ToIntFunction<T>
- ToLongFunction<T>
- ToDoubleFunction<T>

IntFunction<R>, LongFunction<R>, and DoubleFunction<R> take an int, a long, and a double as an argument, respectively, and return a value of type R. ToIntFunction<T>, ToLongFunction<T>, and ToDoubleFunction<T> take an argument of type T and return an int, a long, and a double, respectively. Similar specialized functions exist for other types of generic functions listed in the table.

■ **Tip** Your com.jdojo.lambda.Mapper<T> interface represents the same function type as ToIntFunction<T> in the java.util.function package. You created the Mapper<T> interface to learn how to create and use a generic functional interface. From now on, look at the built-in functional interfaces before creating your own; use them if they meet your needs.

The following snippet of code shows how to use the same lambda expression to represent a function that accepts an int and returns its square, using four variants of the Function<T, R> function type:

```
// Takes an int and returns its square
Function<Integer, Integer> square1 = x -> x * x;
IntFunction<Integer> square2 = x -> x * x;
ToIntFunction<Integer> square3 = x -> x * x;
UnaryOperator<Integer> square4 = x -> x * x;

System.out.println(square1.apply(5));
System.out.println(square2.apply(5));
System.out.println(square3.applyAsInt(5));
System.out.println(square4.apply(5));
```

```
25
25
25
25
```

The Function interface contains the following default and static methods:

- default <V> Function<T,V> andThen(Function<? super R,? extends V> after)
- default <V> Function<V,R> compose(Function<? super V,? extends T> before)
- static <T> Function<T,T> identity()

The andThen() method returns a composed Function that applies this function to the argument, and then applies the specified after function to the result. The compose() function returns a composed function that applies the specified before function to the argument, and then applies this function to the result. The identify() method returns a function that always returns its argument.

The following snippet of code demonstrates how to use default and static methods of the Function interface to compose new functions:

```
// Create two functions
Function<Long, Long> square = x -> x * x;
Function<Long, Long> addOne = x -> x + 1;
```

```
// Compose functions from the two functions
Function<Long, Long> squareAddOne = square.andThen(addOne);
Function<Long, Long> addOneSquare = square.compose(addOne);

// Get an identity function
Function<Long, Long> identity = Function.<Long>identity();

// Test the functions
long num = 5L;
System.out.println("Number: " + num);
System.out.println("Square and then add one: " + squareAddOne.apply(num));
System.out.println("Add one and then square: " + addOneSquare.apply(num));
System.out.println("Identity: " + identity.apply(num));
```

```
Number: 5
Square and then add one: 26
Add one and then square: 36
Identity: 5
```

You are not limited to composing a function that consists of two functions that are executed in a specific order. A function may be composed of as many functions as you want. You can chain lambda expressions to create a composed function in one expression. Note that when you chain lambda expressions, you may need to provide hints to the compiler to resolve the target type ambiguity that may arise. The following is an example of a composed function by chaining three functions. A cast is provided to help the compiler. Without the cast, the compiler will not be able to infer the target type.

```
// Square the input, add one to the result, and square the result
Function<Long, Long> chainedFunction = ((Function<Long, Long>)(x -> x * x))
                         .andThen(x -> x + 1)
                         .andThen(x -> x * x);
System.out.println(chainedFunction.apply(3L));
```

```
100
```

Using the Predicate<T> Interface

A predicate represents a condition that is either true or false for a given input. The Predicate interface contains the following default and static methods that let you compose a predicate based on other predicates using logical NOT, AND, and OR.

- default Predicate<T> negate()
- default Predicate<T> and(Predicate<? super T> other)
- default Predicate<T> or(Predicate<? super T> other)
- static <T> Predicate<T> isEqual(Object targetRef)

The negate() method returns a Predicate that is a logical negation of the original predicate. The and() method returns a short-circuiting logical AND predicate of this predicate and the specified predicate. The or() method returns a short-circuiting logical OR predicate of this predicate and the specified predicate. The isEqual() method returns a predicate that tests if the specified targetRef is equal to the specified argument for the predicate according to Objects.equals(Object o1, Object o2); if two inputs are null, this predicate evaluates to true. You can chain the calls to these methods to create complex predicates. The following snippet of code shows some examples of creating and using predicates:

```
// Create some predicates
Predicate<Integer> greaterThanTen = x -> x > 10;
Predicate<Integer> divisibleByThree = x -> x % 3 == 0;
Predicate<Integer> divisibleByFive = x -> x % 5 == 0;
Predicate<Integer> equalToTen = Predicate.isEqual(null);

// Create predicates using NOT, AND, and OR on other predicates
Predicate<Integer> lessThanOrEqualToTen = greaterThanTen.negate();
Predicate<Integer> divisibleByThreeAndFive = divisibleByThree.and(divisibleByFive);
Predicate<Integer> divisibleByThreeOrFive = divisibleByThree.or(divisibleByFive);

// Test the predicates
int num = 10;
System.out.println("Number: " + num);
System.out.println("greaterThanTen: " + greaterThanTen.test(num));
System.out.println("divisibleByThree: " + divisibleByThree.test(num));
System.out.println("divisibleByFive: " + divisibleByFive.test(num));
System.out.println("lessThanOrEqualToTen: " + lessThanOrEqualToTen.test(num));
System.out.println("divisibleByThreeAndFive: " + divisibleByThreeAndFive.test(num));
System.out.println("divisibleByThreeOrFive: " + divisibleByThreeOrFive.test(num));
System.out.println("equalsToTen: " + equalToTen.test(num));
```

```
Number: 10
greaterThanTen: false
divisibleByThree: false
divisibleByFive: true
lessThanOrEqualToTen: true
divisibleByThreeAndFive: false
divisibleByThreeOrFive: true
equalsToTen: false
```

Using Functional Interfaces

Functional interfaces are used in two contexts by two different types of users:

- By library designers for designing APIs
- By library users for using the APIs

Functional interfaces are used to design APIs by library designers. They are used to declare a parameter's type and return type in method declarations. They are used the same way non-functional interfaces are used. Functional interfaces existed in Java since the beginning, and Java 8 has not changed the way they are used in designing the APIs.

In Java 8, library users use functional interfaces as target types for lambda expressions. That is, when a method in the API takes a functional interface as an argument, the user of the API should use a lambda expression to pass the argument. Using lambda expressions has the benefit of making the code concise and more readable.

In this section, I show you how to design APIs using functional interfaces and how to use lambda expressions to use the APIs. Functional interfaces have been used heavily in designing the Java library for the Collections and Streams APIs that I cover in Chapters 12 and 13.

I use one enum and two classes in subsequent examples. The Gender enum, shown in Listing 5-12, contains two constants to represent the gender of a person. The Person class, shown in Listing 5-13, represents a person; it contains, apart from other methods, a getPersons() method that returns a list of persons.

Listing 5-12. A Gender enum

```
// Gender.java
package com.jdojo.lambda;

public enum Gender {
    MALE, FEMALE
}
```

Listing 5-13. A Person Class

```
// Person.java
package com.jdojo.lambda;

import java.time.LocalDate;
import java.util.ArrayList;
import java.util.List;
import static com.jdojo.lambda.Gender.MALE;
import static com.jdojo.lambda.Gender.FEMALE;

public class Person {
    private String firstName;
    private String lastName;
    private LocalDate dob;
    private Gender gender;

    public Person(String firstName, String lastName, LocalDate dob, Gender gender) {
        this.firstName = firstName;
        this.lastName = lastName;
        this.dob = dob;
        this.gender = gender;
    }

    public String getFirstName() {
        return firstName;
    }

    public void setFirstName(String firstName) {
        this.firstName = firstName;
    }

    public String getLastName() {
        return lastName;
    }
```

```
    public void setLastName(String lastName) {
        this.lastName = lastName;
    }

    public LocalDate getDob() {
        return dob;
    }

    public void setDob(LocalDate dob) {
        this.dob = dob;
    }

    public Gender getGender() {
        return gender;
    }

    public void setGender(Gender gender) {
        this.gender = gender;
    }

    @Override
    public String toString() {
        return firstName + " " + lastName + ", " + gender + ", " + dob;
    }

    // A convenience method
    public static List<Person> getPersons() {
        ArrayList<Person> list = new ArrayList<>();
        list.add(new Person("John", "Jacobs", LocalDate.of(1975, 1, 20), MALE));
        list.add(new Person("Wally", "Inman", LocalDate.of(1965, 9, 12), MALE));
        list.add(new Person("Donna", "Jacobs", LocalDate.of(1970, 9, 12), FEMALE));

        return list;
    }
}
```

The FunctionUtil class in Listing 5-14 is a utility class. Its methods apply a function on a List. List is an interface that is implemented by the ArrayList class. The forEach() method applies an action on each item in the list, typically producing side effects; the action is represented by a Consumer. The filter() method filters a list based on a specified Predicate. The map() method maps each item in the list to a value using a Function. As a library designer, you will design these methods using functional interfaces. Note that the FunctionUtil class contains no mention of lambda expressions. You could have designed this class the same way even before Java 8.

Listing 5-14. A FunctionUtil Class

```
// FunctionUtil.java
package com.jdojo.lambda;

import java.util.ArrayList;
import java.util.List;
import java.util.function.Consumer;
```

```
import java.util.function.Function;
import java.util.function.Predicate;

public class FunctionUtil {
    // Applies an action on each item in a list
    public static <T> void forEach(List<T> list, Consumer<? super T> action) {
        for (T item : list) {
            action.accept(item);
        }
    }

    // Applies a filter to a list and returns the filtered list items
    public static <T> List<T> filter(List<T> list, Predicate<? super T> predicate) {
        List<T> filteredList = new ArrayList<>();
        for (T item : list) {
            if (predicate.test(item)) {
                filteredList.add(item);
            }
        }

        return filteredList;
    }

    // Maps each item in a list to a value
    public static <T, R> List<R> map(List<T> list, Function<? super T, R> mapper) {
        List<R> mappedList = new ArrayList<>();
        for (T item : list) {
            mappedList.add(mapper.apply(item));

        }

        return mappedList;
    }
}
```

You will now use the FunctionUtil class as a library user and use the functional interfaces as target types of lambda expressions. Listing 5-15 shows how to use the FunctionUtil class.

Listing 5-15. Using Functional Interfaces as Target Types of Lambda Expressions as Library Users

```
// FunctionUtilTest.java
package com.jdojo.lambda;

import static com.jdojo.lambda.Gender.MALE;
import java.util.List;

public class FunctionUtilTest {
    public static void main(String[] args) {
        List<Person> list = Person.getPersons();

        // Use the forEach() method to print each person in the list
        System.out.println("Original list of persons:");
        FunctionUtil.forEach(list, p -> System.out.println(p));
```

```
        // Filter only males
        List<Person> maleList = FunctionUtil.filter(list, p -> p.getGender() == MALE);

        System.out.println("\nMales only:");
        FunctionUtil.forEach(maleList, p -> System.out.println(p));

        // Map each person to his/her year of birth
        List<Integer> dobYearList = FunctionUtil.map(list, p -> p.getDob().getYear());

        System.out.println("\nPersons mapped to year of their birth:");
        FunctionUtil.forEach(dobYearList, year -> System.out.println(year));

        // Apply an action to each person in the list. Add one year to each male's dob
        FunctionUtil.forEach(maleList, p -> p.setDob(p.getDob().plusYears(1)));

        System.out.println("\nMales only after adding 1 year to DOB:");
        FunctionUtil.forEach(maleList, p -> System.out.println(p));
    }
}
```

```
Original list of persons:
John Jacobs, MALE, 1975-01-20
Wally Inman, MALE, 1965-09-12
Donna Jacobs, FEMALE, 1970-09-12

Males only:
John Jacobs, MALE, 1975-01-20
Wally Inman, MALE, 1965-09-12

Persons mapped to year of their birth:
1975
1965
1970

Males only after adding 1 year to DOB:
John Jacobs, MALE, 1976-01-20
Wally Inman, MALE, 1966-09-12
```

The program gets a list of persons, applies a filter to the list to get a list of only males, maps persons to the year of their birth, and adds one year to each male's date of birth. It performs each of these actions using lambda expressions. Note the conciseness of the code; it uses only one line of code to perform each action. Most notable is the use of the `forEach()` method. This method takes a `Consumer` function. Then each item is passed to this function. The function can take any action on the item. You passed a `Consumer` that prints the item on the standard output as shown:

```
FunctionUtil.forEach(list, p -> System.out.println(p));
```

Typically, a `Consumer` applies an action on the item it receives to produce side effects. In this case, it simply prints the item, without producing any side effects.

Method References

A lambda expression represents an anonymous function that is treated as an instance of a functional interface. A method reference is a shorthand way to create a lambda expression using an existing method. Using method references makes your lambda expressions more readable and concise; it also lets you use the existing methods as lambda expressions. If a lambda expression contains a body that is an expression using a method call, you can use a method reference in place of that lambda expression.

■ **Tip** A method reference is not a new type in Java. It is not a function pointer as used in some other programming languages. It is simply shorthand for writing a lambda expression using an existing method. It can only be used where a lambda expression can be used.

Let's consider an example before I explain the syntax for method references. Consider the following snippet of code:

```
import java.util.function.ToIntFunction;
...
ToIntFunction<String> lengthFunction = str -> str.length();
String name = "Ellen";
int len = lengthFunction.applyAsInt(name);
System.out.println("Name = " + name + ", length = " + len);
```

```
Name = Ellen, length = 5
```

The code uses a lambda expression to define an anonymous function that takes a `String` as an argument and returns its length. The body of the lambda expression consists of only one method call that is the `length()` method of the `String` class. You can rewrite the lambda expression using a method reference to the `length()` method of the `String` class, as shown:

```
import java.util.function.ToIntFunction;
...
ToIntFunction<String> lengthFunction = String::length;
String name = "Ellen";
int len = lengthFunction.applyAsInt(name);
System.out.println("Name = " + name + ", length = " + len);
```

```
Name = Ellen, length = 5
```

The general syntax for a method reference is

```
<Qualifier>::<MethodName>
```

The `<Qualifier>` depends on the type of the method reference. Two consecutive colons act as a separator. The `<MethodName>` is the name of the method. For example, in the method reference `String::length`, `String` is the qualifier and `length` is the method name.

■ **Tip** A method reference does not call the method when it is declared. The method is called later when the method of its target type is called.

The syntax for method references allows specifying only the method name. You cannot specify the parameter types and return type of the method. Recall that a method reference is shorthand for a lambda expression. The target type, which is always a functional interface, determines the method's details. If the method is an overloaded method, the compiler will choose the most specific method based on the context. See Table 5-3.

Table 5-3. *Types of Method References*

Syntax	Description
`TypeName::staticMethod`	A method reference to a static method of a class, an interface, or an enum
`objectRef::instanceMethod`	A method reference to an instance method of the specified object
`ClassName::instanceMethod`	A method reference to an instance method of an arbitrary object of the specified class
`TypeName.super::instanceMethod`	A method reference to an instance method of the supertype of a particular object
`ClassName::new`	A constructor reference to the constructor of the specified class
`ArrayTypeName::new`	An array constructor reference to the constructor of the specified array type

Using method references may be a little confusing in the beginning. The main point of confusion is the process of mapping the number and type of arguments in the actual method to the method reference. To help understand the syntax, I use a method reference and its equivalent lambda expression in all examples.

static Method References

A static method reference uses a static method of a type as a lambda expression. The type could be a class, an interface, or an enum. Consider the following static method of the `Integer` class:

```
static String toBinaryString(int i)
```

The `toBinaryString()` method represents a function that takes an `int` as an argument and returns a `String`. You can use it in a lambda expression as shown:

```
// Using a lambda expression
Function<Integer,String> func1 = x -> Integer.toBinaryString(x);
System.out.println(func1.apply(17));
```

```
10001
```

The compiler infers the type of x as Integer and the return type of the lambda expression as String, by using the target type Function<Integer,String>. You can rewrite this statement using a static method reference, as shown:

```
// Using a method reference
Function<Integer, String> func2 = Integer::toBinaryString;
System.out.println(func2.apply(17));
```

```
10001
```

The compiler finds a static method reference to the toBinaryString() method of the Integer class on the right side of the assignment operator. The toBinaryString() method takes an int as an argument and returns a String. The target type of the method reference is a function that takes an Integer as an argument and returns a String. The compiler verifies that after unboxing the Integer argument type of the target type to int, the method reference and target type are assignment compatible.

Consider another static method sum() in the Integer class:

```
static int sum(int a, int b)
```

The method reference would be Integer::sum. Let's use it in the same way you used the toBinaryString() method in the previous example.

```
Function<Integer,Integer> func2 = Integer::sum; // A compile-time error
```

```
Error: incompatible types: invalid method reference
        Function<Integer, Integer> func2 = Integer::sum;
method sum in class Integer cannot be applied to given types
required: int,int
found: Integer
reason: actual and formal argument lists differ in length
```

The error message is stating that the method reference Integer::sum is not assignment compatible with the target type Function<Integer,Integer>. The sum(int, int) method takes two int arguments, whereas the target type takes only one Integer argument. The mismatch in the number of arguments caused the compile-time error.

To fix the error, the target type of the method reference Integer::sum should be a functional interface whose abstract method takes two int arguments and returns an int. Using a BiFunction<Integer,Integer, Integer> as the target type will work. The following snippet of code shows how to use a method reference Integer::sum as well as the equivalent lambda expression:

```
// Uses a lambda expression
BiFunction<Integer,Integer,Integer> func1 = (x, y) -> Integer.sum(x, y);
System.out.println(func1.apply(17, 15));

// Uses a method reference
BiFunction<Integer,Integer,Integer> func2 = Integer::sum;
System.out.println(func2.apply(17, 15));
```

```
32
32
```

Let's try using a method reference of the overloaded static method valueOf() of the Integer class. The method has three versions:

- static Integer valueOf(int i)
- static Integer valueOf(String s)
- static Integer valueOf(String s, int radix)

The following snippet of code shows how different target types will use the three different versions of the Integer.valueOf() static method. It is left as an exercise for readers to write the following snippet of code using lambda expressions:

```
// Uses Integer.valueOf(int)
Function<Integer,Integer> func1 = Integer::valueOf;

// Uses Integer.valueOf(String)
Function<String,Integer> func2 = Integer::valueOf;

// Uses Integer.valueOf(String, int)
BiFunction<String,Integer,Integer> func3 = Integer::valueOf;

System.out.println(func1.apply(17));
System.out.println(func2.apply("17"));
System.out.println(func3.apply("10001", 2));
```

```
17
17
17
```

The following is the last example in this category. The Person class, shown in Listing 5-13, contains a getPersons() static method that is declared as follows:

```
static List<Person> getPersons()
```

The method takes no argument and returns a List<Person>. A Supplier<T> represents a function that takes no arguments and returns a result of type T. The following snippet of code uses the method reference Person::getPersons as a Supplier<List<Person>>:

```
Supplier<List<Person>> supplier = Person::getPersons;
List<Person> personList = supplier.get();
FunctionUtil.forEach(personList, p -> System.out.println(p));
```

```
John Jacobs, MALE, 1975-01-20
Wally Inman, MALE, 1965-09-12
Donna Jacobs, FEMALE, 1970-09-12
```

Instance Method References

An instance method is invoked on an object's reference. The object reference on which an instance method is invoked is known as the *receiver* of the method invocation. The receiver of a method invocation can be an object reference or an expression that evaluates to an object's reference. The following snippet of code shows the receiver of the `length()` instance method of the `String` class:

```
String name = "Kannan";

// name is the receiver of the length() method
int len1 = name.length();

// "Hello" is the receiver of the length() method
int len2 = "Hello".length();

// (new String("Kannan")) is the receiver of the length() method
int len3 = (new String("Kannan")).length();
```

In a method reference of an instance method, you can specify the receiver of the method invocation explicitly or you can provide it implicitly when the method is invoked. The former is called a *bound receiver* and the latter is called an *unbound receiver*. The syntax for an instance method reference supports two variants:

- `objectRef::instanceMethod`
- `ClassName::instanceMethod`

Bound Receiver

For a bound receiver, use the `objectRef::instanceMethod` syntax. Consider the following snippet of code:

```
Supplier<Integer> supplier = () -> "Ellen".length();
System.out.println(supplier.get());
```

```
5
```

This statement uses a lambda expression that represents a function that takes no arguments and returns an `int`. The body of the expression uses a `String` object called `"Ellen"` to invoke the `length()` instance method of the `String` class. You can rewrite this statement using an instance method reference with the `"Ellen"` object as the bound receiver and using a `Supplier<Integer>` as the target type, as shown:

```
Supplier<Integer> supplier = "Ellen"::length;
System.out.println(supplier.get());
```

```
5
```

Consider the following snippet of code to represent a `Consumer<String>` that takes a `String` as an argument and returns `void`:

```
Consumer<String> consumer = str -> System.out.println(str);
consumer.accept("Hello");
```

```
Hello
```

This lambda expression invokes the `println()` method on the `System.out` object. This can be rewritten using a method reference with `System.out` as the bound receiver, as shown:

```
Consumer<String> consumer = System.out::println;
consumer.accept("Hello");
```

```
Hello
```

When the method reference `System.out::println` is used, the compiler looks at its target type, which is `Consumer<String>`. It represents a function type that takes a `String` as an argument and returns `void`. The compiler finds a `println(String)` method in the `PrintStream` class of the `System.out` object and uses that method for the method reference.

As the last example in this category, you will use the method reference `System.out::println` to print the list of persons, as shown:

```
List<Person> list = Person.getPersons();
FunctionUtil.forEach(list, System.out::println);
```

```
John Jacobs, MALE, 1975-01-20
Wally Inman, MALE, 1965-09-12
Donna Jacobs, FEMALE, 1970-09-12
```

Unbound Receiver

For an unbound receiver, use the `ClassName::instanceMethod` syntax. Consider the following statement in which the lambda expression takes a `Person` as an argument and returns a `String`:

```
Function<Person,String> fNameFunc = (Person p) -> p.getFirstName();
```

This statement can be rewritten using the instance method reference, as shown:

```
Function<Person,String> fNameFunc = Person::getFirstName;
```

In the beginning, this is confusing for two reasons:

- The syntax is the same as the syntax for a method reference to a static method.
- It raises a question: which object is the receiver of the instance method invocation?

The first confusion can be cleared up by looking at the method name and checking whether it is a static or instance method. If the method is an instance method, the method reference represents an instance method reference.

The second confusion can be cleared up by keeping a rule in mind that the first argument to the function represented by the target type is the receiver of the method invocation. Consider an instance method reference called `String::length` that uses an unbound receiver. The receiver is supplied as the first argument to the `apply()` method, as shown:

```
Function<String,Integer> strLengthFunc = String::length;

String name ="Ellen";

// name is the receiver of String::length
int len = strLengthFunc.apply(name);
System.out.println("name = " + name + ", length = " + len);
```

```
name = Ellen, length = 5
```

The instance method `concat()` of the `String` class has the following declaration:

```
String concat(String str)
```

The method reference `String::concat` represents an instance method reference for a target type whose function takes two `String` arguments and returns a `String`. The first argument will be the receiver of the `concat()` method and the second argument will be passed to the `concat()` method. The following snippet of code shows an example:

```
String greeting = "Hello";
String name = " Laynie";

// Uses a lambda expression
BiFunction<String,String,String> func1 = (s1, s2) -> s1.concat(s2);
System.out.println(func1.apply(greeting, name));

// Uses an instance method reference on an unbound receiver
BiFunction<String,String,String> func2 = String::concat;
System.out.println(func2.apply(greeting, name));
```

```
Hello Laynie
Hello Laynie
```

As the last example in this category, you will use the method reference `Person::getFirstName` that is an instance method reference on an unbound receiver, as shown:

```
List<Person> personList = Person.getPersons();

// Maps each Person object to its first name
List<String> firstNameList = FunctionUtil.map(personList, Person::getFirstName);

// Prints the first name list
FunctionUtil.forEach(firstNameList, System.out::println);
```

```
John
Wally
Donna
```

Supertype Instance Method References

The keyword super is used as a qualifier to invoke the overridden method in a class or an interface. The keyword is available only in an instance context. Use the following syntax to construct a method reference that refers to the instance method in the supertype and the method that's invoked on the current instance:

```
TypeName.super::instanceMethod
```

Consider the Priced interface and the Item class in Listing 5-16 and Listing 5-17. The Priced interface contains a default method that returns 1.0. The Item class implements the Priced interface. It overrides the toString() method of the Object class and the getPrice() method of the Priced interface. I added three constructors to the Item class that display a message on the standard output. I use them in examples in the next section.

Listing 5-16. A Priced Interface with a Default Method of getPrice()

```
// Priced.java
package com.jdojo.lambda;

public interface Priced {
    default double getPrice() {
        return 1.0;
    }
}
```

Listing 5-17. An Item Class That Implements the Priced Interface

```
// Item.java
package com.jdojo.lambda;

import java.util.function.Supplier;

public class Item implements Priced {
    private String name = "Unknown";
    private double price = 0.0;

    public Item() {
        System.out.println("Constructor Item() called.");
    }

    public Item(String name) {
        this.name = name;
        System.out.println("Constructor Item(String) called.");
    }
```

```
    public Item(String name, double price) {
        this.name = name;
        this.price = price;
        System.out.println("Constructor Item(String, double) called.");
    }

    public String getName() {
        return name;
    }

    public void setName(String name) {
        this.name = name;
    }

    public void setPrice(double price) {
        this.price = price;
    }

    @Override
    public double getPrice() {
        return price;
    }

    @Override
    public String toString() {
        return "name = " + getName() + ", price = " + getPrice();
    }

    public void test() {
        // Uses the Item.toString() method
        Supplier<String> s1 = this::toString;

        // Uses the Object.toString() method
        Supplier<String> s2 = Item.super::toString;

        // Uses the Item.getPrice() method
        Supplier<Double> s3 = this::getPrice;

        // Uses the Priced.getPrice() method
        Supplier<Double> s4 = Priced.super::getPrice;

        // Uses all method references and prints the results
        System.out.println("this::toString: " + s1.get());
        System.out.println("Item.super::toString: " + s2.get());
        System.out.println("this::getPrice: " + s3.get());
        System.out.println("Priced.super::getPrice: " + s4.get());
    }
}
```

The `test()` method in the `Item` class uses four method references with a bound receiver. The receiver is the `Item` object on which the `test()` method is called.

- The method reference `this::toString` refers to the `toString()` method of the `Item` class.
- The method reference `Item.super::toString` refers to the `toString()` method of the `Object` class, which is the superclass of the `Item` class.
- The method reference `this::getPrice` refers to the `getPrice()` method of the `Item` class.
- The method reference `Priced.super::getPrice` refers to the `getPrice()` method of the `Priced` interface, which is the superinterface of the `Item` class.

The program in Listing 5-18 creates an object of the `Item` class and calls its `test()` method. The output shows the method being used by the four method references.

Listing 5-18. Testing the Item Class

```
// ItemTest.java
package com.jdojo.lambda;

public class ItemTest {
    public static void main(String[] args) {
        Item apple = new Item("Apple", 0.75);
        apple.test();
    }
}
```

```
Constructor Item(String, double) called.
this::toString: name = Apple, price = 0.75
Item.super::toString: com.jdojo.lambda.Item@24d46ca6
this::getPrice: 0.75
Priced.super::getPrice: 1.0
```

Constructor References

Sometimes the body of a lambda expression may be just an object creation expression. Consider the following two statements that use a `String` object creation expression as the body for lambda expressions:

```
Supplier<String> func1 = () -> new String();
Function<String,String> func2 = str -> new String(str);
```

You can rewrite these statements by replacing the lambda expressions with constructor references as shown:

```
Supplier<String> func1 = String::new;
Function<String,String> func2 = String::new;
```

The syntax for using a constructor is as follows:

- `ClassName::new`
- `ArrayTypeName::new`

The `ClassName` in `ClassName::new` is the name of the class that can be instantiated; it cannot be the name of an abstract class. The keyword `new` refers to the constructor of the class. A class may have multiple constructors. The syntax does not provide a way to refer to a specific constructor. The compiler selects a specific constructor based on the context. It looks at the target type and the number of arguments in the abstract method of the target type. The constructor whose number of arguments matches the number of arguments in the abstract method of the target type is chosen. Consider the following snippet of code that uses three constructors of the `Item` class, shown in Listing 5-17, in lambda expressions:

```
Supplier<Item> func1 = () -> new Item();
Function<String,Item> func2 = name -> new Item(name);
BiFunction<String,Double,Item> func3 = (name, price) -> new Item(name, price);

System.out.println(func1.get());
System.out.println(func2.apply("Apple"));
System.out.println(func3.apply("Apple", 0.75));
```

```
Constructor Item() called.
name = Unknown, price = 0.0
Constructor Item(String) called.
name = Apple, price = 0.0
Constructor Item(String, double) called.
name = Apple, price = 0.75
```

The following snippet of code replaces the lambda expressions with a constructor reference `Item::new`. The output shows the same constructors as before.

```
Supplier<Item> func1 = Item::new;
Function<String,Item> func2 = Item::new;
BiFunction<String,Double,Item> func3 = Item::new;

System.out.println(func1.get());
System.out.println(func2.apply("Apple"));
System.out.println(func3.apply("Apple", 0.75));
```

```
Constructor Item() called.
name = Unknown, price = 0.0
Constructor Item(String) called.
name = Apple, price = 0.0
Constructor Item(String, double) called.
name = Apple, price = 0.75
```

When the statement

```
Supplier<Item> func1 = Item::new;
```

is executed, the compiler finds that the target type Supplier<Item> does not accept an argument. Therefore, it uses the no-args constructor of the Item class.

When the statement

```
Function<String,Item> func2 = Item::new;
```

is executed, the compiler finds that the target type Function<String,Item> takes a String argument. Therefore, it uses the constructor of the Item class that takes a String argument.

When the statement

```
BiFunction<String,Double,Item> func3 = Item::new;
```

is executed, the compiler finds that the target type BiFunction<String,Double,Item> takes two arguments: a String and a Double. Therefore, it uses the constructor of the Item class that takes a String and a double argument.

The following statement generates a compile-time error, as the compiler does not find a constructor in the Item class that accepts a Double argument:

```
Function<Double,Item> func4 = Item::new; // A compile-time error
```

Arrays in Java do not have constructors. There is special syntax to use constructor references for arrays. Array constructors are treated to have one argument of int type that is the size of the array. The following snippet of code shows the lambda expression and its equivalent constructor reference for an int array:

```
// Uses a lambda expression
IntFunction<int[]> arrayCreator1 = size -> new int[size];
int[] empIds1 = arrayCreator1.apply(5); // Creates an int array of five elements

// Uses an array constructor reference
IntFunction<int[]> arrayCreator2 = int[]::new;
int[] empIds2 = arrayCreator2.apply(5); // Creates an int array of five elements
```

You can also use a Function<Integer,R> type to use an array constructor reference, where R is the array type.

```
// Uses an array constructor reference
Function<Integer,int[]> arrayCreator3 = int[]::new;
int[] empIds3 = arrayCreator3.apply(5); // Creates an int array of five elements
```

The syntax for the constructor reference for arrays supports creating an array of multiple dimensions. However, you can specify the length for only the first dimension. The following statement creates a two-dimensional int array with the first dimension having the length of 5:

```
// Uses an array constructor reference
IntFunction<int[][]> TwoDimArrayCreator = int[][]::new;
int[][] matrix = TwoDimArrayCreator.apply(5); // Creates an int[5][] array
```

You might be tempted to use a `BiFunction<Integer,Integer,int[][]>` to use a constructor reference for a two-dimensional array to supply the length for both dimensions. However, the syntax is not supported. Array constructors are supposed to accept only one parameter—the length of the first dimension. The following statement generates a compile-time error:

```
BiFunction<Integer,Integer,int[][]> arrayCreator = int[][]::new;
```

Generic Method References

Typically, the compiler figures out the actual type for generic type parameters when a method reference refers to a generic method. Consider the following generic method in the `java.util.Arrays` class:

```
static <T> List<T> asList(T... a)
```

The `asList()` method takes a varargs argument of type `T` and returns a `List<T>`. You can use `Arrays::asList` as a method reference. The syntax for the method reference allows you to specify the actual type parameter for the method just after the two consecutive colons. For example, if you are passing `String` objects to the `asList()` method, its method reference can be written as `Arrays::<String>asList`.

■ **Tip** The syntax for a method reference also supports specifying the actual type parameters for generic types. The actual type parameters are specified just before the two consecutive colons. For example, the constructor reference `ArrayList<Long>::new` specifies `Long` as the actual type parameter for the generic `ArrayList<T>` class.

The following snippet of code contains an example of specifying the actual type parameter for the generic method `Arrays.asList()`. In the code, `Arrays::asList` will work the same, as the compiler will infer `String` as the type parameter for the `asList()` method by examining the target type.

```
import java.util.Arrays;
import java.util.List;
import java.util.function.Function;
...
Function<String[],List<String>> asList = Arrays::<String>asList;

String[] namesArray = {"Jim", "Ken", "Li"};
List<String> namesList = asList.apply(namesArray);
for(String name : namesList) {
    System.out.println(name);
}
```

```
Jim
Ken
Li
```

Lexical Scoping

A scope is the part of a Java program within which a name can be used without a qualifier. Classes and methods define their own scope. Scopes may be nested. For example, a method scope does not exist independently, as a method is always part of another construct, for example a class; an inner class appears inside the scope of another class; a local and an anonymous class appear inside the scope of a method.

Even though a lambda expression looks like a method declaration, it does not define a scope of its own. It exists in its enclosing scope. This is known as *lexical scoping* for lambda expressions. For example, when a lambda expression is used inside a method, the lambda expression exists in the scope of the method.

The meanings of the keywords `this` and `super` are the same inside the lambda expression and its enclosing method. Note that this is different from the meanings of these keywords inside a local and anonymous inner class in which the keyword `this` refers to the current instance of the local and anonymous inner class, not its enclosing class.

Listing 5-19 contains code for a functional interface named `Printer` that you will use to print messages in the examples in this section.

Listing 5-19. A Printer Functional Interface

```
// Printer.java
package com.jdojo.lambda;

@FunctionalInterface
public interface Printer {
    void print(String msg);
}
```

The program in Listing 5-20 creates two instances of the `Printer` interface: one using a lambda expression in the `getLambdaPrinter()` method and one using an anonymous inner class in the `getAnonymousPrinter()` method. Both instances use the keyword `this` inside the `print()` method. Both methods print the class name that the keyword `this` refers to. The output shows that the keyword `this` has the same meaning inside the `getLambdaPrinter()` method and the lambda expression. However, the keyword `this` has different meanings inside the `getAnonymousPrinter()` method and the anonymous class.

Listing 5-20. Testing Scope of a Lambda Expression and an Anonymous Class

```
// ScopeTest.java
package com.jdojo.lambda;

public class ScopeTest {
    public static void main(String[] args) {
        ScopeTest test = new ScopeTest();
        Printer lambdaPrinter = test.getLambdaPrinter();
        lambdaPrinter.print("Lambda Expressions");

        Printer anonymousPrinter = test.getAnonymousPrinter();
        anonymousPrinter.print("Anonymous Class");
    }

    public Printer getLambdaPrinter() {
        System.out.println("getLambdaPrinter(): " + this.getClass());
```

```
        // Uses a lambda expression
        Printer printer = msg -> {
            // Here, this refers to the current object of the ScopeTest class
            System.out.println(msg + ": " + this.getClass());
        };

        return printer;
    }

    public Printer getAnonymousPrinter() {
        System.out.println("getAnonymousPrinter(): " + this.getClass());

        // Uses an anonymous class
        Printer printer = new Printer() {
            @Override
            public void print(String msg) {
                // Here, this refers to the current object of the anonymous class
                System.out.println(msg + ": " + this.getClass());
            }
        };

        return printer;
    }
}
```

```
getLambdaPrinter(): class com.jdojo.lambda.ScopeTest
Lambda Expressions: class com.jdojo.lambda.ScopeTest
getAnonymousPrinter(): class com.jdojo.lambda.ScopeTest
Anonymous Class: class com.jdojo.lambda.ScopeTest$1
```

Lexical scoping of a lambda expression means that variables declared in the lambda expression, including its parameters, exist in the enclosing scope. Simple names in a scope must be unique. It means that a lambda expression cannot redefine variables with the name that already exists in the enclosing scope.

The following code for a lambda expression inside the `main()` method generates a compile-time error, as its parameter name `msg` is already defined in the `main()` method's scope:

```
public class Test {
    public static void main(String[] args) {
        String msg = "Hello";

        // A compile-time error. The msg variable is already defined and
        // the lambda parameter is attempting to redefine it.
        Printer printer = msg -> System.out.println(msg);
    }
}
```

The following code generates a compile-time error for the same reason that the local variable named msg is in scope inside the body of the lambda expression and the lambda expression is attempting to declare a local variable with the same name msg:

```
public class Test {
    public static void main(String[] args) {
        String msg = "Hello";

        Printer printer = msg1 -> {
            String msg = "Hi"; // A compile-time error
            System.out.println(msg1);
        };
    }
}
```

Variable Capture

Like a local and anonymous inner class, a lambda expression can access *effectively final* local variables. A local variable is effectively final in the following two cases:

- It is declared final.
- It is not declared final, but initialized only once.

In the following snippet of code, the msg variable is effectively final, as it has been declared final. The lambda expression accesses the variable inside its body.

```
public Printer test() {
    final String msg = "Hello"; // msg is effectively final

    Printer printer = msg1 -> System.out.println(msg + " " + msg1);
    return printer;
}
```

In the following snippet of code, the msg variable is effectively final, as it is initialized once. The lambda expression accesses the variables inside its body.

```
public Printer test() {
    String msg = "Hello"; // msg is effectively final

    Printer printer = msg1 -> System.out.println(msg + " " + msg1);
    return printer;
}
```

The following snippet of code is a slight variation of the previous example. The msg variable is effectively final, as it has been initialized only once.

```
public Printer test() {
    String msg;
    msg = "Hello"; // msg is effectively final
```

```
    Printer printer = msg1 -> System.out.println(msg + " " + msg1);
    return printer;
}
```

In the following snippet of code, the msg variable is not effectively final, as it is assigned a value twice. The lambda expression is accessing the msg variable that generates a compile-time error.

```
public Printer test() {
    // msg is not effectively final as it is changed later
    String msg = "Hello";

    // A compile-time error
    Printer printer = msg1 -> System.out.println(msg + " " + msg1);

    msg = "Hi"; // msg is changed making it effectively non-final

    return printer;
}
```

The following snippet of code generates a compile-time error because the lambda expression accesses the msg variable that is declared lexically after its use. In Java, forward referencing of variable names in method's scope is not allowed. Note that the msg variable is effectively final.

```
public Printer test() {
    // A compile-time error. The msg variable is not declared yet.
    Printer printer = msg1 -> System.out.println(msg + " " + msg1);

    String msg = "Hello";  // msg is effectively final

    return printer;
}
```

Can you guess why the following snippet of code generates a compile-time error?

```
public Printer test() {
    String msg = "Hello";

    Printer printer = msg1 ->  {
        msg = "Hi " + msg1; // A compile-time error. Attempting to modify msg.
        System.out.println(msg);
    };

    return printer;
}
```

The lambda expression accesses the local variable msg. Any local variable accessed inside a lambda expression must be effectively final. The lambda expression attempts to modify the msg variable inside its body, and that causes the compile-time error.

■ **Tip** A lambda expression can access instance and class variables of a class whether they are effectively final or not. If instance and class variables are not final, they can be modified inside the body of the lambda expressions. A lambda expression keeps a copy of the local variables used in its body. If the local variables are reference variables, a copy of the references is kept, not a copy of the objects.

The program in Listing 5-21 demonstrates how to access the local and instance variables inside lambda expressions.

Listing 5-21. Accessing Local and Instance Variables Inside Lambda Expressions

```
// VariableCapture.java
package com.jdojo.lambda;

public class VariableCapture {
    private int counter = 0;

    public static void main(String[] args) {
        VariableCapture vc1 = new VariableCapture();
        VariableCapture vc2 = new VariableCapture();

        // Create lambdas
        Printer p1 = vc1.createLambda(1);
        Printer p2 = vc2.createLambda(100);

        // Execute the lambda bodies
        p1.print("Lambda #1");
        p2.print("Lambda #2");
        p1.print("Lambda #1");
        p2.print("Lambda #2");
        p1.print("Lambda #1");
        p2.print("Lambda #2");
    }

    public Printer createLambda(int incrementBy) {
        Printer printer = msg -> {
            // Accesses instance and local variables
            counter += incrementBy;
            System.out.println(msg + ": counter = " + counter);
        };

        return printer;
    }
}
```

```
Lambda #1: counter = 1
Lambda #2: counter = 100
Lambda #1: counter = 2
Lambda #2: counter = 200
Lambda #1: counter = 3
Lambda #2: counter = 300
```

The createLambda() method uses a lambda expression to create an instance of the Printer functional interface. The lambda expression uses the method's parameter incrementBy. Inside the body, it increments the instance variable counter and prints its value. The main() method creates two instances of the VariableCapture class and calls the createLambda() method on those instances by passing 1 and 100 as incrementBy values. The print() methods of the Printer objects are called three times for both instances. The output shows that the lambda expression captures the incrementBy value and increments the counter instance variable every time it is called.

Jumps and Exits

Statements such as break, continue, return, and throw are allowed inside the body of a lambda expression. These statements indicate jumps inside a method and exits from a method. Inside a lambda expression, they indicate jumps inside the body of the lambda expression and exits from the body of the lambda expressions. They indicate local jumps and exits in the lambda expressions. Non-local jumps and exits in lambda expressions are not allowed. The program in Listing 5-22 demonstrates the valid use of the break and continue statements inside the body of a lambda expression.

Listing 5-22. Using Break and Continue Statements Inside the Body of a Lambda Expression

```
// LambdaJumps.java
package com.jdojo.lambda;

import java.util.function.Consumer;

public class LambdaJumps {
    public static void main(String[] args) {
        Consumer<int[]> printer = ids -> {
            int printedCount = 0;
            for (int id : ids) {
                if (id % 2 != 0) {
                    continue;
                }

                System.out.println(id);
                printedCount++;

                // Break out of the loop after printing 3 ids
                if (printedCount == 3) {
                    break;
                }
            }
        };
```

```
        // Print an array of 8 integers
        printer.accept(new int[]{1, 2, 3, 4, 5, 6, 7, 8});
    }
}
```

```
2
4
6
```

In the following snippet of code, the break statement is inside a for loop statement and it is also inside the body of a lambda statement. If this break statement is allowed, it will jump out of the body of the lambda expression. This is the reason that the code generates a compile-time error.

```
public void test() {
    for(int i = 0; i < 5; i++) {
        Consumer<Integer> evenIdPrinter = id -> {
            if (id < 0) {
                // A compile-time error. Attempting to break out of the lambda body
                break;
            }
        };
    }
}
```

Recursive Lambda Expressions

Sometimes a function may invoke itself from its body. Such a function is called a *recursive function*. A lambda expression represents a function. However, a lambda expression does not support recursive invocations. If you need a recursive function, you need to use a method reference or an anonymous inner class.

The program in Listing 5-23 shows how to use a method reference when a recursive lambda expression is needed. It defines a recursive method called factorial() that computes the factorial of an integer. In the main() method, it uses the method reference RecursiveTest::factorial in place of a lambda expression.

Listing 5-23. Using a Method Reference When a Recursive Lambda Expression Is Needed

```
// RecursiveTest.java
package com.jdojo.lambda;

import java.util.function.IntFunction;

public class RecursiveTest {
    public static void main(String[] args) {
        IntFunction<Long> factorialCalc = RecursiveTest::factorial;

        int n = 5;
        long fact = factorialCalc.apply(n);
        System.out.println("Factorial of " + n + " is " + fact);
    }
```

```
    public static long factorial(int n) {
        if (n < 0) {
            String msg = "Number must not be negative.";
            throw new IllegalArgumentException(msg);
        }

        if (n == 0) {
            return 1;
        } else {
            return n * factorial(n - 1);
        }
    }
}
```

```
factorial of 5 is 120
```

You can achieve the same results using an anonymous inner class as shown:

```
IntFunction<Long> factorialCalc = new IntFunction<Long>() {
    @Override
    public Long apply(int n) {
        if (n < 0) {
            String msg = "Number must not be negative.";
            throw new IllegalArgumentException(msg);
        }

        if (n == 0) {
            return 1L;
        } else {
            return n * this.apply(n - 1);
        }
    }
};
```

Comparing Objects

The Comparator interface is a functional interface with the following declaration:

```
package java.util;

@FunctionalInterface
public interface Comparator<T> {
    int compare(T o1, T o2);

    /* Other methods are not shown. */
}
```

The Comparator<T> interface contains many default and static methods that can be used along with lambda expressions to create its instances. It is worth exploring the API documentation for the interface. In this section, I discuss the following two methods of the Comparator interface:

- static <T,U extends Comparable<? super U>> Comparator<T> comparing(Function<? super T,? extends U> keyExtractor)
- default <U extends Comparable<? super U>> Comparator<T> thenComparing(Function<? super T,? extends U> keyExtractor)

The comparing() method takes a Function and returns a Comparator. The Function should return a Comparable that is used to compare two objects. You can create a Comparator object to compare Person objects based on their first names, as shown:

```
Comparator<Person> firstNameComp = Comparator.comparing(Person::getFirstName);
```

The thenComparing() method is a default method. It is used to specify a secondary comparison if two objects are the same in sorting order based on the primary comparison. The following statement creates a Comparator<Person> that sorts Person objects based on their last names, first names, and DOBs:

```
Comparator<Person> lastFirstDobComp =
    Comparator.comparing(Person::getLastName)
              .thenComparing(Person::getFirstName)
              .thenComparing(Person::getDob);
```

The program in Listing 5-24 shows how to use the method references to create a Comparator object to sort Person objects. It uses the sort() default method of the List interface to sort the list of persons. The sort() method takes a Comparator as an argument. Thanks to lambda expressions and default methods in interfaces for making the sorting task so easy!

Listing 5-24. Sorting a List of Person Objects

```
// ComparingObjects.java
package com.jdojo.lambda;

import java.util.Comparator;
import java.util.List;

public class ComparingObjects {
    public static void main(String[] args) {
        List<Person> persons = Person.getPersons();

        // Sort using the first name
        persons.sort(Comparator.comparing(Person::getFirstName));

        // Print the sorted list
        System.out.println("Sorted by the first name:");
        FunctionUtil.forEach(persons, System.out::println);

        // Sort using the last name, first name, and then DOB
        persons.sort(Comparator.comparing(Person::getLastName)
                               .thenComparing(Person::getFirstName)
                               .thenComparing(Person::getDob));
```

```
        // Print the sorted list
        System.out.println("\nSorted by the last name, first name, and dob:");
        FunctionUtil.forEach(persons, System.out::println);
    }
}
```

```
Sorted by the first name:
Donna Jacobs, FEMALE, 1970-09-12
John Jacobs, MALE, 1975-01-20
Wally Inman, MALE, 1965-09-12

Sorted by the last name, first name, and dob:
Wally Inman, MALE, 1965-09-12
Donna Jacobs, FEMALE, 1970-09-12
John Jacobs, MALE, 1975-01-20
```

Summary

A lambda expression is an unnamed block of code (or an unnamed function) with a list of formal parameters and a body. A lambda expression provides a concise way, as compared to anonymous inner classes, to create instances of functional interfaces. Lambda expressions and default methods in interfaces have given new life to the Java programming languages as far as expressiveness and fluency in Java programming go. The Java collection library has benefited the most from lambda expressions.

The syntax for defining lambda expressions is similar to declaring a method. A lambda expression may have a list of formal parameters and a body. A lambda expression is evaluated to an instance of a functional interface. The body of the lambda expression is not executed when the expression is evaluated. The body of the lambda expression is executed when the method of the functional interface is invoked.

One of the design goals of lambda expressions was to keep it concise and readable. The lambda expression syntax supports shorthand for common use-cases. Method references are shorthand to specify lambda expressions that use existing methods.

A poly expression is an expression whose type depends on the context of its use. A lambda expression is always a poly expression. A lambda expression cannot be used by itself. Its type is inferred by the compiler from the context. A lambda expression can be used in assignments, method invocations, returns, and casts.

When a lambda expression occurs inside a method, it is lexically scoped. That is, a lambda expression does not define a scope of its own; rather, it occurs in the method's scope. A lambda expression may use the effectively final local variables of a method. A lambda expression may use the statements such as `break`, `continue`, `return`, and `throw`. The `break` and `continue` statements specify local jumps inside the body of the lambda expression. Attempting to jump outside the body of the lambda expression generates a compile-time error. The `return` and `throw` statements exit the body of the lambda expression.

QUESTIONS AND EXERCISES

1. What are lambda expressions and how are they related to functional interfaces?

2. How does a lambda expression differ from an anonymous class? Can you always replace a lambda expression with an anonymous class and vice versa?

3. Are the following two lambda expressions different?

   a. `(int x, int y) -> { return x + y; }`

   b. `(int x, int y) -> x + y`

4. If someone shows you the following lambda expressions, explain the possible functions they may represent.

   a. `(int x, int y) -> x + y`

   b. `(x, y) -> x + y`

   c. `(String msg) -> { System.out.println(msg); }`

   d. `() -> {}`

5. What kind of function the following lambda expression may represent?

   `x -> x;`

6. Will the following declaration of a `MathUtil` interface compile? Explain your answer.

```
@FunctionalInterface
public interface Operations {
    int factorial(int n);
    int abs(int n);
}
```

7. Will the following statement compile? Explain your answer.

```
Object obj = x -> x + 1;
```

8. Will the following statements compile? Explain your answer.

```
Function<Integer,Integer> f = x -> x + 1;
Object obj = f;
```

9. What will be the output when you run the following `Scope` class?

```
// Scope.java
package com.jdojo.lambda.exercises;

import java.util.function.Function;

public class Scope {
```

```
    private static long n = 100;
    private static Function<Long,Long> f = n -> n + 1;

    public static void main(String[] args) {
        System.out.println(n);
        System.out.println(f.apply(n));
        System.out.println(n);
    }
}
```

10. Why does the following method declaration not compile?

```
public static void test() {
    int n = 100;
    Function<Integer,Integer> f = n -> n + 1;
    System.out.println(f.apply(100));
}
```

11. What will be the output when the following `Capture` class is run?

```
// Capture.java
package com.jdojo.lambda.exercises;

import java.util.function.Function;

public class Capture {
    public static void main(String[] args) {
        test();
        test();
    }

    public static void test() {
        int n = 100;
        Function<Integer,Integer> f = x -> n + 1;
        System.out.println(f.apply(100));
    }
}
```

12. Assume that there is a `Person` class, which contains four constructors. One of the constructors is a no-args constructor. Given a constructor reference, `Person::new`, can you tell which constructor of the `Person` it refers to?

13. Will the following declaration of the `FeelingLucky` interface compile? Notice that it has been annotated with `@FunctionalInterface`.

```
@FunctionalInterface
public interface FeelingLucky {
    void gamble();

    public static void hitJackpot() {
```

```
            System.out.println("You have won 80M dollars.");
        }
    }
```

14. Why does the following declaration of the `Mystery` interface not compile?

```
@FunctionalInterface
public interface Mystery {
    @Override
    String toString();
}
```

15. What will be the output when the following `PredicateTest` class is run?

```
// PredicateTest.java
package com.jdojo.lambda.exercises;

import java.util.function.Predicate;

public class PredicateTest {
   public static void main(String[] args) {
       int[] nums = {1, 2, 3, 4, 5};
       filterThenPrint(nums, n -> n%2 == 0);
       filterThenPrint(nums, n -> n%2 == 1);
   }

   static void filterThenPrint(int[] nums, Predicate<Integer> p) {
       for(int x : nums) {
           if(p.test(x)) {
               System.out.println(x);
           }
       }
   }
}
```

16. What will be the output when the following `SupplierTest` class is run? Explain your answer.

```
// SupplierTest.java
package com.jdojo.lambda.exercises;

import java.util.function.Supplier;
public class SupplierTest {
    public static void main(String[] args) {
        Supplier<Integer> supplier = () -> {
            int counter = 0;
            return ++counter;
        };
```

```
            System.out.println(supplier.get());
            System.out.println(supplier.get());
        }
    }
```

17. What will be the output when the following `ConsumerTest` class is run?

```
// ConsumerTest.java
package com.jdojo.lambda.exercises;

import java.util.function.Consumer;

public class ConsumerTest {
    public static void main(String[] args) {
         Consumer<String> c1 = System.out::println;
         Consumer<String> c2 = s -> {};

         consume(c1, "Hello");
         consume(c2, "Hello");
    }

    static <T> void consume(Consumer<T> consumer, T item) {
        consumer.accept(item);
    }
}
```

CHAPTER 6

Threads

In this chapter, you will learn:

- What threads are
- How to create threads in Java
- How to execute your code in separate threads
- What the Java Memory Model is
- The lifecycle of threads
- How to use object monitors to synchronize access to a critical section by threads
- How to interrupt, stop, suspend, and resume threads
- Atomic variables, explicit locks, synchronizer, executor framework, fork/join framework, and thread-local variables

All example programs in this chapter are members of a `jdojo.threads` module, as declared in Listing 6-1.

Listing 6-1. The Declaration of a jdojo.threads Module

```
// module-info.java
module jdojo.threads {
    exports com.jdojo.threads;
}
```

What Is a Thread?

Threads are a vast topic. They deserve an entire book. This chapter does not discuss the concept of threads in detail. Rather, it discusses how to work with threads using Java constructs. Before I define the term *thread*, it is necessary to understand the meaning of some related terms, such as program, process, multitasking, sequential programming, concurrent programming, etc.

A *program* is an algorithm expressed in a programming language. A *process* is a running instance of a program with all system resources allocated by the operating system to that instance of the program. Typically, a process consists of a unique identifier, a program counter, executable code, an address space, open handles to system resources, a security context, and many other things. A *program counter*, also called an *instruction pointer*, is a value maintained in the CPU register that keeps track of the instruction being executed by the CPU. It is automatically incremented at the end of the execution of an instruction. You can

K. Sharan, *Java Language Features*, https://doi.org/10.1007/978-1-4842-3348-1_6

also think of a process as a unit of activity (or a unit of work, or a unit of execution, or a path of execution) within an operating system. The concept of process allows one computer system to support multiple units of executions.

Multitasking is the ability of an operating system to execute multiple tasks (or processes) at once. On a single CPU machine, multitasking is not possible in a true sense because one CPU can execute instructions for only one process at a time. In such a case, the operating system achieves multitasking by dividing the single CPU's time among all running processes and switching between processes quickly enough to give an impression that all processes are running simultaneously. The switching of the CPU among processes is called a *context switch*. In a context switch, the running process is stopped, its state is saved, the state of the process that is going to get the CPU is restored, and the new process is run. It is necessary to save the state of the running process before the CPU is allocated to another process, so when this process gets the CPU again, it can start its execution from the same point where it left. Typically, the state of a process consists of a program counter, register values used by the process, and any other pieces of information that are necessary to restore the process later. An operating system stores a process state in a data structure, which is called a *process control block* or a *switchframe*. A context switch is rather an expensive task.

There are two types of multitasking: cooperative and preemptive. In cooperative multitasking, the running process decides when to release the CPU so that other processes can use the CPU. In preemptive multitasking, the operating system allocates a time slice to each process. Once a process has used up its time slice, it is preempted, and the operating system assigns the CPU to another process. In cooperative multitasking, a process may monopolize the CPU for a long time and other processes may not get a chance to run. In preemptive multitasking, the operating system makes sure all processes get CPU time. UNIX, OS/2, and Windows (except Windows 3.x) use preemptive multitasking. Windows 3.x used cooperative multitasking.

Multiprocessing is the ability of a computer to use more than one processor simultaneously. *Parallel processing* is the ability of a system to simultaneously execute the same task on multiple processors. You may note that, for parallel processing, the task must be split up into subtasks, so that the subtasks can be executed on multiple processors simultaneously. Let's consider a program that consists of six instructions:

```
Instruction-1
Instruction-2
Instruction-3
Instruction-4
Instruction-5
Instruction-6
```

To execute this program completely, the CPU has to execute all six instructions. Suppose the first three instructions depend on each other. Assume that `Instruction-2` uses the result of `Instruction-1`; `Instruction-3` uses the result of `Instruction-2`. Assume that the last three instructions also depend on each other the same way the first three depend on each other. Suppose the first three and the last three instructions, as two groups, do not depend on each other. How would you like to execute these six instructions to get the best result? One of the ways to execute them is sequentially as they appear in the program. This gives you one sequence of execution in your program. Another way of executing them is to have two sequences of executions. One sequence of execution will execute `Instruction-1`, `Instruction-2`, and `Instruction-3`, and at the same time, another sequence of execution will execute `Instruction-4`, `Instruction-5`, and `Instruction-6`. The phrases "unit of execution" and "sequence of execution" mean the same; I use them interchangeably. These two scenarios are depicted in Figure 6-1.

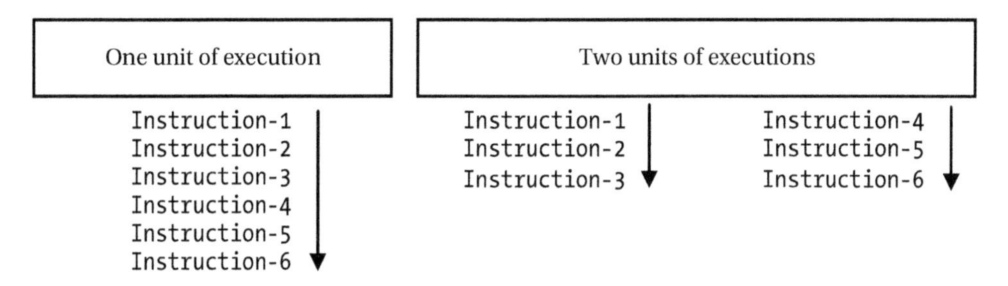

Figure 6-1. *Dividing a program into multiple units of execution*

Note that a process is also a unit of execution. Therefore, the two sets of instructions can be run as two processes to achieve concurrency in their execution. So far, we have assumed that the two sets of instructions are independent of each other. Suppose this assumption still holds true. What if the two sets of instructions access a shared memory; or, when both sets of instructions finish running, you need to combine the results from both to compute the final result? Processes are generally not allowed to access another process's address space. They must communicate using inter-process communication facilities such as sockets, pipes, etc. The very nature of a process—that it runs independent of other processes—may pose problems when multiple processes need to communicate or share resources. All modern operating systems let you solve this problem by allowing you to create multiple units of execution within a process, where all units of execution can share address space and resources allocated to the process. Each unit of execution within a process is called a *thread.*

Every process has at least one thread. A process can create multiple threads, if needed. The resources available to the operating system and its implementation determine the maximum number of threads a process can create. All threads within a process share all resources including the address space; they can also communicate with each other easily because they operate within the same process and they share the same memory. Each thread within a process operates independent of the other threads within the same process.

A thread maintains two things: a program counter and a stack. The program counter lets a thread keep track of the instruction that it is currently executing. It is necessary to maintain a separate program counter for each thread because each thread within a process may be executing different instructions at the same time. Each thread maintains its own stack to store the values of the local variables. A thread can also maintain its private memory, which cannot be shared with other threads, even if they are in the same process. The private memory maintained by a thread is called *thread-local storage (TLS)*. Figure 6-2 depicts threads represented within a process.

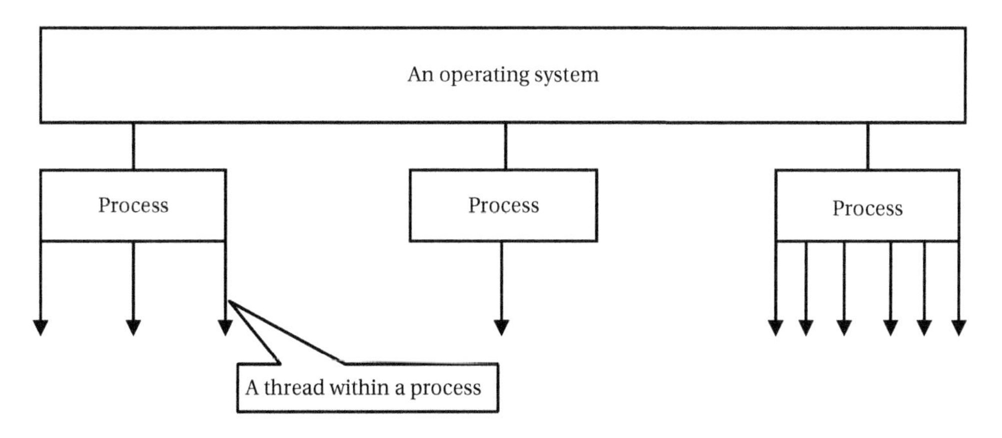

Figure 6-2. *Processes and threads*

In all modern operating systems, threads are scheduled on the CPU for execution, not the processes. Therefore, the CPU context switch occurs between the threads. The context switch between threads is less expensive compared to the context switch between processes. Because of the ease of communication, sharing resources among threads within a process, and a cheaper context switch, it is preferred to split a program into multiple threads, rather than multiple processes. Sometimes a thread is also called a *lightweight process*. The program with six instructions as discussed previously can also be split into two threads within a process, as depicted in Figure 6-3. On a multi-processor machine, multiple threads of a process may be scheduled on different processors, thus providing true concurrent executions of a program. A program that uses multiple threads is called a *multi-threaded program*.

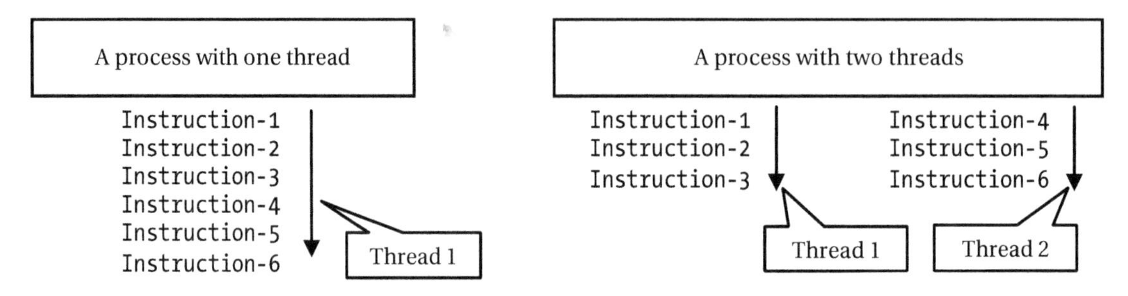

Figure 6-3. *Dividing the program logic to use two threads within a process*

You can think of the relationship between a process and threads as

```
Process = address space + resources + threads
```

where threads are units of execution within the process; they maintain their own unique program counter and stack; they share the process address space and resources; they are scheduled on a CPU independently and may execute on different CPUs, if available.

Creating Threads in Java

The Java API makes it easy to work with threads. It lets you represent a thread as an object. An object of the `java.lang.Thread` class represents a thread. Creating and using a thread in Java is as simple as creating an object of the `Thread` class and using that object in a program. Let's start with the simplest example of creating a thread in Java. There are at least two steps involved in working with a thread:

- Creating an object of the `Thread` class
- Invoking the `start()` method of the `Thread` class to start the thread

Creating an object of the `Thread` class is the same as creating an object of any other classes in Java. In its simplest form, you can use the no-args constructor of the `Thread` class to create a `Thread` object.

```
// Creates a thread object
Thread simplestThread = new Thread();
```

Creating an object of the Thread class allocates memory for that object on the heap. It does not start or run the thread. You must call the start() method of the Thread object to start the thread:

```
// Starts the thread
simplestThread.start();
```

The start() method returns after doing some housekeeping work. It puts the thread in the runnable state. In this state, the thread is ready to receive the CPU time. Note that invoking the start() method of a Thread object does not guarantee "when" this thread will start getting the CPU time. That is, it does not guarantee when the thread will start running. It just schedules the thread to receive the CPU time.

Let's write a simple Java program with these two statements, as shown in Listing 6-2. The program will not do anything useful. However, it will get you started using threads.

Listing 6-2. The Simplest Thread in Java

```
// SimplestThread.java
package com.jdojo.threads;

public class SimplestThread {
    public static void main(String[] args) {
        // Creates a thread object
        Thread simplestThread = new Thread();

        // Starts the thread
        simplestThread.start();
    }
}
```

When you run the SimplestThread class, you do not see any output. The program will start and finish silently. Even though you did not see any output, here are a few things the JVM did when the two statements in the main() method were executed:

- When the second statement, simplestThread.start(), is executed, the JVM scheduled this thread for execution.
- At some point in time, this thread got the CPU time and started executing. What code does a thread in Java start executing when it gets the CPU time?
- A thread in Java always starts its execution in a run() method. You can define the run() method to be executed by a thread when you create an object of the Thread class. In your case, you created an object of the Thread class using its no-args constructor. When you use the no-args constructor of the Thread class to create its object (as in new Thread()), the run() method of the Thread class is called when the thread starts its execution. The following sections in this chapter explain how to define your own run() method for a thread.
- The run() method of the Thread class checks how the object of the Thread class was created. If the thread object was created using the no-args constructor of the Thread class, it does not do anything, and immediately returns. Therefore, in your program, when the thread got the CPU time, it called the run() method of the Thread class, which did not execute any meaningful code, and returned.
- When the CPU finishes executing the run() method, the thread is dead, which means the thread will not get the CPU time again.

Figure 6-4 depicts how the simplest thread example works.

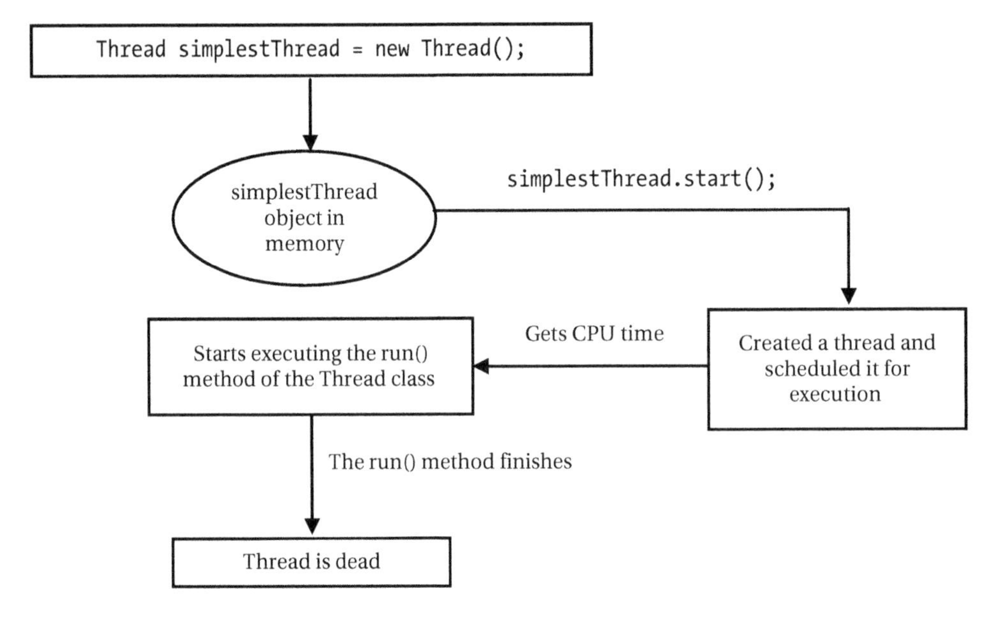

Figure 6-4. *The simplest thread execution*

There are two important points to add to the current discussion.

- When a thread is dead, it does not mean the thread object is garbage collected. Note that a thread is a unit of execution. "A thread is dead" means that the unit of execution that the thread represented has finished its work. However, the thread object representing the unit of execution still exists in memory. After the thread is dead, the object will be garbage collected based on the same garbage collection rules that are used for any other Java objects. Some restrictions exist that dictate the methods you can call on a dead thread. For example, you cannot call its `start()` method again. That is, a thread object can be started only once. However, you can still check if the thread is dead by calling the `isAlive()` method of the thread object.
- The thread does not get the CPU time in one go to execute the `run()` method. The operating system decides on the amount of time to allocate and when to allocate that time to the thread. This means that the multiple context switches may occur before the thread finishes executing the `run()` method.

Specifying Your Code for a Thread

There are three ways you can specify your code to be executed by a thread:

- By inheriting your class from the `Thread` class
- By implementing the `Runnable` interface in your class
- By using the method reference to a method that takes no parameters and returns `void`

■ **Tip** Inheriting your class from the Thread class may not be possible if your class already inherits from another class. In that case, you need to use the second method. You can use the third method from Java 8. Before Java 8, it was common to use an anonymous class to define a thread object where the anonymous class would either inherit from the Thread class or implement the Runnable interface.

Inheriting Your Class from the Thread Class

When you inherit your class from the Thread class, you should override the run() method and provide the code to be executed by the thread.

```
public class MyThreadClass extends Thread {
    @Override
    public void run() {
        System.out.println("Hello Java threads!");
    }
    // More code goes here }
```

The steps to create a thread object and start the thread are the same.

```
MyThreadClass myThread = new MyThreadClass();
myThread.start();
```

The thread will execute the run() method of the MyThreadClass class.

Implementing the Runnable Interface

You can create a class that implements the java.lang.Runnable interface. Runnable is a functional interface and it is declared in the java.lang package as follows:

```
@FunctionalInterface
public interface Runnable {
    void run();
}
```

From Java 8, you can use a lambda expression to create an instance of the Runnable interface.

```
Runnable aRunnableObject = () -> System.out.println("Hello Java threads!");
```

Create an object of the Thread class using the constructor that accepts a Runnable object.

```
Thread myThread = new Thread(aRunnableObject);
```

Start the thread by calling the start() method of the thread object.

```
myThread.start();
```

The thread will execute the code contained in the body of the lambda expression.

Using a Method Reference

From Java 8, you can use the method reference of a method (static or instance) that takes no parameters and returns void as the code to be executed by a thread. The following code declares a ThreadTest class that contains an execute() method. The method contains the code to be executed in a thread.

```
public class ThreadTest {
    public static void execute() {
        System.out.println("Hello Java threads!");
    }
}
```

The following snippet of code uses the method reference of the execute() method of the ThreadTest class to create a Runnable object:

```
Thread myThread = new Thread(ThreadTest::execute);
myThread.start();
```

The thread will execute the code contained in the execute() method of the ThreadTest class.

A Quick Example

Let's look at a simple example to print integers from 1 to 500 in a new thread. Listing 6-3 contains the code for the PrinterThread class that performs this task. When the class is run, it prints integers from 1 to 500 on the standard output.

Listing 6-3. Printing Integers from 1 to 500 in a New Thread

```
// PrinterThread.java
package com.jdojo.threads;

public class PrinterThread {
    public static void main(String[] args) {
        // Create a Thread object
        Thread t = new Thread(PrinterThread::print);

        // Start the thread
        t.start();
    }

    public static void print() {
        for (int i = 1; i <= 500; i++) {
            System.out.print(i + " ");
        }
    }
}
```

```
1 2 3 4 5 6 7 8 9 10 11 12 13 14  ... 497 498 499 500
```

I used a method reference to create the thread object in the example. You can use any of the other ways discussed earlier to create a thread object.

Using Multiple Threads in a Program

Using multiple threads in a Java program is as simple as creating multiple Thread objects and calling their start() method. Java does not have any upper limit on the number of threads that can be used in a program. It is limited by the operating system and the memory available to the program. Listing 6-4 uses two threads. Both threads print integers from 1 to 500. The code prints a new line after each integer. However, the output shows a space after each integer to keep the output short. Only partial output is shown.

Listing 6-4. Running Multiple Threads in a Program

```
// MultiPrinterThread.java
package com.jdojo.threads;

public class MultiPrinterThread {
    public static void main(String[] args) {
        // Create two Thread objects
        Thread t1 = new Thread(MultiPrinterThread::print);
        Thread t2 = new Thread(MultiPrinterThread::print);

        // Start both threads
        t1.start();
        t2.start();
    }

    public static void print() {
        for (int i = 1; i <= 500; i++) {
            System.out.println(i);
        }
    }
}
```

```
1  2  3  4  5  1  2  3  4  5  6  7  8  9  10  11  12  13  14  15  16  17  18  19  20  21
22  23  24  25  26  6  7  27  28  8  9  10  11  12  29  30  31  13  14  32  15  16  17
...  496  497  498  499  500  424  425 ... 492  493  494  495  496  497  498  499  500
```

You will find some interesting things in the output. Every time you run this program, you may get different output. However, the nature of the output on your computer can be compared to the output shown here. On a very fast machine, the output may print 1 to 500 and 1 to 500. However, let's focus the discussion assuming that your output is like the one shown.

The program created two threads. Each thread prints integers from 1 to 500. It starts the thread t1 first and the thread t2 second. You might expect that the thread t1 will start first to print integers from 1 to 500, and then the thread t2 will start to print integers from 1 to 500. However, it is obvious from the output that the program did not run the way you might have expected.

The start() method of the Thread class returns immediately. That is, when you call the start() method of a thread, the JVM takes note of your instruction to start the thread. However, it does not start the thread right away. It has to do some housekeeping before it can really start a thread. When a thread starts, it is up to the operating system to decide when and how much CPU time it will give to that thread. Therefore, as soon as the t1.start() and t2.start() methods return, your program enters the indeterminate realm. That is, both threads will start running; however, you do not know when they will start running and in what sequence they will run to execute their code. When you start multiple threads, you do not even know which thread will start running first. Looking at the output, you can observe that one of the threads started and it got enough CPU time to print integers from 1 to 5 before it was preempted. Another thread got CPU time to print from 1 to 26 before it was preempted. The second time, the first thread (the thread that started printing integers first) got the CPU time and it printed only two integers, 6 and 7, and so on. You can see that both threads got CPU time. However, the amount of CPU time and the sequence in which they got the CPU time are unpredictable. Each time you run this program, you may get different output. The only guarantee that you get from this program is that all integers between 1 and 500 will be printed twice in some order.

Issues in Using Multiple Threads

Some issues are involved when you use multiple threads in a program. You need to consider these issues only if multiple threads have to coordinate based on some conditions or some shared resources.

In the previous sections, the examples involving threads were trivial. They simply printed some integers on the standard output. Let's look at a different kind of example that uses multiple threads, which access and modify the value of a variable. Listing 6-5 shows the code for the BalanceUpdate class.

Listing 6-5. Multiple Threads Modifying the Same Variable

```
// BalanceUpdate.java
package com.jdojo.threads;

public class BalanceUpdate {
    // Initialize balance to 100
    private static int balance = 100;

    public static void main(String[] args) {
        startBalanceUpdateThread(); // Thread to update the balance value
        startBalanceMonitorThread(); // Thread to monitor the balance value
    }

    public static void updateBalance() {
        // Add 10 to balance and subtract 10 from balance
        balance = balance + 10;
        balance = balance - 10;
    }

    public static void monitorBalance() {
        int b = balance;
        if (b != 100) {
            System.out.println("Balance changed: " + b);
            System.exit(0); // Exit the program
        }
    }

    public static void startBalanceUpdateThread() {
        // Start a new thread that calls the updateBalance() method in an infinite loop
        Thread t = new Thread(() -> {
```

```
            while (true) {
                updateBalance();
            }
        });

        t.start();
    }

    public static void startBalanceMonitorThread() {
        // Start a thread that monitors the balance value
        Thread t = new Thread(() -> {
            while (true) {
                monitorBalance();
            }
        });

        t.start();
    }
}
```

```
Balance changed: 110
```

A brief description of each component of this class follows:

- `balance`: It is a static variable of type `int`. It is initialized to 100.
- `updateBalance()`: It is a static method that adds 10 to the static variable balance and subtracts 10 from it. Upon completion of this method, the value of the static variable `balance` is expected to remain the same as 100.
- `startBalanceUpdateThread()`: It starts a new thread that keeps calling the `updateBalance()` method in an infinite loop. That is, once you call this method, a thread keeps adding 10 to the `balance` variable and subtracting 10 from it.
- `startBalanceMonitorThread()`: It starts a new thread that monitors the value of the `balance` static variable by repeatedly calling the `monitorBalance()` method. When the thread detects that the value of the `balance` variable is other than 100, it prints the current value and exits the program.
- `main()`: This method is used to run the program. It starts a thread that updates the `balance` class variable in a loop using the `updateBalance()` method. It also starts another thread that monitors the value of the `balance` class variable.

The program consists of two threads. One thread calls the `updateBalance()` method, which adds 10 to `balance` and subtracts 10 from it. That is, after this method finishes executing, the value of the `balance` variable is expected to remain unchanged. Another thread monitors the value of the `balance` variable. When it detects that the value of the `balance` variable is anything other than 100, it prints the new value and exits the program. Specifying zero in `System.exit(0)` method call indicates that you want to terminate the program normally.

Intuitively, the balance monitor thread should not print anything because the `balance` should always be `100` and the program should never end because both threads are using infinite loops. However, that is not the case. If you run this program, you will find, in a short time, the program prints the `balance` value other than `100` and exits.

Suppose on a particular machine the statement "balance = balance + 10;" is implemented as the following machine instructions assuming register-1 as a CPU register:

```
register-1 = balance;
register-1 = register-1 + 10;
balance = register-1;
```

Similarly, assume that the statement "balance = balance - 10;" is implemented as the following machine instructions assuming register-2 as another CPU register:

```
register-2 = balance;
register-2 = register-2 - 10;
balance = register-2;
```

When the updateBalance() method is invoked, the CPU has to execute six instructions to add 10 to and subtract 10 from the balance variable. When the balance update thread is in the middle of executing any of the first three instructions, the balance monitor thread will read the balance value as 100. When the balance update thread has finished executing the third instruction, the balance monitor thread will read its value as 110. The value 110 for the balance variable will be restored to 100 only when the balance update thread executes the sixth instruction. Note that if the balance monitor thread reads the value of the balance variable any time after the execution of the third instruction and before the execution of the sixth instruction by the balance update thread, it will read a value that is not the same as the value that existed at the start of the updateBalance() method execution. Table 6-1 shows how the value of the balance variable will be modified and read by the two threads.

In your program, the monitor thread was able to read the value of the balance variable as 110 because you allowed two threads to modify and read the value of the balance variable concurrently. If you allowed only one thread at a time to work with (modify or read) the balance variable, the balance monitor thread would never read the value of the balance variable other than 100.

Table 6-1. *Instruction Executions for Multiple Threads*

Statement (Suppose Balance Value is 100 to Start With)	Instructions Being Executed by the Balance Update Thread	The Value of Balance Read by the Balance Monitor Thread
balance = balance + 10;	register-1 = balance;	100
	register-1 = register-1 + 10;	100
	balance = register-1;	Before execution: 100 After execution: 110
balance = balance - 10;	register-2 = balance;	110
	register-2 = register-2 - 10;	110
	balance = register-2;	Before execution: 110 After execution: 100

The situation where multiple threads manipulate and access a shared data concurrently and the outcome depends on the order in which the execution of threads take place is known as a *race condition*. A race condition in a program may lead to unpredictable results. Listing 6-5 is an example of a race condition where the program output depends on the sequence of execution of the two threads.

To avoid a race condition in a program, you need to make sure that only one of the racing threads works with the shared data at a time. To solve this problem, you need to synchronize the access to the two methods updateBalance() and monitorBalance() of the BalanceUpdate class. That is, only one thread should access one of these two methods at a time. In other words, if one thread is executing the updateBalance() method, another thread that wants to execute the monitorBalance() method must wait until the thread executing the updateBalance() method is finished. Similarly, if one thread is executing the monitorBalance() method, another thread that wants to execute the updateBalance() method must wait until the thread executing the monitorBalance() method is finished. This will ensure that when a thread is in the process of updating the balance variable, no other threads will read the inconsistent value of the balance variable and if a thread is reading the balance variable, no other threads will update the balance variable at the same time.

This kind of problem that needs synchronizing the access of multiple threads to a section of code in a Java program can be solved using the synchronized keyword. To understand the use of the synchronized keyword, I need to discuss the Java Memory Model in brief, and the lock and wait sets of an object.

Java Memory Model

All program variables (instance fields, static fields, and array elements) in a program are allocated memory from the main memory of a computer. Each thread has a working memory (processor cache or registers). The Java Memory Model (JMM) describes how, when, and in what order program variables are stored to, and read from, the main memory. The JMM is described in the Java Language Specification in detail. You may visualize the JMM as depicted in Figure 6-5.

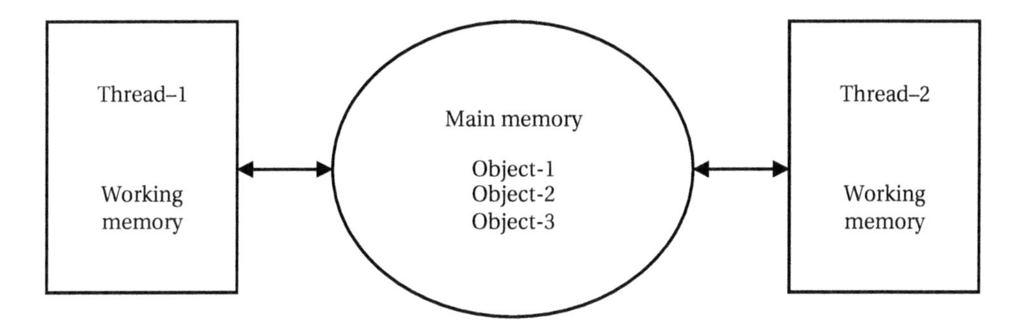

Figure 6-5. *The Java Memory Model*

Figure 6-5 shows two threads sharing the main memory. Let's assume that you have a Java program that is running two threads, thread-1 and thread-2, and each thread is running on different processors. Suppose thread-1 reads the value of an instance variable of object-1 in its working memory, updates the value, and does not write the updated value back to the main memory. Let's run through a few possible scenarios.

- What happens if thread-2 tries to read the value of the same instance variable of object-1 from the main memory? Would thread-2 read the old value from the main memory, or would it be able to read the updated value from the working memory of thread-1?
- Suppose thread-1 is in the middle of writing the updated value to the main memory, and at the same time, thread-2 is trying to read the same value from the main memory. Would thread-2 read the old value or some garbage value from the main memory because the value is not written back to the main memory completely?

The JMM answers all such questions. In essence, the JMM describes three important aspects of the execution of instructions in a Java program. They are as follows:

- Atomicity
- Visibility
- Ordering

Atomicity

The JMM describes actions that should be executed atomically. It describes atomicity rules about read and write actions on instance variables, static variables, and array elements. It guarantees that read and write on an object's field of any type, except `long` and `double`, are always atomic. However, if a field of type `long` or `double` is declared `volatile` (I discuss the `volatile` keyword in detail later in this chapter), read and write on that field are also guaranteed to be atomic.

Visibility

The JMM describes the conditions under which the effects produced by actions in one thread are visible to other threads. Mainly, it determines when a thread writes a value to a field, at what point the new value of that field can be visible to other threads. I discuss more about the visibility aspect of the JMM when I discuss locks, synchronization, and volatile variables later in this chapter. For completeness, the following are some of the visibility rules:

- When a thread reads the value of a field for the first time, it will read either the initial value of the field or some value that was written to that field by some other thread.
- A write to a volatile variable is always written to the main memory. A read on a volatile variable is always read from the main memory. That is, a volatile variable is never cached in the working memory of a thread. In effect, any write to a volatile variable is flushed to the main memory, immediately making the new value visible to other threads.
- When a thread terminates, the working memory of the thread is written to the main memory immediately. That is, after a thread terminates, all variables' values visible only to the terminated thread are made visible to all threads.
- When a thread enters a synchronized block, that thread reloads the values of all variables in its working memory. When a thread leaves a synchronized block, it writes all variables values from its working memory to the main memory.

Ordering

The JMM describes in what order actions are performed within a thread and among threads. It guarantees that all actions performed within a thread are ordered. Actions in different threads are not guaranteed to be performed in any order. You may achieve some ordering while working with multiple threads by using the synchronization technique described later in this chapter.

■ **Tip** Each thread in a Java program uses two kinds of memory: working memory and main memory. A thread cannot access the working memory of another thread. Main memory is shared among the threads. Threads communicate with each other using the main memory. Every thread has its own stack, which is used to store local variables.

Object's Monitor and Threads Synchronization

In a multi-threaded program, a section of code that may have undesirable effects on the outcome of the program if executed by multiple threads concurrently is called a *critical section*. Often, the undesirable effects result from the concurrent use of a resource by multiple threads in the critical section. It is necessary to control the access to a critical section in a program so only one thread can execute the critical section at a time.

In a Java program, a critical section can be a block of statements or a method. Java has no built-in mechanism to identify a critical section in a program. However, Java has many built-in constructs that allow programmers to declare a critical section, and to control and coordinate access to it. It is the programmer's responsibility to identify critical sections in a program and control the access to those critical sections by multiple threads. Controlling and coordinating the access to a critical section by multiple threads is known as *thread synchronization*. Thread synchronization is always a challenging task when writing a multi-threaded program. In Listing 6-5, the `updateBalance()` and `monitorBalance()` methods are critical sections and you must synchronize the threads' access to these two methods to get a consistent output. Two kinds of thread synchronizations are built into the Java programming language:

- Mutual exclusion synchronization
- Conditional synchronization

In mutual exclusion synchronization, only one thread is allowed to have access to a section of code at a point in time. Listing 6-5 is an example of a program where mutual exclusion synchronization is needed so that only one thread can execute `updateBalance()` and `monitorBalance()` at a point in time. In this case, you can think of the mutual exclusion as an exclusive access to the `balance` variable by a thread.

The conditional synchronization allows multiple threads to work together to achieve a result. For example, consider a multi-threaded program to solve a *producer/consumer* problem. There are two threads in a program: one thread produces data (the producer thread) and another thread consumes the data (the consumer thread). The consumer thread must wait until the producer thread produces data and makes it available for consuming. The producer thread must notify the consumer thread when it produces data so the consumer thread can consume it. In other words, producer and consumer threads must coordinate/cooperate with each other to accomplish the task. During conditional synchronization, mutual exclusion synchronization may also be needed. Suppose the producer thread produces data one byte at a time and puts the data into a buffer whose capacity is also one byte. The consumer thread consumes data from the same buffer. In this case, only one of the threads should have access to the buffer at a time (a mutual exclusion). If the buffer is full, the producer thread must wait for the consumer thread to empty the buffer; if the buffer is empty, the consumer thread must wait for the producer thread to produce a byte of data and put it into the buffer (a conditional synchronization).

The mutual exclusion synchronization is achieved through a lock. A lock supports two operations: `acquire` and `release`. A thread that wants exclusive access to a resource must acquire the lock associated with that resource. As long as a thread possesses the lock to a resource, other threads cannot acquire the same lock. Once the thread that possesses the lock is finished with the resource, it releases the lock so another thread can acquire it.

The conditional synchronization is achieved through condition variables and three operations: `wait`, `signal`, and `broadcast`. Condition variables define the conditions on which threads are synchronized. The `wait` operation makes a thread wait on a condition to become true so it can proceed. The `signal` operation wakes up one of the threads that was waiting on the condition variables. The `broadcast` operation wakes up all threads that were waiting on the condition variables. Note that the difference between the `signal` operation and `broadcast` operation is that the former wakes up only one waiting thread, whereas the latter wakes up all waiting threads.

A *monitor* is a programming construct that has a lock, condition variables, and associated operations on them. Thread synchronization in a Java program is achieved using monitors. Every object in a Java program has an associated monitor.

A critical section in a Java program is defined with respect to an object's monitor. A thread must acquire the object's monitor before it can start executing the piece of code declared as a critical section. The `synchronized` keyword is used to declare a critical section. There are two ways to use the `synchronized` keyword:

- To declare a method as a critical section
- To declare a block of statements as a critical section

You can declare a method as a critical section by using the keyword `synchronized` before the method's return type, as shown:

```
public class CriticalSection {
    public synchronized void someMethod_1() {
        // Method code goes here
    }

    public static synchronized void someMethod_2() {
        // Method code goes here
    }
}
```

■ **Tip** You can declare both an instance method and a static method as synchronized. A constructor cannot be declared as synchronized. A constructor is called only once by only one thread, which is creating the object. So it makes no sense to synchronize access to a constructor.

In the case of a synchronized instance method, the entire method is a critical section and it is associated with the monitor of the object for which this method is executed. That is, a thread must acquire the object's monitor lock before executing the code inside a synchronized instance method of that object. For example,

```
// Create an object called cs1
CriticalSection cs1 = new CriticalSection();

// Execute the synchronized instance method. Before this method execution starts, the thread
// that is executing this statement must acquire the monitor lock of the cs1 object
cs1.someMethod_1();
```

In case of a synchronized static method, the entire method is a critical section and it is associated with the class object that represents that class. That is, a thread must acquire the class object's monitor lock before executing the code inside a synchronized static method of that class. For example,

```
// Execute the synchronized static method. Before this method execution starts, the thread that
// is executing this statement must acquire the monitor lock of the CriticalSection.class object
CriticalSection.someMethod_2();
```

The syntax for declaring a block of code as a critical section is as follows:

```
synchronized(<objectReference>) {
    // one or more statements of the critical section
}
```

The <objectReference> is the reference of the object whose monitor lock will be used to synchronize the access to the critical section. This syntax is used to define part of a method body as a critical section. This way, a thread needs to acquire the object's monitor lock only, while executing a smaller part of the method's code, which is declared as a critical section. Other threads can still execute other parts of the body of the method concurrently. Additionally, this method of declaring a critical section lets you declare a part or whole of a constructor as a critical section. Recall that you cannot use the keyword synchronized in the declaration part of a constructor. However, you can use it inside a constructor's body to declare a block of code as synchronized. The following snippet of code illustrates the use of the keyword synchronized:

```
public class CriticalSection2 {
    public synchronized void someMethod10() {
        // Method code goes here. Only one thread can execute here at a time.
    }

    public void someMethod11() {
        synchronized(this) {
            // Method code goes here. Only one thread can execute here at a time.
        }
    }

    public void someMethod12() {
        // Some statements go here. Multiple threads can execute here at a time.

        synchronized(this) {
            // Some statements go here. Only one thread can execute here at a time.
        }

        // Some statements go here. Multiple threads can execute here at a time.
    }

    public static synchronized void someMethod20() {
        // Method code goes here. Only one thread can execute here at a time.
    }
```

```
    public static void someMethod21() {
        synchronized(CriticalSection2.class) {
            // Method code goes here. Only one thread can execute here at a time.
        }
    }

    public static void someMethod_22() {
        // Some statements go here: section_1. Multiple threads can execute here at a time.

        synchronized(CriticalSection2.class) {
            // Some statements go here: section_2. Only one thread can execute here at a time.
        }

        // Some statements go here: section_3.  Multiple threads can execute here at a time
    }
}
```

The CriticalSection2 class has six methods: three instance methods and three class methods. The someMethod10() method is synchronized as the synchronized keyword is used in the method declaration. The someMethod11() method differs from the someMethod10() method only in the way it uses the synchronized keyword. It puts the entire method body inside the synchronized keyword as a block, which has practically the same effect as declaring the method synchronized. The method someMethod12() is different. It declares only part of the method's body as a synchronized block. There can be more than one thread that can execute someMethod12() concurrently. However, only one of them can be executing inside the synchronized block at one point in time. Other sets of methods—someMethod20(), someMethod21() and someMethod22()—are class methods, and they will behave the same way, except that class's object monitor will be used to achieve the thread synchronization.

The process of acquiring and releasing an object's monitor lock is handled by the JVM. The only thing you need to do is declare a method (or a block) as synchronized. Before entering a synchronized method or block, the thread acquires the monitor lock of the object. On exiting the synchronized method or block, it releases the object's monitor lock. A thread that has acquired an object's monitor lock can acquire it again as many times as it wants. However, it must release the object's monitor lock as many times as it had acquired it in order for another thread to acquire the same object's monitor lock. Let's consider the following code for a MultiLocks class:

```
public class MultiLocks {
    public synchronized void method1() {
        // Some statements go here

        this.method2();

        // Some statements go here
    }

    public synchronized void method2() {
        // Some statements go here
    }

    public static synchronized void method3() {
        // Some statements go here
```

```
        MultiLocks.method4();

        // Some statements go here
    }

    public static synchronized void method4() {
        // Some statements go here
    }
}
```

The MultiLocks class has four methods and all of them are synchronized. Two of them are instance methods, which are synchronized using the reference of the object on which the method call will be made. Two of them are class methods, which are synchronized using the reference of the class object of the MultiLocks class. If a thread wants to execute method1() or method2(), it must first acquire the monitor lock of the object on which the method is called. You are calling method2() from inside the method method1(). Since a thread that is executing method1() must already have acquired the object's monitor lock and a call to method2() requires the acquisition of the same lock, that thread will reacquire the same object's monitor lock automatically when it executes method2() from inside method1() without competing with other threads to acquire the object's monitor lock.

Therefore, when a thread executes method2() from inside method1(), it will have acquired the object's monitor lock twice. When it exits method2(), it will release the lock once; when it exits method1(), it will release the lock the second time; and then the object's monitor lock will be available for other threads for acquisition. The same argument applies to the call to method4() from inside method3() except that, in this case, the MultiLocks class object's monitor lock is involved in the synchronization. Consider calling method3() from method1(), like so:

```
public class MultiLocks {
    public synchronized void method1() {
        // Some statements go here

        this.method2();
        MultiLocks.method3();

        // Some statements go here
    }

    // Rest of the code remains the same as shown before
}
```

Suppose you call method1(), like so:

```
MultiLocks ml = new MultiLocks();
ml.method1();
```

When ml.method1()is executed, the executing thread must acquire the monitor lock of the object ml. However, the executing thread must acquire the monitor lock of the MultiLocks.class object to execute the MultiLocks.method3() method. Note that ml and MultiLocks.class are two different objects. The thread that wants to execute the MultiLocks.method3() method from the method1() method must possess both objects' monitor locks at the same time.

You can apply the same arguments to work with synchronized blocks. For example, you can have a snippet of code like this

```
synchronized (objectReference) {
    // Trying to synchronize again on the same object is ok
    synchronized(objectReference) {
        // Some statements go here
    }
}
```

It is time to take a deeper look into the workings of threads synchronization using an object's monitor. Figure 6-6 depicts how multiple threads can use an object's monitor.

I use a doctor-patient analogy while discussing threads synchronization. Suppose a doctor has a clinic to treat patients. We know that it is very important to allow only one patient access to the doctor at a time. Otherwise, the doctor may mix up one patient's symptoms with another patient's symptoms; a patient with fever may get a prescription for a headache! Therefore, we will assume that only one patient can have access to the doctor at any point in time. It is the same assumption that only one thread (patient) can have access to an object's monitor (doctor) at a time.

Any patient who wants an access to the doctor must sign in and wait in the waiting room. Similarly, each object monitor has an *entry set* (waiting room for newcomers) and any thread that wants to acquire the object's monitor lock must enter the entry set first. If the patient signs in, he may get access to the doctor immediately, if the doctor is not treating a patient and there were no patients waiting for his turn in the waiting room. Similarly, if the entry set of an object's monitor is empty and there is no other thread that possesses the object's monitor lock, the thread entering the entry set acquires the object's monitor lock immediately. However, if there were patients waiting in the waiting room or one being treated by the doctor, the patient who signs in is blocked and he must wait for the doctor to become available again. Similarly, if a thread enters the entry set, and other threads are already blocked in the entry set, or another thread already possesses the object's monitor lock, the thread that just signed in is said to be blocked and must wait in the entry set.

A thread entering the entry set is shown by the arrow labeled `Enter`. A thread itself is shown in Figure 6-6 using a circle. A circle with the text `B` shows a thread that is blocked in the entry set. A circle with the text `R` shows a thread that has acquired the object's monitor.

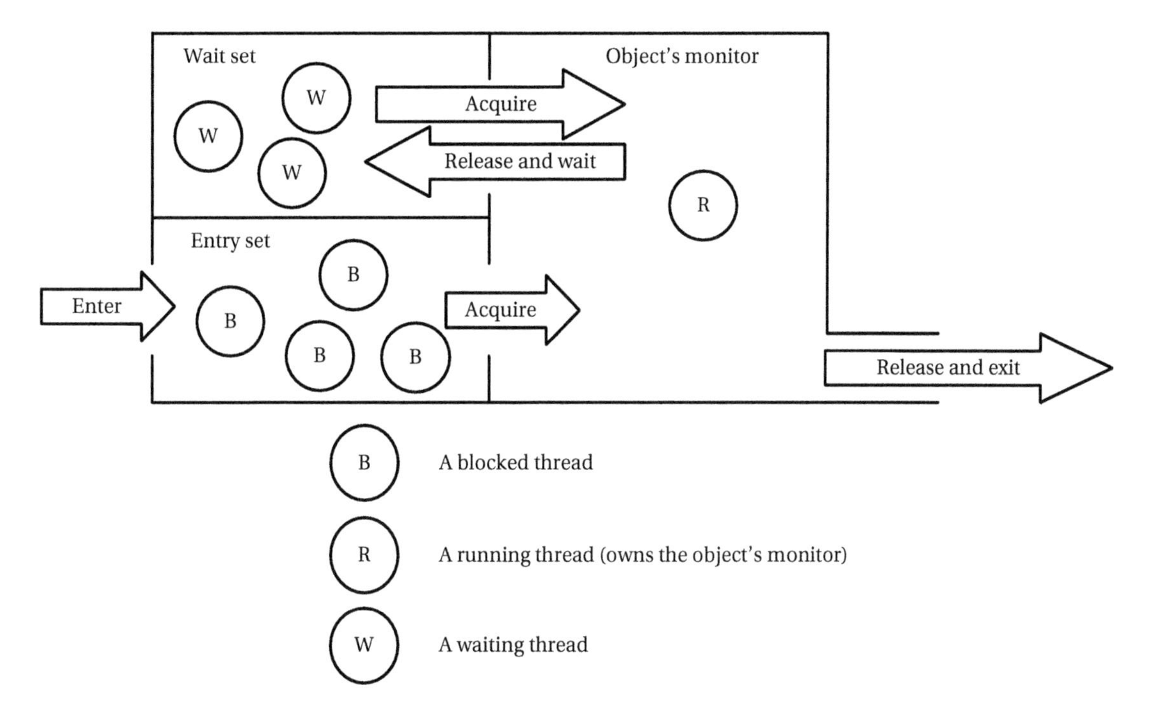

Figure 6-6. *Multiple threads using an object's monitor*

What happens to the threads that are blocked in the entry set? When do they get a chance to acquire the object's monitor? You can think about the patients blocked in the waiting room and getting their turn to be treated by the doctor. Many factors decide which patient will be treated next. First, the patient being treated must free the doctor before another patient can have access to the doctor. In Java, the thread that has the ownership of the object's monitor must release the object's monitor before any threads that are blocked in the entry set can have the ownership of the object's monitor. A patient may free the doctor for one of two reasons:

- The patient is done with his treatment and he is ready to go home. This is a straightforward case of a patient freeing the doctor after his treatment is over.
- A patient is in the middle of his treatment. However, he must wait for some time in order for the doctor to resume his treatment. Let's assume that the clinic has a special waiting room (separate from the one where patients who just signed in wait) for those patients who are in the middle of their treatment. This case needs some explanation. Let's say that the doctor is an eye specialist and he has some patients in his clinic. The patient who is being treated needs an eye examination for which his pupils must be dilated first. It takes about 30 minutes after the patient receives eye drops for full pupil dilation, which is required for the examination. Should the doctor be waiting for 30 minutes for the patient's pupils to dilate? Should this patient release the doctor for 30 minutes and let other patient have access to the doctor? You would agree that if doctor's time can be used to treat other patients while this

patient's pupils are being dilated, it is fine for this patient to release the doctor. What should happen when this patient's pupils are dilated, however, and the doctor is still busy treating another patient? The doctor cannot leave any patient in the middle of treatment. Therefore, the patient who released the doctor and waited for some condition to be true (here dilation process to complete) must wait until doctor is free again. I explain this issue more later in this chapter and I try to correlate this situation with threads and the object's monitor lock.

I must discuss another issue in the context of the doctor-patient example before I can compare this with the monitor-threads case. When the doctor is free and only one patient is waiting to get access to him, there is no problem. The sole patient waiting for the doctor will get access to him immediately. However, what happens when the doctor becomes available and there is more than one patient waiting to get access to him? Which one of the waiting patients should get access to the doctor first? Should it be the patient who came first (First In, First Out or FIFO)? Should it be the patient who came in last (Last In, First Out or LIFO)? Should it be the patient who needs the least (or the most) amount of time for his treatment? Should it be the patient who is in the most serious condition? The answer depends on the policy followed by the clinic management.

Similar to a patient in the doctor-patient example, a thread can also release an object's monitor lock for two reasons:

- At this time, the thread has completed the work for which it had acquired the object's monitor lock. The arrow labeled "Release and Exit" in Figure 6-6 indicates this scenario in the diagram. When a thread simply exits a synchronized method/block, it releases the object's monitor lock it had acquired.
- The thread is in the middle of a task and it needs to wait for some condition to be true to complete its remaining task. Let's consider the producer/consumer problem. Suppose the producer acquires the buffer object's monitor lock and wants to write some data into the buffer. However, it finds that the buffer is full and the consumer must consume the data and make the buffer empty before it can write to it. In this case, the producer must release the buffer object's monitor lock and wait until the consumer acquires the lock and empties the buffer. The same logic applies for the consumer when it acquires the buffer's monitor lock and finds that buffer is empty. At that time, the consumer must release the lock and wait until the producer produces some data. This kind of temporarily releasing of the object's monitor lock and waiting for some condition to occur is shown in the diagram labeled as the "Release and Wait" arrow. An object can have multiple threads that can be in "Release and Wait" state at the same time. All threads that have released the object's monitor lock and are waiting for some conditions to occur are put in a set called a *wait set*.

How is a thread placed in the wait set? Note that a thread can be placed in the wait set of an object monitor only if it once acquired the object's monitor lock. Once a thread has acquired the object's monitor lock, it must call the `wait()` method of the object in order to place itself into the wait set. This means a thread must always call the `wait()` method from inside a `synchronized` method or a block. The `wait()` method is defined in the `java.lang.Object` class and it is declared final; that is, no other class in Java can override this method. You must consider the following two rules before you call the `wait()` method of an object.

Rule #1

The call to the `wait()` method must be placed inside a synchronized method (static or non-static) or a synchronized block.

Rule #2

The `wait()` method must be called on the object whose monitor the current thread has acquired. It throws a `java.lang.InterruptedException`. The code that calls this method must handle this exception. The `wait()` method throws an `IllegalMonitorStateException` when the current thread is not the owner of the object's monitor. The following snippet of code does not place the `wait()` method call inside a `try-catch` to keep the code simple and readable. For example, inside a synchronized non-static method, the call to the `wait()` method may look like the following:

```
public class WaitMethodCall {
    // Object that is used to synchronize a block
    private Object objectRef = new Object();

    public synchronized void someMethod_1() {
        // The thread running here has already acquired the monitor lock on
        // the object represented by the reference this because it is a
        // synchronized non-static method

        // other statements go here

        while (some condition is true) {
            // It is ok to call the wait() method on this, because the
            // current thread possesses monitor lock on this
            this.wait();
        }
        // other statements go here
    }

    public static synchronized void someMethod_2() {
        // The thread executing here has already acquired the monitor lock on
        // the class object represented by the WaitMethodCall.class reference
        // because it is a synchronized static method

        while (some condition is true) {
            // It is ok to call the wait() method on WaitMethodCall.class
            // because the current thread possesses monitor lock on
            // WaitMethodCall.class object
            WaitMethodCall.class.wait();
        }
        // other statements go here
    }

    public void someMethod_3() {
        // other statements go here

        synchronized(objectRef) {
            // Current thread possesses monitor lock of objectRef

            while (some condition is true) {
                // It is ok to call the wait() method on objectRef because
                // the current thread possesses monitor lock on objectRef
```

```
                objectRef.wait();
            }
        }
        // other statements go here
    }
}
```

Note that objectRef is an instance variable and it is of the type java.lang.Object. Its only use is to synchronize threads' access to a block inside the someMethod_3() method. Since it is declared an instance variable, all threads calling someMethod_3() will use its monitor to execute the synchronized block. A common mistake made by beginners is to declare objectRef as a local variable inside a method and use it to in a synchronized block. The following snippet of code shows such a mistake:

```
public void wrongSynchronizationMethod {
    // This objectRef is created every time a thread calls this method
    Object objectRef = new Object();

    // It is a blunder to use objectRef for synchronization below
    synchronized(objectRef) {
        // In fact, this block works as if there is no synchronization, because every
        // thread  creates a new objectRef and acquires its monitor lock immediately.
    }
}
```

With this snippet of code in mind, you must use an object reference that is common to all threads to synchronize access to a block.

Let's get back to the question of which patient will get access to the doctor when he becomes available again. Will it be a patient from the waiting room who is waiting after signing in or a patient from another waiting room who was waiting in the middle of his treatment? Before you answer this question, let's make it clear that there is a difference between the patients in the waiting room who are waiting after signing in and the patients waiting for some condition (e.g., dilation to complete) to occur in another waiting room. After signing in, patients wait on the availability of the doctor, whereas patients in the middle of their treatments wait on a particular condition to occur. For patients in the second category, a particular condition must hold before they can seek access to the doctor, whereas patients in the first category are ready to grab access to the doctor as soon as possible. Therefore, someone must notify a patient in the second category that a particular condition has occurred and it is time for him to seek access to the doctor again to continue his treatment. Let's assume that this notification must come from a patient being currently treated by the doctor. That is, the patient who currently has access to the doctor notifies the patients waiting in the middle of their treatments to get ready to gain access to the doctor again. Note that it is just a notification that some condition has occurred and it is delivered only to the patients waiting in the middle of their treatments. Whether the patient in the middle of his treatment will get access to the doctor right after the current patient is done with the doctor is not guaranteed. It only guarantees that the condition on which a patient was waiting holds at the time of notification and the waiting patient may try to get access to the doctor to continue his treatment. Let's correlate this example to monitor-threads example.

The threads in the entry set are blocked and they are ready to grab access to the monitor as soon as possible. The threads in the wait set are waiting for some condition to occur. A thread that has ownership of the monitor must notify the threads waiting in the wait set about the fulfillment of the conditions on which they are waiting. In Java, the notification is made by calling the notify() and notifyAll() methods of the Object class. Like the wait() method, the notify() and notifyAll() methods are also declared final. Like the wait() method, these two methods must be called by a thread using an object whose monitor has already been acquired by the thread. If a thread calls these methods on an object before acquiring the object's monitor, an IllegalMonitorStateException is thrown. The call to the notify() method wakes up one thread from the wait set, whereas the call to the notifyAll() method wakes up all threads in the wait set. In case of the notify() method call, the thread that is woken up is chosen arbitrarily. Note that when a thread calls the notify() or notifyAll() method, it still holds the lock on the object's monitor. Threads in the wait set are only woken up by the notify() or notifyAll() call. They do not acquire the object's monitor lock immediately. When the thread that called the notify() or notifyAll() method releases the object's monitor lock by "Release and Exit" or "Release and Wait," the woken up threads in the wait set compete with the threads in the entry set to acquire the object's monitor again. Therefore, a call to the notify() and notifyAll() serves only as a wakeup call for threads in the wait set and it does not guarantee access to the object's monitor.

■ **Tip** There is no way to wake up a specific thread in the wait set. The call to notify() chooses a thread arbitrarily, whereas the call to notifyAll() wakes up all threads. Use notifyAll() when you are in doubt about which method to use.

The following snippet of code shows pseudocode for using the notifyAll() method along with the wait() method. You may observe that the call to the wait() and notify() methods are made on the same object, because if objectRef.wait() puts a thread in the wait set of the objectRef object, the objectRef.notify() or objectRef.notifyAll() method will wake that thread from the wait set of the objectRef object.

```
public class WaitAndNotifyMethodCall {
    private Object objectRef = new Object();

    public synchronized void someMethod_1() {
        while (some condition is true) {
            this.wait();
        }

        if (some other condition is true) {
            // Notify all waiting threads
            this.notifyAll();
        }
    }

    public static synchronized void someMethod_2() {
        while (some condition is true) {
            WaitAndNotifyMethodCall.class.wait();
        }

        if (some other condition is true) {
            // Notify all waiting threads
            WaitAndNotifyMethodCall.class.notifyAll();
        }
    }
```

```
    public void someMethod_3() {
        synchronized(objectRef) {
            while (some condition is true) {
                objectRef.wait();
            }

            if (some other condition is true) {
                // Notify all waiting threads
                objectRef.notifyAll();
            }
        }
    }
}
```

Once a thread is woken up in the wait set, it has to compete with the threads in the entry set to acquire the monitor lock of the object. After a thread is woken up in the wait set and acquires the object's monitor lock, it has choices: to do some work and release the lock by invoking the `wait()` method (release and wait) again, or release the lock by exiting the synchronized section (release and exit). One important point to remember about the call to the `wait()` method is that, typically, a call to the `wait()` method is placed inside a loop. Here is the reason why it is necessary to do so. A thread looks for a condition to hold. It waits by calling the `wait()` method and placing itself in the wait set if that condition does not hold. The thread wakes up when it is notified by another thread, which calls the `notify()` or `notifyAll()` method. When the thread that woke up acquires the lock, the condition that held at the time of notification may not still hold. Therefore, it is necessary to check for the condition again, when the thread wakes up and acquires the lock, to make sure the condition it was looking for is true, and it can continue its work. For example, consider the producer/consumer problem. Suppose there is one producer and many consumers. Suppose a consumer calls the `wait()` method as follows:

```
if (buffer is empty) {
    buffer.wait();
}

buffer.consume();
```

Suppose the buffer is empty and all consumers are waiting in the wait set. The producer produces some data and it calls the `buffer.notifyAll()` method to wake up all consumer threads in the wait set. All consumer threads wake up; however, only one will get a chance to acquire the monitor lock next. The first one acquires the lock and executes the `buffer.consume()` method to empty the buffer. When the next consumer acquires the monitor lock, it will also execute the `buffer.consume()` statement. However, the consumer that woke up and acquired the lock before this one had already emptied the buffer. The logical mistake in the previous snippet of code is that the call to the `wait()` method is placed inside an `if` statement instead of inside a loop. That is, after a thread wakes up, it is not checking if the buffer contains some data or not, before trying to consume the data. The corrected snippet of code is the following:

```
while (buffer is empty) {
    buffer.wait();
}

buffer.consume();
```

I answer one more question before you can see this big discussion about thread synchronization in action. The question is, "Which thread gets a chance to acquire the object's monitor lock when there are some blocked threads in the entry set and some woken up threads in the wait set?" Note that the threads that are in the wait set do not compete for the object's monitor until they are woken up by the `notify()` or `notifyAll()` call. The answer to this question is that it depends on the scheduler's algorithm of the operating system.

Listing 6-6 contains the code for the `BalanceUpdateSynchronized` class, which is a modified version of the `BalanceUpdate` class listed in Listing 6-5. The only difference between the two classes is the use of the `synchronized` keyword to declare the `updateBalance()` and `monitorBalance()` methods in the new class, so only one thread can enter one of the methods at a time. When you run the new class, you will not see any output because the `monitorBalance()`method will never see the value of the `balance` variable other than 100. You will need to terminate the program manually, for example, using Ctrl+C on Windows.

Listing 6-6. Synchronized Balance Update

```
// BalanceUpdateSynchronized.java
package com.jdojo.threads;

public class BalanceUpdateSynchronized {
    // Initialize balance to 100
    private static int balance = 100;

    public static void main(String[] args) {
        startBalanceUpdateThread(); // Thread to update the balance value
        startBalanceMonitorThread(); // Thread to monitor the balance value
    }

    public static synchronized void updateBalance() {
        // Add 10 to balance and subtract 10 from balance
        balance = balance + 10;
        balance = balance - 10;
    }

    public static synchronized void monitorBalance() {
        int b = balance;
        if (b != 100) {
            System.out.println("Balance changed: " + b);
            System.exit(1); // Exit the program
        }
    }

    public static void startBalanceUpdateThread() {
        // Start a new thread that calls the updateBalance() method in an infinite loop
        Thread t = new Thread(() -> {
            while (true) {
                updateBalance();
            }
        });
        t.start();
    }
```

```
    public static void startBalanceMonitorThread() {
        // Start a thread that monitors the balance value
        Thread t = new Thread(() -> {
            while (true) {
                monitorBalance();
            }
        });
        t.start();
    }
}
```

I show examples of using the `wait()` and `notify()` methods in the next section, which discusses the producer/consumer problem. The `wait()` method in the `Object` class is overloaded and it has three versions:

- `wait()`: The thread waits in the object's wait set until another thread calls the `notify()` or `notifyAll()` method on the same object.
- `wait(long timeinMillis)`: The thread waits in the object's wait set until another thread calls the `notify()` or `notifyAll()` method on the same object or the specified amount of `timeinMillis` time has elapsed.
- `wait(long timeinMillis, long timeinNanos)`: This version lets you specify time in milliseconds and nanoseconds.

The Producer/Consumer Synchronization Problem

The producer/consumer is a typical thread synchronization problem that uses the `wait()` and `notify()` methods. I keep it simple. The problem statement goes like this:

> *There are four classes: Buffer, Producer, Consumer, and ProducerConsumerTest. An object of the Buffer class will have an integer data element that will be produced by the producer and consumed by the consumer. Therefore, in this example, a Buffer object can hold only one integer at a point in time. Your goal is to synchronize the access to the buffer, so the Producer produces a new data element only when the Buffer is empty and the Consumer consumes the buffer's data only when it is available. The ProducerConsumerTest class is used to test the program.*

Listing 6-7, Listing 6-8, Listing 6-9, and Listing 6-10 contain the code for the four classes.

Listing 6-7. A Buffer Class for Producer/Consumer Synchronization

```
// Buffer.java
package com.jdojo.threads;

public class Buffer {
    private int data;
    private boolean empty;
```

```
    public Buffer() {
        this.empty = true;
    }

    public synchronized void produce(int newData) {
        // Wait until the buffer is empty
        while (!this.empty) {
            try {
                this.wait();
            } catch (InterruptedException e) {
                e.printStackTrace();
            }
        }

        // Store the new data produced by the producer
        this.data = newData;

        // Set the empty flag to false, so the consumer may consume the data
        this.empty = false;

        // Notify the waiting consumer in the wait set
        this.notify();

        System.out.println("Produced: " + newData);
    }

    public synchronized int consume() {
        // Wait until the buffer gets some data
        while (this.empty) {
            try {
                this.wait();
            } catch (InterruptedException e) {
                e.printStackTrace();
            }
        }

        // Set the empty flag to true, so that the producer can store new data
        this.empty = true;

        // Notify the waiting producer in the wait set
        this.notify();

        System.out.println("Consumed: " + data);

        return data;
    }
}
```

Listing 6-8. A Producer Class for Producer/Consumer Synchronization

```
// Producer.java
package com.jdojo.threads;

import java.util.Random;

public class Producer extends Thread {
    private final Buffer buffer;

    public Producer(Buffer buffer) {
        this.buffer = buffer;
    }

    @Override
    public void run() {
        Random rand = new Random();
        while (true) {
            // Generate a random integer and store it in the buffer
            int n = rand.nextInt();
            buffer.produce(n);
        }
    }
}
```

Listing 6-9. A Consumer Class for Producer/Consumer Synchronization

```
// Consumer.java
package com.jdojo.threads;

public class Consumer extends Thread {
    private final Buffer buffer;

    public Consumer(Buffer buffer) {
        this.buffer = buffer;
    }

    @Override
    public void run() {
        int data;
        while (true) {
            // Consume the data from the buffer. We are not using the consumed
            // data for any other purpose here
            data = buffer.consume();
        }
    }
}
```

Listing 6-10. A ProducerConsumerTest Class to Test the Producer/Consumer Synchronization

```
// ProducerConsumerTest.java
package com.jdojo.threads;

public class ProducerConsumerTest {
    public static void main(String[] args) {
        // Create Buffer, Producer and Consumer objects
        Buffer buffer = new Buffer();
        Producer p = new Producer(buffer);
        Consumer c = new Consumer(buffer);

        // Start the producer and consumer threads
        p.start();
        c.start();
    }
}
```

```
Produced: 1872733184
Consumed: 1872733184
...
```

When you run the ProducerConsumerTest class, you may get different output. However, your output will look similar in the sense that two lines printed will be always of the following form, where XXX indicates an integer:

```
Produced: XXX
Consumed: XXX
```

In this example, the Buffer class needs some explanation. It has two instance variables:

- `private int data`
- `private boolean empty`

The producer uses the data instance variable to store the new data. The consumer reads it. The empty instance variable is used as an indicator whether the buffer is empty or not. In the constructor, it is initialized to true, indicating that the new buffer is empty.

It has two synchronized methods: produce() and consume(). Both methods are declared synchronized because the goal is to protect the Buffer object to be used by multiple threads concurrently. If the producer is producing new data by calling the produce() method, the consumer must wait to consume the data until the producer is done and vice versa. The producer thread calls the produce() method, passing the newly generated data to it. However, before the new data is stored in the data instance variable, the producer makes sure that the buffer is empty. If the buffer is not empty, it calls the this.wait() method to place itself in the wait set of the buffer object until the consumer notifies it using the this.notify() method inside the consume() method.

Once the producer thread detects that the buffer is empty, it stores the new data in the data instance variable, sets the empty flag to false, and calls this.notify() to wake up the consumer thread in the wait set to consume the data. At the end, it also prints a message on the console that data has been produced.

The consume() method of the Buffer class is similar to its counterpart, the produce() method. The only difference is that the consumer-thread calls this method and it performs logic that's opposite of the produce() method. For example, it checks if the buffer is not empty before consuming the data.

The Producer and Consumer classes inherit from the Thread class. They override the run() method of the Thread class. Both of them accept an object of the Buffer class in their constructor to use it in their run() method. The Producer class generates a random integer in its run() method inside an infinite loop and keeps writing it to the buffer. The Consumer class keeps consuming data from the buffer in an infinite loop.

The ProducerConsumerTest class creates all three objects (a buffer, a producer, and a consumer) and starts the producer and consumer threads. Since both classes (Producer and Consumer) use infinite loops inside the run() method, you have to terminate the program forcibly, such as by pressing Ctrl+C, if you are running this program from a Windows command prompt.

Which Thread Is Executing?

The Thread class has some useful static methods; one of them is the currentThread() method. It returns the reference of the Thread object that calls this method. Consider the following statement:

```
Thread t = Thread.currentThread();
```

The statement will assign the reference of the thread object that executes this statement to the variable t. Note that a statement in Java can be executed by different threads at different points in time during the execution of a program. Therefore, t may be assigned the reference of a different Thread object when the statement is executed at different times in the same program. Listing 6-11 demonstrates the use of the currentThread() method. You may get the same text in the output, but in a different order.

Listing 6-11. Using the Thread.currentThread() Method

```
// CurrentThread.java
package com.jdojo.threads;

public class CurrentThread extends Thread {
    public CurrentThread(String name) {
        super(name);
    }

    @Override
    public void run() {
        Thread t = Thread.currentThread();
        String threadName = t.getName();
        System.out.println("Inside run() method: " + threadName);
    }

    public static void main(String[] args) {
        CurrentThread ct1 = new CurrentThread("Thread #1");
        CurrentThread ct2 = new CurrentThread("Thread #2");
        ct1.start();
        ct2.start();

        // Let's see which thread is executing the following statement
        Thread t = Thread.currentThread();
        String threadName = t.getName();
        System.out.println("Inside main() method: " + threadName);
    }
}
```

```
Inside main() method: main
Inside run() method: Thread #1
Inside run() method: Thread #2
```

Two different threads call the `Thread.currentThread()` method inside the `run()` method of the `CurrentThread` class. The method returns the reference of the thread executing the call. The program simply prints the name of the thread that is executing. It is interesting to note that when you called the `Thread.currentThread()` method inside the `main()` method, a thread named `main` executed the code. When you run a class, the JVM starts a thread named `main`, which is responsible for executing the `main()` method.

Letting a Thread Sleep

The `Thread` class contains a static `sleep()` method, which makes a thread sleep for a specified duration. It accepts a timeout as an argument. You can specify the timeout in milliseconds, milliseconds, and nanoseconds. The thread that executes this method sleeps for the specified amount of time. A sleeping thread is not scheduled by the operating system scheduler to receive the CPU time. If a thread has the ownership of an object's monitor lock before it goes to sleep, it continues to hold those monitor locks. The `sleep()` method may throw an `InterruptedException` and your code should be ready to handle it. Listing 6-12 demonstrates the use of the `sleep()` method.

Listing 6-12. A Sleeping Thread

```
// LetMeSleep.java
package com.jdojo.threads;

public class LetMeSleep {
    public static void main(String[] args) {
        try {
            System.out.println("I am going to sleep for 5 seconds.");
            Thread.sleep(5000); // The "main" thread will sleep
            System.out.println("I woke up.");
        } catch (InterruptedException e) {
            System.out.println("Someone interrupted me in my sleep.");
        }
        System.out.println("I am done.");
    }
}
```

```
I am going to sleep for 5 seconds.
I woke up.
I am done.
```

■ **Tip** The `TimeUnit` enum in the `java.util.concurrent` package represents a measurement of time in various units such as milliseconds, seconds, minutes, hours, days, etc. It has some convenience methods. One of them is the `sleep()` method. The `Thread.sleep()` method accepts time in milliseconds. If you want a thread to sleep for five seconds, you need to call this method as `Thread.sleep(5000)` by converting the seconds into milliseconds. You can use the `sleep()` method of `TimeUnit` instead to avoid the time duration conversion, like so:

```
TimeUnit.SECONDS.sleep(5); // Same as Thread.sleep(5000);
```

I Will Join You in Heaven

I can rephrase this section heading as "I will wait until you die." That's right. A thread can wait for another thread to die (or terminate). Suppose there are two threads, `t1` and `t2`. If the thread `t1` executes `t2.join()`, thread `t1` starts waiting until thread `t2` is terminated. In other words, the call `t2.join()` blocks until `t2` terminates. Using the `join()` method in a program is useful if one of the threads cannot proceed until another thread has finished executing.

Listing 6-13 has an example where you want to print a message on the standard output when the program has finished executing. The message to print is `"We are done."`

Listing 6-13. An Incorrect Way of Waiting for a Thread to Terminate

```
// JoinWrong.java
package com.jdojo.threads;

public class JoinWrong {
    public static void main(String[] args) {
        Thread t1 = new Thread(JoinWrong::print);
        t1.start();
        System.out.println("We are done.");
    }

    public static void print() {
        for (int i = 1; i <= 5; i++) {
            try {
                System.out.println("Counter: " + i);
                Thread.sleep(1000);
            } catch (InterruptedException e) {
                e.printStackTrace();
            }
        }
    }
}
```

```
We are done.
Counter: 1
Counter: 2
Counter: 3
Counter: 4
Counter: 5
```

In the `main()` method, a thread is created and started. The thread prints integers from 1 to 5. It sleeps for one second after printing an integer. In the end, the `main()` method prints a message. It seems that this program should print the numbers from 1 to 5, followed by your last message. However, if you look at the output, it is in the reverse order. What is wrong with this program?

The JVM starts a new thread called `main` that is responsible for executing the `main()` method of the class that you run. In your case, the `main()` method of the `JoinWrong` class is executed by the `main` thread. This thread will execute the following statements:

```
Thread t1 =  new Thread(JoinWrong::print);
t1.start();
System.out.println("We are done.");
```

When the `t1.start()` method call returns, you have one more thread running in your program (`thread t1`) in addition to the `main` thread. The `t1` thread is responsible for printing the integers from 1 to 5, whereas the `main` thread is responsible for printing the message `"We are done."` Since there are two threads responsible for two different tasks, it is not guaranteed which task will finish first. What is the solution? You must make your `main` thread wait on the thread `t1` to terminate. This can be achieved by calling the `t1.join()` method inside the `main()` method.

Listing 6-14 contains the correct version of Listing 6-13 by using the `t1.join()` method call before printing the final message. When the `main` thread executes the `join()` method call, it waits until the `t1` thread is terminated. The `join()` method of the `Thread` class may throw an `InterruptedException`, and your code should be ready to handle it.

Listing 6-14. A Correct Way of Waiting for a Thread to Terminate

```
// JoinRight.java
package com.jdojo.threads;

public class JoinRight {
    public static void main(String[] args) {
        Thread t1 = new Thread(JoinRight::print);
        t1.start();

        try {
            t1.join(); // "main" thread waits until t1 is terminated
        } catch (InterruptedException e) {
            e.printStackTrace();
        }

        System.out.println("We are done.");
    }
```

```
    public static void print() {
        for (int i = 1; i <= 5; i++) {
            try {
                System.out.println("Counter: " + i);
                Thread.sleep(1000);
            } catch (InterruptedException e) {
                e.printStackTrace();
            }
        }
    }
}
```

```
Counter: 1
Counter: 2
Counter: 3
Counter: 4
Counter: 5
We are done.
```

The `join()` method of the `Thread` class is overloaded. Its other two versions accept a timeout argument. If you use the `join()` method with a timeout, the caller thread will wait until the thread on which it is called is terminated or the timeout has elapsed. If you replace the `t1.join()` statement in the `JoinRight` class with `t1.join(1000)`, you will find that the output is not in the same order because the `main` thread will wait only for a second for the `t1` thread to terminate before it prints the final message.

Can a thread join multiple threads? The answer is yes. A thread can join multiple threads like so:

```
t1.join(); // Join t1
t2.join(); // Join t2
t3.join(); // Join t3
```

You should call the `join()` method of a thread after it has been started. If you call the `join()` method on a thread that has not been started, it returns immediately. Similarly, if you invoke the `join()` method on a thread that is already terminated, it returns immediately.

Can a thread join itself? The answer is yes and no. Technically, it is allowed for a thread to join itself. However, a thread should not join itself in most circumstances. In such a case, a thread waits to terminate itself. In other words, the thread waits forever.

```
// "Bad" call (not if you know what you are doing) to join. It waits forever
// until another thread interrupts it.
Thread.currentThread().join();
```

If you write this statement, make sure that your program interrupts the waiting thread using some other threads. In such a case, the waiting thread will return from the `join()` method call by throwing an `InterruptedException`.

Be Considerate to Others and Yield

A thread may voluntarily give up the CPU by calling the static `yield()` method of the `Thread` class. The call to the `yield()` method is a hint to the scheduler that it may pause the running thread and give the CPU to other threads. A thread may want to call this method only if it executes in a long loop without waiting or blocking. If a thread frequently waits or blocks, the `yield()` method call is not very useful because this thread does not monopolize the CPU and other threads will get the CPU time when this thread is blocked or waiting. It is advisable not to depend on the `yield()` method because it is just a hint to the scheduler. It is not guaranteed to give a consistent result across different platforms. A thread that calls the `yield()` method continues to hold the monitor locks. Note that there is no guarantee as to when the thread that yields will get the CPU time again. You may use it like so:

```
// The run() method of a thread class
public void run() {
    while(true) {
        // do some processing here...
        Thread.yield(); // Let's yield to other threads
    }
}
```

Lifecycle of a Thread

A thread is always in one of the following six states:

- New
- Runnable
- Blocked
- Waiting
- Timed-waiting
- Terminated

All these states of a thread are JVM states. They do not represent the states assigned to a thread by an operating system.

When a thread is created and its `start()` method is not yet called, it is in the new state.

```
Thread t = new SomeThreadClass(); // t is in the new state
```

A thread that is ready to run or running is in the runnable state. In other words, a thread that is eligible for getting the CPU time is in a runnable state.

■ **Tip** The JVM combines two OS-level thread states: ready-to-run and running into a state called the runnable state. A thread in the ready-to-run OS state means it is waiting for its turn to get the CPU time. A thread in the running OS state means it is running on the CPU.

A thread is said to be in a blocked state if it was trying to enter (or re-enter) a synchronized method or block but the monitor is being used by another thread. A thread in the entry set that is waiting to acquire a monitor lock is in the blocked state. A thread in the wait set that is waiting to reacquire the monitor lock after it has been woken up is also in a blocked state.

A thread may place itself in a waiting state by calling one of the methods listed in Table 6-2. A thread may place itself in a timed-waiting state by calling one of the methods listed in Table 6-3. I discuss the `parkNanos()` and `parkUntil()` methods later in this chapter.

***Table 6-2.** Methods That Place a Thread in Waiting State*

Method	Description
`wait()`	This is the `wait()` method of the `Object` class, which a thread may call if it wants to wait for a specific condition to hold. Recall that a thread must own the monitor's lock of an object to call the `wait()` method on that object. Another thread must call the `notify()` or `notifyAll()` method on the same object in order for the waiting thread to transition to the runnable state.
`join()`	This is the `join()` method of the `Thread` class. A thread that calls this method wants to wait until the thread on which this method is called terminates.
`park()`	This is the `park()` method of the `LockSupport` class, which is in the `java.util.concurrent.locks` package. A thread that calls this method may wait until a permit is available by calling the `unpark()` method on a thread. I cover the `LockSupport` class later in this chapter.

***Table 6-3.** Methods That Place a Thread in a Timed-Waiting State*

Method	Description
`sleep()`	This method is in the `Thread` class.
`wait (long millis)` `wait(long millis, int nanos)`	These methods are in the `Object` class.
`join(long millis)` `join(long millis, int nanos)`	These methods are in the `Thread` class.
`parkNanos (long nanos)` `parkNanos (Object blocker, long nanos)`	These methods are in the `LockSupport` class, which is in the `java.util.concurrent.locks` package.
`parkUntil (long deadline)` `parkUntil (Object blocker, long nanos)`	These methods are in the `LockSupport` class, which is in the `java.util.concurrent.locks` package.

A thread that has completed its execution is said to be in the terminated state. A thread is terminated when it exits its `run()` method or its `stop()` method is called. A terminated thread cannot transition to any other state. You can use the `isAlive()` method of a thread after it has been started to know if it is alive or terminated.

You can use the `getState()` method of the `Thread` class to get the state of a thread at any time. This method returns one of the constants of the `Thread.State` enum type. Listing 6-15 and Listing 6-16 demonstrate the transition of a thread from one state to another. The output of Listing 6-16 shows some of the states the thread transitions to during its lifecycle.

Listing 6-15. A ThreadState Class

```
// ThreadState.java
package com.jdojo.threads;

public class ThreadState extends Thread {
    private boolean keepRunning = true;
    private boolean wait = false;
    private final Object syncObject;

    public ThreadState(Object syncObject) {
        this.syncObject = syncObject;
    }

    @Override
    public void run() {
        while (keepRunning) {
            synchronized (syncObject) {
                if (wait) {
                    try {
                        syncObject.wait();
                    } catch (InterruptedException e) {
                        e.printStackTrace();
                    }
                }
            }
        }
    }

    public void setKeepRunning(boolean keepRunning) {
        this.keepRunning = keepRunning;
    }

    public void setWait(boolean wait) {
        this.wait = wait;
    }
}
```

Listing 6-16. A ThreadStateTest Class to Demonstrate the States of a Thread

```
// ThreadStateTest.java
package com.jdojo.threads;

public class ThreadStateTest {
    public static void main(String[] args) {
        Object syncObject = new Object();
        ThreadState ts = new ThreadState(syncObject);
        System.out.println("Before start()-ts.isAlive(): " + ts.isAlive());
        System.out.println("#1: " + ts.getState());
```

```
        // Start the thread
        ts.start();
        System.out.println("After start()-ts.isAlive(): " + ts.isAlive());
        System.out.println("#2: " + ts.getState());
        ts.setWait(true);

        // Make the current thread sleep, so the thread starts waiting
        sleepNow(100);

        synchronized (syncObject) {
            System.out.println("#3: " + ts.getState());
            ts.setWait(false);

            // Wake up the waiting thread
            syncObject.notifyAll();
        }

        // Make the current thread sleep, so ts thread wakes up
        sleepNow(2000);
        System.out.println("#4: " + ts.getState());
        ts.setKeepRunning(false);

        // Make the current thread sleep, so the ts thread will wake up
        sleepNow(2000);
        System.out.println("#5: " + ts.getState());
        System.out.println("At the end. ts.isAlive(): " + ts.isAlive());
    }

    public static void sleepNow(long millis) {
        try {
            Thread.currentThread().sleep(millis);
        } catch (InterruptedException e) {
        }
    }
}
```

```
Before start()-ts.isAlive(): false
#1: NEW
After start()-ts.isAlive(): true
#2: RUNNABLE
#3: WAITING
#4: RUNNABLE
#5: TERMINATED
At the end. ts.isAlive(): false
```

Priority of a Thread

A thread has a priority. The priority is indicated by an integer between 1 and 10. A thread with the priority of 1 is said to have the lowest priority. A thread with the priority of 10 is said to have the highest priority. There are three constants defined in the Thread class to represent three different thread priorities, as listed in Table 6-4.

Table 6-4. *Thread's Priority Constants Defined in the Thread Class*

Thread Priority Constants	Integer Value
MIN_PRIORITY	1
NORM_PRIORITY	5
MAX_PRIORITY	10

The priority of a thread is a hint to the scheduler that indicates the importance (or the urgency) with which it should schedule the thread. The higher priority of a thread indicates that the thread is of higher importance and the scheduler should give priority in giving the CPU time to that thread. Note that the priority of a thread is just a hint to the scheduler; it is up to the scheduler to respect that hint. It is not recommended to depend on the thread priority for the correctness of a program. For example, if there are ten maximum priority threads and one minimum priority thread, that does not mean that the scheduler will schedule the minimum priority thread after all ten maximum priority threads have been scheduled and finished. This scheduling scheme will result in a *thread starvation*, where a lower priority thread will have to wait indefinitely or for a long time to get CPU time.

The setPriority() method of the Thread class sets a new priority for the thread. The getPriority() method returns the current priority for a thread. When a thread is created, its priority is set by default to the priority of the thread that creates the new thread.

Listing 6-17 demonstrates how to set and get the priority of a thread. It also demonstrates how a new thread gets the priority of the thread that creates it. In the example, threads t1 and t2 get the priority of the main thread at the time they are created.

Listing 6-17. Setting and Getting a Thread's Priority

```
// ThreadPriority.java
package com.jdojo.threads;

public class ThreadPriority {
    public static void main(String[] args) {
        // Get the reference of the current thread
        Thread t = Thread.currentThread();
        System.out.println("main Thread Priority: " + t.getPriority());

        // Thread t1 gets the same priority as the main thread at this point
        Thread t1 = new Thread();
        System.out.println("Thread(t1) Priority: " + t1.getPriority());

        t.setPriority(Thread.MAX_PRIORITY);
        System.out.println("main Thread Priority: " + t.getPriority());

        // Thread t2 gets the same priority as main thread at this point, which is
        // Thread.MAX_PRIORITY (10)
```

```
        Thread t2 = new Thread();
        System.out.println("Thread(t2) Priority: " + t2.getPriority());

        // Change thread t2 priority to minimum
        t2.setPriority(Thread.MIN_PRIORITY);
        System.out.println("Thread(t2) Priority: " + t2.getPriority());
    }
}
```

```
main Thread Priority: 5
Thread(t1) Priority: 5
main Thread Priority: 10
Thread(t2) Priority: 10
Thread(t2) Priority: 1
```

Is It a Demon or a Daemon?

A thread can be a daemon thread or a user thread. The word "daemon" is pronounced the same as "demon." However, the word daemon in a thread's context has nothing to do with a demon!

A daemon thread is a kind of a service provider thread, whereas a user thread (or non-daemon thread) is a thread that uses the services of daemon threads. A service provider should not exist if there is no service consumer. The JVM applies this logic. When the JVM detects that all threads in an application are only daemon threads, it exits the application. Note that if there are only daemon threads in an application, the JVM does not wait for those daemon threads to finish before exiting the application.

You can make a thread a daemon thread by using the `setDaemon()` method by passing `true` as an argument. You must call the `setDaemon()` method of a thread before you start the thread. Otherwise, an `IllegalThreadStateException` is thrown. You can use the `isDaemon()` method to check if a thread is a daemon thread.

■ **Tip** The JVM starts a garbage collector thread to collect all unused object's memory. The garbage collector thread is a daemon thread.

When a thread is created, its daemon property is the same as the thread that creates it. In other words, a new thread inherits the daemon property of its creator thread.

Listing 6-18 creates a thread and sets the thread as a daemon thread. The thread prints an integer and sleeps for some time in an infinite loop. At the end of the `main()` method, the program prints a message to the standard output stating that it is exiting the `main()` method. Since thread `t` is a daemon thread, the JVM will terminate the application when the `main()` method is finished executing. You can see this in the output. The application prints only one integer from the thread before it exits. You may get different output when you run this program.

Listing 6-18. A Daemon Thread Example

```
// DaemonThread.java
package com.jdojo.threads;

public class DaemonThread {
    public static void main(String[] args) {
        Thread t = new Thread(DaemonThread::print);
        t.setDaemon(true);
        t.start();
        System.out.println("Exiting main method");
    }

    public static void print() {
        int counter = 1;
        while (true) {
            try {
                System.out.println("Counter: ^^" + counter++);
                Thread.sleep(2000); // sleep for 2 seconds
            } catch (InterruptedException e) {
                e.printStackTrace();
            }
        }
    }
}
```

```
Exiting main method
Counter:1
```

Listing 6-19 is the same program as Listing 6-18, except that it sets the thread as a non-daemon thread. Since this program has a non-daemon (or a user) thread, the JVM will keep running the application, even after the `main()` method finishes. You have to stop this application manually because the thread runs in an infinite loop.

Listing 6-19. A Non-Daemon Thread Example

```
// NonDaemonThread.java
package com.jdojo.threads;

public class NonDaemonThread {
    public static void main(String[] args) {
        Thread t = new Thread(NonDaemonThread::print);

        // t is already a non-daemon thread because the "main" thread that runs
        // the main() method is a non-daemon thread. You can verify it by using
        // t.isDaemon() method. It will return false. Still we will use
        // the following statement to make it clear that we want t to be
        // a non-daemon thread.
        t.setDaemon(false);
        t.start();
        System.out.println("Exiting main method");
    }
```

```
    public static void print() {
        int counter = 1;
        while (true) {
            try {
                System.out.println("Counter: " + counter++);
                Thread.sleep(2000); // sleep for 2 seconds
            } catch (InterruptedException e) {
                e.printStackTrace();
            }
        }
    }
}
```

```
Exiting main method
Counter: 1
Counter: 2
...
```

Am I Interrupted?

You can interrupt a thread that is alive by using the `interrupt()` method. This method invocation on a thread is just an indication to the thread that some other part of the program is trying to draw its attention. It is up to the thread how it responds to the interruption. Java implements the interruption mechanism using an `interrupted` status flag for every thread.

A thread could be in one of the two states when it is interrupted: running or blocked. If a thread is interrupted when it is running, its `interrupted` status is set by the JVM. The running thread can check its `interrupted` status by calling the `Thread.interrupted()` static method, which returns `true` if the current thread was interrupted. The call to the `Thread.interrupted()` method clears the `interrupted` status of a thread. That is, if you call this method again on the same thread and if the first call returned `true`, the subsequent calls will return `false`, unless the thread is interrupted after the first call but before the subsequent calls.

Listing 6-20 shows the code that interrupts the `main` thread and prints the interrupted status of the thread. Note that the second call to the `Thread.interrupted()` method returns `false`, as indicated in the output `#3: false`. This example also shows that a thread can interrupt itself. The `main` thread that is responsible for running the `main()` method is interrupting itself in this example.

Listing 6-20. A Simple Example of Interrupting a Thread

```
// SimpleInterrupt.java
package com.jdojo.threads;

public class SimpleInterrupt {
    public static void main(String[] args) {
        System.out.println("#1: " + Thread.interrupted());

        // Now interrupt the main thread
        Thread.currentThread().interrupt();
```

```
        // Check if it has been interrupted
        System.out.println("#2: " + Thread.interrupted());

        // Check again if it has been interrupted
        System.out.println("#3: " + Thread.interrupted());
    }
}
```

```
#1: false
#2: true
#3: false
```

Let's look at another example of the same kind. This time, one thread will interrupt another thread. Listing 6-21 starts a thread that increments a counter until the thread is interrupted. At the end, the thread prints the value of the counter. The `main()` method starts the thread; it sleeps for one second to let the counter thread do some work; it interrupts the thread. Since the thread checks whether it has been interrupted or not before continuing in the `while` loop, it exits the loop once it is interrupted. You may get different output when you run this program.

Listing 6-21. A Thread Interrupting Another Thread

```
// SimpleInterruptAnotherThread.java
package com.jdojo.threads;

public class SimpleInterruptAnotherThread {
    public static void main(String[] args) {
        Thread t = new Thread(SimpleInterruptAnotherThread::run);
        t.start();

        try {
            // Let the main thread sleep for 1 second
            Thread.currentThread().sleep(1000);
        } catch (InterruptedException e) {
            e.printStackTrace();
        }

        // Now interrupt the thread
        t.interrupt();
    }

    public static void run() {
        int counter = 0;

        while (!Thread.interrupted()) {
            counter++;
        }

        System.out.println("Counter: " + counter);
    }
}
```

```
Counter: 1313385352
```

The Thread class has a non-static `isInterrupted()` method that can be used to test if a thread has been interrupted. When you call this method, unlike the `interrupted()` method, the `interrupted` status of the thread is not cleared. Listing 6-22 demonstrates the difference between these methods.

Listing 6-22. Difference Between the interrupted() and isInterrupted() Methods

```
// SimpleIsInterrupted.java
package com.jdojo.threads;

public class SimpleIsInterrupted {
    public static void main(String[] args) {
        // Check if the main thread is interrupted
        System.out.println("#1: " + Thread.interrupted());

        // Now interrupt the main thread
        Thread mainThread = Thread.currentThread();
        mainThread.interrupt();

        // Check if it has been interrupted
        System.out.println("#2: " + mainThread.isInterrupted());

        // Check if it has been interrupted
        System.out.println("#3: " + mainThread.isInterrupted());

        // Now check if it has been interrupted using the static method
        // which will clear the interrupted status
        System.out.println("#4: " + Thread.interrupted());

        // Now, isInterrupted() should return false, because previous
        // statement Thread.interrupted() has cleared the flag
        System.out.println("#5: " + mainThread.isInterrupted());
    }
}
```

```
#1: false
#2: true
#3: true
#4: true
#5: false
```

You may interrupt a blocked thread. Recall that a thread may block itself by executing one of the `sleep()`, `wait()`, and `join()` methods. If a thread blocked on these three methods is interrupted, an `InterruptedException` is thrown and the `interrupted` status of the thread is cleared because the thread has already received an exception to signal the interruption.

Listing 6-23 starts a thread that sleeps for one second and prints a message until it is interrupted. The main thread sleeps for five seconds, so the sleeping thread gets a chance to sleep and print messages a few times. When the main thread wakes up, it interrupts the sleeping thread. You may get different output when you run the program.

Listing 6-23. Interrupting a Blocked Thread

```
// BlockedInterrupted.java
package com.jdojo.threads;

public class BlockedInterrupted {
    public static void main(String[] args) {
        Thread t = new Thread(BlockedInterrupted::run);
        t.start();

        // main thread sleeps for 5 seconds
        try {
            Thread.sleep(5000);
        } catch (InterruptedException e) {
            e.printStackTrace();
        }

        // Interrupt the sleeping thread
        t.interrupt();
    }

    public static void run() {
        int counter = 1;
        while (true) {
            try {
                Thread.sleep(1000);
                System.out.println("Counter: " + counter++);
            } catch (InterruptedException e) {
                System.out.println("I got interrupted!");

                // Terminate the thread by returning
                return;
            }
        }

    }
}
```

```
Counter: 1
Counter: 2
Counter: 3
Counter: 4
I got interrupted!
```

If a thread is blocked on an I/O, interrupting a thread does not really do anything if you are using the old I/O API. However, if you are using the new I/O API, your thread will receive a ClosedByInterruptException, which is declared in the java.nio.channels package. I discuss I/O in detail in subsequent chapters.

Threads Work in a Group

A thread is always a member of a thread group. By default, the thread group of a thread is the group of its creator thread. The JVM creates a thread group called main and a thread in this group called main, which is responsible for running the main() method of the main class at startup. A thread group in a Java program is represented by an object of the ThreadGroup class. The getThreadGroup() method of the Thread class returns the reference to the ThreadGroup of a thread. Listing 6-24 demonstrates that, by default, a new thread is a member of the thread group of its creator thread.

Listing 6-24. Determining the Default Thread Group of a Thread

```
// DefaultThreadGroup.java
package com.jdojo.threads;

public class DefaultThreadGroup {
    public static void main(String[] args) {
        // Get the current thread, which is called "main"
        Thread t1 = Thread.currentThread();

        // Get the thread group of the main thread
        ThreadGroup tg1 = t1.getThreadGroup();

        System.out.println("Current thread's name: " + t1.getName());
        System.out.println("Current thread's group name: " + tg1.getName());

        // Creates a new thread. Its thread group is the same that of the main thread.
        Thread t2 = new Thread("my new thread");

        ThreadGroup tg2 = t2.getThreadGroup();
        System.out.println("New thread's name: " + t2.getName());
        System.out.println("New thread's group name: " + tg2.getName());
    }
}
```

```
Current thread's name: main
Current thread's group name: main
New thread's name: my new thread
New thread's group name: main
```

You can also create a thread group and place a new thread in that thread group. To place a new thread in your thread group, you must use one of the constructors of the Thread class that accepts a ThreadGroup object as an argument. The following snippet of code places a new thread in a particular thread group:

```
// Create a new ThreadGroup
ThreadGroup myGroup = new ThreadGroup("My Thread Group");
```

```
// Make the new thread a member of the myGroup thread group
Thread t = new Thread(myGroup, "myThreadName");
```

Thread groups are arranged in a tree-like structure. A thread group can contain another thread group. The getParent() method of the ThreadGroup class returns the parent thread group of a thread group. The parent of the top-level thread group is null.

The activeCount() method of the ThreadGroup class returns an estimate of the number of active threads in the group. The enumerate(Thread[] list) method of the ThreadGroup class can be used to get the threads in a thread group.

A thread group in a Java program can be used to implement a group-based policy that applies to all threads in a thread group. For example, by calling the interrupt() method of a thread group, you can interrupt all threads in the thread group and its subgroups.

Volatile Variables

I discussed the use of the synchronized keyword in previous sections. Two things happen when a thread executes a synchronized method/block.

- The thread must obtain the monitor lock of the object on which the method/block is synchronized.
- The thread's working copy of the shared variables is updated with the values of those variables in the main memory just after the thread gets the lock. The values of the shared variables in the main memory are updated with the thread's working copy value just before the thread releases the lock. That is, at the start and at the end of a synchronized method/block, the values of the shared variables in thread's working memory and the main memory are synchronized.

What can you do to achieve only the second point without using a synchronized method/block? That is, how can you keep the values of variables in a thread's working memory in sync with their values in the main memory? The answer is the keyword volatile. You can declare a variable volatile like so:

```
volatile boolean flag = true;
```

For every read request for a volatile variable, a thread reads the value from the main memory. For every write request for a volatile variable, a thread writes the value to the main memory. In other words, a thread does not cache the value of a volatile variable in its working memory. Note that using a volatile variable is useful only in a multi-threaded environment for variables that are shared among threads. It is faster and cheaper than using a synchronized block.

You can declare only a class member variable (instance or static fields) as volatile. You cannot declare a local variable as volatile because a local variable is always private to the thread, which is never shared with other threads. You cannot declare a volatile variable final because the volatile keyword is used with a variable that changes.

You can use a volatile variable to stop a thread by using the variable's value as a flag. If the flag is set, the thread can keep running. If another thread clears the flag, the thread should stop. Since two threads share the flag, you need to declare it volatile, so that on every read the thread will get its updated value from the main memory.

Listing 6-25 demonstrates the use of a volatile variable. If the keepRunning variable is not declared volatile, the JVM is free to run the while loop in the run() method forever, as the initial value of keepRunning is set to true and a thread can cache this value in its working memory. Since the keepRunning variable is declared volatile, the JVM will read its value from the main memory every time it is used. When another thread updates the keepRunning variable's value to false using the stopThread() method, the next iteration of the while loop will read its updated value and stop the loop. Your program may work the same way as in Listing 6-25 even if you do not declare the keepRunning as volatile. However, according to the JVM specification, this behavior is not guaranteed. If the JVM specification is implemented correctly, using a volatile variable in this way ensures the correct behavior for your program.

Listing 6-25. Using a volatile Variable in a Multi-Threaded Program

```
// VolatileVariable.java
package com.jdojo.threads;

public class VolatileVariable extends Thread {
    private volatile boolean keepRunning = true;

    @Override
    public void run() {
        System.out.println("Thread started...");

        // keepRunning is volatile. So, for every read, the thread reads its
        // latest value from the main memory
        while (keepRunning) {
            try {
                System.out.println("Going to sleep ...");
                Thread.sleep(1000);
            } catch (InterruptedException e) {
                e.printStackTrace();
            }
        }

        System.out.println("Thread stopped...");
    }

    public void stopThread() {
        this.keepRunning = false;
    }

    public static void main(String[] args) {
        // Create the thread
        VolatileVariable vv = new VolatileVariable();

        // Start the thread
        vv.start();

        // Let the main thread sleep for 3 seconds
        try {
            Thread.sleep(3000);
        } catch (InterruptedException e) {
            e.printStackTrace();
        }
```

```
        // Stop the thread
        System.out.println("Going to set the stop flag to true...");
        vv.stopThread();
    }
}
```

```
Thread started...
Going to sleep ...
Going to sleep ...
Going to sleep ...
Going to set the stop flag to true...
Thread stopped...
```

■ **Tip** A volatile variable of `long` and `double` types is treated atomically for read and write purposes. Recall that a non-volatile variable of `long` and `double` types is treated non-atomically. That is, if two threads are writing two different values, say `v1` and `v2` to a non-volatile `long` or `double` variable, respectively, your program may see a value for that variable that is neither `v1` nor `v2`. However, if that `long` or `double` variable is declared volatile, your program sees the value `v1` or `v2` at a given point in time. You cannot make array elements volatile.

Stopping, Suspending, and Resuming Threads

The `stop()`, `suspend()`, and `resume()` methods in the `Thread` class let you stop a thread, suspend a thread, and resume a suspended thread, respectively. These methods have been deprecated because their use is error-prone.

You can stop a thread by calling the `stop()` method. When the `stop()` method of a thread is called, the JVM throws a `ThreadDeath` error. Because of throwing this error, all monitors locked by the thread being stopped are unlocked. Monitor locks are used to protect some important shared resources (typically Java objects). If any of the shared resources protected by the monitors were in inconsistent states when the thread was stopped, other threads may see that inconsistent state of those resources. This will result in incorrect behavior of the program. This is the reason why the `stop()` method has been deprecated; you are advised not to use it in your program.

How can you stop a thread without using its `stop()` method? You can stop a thread by setting a flag that the running thread will check regularly. If the flag is set, the thread should stop executing. This way of stopping a thread was illustrated in Listing 6-25 in the previous section.

You can suspend a thread by calling its `suspend()` method. To resume a suspended thread, you need to call its `resume()` method. However, the `suspend()` method has been deprecated because it is error-prone and it may cause a deadlock. Let's assume that the suspended thread holds the monitor lock of an object. The thread that will resume the suspended thread is trying to obtain the monitor lock of the same object. This will result in a deadlock. The suspended thread will remain suspended because there is no thread that will resume it, and the thread that will resume it will remain blocked because the monitor lock it is trying to obtain is held by the suspended thread. This is the why the `suspend()` method has been deprecated. The `resume()` method is also deprecated because it is called in conjunction with the `suspend()` method. You can use a similar technique to simulate the `suspend()` and `resume()` methods of the `Thread` class in your program as you did to simulate the `stop()` method.

Listing 6-26 demonstrates how to simulate the `stop()`, `suspend()`, and `resume()` methods of the `Thread` class in your thread.

Listing 6-26. Stopping, Suspending, and Resuming a Thread

```
// StopSuspendResume.java
package com.jdojo.threads;

public class StopSuspendResume extends Thread {
    private volatile boolean keepRunning = true;
    private boolean suspended = false;

    public synchronized void stopThread() {
        this.keepRunning = false;

        // Notify the thread in case it is suspended when this method
        // is called, so  it will wake up and stop.
        this.notify();
    }

    public synchronized void suspendThread() {
        this.suspended = true;
    }

    public synchronized void resumeThread() {
        this.suspended = false;
        this.notify();
    }

    @Override
    public void run() {
        System.out.println("Thread started...");
        while (keepRunning) {
            try {
                System.out.println("Going to sleep...");
                Thread.sleep(1000);

                // Check for a suspended condition must be made inside a
                // synchronized block to call the wait() method
                synchronized (this) {
                    while (suspended) {
                        System.out.println("Suspended...");
                        this.wait();
                        System.out.println("Resumed...");
                    }
                }
            } catch (InterruptedException e) {
                e.printStackTrace();
            }
        }
        System.out.println("Thread stopped...");
    }
```

```
    public static void main(String[] args) {
        StopSuspendResume t = new StopSuspendResume();

        // Start the thread
        t.start();

        // Sleep for 2 seconds
        try {
            Thread.sleep(2000);
        } catch (InterruptedException e) {
            e.printStackTrace();
        }

        // Suspend the thread
        t.suspendThread();

        // Sleep for 2 seconds
        try {
            Thread.sleep(2000);
        } catch (InterruptedException e) {
            e.printStackTrace();
        }

        // Resume the thread
        t.resumeThread();

        try {
            Thread.sleep(2000);
        } catch (InterruptedException e) {
            e.printStackTrace();
        }

        // Stop the thread
        t.stopThread();
    }
}
```

```
Thread started...
Going to sleep...
Going to sleep...
Going to sleep...
Suspended...
Resumed...
Going to sleep...
Going to sleep...
Going to sleep...
Thread stopped...
```

Note that you have two instance variables in the StopSuspendResume class. The suspended instance variable is not declared volatile. It is not necessary to declare it volatile because it is always accessed inside a synchronized method/block. The following code in the run() method is used to implement the suspend and resume features:

```
synchronized (this) {
    while (suspended) {
        System.out.println("Suspended...");
        this.wait();
        System.out.println("Resumed...");
    }
}
```

When the suspended instance variable is set to true, the thread calls the wait() method on itself to wait. Note the use of the synchronized block. It uses this as the object to synchronize. This is the reason that you can call this.wait() inside the synchronized block because you have obtained the lock on this object before entering the synchronized block. Once the this.wait() method is called, the thread releases the lock on this object and keeps waiting until another thread calls the resumeThread() method to notify it. I also use the this.notify() method call inside the stopThread() method because if the thread is suspended when the stopThread() method is called, the thread will not stop; rather, it will remain suspended.

The thread in this example sleeps for only one second in its run() method. Suppose your thread sleeps for an extended period. In such a case, calling the stopThread() method will not stop the thread immediately because the thread will stop only when it wakes up and checks its keepRunning instance variable value in its next loop iteration. In such cases, you can use the interrupt() method inside the stopThread() method to interrupt sleeping/waiting threads, and when an InterruptedException is thrown, you need to handle it appropriately.

If you use the technique used in Listing 6-26 to stop a thread, you may run into problems in some situations. The while loop inside the run() method depends on the keepRunning instance variable, which is set in the stopThread() method. The example in this listing is simple. It is just meant to demonstrate the concept of how to stop, suspend, and resume a thread. Suppose inside the run() method, your code waits for other resources like calling a method someBlockingMethodCall() as shown:

```
while (keepRunning) {
    try {
        someBlockingMethodCall();
    } catch (InterruptedException e) {
        e.printStackTrace();
    }
}
```

If you call the stopThread() method while this thread is blocked on the method call someBlockingMethodCall(), this thread will not stop until it returns from the blocked method call or it is interrupted. To overcome this problem, you need to change the strategy for how to stop a thread. It is a good idea to rely on the interruption technique of a thread to stop it prematurely. The stopThread() method can be changed as follows:

```
public void stopThread() {
    // interrupt this thread
    this.interrupt();
}
```

In addition, the while loop inside the run() method should be modified to check if the thread is interrupted. You need to modify the exception handling code to exit the loop if this thread is interrupted while it is blocked. The following snippet of code illustrates this logic:

```
public void run() {
    while (Thread.currentThread().isInterrupted())) {
        try {
            // Do the processing
        } catch (InterruptedException e) {
            // Stop the thread by exiting the loop
            break;
        }
    }
}
```

Spin-Wait Hints

Sometimes, one thread may have to wait for another thread to update a volatile variable. When the volatile variable is updated with a certain value, the first thread may proceed. If the wait could be longer, it is suggested that the first thread relinquish the CPU by sleeping or waiting and it be notified when it can resume work. However, making a thread sleep or wait has latency. For a short time wait and to reduce latency, it is common for a thread to wait in a loop by checking for a certain condition to be true. Consider the code in a class that uses a loop to wait for a volatile variable named dataReady to be true:

```
volatile boolean dataReady;
...

@Override
public void run() {
    // Wait in a loop until data is ready
    while (!dataReady) {
        // No code
    }

    processData();
}

private void processData() {
    // Data processing logic goes here
}
```

The while loop in this code is called a spin-loop, busy-spin, busy-wait, or spin-wait. The while loop keeps looping until the value of the dataReady variable becomes true.

While spin-wait is discouraged because of its unnecessary use of resources, it is commonly needed. In this example, the advantage is that the thread will start processing data as soon as the dataReady variable becomes true. However, you pay for performance and power consumption because the thread is actively looping.

Certain processors can be hinted that a thread is in a spin-wait and, if possible, can optimize the resource usage. For example, x86 processors support a PAUSE instruction to indicate a spin-wait. The instruction delays the execution of the next instruction for the thread for a finite small amount of time, thus improving resource usage.

JDK9 added a new static `onSpinWait()` method to the `Thread` class. It is a pure hint to the processor that the caller thread is momentarily not able to proceed, so resource usage can be optimized. A possible implementation of this method may be no-op when the underlying platform does not support such hints.

Listing 6-27 contains sample code. Note that your program's semantics do not change by using a spin-wait hint. It may perform better if the underlying hardware supports the hint.

Listing 6-27. Sample Code for Using a Spin-Wait Hint to the Processor Using the static Thread.onSpinWait() Method

```
// SpinWaitTest.java
package com.jdojo.misc;

public class SpinWaitTest implements Runnable {
    private volatile boolean dataReady = false;

    @Override
    public void run() {
        // Wait while data is ready
        while (!dataReady) {
            // use a spin-wait hint
            Thread.onSpinWait();
        }

        processData();
    }

    private void processData() {
        // Data processing logic goes here
    }

    public void setDataReady(boolean dataReady) {
        this.dataReady = dataReady;
    }
}
```

Handling an Uncaught Exception in a Thread

You can handle an uncaught exception thrown in your thread. It is handled using an object of a class that implements the nested `Thread.UncaughtExceptionHandler` interface. The interface contains one method:

```
void uncaughtException(Thread t, Throwable e);
```

Here, `t` is the thread object reference that throws the exception and `e` is the uncaught exception thrown. Listing 6-28 contains the code for a class whose object can be used as an uncaught exception handler for a thread.

Listing 6-28. An Uncaught Exception Handler for a Thread

```
// CatchAllThreadExceptionHandler.java
package com.jdojo.threads;

public class CatchAllThreadExceptionHandler implements Thread.UncaughtExceptionHandler {
    @Override
    public void uncaughtException(Thread t, Throwable e) {
        System.out.println("Caught Exception from Thread: " + t.getName());
    }
}
```

The class simply prints a message and the thread name stating that an uncaught exception from a thread has been handled. Typically, you may want to do some cleanup work or log the exception to a file or a database in the `uncaughtException()` method of the handler. The `Thread` class contains two methods to set an uncaught exception handler for a thread: one is a `static setDefaultUncaughtExceptionHandler()` method and another is a non-static `setUncaughtExceptionHandler()` method. Use the `static` method to set a default handler for all threads in your application. Use the non-static method to set a handler for a particular thread. When a thread has an uncaught exception, the following steps are taken:

- If the thread sets an uncaught exception handler using the `setUncaughtExceptionHandler()` method, the `uncaughtException()` method of that handler is invoked.
- If a thread does not have an uncaught exception handler set, its thread group's `uncaughtException()` method is called. If the thread group has a parent thread group, it calls the `uncaughtException()` method of its parent. Otherwise, it checks if there is a default uncaught exception handler set. If it finds a default uncaught exception handler, it calls the `uncaughtException()` method on it. If it does not find a default uncaught exception handler, a message is printed on the standard error stream. It does not do anything if it does not find a default uncaught exception handler and a `ThreadDeath` exception is thrown.

Listing 6-29 demonstrates how to set a handler for uncaught exceptions in a thread. It creates an object of class `CatchAllThreadExceptionHandler` and sets it as a handler for the uncaught exceptions for the main thread. The `main` thread throws an unchecked exception in its last statement. The output shows that the handler handles the exception thrown in the `main()` method.

Listing 6-29. Setting an Uncaught Exception Handler for a Thread

```
// UncaughtExceptionInThread.java
package com.jdojo.threads;

public class UncaughtExceptionInThread {
    public static void main(String[] args) {
        CatchAllThreadExceptionHandler handler = new CatchAllThreadExceptionHandler();

        // Set an uncaught exception handler for the main thread
        Thread.currentThread().setUncaughtExceptionHandler(handler);

        // Throw an exception
        throw new RuntimeException();
    }
}
```

```
Caught Exception from Thread: main
```

Thread Concurrency Packages

Although Java had support for multi-threading built into the language from the very beginning, it was not easy to develop a multi-threaded Java program that used an advanced level of concurrency constructs. For example, the `synchronized` keyword, used to lock an object's monitor, has existed since the beginning. However, a thread that tries to lock an object's monitor simply blocks if the lock is not available. In this case, developers had no choice but to back out. Wouldn't it be nice to have a construct that is based on a "try and lock" philosophy rather than a "lock or block" philosophy? In this strategy, if an object's monitor lock is not available, the call to lock the monitor returns immediately.

The `java.util.concurrent` package and its two subpackages, `java.util.concurrent.atomic` and `java.util.concurrent.locks`, include very useful concurrency constructs. You use them only when you are developing an advanced level multi-threaded program. I don't cover all concurrency constructs in this section because describing everything available in these packages could take more than a hundred pages. I briefly cover some of the most useful concurrency constructs available in these packages. You can broadly categorize these concurrency features into four categories:

- Atomic variables
- Locks
- Synchronizers
- Concurrent collections (refer to Chapter 12 for concurrent collections)

Atomic Variables

Typically, when you need to share an updateable variable among threads, synchronization is used. Synchronization among multiple threads used to be achieved using the `synchronized` keyword and it was based on an object's monitor. If a thread is not able to acquire an object's monitor, that thread is suspended and it has to be resumed later. This way of synchronization (suspending and resuming) uses a great deal of system resources. The problem is not in the locking and unlocking the mechanism of the monitor lock; rather it is in suspending and resuming threads. If there is no contention for acquiring a lock, using the `synchronized` keyword to synchronize threads does not hurt much.

An atomic variable uses a lock-free synchronization of a single variable. Note that if your program needs to synchronize on more than one shared variable, you still need to use the old synchronization methods. By lock-free synchronization, I mean that multiple threads can access a shared variable safely using no object monitor lock. JDK takes advantage of a hardware instruction called "*compare-and-swap*" (CAS) to implement the lock-free synchronization for one variable.

CAS is based on three operands: a memory location `M`, an expected old value `V`, and a new value `N`. If the memory location `M` contains a value `V`, CAS updates it atomically to `N`; otherwise, it does not do anything. CAS always returns the current value at the location `M` that existed before the CAS operation started. The pseudocode for CAS is as follows:

```
CAS(M, V, N) {
    currentValueAtM = get the value at Location M;
```

```
    if (currentValueAtM == V) {
        set value at M to N;
    }

    return currentValueAtM;
}
```

The CAS instruction is lock free. It is directly supported in most modern computer hardware. However, CAS is not always guaranteed to succeed in a multi-threaded environment. CAS takes an optimistic approach by assuming that there are no other threads updating the value at location M; if the location M contains value V, update it to N; if the value at location M is not V, do not do anything. Therefore, if multiple threads attempt to update the value at location M to different values simultaneously, only one thread will succeed and the others will fail.

The synchronization using locks takes a pessimistic approach by assuming that other threads may be working with location M and acquires a lock before it starts working at location M, so that other threads will not access location M while one is working with it. In case CAS fails, the caller thread may try the action again or give up; the caller thread using CAS never blocks. However, in case of synchronization using a lock, the caller thread may have to be suspended and resumed if it could not acquire the lock. Using synchronization, you also run the risk of a *deadlock*, a *livelock*, and other synchronization-related failures.

Atomic variable classes are named like AtomicXxx and can be used to execute multiple instructions on a single variable atomically without using any lock. Here, Xxx is replaced with different words to indicate different classes that are used for different purposes; for example, the AtomicInteger class is used to represent an int variable, which is supposed to be manipulated atomically. Twelve classes in the Java class library support read-modify-write operations on a single variable atomically. They are in the java.util.concurrent.atomic package. They can be categorized in four categories, which are discussed in the following sections.

Scalar Atomic Variable Classes

The AtomicInteger, AtomicLong, and AtomicBoolean classes support operations on primitive data types int, long, and boolean, respectively.

If you need to work with other primitive data types, use the AtomicInteger class. You can use it directly to work with the byte and short data types. Use it to work with the float data type by using the Float.floatToIntBits() method to convert a float value to the int data type and the AtomicInteger.floatValue() method to convert an int value to the float data type.

You can use the AtomicLong class to work with the double data type by using the Double.doubleToLongBits() method to convert a double value to the long data type and the AtomicLong.doubleValue() method to convert the long value to the double data type.

The AtomicReference<V> class is used to work with a reference data type when a reference variable needs to be updated atomically.

Atomic Arrays Classes

There are three classes—called AtomicIntegerArray, AtomicLongArray, and AtomicReferenceArray <E>—that represent an array of int, long, and reference types whose elements can be updated atomically.

Atomic Field Updater Classes

There are three classes—called AtomicLongFieldUpdater, AtomicIntegerFieldUpdater, and AtomicReferenceFieldUpdater<T,V>—that can be used to update a volatile field of a class atomically using reflection. These classes have no constructors. To get a reference to an object of these classes, you need to use their factory method called newUpdater().

Atomic Compound Variable Classes

CAS works by asking "Is the value at location M still V?" If the answer is yes, it updates the value at location M from V to N. In a typical scenario, one thread may read the value from location M as V. By the time this thread tries to update the value from V to N, another thread has changed the value at location M from V to P, and back from P to V. Therefore, the call CAS(M, V, N) will succeed because the value at location M is still V, even though it was changed (V to P and back to V) twice after the thread read the value V last time. In some cases, it is fine. The thread that wants to update the value at location M does not care if the old value V that it read last time was updated before its own update as long as the value at location M is V at the time it is updating the value to N. However, in some cases, it is not acceptable. If a thread reads the value V from a location M, this thread wants to make sure that after it read the value, no other thread has updated the value. In such cases, CAS needs to ask "Has the value at location M changed since I last read it as V?" To achieve this functionality, you need to store a pair of values: the value you want to work with and its version number. Each update will also update the version number. The AtomicMarkableReference and AtomicStampedReference classes fall into this category of atomic compound variable class.

Let's look at a simple example that uses an atomic class. If you want to write a class to generate a counter using built-in Java synchronization, it will resemble the code shown in Listing 6-30.

Listing 6-30. A Counter Class That Uses Synchronization

```
// SynchronizedCounter.java
package com.jdojo.threads;

public class SynchronizedCounter {
    private long value;

    public synchronized long next() {
        return ++value;
    }
}
```

You would rewrite the SynchronizedCounter class using the AtomicLong class, as shown in Listing 6-31.

Listing 6-31. A Counter Class Using Atomic Variable

```
// AtomicCounter.java
package com.jdojo.threads;

import java.util.concurrent.atomic.AtomicLong;

public class AtomicCounter {
    private final AtomicLong value = new AtomicLong(0L);
```

```
    public long next() {
        return value.incrementAndGet();
    }
}
```

Note that the AtomicCounter class does not use any explicit synchronization. It takes advantage of CAS hardware instruction. The call to the incrementAndGet() method inside the next() method of the AtomicCounter class is performed atomically for you.

You can also use an object of the AtomicLong class as a thread-safe counter object like so:

```
AtomicLong aCounter = new AtomicLong(0L);
```

Then you can use the aCounter.incrementAndGet() method to generate a new counter. The incrementAndGet() method of the AtomicLong class increments its current value and returns the new value. You also have its counterpart method called getAndIncrement(), which increments its value and returns its previous value.

The AtomicXxx variable classes have a compareAndSet() method. It is a variant of compare and swap (CAS). The only difference is that the compareAndSet() method returns a boolean. It returns true if it succeeds; otherwise it returns false. The following is the pseudocode representation of the compareAndSet() method:

```
compareAndSet(M, V, N) {
    // Call CAS (see CAS pseudocode) if CAS succeeded, return true;
    // otherwise, return false.
    return (CAS(M, V, N) == V)
}
```

Explicit Locks

The explicit locking mechanism can be used to coordinate access to shared resources in a multi-threaded environment without using the synchronized keyword. The Lock interface, which is declared in the java.util.concurrent.locks package, defines the explicit locking operations. The ReentrantLock class, in the same package, is the concrete implementation of the Lock interface. The Lock interface contains the following methods:

- void lock();
- Condition newCondition();
- void lockInterruptibly() throws InterruptedException;
- boolean tryLock();
- boolean tryLock(long time, TimeUnit unit) throws InterruptedException;
- void unlock();

The use of the lock() method to acquire a lock behaves the same as the use of the synchronized keyword. The use of the synchronized keyword requires that a thread should acquire and release an object's monitor lock in the same block of code. When you use the synchronized keyword to acquire an object's monitor lock, the lock is released by the JVM when the program leaves the block in which the lock was acquired. This feature makes working with intrinsic locks very simple and less error prone. However, in the case of the Lock interface, the restriction of acquiring and releasing the lock in the same block of code does not apply. This makes it a little flexible to use; however, it is more error prone because the responsibility of acquiring as well as releasing the lock is on the developer. It is not difficult to acquire the lock and forget to release it, resulting in hard-to-find bugs. You must make sure that you release the lock by calling the `unlock()` method of the `Lock` interface after you are done with the lock. You can use the `lock()` and `unlock()` methods in their simplest form, shown in Listing 6-32.

Listing 6-32. Using an Explicit Lock in its Simplest Form

```
// SimpleExplicitLock.java
package com.jdojo.threads;

import java.util.concurrent.locks.Lock;
import java.util.concurrent.locks.ReentrantLock;

public class SimpleExplicitLock {
    // Instantiate the lock object
    private final Lock myLock = new ReentrantLock();

    public void updateResource() {
        // Acquire the lock
        myLock.lock();

        try {
            // Logic for updating/reading the shared resource goes here
        } finally {
            // Release the lock
            myLock.unlock();
        }
    }
}
```

Note the use of a `try-finally` block to release the lock in the `updateResource()` method. The use of a `try-finally` block is necessary in this case because no matter how you finish returning from this method after you call `myLock.lock()`, you would like to release the lock. This can be assured only if you place the call to the `unlock()` method inside the `finally` block.

You may wonder why you would use the code structure listed in Listing 6-32 when you could have used the `synchronized` keyword to achieve the same effect, like so:

```
public void updateResource() {
    // Acquire the lock and the lock will be released automatically by the
    // JVM when your code exits the block
    synchronized (this) {
        // Logic for updating/reading the shared resource goes here
    }
}
```

You are correct in thinking that using the `synchronized` keyword would have been better in this case. It is much simpler and less error prone to use the `synchronized` keyword in such situations. The power of using the new `Lock` interface becomes evident when you come across situations where using the `synchronized` keyword is not possible or very cumbersome. For example, if you want to acquire the lock in the `updateResource()` method and release it in some other methods, you cannot use the `synchronized` keyword. If you need to acquire two locks to work with a shared resource and if only one lock is available, you want to do something else rather than waiting for the other lock to become available. If you use the synchronized keyword or the lock() method of the Lock interface to acquire a lock, the call blocks if the lock is not available immediately, which gives you no option to back off once you asked for the lock. Such blocked threads cannot be interrupted either. The two methods of the Lock interface, tryLock() and lockInterruptibly(), give you the ability to try to acquire a lock (rather than acquire a lock or block). The thread that has acquired the lock can be interrupted if it is blocked. The syntax to acquire and release a lock using the Lock interface should use a try-finally or a try-catch-finally block structure, to avoid unintended bugs, by placing the unlock() call in a finally block.

You will solve a classic synchronization problem known as the dining-philosophers problem using the explicit lock constructs. The problem goes like this: five philosophers spend all of their time either thinking or eating. They sit around a circular table with five chairs and five forks, as shown in Figure 6-7. There are only five forks and all five philosophers need to pick the two nearest (one from his left and one from his right) forks to eat.

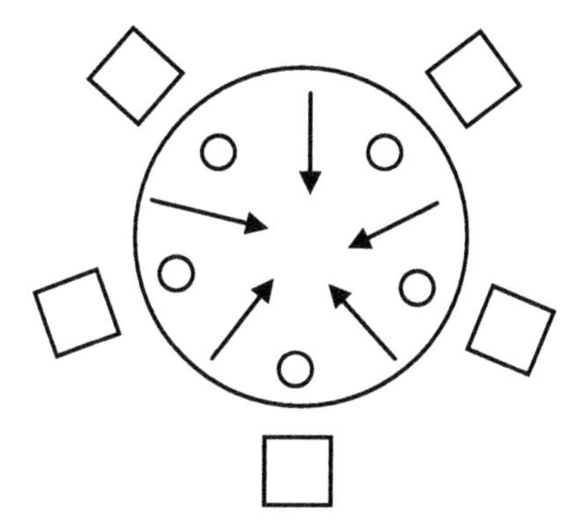

Figure 6-7. *Five philosophers at a dining table*

Once a philosopher finishes eating, he puts down both forks and starts thinking. A philosopher cannot pick up a fork if his neighbor is using it. What happens if each of the five philosophers picks up one fork from his right and waits for his left fork to be released by his neighbor? This would be a deadlock situation and no philosopher would be able to eat. This deadlock condition can be avoided easily by using the tryLock() method of the Lock interface. This method returns immediately and it never blocks. If the lock is available, it gets the lock and returns true. If the lock is not available, it returns false. The class in Listing 6-33 can be used to model the philosophers assuming that an object of the ReentrantLock class represents a fork.

Listing 6-33. A Philosopher Class to Represent a Philosopher

```
// Philosopher.java
package com.jdojo.threads;

import java.util.concurrent.locks.Lock;

public class Philosopher {
    private final Lock leftFork;
    private final Lock rightFork;
    private final String name; // Philosopher's name

    public Philosopher(Lock leftFork, Lock rightFork, String name) {
        this.leftFork = leftFork;
```

```
        this.rightFork = rightFork;
        this.name = name;
    }

    public void think() {
        System.out.println(name + " is thinking...");
    }

    public void eat() {
        // Try to get the left fork
        if (leftFork.tryLock()) {
            try {
                // try to get the right fork
                if (rightFork.tryLock()) {
                    try {
                        // Got both forks. Eat now
                        System.out.println(name + " is eating...");
                    } finally {
                        // release the right fork
                        rightFork.unlock();
                    }
                }
            } finally {
                // release the left fork
                leftFork.unlock();
            }
        }
    }
}
```

To create philosophers, you would use code like:

```
Lock fork1 = new ReentrantLock();
Lock fork2 = new ReentrantLock();
...
Lock fork5 = new ReentrantLock();

Philosopher p1 = new Philosopher(fork1, fork2, "John");
Philosopher p2 = new Philosopher(fork2, fork3, "Wallace");
...
Philosopher p5 = new Philosopher(fork5, fork1, "Charles");
```

It is left for the reader as an exercise to complete the code and run all five philosophers in five different threads to simulate the dining-philosophers problem. You can also think about how to use the `synchronized` keyword to solve the same problem. Read the code in the `eat()` method carefully. It tries to get the left and right forks one at a time. If you can get only one fork and not the other, you put down the one you got so others can have it. The code in the `eat()` method has only the logic to get the forks. In a real program, if you cannot get both forks, you would like to wait for some time and try again to pick up the forks. You will have to write that logic.

You can specify the fairness of a lock when you instantiate the ReentrantLock class. The fairness indicates the way of allocating the lock to a thread when multiple threads are waiting to get the lock. In a fair lock, threads acquire the lock in the order they request it. In a non-fair lock, jumping ahead by a thread is allowed. For example, in a non-fair lock, if some threads are waiting for a lock and another thread, which requests the same lock later, gets the lock before the waiting threads, if the lock becomes available at the time the second thread requested it. This may sound a little strange because it is not fair to the waiting threads to leave them waiting and granting the lock to the thread that requested it later. However, it has a performance gain. The overhead of suspending and resuming a thread is reduced using non-fair locking. The tryLock() method of the ReentrantLock class always uses a non-fair lock. You can create fair and non-fair locks as follows:

```
Lock nonFairLock1 = new ReentrantLock();       // A non-fair lock (Default is non-fair)
Lock nonFairLock2 = new ReentrantLock(false);  // A non-fair lock
Lock fairLock2 = new ReentrantLock(true);      // A fair lock
```

A ReentrantLock provides a mutually exclusive locking mechanism. That is, only one thread can own the ReentrantLock at a time. If you have a data structure guarded by a ReentrantLock, a writer thread as well as a reader thread must acquire the lock one at a time to modify or to read the data. This restriction of ReentrantLock, to be owned by only one thread at a time, may downgrade the performance if your data structure is read frequently and modified infrequently. In such situations, you may want multiple reader threads to have concurrent access to the data structure. However, if the data structure is being modified, only one writer thread should have the access to the data structure. The Read-Write lock allows you to implement this kind of locking mechanism using an instance of the ReadWriteLock interface. It has two methods: one to get the reader lock and another to get the writer lock, as shown:

```
public interface ReadWriteLock {
    Lock readLock();
    Lock writeLock();
}
```

A ReentrantReadWriteLock class is an implementation of the ReadWriteLock Interface. Only one thread can hold the write lock of ReentrantReadWriteLock, whereas multiple threads can hold its read lock. Listing 6-34 demonstrates the usage of ReentrantReadWriteLock. Note that in the getValue() method, you use read lock so multiple threads can read the data concurrently. The setValue() method uses a write lock so only one thread can modify the data at a given time.

■ **Tip** The ReadWriteLock allows you have a read and a write version of the same lock. Multiple threads can own a read lock as long as another thread does not own the write lock. However, only one thread can own the write lock at a time.

Listing 6-34. Using a ReentrantReadWriteLock to Guard a Read-Mostly Data Structure

```
// ReadMostlyData.java
package com.jdojo.threads;

import java.util.concurrent.locks.Lock;
import java.util.concurrent.locks.ReentrantReadWriteLock;
```

```
public class ReadMostlyData {
    private int value;
    private final ReentrantReadWriteLock rwLock = new ReentrantReadWriteLock();
    private final Lock rLock = rwLock.readLock();
    private final Lock wLock = rwLock.writeLock();

    public ReadMostlyData(int value) {
        this.value = value;
    }

    public int getValue() {
        // Use the read lock, so multiple threads may read concurrently
        rLock.lock();
        try {
            return this.value;
        } finally {
            rLock.unlock();
        }
    }

    public void setValue(int value) {
        // Use the write lock, so only one thread can write at a time
        wLock.lock();
        try {
            this.value = value;
        } finally {
            wLock.unlock();
        }
    }
}
```

Synchronizers

I discussed how to coordinate access to a critical section by multiple threads using a mutually exclusive mechanism of intrinsic locks and explicit locks. Some classes known as synchronizers are used to coordinate the control flow of a set of threads in a situation that needs other than mutually exclusive access to a critical section. A synchronizer object is used with a set of threads. It maintains a state, and depending on its state, it lets a thread pass through or forces it to wait. This section discusses the following types of synchronizers:

- Semaphores
- Barriers
- Phasers
- Latches
- Exchangers

Other classes can also act as synchronizers, such as a blocking queue.

Semaphores

A semaphore is used to control the number of threads that can access a resource. A synchronized block also controls the access to a resource that is the critical section. So, how is a semaphore different from a synchronized block? A synchronized block allows only one thread to access a resource (a critical section), whereas a semaphore allows N threads (N can be any positive number) to access a resource.

If N is set to one, a semaphore can act as a synchronized block to allow a thread to have mutually exclusive access to a resource. A semaphore maintains a number of virtual permits. To access a resource, a thread acquires a permit and it releases the permit when it is done with the resource. If a permit is not available, the requesting thread is blocked until a permit becomes available. You can think of a semaphore's permit as a token.

Let's discuss a daily life example of using a semaphore. Suppose there is a restaurant with three dining tables. Only three people can eat in that restaurant at a time. When a person arrives at the restaurant, he must take a token for a table. When he is done eating, he will return the token. Each token represents a dining table. If a person arrives at the restaurant when all three tables are in use, he must wait until a table becomes available. If a table is not available immediately, you have a choice to wait until one becomes available or to go to another restaurant. Let's simulate this example using a semaphore. You will have a semaphore with three permits. Each permit will represent a dining table. The `Semaphore` class in the `java.util.concurrent` package represents the semaphore synchronizer. You create a semaphore using one of its constructors:

```
final int MAX_PERMITS = 3;
Semaphore s = new Semaphores(MAX_PERMITS);
```

Another constructor for the `Semaphore` class takes fairness as the second argument:

```
final int MAX_PERMITS = 3;
Semaphore s = new Semaphores(MAX_PERMITS, true); // A fair semaphore
```

The fairness of a semaphore has the same meaning as that for locks. If you create a fair semaphore, in the situation of multiple threads asking for permits, the semaphore will guarantee first in, first out (FIFO). That is, the thread that asked for the permit first will get the permit first.

To acquire a permit, use the `acquire()` method. It returns immediately if a permit is available. It blocks if a permit is not available. The thread can be interrupted while it is waiting for the permit to become available. Other methods of the `Semaphore` class let you acquire one or multiple permits in one go.

To release a permit, use the `release()` method.

Listing 6-35 contains the code for a `Restaurant` class. It takes the number of tables available in a restaurant as an argument in its constructor and creates a semaphore, which has the number of permits that is equal to the number of tables. A customer uses its `getTable()` and `returnTable()` methods to get and return a table, respectively. Inside the `getTable()` method, you acquire a permit. If a customer calls the `getTable()` method and no table is available, he must wait until one becomes available. This class depends on a `RestaurantCustomer` class that is declared in Listing 6-36.

Listing 6-35. A Restaurant Class, Which Uses a Semaphore to Control Access to Tables

```
// Restaurant.java
package com.jdojo.threads;

import java.util.concurrent.Semaphore;

public class Restaurant {
    private final Semaphore tables;
```

```
    public Restaurant(int tablesCount) {
        // Create a semaphore using number of tables we have
        this.tables = new Semaphore(tablesCount);
    }

    public void getTable(int customerID) {
        try {
            System.out.println("Customer #" + customerID
                    + " is trying to get a table.");

            // Acquire a permit for a table
            tables.acquire();

            System.out.println("Customer #" + customerID + " got a table.");
        } catch (InterruptedException e) {
            e.printStackTrace();
        }
    }

    public void returnTable(int customerID) {
        System.out.println("Customer #" + customerID + " returned a table.");
        tables.release();
    }

    public static void main(String[] args) {
        // Create a restaurant with two dining tables
        Restaurant restaurant = new Restaurant(2);

        // Create five customers
        for (int i = 1; i <= 5; i++) {
            RestaurantCustomer c = new RestaurantCustomer(restaurant, i);
            c.start();
        }
    }
}
```

```
Customer #4 is trying to get a table.
Customer #5 is trying to get a table.
Customer #1 is trying to get a table.
Customer #3 is trying to get a table.
...
```

Listing 6-36 contains the code for a RestaurantCustomer class whose object represents a customer in a restaurant. The run() method of the customer thread gets a table from the restaurant, eats for a random amount of time, and returns the table to the restaurant. When you run the Restaurant class, you may get similar but not the same output. You may observe that you have created a restaurant with only two tables and five customers are trying to eat. At any given time, only two customers are eating, as shown by the output.

Listing 6-36. A RestaurantCustomer Class to Represent a Customer in a Restaurant

```
// RestaurantCustomer.java
package com.jdojo.threads;

import java.util.Random;

class RestaurantCustomer extends Thread {
    private final Restaurant r;
    private final int customerID;
    private static final Random random = new Random();

    public RestaurantCustomer(Restaurant r, int customerID) {
        this.r = r;
        this.customerID = customerID;
    }

    @Override
    public void run() {
        r.getTable(this.customerID); // Get a table

        try {
            // Eat for some time. Use number between 1 and 30 seconds
            int eatingTime = random.nextInt(30) + 1;
            System.out.println("Customer #" + this.customerID
                    + " will eat for " + eatingTime + " seconds.");

            Thread.sleep(eatingTime * 1000);

            System.out.println("Customer #" + this.customerID
                    + " is done eating.");
        } catch (InterruptedException e) {
            e.printStackTrace();
        } finally {
            r.returnTable(this.customerID);
        }
    }
}
```

A semaphore is not limited to the number of permits it was created with. Each `release()` method adds one permit to it. Therefore, if you call the `release()` method more than the times you call its `acquire()` method, you end up having more permits than the one you started with. A permit is not acquired on a per thread basis. One thread can acquire a permit from a semaphore and another can return it. This leaves the burden of the correct usage of acquiring and releasing a permit on the developers. A semaphore has other methods to acquire a permit, which will let you back off instead of forcing you to wait if a permit is not immediately available, such as the `tryAcquire()` and `acquireUninterruptibly()` methods.

Barriers

A barrier is used to make a group of threads meet at a barrier point. A thread from a group arriving at the barrier waits until all threads in that group arrive. Once the last thread from the group arrives at the barrier, all threads in the group are released. You can use a barrier when you have a task that can be divided into subtasks; each subtask can be performed in a separate thread and each thread must meet at a common point to combine their results. Figure 6-8 through Figure 6-11 depict how a barrier synchronizer lets a group of three threads meet at the barrier point and lets them proceed.

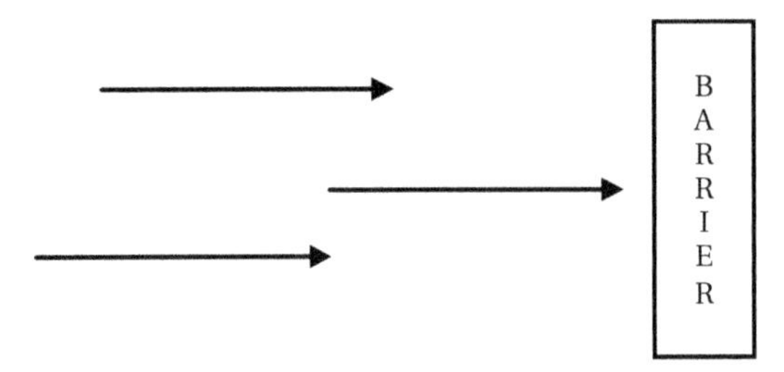

Figure 6-8. *Three threads arriving at a barrier*

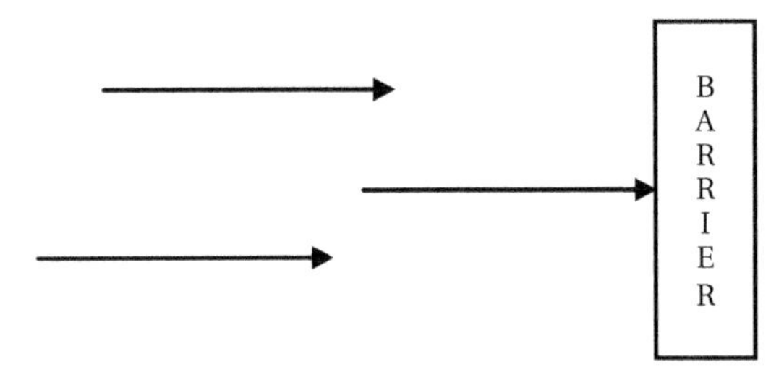

Figure 6-9. *One thread waits for the two other threads to arrive at the barrier*

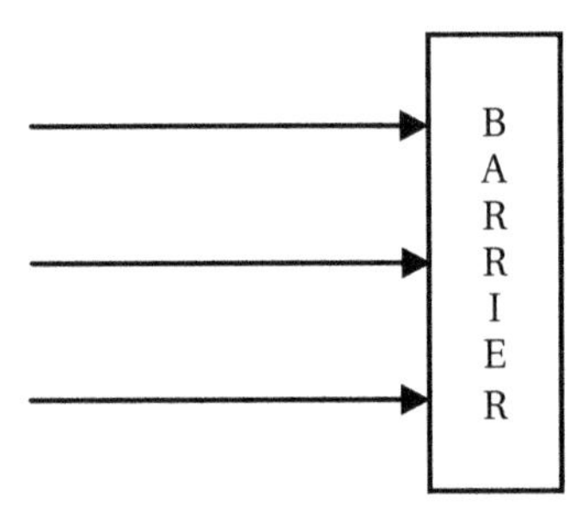

Figure 6-10. *All three threads arrive at the barrier and are then released at once*

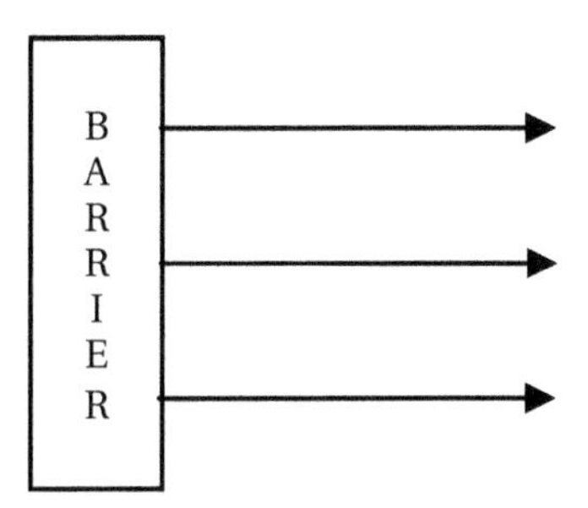

Figure 6-11. *All three threads pass the barrier successfully*

The `CyclicBarrier` class in the `java.util.concurrent` package provides the implementation of the barrier synchronizer. It is called a cyclic barrier because once all waiting threads at the barrier point are released, you can reuse the barrier by calling its `reset()` method. It also allows you to associate a barrier action to it, which is a `Runnable` task (an object of a class that implements the `Runnable` interface). The barrier action is executed just before all threads are released. You can think of the barrier action as a "party time" when all threads meet at the barrier, but before they are released. Here are the steps you need to perform to use a barrier in a program:

1. Create an object of the `CyclicBarrier` class with the number of threads in the group.

   ```
   CyclicBarrier barrier = new CyclicBarrier(5); // 5 threads
   ```

   If you want to execute a barrier action when all threads meet at the barrier, you can use another constructor of the `CyclicBarrier` class.

   ```
   // Assuming a BarrierAction class implements the Runnable interface
   Runnable barrierAction = new BarrierAction();
   CyclicBarrier barrier = new CyclicBarrier(5, barrierAction);
   ```

2. When a thread is ready to wait at the barrier, the thread executes the `await()` method of the `CyclicBarrier` class. The `await()` method comes in two flavors. One lets you wait for all other threads unconditionally and the other lets you specify a timeout.

The program in Listing 6-37 demonstrates how to use a cyclic barrier. You may get different output. However, the sequence of events will be the same: all three threads will work for some time, wait at the barrier for others to arrive, have a party time, and pass the barrier.

Listing 6-37. A Class That Demonstrates How to Use a CyclicBarrier in a Program

```
// MeetAtBarrier.java
package com.jdojo.threads;

import java.util.Random;
import java.util.concurrent.CyclicBarrier;
import java.util.concurrent.BrokenBarrierException;

public class MeetAtBarrier extends Thread {
    private final CyclicBarrier barrier;
```

```
    private final int ID;
    private static final Random random = new Random();

    public MeetAtBarrier(int ID, CyclicBarrier barrier) {
        this.ID = ID;
        this.barrier = barrier;
    }

    @Override
    public void run() {
        try {
            // Generate a random number between 1 and 30 to wait
            int workTime = random.nextInt(30) + 1;

            System.out.println("Thread #" + ID + " is going to work for "
                    + workTime + " seconds");

            // Yes. Sleeping is working for this thread!!!
            Thread.sleep(workTime * 1000);

            System.out.println("Thread #" + ID + " is waiting at the barrier...");

            // Wait at barrier for other threads in group to arrive
            this.barrier.await();

            System.out.println("Thread #" + ID + " passed the barrier...");
        } catch (InterruptedException e) {
            e.printStackTrace();
        } catch (BrokenBarrierException e) {
            System.out.println("Barrier is broken...");
        }
    }

    public static void main(String[] args) {
        // Create a barrier for a group of three threads with a barrier action
        String msg = "We are all together. It's party time...";
        Runnable barrierAction = () -> System.out.println(msg);
        CyclicBarrier barrier = new CyclicBarrier(3, barrierAction);

        for (int i = 1; i <= 3; i++) {
            MeetAtBarrier t = new MeetAtBarrier(i, barrier);
            t.start();
        }
    }
}
```

```
Thread #2 is going to work for 15 seconds
Thread #3 is going to work for 2 seconds
Thread #1 is going to work for 30 seconds
Thread #3 is waiting at the barrier...
Thread #2 is waiting at the barrier...
```

```
Thread #1 is waiting at the barrier...
We are all together. It's party time...
Thread #3 passed the barrier...
Thread #2 passed the barrier...
Thread #1 passed the barrier...
```

You might have noticed that inside the run() method of the MeetAtBarrier class, you are catching BrokenBarrierException. If a thread times out or it is interrupted while waiting at the barrier point, the barrier is considered *broken*. The thread that times out is released with a TimeoutException, whereas all waiting threads at the barrier are released with a BrokenBarrierException.

■ **Tip** The await() method of the CyclicBarrier class returns the arrival index of the thread calling it. The last thread to arrive at the barrier has an index of zero and the first has an index of the number of threads in the group minus one. You can use this index to do any special processing in your program. For example, the last thread to arrive at the barrier may log the time when a particular round of computation is finished by all participating threads.

Phasers

The Phaser class in the java.util.concurrent package provides an implementation for another synchronization barrier called *phaser*. A Phaser provides functionality similar to the CyclicBarrier and CountDownLatch synchronizers. I cover the CountDownLatch synchronizer in the next section. However, it is more powerful and flexible. It provides the following features:

- Like a CyclicBarrier, a Phaser is also reusable.
- Unlike a CyclicBarrier, the number of parties to synchronize on a Phaser can change dynamically. In a CyclicBarrier, the number of parties is fixed at the time the barrier is created. However, in a Phaser, you can add or remove parties at any time.
- A Phaser has an associated phase number, which starts at zero. When all registered parties arrive at a Phaser, the Phaser advances to the next phase and the phase number is incremented by one. The maximum value of the phase number is Integer.MAX_VALUE. After its maximum value, the phase number restarts at zero.
- A Phaser has a termination state. All synchronization methods called on a Phaser in a termination state return immediately without waiting for an advance. The Phaser class provides different ways to terminate a phaser.
- A Phaser has three types of parties count: a registered parties count, an arrived parties count, and an unarrived parties count. The registered parties count is the number of parties that are registered for synchronization. The arrived parties count is the number of parties that have arrived at the current phase of the phaser. The unarrived parties count is the number of parties that have not yet arrived at the current phase of the phaser. When the last party arrives, the phaser advances to the next phase. Note that all three types of party counts are dynamic.

- Optionally, a Phaser lets you execute a phaser action when all registered parties arrive at the phaser. Recall that a CyclicBarrier lets you execute a barrier action, which is a Runnable task. Unlike a CyclicBarrier, you specify a phaser action by writing code in the onAdvance() method of your Phaser class. It means you need to use your own phaser class by inheriting it from the Phaser class and override the onAdvance() method to provide a Phaser action. I discuss an example of this kind shortly.

Figure 6-12 shows a phaser with three phases. It synchronizes on a different number of parties in each phase. An arrow in the figure represents a party.

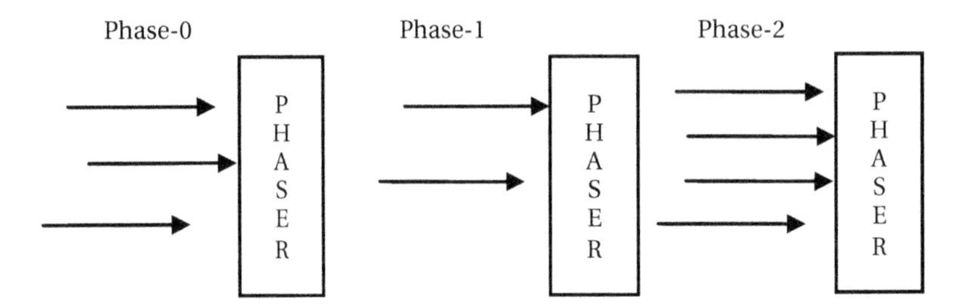

Figure 6-12. *A Phaser with three phases with a different number of parties in each phase*

There are several steps to work with a Phaser. You can create a Phaser with no initially registered party using its default constructor.

```
// A phaser with no registered parties
Phaser phaser = new Phaser();
```

Another constructor lets you register parties when the Phaser is created.

```
// A phaser with 5 registered parties
Phaser phaser = new Phaser(5);
```

A Phaser may be arranged in a tree-like structure. Other constructors let you create a Phaser by specifying the parent of the newly created Phaser. Once you have created a Phaser, the next step is to register parties that are interested in synchronizing on the phaser. You can register a party in the following ways:

- By specifying the number of parties to register in the constructor of the Phaser class when you create a Phaser object
- By using the register() method of the Phaser class to register one party at a time
- By using the bulkRegister(int parties) method of the Phaser class to register the specified number of parties in bulk

The registered parties of a Phaser may change at any time by registering new parties or deregistering the already registered parties. You can deregister a registered party using the arriveAndDeregister() method of the Phaser class. This method lets a party arrive at the Phaser and deregister without waiting for other parties to arrive. If a party is deregistered, the number of parties is reduced by one in the next phase of the Phaser.

Typically, a party in a Phaser means a thread. However, a Phaser does not associate the registration of a party with a specific thread. It simply maintains a count that is increased by one when a party is registered and decreased by one when a party is deregistered.

The most important part of a Phaser is the way multiple parties synchronize on it. A typical way to synchronize on a Phaser is to let the registered number of parties arrive and wait at the Phaser for other registered parties to arrive. Once the last registered party arrives at the Phaser, all parties advance to the next phase of the Phaser.

The arriveAndAwaitAdvance() method of the Phaser class lets a party arrive at the Phaser and waits for other parties to arrive before it can proceed.

The arriveAndDeregister() method of the Phaser class lets a party arrive at the Phaser and deregister without waiting for other parties to arrive. Upon deregistration, the number of parties required to advance to the future phase reduces by one. Typically, the arriveAndDeregister() method is used by a controller party whose job is to control the advance of other parties without participating in the advance itself. Typically, the controller party registers itself with the Phaser and waits for some conditions to occur; when the required condition occurs, it arrives and deregisters itself from the Phaser so parties can synchronize on the Phaser and advance.

Let's walk through an example of using a Phaser to synchronize a group of tasks so they can all start at the same time. An instance of the StartTogetherTask class, shown in Listing 6-38, represents a task in this example.

Listing 6-38. A StartTogetherTask Class to Represent Tasks That Start Together by Synchronizing on a Phaser

```
// StartTogetherTask.java
package com.jdojo.threads;

import java.util.Random;
import java.util.concurrent.Phaser;

public class StartTogetherTask extends Thread {
    private final Phaser phaser;
    private final String taskName;
    private static Random rand = new Random();

    public StartTogetherTask(String taskName, Phaser phaser) {
        this.taskName = taskName;
        this.phaser = phaser;
    }

    @Override
    public void run() {
        System.out.println(taskName + ":Initializing...");

        // Sleep for some time between 1 and 5 seconds
        int sleepTime = rand.nextInt(5) + 1;
        try {
            Thread.sleep(sleepTime * 1000);
        } catch (InterruptedException e) {
            e.printStackTrace();
        }
```

```
        System.out.println(taskName + ":Initialized...");

        // Wait for all parties to arrive to start the task
        phaser.arriveAndAwaitAdvance();
        System.out.println(taskName + ":Started...");
    }
}
```

The StartTogetherTask class inherits from the Thread class. Its constructor accepts a task name and a Phaser instance. In its run() method, it prints a message that it is initializing. It fakes its initialization by sleeping for a random period of 1 to 5 seconds. After that, it prints a message that it is initialized. At this stage, it waits on a Phaser advance by calling the arriveAndAwaitAdvance() method of the Phaser. This method will block until all registered parties arrive at the Phaser. When this method returns, it prints a message that the task has started. Listing 6-39 contains the code to test three tasks of StartTogetherTask type.

Listing 6-39. Testing Some Objects of the StartTogetherTask Class with a Phaser

```
// StartTogetherTaskTest.java
package com.jdojo.threads;

import java.util.concurrent.Phaser;

public class StartTogetherTaskTest {
    public static void main(String[] args) {
        // Start with 1 registered party
        Phaser phaser = new Phaser(1);

        // Let's start three tasks
        final int TASK_COUNT = 3;

        for (int i = 1; i <= TASK_COUNT; i++) {
            // Register a new party with the phaser for each task
            phaser.register();

            // Now create the task and start it
            String taskName = "Task #" + i;
            StartTogetherTask task = new StartTogetherTask(taskName, phaser);
            task.start();
        }

        // Now, deregister the self, so all tasks can advance
        phaser.arriveAndDeregister();
    }
}
```

```
Task #3:Initializing...
Task #2:Initializing...
Task #1:Initializing...
Task #3:Initialized...
Task #1:Initialized...
Task #2:Initialized...
Task #2:Started...
Task #1:Started...
Task #3:Started...
```

First, the program creates a Phaser object by specifying 1 as the initially registered party.

```
// Start with 1 registered party
Phaser phaser = new Phaser(1);
```

You register a task with the Phaser one at a time. If a task (or a party) is registered and started before other tasks are registered, the first task will advance the phaser because there will be one registered party and it will arrive at the phaser by itself. Therefore, you need to start with one registered party in the beginning. It acts like the controller party for other tasks.

You create three tasks in a loop. Inside the loop, you register a party (that represents a task) with the Phaser, create a task, and start it. Once you are done setting up the tasks, you call the arriveAndDeregister() method of the Phaser. This takes care of one extra party that you had registered when you created the Phaser. This method makes a party arrive at the Phaser and deregister without waiting for other registered parties to arrive. After this method call is over, it is up to the three tasks to arrive at the Phaser and advance. Once all three tasks arrive at the Phaser, they will all advance at the same time, thus making them start at the same time. You may get different output. However, the last three messages in the output will always be about starting the three tasks.

If you do not want to use an additional party to act as a controller, you need to register all tasks in advance to make this program work correctly. You can rewrite the code in the main() method of the StartTogetherTaskTest class as follows:

```
public static void main(String[] args) {
    // Start with 0 registered party
    Phaser phaser = new Phaser();

    // Let's start three tasks
    final int TASK_COUNT = 3;

    // Initialize all tasks in one go
    phaser.bulkRegister(TASK_COUNT);

    for(int i = 1; i <= TASK_COUNT; i++) {
        // Now create the task and start it
        String taskName = "Task #" + i;
        StartTogetherTask task = new StartTogetherTask(taskName, phaser);
        task.start();
    }
}
```

This time, you create a Phaser with no registered party. You register all the parties using the bulkRegister() method in one go. Note that you do not register a party inside the loop anymore. The new code has the same effect as the old one. It is just a different way to write the same logic.

Like a CyclicBarrier, a Phaser lets you execute an action upon a phase advance using its onAdvance() method. You will need to create your own phaser class by inheriting it from the Phaser class and override the onAdvance() method to write your custom Phaser action. On each phase advance, the onAdvance() method of the phaser is invoked. The onAdvance() method in the Phaser class is declared as follows. The first argument is the phase number and the second is the number of registered parties.

```
protected boolean onAdvance(int phase, int registeredParties)
```

Besides defining a phase advance action, the onAdvance() method of the Phaser class also controls the termination state of a Phaser. A Phaser is terminated if its onAdvance() method returns true. You can use the isTerminated() method of the Phaser class to check if a phaser is terminated or not. You can also terminate a phaser using its forceTermination() method.

Listing 6-40 demonstrates how to add a Phaser action. This is a trivial example. However, it demonstrates the concept of adding and executing a Phaser action. It uses an anonymous class to create a custom Phaser class. The anonymous class overrides the onAdvance() method to define a Phaser action. It simply prints a message in the onAdvance() method as the Phaser action. It returns false, which means the phaser will not be terminated from the onAdvance() method. Later, it registers the self as a party and triggers a phase advance using the arriveAndDeregister() method. On every phase advance, the Phaser action that is defined by the onAdvance() method is executed.

Listing 6-40. Adding a Phaser Action to a Phaser

```
// PhaserActionTest.java
package com.jdojo.threads;

import java.util.concurrent.Phaser;

public class PhaserActionTest {
    public static void main(String[] args) {
        // Create a Phaser object using an anonymous class and override its
        // onAdvance() method to define a phaser action
        Phaser phaser = new Phaser() {
            @Override
            protected boolean onAdvance(int phase, int parties) {
                System.out.println("Inside onAdvance(): phase = "
                        + phase + ", Registered Parties = " + parties);

                // Do not terminate the phaser by returning false
                return false;
            }
        };

        // Register the self (the "main" thread) as a party
        phaser.register();

        // Phaser is not terminated here
        System.out.println("#1: isTerminated(): " + phaser.isTerminated());
```

```
        // Since we have only one party registered, this arrival will advance
        // the phaser and registered parties reduces to zero
        phaser.arriveAndDeregister();

        // Trigger another phase advance
        phaser.register();
        phaser.arriveAndDeregister();

        // Phaser is still not terminated
        System.out.println("#2: isTerminated(): " + phaser.isTerminated());

        // Terminate the phaser
        phaser.forceTermination();

        // Phaser is terminated
        System.out.println("#3: isTerminated(): " + phaser.isTerminated());
    }
}
```

```
#1: isTerminated(): false
Inside onAdvance(): phase = 0, Registered Parties = 0
Inside onAdvance(): phase = 1, Registered Parties = 0
#2: isTerminated(): false
#3: isTerminated(): true
```

Let's consider using a Phaser to solve a complex task. This time, the Phaser works in multiple phases by synchronizing multiple parties in each phase. Multiple tasks generate random integers in each phase and add them to a List. After the Phaser is terminated, you compute the sum of all the randomly generated integers.

Listing 6-41 contains the code for a task. Let's call this task AdderTask. In its run() method, it creates a random integer between 1 and 10, adds the integer to a List, and waits for a Phaser to advance. It keeps adding an integer to the list in each phase of the Phaser until the Phaser is terminated.

Listing 6-41. An AdderTask Class Whose Instances Can Be Used with a Phaser to Generate Some Integers

```
// AdderTask.java
package com.jdojo.threads;

import java.util.List;
import java.util.Random;
import java.util.concurrent.Phaser;

public class AdderTask extends Thread {
    private final Phaser phaser;
    private final String taskName;
    private final List<Integer> list;
    private static Random rand = new Random();
```

```
    public AdderTask(String taskName, Phaser phaser, List<Integer> list) {
        this.taskName = taskName;
        this.phaser = phaser;
        this.list = list;
    }

    @Override
    public void run() {
        do {
            // Generate a random integer between 1 and 10
            int num = rand.nextInt(10) + 1;

            System.out.println(taskName + " added " + num);

            // Add the integer to the list
            list.add(num);

            // Wait for all parties to arrive at the phaser
            phaser.arriveAndAwaitAdvance();
        } while (!phaser.isTerminated());
    }
}
```

Listing 6-42 creates a Phaser by inheriting an anonymous class from the Phaser class. In its onAdvance() method, it terminates the phaser after the second advance, which is controlled by the PHASE_COUNT constant, or if the registered parties reduces to zero. You use a synchronized List to gather the random integers generated by the adder tasks. You plan to use three adder tasks, so you register four parties (one more than the number of tasks) with the phaser. The additional party will be used to synchronize each phase. It waits for each phase advance until the Phaser is terminated. At the end, the sum of the random integers generated by all adder tasks is computed and displayed on the standard output. You may get different output.

Listing 6-42. A Program to Use Multiple AdderTask Tasks with a Phaser

```
// AdderTaskTest.java
package com.jdojo.threads;

import java.util.List;
import java.util.ArrayList;
import java.util.Collections;
import java.util.concurrent.Phaser;

public class AdderTaskTest {
    public static void main(String[] args) {
        final int PHASE_COUNT = 2;
        Phaser phaser
                = new Phaser() {
            @Override
            public boolean onAdvance(int phase, int parties) {
                // Print the phaser details
                System.out.println("Phase:" + phase
                        + ", Parties:" + parties
```

```
                + ", Arrived:" + this.getArrivedParties());
            boolean terminatePhaser = false;

            // Terminate the phaser when we reach the PHASE_COUNT
            // or there is no registered party
            if (phase >= PHASE_COUNT - 1 || parties == 0) {
                terminatePhaser = true;
            }

            return terminatePhaser;
        }
    };

    // Use a synchronized List
    List<Integer> list = Collections.synchronizedList(new ArrayList<>());

    // Let's start three tasks
    final int ADDER_COUNT = 3;

    // Register parties one more than the number of adder tasks.
    // The extra party will synchronize to compute the result of
    // all generated integers by all adder tasks
    phaser.bulkRegister(ADDER_COUNT + 1);

    for (int i = 1; i <= ADDER_COUNT; i++) {
        // Create the task and start it
        String taskName = "Task #" + i;
        AdderTask task = new AdderTask(taskName, phaser, list);
        task.start();
    }

    // Wait for the phaser to terminate, so we can compute the sum
    // of all generated integers by the adder tasks
    while (!phaser.isTerminated()) {
        phaser.arriveAndAwaitAdvance();
    }

    // Phaser is terminated now. Compute the sum
    int sum = 0;
    for (Integer num : list) {
        sum = sum + num;
    }

    System.out.println("Sum = " + sum);
  }
}
```

```
Task #2 added 2
Task #1 added 2
Task #3 added 5
Phase:0, Parties:4, Arrived:4
Task #3 added 5
Task #1 added 1
Task #2 added 7
Phase:1, Parties:4, Arrived:4
Sum = 22
```

Latches

A latch works similar to a barrier in the sense that it also makes a group of threads wait until it reaches its terminal state. Once a latch reaches its terminal state, it lets all threads pass through. Unlike a barrier, it is a one-time object. Once it has reached its terminal state, it cannot be reset and reused. A latch can be used in situations where a number of activities cannot proceed until a certain number of one-time activities have completed. For example, a service should not start until all services that it depends on have started.

The CountDownLatch class in the java.util.concurrent package provides the implementation of a latch. It is initialized to a count using its constructor. All threads that call the await() method of the latch object are blocked until latch's countDown() method is called as many times as its count is set. When the number of calls to the countDown() method is the same as its count, it reaches its terminal state and all blocked threads are released. Once a latch reaches its terminal state, its await() method returns immediately. You can think of the count that is set for the latch as the same as the number of events that a group of thread will wait to occur. Each occurrence of an event will call its countDown() method.

Listing 6-43 and Listing 6-44 contain classes that represent a helper service and a main service, respectively. The main service depends on helper services to start. After all helper services have started, only then can the main service start.

Listing 6-43. A Class to Represent a Helper Service

```
// LatchHelperService.java
package com.jdojo.threads;

import java.util.concurrent.CountDownLatch;
import java.util.Random;

public class LatchHelperService extends Thread {
    private final int ID;
    private final CountDownLatch latch;
    private final Random random = new Random();

    public LatchHelperService(int ID, CountDownLatch latch) {
        this.ID = ID;
        this.latch = latch;
    }

    @Override
    public void run() {
        try {
```

```
            int startupTime = random.nextInt(30) + 1;

            System.out.println("Service #" + ID + " starting in "
                    + startupTime + " seconds...");

            Thread.sleep(startupTime * 1000);

            System.out.println("Service #" + ID + " has started...");
        } catch (InterruptedException e) {
            e.printStackTrace();
        } finally {
            // Count down on the latch to indicate that it has started
            this.latch.countDown();
        }
    }
}
```

Listing 6-44. A Class to Represent the Main Service That Depends on Helper Services to Start

```
// LatchMainService.java
package com.jdojo.threads;

import java.util.concurrent.CountDownLatch;

public class LatchMainService extends Thread {
    private final CountDownLatch latch;

    public LatchMainService(CountDownLatch latch) {
        this.latch = latch;
    }

    @Override
    public void run() {
        try {
            System.out.println("Main service is waiting for helper services to start...");
            latch.await();
            System.out.println("Main service has started...");
        } catch (InterruptedException e) {
            e.printStackTrace();
        }
    }
}
```

Listing 6-45 lists a program to test the concept of helper and main services with a latch. You create a latch that is initialized to two. The main service thread is started first and it calls latch's `await()` method to wait for the helper service to start. Once both helper threads call the `countDown()` method of the latch, the main service starts. The output explains the sequence of events clearly.

Listing 6-45. A Class to Test the Concept of a Latch with Helper and Main Services

```
// LatchTest.java
package com.jdojo.threads;

import java.util.concurrent.CountDownLatch;

public class LatchTest {
    public static void main(String[] args) {
        // Create a countdown latch with 2 as its counter
        CountDownLatch latch = new CountDownLatch(2);

        // Create and start the main service
        LatchMainService ms = new LatchMainService(latch);
        ms.start();

        // Create and start two helper services
        for (int i = 1; i <= 2; i++) {
            LatchHelperService lhs = new LatchHelperService(i, latch);
            lhs.start();
        }
    }
}
```

```
Main service is waiting for helper services to start...
Service #1 starting in 12 seconds...
Service #2 starting in 2 seconds...
Service #2 has started...
Service #1 has started...
Main service has started...
```

Exchangers

An exchanger is another form of a barrier. Like a barrier, an exchanger lets two threads wait for each other at a synchronization point. When both threads arrive, they exchange an object and continue their activities. This is useful in building a system where two independent parties need to exchange information from time to time. Figure 6-13 through Figure 6-15 depict how an exchanger works with two threads and lets them exchange an object.

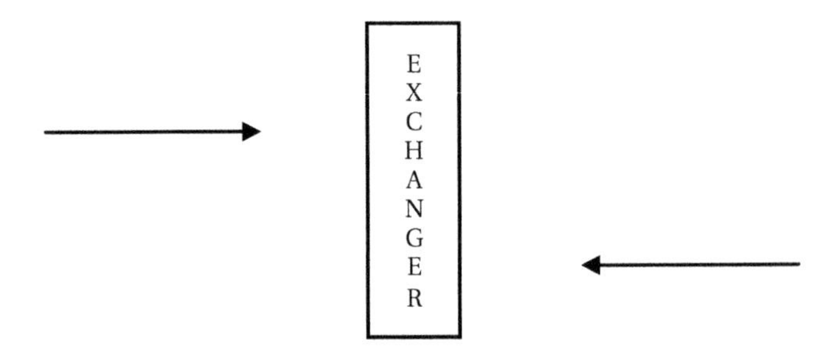

Figure 6-13. *Two threads perform their work independently*

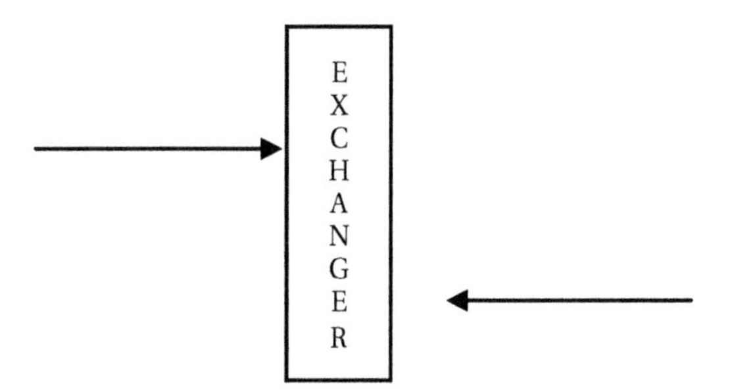

Figure 6-14. *One thread arrives at the exchange point and waits for another thread to arrive*

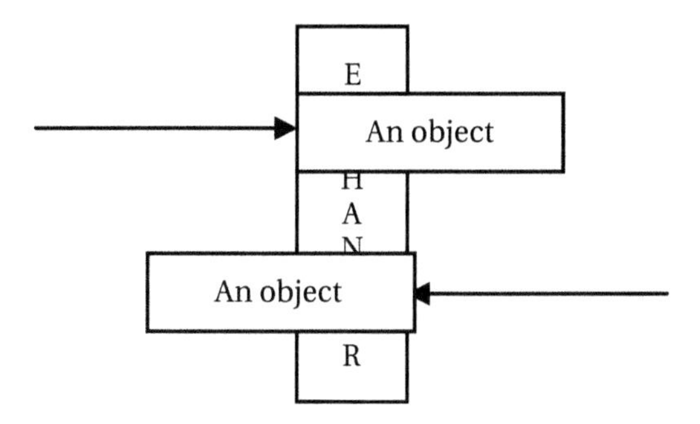

Figure 6-15. *Two threads meet at exchange point and exchange objects*

The Exchanger<V> class provides an implementation for an exchanger synchronizer. It has one constructor, which takes no arguments. The type parameter V is the type of Java object that will be exchanged between two parties. You can create an exchanger that will let two threads exchange a Long as follows:

```
Exchanger<Long> exchanger = new Exchanger<>();
```

The Exchanger class has only one method, exchange(). When a thread is ready to exchange an object with another thread, it calls the exchange() method of the exchanger and waits for another thread to exchange the object. A thread that is waiting to exchange an object may be interrupted. Another overloaded version of the exchange() method accepts a timeout period. If the timeout period is specified, the thread calling this method will wait for another thread to exchange an object until the timeout period is elapsed. The exchange() method takes the object to pass on to another thread as an argument and it returns the object passed by another thread. You call the exchange() method like so:

```
objectReceived = exchanger.exchange(objectedPassed);
```

Listing 6-46, Listing 6-47, and Listing 6-48 demonstrate the use of an exchanger in building a producer/consumer system that exchanges a buffer, which is an ArrayList of Integer objccts. To declare an array list of integer objects, you have to declare it as follows:

```
ArrayList<Integer> buffer = new ArrayList<Integer>();
```

In Listing 6-48, you have created an exchanger as

```
Exchanger<ArrayList<Integer>> exchanger = new Exchanger<ArrayList<Integer>>();
```

The type declaration Exchanger<ArrayList<Integer>> indicates that the exchanger will let two threads exchange objects of type ArrayList<Integer>. You can also note that the type declarations in the ExchangerProducer and ExchangerConsumer classes match the previous declaration. The producer fills up the data and waits for some time to give the users the impression that it is really filling up data. It waits for the consumer to exchange the filled buffer with an empty buffer from the consumer. The consumer does the opposite. It waits for the producer to exchange the buffer. When it gets a full buffer from the producer, it empties the buffer and again waits for the producer to exchange its empty buffer for a full one. Since the producer and consumer run in infinite loops, the program will not end. You will have to end the program manually. You will get a similar output to that shown in Listing 6-48.

Listing 6-46. A Producer Thread That Will Use an Exchanger to Exchange Data with a Consumer

```
// ExchangerProducer.java
package com.jdojo.threads;

import java.util.concurrent.Exchanger;
import java.util.ArrayList;
import java.util.Random;

public class ExchangerProducer extends Thread {
    private final Exchanger<ArrayList<Integer>> exchanger;
    private ArrayList<Integer> buffer = new ArrayList<>();
    private final int bufferLimit;
    private final Random random = new Random();
    private int currentValue = 0; // to produce values

    public ExchangerProducer(Exchanger<ArrayList<Integer>> exchanger,
            int bufferLimit) {
        this.exchanger = exchanger;
        this.bufferLimit = bufferLimit;
    }

    @Override
    public void run() {
        // keep producing integers
        while (true) {
            try {
                System.out.println("Producer is filling the buffer with data...");

                // Wait for some time by sleeping
                int sleepTime = random.nextInt(20) + 1;
                Thread.sleep(sleepTime * 1000);

                // Fill the buffer
                this.fillBuffer();
                System.out.println("Producer has produced:" + buffer);
```

```
                // Let's wait for the consumer to exchange data
                System.out.println("Producer is waiting to exchange the data...");
                buffer = exchanger.exchange(buffer);
            } catch (InterruptedException e) {
                e.printStackTrace();
            }
        }
    }

    public void fillBuffer() {
        for (int i = 1; i <= bufferLimit; i++) {
            buffer.add(++currentValue);
        }
    }
}
```

Listing 6-47. A Consumer Thread That Will Use an Exchanger to Exchange Data with a Producer

```
// ExchangerConsumer.java
package com.jdojo.threads;

import java.util.concurrent.Exchanger;
import java.util.ArrayList;
import java.util.Random;

public class ExchangerConsumer extends Thread {
    private final Exchanger<ArrayList<Integer>> exchanger;
    private ArrayList<Integer> buffer = new ArrayList<>();
    private final Random random = new Random();

    public ExchangerConsumer(Exchanger<ArrayList<Integer>> exchanger) {
        this.exchanger = exchanger;
    }

    @Override
    public void run() {
        // keep consuming the integers
        while (true) {
            try {
                // Let's wait for the consumer to exchange data
                System.out.println("Consumer is waiting to exchange the data...");

                buffer = exchanger.exchange(buffer);
                System.out.println("Consumer has received:" + buffer);
                System.out.println("Consumer is emptying data from the buffer...");

                // Wait for some time by sleeping
                int sleepTime = random.nextInt(20) + 1;

                // Sleep for some time
                Thread.sleep(sleepTime * 1000);
```

```
                // Empty the buffer
                this.emptyBuffer();
            } catch (InterruptedException e) {
                e.printStackTrace();
            }
        }
    }

    public void emptyBuffer() {
        buffer.clear();
    }
}
```

Listing 6-48. A Class to Test a Producer/Consumer System with an Exchanger

```
// ExchangerProducerConsumerTest.java
package com.jdojo.threads;

import java.util.concurrent.Exchanger;
import java.util.ArrayList;

public class ExchangerProducerConsumerTest {
    public static void main(String[] args) {
        Exchanger<ArrayList<Integer>> exchanger = new Exchanger<>();

        // The producer will produce 5 integers at a time
        ExchangerProducer producer = new ExchangerProducer(exchanger, 5);
        ExchangerConsumer consumer = new ExchangerConsumer(exchanger);

        producer.start();
        consumer.start();
    }
}
```

```
Producer is filling the buffer with data...
Consumer is waiting to exchange the data...
Producer has produced:[1, 2, 3, 4, 5]
Producer is waiting to exchange the data...
Producer is filling the buffer with data...
Consumer has received:[1, 2, 3, 4, 5]
Consumer is emptying data from the buffer...
...
```

The Executor Framework

A task is a logical unit of work, and typically a thread is used to represent and execute a task. Many aspects of task execution should be considered before modeling it in a program. A few aspects of a task are as follows:

- How it is created.
- How it is submitted for execution.

- How it is executed. Is it executed synchronously or asynchronously?
- The time at which it is executed. Is it executed immediately upon submission or queued?
- Which thread executes it? Is it executed in the thread that submits it or in another thread?
- How do we get the result of a task when it is finished executing?
- How do we know the error that occurs during its execution?
- Does it depend on other tasks to finish its execution?

A task may be represented as a Runnable. If you want to manage tasks using threads, follow the steps described next. You can create a class to represent a task.

```
public class MyTask implements Runnable {
    public void run() {
        // Task processing logic goes here
    }
}
```

You create tasks as follows:

```
MyTask task1 = new MyTask();
MyTask task2 = new MyTask();
MyTask task3 = new MyTask();
```

To execute the tasks, you use threads as follows:

```
Thread t1 = new Thread(task1);
Thread t2 = new Thread(task2);
Thread t3 = new Thread(task3);
t1.start();
t2.start();
t3.start();
```

If you want to get the result of a task execution, you have to write additional code. You may notice that managing tasks like this is difficult, if not impossible. There is another aspect of tasks execution that is very important: how many threads should be created to execute a group of tasks? One approach would be to create a thread per task. Creating a thread per task has the following disadvantages:

- Creating and destroying threads requires overhead and takes time, which in turn delays the start of the execution of the tasks.
- Each thread consumes resources. If the number of threads is more than the available CPUs, other threads will be sitting idle and will consume resources.
- Each platform has a limit on how many maximum threads it can support. If an application exceeds that limit, it may even crash!

Another approach is to create one thread and let it handle the execution of all tasks. This is another extreme case, which has the following disadvantages:

- Having one thread executing all tasks makes it a sequential executor.
- This policy is deadlock-prone if one task submits another task and it depends on the result of the task it has submitted.
- If you have long-running tasks, other tasks waiting for their execution seem to be unresponsive because of the long time it will take to start the pending tasks.

The executor framework attempts to solve all of these problems of task's execution. The framework provides a way to separate task submission from task execution. You create a task and submit it to an executor. The executor takes care of the execution details of the task. It provides configurable policies to control many aspects of the task execution.

The `Executor` interface in the `java.util.concurrent` package is the foundation for the executor framework. The interface contains only one method, as shown:

```
public interface Executor {
    void execute (Runnable command);
}
```

You can use the executor framework to execute the previously mentioned three tasks as follows:

```
// Get an executor instance.
Executor executor = Executors.newCachedThreadPool();

// Submit three tasks to the executor
executor.execute(task1);
executor.execute(task2);
executor.execute(task3);
```

Note that when you used an executor, you did not create three threads to execute the three tasks. The executor will decide that for you. You just called the `execute()` method of the executor to submit a task. The executor will manage the threads that will execute the tasks and other details about the task execution.

The executor framework provides a class library to select the policies on the thread usage to execute the tasks. You can choose to run all tasks in one thread, in a fixed number of threads, or in a variable number of threads. In fact, you can choose a thread pool to execute your tasks, and the thread pool is configurable as to how many threads will be in the pool and how those threads will be maintained. In any case, all threads in the pool are reused as they become available. Using a thread pool to execute the submitted tasks has two important advantages:

- The overhead of creating new threads and destroying them when you are done with them is reduced. The executor reuses the threads from the thread pool.
- If a thread is available in the thread pool at the time of a task submission, the task may start immediately. This eliminates the time delay between the thread creation and the task execution.

It is important to mention another interface called `ExecutorService` at this point. It provides some advanced features of an executor, which include managing the shutdown of the executor and checking the status of the submitted tasks. It inherits from the `Executor` interface. Some of the important methods of this interface are `shutdown()`, `shutdownNow()`, `submit()`, and `awaitTermination()`. I discuss them shortly.

It is important that you shut down the executor when it is no longer needed. The executor framework creates non-daemon threads to execute the tasks. Generally, when a thread is done executing a task, it is not destroyed. Rather it is kept in the thread pool for reuse in the future—whether a thread is destroyed or kept depends on the thread pool configuration. A Java application will not exit if some non-daemon threads are still alive. Therefore, if you forget to shut down the executor, your application may never exit.

How does an executor handle a task execution? To avoid a detailed and lengthy discussion, here is a simple explanation. You specify the type of thread pool that the executor should use to manage the tasks at the time you create the executor. All tasks that you submit to an executor are queued in a queue known as the *work queue*. As a thread becomes available, it removes a task from the work queue and executes it. When a thread is done executing a task, depending on your thread pool type, your executor either destroys the thread or puts it back into the pool so it can be reused to execute another task. You have a number of options to decide on what kind of thread pool to use for an executor:

- You can use one of the factory methods of the `Executors` class to get an executor, which has a preconfigured thread pool and lets you reconfigure it, if you desire so. You will use this approach to get an executor in your examples. You can also use this class to get a preconfigured executor that cannot be reconfigured. The commonly used methods of the `Executors` class to get an executor service are as follows:
    - `newCachedThreadPool()`: It returns an `ExecutorService` object. The thread pool reuses the previously created threads if they are available. Otherwise, it creates a new thread to execute a task. It destroys and removes idle threads from the pool. The thread pool has characteristics of expanding and shrinking depending on the workload.
    - `newFixedThreadPool(int nThreads)`: It returns an `ExecutorService` object. The thread pool maintains a fixed number of threads. At any time, the thread pool will have the maximum `nThread` number of threads. If a task arrives in the work queue and all threads are busy executing other tasks, the task has to wait for its execution until a thread becomes available. If a thread is terminated because of an unexpected failure during a task execution, it is replaced with a new thread.
    - `newSingleThreadExecutor()`: It returns an `ExecutorService` object. The thread pool maintains only one thread to execute all tasks. It guarantees that only one task will be executed at a time. If the lone thread dies unexpectedly, it is replaced with a new one.
- You can instantiate the `ThreadPoolExecutor` class and configure the thread pool.
- You can create your own executor from scratch.

Listing 6-49 contains the complete code for a `RunnableTast` class.

Listing 6-49. A Runnable Task

```
// RunnableTask.java
package com.jdojo.threads;

import java.util.Random;

public class RunnableTask implements Runnable {
    private final int taskId;
    private final int loopCounter;
    private final Random random = new Random();
```

```
    public RunnableTask(int taskId, int loopCounter) {
        this.taskId = taskId;
        this.loopCounter = loopCounter;
    }

    @Override
    public void run() {
        for (int i = 1; i <= loopCounter; i++) {
            try {
                int sleepTime = random.nextInt(10) + 1;
                System.out.println("Task #" + this.taskId
                        + " - Iteration #" + i
                        + " is going to sleep for "
                        + sleepTime + " seconds.");

                Thread.sleep(sleepTime * 1000);
            } catch (InterruptedException e) {
                System.out.println("Task #" + this.taskId
                        + " has been interrupted.");
                break;
            }
        }
    }
}
```

An object of the RunnableTask class represents a task in your program. You will have a task that will sleep for some time and print a message on the standard output. The time to sleep will be determined randomly between 1 and 10 seconds. Every task will be assigned a task ID and a loop counter. The task ID is used to identify the task. The loop counter is used to control the loop inside the run() method. Listing 6-50 contains the complete code to test the Runnable task class.

Listing 6-50. A Class to Test an Executor to Run Some Runnable Tasks

```
// RunnableTaskTest.java
package com.jdojo.threads;

import java.util.concurrent.Executors;
import java.util.concurrent.ExecutorService;

public class RunnableTaskTest {
    public static void main(String[] args) {
        final int THREAD_COUNT = 3;
        final int LOOP_COUNT = 3;
        final int TASK_COUNT = 5;

        // Get an executor with three threads in its thread pool
        ExecutorService exec = Executors.newFixedThreadPool(THREAD_COUNT);
```

```
        // Create five tasks and submit them to the executor
        for (int i = 1; i <= TASK_COUNT; i++) {
            RunnableTask task = new RunnableTask(i, LOOP_COUNT);
            exec.submit(task);
        }

        // Let's shutdown the executor
        exec.shutdown();
    }
}
```

```
Task #1 - Iteration #1 is going to sleep for 9 seconds.
Task #2 - Iteration #1 is going to sleep for 2 seconds.
Task #3 - Iteration #1 is going to sleep for 7 seconds.
Task #2 - Iteration #2 is going to sleep for 5 seconds.
Task #2 - Iteration #3 is going to sleep for 7 seconds.
Task #3 - Iteration #2 is going to sleep for 2 seconds.
...
```

The RunnableTaskTest class creates an Executor with three threads. It creates five instances of the RunnableTask class—each task making three iterations in its run() method. All five tasks are submitted to the Executor. You have used an executor with its thread pool with a fixed number of threads. Your executor will have only three threads in its thread pool to execute only three tasks at a time. When the executor is done with one of the first three tasks, it starts the fourth one. Note the exec.shutdown() method call to shut down the executor after submitting all tasks. The shutdownNow() method call of executor attempts to stop the executing tasks by interrupting it and discards the pending tasks. It returns the list of all pending tasks that were discarded. If you replace the exec.shutdown() to exec.shutdownNow() in the main() method, you may get an output similar to the one shown:

```
Task #1 - Iteration #1 is going to sleep for 7 seconds.
Task #2 - Iteration #1 is going to sleep for 10 seconds.
Task #3 - Iteration #1 is going to sleep for 9 seconds.
Task #2 has been interrupted.
Task #3 has been interrupted.
Task #1 has been interrupted.
```

Result-Bearing Tasks

How do you get the result of a task when it is complete? The task that can return a result upon its execution has to be represented as an instance of the Callable<V> interface:

```
public interface Callable<V> {
    V call() throws Exception;
}
```

The type parameter V is the type of the result of the task. Note that the run() method of the Runnable interface cannot return a value and it cannot throw any checked exception. The call() method of the Callable interface can return a value of any type. It also allows you to throw an exception.

Let's redo your RunnableTask class from Listing 6-49 as CallableTask, which is shown in Listing 6-51.

Listing 6-51. A Callable Task

```
// CallableTask.java
package com.jdojo.threads;

import java.util.Random;
import java.util.concurrent.Callable;

public class CallableTask implements Callable<Integer> {
    private final int taskId;
    private final int loopCounter;
    private final Random random = new Random();

    public CallableTask(int taskId, int loopCounter) {
        this.taskId = taskId;
        this.loopCounter = loopCounter;
    }

    @Override
    public Integer call() throws InterruptedException {
        int totalSleepTime = 0;

        for (int i = 1; i <= loopCounter; i++) {
            try {
                int sleepTime = random.nextInt(10) + 1;

                System.out.println("Task #" + this.taskId
                        + " - Iteration #" + i
                        + " is going to sleep for "
                        + sleepTime + " seconds.");

                Thread.sleep(sleepTime * 1000);
                totalSleepTime = totalSleepTime + sleepTime;
            } catch (InterruptedException e) {
                System.out.println("Task #" + this.taskId
                        + " has been interrupted.");
                throw e;
            }
        }

        return totalSleepTime;
    }
}
```

The call() method of the task returns the sum of all its sleeping periods. Listing 6-52 illustrates the use of the Callable task. You may get different output every time you run the program.

Listing 6-52. A Class to Demonstrate How to Use a Callable Task with an Executor

```
// CallableTaskTest.java
package com.jdojo.threads;

import java.util.concurrent.Executors;
import java.util.concurrent.ExecutorService;
import java.util.concurrent.Future;
import java.util.concurrent.ExecutionException;

public class CallableTaskTest {
    public static void main(String[] args) {
        // Get an executor with three threads in its thread pool
        ExecutorService exec = Executors.newFixedThreadPool(3);

        // Create the callable task with loop counter as 3
        CallableTask task = new CallableTask(1, 3);

        // Submit the callable task to executor
        Future<Integer> submittedTask = exec.submit(task);

        try {
            Integer result = submittedTask.get();
            System.out.println("Task's total sleep time: " + result + " seconds");
        } catch (ExecutionException e) {
            System.out.println("Error in executing the task.");
        } catch (InterruptedException e) {
            System.out.println("Task execution has been interrupted.");
        }

        // Let's shutdown the executor
        exec.shutdown();
    }
}
```

```
Task #1 - Iteration #1 is going to sleep for 6 seconds.
Task #1 - Iteration #2 is going to sleep for 5 seconds.
Task #1 - Iteration #3 is going to sleep for 4 seconds.
Task's total sleep time: 15 seconds
```

I explain the logic in the two listings step by step:

The CallableTask class defines the call() method, which contains the logic for task processing. It sums up all the sleep times for the task and returns it.

The CallableTaskTest class uses an executor with three threads in its thread pool.

The ExecutorService.submit() method returns a Future<V> object. Future is an interface that lets you track the progress of the task that you submit. It contains the following methods:

- boolean cancel(boolean mayInterruptIfRunning)
- V get() throws InterruptedException, ExecutionException

- `V get(long timeout, TimeUnit unit) throws InterruptedException, ExecutionException, TimeoutException`
- `boolean isCancelled()`
- `boolean isDone()`

The `get()` method returns the result of the task execution, which is the same as the returned value from the `call()` method of a `Callable` object. If the task has not yet finished executing, the `get()` method blocks. You can use another version of the `get()` method to specify a timeout period for waiting for the result of a task execution.

The `cancel()` method cancels a submitted task. Its call has no effect on a completed task. It accepts a `boolean` argument to indicate if the executor should interrupt the task if the task is still running. If you use `cancel(true)` to cancel a task, make sure the task responds to the interruption properly.

The `isDone()` method tells you if the task has finished executing. It returns `true` if the task is finished executing normally, it has been cancelled, or it had an exception during its execution.

In the `CallableTaskTest` class, you keep the returned `Future` object in the `submittedTask` variable. The `Future<Integer>` declaration indicates that your task returns an `Integer` object as its result.

```
Future<Integer> submittedTask = exec.submit(task);
```

Another important method call is the `get()` method on `submittedTask`.

```
Integer result = submittedTask.get();
```

I placed the call to the `get()` method in a `try-catch` block because it may throw an exception. If the task has not finished executing, the `get()` method will block. The program prints the result of the task execution, which is the total time that the task spent sleeping during its execution.

Finally, you shut down the executor using its `shutdown()` method.

Scheduling a Task

The executor framework lets you schedule a task that will run in the future. You can run a task to execute after a given delay or periodically. Scheduling a task is done using an instance of the `ScheduledExecutorService` interface, which you can get using one of the static factory methods of the `Executors` class. You can also use the concrete implementation of this interface, which is the `ScheduledThreadPoolExecutor` class. To get an instance of the `ScheduledExecutorService` interface, use the following snippet of code:

```
// Get scheduled executor service with 3 threads
ScheduledExecutorService sexec = Executors.newScheduledThreadPool(3);
```

To schedule a task (say `task1`) after a certain delay (say 10 seconds), use

```
sexec.schedule(task1, 10, TimeUnit.SECONDS);
```

To schedule a task (say `task2`) after a certain delay (say 10 seconds), and repeat after a certain period (say 25 seconds), use

```
sexec.scheduleAtFixedRate(task2, 10, 25, TimeUnit.SECONDS);
```

After a 10 second delay, `task2` will execute for the first time. Subsequently, it will keep executing after `10 + 25` seconds, `10 + 2 * 25` seconds, `10 + 3 * 25` seconds, and so on.

You can also schedule a task with a set delay period between the end of an execution and the start of the next execution. To schedule `task3` for the first time after 40 seconds, and every 60 seconds after every execution finishes, use

```
sexec.scheduleWithFixedDelay(task3, 40, 60, TimeUnit.SECONDS);
```

The `ScheduledExecutorService` interface does not provide a method to schedule a task using an absolute time. However, you can schedule a task to execute at an absolute time using the following technique. Suppose `scheduledDateTime` is the date and time at which you want to execute the task.

```
import java.time.LocalDateTime;
import static java.time.temporal.ChronoUnit.SECONDS;
import java.util.concurrent.TimeUnit;
...
LocalDateTime scheduledDateTime = get the scheduled date and time for the task...

// Compute the delay from the time you schedule the task
long delay = SECONDS.between(LocalDateTime.now(), scheduledDateTime);

// Schedule the task
sexec.schedule(task, delay, TimeUnit.MILLISECONDS);
```

■ **Tip** The `submit()` method of `ExecutorService` submits the task for immediate execution. You can submit a task for immediate execution using the `ScheduledExecutorService.schedule()` method by specifying an initial delay of zero. A negative initial delay schedules a task for immediate execution.

Listing 6-53 contains the code for a `Runnable` task. It simply prints the date and time when it is run.

Listing 6-53. A Scheduled Task

```
// ScheduledTask.java
package com.jdojo.threads;

import java.time.LocalDateTime;

public class ScheduledTask implements Runnable {
    private final int taskId;

    public ScheduledTask(int taskId) {
        this.taskId = taskId;
    }

    @Override
    public void run() {
        LocalDateTime now = LocalDateTime.now();
        System.out.println("Task #" + this.taskId + " ran at " + now);
    }
}
```

Listing 6-54 demonstrates how to schedule a task. The second task has been scheduled to run repeatedly. To let it run a few times, make the main thread sleep for 60 seconds before you shut down the executor. Shutting down an executor discards any pending tasks. A good way to stop a scheduled task that repeats is to cancel it after a certain delay using another scheduled task. You may get different output when you run the ScheduledTaskTest class.

Listing 6-54. A Class to Test Scheduled Task Executions Using the Executor Framework

```
// ScheduledTaskTest.java
package com.jdojo.threads;

import java.util.concurrent.Executors;
import java.util.concurrent.ScheduledExecutorService;
import java.util.concurrent.TimeUnit;

public class ScheduledTaskTest {
    public static void main(String[] args) {
        // Get an executor with 3 threads
        ScheduledExecutorService sexec = Executors.newScheduledThreadPool(3);

        // Task #1 and Task #2
        ScheduledTask task1 = new ScheduledTask(1);
        ScheduledTask task2 = new ScheduledTask(2);

        // Task #1 will run after 2 seconds
        sexec.schedule(task1, 2, TimeUnit.SECONDS);

        // Task #2 runs after 5 seconds delay and keep running every 10 seconds
        sexec.scheduleAtFixedRate(task2, 5, 10, TimeUnit.SECONDS);

        // Let the current thread sleep for 60 seconds and shut down the
        // executor that will cancel the task #2 because it is scheduled
        // to run after every 10 seconds
        try {
            TimeUnit.SECONDS.sleep(60);
        } catch (InterruptedException e) {
            e.printStackTrace();
        }

        // Shut down the executor
        sexec.shutdown();
    }
}
```

```
Task #1 ran at 2017-10-07T10:47:48.800387200
Task #2 ran at 2017-10-07T10:47:51.753682400
Task #2 ran at 2017-10-07T10:48:01.754210400
Task #2 ran at 2017-10-07T10:48:11.754739100
Task #2 ran at 2017-10-07T10:48:21.755259400
Task #2 ran at 2017-10-07T10:48:31.755795600
Task #2 ran at 2017-10-07T10:48:41.756322800
```

Handling Uncaught Exceptions in a Task Execution

What happens when an uncaught exception occurs during a task execution? The executor framework handles occurrences of such uncaught exception nicely for you. If you execute a `Runnable` task using the `execute()` method of an `Executor`, any uncaught runtime exceptions will halt the task execution, and the exception stack trace will be printed on the console, as shown in the output of Listing 6-55.

Listing 6-55. Printing the Runtime Stack Trace from the execute() Method of the Executor

```
// BadRunnableTask.java
package com.jdojo.threads;

import java.util.concurrent.ExecutorService;
import java.util.concurrent.Executors;

public class BadRunnableTask {
    public static void main(String[] args) {
        Runnable badTask = () -> {
            throw new RuntimeException("The task threw an exception...");
        };

        ExecutorService exec = Executors.newSingleThreadExecutor();
        exec.execute(badTask);
        exec.shutdown();
    }
}
```

```
Exception in thread "pool-1-thread-1" java.lang.RuntimeException: The task threw an
exception...
       at jdojo.threads/com.jdojo.threads.BadRunnableTask.lambda$main$0(BadRunnableTask.java:10)
       at java.base/java.util.concurrent.ThreadPoolExecutor.runWorker(ThreadPoolExecutor.java:1167)
       at java.base/java.util.concurrent.ThreadPoolExecutor$Worker.run(ThreadPoolExecutor.java:641)
       at java.base/java.lang.Thread.run(Thread.java:844)
```

If you are submitting a task using the `submit()` method of the `ExecutorService`, the executor framework handles the exception and indicates that to you when you use the `get()` method to get the result of the task execution. The `get()` method of the `Future` instance throws an `ExecutionException`, wrapping the actual exception as its cause. Listing 6-56 illustrates this kind of example. You can use the `get()` method of the `Future` instance even if you submit a `Runnable` task. On successful execution of the task, the `get()` method will return `null`. If an uncaught exception is thrown during the task execution, it throws an `ExecutionException`.

Listing 6-56. Future's get() Method Throws ExecutionException, Wrapping the Actual Exception Thrown in Task Execution as Its Cause

```
// BadCallableTask.java
package com.jdojo.threads;

import java.util.concurrent.ExecutorService;
import java.util.concurrent.Executors;
import java.util.concurrent.Callable;
import java.util.concurrent.Future;
import java.util.concurrent.ExecutionException;
```

```
public class BadCallableTask {
    public static void main(String[] args) {
        Callable<Object> badTask = () -> {
            throw new RuntimeException("The task threw an exception...");
        };

        // Create an executor service
        ExecutorService exec = Executors.newSingleThreadExecutor();

        // Submit a task
        Future submittedTask = exec.submit(badTask);

        try {
            // The get method should throw ExecutionException
            Object result = submittedTask.get();
        } catch (ExecutionException e) {
            System.out.println("Execution exception has occurred: "
                    + e.getMessage());
            System.out.println("Execution exception cause is: "
                    + e.getCause().getMessage());
        } catch (InterruptedException e) {
            e.printStackTrace();
        }

        exec.shutdown();
    }
}
```

```
Execution exception has occurred: java.lang.RuntimeException: The task threw an exception...
Execution exception cause is: The task threw an exception...
```

Executor's Completion Service

In the previous sections, I explained how to fetch the result of a task execution using a `Future` object. To fetch the result of a submitted task, you must keep the reference of the `Future` object returned from the executor, as demonstrated in Listing 6-52. However, if you have a number of tasks that you have submitted to an executor and you want to know their results as they become available, you need to use the completion service of the executor. It is represented by an instance of the `CompletionService<V>` interface. It combines an executor and a blocking queue to hold the completed tasks references. The `ExecutorCompletionService<V>` class is a concrete implementation of the `CompletionService<V>` interface. Here are the steps to use it:

1. Create an executor object.

   ```
   ExecutorService exec = Executors.newScheduledThreadPool(3);
   ```

2. Create an object of `ExecutorCompletionService` class, passing the executor created in the previous step to its constructor.

   ```
   ExecutorCompletionService CompletionService = new ExecutorCompletionService(exec);
   ```

The executor completion service uses a blocking queue internally to hold the completed task. You can also use your own blocking queue to hold the completed tasks.

3. The `take()` method of the completion service returns the reference of a completed task. It blocks if no completed task is present. If you do not want to wait, in case there is no completed task, you can use the `poll()` method, which returns `null` if there is no completed task in the queue. Both methods remove the completed task from the queue if they find one.

Listing 6-57, Listing 6-58, and Listing 6-59 illustrate the use of the completion service. An instance of the `TaskResult` class represents the result of a task. It was necessary to have a custom object like a `TaskResult` to represent the result of a task because the completion service just tells you that a task is completed and you get its result. It does not tell you which task is completed. To identify the task that was completed, you need to identify the task in the result of the task. Your `SleepingTask` returns a `TaskResult` from its `call()` method by embedding the task ID and the total sleeping time for the task.

Listing 6-57. A Class to Represent the Result of a Task

```
// TaskResult.java
package com.jdojo.threads;

public class TaskResult {
    private final int taskId;
    private final int result;

    public TaskResult(int taskId, int result) {
        this.taskId = taskId;
        this.result = result;
    }

    public int getTaskId() {
        return taskId;
    }

    public int getResult() {
        return result;
    }

    @Override
    public String toString() {
        return "Task Name: Task #" + taskId + ", Task Result:" + result + " seconds";
    }
}
```

Listing 6-58. A Class Whose Object Represents a Callable Task and Produces a TaskResult as Its Result

```
// SleepingTask.java
package com.jdojo.threads;

import java.util.Random;
import java.util.concurrent.Callable;
```

```
public class SleepingTask implements Callable<TaskResult> {
    private int taskId;
    private int loopCounter;
    private Random random = new Random();

    public SleepingTask(int taskId, int loopCounter) {
        this.taskId = taskId;
        this.loopCounter = loopCounter;
    }

    @Override
    public TaskResult call() throws InterruptedException {
        int totalSleepTime = 0;

        for (int i = 1; i <= loopCounter; i++) {
            try {
                int sleepTime = random.nextInt(10) + 1;

                System.out.println("Task #" + this.taskId + " - Iteration #" + i
                        + " is going to sleep for " + sleepTime + " seconds.");

                Thread.sleep(sleepTime * 1000);

                totalSleepTime = totalSleepTime + sleepTime;
            } catch (InterruptedException e) {
                System.out.println("Task #" + this.taskId
                        + " has been interrupted.");
                throw e;
            }
        }

        return new TaskResult(taskId, totalSleepTime);
    }
}
```

Listing 6-59. A Class to Test the Completion Service

```
// CompletionServiceTest.java
package com.jdojo.threads;

import java.util.concurrent.Future;
import java.util.concurrent.Executors;
import java.util.concurrent.ExecutorService;
import java.util.concurrent.ExecutionException;
import java.util.concurrent.ExecutorCompletionService;

public class CompletionServiceTest {
    public static void main(String[] args) {
        // Get an executor with three threads in its thread pool
        ExecutorService exec = Executors.newFixedThreadPool(3);
```

```
        // Completed task returns an object of the TaskResult class
        ExecutorCompletionService<TaskResult> completionService
                = new ExecutorCompletionService<>(exec);

        // Submit five tasks and each task will sleep three times for a
        // random period between 1 and 10 seconds
        for (int i = 1; i <= 5; i++) {
            SleepingTask task = new SleepingTask(i, 3);
            completionService.submit(task);
        }

        // Print the result of each task as they are completed
        for (int i = 1; i <= 5; i++) {
            try {
                Future<TaskResult> completedTask = completionService.take();
                TaskResult result = completedTask.get();
                System.out.println("Completed a task - " + result);
            } catch (ExecutionException ex) {
                System.out.println("Error in executing the task.");
            } catch (InterruptedException ex) {
                System.out.println("Task execution has been interrupted.");
            }
        }

        // Let's shut down the executor
        exec.shutdown();
    }
}
```

```
Task #3 - Iteration #1 is going to sleep for 3 seconds.
...
Task #4 - Iteration #1 is going to sleep for 5 seconds.
Completed a task - Task Name: Task #2, Task Result:15 seconds
...
Completed a task - Task Name: Task #4, Task Result:15 seconds
Completed a task - Task Name: Task #5, Task Result:18 seconds
```

The Fork/Join Framework

The fork/join framework is an implementation of the executor service whose focus is to solve those problems efficiently, which may use the divide-and-conquer algorithm by taking advantage of the multiple processors or multiple cores on a machine. The framework helps solve the problems that involve parallelism. Typically, the fork/join framework is suitable in a situation where

- A task can be divided in multiple subtasks that can be executed in parallel.
- When subtasks are finished, the partial results can be combined to get the final result.

The fork/join framework creates a pool of threads to execute the subtasks. When a thread is waiting on a subtask to finish, the framework uses that thread to execute other pending subtasks of other threads. The technique of an idle thread executing other thread's task is called *work-stealing*. The framework uses the work-stealing algorithm to enhance the performance. The following four classes in the `java.util.concurrent` package are central to learning the fork/join framework:

- `ForkJoinPool`
- `ForkJoinTask<V>`
- `RecursiveAction`
- `RecursiveTask<V>`

An instance of the `ForkJoinPool` class represents a thread pool. An instance of the `ForkJoinTask` class represents a task. The `ForkJoinTask` class is an `abstract` class. It has two concrete subclasses: `RecursiveAction` and `RecursiveTask`. Java 8 added an abstract subclass of the `ForkJoinTask` class that is called `CountedCompleter<T>`. The framework supports two types of tasks:

- A task that does not yield a result and a task that yields a result. An instance of the `RecursiveAction` class represents a task that does not yield a result.
- An instance of the `RecursiveTask` class represents a task that yields a result.

A `CountedCompleter` task may or may not yield a result. Both classes, `RecursiveAction` and `RecursiveTask`, provide an abstract `compute()` method. Your class whose object represents a fork/join task should inherit from one of these classes and provide an implementation for the `compute()` method. Typically, the logic inside the `compute()` method is written similar to the following:

```
if (Task is small) {
    Solve the task directly.
} else {
    Divide the task into subtasks.
    Launch the subtasks asynchronously (the fork stage).
    Wait for the subtasks to finish (the join stage).
    Combine the results of all subtasks.
}
```

The following two methods of the `ForkJoinTask` class provide two important features during a task execution:

- The `fork()` method launches a new subtask from a task for an asynchronous execution.
- The `join()` method lets a task wait for another task to complete.

Steps in Using the Fork/Join Framework

Using the fork/join framework involves the following five steps.

Step 1: Declaring a Class to Represent a Task

Create a class inheriting from the RecursiveAction or RecursiveTask class. An instance of this class represents a task that you want to execute. If the task yields a result, you need to inherit it from the RecursiveTask class. Otherwise, you will inherit it from the RecursiveAction class. The RecursiveTask is a generic class. It takes a type parameter, which is the type of the result of your task. A MyTask class that returns a Long result may be declared as follows:

```
public class MyTask extends RecursiveTask<Long> {
    // Code for your task goes here
}
```

Step 2: Implementing the compute() Method

The logic to execute your task goes inside the compute() method of your class. The return type of the compute() method is the same as the type of the result that your task returns. The declaration for the compute() method of the MyTask class look like the following:

```
public class MyTask extends RecursiveTask<Long> {
    public Long compute() {
        // Logic for the task goes here
    }
}
```

Step 3: Creating a Fork/Join Thread Pool

You can create a pool of worker threads to execute your task using the ForkJoinPool class. The default constructor of this class creates a pool of threads, which has the same parallelism as the number of processors available on the machine.

```
ForkJoinPool pool = new ForkJoinPool();
```

Other constructors let you specify the parallelism and other properties of the pool.

Step 4: Creating the Fork/Join Task

You need to create an instance of your task.

```
MyTask task = MyTask();
```

Step 5: Submitting the Task to the Fork/Join Pool for Execution

You need to call the invoke() method of the ForkJoinPool class, passing your task as an argument. The invoke() method will return the result of the task if your task returns a result. The following statement will execute your task:

```
long result = pool.invoke(task);
```

A Fork/Join Example

Let's consider a simple example of using the fork/join framework. Your task will generate a few random integers and compute their sum. Listing 6-60 shows the complete code for your task.

Listing 6-60. A ForkJoinTask Class to Compute the Sum of a Few Random Integers

```
// RandomIntSum.java
package com.jdojo.threads;

import java.util.ArrayList;
import java.util.List;
import java.util.Random;
import java.util.concurrent.RecursiveTask;

public class RandomIntSum extends RecursiveTask<Long> {
    private static final Random randGenerator = new Random();
    private final int count;

    public RandomIntSum(int count) {
        this.count = count;
    }

    @Override
    protected Long compute() {
        long result = 0;

        if (this.count <= 0) {
            return 0L; // We do not have anything to do
        }

        if (this.count == 1) {
            // Compute the number directly and return the result
            return (long) this.getRandomInteger();
        }

        // Multiple numbers. Divide them into many single tasks. Keep the
        // references of all tasks to call their join() method later
        List<RecursiveTask<Long>> forks = new ArrayList<>();

        for (int i = 0; i < this.count; i++) {
            RandomIntSum subTask = new RandomIntSum(1);
            subTask.fork(); // Launch the subtask

            // Keep the subTask references to combine the results later
            forks.add(subTask);
        }
```

```
        // Now wait for all subtasks to finish and combine the results
        for (RecursiveTask<Long> subTask : forks) {
            result = result + subTask.join();
        }

        return result;
    }

    public int getRandomInteger() {
        // Generate the next random integer between 1 and 100
        int n = randGenerator.nextInt(100) + 1;

        System.out.println("Generated a random integer: " + n);
        return n;
    }
}
```

The RandomIntSum class inherits from the RecursiveTask<Long> class because it yields a result of the type Long. The result is the sum of all random integers. It declares a randGenerator instance variable that is used to generate random numbers. The count instance variable stores the number of random numbers that you want to use. The value for the count instance variable is set in the constructor.

The getRandomInteger() method generates a random integer between 1 and 100, prints the integer value on the standard output, and returns the random integer.

The compute() method contains the main logic to perform the task. If the number of random numbers to use is one, it computes the result and returns it to the caller. If the number of random number is more than one, it launches as many subtasks as the number of random numbers. Note that if you use ten random numbers, it will launch ten subtasks because each random number can be computed independently. Finally, you need to combine the results from all subtasks. Therefore, you need to keep the references of the subtask for later use. You used a List to store the references of all subtasks. Note the use of the fork() method to launch a subtask. The following snippet of code performs this logic:

```
List<RecursiveTask<Long>> forks = new ArrayList<>();
for(int i = 0; i < this.count; i++) {
    RandomIntSum subTask = new RandomIntSum(1);
    subTask.fork(); // Launch the subtask

    // Keep the subTask references to combine the results at the end
    forks.add(subTask);
}
```

Once all subtasks are launched, you need to wait for all subtasks to finish and combine all random integers to get the sum. The following snippet of code performs this logic. Note the use of the join() method, which will make the current task wait for the subtask to finish.

```
for(RecursiveTask<Long> subTask : forks) {
    result = result + subTask.join();
}
```

Finally, the compute() method returns the result, which is the sum of all the random integers. Listing 6-61 has the code to execute a task, which is an instance of the RandomIntSum class. You may get different output.

Listing 6-61. Using a Fork/Join Pool to Execute a Fork/Join Task

```
// ForkJoinTest.java
package com.jdojo.threads;

import java.util.concurrent.ForkJoinPool;

public class ForkJoinTest {
    public static void main(String[] args) {
        // Create a ForkJoinPool to run the task
        ForkJoinPool pool = new ForkJoinPool();

        // Create an instance of the task
        RandomIntSum task = new RandomIntSum(3);

        // Run the task
        long sum = pool.invoke(task);

        System.out.println("Sum is " + sum);
    }
}
```

```
Generated a random integer: 26
Generated a random integer: 5
Generated a random integer: 68
Sum is 99
```

This is a very simple example of using the fork/join framework. You are advised to explore the fork/join framework classes to know more about the framework. Inside the `compute()` method of your task, you can have complex logic to divide tasks into subtasks. Unlike in this example, you may not know in advance how many subtasks you need to launch. You may launch a subtask that may launch another subtask and so on.

Thread-Local Variables

A thread-local variable provides a way to maintain a separate value for a variable for each thread. The `ThreadLocal<T>` class in the `java.lang` package provides the implementation of a thread-local variable. It has five methods:

- `T get()`
- `protected T initialValue()`
- `void remove()`
- `void set(T value)`
- `static <S> ThreadLocal<S> withInitial(Supplier<? extends S> supplier)`

The `get()` and `set()` methods are used to get and set the value for a thread-local variable, respectively. The `initialValue()` method is used to set the initial value of the variable, and it has a `protected` access. To use it, you need to subclass the `ThreadLocal` class and override this method. You can remove the value by using the `remove()` method. The `withInitial()` method lets you create a `ThreadLocal` with an initial value.

Let's create a CallTracker class, shown in Listing 6-62, to keep track of the number of times a thread calls its call() method.

Listing 6-62. A Class That Uses a ThreadLocal Object to Track Calls to Its Method

```
// CallTracker.java
package com.jdojo.threads;

public class CallTracker {
    // threadLocal variable is used to store counters for all threads
    private static final ThreadLocal<Integer> threadLocal = new ThreadLocal<Integer>();

    public static void call() {
        Integer counterObject = threadLocal.get();

        // Initialize counter to 1
        int counter = 1;

        if (counterObject != null) {
            counter = counterObject + 1;
        }

        // Set the new counter
        threadLocal.set(counter);

        // Print how many times this thread has called this method
        String threadName = Thread.currentThread().getName();
        System.out.println("Call counter for " + threadName + " = " + counter);
    }
}
```

The get() method of the ThreadLocal class works on a thread basis. It returns the value set by the set() method by the same thread, which is executing the get() method. If a thread calls the get() method the very first time, it returns null. The program sets the call counter for the caller thread to 1 if it is its first call. Otherwise, it increments the call counter by 1. It sets the new counter back in the threadLocal object. In the end, the call() method prints a message about how many times the current thread has called this method.

Listing 6-63 uses the CallTracker class in three threads. Each thread calls this method a random number of times between 1 and 5. You can observe in the output that the counter is maintained for each thread's call separately. You may get different output.

Listing 6-63. A Test Class for the CallTracker Class

```
// CallTrackerTest.java
package com.jdojo.threads;

import java.util.Random;

public class CallTrackerTest {
    public static void main(String[] args) {
        // Let's start three threads to the CallTracker.call() method
        new Thread(CallTrackerTest::run).start();
```

```
        new Thread(CallTrackerTest::run).start();
        new Thread(CallTrackerTest::run).start();
    }

    public static void run() {
        Random random = new Random();

        // Generate a random value between 1 and 5
        int counter = random.nextInt(5) + 1;

        // Print the thread name and the generated random number by the thread
        System.out.println(Thread.currentThread().getName()
                + " generated counter: " + counter);

        for (int i = 0; i < counter; i++) {
            CallTracker.call();
        }
    }
}
```

```
Thread-0 generated counter: 4
Thread-1 generated counter: 2
Thread-2 generated counter: 3
Call counter for Thread-0 = 1
Call counter for Thread-2 = 1
Call counter for Thread-1 = 1
Call counter for Thread-2 = 2
Call counter for Thread-0 = 2
Call counter for Thread-2 = 3
Call counter for Thread-1 = 2
Call counter for Thread-0 = 3
Call counter for Thread-0 = 4
```

The `initialValue()` method sets the initial value of the thread-local variable for each thread. If you have set the initial value, the call to the `get()` method, before you call the `set()` method, will return that initial value. It is a `protected` method. You must override it in a subclass. You can set the initial value for the call counter to 1000 by using an anonymous class as shown:

```
// Create an anonymous subclass ThreadLocal class and override its initialValue()
// method to return 1000 as the initial value
private static ThreadLocal<Integer> threadLocal = new ThreadLocal<Integer>() {
                        @Override
                        public Integer initialValue() {
                            return 1000;
                        }
                    };
```

Sub-classing the ThreadLocal class just to have an instance of ThreadLocal with an initial value was overkill. Finally, the class designers realized it (in Java 8) and provided a factory method called withInitial() in the ThreadLocal class that can specify an initial value. The method is declared as follows:

```
public static <S> ThreadLocal<S> withInitial(Supplier<? extends S> supplier)
```

The specified supplier provides the initial value for the ThreadLocal. The get() method of the supplier is used to get the initial value. You can rewrite this logic and replace the anonymous class with a lambda expression as follows:

```
// Create a ThreadLocal with an initial value of 1000
ThreadLocal<Integer> threadLocal = ThreadLocal.withInitial(() -> 1000);
```

Having a Supplier as the supplier for the initial value, you can generate the initial value lazily and based on some logic. The following statement creates a ThreadLocal with the initial value as the second part of the current time when the initial value is retrieved:

```
// Return the second part of the current time as the initial value
ThreadLocal<Integer> threadLocal = ThreadLocal.withInitial(() -> LocalTime.now().getSecond());
```

You can use the remove() method to reset the value of the thread-local variable for a thread. After the call to the remove() method, the first call to the get() method works as if it were called the first time by returning the initial value.

The typical use of a thread-local variable is to store user ID, transaction ID, or transaction context for a thread. The thread sets those values in the beginning, and any code during the execution of that thread can use those values. Sometimes a thread may start child threads that may need to use the value set for a thread-local variable in the parent thread. You can achieve this by using an object of the InheritableThreadLocal<T> class, which is inherited from the ThreadLocal class. The child thread inherits its initial value from the parent thread. However, the child thread can set its own value using the set() method.

Setting Stack Size of a Thread

Each thread in a JVM is allocated its own stack. A thread uses its stack to store all local variables during its execution. Local variables are used in constructors, methods, or blocks (static or non-static). The stack size of each thread will limit the number of threads that you can have in a program. Local variables are allocated memory on stack during their scope. Once they are out of scope, the memory used by them is reclaimed. It is essential to optimize the stack size of a thread in your program if it uses too many threads. If the stack size is too big, you can have a fewer number of threads in your program. The number of threads will be limited by the available memory to the JVM. If the stack size is too small to store all local variables used at a time, you may encounter a StackOverflowError. To set the stack size for each thread, you can use a non-standard JVM option called -Xss<size>, where <size> is the size of the thread stack. To set the stack size to 512 KB, you can use a command, like so:

```
java -Xss512k <other-arguments>
```

Summary

A thread is a unit of execution in a program. An instance of the Thread class represents a thread in a Java program. The thread starts its execution in the run() method of the Thread class or its subclass. To execute your code in a thread, you need to subclass the Thread class and override its run() method; you can also use an instance of the Runnable interface as the target for a thread. Beginning with Java 8, you can use a method reference of any method that takes no parameters and returns void as the target for a thread. A thread is scheduled by using the start() method of the Thread class.

There are two types of threads: daemon and non-daemon. A non-daemon thread is also known as a user thread. The JVM exits when only threads running in the JVM are all daemon threads.

Each thread in Java has a priority that is an integer between 1 and 10, 1 being the lowest priority and 10 being the highest priority. The priority of a thread is a hint, which can be ignored, to the operating system about its importance for getting the CPU time.

In a multi-threaded program, a section of code that may have undesirable effects on the outcome of the program if executed by multiple threads concurrently is called a *critical section*. You can mark a critical section in a Java program using the synchronized keyword. Methods can also be declared as synchronized. Only one synchronized instance method of an object can be executed at a time by any threads. Only one synchronized class method of a class can be executed at a time by any threads.

A thread in a Java program goes through a set of states that determines its lifecycle. A thread can be in any one of these states: new, runnable, blocked, waiting, timed-waiting, or terminated. States are represented by constants of the Thread.State enum. Use the getState() method of the Thread class to get the current state of the thread.

A thread can be interrupted, stopped, suspended, and resumed. A stopped thread or a thread that has finished executing cannot be restarted.

Atomic variables, explicit locks, the synchronizer, the executor framework, and the fork/join framework are provided as class libraries to the Java developers to assist in developing concurrent applications. Atomic variables are variables that can be atomically updated without using explicit synchronization. Explicit locks have features that let you acquire locks and back off if the locks are not available. The executor framework helps schedule tasks. The fork/join framework is written on top of the executor framework to assist in working with tasks that can be divided in subtasks and finally their results can be combined.

Thread-local variables are implemented through the ThreadLocal<T> class. They store values based on threads. They are suitable for values that are local to threads and that cannot be seen by other threads.

QUESTIONS AND EXERCISES

1. What is a thread? Can threads share memory? What is thread local storage?
2. What is a multi-threaded program?
3. What is the name of the class whose objects represent threads in Java programs?
4. Suppose you create an object of the Thread class:

   ```
   Thread t = new Thread();
   ```

   What do you need to do next so that this Thread object will get CPU time?
5. What is a race condition when using multiple threads? How do you avoid a race condition in your program?
6. What is a critical section in a program?

7. What is the effect of using the `synchronized` keyword in a method's declaration?
8. What is thread synchronization? How is thread synchronization achieved in a Java program?
9. What are an entry set and a wait set of an object?
10. Describe the user of the `wait()`, `notify()`, and `notifyAll()` methods in thread synchronization.
11. What method of the `Thread` class do you use to check if a thread is terminated or alive?
12. Describe the following six states of a thread: `New`, `Runnable`, `Blocked`, `Waiting`, `Timed-waiting`, and `Terminated`. What method in the `Thread` class returns the state of a thread?
13. Can you restart a thread by calling its `start()` method after the thread is terminated?
14. What is thread starvation?
15. What is a daemon thread? What happens when the JVM detects that there are only daemon threads running in the application? Are the main thread and garbage collector thread daemon threads?
16. How do you interrupt a thread? What is the difference in calling the instance `isInterrupted()` method and static `interrupted()` method of the `Thread` class? What happens when a blocked thread is interrupted?
17. What is a thread group? What is the default thread group of a thread? How do you get an estimate of active threads in a thread group?
18. Describe the use of volatile variables in Java programs.
19. What is the difference between using an `AtomicLong` variable and a `long` variable with a synchronized getter and setter?
20. What are semaphores, barriers, phasers, latches, and exchangers? Name the classes in Java that represent instances of these synchronizers.
21. What is the Executor framework? What is the difference between an instance of the `Executor` interface and an instance of the `ExecutorService` interface? What class do you use to get a preconfigured `Executor` instance?
22. If you want to submit a result-bearing task to an `Executor`, the task needs to be an instance of which interface: `Runnable` or `Callable<T>`?
23. What does an instance of the `Future<T>` interface represent?
24. What is the difference in using the `shutdown()` and `shutdownNow()` methods to shut down an executor?
25. What is the Fork/Join framework?
26. Describe the use of the `ThreadLocal<T>` class.

27. What JVM option do you use to set the Java thread's stack size?

28. Create a class inheriting it from the Thread class. When an instance of the class is run as a thread, it should print text like 1<name> 2<name>, ...N<name> where <name> is the name of the thread you specify and N is the upper limit on the number of integers starting from 1 to be printed. For example, if you create an instance of your class with 100 and "A", it should print 1A 2A 3A...100A. Create three threads of your class and run them simultaneously.

29. Create a class named BankAccount. An instance of this class represents a bank account. It should contain three methods—deposit(), withdraw(), and balance(). They deposit, withdraw, and return the balance in the account. Its balance instance variable should store the balance in the account and it is initialized to 100. The balance in the account must not go below 100. Do not use any thread synchronization constructs or keywords in this class. Create an instance of the BankAccount class. Pass this instance to four threads—two threads should deposit money and two should withdraw money. The deposit and withdrawal amount should be selected randomly between 1 and 10. Start another thread, a monitor thread, that keeps calling the balance() method to check if the balance goes below 100. When the balance goes below 100, it should print a message and exit the application.

30. Create another copy of the BankAccount class and name it Account. Use thread synchronization to guard the access to the balance instance variable in the Account class, so its value never goes below 100. Run the same number of threads as in the previous exercise for five minutes. This time, the monitor thread should not print any message. After five minutes, all your threads should be interrupted and your threads should respond to the interruption by finishing its task. This way, your application should exit normally after five minutes.

CHAPTER 7

Input/Output

In this chapter, you will learn:

- What input/output is
- How to work with a `File` object to represent an abstract pathname for a file or a directory in a file system
- The decorator pattern
- Byte-based and character-based input/output streams
- Reading data from a file and writing data to a file
- Reading and writing primitive type and reference type data to input/output streams
- Object serialization and deserialization
- How to develop custom input/output stream classes
- Using the `Console` and `Scanner` classes to interact with the console
- The `StringTokenizer` and `StreamTokenizer` classes to split text into tokens based on delimiters

All example programs in this chapter are members of a `jdojo.io` module, as declared in Listing 7-1.

Listing 7-1. The Declaration of a jdojo.io Module

```
// module-info.java
module jdojo.io {
    exports com.jdojo.io;
}
```

What Is Input/Output?

Input/output (I/O) deals with reading data from a source and writing data to a destination. Data is read from the input source (or simply input) and written to the output destination (or simply output). For example, your keyboard works as a standard input, letting you read data entered using the keyboard into your program. You have been using the `System.out.println()` method to print text on the standard output from the very first Java program without your knowledge that you have been performing I/O.

Typically, you read data stored in a file or you write data to a file using I/O. However, your input and output are not limited to only files. You may read data from a `String` object and write it to another `String` object. In this case, the input is a `String` object; the output is also a `String` object. You may read data from

K. Sharan, *Java Language Features*, https://doi.org/10.1007/978-1-4842-3348-1_7

a file and write it to a String object, which will use a file as an input and a String object as an output. Many combinations for input and output are possible. Input and output do not have to be used together all the time. You may use only input in your program, such as reading the contents of a file into a Java program. You may use only output in your program, such as writing the result of a computation to a file.

The java.io and java.nio (nio stands for New I/O) packages contain Java classes that deal with I/O. The java.io package has an overwhelming number of classes to perform I/O. It makes learning Java I/O a little complex. The situation where the number of classes increases to an unmanageable extent is called a *class explosion* and the java.io package is a good example of that. It is no wonder that there are some books in the market that deal only with Java I/O. These books describe all Java I/O classes one by one. This chapter looks at Java I/O from a different perspective. First, you will look at the design pattern that was used to design the Java I/O classes. Once you understand the design pattern, it is easy to understand how to use those classes to perform I/O. After all, I/O is all about reading and writing data and it should not be that hard to understand! Before you start looking at the design pattern for the I/O classes, you will learn how to deal with files in the next section.

Working with Files

How do you refer to a file in your computer? You refer to it by its pathname. A file's pathname is a sequence of characters by which you can identify it uniquely in a file system. A pathname consists of a file name and its unique location in the file system. For example, on a Windows platform, C:\users\dummy.txt is the pathname for a file named dummy.txt, which is located in the directory named users, which in turn is located in the root directory in the C: drive. On a UNIX platform, /users/dummy is the pathname for a file named dummy, which is located in the directory named users, which in turn is located in the root directory.

A pathname can be either absolute or relative. An absolute pathname points to the same location in a file system irrespective of the current working directory. For example, on a Windows platform, C:\users\dummy.txt is an absolute pathname.

A relative pathname is resolved with respect to the working directory. Suppose dummy.txt is your pathname. If the working directory is C:\, this pathname points to C:\dummy.txt. If the working directory is C:\users, it points to C:\users\dummy.txt. Note that if you specify a relative pathname for a file, it points to a different file depending on the current working directory. A pathname that starts with a root is an absolute pathname. The forward slash (/) is the root on the UNIX platform and a drive letter followed with a backslash such as A:\ or C:\ defines the root for the Windows platform.

Tip The pathname syntax is platform-dependent. Programs using platform-dependent syntax to represent pathnames may not work correctly on other platforms. In this chapter, most of the time I use the term "file" to mean a file or a directory.

Creating a File Object

An object of the File class is an abstract representation of a pathname of a file or a directory in a platform-independent manner. Using the following constructors of the File class, you can create a File object from a pathname, a parent pathname and a child pathname, and a URI:

- File(String pathname)
- File(File parent, String child)

- `File(String parent, String child)`
- `File(URI uri)`

If you have a file pathname called "`dummy.txt`", you can create a `File` object, like so:

```
File dummyFile = new File("dummy.txt");
```

Note that a file named `dummy.txt` does not have to exist to create a `File` object using this statement. The `dummyFile` object represents an abstract pathname, which may or may not point to a real file in a file system.

The `File` class contains several methods to work with files and directories. Using a `File` object, you can create a new file, delete an existing file, rename a file, change permissions on a file, and so on. You will see all these operations on a file in action in subsequent sections.

■ **Tip** The `File` class contains two methods, `isFile()` and `isDirectory()`. Use these methods to determine whether a `File` object represents a file or a directory.

Knowing the Current Working Directory

The concept of the current working directory is related to operating systems, not to the Java programming language or Java I/O. When a process starts, it uses the current working directory to resolve the relative paths of files. When you run a Java program, the JVM runs as a process, and therefore it has a current working directory. The value for the current working directory for a JVM is set depending on how you run the `java` command. You can get the current working directory for the JVM by reading the `user.dir` system property as follows:

```
String workingDir = System.getProperty("user.dir");
```

At this point, you may be tempted to use the `System.setProperty()` method to change the current working directory for the JVM in a running Java program. The following snippet of code will not generate any errors; it will not change the current working directory either:

```
System.setProperty("user.dir", "C:\\kishori");
```

After you try to set the current working directory in your Java program, the `System.getProperty("user.dir")` will return the new value. However, to resolve the relative file paths, the JVM will continue to use the current working directory that was set when the JVM was started, not the one changed using the `System.setProperty()` method.

■ **Tip** Java designers found it too complex to allow changing the current working directory for the JVM in the middle of a running Java program. For example, if it were allowed, the same relative pathname would resolve to different absolute paths at different times in the same running JVM, giving rise to inconsistent behavior of the program.

You can also specify the current working directory for the JVM as the user.dir property value as a JVM option. To specify C:\test as the user.dir system property value on Windows, you run your program like so:

```
java -Duser.dir=C:\test <other-arguments>
```

Checking for a File's Existence

You can check if the abstract pathname of a File object exists using the exists() method of the File class:

```
// Create a File object
File dummyFile = new File("dummy.txt");

// Check for the file's existence
boolean fileExists = dummyFile.exists();
if (fileExists) {
    System.out.println("The dummy.txt file exists.");
} else {
    System.out.println("The dummy.txt file does not exist.");
}
```

I have used dummy.txt as the file name that is a relative path for this file. Where in the file system does the exists() method look for this file for its existence? There could be no file with this name or there could be multiple files with this name. When a relative file path is used, the JVM prepends the current working directory to the file path and uses the resulting absolute path for all file-related actual operations. Note that the absolute path is constructed in a platform-dependent way. For example, if the current working directory on Windows is C:\ksharan, the file name will be resolved to C:\ksharan\dummy.txt; if the current working directory on UNIX is /users/ksharan, the file name will be resolved to /users/ksharan/dummy.txt.

Which Path Do You Want to Go?

In addition to a relative path, a file has an absolute path and a canonical path. The absolute path identifies the file uniquely on a file system. A canonical path is the simplest path that uniquely identifies the file on a file system. The only difference between the two paths is that the canonical path is simplest in its form. For example, on Windows, if you have pathname dummy.txt whose absolute pathname is C:\users\dummy.txt, the pathname C:\users\sharan\..\dummy.txt also represents an absolute pathname for the same file. The two consecutive dots in the pathname represent one level up in the file hierarchy. Among the two absolute paths, the second one is not the simplest one. The canonical path for dummy.txt is the simplest absolute path, which is C:\users\dummy.txt.

The getAbsolutePath() and getCanonicalPath() methods in the File class return the absolute and canonical paths, respectively. Note that in a Java program you need to use double backslashes in a string literal to represent one backward slash; for example, the path C:\users\sharan needs to be written as "C:\\users\\sharan" as a string.

■ **Tip** The getAbsoluteFile() and getCanonicalFile() methods of the File class returns the absolute and canonical paths, respectively, as a File, whereas the getAbsolutePath() and getCanonicalPath() methods return the same paths as a String.

Different platforms use different name-separate character to separate parts in a pathname. For example, Windows uses a backslash (\) as name-separator, whereas UNIX-like operating systems use a slash (/). The File class defines two constants, File.separator and File.separatorChar, to represent a platform-dependent name-separator as a String and as a char, respectively. For example, on Windows, the value of the File.separator is "\\" and the value of File.separatorChar is '\\' and on UNIX their values are "/" and '/'. The benefit of using these constants in your program is that Java will use the appropriate file-separator character in your file pathname depending on the operating system in which your program is executed.

Listing 7-2 illustrates how to get the absolute and canonical paths of a file. You may get different output when you run the program. All examples in this chapters were run on Windows and the output will show Windows pathnames, unless specified otherwise.

Listing 7-2. Getting the Absolute and Canonical Paths of a File

```
// FilePath.java
package com.jdojo.io;

import java.io.File;
import java.io.IOException;

public class FilePath {
    public static void main(String[] args) {
        String workingDir = System.getProperty("user.dir");
        System.out.println("Working Directory: " + workingDir);

        System.out.println("----------------------");

        String pathname = "dummy.txt";
        printFilePath(pathname);

        System.out.println("----------------------");

        pathname = ".." + File.separator + "notes.txt";
        printFilePath(pathname);
    }

    public static void printFilePath(String pathname) {
        File f = new File(pathname);
        System.out.println("File Name: " + f.getName());
        System.out.println("File exists: " + f.exists());
        System.out.println("Absolute Path: " + f.getAbsolutePath());

        try {
            System.out.println("Canonical Path: " + f.getCanonicalPath());
        } catch (IOException e) {
            e.printStackTrace();
        }
    }
}
```

```
Working Directory: C:\Java9LanguageFeatures
----------------------
File Name: dummy.txt
File exists: false
Absolute Path: C:\Java9LanguageFeatures\dummy.txt
Canonical Path: C:\Java9LanguageFeatures\dummy.txt
----------------------
File Name: notes.txt
File exists: false
Absolute Path: C:\Java9LanguageFeatures\..\notes.txt
Canonical Path: C:\notes.txt
```

You have to deal with two "devils" when you work with I/O in Java. If you do not specify the absolute pathname, your absolute path will be decided by the Java runtime and the operating system. If you specify the absolute pathname, your code may not run on different operating systems. One way to handle this situation is to use a configuration file, where you specify a different file pathname for different operating systems, and you pass the configuration file path to your program at startup.

The canonical path of a file is system-dependent and the call to the getCanonicalPath() may throw an IOException. You must place this method call inside a try-catch block or throw an IOException from the method in which you invoke this method. Some of the I/O method calls throw an IOException in situations when the requested I/O operation fails.

Creating, Deleting, and Renaming Files

You can create a new file using the createNewFile() method of the File class:

```
// Create a File object to represent the abstract pathname
File dummyFile = new File("dummy.txt");

// Create the file in the file system
boolean fileCreated = dummyFile.createNewFile();
```

The createNewFile() method creates a new, empty file if the file with the specified name does not already exist. It returns true if the file is created successfully; otherwise, it returns false. The method throws an IOException if an I/O error occurs.

You can also create a temporary file in the default temporary file directory or a directory of your choice using the following createTempFile() static method of the File class:

- File createTempFile(String prefix, String suffix) throws IOException
- File createTempFile(String prefix, String suffix, File directory) throws IOException

The method accepts a prefix (at least three characters in length) and a suffix to generate the temporary file name. The following snippet of code shows examples of using both versions of the method:

```
// Create a temporary file in the default temporary directory
File tempFile1 = File.createTempFile("kkk", ".txt");

// Create a temporary file in the existing C:\kishori\temp directory
File tempDir = new File("C:\\kishori\\temp");
File tempFile2 = File.createTempFile("kkk", ".txt", tempDir);
```

You can use the mkdir() or mkdirs() method to create a new directory. The mkdir() method creates a directory only if the parent directories specified in the pathname already exists. For example, if you want to create a new directory called home in the users directory in the C: drive on Windows, you construct the File object representing this pathname like so:

```
File newDir = new File("C:\\users\\home");
```

Now the newDir.mkdir() method will create the home directory only if the C:\users directory already exists. However, the newDir.mkdirs() method will create the users directory if it does not exist in the C: drive, and hence, it will create the home directory under the C:\users directory.

Deleting a file is easy. You need to use the delete() method of the File class to delete a file/directory. A directory must be empty before you can delete it. The method returns true if the file/directory is deleted; otherwise, it returns false. You can also delay the deletion of a file until the JVM terminates by using the deleteOnExit() method. This is useful if you create temporary files in your program that you want to delete when your program exits.

```
File dummyFile = new File("dummy.txt");

// To delete the dummy.txt file immediately
dummyFile.delete();

// To delete the dummy.txt file when the JVM terminates
dummyFile.deleteOnExit();
```

■ **Tip** The call to the deleteOnExit() method is final. That is, once you call this method, there is no way for you to change your mind and tell the JVM not to delete this file when it terminates. You can use the delete() method to delete the file immediately even after you have requested the JVM to delete the same file on exit.

To rename a file, you can use the renameTo() method, which takes a File object to represent the new file:

```
// Rename old-dummy.txt to new_dummy.txt
File oldFile = new File("old_dummy.txt");
File newFile = new File("new_dummy.txt");

boolean fileRenamed = oldFile.renameTo(newFile);
if (fileRenamed) {
    System.out.println(oldFile + " renamed to " + newFile);
} else {
    System.out.println("Renaming " + oldFile + " to " + newFile + " failed.");
}
```

The renameTo() method returns true if renaming the file succeeds; otherwise, it returns false. You are advised to check the return value of this method to make sure the renaming succeeded because the behavior of this method is very system-dependent.

■ **Tip** The `File` object is immutable. Once created, it always represents the same pathname, which is passed to its constructor. When you rename a file, the old `File` object still represents the original pathname. An important point to remember is that a `File` object represents a pathname, not an actual file in a file system.

Listing 7-3 illustrates the use of some of the methods described in this section. You may get different output; the output is shown when the program ran on Windows. When you run the program the second time, you may get different output because it may not be able to rename the file if it already existed from the first run.

Listing 7-3. Creating, Deleting, and Renaming a File

```
// FileCreateDeleteRename.java
package com.jdojo.io;

import java.io.File;
import java.io.IOException;

public class FileCreateDeleteRename {
    public static void main(String[] args) {
        try {
            File newFile = new File("my_new_file.txt");
            System.out.println("Before creating the new file:");
            printFileDetails(newFile);

            // Create a new file
            boolean fileCreated = newFile.createNewFile();
            if (!fileCreated) {
                System.out.println(newFile + " could not be created.");
            }

            System.out.println("After creating the new file:");
            printFileDetails(newFile);

            // Delete the new file
            newFile.delete();

            System.out.println("After deleting the new file:");
            printFileDetails(newFile);

            // Let's recreate the file
            newFile.createNewFile();

            System.out.println("After recreating the new file:");
            printFileDetails(newFile);

            // Let's tell the JVM to delete this file on exit
            newFile.deleteOnExit();

            System.out.println("After using deleteOnExit() method:");
            printFileDetails(newFile);
```

```
            // Create a new file and rename it
            File firstFile = new File("my_first_file.txt");
            File secondFile = new File("my_second_file.txt");

            fileCreated = firstFile.createNewFile();
            if (fileCreated || firstFile.exists()) {
                System.out.println("Before renaming file:");
                printFileDetails(firstFile);
                printFileDetails(secondFile);

                boolean renamedFlag = firstFile.renameTo(secondFile);
                if (!renamedFlag) {
                    System.out.println("Could not rename " + firstFile);
                }

                System.out.println("After renaming file:");
                printFileDetails(firstFile);
                printFileDetails(secondFile);
            }
        } catch (IOException e) {
            e.printStackTrace();
        }
    }

    public static void printFileDetails (File f) {
        System.out.println("Absolute Path: " + f.getAbsoluteFile());
        System.out.println("File exists: " + f.exists());
        System.out.println("------------------------------");
    }
}
```

```
Before creating the new file:
Absolute Path: C:\Java9LanguageFeatures\my_new_file.txt
File exists: false
------------------------------
After creating the new file:
Absolute Path: C:\Java9LanguageFeatures\my_new_file.txt
File exists: true
------------------------------
After deleting the new file:
Absolute Path: C:\Java9LanguageFeatures\my_new_file.txt
File exists: false
------------------------------
After recreating the new file:
Absolute Path: C:\Java9LanguageFeatures\my_new_file.txt
File exists: true
------------------------------
After using deleteOnExit() method:
Absolute Path: C:\Java9LanguageFeatures\my_new_file.txt
File exists: true
------------------------------
```

```
Before renaming file:
Absolute Path: C:\Java9LanguageFeatures\my_first_file.txt
File exists: true
------------------------------
Absolute Path: C:\Java9LanguageFeatures\my_second_file.txt
File exists: false
------------------------------
After renaming file:
Absolute Path: C:\Java9LanguageFeatures\my_first_file.txt
File exists: false
------------------------------
Absolute Path: C:\Java9LanguageFeatures\my_second_file.txt
File exists: true
------------------------------
```

Working with File Attributes

The `File` class contains methods that let you get/set attributes of files and directories in a limited ways. You can set a file as read-only, readable, writable, and executable using the `setReadOnly()`, `setReadable()`, `setWritable()`, and `setExecutable()` methods, respectively. You can use the `lastModified()` and `setLastModified()` methods to get and set the last modified date and time of a file. You can check if a file is hidden using the `isHidden()` method. Note that the `File` class does not contain a `setHidden()` method, as the definition of a hidden file is platform-dependent.

> **Tip** I discuss working with file attributes using the New Input/Output 2 (NIO.2) API in Chapter 10. NIO.2 has extensive support for file attributes.

Copying a File

The `File` class does not provide a method to copy a file. To copy a file, you must create a new file, read the content from the original file, and write it into the new file. I discuss how to copy the contents of a file into another file later in this chapter, after I discuss the input and output streams. The NIO 2.0 API, which was added in Java 7, provides a direct way to copy a file contents and its attributes. Refer to Chapter 10 for more details.

Knowing the Size of a File

You can get the size of a file in bytes using the `length()` method of the `File` class.

```
File myFile = new File("myfile.txt");
long fileLength = myFile.length();
```

If a `File` object represents a non-existent file, the `length()` method returns zero. If it is a directory name, the return value is not specified. Note that the return type of the `length()` method is `long`, not `int`.

Listing Directories and Files

You can get a list of the available root directories in a file system by using the `listRoots()` static method of the `File` class. It returns an array of `File` objects.

```
// Get the list of all root directories
File[] roots = File.listRoots();
```

Root directories are different across platforms. On Windows, you have a root directory for each drive (e.g., `C:\`, `A:\`, `D:\`, etc.). On UNIX, you have a single root directory represented by a slash (`/`).

Listing 7-4 illustrates how to get the root directories on a machine. The output is shown when this program ran on Windows. You may get different output when you run this program on your machine. The output will depend on the operating system and the drives that are attached to your machine.

Listing 7-4. Listing All Available Root Directories on a Machine

```
// RootList.java
package com.jdojo.io;

import java.io.File;

public class RootList {
    public static void main(String[] args) {
        File[] roots = File.listRoots();
        System.out.println("List of root directories:");
        for (File f : roots) {
            System.out.println(f.getPath());
        }
    }
}
```

```
List of root directories:
C:\
E:\
```

You can list all files and directories in a directory by using the `list()` or `listFiles()` methods of the `File` class. The only difference between them is that the `list()` method returns an array of `String`, whereas the `listFiles()` method returns an array of `File`. You can also use a file filter with these methods to exclude some files and directories from the returned results.

Listing 7-5 illustrates how to list the files and directories in a directory. Note that the `list()` and `listFiles()` methods do not list the files and directories recursively. You need to write the logic to list files recursively. You need to change the value of the `dirPath` variable in the `main()` method. You may get different output. The output shows the results when the program ran on Windows.

Listing 7-5. Listing All Files and Directories in a Directory

```
// FileLists.java
package com.jdojo.io;

import java.io.File;

public class FileLists {
    public static void main(String[] args) {
        // Change the dirPath value to list files from your directory
        String dirPath = "C:\\";

        File dir = new File(dirPath);
        File[] list = dir.listFiles();

        for (File f : list) {
            if (f.isFile()) {
                System.out.println(f.getPath() + " (File)");
            } else if (f.isDirectory()) {
                System.out.println(f.getPath() + " (Directory)");
            }
        }
    }
}
```

```
C:\gradle (Directory)
C:\hiberfil.sys (File)
C:\Java9LanguageFeatures (Directory)
C:\virtualbox (Directory)
C:\VS_EXPBSLN_x64_enu.CAB (File)
C:\Windows (Directory)
...
```

Suppose you wanted to exclude all files from the list with an extension `.SYS`. You can do this by using a file filter that is represented by an instance of the functional interface `FileFilter`. It contains an `accept()` method that takes the `File` being listed as an argument and returns `true` if the `File` should be listed. Returning `false` does not list the file. The following snippet of code creates a file filter that will filter files with the extension `.SYS`:

```
// Create a file filter to exclude any .SYS file
FileFilter filter = file -> {
    if (file.isFile()) {
        String fileName = file.getName().toLowerCase();
        if (fileName.endsWith(".sys")) {
            return false;
        }
    }
    return true;
};
```

Using lambda expressions makes it easy to build the file filters. The following snippet of code creates two file filters—one filters only files and another only directories:

```
// Filters only files
FileFilter fileOnlyFilter = File::isFile;

// Filters only directories
FileFilter dirOnlyFilter = File::isDirectory;
```

Listing 7-6 illustrates how to use a file filter. The program is the same as in Listing 7-5 except that it uses a filter to exclude all .SYS files from the list. You can compare the output of these two listings to see the effect of the filter.

Listing 7-6. Using FileFilter to Filter Files

```
// FilteredFileList.java
package com.jdojo.io;

import java.io.File;
import java.io.FileFilter;

public class FilteredFileList {
    public static void main(String[] args) {
        // Change the dirPath value to list files from your directory
        String dirPath = "C:\\";
        File dir = new File(dirPath);

        // Create a file filter to exclude any .SYS file
        FileFilter filter = file -> {
            if (file.isFile()) {
                String fileName = file.getName().toLowerCase();
                if (fileName.endsWith(".sys")) {
                    return false;
                }
            }
            return true;
        };

        // Pass the filter object to listFiles() method to exclude the .sys files
        File[] list = dir.listFiles(filter);

        for (File f : list) {
            if (f.isFile()) {
                System.out.println(f.getPath() + " (File)");
            } else if (f.isDirectory()) {
                System.out.println(f.getPath() + " (Directory)");
            }
        }
    }
}
```

```
C:\gradle (Directory)
C:\Java9LanguageFeatures (Directory)
C:\virtualbox (Directory)
C:\VS_EXPBSLN_x64_enu.CAB (File)
C:\Windows (Directory)
...
```

The Decorator Pattern

Suppose you need to design classes for a bar that sells alcoholic drinks. The available drinks are rum, vodka, and whiskey. It also sells two drink flavorings: honey and spices. You have to design classes for a Java application so that when a customer orders a drink, the application will let the user print a receipt with the drink name and its price.

What are the things that you need to maintain in the classes to compute the price of a drink and get its name? You need to maintain the name and price of all ingredients of the drink separately. When you need to print the receipt, you will concatenate the names of all ingredients and add up the prices for all ingredients. One way to design the classes for this application would be to have a `Drink` class with two instance variables: `name` and `price`. There would be a class for each kind of drink; the class would inherit from the `Drink` class. Some of the possible classes would be as follows:

- `Drink`
- `Rum`
- `Vodka`
- `Whiskey`
- `RumWithHoney`
- `RumWithSpices`
- `VodkaWithHoney`
- `VodkaWithSpices`
- `WhiskeyWithHoney`
- `WhiskeyWithSpices`
- `WhiskeyWithHoneyAndSpices`

Note that we have already listed 11 classes and the list is not complete yet. Consider ordering whiskey with two servings of honey. You can see that the number of classes involved is huge. If you add some more drinks and flavorings, the classes will increase tremendously. With this class design, you will have a problem maintaining the code. If the price of honey changes, you will need to revisit every class that has honey in it and change its price. This design will produce a class explosion. Fortunately, there is a design pattern to deal with such a problem. It is called the *decorator* pattern. Typically, classes are organized as shown in Figure 7-1 to use the decorator pattern.

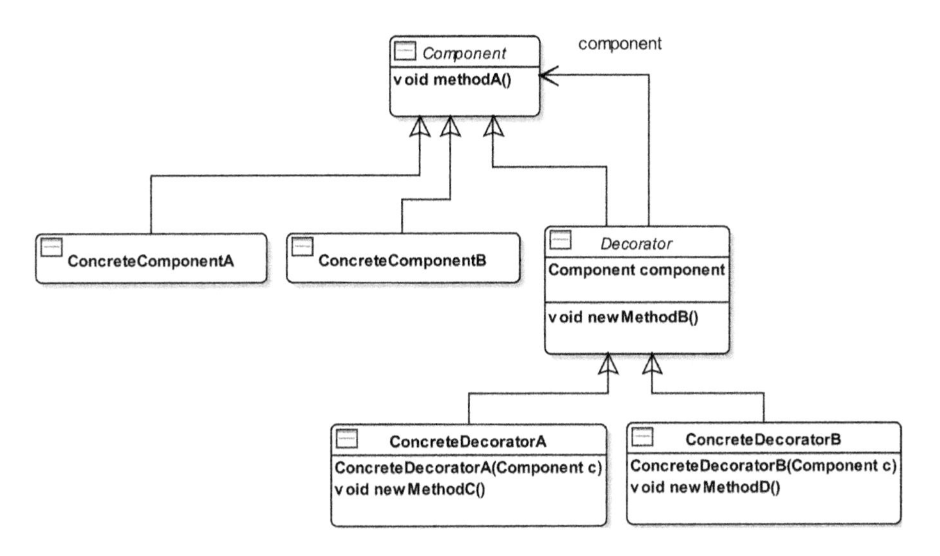

Figure 7-1. *A generic class diagram based on the decorator pattern*

The decorator pattern requires you to have a common abstract superclass from which you inherit your concrete component classes and an abstract decorator class. Name the common superclass `Component`. You can use an interface instead of an abstract class. Concrete components, shown as `ConcreteComponentA` and `ConcreteComponentB` in the class diagram, are inherited from the `Component` class. The `Decorator` class is the abstract decorator class, which is inherited from the `Component` class. Concrete decorators, shown as `ConcreteDecoratorA` and `ConcreteDecoratorB` in the class diagram, are inherited from the `Decorator` class. The `Decorator` class keeps a reference to its superclass `Component`. The reference of a concrete component is passed to a concrete decorator as an argument in its constructor as follows:

```
ConcreteComponentA ca = new ConcreteComponentA();
ConcreteDecoratorA cd = new ConcreteDecoratorA(ca);
```

When a method is called on a concrete decorator, it takes some actions and calls the method on the component it encloses. The decorator may decide to take its action before and/or after it calls the method on the component. This way, a decorator extends the functionality of a component. This pattern is called a decorator pattern because the decorator class adds functionality to (or decorates) the component it encloses. It is also known as the *wrapper* pattern for the same reason: it encloses (wraps) the component that it decorates.

The decorator has the same interface as the concrete components because both of them are inherited from the common superclass, `Component`. Therefore, you can use a `Decorator` object wherever a `Component` object is expected. Sometimes decorators add functionality by adding new methods that are not present in the component, as shown in the class diagram: `newMethodB()`, `newMethodC()` and `newMethodD()`.

Let's apply this discussion about the generic class diagram of the decorator pattern to model classes for your drink application. The class diagram is shown in Figure 7-2.

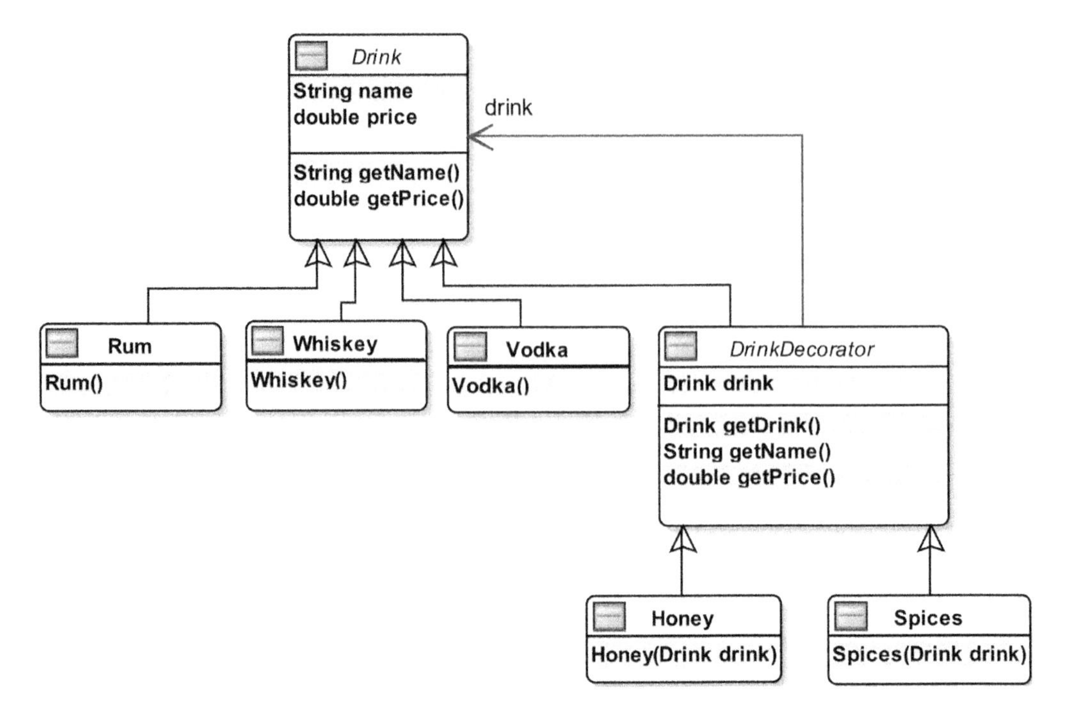

Figure 7-2. *The class diagram for the drink application based on the decorator pattern*

In the drink application, `Rum`, `Vodka`, and `Whiskey` are the concrete components (main drinks). `Honey` and `Spices` are the two decorators that are added to decorate (or to change the flavor) of the main drinks.

The `Drink` class, shown in Listing 7-7, serves as the abstract common ancestor class for the main drinks and decorators. The `name` and `price` instance variables in the `Drink` class hold the name and price of a drink; the class also contains the getters for these instance variables. These methods define the common interface for the main drinks as well as the flavors.

Listing 7-7. An Abstract Drink Class to Model the Abstract Component in the Decorator Pattern

```
// Drink.java
package com.jdojo.io;

public abstract class Drink {
    protected String name;
    protected double price;

    public String getName() {
        return name;
    }

    public double getPrice() {
        return price;
    }
}
```

Listing 7-8 contains the code for the Rum class that inherits from the Drink class. It sets the name and price in its constructor. Listing 7-9 and Listing 7-10 list the Vodka and Whiskey classes, respectively. The three classes are similar.

Listing 7-8. A Rum Class

```
// Rum.java
package com.jdojo.io;

public class Rum extends Drink {
    public Rum() {
        this.name = "Rum";
        this.price = 0.9;
    }
}
```

Listing 7-9. A Vodka Class

```
// Vodka.java
package com.jdojo.io;

public class Vodka extends Drink {
    public Vodka() {
        this.name = "Vodka";
        this.price = 1.2;
    }
}
```

Listing 7-10. A Whiskey Class

```
// Whiskey.java
package com.jdojo.io;

public class Whiskey extends Drink {
    public Whiskey() {
        this.name = "Whisky";
        this.price = 1.5;
    }
}
```

The DrinkDecorator, shown in Listing 7-11, is the abstract decorator class that is inherited from the Drink class. The concrete decorators Honey and Spices inherit from the DrinkDecorator class. It has an instance variable named drink, which is of the type Drink. This instance variable represents the Drink object that a decorator will decorate. It overrides the getName() and getPrice() methods for decorators. In its getName() method, it gets the name of the drink it is decorating and appends its own name to it. This is what I mean by adding functionality to a component by a decorator. The getPrice() method works the same way. It gets the price of the drink it decorates and adds its own price to it.

Listing 7-11. An Abstract DrinkDecorator Class

```
// DrinkDecorator.java
package com.jdojo.io;

public abstract class DrinkDecorator extends Drink {
    protected Drink drink;

    @Override
    public String getName() {
        // Append its name after the name of the drink it is decorating
        return drink.getName() + ", " + this.name;
    }

    @Override
    public double getPrice() {
        // Add its price to the price of the drink it is decorating/
        return drink.getPrice() + this.price;
    }

    public Drink getDrink() {
        return drink;
    }
}
```

Listing 7-12 lists a concrete decorator, the Honey class, which inherits from the DrinkDecorator class. It accepts a Drink object as an argument in its constructor. It requires that before you can create an object of the Honey class, you must have a Drink object. In its constructor, it sets its name, price, and the drink it will work with. It will use the getName() and getPrice() methods of its superclass DrinkDecorator class.

Listing 7-12. A Honey Class, a Concrete Decorator

```
// Honey.java
package com.jdojo.io;

public class Honey extends DrinkDecorator{
    public Honey(Drink drink) {
        this.drink = drink;
        this.name = "Honey";
        this.price = 0.25;
    }
}
```

Listing 7-13 lists another concrete decorator, the Spices class, which is implemented the same way as the Honey class.

Listing 7-13. A Spices Class, a Concrete Decorator

```
// Spices.java
package com.jdojo.io;

public class Spices extends DrinkDecorator {
    public Spices(Drink drink) {
        this.drink = drink;
        this.name = "Spices";
        this.price = 0.10;
    }
}
```

It is the time to see the drink application in action. Let's order whiskey with honey. How will you construct the objects to order whiskey with honey? It's simple. You always start by creating the concrete component. Concrete decorators are added to the concrete component. Whiskey is your concrete component and honey is your concrete decorator. You always work with the last component object you created in the series. Typically, the last component that you created is one of the concrete decorators unless you are dealing with only a concrete component.

```
// Create a Whiskey object
Whiskey w = new Whiskey();

// Add Honey to the Whiskey. Pass the object w in Honey's constructor
Honey h = new Honey(w);

// At this moment onwards, we will work with the last component we have
// created, which is h (a honey object). To get the name of the drink,
// call the getName() method on the honey object
String drinkName = h.getName();
```

Note that the Honey class uses the getName() method, which is implemented in the DrinkDecorator class. It will get the name of the drink, which is Whiskey in your case, and add its own name. The h.getName() method will return "Whiskey, Honey".

```
// Get the price
double drinkPrice = h.getPrice();
```

The h.getPrice() method will return 1.75. It will get the price of whiskey, which is 1.5 and add the price of honey, which is 0.25.

You do not need a two-step process to create a whiskey with honey drink. You can use the following one statement to create it:

```
Drink myDrink = new Honey(new Whiskey());
```

By using this coding style, you get a feeling that Honey is really enclosing (or decorating) Whiskey. You ordered a drink: whiskey with honey. Therefore, it is better to store the reference of the final drink to a Drink variable (Drink myDrink) rather than a Honey variable (Honey h). However, if the Honey class implemented some additional methods than those inherited from the Drink class and you intended to use one of those additional methods, you need to use a variable of the Honey class to store the final reference.

```
// If our Honey class has additional methods, which are not defined in the Drink
// class, store the reference in Honey type variable
Honey h = new Honey(new Whiskey());
```

How would you order a drink of whiskey with two servings of honey? It's simple. Create a Whiskey object, enclose it in a Honey object, and enclose the Honey object in another Honey object, like so:

```
// Create a drink of whiskey with double honey
Drink myDrink = new Honey(new Honey(new Whiskey()));
```

Similarly, you can create a drink of vodka with honey and spices, and get its name and price as follows:

```
// Create a drink of vodka with honey and spices
Drink myDrink = new Spices(new Honey(new Vodka()));
String drinkName = myDrink.getName();
double drinkPrice = myDrink.getPrice();
```

Sometimes reading the construction of objects based on the decorator pattern may be confusing because of several levels of object wrapping in the constructor call. You need to read the object's constructor starting from the innermost level. The innermost level is always a concrete component and all subsequent levels will be concrete decorators. In the previous example of vodka with honey and spices, the innermost level is the creation of vodka, new Vodka(), which is wrapped in honey, new Honey(new Vodka()), which in turn is wrapped in spices, new Spices(new Honey(new Vodka())). Figure 7-3 depicts how these three objects are arranged. Listing 7-14 demonstrates how to use your drink application.

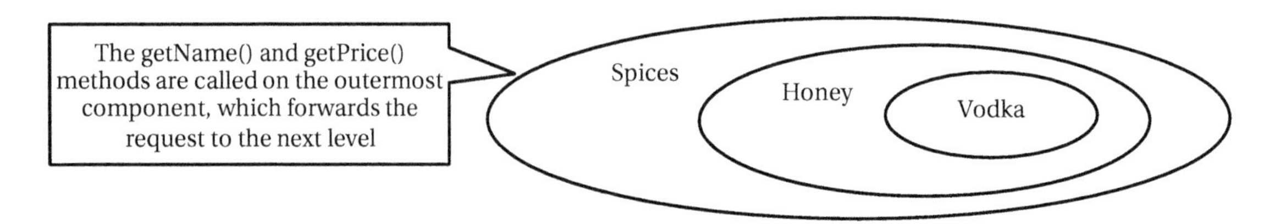

Figure 7-3. *The arrangement of components in the decorator pattern*

Listing 7-14. Testing the Drink Application

```
// DrinkTest.java
package com.jdojo.io;

public class DrinkTest {
    public static void main(String[] args) {
        // Have Whiskey only
        Drink d1 = new Whiskey();
        printReceipt(d1);

        // Have Whiskey with Honey
        Drink d2 = new Honey(new Whiskey());
        printReceipt(d2);
```

```
        // Have Vodka with Spices
        Drink d3 = new Spices(new Vodka());
        printReceipt(d3);

        // Have Rum with double Honey and Spices
        Drink d4 = new Spices(new Honey(new Honey(new Rum())));
        printReceipt(d4);
    }

    public static void printReceipt(Drink drink) {
        String name = drink.getName();
        double price = drink.getPrice();
        System.out.println(name + " - $" + price);
    }
}
```

```
Whisky - $1.5
Whisky, Honey - $1.75
Vodka, Spices - $1.3
Rum, Honey, Honey, Spices - $1.5
```

You need to consider the other aspects of the decorator pattern:

- The abstract `Component` class (the `Drink` class in the example) can be replaced with an interface. Note that you have included two instance variables in the `Drink` class. If you want to replace the `Drink` class with an interface, you must move these two instance variables down the class hierarchy.
- You may add any number of new methods in abstract decorators and concrete decorators to extend the behavior of its component.
- With the decorator pattern, you end up with lots of small classes, which may make your application hard to learn. However, once you understand the class hierarchy, it is easy to customize and use them.
- The goal of the decorator pattern is achieved by having a common superclass for the concrete components and concrete decorators. This makes it possible for a concrete decorator to be treated as a component, which in turn allows for wrapping a decorator inside another decorator. While constructing the class hierarchy, you can introduce more classes or remove some. For example, you could have introduced a class named `MainDrink` between the `Drink` class, and the `Rum`, `Vodka`, and `Whiskey` classes.
- The concrete decorator need not be inherited from an abstract decorator class. Sometimes you may want to inherit a concrete decorator directly from the abstract `Component` class. For example, the `ObjectInputStream` class is inherited from the `InputStream` class in the `java.io` package, not from the `FilterInputStream` class. Refer to Figure 7-5 for details. The main requirement for a concrete decorator is that it should have the abstract component as its immediate or non-immediate superclass and it should accept an abstract component type argument in its constructor.

Input/Output Streams

The literal meaning of the word stream is "an unbroken flow of something." In Java I/O, a stream means an unbroken flow (or sequential flow) of data. The data in the stream could be bytes, characters, objects, etc.

A river is a stream of water where the water flows from a source to its destination in an unbroken sequence. Similarly, in Java I/O, the data flows from a source known as a *data source* to a destination known as a *data sink*. The data is read from a data source to a Java program. A Java program writes data to a data sink. The stream that connects a data source and a Java program is called an *input stream*. The stream that connects a Java program and a data sink is called an *output stream*. In a natural stream, such as a river, the source and the destination are connected through the continuous flow of water. However, in Java I/O, a Java program comes between an input stream and an output stream. Data flows from a data source through an input stream to a Java program. The data flows from the Java program through an output stream to a data sink. In other words, a Java program reads data from the input stream and writes data to the output stream. Figure 7-4 depicts the flow of data from an input stream to a Java program and from a Java program to an output stream.

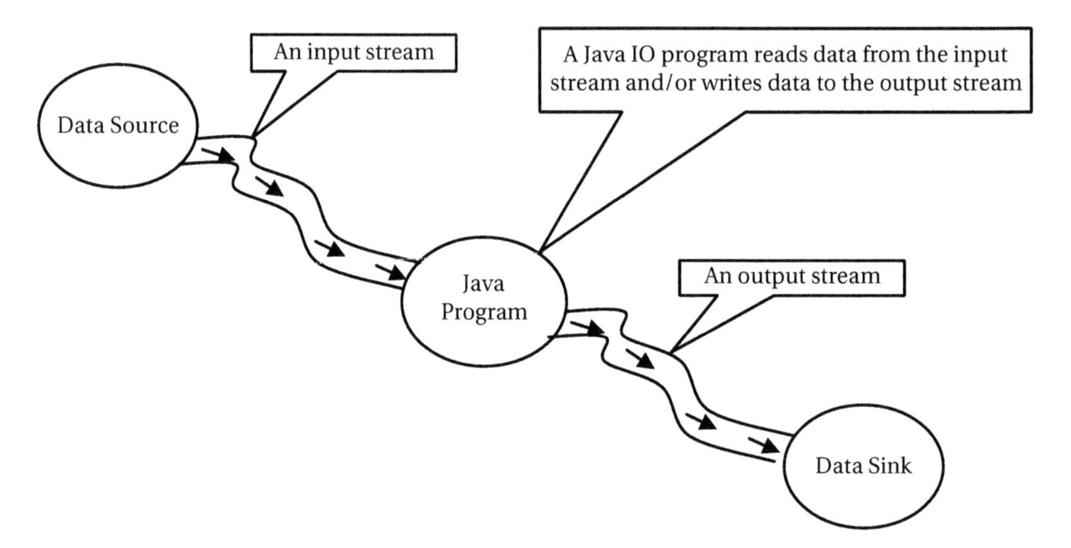

Figure 7-4. *Flow of data using an input/output stream in a Java program*

To read data from a data source into a Java program, you need to perform the following steps:

- Identify the data source. It may be a file, a string, an array, a network connection, etc.
- Construct an input stream using the data source.
- Read the data from the input stream. Typically, you read the data in a loop until you have read all the data from the input stream. The methods of an input stream return a special value to indicate the end of the input stream.
- Close the input stream. Note that constructing an input stream itself opens it for reading. There is no explicit step to open an input stream. However, you must close the input stream when you are done reading data from it. From Java 7, you can use a `try-with-resources` block, which closes the input stream automatically.

To write data to a data sink from a Java program, you need to perform the following steps:

1. Identify the data sink. That is, identify the destination where data will be written. It may be a file, a string, an array, a network connection, etc.
2. Construct an output stream using the data sink.
3. Write the data to the output stream.
4. Close the output stream. Note that constructing an output stream itself opens it for writing. There is no explicit step to open an output stream. However, you must close the output stream when you are done writing data to it. From Java 7, you can use a `try-with-resources` block, which closes the output stream automatically.

Input/output stream classes in Java are based on the decorator pattern. By now, you know that a class design based on the decorator pattern results in several small classes. So is the case with Java I/O. There are many classes involved in Java I/O. Learning each class at a time is no easy task. However, learning these classes can be made easy by comparing them with the class arrangements in the decorator pattern. I compare the Java I/O classes with the decorator pattern later. In the next two sections, you will see input/output streams in action using simple programs, which will read data from a file and write data to a file.

Reading from a File Using an Input Stream

In this section, I show you how to read data from a file. The data will be displayed on the standard output. You have a file called `luci1.txt`, which contains the first stanza from the poem *Lucy* by William Wordsworth (1770-1850). One stanza from the poem is as follows:

```
STRANGE fits of passion have I known:
And I will dare to tell,
But in the lover's ear alone,
What once to me befell.
```

You can create a `luci1.txt` file with this text and save it in your current working directory. The following steps are needed to read from the file:

1. Identify the data source, which is the file path for the `luci1.txt` file in this case.
2. Create an input stream using the file.
3. Read the data from the file using the input stream.
4. Close the input stream.

Identifying the Data Source

Your data source could be simply the file name as a string or a `File` object representing the pathname of the file. Let's assume that the `luci1.txt` file is in the current working directory.

```
// The data source
String srcFile = "luci1.txt";
```

Creating the Input Stream

To read from a file, you need to create an object of the FileInputStream class, which will represent the input stream:

```
// Create a file input stream
FileInputStream fin = new FileInputStream(srcFile);
```

When the data source for an input stream is a file, Java wants you to make sure that the file exists when you construct the file input stream. The constructor of the FileInputStream class throws a FileNotFoundException if the file does not exist. To handle this exception, you need to place your code in a try-catch block, like so:

```
try {
    // Create a file input stream
    FileInputStream fin = new FileInputStream(srcFile);
} catch (FileNotFoundException e){
    // The error handling code goes here
}
```

Reading the Data

The FileInputStream class has an overloaded read() method to read data from the file. You can read one byte or multiple bytes at a time using the different versions of this method. Be careful when using the read() method. Its return type is int, although it returns a byte value. It returns -1 if the end of the file is reached, indicating that there are no more bytes to read. You need to convert the returned int value to a byte to get the byte read from the file. You can read a byte at a time in a loop, like so:

```
int data;
byte byteData;

// Read the first byte
data = fin.read();
while (data != -1) {
    // Display the read data on the console. Note the cast from int to byte
    byteData = (byte) data;

    // Cast the byte data to char to display the data
    System.out.print((char) byteData);

    // Try reading another byte
    data = fin.read();
}
```

You can rewrite the previous file-reading logic in a compact form, like so:

```
byte byteData;
while ((byteData = (byte) fin.read()) != -1){
    System.out.print((char) byteData);
}
```

I use the compact form of reading the data from an input stream in subsequent examples. You need to place the code for reading data from an input stream in a try-catch block because it may throw an IOException.

Closing the Input Stream

Finally, you need to close the input stream using its close() method:

```
// Close the input stream
fin.close();
```

The close() method may throw an IOException, and because of that, you need to enclose this call inside a try-catch block.

```
try {
    // Close the input stream
    fin.close();
} catch (IOException e) {
    e.printStackTrace();
}
```

Typically, you construct an input stream inside a try block and close it in a finally block to make sure it is always closed after you are done with it.

All input/output streams are auto closeable. You can use a try-with-resources to create their instances, so they will be closed automatically regardless of an exception being thrown, avoiding the need to call their close() method explicitly. The following snippet of code shows using a try-with-resources to create a file input stream:

```
String srcFile = "luci1.txt";
try (FileInputStream fin = new FileInputStream(srcFile)) {
    // Use fin to read data from the file here
} catch (FileNotFoundException e) {
    // Handle the exception here
}
```

A Utility Class

You will frequently need to perform things such as closing an input/output stream and printing a message on the standard output when a file is not found, etc. Listing 7-15 contains the code for a FileUtil class that you will use in the example programs.

Listing 7-15. A Utility Class Containing Convenience Methods to Work with I/O Classes

```
// FileUtil.java
package com.jdojo.io;

import java.io.Closeable;
import java.io.IOException;
```

```
public class FileUtil {
    // Prints the location details of a file
    public static void printFileNotFoundMsg(String fileName) {
        String workingDir = System.getProperty("user.dir");
        System.out.println("Could not find the file '"
                + fileName + "' in '" + workingDir + "' directory ");
    }

    // Closes a Closeable resource such as an input/output stream
    public static void close(Closeable resource) {
        if (resource != null) {
            try {
                resource.close();
            } catch (IOException e) {
                e.printStackTrace();
            }
        }
    }
}
```

Completing the Example

Listing 7-16 illustrates the steps involved in reading the file luci1.txt. If you receive an error message indicating that the file does not exist, it will also print the directory where it is expecting the file. You may use an absolute path of the source file instead of a relative path by replacing the statement

```
String srcFile = "luci1.txt";
```

with an absolute path like c:\smith\luci1.txt on Windows or /users/smith/luci1.txt on UNIX. Note that you must use c:\\smith\\luci1.txt (two backslashes to escape a backslash) when you construct a string that contains a backslash.

```
String srcFile = "absolute path of luci1.txt file";
```

By simply using luci1.txt as the data source file path, the program expects that the file is present in your current working directory when you run the program.

Listing 7-16. Reading a Byte at a Time from a File Input Stream

```
// SimpleFileReading.java
package com.jdojo.io;

import java.io.FileInputStream;
import java.io.FileNotFoundException;
import java.io.IOException;

public class SimpleFileReading {
    public static void main(String[] args) {
        String dataSourceFile = "luci1.txt";
        try (FileInputStream fin = new FileInputStream(dataSourceFile)) {
```

```
            byte byteData;
            while ((byteData = (byte) fin.read()) != -1) {
                System.out.print((char) byteData);
            }
        } catch (FileNotFoundException e) {
            FileUtil.printFileNotFoundMsg(dataSourceFile);
        } catch (IOException e) {
            e.printStackTrace();
        }
    }
}
```

```
STRANGE fits of passion have I known:
And I will dare to tell,
But in the lover's ear alone,
What once to me befell.
```

Writing Data to a File Using an Output Stream

In this section, I show you how to write a stanza from the poem *Lucy* by William Wordsworth to a file named `luci2.txt`. The stanza is as follows:

```
When she I loved look'd every day
Fresh as a rose in June,
I to her cottage bent my way,
Beneath an evening moon.
```

The following steps are needed to write to the file:

1. Identify the data sink, which is the file to which the data will be written.
2. Create an output stream using the file.
3. Write the data to the file using the output stream.
4. Flush the output stream.
5. Close the output stream.

Identifying the Data Sink

Your data sink could be simply the file path as a string or a `File` object representing the pathname of the file. Let's assume that the `luci2.txt` file is in the current working directory.

```
// The data sink
String destFile = "luci2.txt";
```

Creating the Output Stream

To write to a file, you need to create an object of the FileOutputStream class, which will represent the output stream.

```
// Create a file output stream
FileOutputStream fos = new FileOutputStream(destFile);
```

When the data sink for an output stream is a file, Java tries to create the file if the file does not exist. Java may throw a FileNotFoundException if the file name that you have used is a directory name, or if it could not open the file for any reason. You must be ready to handle this exception by placing your code in a try-catch block, as shown:

```
try {
    FileOutputStream fos = new FileOutputStream(srcFile);
} catch (FileNotFoundException e){
    // Error handling code goes here
}
```

If your file contains data at the time of creating a FileOutputStream, the data will be erased. If you want to keep the existing data and append the new data to the file, you need to use another constructor of the FileOutputStream class, which accepts a boolean flag for appending the new data to the file.

```
// To append data to the file, pass true in the second argument
FileOutputStream fos = new FileOutputStream(destFile, true);
```

Writing the Data

Write data to the file using the output stream. The FileOutputStream class has an overloaded write() method to write data to a file. You can write one byte or multiple bytes at a time using the different versions of this method. You need to place the code for writing data to the output stream in a try-catch block because it may throw an IOException if data cannot be written to the file.

Typically, you write binary data using a FileOutputStream. If you want to write a string such as "Hello" to the output stream, you need to convert the string to bytes. The String class has a getBytes() method that returns an array of bytes that represents the string. You write a string to the FileOutputStream as follows:

```
String text = "Hello";
byte[] textBytes = text.getBytes();
fos.write(textBytes);
```

You want to write four lines of text to luci2.txt. You need to insert a new line after every line for the first three lines of text. A new line is different on different platforms. You can get a new line for the platform on which your program is running by reading the line.separator system variable as follows:

```
// Get the new line for the platform
String lineSeparator = System.getProperty("line.separator");
```

Note that a line separator may not necessarily be one character. To write a line separator to a file output stream, you need to convert it to a byte array and write that byte array to the file as follows:

```
fos.write(lineSeparator.getBytes());
```

Flushing the Output Stream

You need to flush the output stream using the `flush()` method:

```
// Flush the output stream
fos.flush();
```

Flushing an output stream indicates that if any written bytes were buffered, they may be written to the data sink. For example, if the data sink is a file, you write bytes to a `FileOutputStream`, which is an abstraction of a file. The output stream passes the bytes to the operating system, which is responsible for writing them to the file. For a file output stream, if you call the `flush()` method, the output stream passes the bytes to the operating system for writing. It is up to the operating system when it writes the bytes to the file. If an implementation of an output stream buffers the written bytes, it flushes the bytes automatically when its buffer is full or when you close the output stream by calling its `close()` method.

Closing the Output Stream

Closing an output stream is similar to closing an input stream. You need to close the output stream using its `close()` method.

```
// Close the output stream
fos.close();
```

The `close()` method may throw an `IOException`. Use a `try-with-resources` to create an output stream if you want it to be closed automatically.

Completing the Example

Listing 7-17 illustrates the steps involved in writing to a file named `luci2.txt`. If the file does not exist in your current directory, the program will create it. If it exists, it will be overwritten. The file path displayed in the output may be different when you run the program.

Listing 7-17. Writing Bytes to a File Output Stream

```
// SimpleFileWriting.java
package com.jdojo.io;

import java.io.File;
import java.io.FileNotFoundException;
import java.io.FileOutputStream;
import java.io.IOException;

public class SimpleFileWriting {
    public static void main(String[] args) {
        String destFile = "luci2.txt";

        // Get the line separator for the current platform
        String lineSeparator = System.getProperty("line.separator");
```

```
        String line1 = "When she I loved look'd every day";
        String line2 = "Fresh as a rose in June,";
        String line3 = "I to her cottage bent my way,";
        String line4 = "Beneath an evening moon.";

        try (FileOutputStream fos = new FileOutputStream(destFile)) {
            // Write all four lines to the output stream as bytes
            fos.write(line1.getBytes());
            fos.write(lineSeparator.getBytes());

            fos.write(line2.getBytes());
            fos.write(lineSeparator.getBytes());

            fos.write(line3.getBytes());
            fos.write(lineSeparator.getBytes());

            fos.write(line4.getBytes());

            // Flush the written bytes to the file
            fos.flush();

            // Display the output file path
            System.out.println("Text has been written to "
                    + (new File(destFile)).getAbsolutePath());
        } catch (FileNotFoundException e1) {
            FileUtil.printFileNotFoundMsg(destFile);
        } catch (IOException e2) {
            e2.printStackTrace();
        }
    }
}
```

```
Text has been written to C:\Java9LanguageFeatures\luci2.txt
```

Input Stream Meets the Decorator Pattern

Figure 7-5 depicts the class diagram that includes some commonly used input stream classes. You can refer to the API documentation of the `java.io` package for the complete list of the input stream classes. The comments in the class diagram compare input stream classes with the classes in the decorator pattern. Notice that the class diagram for the input streams is similar to the class diagram for your drink application, which was also based on the decorator pattern. Table 7-1 compares the classes in the decorator pattern, the drink application, and the input streams.

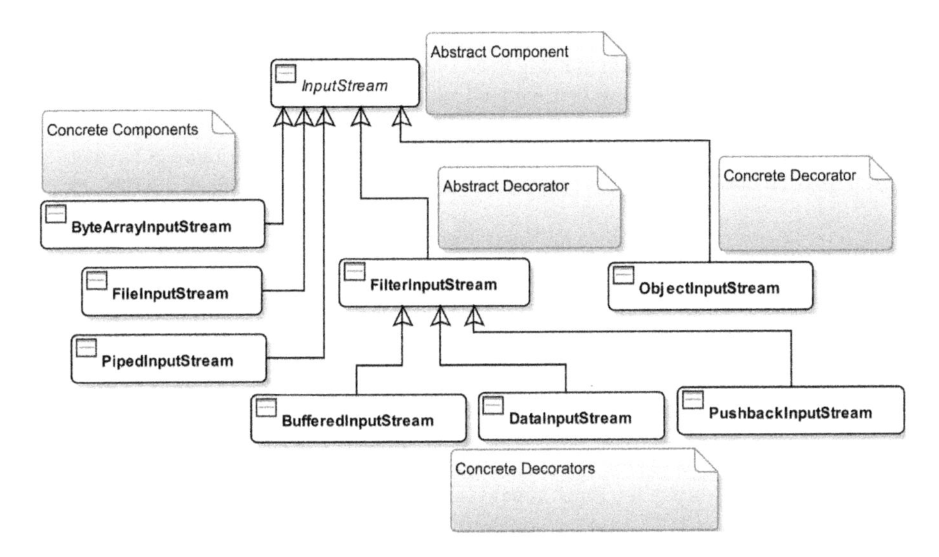

***Figure 7-5.** Commonly used classes for input streams compared with the decorator pattern*

***Table 7-1.** Comparing the Class Design in the Decorator Pattern, the Drink Application, and Input Streams*

Decorator Pattern	Drink Application	Input Stream
`Component`	`Drink`	`InputStream`

`ConcreteComponentA`
`ConcreteComponentB`
	`Rum`
	`Vodka`
	`Whisky`
		`FileInputStream`
		`ByteArrayInputStream`
		`PipedInputStream`

`Decorator`	`DrinkDecorator`	`FilterInputStream`

`ConcreteDecoratorA`
`ConcreteDecoratorB`
	`Honey`
	`Spices`
		`BufferedInputStream`
		`PushbackInputStream`
		`DataInputStream`
		`ObjectInputStream`

The abstract base component is the `InputStream` class, which is similar to the `Drink` class. You have concrete component classes of `FileInputStream`, `ByteArrayInputStream`, and `PipedInputStream`, which are similar to the `Rum`, `Vodka`, and `Whiskey` classes. You have a `FilterInputStream` class, which is similar to the `DrinkDecorator` class. Notice the decorator class in the input stream family does not use the word "Decorator" in its class name; it is named as `FilterInputStream` instead. It is also not declared abstract as you had declared the `DrinkDecorator` class. Not declaring it abstract seems to be an inconsistency in the class design. You have concrete decorator classes of `BufferedInputStream`, `DataInputStream`, and `PushbackInputStream`, which are similar to the `Honey` and `Spices` classes in the drink application. One noticeable difference is that the `ObjectInputStream` class is a concrete decorator and it is inherited from the abstract component `InputStream`, not from the abstract decorator `FilterInputStream`. Note that the requirement for a concrete decorator is that it should have the abstract component class in its immediate or non-immediate superclass and it should have a constructor that accepts an abstract component as its argument. The `ObjectInputStream` class fulfills these requirements.

Once you understand that the class design for input streams in Java I/O is based on the decorator pattern, it should be easy to construct an input stream using these classes. The superclass `InputStream` contains the basic methods to read data from an input stream, which are supported by all concrete component classes as well as all concrete decorator classes. The basic operation on an input stream is to read data from it. Some important methods defined in the `InputStream` class are listed in Table 7-2. Note that you have already used two of these methods, `read()` and `close()`, in the `SimpleFileReading` class to read data from a file.

Table 7-2. *Some Important Methods of the InputStream Class*

Method	Description
`int read()`	Reads one byte from the input stream and returns the read byte as an `int`. It returns -1 when the end of the input stream is reached.
`int read(byte[] buffer)`	Reads maximum up to the length of the specified `buffer`. It returns the number of bytes read in the `buffer`. It returns -1 if the end of the input stream is reached.
`int read(byte[] buffer, int offset, int length)`	Reads maximum up to the specified `length` bytes. The data is written in the `buffer` starting from the `offset` index. It returns the number of bytes read or -1 if the end of the input stream is reached.
`byte[] readAllBytes()`	Reads all remaining bytes from the input stream and returns the read bytes in a `byte[]`.This method was added to the `InputStream` class in JDK9.
`int readNBytes(byte[] buffer, int offset, int length)`	Reads the requested number of bytes, as specified by `length`, from the input stream into the given byte array. It returns the actual number of bytes read into the `buffer`. The read data is stored in the buffer starting at `offset`. This method was added to the `InputStream` class in JDK9.
`void close()`	Closes the input stream.
`int available()`	Returns the estimated number of bytes that can be read from this input stream without blocking.
`long transferTo(OutputStream out)`	Reads all bytes from this input stream and writes the bytes to the specified output stream. It returns the number of bytes transferred. This method was added to the `InputStream` class in JDK9.

■ **Tip** All methods in `InputStream` that read data block until the input data is available for reading, the end of the input stream is reached, or an exception is thrown.

Let's briefly discuss the four input stream concrete decorators: `BufferedInputStream`, `PushbackInputStream`, `DataInputStream`, and `ObjectInputStream`. I discuss `BufferedInputStream` and `PushbackInputStream` in this section. I discuss `DataInputStream` in the "Reading and Writing Primitive Data Types" section. I discuss `ObjectInputStream` in the "Object Serialization" section.

BufferedInputStream

A BufferedInputStream adds functionality to an input stream by buffering the data. It maintains an internal buffer to store bytes read from the underlying input stream. When bytes are read from an input stream, the BufferedInputStream reads more bytes than requested and buffers them in its internally maintained buffer. When a byte read is requested, it checks if the requested byte already exists in its buffer. If the requested byte exists in its buffer, it returns the byte from its buffer. Otherwise, it reads some more bytes in its buffer and returns only the requested bytes. It also adds support for the mark and reset operations on an input stream to let you reread bytes from an input stream. The main benefit of using BufferedInputStream is faster speed because of buffering. Listing 7-18 shows how to use a BufferedInputStream to read contents of a file.

Listing 7-18. Reading from a File Using a BufferedInputStream for Faster Speed

```
// BufferedFileReading.java
package com.jdojo.io;

import java.io.BufferedInputStream;
import java.io.FileInputStream;
import java.io.FileNotFoundException;
import java.io.IOException;

public class BufferedFileReading {
    public static void main(String[] args) {
        String srcFile = "luci1.txt";

        try (BufferedInputStream bis
                = new BufferedInputStream(new FileInputStream(srcFile))) {
            // Read one byte at a time and display the read data
            byte byteData;
            while ((byteData = (byte) bis.read()) != -1) {
                System.out.print((char) byteData);
            }
        } catch (FileNotFoundException e1) {
            FileUtil.printFileNotFoundMsg(srcFile);
        } catch (IOException e2) {
            e2.printStackTrace();
        }
    }
}
```

```
STRANGE fits of passion have I known:
And I will dare to tell,
But in the lover's ear alone,
What once to me befell.
```

The code in the BufferedFileReading class reads the text in the luci1.txt file. The only difference between SimpleFileReading in Listing 7-14 and BufferedFileReading in Listing 7-18 is that the latter uses a decorator BufferedInputStream for a FileInputStream and the former simply uses a FileInputStream. In SimpleFileReading, you constructed the input stream as follows:

```
String srcFile = "luci1.txt";
FileInputStream fis = new FileInputStream(srcFile);
```

In BufferedFileReading, you constructed the input stream as follows:

```
String srcFile = "luci1.txt";
BufferedInputStream bis = new BufferedInputStream(new FileInputStream(srcFile));
```

You may not find any noticeable speed gain using BufferedFileReading over SimpleFileReading in this example because the file size is small. You are reading one byte at a time in both examples to keep the code simpler to read. You should be using another version of the read() method of the input stream so you can read more bytes at a time. Using the readAllBytes() method, which was added to the InputStream in JDK9, you can read the entire contents of the file in one go.

PushbackInputStream

A PushbackInputStream adds functionality to an input stream that lets you unread bytes (or push back the read bytes) using its unread() method. There are three versions of the unread() method.

- void unread(byte[] buffer)
- void unread(byte[] buffer, int offset, int length)
- void unread(int buffer)

The unread(int buffer) method lets you push back one byte at a time and other two methods let you push back multiple bytes at a time. If you call the read() method on the input stream after you have called its unread() method, you will first read those bytes that you have pushed back. Once all unread bytes are read again, you start reading fresh bytes from the input stream. For example, suppose your input stream contains a string of bytes, HELLO. If you read two bytes, you would have read HE. If you call unread((byte) 'E') to push back the last byte you have read, the subsequent read will return E and the next reads will read LLO.

Listing 7-19 illustrates the use of the PushbackInputStream. The program reads the first stanza of the poem *Lucy* by William Wordsworth from the luci1.txt in the current working directory. It reads each byte from the file twice, as shown in the output. For example, STRANGE is read as SSTTRRAANNGGEE. You may notice a blank line between two lines because each new line is read twice.

Listing 7-19. Using the PushbackInputStream Class

```
// PushbackFileReading.java
package com.jdojo.io;

import java.io.PushbackInputStream;
import java.io.FileInputStream;
import java.io.FileNotFoundException;
import java.io.IOException;
```

```
public class PushbackFileReading {
    public static void main(String[] args) {
        String srcFile = "luci1.txt";

        try (PushbackInputStream pis
                = new PushbackInputStream(new FileInputStream(srcFile))) {

            // Read one byte at a time and display it
            byte byteData;
            while ((byteData = (byte) pis.read()) != -1) {
                System.out.print((char) byteData);

                // Unread the last byte that we have just read
                pis.unread(byteData);

                // Reread the byte we unread (or pushed back)
                byteData = (byte) pis.read();
                System.out.print((char) byteData);
            }
        } catch (FileNotFoundException e1) {
            FileUtil.printFileNotFoundMsg(srcFile);
        } catch (IOException e2) {
            e2.printStackTrace();
        }
    }
}
```

```
SSTTRRAANNGGEE ffiittss ooff ppaassssiioonn hhaavvee II kknnoowwnn::
AAnndd II wwiillll ddaarree ttoo tteellll,,

BBuutt iinn tthhee lloovveerr''ss eeaarr aalloonnee,,

WWhhaatt oonnccee ttoo mmee bbeeffeellll..
```

Output Stream Meets the Decorator Pattern

Figure 7-6 depicts the class diagram that includes some commonly used output stream classes. You can refer to the API documentation of the `java.io` package for the complete list of the output stream classes. The comments in the class diagram compare the output stream classes with the classes required to implement the decorator pattern. Notice that the class diagram for the output stream is similar to that of the input stream and the drink application.

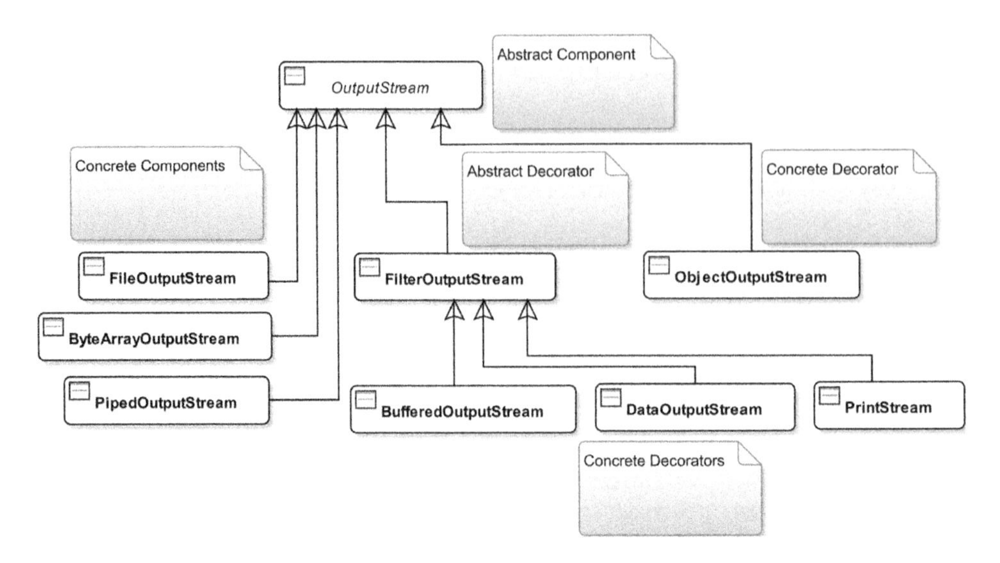

Figure 7-6. *Some commonly used classes for output streams compared with the decorator pattern*

Most of the time, if you know the name of the input stream class, you can get the corresponding output stream class by replacing the word "Input" in the class name with the word "Output." For example, for the `FileInputStream` class, you have a corresponding `FileOutputStream` class; for the `BufferedInputStream` class, you have a corresponding `BufferedOutputStream` class, and so on. You may not find a corresponding output stream class for every input stream class; for example, `PushbackInputStream` class has no corresponding output stream class. You may find some new classes that are not in the input stream class hierarchy because they do not make sense while reading data; for example, you have a new concrete decorator class `PrintStream` in the output stream class hierarchy. Table 7-3 compares the classes in the decorator pattern, your drink application, and the output streams.

Table 7-3. *Comparing Classes in the Decorator Pattern, the Drink Application, and the Output Streams*

Decorator Pattern	Drink Application	Output Stream
`Component`	`Drink`	`OutputStream`

`ConcreteComponentA`
`ConcreteComponentB`
	`Rum`
	`Vodka`
	`Whisky`
		`FileOutputStream`
		`ByteArrayOutputStream`
		`PipedOutputStream`

`Decorator`	`DrinkDecorator`	`FilterOutputStream`

`ConcreteDecoratorA`
`ConcreteDecoratorB`
	`Honey`
	`Spices`
		`BufferedOutputStream`
		`DataOutputStream`
		`ObjectOutputStream`

There are three important methods defined in the abstract superclass `OutputStream`: `write()`, `flush()`, and `close()`. The `write()` method is used to write bytes to an output stream. It has three versions that let you write one byte or multiple bytes at a time. You used it to write data to a file in the `SimpleFileWriting` class in Listing 7-17. The `flush()` method is used to flush any buffered bytes to the data sink. The `close()` method closes the output stream.

The technique to use concrete decorators with the concrete component classes for the output stream is the same as for the input stream classes. For example, to use the BufferedOutputStream decorator for better speed to write to a file, use the following statement:

```
BufferedOutputStream bos = new BufferedOutputStream(
                             new FileOutputStream("your output file path")
                           );
```

To write data to a ByteArrayOutputStream, use the following statements:

```
ByteArrayOutputStream baos = new ByteArrayOutputStream();
baos.write(buffer); // Here, buffer is a byte array
```

ByteArrayOutputStream provides some important methods: reset(), size(), toString(), and writeTo(). The reset() method discards all bytes written to it; the size() method returns the number of bytes written to the stream; the toString() method returns the string representation of the bytes in the stream; the writeTo() method writes the bytes in the stream to another output stream. For example, if you have written some bytes to a ByteArrayOutputStream called baos and want to write its content to a file represented by FileOutputStream named fos, you would use the following statement:

```
// All bytes written to baos is written to fos
baos.writeTo(fos);
```

I don't cover any more examples of writing to an output stream in this section. You can use SimpleFileWriting class in Listing 7-17 as an example to use any other type of output stream. You can use any output stream's concrete decorators by using them as an enclosing object for a concrete component or another concrete decorator. I discuss the DataOutputStream, ObjectOutputStream, and PrintStream classes with examples in subsequent sections.

PrintStream

The PrintStream class is a concrete decorator for the output stream as shown in Figure 7-6. It adds the following functionality to an output stream:

- It contains methods that let you print any data type values, primitive or object, in a suitable format for printing.
- Its methods to write data to the output stream do not throw an IOException. If a method call throws an IOException, it sets an internal flag, rather than throwing the exception to the caller. The flag can be checked using its checkError() method, which returns true if an IOException occurs during the method execution.
- It has an auto-flush capability. You can specify in its constructor that it should flush the contents written to it automatically. If you set the auto-flush flag to true, it will flush its contents when a byte array is written, one of its overloaded println() methods is used to write data, a new line character is written, or a byte (\n) is written.

Some of the important methods in PrintStream class are as follows:

- void print(Xxx arg)
- void println(Xxx arg)
- PrintStream printf(String format, Object... args)
- PrintStream printf(Locale l, String format, Object... args)

Here, Xxx is any primitive data type (int, char, float, etc.), String, or Object.

The print(Xxx arg) method writes the specified arg value to the output stream in a printable format. For example, you can use print(10) to write an integer to an output stream. Xxx also includes two reference types: String and Object. If your argument is an object, the toString() method on that object is called, and the returned string is written to the output stream. If the object type argument is null, a string "null" is written to the output stream. Note that all input and output streams are byte based. When I mention that the print stream writes a "null" string to the output stream, it means that the print stream converts the string "null" into bytes and writes those bytes to the output stream. The character-to-byte conversion is done based on the platform's default character encoding. You can also provide the character encoding to use for such conversions in some of the constructors of the PrintStream class.

The println(XXX arg) method works like the print(XXX arg) method with one difference. It appends a line separator string to the specified arg. That is, it writes an arg value and a line separator to the output stream. The method println() with no argument is used to write a line separator to the output stream. The line separator is platform-dependent and it is determined by the system property named line.separator.

The printf() method is used to write a formatted string to the output stream. For example, if you want to write a string in the form "Today is: <today-date>" to a output stream, you can use its printf() method as follows:

```
// Assuming that date format is mm/dd/yyyy and ps is the PrintStream object reference
ps.printf("Today is: %1$tm/%1$td/%1$tY", java.time.LocalDate.now());
```

Listing 7-20 illustrates how to use a PrintStream to write to a file. It writes another stanza from the poem *Lucy* by William Wordsworth to a file named luci3.txt. The contents of the file after you run this program would be as follows:

```
Upon the moon I fix'd my eye,
All over the wide lea;
With quickening pace my horse drew nigh
Those paths so dear to me.
```

Listing 7-20. Using the PrintStream Class to Write to a File

```
// FileWritingWithPrintStream.java
package com.jdojo.io;

import java.io.File;
import java.io.FileNotFoundException;
import java.io.PrintStream;

public class FileWritingWithPrintStream {
    public static void main(String[] args) {
        String destFile = "luci3.txt";
```

```
        try (PrintStream ps = new PrintStream(destFile)) {
            // Write data to the file. println() appends a new line
            // and print() does not append a new line
            ps.println("Upon the moon I fix'd my eye,");
            ps.println("All over the wide lea;");
            ps.println("With quickening pace my horse drew nigh");
            ps.print("Those paths so dear to me.");

            // flush the print stream
            ps.flush();

            System.out.println("Text has been written to "
                    + (new File(destFile).getAbsolutePath()));
        } catch (FileNotFoundException e1) {
            FileUtil.printFileNotFoundMsg(destFile);
        }
    }
}
```

```
Text has been written to C:\Java9LanguageFeatures\luci3.txt
```

Listing 7-20 is very similar in structure to Listing 7-17. It creates a `PrintStream` object using the data sink file name. You can also create a `PrintStream` object using any other `OutputStream` object. You may notice that you do not have to handle the `IOException` in the `catch` block because unlike another output stream, a `PrintStream` object does not throw this exception. In addition, you use the `println()` and `print()` methods to write the four lines of text without worrying about converting them to bytes. If you want to use auto-flush in this program, you need to create the `PrintStream` object using another constructor as follows:

```
boolean autoFlush = true;
PrintStream ps = new PrintStream(new FileOutputStream(destFile), autoFlush);
```

Using Pipes

A pipe connects an input stream and an output stream. A piped I/O is based on the producer-consumer pattern. The producer produces data and the consumer consumes the data, without caring about each other. It works similar to a physical pipe, where you inject something at one end and gather it at the other end. In a piped I/O, you create two streams representing two ends of the pipe. A `PipedOutputStream` object represents one end and a `PipedInputStream` object the other end. You connect the two ends using the `connect()` method on the either object. You can also connect them by passing one object to the constructor when you create another object. You can imagine the logical arrangement of a piped input stream and a piped output stream as depicted in Figure 7-7.

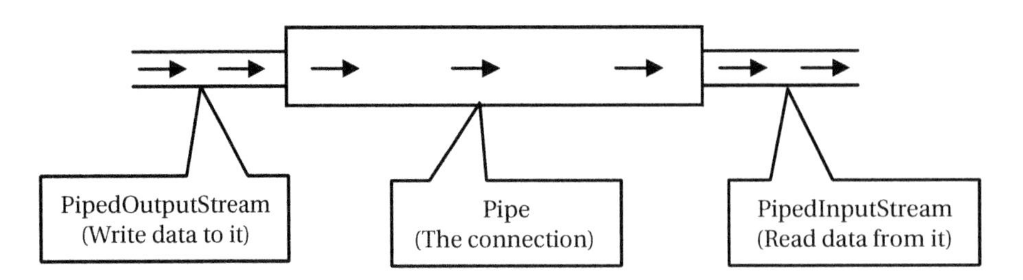

Figure 7-7. *The logical arrangement of piped input and output streams*

The following snippet of code shows two ways of creating and connecting the two ends of a pipe:

```
// Method #1: Create piped input and output streams and connect them
PipedInputStream pis = new PipedInputStream();
PipedOutputStream pos = new PipedOutputStream();
pis.connect(pos); /* Connect the two ends */

// Method #2: Create piped input and output streams and connect them
PipedInputStream pis = new PipedInputStream();
PipedOutputStream pos = new PipedOutputStream(pis);
```

You can produce and consume data after you connect the two ends of the pipe. You produce data by using one of the `write()` methods of the `PipedOutputStream` object. Whatever you write to the piped output stream automatically becomes available to the piped input stream object for reading. You use the `read()` method of `PipedInputStream` to read data from the pipe. The piped input stream is blocked if data is not available when it attempts to read from the pipe.

Have you wondered where the data is stored when you write it to a piped output stream? Similar to a physical pipe, a piped stream has a buffer with a fixed capacity to store data between the time it is written to and read from the pipe. You can set the pipe capacity when you create it. If a pipe's buffer is full, an attempt to write on the pipe blocks.

```
// Create piped input and output streams with the buffer capacity of 2048 bytes
PipedOutputStream pos = new PipedOutputStream();
PipedInputStream pis = new PipedInputStream(pos, 2048);
```

■ **Tip** Typically, a pipe is used to transfer data from one thread to another. One thread will produce data and another thread will consume the data. Note that the synchronization between two threads is taken care of by the blocking read and write.

Listing 7-21 demonstrates how to use a piped I/O. The `main()` method creates and connects a piped input and a piped output stream. The piped output stream is passed to the `produceData()` method, producing numbers from 1 to 50. The thread sleeps for a half second after producing a number. The `consumeData()` method reads data from the piped input stream. I used a quick and dirty way of handling the exceptions to keep the code smaller and readable. Data is produced and read in two separate threads.

Listing 7-21. Using Piped Input and Output Streams

```
// PipedStreamTest.java
package com.jdojo.io;

import java.io.PipedInputStream;
import java.io.PipedOutputStream;

public class PipedStreamTest {
    public static void main(String[] args) throws Exception {
        // Create and connect piped input and output streams
        PipedInputStream pis = new PipedInputStream();
        PipedOutputStream pos = new PipedOutputStream();
        pos.connect(pis);

        // Creates and starts two threads, one to produce data (write data)
        // and one to consume data (read data)
        Runnable producer = () -> produceData(pos);
        Runnable consumer = () -> consumeData(pis);
        new Thread(producer).start();
        new Thread(consumer).start();
    }

    public static void produceData(PipedOutputStream pos) {
        try {
            for (int i = 1; i <= 50; i++) {
                pos.write((byte) i);
                pos.flush();
                System.out.println("Writing: " + i);
                Thread.sleep(500);
            }
            pos.close();
        } catch (Exception e) {
            e.printStackTrace();
        }
    }

    public static void consumeData(PipedInputStream pis) {
        try {
            int num = -1;
            while ((num = pis.read()) != -1) {
                System.out.println("Reading: " + num);
            }
            pis.close();
        } catch (Exception e) {
            e.printStackTrace();
        }
    }
}
```

```
Writing: 1
Reading: 1
...
Writing: 50
Reading: 50
```

Reading and Writing Primitive Data Types

An object of the DataInputStream class is used to read values of the primitive data types in a machine-independent way from an input stream. An object of the DataOutputStream class is used to write values of the primitive data type in a machine-independent way to an output stream.

The DataInputStream class contains readXxx() methods to read a value of data type Xxx, where Xxx is a primitive data type such as int, char, etc. For example, to read an int value, it contains a readInt() method; to read a char value, it has a readChar() method, etc. It also supports reading strings using the readUTF() method.

The DataOutputStream class contains a writeXxx(Xxx value) method corresponding to each the readXxx() method of the DataInputStream class, where Xxx is a Java primitive data type. It supports writing a string to an output stream using the writeUTF(String text) method.

The DataInputStream and DataOutputStream classes are concrete decorators, which provide you a convenient way to read and write values of the primitive data types and strings using input and output streams, respectively. You must have an underlying concrete component linked to a data source or a data sink to use these classes. For example, to write values of the primitive data types to a file named primitives.dat, you construct an object of DataOutputStream as follows:

```
DataOutputStream dos = new DataOutputStream(new FileOutputStream("primitives.dat"));
```

Listing 7-22 writes an int value, a double value, a boolean value, and a string to a file named primitives.dat. The file path in the output may be different when you run this program.

Listing 7-22. Writing Java Primitive Values and Strings to a File

```
// WritingPrimitives.java
package com.jdojo.io;

import java.io.DataOutputStream;
import java.io.File;
import java.io.FileNotFoundException;
import java.io.FileOutputStream;
import java.io.IOException;

public class WritingPrimitives {
    public static void main(String[] args) {
        String destFile = "primitives.dat";

        try (DataOutputStream dos = new DataOutputStream(
                new FileOutputStream(destFile))) {
```

```
            // Write some primitive values and a string
            dos.writeInt(765);
            dos.writeDouble(6789.50);
            dos.writeBoolean(true);
            dos.writeUTF("Java Input/Output is cool!");

            // Flush the written data to the file
            dos.flush();

            System.out.println("Data has been written to "
                    + (new File(destFile)).getAbsolutePath());
        } catch (FileNotFoundException e) {
            FileUtil.printFileNotFoundMsg(destFile);
        } catch (IOException e) {
            e.printStackTrace();
        }
    }
}
```

```
Data has been written to C:\Java9LanguageFeatures\primitives.dat
```

Listing 7-23 reads those primitive values back. Note that you must read the values in the same order using a `DataInputStream` as they were written using the `DataOutputStream`. You need to run the `WritingPrimitives` class before you run the `ReadingPrimitives` class.

Listing 7-23. Reading Primitive Values and Strings from a File

```
// ReadingPrimitives.java
package com.jdojo.io;

import java.io.IOException;
import java.io.FileInputStream;
import java.io.FileNotFoundException;
import java.io.DataInputStream;

public class ReadingPrimitives {
    public static void main(String[] args) {
        String srcFile = "primitives.dat";

        try (DataInputStream dis = new DataInputStream(
                new FileInputStream(srcFile))) {
            // Read the data in the same order they were written
            int intValue = dis.readInt();
            double doubleValue = dis.readDouble();
            boolean booleanValue = dis.readBoolean();
            String msg = dis.readUTF();

            System.out.println(intValue);
            System.out.println(doubleValue);
            System.out.println(booleanValue);
            System.out.println(msg);
```

```
        } catch (FileNotFoundException e) {
            FileUtil.printFileNotFoundMsg(srcFile);
        } catch (IOException e) {
            e.printStackTrace();
        }
    }
}
```

```
765
6789.5
true
Java Input/Output is cool!
```

Object Serialization

You create an object using the new operator. For example, if you have a Person class that accepts a person's name, gender, and height as arguments in its constructor, you can create a Person object as follows:

```
Person john = new Person("John", "Male", 6.7);
```

What would you do if you wanted to save the object john to a file and later restore it in memory without using the new operator again? You have not learned how to do it yet. This is the subject of the discussion in this section.

The process of converting an object in memory to a sequence of bytes and storing the sequence of bytes in a storage medium such as a file is called *object serialization*. You can store the sequence of bytes to permanent storage such as a file or a database. You can also transmit the sequence of bytes over a network. The process of reading the sequence of bytes produced by a serialization process and restoring the object back in memory is called *object deserialization*. The serialization of an object is also known as *deflating* or *marshaling* the object. The deserialization of an object is also known as *inflating* or *unmarshaling* the object. You can think of serialization as writing an object from memory to a storage medium and deserialization as reading an object into memory from a storage medium.

An object of the ObjectOutputStream class is used to serialize an object. An object of the ObjectInputStream class is used to deserialize an object. You can also use objects of these classes to serialize values of the primitive data types such as int, double, boolean, etc.

The ObjectOutputStream and ObjectInputStream classes are the concrete decorator classes for output and input streams, respectively. However, they are not inherited from their abstract decorator classes. They are inherited from their respective abstract component classes. ObjectOutputStream is inherited from OutputStream and ObjectInputStream is inherited from InputStream. This seems to be an inconsistency. However, this still fits into the decorator pattern.

Your class must implement the Serializable or Externalizable interface to be serialized or deserialized. The Serializable interface is a marker interface. If you want the objects of a Person class to be serialized, you need to declare the Person class as follows:

```
public class Person implements Serializable {
    // Code for the Person class goes here
}
```

Java takes care of the details of reading/writing a Serializable object from/to a stream. You just need to pass the object to write/read to/from a stream to one of the methods of the stream classes.

Implementing the Externalizable interface gives you more control in reading and writing objects from/to a stream. It inherits the Serializable interface. It is declared as follows:

```
public interface Externalizable extends Serializable {
    void readExternal(ObjectInput in) throws IOException, ClassNotFoundException;
    void writeExternal(ObjectOutput out) throws IOException;
}
```

The readExternal() method is called when you read an object from a stream. The writeExternal() method is called when you write an object to a stream. You have to write the logic to read and write the object's fields inside the readExternal() and writeExternal() methods, respectively. Your class implementing the Externalizable interface looks like the following:

```
public class Person implements Externalizable {
    public void readExternal(ObjectInput in) throws IOException, ClassNotFoundException {
        // Write the logic to read the Person object fields from the stream
    }

    public void writeExternal(ObjectOutput out) throws IOException {
        // Write the logic to write Person object fields to the stream
    }
}
```

Serializing Objects

To serialize an object, you need to perform the following steps:

1. Have the references of the objects to be serialized.
2. Create an object output stream for the storage medium to which the objects will be written.
3. Write objects to the output stream.
4. Close the object output stream.

Create an object of the ObjectOutputStream class by using it as a decorator for another output stream that represents the storage medium to save the object. For example, to save an object to a person.ser file, create an object output stream as follows:

```
// Create an object output stream to write objects to a file
ObjectOutputStream oos = new ObjectOutputStream(new FileOutputStream("person.ser"));
```

To save an object to a ByteArrayOutputStream, you construct an object output stream as follows:

```
// Creates a byte array output stream to write data to
ByteArrayOutputStream baos = new ByteArrayOutputStream();

// Creates an object output stream to write objects to the byte array output stream
ObjectOutputStream oos = new ObjectOutputStream(baos);
```

Use the `writeObject()` method of the `ObjectOutputStream` class to serialize the object by passing the object reference as an argument, like so:

```
// Serializes the john object
oos.writeObject(john);
```

Finally, use the `close()` method to close the object output stream when you are done writing all objects to it:

```
// Close the object output stream
oos.close();
```

Listing 7-24 defines a `Person` class that implements the `Serializable` interface. The `Person` class contains three fields: `name`, `gender`, and `height`. It overrides the `toString()` method and returns the `Person` description using the three fields. I have not added getters and setters for the fields in the `Person` class to keep the class short and simple.

Listing 7-24. A Person Class That Implements the Serializable Interface

```
// Person.java
package com.jdojo.io;

import java.io.Serializable;

public class Person implements Serializable {
    private String name = "Unknown";
    private String gender = "Unknown";
    private double height = Double.NaN;

    public Person(String name, String gender, double height) {
        this.name = name;
        this.gender = gender;
        this.height = height;
    }

    @Override
    public String toString() {
        return "Name: " + this.name + ", Gender: " + this.gender
                + ", Height: " + this.height;
    }
}
```

Listing 7-25 demonstrates how to write `Person` objects to a `person.ser` file. The output displays the objects written to the file and the absolute path of the file, which may be different on your machine.

Listing 7-25. Serializing an Object

```
// PersonSerializationTest.java
package com.jdojo.io;

import java.io.File;
import java.io.FileOutputStream;
```

```
import java.io.IOException;
import java.io.ObjectOutputStream;

public class PersonSerializationTest {
    public static void main(String[] args) {
        // Create three Person objects
        Person john = new Person("John", "Male", 6.7);
        Person wally = new Person("Wally", "Male", 5.7);
        Person katrina = new Person("Katrina", "Female", 5.4);

        // The output file
        File fileObject = new File("person.ser");

        try (ObjectOutputStream oos
                = new ObjectOutputStream(new FileOutputStream(fileObject))) {

            // Write (or serialize) the objects to the object output stream
            oos.writeObject(john);
            oos.writeObject(wally);
            oos.writeObject(katrina);

            // Display the serialized objects on the standard output
            System.out.println(john);
            System.out.println(wally);
            System.out.println(katrina);

            // Print the output path
            System.out.println("Objects were written to "
                    + fileObject.getAbsolutePath());
        } catch (IOException e) {
            e.printStackTrace();
        }
    }
}
```

```
Name: John, Gender: Male, Height: 6.7
Name: Wally, Gender: Male, Height: 5.7
Name: Katrina, Gender: Female, Height: 5.4
Objects were written to C:\Java9LanguageFeatures\person.ser
```

Deserializing Objects

It is time to read the objects back from the `person.ser` file. Reading a serialized object is the opposite of serializing it. To deserialize an object, you need to perform the following steps:

1. Create an object input stream for the storage medium from which objects will be read.
2. Read the objects.
3. Close the object input stream.

Create an object of the ObjectInputStream class by using it as a decorator for another input stream that represents the storage medium where serialized objects were stored. For example, to read an object from a person.ser file, create an object input stream as follows:

```
// Create an object input stream to read objects from a file
ObjectInputStream ois = new ObjectInputStream(new FileInputStream("person.ser"));
```

To read objects from a ByteArrayInputStream, create an object output stream as follows:

```
// Create an object input stream to read objects from a byte array input stream
ObjectInputStream ois = new ObjectInputStream(Byte-Array-Input-Stream-Reference);
```

Use the readObject() method of the ObjectInputStream class to deserialize the object, like so:

```
// Read an object from the stream
Object obj = oos.readObject();
```

Make sure to call the readObject() method to read objects in the same order you called the writeObject() method to write objects. For example, if you wrote three pieces of information in the order object-1, a float, and object-2, you must read them in the same order: object-1, a float, and object-2.

Finally, close the object input stream as follows:

```
// Close the object input stream
ois.close();
```

Listing 7-26 demonstrates how to read objects from the person.ser file. Make sure that the person.ser file exists in your current directory. Otherwise, the program will print an error message with the expected location of this file.

Listing 7-26. Reading Objects from a File

```
// PersonDeserializationTest.java
package com.jdojo.io;

import java.io.File;
import java.io.FileInputStream;
import java.io.FileNotFoundException;
import java.io.IOException;
import java.io.ObjectInputStream;

public class PersonDeserializationTest {
    public static void main(String[] args) {
        // The input file
        File fileObject = new File("person.ser");

        try (ObjectInputStream ois
                = new ObjectInputStream(new FileInputStream(fileObject))) {

            // Read (or deserialize) the three objects
            Person john = (Person) ois.readObject();
            Person wally = (Person) ois.readObject();
            Person katrina = (Person) ois.readObject();
```

```
            // Let's display the objects that are read
            System.out.println(john);
            System.out.println(wally);
            System.out.println(katrina);

            // Print the input path
            System.out.println("Objects were read from "
                    + fileObject.getAbsolutePath());
        } catch (FileNotFoundException e) {
            FileUtil.printFileNotFoundMsg(fileObject.getPath());
        } catch (ClassNotFoundException | IOException e) {
            e.printStackTrace();
        }
    }
}
```

```
Name: John, Gender: Male, Height: 6.7
Name: Wally, Gender: Male, Height: 5.7
Name: Katrina, Gender: Female, Height: 5.4
Objects were read from C:\Java9LanguageFeatures\person.ser
```

Externalizable Object Serialization

In the previous sections, I showed you how to serialize and deserialize Serializable objects. In this section, I show you how to serialize and deserialize Externalizable objects. I have modified the Person class to implement the Externalizable interface. I named the new class PersonExt and it's shown in Listing 7-27.

Listing 7-27. A PersonExt Class That Implements the Externalizable Interface

```
// PersonExt.java
package com.jdojo.io;

import java.io.Externalizable;
import java.io.IOException;
import java.io.ObjectInput;
import java.io.ObjectOutput;

public class PersonExt implements Externalizable {
    private String name = "Unknown";
    private String gender = "Unknown";
    private double height = Double.NaN;

    // You must define a no-arg constructor for this class. It is
    // used to construct the object during deserialization process
    // before the readExternal() method of this class is called.
    public PersonExt() {
    }
```

```
    public PersonExt(String name, String gender, double height) {
        this.name = name;
        this.gender = gender;
        this.height = height;
    }

    // Override the toString() method to return the person description
    @Override
    public String toString() {
        return "Name: " + this.name + ", Gender: " + this.gender
                + ", Height: " + this.height;
    }

    @Override
    public void readExternal(ObjectInput in) throws IOException, ClassNotFoundException {
        // Read name and gender in the same order they were written
        this.name = in.readUTF();
        this.gender = in.readUTF();
    }

    @Override
    public void writeExternal(ObjectOutput out) throws IOException {
        // Write only the name and gender to the stream
        out.writeUTF(this.name);
        out.writeUTF(this.gender);
    }
}
```

Java will pass the reference of the object output stream and object input stream to the `writeExternal()` and `readExternal()` methods of the `PersonExt` class, respectively.

In the `writeExternal()` method, you write the `name` and `gender` fields to the object output stream. Note that the `height` field is not written to the object output stream. It means that you will not get the value of the `height` field back when you read the object from the stream in the `readExternal()` method. The `writeUTF()` method is used to write strings (`name` and `gender`) to the object output stream.

In the `readExternal()` method, you read the `name` and `gender` fields from the stream and set them in the `name` and `gender` instance variables.

Listing 7-28 and Listing 7-29 contain the serialization and deserialization logic for `PersonExt` objects.

Listing 7-28. Serializing PersonExt Objects That Implement the Externalizable Interface

```
// PersonExtSerializationTest.java
package com.jdojo.io;

import java.io.File;
import java.io.FileOutputStream;
import java.io.IOException;
import java.io.ObjectOutputStream;

public class PersonExtSerializationTest {
    public static void main(String[] args) {
        // Create three Person objects
        PersonExt john = new PersonExt("John", "Male", 6.7);
```

```
        PersonExt wally = new PersonExt("Wally", "Male", 5.7);
        PersonExt katrina = new PersonExt("Katrina", "Female", 5.4);

        // The output file
        File fileObject = new File("personext.ser");

        try (ObjectOutputStream oos = new ObjectOutputStream(
                new FileOutputStream(fileObject))) {

            // Write (or serialize) the objects to the object output stream
            oos.writeObject(john);
            oos.writeObject(wally);
            oos.writeObject(katrina);

            // Display the serialized objects on the standard output
            System.out.println(john);
            System.out.println(wally);
            System.out.println(katrina);

            // Print the output path
            System.out.println("Objects were written to "
                    + fileObject.getAbsolutePath());
        } catch (IOException e1) {
            e1.printStackTrace();
        }
    }
}
```

```
Name: John, Gender: Male, Height: 6.7
Name: Wally, Gender: Male, Height: 5.7
Name: Katrina, Gender: Female, Height: 5.4
Objects were written to C:\Java9LanguageFeatures\personext.ser
```

Listing 7-29. Deserializing PersonExt Objects That Implement the Externalizable Interface

```
// PersonExtDeserializationTest.java
package com.jdojo.io;

import java.io.File;
import java.io.FileInputStream;
import java.io.FileNotFoundException;
import java.io.IOException;
import java.io.ObjectInputStream;

public class PersonExtDeserializationTest {
    public static void main(String[] args) {
        // The input file
        File fileObject = new File("personext.ser");
```

```
        try (ObjectInputStream ois
                = new ObjectInputStream(new FileInputStream(fileObject))) {

            // Read (or deserialize) the three objects
            PersonExt john = (PersonExt) ois.readObject();
            PersonExt wally = (PersonExt) ois.readObject();
            PersonExt katrina = (PersonExt) ois.readObject();

            // Let's display the objects that are read
            System.out.println(john);
            System.out.println(wally);
            System.out.println(katrina);

            // Print the input path
            System.out.println("Objects were read from "
                    + fileObject.getAbsolutePath());
        } catch (FileNotFoundException e) {
            FileUtil.printFileNotFoundMsg(fileObject.getPath());
        } catch (ClassNotFoundException | IOException e) {
            e.printStackTrace();
        }
    }
}
```

```
Name: John, Gender: Male, Height: NaN
Name: Wally, Gender: Male, Height: NaN
Name: Katrina, Gender: Female, Height: NaN
Objects were read from C:\Java9LanguageFeatures\personext.ser
```

The output of Listing 7-29 demonstrates that the value of the height field is the default value (`Double.NaN`) after you deserialize a `PersonExt` object. Here are the steps to take to serialize and deserialize an object using `Externalizable` interface:

1. When you call the `writeObject()` method to write an `Externalizable` object, Java writes the identity of the object to the output stream, and calls the `writeExternal()` method of its class. You write the data related to the object to the output stream in the `writeExternal()` method. You have full control over what object-related data you write to the stream in this method. If you want to store some sensitive data, you may want to encrypt it before you write it to the stream and decrypt the data when you read it from the stream.

2. When you call the `readObject()` method to read an `Externalizable` object, Java reads the identity of the object from the stream. Note that for an `Externalizable` object, Java writes only the object's identity to the output stream, not any details about its class definition. It uses the object class's no-args constructor to create the object. This is the reason that you must provide a no-args constructor for an `Externalizable` object. It calls the object's `readExternal()` method, so you can populate object's fields values.

For a `Serializable` object, the JVM serializes only instance variables that are not declared as transient. I discuss serializing transient variables in the next section. For an `Externalizable` object, you have full control over what pieces of data are serialized.

Serializing transient Fields

The keyword transient is used to declare a class's field. As the literal meaning of the word "transient" implies, a transient field of a Serializable object is not serialized. The following code for an Employee class declares the ssn and salary fields as transient:

```
public class Employee implements Serializable {
    private String name;
    private String gender;
    private transient String ssn;
    private transient double salary;
}
```

The transient fields of a Serializable object are not serialized when you use the writeObject() method of the ObjectOutputStream class.

Note that if your object is Externalizable, not Serializable, declaring a field transient has no effect because you control what fields are serialized in the writeExternal() method. If you want transient fields of your class to be serialized, you need to declare the class Externalizable and write the transient fields to the output stream in the writeExternal() method of your class. I don't cover any examples of serializing transient fields because the logic is the same as shown in Listing 7-27, except that you declare some instance variables as transient and write them to the output stream in the writeExternal() method.

Advanced Object Serialization

The following sections discuss advanced serialization techniques. They are designed for experienced developers. If you are a beginner or an intermediate level developer, you may skip the following sections; you should, however, revisit them after you gain more experience with Java I/O.

Writing an Object Multiple Times to a Stream

The JVM keeps track of object references it writes to the object output stream using the writeObject() method. Suppose you have a PersonMutable object named john and you use an ObjectOutputStream object oos to write it to a file as follows:

```
PersonMutable john = new PersonMutable("John", "Male", 6.7);
oos.writeObject(john);
```

At this time, Java makes a note that the object john has been written to the stream. You may want to change some attributes of the john object and write it to the stream again as follows:

```
john.setName("John Jacobs");
john.setHeight(5.9);
oos.writeObject(john);
```

At this time, Java does not write the john object to the stream. Rather, the JVM back references it to the john object that you wrote the first time. That is, all changes made to the name and height fields are not written to the stream separately. Both writes for the john object share the same object in the written stream. When you read the objects back, both objects will have the same name, gender, and height.

An object is not written more than once to a stream to keep the size of the serialized objects smaller. Listing 7-30 shows this process. The `MultipleSerialization` class as shown in Listing 7-31, in its `serialize()` method, writes an object, changes object's attributes and serializes the same object again. It reads the objects in its `deserialize()` method. The output shows that Java did not write the changes made to the object when it wrote the object the second time.

Listing 7-30. A MutablePerson Class Whose Name and Height Can Be Changed

```
// MutablePerson.java
package com.jdojo.io;

import java.io.Serializable;

public class MutablePerson implements Serializable {
    private String name = "Unknown";
    private String gender = "Unknown";
    private double height = Double.NaN;

    public MutablePerson(String name, String gender, double height) {
        this.name = name;
        this.gender = gender;
        this.height = height;
    }

    public void setName(String name) {
        this.name = name;
    }

    public String getName() {
        return name;
    }

    public void setHeight(double height) {
        this.height = height;
    }

    public double getHeight() {
        return height;
    }

    @Override
    public String toString() {
        return "Name: " + this.name + ", Gender: " + this.gender
                + ", Height: " + this.height;
    }
}
```

Listing 7-31. Writing an Object Multiple Times to the Same Output Stream

```
// MultipleSerialization.java
package com.jdojo.io;

import java.io.File;
import java.io.FileInputStream;
import java.io.FileOutputStream;
import java.io.IOException;
import java.io.ObjectInputStream;
import java.io.ObjectOutputStream;

public class MultipleSerialization {
    public static void main(String[] args) {
        String fileName = "mutableperson.ser";

        // Write the same object twice to the stream
        serialize(fileName);

        System.out.println("--------------------------------------");

        // Read the two objects back
        deserialize(fileName);
    }

    public static void serialize(String fileName) {
        // Create a MutablePerson objects
        MutablePerson john = new MutablePerson("John", "Male", 6.7);

        File fileObject = new File(fileName);
        try (ObjectOutputStream oos
                = new ObjectOutputStream(new FileOutputStream(fileObject))) {

            // Let's display the objects we have serialized on the console
            System.out.println("Objects are written to "
                    + fileObject.getAbsolutePath());

            // Write the john object first time to the stream
            oos.writeObject(john);
            System.out.println(john); // Display what we wrote

            // Change john object's name and height
            john.setName("John Jacobs");
            john.setHeight(6.9);

            // Write john object again with changed name and height
            oos.writeObject(john);
            System.out.println(john); // display what we wrote again
        } catch (IOException e1) {
            e1.printStackTrace();
        }
    }
```

```
    public static void deserialize(String fileName) {
        // personmutable.ser file must exist in the current directory
        File fileObject = new File(fileName);

        try (ObjectInputStream ois
                = new ObjectInputStream(new FileInputStream(fileObject))) {

            // Read the two objects that were written in the serialize() method
            MutablePerson john1 = (MutablePerson) ois.readObject();
            MutablePerson john2 = (MutablePerson) ois.readObject();

            // Display the objects
            System.out.println("Objects are read from "
                    + fileObject.getAbsolutePath());
            System.out.println(john1);
            System.out.println(john2);
        } catch (IOException | ClassNotFoundException e) {
            e.printStackTrace();
        }
    }
}
```

```
Objects are written to C:\Java9LanguageFeatures\mutableperson.ser
Name: John, Gender: Male, Height: 6.7
Name: John Jacobs, Gender: Male, Height: 6.9
--------------------------------------
Objects are read from C:\Java9LanguageFeatures\mutableperson.ser
Name: John, Gender: Male, Height: 6.7
Name: John, Gender: Male, Height: 6.7
```

If you do not want Java to share an object reference, use the `writeUnshared()` method instead of the `writeObject()` method of the `ObjectOutputStream` class to serialize an object. An object written using the `writeUnshared()` method is not shared or back referenced by any subsequent call to the `writeObject()` method or the `writeUnshared()` method on the same object. You should read the object that was written using the `writeUnshared()` or the `readUnshared()` methods of the `ObjectInputStream` class. If you replace the call to `writeObject()` with `writeUnshared()` and the call to `readObject()` with `readUnshared()` in the `MutipleSerialization` class, you get the changed state of the object back when you read the object the second time.

You can control the serialization of a `Serializable` object in another way by defining a field named `serialPersistentFields`, which is an array of `ObjectStreamField` objects. This field must be declared `private`, `static`, and `final`. This field declares that all the fields mentioned in the array are serializable. Note that this is just the opposite of using the `transient` keyword with a field. When you use the `transient` keyword, you state that this field is not serializable, whereas by declaring a `serialPersistentFields` array, you state that these fields are serializable. The declaration of `serialPersistentFields` takes precedence over the declaration of transient fields in a class. For example, if you declare a field transient and include that field in the `serialPersistentFields` field, that field will be serialized. The following snippet of code shows how to declare a `serialPersistentFields` field in a `Person` class:

```
public class Person implements Serializable {
    private String name;
    private String gender;
    private double height;

    // Declare that only name and height fields are serializable
    private static final ObjectStreamField[] serialPersistentFields
        = {new ObjectStreamField("name", String.class),
           new ObjectStreamField("height", double.class)};
}
```

Class Evolution and Object Serialization

Your class may evolve (or change) over time. For example, you may remove an existing field or a method from a class. You may add new fields or methods to a class. During an object serialization, Java uses a number that is unique for the class of the object you serialize. This unique number is called the *serial version unique ID* (SUID). Java computes this number by computing the hash code of the class definition. If you change the class definition such as by adding new fields, the SUID for the class will change. When you serialize an object, Java also saves the class information to the stream. When you deserialize the object, Java computes the SUID for the class of the object being deserialized by reading the class definition from the stream. It compares the SUID computed from the stream with the SUID of the class loaded into the JVM.

If you change the definition of the class after you serialize an object of that class, the two numbers will not match and you will get a `java.io.InvalidClassException` during the deserialization process. If you never serialize the objects of your class or you never change your class definition after you serialize the objects and before you deserialize them, you do not need to worry about the SUID of your class. What should you do to make your objects deserialize properly, even if you change your class definition, after serializing objects of your class? You should declare a `private`, `static`, and `final` instance variable in your class that must be of the `long` type and named `serialVersionUID`.

```
public class MyClass {
    // Declare the SUID field.
    private static final long serialVersionUID = 801890L;

    // More code goes here
}
```

The `MyClass` uses 801890 as the value for `serialVersionUID`. This number was chosen arbitrarily. It does not matter what number you choose for this field. The JDK ships with a `serialver` tool that you can use to generate the value for the `serialVersionUID` field of your class. You can use this tool at the command prompt as follows:

```
serialver -classpath <class-path> <your-class-name>
```

When you run this tool with your class name, it prints the declaration of the `serialVersionUID` field for your class with the generated SUID for it. You just need to copy and paste that declaration into your class declaration.

■ **Tip** Suppose you have a class that does not contain a `serialVersionUID` field and you have serialized its object. If you change your class and try to deserialize the object, the Java runtime will print an error message with the expected `serialVersionUID`. You need to add the `serialVersionUID` field in your class with the same value and try deserializing the objects.

Stopping Serialization

How do you stop the serialization of objects of your class? Not implementing the `Serializable` interface in your class seems to be an obvious answer. However, it is not a valid answer in all situations. For example, if you inherit your class from an existing class that implements the `Serializable` interface, your class implements the `Serializable` interface implicitly. This makes your class automatically serializable. To stop objects of your class from being serialized all the time, you can add the `writeObject()` and `readObject()` methods in your class. These methods should simply throw an exception.

Listing 7-32 contains partial code for a class named `NotSerializable`. The class implements the `Serializable` interface and still it is not serializable because it throws an exception in the `readObject()` and `writeObject()` methods.

Listing 7-32. Stopping a Class from Serializing

```
// NotSerializable.java
package com.jdojo.io;

import java.io.IOException;
import java.io.ObjectInputStream;
import java.io.ObjectOutputStream;
import java.io.Serializable;

public class NotSerializable implements Serializable {
    // Instance variables go here

    private void readObject(ObjectInputStream ois)
            throws IOException, ClassNotFoundException {
        // Throw an exception
        throw new IOException("Not meant for serialization!!!");
    }

    private void writeObject(ObjectOutputStream os) throws IOException {
        // Throw an exception
        throw new IOException("Not meant for serialization!!!");
    }

    // Other code for the class goes here
}
```

Readers and Writers

Input and output streams are byte-based streams. In this section, I discuss readers and writers, which are character-based streams. A reader is used to read character-based data from a data source. A writer is used to write character-based data to a data sink.

Figure 7-8 and Figure 7-9 show some classes, and the relationship between them, for the `Reader` and `Writer` stream families. Recall that the input and output stream class names end with the words "InputStream" and "OutputStream," respectively. The `Reader` and `Writer` class names end with the words "Reader" and "Writer," respectively.

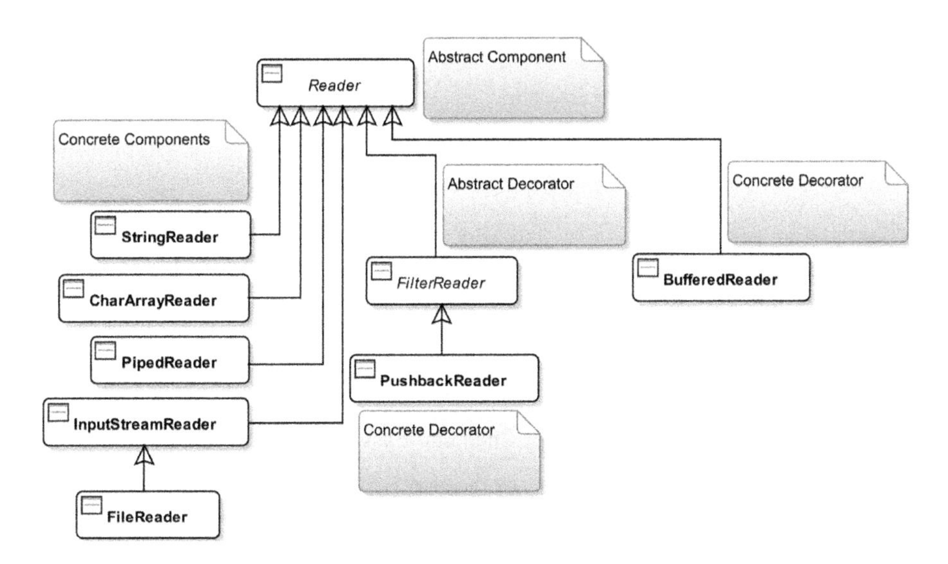

Figure 7-8. *Commonly used classes for Reader streams compared with the decorator pattern*

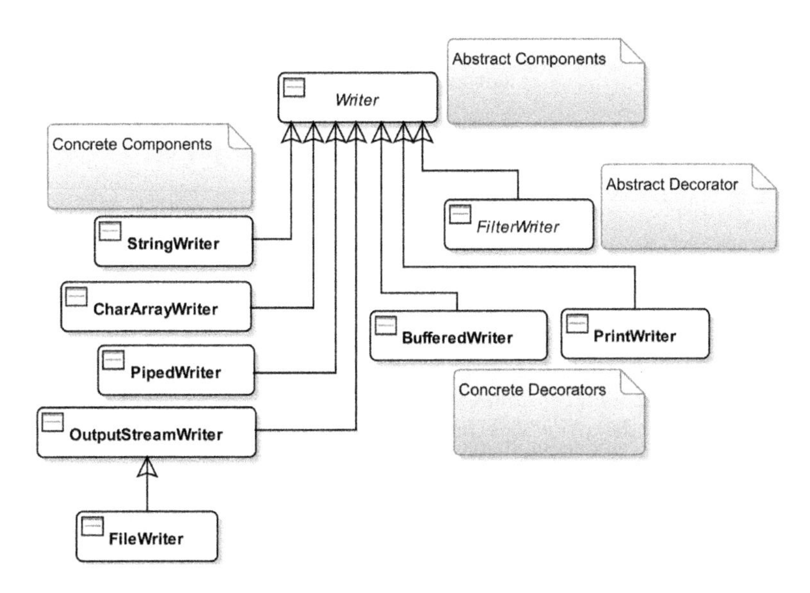

Figure 7-9. *Commonly used classes for Writer streams compared with the decorator pattern*

Table 7-4 and Table 7-5 compare classes in byte-based and character-based input/output streams.

Table 7-4. *Comparing Classes in Byte-based and Character-based Input Streams*

Byte-Based Input Stream Class	Character-Based Input Stream Class
`InputStream`	`Reader`
`ByteArrayInputStream`	`CharArrayReader`
`StringBufferInputStream`	`StringReader`
`PipedInputStream`	`PipedReader`
`FileInputStream`	`FileReader`
No corresponding class	`InputStreamReader`
`FilterInputStream`	`FilterReader`
`BufferedInputStream`	`BufferedReader`
`PushbackInputStream`	`PushbackReader`
`DataInputStream`	No corresponding class
`ObjectInputStream`	No corresponding class

Table 7-5. *Comparing Classes from Byte-Based Output Streams and Character-Based Output Streams*

Byte-Based Output Stream Class	Character-Based Output Stream Class
`OutputStream`	`Writer`
`ByteArrayOutputStream`	`CharArrayWriter`
No corresponding class	`StringWriter`
`PipedOutputStream`	`PipedWriter`
`FileOutputStream`	`FileWriter`
No corresponding class	`OutputStreamWriter`
`FilterOutputStream`	`FilterWriter`
`BufferedOutputStream`	`BufferedWriter`
`DataOutputStream`	No corresponding class
`ObjectOutputStream`	No corresponding class
`PrintStream`	`PrintWriter`

Some classes in the byte-based input/output streams do not have the corresponding character-based classes and vice versa. For example, reading and writing primitive data and objects are always byte-based; therefore, you do not have any classes in the reader/writer class family corresponding to the data/object input/output streams.

I discussed how to use the byte-based input/output classes in detail in the previous sections. You will find the classes in the reader/writer and the input/output categories similar. They are also based on the decorator pattern.

In the reader class hierarchy, BufferedReader, which is a concrete decorator, is directly inherited from the Reader class instead of the abstract decorator FilterReader class. In the writer class hierarchy, all concrete decorators have been inherited from the Writer class instead of the FilterWriter. No concrete decorator inherits the FilterWriter class.

The two classes, InputStreamReader and OutputStreamWriter, in the reader/writer class family provide the bridge between the byte-based and character-based streams. If you have an instance of InputStream and you want to get a Reader from it, you can get that by using the InputStreamReader class. That is, you need to use the InputStreamReader class if you have a stream that supplies bytes and you want to read characters by getting those bytes decoded into characters for you. For example, if you have an InputStream object called iso, and you want to get a Reader object instance, you can do so as follows:

```
// Create a Reader object from an InputStream object using the platform default encoding
Reader reader = new InputStreamReader(iso);
```

If you know the encoding used in the byte-based stream, you can specify it while creating a Reader object as follows:

```
// Create a Reader object from an InputStream using the "US-ASCII" encoding
Reader reader = new InputStreamReader(iso, "US-ASCII");
```

Similarly, you can create a Writer object to spit out characters from a bytes-based output stream as follows, assuming that oso is an OutputStream object:

```
// Create a Writer object from OutputStream using the platform default encoding
Writer writer = new OutputStreamWriter(oso);

// Create a Writer object from OutputStream using the "US-ASCII" encoding
Writer writer = new OutputStreamWriter(oso, "US-ASCII");
```

You do not have to write only a character at a time or a character array when using a writer. It has methods that let you write a String and a CharSequence object.

Let's write another stanza from the poem *Lucy* by William Wordsworth to a file and read it back into the program. This time, you will use a BufferedWriter to write the text and a BufferedReader to read the text back. Here are the four lines of text in the stanza:

```
And now we reach'd the orchard-plot;
And, as we climb'd the hill,
The sinking moon to Lucy's cot
Came near and nearer still.
```

The text is saved in a luci4.txt file in the current directory. Listing 7-33 illustrates how to use a Writer object to write the text to this file. You may get different output when you run the program because it prints the path of the output file, which depends on the current working directory.

Listing 7-33. Using a Writer Object to Write Text to a File

```
// FileWritingWithWriter.java
package com.jdojo.io;

import java.io.BufferedWriter;
import java.io.File;
import java.io.FileNotFoundException;
```

```
import java.io.FileWriter;
import java.io.IOException;

public class FileWritingWithWriter {
    public static void main(String[] args) {
        // The output file
        String destFile = "luci4.txt";

        try (BufferedWriter bw = new BufferedWriter(new FileWriter(destFile))) {
            // Write the text to the writer
            bw.append("And now we reach'd the orchard-plot;");
            bw.newLine();
            bw.append("And, as we climb'd the hill,");
            bw.newLine();
            bw.append("The sinking moon to Lucy's cot");
            bw.newLine();
            bw.append("Came near and nearer still.");

            // Flush the written text
            bw.flush();

            System.out.println("Text was written to "
                    + (new File(destFile)).getAbsolutePath());
        } catch (FileNotFoundException e1) {
            FileUtil.printFileNotFoundMsg(destFile);
        } catch (IOException e2) {
            e2.printStackTrace();
        }
    }
}
```

```
Text was written to C:\Java9LanguageFeatures\luci4.txt
```

If you compare the code in this listing to any other listings that write data to a stream, you will not find any basic differences. The differences lie only in using classes to construct the output stream. In this case, you used the `BufferedWriter` and `FileWriter` classes to construct a `Writer` object. You used the `append()` method of the `Writer` class to write the strings to the file. You can use the `write()` method or the `append()` method to write a string using a `Writer` object. However, the `append()` method supports writing any `CharSequence` object to the stream, whereas the `write()` method supports writing only characters or a string. The `BufferedWriter` class provides a `newLine()` method to write a platform-specific new line to the output stream.

How would you read the text written to the file `luci4.txt` using a `Reader` object? It's simple. Create a `BufferedReader` object by wrapping a `FileReader` object and read one line of text at a time using its `readLine()` method. The `readLine()` method considers a linefeed (`'\n'`), a carriage return (`'\r'`), and a carriage return immediately followed by a linefeed as a line terminator. It returns the text of the line excluding the line terminator. It returns `null` when the end of the stream is reached. The following is the snippet of code to read the text from the `luci4.txt` file. You can write the full program as an exercise.

```
String srcFile = "luci4.txt";
BufferedReader br = new BufferedReader(new FileReader(srcFile));
String text = null;

while ((text = br.readLine()) != null) {
   System.out.println(text);
}

br.close();
```

Converting a byte-based stream to a character-based stream is straightforward. If you have an `InputStream` object, you can get a `Reader` object by wrapping it inside an `InputStreamReader` object, like so:

```
InputStream is = /* Create your InputStream object here */
Reader reader = new InputStreamReader(is);
```

If you want to construct a `BufferedReader` object from an `InputStream` object, you can do that as follows:

```
InputStream is = /* Create your InputStream object here */
BufferedReader br = new BufferedReader(new InputStreamReader(is));
```

You can construct a `Writer` object from an `OutputStream` object as follows:

```
OutputStream os = /* Create your OutputStream object here */
Writer writer = new OutputStreamWriter(os);
```

Custom Input/Output Streams

Can you have your own I/O classes? The answer is yes. How difficult is it to have your own I/O classes? It is not that difficult if you understand the decorator pattern. Having your own I/O class is just a matter of adding a concrete decorator class in the I/O class hierarchy. In this section, you add a new reader class named `LowerCaseReader`. It will read characters from a character-based stream and convert all characters to lowercase.

The `LowerCaseReader` class is a concrete decorator class in the `Reader` class family. It should inherit from the `FilterReader` class. It needs to provide a constructor that will accept a `Reader` object.

```
public class LowerCaseReader extends FilterReader {
    public LowerCaseReader(Reader in) {
        // Code for the constructor goes here
    }

    // More code goes here
}
```

There are two versions of the `read()` method in the `FilterReader` class to read characters from a character-based stream. You need to override just one version of the `read()` method as follows. All other versions of the `read()` method delegate the reading job to this one.

```
public class LowerCaseReader extends FilterReader {
    public LowerCaseReader(Reader in) {
        // Code for the constructor goes here
    }

    @Override
    public int read(char[] cbuf, int off, int len) throws IOException {
        // Code goes here
    }
}
```

That is all it takes to have your own reader class. You can provide additional methods in your class, if needed. For example, you may want to have a `readLine()` method that will read a line in lowercase. Alternatively, you can also use the `readLine()` method of the `BufferedReader` class by wrapping an object of `LowerCaseReader` in a `BufferedReader` object. Using the new class is the same as using any other reader class. You can wrap a concrete reader component such as a `FileReader` or a concrete decorator such as a `BufferedReader` inside a `LowerCaseReader` object. Alternatively, you can wrap a `LowerCaseReader` object inside any other concrete reader decorator such as a `BufferedReader`. Listing 7-34 contains the complete code for the `LowerCaseReader` class.

Listing 7-34. A Custom Java I/O Reader Class Named LowerCaseReader

```
// LowerCaseReader.java
package com.jdojo.io;

import java.io.Reader;
import java.io.FilterReader;
import java.io.IOException;

public class LowerCaseReader extends FilterReader {
    public LowerCaseReader(Reader in) {
        super(in);
    }

    @Override
    public int read(char[] cbuf, int off, int len) throws IOException {
        int count = super.read(cbuf, off, len);
        if (count != -1) {
            // Convert all read characters to lowercase
            int limit = off + count;
            for (int i = off; i < limit; i++) {
                cbuf[i] = Character.toLowerCase(cbuf[i]);
            }
        }
        return count;
    }
}
```

Listing 7-35 shows how to use your new class. It reads from the file `luci4.txt`. It reads the file twice: the first time by using a `LowerCaseReader` object and the second time by wrapping a `LowerCaseReader` object inside a `BufferedReader` object. Note that while reading the `licu4.txt` file the second time, you are taking advantage of the `readLine()` method of the `BufferedReader` class. The `luci4.txt` file should exist in your current working directory. Otherwise, you will get an error when you run the test program.

Listing 7-35. Testing the Custom Reader Class, LowerCaseReader

```
// LowerCaseReaderTest.java
package com.jdojo.io;

import java.io.FileReader;
import java.io.BufferedReader;
import java.io.FileNotFoundException;
import java.io.IOException;

public class LowerCaseReaderTest {
    public static void main(String[] args) {
        String fileName = "luci4.txt";
        try (LowerCaseReader lcr
                = new LowerCaseReader(new FileReader(fileName))) {
            System.out.println("Reading luci4.txt using LowerCaseReader:");

            int c;
            while ((c = lcr.read()) != -1) {
                System.out.print((char) c);
            }
        } catch (FileNotFoundException e) {
            FileUtil.printFileNotFoundMsg(fileName);
        } catch (IOException e) {
            e.printStackTrace();
        }

        try (BufferedReader br = new BufferedReader(
                new LowerCaseReader(new FileReader(fileName)))) {

            System.out.println("\n\nReading luci4.txt using "
                    + "LowerCaseReader and BufferedReader:");

            String str;
            while ((str = br.readLine()) != null) {
                System.out.println(str);
            }
        } catch (FileNotFoundException e) {
            FileUtil.printFileNotFoundMsg(fileName);
        } catch (IOException e) {
            e.printStackTrace();
        }
    }
}
```

```
Reading luci4.txt using LowerCaseReader:
And now we reach'd the orchard-plot;
And, as we climb'd the hill,
The sinking moon to Lucy's cot
Came near and nearer still.

Reading luci4.txt using LowerCaseReader and BufferedReader:
and now we reach'd the orchard-plot;
and, as we climb'd the hill,
the sinking moon to lucy's cot
came near and nearer still.
```

Random Access Files

A FileInputStream lets you read data from a file, whereas a FileOutputStream lets you write data to a file. A random access file is a combination of both. Using a random access file, you can read from a file as well as write to the file. Reading and writing using the file input and output streams are sequential processes. Using a random access file, you can read or write at any position within the file, hence the name random access.

An object of the RandomAccessFile class facilitates the random file access. It lets you read/write bytes and all primitive types values from/to a file. It also lets you work with strings using its readUTF() and writeUTF() methods. The RandomAccessFile class is not in the class hierarchy of the InputStream and OutputStream classes.

A random access file can be created in four different access modes. You need to provide one of the access modes in its constructor. The access mode value is a string. They are listed as follows:

- "r": The file is opened in a read-only mode. You will receive an IOException if you attempt to write to the file in this mode.
- "rw": The file is opened in a read-write mode. The file is created if it does not exist.
- "rws": The same as the "rw" mode, except that any modifications to the file's content and its metadata are written to the storage device immediately.
- "rwd": The same as the "rw" mode, except that any modifications to the file's content are written to the storage device immediately.

You create an instance of the RandomAccessFile class by specifying the file name and the access mode as shown:

```
RandomAccessFile raf = new RandomAccessFile("randomtest.txt", "rw");
```

A random access file has a file pointer that is advanced when you read data from it or write data to it. The file pointer is a kind of cursor where your next read or write will start. Its value indicates the distance of the cursor from the beginning of the file in byes. You can get the value of file pointer by using its getFilePointer() method. When you create an object of the RandomAccessFile class, the file pointer is set to zero, which indicates the beginning of the file. You can set the file pointer at a specific location in the file using the seek() method.

The length() method of a RandomAccessFile returns the current length of the file. You can extend or truncate a file by using its setLength() method. If you extend a file using this method, the contents of the extended portion of the file are not defined.

Reading from and writing to a random access file is performed the same way you have been reading/writing from/to any input and output streams. Listing 7-36 demonstrates the use of a random access file. When you run this program, it writes two things to a file: the file read counter, which keeps track of how many times a file has been read using this program, and a text message of "Hello World!". The program increments the counter value in the file every time it reads the file. The counter value keeps incrementing when you run this program repeatedly. You may get different output every time you run this program

Listing 7-36. Reading and Writing Files Using a RandomAccessFile Object

```
// RandomAccessFileReadWrite.java
package com.jdojo.io;

import java.io.File;
import java.io.IOException;
import java.io.RandomAccessFile;

public class RandomAccessFileReadWrite {
    public static void main(String[] args) throws IOException {
        String fileName = "randomaccessfile.txt";
        File fileObject = new File(fileName);

        if (!fileObject.exists()) {
            initialWrite(fileName);
        }

        // Read the file twice
        readFile(fileName);
        readFile(fileName);
    }

    public static void readFile(String fileName) throws IOException {
        // Open the file in read-write mode
        try (RandomAccessFile raf = new RandomAccessFile(fileName, "rw")) {
            int counter = raf.readInt();
            String msg = raf.readUTF();

            System.out.println("File Read Counter: " + counter);
            System.out.println("File Text: " + msg);
            System.out.println("----------------------------");

            // Increment the file read counter by 1
            incrementReadCounter(raf);
        }
    }

    public static void incrementReadCounter(RandomAccessFile raf) throws IOException {
        // Read the current file pointer position so that we can restore it at the end
        long currentPosition = raf.getFilePointer();

        // Set the file pointer in the beginning
        raf.seek(0);
```

```
        // Read the counter and increment it by 1
        int counter = raf.readInt();
        counter++;

        // Set the file pointer to zero again to overwrite the value of the counter
        raf.seek(0);
        raf.writeInt(counter);

        // Restore the file pointer
        raf.seek(currentPosition);
    }

    public static void initialWrite(String fileName) throws IOException {
        // Write the file read counter as zero. Open the file in read-write mode.
        try (RandomAccessFile raf = new RandomAccessFile(fileName, "rw")) {
            // Write the file read counter as zero
            raf.writeInt(0);

            // Write a message
            raf.writeUTF("Hello world!");
        }
    }
}
```

```
File Read Counter: 0
File Text: Hello world!
----------------------------
File Read Counter: 1
File Text: Hello world!
----------------------------
```

Copying the Contents of a File

After you learn about input and output streams, it is simple to write code that copies the contents of a file to another file. You need to use the byte-based input and output streams (`InputStream` and `OutputStream` objects) so that your file copy program will work on all kinds of files. The main logic in copying a file is to keep reading from the input stream until the end of file and keep writing to the output stream as data is read from the input stream. The following snippet of code shows this file-copy logic:

```
// Copy the contents of a file
int count = -1;
byte[] buffer = new byte[1024];
while ((count = in.read(buffer)) != -1) {
    out.write(buffer, 0, count);
}
```

Starting from JDK9, you can copy the contents of a file to another file using the `transferTo(OutputStream out)` method of the `InputStream` class. The following snippet of code copies the contents of the `luci1.txt` file to the `luci1_copy.txt` file. The exception handling logic is not shown.

```
FileInputStream fis = new FileInputStream("luci1.txt");
FileOutputStream fos = new FileOutputStream("luci1_copy.txt");
fis.transferTo(fos);
fos.close();
fis.close();
```

■ **Tip** The file-copy logic copies only the file's contents. You will have to write logic to copy a file's attributes. The NIO 2.0 API, covered in Chapter 10, provides a `copy()` method in the `java.nio.file.Files` class to copy the contents and attributes of a file to another file. Use the `Files.copy()` method to copy a file.

Standard Input/Output/Error Streams

A standard input device is a device defined and controlled by the operating system from where your Java program may receive inputs. Similarly, the standard output and error are other operating system-defined (and controlled) devices where your program can send outputs. Typically, a keyboard is a standard input device, and a monitor acts as a standard output and a standard error device. Figure 7-10 depicts the interaction between the standard input, output, and error devices, and a Java program.

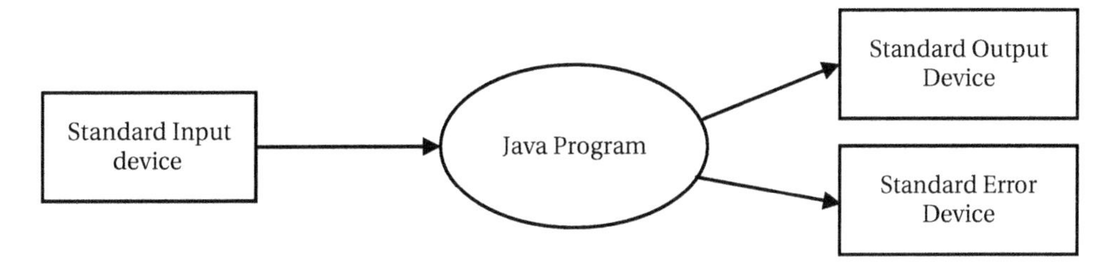

Figure 7-10. *Interaction between a Java program and standard input, output, and error devices*

What happens when you use the following statement to print a message?

```
System.out.println("This message goes to the standard output device!");
```

Typically, your message is printed on the console. In this case, the monitor is the standard output device and the Java program lets you send some data to the standard output device using a high-level `println()` method call. You saw a similar kind of `println()` method call in the previous section when you used the `PrintStream` class that is a concrete decorator class in the `OutputStream` class family. Java makes interacting with a standard output device on a computer easier. It creates an object of the `PrintStream` class and gives you access to it through a public static variable named `out` in the `System` class. Look at the code for the `System` class; it declares three public static variables (one for each device: standard input, output, and error) as follows:

```
public class System {
    public static PrintStream out; // the standard output
    public static InputStream in;  // the standard input
    public static PrintStream err; // the standard error

    // More code for the System class goes here
}
```

The JVM initializes the three variables to appropriate values. You can use the System.out and System.err object references wherever you can use an OutputStream object. You can use the System.in object wherever you can use an InputStream object.

Java lets you use these three objects in the System class in one more way. If you do not want the three objects to represent the standard input, output, and error devices, you can supply your own devices; Java will redirect the data flow to/from these objects to your devices.

Suppose, whenever you call the System.out.println() method to print a message on the console, you want to send all messages to a file instead. You can do so very easily. After all, System.out is just a PrintStream object and you know how to create a PrintStream object using a FileOutputStream object (refer to Listing 7-20) to write to a file. The System class provides three static setter methods, setOut(), setIn(), and setErr(), to replace these three standard devices with your own devices. To redirect all standard output to a file, you need to call the setOut() method by passing a PrintStream object that represents your file. If you want to redirect the output to a file named stdout.txt in your current directory, you do so by executing the following piece of code:

```
// Redirect all standard outputs to the stdout.txt file
PrintStream ps = new PrintStream(new FileOutputStream("stdout.txt"));
System.setOut(ps);
```

Listing 7-37 demonstrates how to redirect the standard output to a file. You may get different output on the console. After you run this program, you will see the following two messages in the stdout.txt file in your current working directory:

```
Hello world!
Java I/O is cool!
```

You may get different output when you run the program, as it prints the path to the stdout.txt file using your current working directory.

Listing 7-37. Redirecting Standard Outputs to a File

```
// CustomStdOut.java
package com.jdojo.io;

import java.io.PrintStream;
import java.io.FileOutputStream;
import java.io.File;

public class CustomStdOut {
    public static void main(String[] args) throws Exception {
        // Create a PrintStream for file stdout.txt
        File outFile = new File("stdout.txt");
        PrintStream ps = new PrintStream(new FileOutputStream(outFile));

        //Print a message on console
        System.out.println("Messages will be redirected to "
                + outFile.getAbsolutePath());

        // Set the standard out to the file
        System.setOut(ps);
```

```
        // The following messages will be sent to the stdout.txt file
        System.out.println("Hello world!");
        System.out.println("Java I/O is cool!");
    }
}
```

```
Messages will be redirected to C:\Java9LanguageFeatures\stdout.txt
```

Generally, you use System.out.println() calls to log debugging messages. Suppose you have been using this statement all over your application and it is time to deploy your application to production. If you do not take out the debugging code from your program, it will keep printing messages on the user's console. You do not have time to go through all your code to remove the debugging code. Can you think of an easy solution? There is a simple solution to swallow all your debugging messages. You can redirect your debugging messages to a file as you did in Listing 7-37. Another solution is to create your own concrete component class in the OutputStream class family. Let's call the new class DummyStandardOutput, as shown in Listing 7-38.

Listing 7-38. A Dummy Output Stream Class That Will Swallow All Written Data

```
// DummyStandardOutput.java
package com.jdojo.io;

import java.io.OutputStream;
import java.io.IOException;

public class DummyStandardOutput extends OutputStream {
    @Override
    public void write(int b) throws IOException {
        // Do not do anything. Swallow whatever is written
    }
}
```

You need to inherit the DummyStandardOutput class from the OutputStream class. The only code you have to write is to override the write(int b) method and do not do anything in this method. Then, create a PrintStream object by wrapping an object of the new class and set it as the standard output using the System.setOut() method shown in Listing 7-39. If you do not want to go for a new class, you can use an anonymous class to achieve the same result, as follows:

```
System.setOut(new PrintStream(new OutputStream() {
            @Override
            public void write(int b) {
                // Do nothing
            }
        }));
```

Listing 7-39. Swallowing All Data Sent to the Standard Output

```
// SwallowOutput.java
package com.jdojo.io;

import java.io.PrintStream;

public class SwallowOutput {
    public static void main(String[] args) {
        PrintStream ps = new PrintStream(new DummyStandardOutput());

        // Set the dummy standard output
        System.setOut(ps);

        // The following messages are not going anywhere
        System.out.println("Hello world!");
        System.out.println("Is someone listening?");
        System.out.println("No. We are all taking a nap!!!");
    }
}
```

```
(No output will be printed.)
```

You can use the `System.in` object to read data from a standard input device (usually a keyboard). You can also set the `System.in` object to read from any other `InputStream` object of your choice, such as a file. You can use the `read()` method of the `InputStream` class to read bytes from this stream. `System.in.read()` reads a byte at a time from the keyboard. Note that the `read()` method of the `InputStream` class blocks until data is available for reading. When a user enters data and presses the Enter key, the entered data becomes available, and the `read()` method returns one byte of data at a time. The last byte read will represent a new line character. When you read a new line character from the input device, you should stop further reading or the `read()` call will block until the user enters more data and presses the Enter key again. Listing 7-40 illustrates how to read data entered using the keyboard.

Listing 7-40. Reading from the Standard Input Device

```
// EchoStdin.java
package com.jdojo.io;

import java.io.IOException;

public class EchoStdin {
    public static void main(String[] args) throws IOException {
        // Prompt the user to type a message
        System.out.print("Please type a message and press enter: ");

        // Display whatever user types in
        int c;
        while ((c = System.in.read()) != '\n') {
            System.out.print((char) c);
        }
    }
}
```

Since System.in is an instance of InputStream, you can use any concrete decorator to read data from the keyboard; for example, you can create a BufferedReader object and read data from the keyboard one line at a time as a string. Listing 7-41 illustrates how to use the System.in object with a BufferedReader. Note that this is the kind of situation when you will need to use the InputStreamReader class to get a character-based stream (BufferedReader) from a byte-based stream (System.in). The program keeps prompting the user to enter some text until the user enters Q or q to quit the program.

Listing 7-41. Using System.in with a BufferedReader

```
// EchoBufferedStdin.java
package com.jdojo.io;

import java.io.BufferedReader;
import java.io.InputStreamReader;
import java.io.IOException;

public class EchoBufferedStdin {
    public static void main(String[] args) throws IOException {
        // Get a BufferedReader, which wraps the System.in object. Note the use
        // of InputStreamReader, the bridge class between the byte-based and
        // the character-based stream
        BufferedReader br = new BufferedReader(new InputStreamReader(System.in));

        String text;
        while (true) {
            // Prompt user to type some text
            System.out.print("Please type a message (Q/q to quit) "
                    + "and press enter: ");

            // Read the text
            text = br.readLine();
            if (text.equalsIgnoreCase("q")) {
                System.out.println("You have decided to exit the program");
                break;
            } else {
                System.out.println("You typed: " + text);
            }
        }
    }
}
```

If you want your standard input to come from a file, you have to create an input stream object to represent that file and set that object using the System.setIn() method as follows:

```
FileInputStream fis = new FileInputStream("stdin.txt");
System.setIn(fis); // Now System.in.read() will read from stdin.txt file
```

The standard error device (generally the console) is used to display error messages. Its use in your program is the same as a standard output device. Instead of System.out for a standard output device, Java provides another PrintStream object called System.err. You use it as follows:

```
System.err.println("This is an error message.");
```

Console and Scanner Classes

Although Java gives you three objects to represent the standard input, output, and error devices, it is not easy to use them for reading numbers from the standard input. The purpose of the Console class is to make the interaction between a Java program and the console easier. I discuss the Console class in this section. I also discuss the Scanner class used for parsing the text read from the console.

The Console class is a utility class in the java.io package that gives access to the system console, if any, associated with the JVM. The console is not guaranteed to be accessible in a Java program on all machines. For example, if your Java program runs as a service, no console will be associated to the JVM and you will not have access to it either. You get the instance of the Console class by using the static console() method of the System class as follows:

```
Console console = System.console();
if (console != null) {
    console.printf("Console is available.");
}
```

The Console class contains a printf() method that displays formatted string on the console. You also have a printf() method in the PrintStream class to write the formatted data. Refer to Chapter 17 of the first volume of this series for more details on using the printf() method and how to use the Formatter class to format text, numbers, and dates.

Listing 7-42 illustrates how to use the Console class. If the console is not available, it prints a message and exits. If you run this program using an IDE such as NetBeans, the console may not be available. Try to run this program using a command prompt. The program prompts the user to enter a user name and a password. If the user enters password *letmein*, the program prints a message. Otherwise, it prints that the password is not valid. The program uses the readLine() method to read a line of text from the console and the readPassword() method to read the password. When the user enters a password, it is not visible; the program receives it in a character array.

Listing 7-42. Using the Console Class to Enter a User Name and Password

```
// ConsoleLogin.java
package com.jdojo.io;

import java.io.Console;

public class ConsoleLogin {
    public static void main(String[] args) {
        Console console = System.console();
        if (console != null) {
            console.printf("Console is available.%n");
        } else {
            System.out.println("Console is not available.%n");
            return; // A console is not available
        }

        String userName = console.readLine("User Name: ");
        char[] passChars = console.readPassword("Password: ");
        String passString = new String(passChars);
        if (passString.equals("letmein")) {
            console.printf("Hello %s", userName);
```

```
        } else {
            console.printf("Invalid password");
        }
    }
}
```

If you want to read numbers from the standard input, you have to read it as a string and parse it to a number. The Scanner class in java.util package reads and parses text, based on a pattern, into primitive types and strings. The text source can be an InputStream, a file, a String object, or a Readable object. You can use a Scanner to read primitive type values from the standard input System.in. It contains many methods, which are named liked hasNextXxx() and nextXxx(), where Xxx is a data type, such as int, double, etc. The hasNextXxx() method checks if the next token from the source can be interpreted as a value of the Xxx type. The nextXxx() method returns a value of a particular data type.

Listing 7-43 illustrates how to use the Scanner class by building a trivial calculator to perform addition, subtraction, multiplication, and division.

Listing 7-43. Using the Scanner Class to Read Inputs from the Standard Input

```
// Calculator.java
package com.jdojo.io;

import java.util.Scanner;

public class Calculator {
    public static void main(String[] args) {
        // Read three tokens from the console: operand-1 operation operand-2
        String msg = "You can evaluate an arithmetic expression.\n"
                + "Expression must be in the form: a op b\n"
                + "a and b are two numbers and op is +, -, * or /."
                + "\nPlease enter an expression and press Enter: ";
        System.out.print(msg);

        // Build a scanner for the standard input
        Scanner scanner = new Scanner(System.in);

        try {
            double n1 = scanner.nextDouble();
            String operation = scanner.next();
            double n2 = scanner.nextDouble();

            double result = calculate(n1, n2, operation);
            System.out.printf("%s %s %s = %.2f%n", n1,
                    operation, n2, result);
        } catch (Exception e) {
            System.out.println("An invalid expression.");
        }
    }

    public static double calculate(double op1, double op2, String operation) {
        switch (operation) {
            case "+":
                return op1 + op2;
```

```
                case "-":
                    return op1 - op2;
                case "*":
                    return op1 * op2;
                case "/":
                    return op1 / op2;
            }

            return Double.NaN;
        }
    }
```

```
You can evaluate an arithmetic expression.
Expression must be in the form: a op b
a and b are two numbers and op is +, -, * or /.
Please enter an expression and press Enter: 10 + 19
10.0 + 19.0 = 29.00
```

StringTokenizer and StreamTokenizer

Java has some utility classes that let you break a string into parts called tokens. A token in this context is a part of the string. You define the sequence of characters that are considered tokens by defining delimiter characters. Suppose you have a string "This is a test, which is simple". If you define a space as a delimiter, this string contains seven tokens:

- This
- is
- a
- test,
- which
- is
- simple

If you define a comma as a delimiter, the same string contains two tokens:

- This is a test
- which is simple

The `StringTokenizer` class is in the `java.util` package. The `StreamTokenizer` class is in the `java.io` package. A `StringTokenizer` lets you break a string into tokens, whereas a `StreamTokenizer` gives you access to the tokens in a character-based stream.

A StringTokenizer object lets you break a string into tokens based on your definition of delimiters. It returns one token at a time. You also have the ability to change the delimiter anytime. You can create a StringTokenizer by specifying the string and accepting the default delimiters, which are a space, a tab, a new line, a carriage return, and a line-feed character (" \t\n\r\f") as follows:

```
// Create a string tokenizer
StringTokenizer st = new StringTokenizer("here is my string");
```

You can specify your own delimiters when you create a StringTokenizer as follows:

```
// Have a space, a comma, and a semi-colon as delimiters
String delimiters = " ,;";
StringTokenizer st = new StringTokenizer("my text...", delimiters);
```

You can use the hasMoreTokens() method to check if you have more tokens and the nextToken() method to get the next token from the string.

You can also use the split() method of the String class to split a string into tokens based on delimiters. The split() method accepts a regular expression as a delimiter. Listing 7-44 illustrates how to use the StringTokenizer and the split() method of the String class.

Listing 7-44. Breaking a String into Tokens Using a StringTokenizer and the String.split() Method

```
// StringTokens.java
package com.jdojo.io;

import java.util.StringTokenizer;

public class StringTokens {
    public static void main(String[] args) {
        String str = "This is a test, which is simple";
        String delimiters = " ,"; // a space and a comma
        StringTokenizer st = new StringTokenizer(str, delimiters);

        System.out.println("Tokens using a StringTokenizer:");
        while (st.hasMoreTokens()) {
            String token = st.nextToken();
            System.out.println(token);
        }

        // Split the same string using String.split() method
        System.out.println("\nTokens using the String.split() method:");
        String regex = "[ ,]+"; // a space or a comma
        String[] s = str.split(regex);
        for (String item : s) {
            System.out.println(item);
        }
    }
}
```

```
Tokens using a StringTokenizer:
This
is
a
test
which
is
simple

Tokens using the String.split() method:
This
is
a
test
which
is
simple
```

The StringTokenizer and the split() method of the String class return each token as a string. Sometimes you may want to distinguish between tokens based on their types; your string may contain comments. You can have these sophisticated features while breaking a character-based stream into tokens using the StreamTokenizer class. Listing 7-45 illustrates how to use a StreamTokenizer.

Listing 7-45. Reading Tokens from a Character-Based Stream

```
// StreamTokenTest.java
package com.jdojo.io;

import java.io.StreamTokenizer;
import static java.io.StreamTokenizer.*;
import java.io.StringReader;
import java.io.IOException;

public class StreamTokenTest {
    public static void main(String[] args) throws Exception {
        String str = "This is a test, 200.89 which is simple 50";
        StringReader sr = new StringReader(str);
        StreamTokenizer st = new StreamTokenizer(sr);

        try {
            while (st.nextToken() != TT_EOF) {
                switch (st.ttype) {
                    case TT_WORD:
                        /* a word has been read */
                        System.out.println("String value: "
                                + st.sval);
                        break;
```

```
                    case TT_NUMBER:
                        /* a number has been read */
                        System.out.println("Number value: "
                                + st.nval);
                        break;
                }
            }
        } catch (IOException e) {
            e.printStackTrace();
        }
    }
}
```

```
String value: This
String value: is
String value: a
String value: test
Number value: 200.89
String value: which
String value: is
String value: simple
Number value: 50.0
```

The program uses a `StringReader` object as the data source. You can use a `FileReader` object or any other `Reader` object as the data source. The syntax to get the tokens is not easy to use. The `nextToken()` method of `StreamTokenizer` is called repeatedly. It populates three fields of the `StreamTokenizer` object: `ttype`, `sval`, and `nval`. The `ttype` field indicates the type of the token that was read. The following are the four possible values for the `ttype` field:

- `TT_EOF`: End of the stream has been reached.
- `TT_EOL`: End of line has been reached.
- `TT_WORD`: A word (a string) has been read as a token from the stream.
- `TT_NUMBER`: A number has been read as a token from the stream.

If `ttype` is equal to `TT_WORD`, the string value is stored in the field `sval` field. If `ttype` is `TT_NUMBER`, the number value is stored in the `nval` field.

`StreamTokenizer` is a powerful class to break a stream into tokens. It creates tokens based on a predefined syntax. You can reset the entire syntax by using its `resetSyntax()` method. You can specify your own set of characters that can make up a word by using its `wordChars()` method. You can specify your custom whitespace characters using its `whitespaceChars()` method.

Summary

Reading data from a data source and writing data to a data sink is called input/output. A stream represents a data source or data sink for serial reading or writing. The Java I/O API contains several classes to support input and output streams. Java I/O classes are in the `java.io` and `java.nio` packages. The input/output stream classes in Java are based on the decorator pattern.

You refer to a file in your computer by its pathname. A file's pathname is a sequence of characters by which you can identify it uniquely in a file system. A pathname consists of a file name and its unique location in the file system. An object of the `File` class is an abstract representation of a pathname of a file or directory in a platform-independent manner. The pathname represented by a `File` object may or may not exist in the file system. The `File` class provides several methods to work with files and directories.

Java I/O supports two types of streams: byte-based streams and character-based streams. Byte-based streams are inherited from the `InputStream` or `OutputStream` classes. Character-based stream classes are inherited from the `Reader` or `Writer` classes.

The process of converting an object in memory to a sequence of bytes and storing the sequence of bytes in a storage medium such as a file is called *object serialization*. The process of reading the sequence of bytes produced by a serialization process and restoring the object back in memory is called *object deserialization*. Java supports serialization and deserialization of object through the `ObjectInputStream` and `ObjectOutputStream` classes. An object must implement the `Serializable` interface to be serialized.

The Java I/O API provides the `Console` and `Scanner` classes to interact with the console.

You can use the `StringTokenizer` and `StreamTokenizer` classes to split text into tokens based on delimiters. The `String` class contains a convenience `split()` method to split a string into tokens based on a regular expression.

QUESTIONS AND EXERCISES

1. What does an instance of the `File` class represent?
2. Explain the effect of the following statement:

   ```
   File file = new File("test.txt");
   ```

   Will this statement create a file named `test.txt` in the current directory if the file does not already exist?

3. What is the difference in using the `delete()` and `deleteOnExit()` methods of the `File` class?

4. What is the difference in using the `mkdir()` and `mkdirs()` methods of the `File` class?

5. Complete the code for the following method named `isExistentDirectory()`. It accepts a pathname as a parameter. It returns `true` if the specified pathname represents an existing directory and returns `false` otherwise.

   ```
   public static boolean isExistentDirectory(String pathname) {
       /* your code goes here */
   }
   ```

6. What classes in the `java.io` package would you use if you need to read and write values of primitive data types such as `int` and `float`?

7. What classes in the `java.io` package would you use if you need to serialize and deserialize objects to a file?

8. In the context of object serialization, what is the difference between implementing the `Serializable` and `Externalizable` interfaces in a class?

9. In the context of object serialization, what is the significance of declaring instance variables in a class as `transient`?
10. Is there a way to serialize `transient` instance variables while serializing objects?
11. How will you stop the objects of your class from being serialized?
12. What is `serialVersionUID` in the context of object serialization?
13. Suppose you have an existing text file named `test.txt` in your current directory. Write the code to append `"Hello"` to this file.
14. Which class in the `java.io` package would you if you need to read from and write to a file at the same time?
15. What is the difference between the `InputStream` and `Reader` classes while performing I/O?
16. Write a program using the `Console` and `Scanner` classes. The program prompts the user for an integer. When the user enters an integer, the program prints whether the integer is odd or even and the program prompts the user for another integer. The user can enter `Q` or `q` to exit the program any time.
17. Write a program that will read the contents of a file and it will print the number of times all vowels (a, e, i, o, and u) occurs in the file. Count should be case-insensitive. That is, both 'A' and 'a' are counted as 'a'. You need to prompt the user to specify the pathname to the file. Include error handling in your code such as for the case when the specified file does not exist.

CHAPTER 8

Working with Archive Files

In this chapter, you will learn:

- What archive files are
- What data compression is and how to compress and decompress data
- How to compute checksum for data using different algorithms
- How to create files in ZIP, GZIP, and JAR file formats and read data from them
- How to use the `jar` command-line tool to work with JAR files

All example programs in this chapter are a member of a `jdojo.archives` module, as declared in Listing 8-1.

Listing 8-1. The Declaration of a jdojo.archives Module

```
// module-info.java
module jdojo.archives {
    exports com.jdojo.archives;
}
```

What Is an Archive File?

An archive file consists of one or more files. It also contains metadata that may include the directory structure of the files, comments, error detection and recovery information, etc. An archive file may also be encrypted. Typically, but not necessarily, an archive file is stored in a compressed format. An archive file is created using file archiver software. For example, the WinZip, 7-zip, etc. Utilities are used to create a file archive in a ZIP format on Microsoft Windows; the `tar` utility is used to create archive files on UNIX-based operating systems. An archive file makes it easier to store and transmit multiple files as one file. This chapter discusses in detail how to work with archive files using the Java I/O API and the `jar` command-line utility that is included in the JDK.

Data Compression

Data compression is the process of applying an encoding algorithm to the given data to represent it in a smaller size. Suppose you have a string, `777778888`. One way to encode it is `5748`, which can be interpreted as "five sevens and four eights." By this encoding, you have reduced the length of the string from nine characters to four characters. The algorithm you applied to compress `777778888` as `5748` is called

K. Sharan, *Java Language Features*, https://doi.org/10.1007/978-1-4842-3348-1_8

Run Length Encoding (RLE). The RLE encodes the data by replacing the repeated sequence of data by the counter number and one copy of data. The RLE is easy to implement. It is suitable only in situations where you have more repeated data.

The reverse of data compression is called data decompression. Here, you apply an algorithm to the compressed data to get back the original data.

There are two types of data compression: lossless and lossy. In lossless data compression, you get your original data back when you decompress the data. For example, if you decompress `5748`, you can get your original data (`777778888`) back without losing any information. You can get the information back in this example because RLE is a lossless data compression algorithm. Other lossless data compression algorithms are LZ77, LZ78, LZW, Huffman coding, Dynamic Markov Compression (DMC), etc.

In lossy data compression, you lose some of the data during the compression process and you will not be able to recover the original data fully when you decompress the compressed data. Lossy data compression is acceptable in some situations, such as viewing pictures, audios, and videos, where the audience will not see a noticeable difference when they use the decompressed data. Compared to the lossless data compression, lossy data compression achieves a higher compression ratio at the cost of the lower data quality. Examples of lossy data compression algorithms are Discrete Cosine Transform (DCT), A-Law Compander, Mu-Law Compander, Vector Quantization, etc.

DEFLATE is a lossless data compression algorithm, which is used for compressing data in ZIP and GZIP file formats. GZIP is an abbreviation for GNU ZIP. GNU is a recursive acronym for GNU's Not UNIX. The ZIP file format is used for data compression and file archival. A file archival is the process of combining multiple files into one file for convenience of storage. Typically, you compress multiple files and put them together in an archive file.

You may have worked with files with an extension of `.zip`. A ZIP file uses the ZIP file format. It combines multiple files into one `.zip` file by, optionally, compressing them.

If you are a UNIX user, you must have worked with a `.tar` or `.tar.gz` file. Typically, on UNIX, you use a two-step process to create a compressed archive file. First, you combine multiple files into a `.tar` archive file using the tar file format (tar stands for **T**ape **Ar**chive), and then you compress that archive file using the GZIP file format to get a `.tar.gz` or `.tgz` file. A `.tar.gz` or `.tgz` file is also called a tarball. A tarball is more compressed as compared to a ZIP file. A ZIP file compresses multiple files separately and archives them. A tarball archives the multiple files first and then compresses them. Because a tarball compresses the combined files together, it takes advantage of data repetition among all files during compression, resulting in a better compression than a ZIP file.

ZLIB is a general-purpose lossless data compression library. It is free and not covered by any patents. Java provides support for data compression using the ZLIB library. `Deflater` and `Inflater` are two classes in the `java.util.zip` package that support general-purpose data compression/decompression functionality in Java using the ZLIB library. Java provides classes to support ZIP and GZIP file formats. It also supports another file format called the JAR file format, which is a variation of the ZIP file format. I discuss examples of the file formats supported by Java in the next few sections.

Checksum

A checksum is an integer that is computed by applying an algorithm on a stream of bytes. Sometimes, the algorithm to compute an integer from a stream of bytes is also known as checksum. Typically, it is used to check for errors during data transmission. The sender computes a checksum for a packet of data and sends that checksum with the packet to the receiver. The receiver computes the checksum for the packet of data it receives and compares it with the checksum it received from the sender. If the two match, the receiver may assume that there were no errors during the data transmission. The sender and the receiver must agree to compute the checksum for the data by applying the same algorithm. Otherwise, the checksum will not match. Using a checksum is not a data security measure to authenticate the data. It is used as an error-detection method. A hacker can alter some bits of the data and you may still get the same checksum as for the original data.

Let's discuss an algorithm to compute a checksum. The algorithm is called Adler-32 after its inventor Mark Adler. Its name has the number 32 in it because it computes a checksum by computing two 16-bit checksums and concatenating them into a 32-bit integer. Let's call the two 16-bit checksums A and B, and the final checksum C. A is the sum of all bytes plus one in the data. B is the sum of individual values of A from each step. In the beginning, A is set to 1 and B is set to 0. A and B are computed based on modulus 65521. That is, if the value of A or B exceeds 65521, their values become their current values modulo 65521. The final checksum is computed as follows:

```
C = B * 65536 + A
```

The final checksum is computed by concatenating the 16-bit B and A values. You need to multiply the value of B by 65536 and add the value of A to it to get the decimal value of that 32-bit final checksum number.

Let's apply the Adler-32 checksum algorithm to compute a checksum for a string HELLO, as shown in Table 8-1.

Table 8-1. *Computing the Adler-32 checksum for the String HELLO*

Character	ASCII Value (Base 10)	A	B
H	72	1 + 72 = 73	0 + 73 = 73
E	69	73 + 69 = 142	73 + 142 = 215
L	76	142 + 76 = 218	215 + 218 = 433
L	76	218 + 76 = 294	433 + 294 = 727
O	79	294 + 79 = 373	727 + 373 = 1100

```
C = B * 65536 + A
  = 1100 * 65536 + 373
  = 72089973
```

Java provides an Adler32 class in the java.util.zip package to compute the Adler-32 checksum for bytes of data. You need to call the update() method of this class to pass bytes to it. Once you have passed all bytes to it, call its getValue() method to get the checksum. CRC32 (**C**yclic **R**edundancy **C**heck 32-bit) is another algorithm to compute a 32-bit checksum. There is also another class named CRC32 in the same package, which lets you compute a checksum using the CRC32 algorithm.

■ **Tip** Java 9 added a CRC32C class in the java.util.zip package. The class lets you compute CRC-32C of a stream of bytes. CRC-32C is defined in RFC 3720 at http://www.ietf.org/rfc/rfc3720.txt.

Listing 8-2 illustrates how to use the Adler32, CRC32, and CRC32C classes to compute checksums.

Listing 8-2. Computing Adler32, CRC32, and CRC32C Checksums

```
// ChecksumTest.java
package com.jdojo.archives;

import java.util.zip.Adler32;
import java.util.zip.CRC32;
import java.util.zip.CRC32C;
import java.util.zip.Checksum;
```

```
public class ChecksumTest {
    public static void main(String[] args) throws Exception {
        String str = "HELLO";
        byte[] data = str.getBytes("UTF-8");
        System.out.println("Adler32, CRC32, and CRC32C checksums for " + str);

        // Compute Adler32 checksum
        Checksum ad = new Adler32();
        ad.update(data);
        long adler32Checksum = ad.getValue();
        System.out.println("Adler32: " + adler32Checksum);

        // Compute CRC32 checksum
        Checksum crc32 = new CRC32();
        crc32.update(data);
        long crc32Checksum = crc32.getValue();
        System.out.println("CRC32: " + crc32Checksum);

        // Compute CRC32C checksum
        Checksum crc32c = new CRC32C();
        crc32c.update(data);
        long crc32cChecksum = crc32c.getValue();
        System.out.println("CRC32C: " + crc32cChecksum);
    }
}
```

```
Adler32, CRC32, and CRC32C checksums for HELLO
Adler32: 72089973
CRC32: 3242484790
CRC32C: 3901656152
```

Adler32 is faster than CRC32. However, CRC32 gives a more robust checksum. Checksum is frequently used to check for data corruption. CheckedInputStream and CheckedOutputStream are two concrete decorator classes in the InputStream/OutputStream class family. They are in the java.util.zip package. They work with a Checksum object. Note that Checksum is an interface, and the Adler32 and CRC32 classes implement that interface. CheckedInputStream computes a checksum as you read data from a stream and CheckedOutputStream computes the checksum as you write data to a stream. The ZipEntry class lets you compute the CRC32 checksum for an entry in a ZIP file using its getCrc() method.

Compressing Byte Arrays

You can use the Deflater and Inflater classes in the java.util.zip package to compress and decompress data in a byte array, respectively. These classes are the basic building blocks for compression and decompression in Java. You may not use them directly very often. You have other high-level, easy-to-use classes in Java to deal with data compression. Those classes are DeflaterInputStream, DeflaterOutputStream, GZIPInputStream, ZipFile, GZIPOutputStream, ZipInputStream, and ZipOutputStream. I discuss these classes in detail in subsequent sections.

Using the Deflater and Inflater classes is not straightforward. You need to use the following steps to compress data in a byte array.

1. Create a Deflater object.
2. Set the input data to be compressed using the setInput() method.
3. Call the finish() method indicating that you have supplied all input data.
4. Call the deflate() method to compress the input data.
5. Call the end() method to end the compression process.

You can create an object of the Deflater class using one of its constructors.

```
// Uses the no-args constructor
Deflater compressor = new Deflater();
```

Other constructors of the Deflater class let you specify the level of compression. You can specify the compression level using one of the constants in the Deflater class. Those constant are BEST_COMPRESSION, BEST_SPEED, DEFAULT_COMPRESSION, and NO_COMPRESSION. There is a trade-off in choosing between the best compression and the best speed. The best speed means lower compression ratio and the best compression means slower compression speed.

```
// Uses the best compression
Deflater compressor = new Deflater(Deflater.BEST_COMPRESSION);
```

By default, the compressed data will be in the ZLIB format. If you want the compressed data to be in GZIP or PKZIP format, you need to specify that by using the boolean flag as true in the constructor.

```
// Uses the best speed compression and GZIP format
Deflater compressor = new Deflater(Deflater.BEST_SPEED, true);
```

You can supply the input data to the Deflater object in a byte array.

```
byte[] input = /* get a data filled byte array */;
compressor.setInput(input);
```

You call the finish() method to indicate that you have supplied all the input data.

```
compressor.finish();
```

You call the deflate() method to compress the input data. It accepts a byte array as its argument. It fills the byte array with the compressed data and returns the number of bytes in the byte array it has filled. After every call to the deflate() method, you need to call the finished() method to check if the compression process is over. Typically, you would place this check in a loop as follows:

```
// Try to read the compressed data 1024 bytes at a time
byte[] readBuffer = new byte[1024];
int readCount = 0;

while(!compressor.finished()) {
    readCount = compressor.deflate(readBuffer);
```

```
    /* At this point, the readBuffer array has the compressed data
       from index 0 to readCount - 1.
    */
}
```

You call the end() method to release any resources the Deflater object has held.

```
// Indicates that the compression process is over
compressor.end();
```

The following steps are used to decompress data in a byte array. The steps are just the reverse of what you did to compress a byte array.

1. Create an Inflater object.
2. Set the input data to be decompressed using the setInput() method.
3. Call the inflate() method to decompress the input data.
4. Call the end() method to end the decompression process.

You can create an object of the Inflater class using one of its constructors.

```
// Uses the no-args constructor
Inflater decompressor = new Inflater();
```

If the compressed data is in GZIP or PKZIP format, you use another constructor and pass true as its argument.

```
// Creates a decompressor to decompress data that is in GZIP or PKZIP format
Inflater decompressor = new Inflater(true);
```

You set the input for the decompressor, which is the compressed data in a byte array.

```
byte[] input = /* get the compressed data in the byte array */;
decompressor.setInput(input);
```

You call the inflate() method to decompress the input data. It accepts a byte array as its argument. It fills the byte array with the decompressed data and returns the number of bytes in the byte array. After every call to this method, you need to call the finished() method to check if the compression process is over. Typically, you use a loop, as follows:

```
// Try to read the decompressed data 1024 bytes at a time
byte[] readBuffer = new byte[1024];
int readCount = 0;

while(!decompressor.finished()) {
    readCount = decompressor.inflate(readBuffer);

    /* At this point, the readBuffer array has the decompressed
       data from index 0 to readCount - 1.
    */
}
```

You need to call the end() method to release any resources held by the Inflater object.

```
// Indicates that the decompression process is over
decompressor.end();
```

Listing 8-3 illustrates how to use the Deflater and Inflater classes. The compress() and decompress() methods accept the inputs and return the compressed and decompressed data, respectively. In this example, I tried to compress a small string of Hello world!. It is 12 bytes in length. It became 20 bytes after I compressed it. The goal of compression is to reduce, not to increase, the size of data. However, you cannot achieve reducing the data size just because you have attempted to compress it. The output of the program in Listing 8-3 is one such example. When you compress the data, the compressed format has to add some information to it to do some housekeeping. If the data you are attempting to compress is very small in size, as was the case in this example, or if it is already compressed, the compressed size of the data may increase because of additional information added by the compression process.

Listing 8-3. Compressing and Decompressing a Byte Array Using the Deflater and Inflater Classes

```
// DeflateInflateTest.java
package com.jdojo.archives;

import java.io.ByteArrayOutputStream;
import java.io.IOException;
import java.util.zip.DataFormatException;
import java.util.zip.Deflater;
import java.util.zip.Inflater;
import static java.util.zip.Deflater.BEST_COMPRESSION;

public class DeflateInflateTest {
    public static void main(String[] args) throws Exception {
        String input = "Hello world!";
        byte[] uncompressedData = input.getBytes("UTF-8");

        // Compress the data
        byte[] compressedData = compress(uncompressedData, BEST_COMPRESSION, false);

        // Decompress the data
        byte[] decompressedData = decompress(compressedData, false);

        String output = new String(decompressedData, "UTF-8");

        // Display the statistics
        System.out.println("Input String: " + input);
        System.out.println("Uncompressed data length: " + uncompressedData.length);
        System.out.println("Compressed data length: " + compressedData.length);
        System.out.println("Decompressed data length: " + decompressedData.length);
        System.out.println("Output String: " + output);
    }

    public static byte[] compress(byte[] input, int compressionLevel,
          boolean GZIPFormat) throws IOException {
```

```
        // Create a Deflater object to compress data
        Deflater compressor = new Deflater(compressionLevel, GZIPFormat);

        // Set the input for the compressor
        compressor.setInput(input);

        // Call the finish() method to indicate that we have
        // no more input for the compressor object
        compressor.finish();

        // Compress the data
        ByteArrayOutputStream bao = new ByteArrayOutputStream();
        byte[] readBuffer = new byte[1024];

        while (!compressor.finished()) {
            int readCount = compressor.deflate(readBuffer);
            if (readCount > 0) {
                // Write compressed data to the output stream
                bao.write(readBuffer, 0, readCount);
            }
        }

        // End the compressor
        compressor.end();

        // Return the written bytes from output stream
        return bao.toByteArray();
    }
    public static byte[] decompress(byte[] input, boolean GZIPFormat)
            throws IOException, DataFormatException {

        // Create an Inflater object to compress the data
        Inflater decompressor = new Inflater(GZIPFormat);

        // Set the input for the decompressor
        decompressor.setInput(input);

        // Decompress data
        ByteArrayOutputStream bao = new ByteArrayOutputStream();
        byte[] readBuffer = new byte[1024];

        while (!decompressor.finished()) {
            int readCount = decompressor.inflate(readBuffer);
            if (readCount > 0) {
                // Write the data to the output stream
                bao.write(readBuffer, 0, readCount);
            }
        }

        // End the decompressor
        decompressor.end();
```

```
        // Return the written bytes from the output stream
        return bao.toByteArray();
    }
}
```

```
Input String: Hello world!
Uncompressed data length: 12
Compressed data length: 20
Decompressed data length: 12
Output String: Hello world!
```

You can use DeflaterInputStream and DeflaterOutputStream to compress data in the input and output streams. There are also InflaterInputStream and InflaterOutputStream classes for decompressing data in the input and output streams. The four classes are concrete decorators in the InputStream and OutputStream class families. Refer to Chapter 7 for more details on the decorator pattern and the concrete decorator classes.

Working with ZIP File Format

The Java API has direct support for the ZIP file format. Typically, you would be using the following four classes from the java.util.zip package:

- ZipEntry
- ZipInputStream
- ZipOutputStream
- ZipFile

A ZipEntry object represents an entry in an archive file in a ZIP file format. If you archived 10 files in a file called test.zip, each file in the archive is represented by a ZipEntry object in your program. A zip entry may be compressed or uncompressed. When you read all files from a ZIP file, you read each of them as a ZipEntry object. When you want to add a file to a ZIP file, you add a ZipEntry object to the ZIP file. The ZipEntry class has methods to set and get information about an entry in a ZIP file.

ZipInputStream is a concrete decorator class in the InputStream class family; you use it to read data from a ZIP file for each entry. ZipOutputStream is a concrete decorator class in the OutputStream class family; you use its class to write data to a ZIP file for each entry.

ZipFile is a utility class to read the entries from a ZIP file. You have the option to use the ZipInputStream class or the ZipFile class when you want to read entries from a ZIP file.

Creating ZIP Files

The following are the steps to create a ZIP file:

1. Create a ZipOutputStream object.
2. Create a ZipEntry object to represent an entry in the ZIP file.
3. Add the ZipEntry to the ZipOutputStream.
4. Write the contents of the entry to the ZipOutputStream.
5. Close the ZipEntry.

6. Repeat the last four steps for each zip entry you want to add to the archive.

7. Close the ZipOutputStream.

You can create an object of ZipOutputStream using the name of the ZIP file. You need to create a FileOutputStream object and wrap it inside a ZipOutputStream object as follows:

```
// Create a zip output stream
ZipOutputStream zos = new ZipOutputStream(new FileOutputStream("ziptest.zip"));
```

You may use any other output stream concrete decorator to wrap your FileOutputStream object. For example, you may want to use BufferedOutputStream for a better speed as follows:

```
ZipOutputStream zos = new ZipOutputStream(new BufferedOutputStream(
                new FileOutputStream("ziptest.zip")));
```

Optionally, you can set the compression level for the ZIP file entries. By default, the compression level is set to DEFAULT_COMPRESSION. For example, the following statement sets the compression level to BEST_COMPRESSION:

```
// Set the compression level for zip entries
zos.setLevel(Deflater.BEST_COMPRESSION);
```

You create a ZipEntry object using the file path for each entry and add the entry to the ZipOutputStream object using its putNextEntry() method, like so:

```
ZipEntry ze = new ZipEntry("test1.txt")
zos.putNextEntry(ze);
```

Optionally, you can set the storage method for the ZIP entry to indicate if the ZIP entry is stored compressed or uncompressed. By default, a ZIP entry is stored in a compressed form.

```
// To store the zip entry in a compressed form
ze.setMethod(ZipEntry.DEFLATED);

// To store the zip entry in an uncompressed form
ze.setMethod(ZipEntry.STORED);
```

Write the content of the entry you have added in the previous step to the ZipOutputStream object. Since a ZipEntry object represents a file, you need to read the file by creating a FileInputStream object.

```
// Create an input stream to read data for the entry file
BufferedInputStream bis = new BufferedInputStream(new FileInputStream("test1.txt"));
byte[] buffer = new byte[1024];
int count;

// Write the data for the entry
while((count = bis.read(buffer)) != -1) {
    zos.write(buffer, 0, count);
}

bis.close();
```

Now, close the entry using the `closeEntry()` method of the `ZipOutputStream`.

```
// Close the zip entry
zos.closeEntry();
```

Repeat the previous steps for each entry that you want to add to the ZIP file. Finally, you need to close the `ZipOutputStream`.

```
// Close the zip entry
zos.close()
```

Listing 8-4 demonstrates how to create a ZIP file. It adds two files called `test1.txt` and `notes\test2.txt` to the `ziptest.zip` file. The program expects these files in the current working directory. If the files do not exist, the program prints an error message with the path of the expected files and exits. When the program finishes successfully, a `ziptest.zip` file is created in the current directory that you can open using a ZIP file utility, such as WinZip on Windows. The program prints the path of the newly created ZIP file. You may get a different output when you run the program.

Listing 8-4. Creating a ZIP File

```
// ZipUtility.java
package com.jdojo.archives;

import java.util.zip.ZipOutputStream;
import java.util.zip.ZipEntry;
import java.io.FileOutputStream;
import java.io.IOException;
import java.io.BufferedInputStream;
import java.io.FileInputStream;
import java.io.BufferedOutputStream;
import java.io.File;
import java.util.zip.Deflater;

public class ZipUtility {
    public static void main(String[] args) {
        // We want to create a ziptest.zip file in the current directory.
        // We want to add two files to this zip file.
        // Both file paths are relative to the current directory.
        String zipFileName = "ziptest.zip";
        String[] entries = new String[2];
        entries[0] = "test1.txt";
        entries[1] = "notes" + File.separator + "test2.txt";
        zip(zipFileName, entries);
    }

    public static void zip(String zipFileName, String[] zipEntries) {
        // Get the current directory for later use
        String currentDirectory = System.getProperty("user.dir");

        try (ZipOutputStream zos
                = new ZipOutputStream(
                        new BufferedOutputStream(
                                new FileOutputStream(zipFileName)))) {
```

```
            // Set the compression level to best compression
            zos.setLevel(Deflater.BEST_COMPRESSION);

            // Add each entry to the ZIP file
            for (String zipEntry : zipEntries) {
                // Make sure the entry file exists
                File entryFile = new File(zipEntry);
                if (!entryFile.exists()) {
                    System.out.println("The entry file " + entryFile.getAbsolutePath()
                            + " does not exist");
                    System.out.println("Aborted processing.");
                    System.exit(1);
                }

                // Create a ZipEntry object
                ZipEntry ze = new ZipEntry(zipEntry);

                // Add the zip entry object to the ZIP file
                zos.putNextEntry(ze);

                // Add the contents of the entry to the ZIP file
                addEntryContent(zos, zipEntry);

                // We are done with the current entry
                zos.closeEntry();
            }

            System.out.println("Output has been written to "
                    + currentDirectory + File.separator + zipFileName);
        } catch (IOException e) {
            e.printStackTrace();
        }
    }

    public static void addEntryContent(ZipOutputStream zos, String entryFileName) {
        // Create an input stream to read data from the entry file
        try (BufferedInputStream bis = new BufferedInputStream(
                        new FileInputStream(entryFileName))) {
            byte[] buffer = new byte[1024];
            int count;
            while ((count = bis.read(buffer)) != -1) {
                zos.write(buffer, 0, count);
            }
        } catch (IOException e) {
            e.printStackTrace();
        }
    }
}
```

```
Output has been written to C:\Java9LanguageFeatures\ziptest.zip
```

Reading the Contents of ZIP Files

Reading contents of a ZIP file is just the opposite of writing contents to it. Here are the steps to read the contents (or extract entries) of a ZIP file.

1. Create a ZipInputStream object.
2. Get a ZipEntry from the input stream calling the getNextEntry() method of the ZipInputStream object.
3. Read the data for the ZipEntry from the ZipInputStream object.
4. Repeat the last two steps to read another ZIP entry from the archive.
5. Close the ZipInputStream.

You can create a ZipInputStream object using the ZIP file name as follows:

```
ZipInputStream zis = new ZipInputStream(
                          new BufferedInputStream(
                             new FileInputStream(zipFileName)));
```

The following snippet of code gets the next entry from the input stream:

```
ZipEntry entry = zis.getNextEntry();
```

Now, you can read the data from the ZipInputStream object for the current ZIP entry. You can save the data for the ZIP entry in a file or any other storage medium. You can check if the ZIP entry is a directory by using the isDirectory() method of the ZipEntry class.

Listing 8-5 illustrates how to read contents of a ZIP file. The example does not check for some of the errors. It does not check if a file already exists before overwriting it. It also assumes that all entries are files. The program expects a ziptest.zip file in your current working directory. It extracts all files from the ZIP file and outputs the path of the directory containing the extracted files. You may get a different output.

Listing 8-5. Reading Contents of a ZIP File

```
// UnzipUtility.java
package com.jdojo.archives;

import java.util.zip.ZipEntry;
import java.io.FileOutputStream;
import java.io.FileNotFoundException;
import java.io.IOException;
import java.io.BufferedInputStream;
import java.io.FileInputStream;
import java.io.BufferedOutputStream;
import java.io.File;
import java.util.zip.ZipInputStream;

public class UnzipUtility {
    public static void main(String[] args) {
        String zipFileName = "ziptest.zip";
        String unzipdirectory = "extracted";
        unzip(zipFileName, unzipdirectory);
    }
```

```
    public static void unzip(String zipFileName, String unzipdir) {
        try (ZipInputStream zis = new ZipInputStream(
                new BufferedInputStream(
                        new FileInputStream(zipFileName)))) {

            // Read each entry from the ZIP file
            ZipEntry entry;
            while ((entry = zis.getNextEntry()) != null) {
                // Extract the entry's contents
                extractEntryContent(zis, entry, unzipdir);
            }

            System.out.println("ZIP file's contents have been extracted to "
                    + (new File(unzipdir)).getAbsolutePath());
        } catch (IOException e) {
            e.printStackTrace();
        }
    }

    public static void extractEntryContent(ZipInputStream zis,
            ZipEntry entry,
            String unzipdir)
            throws IOException, FileNotFoundException {

        String entryFileName = entry.getName();
        String entryPath = unzipdir + File.separator + entryFileName;

        // Create the entry file by creating necessary directories
        createFile(entryPath);

        // Create an output stream to extract the contents of the
        // zip entry and write to the new file
        try (BufferedOutputStream bos = new BufferedOutputStream(
                                          new FileOutputStream(entryPath))) {
            byte[] buffer = new byte[1024];
            int count;
            while ((count = zis.read(buffer)) != -1) {
                bos.write(buffer, 0, count);
            }
        }
    }

    public static void createFile(String filePath) throws IOException {
        File file = new File(filePath);
        File parent = file.getParentFile();

        // Create all parent directories if they do not exist
        if (!parent.exists()) {
            parent.mkdirs();
        }
```

```
            file.createNewFile();
        }
    }
```

```
ZIP file's contents have been extracted to C:\Java9LanguageFeatures\extracted
```

It is easier to use the ZipFile class to read the contents of a ZIP file or list its entries. For example, a ZipFile allows random access to ZIP entries, whereas a ZipInputStream allows sequential access. The entries() method of a ZipFile object returns an enumeration of all ZIP entries in the file. The getInputStream() method returns the input stream to read the content of a ZipEntry object. The following snippet of code shows how to use the ZipFile class. You can rewrite the code in Listing 8-5 using the ZipFile class instead of the ZipOutputStream class as an exercise. The ZipFile class comes in handy when you just want to list the entries in a ZIP file.

```
import java.io.InputStream;
import java.util.Enumeration;
import java.util.zip.ZipEntry;
import java.util.zip.ZipFile;
...
// Create a ZipFile object using the ZIP file name
ZipFile zf = new ZipFile("ziptest.zip");

// Get the enumeration for all zip entries and loop through them
Enumeration<? extends ZipEntry> e = zf.entries();

ZipEntry entry;
while (e.hasMoreElements()) {
    entry = e.nextElement();

    // Get the input stream for the current zip entry
    InputStream is = zf.getInputStream(entry);

    /* Read data for the entry using the is object */

    // Print the name of the entry
    System.out.println(entry.getName());
}
```

Java 8 added a new stream() method to the ZipFile class that returns a Stream<? extends ZipEntry>. I cover the Stream class in Chapter 13. Let's rewrite the previous snippet of code using the Stream class and a lambda expression:

```
import java.io.IOException;
import java.io.InputStream;
import java.util.stream.Stream;
import java.util.zip.ZipEntry;
import java.util.zip.ZipFile;
...
```

```
// Create a ZipFile object using the ZIP file name
ZipFile zf = new ZipFile("ziptest.zip");

// Get the Stream of all zip entries and apply some actions on each of them
Stream<? extends ZipEntry> entryStream = zf.stream();
entryStream.forEach(entry -> {
    try {
        // Get the input stream for the current zip entry
        InputStream is = zf.getInputStream(entry);

        /* Read data for the entry using the is object */
    } catch(IOException e) {
        e.printStackTrace();
    }

    // Print the name of the entry
    System.out.println(entry.getName());
});
```

Working with the GZIP File Format

The GZIPInputStream and GZIPOutputStream classes are used to work with the GZIP file format. They are concrete decorator classes in the InputStream and OutputStream class families. Their usage is similar to any other concrete decorator classes for I/O. You need to wrap your OutputStream object in an object of GZIPOutputStream to apply GZIP compression to your data. You need to wrap your InputStream object in a GZIPInputStream object to apply GZIP decompression. The following snippet of code illustrates how to use these classes to compress and decompress data:

```
// Create a GZIPOutputStream object to compress data in GZIP format
// and write it to gziptest.gz file.
GZIPOutputStream gos = new GZIPOutputStream(new FileOutputStream("gziptest.gz"));

// Write uncompressed data to GZIP output stream and it will be
// compressed and written to gziptest.gz file
gos.write(byteBuffer);
```

If you want buffered writing for better speed, you should wrap the GZIPOutputStream in a BufferedOutputStream and write the data to the BufferedOutputStream.

```
BufferedOutputStream bos = new BufferedOutputStream(new GZIPOutputStream(
                                    new FileOutputStream("gziptest.gz")));
```

How would you compress an object while serializing it? It is simple. Just wrap the GZIPOutputStream in an ObjectOutputStream object. When you write an object to your ObjectOutputStream, its serialized form will be compressed using a GZIP format.

```
ObjectOutputStream oos = new ObjectOutputStream(new GZIPOutputStream(
                                   new FileOutputStream("gziptest.ser")));
```

Apply the reverse logic to read the compressed data in GZIP format for decompressing. The following snippet of code shows how to construct an InputStream object to decompress data, which is in GZIP format:

```
// Decompress data in GZIP format from gziptest.gz file and read it
GZIPInputStream gis = new GZIPInputStream(new FileInputStream("gziptest.gz"));

/* Read uncompressed data from GZIP input stream, e.g., gis.read(byteBuffer);*/

// Construct a BufferedInputStream to read data, which is in GZIP format
BufferedInputStream bis = new BufferedInputStream (new GZIPInputStream(
                                 new FileInputStream(gziptest.gz")));

// Construct an ObjectInputStream to read compressed object
ObjectInputStream ois = new ObjectInputStream (new GZIPInputStream(
                new FileInputStream("gziptest.ser")));
```

Working with the JAR File Format

JAR (**J**ava **Ar**chive) is a file format based on the ZIP file format. It is used to bundle resources, class files, sound files, images, etc. for a Java application or applet. It also provides data compression. Originally, it was developed to bundle resources for an applet to reduce download time over an HTTP connection.

You can think of a JAR file as a special kind of ZIP file. A JAR file provides many features that are not available in a ZIP file. You can digitally sign the contents of a JAR file to provide security. It provides a platform-independent file format. You can use the JAR API to manipulate a JAR file in a Java program.

A JAR file can have an optional META-INF directory to contain files and directories containing information about application configuration. Table 8-2 lists the entries in a META-INF directory.

Table 8-2. *Contents of the META-INF Directory of a JAR File*

Name	Type	Purpose
MANIFEST.MF	File	Contains extension and package related data.
INDEX.LIST	File	Contains location information of packages. Class loaders use it to speed up the class searching and loading process.
X.SF	File	X is the base file name. It stores the signature for the JAR file.
X.DSA	File	X is the base file name. It stores the digital signature of the corresponding signature file.
/services	Directory	Contains all service provider configuration files. This directory is not needed if your application is developed using the module system in JDK9, which lets you configure services in module declaration.
versions	Directory	Contains files specific to a JDK versions in a multi-release JAR file. I cover multi-release JARs in Chapter 11 of the third volume of this series.

The JDK ships with a jar tool to create and manipulate JAR files. You can also create and manipulate a JAR file using the Java API using classes in the java.util.jar package. Most of the classes in this package are similar to the classes in the java.util.zip package. In fact, most of the classes in this package are inherited from the classes that deal with the ZIP file format. For example, the JarFile class inherits from the ZipFile class; the JarEntry class inherits from the ZipEntry class; the JarInputStream class inherits from the ZipInputStream class; the JarOutputStream class inherits from the ZipOutputStream class, etc. The JAR API has some new classes to deal with a manifest file. The Manifest class represents a manifest file. I discuss how to use the JAR API later in this chapter. I discuss the jar tool in this section.

■ **Tip** JDK9 added a few methods to the JarFile class to work with multi-release JAR files, which were introduced in JDK9. For example, the isMultiRelease() method returns true if a JarFile represents a multi-release JAR.

To create a JAR file using the jar tool, many command-line options are available. There are four basic operations that you perform using the jar tool.

- Create a JAR file.
- Update a JAR file.
- Extract entries from a JAR file.
- List the contents of a JAR file.

Table 8-3 lists the command-line options for the jar tool. Chapter 3 of the first volume of this series explains a few of these options. The GNU-style options were added in JDK9. For the complete list of all options for the jar tool and the tool's usage, run the tool with the --help or --help-extra option, like so:

```
C:\Java9LanguageFeatures>jar --help
```

Table 8-3. *Command-line Options for the jar Tool*

Option	Description
-c, --create	Create a new JAR file.
-u, --update	Update an existing JAR file.
-x, --extract	Extract a named file or all files from a JAR file.
-t, --list	List the table of contents of a JAR file.
-f, --file=FILE	Specify the JAR file name.
-m , --manifest=FILE	Include the manifest information from the specified file.
-M, --no-manifest	Do not create a manifest file.
-i, --generate-index=FILE	Generate index information for the specified JAR file. It creates an INDEX.LIST file in JAR file under the META-INF directory.
-0, --no-compress	Do not compress the entries in the JAR file. Only store them. The option value is zero, which means zero compression.
-e, --main-class=CLASSNAME	Add the specified class name as the value for the Main-Class entry in the main section of the manifest file.
-v, --verbose	Generate verbose output on the standard output.
-C DIR	Change to the specified directory and include the following files in a JAR file. Note that the option is in uppercase (C). The lowercase (-c) is used to indicate the create JAR file option.

(*continued*)

Table 8-3. *(continued)*

Option	Description
`--release VERSION`	Place all following files in a versioned directory of the JAR (i.e., `META-INF/versions/VERSION/`).
`-d, --describe-module`	Print the module descriptor, or automatic module name.
`--module-version=VERSION`	The module version when creating a modular JAR or updating a non-modular JAR.
`--hash-modules=PATTERN`	Compute and record the hashes of modules matched by the given pattern and that depend directly or indirectly on a modular JAR being created or a non-modular JAR being updated.
`-p, --module-path`	Location of module dependence for generating the hash.
`--version`	Print the program version.
`-h, --help[:compat], --help-extra`	Print help for the `jar` tool.

Creating a JAR File

Use the following command to create a `test.jar` JAR file with two class files called `A.class` and `B.class`:

```
jar --create --file test.jar A.class B.class
```

If you get an error such as "`jar is not recognized as a command`" when you run this command, you need to use the full path of the `jar` command or add the directory containing the `jar` command to the `PATH` environment variable on your machine. On Windows, if you install the JDK in the `C:\java9` directory, the `jar` command is stored in the `C:\java9\bin` directory.

In the previous command, the `--create` option indicates that you are creating a new JAR file and the `--file test.jar` option indicates that you are specifying the new JAR file name as `test.jar`. At the end of the command, you can specify one or more file names or directory names to include in the JAR file.

To view the contents of the `test.jar` file, you can execute the following command:

```
jar --list --file test.jar
```

```
META-INF/
META-INF/MANIFEST.MF
A.class
B.class
```

The `--list` option in this command indicates that you are interested in the table of contents of a JAR file. The `--file` option specifies the JAR file name, which is `test.jar` in this case. Note that when you created the `test.jar` file, the `jar` tool automatically created two extra entries for you: one directory called `META-INF` and a file named `MANIFEST.MF` in the `META-INF` directory. You see these entries when you list the contents of the JAR file.

The following command will create a `test.jar` file by including everything in the current working directory. Note the use of an asterisk as the wildcard character to denote everything in the current working directory.

```
jar --create --file test.jar *
```

The following command will create a JAR file with all class files in the book/archives directory and all images from the book/images directory. Here, book is a subdirectory in the current working directory.

```
jar --create --file test.jar book/archives/*.class book/images
```

You can specify a manifest file using the command-line option while creating a JAR file. The manifest file you specify will be a text file that contains all manifest entries for your JAR file. Note that your manifest file must have a blank line at the end of the file. Otherwise, the last entry in the manifest file will not be processed. I discuss the contents of a manifest file in detail shortly.

The following command will use a manifest.txt file while creating the test.jar file, including all files and sub-directories in the current directory. Note the use of the option m.

```
jar --create --file test.jar --manifest manifest.txt *
```

Updating a JAR File

Use the option --update to update an existing JAR file entries or its manifest file. The following command will add a C.class file to an existing test.jar file:

```
jar --update --file test.jar C.class
```

Suppose you have a test.jar file and you want to change the Main-Class entry in its manifest file to pkg.HelloWorld class. You can do that by using the following command:

```
jar --update --file test.jar --main-class pkg.HelloWorld
```

Indexing a JAR File

You can generate an index file for your JAR file. It is used to speed up class loading. Use the --generate-index option with the jar command in a separate command, after you have created a JAR file:

```
jar --generate-index test.jar
```

This command will add a META-INF/INDEX.LIST file to the test.jar file. You can verify it by listing the table of contents of the test.jar file using the following command:

```
jar --list --file test.jar
```

```
META-INF/INDEX.LIST
META-INF/
META-INF/MANIFEST.MF
A.class
B.class
manifest.txt
```

The generated INDEX.LIST file contains location information for all packages in all JAR files listed in the Class-Path attribute of the test.jar file. You can include an attribute called Class-Path in the manifest file of a JAR file. It is a space-separated list of JAR files. The attribute value is used to search and load classes when you run the JAR file.

Extracting an Entry from a JAR File

You can extract all or some entries from a JAR file using the option --extract with the jar command. To extract all entries from a test.jar file, you use

```
jar --extract --file test.jar
```

This command extracts all entries from test.jar file in the current working directory. It creates the same directory structure as in the test.jar file. Any existing file during the extraction of an entry is overwritten. The JAR file, test.jar in this example, is unchanged by this command.

To extract individual entries from a JAR file, you need to list them at the end of the command. The entries should be separated by a space. The following command will extract A.class and book/HelloWorld.class entries from a test.jar file:

```
jar --extract --file test.jar A.class book/HelloWorld.class
```

To extract all class files from a book directory, you can use the following command:

```
jar --extract --file test.jar book/*.class
```

Listing the Contents of a JAR File

Use the option t with the jar command to list the table of contents of a JAR file on the standard output:

```
jar --list --file test.jar
```

The Manifest File

A JAR file differs from a ZIP file in that it may optionally contain a manifest file named MANIFEST.MF in the META-INF directory. The manifest file contains information about the JAR file and its entries. It can contain information about the CLASSPATH setting for the JAR file. Its main entry class is a class with the "public static void main(String[])" method to start a stand-alone application, version information about packages, etc.

A manifest file is divided into sections separated by a blank line. Each section contains name-value pairs. A new line separates each name-value pair. A colon separates a name and its corresponding value. A manifest file must end with a new line. The following is a sample of the content of a manifest file:

```
Manifest-Version: 1.0
Created-By: 1.8.0_20-ea-b05 (Oracle Corporation)
Main-Class: com.jdojo.intro.Welcome
Multi-Release: true
```

This manifest file has one section with four attributes:

- Manifest-Version
- Created-By
- Main-Class
- Multi-Release

There are two kinds of sections in a manifest file: the main section and the individual section. A blank line must separate any two sections. Entries in the main section apply to the entire JAR file. Entries in the individual section apply to a particular entry. An attribute in an individual section overrides the same attribute in the main section. An individual entry starts with a Name attribute, whose value is the name of the entry in the JAR file and is followed by other attributes for that entry. For example, suppose you have a manifest file with the following contents:

```
Manifest-Version: 1.0
Created-By: 1.6.0 (Sun Microsystems Inc.)
Main-Class: com.jdojo.chapter2.Welcome
Sealed: true

Name: book/data/
Sealed: false

Name: images/logo.bmp
Content-Type: image/bmp
```

The manifest file contains three sections: one main section and two individual sections. The first individual section indicates that the package book/data is not sealed. This individual section attribute of Sealed: false will override the main section's attribute of Sealed: true. Another individual section is for an entry called images/logo.bmp. It states that the content type of the entry is an image of bmp type.

The jar command can create a default manifest file and add it to the JAR file. The default manifest file contains only two attributes: Manifest-Version and Created-By. You can use the option --no-manifest to tell the jar tool to omit the default manifest file. The following command will create a test.jar file without adding a default manifest file:

```
jar --create --no-manifest --file test.jar book/*.class
```

The jar command gives you an option to customize the contents of the manifest file. You can use the --manifest option to specify your file that contains the contents for the manifest file. The jar command will read the name-value pairs from the specified manifest file and add them to the MANIFEST.MF file. Suppose you have a file named manifest.txt with one attribute entry in it. Make sure to add a new line at the end of the file. The file's contents are as follows:

```
Main-Class: com.jdojo.intro.Welcome
```

To add the Main-Class attribute value from manifest.txt file in a new test.jar file by including all class files in the current working directory, you execute the following command:

```
jar --create --manifest manifest.txt --file test.jar *.class
```

This command will add a manifest file with the following contents to the test.jar file:

```
Manifest-Version: 1.0
Created-By: 9.0.1 (Oracle Corporation)
Main-Class: com.jdojo.intro.Welcome
```

If you do not specify the Manifest-Version and Created-By attributes in your manifest file, the tool adds them. The Manifest-Version defaults to 1.0 and the Created-By defaults to the JDK version you use.

You can also add the Main-Class attribute value in the manifest file without creating your own manifest file. Use the option --main-class with the jar tool when you create/update a JAR file. The following command will add com.jdojo.intro.Welcome as the value of the Main-Class in the MANIFEST.MF file in the test.jar file:

```
jar --create --main-class com.jdojo.intro.Welcome --file test.jar *.class
```

You can set the CLASSPATH for a JAR file in its manifest file. The attribute name is called Class-Path, which you must specify in a custom manifest file. It is a space-separated list of JAR files, ZIP files, and directories. The Class-Path attribute in a manifest file looks like this

```
Class-Path: chapter8.jar file:/c:/book/ http://www.jdojo.com/jutil.jar
```

This entry has three items for the CLASSPATH: a JAR file named chapter8.jar, a directory using the file protocol file:/c:/book/, and another JAR file using the HTTP protocol http://www.jdojo.com/jutil.jar. Note that the directory name must end with a forward slash. Suppose this Class-Path setting is included in the manifest file for the test.jar file. When you run the test.jar file using the following java command, this CLASSPATH will be used to search and load classes.

```
java -jar test.jar
```

When you run a JAR file with the -jar option using the java command, any CLASSPATH setting outside the manifest file of the JAR file (test.jar file in this case) is ignored. Another use of the Class-Path attribute is to generate an index of all packages using the --generate-index option of the jar tool.

Sealing a Package in a JAR File

You can seal a package in a JAR file. Sealing a package in a JAR file means that all classes declared in that package must be archived in the same JAR file. Typically, you seal a package to easily maintain versions of the package. If you change anything in the package, you just recreate a JAR file. To seal a package in a JAR file, you need to include two attributes: Name and Sealed. The value for the Name attribute is the name of the package and the Sealed attribute has a true value. The following entries in a manifest file will seal a package named com.jdojo.archives. Note that the package name must end with a forward slash (/).

```
Name: com/jdojo/archives/
Sealed: true
```

By default, packages in a JAR file are not sealed. If you want to seal the JAR file itself, you can include a Sealed attributed, as shown:

```
Sealed: true
```

Sealing the JAR file will seal all packages in that JAR file. However, you can override it by not sealing a package individually. The following entries in a manifest file will seal all packages in the JAR file, except the book/chapter8/ package:

```
Sealed: true

Name: book/chapter8/
Sealed: false
```

Using the JAR API

Using JAR API is very similar to using the ZIP API, except that the JAR API includes classes for working with a manifest file. An object of the Manifest class represents a manifest file. You create a Manifest object in your code as follows:

```
Manifest manifest = new Manifest();
```

There are two things you can do with a manifest file: read entries from it and write entries to it. There are separate ways to deal with entries in the main and individual sections. To add an entry into a main section, get an instance of the Attributes class using the getMainAttributes() method of the Manifest class and keep adding a name-value pair to it using its put() method. The following snippet of code adds some attributes to the main section of a Manifest object. The known attribute names are defined as constants in the Attributes.Name class. For example, the constant Attributes.Name.MANIFEST_VERSION represents the Manifest-Version attribute name.

```
// Create a Manifest object
Manifest manifest = new Manifest();

/* Add main attributes
   1. Manifest Version
   2. Main-Class
   3. Sealed
*/
Attributes mainAttribs = manifest.getMainAttributes();
mainAttribs.put(Attributes.Name.MANIFEST_VERSION, "1.0");
mainAttribs.put(Attributes.Name.MAIN_CLASS, "com.jdojo.intro.Welcome");
mainAttribs.put(Attributes.Name.SEALED, "true");
```

Adding an individual entry to the manifest file is a little more complex than adding the main entry. Suppose you want to add the following individual entry to a manifest file:

```
Name: "com/jdojo/archives/"
Sealed: false
```

You need to perform the following steps.

1. Get the Map object that stores the individual entries for a manifest.
2. Create an Attributes object.
3. Add the name-value pair to the Attributes object. You can add as many name-value pairs as you want.
4. Add the Attributes object to the attribute Map using the name of the individual section as the key.

The following snippet of code shows you how to add an individual entry to a Manifest object:

```
// Get the Attribute map for the Manifest
Map<String,Attributes> attribsMap = manifest.getEntries();

// Create an Attributes object
Attributes attribs = new Attributes();
```

```
// Create an Attributes.Name object for the "Sealed" attribute
Attributes.Name name = new Attributes.Name("Sealed");

// Add the "name: value" pair (Sealed: false) to the attributes objects
attribs.put(name, "false");

// Add the Sealed: false attribute to the attributes map
attribsMap.put("com/jdojo/archives/", attribs);
```

If you want to add a manifest file to a JAR file, you can specify it in one of the constructors of the `JarOutputStream` class. For example, the following snippet of code creates a JAR output stream to create a `test.jar` file with a `Manifest` object:

```
// Create a Manifest object
Manifest manifest = new Manifest();

// Create a JarOutputStream with a Manifest object
JarOutputStream jos = new JarOutputStream(new BufferedOutputStream(
                          new FileOutputStream("test.jar")), manifest);
```

Listing 8-6 contains the code to create a JAR file that includes a manifest file. The code is similar to creating a ZIP file. The `main()` method contains the file names used to create the JAR file. All files are expected to be in the current working directory.

- It creates a JAR file named `jartest.jar`.
- It adds the `images/logo.bmp` and `com/jdojo/archives/Test.class` files to the `jartest.jar` file.

If the input files do not exist in your current working directory, you will get an error message when you run the program. If you want to add other files to the JAR file, change the code in the `main()` method accordingly.

Listing 8-6. Creating a JAR File Using the JAR API

```
// JARUtility.java
package com.jdojo.archives;

import java.util.jar.Manifest;
import java.util.jar.Attributes;
import java.util.Map;
import java.util.jar.JarOutputStream;
import java.io.FileOutputStream;
import java.io.IOException;
import java.io.BufferedInputStream;
import java.io.FileInputStream;
import java.io.FileNotFoundException;
import java.io.File;
import java.util.zip.Deflater;
import java.io.BufferedOutputStream;
import java.util.jar.JarEntry;
```

```
public class JARUtility {
    public static void main(String[] args) throws Exception {
        // Create a Manifest object
        Manifest manifest = getManifest();

        // Store jar entries in a String array
        String jarFileName = "jartest.jar";
        String[] entries = new String[2];
        entries[0] = "images/logo.bmp";
        entries[1] = "com/jdojo/archives/Test.class";

        createJAR(jarFileName, entries, manifest);
    }

    public static void createJAR(String jarFileName, String[] jarEntries, Manifest manifest)
{
        // Get the current directory for later use
        String currentDirectory = System.getProperty("user.dir");

        // Create the JAR file
        try (JarOutputStream jos = new JarOutputStream(
                                   new BufferedOutputStream(
                                    new FileOutputStream(jarFileName)
                                   ), manifest)) {

            // Set the compression level to best compression
            jos.setLevel(Deflater.BEST_COMPRESSION);

            // Add each entry to JAR file
            for (String jarEntry : jarEntries) {
                // Make sure the entry file exists
                File entryFile = new File(jarEntry);

                if (!entryFile.exists()) {
                    System.out.println("The entry file " + entryFile.getAbsolutePath()
                            + " does not exist");
                    System.out.println("Aborted processing.");
                    System.exit(1);
                }

                // Create a JarEntry object
                JarEntry je = new JarEntry(jarEntry);

                // Add jar entry object to JAR file
                jos.putNextEntry(je);

                // Add the entry's contents to the JAR file
                addEntryContent(jos, jarEntry);

                // Inform the JAR output stream that we are done
                // working with the current entry
```

```
            jos.closeEntry();
        }

        System.out.println("Output has been written to "
                + currentDirectory + File.separator + jarFileName);
    } catch (IOException e) {
        e.printStackTrace();
    }
}

public static void addEntryContent(JarOutputStream jos, String entryFileName)
        throws IOException, FileNotFoundException {

    // Create an input stream to read data from the entry file
    try (BufferedInputStream bis = new BufferedInputStream(
                                    new FileInputStream(entryFileName))) {
        byte[] buffer = new byte[1024];
        int count;
        while ((count = bis.read(buffer)) != -1) {
            jos.write(buffer, 0, count);
        }
    }
}

public static Manifest getManifest() {
    Manifest manifest = new Manifest();

    /* Add main attributes
     1. Manifest Version
     2. Main-Class
     3. Sealed
     */
    Attributes mainAttribs = manifest.getMainAttributes();
    mainAttribs.put(Attributes.Name.MANIFEST_VERSION, "1.0");
    mainAttribs.put(Attributes.Name.MAIN_CLASS, "com.jdojo.archives.Test");
    mainAttribs.put(Attributes.Name.SEALED, "true");

    /* Add two individual sections */
    /* Do not seal the com/jdojo/archives/ package. Note that you have sealed the whole
       JAR file and to exclude this package you we must add a Sealed: false attribute
       for this package separately.
     */
    Map<String, Attributes> attribsMap = manifest.getEntries();

    // Create an attribute "Sealed : false" and
    // add it for individual entry "Name: com/jdojo/archives/"
    Attributes a1 = getAttribute("Sealed", "false");
    attribsMap.put("com/jdojo/archives/", a1);

    // Create an attribute "Content-Type: image/bmp" and add it for images/logo.bmp
    Attributes a2 = getAttribute("Content-Type", "image/bmp");
    attribsMap.put("images/logo.bmp", a2);
```

```
        return manifest;
    }

    public static Attributes getAttribute(String name, String value) {
        Attributes a = new Attributes();
        Attributes.Name attribName = new Attributes.Name(name);
        a.put(attribName, value);
        return a;
    }
}
```

You can read the entries from a JAR file using similar code that reads entries from a ZIP file. To read the entries from a manifest file of a JAR file, you need to get the object of the `Manifest` class using the `getManifest()` class of `JarInputStream` as follows:

```
// Create a JAR input stream object
JarInputStream jis = new JarInputStream(new FileInputStream("jartest.jar"));

// Get the manifest file from the JAR file. Will return null if
// there is no manifest file in the JAR file.
Manifest manifest = jis.getManifest();

if (manifest != null) {
    // Get the attributes from main section
    Attributes mainAttributes = manifest.getMainAttributes();
    String mainClass = mainAttributes.getValue("Main-Class");

    // Get the attributes from individual section
    Map<String, Attributes> entries = manifest.getEntries();
}
```

This section does not include code examples on reading entries from a JAR file. Refer to the code in the `UnzipUtility` class, which has the code to read entries from a ZIP file. The code to read from a JAR file would be similar, except you would be using JAR-related classes from the `java.util.jar` package instead of the ZIP-related classes from the `java.util.zip` package.

Accessing Resources from a JAR File

How would you access the resources stored in a JAR file? For example, how would you access a file named `images/logo.bmp` in a JAR file, so that you can display the BMP file as an image in your Java application? You can construct a URL object by using the reference of a resource in a JAR file. The JAR file URL syntax is of the form

```
jar:<url>!/{entry}
```

The following URL refers to an `images/logo.bmp` JAR entry in a `test.jar` file on `www.jdojo.com` using the HTTP protocol:

```
jar:http://www.jdojo.com/test.jar!/images/logo.bmp
```

The following URL refers to an `images/logo.bmp` JAR entry in a `test.jar` file on the local file system in the `C:\jarfiles\` directory using the `file` protocol:

```
jar:file:/C:/jarfiles/test.jar!/images/logo.bmp
```

Summary

An archive file consists of one or more files. Optionally, the files in an archive file may be compressed. It also contains metadata that may include the directory structure of the files, comments, error detection and recovery information, etc. An archive file may be encrypted as well.

A checksum is a number that is computed by applying an algorithm on a stream of bytes. Typically, it is used when data is transmitted across the network to check for errors during data transmission. The sender and receiver use the same algorithm to compute the checksum for the transmitted data. A mismatch signals an error in data transmission. Java contains the `Adler32` and `CRC32` classes to compute checksum for data using the Adler32 and CRC32 algorithms, respectively. Java provides `Deflater` and `Inflater` classes to work with data compression and decompression.

The JDK supports creating and manipulating archive files in ZIP, GZIP, and JAR formats through APIs and tools. The APIs are in the `java.util.zip` and `java.util.jar` packages. In addition to the JAR API to work with JAR files, the JDK provides a `jar` command-line tool that can be used create, read, and update JAR files. The `jar` tool is located in the `JDK_HOME\bin` directory.

QUESTIONS AND EXERCISES

1. What is an archive file?
2. What is the difference between lossless and lossy data compression? Name one algorithm of each type.
3. What is use of the `Deflater` and `Inflater` classes?
4. What is checksum? Name three algorithms to compute checksum and their corresponding Java classes.
5. What do instances of the following classes represent: `ZipEntry`, `ZipFile`, `ZipInputStream`, and `ZipOutputStream`?
6. What is the difference between a ZIP file and a JAR file?
7. What types of content are stored in the `versions` directory of a JAR file?
8. What is a manifest file and how do you represent a manifest file in a Java program?
9. What is the name of the command-line tool that is used to work with JAR files?
10. Name the options that you use with the `jar` tool to create a new JAR and to update an existing JAR.
11. Write the command to list the table of contents for a JAR file named `test.jar`.
12. What do instances of the following classes represent: `JarEntry`, `JarFile`, `JarInputStream`, and `JarOutputStream`?

CHAPTER 9

New Input/Output

In this chapter, you will learn:

- What the new input/output is
- How to create different types of buffers
- How to read data from buffers and write data to buffers
- How to manipulate position, limit, and mark properties of a buffer
- How to create different types of views of a buffer
- How to encode/decode data in a buffer using different charsets
- What channels are and how to use channels to read/write the file contents
- How to use memory-mapped files for faster I/O
- How to use file locks
- How to know the byte order of a machine and how to deal with byte order when using buffers

All example programs in this chapter are a member of a `jdojo.nio` module, as declared in Listing 9-1.

Listing 9-1. The Declaration of a jdojo.nio Module

```
// module-info.java
module jdojo.nio {
    exports com.jdojo.nio;
}
```

What Is NIO?

The stream-based I/O uses streams to transfer data between a data source/sink and a Java program. The Java program reads from or writes to a stream one byte at a time. This approach to performing I/O operations is slow. The new input/output (NIO) solves the slow speed problem in the old stream based I/O.

In NIO, you deal with channels and buffers for I/O operations. A channel is like a stream. It represents a connection between a data source/sink and a Java program for data transfer. There is one difference between a channel and a stream. A stream can be used for one-way data transfer. That is, an input stream can only transfer data from a data source to a Java program; an output stream can only transfer data from a Java program to a data sink. However, a channel provides a two-way data transfer facility. You can use a

K. Sharan, *Java Language Features*, https://doi.org/10.1007/978-1-4842-3348-1_9

channel to read data as well as to write data. You can obtain a read-only channel, a write-only channel, or a read-write channel, depending on your needs.

In stream-based I/O, the basic unit of data transfer is a byte. In channel-based NIO, the basic unit of data transfer is a buffer. A buffer is a bounded data container. That is, a buffer has a fixed capacity that determines the upper limit of the data it may contain. In stream-based I/O, you write data directly to the stream. In channel-based I/O, you write data into a buffer; you pass that buffer to the channel, which writes the data to the data sink. Similarly, when you want to read data from a data source, you pass a buffer to a channel. The channel reads data from the data source into the buffer. You read data from the buffer. Figure 9-1 depicts the interaction between a channel, a buffer, a data source, a data sink, and a Java program. It is evident that the most important parts in this interaction are reading from a buffer and writing into a buffer. I discuss buffers and channels in detail in subsequent sections.

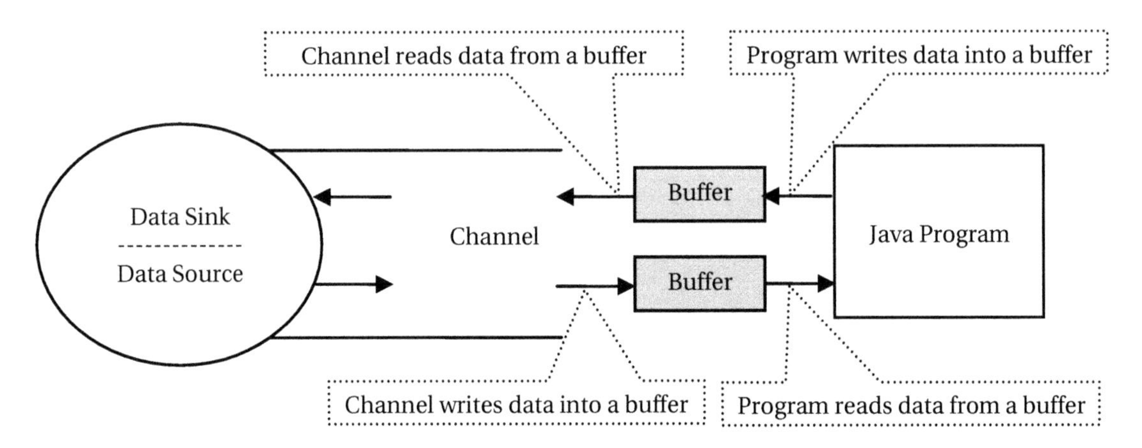

Figure 9-1. *Interaction between a channel, buffers, a Java program, a data source, and a data sink*

Buffers

A buffer is a fixed-length data container. There is a separate buffer type to hold data for each type of primitive value, except for `boolean` type values. A buffer is an object in your program. You have a separate class to represent each type of buffer. All buffer classes are inherited from an abstract `Buffer` class. Buffer classes that hold primitive values are as follows:

- `ByteBuffer`
- `ShortBuffer`
- `CharBuffer`
- `IntBuffer`
- `LongBuffer`
- `FloatBuffer`
- `DoubleBuffer`

An object of an XxxBuffer class is used to hold data of the Xxx primitive data type. For example, a ByteBuffer holds byte values; a ShortBuffer holds short values; a CharBuffer is holds characters, and so on. The following are the four important properties of a buffer, which you must understand to use it effectively:

- Capacity
- Position
- Limit
- Mark

The capacity of a buffer is the maximum number of elements that it can hold. The capacity of a buffer is fixed when the buffer is created. You can think of the capacity of a buffer as the length of an array. Once you create an array, its length is fixed. Similarly, once you create a buffer, its capacity is fixed. However, a buffer is not necessarily backed by an array. You can check if a buffer is backed by an array by calling its hasArray() method, which returns true if the buffer is backed by an array. You can get access to the backing array of a buffer by using the array() method of the buffer object. Once you get access to the backing array of a buffer, any changes made to that array will be reflected in the buffer. A buffer has a capacity() method that returns its capacity as an int.

You can create a buffer of a particular kind in many ways. You can create a buffer by using the allocate() factory method of a particular buffer class as follows:

```
// Create a byte buffer with the capacity as 8
ByteBuffer bb = ByteBuffer.allocate(8);

// Assigns 8 to the capacity variable
int capacity = bb.capacity();

// Create a character buffer with the capacity as 1024
CharBuffer cb = CharBuffer.allocate(1024);
```

A byte buffer gets special treatment in NIO. It has an extra method called allocateDirect() that creates a byte buffer for which the memory is allocated from the operating system memory, not from the JVM heap. This avoids copying the contents to intermediate buffers during I/O operations. A direct buffer has an additional creation cost. However, it is faster during the I/O operations. You should use a direct byte buffer when a buffer is long-lived. You can use the isDirect() method of the ByteBuffer class to check if a buffer is direct or non-direct.

```
// Create a direct byte buffer of 512 bytes capacity
ByteBuffer bbd = ByteBuffer.allocateDirect(512);
```

Another way to create a buffer is to wrap an array using the buffer's static wrap() method:

```
// Create an array of bytes
byte[] byteArray = new byte[512];

// Create a byte buffer by wrapping the byteArray
ByteBuffer bb = ByteBuffer.wrap(byteArray);
```

You can use the same technique to create a buffer to store other primitive values. I discuss other ways of creating a buffer later in this section.

When you create a buffer, all elements of the buffer are initialized to a value of zero. Each element of a buffer has an index. The first element has an index of 0 and the last element has an index of `capacity - 1`.

Position and limit are two properties of a buffer. When a buffer is created, its position is set to 0 and its limit is equal to its capacity. A buffer's position is the index of the next element to be read or written. A buffer's limit is the index of the first element that should not be read or written. So, a read/write operation start at the buffer's position (inclusive) and may continue up to the buffer's limit (exclusive).

Figure 9-2 shows the state of a buffer with a capacity of 8 just after its creation. All its elements have a value of 0. Its position is set to zero. Its limit is set to 8, which is equal to its capacity. In the figure, `P` and `L` denote the position and the limit of the buffer, respectively. Note that the figure shows the index at 8, which is out of range for the buffer, to show the value of the limit.

Buffer Elements ->	0	0	0	0	0	0	0	0	
Element's Index ->	0	1	2	3	4	5	6	7	8
	P								L

Figure 9-2. *A buffer of capacity 8 after its creation*

You can get/set the position of a buffer using its overloaded `position()` method. The `position()` method returns the current value of the position of a buffer. The `position(int newPosition)` method sets the position of the buffer to the specified `newPosition` value and returns the reference of the buffer.

You can get/set the limit of a buffer using its overloaded `limit()` method. The `limit()` method returns the current value of the limit of a buffer. The `limit(int newLimit)` method sets the limit of a buffer to the specified `newLimit` value and returns the reference of the buffer.

You can bookmark a position of a buffer by using the `mark()` method. When you call the `mark()` method, the buffer stores the current value of its position as its mark value. You can set the position of a buffer to its previously bookmarked value by using the `reset()` method. The buffer's mark is not defined when it is created. You must call the `reset()` method on a buffer only when its mark is defined. Otherwise, the `reset()` method throws an `InvalidMarkException`.

The following invariant must hold during the lifetime of a buffer:

```
0 <= mark <= position <= limit <= capacity
```

Since the capacity of a buffer never changes and mark has limited use through the `mark()` and `reset()` methods, I limit the discussion only to the position and limit properties of a buffer. There are some indirect consequences of changing the position and limit values. Since the mark cannot be greater than the position, the mark is discarded if the position is set less than the current mark value. If you set the limit less than the position, the position is automatically set equal to the limit value.

So far, you have read a great deal on buffers. It's time to see a buffer in action. Listing 9-2 contains the code to create a new buffer and display its four properties.

Listing 9-2. Mark, Position, Limit, and Capacity of a New Buffer

```
// BufferInfo.java
package com.jdojo.nio;

import java.nio.ByteBuffer;
import java.nio.InvalidMarkException;
```

```
public class BufferInfo {
    public static void main(String[] args) {
        // Create a byte buffer of capacity 8
        ByteBuffer bb = ByteBuffer.allocate(8);

        System.out.println("Capacity: " + bb.capacity());
        System.out.println("Limit: " + bb.limit());
        System.out.println("Position: " + bb.position());

        // The mark is not set for a new buffer. Calling the reset() method
        // throws a runtime exception if the mark is not set. If the mark is set,
        // the position is set to the mark value.
        try {
            bb.reset();
            System.out.println("Mark: " + bb.position());
        } catch (InvalidMarkException e) {
            System.out.println("Mark is not set");
        }
    }
}
```

```
Capacity: 8
Limit: 8
Position: 0
Mark is not set
```

Reading from and Writing to a Buffer

There are two ways to read data from a buffer:

- Using absolute position
- Using relative position

In an absolute position read, you specify the index in the buffer from which you want to read the data. The position of the buffer is unchanged after an absolute position read.

In a relative position read, you specify how many data elements you want to read. The current position of the buffer determines which data elements will be read. In a relative position read, the read starts at the current position of the buffer and the position is incremented by one after reading each data element.

The `get()` method is used to read data from a buffer. The `get()` method is overloaded. It has four versions. Just replace the data type `byte` with another data type for other primitive type buffers in the following methods:

- `get(int index)`: Returns the data at the given index. For example, `get(2)` will return the data at index 2 from the buffer. It is an absolute way of reading data from a buffer because you provide the absolute position of the element from which you want to read the data. This method does not change the current position of the buffer.
- `get()`: Returns the data from the current position in the buffer and increases the position by 1. For example, if position is set at index 2, calling the `get()` method will return the value at index 2 from the buffer and set the position to 3. It is a relative way of reading data from a buffer because you read the data relative to the current position.

- `get(byte[] destination, int offset, int length)`: Reads data from a buffer in bulk. It reads `length` number of bytes from the current position of the buffer and puts them in the specified `destination` array starting at the specified `offset`. If it cannot read the `length` number of bytes from the buffer, it throws a `BufferUnderflowException`. If there is no exception, it increases the current position by `length`. It is a relative read from a buffer.
- `get(byte[] destination)`: Fills the specified `destination` array by reading data from the current position of the buffer and increments the current position by one each time it reads a data element. If there is not enough data to fill the array, it will throw a `BufferUnderflowException`. It is a relative way of reading data from a buffer. This method call is the same as calling `get(byte[] destination, 0, destination.length)`.

Writing data to a buffer is the opposite of reading data from it. The `put()` method is used to write data to a buffer. The `put()` method has five versions: one for absolute position write and four for relative position write. The absolute version of the `put()` method does not affect the position of the buffer. The relative versions of the `put()` method write the data and advance the position of the buffer by one for each written element. Different buffer classes have different versions of the `put()` method; however, there are five versions that are common among all types of buffers. The following are the five versions of the `put()` method for `ByteBuffer`. These methods throw a `ReadOnlyBufferException` when the buffer is read-only. Just replace the data type `byte` with another data type for other primitive type buffers in the following methods.

- `put(int index, byte b)`: Writes the specified `b` data at the specified `index`. The call to this method does not change the current position of the buffer.
- `put(byte b)`: It is a relative `put()` method that writes the specified byte at the current position of the buffer and increments the position by 1. It throws a `BufferOverflowException` if there is not enough room in the buffer to the specified byte.
- `put(byte[] source, int offset, int length)`: Writes the `length` number of bytes from the `source` array starting at `offset` to the buffer starting at the current position. The position of the buffer is incremented by `length`. It throws a `BufferOverflowException` if there is not enough room in the buffer to write all bytes.
- `put(byte[] source)`: It is the same as calling `put(byte[] source, 0, source.length)`.
- `ByteBuffer put(ByteBuffer src)`: Reads the remaining bytes from the specified byte buffer `src` and writes them to the buffer. If the remaining space in the target buffer is less than the remaining bytes in the source buffer, a runtime `BufferOverflowException` is thrown.

Let's have some pictorial views of the state of a buffer and its properties after each read and write. Figure 9-3 through Figure 9-6 depict how the position of a buffer with a capacity of 8 is advanced after each write in the buffer. After the eighth write in the buffer, the position and the limit become equal. If you attempt to write a ninth time, you would get a `BufferOverflowException`. Note that I have used a relative write using the `put(byte b)` method.

Buffer Elements >>	0	0	0	0	0	0	0	0	
Element's Index >>	0	1	2	3	4	5	6	7	8
	P								L

Figure 9-3. *Buffer state with capacity 8 after creation; buffer state is (position=0, limit=8)*

Buffer Elements >>	50	0	0	0	0	0	0	0	
Element's Index >>	0	1	2	3	4	5	6	7	8
		P							L

Figure 9-4. *Buffer state after calling put((byte)50); buffer state is (position= 1, limit=8)*

Buffer Elements >>	50	51	0	0	0	0	0	0	
Element's Index >>	0	1	2	3	4	5	6	7	8
			P						L

Figure 9-5. *Buffer state after calling put((byte)51); buffer state is (position= 2, limit=8)*

Buffer Elements >>	50	51	52	53	54	55	56	57	
Element's Index >>	0	1	2	3	4	5	6	7	8
									L P

Figure 9-6. *Buffer state after calling put((byte)52), put((byte)53), put((byte)54), put((byte)55), put((byte)56), and put((byte)57); buffer state is (position= 8, limit=8)*

Let's read the data that you have just written into the buffer whose state is shown in Figure 9-6. Note that the position of the buffer is 8 and its limit is also 8. If you call the `get()` method (a relative read) to read data from this buffer, you would get a `BufferUnderflowException`. You have just filled the buffer with data. However, when you attempt to read the data, you get an exception because the `get()` method returns data from the current position of the buffer, which is out of range in this case. The `get()` method will return data only if the position of the buffer is in the range of 0 and 7. Let's not lose hope and try to read the data using an absolute position with the `get(int index)` method. If you call `get(0), get(1) ... get(7)`, you will be surprised to know that you can read all the data you had written. Listing 9-3 demonstrates this.

Listing 9-3. Writing to and Reading from a Buffer

```
// BufferReadWrite.java
package com.jdojo.nio;

import java.nio.ByteBuffer;
```

```
public class BufferReadWrite {
    public static void main(String[] args) {
        // Create a byte buffer with a capacity of 8
        ByteBuffer bb = ByteBuffer.allocate(8);

        // Print the buffer info
        System.out.println("After creation:");
        printBufferInfo(bb);

        // Populate buffer elements from 50 to 57
        for (int i = 50; i < 58; i++) {
            bb.put((byte) i);
        }

        // Print the buffer info
        System.out.println("After populating data:");
        printBufferInfo(bb);
    }

    public static void printBufferInfo(ByteBuffer bb) {
        int limit = bb.limit();
        System.out.println("Position = " + bb.position() + ", Limit = " + limit);

        // Use absolute reading without affecting the position
        System.out.print("Data: ");
        for (int i = 0; i < limit; i++) {
            System.out.print(bb.get(i) + " ");
        }
        System.out.println();
    }
}
```

```
After creation:
Position = 0, Limit = 8
Data: 0 0 0 0 0 0 0 0
After populating data:
Position = 8, Limit = 8
Data: 50 51 52 53 54 55 56 57
```

Now you understand that there is a big difference in using relative and absolute methods for reading from and writing to a buffer. Both methods have a working range. The data must be read and written in the working range. The working range for relative and absolute methods is different.

The working range for a relative read/write are the indices between position and limit -1 of the buffer, where position is less than limit -1. That is, you can read/write data using the relative `get()` and `put()` methods if the position of the buffer is less than its limit.

The working range for the absolute read/write is the index between zero and limit -1. So, how do you read all the data from a buffer using a relative position read, after you have finished writing data into the buffer? One way to accomplish this is to set the limit of the buffer equal to its position and set its position to 0. The following snippet of code shows this technique:

```
// Create a byte buffer of capacity 8 and populate its elements
ByteBuffer bb = ByteBuffer.allocate(8);
for(int i = 50; i < 58; i++) {
    bb.put((byte)i);
}

// Set the limit the same as the position and set the position to 0
bb.limit(bb.position());
bb.position(0);

// Now bb is set to read all data using relative get() method
int limit = bb.limit();
for(int i = 0; i < limit; i++) {
    byte b = bb.get(); // Uses a relative read
    System.out.println(b);
}
```

```
50
51
52
53
54
55
56
57
```

The Buffer class has a method to accomplish just what you have coded in this snippet of code. You can set the limit of the buffer to its position and set the position to 0 by using its flip() method. Figure 9-7 shows the state of a buffer, which has a capacity of 8, after it has been created and after its two elements at index 0 and 1 have been written. Figure 9-8 shows the state of the buffer after its flip() method is called. The flip() method discards the mark of a buffer if it is defined.

Buffer Elements >>	50	51	0	0	0	0	0	0	
Element's Index >>	0	1	2	3	4	5	6	7	8
			P						L

***Figure 9-7.** Buffer's state just after you have written two elements at indexes 0 and 1*

Buffer Elements >>	50	51	0	0	0	0	0	0	
Element's Index >>	0	1	2	3	4	5	6	7	8
	P		L						

Figure 9-8. *Buffer's state after writing two elements at indexes 0 and 1 and calling the flip() method*

In the previous snippet of code, you used a `for` loop to read the data from the buffer. The index of the `for` loop runs from zero to limit -1. However, there is an easier way to read/write data from/to a buffer using a relative read/write method. The `hasRemaining()` method of a buffer returns `true` if you can use relative `get()` or `put()` method on the buffer to read/write at least one element. You can also get the maximum number of elements you can read/write using relative `get()` or `put()` methods by using its `remaining()` method. Listing 9-4 demonstrates the use of these methods.

Listing 9-4. Using the flip() and hasRemaining() Methods of a Buffer Between Relative Reads and Writes

```
// BufferReadWriteRelativeOnly.java
package com.jdojo.nio;

import java.nio.ByteBuffer;

public class BufferReadWriteRelativeOnly {
    public static void main(String[] args) {
        // Create a byte buffer of capacity 8
        ByteBuffer bb = ByteBuffer.allocate(8);

        // Print the buffer info
        System.out.println("After creation:");
        printBufferInfo(bb);

        // Must call flip() to reset the position to zero because the printBufferInfo()
        // method uses relative get() method, which increments the position.
        bb.flip();

        // Populate buffer elements from 50 to 57
        int i = 50;
        while (bb.hasRemaining()) {
            bb.put((byte) i++);
        }

        // Call flip() again to reset the position to zero,
        // because the above put() call incremented the position
        bb.flip();

        // Print the buffer info
        System.out.println("After populating data:");
        printBufferInfo(bb);
    }
```

```
    public static void printBufferInfo(ByteBuffer bb) {
        int limit = bb.limit();
        System.out.println("Position = " + bb.position() + ", Limit = " + limit);

        // We use relative method of reading the data, so it affects the
        // the position of the buffer
        System.out.print("Data: ");
        while (bb.hasRemaining()) {
            System.out.print(bb.get() + " ");
        }

        System.out.println();
    }
}
```

```
After creation:
Position = 0, Limit = 8
Data: 0 0 0 0 0 0 0 0
After populating data:
Position = 0, Limit = 8
Data: 50 51 52 53 54 55 56 57
```

Apart from the flip() method, there are three more methods of a buffer that change its mark, position, and/or limit. They are clear(), reset(), and rewind().

The clear() method of a buffer sets the position to zero, limit to its capacity, and discards its mark. That is, it sets the buffer's properties as if the buffer has just been created. Note that it does not change any data in the buffer. Figure 9-9 and Figure 9-10 show the mark, position, and limit of a buffer before and after calling the clear() method. Typically, you call the clear() method on a buffer before you start filling it with fresh data.

Buffer Elements >>	50	51	52	53	54	0	0	0	
Element's Index >>	0	1	2	3	4	5	6	7	8
		M	P			L			

***Figure 9-9.** Buffer's state before calling its clear() method*

Buffer Elements >>	50	51	52	53	54	0	0	0	
Element's Index >>	0	1	2	3	4	5	6	7	8
	P								L

***Figure 9-10.** Buffer's state after calling its clear() method; the clear() method discarded the mark*

The `reset()` method sets the position of a buffer equal to its mark. If a mark is not defined, it throws an `InvalidMarkException`. It does not affect the limit and data of the buffer. Typically, it is called to revisit (for rereading or rewriting) the buffer's elements starting from the previously marked position and up to the current position. The mark of the buffer remains unchanged by the `reset()` method. Figure 9-11 and Figure 9-12 show the states of a buffer before and after its `reset()` method is called.

Buffer Elements >>	50	51	52	53	54	0	0	0	
Element's Index >>	0	1	2	3	4	5	6	7	8
		M	P			L			

***Figure 9-11.** Buffer's state before calling its reset() method*

Buffer Elements >>	50	51	52	53	54	55	56	57	
Element's Index >>	0	1	2	3	4	5	6	7	8
		M P				L			

***Figure 9-12.** Buffer's state after calling its reset() method*

The `rewind()` method sets the position of the buffer to zero and discards its mark. It does not affect the limit. Typically, you call this method between multiple read/write operations to use the same number of data elements in the buffer multiple times. Figure 9-13 and Figure 9-14 show the state of a buffer before and after calling its `rewind()` method.

Buffer Elements >>	50	51	52	53	54	0	0	0	
Element's Index >>	0	1	2	3	4	5	6	7	8
			P			L			

***Figure 9-13.** Buffer's state before calling its rewind() method*

Buffer Elements >>	50	51	52	53	54	0	0	0	
Element's Index >>	0	1	2	3	4	5	6	7	8
	P					L			

***Figure 9-14.** Buffer's state after calling its rewind() method*

Read-Only Buffers

A buffer can be read-only or read-write. You can only read the contents of a read-only buffer. Any attempt to change the contents of a read-only buffer results in a `ReadOnlyBufferException`. Note that the properties of a read-only buffer such as its position, limit, and mark can be changed during the read operations, but not its data.

You may want to get a read-only buffer from a read-write buffer, so you can pass it as an argument to a method to make sure the method does not modify buffer's contents. You can get a read-only buffer by calling the `asReadOnlyBuffer()` method of the specific buffer class. You can check if a buffer is read-only by calling the `isReadOnly()` method as follows:

```
// Create a buffer that is read-write by default
ByteBuffer bb = ByteBuffer.allocate(1024);
boolean readOnly = bb.isReadOnly(); // Assigns false to readOnly

// Get a read-only buffer
ByteBuffer bbReadOnly = bb.asReadOnlyBuffer();
readOnly = bbReadOnly.isReadOnly(); // Assigns true to readOnly
```

The read-only buffer returned by the `asReadOnlyBuffer()` method is a different view of the same buffer. That is, the new read-only buffer shares data with its original buffer. Any modifications to the contents of the original buffer are reflected in the read-only buffer. A read-only buffer has the same value of position, mark, limit, and capacity as its original buffer at the time of creation and it maintains them independently afterwards.

Different Views of a Buffer

You can obtain different views of a buffer. A view of a buffer shares data with the original buffer and maintains its own position, mark, and limit. I discussed getting a read-only view of a buffer in the previous section that does not let its contents be modified. You can also duplicate a buffer, in which case they share contents, but maintain mark, position, and limit independently. Use the `duplicate()` method of a buffer to get a copy of the buffer as follows:

```
// Create a buffer
ByteBuffer bb = ByteBuffer.allocate(1024);

// Create a duplicate view of the buffer
ByteBuffer bbDuplicate = bb.duplicate();
```

You can also create a sliced view of a buffer. That is, you can create a view of a buffer that reflects only a portion of the contents of the original buffer. You use the `slice()` method of a buffer to create its sliced view as follows:

```
// Create a buffer
ByteBuffer bb = ByteBuffer.allocate(8);

// Set the position and the limit before getting a slice
bb.position(3);
bb.limit(6);

// bbSlice buffer will share data of bb from index 3 to 5.
// bbSlice will have position set to 0 and its limit set to 3.
ByteBuffer bbSlice = bb.slice();
```

■ **Tip** JDK9 added the `duplicate()` and `slice()` methods to the `Buffer` class, which is the superclass of other buffer types. In JDK8, these methods were in subclasses of the `Buffer` class. The return type of these methods in the `Buffer` class is `Buffer`, whereas subclasses override these methods and their return types are specific subclass types. For example, the return types of these methods in the `ByteBuffer` class are `ByteBuffer`.

You can also get a view of a byte buffer for different primitive data types. For example, you can get a character view, a float view, etc. of a byte buffer. The `ByteBuffer` class contains methods such as `asCharBuffer()`, `asLongBuffer()`, `asFloatBuffer()`, etc. to obtain a view for other primitive data types.

```
// Create a byte buffer
ByteBuffer bb = ByteBuffer.allocate(8);

// Create a char view of the byte buffer
CharBuffer cb = bb.asCharBuffer();

// Create a float view of the byte buffer
FloatBuffer fb = bb.asFloatBuffer();
```

Character Set

A character is not always stored in one byte. The number of bytes used to store a character depends on the coded character set and the character-encoding scheme. A coded-character set is a mapping between a set of abstract characters and a set of integers. A character-encoding scheme is a mapping between a coded-character set and a set of octet sequence. Refer to Appendix A in the first volume of this series for more details on character set and character encoding.

An instance of the `java.nio.charset.Charset` class represents a character set and a character-encoding scheme. Examples of some character set names are US-ASCII, ISO-8859-1, UTF-8, UTF-16BE, UTF-16LE, and UTF-16.

The process of converting a character into a sequence of bytes based on an encoding scheme is called *character encoding*. The process of converting a sequence of bytes into a character based on an encoding scheme is called *decoding*.

In NIO, you can convert a Unicode character to a sequence of bytes and vice versa using an encoding scheme. The `java.nio.charset` package provides classes to encode/decode a `CharBuffer` to a `ByteBuffer` and vice versa. An object of the `Charset` class represents the encoding scheme. The `CharsetEncoder` class performs the encoding. The `CharsetDecoder` class performs the decoding. You can get an object of the `Charset` class using its `forName()` method by passing the name of the character set as its argument.

The `String` and `InputStreamReader` classes support character encoding and decoding. When you use `str.getBytes("UTF-8")`, you are encoding the Unicode-characters stored in the string object `str` to a sequence of bytes using the UTF-8 encoding-scheme. When you use the constructor of the `String` class `String(byte[] bytes, Charset charset)` to create a `String` object, you are decoding the sequence of bytes in the `bytes` array from the specified character set to the Unicode-character set. You are also decoding a sequence of bytes from an input stream into Unicode-characters when you create an object of the `InputStreamReader` class using a character set.

For simple encoding and decoding tasks, you can use the encode() and decode() methods of the Charset class. Let's encode a sequence of characters in the string Hello stored in a character buffer and decode it using the UTF-8 encoding-scheme. The snippet of code to achieve this is as follows:

```
// Get a Charset object for UTF-8 encoding
Charset cs = Charset.forName("UTF-8");

// Character buffer to be encoded
CharBuffer cb = CharBuffer.wrap("Hello");

// Encode character buffer into a byte buffer
ByteBuffer encodedData = cs.encode(cb);

// Decode the byte buffer back to a character buffer
CharBuffer decodedData = cs.decode(encodedData);
```

The encode() and decode() methods of the Charset class are easy to use. However, they cannot be used in all situations. They require you to know the inputs in advance. Sometimes you do not know the data to be encoded/decoded in advance.

CharsetEncoder and CharsetDecoder classes provide much more power during the encoding and decoding process. They accept a chunk of input to be encoded or decoded. The encode() and decode() methods of the Charset class return the encoded and decoded buffers to you. However, CharsetEncoder and CharsetDecoder will let you use your buffers for input and output data. The power comes with a little complexity! If you want more powerful encoding/decoding, you need to use the following five classes instead of just the Charset class:

- Charset
- CharsetEncoder
- CharsetDecoder
- CoderResult
- CodingErrorAction

You still need to use the Charset class to represent a character set. A CharsetEncoder object lets you encode characters into a sequence of bytes using its encode() method. A sequence of bytes is decoded using the decode() method of a CharsetDecoder object. The newEncoder() method of a Charset object returns an instance of the CharsetEncoder class, whereas its newDecoder() method returns an instance of the CharsetDecoder class.

```
// Get encoder and decoder objects from a Charset object
Charset cs = Charset.forName("UTF-8");
CharsetEncoder encoder = cs.newEncoder();
CharsetDecoder decoder = cs.newDecoder();
```

Two buffers, an input buffer and an output buffer, are needed for encoding and decoding. A character buffer supplies the input characters to the encoding process and receives the decoded characters from the decoding process. The encoding process writes the encoded result into a byte buffer and the decoding process reads its input from a byte buffer. The following snippet of code illustrates the few steps in using an encoder and a decoder:

```
// Encode characters, which are in the inputChars buffer.
// The outputBytes buffer receives encoded bytes.
CharBuffer inputChars = /* get input characters to be encoded */;
ByteBuffer outputBytes = /* get the output buffer for the encoded data */;

boolean eoi = true; // Indicates the end of the input
CoderResult result = encoder.encode(inputChars, outputBytes, eoi);

// Decode bytes, which are in the inputBytes buffer.
// The outputChars buffer receives the decoded characters.
ByteBuffer inputBytes = /* get the input bytes to be decoded */;
CharBuffer outputChars = /* get the output buffer for the decoded characters */;

boolean eoi = true; // Indicates the end of the input
CoderResult result = decoder.decode(inputBytes, outputChars, eoi);
```

Consider a situation of encoding 16 characters stored in a character buffer using a 4-byte buffer. The encoding process cannot encode all characters in one call to the encode() method. There must be a way to read all encoded output repeatedly. You can apply the same argument for the decoding process. You can pass an input to the encoding/decoding process and receive an output from them in chunks. The encoder's encode() method and decoder's decode() method return an object of the CoderResult class, which contains the status of the encoding/decoding process. There are two important results that this object can indicate:

- Underflow
- Overflow

An *underflow* indicates that the process needs more input. You can test for this condition by using the isUnderflow() method of the CoderResult object. You can also test this condition by comparing the return value of the encode() or decode() method with CoderResult.UNDERFLOW object as follows:

```
CoderResult result = encoder.encode(input, output, eoi);
if (result == CoderResult.UNDERFLOW) {
    // Supply some more input
}
```

An *overflow* indicates that the process has produced more output than the capacity of the output buffer. You need to empty the output buffer and call the encode()/decode() method again to get more output. You can test for this condition by using the isOverflow() method of the CoderResult object. You can also test for this condition by comparing the return value of the encode() or decode() method with CoderResult.OVERFLOW object as follows:

```
CoderResult result = encoder.encode(input, output, eoi);
if (result == CoderResult.OVERFLOW) {
    // Empty output buffer to make some room for more output
}
```

■ **Tip** Apart from reporting buffer underflow and overflow, a `CoderResult` object is also capable of reporting a malformed-input error and an unmappable-character error. You can also customize the default action of the encoding/decoding engine for these error conditions by using their `onMalformedInput()` and `onUnmappableCharacter()` methods.

The last argument to the `encode()`/`decode()` method is a `boolean` value, which indicates the end of the input. You should pass `true` for the end of the input argument when you pass the last chunk of data for encoding or decoding.

After passing the last chunk of data, you need to call the `flush()` method to flush the internal buffer of the engine. It returns an object of `CoderResult` that can indicate underflow or overflow. If there is an overflow, you need to empty the output buffer and call the `flush()` method again. You need to keep calling the `flush()` method until its return value indicates an underflow. The `flush()` method call should be placed in a loop, so you get all of the encoded/decoded data.

The `DataSourceSink` class in Listing 9-5 serves as a data source and a data sink. I created this class only for illustration purposes; you would not need a class like this in a real-world application. It supplies a stanza from the poem *Lucy* by William Wordsworth in a character buffer. The `getCharData()` method fills the character buffer. It returns -1 when there are no more characters to supply. You use this method during the encoding process. The `storeByteData()` method is used to accumulate the encoded bytes during the encoding process. The `getByteData()` method is used during the decoding process to supply the encoded bytes in chunks that you accumulate during the encoding process.

Listing 9-5. A Data Source and Sink that Supplies Character Data and Stores and Supplies Byte Data

```
// DataSourceSink.java
package com.jdojo.nio;

import java.nio.ByteBuffer;
import java.nio.CharBuffer;

public class DataSourceSink {
    private CharBuffer cBuffer = null;
    private ByteBuffer bBuffer = null;

    public DataSourceSink() {
        String text = this.getText();
        cBuffer = CharBuffer.wrap(text);
    }

    public int getByteData(ByteBuffer buffer) {
        if (!bBuffer.hasRemaining()) {
            return -1;
        }

        int count = 0;
        while (bBuffer.hasRemaining() && buffer.hasRemaining()) {
            buffer.put(bBuffer.get());
            count++;
        }
```

```
        return count;
    }

    public int getCharData(CharBuffer buffer) {
        if (!cBuffer.hasRemaining()) {
            return -1;
        }

        int count = 0;
        while (cBuffer.hasRemaining() && buffer.hasRemaining()) {
            buffer.put(cBuffer.get());
            count++;
        }

        return count;
    }

    public void storeByteData(ByteBuffer byteData) {
        if (this.bBuffer == null) {
            int total = byteData.remaining();
            this.bBuffer = ByteBuffer.allocate(total);
            while (byteData.hasRemaining()) {
                this.bBuffer.put(byteData.get());
            }
            this.bBuffer.flip();
        } else {
            this.bBuffer = this.appendContent(byteData);
        }
    }

    private ByteBuffer appendContent(ByteBuffer content) {
        // Create a new buffer to accommodate new data
        int count = bBuffer.limit() + content.remaining();
        ByteBuffer newBuffer = ByteBuffer.allocate(count);

        // Set the position of bBuffer that has some data
        bBuffer.clear();
        newBuffer.put(bBuffer);
        newBuffer.put(content);
        bBuffer.clear();
        newBuffer.clear();
        return newBuffer;
    }

    public final String getText() {
        String newLine = System.getProperty("line.separator");
        StringBuilder sb = new StringBuilder();
        sb.append("My horse moved on; hoof after hoof");
        sb.append(newLine);
        sb.append("He raised, and never stopped:");
        sb.append(newLine);
```

```
        sb.append("When down behind the cottage roof,");
        sb.append(newLine);
        sb.append("At once, the bright moon dropped.");

        return sb.toString();
    }
}
```

Listing 9-6 demonstrates how to use a character set encoder/decoder. The encode() and decode() methods of the CharEncoderDecoder class have the encoding and decoding logic. This example displays the decoded characters on the standard output.

Listing 9-6. Charset Encoder and Decoder Using a DataSourceSink as a Data Supplier/Consumer for Encoding/Decoding

```
// CharEncoderDecoder.java
package com.jdojo.nio;

import java.nio.ByteBuffer;
import java.nio.CharBuffer;
import java.nio.charset.Charset;
import java.nio.charset.CharsetDecoder;
import java.nio.charset.CharsetEncoder;
import java.nio.charset.CoderResult;

public class CharEncoderDecoder {
    public static void main(String[] args) throws Exception {
        DataSourceSink dss = new DataSourceSink();

        // Display the text we are going to encode
        System.out.println("Original Text:");
        System.out.println(dss.getText());
        System.out.println("--------------------");

        // Encode the text using UTF-8 encoding. We will store
        // encoded bytes in the dss object during the encoding process
        encode(dss, "UTF-8");

        // Decode bytes stored in the dss object using UTF-8 encoding
        System.out.println("Decoded Text:");
        decode(dss, "UTF-8");
    }

    public static void encode(DataSourceSink ds, String charset) {
        CharsetEncoder encoder = Charset.forName(charset).newEncoder();

        CharBuffer input = CharBuffer.allocate(8);
        ByteBuffer output = ByteBuffer.allocate(8);

        // Initialize variables for loop
        boolean endOfInput = false;
        CoderResult result = CoderResult.UNDERFLOW;
```

```
        while (!endOfInput) {
            if (result == CoderResult.UNDERFLOW) {
                input.clear();
                endOfInput = (ds.getCharData(input) == -1);
                input.flip();
            }

            // Encode the input characters
            result = encoder.encode(input, output, endOfInput);

            // Drain output when
            // 1. It is an overflow. Or,
            // 2. It is an underflow and it is the end of the input
            if (result == CoderResult.OVERFLOW
                    || (endOfInput && result == CoderResult.UNDERFLOW)) {
                output.flip();
                ds.storeByteData(output);
                output.clear();
            }
        }

        // Flush the internal state of the encoder
        while (true) {
            output.clear();
            result = encoder.flush(output);
            output.flip();
            if (output.hasRemaining()) {
                ds.storeByteData(output);
                output.clear();
            }

            // Underflow means flush() method has flushed everything
            if (result == CoderResult.UNDERFLOW) {
                break;
            }
        }
    }

    public static void decode(DataSourceSink dss, String charset) {
        CharsetDecoder decoder = Charset.forName(charset).newDecoder();
        ByteBuffer input = ByteBuffer.allocate(8);
        CharBuffer output = CharBuffer.allocate(8);

        boolean endOfInput = false;
        CoderResult result = CoderResult.UNDERFLOW;

        while (!endOfInput) {
            if (result == CoderResult.UNDERFLOW) {
                input.clear();
                endOfInput = (dss.getByteData(input) == -1);
                input.flip();
            }
```

```
            // Decode the input bytes
            result = decoder.decode(input, output, endOfInput);

            // Drain output when
            // 1. It is an overflow. Or,
            // 2. It is an underflow and it is the end of the input
            if (result == CoderResult.OVERFLOW
                    || (endOfInput && result == CoderResult.UNDERFLOW)) {

                output.flip();
                while (output.hasRemaining()) {
                    System.out.print(output.get());
                }
                output.clear();
            }
        }

        // Flush the internal state of the decoder
        while (true) {
            output.clear();
            result = decoder.flush(output);
            output.flip();
            while (output.hasRemaining()) {
                System.out.print(output.get());
            }

            if (result == CoderResult.UNDERFLOW) {
                break;
            }
        }
    }
}
```

```
Original Text:
My horse moved on; hoof after hoof
He raised, and never stopped:
When down behind the cottage roof,
At once, the bright moon dropped.
--------------------
Decoded Text:
My horse moved on; hoof after hoof
He raised, and never stopped:
When down behind the cottage roof,
At once, the bright moon dropped.
```

You can get the list of all available character sets supported by the JVM using the static `availableCharsets()` method of the `Charset` class, which returns a `SortedMap<String,Charset>` whose keys are character set names and values are `Charset` objects.

■ **Tip** You can create your own character encoder/decoder by using the `CharsetProvider` class in `java.nio.charset.spi` package. You need to explore the `java.nio.charset` and `java.nio.charset.spi` packages for details on how to create and install your own character set. This book does not cover how to create and install a custom character set.

Listing 9-7 demonstrates how to list all character sets supported by the JVM. A partial output is shown. You may get a different output.

Listing 9-7. List of Available Character Sets Supported by Your JVM

```
// AvailableCharsets.java
package com.jdojo.nio;

import java.util.Map;
import java.nio.charset.Charset;
import java.util.Set;

public class AvailableCharsets {
    public static void main(String[] args) {
        Map<String, Charset> map = Charset.availableCharsets();
        Set<String> keys = map.keySet();
        System.out.println("Available Character Set Count: " + keys.size());

        for(String charsetName : keys) {
            System.out.println(charsetName);
        }
    }
}
```

```
Available Character Set Count: 170
Big5
ISO-8859-1
US-ASCII
UTF-16
UTF-16BE
UTF-16LE
UTF-32
UTF-32BE
UTF-32LE
UTF-8
windows-1250
x-iso-8859-11
...
```

Channels

A channel is an open connection between a data source/data sink and a Java program to perform some I/O operations. The `Channel` interface is in the `java.nio.channels` package. It is used as a base to implement channels in Java. It declares only two methods: `close()` and `isOpen()`. When a channel is created, it is open and its `isOpen()` method returns `true`. Once you are finished using a channel, you should call its `close()` method to close it. At that point, `isOpen()` returns `false`. Figure 9-15 depicts the class diagram for the `Channel` interface.

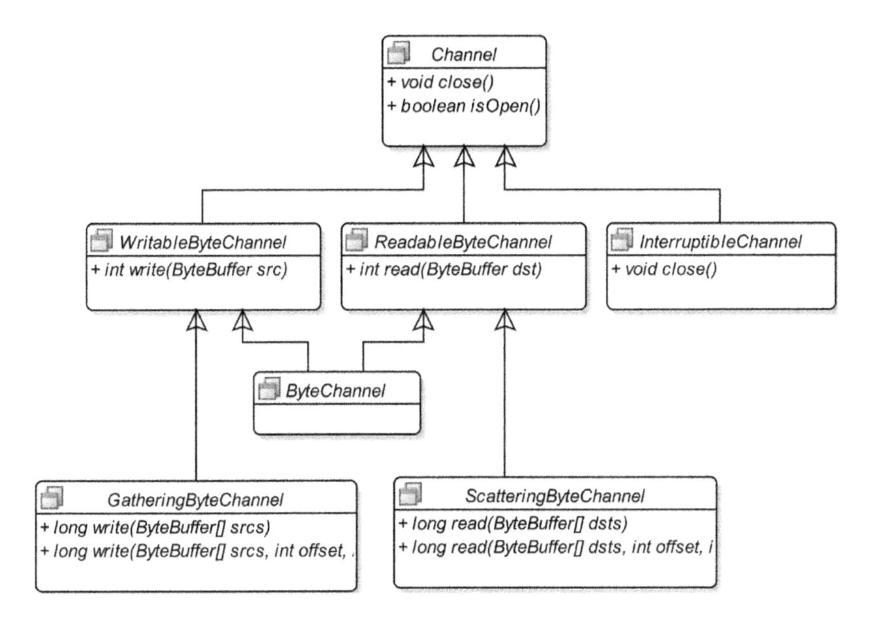

Figure 9-15. *A class diagram for the channel interface*

Java program interacts with a channel for an I/O operation using byte buffers. That is, even if you have many different kinds of buffers, you will need to convert them to a byte buffer before you can pass them to a channel for reading/writing data.

A `ReadableByteChannel` is used to read data from a data source into a byte buffer using its `read()` method. A `WritableByteChannel` is used to write data from a byte buffer to a data sink using its `write()` method. A `ByteChannel` is capable of both reading and writing byte data.

A `ScatteringByteChannel` reads data from a data source into multiple byte buffers. It is useful to read data from a known file format or a similar data source, where data is supplied in some fixed-length headers followed by a variable length body. For example, suppose a file has a 256-byte fixed-length header and a variable length body. An object of the `ScatteringByteChannel` class is used to read data from this kind of file using two byte buffers. The first byte buffer will be of capacity 256. The second buffer will be of a size of your choice. When you pass these two buffers to this channel, the fixed-length header of 256 bytes will be read in the first buffer. The second buffer will have the file data and you may have to use the second buffer multiple times to read the rest of bytes from the file. The advantage of using this channel is separating the fixed-length header data from other data.

A `GatheringByteChannel` performs just the opposite of what a `ScatteringByteChannel` performs. It writes data from multiple byte buffers to a data sink. It is used to write data in a format that is grouped in some fixed-length headers, followed by a variable length body.

An InterruptibleChannel channel can be closed asynchronously. If a thread is blocked on an I/O operation on this channel, another thread can call its close() method to close it. The blocked thread will receive an AsynchronousCloseException. If a thread is blocked on an I/O operation on this channel, another thread can call the interrupt() method on the blocked thread. This channel is closed, and the blocked thread receives a ClosedByInterruptException exception.

Typically, you do not deal with these channel interfaces directly in your programs. You deal with concrete channel classes that implement one or more of these interfaces. Unlike I/O streams, you do not create a channel directly. You get it indirectly by calling a method. To obtain a channel for a data source and a data sink, you need to create an object of InputStream and OutputStream—using old ways of working with I/O using classes in the java.io package. The Channels class in the java.nio.channels package is a utility class that has many static methods to convert streams into channels and vice versa. The Channels class also provides methods to convert readers/writers to channels and vice versa. For example, if you have an input stream object named myInputStream, you can obtain a ReadableByteChannel as follows:

```
ReadableByteChannel rbc = Channels.newChannel(myInputStream);
```

If you have a ReadableByteChannel named rbc, you can obtain the underlying InputStream object as follows:

```
// Get the InputStream of the ReadableByteChannel
InputStream myInputStream = Channels.newInputStream(rbc);
```

The FileInputStream and FileOutputStream classes contain methods to work with channels. They have a method called getChannel(), which returns a FileChannel object. A FileChannel is used to read and write data to a file. A FileChannel obtained from a FileInputStream is opened in a read-only mode. A FileChannel obtained from a FileOutputStream object is opened in a write-only mode. If you obtain a FileChannel from a RandomAccessFile, it is opened in a read-only, write-only, or read-write mode, depending on the way you create that RandomAccessFile object. The following snippet of code obtains FileChannel objects for different kinds of file streams:

```
FileInputStream fis = new FileInputStream("luci1.txt");
FileChannel fcReadOnly = fis.getChannel(); // A read-only channel

FileOutputStream fos = new FileOutputStream("luci1.txt");
FileChannel fcWriteOnly = fos.getChannel(); // A write-only channel

// Open file in a read-only mode
RandomAccessFile raf1 = new RandomAccessFile("luci1.txt", "r");
FileChannel rafReadOnly = raf1.getChannel(); // A read-only channel

// Open file in a read-write mode
RandomAccessFile raf2 = new RandomAccessFile("luci1.txt", "rw");
FileChannel rafReadWrite = raf2.getChannel(); // A read-write channel
```

■ **Tip** You can also obtain a FileChannel using the FileChannel.open() static method. This avoids the need to create an input/output stream to create a FileChannel. The new open() method uses a Path object, which is part of NIO 2. Refer to Chapter 9 on NIO 2 for more details on using a Path object.

Reading/Writing Files

I covered the basic concepts of buffers and channels. A FileChannel maintains a position as a buffer does. The read() and write() methods for FileChannel come in two varieties: relative position read/write and absolute position read/write. The meanings of relative and absolute position read/write are the same as in the context of a buffer read/write. When you open a FileChannel, its position is set to 0, which is the beginning of the file. When you read from a FileChannel using a relative read() method, its position is incremented by the number of bytes read. An absolute position read from a FileChannel does not affect its position. You can get the current value of the position of a FileChannel using its position() method. You can set its position to a new position using its position(int newPosition) method. You need to follow a few easy steps to read data from a file and to write data to a file using NIO.

The steps to read data from a file using buffer and channel are as follows:

1. Create an object of the FileInputStream class.
2. Get a FileChannel object using the getChannel() method of the FileInputStream object that you created in the previous step.
3. Create a ByteBuffer object to read data from the file.
4. Call the read() method of the FileChannel object by passing a ByteBuffer object. Make sure that before you pass the ByteBuffer, the buffer's position and limit are set appropriately. A simple rule of thumb is to always call the clear() method on the ByteBuffer before passing it to a channel to read data into it. The read() method of a channel returns the number of bytes read into the buffer.
5. Call the flip() method of the ByteBuffer, so you can read data into your program from the buffer. The previous step will change the position of the buffer because the channel reads data into it. You may need to use a CharsetDecoder object to decode the ByteBuffer into a character buffer if the bytes you have read represent characters.
6. Read data from the ByteBuffer into your program.
7. Repeat the process of reading data from the FileChannel into the ByteBuffer by calling its read() method until the read() method returns 0 or -1.
8. Close the channel using its close() method.

■ **Tip** Like input/output streams, channels are also AutoCloseable. If you use a try-with-resources statement to obtain a channel, the channel will be closed automatically, thus avoiding a need for you to call the close() method of the channel explicitly.

Listing 9-8 puts all of these steps together. It reads text from a file named luci1.txt. The file should be in your current working directory. If the file does not exist, the program prints a message with the full path where the file is expected to exist. If you do not have this file, create it and enter the following text in the file, before you run the program:

```
STRANGE fits of passion have I known:
And I will dare to tell,
But in the lover's ear alone,
What once to me befell.
```

You need to pay close attention to the call to the `clear()` and `flip()` methods on a buffer. When you call the `read()` or `write()` method of a channel, it performs a relative position read/write on the buffer. Therefore, you must call the `flip()` method of the buffer to read data from it after the channel writes data into the buffer.

Listing 9-8. Reading from a File Using a Buffer and a Channel

```
// FileChannelRead.java
package com.jdojo.nio;

import java.io.File;
import java.io.FileInputStream;
import java.io.IOException;
import java.nio.ByteBuffer;
import java.nio.channels.FileChannel;

public class FileChannelRead {
    public static void main(String[] args) {
        // The input file to read from
        File inputFile = new File("luci1.txt");

        // Make sure the input file exists
        if (!inputFile.exists()) {
            System.out.println("The input file " + inputFile.getAbsolutePath()
                    + " does not exist.");
            System.out.println("Aborted the file reading process.");
            System.exit(1);
        }

        // Obtain channel for luci1.txt file to read from it
        try (FileChannel fileChannel = new FileInputStream(inputFile).getChannel()) {
            // Create a buffer
            ByteBuffer buffer = ByteBuffer.allocate(1024);

            // Read all data from the channel
            while (fileChannel.read(buffer) > 0) {
                // Flip the buffer before we can read data from it
                buffer.flip();

                // Display the read data as characters on the console.
                // Note that we are assuming that a byte represents a
                // character, which is not true all the time. In a
                // real world application, you should use
                // CharsetDecoder to decode the bytes into character
                // before you display/use them.
                while (buffer.hasRemaining()) {
                    byte b = buffer.get();

                    // Assuming a byte represents a character
                    System.out.print((char) b);
                }
```

```
                // Clear the buffer before the next read into it
                buffer.clear();
            }
        } catch (IOException e) {
            e.printStackTrace();
        }
    }
}
```

```
STRANGE fits of passion have I known:
And I will dare to tell,
But in the lover's ear alone,
What once to me befell.
```

The steps to write data to a file using a buffer and a channel are as follows:

1. Create an object of the `FileOutputStream` class.
2. Get a `FileChannel` object using the `getChannel()` method of the `FileOutputStream` object that you created in the previous step.
3. Create a `ByteBuffer` object to write data to the file.
4. Fill the `ByteBuffer` with data.
5. Call the `flip()` method of the buffer to get it ready to be read by the channel.
6. Call the `write()` method of the `FileChannel` object by passing the `ByteBuffer` object filled with data.
7. Close the channel by calling its `close()` method.

Listing 9-9 puts all these steps together to write the following text to a `luci5.txt` file:

```
In one of those sweet dreams I slept,
Kind Nature's gentlest boon!
And all the while my eyes I kept
On the descending moon.
```

The code creates a string from the text inserting a platform-dependent new line character between two lines. It converts the text into a byte array, creates a `ByteBuffer` by wrapping the byte array, and writes the buffer to the file channel. Note that you do not need to use the `flip()` method on the buffer because, before passing it to the channel for writing, your buffer object was just created with the text, and its position and limit were set appropriately by the `wrap()` method. The program prints the path of the file in which the text was written that may be different on your machine.

Listing 9-9. Writing to a File Using a Buffer and a Channel

```
// FileChannelWrite.java
package com.jdojo.nio;

import java.io.File;
import java.nio.channels.FileChannel;
import java.io.IOException;
import java.nio.ByteBuffer;
import java.io.FileOutputStream;
```

```
public class FileChannelWrite {
    public static void main(String[] args) {
        // The output file to write to
        File outputFile = new File("luci5.txt");

        try (FileChannel fileChannel = new FileOutputStream(outputFile).getChannel()) {

            // Get the text as string
            String text = getText();

            // Convert text into byte array
            byte[] byteData = text.getBytes("UTF-8");

            // Create a ByteBuffer using the byte array
            ByteBuffer buffer = ByteBuffer.wrap(byteData);

            // Write bytes to the file
            fileChannel.write(buffer);

            System.out.println("Data has been written to "
                    + outputFile.getAbsolutePath());
        } catch (IOException e1) {
            e1.printStackTrace();
        }
    }

    public static String getText() {
        String lineSeparator = System.getProperty("line.separator");
        StringBuilder sb = new StringBuilder();
        sb.append("In one of those sweet dreams I slept,");
        sb.append(lineSeparator);
        sb.append("Kind Nature's gentlest boon!");
        sb.append(lineSeparator);
        sb.append("And all the while my eyes I kept");
        sb.append(lineSeparator);
        sb.append("On the descending moon.");

        return sb.toString();
    }
}
```

```
Data has been written to C:\Java9LanguageFeatures\luci5.txt
```

A file has two kinds of data associated with it. One is its contents and the other is metadata such as creation time, last-modified time, etc. When you write data to a file channel, the data may not be actually written to the storage device (for example, the hard disk) immediately. To write the data to the storage device immediately, after a call to the `write()` method on a file channel, you can call its `force(boolean` metaData) method. It guarantees that the file's contents and metadata are written to its storage device. If you call force(false), only the file's metadata is written to the storage device. If you call force(true), both the file's content and its metadata are written to the storage device. In fact, this is guaranteed only if the storage device is local. Otherwise, the JVM tries its best to write the data to the storage device.

■ **Tip** A file channel works only with byte buffers. In the examples in this section, I assumed that a character is represented in a byte, which is true only when you are using an encoding such as US-ASCII or UTF-8 for English alphabets. Refer to the "Character Set" section on how to encode a character buffer into a byte buffer and how to decode a byte buffer into a character buffer.

Memory-Mapped File I/O

There is another way to perform I/O on a file, which is by mapping a region of the file into physical memory and treating it as a memory array. This is the fastest way available to perform file I/O in Java. Using a special kind of byte buffer called MappedByteBuffer lets you perform memory-mapped file I/O.

For memory-mapped file I/O, start by obtaining a FileChannel for the file, and use the map() method of the FileChannel to get a MappedByteBuffer. Read or write directly to the mapped byte buffer instead of using the read() or write() method of the FileChannel. When you read from the mapped byte buffer, you read from the file's region you have mapped. When you write to the mapped byte buffer, you write to the mapped region of the file. If you want to write the written data to the mapped byte buffer immediately to the storage device, you need to use the force() method of the mapped byte buffer. There is no boolean argument to force() related to metadata.

Once you obtain the mapped byte buffer from a FileChannel, closing the channel has no effect on your buffer. You can keep reading/writing the mapped byte buffer, even after the FileChannel is closed.

You can map a region of a file in a read-only, read-write, or private mode. In a read-only mode, you can only read from the mapped byte buffer. In a read-write mode, you can read from as well as write to the mapped byte buffer. The private mode needs a little explanation. This mode is also called a *copy-on-write* mode. When multiple programs map the same region of a file, a separate copy of that region is not created for each program. Rather, all programs share the same region of the file. When a program modifies the mapped region, a separate copy of that region is created only for that program, which is its private copy. Any modification to the private copy is not visible to other programs.

The following snippet of code maps the entire luci5.txt file in read-only mode. It reads the file and displays the contents on the standard output.

```
FileInputStream fis = new FileInputStream("luci5.txt");
FileChannel fc = fis.getChannel();

long startRegion = 0;
long endRegion = fc.size();
MappedByteBuffer mbb = fc.map(FileChannel.MapMode.READ_ONLY, startRegion, endRegion);
while(mbb.hasRemaining()) {
   System.out.print((char) mbb.get());
}

fc.close();
```

File Locking

NIO supports file locking to synchronize access to a file. You have the ability to lock a region of a file or the entire file. The file locking mechanism is handled by the operating system and, therefore, its exact effect is platform-dependent. On some operating systems, a file lock is advisory, whereas on some, it is mandatory. Since it is handled by the operating system, its effect is visible to other programs as well as to Java programs running in other JVMs.

Tip An advisory lock lets other users use the file on which you have acquired the lock, but prevents them from acquiring a lock on the same file. A mandatory lock forces the user to acquire a lock on the file before the file can be used.

There are two kinds of file locking: *exclusive* and *shared*. Only one program can hold an exclusive lock on a region of a file. Multiple programs can hold shared locks on the same region of a file. You cannot mix an exclusive lock and a shared lock on the same region of a file. If a program has a shared lock on a region, another program must wait to get an exclusive lock on that region and vice versa. Some operating systems do not support a shared file lock, and, in that case, the request for a shared file lock is converted to a request for an exclusive file lock.

An object of the `FileLock` class, which is in the `java.nio.channels` package, represents a file lock. You acquire a lock on a file by using the `lock()` or `tryLock()` method of the `FileChannel` class. The `lock()` method blocks if the lock on the requested region of the file is not available. The `tryLock()` method does not block; it returns immediately. It returns an object of the `FileLock` class if the lock was acquired; otherwise, it returns `null`.

Both `lock()` and `tryLock()` methods have two versions: one without an argument and another with three arguments. The version without an argument locks the entire file. The version with three arguments accepts the starting position of the region to lock, the number of bytes to lock, and a `boolean` flag to indicate if the lock is shared. The `isShared()` method of the `FileLock` object returns `true` if the lock is shared; otherwise, it returns `false`.

The following snippet of code shows different ways of obtaining locks on a file. The exception handling code is omitted for clarity.

```
// Create a random access file and obtain a channel for it
RandomAccessFile raf = new RandomAccessFile("test.txt", "rw");
FileChannel fileChannel = raf.getChannel();

// Get an exclusive lock on the file
FileLock lock = fileChannel.lock();

// Get an exclusive lock on first 10 bytes
FileLock lock = fileChannel.lock(0, 10, false);

// Try to get an exclusive lock on the entire file
FileLock lock = fileChannel.tryLock();
if (lock == null) {
    // Could not get the lock
} else {
    // Got the lock
}
```

```
// Try to lock 100 bytes starting from the 11th byte in a shared mode
FileLock lock = fileChannel.tryLock(11, 100, true);
if (lock == null) {
    // Could not get the lock
} else {
    // Got the lock
}
```

The region of a file that you lock may not be contained in the range of the file size. Suppose you have a file with a size of 100 bytes. When you request a lock on this file, you can specify that you want to lock a region of this file starting at byte 11 and covering 5000 bytes. Note that this file contains only 100 bytes; you are locking 5000 bytes. In such a case, if the file size grows beyond 100 bytes, your lock covers the additional region of the file. Suppose you locked the entire file, which is 100 bytes in size. If this file grows to 150 bytes, your lock does not cover the last 50 bytes that was added after you acquired the lock. The `lock()` and `tryLock()` methods of the `FileChannel` object, where you do not specify any argument, lock a region from 0 to `Long.MAX_VALUE` of the file. The two method calls—`fc.lock()` and `fc.lock(0, Long.MAX_VALUE, false)`—have the same effect.

When you are done with the file lock, you need to release it by using the `release()` method. A file lock is released in three ways: by calling its `release()` method, by closing the file channel it is obtained from, and by shutting down the JVM. It is good practice to use a `try-catch-finally` block to acquire and release a file lock as follows:

```
RandomAccessFile raf = new RandomAccessFile("test.txt", "rw");
FileChannel fileChannel = raf.getChannel();
FileLock lock = null;

try {
    lock = fileChannel.lock(0, 10, true);

    /* Work with the file here */
} catch(IOException e) {
    // Handle the exception
} finally {
    if (lock != null) {
        try {
            lock.release();
        } catch(IOException e) {
            // Handle the exception
        }
    }
}
```

Copying the Contents of a File

You can use buffers and channels to copy a file much faster. Copying the contents of a file to another file is just one method call when you use a `FileChannel`. Get the `FileChannel` object for the source file and the destination file, and call the `transferTo()` method on the source `FileChannel` object or call the `transferFrom()` method on the sink `FileChannel` object. The following snippet of code shows how to copy the `luci5.txt` file to `luci5_copy.txt`:

```
// Obtain the source and sink channels
FileChannel sourceChannel = new FileInputStream(sourceFile).getChannel();
FileChannel sinkChannel = new FileOutputStream(sinkFile).getChannel();

// Copy source file contents to the sink file
sourceChannel.transferTo(0, sourceChannel.size(), sinkChannel);

// Instead of using the transferTo() method on the source channel,
// you can also use the transferFrom() method on the sink channel
sinkChannel.transferFrom(sourceChannel, 0, sourceChannel.size());
```

Listing 9-10 contains the complete code. The program prints the path of the source and destination files when the file copy succeeds.

Listing 9-10. Copying a File's Contents Using a FileChannel

```
// FastestFileCopy.java
package com.jdojo.nio;

import java.io.IOException;
import java.io.File;
import java.io.FileInputStream;
import java.io.FileOutputStream;
import java.nio.channels.FileChannel;

public class FastestFileCopy {
    public static void main(String[] args) {
        File sourceFile = new File("luci5.txt");
        File sinkFile = new File("luci5_copy.txt");
        try {
            copy(sourceFile, sinkFile, false);
            System.out.println(sourceFile.getAbsoluteFile()
                    + " has been copied to " + sinkFile.getAbsolutePath());
        } catch (IOException e) {
            System.out.println(e.getMessage());
        }
    }

    public static void copy(File sourceFile,
            File sinkFile, boolean overwrite) throws IOException {
```

```
        // Perform some error checks
        if (!sourceFile.exists()) {
            throw new IOException("Source file "
                    + sourceFile.getAbsolutePath() + " does not exist.");
        }

        if (sinkFile.exists() && !overwrite) {
            throw new IOException("Destination file "
                    + sinkFile.getAbsolutePath() + " already exists.");
        }

        // Obtain source and sink file channels in a
        // try-with-resources block, so they are closed automatically.
        try (FileChannel srcChannel = new FileInputStream(sourceFile).getChannel();
             FileChannel sinkChannel = new FileOutputStream(sinkFile).getChannel()) {
            // Copy source file contents to the sink file
            srcChannel.transferTo(0, srcChannel.size(), sinkChannel);
        }
    }
}
```

Knowing the Byte Order of a Machine

If you ever wanted to know the byte order (also called endian-ness) of your machine, you need to use the `nativeOrder()` method of the `ByteOrder` class, as shown in Listing 9-11. The byte order of a machine/buffer is discussed in detail in the next section. The program prints the byte order of the machine on which it is run. You may get a different output.

Listing 9-11. Knowing the Endian-ness (Byte Order) of Your Machine

```
// MachineByteOrder.java
package com.jdojo.nio;

import java.nio.ByteOrder;

public class MachineByteOrder {
    public static void main(String args[]) {
        ByteOrder b = ByteOrder.nativeOrder();
        if (b.equals(ByteOrder.BIG_ENDIAN)) {
            System.out.println("Big endian");
        } else {
            System.out.println("Little endian");
        }
    }
}
```

```
Little endian
```

Byte Buffer and Its Byte Order

A byte order is the order in which bytes of a multi-byte value are stored. Suppose you have a short value 300 stored in a variable as follows:

```
short s = 300;
```

A short value is stored in two bytes. The value 300 can be represented in 16-bits as 0000000100101100, where the right-most bit is the least significant bit and the left-most bit is the most significant bit. You can split the 16-bit into two bytes as 00000001 and 00101100. At the byte level, you can think of 00000001 as the most significant byte and 00101100 as the least significant byte. If you consider two bytes separately for a short value, you may store them as either 00000001 followed by 00101100 or 00101100 followed by 00000001. As long as you know the order of the bytes in which they are stored, you can compute the correct value 300 using either form of the 16 bits: 0000000100101100 or 0010110000000001.

A byte order is called *big endian* if the bytes of a multi-byte value are stored from the most significant byte to the least significant byte. If the bytes of a multi-byte value are stored from the least significant byte to the most significant byte, it is known as little endian. To remember the two definitions easily, you can replace the word "big" with "most significant," "little" with "least significant," and "endian" with "first". That is, remember "big endian" as "most significant first" and "little endian" as "least significant first."

If you store a short value of 300 as 0000000100101100, you are using the big endian byte order. In the little endian byte order, you would store 300 as 0010110000000001, which seems backwards for representing a 16-bit value.

When you deal with byte data in a byte buffer, you may be considering each byte as an independent byte. A byte in a byte buffer may be part of a bigger value. When a byte value in a byte buffer is independent, the byte order is not a consideration. When a byte in a byte buffer is part of a bigger value (e.g., two bytes of a short value 300), the byte order becomes very important in reading. If you read two bytes from a byte buffer to compute a short value, you must know how those two bytes are stored. Suppose you read two bytes as 0000000100101100. If it is in a big endian byte order, it represents a value of 300. If it is in a little endian byte order, it represents a value of 11265.

Java uses a big-endian byte order to store data. By default, a byte buffer uses a big endian byte order. An instance of the `java.nio.ByteOrder` class represents a byte order. You will not need to instantiate this class because you always use the value that represents a byte order; you don't create a new byte order. In fact, this class has no `public` constructor. You can use two constants, `BIG_ENDIAN` and `LITTLE_ENDIAN`, which are defined in the `ByteOrder` class to represent these byte orders.

■ **Tip** A byte order is meaningful only in a multi-byte value stored in a byte buffer. You may also need to deal with byte orders when you are dealing with two different systems that use different byte orders.

Listing 9-12 demonstrates how to get and set byte order for a byte buffer. You use the `order()` method of the `ByteBuffer` class to get or set the byte order. The program stores a short value of 300 in two bytes of a byte buffer. It displays the values stored in the first and the second bytes using both big endian and little endian byte orders. The output shows the values of bytes in decimal as 1 and 44, whose binary equivalents are 00000001 and 00101100, respectively.

Listing 9-12. Setting the Byte Order of a Byte Buffer

```
// ByteBufferOrder.java
package com.jdojo.nio;

import java.nio.ByteBuffer;
import java.nio.ByteOrder;

public class ByteBufferOrder {
    public static void main(String[] args) {
        ByteBuffer bb = ByteBuffer.allocate(2);
        System.out.println("Default Byte Order: " + bb.order());
        bb.putShort((short) 300);
        bb.flip();
        showByteOrder(bb);

        // Repopulate the buffer in little endian byte order
        bb.clear();
        bb.order(ByteOrder.LITTLE_ENDIAN);
        bb.putShort((short) 300);
        bb.flip();
        showByteOrder(bb);
    }

    public static void showByteOrder(ByteBuffer bb) {
        System.out.println("Byte Order: " + bb.order());
        while (bb.hasRemaining()) {
            System.out.print(bb.get() + "  ");
        }
        System.out.println();
    }
}
```

```
Default Byte Order: BIG_ENDIAN
Byte Order: BIG_ENDIAN
1  44
Byte Order: LITTLE_ENDIAN
44  1
```

Summary

New input/output (NIO) provides faster I/O compared to the stream-based input/output. NIO uses buffers and channels for I/O operations. A channel represents a connection between a data source/sink and a Java program for data transfer. A buffer contains data to be written to a file or data that is read from a file. Buffers for holding different types of primitive values are supported as instances of separate classes. You can use only a `ByteBuffer` for file I/O operations. NIO also supports memory-mapped file I/O that is the fastest way to read/write files.

A buffer maintains several properties that are affected by reading its data or writing data to it. The position property of a buffer is the index in the buffer that is the starting position to be read or written in the next read/write operation. The limit property of a buffer is the index in the buffer that is the starting index indicating the invalid read/write position. The buffer's position may change as you read from the buffer or write to the buffer.

Buffer-related classes contain methods to manipulate those properties directly as well. A buffer supports absolute read/write and relative read/write. In absolute read/write, the buffer's position is unaffected. In a relative read/write, the position property of the buffer is automatically advanced.

Byte buffers support different views. You can use a view of a buffer to access the data buffer's data as different primitive type values or to see only part of the buffer's data.

A character is not always stored in one byte. The number of bytes used to store a character depends on the coded character set and the character-encoding scheme. A coded-character set is a mapping between a set of abstract characters and a set of integers. A character-encoding scheme is a mapping between a coded-character set and a set of octet sequence. An instance of the `java.nio.charset.Charset` class represents a character set and a character-encoding scheme. Examples of some character set names are US-ASCII, ISO-8859-1, UTF-8, UTF-16BE, UTF-16LE, and UTF-16. The process of converting a character into a sequence of bytes based on an encoding scheme is called *character encoding*. The process of converting a sequence of bytes into a character based on an encoding scheme is called *decoding*. In NIO, you can convert a Unicode character to a sequence of bytes and vice versa using an encoding scheme. The `java.nio.charset` package provides classes to encode/decode a `CharBuffer` to a `ByteBuffer` and vice versa. An object of the `Charset` class represents the encoding scheme. The `CharsetEncoder` class performs the encoding. The `CharsetDecoder` class performs the decoding. You can get an object of the `Charset` class using its `forName()` method by passing the name of the character set as its argument.

A `FileChannel`, along with buffers, are used to read/write files. You can obtain a `FileChannel` from an `InputStream`, an `OutputStream`, or using the factory method of the `FileChannel` class. You can also lock a file in exclusive or shared mode using the `lock()` method of the `FileChannel` class.

The byte order is the order in which bytes of a multi-byte value are stored. A byte order is called *big endian* if the bytes of a multi-byte value are stored from the most significant byte to the least significant byte. If the bytes of a multi-byte value are stored from the least significant byte to the most significant byte, it is known as little endian. You need to deal with the byte order of a byte buffer if the buffer represents multi-byte data. The `java.nio.ByteOrder` class represents the byte order. It contains two constants, `BIG_ENDIAN` and `LITTLE_ENDIAN`, to represent big-endian and little-endian byte orders, respectively.

QUESTIONS AND EXERCISES

1. What is new input/output?
2. What is a buffer? Name three classes that represent three different types of buffers.
3. Define the capacity, position, and limit of a buffer. Write the invariant that must be true all the time for these three properties of a buffer.
4. What is the difference between relative read and absolute read from a buffer?
5. After you have written into a `Buffer`, what method do you need to call on the `Buffer` before you start reading the written data using a relative read?
6. What is the difference between the `remaining()` and `hasRemaining()` methods of the `Buffer` class?
7. What is the effect of calling the `clear()` method of a `Buffer`?
8. What is the effect of calling the `reset()` method of a `Buffer`?
9. What is the effect of calling the `rewind()` method of a `Buffer`?

10. Write the output when the following code for a `TestReadOnlyBufferTest` class is run. This exercise is to test your knowledge about the properties of a read-only buffer.

```
// ReadOnlyBufferTest.java
package com.jdojo.nio;

import java.nio.IntBuffer;

public class ReadOnlyBufferTest {
    public static void main(String[] args) {
        // Create an IntBuffer of capacity 1
        IntBuffer data = IntBuffer.allocate(1);
        System.out.println(data.isReadOnly());

        // Get a read-only copy of the IntBuffer
        IntBuffer copy = data.asReadOnlyBuffer();
        System.out.println(copy.isReadOnly());

        // Print the contents of the read-only buffer
        System.out.println(copy.get());

        // Write into the original buffer
        data.put(64);

        // Print the contents of the read-only buffer again
        copy.rewind();
        System.out.println(copy.get());
    }
}
```

11. Suppose you have an `IntBuffer`. What is the difference between creating two copies of the `IntBuffer`, one by using the `asReadOnlyBuffer()` method and another by using the `duplicate()` method?

12. What do instances of the following classes represent: `Charset`, `CharsetEncoder`, and `CharsetDecoder`?

13. What is a channel? What is the fully qualified name of the interface that every implementation of a channel implements? If you have a reference to a channel, how would you tell if the channel is open?

14. When do you use instances of the `GatheringByteChannel` and `ScatteringByteChannel` classes?

15. Suppose you have a file named `test.txt` in your current directory. Write a snippet of code to get a `FileChannel` for this file in read-write mode.

16. What is memory-mapped file I/O? Name a class whose instances are used to work with memory-mapped file I/O.

17. What is the difference in using the `lock()` and `tryLock()` methods of the `FileChannel` class while locking a region of a file?

18. Write a snippet of code that prints the byte order (little-endian or big-endian) of the current machine.

CHAPTER 10

New Input/Output 2

In this chapter, you will learn:

- What New Input/Output 2 is
- How to work with a file system and file store
- How to represent a platform-dependent abstract pathname using a Path
- How to perform different file operations on a Path object
- How to traverse a file tree
- How to manage file attributes
- How to watch a directory for changes
- How to perform asynchronous file I/O operations

All example programs in this chapter are members of a jdojo.nio2 module, as declared in Listing 10-1. The JDK9 module system discourages including digits at the end of a module name. However, jdojo.nio2 (note the 2 at the end of the name) is the best name that I can give to this module, as it contains examples for the New Input/Output 2 topic.

Listing 10-1. The Declaration of a jdojo.nio2 Module

```
// module-info.java
module jdojo.nio2 {
    exports com.jdojo.nio2;
}
```

What Is New Input/Output 2?

Java 7 introduced the New Input/Output 2 (NIO.2) API, which provides a new I/O API. It provides many features that were lacking in the original File I/O API. The features provided in NIO.2 are essential for working with a file system efficiently. It adds three packages to the Java class library: java.nio.file, java.nio.file.attribute, and java.nio.file.spi. The following are some of the new features of NIO.2:

- It lets you deal with all file systems in a uniform way. The file system support provided by NIO.2 is extensible. You can use the default implementation for a file system or you can choose to implement your own file system.

K. Sharan, *Java Language Features*, https://doi.org/10.1007/978-1-4842-3348-1_10

- It supports basic file operations (copy, move, and delete) on all file systems. It supports an atomic file move operation. It has improved exception handling support.
- It has support for symbolic links. Whenever applicable, operations on a symbolic link are redirected to the target file.
- One of the most important additions to NIO.2 is the support for accessing the attributes of file systems and files.
- It lets you create a watch service to watch for any events on a directory such as adding a new file or a subdirectory, deleting a file, etc. When such an event occurs on the directory, your program receives a notification through the watch service.
- It added an API that lets you walk through a file tree. You can perform a file operation on a node as you walk through the file tree.
- It supports asynchronous I/O on network sockets and files.
- It supports multicasting using a `DatagramChannel`.

Working with a File System

An object of the `FileSystem` class represents a file system in a Java program. A `FileSystem` object is used to perform two tasks:

- To act as an interface between a Java program and a file system.
- To act as a factory for creating many types of file system-related objects and services.

A `FileSystem` object is platform-dependent. You do not create an object of the `FileSystem` class directly. To obtain the default `FileSystem` object for a platform, you need to use the `getDefault()` static method of the `FileSystems` class as follows:

```
// Create the platform-specific default file system object
FileSystem fs = FileSystems.getDefault();
```

Typically, a file system consists of one or more file stores. A file store provides storage for files. The `getFileStores()` method of the `FileSystem` class returns an `Iterable<FileStore>`, which you can use to iterate over all file stores of a file system.

A file system may be represented differently on different platforms. One platform may represent a file system in a single hierarchy of files with one top-level root directory, whereas another may represent it in multiple hierarchies of files with multiple top-level directories. The `getRootDirectories()` method of the `FileSystem` class returns an `Iterable<Path>`, which can be used to iterate over paths to all top-level directories in the file system. I discuss the `Path` class in detail in the next section.

You can use the `isReadOnly()` method of the `FileSystem` object to test if it only allows read-only access to the file stores. You will work with the `FileSystem` class in subsequent sections to create the file system-related objects and services.

Listing 10-2 demonstrates how to use a `FileSystem` object. It uses the default file system for the platform. The output shows the file system information when the program was run on Windows; you may get different output when you run the program.

Listing 10-2. Retrieving Information About a File System

```
// FileSystemTest.java
package com.jdojo.nio2;

import java.nio.file.FileStore;
import java.nio.file.FileSystem;
import java.nio.file.FileSystems;
import java.nio.file.Path;
import java.io.IOException;

public class FileSystemTest {
    public static void main(String[] args) {
        // Get the reference to the default file system
        FileSystem fs = FileSystems.getDefault();

        System.out.println("Read-only file system: " + fs.isReadOnly());
        System.out.println("File name separator: " + fs.getSeparator());

        System.out.println("\nAvailable file-stores are");

        for (FileStore store : fs.getFileStores()) {
            printDetails(store);
        }

        System.out.println("\nAvailable root directories are");

        for (Path root : fs.getRootDirectories()) {
            System.out.println(root);
        }
    }

    public static void printDetails(FileStore store) {
        try {
            String desc = store.toString();
            String type = store.type();
            long totalSpace = store.getTotalSpace();
            long unallocatedSpace = store.getUnallocatedSpace();
            long availableSpace = store.getUsableSpace();
            System.out.println(desc + ", Total: " + totalSpace
                    + ", Unallocated: " + unallocatedSpace
                    + ", Available: " + availableSpace);
        } catch (IOException e) {
            e.printStackTrace();
        }
    }
}
```

```
Read-only file system: false
File name separator: \

Available file-stores are
OS (C:), Total: 985563918336, Unallocated: 828183392256, Available: 828183392256

Available root directories are
C:\
E:\
```

Working with Paths

Typically, a file system stores objects (files, directories, symbolic links, etc.) in a hierarchical fashion. A file system uses one or more root nodes that serve as the root of the hierarchy. An object in a file system has a path, which is typically represented as a string, such as `C:\home\test.txt` on Windows, and `/home/test.txt` on UNIX-like operating systems. A path string may contain multiple components separated by a special character called a *separator* or *delimiter*. For example, the path `C:\home\test.txt` consists of three components: `C:\` as the root, home as a directory, and `test.txt` as a file name. A backslash is a path separator on Windows. UNIX-like operating systems use a forward slash (/) as the path separator. Note that path representation is platform-dependent.

A path can be absolute or relative. If a path starts with a root node, it is an absolute path. A relative path does not start with a root node. No additional information is needed to locate an object referred in a file system by an absolute path. Additional information is needed to locate an object referred in a file system by a relative path. For example, on Windows, the path `C:\home\test.txt` is an absolute path because it starts with the root node `C:\`, whereas the path `luci1.txt` is a relative path. To locate the `luci1.txt` file, you need more information, such as the path of the directory in which it exists.

A `Path` object is a programmatic representation of a path of an object in a file system such as a file, a directory, and a symbolic link. A file system path is platform-dependent, so is a `Path` object.

`Path` is an interface in the `java.nio.file` package. When you work with a `Path` object, it is most likely that you will also need to work with its two companion classes: `Paths` and `Files`. A path does not have to exist in a file system to create a `Path` object to represent it in a Java program.

■ **Tip** As a developer, you will be using `Path` objects most of the time when working with NIO.2 API. The Path API meets most of the file I/O-related needs of a developer. It has been designed to work with the old `java.io.File` API. You can get a `Path` object from a `File` object using the `toPath()` method of the `File` class. You can get a `File` object from a `Path` object using the `toFile()` method of a `Path` object.

You can perform two kinds of operations on a `Path` object:

- Path-related operations
- File I/O operations

The methods in the `Path` interface let you perform the following path-related operations:

- Accessing the components of a path such as the file name, root name, etc.
- Comparing and testing paths. For example, checking if a path ends with `.txt`, comparing if two paths are identical, checking if a path is absolute or relative, etc.
- Combining and resolving paths.

The Path interface does not include any methods to perform file I/O operations. You need to use the Files class to perform the file I/O operations on a Path object. The Files class consists of all static methods. I cover using the Files class shortly. First I cover the details of using the Path interface.

Creating a Path Object

The getPath() method of the FileSystem class acts as a factory method to create Path objects. The following snippet of code creates a Path object for the file path C:\poems\luci1.txt on Windows:

```
Path p1 = FileSystems.getDefault().getPath("C:\\poems\\luci1.txt");
```

You can pass components of a path separately to the getPath() method when constructing a Path object. Java will take care of using the appropriate platform-dependent file name separators. The following statement creates a Path object to represent the C:\poems\luci1.txt path on Windows:

```
Path p2 = FileSystems.getDefault().getPath("C:", "poems", "luci1.txt");
```

The Path API includes a utility class called Paths whose sole job is to create a Path object from the components of a path string or a URI. The Paths class contains the following two static methods:

- Path get(String first, String... more)
- Path get(URI uri)

Both methods in the Paths class internally delegate the call to the default FileSystem. The following snippet of code creates Path objects to represent the same path, C:\poems\luci1.txt:

```
Path p3 = Paths.get("C:\\poems\\luci1.txt");
Path p4 = Paths.get("C:", "poems", "luci1.txt");
```

■ **Tip** You can create a Path object from an empty path such as Paths.get(""). A Path object with an empty path refers to the default directory of the file system. A default directory is the same as the current working directory.

Accessing Components of a Path

A path in a file system consists of one or more components. The methods of the Path interface let you access those components.

The getNameCount() method returns the number of components in a Path excluding the root. For example, the C:\poems\luci1.txt path consists of three components: the root named C:, and two components named poems and luci1.txt. In this case, the getNameCount() method returns 2. The getName(int index) method returns the component name at the specified index. The component closest to the root has an index of 0. The component farthest from the root has an index of count - 1. In the path C:\poems\luci1.txt, the index of the poems component is 0 and the index of the luci1.txt component is 1.

The getParent() method returns the parent of a path. If a path does not have a parent, it returns null. The parent of a path is the path itself without the farthest component from the root. For example, the parent of the C:\poems\luci.txt path is C:\poems. The relative path test.txt has no parent.

The getRoot() method returns the root of the path. If a path does not have a root, it returns null. For example, the C:\poems\luci1.txt path on Windows has C:\ as its root.

The `getFileName()` method returns the file name denoted by the path. If a path has no file name, it returns `null`. The file name is the farthest component from the root. For example, in the `C:\poems\luci1.txt` path, `luci1.txt` is the file name.

You can check if a path represents an absolute path by using the `isAbsolute()` method.

■ **Tip** A path does not have to exist in the file system to get information about its components. The `Path` API uses the information provided in the path string to give you all these pieces of information about the path's components.

Listing 10-3 demonstrates how to access components of a `Path` object. One of the paths used in this example is a Windows-based path. If you are not running the program on Windows, change the path in the `main()` method to represent a valid path on your platform. You may get different output when you run the program.

Listing 10-3. Demonstrating How to Access Components of a Path

```
// PathComponentsTest.java
package com.jdojo.nio2;

import java.nio.file.Path;
import java.nio.file.Paths;

public class PathComponentsTest {
    public static void main(String[] args) {
        Path p1 = Paths.get("C:\\poems\\luci1.txt");
        printDetails(p1);

        System.out.println("----------------------");

        Path p2 = Paths.get("luci1.txt");
        printDetails(p2);
    }

    public static void printDetails(Path p) {
        System.out.println("Details for path: " + p);

        int count = p.getNameCount();
        System.out.println("Name count: " + count);

        for (int i = 0; i < count; i++) {
            Path name = p.getName(i);
            System.out.println("Name at index " + i + " is " + name);
        }

        Path parent = p.getParent();
        Path root = p.getRoot();
        Path fileName = p.getFileName();
        System.out.println("Parent: " + parent + ", Root: " + root
                + ", File Name: " + fileName);
```

```
        System.out.println("Absolute Path: " + p.isAbsolute());
    }
}
```

```
Details for path: C:\poems\luci1.txt
Name count: 2
Name at index 0 is poems
Name at index 1 is luci1.txt
Parent: C:\poems, Root: C:\, File Name: luci1.txt
Absolute Path: true
----------------------
Details for path: luci1.txt
Name count: 1
Name at index 0 is luci1.txt
Parent: null, Root: null, File Name: luci1.txt
Absolute Path: false
```

Comparing Paths

You can compare two Path objects for equality based on their textual representation. The equals() method tests for the equality of two Path objects by comparing their string forms. Whether the equality test is case-sensitive depends on the file system. For example, the path comparison for equality is case-insensitive on Windows. The following snippet of code shows how to compare paths on Windows:

```
Path p1 = Paths.get("C:\\poems\\luci1.txt");
Path p2 = Paths.get("C:\\POEMS\\LUCI1.TXT");
Path p3 = Paths.get("C:\\poems\\..\\poems\\luci1.txt");
boolean b1 = p1.equals(p2); // Returns true on Windows
boolean b2 = p1.equals(p3); // Returns false on Windows
```

In this snippet of code, p1.equals(p3) returns false, even though p1 and p3 refer to the same file; this is so because the equals() method compares two paths textually without resolving the actual file references.

■ **Tip** The Path.equals() method does not test a Path for existence in the file system.

The Path interface implements the java.lang.Comparable interface. You can use its compareTo() method to compare it with another Path object textually. The compareTo() method returns an int value, which is 0, less than 0, or greater than 0, when the two paths are equal, the path is less than the specified path, or the path is greater than the specified path, respectively. It is useful in sorting multiple paths in the textual order. The file system is not accessed when paths are compared using the compareTo() method. The ordering used by this method to compare two paths is platform-dependent. The following snippet of code shows examples of using the compareTo() method on Windows:

```
Path p1 = Paths.get("C:\\poems\\luci1.txt");
Path p2 = Paths.get("C:\\POEMS\\Luci1.txt");
Path p3 = Paths.get("C:\\poems\\..\\poems\\luci1.txt");
int v1 = p1.compareTo(p2); // Assigns 0 to v1
int v2 = p1.compareTo(p3); // Assigns 30 to v2
```

You can use the endsWith()and startsWith() methods to test if a path ends with and starts with a given path, respectively. It is important to note that these methods do not test if a path ends and starts with a text, respectively. They test if a path ends and starts with components of another path, respectively. The following snippet of code shows some examples of using these methods with paths on Windows:

```
Path p1 = Paths.get("C:\\poems\\luci1.txt");
Path p2 = Paths.get("luci1.txt");
Path p3 = Paths.get("poems\\luci1.txt");
Path p4 = Paths.get(".txt");

// Using endsWith()
boolean b1 = p1.endsWith(p2); // Assigns true to b1
boolean b2 = p1.endsWith(p3); // Assigns true to b2
boolean b3 = p1.endsWith(p4); // Assigns false to b3

// Using startsWith()
Path p5 = Paths.get("C:\\");
Path p6 = Paths.get("C:\\poems");
Path p7 = Paths.get("C:\\poem");

boolean b4 = p1.startsWith(p5); // Assigns true to b4
boolean b5 = p1.startsWith(p6); // Assigns true to b5
boolean b6 = p1.startsWith(p7); // Assigns false to b6
```

The endsWith() method compares the components, not the text, of a path with the specified path. For example, the path C:\poems\luci1.txt ends with luci1.txt, poems\luci1.txt, and C:\poems\luci1.txt. The same logic is used by the startsWith() method, though in the reverse order.

You can use the isSameFile(Path p1, Path p2) method of the Files class to check if two paths refer to the same file. If p1.equals(p2) returns true, this method returns true without verifying the existence of the paths in the file system. Otherwise, it checks with the file system, if both paths locate the same file. The file system implementation may require this method to access or open both files. The isSameFile() method throws an IOException when an I/O error occurs. Listing 10-4 demonstrates how the isSameFile() method works.

Listing 10-4. Checking If Two Paths Will Locate the Same File

```
// SameFileTest.java
package com.jdojo.nio2;

import java.io.IOException;
import java.nio.file.Files;
import java.nio.file.Path;
import java.nio.file.Paths;

public class SameFileTest {
    public static void main(String[] args) {
        // Assume that C:\poems\luci1.txt file exists
        Path p1 = Paths.get("C:\\poems\\luci1.txt");
        Path p2 = Paths.get("C:\\poems\\..\\poems\\luci1.txt");

        // Assume that C:\abc.txt file does not exist
        Path p3 = Paths.get("C:\\abc.txt");
        Path p4 = Paths.get("C:\\abc.txt");
```

```
        try {
            boolean isSame = Files.isSameFile(p1, p2);
            System.out.println("p1 and p2 are the same: " + isSame);

            isSame = Files.isSameFile(p3, p4);
            System.out.println("p3 and p4 are the same: " + isSame);
        } catch (IOException e) {
            e.printStackTrace();
        }
    }
}
```

```
p1 and p2 are the same: true
p3 and p4 are the same: true
```

Let's assume that the file denoted by the `C:\poems\luci1.txt` path exists. Since paths `p1` and `p2` are not equal using the `equals()` method, the `isSameFile()` method looks for these two paths in the file system for existence. It returns `true`, because `p1` and `p2` will resolve to the same file in the file system. Assume that the file denoted by the `C:\abc.txt` path does not exist. The `isSameFile(p3, p4)` method call returns `true` because both paths are textually equal. The output depends on the existence and non-existence of these files. The program may print the stack trace of an error if it does not find files at the same location. Change the file paths in the program to play with these methods. If you are running the program on the platform other than Windows, you must change the file path to conform to the path syntax used on your platform.

Normalizing, Resolving, and Relativizing Paths

In a file system, it is common to use a dot and two dots to represent the current directory and the parent directory, respectively. Sometimes it is also acceptable to specify more than one consecutive delimiter between a file name and a directory name. The `normalize()` method of the `Path` interface returns a `Path` after removing these extra characters. This method does not access the file system. Sometimes a normalized path may not locate the same file as the original path if the original path contained a symbolic link. The following snippet of code shows some examples of normalizing paths on Windows. Change the paths to conform to your platform if you run this code on other platforms.

```
Path p1 = Paths.get("C:\\poems\\..\\\\poems\\luci1.txt");
Path p1n = p1.normalize();
System.out.println(p1 + " normalized to " + p1n);

Path p2 = Paths.get("C:\\poems\\luci1.txt");
Path p2n = p2.normalize();
System.out.println(p2 + " normalized to " + p2n);

Path p3 = Paths.get("a\\..\\.\\test.txt");
Path p3n = p3.normalize();
System.out.println(p3 + " normalized to " + p3n);
```

```
C:\poems\..\poems\luci1.txt normalized to C:\poems\luci1.txt
C:\poems\luci1.txt normalized to C:\poems\luci1.txt
a\..\.\test.txt normalized to test.txt
```

You can combine two paths using the resolve(Path p) method of the Path interface. If the specified path is an absolute path, it returns the specified path. It returns the path if the specified path is an empty path. In other cases, it simply combines the two paths and returns the result, so the returned path ends with the specified path. The path on which this method is invoked is assumed to be a directory. The following snippet of code shows some examples of resolving paths on Windows. Change the paths to conform to your platform if you run this code on other platforms.

```
Path p1 = Paths.get("C:\\poems");
Path p2 = Paths.get("luci1.txt");
System.out.println(p1.resolve(p2));

Path p3 = Paths.get("C:\\test.txt");
System.out.println(p1.resolve(p3));

Path p4 = Paths.get("");
System.out.println(p1.resolve(p4));

Path p5 = Paths.get("poems\\Luci");
Path p6 = Paths.get("luci4.txt");
System.out.println(p5.resolve(p6));
```

```
C:\poems\luci1.txt
C:\test.txt
C:\poems
poems\Luci\luci4.txt
```

Relativizing is the process of getting a relative path for a given path against another path. The relativize(Path p) method of the Path interface does this job. The relative path that is returned from this method, when resolved against the same path against which the path was relativized, returns the same given path. A relative path cannot be obtained if one of the paths has a root element. Whether a relative path can be obtained is platform-dependent if both paths have root elements. The following snippet of code shows some examples of getting relative paths. When there is no common sub-path between the two paths, it is assumed that both paths locate sibling objects. For example, when getting a relative path for Doug against Bobby, it is assumed that Doug and Bobby are siblings. The output is shown when the program was run on Windows. On other platforms, you may get a slightly different output.

```
Path p1 = Paths.get("poems");
Path p2 = Paths.get("poems", "recent", "Luci");
System.out.println(p1.relativize(p2));
System.out.println(p2.relativize(p1));

Path p3 = Paths.get("Doug");
Path p4 = Paths.get("Bobby");
System.out.println(p3.relativize(p4));
System.out.println(p4.relativize(p3));
```

```
recent\Luci
..\..
..\Bobby
..\Doug
```

Symbolic Links

A *symbolic link* is a special type of file that contains a reference to another file or directory. A symbolic link is also known as *symlink* or *soft link*. The file referenced by a symbolic link is known as the target file for the symbolic link. Some operating systems that support symbolic links are UNIX-like operating systems (Linux, Mac OS X, etc.), Windows 10, etc.

Operations on a symbolic link are transparent to the application. When an operation is performed on a symbolic link, the operating system performs the operation on the target of the link. For example, performing a read/write operation on a symbolic link performs a read/write on its target. However, the delete, move, and rename operations are performed directly on the link, rather than on its target. Sometimes it is possible to have a circular reference in a symbolic link, where the target of a symbolic link points back to the original link.

The NIO.2 API fully supports symbolic links. It has safeguards in place to detect a circular reference in a symbolic link. You can work with symbolic links using the `java.nio.file.Files` class. You can use its `isSymbolicLink(Path p)` method to check if the file denoted by the specified path is a symbolic link. The `createSymbolicLink()` method of the `Files` class is used to create a symbolic link.

■ **Tip** The `createSymbolicLink()` method in the `Files` class is an optional operation, which may not be supported on all platforms.

The following snippet of code shows how to create a symbolic link for a file on Windows. When I use Windows, the administrative privilege is required to create symbolic links. If you do not have this privilege, you will get an exception with an appropriate error message indicating this.

```
Path existingFilePath = Paths.get("C:\\poems\\luci1.txt");
Path symLinkPath = Paths.get("C:\\luci1_link.txt");
try {
    Files.createSymbolicLink(symLinkPath, existingFilePath);
} catch (IOException e) {
    e.printStackTrace();
}
```

The NIO.2 API follows the symbolic link by default. In some cases, you can specify whether you want to follow a symbolic link or not. The option not to follow a symbolic link is indicated by using the enum constant `LinkOption.NOFOLLOW_LINKS`. The `LinkOption` enum is in the `java.nio.file` package. Methods supporting this option let you pass an argument of the `LinkOption` type.

■ **Tip** The NIO.2 API also supports regular links (also known as hard links). You can use the `createLink(Path newLink, Path existingPath)` method of the `Files` class to create a hard link.

Different Forms of a Path

You can get different types of representations for a path. Suppose you create a `Path` object as follows:

```
// Create a Path object to represent a relative path
Path p1 = Paths.get("test.txt");
```

Here, p1 represents a relative path. You can get the absolute path that is represented by p1 using its toAbsolutePath() method as follows:

```
// Get the absolute path represented by p1
Path p1AbsPath = p1.toAbsolutePath();
```

Now the p1AbsPath is the absolute path for p1. For example, on Windows, p1AbsPath may look like C:\testapp\test.txt. If a path is not an absolute path, the toAbsolutePath() method uses a platform-dependent default directory to resolve the path to give you the absolute path. If the path is an absolute path, the toAbsolutePath() method returns the same path.

You can use the toRealPath() method to get the real path of an existing file. It returns a canonical path to an existing file. If the path represents a symbolic link, it returns the real path of the target file. You can pass a link option to this method indicating whether you do not want to follow the symbolic link to its target. If the file represented by the path does not exist, the toRealPath() throws an IOException. The following snippet of code demonstrates how to get the real path from a Path object:

```
import java.io.IOException;
import java.nio.file.LinkOption;
import java.nio.file.Path;
import java.nio.file.Paths;
...
try {
    Path p2 = Paths.get("test2.txt");

    // Follow link for p2 if it is a symbolic link
    Path p2RealPath = p2.toRealPath();

    System.out.println("p2RealPath:" + p2RealPath);
} catch (IOException e) {
    e.printStackTrace();
}

try {
    Path p3 = Paths.get("test3.txt");

    // Do not follow link for p3, if it is a symbolic link
    Path p3RealPath = p3.toRealPath(LinkOption.NOFOLLOW_LINKS);

    System.out.println("p3RealPath:" + p3RealPath);
} catch (IOException e) {
    e.printStackTrace();
}
```

You can use the toUri() method of a Path object to get its URI representation. A URI representation of a path is highly platform-dependent. Typically, a URI form of a path can be used in a browser to open the file indicated by the path. The following snippet of code shows how to get the URI form of a path. The output was generated on Windows. You may get different output.

```
Path p2 = Paths.get("test2.txt");
java.net.URI p2UriPath = p2.toUri();
System.out.println("Absolute Path: " + p2.toAbsolutePath());
System.out.println("URI Path: " + p2UriPath);
```

```
Absolute Path: C:\java_code\testapp\test2.txt
URI Path: file:///C:/java_code/testapp/test2.txt
```

Performing File Operations on a Path

The `java.nio.file.Files` class consists of all static methods that let you perform most of the file operations on a `Path` object.

Creating New Files

The `Files` class provides several methods to create regular files, directories, symbolic links, and temporary files/directories. These methods throw an `IOException` when an I/O error occurs during the file creation; for example, they throw a `java.nio.file.FileAlreadyExistsException` if you attempt to create a file that already exists. Most of the methods accept a varargs parameter of the `FileAttribute` type, which lets you specify the file attributes. I discuss file attributes shortly.

You can use the `createFile()` method to create a new regular file. The new file, if created, is empty. The file creation fails in case the file already exists, or the parent directory does not exist. Listing 10-5 shows how to create a new file. It attempts to create a `text.txt` file in your default directory. The program prints the details of the file creation status.

Listing 10-5. Creating a New File

```java
// CreateFileTest.java
package com.jdojo.nio2;

import java.io.IOException;
import java.nio.file.FileAlreadyExistsException;
import java.nio.file.Files;
import java.nio.file.NoSuchFileException;
import java.nio.file.Path;
import java.nio.file.Paths;

public class CreateFileTest {
    public static void main(String[] args) {
        Path p1 = Paths.get("test.txt");
        try {
            Files.createFile(p1);
            System.out.format("File created: %s%n", p1.toRealPath());
        } catch (FileAlreadyExistsException e) {
            System.out.format("File %s already exists.%n",
                    p1.normalize());
        } catch (NoSuchFileException e) {
            System.out.format("Directory %s does not exists.%n",
                    p1.normalize().getParent());
        } catch (IOException e) {
            e.printStackTrace();
        }
    }
}
```

The createDirectory() and createDirectories() methods are used to create a new directory. If the parent directory of the new directory does not exist, the createDirectory() method fails. The createDirectories() method creates a non-existent parent directory. You can use the createTempDirectory() and createTempFile() methods to create a temporary directory and a temporary file, respectively.

The following snippet of code shows how to create temporary files and directories. The output was generated when the program ran on Windows 10. The name generation for a temporary directory/file is implementation-dependent. Attempts are made to use the supplied prefix and suffix for the temporary file/directory. You need to change the paths to conform to your platform and you may get different output.

```
try {
    String dirPrefix = "KDir";
    Path tDir = Files.createTempDirectory(dirPrefix);
    System.out.println("Temp directory: " + tDir);

    String fPrefix = "KF_";
    String fSuffix = ".txt";
    Path tFile1 = Files.createTempFile(fPrefix, fSuffix);
    System.out.println("Temp file1: " + tFile1);
} catch (IOException e) {
    e.printStackTrace();
}
```

```
Temp directory: C:\Users\ksharan\KDir15281773985593265118
Temp file1: C:\Users\ksharan\KF_1825194228632364 1819.txt
```

A temporary file/directory is not automatically deleted. You may want to use the deleteOnExit() method of the java.io.File class to delete the file when the JVM exits.

```
Path tempFile = Files.createTempFile("myTempFile", ".txt");

// Delete the file when the JVM exits
tempFile.toFile().deleteOnExit();
```

Deleting Files

The Files class contains the following two methods to delete a file, a directory, and a symbolic link:

- void delete(Path path) throws IOException
- boolean deleteIfExists(Path path) throws IOException

The delete() method throws an IOException if the deletion fails. For example, it throws a NoSuchFileException if the file being deleted does not exist and throws a DirectoryNotEmptyException if the directory being deleted is not empty.

The deleteIfExists() method does not throw a NoSuchFileException if the file being deleted does not exist. It returns true if it deletes the file. Otherwise, it returns false. It throws a DirectoryNotEmptyException if the directory being deleted is not empty.

The following snippet of code shows how to delete a file and handle exceptions:

```
// Create a Path object on Windows
Path p = Paths.get("C:\\poems\\luci1.txt");

try {
    // Delete the file
    Files.delete(p);
    System.out.println(p + " deleted successfully.");
} catch (NoSuchFileException e) {
    System.out.println(p + " does not exist.");
} catch (DirectoryNotEmptyException e) {
    System.out.println("Directory " + p + " is not empty.");
} catch (IOException e) {
    e.printStackTrace();
}
```

Checking for Existence of a File

The `Files` class provides the following two methods to check for existence and non-existence of a file:

- `boolean exists(Path path, LinkOption... options)`
- `boolean notExists(Path path, LinkOption... options)`

These two methods are not the opposite of each other. If it is not possible to determine whether a file exists, both methods return `false`. If you need to take an action when a file exists, use the `exists()` method in your logic. If you need to take an action when a file does not exist, use the `notExists()` method.

Copying and Moving Files

The `Files` class provides the following three versions of the `copy()` method to copy contents and attributes of a file to another file:

- `long copy(InputStream in, Path target, CopyOption... options)`
- `long copy(Path source, OutputStream out)`
- `Path copy(Path source, Path target, CopyOption... options)`

If the specified `source` file is a symbolic link, the target of the symbolic link is copied, not the symbolic link. If the specified `source` file is a directory, an empty directory at the target location is created without copying the contents of the directory. If the specified `source` and `target` files are the same, the `copy()` method does not do anything.

You can specify one or more of the following copy options with the `copy()` method:

- `StandardCopyOption.REPLACE_EXISTING`
- `StandardCopyOption.COPY_ATTRIBUTES`
- `LinkOption.NOFOLLOW_LINKS`

If the target file already exists, the copy() method throws a FileAlreadyExistsException. You can specify the REPLACE_EXISTING option to replace the existing target file. If the target file is a non-empty directory, specifying the REPLACE_EXISTING option throws a DirectoryNotEmptyException. If the target file is a symbolic link and if it exists, the symbolic link is replaced by specifying the REPLACE_EXISTING option, not the target of the symbolic link.

The COPY_ATTRIBUTES option copies the attributes of the source file to the target file. The file attributes that are copied are highly platform- and file system-dependent. At least, the last-modified-time attribute of the source file is copied to the target file, if supported by both source and target file stores.

If the NOFOLLOW_LINKS option is used, the copy() method copies the symbolic link, not the target of the symbolic link.

Listing 10-6 demonstrates the use of the copy() method to copy a file. It handles the possible exceptions if the copy operation fails. You need to change the paths for the source and target files before running the program.

Listing 10-6. Copying a File, a Directory, and a Symbolic Link Using the Files.copy() Method

```
// CopyTest.java
package com.jdojo.nio2;

import java.nio.file.Path;
import java.nio.file.Paths;
import java.nio.file.Files;
import java.io.IOException;
import java.nio.file.FileAlreadyExistsException;
import java.nio.file.DirectoryNotEmptyException;
import static java.nio.file.StandardCopyOption.REPLACE_EXISTING;
import static java.nio.file.StandardCopyOption.COPY_ATTRIBUTES;

public class CopyTest {
    public static void main(String[] args) {
        // Change the paths for the source and target files before you run the program
        Path source = Paths.get("C:\\poems\\luci1.txt");
        Path target = Paths.get("C:\\poems\\luci1_backup.txt");

        try {
            Path p = Files.copy(source, target, REPLACE_EXISTING, COPY_ATTRIBUTES);
            System.out.println(source + " has been copied to " + p);
        } catch (FileAlreadyExistsException e) {
            System.out.println(target + " already exists.");
        } catch (DirectoryNotEmptyException e) {
            System.out.println(target + " is not empty.");
        } catch (IOException e) {
            e.printStackTrace();
        }
    }
}
```

The move(Path source, Path target, CopyOption... options) method of the Files class lets you move or rename a file. The move operation fails if the specified target file already exists. You can specify the REPLACE_EXISTING option to replace the existing target file. If the file to move is a symbolic link, it moves the symbolic link, not the target of the symbolic link. The move() method can only be used to move an empty directory. A DirectoryNotEmptyException is thrown if the directory is not empty.

Apart from the REPLACE_EXISTING CopyOption, you can use the ATOMIC_MOVE as another CopyOption. If the ATOMIC_MOVE option is used, it throws an AtomicMoveNotSupportedException if the file could not be moved atomically. If ATOMIC_MOVE option is specified, all other options are ignored. The following snippet of code shows how to move a file by handling possible exceptions:

```
import java.io.IOException;
import java.nio.file.AtomicMoveNotSupportedException;
import java.nio.file.DirectoryNotEmptyException;
import java.nio.file.FileAlreadyExistsException;
import java.nio.file.Files;
import java.nio.file.NoSuchFileException;
import java.nio.file.Path;
import java.nio.file.Paths;
import static java.nio.file.StandardCopyOption.ATOMIC_MOVE;
...
// Create source and target paths using the syntax supported by your platform
Path source = Paths.get("C:\\poems\\luci1.txt");
Path target = Paths.get("C:\\poems\\dir2\\luci1.txt");

try {
    // Try moving the source to target atomically
    Path p = Files.move(source, target, ATOMIC_MOVE);
    System.out.println(source + " has been moved to " + p);
} catch (NoSuchFileException e) {
    System.out.println("Source/target does not exist.");
} catch (FileAlreadyExistsException e) {
    System.out.println(target + " already exists. Move failed.");
} catch (DirectoryNotEmptyException e) {
    System.out.println(target + " is not empty. Move failed.");
} catch (AtomicMoveNotSupportedException e){
    System.out.println("Atomic move is not supported. Move failed.");
} catch (IOException e) {
    e.printStackTrace();
}
```

Commonly Used File Attributes

The Files class contains many methods that let you access the commonly used attributes of a file. For example, you can use the Files.isHidden(Path p) method to test if a file represented by the specified Path is hidden. The following methods in the Files class let you access various types of commonly used attributes of a file. Refer to the "Managing File Attributes" section in this chapter for managing advanced file attributes.

- long size(Path)
- boolean isHidden(Path path)
- boolean isRegularFile(Path path, LinkOption... options)
- boolean isDirectory(Path, LinkOption... options)
- boolean isSymbolicLink(Path path)
- FileTime getLastModifiedTime(Path path, LinkOption... options)

Probing the Content Type of a File

You can use the `Files.probeContentType(Path path)` method to probe the content type of a file. The method returns the content type in the string form of the value of a Multipurpose Internet Mail Extension (MIME) content type. If the content type of a file cannot be determined, it returns `null`.

Listing 10-7 shows how to probe the content type of a file. You may get different output when you run this program. The program uses the file path `C:\poems\luci1.txt`. Change this path to the path of the file whose content type you want to know.

Listing 10-7. Probing the Content Type of a File

```
// ProbeFileContent.java
package com.jdojo.nio2;

import java.nio.file.Files;
import java.nio.file.Path;
import java.nio.file.Paths;
import java.io.IOException;

public class ProbeFileContent {
    public static void main(String[] args) {
        Path p = Paths.get("C:\\poems\\luci1.txt");

        try {
            String contentType = Files.probeContentType(p);
            System.out.format("Content type of %s is %s%n", p, contentType);
        } catch (IOException e) {
            e.printStackTrace();
        }
    }
}
```

```
Content type of C:\poems\luci1.txt is text/plain
```

Reading the Contents of a File

The NIO.2 API supports reading the contents of a file in the following three ways:

- As bytes or lines of text
- Using `InputStream` and `BufferedReader` using the `java.io` API
- Using the channel API using a `SeekableByteChannel` object

The `Files` class contains the following methods to read the contents of a file as bytes and lines of text:

- `byte[] readAllBytes(Path path)`
- `List<String> readAllLines(Path path)`
- `List<String> readAllLines(Path, Charset cs)`

All three methods may throw an `IOException`. The `readAllBytes()` method reads all bytes from a file. The `readAllLines()` method reads the entire contents of a file as lines of text. The `readAllLines()` method uses a carriage return, a line feed, and a carriage returned followed by a line feed as a line terminator. The lines that are returned do not contain the line terminator. The version of this method that takes only the `Path` of the source file as an argument assumes the contents of the file in the UTF-8 charset.

■ **Tip** The `readAllBytes()` and `readAllLines()` methods in the `Files` class are intended to read the contents of a small file. Both methods take care of opening/closing the file before/after reading.

The `Files` class provides methods to obtain the `InputStream` and `BufferedReader` objects from a `Path` object. The `newInputStream(Path path, OpenOption... options)` method returns an `InputStream` for the specified path. The `newBufferedReader(Path path)` and `newBufferedReader(Path path, Charset cs)` methods return a `BufferedReader`; the former assumes that the file's contents are in the UTF-8 charset, whereas the latter lets you specify the charset. Refer to Chapter 7 for more details on how to use `InputStream` and `BufferedReader` to read the contents of a file.

The `Files` class provides methods to obtain a `SeekableByteChannel` object from a `Path` using its `newByteChannel(Path path, OpenOption... options)` method. A `SeekableByteChannel` object provides random access to a file using the channel API. It can be used to read from and write to a file. You can cast a `SeekableByteChannel` to a `FileChannel` to use advanced features of the channel API such as locking a region of the file and mapping a region of the file directly into memory. It maintains a current position where you can start reading or writing. Refer to Chapter 9 for more details on how to use channels to read data from a file. I discuss an example of using a `SeekableByteChannel` to read/write the contents of a file later in this chapter.

Many of the methods of the `Files` class that deal with reading from and writing to files accept an optional argument of the `OpenOption` type. This option lets you configure the file being opened. Table 10-1 lists the values with their descriptions for the `OpenOption` type. `OpenOption` is an interface in the `java.nio.file` package. The `StandardOpenOption` enum in the `java.nio.file` package implements the `OpenOption` interface. Therefore, each enum constant in the `StandardOpenOption` represents a value of the `OpenOption` type.

Table 10-1. *List of OpenOption Type Values That Are Enum Constants in the StandardOpenOption Enum*

StandardOpenOption Constant	Description
`APPEND`	Appends the written data to the existing file, if the file is opened for writing.
`CREATE`	Creates a new file if it does not exist.
`CREATE_NEW`	Creates a new file if it does not exist. If the file already exists, it fails the operation.
`DELETE_ON_CLOSE`	Deletes the file when the stream is closed. It is useful when used with a temporary file.
`DSYNC`	Keeps the contents of the file synchronized with the underlying storage.
`READ`	Opens a file with read access.
`SPARSE`	If it is used with the `CREATE_NEW` option, it is a hint to the file system that the new file should be a sparse file. If a sparse file is not supported by a file system, this option is ignored.
`SYNC`	Keeps the content and the metadata of the file synchronized with the underlying storage.
`TRUNCATE_EXISTING`	Truncates the length of an existing file to zero if the file is opened for a write access.
`WRITE`	Opens a file for a write access.

The following snippet of code obtains a SeekableByteChannel object for the luci2.txt file in the default directory. It opens the file for READ and WRITE access. It uses the CREATE option, so the file is created if it does not exist.

```
import java.nio.file.Path;
import java.nio.file.Paths;
import java.nio.file.Files;
import java.nio.channels.SeekableByteChannel;
import static java.nio.file.StandardOpenOption.READ;
import static java.nio.file.StandardOpenOption.WRITE;
import static java.nio.file.StandardOpenOption.CREATE;
...
Path src = Paths.get("luci2.txt");
SeekableByteChannel sbc = Files.newByteChannel(src, READ, WRITE, CREATE);
```

Listing 10-8 demonstrates how to read and display the contents of the luci1.txt file in your default directory. The program displays an error message if the file does not exist.

Listing 10-8. Using the Files.readAllLines() Method to Read Contents of a File

```
// ReadAllLines.java
package com.jdojo.nio2;

import java.nio.file.Files;
import java.nio.file.Path;
import java.nio.file.Paths;
import java.util.List;
import java.nio.charset.Charset;
import java.io.IOException;
import java.nio.file.NoSuchFileException;

public class ReadAllLines {
    public static void main(String[] args) {
        Charset cs = Charset.forName("US-ASCII");
        Path source = Paths.get("luci1.txt");

        try {
            // Read all lines in one go
            List<String> lines = Files.readAllLines(source, cs);

            // Print each line
            for (String line : lines) {
                System.out.println(line);
            }
        } catch (NoSuchFileException e) {
            System.out.println(source.toAbsolutePath() + " does not exist.");
        } catch (IOException e) {
            e.printStackTrace();
        }
    }
}
```

Writing to a File

The NIO.2 API supports writing to a file in the following three ways:

- Writing an array of bytes or a collection of lines of text to a file in one shot.
- Writing to a file using an `OutputStream` and a `BufferedWriter` using the `java.io` API.
- Writing to a file using the channel API using a `SeekableByteChannel` object.

You can use the following `write()` methods of the `Files` class to write contents to a file in one shot:

- `Path write(Path path, byte[] bytes, OpenOption... options)`
- `Path write(Path path, Iterable<? extends CharSequence> lines, OpenOption... options)`
- `Path write(Path path, Iterable<? extends CharSequence> lines, Charset cs, OpenOption... options)`

These methods are designed to write smaller contents to a file. You are advised to use other methods (discussed shortly) to write bigger contents to a file.

The `write()` method opens the file, writes the passed in contents to the file, and closes it. If no open options are present, it opens the file with the `CREATE`, `TRUNCATE_EXISTING`, and `WRITE` options. If you are writing lines of text to a file, it writes a platform-dependent line separator after every line of text. If a charset is not specified when the lines of text are written, the UTF-8 charset is assumed.

Listing 10-9 demonstrates how to write lines of text to a file using the `write()` method. The program writes a few lines of text in a file named `twinkle.txt` in the default directory. It prints the path of the file. You may get different output when you run this program.

Listing 10-9. Writing Lines of Text to a File in One Shot Using the NIO.2 API

```
// WriteLinesTest.java
package com.jdojo.nio2;

import java.io.IOException;
import java.nio.charset.Charset;
import java.nio.file.Files;
import java.nio.file.Path;
import java.nio.file.Paths;
import java.util.ArrayList;
import java.util.List;
import static java.nio.file.StandardOpenOption.WRITE;
import static java.nio.file.StandardOpenOption.CREATE;

public class WriteLinesTest {
    public static void main(String[] args) {
        // Prepare the lines of text to write in a List
        List<String> texts = new ArrayList<>();
        texts.add("Twinkle, twinkle, little star,");
        texts.add("How I wonder what you are.");
        texts.add("Up above the world so high,");
        texts.add("Like a diamond in the sky.");
```

```
        Path dest = Paths.get("twinkle.txt");
        Charset cs = Charset.forName("US-ASCII");
        try {
            Path p = Files.write(dest, texts, cs, WRITE, CREATE);
            System.out.println("Text was written to "
                    + p.toAbsolutePath());
        } catch (IOException e) {
            e.printStackTrace();
        }
    }
}
```

```
Text was written to C:\Java9LanguageFeatures\twinkle.txt
```

The Files class contains a newOutputStream(Path path, OpenOption... options) method that returns an OutputStream for the specified path. The class contains a newBufferedWriter(Path path, Charset cs, OpenOption... options) method that returns a BufferedWriter for the specified path. You can use the java.io API to write contents to a file using OutputStream and BufferedWriter. Refer to Chapter 7 for more details on how to use the java.io API.

You can use the newByteChannel(Path path, OpenOption... options) method to get a SeekableByteChannel for the specified path. You can use the write(ByteBuffer src) method of the SeekableByteChannel to write data to a file. Refer to Chapter 9 for more details on how to use the channel API to write to a file. I discuss an example of using SeekableByteChannel in the next section.

Random Access to a File

A SeekableByteChannel provides random access to a file using the channel API. You can use it to read data from and write data to a file. It is an interface declared in the java.nio.channels package. The FileChannel class in the java.nio.channels package implements this interface. You can get a SeekableByteChannel for a Path using the newByteChannel() method of the Files class as follows:

```
Path src = Paths.get("twinkle2.txt");
SeekableByteChannel seekableChannel =
        Files.newByteChannel(src, READ, WRITE, CREATE, TRUNCATE_EXISTING);
```

A SeekableByteChannel is connected to an entity such as a file. It maintains a current position. When you write to the channel, the data is written at the current position. If you read from it, the data is read from the current position. You can get the current position using its position() method. To set its current position, you need to use its position(long newPosition) method.

You can get the size of the entity of a SeekableByteChannel in bytes using its size() method. As the data is truncated or written to the channel, the size is updated.

The truncate(long size) method of the SeekableByteChannel lets you truncate the size of the entity to the specified size. If the specified size is less than the current size of the entity, it truncates the data to the specified size. If the specified size is greater than or equal to the current size of the entity, this method does not modify the entity.

Use the read(ByteBuffer destination) and write(ByteBuffer source) methods to read data from the channel and write data to the channel, respectively. Make sure to set the current position correctly, before you perform the read and write operations on the channel.

Listing 10-10 shows how to read from and write to a file using a `SeekableByteChannel`. It creates a file named `twinkle2.txt` in the default directory and writes a few lines of text to it. It resets the position to zero after writing the data and reads the text to print it on the standard output. At every step, it prints the size and the current position.

Listing 10-10. A Sample Program That Uses a SeekableByteChannel to Read and Write Data from/to a File

```
// SeekableByteChannelTest.java
package com.jdojo.nio2;

import java.nio.ByteBuffer;
import java.nio.charset.Charset;
import java.io.IOException;
import java.nio.CharBuffer;
import java.nio.channels.SeekableByteChannel;
import java.nio.file.Path;
import java.nio.file.Paths;
import java.nio.file.Files;
import static java.nio.file.StandardOpenOption.READ;
import static java.nio.file.StandardOpenOption.WRITE;
import static java.nio.file.StandardOpenOption.CREATE;
import static java.nio.file.StandardOpenOption.TRUNCATE_EXISTING;

public class SeekableByteChannelTest {
    public static void main(String[] args) {
        Path src = Paths.get("twinkle2.txt");

        // Get the file encoding for the system
        String encoding = System.getProperty("file.encoding");
        Charset cs = Charset.forName(encoding);

        try (SeekableByteChannel seekableChannel
                = Files.newByteChannel(src, READ, WRITE, CREATE, TRUNCATE_EXISTING)) {

            // Print the details
            printDetails(seekableChannel, "Before writing data");

            // First, write some data to the file
            writeData(seekableChannel, cs);

            // Print the details
            printDetails(seekableChannel, "After writing data");

            // Reset the position of the seekable channel to 0,
            // so we can read the data from the beginning
            seekableChannel.position(0);

            // Print the details
            printDetails(seekableChannel, "After resetting position to 0");

            // Read the data from the file
            readData(seekableChannel, cs);
```

```
            // Print the details
            printDetails(seekableChannel, "After reading data");
        } catch (IOException e) {
            e.printStackTrace();
        }
    }

    public static void writeData(SeekableByteChannel seekableChannel,
            Charset cs) throws IOException {
        // Get the platform-dependent line separator
        String separator = System.getProperty("line.separator");

        // Prepare the text to write to the file
        StringBuilder sb = new StringBuilder();
        sb.append("When the blazing sun is gone,");
        sb.append(separator);
        sb.append("When he nothing shines upon,");
        sb.append(separator);
        sb.append("Then you show your little light,");
        sb.append(separator);
        sb.append("Twinkle, twinkle, all the night");
        sb.append(separator);

        // Wrap the text into a char buffer
        CharBuffer charBuffer = CharBuffer.wrap(sb);

        // Encode the char buffer data into a byte buffer
        ByteBuffer byteBuffer = cs.encode(charBuffer);

        // Write the data to the file
        seekableChannel.write(byteBuffer);
    }

    public static void readData(SeekableByteChannel seekableChannel,
            Charset cs) throws IOException {
        ByteBuffer byteBuffer = ByteBuffer.allocate(128);
        String encoding = System.getProperty("file.encoding");

        while (seekableChannel.read(byteBuffer) > 0) {
            byteBuffer.rewind();
            CharBuffer charBuffer = cs.decode(byteBuffer);
            System.out.print(charBuffer);
            byteBuffer.flip();
        }
    }

    public static void printDetails(SeekableByteChannel seekableChannel, String msg) {
        try {
            System.out.println(msg + ": Size = " + seekableChannel.size()
                    + ", Position = " + seekableChannel.position());
```

```
        } catch (IOException e) {
            e.printStackTrace();
        }
    }
}
```

```
Before writing data: Size = 0, Position = 0
After writing data: Size = 128, Position = 128
After resetting position to 0: Size = 128, Position = 0
When the blazing sun is gone,
When he nothing shines upon,
Then you show your little light,
Twinkle, twinkle, all the night
After reading data: Size = 128, Position = 128
```

Traversing a File Tree

NIO.2 provides a FileVisitor API to recursively process all files and directories in a file tree. The API is useful when you want to perform some actions on all or some files or directories in a file tree. For example, you cannot delete a directory until it is empty. Before you delete a directory, you must delete all files and directories underneath it, which can be achieved easily using the FileVisitor API. You need to use the following steps to traverse a file tree:

1. Create a file visitor class by implementing the `java.nio.file.FileVisitor` interface.
2. To start visiting the file tree, use the `walkFileTree()` method of the `Files` class by specifying the starting directory and a file visitor object of the class created in the previous step. One of the methods of the `FileVisitor` interface is called when a file/directory is visited or a file/directory visit fails.

■ **Tip** The NIO.2 API provides the `SimpleFileVisitor` class, which is a basic implementation of the `FileVisitor` interface. The methods in the `SimpleFileVisitor` class do not do anything when a file/directory is visited. When a failure occurs, it rethrows the original exception. You can inherit your file visitor class from the `SimpleFileVisitor` class and override only the methods that fit your needs.

Table 10-2 lists the methods of the `FileVisitor` interface with their descriptions. All methods throw an `IOException` and they all return an enum constant of `FileVisitResult` type. Table 10-3 lists the constants defined by the `FileVisitResult` enum type with their descriptions.

Table 10-2. *Methods of the FileVisitor Interface*

Method	Description
`FileVisitResult preVisitDirectory (T dir, BasicFileAttributes attrs) throws IOException`	This method is called once before visiting entries in a directory.
`FileVisitResult postVisitDirectory (T dir, IOException exc) throws IOException`	This method is called after entries in a directory (and all of their descendants) have been visited. It is invoked even if there are errors during the visit of entries in a directory. If there was any exception thrown during the iteration of a directory, the exception object is passed to this method as the second argument. If the second argument to this method is `null`, there was no exception during the directory iteration.
`FileVisitResult visitFile (T file, BasicFileAttributes attrs) throws IOException`	This method is called when a file in a directory is visited.
`FileVisitResult visitFileFailed (T file, IOException exc) throws IOException`	This method is called when a file or directory could not be visited for any reason.

Table 10-3. *Enum Constants of FileVisitResult and Their Descriptions*

Enum Constant	Description
`CONTINUE`	Continues processing.
`SKIP_SIBLINGS`	Continues processing without visiting the siblings of the file or directory. If it is returned from the `preVisitDirectory()` method, the entries in the current directory are also skipped and the `postVisitDirectory()` method is not called on that directory.
`SKIP_SUBTREE`	Continues processing without visiting entries in the directory. It is meaningful only when returned from the `preVisitDirectory()` method. Otherwise, its effect is the same as `CONTINUE`.
`TERMINATE`	Terminates the file-visiting process.

You do not need to write logic in all four methods of your file visitor class. For example, if you want to copy a directory, you would like the code in the `preVisitDirectory()` method to create a new directory and the `visitFile()` method to copy the file. If you want to delete a directory, you need to delete the entries first. In this case, you will implement the `visitFile()` method to delete the files and the `postVisitDirectory()` method to delete the directory afterward.

Let's implement a file visitor that will print the names of all files and subdirectories of a directory. It will also print the size of the files in bytes. Listing 10-11 contains the complete program. It prints the details of files and subdirectories of the default directory.

Listing 10-11. A Program to the Print the Names of Subdirectories and Files of a Directory

```
// WalkFileTreeTest.java
package com.jdojo.nio2;
```

```
import java.io.IOException;
import java.nio.file.FileVisitor;
import java.nio.file.Path;
import java.nio.file.Paths;
import java.nio.file.SimpleFileVisitor;
import java.nio.file.attribute.BasicFileAttributes;
import java.nio.file.FileVisitResult;
import java.nio.file.Files;
import static java.nio.file.FileVisitResult.CONTINUE;

public class WalkFileTreeTest {
    public static void main(String[] args) {
        // Get the Path object for the default directory
        Path startDir = Paths.get("");

        // Get a file visitor object
        FileVisitor<Path> visitor = getFileVisitor();

        try {
            // Traverse the contents of the startDir
            Files.walkFileTree(startDir, visitor);
        } catch (IOException e) {
            e.printStackTrace();
        }
    }

    public static FileVisitor<Path> getFileVisitor() {
        // Declare a local class DirVisitor that
        // inherits from the SimpleFileVisitor<Path> class
        class DirVisitor<Path> extends SimpleFileVisitor<Path> {
            @Override
            public FileVisitResult preVisitDirectory(Path dir, BasicFileAttributes attrs) {
                System.out.format("%s [Directory]%n", dir);
                return CONTINUE;
            }

            @Override
            public FileVisitResult visitFile(Path file, BasicFileAttributes attrs) {

                System.out.format("%s [File, Size: %s bytes]%n", file, attrs.size());
                return CONTINUE;
            }
        }

        // Create an object of the DirVisitor
        FileVisitor<Path> visitor = new DirVisitor<>();

        return visitor;
    }
}
```

The getFileVisitor() method creates a FileVisitor object whose class inherits from the SimpleFileVisitor class. In the preVisitDirectory() method, it prints the name of the directory and returns FileVisitResult.CONTINUE to indicate that it wants to continue processing the entries in the directory. In the visitFile() method, it prints the name and size of the file and continues the processing. The FileVisitor API traverses a file tree in depth-first order. However, it does not guarantee the order of the visits of the subdirectories of a directory. To traverse a file tree, you need to call the walkFileTree() method of the Files class. The walkFileTree() method will automatically call the method of the visitor object as it walks through the file tree.

The FileVisitor API is very useful whenever you want to take some actions on all entries or some selective entries in a file tree. Operations such as copying a directory tree, deleting a non-empty directory, finding a file, etc. can be implemented easily using the FileVisitor API. Listing 10-12 demonstrates how to use the FileVisitor API to delete a directory tree. You need to specify the path to the directory to be deleted before you run the program. Note that you will not be able to get the contents of the deleted directory back. Therefore, be careful when experimenting with this program and do not delete any useful directory accidently.

Listing 10-12. Using the FileVisitor API to Delete a Directory Tree

```
// DeleteDirectoryTest.java
package com.jdojo.nio2;

import java.io.IOException;
import java.nio.file.FileVisitResult;
import static java.nio.file.FileVisitResult.CONTINUE;
import static java.nio.file.FileVisitResult.TERMINATE;
import java.nio.file.FileVisitor;
import java.nio.file.Files;
import java.nio.file.Path;
import java.nio.file.Paths;
import java.nio.file.SimpleFileVisitor;
import java.nio.file.attribute.BasicFileAttributes;

public class DeleteDirectoryTest {
    public static void main(String[] args) {
        /* WARNING!!!
           Replace YOUR_DIR_PATH_TO_DELETE in the following statement with
           the path of the directory whose contents you want to delete.
           You will not be able to get the contents of the directory back
           after you run this program.
         */
        Path dirToDelete = Paths.get("YOUR_DIR_PATH_TO_DELETE");
        FileVisitor<Path> visitor = getFileVisitor();

        try {
            Files.walkFileTree(dirToDelete, visitor);
        } catch (IOException e) {
            System.out.println(e.getMessage());
        }
    }
```

```
    public static FileVisitor<Path> getFileVisitor() {
        // A inner local class that is used as a file visitor to delete a directory
        class DeleteDirVisitor extends SimpleFileVisitor<Path> {
            @Override
            public FileVisitResult postVisitDirectory(Path dir,
                    IOException e) throws IOException {

                FileVisitResult result = CONTINUE;

                // Now, delete the directory at the end
                if (e != null) {
                    System.out.format("Error deleting %s. %s%n", dir, e.getMessage());
                    result = TERMINATE;
                } else {
                    Files.delete(dir);
                    System.out.format("Deleted directory %s%n", dir);
                }
                return result;
            }

            @Override
            public FileVisitResult visitFile(Path file,
                    BasicFileAttributes attrs) throws IOException {

                // Delete the file that we are visiting
                Files.delete(file);

                System.out.format("Deleted file %s%n", file);
                return CONTINUE;
            }
        }

        // Create an object of the DirVisitor
        FileVisitor<Path> visitor = new DeleteDirVisitor();

        return visitor;
    }
}
```

By default, the `Files.walkFileTree()` method does not follow symbolic links. If you want to follow the symbolic links, you need to use another version of the `walkFileTree()` method that lets you specify the `FileVisitOption.FOLLOW_LINKS` as an option. It also lets you specify the maximum depth, which is the maximum number of levels of a directory to visit. Specifying the depth as 0 visits only the starting file. You can specify `Integer.MAX_VALUE` as the depth to visit all levels. The following snippet of code shows how to use the `walkFileTree()` method to follow a symbolic link:

```
import java.util.Set;
import java.util.EnumSet;
import java.nio.file.Path;
import java.nio.file.Files;
import java.io.IOException;
```

```
import java.nio.file.FileVisitor;
import java.nio.file.FileVisitOption;
import static java.nio.file.FileVisitOption.FOLLOW_LINKS;
...
Path startDir = get the path to the starting directory;
FileVisitor<Path> visitor = get a file visitor;

// Prepare the set of options
Set<FileVisitOption> options = EnumSet.of(FOLLOW_LINKS);

// Visit all levels
int depth = Integer.MAX_VALUE;

// Walk the file tree with all levels and following the symbolic links
Files.walkFileTree(startDir, options, depth, visitor);
```

Matching Paths

The NIO.2 API lets you perform pattern matching on the string form of Path objects using the glob and regex patterns. An instance of the PathMatcher interface is used to perform the match. The PathMatcher interface is a functional interface. It contains the matches(Path path) method, which returns true if the specified path matches the pattern. It is a three-step process to match a pattern to a path:

1. Prepare a glob or regex pattern string.
2. Get a PathMatcher object using the getPathMatcher() method of a FileSystem object.
3. Call the matches() method with a Path object to check if the specified path matches the pattern.

The pattern string consists of two parts, syntax and pattern, separated by a colon:

```
syntax:pattern
```

The value for syntax is either glob or regex. The pattern part follows the syntax that depends on the value of the syntax part. I list the syntax rules for the glob pattern briefly. For the regex pattern syntax rules, refer to Chapter 18 in the first volume of this series. The glob pattern uses the following syntax rules:

- An asterisk (*) matches zero or more characters without crossing directory boundaries.
- Two consecutive asterisks (**) match zero or more characters crossing directory boundaries.
- A question mark (?) matches exactly one character.
- A backslash (\) is used to escape the special meaning of the following character. For example, \\ matches a single backslash, and * matches an asterisk.
- Characters placed inside brackets ([]) are called a bracket expression, which matches a single character. For example, [aeiou] matches a, e, i, o, or u. A dash between two characters specifies a range. For example, [a-z] matches all alphabets between a and z. The exclamation mark (!) after the left bracket is treated as negation. For example, [!tyu] matches all characters except t, y, and u.

- You can use a group of subpatterns by specifying comma-separated subpatterns inside braces ({}). For example, {txt, java, doc} matches txt, java, and doc.
- The matching of the root component of a path is implementation-dependent.

Listing 10-13 demonstrates how to use a PathMatcher object to match a path against a glob pattern. The program uses a glob pattern to match a path on Windows. Change the path syntax to conform to your platform before you run the program.

Listing 10-13. Matching a Path Against a Glob/Regex Pattern

```
// PathMatching.java
package com.jdojo.nio2;

import java.nio.file.FileSystems;
import java.nio.file.Path;
import java.nio.file.PathMatcher;
import java.nio.file.Paths;

public class PathMatching {
    public static void main(String[] args) {
        String globPattern = "glob:**txt";
        PathMatcher matcher = FileSystems.getDefault().getPathMatcher(globPattern);
        Path path = Paths.get("C:\\Java9LanguageFeatures\\luci1.txt");
        boolean matched = matcher.matches(path);
        System.out.format("%s matches %s: %b%n", globPattern, path, matched);
    }
}
```

```
glob:**txt matches C:\Java9LanguageFeatures\luci1.txt: true
```

Managing File Attributes

Through the File class, the java.io API provides support for accessing very basic file attributes such as the last modified time of a file. NIO.2 has extensive support for managing (reading and writing) the file attributes across platforms. The java.nio.attribute package contains the attribute-related classes. It bundles the file attributes in the following six types of views.

- BasicFileAttributeView: This attribute view allows you to manage the basic file attributes such as creation time, last access time, last modified time, size, file type (regular file, directory, symbolic link, or other), and file key (a unique number for a file). It lets you modify the creation time, the last accessed time, and the last modified time of a file. This view is supported on all platforms.
- DosFileAttributeView: It extends the BasicFileAttributeView. As the name suggests, it allows you to access the file attributes that are specific to DOS. It provides the support to check if a file is a hidden file, a system file, an archive file, and a read-only file. It is available only on the systems that support DOS, such as Microsoft Windows.

- PosixFileAttributeView: POSIX stands for Portable Operating System Interface for UNIX. It extends the BasicFileAttributeView and adds support for attributes that are available on the systems that support POSIX standards such as UNIX. Apart from basic file attributes, it lets you manage owner, group, and related access permissions.
- FileOwnerAttributeView: This attribute view lets you manage the owner of a file.
- AclFileAttributeView: ACL stands for Access Control List. It is a list of permissions attached to a file. It lets you manage the ACL for a file.
- UserDefinedFileAttributeView: This view lets you manage a set of user-defined attributes for a file in the form of name-value pairs. Sometimes the user-defined attributes of a file are also known as *extended attributes*. The name of an attribute is a String. The value of an attribute could be of any data type.

Some attribute views are available across platforms and some only on specific platforms. An implementation may provide additional file attribute views.

Checking for a File Attribute View Support

Not all file attribute views are supported on all platforms, except the basic view. You can use the supportsFileAttributeView() method of the FileStore class to check whether a specific file attribute view is supported by a file store. The method accepts the class reference of the type of the file attribute view you want to check for support. If the specified file attribute view is supported, it returns true; otherwise, it returns false. The following snippet of code shows how to check for file attribute support:

```
Path path = /* get a path reference to a file store */;

// Get the file store reference for the path
FileStore fs = Files.getFileStore(path);

// Check if POSIX file attribute is supported by the file store
boolean supported = fs.supportsFileAttributeView(PosixFileAttributeView.class);
if (supported) {
    System.out.println("POSIX file attribute view is supported.");
} else {
    System.out.println("POSIX file attribute view is not supported.");
}
```

Listing 10-14 demonstrates how to check if a file store supports a file attribute view. It checks for the file attribute support for the C: drive on Windows. Change the file store path in the main() method to check for the supported file attribute views by your file store. You may get different output when you run the program.

Listing 10-14. Checking for Supported File Attribute Views by a File Store

```
// SupportedFileAttribViews.java
package com.jdojo.nio2;

import java.io.IOException;
import java.nio.file.FileStore;
import java.nio.file.Files;
import java.nio.file.Path;
```

```
import java.nio.file.Paths;
import java.nio.file.attribute.AclFileAttributeView;
import java.nio.file.attribute.BasicFileAttributeView;
import java.nio.file.attribute.DosFileAttributeView;
import java.nio.file.attribute.FileAttributeView;
import java.nio.file.attribute.FileOwnerAttributeView;
import java.nio.file.attribute.PosixFileAttributeView;
import java.nio.file.attribute.UserDefinedFileAttributeView;

public class SupportedFileAttribViews {
    public static void main(String[] args) {
        // Use C: as the file store path on Windows
        Path path = Paths.get("C:");

        try {
            FileStore fs = Files.getFileStore(path);
            printDetails(fs, AclFileAttributeView.class);
            printDetails(fs, BasicFileAttributeView.class);
            printDetails(fs, DosFileAttributeView.class);
            printDetails(fs, FileOwnerAttributeView.class);
            printDetails(fs, PosixFileAttributeView.class);
            printDetails(fs, UserDefinedFileAttributeView.class);
        } catch (IOException ex) {
            ex.printStackTrace();
        }
    }

    public static void printDetails(FileStore fs,
            Class<? extends FileAttributeView> attribClass) {

        // Check if the file attribute view is supported
        boolean supported = fs.supportsFileAttributeView(attribClass);
        System.out.format("%s is supported: %s%n", attribClass.getSimpleName(), supported);
    }
}
```

```
AclFileAttributeView is supported: true
BasicFileAttributeView is supported: true
DosFileAttributeView is supported: true
FileOwnerAttributeView is supported: true
PosixFileAttributeView is supported: false
UserDefinedFileAttributeView is supported: true
```

Reading and Updating File Attributes

The NIO.2 API provides many ways to work with file attributes. Sometimes it may be confusing to decide the method that you want to use to manage the file attributes.

You may need to work with only one attribute or many attributes of a file at a time. If you need to read or update the value of only one attribute of a file, you need to look at the available methods in the Files class that let you read/update that specific attribute. For example, if you want to check if a file is a directory, use the Files.isDirectory() method. If you want to read the owner of a file, use the Files.getOwner() method. If you want to update the owner of a file, use the Files.setOwner() method. The Files class has the following two static methods that let you read and update a file attribute using the attribute name as a string:

- Object getAttribute(Path path, String attribute, LinkOption...options)
- Path setAttribute(Path path, String attribute, Object value, LinkOption...options)

If you need to read or update multiple attributes of a file, you need to work with a specific file attribute view. The types of attributes determine the file attribute view that you need to use. For most of the file attribute views, you have to work with two interfaces named as XxxAttributes and XxxAttributeView. For example, for the basic file attributes, you have the BasicFileAttributes and BasicFileAttributeView interfaces. The XxxAttributes lets you read the attributes. The XxxAttributeView lets you read as well as update the attributes. If you want only to read the attributes, use XxxAttributes. If you want to read and update attributes, use XxxAttributeView as well as XxxAttributes.

The following two methods of the Files class let you read the file attributes in bulk, which is much more efficient than reading one attribute at a time.

- <A extends BasicFileAttributes> A readAttributes(Path path, Class<A> type, LinkOption... options)
- Map<String,Object> readAttributes(Path path, String attributes, LinkOption... options)

The last argument of both methods lets you specify how a symbolic link is handled. By default, if a file is a symbolic link, the attributes of the target of the symbolic link are read. If you specify NOFOLLOW_LINKS as the option, the attributes of the symbolic link are read, not the attributes of its target.

The first readAttributes() method returns all file attributes of a specified type in an XxxAttributes object. For example, you would write the following snippet of code to read the basic file attributes:

```
// Create the Path object representing the path of the file
Path path = Paths.get("C:\\poems\\luci1.txt");

// Read the basic file attributes
BasicFileAttributes bfa = Files.readAttributes(path, BasicFileAttributes.class);

// Get the last modified time
FileTime lastModifiedTime = bfa.lastModifiedTime();

// Get the size of the file
long size = bfa.size();
```

The second readAttributes() method returns all or some of the attributes of a specific type. The list of attributes to read is supplied in a string form using the following syntax:

```
[view-name:]comma-separated-attributes
```

The view-name is the name of the attribute view that you want to read, such as basic, posix, acl, etc. If view-name is omitted, it defaults to basic. If view-name is present, it is followed by a colon. You can read all attributes of a specific view type by specifying an asterisk (*) as the attributes list. For example, you can specify "basic:*" or "*" to read all basic file attributes. To read the size and the last modified time of the basic view, you would use "basic:size,lastModifiedTime" or "size,lastModifiedTime". To read the owner attribute of a file using an ACL view, you would use a string "acl:owner". To read all posix attributes of a file, you would use "posix:*". The following snippet of code prints the size and the last modified time of the C:\poems\luci1.txt file. Note that the file path uses Windows syntax.

```
// Get a Path object
Path path = Paths.get("C:\\poems\\luci1.txt");

// Prepare the attribute list
String attribList = "basic:size,lastModifiedTime";

// Read the attributes
Map<String, Object> attribs = Files.readAttributes(path, attribList);

// Display the attributes on the standard output
System.out.format("Size:%s, Last Modified Time:%s %n",
        attribs.get("size"), attribs.get("lastModifiedTime"));
```

Listing 10-15 reads the basic file attributes of the luci1.txt file in the current directory and prints some of them on the standard output. You need to change the file path in the main() method to work with another file on your platform. You may get different output when you run this program. If the specified file does not exist, a NoSuchFileException is thrown and the program prints the stack trace of the exception.

Listing 10-15. Reading the Basic File Attributes of a File

```
// BasicFileAttributesTest.java
package com.jdojo.nio2;

import java.io.IOException;
import java.nio.file.Files;
import java.nio.file.Path;
import java.nio.file.Paths;
import java.nio.file.attribute.BasicFileAttributes;

public class BasicFileAttributesTest {
    public static void main(String[] args) {
        // Change the file path to an existing file
        Path path = Paths.get("luci1.txt");

        try {
            // Read basic file attributes
            BasicFileAttributes bfa =
                    Files.readAttributes(path, BasicFileAttributes.class);
```

```
            // Print some of the basic file attributes
            System.out.format("Size: %s bytes %n", bfa.size());
            System.out.format("Creation Time: %s %n", bfa.creationTime());
            System.out.format("Last Access Time: %s %n", bfa.lastAccessTime());
        } catch (IOException e) {
            e.printStackTrace();
        }
    }
}
```

```
Size: 119 bytes
Creation Time: 2017-10-10T23:37:25.684588Z
Last Access Time: 2017-10-10T23:37:25.684588Z
```

You can also read file attributes using a specific view object. You can use the `getFileAttributeView()` method of the `Files` class to get a specific attribute view. It returns `null` if the file attribute view type is not available. The method declaration is as follows:

```
<V extends FileAttributeView> V getFileAttributeView(Path path, Class<V> type,
LinkOption... options)
```

Once you get a view object of a specific view type, you can read all attributes of that view type using the view object's `readAttributes()` method. Note that not all views provide `readAttributes()` method. For example, the `FileOwnerAttributeView` provides only the `getOwner()` method to read the owner attribute of a file. If an attribute view is updateable, the view object provides appropriate setter methods to update the attributes. The following snippet of code reads all basic attributes for the `luci1.txt` file using a basic view object:

```
// Get a Path object
Path path = Paths.get("luci1.txt");

// Get the basic view
BasicFileAttributeView bfv = Files.getFileAttributeView(path, BasicFileAttributeView.class);

// Read all basic attributes through the view
BasicFileAttributes bfa = bfv.readAttributes();
```

The basic view lets you update the last modified time, the last accessed time, and the creation time of a file. The `setTimes()` method lets you update all three types of times. If you pass a `null` value for a time, it means you do not want to update that time. The time you need to pass to the `setTimes()` method is of `FileTime` type.

Listing 10-16 demonstrates how to use the basic file attribute view to read and update basic file attributes. Change the file path in the `main()` method to the path of an existing file whose attributes you want to read. The program uses a file path of `luci1.txt`, which means that the `luci1.txt` file is assumed to be in your current directory.

Listing 10-16. Using Basic File Attribute View to Read and Update Basic File Attributes

```
// BasicFileAttributeViewTest.java
package com.jdojo.nio2;

import java.io.IOException;
import java.nio.file.Files;
import java.nio.file.Path;
import java.nio.file.Paths;
import java.nio.file.attribute.BasicFileAttributeView;
import java.nio.file.attribute.BasicFileAttributes;
import java.nio.file.attribute.FileTime;
import java.time.Instant;

public class BasicFileAttributeViewTest {
    public static void main(String[] args) {
        // Change the path to point to your file
        Path path = Paths.get("luci1.txt");

        try {
            // Get the basic view
            BasicFileAttributeView bfv
                    = Files.getFileAttributeView(path, BasicFileAttributeView.class);

            // Read all basic attributes through the view
            BasicFileAttributes bfa = bfv.readAttributes();

            // Print some basic attributes
            System.out.format("Size: %s bytes %n", bfa.size());
            System.out.format("Creation Time: %s %n", bfa.creationTime());
            System.out.format("Last Access Time: %s %n", bfa.lastAccessTime());

            // Update the create time to the current time
            FileTime newLastModifiedTime = null;
            FileTime newLastAccessTime = null;
            FileTime newCreateTime = FileTime.from(Instant.now());

            // A null for time means you do not want to update that time
            bfv.setTimes(newLastModifiedTime, newLastAccessTime, newCreateTime);
        } catch (IOException e) {
            e.printStackTrace();
        }
    }
}
```

Managing the Owner of a File

There are three ways to manage the owner of a file:

- Using Files.getOwner() and Files.setOwner() methods
- Using Files.getAttribute() and Files.setAttribute() methods using "owner" as the attribute name
- Using the FileOwnerAttributeView

You need to work with UserPrincipal and GroupPrincipal interfaces to manage the owner of a file. The owner of a file could be a user or a group. A UserPrincipal represents a user, whereas a GroupPrincipal represents a group. When you read the owner of a file, you get an instance of UserPrincipal. Use the getName() method on the UserPrincipal object to get the name of the user. When you want to set the owner of a file, you need to get an object of the UserPrincipal from a user name in a string form. To get a UserPrincipal from the file system, you need to use an instance of the UserPrincipalLookupService class, which you can get using the getUserPrincipalLookupService() method of the FileSystem class. The following snippet of code gets a UserPrincipal object for a user whose user ID is ksharan:

```
FileSystem fs = FileSystems.getDefault();
UserPrincipalLookupService upls = fs.getUserPrincipalLookupService();

// Throws a UserPrincipalNotFoundException exception if the user ksharan does not exist
UserPrincipal user = upls.lookupPrincipalByName("ksharan");
System.out.format("User principal name is %s%n", user.getName());
```

You can use method chaining in the previous snippet of code to avoid intermediate variables.

```
UserPrincipal user = FileSystems.getDefault()
                                .getUserPrincipalLookupService()
                                .lookupPrincipalByName("ksharan");
System.out.format("User principal name is %s%n", user.getName());
```

The user principal lookup service is an optional operation for a file system. You need to handle the UnsupportedOperationException that is thrown when the file system does not support it.

To get a GroupPrincipal instance, use the lookupPrincipalByGroupName() method of the user principal lookup service. Once you get a UserPrincipal or GroupPrincipal instance that represents the owner of the file, you can use any of the three methods described at the beginning of this section to update the owner of a file.

Listing 10-17 demonstrates how to read and update the owner of a file using the FileOwnerAttributeView. Change the file path in the main() method to an existing file on your machine before you run the program. The program uses brice as the new user for the file. Change the new user ID to a user who exists on your machine. If the user does not exist on your machine, you may get a UserPrincipalNotFoundException exception. You may get different output when you run the program.

Listing 10-17. Changing the Owner of a File Using the FileOwnerAttributeView

```
// FileOwnerManagement.java
package com.jdojo.nio2;

import java.io.IOException;
import java.nio.file.FileSystem;
import java.nio.file.FileSystems;
import java.nio.file.Files;
import java.nio.file.Path;
import java.nio.file.Paths;
import java.nio.file.attribute.FileOwnerAttributeView;
import java.nio.file.attribute.UserPrincipal;
import java.nio.file.attribute.UserPrincipalLookupService;

public class FileOwnerManagement {
    public static void main(String[] args) throws IOException {
        try {
            // Change the file path to an existing file on your machine
            Path path = Paths.get("luci1.txt");

            FileOwnerAttributeView foav
                    = Files.getFileAttributeView(path, FileOwnerAttributeView.class);

            UserPrincipal owner = foav.getOwner();
            System.out.format("Original owner of %s is %s%n", path, owner.getName());

            FileSystem fs = FileSystems.getDefault();
            UserPrincipalLookupService upls = fs.getUserPrincipalLookupService();

            // Change the file owner to brice
            UserPrincipal newOwner = upls.lookupPrincipalByName("brice");
            foav.setOwner(newOwner);

            UserPrincipal changedOwner = foav.getOwner();
            System.out.format("New owner of %s is %s%n", path, changedOwner.getName());
        } catch (UnsupportedOperationException | IOException e) {
            e.printStackTrace();
        }
    }
}
```

```
Original owner of luci1.txt is kishori\ksharan
New owner of luci1.txt is kishori\brice
```

The following snippet of code uses the `Files.setOwner()` method to update the owner of a file identified with the `luci1.txt` path:

```
UserPrincipal owner = /* get the owner */;
Path path = Paths.get("luci1.txt");
Files.setOwner(path, owner);
```

Managing ACL File Permissions

In this section, I cover managing the file permissions using AclFileAttributeView. Note that ACL type file attributes are supported on Microsoft Windows. An ACL consists of an ordered list of access control entries. Each entry consists of a UserPrincipal, the type of access, and the level of the access to an object. In NIO.2, an instance of the AclEntry class represents an entry in an ACL. You can get and set a List of AclEntry for a file using the getAcl() and setAcl() methods of the AclFileAttributeView. The following snippet of code gets the List of ACL entries for a file named luci1.txt in the current directory:

```
Path path = Paths.get("luci1.txt");
AclFileAttributeView view = Files.getFileAttributeView(path, AclFileAttributeView.class);
List<AclEntry> aclEntries = view.getAcl();
```

The AclEntry class has methods to read various properties of an ACL entry. Its principal() method returns the UserPrincipal to identify the user or the group. Its permissions() method returns a Set<AclEntryPermission> to identify the permissions. Its type() method returns an enum constant of the type AclEntryType such as ALARM, ALLOW, AUDIT, and DENY that indicates the type of the access. Its flags() method returns a Set<AclEntryFlag>, which contains the inheritance flags of the ACL entry.

Listing 10-18 demonstrates how to read ACL entries for file luci1.txt. If the file does not exist in the current directory, a NoSuchFileException is thrown. The program handles the exception and prints the stack trace of the exception. If you run the program on a UNIX-like platform, it will print an error message that the ACL view is not supported. Partial output is shown when the program ran on Windows. You may get different output.

Listing 10-18. Reading ACL Entries and Related Permissions

```
// AclReadEntryTest.java
package com.jdojo.nio2;

import java.io.IOException;
import java.nio.file.Files;
import java.nio.file.Path;
import java.nio.file.Paths;
import java.util.List;
import java.util.Set;
import java.nio.file.attribute.AclEntry;
import java.nio.file.attribute.AclEntryPermission;
import java.nio.file.attribute.AclFileAttributeView;

public class AclReadEntryTest {
    public static void main(String[] args) {
        // Change the path to an existing file on Windows
        Path path = Paths.get("luci1.txt");

        AclFileAttributeView aclView =
                Files.getFileAttributeView(path, AclFileAttributeView.class);
        if (aclView == null) {
            System.out.format("ACL view is not supported.%n");
            return;
        }
```

```
        try {
            List<AclEntry> aclEntries = aclView.getAcl();
            for (AclEntry entry : aclEntries) {
                System.out.format("Principal: %s%n", entry.principal());
                System.out.format("Type: %s%n", entry.type());
                System.out.format("Permissions are:%n");

                Set<AclEntryPermission> permissions = entry.permissions();
                for (AclEntryPermission p : permissions) {
                    System.out.format("%s %n", p);
                }

                System.out.format("------------------------%n");
            }
        } catch (IOException e) {
            e.printStackTrace();
        }
    }
}
```

```
Principal: BUILTIN\Administrators (Alias)
Type: ALLOW
Permissions are:
READ_DATA
READ_ACL
DELETE_CHILD
DELETE
...
------------------------
Principal: NT AUTHORITY\SYSTEM (Well-known group)
Type: ALLOW
Permissions are:
READ_DATA
...
------------------------
```

Updating ACL entries for a file is more involved than reading them. You need to create an AclEntry object using the AclEntry.Builder class. The newBuilder() method of the AclEntry class returns an empty AclEntry.Builder object, which acts as a staging area for a new AclEntry object. You need to call various setter methods such as setPrincipal(), setType(), setPermissions(), etc. on the builder object. When you are finished with setting all properties, call the build() method on the builder object to create an AclEntry object. The following snippet of code demonstrates these steps:

```
// Let's build an ACL entry
UserPrincipal user = /* get a user principal here */;
Set<AclEntryPermission> permissions = /* get permissions here */;

AclEntry newEntry = AclEntry.newBuilder()
                            .setPrincipal(user)
                            .setType(AclEntryType.ALLOW)
                            .setPermissions(permissions)
                            .build();
```

Once you prepare a new AclEntry, you need to add it to the existing ACL entries for the file. The following snippet of code adds the new ACL entry to the existing ones and sets them back using an ACL attribute view:

```
// Get the ACL entry for the path
List<AclEntry> aclEntries = aclView.getAcl();

// Add the ACL entry to the existing list
aclEntries.add(newEntry);

// Update the ACL entries for the file
aclView.setAcl(aclEntries);
```

Listing 10-19 demonstrates how to add a new ACL entry for a user named ksharan. It adds DATA_READ and DATA_WRITE permissions for the user ksharan on the luci1.txt file in the current directory. Make sure that the luci1.txt file and a user with the user ID of ksharan exist on the machine or change the file path and the user name in the program.

Listing 10-19. Updating ACL Entries for a File

```
// AclUpdateEntryTest.java
package com.jdojo.nio2;

import java.io.IOException;
import java.nio.file.FileSystems;
import java.nio.file.Files;
import java.nio.file.Path;
import java.nio.file.Paths;
import java.util.List;
import java.util.Set;
import java.nio.file.attribute.AclEntry;
import java.nio.file.attribute.AclEntryPermission;
import java.nio.file.attribute.AclEntryType;
import java.nio.file.attribute.AclFileAttributeView;
import java.nio.file.attribute.UserPrincipal;
import java.util.EnumSet;
import static java.nio.file.attribute.AclEntryPermission.READ_DATA;
import static java.nio.file.attribute.AclEntryPermission.WRITE_DATA;

public class AclUpdateEntryTest {
    public static void main(String[] args) {
        Path path = Paths.get("luci1.txt");

        AclFileAttributeView aclView
                = Files.getFileAttributeView(path, AclFileAttributeView.class);
        if (aclView == null) {
            System.out.format("ACL view is not supported.%n");
            return;
        }
```

```
        try {
            // Get UserPrincipal for ksharan
            UserPrincipal ksharanUser = FileSystems.getDefault()
                    .getUserPrincipalLookupService()
                    .lookupPrincipalByName("ksharan");

            // Prepare permissions set
            Set<AclEntryPermission> permissions = EnumSet.of(READ_DATA, WRITE_DATA);

            // Let us build an ACL entry
            AclEntry newEntry = AclEntry.newBuilder()
                    .setPrincipal(ksharanUser)
                    .setType(AclEntryType.ALLOW)
                    .setPermissions(permissions)
                    .build();

            // Get the ACL entry for the path
            List<AclEntry> aclEntries = aclView.getAcl();

            // Add the ACL entry for ksharan to the existing list
            aclEntries.add(newEntry);

            // Update the ACL entries
            aclView.setAcl(aclEntries);

            System.out.println("ACL entry added for ksharan successfully");
        } catch (IOException e) {
            e.printStackTrace();
        }
    }
}
```

Managing POSIX File Permissions

In this section, I cover managing file permissions using PosixFileAttributeView. Note that UNIX supports POSIX standard file attributes. POSIX file permissions consist of nine components: three for the owner, three for the group, and three for others. The three types of permissions are read, write, and execute. A typical POSIX file permission in a string form looks like "rw-rw----", which has read and write permissions for the owner and the group. The PosixFilePermission enum type defines nine constants, one for each permission component. The nine constants are named as XXX_YYY, where XXX is OWNER, GROUP, and OTHERS, and YYY is READ, WRITE, and EXECUTE.

PosixFilePermissions is a utility class. It contains methods to convert the POSIX permissions of a file from one form to another. Its toString() method converts a Set of PosixFilePermission enum constants into a string of the rwxrwxrwx form. Its fromString() method converts the POSIX file permissions in a string of the rwxrwxrwx form to a Set<PosixFilePermission>. Its asFileAttribute() method converts a Set<PosixFilePermission> into a FileAttribute object, which you can use in the Files.createFile() method as an argument when creating a new file.

Reading POSIX file permissions is easy. You need to use the readAttributes() method of the PosixFileAttributeView class to get an instance of PosixFileAttributes. The permissions() method of PosixFileAttributes returns all POSIX file permissions in a Set<PosixFilePermission>. The following snippet of code reads and prints POSIX file permissions in the rwxrwxrwx form for a file named luci in the default directory:

```
// Get a Path object for luci file
Path path = Paths.get("luci");

// Get the POSIX attribute view for the file
PosixFileAttributeView posixView =
        Files.getFileAttributeView(path, PosixFileAttributeView.class);

// Here, make sure posixView is not null

// Read all POSIX attributes
PosixFileAttributes attribs = posixView.readAttributes();

// Read the file permissions
Set<PosixFilePermission> permissions = attribs.permissions();

// Convert the file permissions into the rwxrwxrwx string form
String rwxFormPermissions = PosixFilePermissions.toString(permissions);

// Print the permissions
System.out.println(rwxFormPermissions);
```

Updating POSIX file permissions is also easy. You need to get all permissions in a Set<PosixFilePermission>. To update the POSIX file permissions, call the setPermissions() method of PosixFileAttributeView, passing the Set<PosixFilePermission> as an argument. The following snippet of code shows how to set the POSIX file permissions:

```
// Get the permission in a string form
String rwxFormPermissions = "rw-r-----";

// Convert the permission in the string form to a Set<PosixFilePermission>
Set<PosixFilePermission> permissions = PosixFilePermissions.fromString(rwxFormPermissions);

// Update the permissions
posixView.setPermissions(permissions);
```

Alternatively, you can also create a Set of PosixFilePermission enum constants directly and set it as the file permissions, like so:

```
Set<PosixFilePermission> permissions = EnumSet.of(OWNER_READ, OWNER_WRITE, GROUP_READ);
posixView.setPermissions(permissions);
```

Listing 10-20 demonstrates how to read and update POSIX file permissions for a file named luci on UNIX-like platforms. If the file does not exist, the program outputs the stack trace of a NoSuchFileException. If you run the program on a non-UNIX-like platform, it will print a message that POSIX attribute view is not supported. You may get different output when you run this program.

Listing 10-20. Reading and Writing POSIX File Permissions

```
// PosixPermissionsTest.java
package com.jdojo.nio2;

import java.io.IOException;
import java.nio.file.Files;
import java.nio.file.Path;
import java.nio.file.Paths;
import java.util.EnumSet;
import java.util.Set;
import java.nio.file.attribute.PosixFileAttributeView;
import java.nio.file.attribute.PosixFileAttributes;
import java.nio.file.attribute.PosixFilePermission;
import java.nio.file.attribute.PosixFilePermissions;
import static java.nio.file.attribute.PosixFilePermission.OWNER_READ;
import static java.nio.file.attribute.PosixFilePermission.OWNER_WRITE;
import static java.nio.file.attribute.PosixFilePermission.GROUP_READ;

public class PosixPermissionsTest {
    public static void main(String[] args) {
        Path path = Paths.get("luci");
        PosixFileAttributeView posixView =
                Files.getFileAttributeView(path, PosixFileAttributeView.class);
        if (posixView == null) {
            System.out.println("POSIX attribute view is not supported.");
            return;
        }

        readPermissions(posixView);
        updatePermissions(posixView);
    }

    public static void readPermissions(PosixFileAttributeView posixView) {
        try {
            PosixFileAttributes attribs;
            attribs = posixView.readAttributes();
            Set<PosixFilePermission> permissions = attribs.permissions();

            // Convert the set of posix file permissions into rwxrwxrwx form
            String rwxFormPermissions = PosixFilePermissions.toString(permissions);
            System.out.println(rwxFormPermissions);
        } catch (IOException ex) {
            ex.printStackTrace();
        }
    }

    public static void updatePermissions(PosixFileAttributeView posixView) {
        try {
            Set<PosixFilePermission> permissions =
                    EnumSet.of(OWNER_READ, OWNER_WRITE, GROUP_READ);
            posixView.setPermissions(permissions);
```

```
            System.out.println("Permissions set successfully.");
        } catch (IOException ex) {
            ex.printStackTrace();
        }
    }
}
```

```
rw-rw-r--
Permissions set successfully.
```

Watching a Directory for Modifications

NIO.2 supports a watch service that notifies the Java program when registered objects in a file system are modified. Currently, you can watch only directories for modifications. The watch service uses the native file event notification facility of the file system. If a file system does not provide a file event notification facility, it may use other mechanisms such as polling. The following classes and interfaces in the `java.nio.file` package are involved in the implementation of a watch service:

- The `Watchable` interface
- The `WatchService` interface
- The `WatchKey` interface
- The `WatchEvent<T>` interface
- The `WatchEvent.Kind<T>` interface
- The `StandardWatchEventKinds` class

A `Watchable` is a file system object that can be watched for changes. A `Watchable` can be registered with a watch service. A `Path` is a `Watchable`. Therefore, you can register a `Path` with a watch service.

A `WatchService` represents a watch service that watches registered objects for changes. When an object is registered with a `WatchService`, the `WatchService` returns a `WatchKey` that serves as a token for the registration. In other words, a `WatchKey` identifies the registration of an object with a `WatchService`.

A `WatchEvent` represents an event (or a repeated event) on an object registered with a watch service. Its `kind()` method returns the kind of event that occurs on the registered object. Its `context()` method returns a `Path` object that represents the entry on which the event occurs. The `Path` object represents a relative path between the registered directory with the watch service and the entry on which the event occurs. An event may be repeated before it is notified. The `count()` method returns the number of times the event occurs for a specific notification. If it returns a value greater than 1, it is a repeated event.

A `WatchEvent.Kind<T>` represents the kind of event that occurs on a registered object. The `StandardWatchEventKinds` class defines constants to represent the kind of an event.

The `StandardWatchEventKinds` class defines the following four constants to identify the kind of an event. Each constant is of the type `WatchEvent.Kind` type.

- `ENTRY_CREATE`
- `ENTRY_DELETE`
- `ENTRY_MODIFY`
- `OVERFLOW`

The names of the first three constants are self-explanatory. They represent events when an entry is created, deleted, and modified in a registered directory. The last event kind is OVERFLOW, which represents a special kind of event to indicate that event may have been lost or discarded.

The following steps are needed to watch a directory for changes:

1. Create a watch service.
2. Register a directory with the watch service.
3. Retrieve a watch key from the watch service queue.
4. Process the events that occur on the registered directory.
5. Reset the watch key after processing the events.
6. Close the watch service.

Creating a Watch Service

You can create a watch service for the file system as follows:

```
WatchService ws = FileSystems.getDefault()
                             .newWatchService();
```

Registering the Directory with the Watch Service

You need to create a Path object representing the directory you want to watch and invoke its register() method to register it with the watch service. At the time of registration, you need to specify the kinds of events for which you want to register your directory. The register() method will return a WatchKey as a registration token.

```
// Get a Path object for C:\kishori directory to watch
Path dirToWatch = Paths.get("C:\\kishori");

// Register the dirToWatch for create, modify, and delete events
WatchKey token = dirToWatch.register(ws, ENTRY_CREATE, ENTRY_MODIFY, ENTRY_DELETE);
```

You can cancel the registration of a directory with the watch service using the cancel() method of the WatchKey. When a directory is registered, its WatchKey is said to be in the *ready* state. You can register multiple directories with a watch service. Note that the directory must exist at the time of registration.

Retrieving a WatchKey from the Watch Service Queue

When an event occurs on a registered directory, the WatchKey for that registered directory is said to be in the *signaled* state and the WatchKey is queued to the watch service. Another event may occur on a registered directory when its WatchKey is in the *signaled* state. If an event occurs on a directory while its WatchKey is in the *signaled* state, the event is queued to the WatchKey, but the WatchKey itself is not re-queued to the watch service. A WatchKey in the *signaled* state remains in this state until its reset() method is called to change its state to the *ready* state.

You can use the `take()` or `poll()` method of the `WatchService` object to retrieve and remove a signaled and queued `WatchKey`. The `take()` method waits until a `WatchKey` is available. The `poll()` method lets you specify a timeout for the wait. Typically, an infinite loop is used to retrieve a signaled `WatchKey`:

```
while(true) {
    // Retrieve and remove the next available WatchKey from the watch service
    WatchKey key = ws.take();

    // More code goes here
}
```

Processing the Events

Once you retrieve and remove a `WatchKey` from the watch service queue, you can retrieve and remove all pending events for that `WatchKey`. A `WatchKey` may have more than one pending event. The `pollEvents()` method of the `WatchKey` retrieves and removes all its pending events. It returns a `List<WatchEvent>`. Each element in the list represents an event on the `WatchKey`. Typically, you will need to use the `kind()`, `context()`, and `count()` methods of the `WatchEvent` object to know the details of the event. The following snippet of code shows the typical logic for processing an event:

```
while(true) {
    // Retrieve and remove the next available WatchKey
    WatchKey key = ws.take();

    // Process all events of the WatchKey
    for(WatchEvent<?> event : key.pollEvents()) {
        // Process each event here
    }
}
```

Resetting the WatchKey after Processing Events

You must reset the `WatchKey` object by calling its `reset()` method, so it may receive event notifications and be queued to the watch service again. The `reset()` method puts the `WatchKey` into the *ready* state. The `reset()` method returns `true` if the `WatchKey` is still valid. Otherwise, it returns `false`. A `WatchKey` may become invalid if it is cancelled or its watch service is closed.

```
// Reset the WatchKey
boolean isKeyValid = key.reset();
if (!isKeyValid) {
    System.out.println("No longer watching " + dirToWatch);
}
```

Closing the Watch Service

When you are done with the watch service, close it by calling its `close()` method. You will need to handle the `java.io.IOException` when you call its `close()` method.

```
// Close the watch service
ws.close();
```

■ **Tip** The `WatchService` is `AutoCloseable`. If you create an object of the `WatchService` in a `try-with-resources` block, it will be automatically closed when the program exits the block.

Listing 10-21 contains a complete program that watches a `C:\kishori` directory for changes. You can replace the directory path in the `Watcher` class with the directory path that you want to watch for changes. You will need to make changes to the watched directory, such as creating a new file and changing an existing file, after you run the `Watcher` class. The output will show the details of the events that occur on an entry in the watched directory. You may get different output.

Listing 10-21. Implementing a Watch Service to Monitor Changes in a Directory

```
// Watcher.java
package com.jdojo.nio2;

import java.nio.file.WatchEvent.Kind;
import java.io.IOException;
import java.nio.file.FileSystems;
import java.nio.file.Path;
import java.nio.file.Paths;
import java.nio.file.WatchService;
import java.nio.file.WatchEvent;
import java.nio.file.WatchKey;
import static java.nio.file.StandardWatchEventKinds.ENTRY_CREATE;
import static java.nio.file.StandardWatchEventKinds.ENTRY_MODIFY;
import static java.nio.file.StandardWatchEventKinds.ENTRY_DELETE;
import static java.nio.file.StandardWatchEventKinds.OVERFLOW;

public class Watcher {
    public static void main(String[] args) {
        try (WatchService ws = FileSystems.getDefault().newWatchService()) {
            // Get a Path object for C:\kishori directory to watch
            Path dirToWatch = Paths.get("C:\\kishori");

            // Register the path with the watch service for create,
            // modify and delete events
            dirToWatch.register(ws, ENTRY_CREATE, ENTRY_MODIFY, ENTRY_DELETE);

            System.out.println("Watching " + dirToWatch + " for events.");

            // Keep watching for events on the dirToWatch
            while (true) {
                // Retrieve and remove the next available WatchKey
                WatchKey key = ws.take();

                for (WatchEvent<?> event : key.pollEvents()) {
                    Kind<?> eventKind = event.kind();
                    if (eventKind == OVERFLOW) {
                        System.out.println("Event overflow occurred");
                        continue;
                    }
```

```
                    // Get the context of the event, which is the directory
                    // entry on which the event occurred.
                    @SuppressWarnings("unchecked")
                    WatchEvent<Path> currEvent = (WatchEvent<Path>) event;
                    Path dirEntry = currEvent.context();

                    // Print the event details
                    System.out.println(eventKind + " occurred on " + dirEntry);
                }

                // Reset the key
                boolean isKeyValid = key.reset();

                if (!isKeyValid) {
                    System.out.println("No longer watching " + dirToWatch);
                    break;
                }
            }
        } catch (IOException | InterruptedException e) {
            e.printStackTrace();
        }
    }
}
```

```
Watching C:\kishori for events.
ENTRY_DELETE occurred on temp
ENTRY_CREATE occurred on hello.txt
ENTRY_MODIFY occurred on hello.txt
```

Asynchronous File I/O

NIO.2 supports asynchronous file I/O. In a synchronous file I/O, the thread that requests the I/O operation waits until the I/O operation is complete. In an asynchronous file I/O, the Java application requests the system for an I/O operation and the operation is performed by the system asynchronously. When the system is performing the file I/O operation, the application continues doing other work. When the system finishes the file I/O, it notifies the application about the completion of its request.

The asynchronous file I/O model is scalable as compared to the synchronous file I/O model. The requests for an asynchronous file I/O and the completion notification to the application are performed by a pool of threads that are specially created for this purpose. The asynchronous file I/O API has options to let you use the default thread pool or a custom thread pool. It offers enhanced scalability by using a predefined dedicated pool of threads to handle all asynchronous file I/O operations, instead of creating a new thread for each I/O operation.

An instance of the `java.nio.channels.AsynchronousFileChannel` class represents an asynchronous file channel that is used to read, write, and perform other operations on a file asynchronously. Multiple I/O operations can be performed simultaneously on an asynchronous file channel. An asynchronous file channel does not maintain a current position where a read or a write operation starts. You need to provide the position for each read and write operation with each request.

The static open() method of the AsynchronousFileChannel class is used to get an instance of the AsynchronousFileChannel class. The method is overloaded. One version uses the default thread pool to handle the I/O operations and the completion notification. Another version lets you specify an ExecutorService to which the asynchronous tasks will be submitted for handling the I/O operations and the completion notifications. The following snippet of code gets an AsynchronousFileChannel on a file for writing. It creates the file if the file does not exist.

```
// Get a Path object
Path path = Paths.get("rainbow.txt");

// Get an asynchronous file channel for WRITE. Create the file, if it does not exist
AsynchronousFileChannel afc = AsynchronousFileChannel.open(path, WRITE, CREATE);
```

The AsynchronousFileChannel provides two ways to handle the result of an asynchronous file I/O operation.

- Using a java.util.concurrent.Future object.
- Using a java.nio.channels.CompletionHandler object.

Each method of the AsynchronousFileChannel class that supports asynchronous file I/O operation has two versions. One version returns a Future object, which you can use to handle the result of the requested asynchronous operation. The get() method of the Future object returns the number of bytes written to the file channel. The following snippet of code uses the version of the write() method that returns a Future object:

```
// Get the data to write in a ByteBuffer
ByteBuffer dataBuffer = /* get a byte buffer filled with data */;

// Perform the asynchronous write operation
long startPosition = 0;
Future<Integer> result = afc.write(dataBuffer, startPosition);
```

Once you get a Future object, you can use a polling method or a blocked waiting method to handle the result of the asynchronous file I/O. The following snippet of code shows the polling method, where it keeps calling the isDone() method of the Future object to check if the I/O operation is finished:

```
while (!result.isDone()) {
    // Async file I/O is not done yet. Keep working on something else
}

// We are done with the async file I/O. Get the result
int writtenNumberOfBytes = result.get();
```

■ **Tip** Note that the call to the Future.get() method blocks until the result is available. The call to the Future.isDone() method is non-blocking.

Another version of the methods of the AsynchronousFileChannel class that supports asynchronous file I/O lets you pass a CompletionHandler object whose methods are called when the requested asynchronous I/O operation completes or fails. The CompletionHandler interface has two methods: completed() and failed(). The completed() method is called when the requested I/O operation completes successfully. When the requested I/O operation fails, the failed() method is called. The API lets you pass an object of any type to the completed() and failed() methods. Such an object is called an *attachment*. You may want to pass an attachment such as the ByteBuffer or the reference to the channel, etc. to these methods so you can perform additional actions, such as reading the data from the ByteBuffer inside these methods. Pass null as an attachment if you do not have anything useful to pass to these methods as an attachment. Suppose you intend to use an object of the following Attachment class as an attachment to your completion handler:

```
// Used as an attachment
public class Attachment {
    public Path path;
    public ByteBuffer buffer;
    public AsynchronousFileChannel asyncChannel;
}
```

Now you can declare your completion handler class as follows:

```
// A class to handle completion of an asynchronous I/O operation
public class MyHandler implements CompletionHandler<Integer, Attachment> {
    @Override
    public void completed(Integer result, Attachment attach) {
        // Handle completion of the I/O operation
    }

    @Override
    public void failed(Throwable e, Attachment attach) {
        // Handle failure of the I/O operation
    }
}
```

You can use an object of the MyHandler class to handle the completion of an asynchronous file I/O operation. The following snippet of code uses a MyHandler instance as a completion handler for an asynchronous write operation. The completed() or failed() method of the MyHandler instance will be called depending on the result of the I/O operation.

```
// Get a completion handler
MyHandler handler = new MyHandler();

// Get the data to write in a ByteBuffer
ByteBuffer dataBuffer = /* get a data buffer */;

// Prepare the attachment
Attachment attach = new Attachment();
attach.asyncChannel = afc;
attach.buffer = dataBuffer;
attach.path = path;

// Perform the asynchronous write operation
afc.write(dataBuffer, 0, attach, handler);
```

■ **Tip** The `ByteBuffer` used to read or write in an asynchronous file operation should not be used by the application between the time it is used in an asynchronous file I/O request and the time the request is completed. Otherwise, it will have an unpredictable result. You can close `AsynchronousFileChannel` using its `close()` method. All pending operations are completed with `java.nio.channels.AsynchronousCloseException` when its `close()` method is called.

Listing 10-22 demonstrates how to use a `CompletionHandler` object to handle the results of an asynchronous write to a file. After submitting the request for the asynchronous write on a file, the main thread sleeps for five seconds to give the asynchronous operation time to finish. In a real-world application, after submitting an asynchronous file I/O request, you would continue performing other tasks. The program writes some text to a `rainbow.txt` file in the default directory. You may get different output.

Listing 10-22. Using a CompletionHandler Object to Handle the Result of an Asynchronous File Write

```
// AsyncFileWrite.java
package com.jdojo.nio2;

import java.nio.ByteBuffer;
import java.io.IOException;
import java.nio.file.Path;
import java.nio.file.Paths;
import java.nio.channels.CompletionHandler;
import java.nio.channels.AsynchronousFileChannel;
import java.nio.charset.Charset;
import static java.nio.file.StandardOpenOption.WRITE;
import static java.nio.file.StandardOpenOption.CREATE;

public class AsyncFileWrite {
    // Used as an attachment to the CompletionHandler
    private static class Attachment {
        public Path path;
        public ByteBuffer buffer;
        public AsynchronousFileChannel asyncChannel;
    }

    // An inner class to handle completion of the asynchronous write operation
    private static class WriteHandler implements CompletionHandler<Integer, Attachment> {
        @Override
        public void completed(Integer result, Attachment attach) {
            System.out.format("%s bytes written to %s%n",
                    result, attach.path.toAbsolutePath());

            try {
                // Close the channel
                attach.asyncChannel.close();
            } catch (IOException e) {
                e.printStackTrace();
            }
        }
```

```
        @Override
        public void failed(Throwable e, Attachment attach) {
            System.out.format("Write operation on %s file failed."
                    + " The error is:  %s%n", attach.path, e.getMessage());
            try {
                // Close the channel
                attach.asyncChannel.close();
            } catch (IOException e1) {
                e1.printStackTrace();
            }
        }
    }

    public static void main(String[] args) {
        Path path = Paths.get("rainbow.txt");

        try {
            // Get an async channel
            AsynchronousFileChannel afc =
                    AsynchronousFileChannel.open(path, WRITE, CREATE);

            // Get a completion handler
            WriteHandler handler = new WriteHandler();

            // Get the data to write in a ByteBuffer
            ByteBuffer dataBuffer = getDataBuffer();

            // Prepare the attachment
            Attachment attach = new Attachment();
            attach.asyncChannel = afc;
            attach.buffer = dataBuffer;
            attach.path = path;

            // Perform the asynchronous write operation
            afc.write(dataBuffer, 0, attach, handler);

            try {
                // Let the thread sleep for 5 seconds,
                // to allow the asynchronous write is complete
                System.out.println("Sleeping for 5 seconds...");
                Thread.sleep(5000);
            } catch (InterruptedException e) {
                e.printStackTrace();
            }

            System.out.println("Done...");
        } catch (IOException e) {
            e.printStackTrace();
        }
    }
```

```
    public static ByteBuffer getDataBuffer() {
        String lineSeparator = System.getProperty("line.separator");

        StringBuilder sb = new StringBuilder();
        sb.append("My heart leaps up when I behold");
        sb.append(lineSeparator);
        sb.append("A Rainbow in the sky");
        sb.append(lineSeparator);
        sb.append(lineSeparator);
        sb.append("So was it when my life began;");
        sb.append(lineSeparator);
        sb.append("So is it now I am a man;");
        sb.append(lineSeparator);
        sb.append("So be it when I shall grow old,");
        sb.append(lineSeparator);
        sb.append("Or let me die!");
        sb.append(lineSeparator);
        sb.append(lineSeparator);
        sb.append("The Child is father of the man;");
        sb.append(lineSeparator);
        sb.append("And I could wish my days to be");

        String str = sb.toString();
        Charset cs = Charset.forName("UTF-8");
        ByteBuffer bb = ByteBuffer.wrap(str.getBytes(cs));

        return bb;
    }
}
```

```
Sleeping for 5 seconds...
228 bytes written to C:\Java9LanguageFeatures\rainbow.txt
Done...
```

Listing 10-23 demonstrates how to use a `Future` to handle the results of an asynchronous write to a file. It uses a `try-with-resources` clause to open an `AsynchronousFileChannel`. It uses a polling method (`Future.isDone()` method calls) to check if the I/O operation has completed. The program writes some text to a file named `rainbow.txt` in the default directory. You may get different output.

Listing 10-23. Using a Future Object to Handle the Result of an Asynchronous File Write

```
// AsyncFileWriteFuture.java
package com.jdojo.nio2;

import java.util.concurrent.ExecutionException;
import java.util.concurrent.Future;
import java.nio.ByteBuffer;
import java.io.IOException;
import java.nio.file.Path;
import java.nio.file.Paths;
```

```
import java.nio.channels.AsynchronousFileChannel;
import static java.nio.file.StandardOpenOption.WRITE;
import static java.nio.file.StandardOpenOption.CREATE;

public class AsyncFileWriteFuture {
    public static void main(String[] args) {
        Path path = Paths.get("rainbow.txt");

        try (AsynchronousFileChannel afc
                = AsynchronousFileChannel.open(path, WRITE, CREATE)) {

            // Get the data to write in a ByteBuffer
            ByteBuffer dataBuffer = AsyncFileWrite.getDataBuffer();

            // Perform the asynchronous write operation
            Future<Integer> result = afc.write(dataBuffer, 0);

            // Keep polling to see if I/O has finished
            while (!result.isDone()) {
                try {
                    // Let the thread sleep for 2 seconds
                    // before the next polling
                    System.out.println("Sleeping for 2 seconds...");
                    Thread.sleep(2000);
                } catch (InterruptedException e) {
                    e.printStackTrace();
                }
            }

            // I/O is complete
            try {
                int writtenBytes = result.get();
                System.out.format("%s bytes written to %s%n",
                        writtenBytes, path.toAbsolutePath());
            } catch (InterruptedException | ExecutionException e) {
                e.printStackTrace();
            }
        } catch (IOException e) {
            e.printStackTrace();
        }
    }
}
```

```
Sleeping for 2 seconds...
228 bytes written to C:\Java9LanguageFeatures\rainbow.txt
```

Listing 10-24 demonstrates how to use a CompletionHandler object to handle the results of an asynchronous read from a file. The program reads and prints the contents of a rainbow.txt file in the default directory. To read the contents of a different file, change the path of the file in the main() method. You may get different output.

Listing 10-24. Using a CompletionHandler to Handle the Result of an Asynchronous File Read

```
// AsyncFileRead.java
package com.jdojo.nio2;

import java.nio.ByteBuffer;
import java.io.IOException;
import java.nio.file.Path;
import java.nio.file.Paths;
import java.nio.channels.CompletionHandler;
import java.nio.channels.AsynchronousFileChannel;
import java.nio.charset.Charset;
import static java.nio.file.StandardOpenOption.READ;

public class AsyncFileRead {
    // Used as an attachment to the CompletionHandler
    private static class Attachment {
        public Path path;
        public ByteBuffer buffer;
        public AsynchronousFileChannel asyncChannel;
    }

    // An inner class to handle completion of the asynchronous read operation
    private static class ReadHandler implements CompletionHandler<Integer, Attachment> {
        @Override
        public void completed(Integer result, Attachment attach) {
            System.out.format("%s bytes read from %s%n", result, attach.path);
            System.out.format("Read data is:%n");

            byte[] byteData = attach.buffer.array();
            Charset cs = Charset.forName("UTF-8");
            String data = new String(byteData, cs);
            System.out.println(data);

            try {
                // Close the channel
                attach.asyncChannel.close();
            } catch (IOException e) {
                e.printStackTrace();
            }
        }

        @Override
        public void failed(Throwable e, Attachment attach) {
            System.out.format("Read operation on %s file failed."
                    + " The error is: %s%n",
                    attach.path, e.getMessage());
```

```
            try {
                // Close the channel
                attach.asyncChannel.close();
            } catch (IOException e1) {
                e1.printStackTrace();
            }
        }
    }

    public static void main(String[] args) {
        Path path = Paths.get("rainbow.txt");
        try {
            // Get an async channel
            AsynchronousFileChannel afc = AsynchronousFileChannel.open(path, READ);

            // Get a completion handler
            ReadHandler handler = new ReadHandler();

            // Get the data size in bytes to read
            int fileSize = (int) afc.size();
            ByteBuffer dataBuffer = ByteBuffer.allocate(fileSize);

            // Prepare the attachment
            Attachment attach = new Attachment();
            attach.asyncChannel = afc;
            attach.buffer = dataBuffer;
            attach.path = path;

            // Perform the asynchronous read operation
            afc.read(dataBuffer, 0, attach, handler);

            try {
                // Let the thread sleep for five seconds,
                // to allow the asynchronous read to complete
                System.out.println("Sleeping for 5 seconds...");
                Thread.sleep(5000);
            } catch (InterruptedException e) {
                e.printStackTrace();
            }

            System.out.println("Done...");
        } catch (IOException e) {
            e.printStackTrace();
        }
    }
}
```

```
Sleeping for 5 seconds...
228 bytes read from rainbow.txt
Read data is:
My heart leaps up when I behold
A Rainbow in the sky

So was it when my life began;
So is it now I am a man;
So be it when I shall grow old,
Or let me die!

The Child is father of the man;
And I could wish my days to be
Done...
```

Listing 10-25 demonstrates how to use a Future object to handle the results of an asynchronous read from a file. It uses the wait method (a Future.get() method call) to wait for the asynchronous file I/O to complete. The program reads the contents of a rainbow.txt file in the default directory. Change the path of this file if you want to read the contents of a different file. You may get different output.

Listing 10-25. Using a Future Object to Handle the Result of an Asynchronous File Read

```
// AsyncFileReadFuture.java
package com.jdojo.nio2;

import java.util.concurrent.ExecutionException;
import java.util.concurrent.Future;
import java.nio.ByteBuffer;
import java.io.IOException;
import java.nio.file.Path;
import java.nio.file.Paths;
import java.nio.channels.AsynchronousFileChannel;
import java.nio.charset.Charset;
import static java.nio.file.StandardOpenOption.READ;

public class AsyncFileReadFuture {
    public static void main(String[] args) {
        Path path = Paths.get("rainbow.txt");

        try (AsynchronousFileChannel afc = AsynchronousFileChannel.open(path, READ)) {

            // Get a data buffer of the file size to read
            int fileSize = (int) afc.size();
            ByteBuffer dataBuffer = ByteBuffer.allocate(fileSize);

            // Perform the asynchronous read operation
            Future<Integer> result = afc.read(dataBuffer, 0);

            System.out.println("Waiting for reading to be finished...");
            try {
                // Let us wait until reading is finished
                int readBytes = result.get();
```

```
                System.out.format("%s bytes read from %s%n", readBytes, path);
                System.out.format("Read data is:%n");

                // Read the data from the buffer
                byte[] byteData = dataBuffer.array();
                Charset cs = Charset.forName("UTF-8");
                String data = new String(byteData, cs);

                System.out.println(data);
            } catch (InterruptedException | ExecutionException e) {
                e.printStackTrace();
            }
        } catch (IOException ex) {
            ex.printStackTrace();
        }
    }
}
```

```
Waiting for reading to be finished...
228 bytes read from rainbow.txt
Read data is:
My heart leaps up when I behold
A Rainbow in the sky

So was it when my life began;
So is it now I am a man;
So be it when I shall grow old,
Or let me die!

The Child is father of the man;
And I could wish my days to be
```

Summary

The New Input/Output 2 (NIO.2) is a new I/O API that provides improved, comprehensive support for working with platform-dependent file systems. An instance of the `FileSystem` class represents a platform-dependent file system.

An instance of the `Path` class represents an abstract pathname in the file system. It contains several methods to manipulate a path. A `Path` is used with a utility class named `Files` to work with the contents and attributes of the file that it represents. The `Files` class consists of all static convenience methods to work with files, such as for deleting, copying, and moving files.

NIO.2 has extensive support for reading and modifying file attributes. Attribute support is provided through different attribute views. Some views are supported on all platforms and some are platform specific. Some views are optional.

NIO.2 provides a watch service to watch for changes to a directory's contents. The Java program registers a directory with the watch service to get notified for specific events that occur in the directory, such as the creation of a new file/directory, change in the contents of a file, deletion of a file, etc. The watch service notifies the Java program when the event of interest occurs on the registered directories.

NIO.2 provides comprehensive support for asynchronous file I/O. An instance of the `java.nio.channels.AsynchronousFileChannel` class represents an asynchronous file channel that is used to read, write, and perform other operations on a file asynchronously. Multiple I/O operations can be performed simultaneously on an asynchronous file channel.

QUESTIONS AND EXERCISES

1. What are file systems and file stores?
2. How do you obtain an instance of the `FileSystem` class that represents the default file system on the current platform?
3. What is a path, an absolute path, and a relative path in a file system?
4. Instances of both the `File` class and the `Path` interface represent pathnames. Differentiate between the two. How do you get a `File` from a `Path` and vice versa?
5. What is purpose of the `Paths` class? Write a snippet of code to get a `Path` instance using the `Paths` class to represent a file named `test.txt` in the current working directory.
6. Write a snippet of code to print the path string of the current working directory.
7. What is the use of the `startsWith()` and `endsWith()` methods in the `Path` interface?
8. Suppose you have two instances of the `Path` interface named `p1` and `p2`. What is the difference in calling `p1.equals(p2)` and `Files.isSameFile(p1, p2)`?
9. What is a symbolic link? How do you check if a `Path` represents a symbolic link?
10. What methods of the `Files` class are used to create regular files and temporary files?
11. What is the difference between using the `delete()` and `deleteIfExists()` methods of the `Files` class to delete a file?
12. Using the NIO.2 API, how do you check if a file exists?
13. What methods in the `Files` class are used to copy and move a file?
14. Write a program that prints the creation time of a file named `test` in the current directory, changes the creation time of the file to five hours before the original time, and prints the new creation time.
15. How do you know the MIME type of a file?
16. How do you know if a `Path` represents a directory, a regular file, or a symbolic link?
17. What file attribute view is guaranteed to be available on all platforms?
18. What types of file system objects can you watch using the watch service in the NIO.2 API?
19. Briefly explain the uses of the following classes and interfaces: `Watchable`, `WatchService`, `WatchKey`, `WatchEvent<T>`, `WatchEvent.Kind<T>`, and `StandardWatchEventKinds`.
20. What is the purpose of the `AsynchronousFileChannel` class?

CHAPTER 11

Garbage Collection

In this chapter, you will learn:

- What garbage collection is
- How garbage collection is implemented in Java
- How to pass a hint to the JVM to run the garbage collector
- How to implement the finalizers
- Different states of an object based on its reachability and finalization status
- The difference between strong and weak references
- How to use weak references to implement memory-sensitive cache
- How to use `PhantomReference` and `ReferenceQueue` classes to implement cleanup tasks for objects
- How to use the new `Cleaner` class in JDK9 to perform cleanup work for phantom reachable objects

All example programs in this chapter are members of the `jdojo.gc` module, as declared in Listing 11-1.

Listing 11-1. The Declaration of a jdojo.gc Module

```
// module-info.java
module jdojo.gc {
    exports com.jdojo.gc;
}
```

What Is Garbage Collection?

In a programming language, memory management is central to the development of a fast, efficient, and bug-free application. Memory management involves two activities:

- Memory allocation
- Memory reclamation

K. Sharan, *Java Language Features*, https://doi.org/10.1007/978-1-4842-3348-1_11

When a program needs memory, memory is allocated from a memory pool. When the program is finished with the memory, the memory is returned to the memory pool, so it can be reused by some other part of the program in the future. The process of returning memory to the pool is known as *memory reclamation* or *memory recycling*. The memory allocation and reclamation can be accomplished explicitly or implicitly.

In explicit memory allocation, the programmer decides how much memory is needed. The programmer requests that amount of memory from the program runtime environment, known as the *memory allocator* or simply the *allocator*. The allocator allocates the requested memory and marks that memory as in-use, so it will not allocate the same memory block again. Here, we assumed that our request for new memory block to allocator is always fulfilled. This can happen only if we have an infinite amount of memory. However, that is not the case with any computer. Some computers may have megabytes of memory and some may have gigabytes. However, there is always a limit to the memory available on a computer. If we run a program that always allocates memory blocks from the memory pool and never returns the memory back to the pool, we will soon run out of memory and the program will stop.

In explicit memory reclamation, the programmer decides when to return the memory to the memory pool. The allocator is free to allocate the returned memory when it receives a new request for memory allocation. Explicit memory reclamation often leads to subtle bugs in programs. It also complicates the inter-modules interface design. Suppose there are two modules in an application and they are named `m1` and `m2`. Module `m1` allocates a block of memory and the reference to that memory is `r1`. Module `m1` makes a call to module `m2`, passing the reference `r1`. Module `m2` stores the reference `r1` for future use. Which module should be responsible for the reclamation of the memory referenced by `r1`? There could be different scenarios depending on the program flow between the two modules. Suppose module `m1` reclaims the memory immediately after a call to module `m2`. In such a case, you may come across two problems:

- At some point in the program execution, module `m2` tries to access the memory using the reference `r1`. Because module `m1` has already reclaimed the memory referenced by `r1`, the same memory might have been reallocated by the allocator and may have entirely different data stored at that memory location. In such a case, `r1` is called a *dangling reference* because it is referencing a memory location that has already been reclaimed. If you try to read data using a dangling reference, the result would be unpredictable. You cannot have a dangling reference in Java.
- Module `m1` may try to use reference `r1` after it has reclaimed the memory referenced by `r1`. This will also lead to the problem of using a dangling reference.

If module `m2` reclaims the memory referenced by `r1`, you may end up with the same dangling reference problem if any of the modules, `m1` or `m2`, try to use reference `r1`. What happens if none of the modules reclaims the memory and never uses the reference `r1` again? The memory will never be returned to the memory pool and will never be reused. This situation is known as a *memory leak* because the allocator has no knowledge of the memory block, which is not returned to it, even though it is never used again by the program. If memory leaks happen regularly, the program will eventually run out of memory and will cease to function. If your program runs for a short time with small memory leaks, you may not even notice this bug for years or for the entire life of your program!

In a programming language that allows explicit memory management, programmers spend a substantial amount of effort in the memory management aspect of the program. In another kind of memory-related problem, a programmer may allocate a big amount of memory statically, so that he can use it throughout the lifecycle of the program. The static memory allocation may not always succeed, since static memory has an upper limit. The hardest part of the memory management decision is to decide when to reclaim the memory to avoid dangling references and memory leaks.

In implicit memory allocation, a programmer indicates to the runtime system that he wants to allocate memory to store a particular type of data. The runtime system computes the memory needed to store the requested type of data and allocates it to the running program. In implicit/automatic memory reclamation, a programmer does not need to worry about memory reclamation. The runtime system will automatically reclaim all memory blocks, which will never be used by the program again. The process of automatic reclamation of unused memory is known as *garbage collection*. The program that performs garbage collection is known as a *garbage collector* or simply a *collector*. The garbage collector may be implemented as part of the language runtime system or as an add-on library.

Memory Allocation in Java

In Java, programmers deal with objects. The memory required for an object is always allocated on the heap. The memory is allocated implicitly using the `new` operator. Suppose you have a class called `Employee`. You create an object of the `Employee` class.

```
Employee emp = new Employee();
```

Depending on the definition of the `Employee` class, the Java runtime computes how much memory is needed, allocates the needed memory on heap, and stores the reference to that memory block in the `emp` reference variable. Note that when you want to create an `Employee` object, you do not specify how much memory you need. The `new Employee()` part of the previous statement indicates to Java that you want to create an object of the `Employee` class. Java queries the definition of the `Employee` class to compute the memory required to represent an `Employee` object.

Every Java object in memory has two areas: a *header area* and a *data area*. The header area stores bookkeeping information to be used by the Java runtime, for example, the pointer to the object's class, object's garbage collection status, object's locking information, length of an array if the object is an array, etc. The data area is used to store the values of all instance variables of the object. The header area layout is fixed for a particular JVM implementation, whereas the data area layout is dependent on the object type. The Java Hotspot virtual machine uses two machine-words (in 32-bit architecture one word is 4 bytes) for the object header. If the object is an array, it uses three machine-words for its header. One extra word in the header is used to store the value of the array's length. However, most JVMs use three machine-words for an object's header. Figure 11-1 depicts the object layout for the Java Hotspot VM.

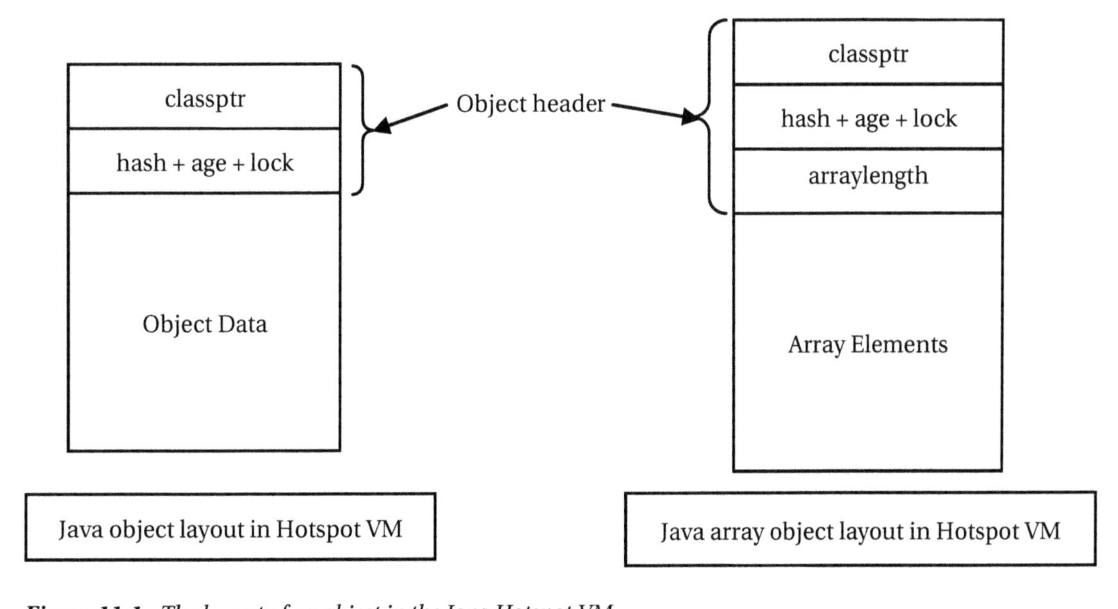

Figure 11-1. *The layout of an object in the Java Hotspot VM*

The Java Hotspot VM uses a variable length object header to save memory on the heap. Since most Java objects are small, one machine-word savings per object for non-array objects is a significant heap space savings. The Java Hotspot VM's object header contains the following information:

- `classptr`: This is the first machine-word in the object layout. It contains a pointer to the class information of the object. The class information includes the object's method table, the object's size, and a pointer to a `Class` structure, which contains information about the class of the object, etc.
- `hash + age + lock`: This is the second machine-word in the object header. It contains the object's hash code, age information, and lock fields. Age information is used in the process of reclaiming the object's memory by the generational garbage collector. The generation garbage collector is a special type of garbage collector that uses the object's age in its algorithm to reclaim an object's memory.
- `arraylength`: This is the third machine-word in the object header. It is included only if the object is an array. It contains the length of the array. In this case, the object's data area contains the array elements.

■ **Note** In Java, all objects are created on heap. Java uses the `new` operator to allocate memory for an object on heap. An array's length is not part of its class definition. It is defined at runtime. It is stored in the object header. You will not find the `length` instance variable in the array's class definition when you perform introspection on an array's object.

Java does not provide any direct means to compute the size of an object. You should not write a Java program that depends on the size of the objects anyway. The size of primitive types—for example, `int`, `long`, `double`, etc.—is fixed for all JVM implementations. The layout and size of an object depend on the JVM implementation. Therefore, any code that depends on the size of objects may work on one platform and not on others.

Garbage Collection in Java

The garbage collector is part of the Java platform. It runs in the background in a low priority thread. It automatically reclaims objects. However, before it reclaims objects, it makes sure that the running program in its current state will never use them again. This way, it ensures that the program will not have any dangling references. An object that cannot be used in the future by the running program is known as a *dead object* or *garbage*. An object that can be used in the future by the running program is known as a *live object*.

There are many algorithms to determine whether an object is live or dead. One of the simplest, but not very efficient, algorithms is based on reference counting, which stores the count of references that refer to an object. When an object's reference is assigned to a reference variable, the reference count is incremented by 1. When a reference variable no longer refers to an object, the reference count is decremented by 1. When the reference count for an object is zero, it becomes garbage (or dead). This algorithm has a lot of overhead of updating the reference count of objects. Another type of algorithm, which is called a *tracing algorithm*, is based on the concept of a root set. A root set includes the following:

- Reference variables in the Java stack for each thread
- static reference variables defined in loaded classes
- Reference variables registered using the Java Native Interface (JNI)

A garbage collector, which is based on the tracing algorithm, starts traversing references starting from the root set. Objects that can be reached (or accessed) from the reference variables in the root set are known as *reachable objects*. A reachable object is considered live. A reachable object from the root set may refer to other objects. These objects are also considered reachable. Therefore, all objects that can be reached directly or indirectly from the root set reference variables are considered live. Other objects are considered dead and are thus eligible for garbage collection.

An object may manage resources other than memory on heap. These resources may include network connections, file handles, memory managed explicitly by native code, etc. For example, an object may open a file when the object is created. File handles that can be opened simultaneously may have an upper limit depending on your operating system. When the object is garbage collected, you may want to close those file handles. The garbage collector gives the dying object a chance to perform the cleanup work. It does this by executing a predefined block of code before the memory for the dying object is reclaimed. The process of performing the cleanup work, before the object is reclaimed by the garbage collector, is known as *finalization*. The block of code that is invoked by the garbage collector to perform finalization is known as the *finalizer*. In Java, you can define an instance method called `finalize()` in a class, which serves as a finalizer for the objects of that class. The Java garbage collector invokes the `finalize()` method of an object before it reclaims the memory occupied by the object.

Invoking the Garbage Collector

Programmers have little control over the timing when the garbage collection is run. The JVM performs the garbage collection whenever it runs low on memory. The JVM tries its best to free up memory of all unreachable objects before it throws a `java.lang.OutOfMemoryError` error. The `gc()` method of the `java.lang.Runtime` class may be used to pass a hint to the JVM that it may run the garbage collection. The call to the `gc()` method is just a hint to the JVM. The JVM is free to ignore the call. Suggesting that the garbage collection should run can be invoked as shown:

```
// Get runtime instance and invoke the garbage collection
Runtime.getRuntime().gc();
```

The `System` class contains a convenience method called `gc()`, which is equivalent to executing the previous statement. You can also use the following statement to run the garbage collector:

```
// Invoke the garbage collection
System.gc();
```

The program in Listing 11-2 demonstrates the use of the `System.gc()` method. The program creates 2,000 objects of the `Object` class in the `createObjects()` method. The references of the new objects are not stored. You cannot refer to these objects again, and hence, they are garbage. When you invoke the `System.gc()` method, you suggest the JVM that it should try to reclaim the memory used by these objects. The memory freed by the garbage collector is displayed in the output section. Note that you will more than likely get a different output when you run this program. The `freeMemory()` method of the `Runtime` class returns the amount of free memory in the JVM.

Listing 11-2. Invoking Garbage Collection

```
// InvokeGC.java
package com.jdojo.gc;

public class InvokeGC {
    public static void main(String[] args) {
        long m1, m2, m3;
```

```
        // Get a runtime instance
        Runtime rt = Runtime.getRuntime();

        for (int i = 0; i < 3; i++) {
            // Get free memory
            m1 = rt.freeMemory();

            // Create some objects
            createObjects(2000);

            // Get free memory
            m2 = rt.freeMemory();

            // Invoke garbage collection
            System.gc();

            // Get free memory
            m3 = rt.freeMemory();

            System.out.println("m1 = " + m1 + ", m2 = " + m2 + ", m3 = "
                    + m3 + "\nMemory freed by gc() = " + (m3 - m2));

            System.out.println("-------------------------");
        }
    }

    public static void createObjects(int count) {
        for (int i = 0; i < count; i++) {
            // Do not store the references of new objects, so they become
            // eligible for garbage collection immediately.
            new Object();
        }
    }
}
```

```
m1 = 130188712, m2 = 130188712, m3 = 7402320
Memory freed by gc() = -122786392
-------------------------
m1 = 6225808, m2 = 6225808, m3 = 7241760
Memory freed by gc() = 1015952
-------------------------
m1 = 7207408, m2 = 7207408, m3 = 7241832
Memory freed by gc() = 34424
-------------------------
```

In general, it is not advisable to invoke the garbage collector programmatically. Invoking the garbage collector has some overhead. It may slow down performance if it is invoked arbitrarily. The Java runtime takes care of reclaiming unused object's memory automatically. You may get an `OutOfMemoryError` in your program. This error may be caused by many reasons. The Java runtime makes all efforts to free up memory, invoking the garbage collector before throwing the OutOfMemoryError error. Therefore, simply invoking the garbage collector programmatically will not make this error go away. To resolve this error, you can look at the following:

- Review your program to make sure that you are not holding onto some object references that you will never use again. Set these references to null after you are done with them. Setting all references to an object to null makes the object eligible for the garbage collection. If you are storing large objects in static variables, those objects will remain in memory until the class itself is unloaded. Generally, the objects stored in static variables will take up memory forever. Review your program and try to avoid storing large objects in static variables.
- Review your code and make sure that you are not caching large amounts of data in objects. You can use weak references to cache large amounts of data in objects. Weak references have an advantage over regular references (regular references are also known as strong references), in that the objects referenced by weak references are garbage collected before the Java runtime throws an OutOfMemoryError. I discuss weak references later in this chapter.
- If none of these solutions works for you, you may try to adjust the heap size.

Object Finalization

Finalization is an action that is automatically performed on an object before the memory used by the object is reclaimed by the garbage collector. The block of code that contains the action to be performed is known as a *finalizer*. The Object class has a finalize() method, which is declared as

```
protected void finalize() throws Throwable
```

Because all Java classes inherit from the Object class, the finalize() method can be invoked on all Java objects. Any class can override and implement its own version of the finalize() method. The finalize() method serves as a finalizer for Java objects. That is, the garbage collector automatically invokes the finalize() method on an object before reclaiming the object's memory. Understanding the correct use of the finalize() method is key to writing a good Java program, which manages resources other than the heap memory.

■ **Note** The finalize() method in the Object class has been deprecated since JDK9. Use other ways clean up resources held by an object. I discuss them in this chapter. I also discuss how to use the finalize() method, even though it is deprecated, for the sake of completeness.

Let's first start with a simple example that demonstrates the fact that the finalize() method is called before an object is garbage collected. Listing 11-3 defines a finalize() method in the Finalizer class. I used the @SuppressWarnings("deprecation") annotation on the finalize() method to suppress the compile-time deprecation warning because the method has been deprecated in JDK9.

Listing 11-3. Using the finalize() Method

```
// Finalizer.java
package com.jdojo.gc;

public class Finalizer {
    // id is used to identify the object
    private final int id;

    // Constructor which takes the id as argument
    public Finalizer(int id){
        this.id = id;
    }

    // This is the finalizer for the object. The JVM will call this method,
    // before the object is garbage collected
    @SuppressWarnings("deprecation")
    @Override
    public void finalize(){
        // Just print a message indicating which object is being garbage collected.
        // Print message when id is a multiple of 100 just to avoid a bigger output.
        if (id % 100 == 0) {
            System.out.println ("finalize() called for " + id ) ;
        }
    }

    public static void main(String[] args) {
        // Create 500000 objects of the Finalizer class
        for(int i = 1; i <= 500000; i++){
            // Do not store reference to the new object
            new Finalizer(i);
        }

        // Invoke the garbage collector
        System.gc();
    }
}
```

```
finalize() called for 63700
finalize() called for 186000
finalize() called for 185000
finalize() called for 184400
...
```

The `finalize()` method prints a message if the object being garbage collected has an ID that's a multiple of 100. The `main()` method creates 500,000 objects of the `Finalizer` class and calls `System.gc()` to invoke the garbage collector.

When the garbage collector determines that an object is unreachable, it marks that object for finalization and places that object in a queue. If you want the Java runtime to finalize all objects that are pending finalization, you can do so by calling the `runFinalization()` method of the `Runtime` class as shown:

```
Runtime rt = Runtime.getRuntime();
rt.runFinalization();
```

The `System` class has a `runFinalization()` convenience method, which is equivalent to calling the `runFinalization()` method of the `Runtime` class. It can be called as shown:

```
System.runFinalization();
```

Invoking the `runFinalization()` method is only a hint to the Java runtime to invoke the `finalize()` method of all objects pending finalization. Technically, you may call the `finalize()` method on an object in your code as many times as you want. However, it is meant for the garbage collector to call an object's `finalize()` method at most one time during the lifetime of the object. The garbage collector's one-time call to the `finalize()` method of an object is not affected by the fact that the `finalize()` method of the object was called programmatically before.

Programmers should not override the `finalize()` method in a class trivially. A `finalize()` method with no code, or one which calls the `finalize()` method of the `Object` class, is an example of a trivially overridden `finalize()` method. The method in the `Object` class does nothing. If your class is a direct subclass of the `Object` class and you do not have any meaningful code in the `finalize()` method of your class, it is better not to include the `finalize()` method in your class at all. Memory reclamation is faster and sooner for the objects, which do not have an implementation of the `finalize()` method compared to those that have an implementation of the `finalize()` method.

Finally or Finalize?

The timing of object finalization is not guaranteed. Finalization of all unreachable objects is also not guaranteed. In short, there is no guarantee when the `finalize()` method of an unreachable object will be called or if it will be called at all. So, what good is the `finalize()` method? The main purpose of a garbage collector in Java is to relieve programmers from the burden of freeing the memory of unused objects to avoid the problem of memory leaks and dangling references. Its secondary job is to run the finalization on the objects with no guarantee about the timing. As a programmer, you should not depend much on the finalization process of garbage collection. You should not code the `finalize()` method or code it with care. If you need to clean up resources for sure when you are done with them, you may use a `try-finally` block. If your resources are `AutoCloseable`, you may use a `try-with-resources` block. A `try-finally` block works as follows:

```
try {
    /* Get your resources and work with them */
} finally {
    /* Release your resources */
}
```

You can acquire resources and use them in a `try` block and release them in the associated `finally` block. A `finally` block is guaranteed to be executed after a `try` block is executed. This way, you can be sure that scarce resources in your program are always freed once you are done with them. However, it may not always be feasible, because of performance issues, to release resources immediately after you are done with them. For example, you may not want to open a network connection every time you need it. You may open a network connection once, use it, and close it when you no longer need it. Sometimes you may not know the exact point in a program from where you will not need that network connection. In such cases, you can code the `finalize()` method as a backup to free the resources if they have not been freed yet. You can call the `finalize()` method programmatically when you know for sure that the resources can be freed. Listing 11-4 contains the code for a `FinalizeAsBackup` class that shows the skeleton of the code that uses such a technique.

Listing 11-4. Template of a Class that Uses the finalize() Method as a Backup to Free Resources

```
// FinalizeAsBackup.java
package com.jdojo.gc;

public class FinalizeAsBackup {
    /* Other codes go here */
    SomeResource sr;
    public void aMethod() {
        sr = Obtain the resources here...;

        /* Do some processing . . . */

        /* Note the conditional freeing of resources */
        if (some condition is true) {
            /* Free resources here calling finalize() */
            this.finalize();
        }
    }

    public void finalize() {
        /* Free the resources if they have not been freed yet */
        if (resources not yet freed ) {
            free resources now;
        }
    }
}
```

The `aMethod()` method of the class gets the resource and stores its reference in the `sr` instance variable. Programmers call the `finalize()` method when they are sure they should free the resources. Otherwise, the garbage collector will call the `finalize()` method and resources will be freed. Note that the `FinalizeAsBackup` class is a template. It contains pseudocode to explain the technique. This class will not compile.

■ **Tip** The moral of the story about using the `finalize()` method is to not use it or use it with care and use it only as a last resort to free resources. You can use a `try-finally` block to free resources. The order in which objects are finalized is not defined. For example, if object `obj1` becomes eligible for garbage collection before object `obj2`, it is not guaranteed that `obj1` will be finalized before `obj2`. When an uncaught exception is thrown, the main program is halted. However, an uncaught exception in a finalizer halts the finalization of only that object, not the entire application.

Object Resurrection

Someone is about to die. God asks him for his last wish. He says, "Give me my life back." God grants his last wish and he gets back his life. When he was about to die the second time God kept quiet and let him die without asking him for his last wish. Otherwise, he would ask for his life repeatedly and he would never die.

The same logic applies to an object's finalization in Java. The call to the finalize() method of an object is like the garbage collector asking the object for its last wish. Generally, the object responds, "I want to clean up all my mess." That is, an object responds to its finalize() method call by performing some cleanup work. It may respond to its finalize() method call by resurrecting itself by placing its reference in a reachable reference variable. Once it is reachable through an already reachable reference variable, it is back to life. The garbage collector marks an object using the object's header bits as finalized, after it calls the object's finalize() method. If an already finalized object becomes unreachable the next time during garbage collection, the garbage collector does not call the object's finalize() method again.

The resurrection of an object is possible because the garbage collector does not reclaim an object's memory just after calling its finalize() method. After calling the finalize() method, it just marks the object as finalized. In the next phase of the garbage collection, it determines again if the object is reachable. If the object is unreachable and finalized, only then will it reclaim the object's memory. If an object is reachable and finalized, it does not reclaim object's memory; this is a typical case of resurrection.

Resurrecting an object in its finalize() method is not a good programming practice. One simple reason is that if you have coded the finalize() method, you expect it to be executed every time an object dies. If you resurrect the object in its finalize() method, the garbage collector will not call its finalize() method again when it becomes unreachable a second time. After resurrection, you might have obtained some resources that you expect to be released in the finalize() method. This will leave subtle bugs in your program. It is also hard for other programmers to understand your program flow if your program resurrects objects in their finalize() methods. Listing 11-5 demonstrates how an object can be resurrected using its finalize() method.

Listing 11-5. Object Resurrection

```
// Resurrect.java
package com.jdojo.gc;

public class Resurrect {
    // Declare a static variable of the Resurrect type
    private static Resurrect res = null;

    // Declare an instance variable that stores the name of the object
    private String name = "";

    public Resurrect(String name) {
        this.name = name;
    }

    public static void main(String[] args) {
        // We will create objects of the Resurrect class and will not store
        // their references, so they are eligible for garbage collection immediately.
        for (int count = 1; count <= 1000; count++) {
            new Resurrect("Object #" + count);
```

```
            // For every 100 objects created invoke garbage collection
            if (count % 100 == 0) {
                System.gc();
                System.runFinalization();
            }
        }
    }

    public void sayHello() {
        System.out.println("Hello from " + name);
    }

    public static void resurrectIt(Resurrect r) {
        // Set the reference r to static variable res, which makes it reachable
        // as long as res is reachable.
        res = r;

        // Call a method to show that we really got the object back
        res.sayHello();
    }

    @SuppressWarnings("deprecation")
    @Override
    public void finalize() {
        System.out.println("Inside finalize(): " + name);

        // Resurrect this object
        Resurrect.resurrectIt(this);
    }
}
```

```
Inside finalize(): Object #82
Hello from Object #82
Inside finalize(): Object #100
Hello from Object #100
Inside finalize(): Object #99
Hello from Object #99
...
```

The `Resurrect` class creates 1,000 objects in the `main()` method. It does not store references of those new objects, so they become garbage as soon as they are created. After creating 100 new objects, it invokes the garbage collector using the `System.gc()` method. It also calls the `System.runFinalization()` method, so the finalizers are run for the garbage objects. When the garbage collector calls the `finalize()` method for an object, that object passes its reference to the `resurrectIt()` method. This method stores the dying object's reference in the static variable `res`, which is reachable. The method `resurrectIt()` also calls the `sayHello()` method on the resurrected object to show which object was resurrected. Note that once another object resurrects itself, you are overwriting the static `res` variable with the recently resurrected object reference. The previously resurrected object becomes garbage again. The garbage collector will reclaim the memory for the previously resurrected object without calling its `finalize()` method again. You may get different output when you run the program.

State of an Object

The state of a Java object is defined based on two criteria:

- Finalization status
- Reachability

Based on the finalization status, an object can be in one of the following three states:

- Unfinalized
- Finalizable
- Finalized

When an object is instantiated, it is in the unfinalized state. For example,

```
Employee john = new Employee();
```

The object referred to by the `john` reference variable is in an unfinalized state after this statement is executed. The finalizer of an unfinalized object had never been invoked automatically by the JVM. An object becomes finalizable when the garbage collector determines that the `finalize()` method can be invoked on the object. A finalized object has its `finalize()` method invoked automatically by the garbage collector.

Based on reachability, an object can be in one of three states:

- Reachable
- Finalizer-reachable
- Unreachable

An object is reachable if it can be accessed through any chain of references from the root set. A finalizer-reachable object can be reached through the finalizer of any finalizable object. A finalizer-reachable object may become reachable if the finalizer from which it is reachable stores its reference in an object that is reachable. This is the situation when an object resurrects. An object may resurrect itself in its `finalize()` method or through another object's `finalize()` method. An unreachable object cannot be reached by any means.

There are nine combinations of object states based on their finalization status and reachability status. One of the nine combinations, finalizable and unreachable, is not possible. The `finalize()` method of a finalizable object may be called in the future. The `finalize()` method can still refer to the object using the `this` keyword. Therefore, a finalizable object cannot also be unreachable. An object can exist in one of the following eight states:

- Unfinalized - Reachable
- Unfinalized - Finalizer-reachable
- Unfinalized - Unreachable
- Finalizable - Reachable
- Finalizable - Finalizer-reachable
- Finalized - Reachable
- Finalized - Finalizer-reachable
- Finalized - Unreachable

Weak References

The concept of weak references in the context of garbage collection is not new to Java. It existed before in other programming languages. So far, the object references I have discussed are strong references. That is, as long as the object reference is in scope, the object it refers to cannot be garbage collected. For example, consider the following object creation and reference assignment statement:

```
Employee john = new Employee("John Jacobs");
```

Here, `john` is a reference to the object created by the expression `new Employee("John Jacobs")`. The memory state that exists after executing this statement is depicted in Figure 11-2.

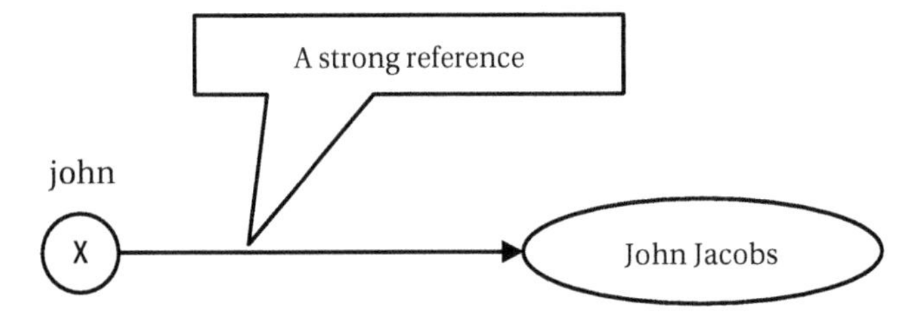

Figure 11-2. *An example of a strong reference*

If at least one strong reference to an object exists, the garbage collector will not reclaim that object. In the previous section, I discussed the object state based on its reachability. By stating that there is a strong reference to an object, I mean that the object is reachable. With the introduction of weak references, now there are three more states of an object based on its reachability:

- Softly reachable
- Weakly reachable
- Phantom reachable

Therefore, when I called an object *reachable* in the last section, I will call it *strongly reachable* now onward. This change in terminology is because of the introduction of three new kinds of object reachability. Before I discuss the three new kinds of object reachability, you need to know about the classes included in the `java.lang.ref` package. There are four classes of interest, as shown in Figure 11-3. I do not discuss the `Reference` class from the diagram.

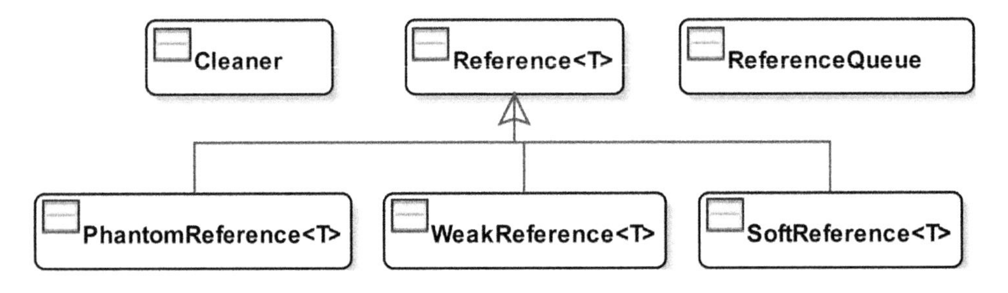

Figure 11-3. *A class diagram for some classes in the java.lang.ref package*

Reference<T> is an abstract class and it is the superclass for the SoftReference<T>, WeakReference<T>, and PhantomReference<T> classes. They are generic classes; their type parameter T is the type of object they reference. The SoftReference, WeakReference, and PhantomReference classes are used to create weak references. Note that by the phrase "weak reference," I mean a reference that is not a strong reference. By the phrase WeakReference, I mean the java.lang.ref.WeakReference class. The ReferenceQueue class is used to place the references of SoftReference, WeakReference, and PhantomReference objects in a queue. Let's look at different ways to create these three types of objects. The constructors for these three classes are shown in Table 11-1.

Table 11-1. *Constructors for the SoftReference, WeakReference, and PhantomReference Classes*

Class	Constructors
SoftReference<T>	SoftReference(T referent) SoftReference(T referent, ReferenceQueue<? super T> q)
WeakReference<T>	WeakReference(T referent) WeakReference(T referent, ReferenceQueue<? super T> q)
PhantomReference<T>	PhantomReference(T referent, ReferenceQueue<? super T> q)

You can create an object of the SoftReference class as follows:

```
Employee john = new Employee ("John Jacobs");
SoftReference<Employee> sr = new SoftReference<>(john);
```

The memory state after executing these two statements is depicted in Figure 11-4.

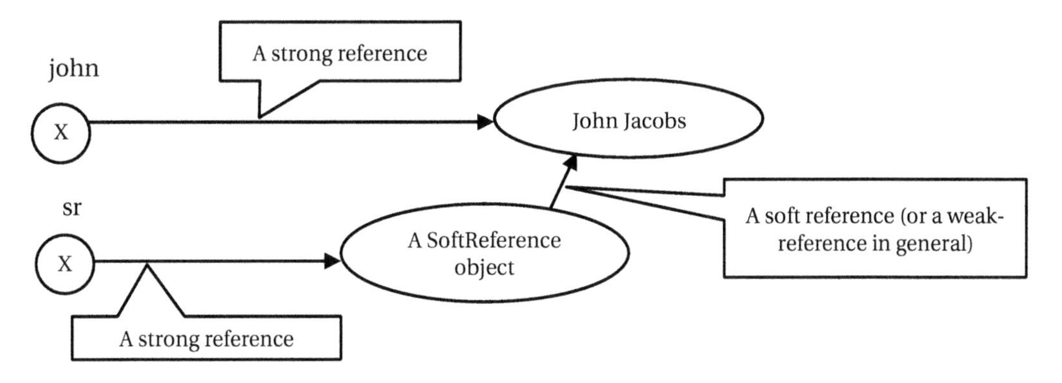

Figure 11-4. *An example of a soft reference*

In Figure 11-4, there are two strong references and one soft reference. All three weak reference classes have two instance variables: referent and queue. They are used to hold the reference of the object and reference queue passed in to the constructors of these classes. A reference to any object stored in the referent instance variable of any of these three classes is known as a weak reference in general—and a soft reference, weak reference, or phantom reference in particular—depending on the class being used. Therefore, the link from a soft reference object to the employee object shown in Figure 11-4 is a weak reference. To be specific, I call it a soft reference because I used an object of the SoftReference class. Any reference that does not involve the referent instance variable of any of these three classes is a strong reference in Java. Therefore, john and sr are strong references.

How are weak references different from strong references? The difference lies in how the garbage collector treats them. Weak references do not prevent the objects they reference from being collected by the garbage collector. That is, if there is a weak reference to an object, the garbage collector can still reclaim the object. However, if there is at least one strong reference to an object, the garbage collector will not reclaim the object. Before you start looking at details of how to use these three reference classes, let's discuss the reachability of an object when these classes are involved in a program.

- *Strongly reachable*: An object is strongly reachable if it can be reached from the root set through at least one chain of references, which does not involve any weak reference.
- *Softly reachable*: An object is softly reachable if it is not strongly reachable and it can be reached from the root set through at least one chain of references, which involves at least one soft reference, but no weak and phantom references.
- *Weakly reachable*: An object is weakly reachable if it is not strongly and softly reachable and it can be reached from the root set through at least one chain of references, which involves at least a weak reference and no phantom references.
- *Phantom reachable*: An object is phantom reachable if it is not strongly, softly, and weakly reachable and it can be reached from the root set through at least one chain of references, which involves at least a phantom reference. A phantom reachable object is finalized, but not reclaimed.

Among the three kinds of weak references, a soft reference is considered stronger than a weak reference and a phantom reference. A weak reference is considered stronger than a phantom reference. Therefore, the rule to identify the reachability of an object is that if an object is not strongly reachable, it is as reachable as the weakest reference in the reference chain leading to that object. That is, if a chain of references to an object involves a phantom reference, the object must be phantom reachable. If a chain of references to an object does not involve a phantom reference, but it involves a weak reference, the object must be weakly reachable. If a chain of references to an object does not involve a phantom reference and a weak reference, but it involves a soft reference, the object must be softly reachable.

How do you determine the reachability of an object when there is more than one chain of references to the object? In such cases, you determine the object's reachability using all possible chains of references and use the strongest one. That is, if an object is softly reachable through one chain of references and phantom reachable through another, the object is considered softly reachable. Figure 11-5 depicts the examples of how an object's reachability is determined. The elliptical shape at the end of every reference chain represents an object. The reachability of the object has been indicated inside the elliptical shape. The rectangles denote references.

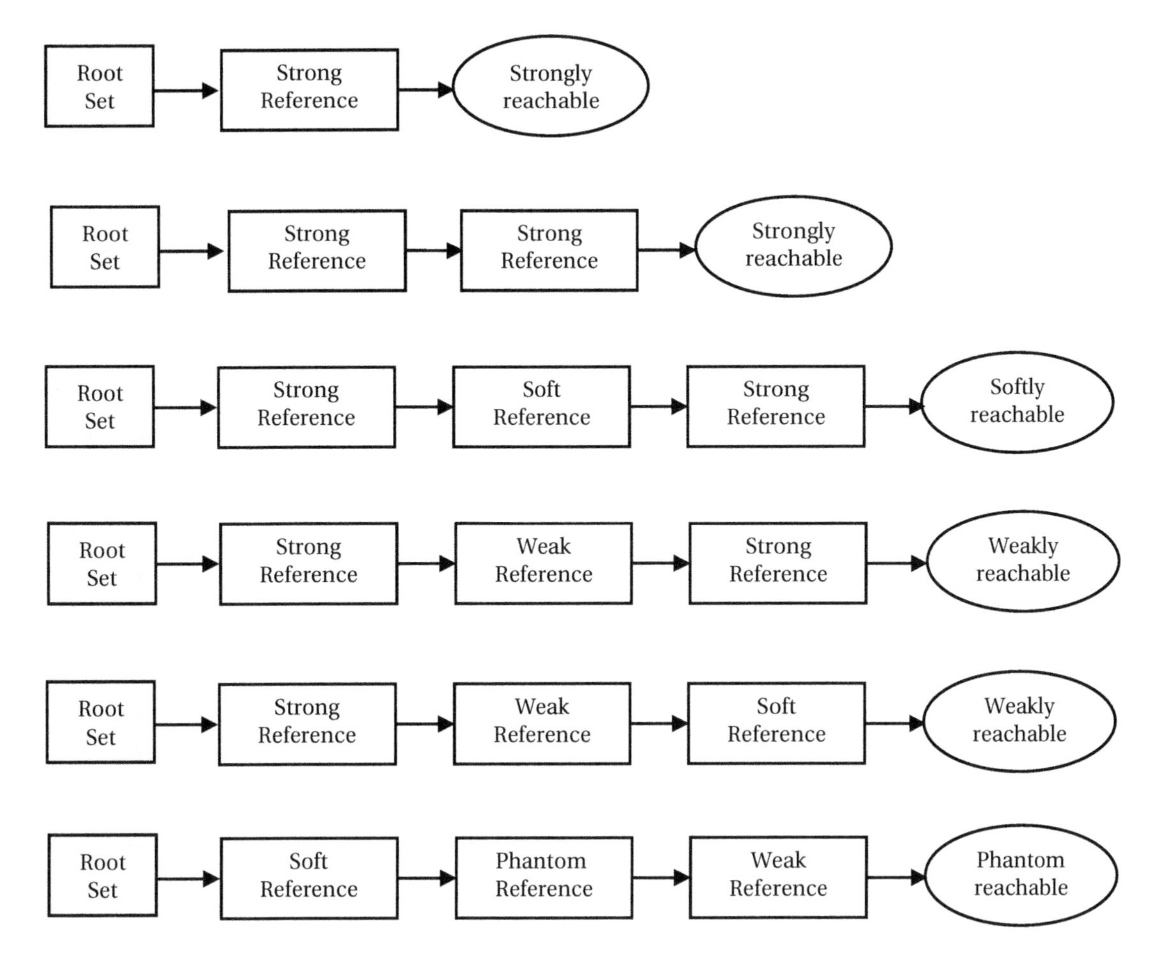

Figure 11-5. *Different kinds of an object's reachability*

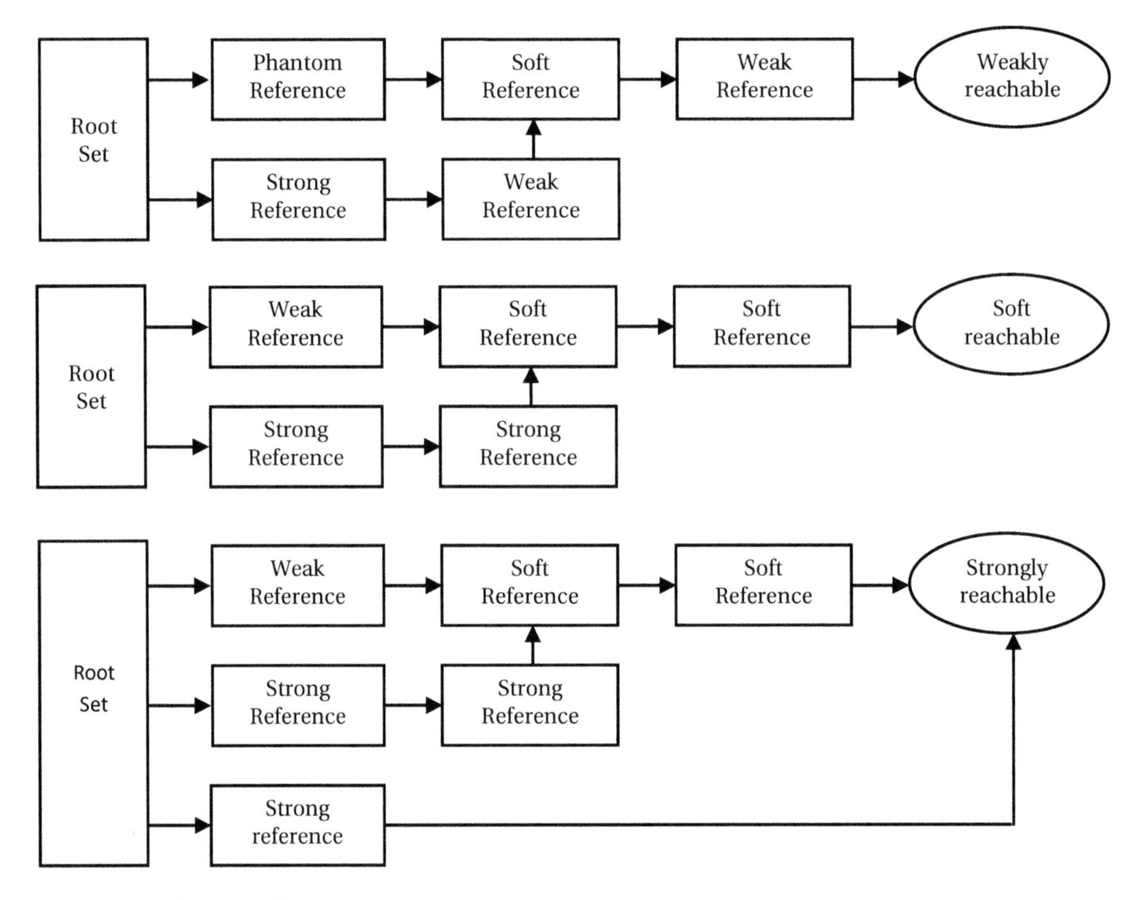

Figure 11-5. *(continued)*

Accessing and Clearing a Referent's Reference

This section uses objects of a trivial class to demonstrate the use of reference classes. This class, called `BigObject`, is shown in Listing 11-6. It has a big array of `long` as an instance variable, so it uses a big chunk of memory. The `id` instance variable is used to track the objects of this class. The `finalize()` method prints a message on the console using the object's `id`.

Listing 11-6. A BigObject Class, Which Uses Big Memory

```
// BigObject.java
package com.jdojo.gc;

public class BigObject {
    // Declare a big array of with room for 20480 long elements.
    private final long[] anArray = new long[20480];

    // Have an id to track the object
    private final long id;
```

```
    public BigObject(long id) {
        this.id = id;
    }

    // Define finalize() to track the object's finalization
    @SuppressWarnings("deprecation")
    @Override
    public void finalize() {
        System.out.println("finalize() called for id: " + id);
    }

    @Override
    public String toString() {
        return "BigObject: id = " + id;
    }
}
```

The object that you pass to the constructors of the `WeakReference`, `SoftReference`, and `PhantomReference` classes is called a *referent*. In other words, the object referred to by the object of these three reference classes is called a referent. To get the reference of the referent of a reference object, you need to call the `get()` method.

```
// Create a big object with id as 101
BigObject bigObj = new BigObject(101);

/* At this point, the big object with id 101 is strongly reachable */

// Create a soft reference object using bigObj as referent
SoftReference<BigObject> sr = new SoftReference<>(bigObj);

/* At this point, the big object with id 101 is still strongly reachable, because bigObj
   is a strong reference referring to it. It also has a soft reference referring to it.
*/

// Set bigObj to null to make the object softly reachable
bigObj = null;

/* At this point, the big object with id 101 is softly reachable, because
   it can be reached only through a soft reference sr.
*/

// Get the reference of referent of soft reference object
BigObject referent = sr.get();

/* At this point, the big object with id 101 again becomes strongly reachable because
   referent is a strong reference. It also has a soft reference referring to it.
*/
```

Figure 11-6 depicts the memory states with all the references after you execute each statement in the previous snippet of code.

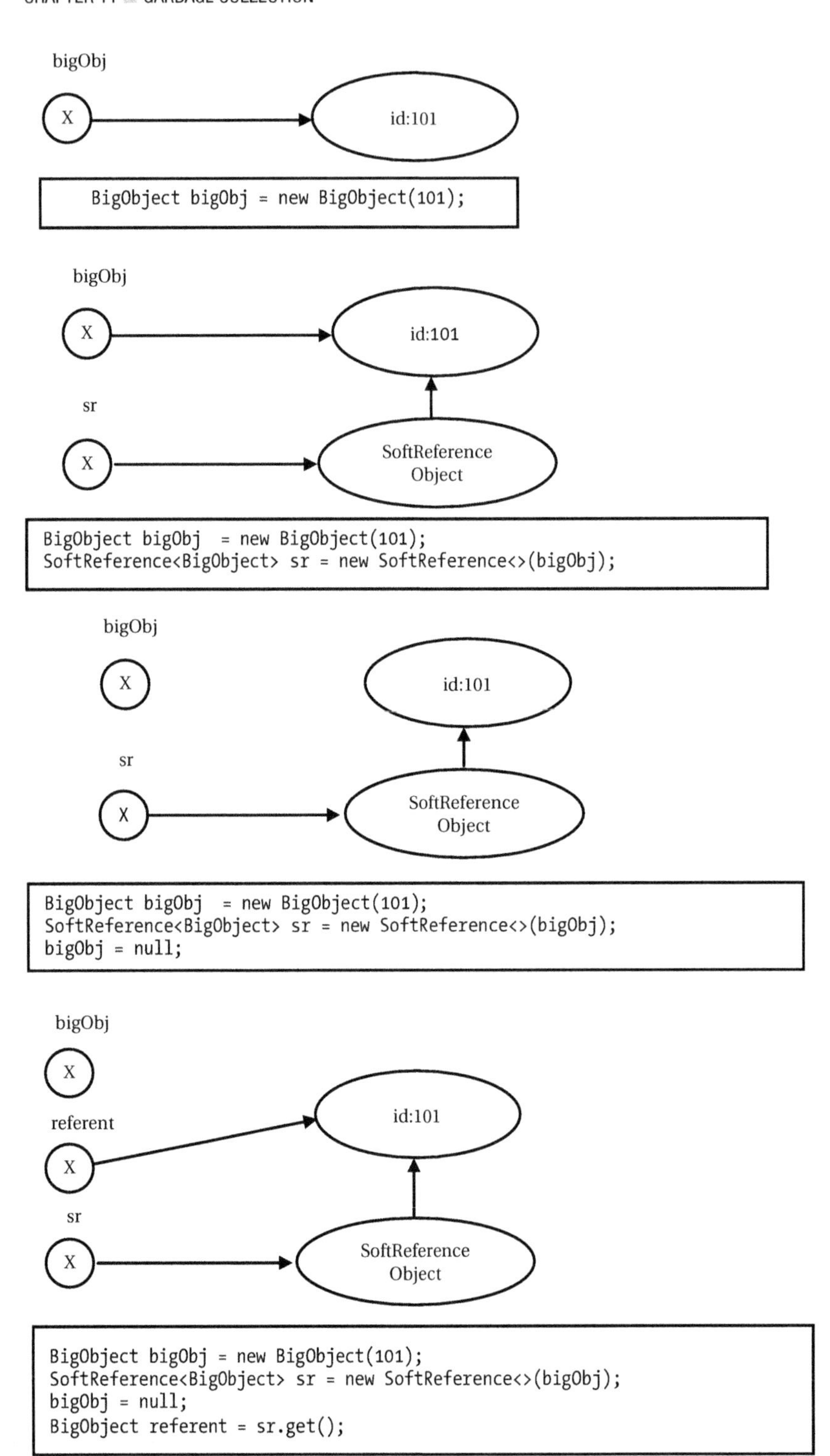

Figure 11-6. *Accessing the referent of a reference object*

The `clear()` method clears the link between the reference (weak, soft, or phantom) object and its referent. The following piece of code illustrates its use:

```
// Create a soft reference object. Use a BigObject with id 976 as its referent.
SoftReference<BigObject> sr1 = new SoftReference<>(new BigObject(976));

/* At this point, the BigObject with id 976 is softly reachable, because it is reachable
   only through a soft reference sr.
*/

// Clear the referent
sr1.clear();

/* At this point, the big object with id 976 is unreachable (to be exact, it is
   finalizer-reachable), because we cleared the only one reference (soft reference)
   we had to the object.
*/
```

The memory state with all references, after each statement in the previous snippet of code is executed, is depicted in Figure 11-7. After the referent's reference is cleared using the `clear()` method, the `get()` method returns `null`. Note that the `get()` method of a `PhantomReference` object always returns `null`.

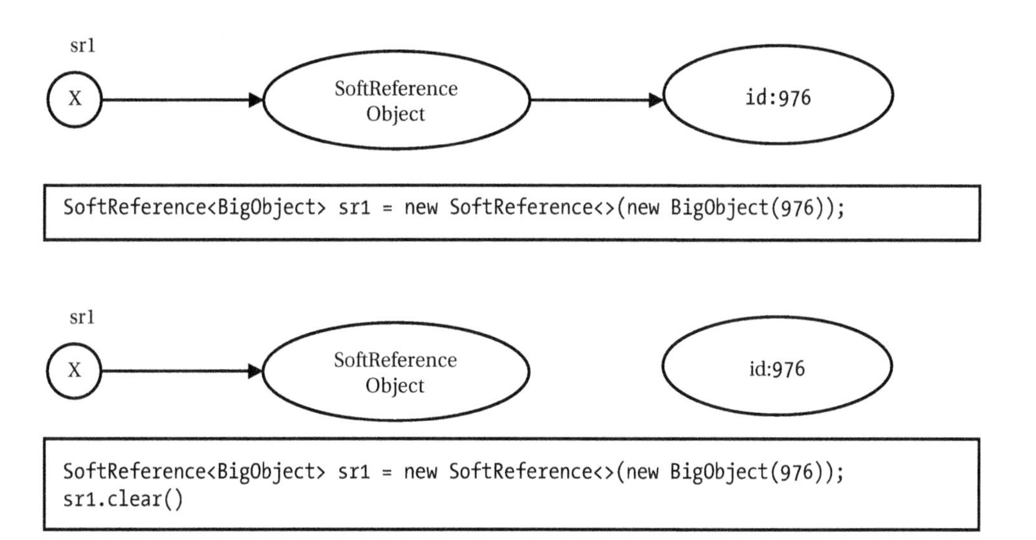

Figure 11-7. *Clearing a referent*

Using the SoftReference Class

A softly reachable object is used to maintain memory-sensitive caches. That is, if you want to maintain a cache of objects as long as the program is not running low on memory, you can use softly reachable objects. When the program runs low on memory, the garbage collector clears the soft references to an object, making the object eligible for reclamation. At that point, your program will lose some or all of its objects from the cache. Java does not guarantee that soft references will not be cleared if the program is not running low on memory. However, it guarantees that all soft references will be cleared before the JVM throws an

OutOfMemoryError. There is also no guarantee of the order in which soft references will be cleared. However, JVM implementations are encouraged to clear the least-recently created/used soft reference first. Listing 11-7 shows the wrong use of soft references to cache data.

Listing 11-7. An Incorrect Use of a Soft Reference

```
// WrongSoftRef.java
package com.jdojo.gc;

import java.lang.ref.SoftReference;
import java.util.ArrayList;

public class WrongSoftRef {
    public static void main(String[] args) {
        // Create a big object with an id 101 for caching
        BigObject bigObj = new BigObject(101);

        // Wrap soft reference inside a soft reference
        SoftReference<BigObject> sr = new SoftReference<>(bigObj);

        // Let us try to create many big objects storing their
        // references in an array list, just to use up big memory.
        ArrayList<BigObject> bigList = new ArrayList<>();
        long counter = 102;
        while (true) {
            bigList.add(new BigObject(counter++));
        }
    }
}
```

```
Exception: java.lang.OutOfMemoryError thrown from the UncaughtExceptionHandler in thread
"main"
```

The intention of the programmer was to cache a big object with an ID of 101 using a soft reference. If the program runs low on memory, the cached big object with ID 101 may be reclaimed. The while loop inside the program is trying to create many big objects to make the program run low on memory. The programmer is expecting that when the program is executed, it should reclaim memory used by the big object with ID 101, before throwing an OutOfMemoryError.

The output shows that the program did not reclaim the memory used by the big object with ID 101. Why did the garbage collector not behave the way it was expected to behave? There is an error in the code for the WrongSoftRef class. The big object with ID 101 is strongly reachable because the bigObj reference to it is a strong reference. You must set the bigObj reference variable to null to make it softly reachable.

Listing 11-8 shows the correct use of soft references. It is clear from the output that the finalize() method of the big object with ID 101 was called and the object was reclaimed before JVM threw an OutOfMemoryError. You still got an OutOfMemoryError because you are creating many new objects inside a while loop and all of them are strongly reachable from the array list. This proves the point that soft references are cleared and the referents are reclaimed by the garbage collector before JVM throws an OutOfMemoryError. You may get a different output. Sometimes, you get an OutOfMemoryError without the object being reclaimed.

Listing 11-8. A Correct Use of a Soft Reference

```
// CorrectSoftRef.java
package com.jdojo.gc;

import java.lang.ref.SoftReference;
import java.util.ArrayList;

public class CorrectSoftRef {
    public static void main(String[] args) {
        // Create a big object with an id 101 for caching
        BigObject bigObj = new BigObject(101);

        // Wrap soft reference inside a soft reference
        SoftReference<BigObject> sr = new SoftReference<>(bigObj);

        // Set bigObj to null, so the big object will be
        // softly reachable and can be reclaimed, if necessary.
        bigObj = null;

        // Let us try to create many big objects storing their
        // references in an array list, just to use up big memory.
        ArrayList<BigObject> bigList = new ArrayList<>();
        long counter = 102;
        while (true) {
            bigList.add(new BigObject(counter++));
        }
    }
}
```

```
finalize() called for id: 101
Exception: java.lang.OutOfMemoryError thrown from the UncaughtExceptionHandler in thread
"main"
```

Listing 11-9 illustrates how to use soft references to implement memory-sensitive caches.

Listing 11-9. Creating a Cache Using Soft References

```
// BigObjectCache.java
package com.jdojo.gc;

import java.lang.ref.SoftReference;

public class BigObjectCache {
    @SuppressWarnings("unchecked")
    private static final SoftReference<BigObject>[] cache = new SoftReference[10];

    public static BigObject getObjectById(int id) {
        // Check for valid cache id
        if (id < 0 || id >= cache.length) {
            throw new IllegalArgumentException("Invalid id");
        }
```

```
        BigObject obj;

        // Check if we have a cache for this id
        if (cache[id] == null) {
            // We have not cached the object yet. Cache and return it.
            obj = createCacheForId(id);
            return obj;
        }

        // Get the BigObject reference using a soft reference
        obj = cache[id].get();

        // Make sure the object has not yet been reclaimed
        if (obj == null) {
            // Garbage collector has reclaimed the object.
            // Cache it again and return the newly cached object.
            obj = createCacheForId(id);
        }

        return obj;
    }

    // Creates cache for a given id
    private static BigObject createCacheForId(int id) {
        BigObject obj = null;
        if (id >= 0 && id < cache.length) {
            obj = new BigObject(id);
            cache[id] = new SoftReference<>(obj);
        }

        return obj;
    }
}
```

It can cache up to 10 objects of the `BigObject` class with IDs from 0 to 9. To get the cached object for a given ID, you need to call the `getObjectById()` method. If that ID has not yet been cached or it was reclaimed by the garbage collector, the method creates and caches the object. This example is very restrictive and its purpose is only to demonstrate the use of the `SoftReference` class to maintain a memory-sensitive cache. You can cache only objects with IDs from 0 to 9. It can be modified to meet specific requirements. For example, you can use an `ArrayList` to cache the objects instead of using an array. You can use the `BigObjectCache` class as shown:

```
// Get the object from cache
BigObject cachedObject = BigObjectCache.getObjectById(5);

/* Do some processing...*/

// You must set the cachedObject to null after you are done with it, so the cached object
// becomes softly reachable and may be reclaimed by the garbage collector.
cachedObject = null;
```

If an object with an ID of 5 is not already in the cache, it will be cached and the new object reference will be assigned to cachedObject. If an object with an ID of 5 is already in the cache, the reference of that object from the cache will be returned and assigned to cachedObject.

Using the ReferenceQueue Class

An object of the ReferenceQueue<T> class is used in conjunction with objects of the SoftReference<T>, WeakReference<T>, and PhantomReference<T> classes if the object needs to be notified when its reachability changes. An object of any of these reference classes can be registered with a reference queue, as shown:

```
ReferenceQueue<BigObject> q = new ReferenceQueue<>();
SoftReference<BigObject> sr = new SoftReference<>(new BigObject(19), q);
WeakReference<BigObject> wr = new WeakReference<>(new BigObject(20), q);
PhantomReference<BigObject> pr = new PhantomReference<>(new BigObject(21), q);
```

It is optional to register the SoftReference and WeakReference objects with a reference queue. However, you must register a PhantomReference object with a reference queue. When a SoftReference or WeakReference is cleared by the garbage collector, the reference of the SoftReference or the WeakReference object is appended to the reference queue. Note the references of the SoftReference and WeakReference are placed in the queue, not the reference of their referent. For example, if the garbage collector clears the soft reference to a BigObject with ID 19 in the previous snippet of code, sr will be placed in the reference queue. In case of a PhantomReference, when its referent becomes phantom reachable, the garbage collector places the PhantomReference object in the reference queue.

Until JDK9, unlike soft and weak references, the garbage collector did not clear the phantom references as it placed them in their reference queue. The program must clear the phantom references by calling the clear() method. From JDK9, all three types of references are cleared before they are enqueued.

There are two ways to determine if a reference object has been placed in its reference queue. You can call the poll() or remove() method on a ReferenceQueue, or you can call the isEnqueued() method on the soft, weak, and phantom references. The poll() method removes a reference from the queue and returns the reference. If there is no reference available in the queue, it returns null. The remove() method works the same as the poll() method, except that if there is no reference available in the queue, it blocks until a reference becomes available. The isEnqueued() method for soft, weak, and phantom references returns true if they are placed in queue. Otherwise, it returns false. Listing 11-10 demonstrates how to use the ReferenceQueue class.

Listing 11-10. Using the ReferenceQueue Class

```
// ReferenceQueueDemo.java
package com.jdojo.gc;

import java.lang.ref.ReferenceQueue;
import java.lang.ref.WeakReference;

public class ReferenceQueueDemo {
    public static void main(String[] args) {
        // Create a reference queue
        ReferenceQueue<BigObject> q = new ReferenceQueue<>();

        // Wrap a BigObject inside a soft reference.
        // Also register the soft reference with the reference queue
        BigObject bigObj = new BigObject(131);
        WeakReference<BigObject> wr = new WeakReference<>(bigObj, q);
```

```
        // Clear the strong reference to the big object
        bigObj = null;

        // Check if weak reference has been queued
        System.out.println("Before calling gc():");
        printMessage(wr, q);

        // Invoke garbage collector. If it runs, it will clear the weak reference
        System.out.println("Invoking garbage collector...");
        System.gc();
        System.out.println("Garbage collector finished...");

        // Check if weak reference has been queued
        System.out.println("After calling gc():");
        printMessage(wr, q);
    }

    public static void printMessage(WeakReference<BigObject> wr,
            ReferenceQueue<BigObject> q) {

        System.out.println("wr.get() = " + wr.get());
        System.out.println("wr.isEnqueued() = " + wr.isEnqueued());
        WeakReference<BigObject> temp = (WeakReference<BigObject>) q.poll();
        if (temp == wr) {
            System.out.println("q.poll() returned wr");
        } else {
            System.out.println("q.poll() = " + temp);
        }
    }
}
```

```
Before calling gc():
wr.get()= BigObject: id = 131
wr.isEnqueued()= false
q.poll()= null
Invoking garbage collector...
Garbage collector finished...
After calling gc():
wr.get()= null
wr.isEnqueued()= true
q.poll() returned wr
finalize() called for id: 131
```

Using the WeakReference Class

The only difference between a softly reachable and a weakly reachable object is that the garbage collector clears and reclaims weakly reachable objects whenever it runs, whereas it uses some algorithm to decide whether it needs to clear and reclaim a softly reachable object or not. In other words, the garbage collector may or may not reclaim a softly reachable object, whereas it always reclaims a weakly reachable object.

You may not see any important use of a weak reference because its referent is reclaimed when the garbage collector is run. Generally, weak references are not used to maintain caches. They are used to associate extra data with an object. Suppose you have a person's details and his address. If you lose his details, you will not be interested in his address. However, as long as the person's details are accessible, you want to keep his address information. This kind of information can be stored using weak references and a Hashtable. A Hashtable stores objects in key-value pairs. While adding a key-value pair to a Hashtable, you need to wrap the key object in a WeakReference object. The key and value are not garbage collected when the key is accessible or in use. When the key object is no longer in use, it will be garbage collected because it was wrapped inside a WeakReference. At that point, you can remove that entry from the Hashtable, so the value object will also be eligible for the garbage collection. The following is a sample snippet of code using Hashtable and WeakReference objects:

```
// Create a Hashtable object
Hashtable ht = new Hashtable();

// Create a reference queue, so  we can check when a key was garbage collected
Referencequeue q = new ReferenceQueue();

// Create key and value objects
key = your key object creation logic goes here
value = your value object creation logic goes here

// Create a weak reference object using the key object as the referent
WeakReference wKey = new WeakReference(key, q);

// Place the key-value pair in the Hashtable. Note that we place key wrapped
// in the weak reference. That is, we will use wKey as key
ht.put(wKey, value);

/* Use key and value objects in your program... */

// When done with the key object, set it to null, so it will not be strongly reachable.
key = null;

/* At this point, if garbage collector is run, weak reference to key object will be cleared
   and the WeakReference, wr, will be placed in reference queue, q.
*/

// Your logic to remove the entry for garbage collected key object will be as follows
if (wr.isEnqueued()) {
    // This will make value object eligible for reclamation
    ht.remove(wr);
}
```

Note that using a WeakReference object to associate extra information with an object using a Hashtable involves some complex code and logic. The java.util.WeakHashMap class provides this functionality without writing any complex logic. You add the key-value pairs to a WeakHashMap without wrapping the key object inside a WeakReference. The WeakHashMap class takes care of creating a reference queue and wrapping the key object in a WeakReference. There is one important point to remember while using a WeakHashMap. The key object is reclaimed when it is not strongly reachable. However, the value object is not reclaimed immediately. The value object is reclaimed after the entry is removed from the map. The WeakHashMap removes the entry after the weak reference to the key has been cleared and one of its methods—put(), remove(), or clear()—is called. Listing 11-11 demonstrates the use of a WeakHashMap. The example uses objects of the BigObject class as keys as well as values. The messages in the output show when the key and value objects are reclaimed by the garbage collector. You may get different output when you run this program.

Listing 11-11. Using a WeakHashMap

```
// WeakHashMapDemo.java
package com.jdojo.gc;

import java.util.WeakHashMap;

public class WeakHashMapDemo {
    public static void main(String[] args) {
        // Create a WeakHashMap
        WeakHashMap<BigObject, BigObject> wmap = new WeakHashMap<>();

        // Add two key-value pairs to WeakHashMap
        BigObject key1 = new BigObject(10);
        BigObject value1 = new BigObject(110);
        BigObject key2 = new BigObject(20);
        BigObject value2 = new BigObject(210);

        wmap.put(key1, value1);
        wmap.put(key2, value2);

        // Print a message
        printMessage("After adding two entries:", wmap);

        /* Invoke gc(). This gc() invocation will not reclaim any of
           the key objects, because we are still having their strong references.
         */
        System.out.println("Invoking gc() first time...");
        System.gc();

        // Print a message
        printMessage("After first gc() call:", wmap);

        // Now remove strong references to keys and values
        key1 = null;
        key2 = null;
        value1 = null;
        value2 = null;

        /* Invoke gc(). This gc() invocation will reclaim two key objects
           with ids 10 and 20. However, the corresponding two value objects
           will still /be strongly referenced by WeakHashMap internally and hence
           will not be reclaimed at this point.
         */
        System.out.println("Invoking gc() second time...");
        System.gc();
```

```
        // Print a message
        printMessage("After second gc() call:", wmap);

        /* Both keys have been reclaimed by now. Just to make value
           objects reclaimable, we will call clear() method on WeakHashMap.
           Usually, you will not call this method here in your program.
         */
        wmap.clear();

        // Invoke gc() so that value object will be reclaimed
        System.out.println("Invoking gc() third time...");
        System.gc();

        // Print message
        printMessage("After calling clear() method:", wmap);
    }

    public static void printMessage(String msgHeader, WeakHashMap wmap) {
        System.out.println(msgHeader);

        // Print the size and content of map */
        System.out.println("Size = " + wmap.size());
        System.out.println("Content = " + wmap);
        System.out.println();
    }
}
```

```
After adding two entries:
Size = 2
Content = {BigObject: id = 20=BigObject: id = 210, BigObject: id = 10=BigObject: id = 110}

Invoking gc() first time...
After first gc() call:
Size = 2
Content = {BigObject: id = 20=BigObject: id = 210, BigObject: id = 10=BigObject: id = 110}

Invoking gc() second time...
After second gc() call:
finalize() called for id: 20
finalize() called for id: 10
Size = 0
Content = {}

Invoking gc() third time...
finalize() called for id: 210
finalize() called for id: 110
After calling clear() method:
Size = 0
Content = {}
```

Using the PhantomReference Class

A PhantomReference object must be created with a ReferenceQueue. When the garbage collector determines that there are only phantom references to an object, it finalizes the object and adds the phantom references to their reference queues.

Until JDK8, phantom references worked a little differently than soft and weak references. Unlike soft and weak references, it did not clear the phantom references to the object automatically. Programs must clear it by calling the clear() method. A garbage collector would not reclaim the object until the program clears the phantom references to that object. Therefore, a phantom reference acted as a strong reference as long as reclaiming of objects is concerned. This behavior has changed in JDK9. In JDK9, phantom references automatically clear references as soft and weak references do.

Why would you use a phantom reference instead of using a strong reference? A phantom reference is used to do post-mortem processing. Unlike the get() method of the soft and weak references, the phantom reference's get() method always returns null. An object is phantom reachable when it has been finalized. If a phantom reference returns the referent's reference from its get() method, it would resurrect the referent. This is why the phantom reference's get() method always returns null.

Listing 11-12 demonstrates the use of a phantom reference to do some post-mortem processing for an object. You may get different output when you run this program.

Listing 11-12. Using PhantomReference Objects

```
// PhantomRef.java
package com.jdojo.gc;

import java.lang.ref.PhantomReference;
import java.lang.ref.ReferenceQueue;

public class PhantomRef {
    public static void main(String[] args) {
        BigObject bigObject = new BigObject(1857);
        ReferenceQueue<BigObject> q = new ReferenceQueue<>();
        PhantomReference<BigObject> pr = new PhantomReference<>(bigObject, q);

        /* You can use BigObject reference here */

        // Set BigObject to null, so garbage collector will find only the
        // phantom reference to it and finalize it.
        bigObject = null;

        // Invoke garbage collector
        printMessage(pr, "Invoking gc() first time:");
        System.gc();
        printMessage(pr, "After invoking gc() first time:");

        // Invoke garbage collector again
        printMessage(pr, "Invoking gc() second time:");
        System.gc();
        printMessage(pr, "After invoking gc() second time:");
    }
```

```
    public static void printMessage(PhantomReference<BigObject> pr, String msg) {
        System.out.println(msg);
        System.out.println("pr.isEnqueued = " + pr.isEnqueued());
        System.out.println("pr.get() = " + pr.get());

        // We will check if pr is queued. If it has been queued,
        // we will clear its referent's reference.
        if (pr.isEnqueued()) {
            // Calling pr.clear() was necessary before JDK9.
            // From JDK9, phantom references are clear automatically
            pr.clear();

            System.out.println("Cleared the referent's reference");
        }
        System.out.println("-----------------------");
    }
}
```

```
Invoking gc() first time:
pr.isEnqueued = false
pr.get() = null
-----------------------
finalize() called for id: 1857
After invoking gc() first time:
pr.isEnqueued = false
pr.get() = null
-----------------------
Invoking gc() second time:
pr.isEnqueued = false
pr.get() = null
-----------------------
After invoking gc() second time:
pr.isEnqueued = true
pr.get() = null
Cleared the referent's reference
-----------------------
```

You can also use phantom references to coordinate the post-mortem processing of more than one object. Suppose you have three objects called obj1, obj2, and obj3. All of them share a network connection. When all three objects become unreachable, you would like to close the shared network connection. You can achieve this by wrapping the three objects in a phantom reference object and using a reference queue. Your program can wait on a separate thread for all three phantom reference objects to be queued. When the last phantom reference is queued, you can close the shared network connection. Post-mortem coordination using a phantom reference is demonstrated in Listing 11-13. Note that the startThread() method of the PhantomRefDemo class creates and starts a thread that waits for three references to be enqueued. Once all three references are enqueued and their referents clears, the thread exits the application. The remove() method of the ReferenceQueue class blocks until there is a phantom reference in the queue. You may get different output when you run this program.

Listing 11-13. Post-Finalization Coordination Using Phantom References

```
// PhantomRefDemo.java
package com.jdojo.gc;

import java.lang.ref.PhantomReference;
import java.lang.ref.Reference;
import java.lang.ref.ReferenceQueue;

public class PhantomRefDemo {
    public static void main(String[] args) {
        final ReferenceQueue<BigObject> q = new ReferenceQueue<>();
        BigObject bigObject1 = new BigObject(101);
        BigObject bigObject2 = new BigObject(102);
        BigObject bigObject3 = new BigObject(103);
        PhantomReference<BigObject> pr1 = new PhantomReference<>(bigObject1, q);
        PhantomReference<BigObject> pr2 = new PhantomReference<>(bigObject2, q);
        PhantomReference<BigObject> pr3 = new PhantomReference<>(bigObject3, q);

        /* This method will start a thread that will wait for the arrival of new
           phantom references in reference queue q
         */
        startThread(q);

        /* You can use bigObject1, bigObject2 and bigObject3 here */

        // Set the bigObject1, bigObject2 and bigObject3 to null,
        // so the objects they are referring to may become phantom reachable.
        bigObject1 = null;
        bigObject2 = null;
        bigObject3 = null;

        /* Let us invoke garbage collection in a loop. One garbage collection will
           just finalize the three big objects with IDs 101, 102 and 103. They may
           not be placed in a reference queue. In another garbage collection run,
           they will become phantom reachable and they will be placed in a queue
           and the waiting thread will remove them from the queue and will clear
           their referent's reference. Note that we exit the application when all
           three objects are cleared inside the run() method of thread. Therefore, the
           following infinite loop is ok for demonstration purposes. If System.gc()
           does not invoke the garbage collector on your machine, you should replace
           the following loop with a loop which would create many big objects keeping
           their references, so the garbage collector would run.
         */
        while (true) {
            System.gc();
        }
    }
```

```
    public static void startThread(final ReferenceQueue<BigObject> q) {
        Thread t = new Thread(() -> {
            try {
                // Wait and clear 3 references
                for(int i = 0; i < 3; i++) {
                    Reference r = q.remove();

                    // Calling r.clear() was necessary before JDK9.
                    // From JDK9, it has no effect.
                    r.clear();
                }

                System.out.println("All three objects have been queued and cleared.");

                /* Typically, you will release the network connection or
                   any resources shared by three objects here.
                */

                // Exit the application
                System.exit(1);
            } catch (InterruptedException e) {
                System.out.println(e.getMessage());
            }
        });

        // Start the thread, which will wait for three phantom references to be queued
        t.start();
    }
}
```

```
finalize() called for id: 103
finalize() called for id: 102
finalize() called for id: 101
All three objects have been queued and cleared.
```

Using the Cleaner Class

In the previous sections, you learned how to use PhantomReference and ReferenceQueue to perform cleanup work for objects when they become phantom reachable. To set up and perform the cleanup work was not easy. JDK9 introduced a new class named Cleaner in the java.lang.ref package. Its use to let you run a cleanup action for an object when the object becomes phantom reachable. The Cleaner class is intended to make setting up and performing the cleanup work easier for you. Here are the steps you need to perform:

1. Create a Cleaner instance using one of its factory methods named create()... You can let the Cleaner use predefined threads to perform the cleanup actions or you can specify your own ThreadFactory in the create() method.

2. Register the object and its cleaning action using the register() method of the Cleaner. A cleaning action is a Runnable.

3. The register() method of the Cleaner class returns an instance of the Cleaner.Cleanable nested interface. The interface contains only one method named clean().

4. Call the clean() method of a Cleanable to unregister the object and perform the cleanup work. Performing the cleanup work is simply calling the run() method of the registered Runnable. Calling the clean() method the second time has no effect because the first call to this method unregisters the object.

5. Typically, the clean() method of a Cleanable is called by one of the threads in the Cleaner. However, if you know the time and place when the cleanup needs to happen, you can perform the cleanup explicitly by calling this method.

6. If you intend to use the objects of your class inside try-with-resources blocks, you need to implement the AutoCloseable interface. You can call the clean() method of the Cleanable representing your registered object from inside the close() method.

Now I walk you through an example on how to use the Cleaner class. You can use one of the following methods of the Cleaner class to create a Cleaner:

- static Cleaner create()
- static Cleaner create(ThreadFactory threadFactory)

Typically, you would create a Cleaner object for the entire application or library and store its reference in a static variable. The following statement creates a Cleaner:

```
Cleaner cleaner = Cleaner.create();
```

Suppose you have the following object that needs cleanup work when it becomes phantom reachable:

```
Object myObject = /* get your object */;
```

The next step is to define a cleaning action, which is a Runnable. There are several ways to create a Runnable such as using a lambda expression, inner class, anonymous inner class, nested inner class, and having a top-level class, which implements the Runnable interface. It does not matter which method you choose to create a Runnable. It is important to make sure that the Runnable does not store the reference of the object whose cleanup work it is supposed to perform. Otherwise, the object will never become phantom reachable and your cleaning action will never be called by the Cleaner. You need to make all resources that need to be cleaned up are accessible to the Runnable. Suppose you have an object that stores a network connection and you want to close the connection as part of the object cleanup. You will need to make the network connection accessible to the Runnable, so it can close the connection when the cleanup work is performed. The following pseudo statement creates a Runnable:

```
Runnable cleaningAction = /* get a Runnable instance */;
```

The following statement registers myObject and its cleaningAction with the Cleaner:

```
Cleaner.Cleanable cleanable = cleaner.register(myObject, cleaningAction);
```

Typically, you will keep the reference of the Cleanable in an instance variable of your object, so you can call its clean() method directly to clean up your object explicitly, if needed. Listing 11-14 contains the code for a CleanBigObject class. Explanation of its parts follows the code.

Listing 11-14. The CleanBigObject Class

```
// CleanBigObject.java
package com.jdojo.gc;

import java.lang.ref.Cleaner;

public class CleanBigObject implements AutoCloseable {
    // Declare a big array of 20KB.
    private final long[] anArray = new long[20480];

    // Have an id to track the object
    private final long id;

    // Let us use a Cleaner
    public static Cleaner cleaner = Cleaner.create();

    // Keep a reference of its cleaning action as a Cleanable
    private final Cleaner.Cleanable cleanable;

    // Declare a cleaning action class, which needs to implement Runnable
    private static class BigObjectCleaner implements Runnable {
        private final long id;
        BigObjectCleaner(long id) {
            this.id = id;
        }

        @Override
        public void run() {
            System.out.println("Cleaning up CleanBigObject: id = " + this.id);
        }
    }

    public CleanBigObject(long id) {
        this.id = id;

        // Register this object with the cleaner
        this.cleanable = cleaner.register(this, new BigObjectCleaner(id));
    }

    @Override
    public void close() {
        // Clean the object explicitly or as part of a try-with-resources block
        cleanable.clean();
    }

     @Override
    public String toString() {
        return "CleanBigObject: id = " + id;
    }
}
```

Here are the different parts of the CleanBigObject class:

- The CleanBigObject class declares a big long array.
- Its id instance variable tracks the ID of each object.
- It creates and stores a Cleaner object in a public class variable. This Cleaner is supposed to be used by the object of this class and other classes to register cleaning actions.
- It declares a private instance variable of type Cleaner.Cleanable, which stores the registered cleaning action for later use such as in its close() method.
- The BigObjectCleaner class is a private nested static class, which implements Runnable; its instances represents a cleaning action for the object of the CleanBigObject class. The constructor of the class accepts the ID of the CleanBigObject. In a real-word application, the constructer would accept the resources to be cleaned. The run() method simply prints a message with the ID of the CleanBigObject that is being cleaned up.
- The constructor of the CleanBigObject class accepts an ID to identify the object. The ID is stored in its instance variable. The constructor registers the object and its cleaning action with the Cleaner.
- The close() method of the CleanBigObject class has been implemented because the class implements the AutoCloseable interface, so you can use the objects of this class in try-with-resources blocks. The method calls the clean() method of the Cleanable that will clean up the CleanBigObject if it has not already been cleaned.
- The toString() method returns a string representation of the object with its ID.

Listing 11-15 contains the code for a CleanerTest class. In its main() method, it creates three objects of the CleanBigObject class and tries to clean up those objects in three different ways. The first example uses a try-with-resources block, so the close() method of the CleanBigObject class is automatically called, which cleans up the object. The second example cleans up the object explicitly by calling its close() method. The third example creates the object without storing its reference and invokes the garbage collection by calling System.gc(). In the end, the program sleeps for two seconds to give the garbage collection time to finish if the previous call to System.gc() makes the JVM run the garbage collection. Note that there is no guarantee that garbage collection will run and, in that case, you may not see the last line in the output.

Listing 11-15. A Test Class to Test the Objects of the CleanBigObject Class

```
// CleanerTest.java
package com.jdojo.gc;

public class CleanerTest {
    public static void main(String[] args) throws InterruptedException {
        // Let us try a CleanBigObject in a try-with-resources block
        try (CleanBigObject cbo1 = new CleanBigObject(1969);) {
            System.out.println(cbo1 + " created inside a try-with-resources block.");
        }

        // Let us create and clean a CleanBigObject explicitly
        CleanBigObject cbo2 = new CleanBigObject(1968);
        System.out.println(cbo2 + " created.");
```

```
        cbo2.close();
        cbo2 = null;

        // Let us create many CleanBigObject and let the Cleaner
        // clean those objects automatically
        new CleanBigObject(1982);
        System.gc();

        // Wait for 2 seconds for the garbage collector to finish
        Thread.sleep(20000);
    }
}
```

```
CleanBigObject: id = 1969 created inside a try-with-resources block.
Cleaning up CleanBigObject: id = 1969
CleanBigObject: id = 1968 created.
Cleaning up CleanBigObject: id = 1968
Cleaning up CleanBigObject: id = 1982
```

Summary

The process of reclaiming the memory of dead objects is known as garbage collection. Garbage collection in Java is automatic. The Java runtime runs garbage collection in a low priority background thread. The JVM does its best to free up memory of dead objects before throwing an OutOfMemoryError. You can pass a hint, although it's not needed in an application, to the JVM by calling Runtime.getRuntime().gc(). You can also use the convenience method System.gc() to pass the same hint to the JVM. The JVM is free to ignore the hint.

The memory occupied by an unreachable object is reclaimed in two phases. The first phase, called finalization, is an action automatically performed on an unreachable object before the memory used by the object is reclaimed by the garbage collector. The block of code that contains the action to be performed is known as a finalizer. A finalizer is implemented using the finalize() method of the object. In the finalize() method, the unreachable object may resurrect itself by storing its reference in a reachable object. In the second phase, if the object is still unreachable, the memory occupied by the object is reclaimed.

At times, you may want to use memory-sensitive objects, which are fine to be kept in memory if enough memory is available. However, if the application runs low on memory, it would be fine to reclaim those objects. Typically, objects cached for a better performance fall into this category of objects. Java provides the SoftReference<T>, WeakReference<T>, and PhantomReference<T> classes in the java.lang.ref package to work with such memory-sensitive objects. These objects may be queued to a ReferenceQueue when their referent's reachability changes, so you can inspect the queue and perform cleanup work.

JDK9 added a new class named Cleaner to the java.lang.ref package. This class offers a better way to clean up objects when the objects become phantom reachable. The Cleaner lets you register objects and their cleaning actions as a Runnable. When a registered object becomes phantom reachable, the Cleaner performs the cleanup work using the registered Runnable for that object. The Cleaner also allows you to clean up the object explicitly. It guarantees that the cleanup will be performed only once in any case.

QUESTIONS AND EXERCISES

1. What is the difference between explicit and implicit memory allocation and memory reclamation?
2. What is a dangling reference?
3. What is memory leak?
4. What is garbage collection and a garbage collector?
5. Show two ways to call the garbage collector in your program.
6. What is the `finalize()` method? How is it used by the garbage collector?
7. What does the Java runtime do before throwing an `OutOfMemoryError`?
8. What is an object resurrection in Java?
9. How do you request that the Java runtime run garbage collection?
10. Describe the uses of the `WeakReference<T>`, `SoftReference<T>`, and `PhantomReference<T>` classes.
11. When do you use a `ReferenceQueue`?
12. How is the `Cleaner` class, which was introduced in JDK9, used?

CHAPTER 12

Collections

In this chapter, you will learn:

- What collections are
- What the Collections framework is and its architecture
- Different ways for traversing elements in a collection
- Different types of collections such as `List`, `Set`, `Queue`, `Map`, etc.
- Applying algorithms to collections
- Obtaining different views of a collection
- Creating empty and singleton collections
- How hash-based collections work internally

All example programs in this chapter are members of a `jdojo.collections` module, as declared in Listing 12-1.

Listing 12-1. The Declaration of a jdojo. collections Module

```
// module-info.java
module jdojo.collections {
    exports com.jdojo.collections;
}
```

What Is a Collection?

A collection is an object that contains a group of objects. A collection is also known as a container. Each object in a collection is called an *element* of the collection.

The concept of collections in Java is no different from the concept of collections in our daily life. You see different kinds of collections every day. Every collection contains a group of objects. What distinguishes one type of collection from that of another type? They are distinguished based on the way they manage their elements. Let's take a few examples of collections from our daily life.

Let's start with a money jar. A money jar is an example of a collection. It contains a group of coins. Do you put a coin in the jar in a specific order? Do you retrieve the coins from the jar in a specific order? Can you put many coins of the same kind in the jar? Can you remove all coins from the jar in one go or must you take them out one at a time?

K. Sharan, *Java Language Features*, https://doi.org/10.1007/978-1-4842-3348-1_12

Can you call an alphabet a collection? Isn't it a collection of letters? Does an alphabet have duplicate letters? No, you can't have duplicate letters in an alphabet. However, you can have duplicate coins in your money jar.

Consider a queue of customers at a counter in a post office. Is the queue of customers not a collection of customers? Definitely, it is. Does this queue follow any specific rule? Yes, it does follow a rule, which is first come, first served. You can rephrase the rule of first come, first served as First In, First Out (FIFO).

Consider a stack of books on your desk. Is it not also a collection of books? Yes, it is. Assuming that you deal with one book at a time, does it follow the rule that the book that was placed on the stack last will be removed first? All right, this rule seems to be the opposite of the rule about the collection of customers in a queue in the post office. This time, the stack of books is following the rule of Last In, First Out (LIFO).

I just mentioned quite a few examples of collections that follow different rules to manage their elements. What would you do if you had to model these collections of objects into a Java program? First, you would categorize all possible kinds of collections that you would deal with in your programs. Then, you would write some reusable generic interfaces and classes that you could use in a situation where you need to deal with collection of objects. The good news is that you do not need to write generic code to manage collections. The designers of the Java language realized the need for it and incorporated a framework in the Java library, which is called the *Collections framework*.

The Collections framework consists of interfaces, implementation classes, and some utility classes that let you handle most types of collections that you would encounter in a Java application. If you encounter a collection type for which Java does not provide an implementation, you can always roll out your own implementation, which will work seamlessly with the Collections framework. The Collections framework is simple, powerful, and an exciting topic to learn. This chapter will explore the different types of collections available in the Collections framework. Figure 12-1 shows five types of collections: a bag, a list, a queue, a stack, and a map.

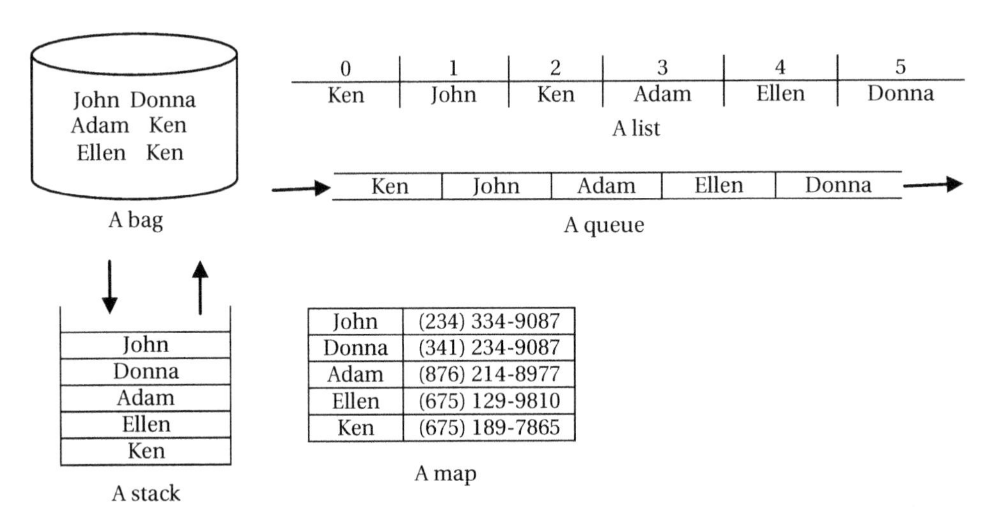

Figure 12-1. *A pictorial view of five different types of collections*

One collection (the map) in the figure stands out: a collection of name-phone pairs. It maps a name to a phone number. At this point, these pictures are not associated with any specific types of collection classes in Java. They are just to help you visualize that Java collections are the same as collections in your daily life. Arrows in some collections indicate the entry and exit of an element to and from the collection. You may observe that some collections enforce that an element must be added in a certain way to the collection and it must exit (be removed) the collection in a certain way. For example, in a queue, elements enter from one end and exit from the other end; in a stack, elements enter and exit from the same end.

Need for a Collection Framework

The support for arrays is built into the Java programming language right from the beginning. Using an array is also one of the most efficient ways to store and retrieve a group of object references and primitive values. Why did we need the Collections framework if we already had arrays in Java? Using an array in Java has the following advantages:

- It can be used to store and retrieve values using indexes, and it is fast.
- It knows its type. It provides compile-time type checking such as you cannot store a `double` value in an `int` array, though if the array is of type `Object`, there is no compile-time type-safety, as any type of objects can be stored in the array.
- You can have arrays of objects as well as primitives.
- You have the helper class named `java.util.Arrays` to help you work with arrays. For example, it provides methods for searching through an array, sorting the array's elements, etc.

Using an array in Java has the following disadvantages:

- Arrays are fixed in size. You must specify the size at the time of creation. Once created, the array size cannot be changed. That is, arrays cannot expand or shrink if you need them to.
- If you store an element in an array at a specific position and later you want to remove it, there is no way to know that the element at that position was removed.
- Compile-time type checking, though an advantage, also becomes a disadvantage. It cannot store different kinds of values. For example, an array of a `Car` class will store only `Car` type objects. A primitive array of `double` will only store values of `double` type.
- You need to write a lot of code if you want to implement a specific type of collection using an array. Suppose you want to have a collection that should not allow duplicate values. Of course, you can develop a new class that uses an array to implement your collection. However, it is a time-consuming task.

The Collections framework provides all the features provided by arrays. It provides many other features that are not provided by arrays. The Collections framework team has already gone through the pain of designing, developing, and testing the interfaces and classes that are needed to use different kinds of collections. All you need to do is to learn those classes and interfaces, and use them in your Java programs. You need to keep the following points in mind when you learn about collections:

- Collections are designed to work only with objects. To work with collections of primitive types, either you wrap and unwrap your primitive values in wrapper objects or you can take advantage of the built-in autoboxing features in Java that will wrap and unwrap the primitive values as needed.
- All collection classes and interfaces in Java are generic. That is, you can specify the type of elements that your collection deals with as the type parameter.

Architecture of the Collection Framework

The Collections framework types are mainly located in the `java.util` package. Types representing concurrent collections are in the `java.util.concurrent` package. The Collections framework consists of three main components:

- Interfaces
- Implementation classes
- Algorithm classes

Interfaces represent specific types of collections in the framework. There is one interface defined for every type of collection; for example, the `List<E>` interface represents a list, the `Set<E>` interface represents a set, the `Map<K,V>` interface represents a map, etc. Using an interface to define a collection (rather than a class) has the following advantages:

- Your code, which is written using interfaces, is not tied to any specific implementation.
- Classes that implement collections defined by interfaces may be changed without forcing you to change your code that was written using interfaces.
- You can have your own implementation for a collection interface to suit specific needs.

The Collections framework provides implementations of collection interfaces, which are called implementation classes. You need to create objects of these classes to have a collection. It is advised to write code using interfaces, rather than using their implementation classes. The following snippet of code shows how to use the implementation class `ArrayList<E>` to create a list and store the reference in a variable of the type `List` that is the interface representing a list:

```
// Create a list of strings using ArrayList as the implementation class
List<String> names = new ArrayList<>();

// Work with the names variable here onward
```

■ **Note** The parameter `E` in all collections types stands for element type in the collections. The type parameters in maps are named `K` and `V`, which stand for type of keys and type of values in the map, respectively.

Sometimes you need to perform different actions on a collection, such as searching through a collection, converting a collection of one type to another type, copying elements from one collection to another, sorting elements of a collection in a specific order, etc. The algorithm classes let you apply these kinds of algorithms to your collections.

Typically, you do not need to develop interfaces or classes in any of these three categories. The Collections framework provides you with all the interfaces and classes you need. You can choose from a variety of collection interfaces and their implementations. Figure 12-2 shows the interfaces that define collections. I discuss each type of collection in detail in subsequent sections.

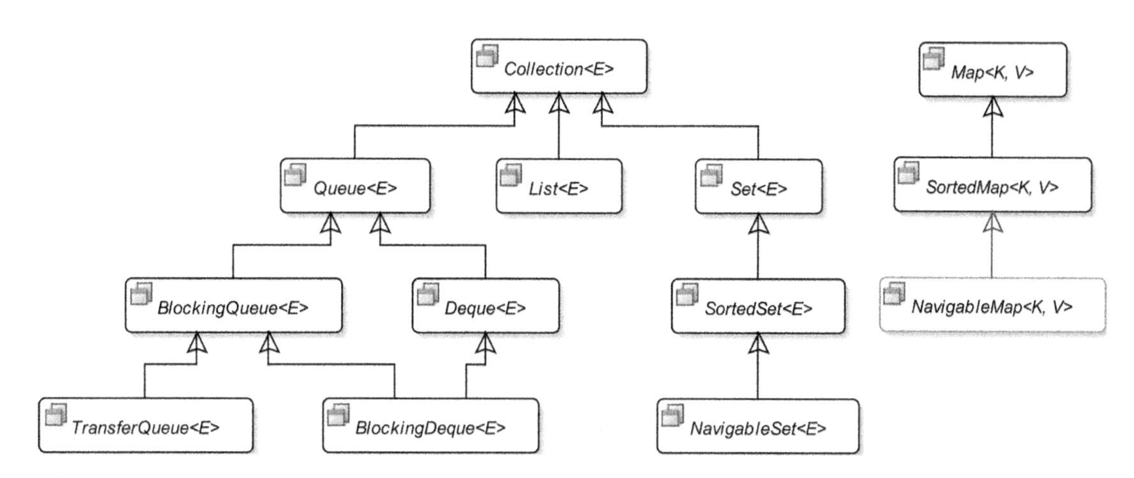

Figure 12-2. *A class diagram, including most interfaces in the Collections framework*

The Collection<E> Interface

The `Collection<E>` interface is the root of the collection interface hierarchy. It defines a generic collection. The Collections framework does not provide an implementation for the `Collection` interface. This is the most generic type of collection. You can use it as an argument type in methods, where you do not care about the collection type of the argument, provided it isn't a map. It declares methods that are inherited by other types of collection interfaces. Non-map collection interfaces inherit from the `Collection` interface and add methods of their own to provide functionalities that are specific to their types. Methods of the `Collection` interface may be classified into the following categories:

- Methods for basic operations
- Methods for bulk (or group) operations
- Methods for aggregate operations
- Methods for array operations
- Methods for comparison operations

Methods in the `Collection` interface are further classified as *optional* and *required*. An implementation class is not required to provide an implementation for the optional methods. If an implementation class chooses not to provide an implementation for optional methods, those methods must throw an `UnsupportedOperationException`.

Methods for Basic Operations

Methods for basic operations let you perform basic operations on a collection such as getting its size (number of elements), adding a new element to it, removing an element from it, checking if an object is an element of this collection, checking if the collection is empty, etc. Some of the methods in the `Collection` interface in this category are as follows:

- `int size()`: Returns the number of elements in the collection.
- `boolean isEmpty()`: Returns `true` if the collection is empty. Otherwise, it returns `false`. This acts the same as checking `size()` for zero.

- `boolean contains(Object o)`: Returns `true` if the collection contains the specified object. Otherwise, it returns `false`.
- `boolean add(E o)`: Adds an element to the collection. It returns `true` if the collection changed. Otherwise, it returns `false`. If the implementation does not allow duplicate elements in a collection, this method will return `false` when you call it with an element that is already in the collection. If a collection is size-constrained and there is no space, the method throws an `IllegalStateException`.
- `boolean remove(Object o)`: Removes the specified object from the collection. Returns `true` if the collection changed because of this call. Otherwise, it returns `false`.
- `Iterator<E> iterator()`: Returns an iterator that can be used to traverse elements in the collection.

Methods for Bulk Operations

Methods for bulk operations let you perform operations on a collection that involves a group of objects such as removing all elements from it, checking if a collection contains all elements from another collection, adding all elements of a collection to another collection, etc. Some of the methods in the `Collection` interface in this category are as follows:

- `boolean addAll(Collection<? extends E> c)`: Adds all elements of the specified collection to this collection. Returns `true` if the collection changes because of this call. Otherwise, it returns `false`.
- `void clear()`: Removes all elements of the collection.
- `boolean containsAll(Collection<?> c)`: Returns `true` if all the elements in the specified collection are also elements of the collection. Otherwise, it returns `false`.
- `boolean removeAll(Collection<?> c)`: Removes all elements from the collection that are elements of the specified collection. Returns `true` if the collection changed as a result of this call. Otherwise, it returns `false`.
- `boolean retainAll(Collection<?> c)`: Retains only those elements that are also elements of the specified collection. That is, it will remove all elements from the collection that are not elements of the specified collection. Returns `true` if the collection changes as a result of this call. Otherwise, it returns `false`.

Methods for Aggregate Operations

Java 8 added support for aggregate operations on collections through streams. A stream is a sequence of elements that supports sequential and parallel aggregate operations such as computing the sum of all elements of a collection whose elements are integers. Streams are a vast topic and I discuss them in Chapter 13. A stream is an instance of the `Stream` interface, which is in the `java.util.stream` package. You can create a `Stream` instance from a collection using the following methods of the `Collection` interface:

- `default Stream<E> stream()`: Returns a sequential `Stream` with the collection as the source of elements for the `Stream`.
- `default Stream<E> parallelStream()`: Returns a possibly parallel `Stream` with the collection as the source of elements for the `Stream`.

Methods for Array Operations

Methods for array operations let you convert a collection into an array. The following are the methods in this category:

- `Object[] toArray()`: Returns the elements of the collections in an array.
- `<T> T[] toArray(T[] a)`: Returns an array of the specified type `T` that contains all elements of the collection. If the specified array's length is equal to or greater than the size of the collection, all elements are copied to the specified array and the same array is returned. Any extra elements in the array are set to null. Otherwise, it creates a new array of type `T` whose length is equal to the size of the collection, copies all elements of the collection to the new array, and returns the new array.

Methods for Comparison Operations

Methods for comparison operations let you compare two collections for equality. The following are the methods in this category:

- `boolean equals(Object o)`: Returns `true` if two collections are equal. Otherwise, it returns `false`. The specific collection type specifies the criteria for equality of two collections.
- `int hashCode()`: Returns the hash code for the collection. Suppose `c1` and `c2` are references of two collections. If `c1.equals(c2)` returns `true`, `c1.hashCode() == c2.hashCode()` must also return `true`.

A Quick Example

Before I discuss different types of collections, I present a quick example of using a list that is a collection of objects. A list is an ordered collection of objects. An instance of the `List<E>` interface represents a list. The `ArrayList<E>` class is an implementation of the `List<E>` interface. The program in Listing 12-2 creates a list to store names and manipulates the list using different methods of the `Collection` interface.

The program uses the `add()` method to add some names to the list. It uses the `remove()` method to remove a name from the list. The `clear()` method is used to remove all names from the list. At every stage, the program prints the size of the list and the elements in the list.

■ **Tip** The `toString()` method of the list (and all types of collections) returns a comma-separated list of elements enclosed in brackets. If a collection is empty, an empty pair of brackets ([]) is returned. The string is very useful for debugging purposes, provided each element has a reasonable `toString()` implementation.

Listing 12-2. Using a List to Store Names

```
// NamesList.java
package com.jdojo.collections;

import java.util.ArrayList;
import java.util.List;
```

```
public class NamesList {
    public static void main(String[] args) {
        // Create a list of strings
        List<String> names = new ArrayList<>();

        // Print the list details
        System.out.printf("After creation: Size = %d, Elements = %s%n",
                names.size(), names);

        // Add some names to the list
        names.add("Ken");
        names.add("Lee");
        names.add("Joe");

        // Print the list details
        System.out.printf("After adding 3 elements: Size = %d, Elements = %s%n",
                names.size(), names);

        // Remove Lee from the list
        names.remove("Lee");

        // Print the list details
        System.out.printf("After removing 1 element: Size = %d, Elements = %s%n",
                names.size(), names);

        // Clear all elements
        names.clear();

        // Print the list details
        System.out.printf("After clearing all elements: Size = %d, Elements = %s%n",
                names.size(), names);
    }
}
```

```
After creation: Size = 0, Elements = []
After adding 3 elements: Size = 3, Elements = [Ken, Lee, Joe]
After removing 1 element: Size = 2, Elements = [Ken, Joe]
After clearing all elements: Size = 0, Elements = []
```

Traversing Elements in Collections

Most often, you need to access all elements of a collection one at a time. Different types of collections store their elements differently. Some collections impose ordering on their elements and some do not. The Collections framework provides the following ways to traverse a collection:

- Using an `Iterator`
- Using a `for-each` loop
- Using the `forEach()` method

■ **Tip** Some collections, such as lists, assign each element an index and they let you access their elements using indexes. You can traverse those collections using a regular `for` loop statement as well.

Using an Iterator

A collection provides an iterator to iterate over all its elements. Sometimes an iterator is also known as a *generator* or a *cursor*. An iterator lets you perform the following three operations on a collection:

- Check if there are elements that have not been yet accessed using this iterator.
- Access the next element in the collection.
- Remove the last accessed element of the collection.

■ **Note** The meaning of the term "next element" of a collection depends on the collection type. The iterator itself does not impose any ordering in which it returns the elements from a collection. However, if the collection imposes ordering on its elements, the iterator will maintain the same ordering. In general, the "next element" means any element in the collection that has not been returned by this iterator yet.

An iterator in Java is an instance of the `Iterator<E>` interface. You can get an iterator for a collection using the `iterator()` method the `Collection` interface. The following snippet of code creates a list of strings and gets an iterator for the list:

```
// Create a list of strings
List<String> names = new ArrayList<>();

// Get an iterator for the list
Iterator<String> nameIterator = names.iterator();
```

The `Iterator<E>` interface contains the following methods:

- `boolean hasNext()`
- `E next()`
- `default void remove()`
- `default void forEachRemaining(Consumer<? super E> action)`

The `hasNext()` method returns `true` if there are more elements in the collection to iterate. Otherwise, it returns `false`. Typically, you call this method before asking the iterator for the next element from the collection.

The `next()` method returns the next element from the collection. You should always call the `hasNext()` method before calling the `next()` method. If you call the `next()` method and the iterator has no more elements to return, it throws a `NoSuchElementException`.

Typically, the hasNext() and next() methods are used together in a loop. The following snippet of code prints all elements of a list using an iterator:

```
List<String> names = /* get a list */;

// Get an iterator for the list
Iterator<String> nameIterator = names.iterator();

// Iterate over all elements in the list
while(nameIterator.hasNext()) {
    // Get the next element from the list
    String name = nameIterator.next();

    // Print the name
    System.out.println(name);
}
```

The remove() method removes the element of the collection that was returned from the last call to the next() method of the iterator. The remove() method can be called only once per call to the next() method. If the remove() method is called more than once per next() method call or before the first call to the next() method, an IllegalStateException is thrown. The support for the remove() method is optional. Calling the remove() method of an iterator may throw an UnsupportedOperationException if the iterator does not support the remove operation.

The following snippet of code iterates over all elements of a list using an iterator and removes the element using the remove() method of the iterator if the element is only two characters long:

```
List<String> names = /* get a list */;

// Get an iterator for the list
Iterator<String> nameIterator = names.iterator();

// Iterate over all elements in the list
while(nameIterator.hasNext()) {
    String name = nameIterator.next();

    // Remove the name if it is two characters
    if (name.length() == 2) {
        nameIterator.remove();
    }
}
```

The forEachRemaining() method takes an action on each element of the collection that has not been accessed by the iterator yet. The action is specified as a Consumer. You can use the following snippet of code to print all elements of a list:

```
List<String> names = /* get a list */;

// Get an iterator for the list
Iterator<String> nameIterator = names.iterator();

// Print the names in the list
nameIterator.forEachRemaining(System.out::println);
```

The code uses method reference `System.out::println` as a `Consumer` for the `forEachRemaining()` method. Notice that using the `forEachRemaining()` method helps shorten the code by eliminating the need for a loop using the `hasNext()` and `next()` methods. Refer to Chapter 5 for more on using the `Consumer` interface and method references.

Listing 12-3 contains a complete program that uses an iterator and the `forEachRemaining()` of the iterator to print all elements of a list to the standard output.

Listing 12-3. Using an Iterator to Iterate Over Elements of a List

```
// NameIterator.java
package com.jdojo.collections;

import java.util.ArrayList;
import java.util.List;

public class NameIterator {
    public static void main(String[] args) {
        // Create a list of strings
        List<String> names = new ArrayList<>();

        // Add some names to the list
        names.add("Ken");
        names.add("Lee");
        names.add("Joe");

        // Print all elements of the names list
        names.iterator()
             .forEachRemaining(System.out::println);
    }
}
```

```
Ken
Lee
Joe
```

The Collections framework supports fail-fast concurrent iterators. You can obtain multiple iterators for a collection and all of them can be used to iterate over the same collection concurrently. If the collection is modified by any means, except using the `remove()` method of the same iterator after the iterator is obtained, the attempt to access the next element using the iterator will throw a `ConcurrentModificationException`. It means that you can have multiple iterators for a collection; however, all iterators must be accessing (reading) elements of the collection. If any of the iterators modify the collection using its `remove()` method, the iterator that modifies the collection will be fine and all other iterators will fail. If the collection is modified outside of all iterators, all iterators will fail.

■ **Tip** An `Iterator` is a one-time object. You cannot reset an iterator. It cannot be reused to iterate over the elements of the collection. If you need to iterate over the elements of the same collection again, you need to obtain a new `Iterator` calling the `iterator()` method of the collection.

Using a for-each Loop

You can use the `for-each` loop to iterate over elements of a collection that hides the logic to set up an iterator for a collection. The general syntax for the `for-each` loop is as follows:

```
Collection<T> yourCollection = /* get a collection */;

for(T element : yourCollection) {
    /* The body of the for-each loop is executed once for each element in yourCollection.
       Each time the body code is executed, the element variable holds the reference of the
       current element in the collection.
    */
}
```

■ **Tip** You can use the `for-each` loop to iterate over any collection whose implementation class implements the `Iterable` interface. The `Collection` interface inherits from the `Iterable` interface, and therefore, you can use the `for-each` loop with all types of collections that implement the `Collection` interface. The `Map` collection type does not inherit from the `Iterable` interface, and therefore, you cannot use the `for-each` loop to iterate over entries in a `Map`.

The `for-each` loop is simple and compact. Behind the scenes, it gets the iterator for your collection and calls the `hasNext()` and `next()` methods for you. You can iterate over all elements of a list of strings as follows:

```
List<String> names = /* get a list */;

// Print all elements of the list using a for-each loop
for(String name : names) {
    System.out.println(name);
}
```

Listing 12-4 contains the complete program that shows how to use the `for-each` loop to iterate over elements of a list of strings. The program is simple and self-explanatory.

Listing 12-4. Using a for-each Loop to Iterate Over Elements of a List

```
// ForEachLoop.java
package com.jdojo.collections;

import java.util.ArrayList;
import java.util.List;

public class ForEachLoop {
    public static void main(String[] args) {
        // Create a list of strings
        List<String> names = new ArrayList<>();

        // Add some names to the list
        names.add("Ken");
        names.add("Lee");
```

```
        names.add("Joe");

        // Print all elements of the names list
        for(String name : names) {
            System.out.println(name);
        }
    }
}
```

```
Ken
Lee
Joe
```

The for-each loop is not a replacement for using an iterator. The compactness of the for-each loop wins over using an iterator in most use-cases. The for-each loop has several limitations, however.

You cannot use the for-each loop everywhere you can use an iterator. For example, you cannot use the for-each loop to remove elements from the collection. The following snippet of code throws a ConcurrentModificationException exception:

```
List<String> names = get a list;
for(String name : names) {
    // Throws a ConcurrentModificationException
    names.remove(name);
}
```

Another limitation of the for-each loop is that you must traverse from the first element to the last element of the collection. It provides no way to start from the middle of the collection. The for-each loop provides no way to visit the previously visited elements, which is allowed by the iterator of some collection types such as lists.

Using the forEach() Method

The Iterable<T> interface contains a new forEach(Consumer<? super T> action) method that you can use in all collection types that inherit from the Collection interface. The method iterates over all elements and applies the action. It works similarly to the forEachRemaining(Consumer<? super E> action) method of the Iterator interface with a difference that the Iterable.forEach() method iterates over all elements, whereas the Iterator.forEachRemaining() method iterates over the elements in the collections that have not yet been retrieved by the Iterator.

■ **Note** Using an Iterator is the fundamental (and a little cumbersome) way of iterating over elements of a collection. It has existed since the beginning of the Java programming language. All other ways, such as the for-each loop, the forEach() method, and the forEachRemaining() method, are syntactic sugar for the Iterator. Internally, they all use an Iterator.

Listing 12-5 shows how to use the forEach() method to print all elements of a list of strings. Notice that using the forEach() method is the most compact way of iterating over elements of a collection.

Listing 12-5. Using the forEach() Method of the Iterable Interface to Iterate Over Elements of a List

```
// ForEachMethod.java
package com.jdojo.collections;

import java.util.ArrayList;
import java.util.List;

public class ForEachMethod {
    public static void main(String[] args) {
        // Create a list of strings
        List<String> names = new ArrayList<>();

        // Add some names to the list
        names.add("Ken");
        names.add("Lee");
        names.add("Joe");

        // Print all elements of the names list
        names.forEach(System.out::println);
    }
}
```

```
Ken
Lee
Joe
```

Using Different Types of Collections

In this section, I discuss different types of collections and their variants, such as sets, lists, queues, maps, etc.

Working with Sets

A set is mathematical concept that represents a collection of unique objects. In mathematics, the ordering of elements in a set is irrelevant. The Collections framework offers three types of sets:

- Mathematical set
- Sorted set
- Navigable set

The following sections cover all types of sets in detail.

Mathematical Set

The `Set<E>` interface models a *set* in mathematics. In mathematics, a set is a collection of unique elements. That is, a set cannot contain duplicate elements. Java allows at most one `null` element in a `Set` because one `null` element is still distinguishable from all other non-null elements and thus, it is unique. Further, the ordering of the elements in a mathematical set is not important. Java follows the same rule; it does not guarantee the ordering of the elements in a `Set`. You can add elements to a `Set` in one order, and when you retrieve them, they may be supplied back in a different order. The only guarantee is that when looping through all elements of a `Set`, you get each element in the `Set` once.

The Collections framework provides the HashSet<E> class as an implementation for the Set<E> interface. The following snippet of code creates a Set<String> and adds three elements to it:

```
Set<String> names = new HashSet<>();
names.add("John");
names.add("Donna");
names.add("Ken");
names.add("Ken"); // Duplicate!!! Has no effect
```

Notice the last statement in the previous snippet of code adds the same name Ken again, which has no effect because the Ken element already exists in the Set.

It is often necessary to create and initialize a Set with a small number of elements. Until Java 9, you did not have the ability to create and initialize a Set at the same time. Notice in the previous snippet of code that you have to write four lines of code to create a Set and add three elements to it.

Java 9 added a static factory method named of() in the Set interface. The method is overloaded. It accepts no elements to any number of elements. One of the versions of the of() method accepts a varargs argument. It creates a Set, adds all specified elements, and returns the reference of the Set. The following statement uses the static of() method of the Set interface to create a Set and initialize it with three elements:

```
// Create an immutable Set of three names
Set<String> names = Set.of("John", "Donna", "Ken");
```

The following statement creates an immutable empty Set:

```
// Create an immutable Set of three names
Set<String> emptyNames = Set.of();
```

Tip The static of() method of the Set interface creates an immutable Set. An attempt to modify the Set throws an UnsupportedOperationException. Unlike the add() method, the of() method throws an IllegalArgumentException if you specify duplicate elements. Unlike the add() method, the of() method throws a NullPointerException if you add a null element. The implementation of the of() method is highly optimized and it is the preferred way of creating an immutable Set with known elements.

Listing 12-6 demonstrates how to create a Set and add elements to it. Note that you can attempt to add duplicate elements to a Set and they are ignored silently. Two elements in a Set are considered equal if comparing them using the equals() method returns true. You may get different output containing the same elements in the Set in a different order.

Listing 12-6. Using the Set Interface with HashSet as Its Implementation Class

```
// SetTest.java
package com.jdojo.collections;

import java.util.HashSet;
import java.util.Set;
```

```
public class SetTest {
    public static void main(String[] args) {
        // Create a set
        Set<String> s1 = new HashSet<>();

        // Add a few elements
        s1.add("John");
        s1.add("Donna");
        s1.add("Ken");
        s1.add("Ken"); // Duplicate!!! No effect

        // Create another set by copying s1
        Set<String> s2 = new HashSet<>(s1);

        // Add a few more elements
        s2.add("Ellen");
        s2.add("Sara");
        s2.add(null); // one null is fine
        s2.add(null); // Duplicate!!! No effect

        // Create an immutable Set using the Set.of() method
        Set<String> s3 = Set.of("Corky", "Paul", "Tom");

        // Create an empty immutable Set using the Set.of() method
        Set<String> s4 = Set.of();

        // Print the sets
        System.out.println("s1: " + s1);
        System.out.println("s1.size(): " + s1.size());

        System.out.println("s2: " + s2);
        System.out.println("s2.size(): " + s2.size());

        System.out.println("s3: " + s3);
        System.out.println("s3.size(): " + s3.size());

        System.out.println("s4: " + s4);
        System.out.println("s4.size(): " + s4.size());
    }
}
```

```
s1: [Donna, Ken, John]
s1.size(): 3
s2: [null, Ellen, Donna, Ken, John, Sara]
s2.size(): 6
s3: [Paul, Corky, Tom]
s3.size(): 3
s4: []
s4.size(): 0
```

I used the toString() method of the Set instances to print the elements of the Set. In a real-world application, you would use an iterator, a for-each loop, or the forEach() method of the Set, as shown:

```
// Create a Set and print its elements using the forEach method
Set<String> names = Set.of(new String[] {"John", "Donna", "Ken"});
names.forEach(System.out::println);
```

```
Ken
Donna
John
```

The Collections framework offers the LinkedHashSet<E> class as another implementation class for the Set<E> interface. The class adds one feature over the HashSet implementation. The HashSet implementation does not guarantee the ordering of elements during iteration. The LinkedHashSet implementation guarantees that the iterator of a Set will return the elements in the same order the elements were inserted (insertion order).

I discuss maintaining ordering of elements in a Set in the next section when I discuss SortedSet. The LinkedHashSet class provides insertion ordering without incurring any overhead.

■ **Tip** A Set has a very useful application. You can use it when you are supplied with an unknown number of objects and you have to keep only unique objects. You can create a Set and add all the objects to it. It will keep only unique objects and ignore the duplicate ones. At the end, you will have only unique objects in your Set.

You can perform *union, intersection,* and *difference* (or *minus*) operations on mathematical sets. You can perform the same operations on sets in Java. For discussing these operations, I assume that you have two sets called s1 and s2. The union of two sets (written as s1 U s2 in mathematics) contains elements from both sets with no duplicates. The intersection of two sets (written as s1 - s2 in mathematics) contains elements that are common to both sets. The difference of two sets, s1 and s2 (written as s1 - s2), is a set that contains all elements of s1 that are not in s2. Here is how you perform these Set operations:

```
// Union of s1 and s2 will be stored in s1
s1.add(s2);

// Intersection of s1 and s2 will be stored in s1
s1.retainAll(s2);

// Difference of s1 and s2 will be stored in s1
s1.removeAll(s2);
```

Note that during the Set operations such as union, intersection, and difference, the set on which you perform the operation is modified. For example, s1 is modified if you perform s1.addAll(s2) to compute the union of s1 and s2. If you want to compute the union of two sets and keep the original set unchanged, you must make a copy of the original set before you perform the union operation, like so:

```
/* Compute the union of two sets by keeping the original set unchanged */
// Make a copy of s1
Set s1Unions2 = new HashSet(s1);
```

```
// Now, s1Unions2 is the union of s1 and s2 and both s1 and s2 are unchanged
s1Unions2.addAll(s2);
```

In mathematics, you can test if the set s1 is a subset of another set s2. Set s1 is a subset of set s2 if set s2 contains all elements that are also present in set s1. You can use the s2.containsAll(s1) method to test if s1 is a subset of s2. This method will return true if s1 is a subset of s2. Otherwise, it will return false.

Listing 12-7 demonstrates how to use the Set interface to perform mathematical set operations.

Listing 12-7. Performing Mathematical Set Operations Using the Set Interface

```
// SetOperations.java
package com.jdojo.collections;

import java.util.HashSet;
import java.util.Set;

public class SetOperations {
    public static void main(String[] args) {
        // Create a set
        Set<String> s1 = new HashSet<>();
        s1.add("John");
        s1.add("Donna");
        s1.add("Ken");

        // Create another set
        Set<String> s2 = new HashSet<>();
        s2.add("Ellen");
        s2.add("Sara");
        s2.add("Donna");

        //Print  the elements of both sets
        System.out.println("s1: " + s1);
        System.out.println("s2: " + s2);

        // Perform set operations
        performUnion(s1, s2);
        performIntersection(s1, s2);
        performDifference(s1, s2);
        testForSubset(s1, s2);
    }

    public static void performUnion(Set<String> s1, Set<String> s2) {
        Set<String> s1Unions2 = new HashSet<>(s1);
        s1Unions2.addAll(s2);
        System.out.println("s1 union s2: " + s1Unions2);
    }

    public static void performIntersection(Set<String> s1, Set<String> s2) {
        Set<String> s1Intersections2 = new HashSet<>(s1);
        s1Intersections2.retainAll(s2);
        System.out.println("s1 intersection s2: " + s1Intersections2);
    }
```

```
    public static void performDifference(Set<String> s1, Set<String> s2) {
        Set<String> s1Differences2 = new HashSet<>(s1);
        s1Differences2.removeAll(s2);

        Set<String> s2Differences1 = new HashSet<>(s2);
        s2Differences1.removeAll(s1);

        System.out.println("s1 difference s2: " + s1Differences2);
        System.out.println("s2 difference s1: " + s2Differences1);
    }

    public static void testForSubset(Set<String> s1, Set<String> s2) {
        System.out.println("s2 is subset s1: " + s1.containsAll(s2));
        System.out.println("s1 is subset s2: " + s2.containsAll(s1));
    }
}
```

```
s1: [Donna, Ken, John]
s2: [Ellen, Donna, Sara]
s1 union s2: [Ellen, Donna, Ken, John, Sara]
s1 intersection s2: [Donna]
s1 difference s2: [Ken, John]
s2 difference s1: [Ellen, Sara]
s2 is subset s1: false
s1 is subset s2: false
```

In this example, I kept the two original sets, s1 and s2, unmodified inside methods that performed some operations on these two sets. However, they could have been modified inside any of these methods. It is not wise to pass a collection to a method like the way I did in this example if you do not want the method to modify your collection. The Collections framework offers a way to get an unmodifiable view of a collection using the java.util.Collections class. I discuss this class and all other features that it offers later in this chapter. The Collections.unmodifiableSet(s1) method will return the unmodifiable version of the s1 set. An attempt to modify an unmodifiable collection results in an UnsupportedOperationException.

Sorted Set

A sorted set is a set that imposes ordering on its elements. An instance of the SortedSet<E> interface represents a sorted set. The SortedSet<E> interface inherits from the Set<E> interface.

The elements in a SortedSet can be sorted in a natural order or using a Comparator. A SortedSet must know how to sort its elements as they are added. The sorted set relies on two things to sort its elements:

- If its elements implement the Comparable interface, it will use the compareTo() method of elements to sort them. This is called sorting in natural order.
- You can supply a Comparator to use a custom sorting. The implementation class for SortedSet is recommended to provide a constructor that will accept a Comparator to use a custom sorting. If a Comparator is specified, the Comparator is used for sorting irrespective of the elements implementing the Comparable interface.

What would happen if the class of the elements of a SortedSet does not implement the Comparable interface and you don't supply a Comparator object? The answer is that, in such cases, you cannot add any elements to a SortedSet. Attempting to add an element results in a ClassCastException.

The TreeSet<E> class is one of the predefined implementation classes for the SortedSet interface in the Collections framework.

The String class implements the Comparable interface. If you are storing only strings in a SortedSet, its elements will be sorted using the natural order using the compareTo() method of the String class. Listing 12-8 demonstrates the use of SortedSet, which uses the natural order to sort its elements.

Listing 12-8. Using a SortedSet That Uses Natural Ordering to Sort Its Elements

```
// SortedSetTest.java
package com.jdojo.collections;

import java.util.SortedSet;
import java.util.TreeSet;

public class SortedSetTest {
    public static void main(String[] args) {
        // Create a sorted set of some names
        SortedSet<String> sortedNames = new TreeSet<>();
        sortedNames.add("John");
        sortedNames.add("Adam");
        sortedNames.add("Eve");
        sortedNames.add("Donna");

        // Print the sorted set of names
        System.out.println(sortedNames);
    }
}
```

```
[Adam, Donna, Eve, John]
```

Let's discuss a real-world example in which you want to store a list of people in a SortedSet. Listing 12-9 contains the code for a Person class. It does not implement the Comparable interface. I use the objects of the Person class in a SortedSet to demonstrate custom sorting.

Listing 12-9. A Person Class

```
// Person.java
package com.jdojo.collections;

public class Person {
    private int id;
    private String name;

    public Person(int id, String name) {
        this.id = id;
        this.name = name;
    }

    public int getId() {
        return id;
    }
```

```
    public void setId(int id) {
        this.id = id;
    }

    public String getName() {
        return name;
    }

    public void setName(String name) {
        this.name = name;
    }

    @Override
    public boolean equals(Object o) {
        if (!(o instanceof Person)) {
            return false;
        }

        // id must be the same for two Persons to be equal
        Person p = (Person) o;

        return this.id == p.getId();
    }

    @Override
    public int hashCode() {
        // A trivial implementation
        return this.id;
    }

    @Override
    public String toString() {
        return "(" + id + ", " + name + ")";
    }
}
```

You cannot add a Person in a SortedSet unless you also supply a Comparator object. The following code throws a ClassCastException:

```
Set<Person> persons = new TreeSet<>();
persons.add(new Person(1, "John"));
persons.add(new Person(2, "Donna"));
```

The following snippet of code creates a SortedSet of persons using a Comparator that sorts the persons using their names:

```
SortedSet<Person> personsSortedByName = new TreeSet<>(Comparator.
comparing(Person::getName));
```

The code uses a method reference to create a lambda expression for creating the Comparator object. Refer to Chapter 5 for more details on the lambda expressions and method references.

If you add two Person objects to the personsSortedByName sorted set with the same name, the second one will be ignored because the supplied Comparator compares names of two Person objects for equality.

```
personsSortedByName.add(new Person(1, "John"));
personsSortedByName.add(new Person(2, "Donna"));
personsSortedByName.add(new Person(3, "Donna")); // A duplicate Person. Will be ignored.
```

Listing 12-10 demonstrates how to use a Comparator object to apply custom sorting in a SortedSet. It uses two custom sorting for Person objects, one by id and one by name. The output shows that one SortedSet is sorted by id and another by name.

Listing 12-10. Using Custom Sorting in a SortedSet

```
// SortedSetComparatorTest.java
package com.jdojo.collections;

import java.util.Comparator;
import java.util.SortedSet;
import java.util.TreeSet;

public class SortedSetComparatorTest {
    public static void main(String[] args) {
        // Create a sorted set sorted by id
        SortedSet<Person> personsById
                = new TreeSet<>(Comparator.comparing(Person::getId));

        // Add some persons to the set
        personsById.add(new Person(1, "John"));
        personsById.add(new Person(2, "Adam"));
        personsById.add(new Person(3, "Eve"));
        personsById.add(new Person(4, "Donna"));
        personsById.add(new Person(4, "Donna")); // A duplicate Person

        // Print the set
        System.out.println("People sorted by id:");
        personsById.forEach(System.out::println);

        // Create a sorted set sorted by name
        SortedSet<Person> personsByName
                = new TreeSet<>(Comparator.comparing(Person::getName));
        personsByName.add(new Person(1, "John"));
        personsByName.add(new Person(2, "Adam"));
        personsByName.add(new Person(3, "Eve"));
        personsByName.add(new Person(4, "Donna"));
        personsByName.add(new Person(4, "Kip")); // Not a duplicate person

        System.out.println("\nPeople sorted by name: ");
        personsByName.forEach(System.out::println);
    }
}
```

```
People sorted by id:
(1, John)
(2, Adam)
(3, Eve)
(4, Donna)

People sorted by name:
(2, Adam)
(4, Donna)
(3, Eve)
(1, John)
(4, Kip)
```

Suppose you have a group of strings and you want to remove duplicates and sort them in ascending order of their length. How difficult will it be to achieve this using your current knowledge of collections? The following snippet of code shows how to do this:

```
// Sort the names based on their length
SortedSet<String> names = new TreeSet<>(Comparator.comparing(String::length));
names.add("Ken");
names.add("Lo");
names.add("Ellen");
names.add("Ken"); // A duplicate that is ignored

// Print the unique sorted names
names.forEach(System.out::println);
```

```
Lo
Ken
Ellen
```

The `SortedSet` interface inherits all methods of the `Set` interface; it also adds some more methods to give you access to its subsets. For example, if you want to get a subset of the `SortedSet`, you can use its `subSet(E fromElement, E toElement)` method to get the elements between `fromElement` (inclusive) and `toElement` (exclusive). Listing 12-11 demonstrates how to use some of the methods of the `SortedSet` interface to get a subset of its elements.

Listing 12-11. Accessing Subsets of a SortedSet

```
// SortedSetSubset.java
package com.jdojo.collections;

import java.util.SortedSet;
import java.util.TreeSet;

public class SortedSetSubset {
    public static void main(String[] args) {
        // Create a sorted set of names
        SortedSet<String> names = new TreeSet<>();
        names.add("John");
```

```
        names.add("Adam");
        names.add("Eve");
        names.add("Donna");

        // Print the sorted set
        System.out.println("Sorted Set: " + names);

        // Print the first and last elements in the sorted set
        System.out.println("First: " + names.first());
        System.out.println("Last: " + names.last());

        SortedSet ssBeforeDonna = names.headSet("Donna");
        System.out.println("Head Set Before Donna: " + ssBeforeDonna);

        SortedSet ssBetwenDonnaAndJohn = names.subSet("Donna", "John");
        System.out.println("Subset between Donna and John (exclusive): "
                + ssBetwenDonnaAndJohn);

        // Note the trick "John" + "\0" to include "John" in the subset
        SortedSet ssBetwenDonnaAndJohn2 = names.subSet("Donna", "John" + "\0");
        System.out.println("Subset between Donna and John (Inclusive): "
                + ssBetwenDonnaAndJohn2);

        SortedSet ssDonnaAndAfter = names.tailSet("Donna");
        System.out.println("Subset from Donna onwards: " + ssDonnaAndAfter);
    }
}
```

```
Sorted Set: [Adam, Donna, Eve, John]
First: Adam
Last: John
Head Set Before Donna: [Adam]
Subset between Donna and John (exclusive): [Donna, Eve]
Subset between Donna and John (Inclusive): [Donna, Eve, John]
Subset from Donna onwards: [Donna, Eve, John]
```

How is a null element stored in a SortedSet? If a SortedSet uses natural order (uses the Comparable interface's compareTo() method), adding a null element will throw a NullPointerException. If you use a Comparator to apply the ordering, it is up to you to allow a null element in the SortedSet. If you allow a null element in the SortedSet, you can decide whether the null element will be placed in the beginning or at the end of the sorted set. The following snippet of code creates a SortedSet using a Comparator that places the null element first:

```
// Sort the names based on their length, placing null first
SortedSet<String> names =
    new TreeSet<>(Comparator.nullsFirst(Comparator.comparing(String::length)));

names.add("Ken");
names.add("Lo");
names.add("Ellen");
names.add(null); // Adds a null
```

```
// Print the names
names.forEach(System.out::println);
```

```
null
Lo
Ken
Ellen
```

Navigable Set

A navigable set is a specialized sorted set that lets you work with its subsets in a variety of ways. An instance of the NavigableSet<E> interface represents a navigable set. The NavigableSet interface inherits from the SortedSet interface and defines some additional methods to extend the functionality provided by the SortedSet. It extends SortedSet in the following ways:

- It lets you navigate the set in reverse order. The reverse order is the opposite order in which your SortedSet would be sorted normally. Its descendingSet() method returns a NavigableSet, which is another view of the same NavigableSet in the reverse order. If you modify the original NavigableSet or the one returned from the descendingSet() method, the modifications will be reflected in both sets.
- It adds another version of the three methods headSet(), tailSet(), and subSet() in SortedSet, which accept a boolean flag to include the element at the beginning or the end of the subset boundary.

The NavigableSet interface provides four methods—lower(), floor(), higher(), and ceiling()—to search for an element based on search criteria. The lower() method returns the greatest element in the NavigableSet that is less than the specified element. The floor() method is similar to the lower() method that returns the greatest element in the NavigableSet that is less than or equal to the specified element. The higher() method returns the least element in the NavigableSet that is greater than the specified element. The ceiling() method is similar to the higher() method in that it returns the least element in the NavigableSet that is greater than or equal to a specified element.

It provides two methods, pollFirst() and pollLast(), that retrieve and remove the first and the last element of the NavigableSet, respectively. If the NavigableSet is empty, they return null.

The TreeSet<E> class is one of the implementation classes for the NavigableSet<E> interface. Since a NavigableSet is also a SortedSet and a SortedSet is also a Set, you can use an object of TreeSet as a set, a sorted set, and a navigable set. If you do not need ordering of the elements in a set, you are better off using a HashSet rather than a TreeSet.

Listing 12-12 demonstrates how to use navigable sets. It uses integers as the elements of the NavigableSet because numbers seem to be more intuitive when you perform methods like higher() and lower(). The output shows how a NavigableSet performs all its operations on its elements.

Listing 12-12. Using a NavigableSet to Get a Subset of a Set

```
// NavigableSetTest.java
package com.jdojo.collections;

import java.util.TreeSet;
import java.util.NavigableSet;
```

```
public class NavigableSetTest {
    public static void main(String[] args) {
        // Create a navigable set and add some integers
        NavigableSet<Integer> ns = new TreeSet<>();
        ns.add(1);
        ns.add(2);
        ns.add(3);
        ns.add(4);
        ns.add(5);

        // Get a reverse view of the navigable set
        NavigableSet reverseNs = ns.descendingSet();

        // Print the normal and reverse views
        System.out.println("Normal view of the Set: " + ns);
        System.out.println("Reverse view of the set: " + reverseNs);

        // Get and print a subset of the navigable set
        System.out.println("\nGetting subset of the set");

        NavigableSet threeOrMore = ns.tailSet(3, true);
        System.out.println("3 or more: " + threeOrMore);

        // Search the navigable set
        System.out.println("\nSearching through the set");

        System.out.println("lower(3): " + ns.lower(3));
        System.out.println("floor(3): " + ns.floor(3));
        System.out.println("higher(3): " + ns.higher(3));
        System.out.println("ceiling(3): " + ns.ceiling(3));

        // Poll the navigable set
        System.out.println("\nPolling elements from the set");

        // Poll elements one by one and look at the set
        System.out.println("pollFirst(): " + ns.pollFirst());
        System.out.println("Navigable Set: " + ns);

        System.out.println("pollLast(): " + ns.pollLast());
        System.out.println("Navigable Set: " + ns);

        System.out.println("pollFirst(): " + ns.pollFirst());
        System.out.println("Navigable Set: " + ns);

        System.out.println("pollFirst(): " + ns.pollFirst());
        System.out.println("Navigable Set: " + ns);

        System.out.println("pollFirst(): " + ns.pollFirst());
        System.out.println("Navigable Set: " + ns);
```

```
        // Since the set is empty, polling will return null
        System.out.println("pollFirst(): " + ns.pollFirst());
        System.out.println("pollLast(): " + ns.pollLast());
    }
}
```

```
Normal view of the Set: [1, 2, 3, 4, 5]
Reverse view of the set: [5, 4, 3, 2, 1]

Getting subset of the set
3 or more: [3, 4, 5]

Searching through the set
lower(3): 2
floor(3): 3
higher(3): 4
ceiling(3): 3

Polling elements from the set
pollFirst(): 1
Navigable Set: [2, 3, 4, 5]
pollLast(): 5
Navigable Set: [2, 3, 4]
pollFirst(): 2
Navigable Set: [3, 4]
pollFirst(): 3
Navigable Set: [4]
pollFirst(): 4
Navigable Set: []
pollFirst(): null
pollLast(): null
```

Working with Lists

A *list* is an ordered collection of objects. Sometimes a list is also known as a *sequence*. An instance of the `List<E>` interface represents a list in the Collections framework. A list can have duplicate elements. You can also store multiple `null` values in a list.

The `List` interface inherits from the `Collection` interface. It adds methods to support access to elements of the `List` using indexes. It also allows you to add an element to the end of the `List` or at any position identified by an integer called the *index*. The index of an element in a `List` is zero-based. That is, the first element of the `List` has an index of 0, the second element has an index of 1, and so on. Figure 12-3 shows a `List` with four elements and their indexes.

Index ->	0	1	2	3
Element ->	John	Richard	Donna	Ken

***Figure 12-3.** A pictorial view of a List with four elements*

A List provides the following additional features over a generic collection:

- It provides access to its elements using indexes. You can use its add(int index, E element), addAll(int index, Collection<? extends E> c), get(int index), remove(int index), and set(int index, E element) methods to add, get, remove, and replace its elements using indexes.
- You can search for the position of an element in the List using indexOf(Object o) or lastIndexOf(Object o) methods. The indexOf() method searches for the specified object in the List from the beginning and returns the index of the first occurrence of the object. The lastIndexOf() method does the same, starting from the end of the list. Both methods return -1 if the List does not contain the specified object.
- It provides a method called subList(int fromIndex, int toIndex) that gives you a sub-list of the original list starting at index fromIndex (inclusive) to index toIndex (exclusive). The sub-list is another view of the original list.
- It provides a specialized iterator for its elements, which is an instance of the ListIterator<E> interface. This iterator lets you iterate over its elements in both directions (forward and backward) at the same time. You can get the ListIterator for a List using its listIterator() method. Note that the Iterator returned from the iterator() method of the Collection interface returns a forward-only iterator.

The following are two of many implementation classes for the List interface:

- ArrayList<E>
- LinkedList<E>

An ArrayList is backed up by an array. A LinkedList is backed up by a linked list. An ArrayList performs better if you access (get and set) the elements of the list frequently. Accessing elements in an ArrayList is faster because the index of an element becomes the index in the backing array, and accessing an element from an array is always fast. Adding or removing elements from a list backed by an ArrayList performs slower, unless done from the end, because an ArrayList has to perform an array copy internally to keep the elements in sequence. The LinkedList performs better as compared to ArrayList for adding and removing elements from the middle of the list. However, it is slower for accessing elements of the list, unless at the head of the list.

You can create and add some elements to a list as follows:

```
// Create a list of strings
List<String> nameList = new ArrayList<>();
nameList.add("John");    // Adds John at the index 0
nameList.add("Richard"); // Adds Richard at the index 1
```

The add(E element) method of the List interface appends the element to the end of the List. The remove(Object o) method of List removes the first occurrence of the element from the beginning of the list.

You can also add elements to a List using positional indexes. Note that the index that you use to access any element must be between 0 and size, where size is the size of the List. You can use add(int index, E element) method to insert the specified element at the specified index. For example, nameList.add(1, "Sara") will insert "Sara" at index 1, which is the second element in the List. When you use an index to add an element to a List, the element at the specified index and elements to the right of the specified index are shifted to the right and their indexes are incremented by 1. Suppose you have a List as shown in Figure 12-3 and you execute the following code:

```
// Add an element at index 1
nameList.add(1, "Sara");
```

Now the List will look as shown in Figure 12-4.

Index ->	0	1	2	3	4
Element ->	John	Sara	Richard	Donna	Ken

Figure 12-4. *The resulting List after a new element is added at index 1 in the List*

■ **Tip** A List does not allow inserting an element at any arbitrary index by using the add(int index, E element) method. If the List is empty, you can use only 0 as the index to add the first element to the list. If you have five elements in a List, you must use indexes between 0 and 5 to add a new element to the List. The index from 0 to 4 will insert an element between existing elements. The index of 5 will append the element to the end of the List. This implies that a List must grow sequentially. You cannot have a sparse List such as a List with a first element and tenth element, leaving second to ninth elements non-populated. This is the reason that a List is also known as a *sequence*.

Java 9 added a static factory method named of() in the List interface. The method is overloaded. It accepts no elements to any number of elements. One of the versions of the of() method accepts a varargs argument. It creates a List, adds all specified elements, and returns the reference of the List. The following statement uses the static of() method of the List interface to create a List and initialize it with three elements:

```
// Create an immutable List of three names
List<String> names = List.of("John", "Donna", "Ken");
```

The following statement creates an immutable empty List:

```
// Create an immutable List of three names
List<String> emptyNames = List.of();
```

■ **Tip** The static of() method of the List interface creates an immutable List. An attempt to modify the List throws an UnsupportedOperationException. Unlike the add() method, the of() method throws a NullPointerException if you add a null element to the List. The implementation of the of() method is highly optimized and it is the preferred way of creating an immutable List with known elements.

Listing 12-13 demonstrates how to use a List. It shows how to add, remove, and iterate over its elements using indexes.

Listing 12-13. Using a List with the ArrayList as Its Implementation

```
// ListTest.java
package com.jdojo.collections;

import java.util.List;
import java.util.ArrayList;

public class ListTest {
    public static void main(String[] args) {
        // Create a List and add a few elements
        List<String> list = new ArrayList<>();
        list.add("John");
        list.add("Richard");
        list.add("Donna");
        list.add("Ken");

        System.out.println("List: " + list);

        int count = list.size();
        System.out.println("Size of List: " + count);

        // Print each element with its index
        for(int i = 0; i < count; i++) {
            String element =  list.get(i);
            System.out.printf("list[%d] = %s%n", i, element);
        }

        List<String> subList = list.subList(1, 3);
        System.out.println("Sub List 1(inclusive) to 3(exclusive): " + subList);

        // Remove "Donna" from the list
        list.remove("Donna"); // Same as list.remove(2);
        System.out.println("List after removing Donna: " + list);

        // Create a List using the static factory method of()
        List<String> names = List.of("Li", "Xi", "Bo", "Da", "Fa", "Bo");
        System.out.println("List using List.of() method: " + names);
    }
}
```

```
List: [John, Richard, Donna, Ken]
Size of List: 4
list[0] = John
list[1] = Richard
list[2] = Donna
list[3] = Ken
Sub List 1(inclusive) to 3(exclusive): [Richard, Donna]
List after removing Donna: [John, Richard, Ken]
List using List.of() method: [Li, Xi, Bo, Da, Fa, Bo]
```

A List lets you iterate over its elements using a specialized iterator represented by an instance of the ListIterator interface. The ListIterator interface inherits from the Iterator interface; it adds a few more methods to give you access to elements in the list from the current position in the backward direction. You can get a list iterator for all elements of the list or a sub-list, like so:

```
List<String> list = new ArrayList<>();

// Populate the list here...

// Get a full list iterator
ListIterator<String> fullIterator = list.listIterator();

// Get a list iterator, which will start at index 5 in the forward direction.
// You can iterate to an index that's less than 5 if you choose to.
ListIterator<String> partialIterator = list.listIterator(5);
```

The hasPrevious() method of the ListIterator returns true if there is an element before the current position in the list iterator. To get the previous element, use its previous() method. You can observe that the hasPrevious() and previous() methods do the same work but in the opposite direction of the hasNext() and next() methods. You can also get to the index of the next and previous elements from the current position using its nextIndex() and previousIndex() methods. The ListIterator interface also contains methods to insert, replace, and remove an element at the current position.

■ **Tip** A ListIterator lets you look ahead or look back in a List. If you use its next() method followed by the previous() method, the iterator goes back to the same position. The call to the next() method moves it one index forward and the call to the previous() method moves it one index backward.

Listing 12-14 demonstrates how to use a ListIterator. It iterates over elements of a List, first in the forward direction and then in the backward direction. You do not need to recreate the ListIterator again to iterate in the backward direction.

Listing 12-14. Iterating Over the Elements in a List in Forward and Backward Directions

```
// ListIteratorTest.java
package com.jdojo.collections;

import java.util.List;
import java.util.ListIterator;

public class ListIteratorTest {
    public static void main(String[] args) {
        List<String> list = List.of("John", "Richard", "Donna", "Ken");
        System.out.println("List: " + list);

        // Get the list iterator
        ListIterator<String> iterator = list.listIterator();

        System.out.println();
        System.out.println("List Iterator in the forward direction:");
```

```
        while (iterator.hasNext()) {
            int index = iterator.nextIndex();
            String element = iterator.next();
            System.out.printf("list[%d] = %s%n", index, element);
        }

        System.out.println("\nList Iterator in the backward direction:");

        // Reuse the iterator to iterate from the end to the beginning
        while (iterator.hasPrevious()) {
            int index = iterator.previousIndex();
            String element = iterator.previous();
            System.out.printf("list[%d] = %s%n", index, element);
        }
    }
}
```

```
List: [John, Richard, Donna, Ken]

List Iterator in the forward direction:
list[0] = John
list[1] = Richard
list[2] = Donna
list[3] = Ken

List Iterator in the backward direction:
list[3] = Ken
list[2] = Donna
list[1] = Richard
list[0] = John
```

Working with Queues

A queue is a collection based on the notion of a real-world queue. A queue is a collection of objects on which some kind of processing is applied one element at a time. A queue has two ends, known as the head and tail. In a simple queue, objects are added to the tail and removed from the head; the object added first will be removed first. However, queues can be categorized based on the way they allow insertion and removal of their elements. In this section, I discuss the following types of queues:

- A *simple queue* allows insertion at the tail and removal from the head.
- A *priority queue* associates a priority with every element of the queue and allows the element with the highest priority to be removed next from the queue.
- A *delay queue* associates a delay with every element of the queue and allows for the removal of the element only when its delay has elapsed.
- A *doubly ended queue* allows for insertion and removal of its elements from the head as well as the tail.
- A *blocking queue* blocks the thread that adds elements to it when it is full and it blocks the thread removing elements from it when it is empty.

- A *transfer queue* is a special type of blocking queue where a handoff of an object occurs between two threads (a producer and a consumer).
- A *blocking doubly ended queue* is a combination of a doubly ended queue and a blocking queue.

Simple Queues

Simple queues are represented by an instance of the `Queue<E>` interface. Typically, you hold a group of objects in a queue for some kind of processing that is applied to one element at a time. For example, the line of customers at a counter in a post office is an example of a queue. You can classify a queue based on many criteria.

How many elements can a queue hold? Sometimes you have an unlimited (at least theoretically) number of elements in a queue, and sometimes it has a predefined capacity. When the length of a queue is unlimited, it is called an *unbounded queue*. When the length of the queue is predefined, it is called a *bounded queue*. The bound of a queue defines its behavior when an element is added to a full bounded queue. Attempting to add an element to a full queue may throw an exception; it may fail silently; it may wait indefinitely (or for a predefined time period) for the queue to have room to accommodate the new element, etc. The exact behavior depends on the type of the queue.

Which element of the queue comes out next? A queue always has an entry point and an exit point for its elements. The exit point is called the *head* of the queue and the entry point is called the *tail*. The head and the tail may be the same. If the head and the tail of a queue are the same, it is called a Last In, First Out (`LIFO`) queue. A `LIFO` queue is also known as a *stack*. The head and the tail of a queue may be different. If a queue follows a rule that the element entering the queue first will leave the queue first (first come, first served rule), it is called a First In, First Out (`FIFO`) queue. Have you ever had a chance to stand in a queue for a long time and as soon as your turn comes, another person, who showed up after you, is served before you, based on a priority? Java also has this kind of queue and it is called a *priority queue*. In a priority queue, you define the priority using a `Comparator` or implement the `Comparable` interface in the elements' class, and the next element in the queue to come out is decided based on the priority of the elements in the queue.

■ **Tip** Typically, a `null` element does not make sense in a `Queue`. After all, the purpose of having a queue is to apply some processing logic on its elements or use the elements to perform some logic. In either case, a `null` value does not make sense. It is up to the implementation of the `Queue` interface to allow or disallow `null` values. The use of `null` elements in a queue is not recommended. If you use `null` elements in a queue, you will not be able to distinguish between the `null` value returned from its method to indicate a special situation and the `null` value of the element.

A queue lets you perform three basic operations:

- Add an element to its tail
- Remove an element from its head
- Peek the element at its head

The `Queue` interface defines two methods for each of the three operations. One method throws an exception if the operation is not possible; the other method returns a value (`false` or `null`) to indicate the failure. The method you use to perform the specific operation depends on your requirements. The `Queue` interface adds six methods to provide the functionality of a `FIFO` queue. They are listed in Table 12-1.

Table 12-1. *Additional Methods Declared by the Queue<E> Interface*

Category	Method	Description
Adding an element to the queue	`boolean add(E e)`	Adds an element to the queue if it is possible and returns `true`. Otherwise, it throws an `IllegalStateException`.
	`boolean offer(E e)`	Adds an element to the queue without throwing an exception if the element cannot not be added. It returns `false` on failure and `true` on success. It is the preferred way to add an element in a bounded queue.
Removing an element from the queue	`E remove()`	Retrieves and removes the head of the queue. It throws an exception if the queue is empty.
	`E poll()`	Performs the same job as the `remove()` method. However, it returns `null` if the queue is empty instead of throwing an exception.
Peeking at the head of the queue	`E element()`	Retrieves the head of the queue without removing it from the queue. It throws an exception if the queue is empty.
	`E peek()`	Performs the same job as the `element()` method. However, it returns `null` if the queue is empty instead of throwing an exception.

The `LinkedList<E>` and `PriorityQueue<E>` are two implementation classes for the `Queue<E>` interface. Note that the `LinkedList` class is also the implementation class for the `List` interface. The `LinkedList` class is a multi-purpose collection implementation class. I mention its name a few more times in this chapter.

Listing 12-15 demonstrates how to use a `LinkedList` as a `FIFO` queue. In fact, it is the `Queue` interface that represents a `FIFO` queue. An instance of the `LinkedList` class can be used as a `FIFO` queue or a `LIFO` queue.

Listing 12-15. Using a FIFO Queue Using LinkedList as the Implementation Class

```
// QueueTest.java
package com.jdojo.collections;

import java.util.Queue;
import java.util.LinkedList;
import java.util.NoSuchElementException;

public class QueueTest {
    public static void main(String[] args) {
        Queue<String> queue = new LinkedList<>();
        queue.add("John");

        // offer() will work the same as add()
        queue.offer("Richard");
        queue.offer("Donna");
        queue.offer("Ken");

        System.out.println("Queue: " + queue);
```

```
        // Let’s remove elements until the queue is empty
        while (queue.peek() != null) {
            System.out.println("Head Element: " + queue.peek());
            queue.remove();
            System.out.println("Removed one element from Queue");
            System.out.println("Queue: " + queue);
        }

        // Now Queue is empty. Try  calling the peek(),
        // element(), poll() and remove() methods
        System.out.println("queue.isEmpty(): " + queue.isEmpty());
        System.out.println("queue.peek(): " + queue.peek());
        System.out.println("queue.poll(): " + queue.poll());

        try {
            String str = queue.element();
            System.out.println("queue.element(): " + str);
        } catch (NoSuchElementException e) {
            System.out.println("queue.element(): Queue is empty.");
        }

        try {
            String str = queue.remove();
            System.out.println("queue.remove(): " + str);
        } catch (NoSuchElementException e) {
            System.out.println("queue.remove(): Queue is empty.");
        }
    }
}
```

```
Queue: [John, Richard, Donna, Ken]
Head Element: John
Removed one element from Queue
Queue: [Richard, Donna, Ken]
Head Element: Richard
Removed one element from Queue
Queue: [Donna, Ken]
Head Element: Donna
Removed one element from Queue
Queue: [Ken]
Head Element: Ken
Removed one element from Queue
Queue: []
queue.isEmpty(): true
queue.peek(): null
queue.poll(): null
queue.element(): Queue is empty.
queue.remove(): Queue is empty.
```

How do you create a LIFO queue? An instance of the Stack<E> class represents a LIFO queue. The Stack class was not designed properly. It inherits from the java.util.Vector class. You can roll out your own representation of a LIFO queue using the LinkedList class easily. I discuss the Deque collection interface in the next section and you will see how to use it as a LIFO queue. You will also develop your own LIFO queue.

Priority Queues

A priory queue is a queue in which each element has an associated priority. The element with the highest priority is removed next from the queue. Java provides PriorityQueue<E> as an implementation class for an unbounded priority queue. You can use natural order of the elements of the queue as its priority. In this case, the elements of the queue must implement the Comparable interface. You can also supply a Comparator, which will determine the priority order of the elements. When you add a new element to a priority queue, it is positioned in the queue based on its priority. How the priority is decided in the queue is up to you to implement.

Let's develop a priority queue based on natural ordering of its elements. Let's extend your Person class to implement the Comparable interface. You will call your new class ComparablePerson. The priority of a ComparablePerson will be decided on two criteria, id and name. If the id is higher, its priority is lower. If persons have the same id, the name will be used to decide the priority based on the alphabetical order of the names. Listing 12-16 contains the code for the ComparablePerson class.

Listing 12-16. A ComparablePerson Class

```
// ComparablePerson.java
package com.jdojo.collections;

public class ComparablePerson extends Person implements Comparable<ComparablePerson> {
    public ComparablePerson(int id, String name) {
        super(id, name);
    }

    @Override
    public int compareTo(ComparablePerson cp) {
        int cpId = cp.getId();
        String cpName = cp.getName();

        if (this.getId() < cpId) {
            return -1;
        }

        if (this.getId() > cpId) {
            return 1;
        }

        if (this.getId() == cpId) {
            return this.getName().compareTo(cpName);
        }

        // Should not reach here
        return 0;
    }
}
```

Listing 12-17 demonstrates how to use a priority queue.

Listing 12-17. Using a Priority Queue

```
// PriorityQueueTest.java
package com.jdojo.collections;

import java.util.Queue;
import java.util.PriorityQueue;

public class PriorityQueueTest {
    public static void main(String[] args) {
        Queue<ComparablePerson> pq = new PriorityQueue<>();
        pq.add(new ComparablePerson(1, "John"));
        pq.add(new ComparablePerson(4, "Ken"));
        pq.add(new ComparablePerson(2, "Richard"));
        pq.add(new ComparablePerson(3, "Donna"));
        pq.add(new ComparablePerson(4, "Adam"));

        System.out.println("Priority queue: " + pq);

        while (pq.peek() != null) {
            System.out.println("Head Element: " + pq.peek());
            pq.remove();
            System.out.println("Removed one element from Queue");
            System.out.println("Priority queue: " + pq);
        }
    }
}
```

```
Priority queue: [(1, John), (3, Donna), (2, Richard), (4, Ken), (4, Adam)]
Head Element: (1, John)
Removed one element from Queue
Priority queue: [(2, Richard), (3, Donna), (4, Adam), (4, Ken)]
Head Element: (2, Richard)
Removed one element from Queue
Priority queue: [(3, Donna), (4, Ken), (4, Adam)]
Head Element: (3, Donna)
Removed one element from Queue
Priority queue: [(4, Adam), (4, Ken)]
Head Element: (4, Adam)
Removed one element from Queue
Priority queue: [(4, Ken)]
Head Element: (4, Ken)
Removed one element from Queue
Priority queue: []
```

There is one important thing that you will notice in the output. When you print the queue, its elements are not ordered the way you would expect. You would expect that the element returned by the next call to the peek() method should be at head of the queue. Note that a queue is never used to iterate over its elements. Rather, it is used to remove one element from it, process that element, and then remove another element.

The PriorityQueue class does not guarantee any ordering of the elements when you use an iterator. Its toString() method uses its iterator to give you the string representation of its elements. This is the reason that when we print the priority queue, its elements are not ordered according to their priority. However, when we use the peek() or remove() method, the correct element is peeked at or removed, which is based on the element's priority. In the previous case, id and name are used to order the elements. Therefore, the element with the least id and name (alphabetical order) has the highest priority.

Using a Comparator in a priority queue is easy. You need to specify your Comparator when you create an object of the PriorityQueue class. Listing 12-18 demonstrates how to use a Comparator to have a priority queue for the list of ComparablePerson. It uses the alphabetical ordering of the name of a ComparablePerson as the criterion to determine its priority. The person whose name comes first in the alphabetical order has higher priority.

Listing 12-18. Using a Comparator Object in a Priority Queue

```
// PriorityQueueComparatorTest.java
package com.jdojo.collections;

import java.util.Queue;
import java.util.PriorityQueue;
import java.util.Comparator;

public class PriorityQueueComparatorTest {
    public static void main(String[] args) {
        Comparator<ComparablePerson> nameComparator
                = Comparator.comparing(ComparablePerson::getName);

        // Create a priority queue with a Comparator
        Queue<ComparablePerson> pq = new PriorityQueue<>(nameComparator);
        pq.add(new ComparablePerson(1, "John"));
        pq.add(new ComparablePerson(4, "Ken"));
        pq.add(new ComparablePerson(2, "Richard"));
        pq.add(new ComparablePerson(3, "Donna"));
        pq.add(new ComparablePerson(4, "Adam"));

        System.out.println("Priority queue: " + pq);

        while (pq.peek() != null) {
            System.out.println("Head Element: " + pq.peek());
            pq.remove();
            System.out.println("Removed one element from Queue");
            System.out.println("Priority queue: " + pq);
        }
    }
}
```

```
Priority queue: [(4, Adam), (3, Donna), (2, Richard), (4, Ken), (1, John)]
Head Element: (4, Adam)
Removed one element from Queue
Priority queue: [(3, Donna), (1, John), (2, Richard), (4, Ken)]
Head Element: (3, Donna)
Removed one element from Queue
```

```
Priority queue: [(1, John), (4, Ken), (2, Richard)]
Head Element: (1, John)
Removed one element from Queue
Priority queue: [(4, Ken), (2, Richard)]
Head Element: (4, Ken)
Removed one element from Queue
Priority queue: [(2, Richard)]
Head Element: (2, Richard)
Removed one element from Queue
Priority queue: []
```

Double Ended Queues

A doubly ended queue or deque is an extended version of a queue to allow insertion and removal of elements from both ends (the head and the tail). An instance of the `Deque<E>` interface represents a doubly ended queue. The name `Deque` does not mean opposite of `Queue`. Rather, it means "**D**ouble **e**nded **que**ue". It is pronounced "deck," not "de queue."

The `Deque<E>` interface extends the `Queue<E>` interface. It declares additional methods to facilitate all the operations for a queue at the head as well as at the tail. It can be used as a `FIFO` queue or a `LIFO` queue. You already know what a `Queue` is and how to use it. A `Deque` is just another version of a queue to represent different kinds of queues, not just a `FIFO` queue. All you have to do in this section is learn about the new methods that the `Deque` interface offers. Table 12-2 lists the new methods that are declared in the `Deque` interface to facilitate insertion, removal, and peeking at either end (head or tail) of a `Deque`. In the method names, first means head and last means tail.

Table 12-2. *New Methods in Deque Interface for Insertion, Removal, and Peek Operations at Both Ends*

Category	Method	Description
Adding an element to the `Deque`	`void addFirst(E)` `void addLast(E)`	The `addXxx()` methods add an element at the head or tail, and they throw an exception if an element cannot be added, such as in a full bounded `Deque`.
	`boolean offerFirst(E)` `boolean offerLast(E)`	The `offerXxx()` methods work the same way as the `addXxx()` methods. However, they do not throw an exception on failure. Rather, they return `false` if the specified element cannot be added to a `Deque`.
Removing an element from the `Deque`	`E removeFirst()` `E removeLast()`	The `removeXxx()` methods retrieve and remove the element from the head or tail of the `Deque`. They throw an exception if the `Deque` is empty.
	`E pollFirst()` `E pollLast()`	The `pollXxx()` methods perform the same job as the `removeXxx()` methods. However, they return `null` if the `Deque` is empty.
Peeking at an element at end of the `Deque`	`E getFirst()` `E getLast()`	The `getXxx()` methods retrieve without removing the element at the head or the tail of the `Deque`. They throw an exception if the `Deque` is empty.
	`E peekFirst()` `E peekLast()`	The `peekXxx()` methods perform the same job as the `getXxx()` methods. However, they return `null` if the `Deque` is empty instead of throwing an exception.

Since Deque inherits from Queue, a Deque can also act like a FIFO queue. Table 12-3 compares the methods in the Queue interface and their equivalent methods in the Deque interface.

Table 12-3. *Method Comparison of the Queue and Deque Interfaces*

Method in Queue	Equivalent Method in Deque
add(e)	addLast(e)
offer(e)	offerLast(e)
remove()	removeFirst()
poll()	pollFirst()
element()	getFirst()
peek()	peekFirst()

Since, in a FIFO queue, you always add an element at the tail (or Last), the add() method in the Queue interface does the same thing as what the addLast() method does in the Deque interface.

You can also use a Deque as a stack (a LIFO queue) using familiar methods such as push(), pop(), and peek(). The push() method pushes (or adds) an element to the top of the stack that is the same as using the method addFirst(). The pop() method pops (or removes) the element from the top of the stack that is the same as calling the removeFirst() method. The peek() method retrieves, but does not remove, the element at the top of the stack; if the stack is empty, it returns null. Calling the peek() method is the same as calling the peekFirst() method. A stack needs four methods to perform its operations: isEmpty(), push(), pop(), and peek(). Table 12-4 lists the stack specific methods in the Deque interface and their alternate versions.

Table 12-4. *Deque Methods Named Specifically to be Used with Stacks*

Stack Specific Methods in Deque	Equivalent Alternate Methods in Deque
isEmpty()	Inherited from the Collection interface
push(E e)	addFirst(E e)
pop()	removeFirst()
peek()	peekFirst()

Looking at the methods that you have seen so far in the Deque interface, you can say that it is a huge interface. A programmer can easily get confused if he does not learn this interface by breaking its methods down into separate categories. The Deque interface contains methods that fall into the following four categories:

- Methods that let you insert, remove, and peek elements at the head and tail of the Deque, as listed in Table 12-2. All these methods are sufficient to use a Deque as any queue you want. However, it offers some more methods with different names to accomplish the same thing.
- Methods that let you use a Deque as a FIFO queue (or simply as a Queue). They are listed in Table 12-3.
- Methods that let you use familiar method names that are used with stacks. Note that these methods are not performing anything new other than insertion, removal, and peeking. They just have different names. They are listed in Table 12-4.

- Some utility methods that help you work with a Deque in specific situations. For example, its descendingIterator() method returns an Iterator that lets you iterate over its elements in reverse order (from tail to head). It also adds two methods called removeFirstOccurrence(Object o) and removeLastOccurrence(Object o) that let you remove the first occurrence (starting from the head and going towards the tail) and last occurrence (starting from the tail and going towards the head) of an object in the Deque, respectively. Now you can relax—there are no more new methods in the Deque to learn.

The ArrayDeque<E> and LinkedList<E> classes are two implementation classes for the Deque interface. The ArrayDeque class is backed by an array, whereas the LinkedList class is backed by a linked list. You should use the ArrayDeque as a Deque implementation if you are using a Deque as a LIFO queue (or a stack). The LinkedList implementation performs better if you use a Deque as a FIFO queue (or simply as a Queue).

Listing 12-19 demonstrates how to use a Deque as a FIFO queue. If you compare this program with the program in Listing 12-15, in this program you have just used Deque-specific methods to perform the same thing as what you accomplished with the methods of the Queue interface. Suppose a method accepts an argument of type Queue. If you pass a Deque to that method, your Deque will be used as a FIFO queue inside that method.

Listing 12-19. Using a Deque as a FIFO Queue

```
// DequeAsQueue.java
package com.jdojo.collections;

import java.util.Deque;
import java.util.LinkedList;
import java.util.NoSuchElementException;

public class DequeAsQueue {
    public static void main(String[] args) {
        // Create a Deque and add elements at its tail using
        // addLast() or offerLast() method
        Deque<String> deque = new LinkedList<>();
        deque.addLast("John");
        deque.offerLast("Richard");
        deque.offerLast("Donna");
        deque.offerLast("Ken");

        System.out.println("Deque: " + deque);

        // Let's remove elements from the Deque until it is empty
        while (deque.peekFirst() != null) {
            System.out.println("Head Element: " + deque.peekFirst());
            deque.removeFirst();
            System.out.println("Removed one element from Deque");
            System.out.println("Deque: " + deque);
        }

        // Now, the Deque is empty. Try to call its peekFirst(),
        // getFirst(), pollFirst() and removeFirst() methods
        System.out.println("deque.isEmpty(): " + deque.isEmpty());
```

```
        System.out.println("deque.peekFirst(): " + deque.peekFirst());
        System.out.println("deque.pollFirst(): " + deque.pollFirst());

        try {
            String str = deque.getFirst();
            System.out.println("deque.getFirst(): " + str);
        } catch (NoSuchElementException e) {
            System.out.println("deque.getFirst(): Deque is empty.");
        }

        try {
            String str = deque.removeFirst();
            System.out.println("deque.removeFirst(): " + str);
        } catch (NoSuchElementException e) {
            System.out.println("deque.removeFirst(): Deque is empty.");
        }
    }
}
```

```
Deque: [John, Richard, Donna, Ken]
Head Element: John
Removed one element from Deque
Deque: [Richard, Donna, Ken]
Head Element: Richard
Removed one element from Deque
Deque: [Donna, Ken]
Head Element: Donna
Removed one element from Deque
Deque: [Ken]
Head Element: Ken
Removed one element from Deque
Deque: []
deque.isEmpty(): true
deque.peekFirst(): null
deque.pollFirst(): null
deque.getFirst(): Deque is empty.
deque.removeFirst(): Deque is empty.
```

Listing 12-20 demonstrates how to use a Deque as a stack (or LIFO queue).

Listing 12-20. Using a Deque as a Stack

```
// DequeAsStack.java
package com.jdojo.collections;

import java.util.ArrayDeque;
import java.util.Deque;
```

```
public class DequeAsStack {
    public static void main(String[] args) {
        // Create a Deque and use it as stack
        Deque<String> deque = new ArrayDeque<>();
        deque.push("John");
        deque.push("Richard");
        deque.push("Donna");
        deque.push("Ken");

        System.out.println("Stack: " + deque);

        // Let's remove all elements from the Deque
        while (deque.peek() != null) {
            System.out.println("Element at top: " + deque.peek());
            System.out.println("Popped: " + deque.pop());
            System.out.println("Stack: " + deque);
        }

        System.out.println("Stack is empty: " + deque.isEmpty());
    }
}
```

```
Stack: [Ken, Donna, Richard, John]
Element at top: Ken
Popped: Ken
Stack: [Donna, Richard, John]
Element at top: Donna
Popped: Donna
Stack: [Richard, John]
Element at top: Richard
Popped: Richard
Stack: [John]
Element at top: John
Popped: John
Stack: []
Stack is empty: true
```

Note that even if the Deque provides all the methods that you need to use it as a stack, it does not give a programmer a collection type that can be truly used as a stack. If you need a stack in a method as its argument, you will need to declare it as a Deque type as shown:

```
public class MyClass {
    public void myMethod(Deque stack){
        /* This method is free to use (or misuse) stack argument
           as a FIFO even though it needs only a LIFO queue.
        */
    }
}
```

The myMethod() is passed a Deque when it needs a stack. If you trust myMethod(), it's fine. Otherwise, it can access elements of the Deque in any way the Deque interface allows. It is not limited to use only as a stack. The only way you can stop the user of your Deque to use it only as a stack is to roll out your own interface and an implementation class. The Stack class works as a stack. However, you are advised not to use the Stack class to work with a stack as it has the same problem that you are trying to solve.

You can create an interface named LIFOQueue with four methods: isEmpty(), push(), pop(), and peek(). You can create an implementation class named ArrayLIFOQueue, which implements the LIFOQueue interface. Your ArrayLIFOQueue class will wrap an ArrayDeque object. All of its methods will be delegated to ArrayDeque. And that is all. Note that by creating a new LIFOQueue interface and its implementation, you are diverting from the Collections framework. Your new interface and classes will be outside of the Collections framework. However, if you do need to implement your own version of a data structure that can be used strictly as a stack, you can do so.

There is another way to create a stack from a Deque. You can convert a Deque to a LIFO Queue using the asLifoQueue() static method of the Collections class. The method signature is as follows:

```
public static <T> Queue<T> asLifoQueue(Deque<T> deque)
```

The following snippet of code creates a stack from a Deque:

```
Deque<String> deque = /^ create a Deque */;

// Get a LIFO queue from Deque
Queue<String> stack = Collections.asLifoQueue(deque);

// Now, you can pass around stack reference, which can be used only as a LIFO queue
```

Blocking Queues

You have seen the behavior of a Queue in two extreme cases:

- When you want to add an element to it when it is full
- When you want to remove an element from it when it is empty

A queue specifies two types of methods to deal with insertion, removal, and peeking in these two extreme cases: one type of method throws an exception whereas the other type of method returns a special value.

A blocking queue extends the behavior of a queue in dealing with these extreme cases. It adds two more sets of methods: one set of methods blocks indefinitely and another set of methods lets you specify a time period to block.

An instance of the BlockingQueue<E> interface represents a blocking queue. The BlockingQueue<E> interface inherits from the Queue<E> interface. Here are two additional features that the BlockingQueue interface offers:

- It adds two methods, put() and offer(), to let you add an element to the blocking queue at its tail. The put() method blocks indefinitely if the blocking queue is full until space becomes available in the queue. The offer() method lets you specify the time period to wait for space to become available in the blocking queue. It returns true if the specified element was added successfully; it returns false if the specified time period elapsed before the space became available for the new element.

- It adds two methods, `take()` and `poll()`, to let you retrieve and remove the head from the blocking queue. The `take()` method blocks indefinitely if the blocking queue is empty. The `poll()` method lets you specify a time period to wait if the blocking queue is empty; it returns `null` if the specified time elapses before an element became available.

If you use methods from the `Queue` interface with a `BlockingQueue`, they would behave as if you are using a `Queue`. A `BlockingQueue` is designed to be thread-safe. Usually it is used in a producer/consumer-like situation where some threads (called producers) add elements to it and some threads (called consumers) remove elements from it.

A blocking queue does not allow a `null` element. A blocking queue can be bounded or unbounded. It adds another method called `remainingCapacity()` that returns the number of elements that can be added to the blocking queue without blocking. You need to be careful in basing your decision on the return value of this method. There may be other threads attempting to add elements to the blocking queue at the same time you call this method. In such cases, when you attempt to add new elements based on the return value of this method, your elements may not be added, even though you know that there is some space available. The real test as to whether an element can be added to a blocking queue or not is to attempt to add one and check the return value of the `put()` or `offer()` method.

There is one more thing that is related to a blocking queue: *fairness*. Fairness is used to handle situations where multiple threads are blocked to perform insertion or removal. If a blocking queue is fair, it will allow the longest waiting thread to perform the operation when a condition arises that allows the operation to proceed. If the blocking queue is not fair, the order in which the blocked threads are allowed to perform the operation is not specified. Specific implementations determine fairness availability.

The `BlockingQueue` interface and all its implementation classes are in the `java.util.concurrent` package. The following are the implementation classes for the `BlockingQueue` interface:

- `ArrayBlockingQueue`: It is a bounded implementation class for `BlockingQueue`. It is backed by an array. It also lets you specify the fairness of the blocking queue in its constructor. By default, it is not fair.

- `LinkedBlockingQueue`: It is another implementation class for `BlockingQueue`. It can be used as a bounded or unbounded blocking queue. It does not allow specifying a fairness rule for the blocking queue.

- `PriorityBlockingQueue`: It is an unbounded implementation class for `BlockingQueue`. It works the same way as `PriorityQueue` for ordering the elements in the blocking queue. It adds the blocking feature to `PriorityQueue`.

- `SynchronousQueue`: It is a special type of implementation of `BlockingQueue`. It does not have any capacity. The `put` operation waits for the `take` operation to take the element being put. It facilitates a kind of handshake between two threads. One thread tries to put an element to the blocking queue that must wait until there is a thread that tries to take the element. It facilitates an exchange of an object between two threads. You can also specify the fairness rule for the queue. For all practical purposes, this blocking queue is always empty. It seems to have an element only when there are two threads: one trying to add an element and one trying to remove an element. Its `isEmpty()` method always returns `true`.

- `DelayQueue`: It is another unbounded implementation class for `BlockingQueue`. It allows an element to be taken out only if a specified delay has passed for that element. If there are multiple elements in the blocking queue whose specified delay has passed, the element whose delay passed earliest will be placed at the head of the blocking queue.

Let's start with an example of a producer/consumer application. Listing 12-21 contains the code for a producer. It accepts a blocking queue and a producer name in its constructor. It generates a string and adds it to the blocking queue after waiting for a random number of seconds between 1 and 5. If the blocking queue is full, it will wait until the space is available in the queue.

Listing 12-21. The Producer Class for a Blocking Queue

```
// BQProducer.java
package com.jdojo.collections;

import java.util.concurrent.BlockingQueue;
import java.util.Random;

public class BQProducer extends Thread {
    private final BlockingQueue<String> queue;
    private final String name;
    private int nextNumber = 1;
    private final Random random = new Random();

    public BQProducer(BlockingQueue<String> queue, String name) {
        this.queue = queue;
        this.name = name;
    }

    @Override
    public void run() {
        while (true) {
            try {
                String str = name + "-" + nextNumber;
                System.out.println(name + " is trying to add: "
                        + str + ". Remaining capacity: "
                        + queue.remainingCapacity());
                this.queue.put(str);
                nextNumber++;
                System.out.println(name + " added: " + str);

                // Sleep between 1 and 5 seconds
                int sleepTime = (random.nextInt(5) + 1) * 1000;
                Thread.sleep(sleepTime);
            } catch (InterruptedException e) {
                e.printStackTrace();
                break;
            }
        }
    }
}
```

Listing 12-22 contains code for a consumer. It does the opposite of what a producer does. It removes elements from the blocking queue. If the blocking queue is empty, it waits indefinitely for an element to become available. Both the producer and consumer run in an infinite loop.

Listing 12-22. The Consumer Class for a Blocking Queue

```
// BQConsumer.java
package com.jdojo.collections;

import java.util.concurrent.BlockingQueue;
import java.util.Random;

public class BQConsumer extends Thread {
    private final BlockingQueue<String> queue;
    private final String name;
    private final Random random = new Random();

    public BQConsumer(BlockingQueue<String> queue, String name) {
        this.queue = queue;
        this.name = name;
    }

    @Override
    public void run() {
        while (true) {
            try {
                System.out.println(name + " is trying to take an element. "
                        + "Remaining capacity: "
                        + queue.remainingCapacity());

                String str = this.queue.take();
                System.out.println(name + " took: " + str);

                // Sleep between 1 and 5 seconds
                int sleepTime = (random.nextInt(5) + 1) * 1000;
                Thread.sleep(sleepTime);
            } catch (InterruptedException e) {
                e.printStackTrace();
                break;
            }
        }
    }
}
```

Listing 12-23 creates a bounded and fair blocking queue. It creates one producer and two consumers. Each producer and consumer is created in a separate thread. Partial output has been shown. You will have to stop the application manually. You may experiment with adding more producers or consumers and adjusting their sleep times. Note that the messages printed in the output may not appear in the order that makes sense; this is typical in a multi-threaded program. A thread performs an action and it is preempted before it can print a message stating that it did perform the action. Meanwhile, you will see messages from another thread.

Listing 12-23. A Class to Run the Producer/Consumer Program

```
// BQProducerConsumerTest.java
package com.jdojo.collections;

import java.util.concurrent.BlockingQueue;
import java.util.concurrent.ArrayBlockingQueue;

public class BQProducerConsumerTest {
    public static void main(String[] args) {
        int capacity = 5;
        boolean fair = true;
        BlockingQueue<String> queue = new ArrayBlockingQueue<>(capacity, fair);

        // Create one producer and two consumer and let them produce
        // and consume indefinitely
        new BQProducer(queue, "Producer1").start();
        new BQConsumer(queue, "Consumer1").start();
        new BQConsumer(queue, "Consumer2").start();
    }
}
```

```
Consumer2 is trying to take an element. Remaining capacity: 5
Consumer1 is trying to take an element. Remaining capacity: 5
Producer1 is trying to add: Producer1-1. Remaining capacity: 5
Consumer2 took: Producer1-1
Producer1 added: Producer1-1
Consumer2 is trying to take an element. Remaining capacity: 5
Producer1 is trying to add: Producer1-2. Remaining capacity: 5
Producer1 added: Producer1-2
Consumer1 took: Producer1-2
Consumer1 is trying to take an element. Remaining capacity: 5
...
```

I do not discuss an example of PriorityBlockingQueue. You can use the PriorityBlockingQueue implementation class to create the blocking queue in Listing 12-23 and the same example will work. Note that a PriorityBlockingQueue is an unbounded queue. You may also want to use a different type of element (other than a string), which will emulate the priority of elements in a better way. Refer to Listing 12-17 for an example of a simple non-blocking priority queue.

Delay Queues

Let's see an example of a DelayQueue. A DelayQueue is one of the implementation classes for the BlockingQueue interface. It lets you implement a queue whose elements must stay in a queue for a certain amount of time (known as a *delay*). How does the DelayQueue know about the amount of time an element has to be kept in the queue? It uses an interface called Delayed to know the time an element must stay in the queue. The interface is in the java.util.concurrent package. Its declaration is as follows:

```
public interface Delayed extends Comparable<Delayed> {
    long getDelay(TimeUnit timeUnit);
}
```

It extends the Comparable interface whose compareTo() method accepts a Delayed object. The DelayQueue calls the getDelay() method of each element to know how long that element must be kept in the queue before it can be taken out. The DelayQueue will pass a TimeUnit to this method. Your job is to convert the delay time of an element to the TimeUnit being passed and return the value. For example, if you want to keep an element in the queue for 10 seconds, your getDelay(TimeUnit timeUnit) method will be implemented as follows:

```
public class DelayClass implement Delayed {
    public long getDelay(TimeUnit timeUnit){
        long delay = timeUnit.convert(10, TimeUnit.SECONDS);
        return delay;
    }
}
```

The element stays in the DelayQueue as long as the delay returned from the getDelay() method is a positive number. When the getDelay() method returns a zero or a negative number, it is time for the element to get out of the queue. However, there must be someone to take the element out of the queue when it is ready to get out. Typically, you would call the take() method to take an element out of the queue. There may be many elements that are ready (whose delay time has expired) to come out of the queue. Which one of the expired elements will be placed as the head of the queue? The queue determines this by calling the compareTo() method of the elements. This method determines the priority of an expired element to be removed from the queue with respect to the other expired elements. Typically, you would decide that the element that expired most recently would be the first one to be removed. However, it is up to you to decide which expired element will be ready to be removed next. You may decide just the opposite, such as the element that has expired earliest should be removed first.

Listing 12-24 contains code for a DelayedJob class, which implements the Delayed interface. Its constructor takes a job name and a scheduled time for the job as arguments. The scheduled time could be in the past, the present, or in the future. It is specified as a number, which represents the milliseconds passed between the specified time and midnight, January 1, 1970 UTC. Its getDelay() method returns the delay time for this job. Its compareTo() method uses the getDelay() method, so that the earliest expired element will be removed first. Its toString() method simply prints its job name and scheduled time.

Listing 12-24. A DelayedJob Class That Implements the Delayed Interface

```
// DelayedJob.java
package com.jdojo.collections;

import java.time.Instant;
import java.util.concurrent.Delayed;
import java.util.concurrent.TimeUnit;
import static java.util.concurrent.TimeUnit.MILLISECONDS;
import static java.time.temporal.ChronoUnit.MILLIS;

public class DelayedJob implements Delayed {
    private final Instant scheduledTime;
    String jobName;

    public DelayedJob(String jobName, Instant scheduledTime) {
        this.scheduledTime = scheduledTime;
        this.jobName = jobName;
    }
```

```
    @Override
    public long getDelay(TimeUnit unit) {
        // Positive delay means it should stay in queue. Zero or negative delay
        // means that it ready to be removed from the queue.
        long delay = MILLIS.between(Instant.now(), scheduledTime);

        // Convert the delay in millis into the specified unit
        long returnValue = unit.convert(delay, MILLISECONDS);
        return returnValue;
    }

    @Override
    public int compareTo(Delayed job) {
        long currentJobDelay = this.getDelay(MILLISECONDS);
        long jobDelay = job.getDelay(MILLISECONDS);

        int diff = 0;
        if (currentJobDelay > jobDelay) {
            diff = 1;
        } else if (currentJobDelay < jobDelay) {
            diff = -1;
        }
        return diff;
    }

    @Override
    public String toString() {
        String str = "(" + this.jobName + ", " + "Scheduled Time: "
                + this.scheduledTime + ")";
        return str;
    }
}
```

The program in Listing 12-25 shows how to use the `DelayedJob` objects as elements in a `DelayQueue`. It adds three jobs ("Print Data", "Populate Data", and "Balance Data") to the queue that are scheduled to run nine, three, and six seconds after the current time on your computer, respectively. Note the sequence of adding these jobs in the queue. I have not added the job to be run first as the first element. It is the job of the `DelayQueue` to arrange the elements in its queue based on their delay time returned from their `getDelay()` method. When you run this program, there will be a delay of about three seconds because no elements will be expired and the `take()` method on the queue will be blocked. When elements start expiring, you will see them getting removed one by one by the `take()` method in the `while` loop. You may get different output when you run the program.

Listing 12-25. Using a DelayQueue with Instances of DelayedJob as Its Element

```
// DelayQueueTest.java
package com.jdojo.collections;

import java.time.Instant;
import java.util.concurrent.BlockingQueue;
import java.util.concurrent.DelayQueue;
```

```
public class DelayQueueTest {
    public static void main(String[] args) throws InterruptedException {
        BlockingQueue<DelayedJob> queue = new DelayQueue<>();
        Instant now = Instant.now();

        // Create three delayed job and add them to the queue
        // Jobs should run in a sequence as
        // 1. Populate Data (After 3 seeconds)
        // 2. Balance Data (After 6 seconds)
        // 3. Print Data (After 9 seconds)
        queue.put(new DelayedJob("Print Data", now.plusSeconds(9)));
        queue.put(new DelayedJob("Populate Data", now.plusSeconds(3)));
        queue.put(new DelayedJob("Balance Data", now.plusSeconds(6)));

        while (queue.size() > 0) {
            System.out.println("Waiting to take a job from the queue...");
            DelayedJob job = queue.take();
            System.out.println("Took Job: " + job);
        }

        System.out.println("Finished running all jobs.");
    }
}
```

```
Waiting to take a job from the queue...
Took Job: (Populate Data, Scheduled Time: 2017-11-13T03:36:23.197963600Z)
Waiting to take a job from the queue...
Took Job: (Balance Data, Scheduled Time: 2017-11-13T03:36:26.197963600Z)
Waiting to take a job from the queue...
Took Job: (Print Data, Scheduled Time: 2017-11-13T03:36:29.197963600Z)
Finished running all jobs.
```

Transfer Queues

The transfer queue extends the functionality of a blocking queue. An instance of the `TransferQueue<E>` interface represents a transfer queue. In a `TransferQueue`, a producer will wait to hand off an element to a consumer. This is a useful feature in a message passing application, where a producer makes sure that its message has been consumed by a consumer. A producer hands off an element to a consumer using the `transfer(E element)` method of the `TransferQueue<E>`. When a producer invokes this method, it waits until a consumer takes its element. If the `TransferQueue` has some elements, all its elements must be consumed before the element added by the `transfer()` method is consumed. The `tryTransfer()` method provides a non-blocking and a timeout version of the method, which lets a producer transfer an element immediately if a consumer is already waiting or has waited a specified amount of time.

The `TransferQueue` has two more methods to get more information about the waiting consumers. The `getWaitingConsumerCount()` method returns the number of waiting consumers. The `hasWaitingConsumer()` method returns `true` if there is a waiting consumer; otherwise, it returns `false`.

The `LinkedTransferQueue<E>` is an implementation class for the `TransferQueue<E>` interface. It provides an unbounded `TransferQueue`. It is based on `FIFO`.

Listing 12-26 contains code for a TQProducer class whose instance represents a producer for a TransferQueue. The producer sleeps for a random number of seconds between 1 and 5. It generates an integer. If the integer is even, it puts it in the queue. If the integer is odd, it tries to hand it off to a consumer using the transfer() method. Note that if the TransferQueue has some elements, the consumer will consume those elements first, before it consumes the element that a producer is trying to hand off using the transfer() method.

Listing 12-26. A TQProducer Class That Represents a Producer for a TransferQueue

```
// TQProducer.java
package com.jdojo.collections;

import java.util.Random;
import java.util.concurrent.TransferQueue;
import java.util.concurrent.atomic.AtomicInteger;

public class TQProducer extends Thread {
    private final String name;
    private final TransferQueue<Integer> tQueue;
    private final AtomicInteger sequence;
    private Random rand = new Random();

    public TQProducer(String name, TransferQueue<Integer> tQueue, AtomicInteger sequence) {
        this.name = name;
        this.tQueue = tQueue;
        this.sequence = sequence;
    }

    @Override
    public void run() {
        while (true) {
            try {
                // Sleep for 1 to 5 random number of seconds
                int sleepTime = rand.nextInt(5) + 1;
                Thread.sleep(sleepTime * 1000);

                // Generate a sequence number
                int nextNum = this.sequence.incrementAndGet();

                // An even number is enqueued. An odd number is handed off
                // to a consumer
                if (nextNum % 2 == 0) {
                    System.out.printf("%s: Enqueuing: %d%n", name, nextNum);
                    tQueue.put(nextNum); // Enqueue
                } else {
                    System.out.printf("%s: Handing off: %d%n", name, nextNum);
                    System.out.printf("%s: has a waiting consumer: %b%n",
                            name, tQueue.hasWaitingConsumer());
                    tQueue.transfer(nextNum); // A hand off
                }
```

```
            } catch (InterruptedException e) {
                e.printStackTrace();
            }
        }
    }
}
```

Listing 12-27 contains the code for a consumer that consumes elements from a `TransferQueue`. It sleeps for one to five seconds randomly and consumes an element from the `TransferQueue`.

Listing 12-27. A TQConsumer Class That Represents a Consumer for a TransferQueue

```
// TQConsumer.java
package com.jdojo.collections;

import java.util.Random;
import java.util.concurrent.TransferQueue;

public class TQConsumer extends Thread {
    private final String name;
    private final TransferQueue<Integer> tQueue;
    private final Random rand = new Random();

    public TQConsumer(String name, TransferQueue<Integer> tQueue) {
        this.name = name;
        this.tQueue = tQueue;
    }

    @Override
    public void run() {
        while (true) {
            try {
                // Sleep for 1 to 5 random number of seconds
                int sleepTime = rand.nextInt(5) + 1;
                Thread.sleep(sleepTime * 1000);

                int item = tQueue.take();
                System.out.printf("%s removed: %d%n", name, item);
            } catch (InterruptedException e) {
                e.printStackTrace();
            }
        }
    }
}
```

Listing 12-28 contains the code to test a `TransferQueue`. You may get different output when you run the program

Listing 12-28. A Class to Test a TransferQueue

```
// TQProducerConsumerTest.java
package com.jdojo.collections;

import java.util.concurrent.LinkedTransferQueue;
import java.util.concurrent.TransferQueue;
import java.util.concurrent.atomic.AtomicInteger;

public class TQProducerConsumerTest {
    public static void main(String[] args) {
        final TransferQueue<Integer> tQueue = new LinkedTransferQueue<>();
        final AtomicInteger sequence = new AtomicInteger();

        // Initialize transfer queue with five items
        for (int i = 0; i < 5; i++) {
            try {
                tQueue.put(sequence.incrementAndGet());
            } catch (InterruptedException e) {
                e.printStackTrace();
            }
        }

        System.out.println("Initial queue: " + tQueue);

        // Create and start a producer and a consumer
        new TQProducer("Producer-1", tQueue, sequence).start();
        new TQConsumer("Consumer-1", tQueue).start();
    }
}
```

```
Initial queue: [1, 2, 3, 4, 5]
Producer-1: Enqueuing: 6
Consumer-1 removed: 1
Consumer-1 removed: 2
Producer-1: Handing off: 7
Producer-1: has a waiting consumer: false
Consumer-1 removed: 3
Consumer-1 removed: 4
Consumer-1 removed: 5
Consumer-1 removed: 6
Consumer-1 removed: 7
Producer-1: Enqueuing: 8
Consumer-1 removed: 8
...
```

The program creates a TransferQueue and adds five elements to it. It creates and starts a producer and a consumer. Its output needs a little explanation. You added five elements initially to make sure the consumer will have some elements to consume from the TransferQueue when the producer tries to transfer an element. The producer got the first go. It puts the integer 6 into the queue. The consumer removed the integer 1 from the queue. At this time, the producer tried to hand off the integer 7 to the consumer, leaving five elements (2, 3, 4, 5, and 6) still queued in the TransferQueue. The consumer must remove all these elements from the TransferQueue, before it will accept the transfer request for the integer 7 from the producer. This is evident from the output. The consumer removes the elements 2, 3, 4, 5, and 6, and then the element 7. Both the producer and the consumer run in infinite loops. You need to stop the program manually.

Blocking Doubly Ended Queues

A blocking, doubly ended queue provides the functionality of a doubly ended queue and a blocking queue. An instance of the BlockingDeque<E> interface represents a blocking, doubly ended queue. It inherits from the Deque<E> and BlockingQueue<E> interfaces. It adds eight more methods to add and remove elements from the head and the tail. These methods block indefinitely or for a specified amount of time, as in the case of a BlockingQueue. The new methods are putXxx(), offerXxx(), takeXxx(), and pollXxx(), where Xxx is First or Last. The method with the suffix First is used to put or take an element from the head of the Deque, whereas the method with the suffix Last is used to put or take an element from its tail. Refer to the "Double Ended Queues" and "Blocking Queue" sections described earlier in this chapter for more details on using these methods.

The LinkedBlockingDeque<E> class is an implementation class for the BlockingDeque<E> interface. It supports bounded as well as unbounded blocking deques.

Working with Maps

A map represents a type of collection that is different from the collections that you have seen so far. It contains key-value mappings. It is easy to visualize a map as a table with two columns. The first column of the table contains keys; the second column contains the values associated with the keys. Table 12-5 shows person names as keys and their phone numbers as values. You can think of this table representing a map that contains mapping between names and phone numbers. Sometimes a map is also known as a *dictionary*. In a dictionary, you have a word and you look up its meanings. Similarly, in a map, you have a key and you look up its value.

Table 12-5. *A Table with Two Columns, Key and Value. Each Row Contains a Key-Value Pair.*

Key	Value
John	(342)113-9878
Richard	(245)890-9045
Donna	(205)678-9823
Ken	(205)678-9823

If you still have problem visualizing a map, you can think of it as a collection in which each element represents a key-value pair as <key,value>. A <key,value> pair is also known as an *entry* in the map. The key and the value must be reference types. You cannot use primitive types (int, double, etc.) for either keys or values in a map.

A map is represented by an instance of the Map<K,V> interface, where the type parameters K and V are the types of keys and values, respectively. The Map interface is not inherited from the Collection interface. A Map does not allow any duplicate keys. Each key is mapped to exactly one value. In other words, each key in a Map has exactly one value. Values do not have to be unique. That is, two keys may map to the same value. A Map allows for at most one null value as its key and multiple null values as its values. However, an implementation class may restrict null as a value in a Map.

The methods in the Map interface may be classified in the following four categories depending on the operations they perform:

- Methods for basic operations
- Methods for bulk operations
- Methods for view operations
- Methods for comparison operations

The methods in the basic operations category let you perform basic operations on a Map, for example, putting an entry into a Map, getting the value for a specified key, getting the number of entries, removing an entry, checking if the Map is empty, etc. Examples of methods in this category are as follows:

- int size()
- boolean isEmpty()
- boolean containsKey(Object key)
- boolean containsValue(Object value)
- V get(Object key)
- V getOrDefault(Object key, V defaultValue)
- V put(K key, V value)
- V putIfAbsent(K key, V value)
- V remove(Object key)
- boolean remove(Object key, Object value)
- boolean replace(K key, V oldValue, V newValue)

The methods in the bulk operations category let you perform bulk operations on a Map, such as copying entries to a Map from another Map and removing all entries from the Map. Examples of methods in this category are as follows:

- void clear()
- void putAll(Map<? extends K, ? extends V> m)
- void replaceAll(BiFunction<? super K,? super V,? extends V> function)

The view operations category contains three methods. Each returns a different view of the Map. You can view all keys in a Map<K,V> as a Set<K>, all values as a Collection<V>, and all <key,value> pairs as a Set<Map.Entry<K,V>>. Note that all keys and all <key,value> pairs are always unique in a Map and that is the reason why you get their Set views. Since a Map may contain duplicate values, you get a Collection view of its values. Examples of methods in this category are as follows:

- Set<K> keySet()
- Collection<V> values()
- Set<Map.Entry<K,V>> entrySet()

The comparison operations methods deal with comparing two Maps for equality. Examples of methods in this category are as follows:

- boolean equals(Object o)
- int hashCode()

The HashMap<K,V>, LinkedHashMap<K,V>, and WeakHashMap<K,V> are three of the available implementation classes for the Map<K,V> interface.

The HashMap allows one null value as a key and multiple null values as the values. The following snippet of code demonstrates how to create and use a Map. A HashMap does not guarantee any specific iteration order of entries in the Map.

```
// Create a map using HashMap as the implementation class
Map<String, String> map = new HashMap<>();

// Put an entry to the map - "John" as the key and "(342)113-9878" as the value
map.put("John", "(342)113-9878");
```

The LinkedHashMap is another implementation class for the Map interface. It stores entries in the Map using a doubly linked list. It defines the iteration ordering as the insertion order of the entries. If you want to iterate over entries in a Map in its insertion order, you need to use LinkedHashMap instead of HashMap as the implementation class.

Listing 12-29 demonstrates how to use a Map. Note that the methods remove() and get() return the value of a key. If the key does not exist in the Map, they return null. You must use the containsKey() method to check if a key exists in a Map or use the getOrDefault() method that lets you specify the default value in case the key does not exist in the map. The toString() method returns a well-formatted string for all entries in the Map. It places all entries inside braces ({}). Each entry is formatted in the key=value format. A comma separates two entries. The toString() method of the Map returns a string like {key1=value1, key2=value2, key3=value3 ...}.

Listing 12-29. Using a Map

```
// MapTest.java
package com.jdojo.collections;

import java.util.HashMap;
import java.util.Map;

public class MapTest {
    public static void main(String[] args) {
        // Create a map and add some key-value pairs
        Map<String, String> map = new HashMap<>();
        map.put("John", "(342)113-9878");
        map.put("Richard", "(245)890-9045");
        map.put("Donna", "(205)678-9823");
        map.put("Ken", "(205)678-9823");

        // Print the details
        printDetails(map);

        // Remove all entries from the map
        map.clear();
```

```
        System.out.printf("%nRemoved all entries from the map.%n%n");

        // Print the details
        printDetails(map);
    }

    public static void printDetails(Map<String, String> map) {
        // Get the value for the "Donna" key
        String donnaPhone = map.get("Donna");

        // Print details
        System.out.println("Map: " + map);
        System.out.println("Map Size: " + map.size());
        System.out.println("Map is empty: " + map.isEmpty());
        System.out.println("Map contains Donna key: " + map.containsKey("Donna"));
        System.out.println("Donna Phone: " + donnaPhone);
        System.out.println("Donna key is removed: " + map.remove("Donna"));
    }
}
```

```
Map: {Donna=(205)678-9823, Ken=(205)678-9823, John=(342)113-9878, Richard=(245)890-9045}
Map Size: 4
Map is empty: false
Map contains Donna key: true
Donna Phone: (205)678-9823
Donna key is removed: (205)678-9823

Removed all entries from the map.

Map: {}
Map Size: 0
Map is empty: true
Map contains Donna key: false
Donna Phone: null
Donna key is removed: null
```

The WeakHashMap class is another implementation for the Map interface. As the name of the class implies, it contains *weak keys*. When there is no reference to the key except in the map, keys are candidates for garbage collection. If a key is garbage collected, its associated entry is removed from the Map. You use a WeakHashMap when you want to maintain a cache of key-value pairs and you do not mind if your key-value pairs are removed from the Map by the garbage collector. The WeakHashMap allows a null key and multiple null values. Refer to Chapter 11 for a complete example of using the WeakHashMap class.

Sometimes you want to iterate over keys, values, or entries of a Map. The keySet(), values(), and entrySet() methods of a map return a Set of keys, a Collection of values, and a Set of entries, respectively. Iterating over elements of a Set or a Collection is the same as described in the "Traversing Elements in Collections" section. The following snippet of code shows how to print all keys of a map:

```
Map<String,String> map = new HashMap<>();
map.put("John", "(342)113-9878");
map.put("Richard", "(245)890-9045");
```

```
map.put("Donna", "(205)678-9823");
map.put("Ken", "(205)678-9823");

// Get the set of keys
Set<String> keys = map.keySet();

// Print all keys using the forEach() method.
// You can also use a for-each loop, an iterator, etc. to do the same.
keys.forEach(System.out::println);
```

```
Donna
Ken
John
Richard
```

Each key-value pair in a map is called an entry. An entry is represented by an instance of the `Map.Entry<K,V>` interface. `Map.Entry<K,V>` is a nested static interface of the `Map<K,V>` interface. It has three commonly used methods called `getKey()`, `getValue()`, and `setValue()`, which returns the key of the entry, returns the value of the entry, and sets a new value in the entry, respectively. A typical iteration over an entry set of a `Map` is written as follows:

```
Map<String, String> map = new HashMap<>();
map.put("John", "(342)113-9878");
map.put("Richard", "(245)890-9045");
map.put("Donna", "(205)678-9823");
map.put("Ken", "(205)678-9823");

// Get the entry Set
Set<Map.Entry<String,String>> entries = map.entrySet();

// Print all key-value pairs using the forEach() method of the Collection interface.
// You can use a for-each loop, an iterator, etc. to do the same.
entries.forEach((Map.Entry<String,String> entry) -> {
    String key = entry.getKey();
    String value = entry.getValue();
    System.out.println("key=" + key + ", value=" + value);
});
```

```
key=Donna, value=(205)678-9823
key=Ken, value=(205)678-9823
key=John, value=(342)113-9878
key=Richard, value=(245)890-9045
```

Java 8 added a `forEach(BiConsumer<? super K,? super V> action)` method to the `Map<K,V>` interface that lets you iterate over all entries in the map in a cleaner way. The method takes a `BiConsumer` instance whose first argument is the key and second argument is the value for the current entry in the map. You can rewrite the previous snippet of code as follows:

```
Map<String, String> map = new HashMap<>();
map.put("John", "(342)113-9878");
map.put("Richard", "(245)890-9045");
```

```
map.put("Donna", "(205)678-9823");
map.put("Ken", "(205)678-9823");

// Use the forEach() method of the Map interface
map.forEach((String key, String value) -> {
    System.out.println("key=" + key + ", value=" + value);
});
```

```
key=Donna, value=(205)678-9823
key=Ken, value=(205)678-9823
key=John, value=(342)113-9878
key=Richard, value=(245)890-9045
```

Listing 12-30 demonstrates how to get three different views of a Map and iterate over the elements in those views.

Listing 12-30. Using Keys, Values, and Entries Views of a Map

```
// MapViews.java
package com.jdojo.collections;

import java.util.HashMap;
import java.util.Map;
import java.util.Set;
import java.util.Collection;

public class MapViews {
    public static void main(String[] args) {
        Map<String, String> map = new HashMap<>();
        map.put("John", "(342)113-9878");
        map.put("Richard", "(245)890-9045");
        map.put("Donna", "(205)678-9823");
        map.put("Ken", "(205)678-9823");

        System.out.println("Map: " + map.toString());

        // Print keys, values, and entries in the map
        listKeys(map);
        listValues(map);
        listEntries(map);
    }

    public static void listKeys(Map<String,String> map) {
        System.out.println("Key Set:");
        Set<String> keys = map.keySet();
        keys.forEach(System.out::println);
        System.out.println();
    }

    public static void listValues(Map<String,String> map) {
        System.out.println("Values Collection:");
        Collection<String> values = map.values();
```

```
        values.forEach(System.out::println);
        System.out.println();
    }

    public static void listEntries(Map<String,String> map) {
        System.out.println("Entry Set:");

        // Get the entry Set
        Set<Map.Entry<String, String>> entries = map.entrySet();
        entries.forEach((Map.Entry<String, String> entry) -> {
            String key = entry.getKey();
            String value = entry.getValue();
            System.out.println("key=" + key + ", value=" + value);
        });
    }
}
```

```
Map: {Donna=(205)678-9823, Ken=(205)678-9823, John=(342)113-9878, Richard=(245)890-9045}
Key Set:
Donna
Ken
John
Richard

Values Collection:
(205)678-9823
(205)678-9823
(342)113-9878
(245)890-9045

Entry Set:
key=Donna, value=(205)678-9823
key=Ken, value=(205)678-9823
key=John, value=(342)113-9878
key=Richard, value=(245)890-9045
```

Java 9 added an overloaded `of()` static factory method to the `Map<K,V>` interface that provides a simple and compact way to create immutable maps. The methods' implementations are fine-tuned for performance. The following are 11 versions of the `of()` method that let you create an immutable `Map` of zero to ten key-value entries:

- `static <K,V> Map<K,V> of()`
- `static <K,V> Map<K,V> of(K k1, V v1)`
- `static <K,V> Map<K,V> of(K k1, V v1, K k2, V v2)`
- `static <K,V> Map<K,V> of(K k1, V v1, K k2, V v2, K k3, V v3)`
- `static <K,V> Map<K,V> of(K k1, V v1, K k2, V v2, K k3, V v3, K k4, V v4)`
- `static <K,V> Map<K,V> of(K k1, V v1, K k2, V v2, K k3, V v3, K k4, V v4, K k5, V v5)`

- `static <K,V> Map<K,V> of(K k1, V v1, K k2, V v2, K k3, V v3, K k4, V v4, K k5, V v5, K k6, V v6)`
- `static <K,V> Map<K,V> of(K k1, V v1, K k2, V v2, K k3, V v3, K k4, V v4, K k5, V v5, K k6, V v6, K k7, V v7)`
- `static <K,V> Map<K,V> of(K k1, V v1, K k2, V v2, K k3, V v3, K k4, V v4, K k5, V v5, K k6, V v6, K k7, V v7, K k8, V v8)`
- `static <K,V> Map<K,V> of(K k1, V v1, K k2, V v2, K k3, V v3, K k4, V v4, K k5, V v5, K k6, V v6, K k7, V v7, K k8, V v8, K k9, V v9)`
- `static <K,V> Map<K,V> of(K k1, V v1, K k2, V v2, K k3, V v3, K k4, V v4, K k5, V v5, K k6, V v6, K k7, V v7, K k8, V v8, K k9, V v9, K k10, V v10)`

Note the positions of the arguments in the `of()` method. The first and the second arguments are the key and the value of the first key-value entry in the map, respectively; the third and the fourth arguments are the key and the value of the second key-value entry in the map, respectively and so on. The following snippet of code shows how to create maps using the `of()` method:

```
// An empty, immutable Map
Map<Integer, String> emptyMap = Map.of();

// A singleton, unmodifiable Map
Map<String, String> singletonMap = Map.of("Ken", "(205)678-9823");

// A immutable Map with two entries
Map<Integer, String> luckyNumbers = Map.of(1, "One", 2, "Two");
```

To create an immutable `Map` with an arbitrary number of entries, Java 9 provided a static method named `ofEntries()` in the `Map` interface, which has the following signature:

```
<K,V> Map<K,V> ofEntries(Map.Entry<? extends K,? extends V>... entries)
```

To use the `ofEntries()` method, you need to box each map entry in a `Map.Entry` instance. Java 9 provides a convenience `entry()` static method in the `Map` interface to create instances of `Map.Entry`. The signature of the `entry()` method is:

```
<K,V> Map.Entry<K,V> entry(K k, V v)
```

To keep the expression readable and compact, you need to use a static import for the `Map.entry` method and use a statement like the following to create an immutable `Map` with an arbitrary number of entries:

```
import java.util.Map;
import static java.util.Map.entry;

// ...

// Use the Map.ofEntries() and Map.entry() methods to create an immutable Map
Map<Integer, String> numberToWord = Map.ofEntries(entry(1, "One"),
                                                  entry(2, "Two"),
                                                  entry(3, "Three"));
```

The returned maps from the `of()` and `ofEntries()` methods of the `Map` interface do not allow `null` in keys or values. A `NullPointerException` is thrown if a key or value in the map is `null`. They are serializable if all keys and values are serializable. Their implementation classes are optimized and there is no guarantee about the implementation class of the returned `Map`. That is, you should not make any assumptions about the implementation classes of the returned maps from these methods.

Listing 12-31 contains a complete program that shows how to use the new `of()`, `ofEntries()`, and `entry()` static methods of the `Map` interface to create immutable maps. You may get different output for maps, which will contain the same elements in a different order.

Listing 12-31. Using the of(), ofEntries(), and entry() static Methods of the Map Interface

```
// MapFactoryMethodTest.java
package com.jdojo.collections;

import java.util.Map;
import static java.util.Map.entry;

public class MapFactoryMethodTest {
    public static void main(String[] args) {
        // Create a few unmodifiable maps
        Map<Integer, String> emptyMap = Map.of();
        Map<Integer, String> luckyNumber = Map.of(19, "Nineteen");
        Map<Integer, String> numberToWord = Map.of(1, "One", 2, "Two", 3, "Three");

        Map<String, String> days = Map.ofEntries(
                entry("Mon", "Monday"),
                entry("Tue", "Tuesday"),
                entry("Wed", "Wednesday"),
                entry("Thu", "Thursday"),
                entry("Fri", "Friday"),
                entry("Sat", "Saturday"),
                entry("Sun", "Sunday"));

        System.out.println("emptyMap = " + emptyMap);
        System.out.println("singletonMap = " + luckyNumber);
        System.out.println("numberToWord = " + numberToWord);
        System.out.println("days = " + days);

        try {
            // Try using a null value
            Map<Integer, String> map = Map.of(1, null);
        } catch (NullPointerException e) {
            System.out.println("Nulls not allowed in Map.of().");
        }

        try {
            // Try using duplicate keys
            Map<Integer, String> map = Map.of(1, "One", 1, "OneAgain");
        } catch (IllegalArgumentException e) {
            System.out.println(e.getMessage());
        }
    }
}
```

```
emptyMap = {}
singletonMap = {19=Nineteen}
numberToWord = {1=One, 3=Three, 2=Two}
days = {Tue=Tuesday, Wed=Wednesday, Mon=Monday, Sun=Sunday, Sat=Saturday, Thu=Thursday,
Fri=Friday}
Nulls not allowed in Map.of().
duplicate key: 1
```

Sorted Maps

A sorted map stores entries in a map in an ordered way. It sorts the map entries on keys based on either natural sort order or a custom sort order. The natural sort order is defined by the `Comparable` interface of the keys. If the keys do not implement the `Comparable` interface, you must use a `Comparator` to sort the entries. If the keys implement the `Comparable` interface and you use a `Comparator`, the `Comparator` is used to sort the keys.

An instance of the `SortedMap<K,V>` interface represented a sorted map. The `SortedMap<K,V>` interface inherits from the `Map<K,V>` interface. A `SortedMap` is to a `Map` what a `SortedSet` is to a `Set`.

The `SortedMap` interface contains methods that let you take advantage of the sorted keys in the map. It has methods that let you get the first and the last key or a sub-map based on a criteria, etc. Those methods are as follows:

- `Comparator<? super K> comparator()`: It returns the `Comparator` used for custom sorting of the keys in the `SortedMap`. If you have not used a `Comparator`, it returns `null` and natural ordering will be used based on the implementation of the Comparable interface for the keys.
- `K firstKey()`: It returns the key of the first entry in the `SortedMap`. If the `SortedMap` is empty, it throws a `NoSuchElementException`.
- `SortedMap<K, V> headMap(K toKey)`: It returns a view of the `SortedMap` whose entries will have keys less than the specified `toKey`. If you add a new entry to the view, its key must be less than the specified `toKey`. Otherwise, it will throw an exception. The view is backed by the original `SortedMap`.
- `K lastKey()`: It returns the key of the last entry in the `SortedMap`. If the `SortedMap` is empty, it throws a `NoSuchElementException`.
- `SortedMap<K, V> subMap(K fromKey, K toKey)`: It returns a view of the `SortedMap` whose entries will have keys ranging from the specified `fromKey` (inclusive) and `toKey` (exclusive). The original `SortedMap` backs the partial view of the `SortedMap`. Any changes made to either map will be reflected in both. You can put new entries in the sub-map whose keys must fall in the range `fromKey` (inclusive) and `toKey` (Exclusive).
- `SortedMap<K, V> tailMap(K fromKey)`: It returns a view of the `SortedMap` whose entries will have keys equal to or greater than the specified `fromKey`. If you add a new entry to the view, its key must be equal to or greater than the specified `fromKey`. Otherwise, it will throw an exception. The original `SortedMap` backs the tail view.

The `TreeMap<K,V>` class is the implementation class for the `SortedMap<K.V>` interface. For basic operations, you work with a `SortedMap` the same way as you work with a `Map`. Listing 12-32 demonstrates how to use a `SortedMap`.

Listing 12-32. Using a SortedMap

```
// SortedMapTest.java
package com.jdojo.collections;

import java.util.SortedMap;
import java.util.TreeMap;

public class SortedMapTest {
    public static void main(String[] args) {
        SortedMap<String, String> sMap = new TreeMap<>();
        sMap.put("John", "(342)113-9878");
        sMap.put("Richard", "(245)890-9045");
        sMap.put("Donna", "(205)678-9823");
        sMap.put("Ken", "(205)678-9823");

        System.out.println("Sorted Map: " + sMap);

        // Get a sub map from Donna (inclusive) to Ken(exclusive)
        SortedMap<String, String> subMap = sMap.subMap("Donna", "Ken");
        System.out.println("Sorted Submap from Donna to Ken(exclusive): " + subMap);

        // Get the first and last keys
        String firstKey = sMap.firstKey();
        String lastKey = sMap.lastKey();
        System.out.println("First Key: " + firstKey);
        System.out.println("Last key: " + lastKey);
    }
}
```

```
Sorted Map: {Donna=(205)678-9823, John=(342)113-9878, Ken=(205)678-9823,
Richard=(245)890-9045}
Sorted Submap from Donna to Ken(exclusive): {Donna=(205)678-9823, John=(342)113-9878}
First Key: Donna
Last key: Richard
```

If you want to use a `Comparator` to sort the entries based keys in a `SortedMap`, you need use the constructor of the `TreeMap` class that takes a `Comparator` as an argument. The following snippet of code shows how to sort entries in a sorted map based on the length of their keys followed by the alphabetical order of the keys ignoring the case:

```
// Sort entries on key's length and then on keys ignoring case
Comparator<String> keyComparator =
    Comparator.comparing(String::length)
              .thenComparing(String::compareToIgnoreCase);
SortedMap<String, String> sMap = new TreeMap<>(keyComparator);
sMap.put("John", "(342)113-9878");
sMap.put("Richard", "(245)890-9045");
sMap.put("Donna", "(205)678-9823");
```

```
sMap.put("Ken", "(205)678-9823");
sMap.put("Zee", "(205)679-9823");

System.out.println("Sorted Map: " + sMap);
```

```
Sorted Map: {Ken=(205)678-9823, Zee=(205)679-9823, John=(342)113-9878,
Donna=(205)678-9823, Richard=(245)890-9045}
```

Refer to the "Sorted Set" section for more details on using a Comparator for sorting keys. A Comparator in a SortedMap works the same way for keys as it works for the elements in a SortedSet.

Navigable Maps

A navigable map is represented by an instance of the NavigableMap<K,V> interface. It extends the SortedMap<K,V> interface by adding some useful features like getting the closest match for a key, getting a view of the map in reverse order, etc. It also adds some methods that are similar to methods added by SortedMap, but they return an entry (a Map.Entry object) rather than just the key. The TreeMap<K,V> class is the implementation class for the NavigableMap<K,V> interface.

Replace Xxx with Entry or Key in methods names of the NavigableMap interface mentioned in this paragraph. The lowerXxx(K key) method returns the greatest entry or key that is lower than the specified key. The floorXxx(K key) method returns the greatest entry or key that is equal to or lower than the specified key. The higherXxx(K key) method returns the least entry or key that is higher than the specified key. The ceilingXxx(K key) method returns the least entry of key that is equal to or higher than the specified key.

The NavigableMap contains two methods called firstEntry() and lastEntry() that return the first and the last entries as Map.Entry objects; they return null if the map is empty. It contains methods to retrieve and remove the first and the last entries from the map using the pollFirstEntry() and pollLastEntry() methods. It adds other versions of the headMap(), tailMap(), and subMap() methods declared in SortedMap, which accept a boolean flag to indicate if you want to include the extreme values in the sub-map returned from these methods. Finally, it adds the descendingKeySet() and descendingMap() methods that give you a view of keys and the map itself in the reverse order. Listing 12-33 shows how to use a NavigableMap.

Listing 12-33. Using a NavigableMap

```
// NavigableMapTest.java
package com.jdojo.collections;

import java.util.TreeMap;
import java.util.NavigableMap;
import java.util.Map.Entry;

public class NavigableMapTest {
    public static void main(String[] args) {
        // Create a sorted map sorted on string keys alphabetically
        NavigableMap<String, String> nMap = new TreeMap<>();
        nMap.put("John", "(342)113-9878");
        nMap.put("Richard", "(245)890-9045");
        nMap.put("Donna", "(205)678-9823");
        nMap.put("Ken", "(205)678-9823");
```

```
        System.out.println("Navigable Map:" + nMap);

        // Get the closest lower and higher matches for Ken
        Entry<String, String> lowerKen = nMap.lowerEntry("Ken");
        Entry<String, String> floorKen = nMap.floorEntry("Ken");
        Entry<String, String> higherKen = nMap.higherEntry("Ken");
        Entry<String, String> ceilingKen = nMap.ceilingEntry("Ken");

        System.out.println("Lower Ken: " + lowerKen);
        System.out.println("Floor Ken: " + floorKen);
        System.out.println("Higher Ken: " + higherKen);
        System.out.println("Ceiling Ken: " + ceilingKen);

        // Get the reverse order view of the map
        NavigableMap<String, String> reverseMap = nMap.descendingMap();
        System.out.println("Navigable Map(Reverse Order):" + reverseMap);
    }
}
```

```
Navigable Map:{Donna=(205)678-9823, John=(342)113-9878, Ken=(205)678-9823,
Richard=(245)890-9045}
Lower Ken: John=(342)113-9878
Floor Ken: Ken=(205)678-9823
Higher Ken: Richard=(245)890-9045
Ceiling Ken: Ken=(205)678-9823
Navigable Map(Reverse Order):{Richard=(245)890-9045, Ken=(205)678-9823,
John=(342)113-9878, Donna=(205)678-9823}
```

Concurrent Maps

Sometimes you need to perform multiple operations on a map atomically when the map is used by multiple threads concurrently. For example, you may want to put a new key-value pair in a map only if the key does not already exist in the map. Your code may look as follows:

```
Map<String,String> map = ...;
String key = ...;
String value = ...;

// Need to lock the entire map
synchronized(map) {
    if (map.containsKey(key)) {
        // Key is already in the map
    } else {
        map.put(key, value); // Add the new key-value
    }
}
```

In this code, you had to lock the entire map just to put a new key-value pair if the key was absent in the map. Locking the map was necessary because you needed to perform two things atomically: testing for a key's existence and putting the key-value if the test fails. When these two operations are being performed on the map by a thread, no other thread can lock the map for any other operations. A ConcurrentMap enables you to perform concurrent operations, like the one I discussed, without resorting to locking the map.

You can choose the level of concurrency when you create a concurrent map using its implementation class. The level of concurrency is specified as the estimated number of threads that would perform the write operations on the map. The map will try to adjust those many threads concurrently. A ConcurrentMap does not lock the entire map. Even if it locks the entire map, other threads will still be able to perform read and write operations on it because it uses a fine-grained synchronization mechanism based on a *compare-and-set* primitive.

The ConcurrentHashMap<K,V> class is an implementation class for the ConcurrentMap<K,V> interface. Both of them are in the java.util.concurrent package.

Listing 12-34 demonstrates the use of the ConcurrentMap. The example simply shows how to create and use some of the methods of a ConcurrentMap. Typically, you should use a ConcurrentMap in a multi-threaded environment. The program does not use multiple threads to access the map. It only demonstrates use of some of the methods of the ConcurrentMap interface.

Listing 12-34. Using a ConcurrentMap

```
// ConcurrentMapTest.java
package com.jdojo.collections;

import java.util.concurrent.ConcurrentHashMap;
import java.util.concurrent.ConcurrentMap;

public class ConcurrentMapTest {
    public static void main(String[] args) {
        ConcurrentMap<String, String> cMap = new ConcurrentHashMap<>();
        cMap.put("one", "one");

        System.out.println("Concurrent Map: " + cMap);

        System.out.println(cMap.putIfAbsent("one", "nine"));
        System.out.println(cMap.putIfAbsent("two", "two"));
        System.out.println(cMap.remove("one", "two"));
        System.out.println(cMap.replace("one", "two"));

        System.out.println("Concurrent Map: " + cMap);
    }
}
```

```
Concurrent Map: {one=one}
one
null
false
one
Concurrent Map: {one=two, two=two}
```

Concurrent and Navigable Maps

A concurrent navigable map is the concurrent and navigable version of the map. An instance of the `ConcurrentNavigableMap<K,V>` interface represents a concurrent and navigable map. The interface inherits from the `ConcurrentMap<K,V>` and `NavigableMap<K,V>` interfaces. The `ConcurrentSkipListMap<K,V>` is the implementation class for the `ConcurrentNavigableMap<K,V>` interface. I discussed both the concurrent map and navigable map. Refer to the examples of both kinds for using the `ConcurrentNavigableMap`.

Applying Algorithms to Collections

The Collections framework lets you apply many types of algorithms on all or a few elements of a collection. It lets you search through a collection for a value; sort and shuffle elements of a collection; get a read-only view of a collection; etc. The good news is that all of these features are provided in one class named `Collections`. Notice that we have a similarly named interfaced called `Collection`, which is the ancestor of most of the collection interfaces defined in the Collections framework. The `Collections` class consists of all static methods. If you want to apply any algorithm to a collection, you need to look at the list of methods in this class before writing your own logic. I discuss many methods in the `Collections` class in the subsequent sections.

Sorting a List

You can use one of the following two static methods in the `Collections` class to sort the elements of a `List`:

- `<T extends Comparable<? super T>> void sort(List<T> list)`: It sorts the elements in a `List` in the *natural order* defined by the `Comparable` interface that is implemented by the elements in the `List`. Each element in the `List` must implement the `Comparable` interface and they must be comparable to each other.
- `<T> void sort(List<T> list, Comparator<? super T> c)`: It lets you pass a `Comparator` to define a custom ordering of the elements.

■ **Tip** Java 8 added a default method named `sort(Comparator<? super E> c)` in the `List<E>` interface. It allows you to sort a `List` without using the `Collections` class.

The following snippet of code demonstrates how to sort a `List`:

```
import java.util.ArrayList;
import java.util.Collections;
import java.util.List;
...
List<String> list = new ArrayList<>();
list.add("John");
list.add("Richard");
list.add("Donna");
list.add("Ken");

System.out.println("List: " + list);
```

```
// Uses Comparable implementation in String to sort the list in natural order
Collections.sort(list);
System.out.println("Sorted List: " + list);
```

```
List: [John, Richard, Donna, Ken]
Sorted List: [Donna, John, Ken, Richard]
```

The following snippet of code sorts the same list in ascending order of the length of their elements using the sort() method in the List interface:

```
import java.util.ArrayList;
import java.util.Comparator;
import java.util.List;
...
List<String> list = new ArrayList<>();
list.add("John");
list.add("Richard");
list.add("Donna");
list.add("Ken");

System.out.println("List: " + list);

// Uses List.sort() method with a Comparator
list.sort(Comparator.comparing(String::length));

System.out.println("Sorted List: " + list);
```

```
List: [John, Richard, Donna, Ken]
Sorted List: [Ken, John, Donna, Richard]
```

The sort() method uses a modified *mergesort* algorithm. It is a stable sort. That is, equal elements will stay at their current positions after the sort operation. Internally, all elements are copied to an array, sorted in the array, and copied back to the List. Sorting is guaranteed to give n*log(n) performance, where n is the number of elements in the List.

Searching a List

You can use one of the following two static binarySearch() methods in the Collections class to search for a specified object in a List.

- `<T> int binarySearch(List<? extends Comparable<? super T>> list, T key)`
- `<T> int binarySearch(List<? extends T> list, T key, Comparator<? super T> c)`

A List must be sorted in ascending order using the natural order or the Comparator before you use the binarySearch() method on the List. If the List is not sorted, the result of the binarySearch() method is not defined. If the object is found in the List, the method returns the index of the object in the List. Otherwise, it returns (-(insertion index)-1), where the insertion index is the index in the List where this object would have been placed, if it were present. This return value makes sure that you will get a negative value only if the key is not found in the List. If you get a negative number as the returned value from this method, you can use the absolute value of the return index as the basis of the insertion point into the list -((return value) + 1). This method uses the binary search algorithm to perform the search. If the List supports random access, the search runs in log(n) time. If the List does not support random access, the search runs in n×log(n) time. The following snippet of code shows how to use this method:

```
List<String> list = new ArrayList<>();
list.add("John");
list.add("Richard");
list.add("Donna");
list.add("Ken");

// Must sort before performing the binary search
Collections.sort(list);
System.out.println("List: " + list);

// Find Donna
int index = Collections.binarySearch(list, "Donna");
System.out.println("Donna in List is at " + index);

// Find Ellen
index = Collections.binarySearch(list, "Ellen");
System.out.println("Ellen in List is at " + index);
```

```
List: [Donna, John, Ken, Richard]
Donna in List is at 0
Ellen in List is at -2
```

Since "Ellen" is not in the List, the binary search returned -2. It means that if you insert "Ellen" in the List, it will be inserted at index 1, which is computed using the expression (-(-2+1)). Note that "Donna" has an index of 0 and "John" has an index of 1. If "Ellen" is added to the list, its index will be the same as the current index for "John" and "John" will be moved to the right at index 2.

Shuffling, Reversing, Swapping, and Rotating a List

In this section, I discuss applying different kinds of algorithms to a List, such as shuffling , reversing, swapping, and rotating its elements.

Shuffling gives you a random permutation of the elements in a List. The concept of shuffling elements of a List is the same as shuffling a deck of cards. You shuffle the elements of a List by using the Collections.shuffle() static method. You can supply a java.util.Random object or the shuffle() method can use a default randomizer. The two versions of the shuffle() methods are as follows:

- void shuffle(List<?> list)
- void shuffle(List<?> list, Random rnd)

Reversing is the algorithm that puts the elements of a List in the reverse order. You can use the following reverse() static method of the Collections class to accomplish this:

```
void reverse(List<?> list)
```

Swapping lets you swap the position of two elements in a List. You can perform swapping using the swap() static method of the Collections class, which is defined as follows:

```
void swap(List<?> list, int i, int j)
```

Here i and j are indexes of two elements to be swapped and they must be between 0 and size - 1, where size is the size of the List. Otherwise, it throws an IndexOutOfBoundsException.

Rotating involves moving all elements of a List forward or backward by a distance. Suppose you have a List as [a, b, c, d]. You need to visualize that the List is a circular list and its first element is next to its last element. If you rotate this List by a distance of 1, the resulting List becomes [d, a, b, c]. If you rotate the [a, b, c, d] list by a distance of 2, the List becomes [c, d, a, b]. You can also rotate a List backward by using a negative distance. If you rotate the [a, b, c, d] list by a distance of -2, the List becomes [c, d, a, b]. You can also rotate only part of a List using a sub-list view. Suppose list is a reference variable of type List and it has [a, b, c, d] elements. Consider executing the following statement:

```
Collections.rotate(list.subList(1, 4), 1);
```

The statement will change the list to [a, d, b, c]. Note that list.subList(1, 4) returns a view of [b, c, d] elements and this statement rotates only the three elements that are in the sub-list.

The following snippet of code shows how to reorder elements of a List using these methods. You may get different output when you run the following code because shuffle() uses a random algorithm to shuffle the elements of the List.

```
List<String> list = new ArrayList<>();
list.add("John");
list.add("Richard");
list.add("Donna");
list.add("Ken");

System.out.println("List: " + list);

// Shuffle
Collections.shuffle(list);
System.out.println("After Shuffling: " + list);

// Reverse the list
Collections.reverse(list);
System.out.println("After Reversing: " + list);

// Swap elements at indexes 1 and 3
Collections.swap(list, 1, 3);
System.out.println("After Swapping (1 and 3): " + list);

// Rotate elements by 2
Collections.rotate(list, 2);
System.out.println("After Rotating by 2: " + list);
```

```
List: [John, Richard, Donna, Ken]
After Shuffling: [Ken, Donna, Richard, John]
After Reversing: [John, Richard, Donna, Ken]
After Swapping (1 and 3): [John, Ken, Donna, Richard]
After Rotating by 2: [Donna, Richard, John, Ken]
```

Creating Different Views of a Collection

You can get a LIFO Queue view of a Deque using the asLifoQueue() static method of the Collections class:

```
<T> Queue<T> asLifoQueue(Deque<T> deque)
```

Some Map implementations have corresponding Set implementations too. For example, for HashMap, you have a HashSet; for TreeMap, you have a TreeSet. If you want to use a Map's implementation as a Set implementation, you can use the newSetFromMap() static method of the Collections class:

```
<E> Set<E> newSetFromMap(Map<E, Boolean> map)
```

Note that the idea is to use the implementation of the Map as a Set, not to share elements between a Map and a Set. This is the reason that the Map must be empty when you use it in this method and you are not supposed to use the Map directly at all. There is a WeakHashMap implementation class for the Map. However, there is no corresponding WeakHashSet implementation class for the Set. Here is how you can get a WeakHashSet:

```
Map<String,Boolean> map = new WeakHashMap<>();      // Do not populate and use the map
Set<String> wSet = Collections.newSetFromMap(map); // You can use wSet
```

Use the weak hash set wSet as a Set and it acts as the WeakHashMap implementation. Since you are not supposed to use the Map object, it is better to use the following statement to create the set using the WeakHashMap implementation class:

```
// Do not keep the reference of the Map
Set<String> wSet = Collections.newSetFromMap(new WeakHashMap<>());
```

When the JVM needs memory, the garbage collection can remove elements from wSet as it does from any WeakHashMap. By using one line of code, you get a Set that has features of a WeakHashMap.

Read-Only Views of Collections

You can get a read-only view (also called unmodifiable view) of a collection. This is useful when you want to pass around your collection without getting it modified. In such cases, you need to pass around a read-only view of your collection. The Collections class offers the following methods to get read-only views of different types of collections:

- `<T> Collection<T> unmodifiableCollection(Collection<? extends T> c)`
- `<T> List<T> unmodifiableList(List<? extends T> list)`
- `<K,V> Map<K,V> unmodifiableMap(Map<? extends K,? extends V> m)`
- `<K,V> NavigableMap<K,V> unmodifiableNavigableMap(NavigableMap<K,? extends V> m)`
- `<T> Set<T> unmodifiableSet(Set<? extends T> s)`
- `<T> NavigableSet<T> unmodifiableNavigableSet(NavigableSet<T> s)`

- <T> SortedSet<T> unmodifiableSortedSet(SortedSet<T> s)
- <K,V> SortedMap<K,V> unmodifiableSortedMap(SortedMap<K,? extends V> m)

Using any of these methods is straightforward. You pass a collection of a specific type and you get a read-only collection of the same type. These methods lets you get a read-only views of an existing modifiable collection. If you already know the elements of a collection, use the of() static method of the List, Set, and Map interfaces to create a read-only List, Set, and Map.

Synchronized View of a Collection

Most collections that are members of the Collections framework discussed in this chapter are not thread-safe and you should not use them in a multi-threaded environment. Note that the collections whose names have the word "concurrent" in them are designed to be thread-safe. You can get a synchronized view of a collection using one of the following static methods of the Collections class. You have one method for each collection type to return the same type of synchronized version of the collection.

- <T> Collection<T> synchronizedCollection(Collection<T> c)
- <T> List<T> synchronizedList(List<T> list)
- <K,V> Map<K,V> synchronizedMap(Map<K,V> m)
- <K,V> NavigableMap<K,V> synchronizedNavigableMap(NavigableMap<K,V> m)
- <T> NavigableSet<T> synchronizedNavigableSet(NavigableSet<T> s)
- <T> Set<T> synchronizedSet(Set<T> s)
- <T> SortedSet<T> synchronizedSortedSet(SortedSet<T> s)
- <K,V> SortedMap<K,V> synchronizedSortedMap (SortedMap<K,V> m)

You need to pay attention when working with a synchronized view of a collection. All reads and writes through the synchronized view will be thread-safe, except when you are iterating over elements of the collection using an iterator. You must synchronize the entire collection during the time you get the iterator and use it. The following snippet of code illustrates this concept:

```
// Suppose you have a Set
Set s = ...; // unsynchronized set

// Get a synchronized view of the Set, s
Set ss = Collections.synchronizedSet(s);

// We need to iterate over elements of ss. Must get a lock on ss first (not on s).
synchronized(ss) {
    Iterator iterator = ss.iterator();

    // use iterator while holding the lock
    while (iterator.hasNext()) {
        Object obj = iterator.next();

        // Do something with obj here
    }
}
```

You need to follow the same logic while iterating over the key, value, or entry views of a synchronized Map. That is, you must get a lock on the synchronized view of the Map while iterating over any of its views.

Checked Collections

Generics provide compile-time type-safety for collections. If the compiler determines that collections may have elements violating its type declaration, it issues an unchecked compile-time warnings. If you ignore the warnings, your code may bypass the generics rules at runtime. Let's consider the following snippet of code:

```
Set<String> s = new HashSet<>();
s.add("Hello");
a.add(123); // A compile-time error
```

You tried to add an Integer to the Set<String>. The compiler made sure that you do not succeed in doing this. Let's bypass the compiler check this time by using the following snippet of code:

```
Set<String> s = new HashSet<>();
s.add("Hello");

Set anythingGoesSet = s;
anythingGoesSet.add(123); // No runtime exception
```

This time, the compiler will issue an unchecked warning for the anythingGoesSet.add(123); statement because it has no way to know that you are adding an incorrect type of object to the Set. The result of this snippet of code is that you declared a Set<String> and you were able to add an Integer to it. You will get a runtime exception when you try to read the Integer object as a String object, and it will be too late to find out which line of code did it!

The Collections class helps you create a checked collection in which you will get a ClassCastException when a piece of code attempts to add an element that violates the rule. This makes debugging easier. When you create a checked collection, you mention the class type of the element it must hold. Adding any other type of element will throw a ClassCastException. You can use the following static methods of the Collections class to get a checked collection of a specific type:

- `<E> Collection<E> checkedCollection(Collection<E> c, Class<E> type)`
- `<E> List<E> checkedList(List<E> list, Class<E> type)`
- `<K,V> Map<K,V> checkedMap(Map<K,V> m, Class<K> keyType, Class<V> valueType)`
- `<K,V> NavigableMap<K,V> checkedNavigableMap(NavigableMap<K,V> m, Class<K> keyType, Class<V> valueType)`
- `<E> NavigableSet<E> checkedNavigableSet(NavigableSet<E> s, Class<E> type)`
- `<E> Queue<E> checkedQueue(Queue<E> queue, Class<E> type)`
- `<E> Set<E> checkedSet(Set<E> s, Class<E> type)`
- `<K,V> SortedMap<K,V> checkedSortedMap(SortedMap<K,V> m, Class<K> keyType, Class<V> valueType)`
- `<E> SortedSet<E> checkedSortedSet(SortedSet<E> s, Class<E> type)`

Here is the solution to the previous example that will throw a `ClassCastException` when an attempt is made to add an `Integer` to the `Set<String>`:

```
// Work with a checked Set of String type
Set<String> checkedSet = Collections.checkedSet(new HashSet<>(), String.class);

Set anythingGoesSet = checkedSet;
anythingGoesSet.add(123); // Throws a ClassCastException
```

■ **Note** Using a checked collection does not stop you from bypassing the compiler. Rather, it helps you identify the offending code easily and exactly at runtime.

Creating Empty Collections

Sometimes you need to call a method that accepts a collection. However, you do not have any elements for the collection to pass. In such cases, you do not need to go through the hassle of creating a collection object. The `Collections` class provides an immutable empty collection object of each type as a return value of its static methods. It also provides methods that return an empty `Iterator`. The following is a partial list of such static methods in the `Collections` class:

- `<T> List<T> emptyList()`
- `<K,V> Map<K,V> emptyMap()`
- `<T> Set<T> emptySet()`
- `<T> Iterator<T> emptyIterator()`
- `<T> ListIterator<T> emptyListIterator()`

Using these methods is straightforward. Suppose there is a method called `m1(Map<String,String> map)`. If you want to pass an empty map to this method, your call would be as follows:

```
m1(Collections.emptyMap());
```

Java 9 added an overloaded static `of()` method to the `List`, `Set`, and `Map` interfaces. The method creates an empty immutable list, set, and map, respectively. You can rewrite the previous statement in Java 9 as follows:

```
m1(Map.of());
```

Creating Singleton Collections

Sometimes you want to create a collection that needs to have one and only one element in it. This kind of situation arises when a method accepts a collection as its argument and you have only one object to pass to that method. Instead of going through the hassle of creating a new collection and adding a lone element to it, you can use one of the three static methods of the `Collections` class, which will create an *immutable* collection with the one specified element. Those methods are as follows:

- `<T> Set<T> singleton(T o)`
- `<T> List<T> singletonList(T o)`
- `<K,V> Map<K,V> singletonMap(K key, V value)`

The following snippet of code creates a singleton set:

```
Set<String> singletonSet = Collections.singleton("Lonely");
```

Java 9 added an overloaded static `of()` method to the `List`, `Set`, and `Map` interfaces. The method creates an empty immutable singleton list, set, and map, respectively. You can rewrite the previous statement in Java 9 as follows:

```
Set<String> singletonSet = Set.of("Lonely");
```

■ **Tip** The implementation of the `of()` method in the `List`, `Set`, and `Map` interfaces are highly optimized. It's better to use this method rather than the methods in the `Collections` class to have an immutable `List`, `Set`, and `Map`.

Understanding Hash-Based Collections

You have used many implementation classes for collections that have the word "hash" in their names, such as `HashSet`, `LinkedHashSet`, `HashMap`, etc. They are known as hash-based collections. They facilitate fast and efficient storage and retrieval of objects. This section discusses the internal workings of hash-based collections in brief.

Let's start with a daily life example. Assume that you have been given many pieces of paper. Each piece of paper has a number written on it. Your task is to organize (or store) those pieces of paper so that you can tell us as quickly as possible whether a specific number exists in the collection of pieces of paper that you were given. You may be given more pieces of paper with a number on them in the future.

One way to organize your numbers is to place them all in one bucket, as shown in Figure 12-5.

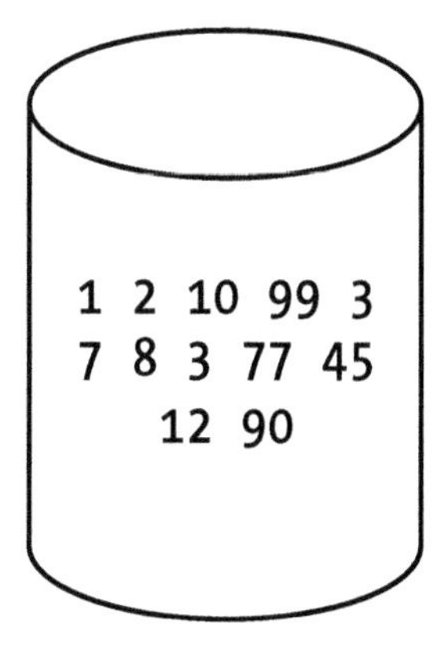

***Figure 12-5.** Placing all numbers in one bucket*

When you are asked to verify the existence of number 89, you will have to look at all of the numbers in your bucket, one at a time, and finally you will say that number 89 does not exist in the collection. In the worst-case scenario, you will have to search the entire bucket to tell if a specific number exists in the bucket. In the best-case scenario, you may find the number on the very first attempt. The average time that it takes you to verify the existence of a number is proportional to the size of the collection. You may realize that organizing your numbers in one bucket is not very efficient for retrieval. As the numbers increase, you will take more time to search through them for a specific number.

Let's try to find a more efficient way to organize the numbers. Let's use more buckets, say four, to store them. Any number that is given to you will be stored in one of the four buckets. If you place a number in one of the four buckets arbitrarily, it poses the same problem in searching. In the worst-case scenario, you will have to search all four buckets for a number because you do not know which bucket contains a specific number. To avoid this inefficiency, let's use an algorithm to place a specific number into a bucket.

To keep the algorithm simple, you will compute the modulus of the number by the number of buckets (four in your case) and place the number in the bucket that corresponds to the modulus value. If you compute a modulus of a number using 4, the value will be 0, 1, 2, or 3. You will name your four buckets as bucket-0, bucket-1, bucket-2, and bucket-3. Which bucket will hold the number 17? The result of 17 modulus 4 is 1. Therefore, the number 17 will go to the bucket-1. Where will number 31 go? The result of 31 modulus 4 is 3. Therefore, the number 31 will go to the bucket-3. Figure 12-6 shows an arrangement in which you have used four buckets to store some numbers based on this algorithm.

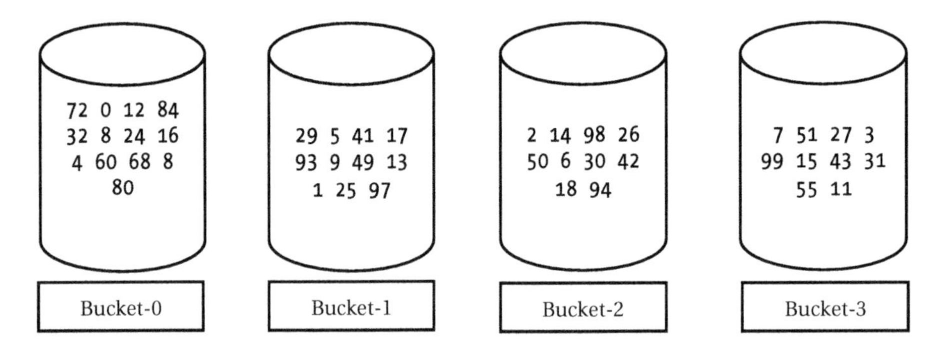

Figure 12-6. *Using four buckets to hold numbers*

Let's walk through the steps to store a number in one of your four buckets. Suppose you are handed the number 94. Which one of the four buckets will store the number 94? First, you evaluate the result of 94 modulus 4, which is 2. Therefore, the number 94 will be stored in the bucket-2. You will follow this logic to decide the bucket for every number that you need to store.

Now, let's walk through the steps of verifying if a number exists in one of the buckets. Suppose you are asked to verify if the number 67 exists in the collection. First, you compute the result of 67 modulus 4, which is 3. According to the logic of storing a number, if the number 67 exists in the collection, it must exist in bucket-3. Once you know the bucket number, you look at each number in the bucket (bucket-3 in this case) for that number. In this case (see Figure 12-6), there are ten numbers in bucket-3 and none of them is 67. After looking at ten numbers in bucket-3, you respond that the number 67 does not exist in the collection. Note that you looked at numbers in only one of the buckets to tell whether the number 67 existed in the collection or not. You did not have to look at numbers in all four buckets. By using an algorithm to store and retrieve a number from the collection, you have shortened the time it takes to search for a number in the collection.

The story is not over yet. Let's consider using four buckets to store numbers where all numbers are a multiple of 4 such as 4, 8, 12, 16, 20, 24, etc. The value of N modulus 4 for all N, which are multiple of 4 is 0. This means that all such numbers will be stored in only one bucket, which is the bucket-0. Is this scenario better than storing all numbers in only one bucket? The answer is no. Using multiple buckets helps in the search process only if the numbers that are stored are uniformly distributed among all buckets. The best-case scenario is when all buckets have only one number in them. In that case, you will be able to tell if a number exists in the collection by just looking at one number in one of the buckets. The search performance may degrade as the size of the collection increases even if numbers are distributed uniformly among the buckets. For example, suppose you have 100 numbers and they are uniformly distributed among four buckets. In the worst-case scenario, you need to search through 25 numbers in a bucket. Suppose the numbers increase to 10,000 and they are still uniformly distributed among the four buckets. Now, in the worst-case scenario, you need to search through 2,500 numbers. To keep your search process fast, you can increase the number of buckets as the numbers in one bucket increases to a point where the time taken to search for a number becomes a performance concern.

The hash-based collections in Java work similar to the collection of numbers that I discussed. Note that a Java collection stores only objects. They do not allow storing of primitive type values. Two methods in the `Object` class are central to the working of hash-based collections. Those methods are `equals()` and `hashCode()`.

Hash-based collections maintain a number of buckets to store objects. When you add an object to a hash-based collection, Java gets the hash code of the object by calling object's `hashCode()` method. Then, it applies an algorithm to the hash code to compute the bucket in which the object should be placed. When you want to check if an object exists in a hash-based collection, Java applies the same logic to compute the bucket in which the object might have been placed. It calls the `hashCode()` method of the object and applies some algorithm to compute the bucket in which it might have been placed. Then, it uses the `equals()` method of the object to compare the object with existing objects in the bucket to check if the object exists in that bucket.

The internal workings of the hash-based collections in Java sound easy. However, it is full of complications for programmers if the `hashCode()` and `equals()` methods are not implemented correctly in the class whose objects are stored in hash-based collections. Let's consider the code for a `BadKey` class, shown in Listing 12-35.

Listing 12-35. A BadKey Class That Is Not a Good Candidate for Keys in Hash-Based Collections

```
// BadKey.java
package com.jdojo.collections;

public class BadKey {
    private int id;

    public BadKey(int id) {
        this.id = id;
    }

    public int getId() {
        return this.id;
    }

    public void setId(int id) {
        this.id = id;
    }

    @Override
    public int hashCode() {
        // Return the value of id as its hash code value
        return id;
    }
```

```
    @Override
    public boolean equals(Object obj) {
        if (obj == this) {
            return true;
        }

        if (obj instanceof BadKey) {
            BadKey bk = (BadKey) obj;
            if (bk.getId() == this.id) {
                return true;
            }
        }

        return false;
    }

    @Override
    public String toString() {
        return String.valueOf(this.id);
    }
}
```

The BadKey class stores an integer value. It is a mutable class. You can modify its state by calling the setId() method and supplying a new value for its id. It overrides the equals() and hashCode() methods of the Object class. The implementation of the hashCode() method is simple. It returns the value of the id instance variable as the hash code. The equals() method checks if the id instance variable's value for two BadKey objects are the same. If two BadKey objects have the same id, they are considered equal.

Consider the program in Listing 12-36. It uses BadKey objects in a Set<BadKey>. Can you spot a problem by looking at the program and the output? Don't worry if you do not see the problem. I will explain it.

Listing 12-36. Using BadKey Objects in a Set

```
// BadKeyTest.java
package com.jdojo.collections;

import java.util.HashSet;
import java.util.Set;

public class BadKeyTest {
    public static void main(String[] args) {
        Set<BadKey> s = new HashSet<>();
        BadKey bk1 = new BadKey(100);
        BadKey bk2 = new BadKey(200);

        // Add two objects bk1 and bk2 to the set
        s.add(bk1);
        s.add(bk2);

        System.out.println("Set contains: " + s);
        System.out.println("Set contains bk1: " + s.contains(bk1));
```

```
        // Set the id for bk1 to 300
        bk1.setId(300);
        System.out.println("Set contains: " + s);
        System.out.println("Set contains bk1: " + s.contains(bk1));
    }
}
```

```
Set contains: [100, 200]
Set contains bk1: true
Set contains: [300, 200]
Set contains bk1: false
```

The program adds two BadKey objects called bk1 and bk2 to the Set. The first line in the output confirms that the set contains the two objects. Then, the value for the id of bk1 object is changed from 100 to 300, which is confirmed by the third line in the output. Since you have not removed the object bk1 from the set, the fourth line of the output is unexpected. The fourth line of the output states that the object bk1 does not exist in the set, whereas the third line of the output states that bk1 object is in the set.

What's wrong? Is the object bk1 in the set or not? The answer is that the object bk1 is in the set until you remove it. If you use a for-each loop or an iterator to access all objects in the set, you will be able to get to it. However, the collection (the set in this case) will not be able to find the object bk1. The reason why the set is not able to find the bk1 object is that the hash code of the object bk1 changed after it was added to the set. Recall that HashSet is a hash-based collection in Java. It uses the hash code of the object to locate the bucket in which the object will be placed. When s.contains(bk1) is executed the second time, the hash code of bk1 will be 300, which is the returned value from its hashCode() method. When the object bk1 was placed in the set, its hash code was 200. Since the hash code of the object bk1 has changed, the set will mistakenly identify a different bucket to locate it. Since the set is looking for the object bk1 in a different bucket than the one in which it was placed, it does not find it. Where is the problem? The problem lies in the hashCode() method of the BadKey class. The BadKey class is a mutable class and the mutable state of this class (the id instance variable) has been used to compute its hash code, which is causing the problem in locating the object in the set.

One way to fix this problem of apparently losing the BadKey objects in the set is to return a constant value from its hashCode() method, say 99. The following is a valid implementation (not a good one, though) of the hashCode() method of the BadKey class:

```
// BadKey.java
package com.jdojo.collections;

public class BadKey {

    // Other code goes here...

    public int hashCode() {
        // Return the same value 99 all the time
        return 99;
    }
}
```

This code will fix the problem of losing the object bk1 in the example shown in Listing 12-36 because hash code for an object of the BadKey class never changes. However, it introduces another issue that is related to the performance of the hash-based collection. If you store objects of the BadKey class in a hash-based collection, say a set, all objects will hash to the same bucket because all objects of the BadKey class will have the same hash code value, which is 99. You fixed one problem and introduced another!

The main issue with the BadKey class is its mutability. It has only one instance variable named id that is mutable. You should consider the following guidelines when you work with mutable objects with hash-based collections:

- You should avoid using objects of a mutable class as elements in a Set and as keys in a Map, if possible. Consider using objects of immutable classes such String, Integer, or your own immutable class as keys for a Map and elements for a Set.
- Implement the equals() and hashCode() methods of your mutable class very carefully. You must return the same value from the hashCode() method of the object of the mutable class. Otherwise, you will lose track of the objects of your mutable class in hash-based collections. If a mutable class has some part of its state that is immutable, use those immutable parts of the class to compute its hash code value so that the hash code value does not change for an object of the mutable class. As a last resort, which is not recommended, consider returning a constant integer from the hashCode() method of your mutable class.
- Make sure that the contracts for the equals() and hashCode() methods are fulfilled.

Summary

A collection is a group of objects. Java provides the Collections framework containing several interfaces and classes for working with a wide range of collection types such as lists, queues, sets, and maps. The Collections framework provides an interface to represent a specific type of collection. Each interface in the framework has at least one implementation class, except the Collection interface. Collection-related interfaces and classes are in the java.util package. Collection classes to be used in multi-threaded programs where synchronization is needed are in the java.util.concurrent package.

The Collections framework contains a Collection interface that is the root for most of the collections. The Collection interface contains most of the methods used with all types of collection (except for the Map-based collections). The interface provides methods for adding elements, removing elements, knowing the size of the collection, etc. Specific subinterfaces of the Collection interface provide additional methods to work with the specific type of collections.

The Collections framework provides a uniform way for traversing elements of all types of collections using iterators. An instance of the Iterator interface represents an iterator. All collections support traversing their elements using the for-each loop and a forEach() method.

In mathematics, a set is a collection of unordered unique elements. An instance of the Set interface represents a set in the Collections framework. HashSet is the implementation class for the mathematical set.

An instance of the SortedSet represents an ordered unique set. TreeSet is the implementation class for the SortedSet interface. Elements in a sorted set can be sorted in natural order or in a custom order using a Comparator.

A queue is a collection of objects used for processing objects one at a time. Objects enter the queue from one end and exit the queue from another end. The Queue interface in the Collections framework represents a queue. The Collections framework provides several implementation classes for the Queue interface to support different types of queues, such as a simple queue, blocking queue, priority queue, delay queue, etc.

A list is an ordered collection of objects. An instance of the List interface represents a list in the Collections framework. ArrayList and LinkedList are two implementation classes for the List interface that are backed up by an array and a linked list, respectively. Each element in the list has an index that starts from 0. The List interface provides methods that let you access its elements sequentially or randomly using indexes of the elements. The Collections framework supports only a dense list; that is, there cannot be a gap between two elements in the list.

A map is another type of collection that stores key-value pairs. Keys in a map must be unique. An instance of the Map interface represents a map in the Collections framework. HashMap is the simple implementation class for the Map interface. The Collections framework also supports sorted, navigable, and concurrent maps. A sorted map stores all key-value pairs sorted based on keys. An instance of the SortedMap interface represents a sorted map. TreeMap is the implementation class for the SortedMap interface. An instance of the NavigableMap and ConcurrentMap represent a navigable map and concurrent map, respectively.

The Collections framework contains a utility class called Collections that contains only static methods. Methods in this class let you apply different types of algorithms to a collection—for example, shuffling elements in a collection, rotating its elements, sorting elements of a list, etc. The class also provides methods to obtain different views of collections, such as read-only view, synchronized view, unmodifiable view, etc.

A hash-based collection uses buckets to store its elements. The number of buckets is determined based on the number of elements in the collection and the required performance. When an element is added to the collection, the element's hash code is used to determine the bucket in which the element will be stored. A reverse process is used when an element is searched in the collection. Hash-based collections provide faster element storage and retrieval.

QUESTIONS AND EXERCISES

1. What is the Collections framework?
2. What is the name of the interface that all collections in the Collections framework, except maps, implement?
3. List the names of different types of operations that you can perform on collections in the Collection Framework.
4. What method in the Collection<E> interface lets you obtain the size of the collection?
5. What methods in the Collection<E> interface let you remove all elements in the collection in one go and one element at a time?
6. What method in the Collection<E> interface would you use to check that the collection contains a given object?
7. How do you check if a collection is empty?
8. Name the method in the Collection<E> interface that lets you convert a collection to an array.
9. Enumerate three ways to iterate over elements of a collection. Can you use a simple for loop statement to iterate over the elements of a collection? What is a fail-fast iterator?
10. Java supports mathematical sets, sorted sets, and navigable sets. Differentiate between the three types of sets and name the interfaces and at least one implementation class for those interfaces representing these three types of sets.
11. How do you traverse the elements in a set?

12. Consider the following two immutable sets of integers:

```
Set<Integer> s1 = Set.of(10, 20, 30, 40);
Set<Integer> s2 = Set.of(10, 15, 20, 25, 30);
```

Write a snippet of code to print the union, intersection, and difference of the two sets, `s1` and `s2`, as computed in mathematics.

13. Spot the problem with the following snippet of code that attempts to create an immutable set of integers:

```
Set<Integer> s1 = Set.of(20, 10, 30, 10);
```

14. Consider the following snippet of code:

```
Set<Integer> s1 = Set.of();
System.out.println("s1.isEmpty(): " + s1.isEmpty());
s1.add(2018);
System.out.println("s1.isEmpty(): " + s1.isEmpty());
```

Will this code compile? If your answer is yes, what will be the output? If you think the code will compile, but will throw a runtime exception, describe the reason for the exception and a way to fix the problem.

15. In your application, you need to work with a sorted range of unique integers. Which interface and implementation class of the set collection family will you use for this purpose?

16. How do you sort the elements in a set in natural order and custom order?

17. What is the difference between a `List` and a `Set`?

18. Consider the following incomplete snippet of code:

```
List<String> list = List.of("Li", "Xi", "Bo", "Da", "Fa", "Bo");
int i1 = /* your code goes here */;
int i2 = /* your code goes here */;
System.out.printf("First and last indexes of Bo are %d and %d.%n", i1, i2);
```

Complete this snippet of code to print the first and the last indexes of the element `"Bo"`. The output should be as follows:

```
First and last indexes of Bo are 2 and 5.
```

19. What is the difference between an `Iterator` and `ListIterator`? Can you use an `Iterator` to traverse elements in a `List`?

20. Suppose you need to use a list in your program in which you need to frequently insert and remove elements from the beginning of the list. What implementation class of the `List` interface would you choose to achieve this?

21. The following snippet of code contains a logical error. Describe the error.

```
List<Integer> list = new ArrayList<>();
list.add(0, 0);
list.add(1, 10);
list.add(2, 20);
list.add(5, 50);
System.out.println(list);
```

22. Consider the following snippet of incomplete code:

```
List<Integer> list = new ArrayList<>();
list.add(10);
list.add(20);
list.add(30);

System.out.println(list);

/* your code goes here */

System.out.println(list);
```

Complete this snippet of code so that each element in the list is replaced by a value, which is double the current value. You are encouraged to use the following `replaceAll()` method of the `List<E>` interface to achieve this:

```
default void replaceAll(UnaryOperator<E> operator)
```

The expected output is as follows:

```
[10, 20, 30]
[20, 40, 60]
```

23. Name the interface whose instances represent simple queues in a Java program.

24. What is the difference between the FIFO and LIFO queues? Name the implementation class that implements a simple FIFO and LIFO queue.

25. What is the difference between using the `add(E e)` and `offer(E e)` methods of the `Queue<E>` interface to insert elements to the queue?

26. What is a priority queue? Name the implementation class for priority queues in Java.

27. Write a complete program that uses a priority queue to store names of a few people. The output of your program should demonstrate that a person with a shorter name has a higher priority in the queue. Add a few names to the queue and remove them one at a time. Print the removed elements and the remaining elements in the queue every time you remove an element.

28. What is the difference between a `Queue` and a `Deque`? Name two implementation classes of the `Deque<E>` interface.

29. Can you use a `Deque` to represent a stack? If your answer is yes, demonstrate it with an example.

30. What is a blocking queue? Name the interface whose instances represent blocking queues. What is fairness of a blocking queue?

31. What is a map? Name the interface whose instances represent maps in Java.

32. Name two implementation classes for the `Map<K,V>` interface in Java.

33. What method do you use to get the number of entries in a `Map`? How do get a `Set` of all keys in a `Map`? How do you get a `Collection` of all values in a `Map`?

34. Consider the following snippet of code that creates a map and populates it with names and their lucky numbers. Complete the code to print the unique names and unique lucky numbers in the map.

```
Map<String,Integer> map = new HashMap<>();
map.put("Bo", 1);
map.put("Co", 8);
map.put("Do", 19);
map.put("Lo", 1);
map.put("Mo", 8);

/* your code goes here */
```

35. Create immutable maps with the following five <key, value> entries of country codes and country names, once using the `of()` method and once using the `ofEntries()` method of the `Map` interface: `<1, "United States">`, `<24, "Austria">`, `<66, "Thailand">`, `<49, "Germany">`, and `<91, "India">`. The keys are integers and values are strings. Print each entry on a separate line.

36. What is the `Collections` class? Name a few purposes for which this class is used.

37. What is wrong with the following snippet of code?

```
List<Integer> list = new ArrayList<>();
list.add(10);
list.add(20);
list.add(5, 50);
```

38. Complete the following snippet of code that sorts a `List<Integer>` using the default `sort()` method in the `List` interface:

```
List<Integer> list = new ArrayList<>();
list.add(40);
list.add(10);
list.add(30);
list.add(20);
```

```
System.out.println("List: " + list);
list.sort(/* your code goes here */);
System.out.println("Sorted List: " + list);
```

The expected output is as follows:

```
List: [40, 10, 30, 20]
Sorted List: [10, 20, 30, 40]
```

39. Consider the following snippet of code that uses a binary search to search for 20 in the list:

```
List<Integer> list = new ArrayList<>();
list.add(40);
list.add(10);
list.add(30);
list.add(20);
System.out.println("List: " + list);

int index = Collections.binarySearch(list, 20);
System.out.println("Index of 20 us in the list is " + index);
```

The current output is as follows:

```
List: [40, 10, 30, 20]
Index of 20 us in the list is -3
```

The output indicates that 20 is not in the list. However, 20 is present in the list. Fix this snippet of code so that 20 is found in the list using the binary search. Describe your findings.

40. What will be the output when you run the following snippet of code:

```
List<Integer> list = new ArrayList<>();
list.add(10);
list.add(20);
list.add(30);
list.add(40);
System.out.println("List: " + list);

Collections.rotate(list, 4);
System.out.println("Rotated List: " + list)
```

41. Write a snippet of code to create a modifiable `Set<Integer>`. Get an unmodifiable view of this set and demonstrate that you can still modify the original modifiable set and those modifications are reflected in the read-only set. Also demonstrate that an attempt to modify the read-only set throws an `UnsupportedOperationException`.

42. What is the advantage of using checked collections?

43. Write a snippet of code to create a singleton immutable `List<String>` with a lone element, `"Hello"`.

44. What are hash-based collections? What kind of special care must be taken with a class if the objects of the class will be stored in hash-based collections?

CHAPTER 13

Streams

In this chapter, you will learn:

- What streams are
- Differences between collections and streams
- How to create streams from different types of data sources
- How to represent an optional value using the `Optional` class
- Applying different types of operations on streams
- Collecting data from streams using collectors
- Grouping and partitioning a stream's data
- Finding and matching data in streams
- How to work with parallel streams

All example programs in this chapter are members of a `jdojo.streams` module, as declared in Listing 13-1.

Listing 13-1. The Declaration of a jdojo.streams Module

```
// module-info.java
module jdojo.streams {
    exports com.jdojo.streams;
}
```

What Are Streams?

An aggregate operation computes a single value from a collection of values. The result of an aggregate operation may be simply a primitive value, an object, or a `void`. Note that an object may represent a single entity such as a person or a collection of values such as a list, a set, a map, etc.

A stream is a sequence of data elements supporting sequential and parallel aggregate operations. Computing the sum of all elements in a stream of integers, mapping all names in a list to their lengths, etc. are examples of aggregate operations on streams.

Looking at the definition of streams, it seems that they are like collections. So, how do streams differ from collections? Both are abstractions for a collection of data elements. Collections focus on storage of data elements for efficient access whereas streams focus on aggregate computations on data elements from a data source that is typically, but not necessarily, collections.

K. Sharan, *Java Language Features*, https://doi.org/10.1007/978-1-4842-3348-1_13

In this section, I discuss the following features of streams, comparing them with collections when necessary:

- Streams have no storage.
- Streams can represent a sequence of infinite elements.
- The design of streams is based on internal iteration.
- Streams are designed to be processed in parallel with no additional work from the developers.
- Streams are designed to support functional programming.
- Streams support lazy operations.
- Streams can be ordered or unordered.
- Streams cannot be reused.

The following sections present brief snippets of code using streams. The code is meant to give you a feel for the Streams API and to compare the Streams API with the Collections API. You do not need to understand the code fully at this point. I explain it later in detail.

Streams Have No Storage

A collection is an in-memory data structure that stores all its elements. All elements must exist in memory before they are added to the collection. A stream has no storage; it does not store elements. A stream pulls elements from a data source on-demand and passes them to a pipeline of operations for processing.

Infinite Streams

A collection cannot represent a group of infinite elements, whereas a stream can. A collection stores all its elements in memory, and therefore, it is not possible to have an infinite number of elements in a collection. Having a collection of an infinite number of elements will require an infinite amount of memory and the storage process will continue forever. A stream pulls its elements from a data source that can be a collection, a function that generates data, an I/O channel, etc. Because a function can generate an infinite number of elements and a stream can pull data from it on demand, it is possible to have a stream representing a sequence of infinite data elements.

Internal Iteration vs. External Iteration

Collections are based on external iteration. You obtain an iterator for a collection and process elements of the collections in serial using the iterator. Suppose you have a list of integers from 1 to 5. You would compute the sum of the squares of all odd integers in the list as follows:

```
List<Integer> numbers = List.of(1, 2, 3, 4, 5);
int sum = 0;
for (int n : numbers) {
    if (n % 2 == 1) {
        int square = n * n;
        sum = sum + square;
    }
}
```

This example uses a for-each loop that performs an external iteration on the list of integers. Simply put, the client code (the for loop in this case) pulls the elements out of collection and applies the logic to get the result. Consider the following snippet of code that uses a stream to compute the sum of the squares of all odd integers in the same list:

```
int sum = numbers.stream()
                 .filter(n -> n % 2 == 1)
                 .map(n -> n * n)
                 .reduce(0, Integer::sum);
```

Did you notice the power and the simplicity of streams? You replaced five statements with just one statement. However, the code brevity is not the point that I want to make. The point is that you did not iterate over the elements in the list when you used the stream. The stream did that for you internally. This is what I meant by internal iteration supported by streams. You specify to a stream what you want by passing an algorithm using lambda expressions to the stream and the stream applies your algorithm to its data element by iterating over its elements *internally* and gives you the result.

Using external iteration, typically, produces sequential code; that is, the code can be executed only by one thread. For example, when you wrote the logic to compute the sum using a for-each loop, the loop must be executed only by one thread. All modern computers come with a multicore processor. Wouldn't it be nice to take advantage of the multicore processor to execute the logic in parallel? The Java library provides a Fork/Join framework to divide a task into subtasks recursively and execute the subtasks in parallel, taking advantage of a multicore processor. However, the Fork/Join framework is not so simple to use, especially for beginners.

Streams come to your rescue! They are designed to process their elements in parallel without you even noticing it! This does not mean that streams automatically decide for you when to process their elements in serial or parallel. You just need to tell a stream that you want to use parallel processing and the stream will take care of the rest. Streams take care of the details of using the Fork/Join framework internally. You can compute the sum of squares of odd integers in the list in parallel, like so:

```
int sum = numbers.parallelStream()
                 .filter(n -> n % 2 == 1)
                 .map(n -> n * n)
                 .reduce(0, Integer::sum);
```

All you had to do was replace the method called stream() with parallelStream()! The Streams API uses multiple threads to filter the odd integers, compute their squares and add them to compute partial sums. Finally, it joins the partial sums to give you the result. In this example, you have only five elements in the list and using multiple threads to process them is overkill. You will not use parallel processing for such a trivial computation. I have presented this example to drive home the point that parallelizing your computation using streams is free; you get it by just using a different method name! The second point is that parallelizing the computation was made possible because of the internal iteration provided by the stream.

Streams are designed to use internal iteration. They provide an iterator() method that returns an Iterator to be used for external iteration of its elements. You will "never" need to iterate elements of a stream yourself using its iterator. If you ever need it, here is how to use it:

```
// Get a list of integers from 1 to 5
List<Integer> numbers = List.of(1, 2, 3, 4, 5);
...

// Get an iterator from the stream
Iterator<Integer> iterator = numbers.stream().iterator();
```

```
while(iterator.hasNext()) {
    int n = iterator.next();
    ...
}
```

Imperative vs. Functional

Collections support imperative programming whereas streams support declarative programming. This is an offshoot of collections supporting external iteration whereas streams support internal iteration. When you use collections, you need to know "what" you want and "how" to get it; this is the feature of imperative programming. When you use streams, you specify only "what" you want in terms of stream operations; the "how" part is taken care by the Streams API. The Streams API supports the functional programming. Operations on a stream produce a result without modifying the data source. Like in the functional programming, when you use streams, you specify "what" operations you want to perform on its elements using the built-in methods provided by the Streams API, typically by passing a lambda expression to those methods, customizing the behavior of those operations.

Stream Operations

A stream supports two types of operations:

- Intermediate operations
- Terminal operations

Intermediate operations are also known as *lazy* operations. Terminal operations are also known as *eager* operations. Operations are known as lazy and eager based on the way they pull the data elements from the data source. A lazy operation on a stream does not process the elements of the stream until another eager operation is called on the stream.

Streams connect through a chain of operations forming a stream pipeline. A stream is inherently lazy until you call a terminal operation on it. An intermediate operation on a stream produces another stream. When you call a terminal operation on a stream, the elements are pulled from the data source and pass through the stream pipeline. Each intermediate operation takes elements from an input stream and transforms the elements to produce an output stream. The terminal operation takes inputs from a stream and produces the result. Figure 13-1 shows a stream pipeline with a data source, three streams, and three operations. The *filter* and *map* operations are intermediate operations and the *reduce* operation is a terminal operation.

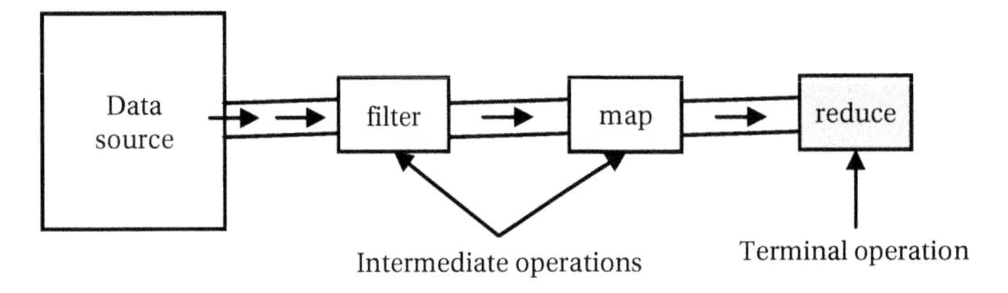

Figure 13-1. *A stream pipeline*

In the figure, the first stream (on the left) pulls data from the data source and becomes the input source for the filter operation. The filter operation produces another stream containing data for which the filter condition is true. The stream produced by the filter operation becomes the input for the map operation. The map operation produces another stream that contains the mapped data. The stream produced by the map operation becomes the input for the reduce operation. The reduce operation is a terminal operation. It computes and returns the result, and then the stream processing is over.

■ **Note** I use the phrase "a stream pulls/consumes elements from its data source" in the preceding discussion. This does not mean that the stream removes the elements from the data source; it only reads them. Streams are designed to support functional programming in which data elements are read and operations on the read data elements produce new data elements. However, the data elements are not modified (or at least should not be modified).

Stream processing does not start until a terminal operation is called. If you just call intermediate operations on a stream, nothing exciting happens, except that they create another stream of objects in memory, without reading data from the data source. This implies that you must use a terminal operation on a stream for it to process the data to produce a result. This is also the reason that the terminal operation is called a result-bearing operation and intermediate operations are also called non-result-bearing operations.

You saw the following code that uses a pipeline of stream operations to compute the sum of the squares of odd integers from 1 to 5:

```
List<Integer> numbers = List.of(1, 2, 3, 4, 5);
int sum = numbers.stream()
                 .filter(n -> n % 2 == 1)
                 .map(n -> n * n)
                 .reduce(0, Integer::sum);
```

Figure 13-2 through Figure 13-5 show the states of the stream pipeline as operations are added. Notice that no data flows through the stream until the reduce operation is called. The last figure shows the integers in the input stream for an operation and the mapped (or transformed) integers produced by the operation. The reduce terminal operation produces the result 35.

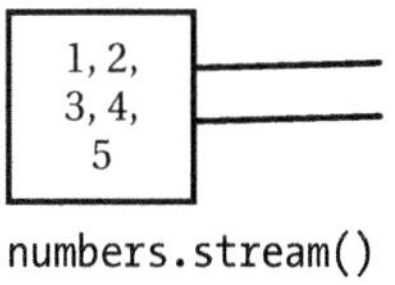

1, 2,
3, 4,
5

`numbers.stream()`

Figure 13-2. *The stream pipeline after the stream object is created*

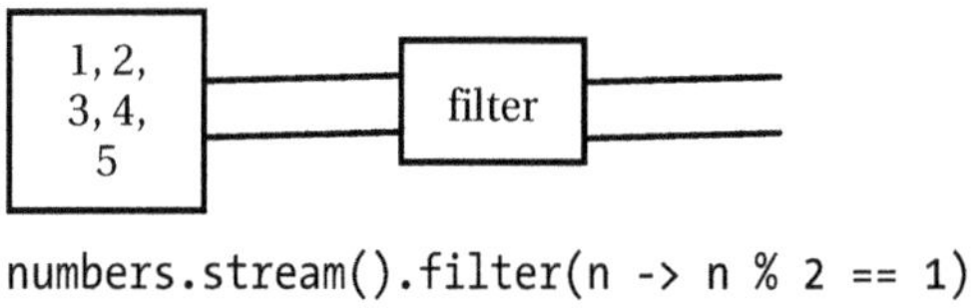

1, 2,
3, 4,
5

filter

`numbers.stream().filter(n -> n % 2 == 1)`

Figure 13-3. *The stream pipeline after the filter operation is called*

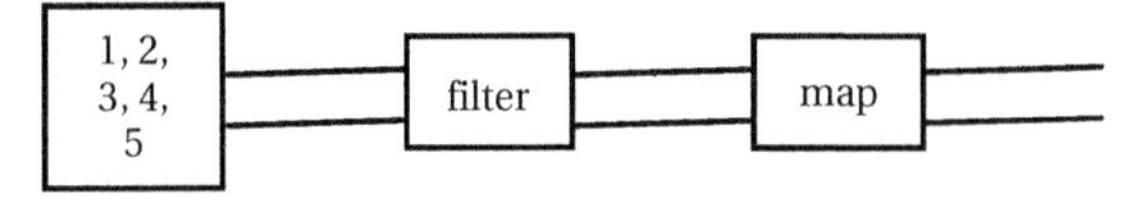


```
numbers.stream().filter(n -> n % 2 == 1).map(n -> n * n)
```

Figure 13-4. *The stream pipeline after the map operation is called*

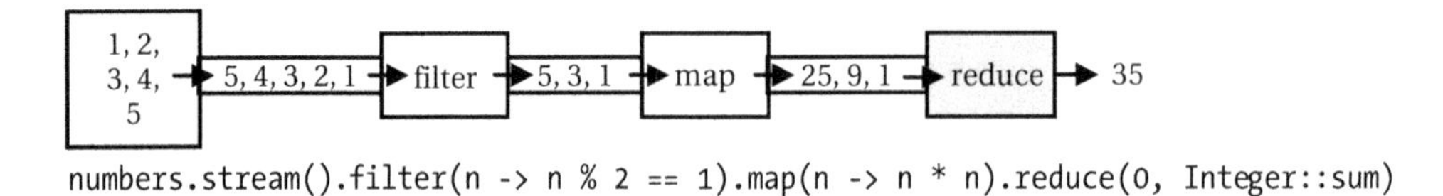

Figure 13-5. *The stream pipeline after the reduce operation is called*

Ordered Streams

A stream can be ordered or unordered. An ordered stream preserves the order of its elements. The Streams API lets you convert an ordered stream into an unordered stream. A stream can be ordered because it represents an ordered data source such as a list or a sorted set. You can also convert an unordered stream into an ordered stream by applying an intermediate operation such as sorting.

A data source is said to have an encounter order if the order in which the elements are traversed by an iterator is predictable and meaningful. For example, arrays and lists always have an encounter order that is from the element at index 0 to the element at the last index. All ordered data sources have an encounter order for their elements. Streams based on data sources having an encounter order also have an encounter order for their elements. Sometimes a stream operation may impose an encounter order on an otherwise unordered stream. For example, a `HashSet` does not have an encounter order for its elements. However, applying a sort operation on a stream based on a `HashSet` imposes an encounter order so that elements are yielded in sorted order.

Streams Are Not Reusable

Unlike collections, streams are not reusable. They are one-shot objects. A stream cannot be reused after calling a terminal operation on it. If you need to perform a computation on the same elements from the same data source again, you must recreate the stream pipeline. A stream implementation may throw an `IllegalStateException` if it detects that the stream is being reused.

Architecture of the Streams API

Figure 13-6 shows a class diagram for the stream-related interfaces. Stream-related interfaces and classes are in the `java.util.stream` package.

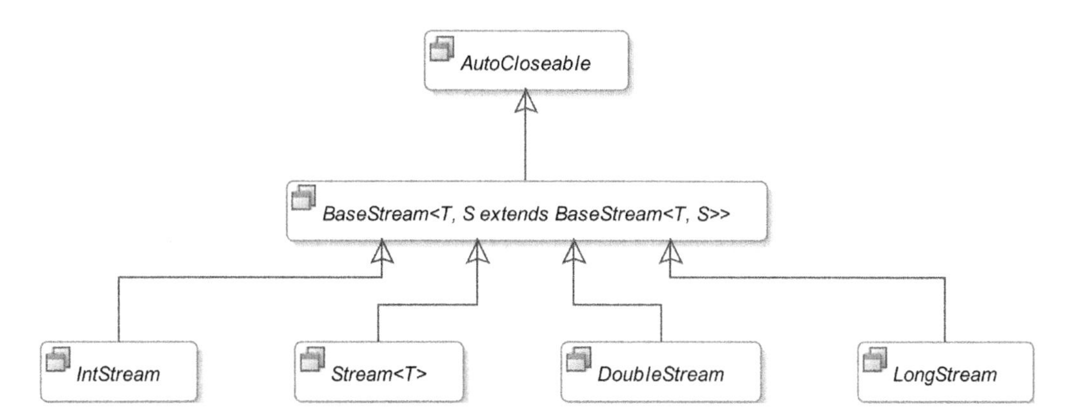

***Figure 13-6.** A class diagram for stream-related interfaces in the Streams API*

All stream interfaces inherit from the `BaseStream` interface, which inherits from the `AutoCloseable` interface from the `java.lang` package. In practice, most streams use collections as their data source, and collections do not need to be closed. When a stream is based on a closeable data source such as a file I/O channel, you may create the instance of the stream using a `try-with-resources` statement to get it closed automatically. Methods common to all types of streams are declared in the `BaseStream` interface as follows.

- `Iterator<T> iterator()`: It returns an iterator for the stream. You will almost never need to use this method in your code. This is a terminal operation. After calling this method, you cannot call any other methods on the stream.
- `S sequential()`: It returns a sequential stream. If the stream is already sequential, it returns itself. Use this method to convert a parallel stream into a sequential stream. This is an intermediate operation.
- `S parallel()`: It returns a parallel stream. If the stream is already parallel, it returns itself. Use this method to convert a parallel stream into a sequential stream. This is an intermediate operation.
- `boolean isParallel()`: It returns `true` if the stream is parallel, `false` otherwise. The result is unpredictable when this method is called after invoking a terminal stream operation method.
- `S unordered()`: It returns an unordered version of the stream. If the stream is already unordered, it returns itself. This is an intermediate operation.
- `void close()`: It closes the stream. You do not need to close collection based streams. Operating on a closed stream throws a `IllegalStateException`.
- `S onClose(Runnable closeHandler)`: It returns an equivalent stream with an additional close handler. Close handlers are run when the `close()` method is called on the stream and are executed in the order they were added.

The `Stream<T>` interface represents a stream of the element type `T`; for example, a `Stream<Person>` represents a stream of `Person` objects. The interface contains methods representing intermediate and terminal operations such as `filter()`, `map()`, `reduce()`, `collect()`, `max()`, `min()`, etc. When you work with streams, you will use these methods most of the time. I discuss each method in detail shortly.

Note that the `Stream<T>` interface takes a type parameter `T`, which means that you can use it only to work with the elements of the reference type. If you have to work with a stream of primitive type such as `int`, `long`, etc., using `Stream<T>` will involve an additional cost of boxing and unboxing the elements when primitive values are needed. For example, adding all elements of a Stream<Integer> will require unboxing all Integer elements to int. The designers of the Streams API realized this and they provided three specialized stream interfaces called IntStream, LongStream, and DoubleStream to work with primitives; these interfaces contain methods to deal with primitive values. Note that you do not have stream interfaces representing other primitive types such as float, short, etc. because the three stream types can be used to work with other primitive type values.

A Quick Example

Let's look at a quick example of using streams. The code reads a list of integers and computes the sum of the squares of all odd integers in the list.

The stream() method in the Collection interface returns a sequential stream where the Collection acts as the data source. The following snippet of code creates a List<Integer> and obtains a Stream<Integer> from the list:

```
// Get a list of integers from 1 to 5
List<Integer> numbersList = List.of(1, 2, 3, 4, 5);

// Get a stream from the list
Stream<Integer> numbersStream = numbersList.stream();
```

The filter() method of the Stream<T> interface takes a Predicate<? super T> as an argument and returns a Stream<T> with elements of the original stream for which the specified Predicate returns true. The following statement obtains a stream of only odd integers:

```
// Get a stream of odd integers
Stream<Integer> oddNumbersStream = numbersStream.filter(n -> n % 2 == 1);
```

Notice the use of the lambda expression as the argument for the filter() method. The lambda expression returns true if the element in the stream is not divisible by 2.

The map() method of the Stream<T> interface takes Function<? super T,? extends R> as an argument. Each element in the stream is passed to this Function and a new stream is generated containing the returned values from the Function. The following statement takes all odd integers and maps them to their squares:

```
// Get a stream of the squares of odd integers
Stream<Integer> squaredNumbersStream = oddNumbersStream.map(n -> n * n);
```

Finally, you need to add the squares of all odd integers to get the result. The reduce(T identity, BinaryOperator<T> accumulator) method of the Stream<T> interface performs a reduction operation on the stream to reduce the stream to a single value. It takes an initial value and an accumulator that is a BinaryOperator<T> as arguments. The first time, the accumulator receives the initial value and the first element of the stream as arguments and returns a value. The second time, the accumulator receives the value returned from its previous call and the second element from the stream. This process continues until all elements of the stream have been passed to the accumulator. The returned value from the last call of the accumulator is returned from the reduce() method. The following snippet of code performs the sum of all integers in the stream:

```
// Sum all integers in the stream
int sum = squaredNumbersStream.reduce(0, (n1, n2) -> n1 + n2);
```

The Integer class contains a static sum() method to perform the sum of two integers. You can rewrite the previous statement using a method reference, like so:

```
// Sum all integers in the stream
int sum = squaredNumbersStream.reduce(0, Integer::sum);
```

In this example, I break down each operation on the stream into a single statement. You cannot use the returned streams from intermediate operations, except to apply other operations on them. Typically, you care about the result of the terminal operation, not the intermediate streams. Streams are designed to support method chaining to avoid temporary variables, which you used in this example. You can combine these statements into one statement as follows:

```
// Sum the squares of all odd integers in the numbers list
int sum = numbersList.stream()
                     .filter(n -> n % 2 == 1)
                     .map(n -> n * n)
                     .reduce(0, Integer::sum);
```

I chain all method calls on streams to form only one statement in subsequent examples. Listing 13-2 contains the complete program for this example. Note that you are working with only integers in this example. For better performance, you could have used an IntStream in this example. I show you how to use an IntStream later.

Listing 13-2. Computing the Sum of the Squares of All Odd Integers From 1 to 5

```
// SquaredIntsSum.java
package com.jdojo.streams;

import java.util.List;

public class SquaredIntsSum {
    public static void main(String[] args) {
        // Get a list of integers from 1 to 5
        List<Integer> numbers = List.of(1, 2, 3, 4, 5);

        // Compute the sum of the squares of all odd integers in the list
        int sum = numbers.stream()
                         .filter(n -> n % 2 == 1)
                         .map(n -> n * n)
                         .reduce(0, Integer::sum);

        System.out.println("Sum = " + sum);
    }
}
```

```
Sum = 35
```

I show many examples of performing aggregate operations on different types of streams. Most of the time, it is easier to explain the stream operations using streams of numbers and strings. I show some real-world examples of using streams by using a stream of Person objects. Listing 13-3 contains the declaration for the Person class.

Listing 13-3. A Person Class

```
// Person.java
package com.jdojo.streams;

import java.time.LocalDate;
import java.time.Month;
import java.util.List;

public class Person {
    // An enum to represent the gender of a person
    public static enum Gender {
        MALE, FEMALE
    }

    private long id;
    private String name;
    private Gender gender;
    private LocalDate dob;
    private double income;

    public Person(long id, String name, Gender gender, LocalDate dob, double income) {
        this.id = id;
        this.name = name;
        this.gender = gender;
        this.dob = dob;
        this.income = income;
    }

    public long getId() {
        return id;
    }

    public void setId(long id) {
        this.id = id;
    }

    public String getName() {
        return name;
    }

    public void setName(String name) {
        this.name = name;
    }

    public Gender getGender() {
        return gender;
    }

    public boolean isMale() {
        return this.gender == Gender.MALE;
    }
```

```
    public boolean isFemale() {
        return this.gender == Gender.FEMALE;
    }

    public void setGender(Gender gender) {
        this.gender = gender;
    }

    public LocalDate getDob() {
        return dob;
    }

    public void setDob(LocalDate dob) {
        this.dob = dob;
    }

    public double getIncome() {
        return income;
    }

    public void setIncome(double income) {
        this.income = income;
    }

    public static List<Person> persons() {
        Person ken = new Person(1, "Ken", Gender.MALE,
                LocalDate.of(1970, Month.MAY, 4), 6000.0);
        Person jeff = new Person(2, "Jeff", Gender.MALE,
                LocalDate.of(1970, Month.JULY, 15), 7100.0);
        Person donna = new Person(3, "Donna", Gender.FEMALE,
                LocalDate.of(1962, Month.JULY, 29), 8700.0);
        Person chris = new Person(4, "Chris", Gender.MALE,
                LocalDate.of(1993, Month.DECEMBER, 16), 1800.0);
        Person laynie = new Person(5, "Laynie", Gender.FEMALE,
                LocalDate.of(2012, Month.DECEMBER, 13), 0.0);
        Person lee = new Person(6, "Li", Gender.MALE,
                LocalDate.of(2001, Month.MAY, 9), 2400.0);

        // Create a list of persons
        List<Person> persons = List.of(ken, jeff, donna, chris, laynie, lee);

        return persons;
    }

    @Override
    public String toString() {
        String str = String.format("(%s, %s, %s, %s, %.2f)",
                id, name, gender, dob, income);
        return str;
    }
}
```

The Person class contains a static Gender enum to represent the gender of a person. The class declares five instance variables (id, name, gender, dob, and income), getters, and setters. The isMale() and isFemale() methods have been declared to be used as method references in lambda expressions. You will use a list of people frequently, and, for that purpose, the class contains a static method called persons() to get a list of people.

Creating Streams

There are many ways to create streams. Many existing classes in the Java libraries have received new methods that return a stream. Based on the data source, stream creation can be categorized as follows:

- Streams from values
- Empty streams
- Streams from functions
- Streams from arrays
- Streams from collections
- Streams from files
- Streams from other sources

Streams from Values

The Stream interface contains the following three static methods to create a sequential Stream from a single value and multiple values:

- `<T> Stream<T> of(T t)`
- `<T> Stream<T> of(T...values)`
- `<T> Stream<T> ofNullable(T t)`

The following snippet of code creates two streams:

```
// Creates a stream with one string element
Stream<String> stream = Stream.of("Hello");

// Creates a stream with four string elements
Stream<String> stream = Stream.of("Ken", "Jeff", "Chris", "Ellen");
```

The ofNullable() method was added to the Stream interface in Java 9. It returns a stream with a single value if the specified value is non-null. Otherwise, it returns an empty stream.

```
String str = "Hello";

// Stream s1 will have one element "Hello"
Stream<String> s1 = Stream.ofNullable(str);

str = null;

// Stream s2 is an empty stream because str is null
Stream<String> s2 = Stream.ofNullable(str);
```

You created a List<Integer> and called its stream() method to get a stream object in Listing 13-2. You can rewrite that example using the Stream.of() method as follows:

```
import java.util.stream.Stream;
...
// Compute the sum of the squares of all odd integers in the list
int sum = Stream.of(1, 2, 3, 4, 5)
                .filter(n -> n % 2 == 1)
                .map(n -> n * n)
                .reduce(0, Integer::sum);

System.out.println("Sum = " + sum);
```

```
Sum = 35
```

Note that the second version of the of() method takes a varargs argument and you can use it to create a stream from an array of objects as well. The following snippet of code creates a stream from a String array.

```
String[] names  = {"Ken", "Jeff", "Chris", "Ellen"};

// Creates a stream of four strings in the names array
Stream<String> stream = Stream.of(names);
```

■ **Tip** The Stream.of() method creates a stream whose elements are of reference type. If you want to create a stream of primitive values from an array of primitive types, you need to use the Arrays.stream() method, which I explain shorty.

The following snippet of code creates a stream of strings from a String array returned from the split() method of the String class:

```
String str  = "Ken,Jeff,Chris,Ellen";

// The stream will contain 4 elements: "Ken", "Jeff", "Chris", and "Ellen"
Stream<String> stream = Stream.of(str.split(","));
```

The Stream interface also supports creating a stream using the builder pattern using the Stream.Builder<T> interface whose instance represents a stream builder. The builder() static method of the Stream interface returns a stream builder.

```
// Gets a stream builder
Stream.Builder<String> builder = Stream.builder();
```

The Stream.Builder<T> interface contains the following methods:

- void accept(T t)
- Stream.Builder<T> add(T t)
- Stream<T> build()

The accept() and add() methods add elements to the stream being built. You might wonder about the existence of two methods in the builder to add elements. The Stream.Builder<T> interface inherits from the Consumer<T> interface, and therefore it inherits the accept() method from the Consumer<T> interface. You can pass a builder's instance to a method that accepts a consumer and the method can add elements to the builder using the accept() method.

The add() method returns the reference to the builder that makes it suitable for adding multiple elements using method chaining. Once you are done adding elements, call the build() method to create the stream. You cannot add elements to the stream after you call the build() method; doing so results in an IllegalStateException runtime exception. The following snippet of code uses the builder pattern to create a stream of four strings:

```
Stream<String> stream = Stream.<String>builder()
                              .add("Ken")
                              .add("Jeff")
                              .add("Chris")
                              .add("Ellen")
                              .build();
```

Note that the code specifies the type parameter as String when it obtains the builder Stream.<String>builder(). The compiler fails to infer the type parameter if you do not specify it. If you obtain the builder separately, the compiler will infer the type as String, as shown:

```
// Obtain a builder
Stream.Builder<String> builder = Stream.builder();

// Add elements and build the stream
Stream<String> stream = builder.add("Ken")
                               .add("Jeff")
                               .add("Chris")
                               .add("Ellen")
                               .build();
```

The IntStream interfaces contain four static methods that let you create IntStream from values:

- IntStream of(int value)
- IntStream of(int... values)
- IntStream range(int start, int end)
- IntStream rangeClosed(int start, int end).

The of() methods let you create a IntStream by specifying individual values. The range() and rangeClosed() methods produce an IntStream that contains ordered integers between the specified start and end. The specified end is exclusive in the range() method, whereas it is inclusive in the rangeClosed() method. The following snippet of code uses both methods to create an IntStream having integers 1, 2, 3, 4, and 5 as their elements:

```
// Create an IntStream containing 1, 2, 3, 4, and 5
IntStream oneToFive = IntStream.range(1, 6);

// Create an IntStream containing 1, 2, 3, 4, and 5
IntStream oneToFive = IntStream.rangeClosed(1, 5);
```

The `LongStream` interface also contains `range()` and `rangeClosed()` methods, which take arguments of type `long` and return a `LongStream`. The `LongStream` and `DoubleStream` interfaces also contain `of()` methods, which work with the `long` and `double` values and return a `LongStream` and a `DoubleStream`, respectively.

Empty Streams

An empty stream is a stream with no elements. The `Stream` interface contains an `empty()` static method to create an empty sequential stream.

```
// Creates an empty stream of strings
Stream<String> stream = Stream.empty();
```

The `IntStream`, `LongStream`, and `DoubleStream` interfaces also contain an `empty()` static method to create an empty stream of primitive types. Here is one example:

```
// Creates an empty stream of integers
IntStream numbers = IntStream.empty();
```

Streams from Functions

An infinite stream is a stream with a data source *capable* of generating an infinite number of elements. Note that I am saying that the data source should be "capable of generating" an infinite number of elements, not that the data source should have or contain an infinite number of elements. It is impossible to store an infinite number of elements of any kind because of memory and time constraints. However, it is possible to have a function that can generate an infinite number of values on demand. The `Stream` interface contains the following two static methods to generate an infinite stream:

- `<T> Stream<T> iterate(T seed, Predicate<? super T> hasNext, UnaryOperator<T> next)`
- `<T> Stream<T> iterate(T seed, UnaryOperator<T> f)`
- `<T> Stream<T> generate(Supplier<? extends T> s)`

The `iterate()` method creates a sequential ordered stream, whereas the `generate()` method creates a sequential unordered stream. The following sections show you how to use these methods.

The stream interfaces for primitive values `IntStream`, `LongStream`, and `DoubleStream` also contain `iterate()` and `generate()` static methods that take parameters specific to their primitive types. For example, these methods are defined as follows in the `IntStream` interface:

- `static IntStream iterate(int seed, IntPredicate hasNext, IntUnaryOperator next)`
- `IntStream iterate(int seed, IntUnaryOperator f)`
- `IntStream generate(IntSupplier s)`

Using the Stream.iterate() Method

The first version of the `iterate()` method is declared as follows:

```
static <T> Stream<T> iterate(T seed, Predicate<? super T> hasNext, UnaryOperator<T> next)
```

The method takes three arguments: a seed, a predicate, and a function. It produces elements by iteratively applying the next function as long as the hasNext predicate is true. The seed argument is the initial element. Calling this method is similar to using a for loop as follows:

```
for (int index = seed; hasNext.test(index); index = next.applyAsInt(index)) {
    // index is the next element in the stream
}
```

The following snippet of code produces a stream of integers from 1 to 10:

```
Stream<Integer> nums = Stream.iterate(1, n -> n <= 10, n -> n + 1);
```

The second version of the iterate() method is declared as follows:

```
static <T> Stream<T> iterate(T seed, UnaryOperator<T> f)
```

The method takes two arguments: a seed and a function. The first argument is a seed that is the first element of the stream. The second element is generated by applying the function to the first element. The third element is generated by applying the function on the second element and so on. Its elements are seed, f(seed), f(f(seed)), f(f(f(seed))), and so on. The following statement creates an infinite stream of natural numbers and an infinite stream of all odd natural numbers:

```
// Creates a stream of natural numbers
Stream<Long> naturalNumbers = Stream.iterate(1L, n -> n + 1);

// Creates a stream of odd natural numbers
Stream<Long> oddNaturalNumbers = Stream.iterate(1L, n -> n + 2);
```

What do you do with an infinite stream? You understand that it is not possible to consume all elements of an infinite stream. This is simply because the stream processing will take forever to complete. Typically, you convert the infinite stream into a fixed-size stream by applying a limit operation that truncates the input stream to be no longer than a specified size. The limit operation is an intermediate operation that produces another stream. You apply the limit operation using the limit(long maxSize) method of the Stream interface. The following snippet of code creates a stream of the first 10 natural numbers:

```
// Creates a stream of the first 10 natural numbers
Stream<Long> tenNaturalNumbers = Stream.iterate(1L, n -> n + 1)
                                       .limit(10);
```

You can apply a forEach operation on a stream using the forEach(Consumer<? super T> action) method of the Stream interface. The method returns void. It is a terminal operation. The following snippet of code prints the first five odd natural numbers on the standard output:

```
Stream.iterate(1L, n -> n + 2)
      .limit(5)
      .forEach(System.out::println);
```

```
1
3
5
7
9
```

Let's look at a realistic example of creating an infinite stream of prime numbers. Listing 13-4 contains a utility class called `PrimeUtil`. The class contains two utility methods. The `next()` instance method returns the next prime number after the last found prime number. The `next(long after)` static method returns the prime number after the specified number. The `isPrime()` static method checks if a number is a prime number.

Listing 13-4. A Utility Class to Work with Prime Numbers

```
// PrimeUtil.java
package com.jdojo.streams;

public class PrimeUtil {
    // Used for a stateful PrimeUtil
    private long lastPrime = 0L;

    // Computes the prime number after the last generated prime
    public long next() {
        lastPrime = next(lastPrime);
        return lastPrime;
    }

    // Computes the prime number after the specified number
    public static long next(long after) {
        long counter = after;

        // Keep looping until you find the next prime number
        while (!isPrime(++counter));

        return counter;
    }

    // Checks if the specified number is a prime number
    public static boolean isPrime(long number) {
        // <= 1 is not a prime number
        if (number <= 1) {
            return false;
        }

        // 2 is a prime number
        if (number == 2) {
            return true;
        }

        // Even numbers > 2 are not prime numbers
        if (number % 2 == 0) {
            return false;
        }
```

```
        long maxDivisor = (long) Math.sqrt(number);
        for (int counter = 3; counter <= maxDivisor; counter += 2) {
            if (number % counter == 0) {
                return false;
            }
        }

        return true;
    }
}
```

The following snippet of code creates an infinite stream of prime numbers and prints the first five prime numbers on the standard output:

```
Stream.iterate(2L, PrimeUtil::next)
      .limit(5)
      .forEach(System.out::println);
```

```
2
3
5
7
11
```

There is another way to get the first five prime numbers. You can generate an infinite stream of natural numbers, apply a filter operation to pick only the prime numbers, and limit the filtered stream to five. The following snippet of code shows this logic using the `isPrime()` method of the `PrimeUtil` class:

```
// Print the first 5 prime numbers
Stream.iterate(2L, n -> n + 1)
      .filter(PrimeUtil::isPrime)
      .limit(5)
      .forEach(System.out::println);
```

```
2
3
5
7
11
```

Sometimes you may want to discard some elements of a stream. This is accomplished using the skip operation. The `skip(long n)` method of the `Stream` interface discards (or skips) the first `n` elements of the stream. This is an intermediate operation. The following snippet of code uses this operation to print five prime numbers, skipping the first 100 prime numbers:

```
Stream.iterate(2L, PrimeUtil::next)
      .skip(100)
      .limit(5)
      .forEach(System.out::println);
```

```
547
557
563
569
571
```

Using everything you have learned about streams, can you write a stream pipeline to print five prime numbers that are greater than 3000? This is left as an exercise for the readers.

Using the generate() Method

The `generate(Supplier<? extends T> s)` method uses the specified `Supplier` to generate an infinite sequential unordered stream. The following snippet of code prints five random numbers greater than or equal to 0.0 and less than 1.0 using the `random()` static method of the `Math` class. You may get different output.

```
Stream.generate(Math::random)
      .limit(5)
      .forEach(System.out::println);
```

```
0.05958352209327644
0.8122226657626394
0.5073323815997652
0.9327951597282766
0.4314430923877808
```

If you want to use the `generate()` method to generate an infinite stream in which the next element is generated based on the value of the previous element, you need to use a `Supplier` that stores the last generated element. Note that a `PrimeUtil` object can act as a `Supplier` whose `next()` instance method remembers the last generated prime number. The following snippet of code prints five prime numbers after skipping the first 100:

```
Stream.generate(new PrimeUtil()::next)
      .skip(100)
      .limit(5)
      .forEach(System.out::println);
```

```
547
557
563
569
571
```

Java 8 added many methods to the `Random` class in the `java.util` package to work with streams. Methods like `ints()`, `longs()`, and `doubles()` return infinite `IntStream`, `LongStream`, and `DoubleStream`, respectively, which contain random numbers of the `int`, `long`, and `double` types. The following snippet of code prints five random `int` values from an `IntStream` returned from the `ints()` method of the `Random` class:

```
// Print five random integers
new Random().ints()
            .limit(5)
            .forEach(System.out::println);
```

```
-1147567659
285663603
-412283607
412487893
-22795557
```

You may get different output every time you run the code. You can use the `nextInt()` method of the `Random` class as the `Supplier` in the `generate()` method to achieve the same result.

```
// Print five random integers
Stream.generate(new Random()::nextInt)
      .limit(5)
      .forEach(System.out::println);
```

If you want to work with only primitive values, you can use the `generate()` method of the primitive type stream interfaces. For example, the following snippet of code prints five random integers using the `generate()` static method of the `IntStream` interface:

```
IntStream.generate(new Random()::nextInt)
         .limit(5)
         .forEach(System.out::println);
```

How would you generate an infinite stream of repeating values? For example, how would you generate an infinite stream of zeroes? The following snippet of code shows you how to do this:

```
IntStream zeroes = IntStream.generate(() -> 0);
```

Streams from Arrays

The `Arrays` class in the `java.util` package contains an overloaded `stream()` static method to create sequential streams from arrays. You can use it to create an `IntStream` from an `int` array, a `LongStream` from a `long` array, a `DoubleStream` from a `double` array, and a `Stream<T>` from an array of the reference type `T`. The following snippet of code creates an `IntStream` and a `Stream<String>` from an `int` array and a `String` array:

```
// Creates a stream from an int array with elements 1, 2, and 3
IntStream numbers = Arrays.stream(new int[]{1, 2, 3});

// Creates a stream from a String array with elements "Ken", and "Jeff"
Stream<String> names = Arrays.stream(new String[] {"Ken", "Jeff"});
```

■ **Tip** You can create a stream from a reference type array using two methods: `Arrays.stream(T[] t)` and `Stream.of(T...t)` method. Providing two methods in the library to accomplish the same thing is intentional.

Streams from Collections

The `Collection` interface contains the `stream()` and `parallelStream()` methods that create sequential and parallel streams from a `Collection`, respectively. The following snippet of code creates streams from a set of strings:

```
import java.util.HashSet;
import java.util.Set;
import java.util.stream.Stream;
...
// Create and populate a set of strings
Set<String> names = Set.of("Ken", "jeff");

// Create a sequential stream from the set
Stream<String> sequentialStream = names.stream();

// Create a parallel stream from the set
Stream<String> parallelStream = names.parallelStream();
```

Streams from Files

Java 8 added many methods to the classes in the `java.io` and `java.nio.file` packages to support I/O operations using streams. For example,

- You can read text from a file as a stream of strings in which each element represents one line of text from the file.
- You can obtain a stream of `JarEntry` from a `JarFile`.
- You can obtain the list of entries in a directory as a stream of `Path`.
- You can obtain a stream of `Path` that is a result of a file search in a specified directory.
- You can obtain a stream of `Path` that contains the file tree of a specified directory.

I show some examples of using streams with file I/O in this section. Refer to the API documentation for the `java.nio.file.Files`, `java.io.BufferedReader`, and `java.util.jar.JarFile` classes for more details on the stream-related methods.

The `BufferedReader` and `Files` classes contain a `lines()` method that reads a file lazily and returns the contents as a stream of strings. Each element in the stream represents one line of text from the file. The file needs to be closed when you are done with the stream. Calling the `close()` method on the stream will close the underlying file. Alternatively, you can create the stream in a `try-with-resources` statement so the underlying file is closed automatically.

The program in Listing 13-5 shows how to read contents of a file using a stream. It also walks the entire file tree for the current working directory and prints the entries in the directory. The program assumes that you have the `luci1.txt` file, which is supplied with the source code, in the current working directory. If the file does not exist, an error message with the absolute path of the expected file is printed. You may get different output when you run the program.

Listing 13-5. Performing File I/O Using Streams

```
// IOStream.java
package com.jdojo.streams;

import java.io.IOException;
import java.nio.file.Files;
import java.nio.file.Path;
import java.nio.file.Paths;
import java.util.stream.Stream;

public class IOStream {
    public static void main(String[] args) {
        // Read the contents of the file luci1.txt
        readFileContents("luci1.txt");

        // Print the file tree for the current working directory
        listFileTree();
    }

    public static void readFileContents(String filePath) {
        Path path = Paths.get(filePath);
        if (!Files.exists(path)) {
            System.out.println("The file "
                    + path.toAbsolutePath() + " does not exist.");
            return;
        }

        try (Stream<String> lines = Files.lines(path)) {
            // Read and print all lines
            lines.forEach(System.out::println);
        } catch (IOException e) {
            e.printStackTrace();
        }
    }

    public static void listFileTree() {
        Path dir = Paths.get("");
        System.out.printf("%nThe file tree for %s%n", dir.toAbsolutePath());

        try (Stream<Path> fileTree = Files.walk(dir)) {
            fileTree.forEach(System.out::println);
        } catch (IOException e) {
            e.printStackTrace();
        }
    }
}
```

```
STRANGE fits of passion have I known:
And I will dare to tell,
But in the lover's ear alone,
What once to me befell.
```

```
The file tree for C:\Java9LanguageFeatures
build
build\modules
build\modules\com
build\modules\com\jdojo
...
```

Streams from Other Sources

Java 8 added methods in many other classes to return the contents they represent in a stream. Two such methods that you may use frequently are explained next.

- The `chars()` method in the `CharSequence` interface returns an `IntStream` whose elements are `int` values representing the characters of the `CharSequence`. You can use the `chars()` method on a `String`, a `StringBuilder`, and a `StringBuffer` to obtain a stream of characters of their contents as these classes implement the `CharSequence` interface.
- The `splitAsStream(CharSequence input)` method of the `java.util.regex.Pattern` class returns a stream of `String` whose elements match the pattern.

Let's look at an example in both categories. The following snippet of code creates a stream of characters from a string, filters out all digits and whitespace, and prints the remaining characters:

```
String str = "5 apples and 25 oranges";
str.chars()
   .filter(n -> !Character.isDigit((char)n) && !Character.isWhitespace((char)n))
   .forEach(n -> System.out.print((char)n));
```

```
applesandoranges
```

The following snippet of code obtains a stream of strings by splitting a string using a regular expression (","). The matched strings are printed on the standard output.

```
String str = "Ken,Jeff,Lee";
Pattern.compile(",")
       .splitAsStream(str)
       .forEach(System.out::println);
```

```
Ken
Jeff
Lee
```

Representing an Optional Value

In Java, null is used to represent "nothing" or an "empty" result. Most often, a method returns null if it does not have a result to return. This has been a source of frequent NullPointerException in Java programs. Consider printing a person's year of birth, like so:

```
Person ken = new Person(1, "Ken", Person.Gender.MALE, null, 6000.0);
int year = ken.getDob().getYear(); // Throws a NullPointerException
System.out.println("Ken was born in the year " + year);
```

The code throws a NullPointerException at runtime. The problem is in the return value of the ken.getDob() method that returns null. Calling the getYear() method on a null reference results in the NullPointerException. So, what is the solution? In fact, there is no real solution to this. Java 8 introduced an Optional<T> class in the java.util package to deal with NullPointerException gracefully. Methods that may return nothing should return an Optional instead of null.

An Optional is a container object that may or may not contain a non-null value. Its isPresent() method returns true if it contains a non-null value, and false otherwise. Its get() method returns the non-null value if it contains a non-null value, and throws a NoSuchElementException otherwise. This implies that when a method returns an Optional, you must, as a practice, check if it contains a non-null value before asking it for the value. If you use the get() method before making sure it contains a non-null value, you may get a NoSuchElementException instead of getting a NullPointerException. This is why I said in the previous paragraph that there is no real solution to the NullPointerException. However, returning an Optional is certainly a better way to deal with null, as developers will get used to using the Optional objects in the way they are designed to be used.

How do you create an Optional<T> object? The Optional<T> class provides the following static factory methods to create its objects:

- <T> Optional<T> empty(): Returns an empty Optional. That is, the Optional returned from this method does not contain a non-null value.
- <T> Optional<T> of(T value): Returns an Optional containing the specified value as the non-null value. If the specified value is null, it throws a NullPointerException.
- <T> Optional<T> ofNullable(T value): Returns an Optional containing the specified value if the value is non-null. If the specified value is null, it returns an empty Optional.

The following snippet of code shows how to create Optional objects:

```
// Create an empty Optional
Optional<String> empty = Optional.empty();

// Create an Optional for the string "Hello"
Optional<String> str = Optional.of("Hello");

// Create an Optional with a String that may be null
String nullableString = ""; // get a string that may be null...
Optional<String> str2 = Optional.of(nullableString);
```

The following snippet of code prints the value in an Optional if it contains a non-null value:

```
// Create an Optional for the string "Hello"
Optional<String> str = Optional.of("Hello");

// Print the value in Optional
if (str.isPresent()) {
    String value = str.get();
    System.out.println("Optional contains " + value);
} else {
    System.out.println("Optional is empty.");
}
```

```
Optional contains Hello
```

You can use the ifPresent(Consumer<? super T> action) method of the Optional class to take an action on the value contained in the Optional. If the Optional is empty, this method does not do anything. You can rewrite the previous code to print the value in an Optional as follows. Note that if the Optional were empty, the code would not print anything.

```
// Create an Optional for the string "Hello"
Optional<String> str = Optional.of("Hello");

// Print the value in the Optional, if present
str.ifPresent(value -> System.out.println("Optional contains " + value));
```

```
Optional contains Hello
```

The following are four methods to get the value of an Optional:

- T get(): Returns the value contained in the Optional. If the Optional is empty, it throws a NoSuchElementException.
- T orElse(T defaultValue): Returns the value contained in the Optional. If the Optional is empty, it returns the specified defaultValue.
- T orElseGet(Supplier<? extends T> defaultSupplier): Returns the value contained in the Optional. If the Optional is empty, it returns the value returned from the specified defaultSupplier.
- <X extends Throwable> T orElseThrow(Supplier<? extends X> exceptionSupplier) throws X extends Throwable: Returns the value contained in the Optional. If the Optional is empty, it throws the exception returned from the specified exceptionSupplier.

The Optional<T> class describes a non-null reference type value or its absence. The java.util package contains three more classes named OptionalInt, OptionalLong, and OptionalDouble to deal with optional primitive values. They contain similarly named methods that apply to primitive data types, except for getting their values. They do not contain a get() method. To return their values, the OptionalInt class contains a getAsInt(), the OptionalLong class contains a getAsLong(), and the OptionalDouble class contains a getAsDouble() method. Like the get() method of the Optional class, the getters for primitive optional classes also throw a NoSuchElementException when they are empty. Unlike the Optional class, they do not contain an ofNullable() factory method because primitive values cannot be null. The following snippet of code shows how to use the OptionalInt class:

```
// Create an empty OptionalInt
OptionalInt empty = OptionalInt.empty();

// Use an OptionalInt to store 287
OptionalInt number = OptionalInt.of(287);

if (number.isPresent()){
    int value = number.getAsInt();
    System.out.println("Number is " + value);
} else {
    System.out.println("Number is absent.");
}
```

```
Number is 287
```

Several methods in the Streams API return an instance of the Optional, OptionalInt, OptionalLong, and OptionalDouble when they do not have anything to return. For example, all types of streams let you compute the maximum element in the stream. If the stream is empty, there is no maximum element. Note that in a stream pipeline, you may start with a non-empty stream and end up with an empty stream because of filtering or other operations such as limit, skip, etc. For this reason, the max() method in all stream classes returns an optional object. The program in Listing 13-6 shows how to get the maximum integer from IntStream.

Listing 13-6. Working with Optional Values

```
// OptionalTest.java
package com.jdojo.streams;

import java.util.Comparator;
import java.util.Optional;
import java.util.OptionalInt;
import java.util.stream.IntStream;
import java.util.stream.Stream;

public class OptionalTest {
    public static void main(String[] args) {
        // Get the maximum of odd integers from the stream
        OptionalInt maxOdd = IntStream.of(10, 20, 30)
                                      .filter(n -> n % 2 == 1)
                                      .max();
        if (maxOdd.isPresent()) {
            int value = maxOdd.getAsInt();
            System.out.println("Maximum odd integer is " + value);
        } else {
            System.out.println("Stream is empty.");
        }
```

```
        // Get the maximum of odd integers from the stream
        OptionalInt numbers = IntStream.of(1, 10, 37, 20, 31)
                                       .filter(n -> n % 2 == 1)
                                       .max();
        if (numbers.isPresent()) {
            int value = numbers.getAsInt();
            System.out.println("Maximum odd integer is " + value);
        } else {
            System.out.println("Stream is empty.");
        }

        // Get the longest name
        Optional<String> name = Stream.of("Ken", "Ellen", "Li")
                                      .max(Comparator.comparingInt(String::length));
        if (name.isPresent()) {
            String longestName = name.get();
            System.out.println("Longest name is " + longestName);
        } else {
            System.out.println("Stream is empty.");
        }
    }
}
```

```
Stream is empty.
Maximum odd integer is 37
Longest name is Ellen
```

Java 9 added the following methods to the `Optional<T>` class:

- `void ifPresentOrElse(Consumer<? super T> action, Runnable emptyAction)`
- `Optional<T> or(Supplier<? extends Optional<? extends T>> supplier)`
- `Stream<T> stream()`

Before I describe these methods and present a complete program showing their use, consider the following list of an `Optional<Integer>`:

```
List<Optional<Integer>> optionalList = List.of(Optional.of(1),
                                               Optional.empty(),
                                               Optional.of(2),
                                               Optional.empty(),
                                               Optional.of(3));
```

The list contains five `Optional` elements, two of which are empty and three contain values as 1, 2, and 3. I refer to this list in the subsequent discussion.

The `ifPresentOrElse()` method lets you provide two alternate courses of actions. If a value is present, it performs the specified `action` with the value. Otherwise, it performs the specified `emptyAction`. The following snippet of code iterates over all the elements in the list using a stream to print the value if `Optional` contains a value and an `"Empty"` string if `Optional` is empty:

```
optionalList.stream()
            .forEach(p -> p.ifPresentOrElse(System.out::println,
                                            () -> System.out.println("Empty")));
```

```
1
Empty
2
Empty
3
```

The `or()` method returns the `Optional` itself if the `Optional` contains a non-null value. Otherwise, it returns the `Optional` returned by the specified `supplier`. The following snippet of code creates a stream from a list of `Optional` and uses the `or()` method to map all empty `Optionals` to an `Optional` with a value of zero.

```
optionalList.stream()
            .map(p -> p.or(() -> Optional.of(0)))
            .forEach(System.out::println);
```

```
Optional[1]
Optional[0]
Optional[2]
Optional[0]
Optional[3]
```

The `stream()` method returns a sequential stream of elements containing the value present in the `Optional`. If the `Optional` is empty, it returns an empty stream. Suppose you have a list of `Optional` and you want to collect all present values in another list. You can achieve this in Java 8 as follows:

```
// Print the values in all non-empty Optionals
optionalList.stream()
            .filter(Optional::isPresent)
            .map(Optional::get)
            .forEach(System.out::println);
```

```
1
2
3
```

You had to use a filter to filter out all empty `Optionals` and map the remaining `Optionals` to their values. With the new `stream()` method in JDK9, you can combine the `filter()` and `map()` operations into one `flatMap()` operation as shown. I discuss flattening streams in detail in the "Flattening Streams" section later in this chapter.

```
// Print the values in all non-empty Optionals
optionalList.stream()
            .flatMap(Optional::stream)
            .forEach(System.out::println);
```

```
1
2
3
```

Applying Operations to Streams

Table 13-1 lists some of the commonly used stream operations, their types, and descriptions. The `Stream` interface contains a method with the same name as the name of the operation in the table. You have seen some of these operations in previous sections. Subsequent sections cover them in detail.

Table 13-1. *List of Commonly Used Stream Operations Supported by the Streams API*

Operation	Type	Description
`distinct`	Intermediate	Returns a stream consisting of the distinct elements of this stream. Elements `e1` and `e2` are considered equal if `e1.equals(e2)` returns `true`.
`filter`	Intermediate	Returns a stream consisting of the elements of this stream that match the specified predicate.
`flatMap`	Intermediate	Returns a stream consisting of the results of applying the specified function to the elements in this stream. The function produces a stream for each input element and the output streams are flattened. Performs one-to-many mapping.
`limit`	Intermediate	Returns a stream consisting of the elements in this stream, truncated to be no longer than the specified size.
`map`	Intermediate	Returns a stream consisting of the results of applying the specified function to the elements in this stream. Performs one-to-one mapping.
`peek`	Intermediate	Returns a stream whose elements consist of this stream. It applies the specified action as it consumes elements of this stream. It is mainly used for debugging purposes.
`skip`	Intermediate	Discards the first `N` elements in the stream and returns the remaining stream. If this stream contains fewer than `N` elements, an empty stream is returned.
`dropWhile`	Intermediate	Returns the elements of the stream, discarding the elements from the beginning for which a predicate is true. This operation was added to the Streams API in Java 9.
`takeWhile`	Intermediate	Returns elements from the beginning of the stream, which match a predicate, discarding the rest of the elements. This operation was added to the Streams API in Java 9.
`sorted`	Intermediate	Returns a stream consisting of the elements in this stream, sorted according to natural order or the specified `Comparator`. For an ordered stream, the sort is stable.

(*continued*)

Table 13-1. (*continued*)

Operation	Type	Description
allMatch	Terminal	Returns true if all elements in the stream match the specified predicate, false otherwise. Returns true if the stream is empty.
anyMatch	Terminal	Returns true if any element in the stream matches the specified predicate, false otherwise. Returns false if the stream is empty.
findAny	Terminal	Returns any element from the stream. An empty Optional is returned for an empty stream.
findFirst	Terminal	Returns the first element of the stream. For an ordered stream, it returns the first element in the encounter order; for an unordered stream, it returns any element.
noneMatch	Terminal	Returns true if no elements in the stream match the specified predicate, false otherwise. Returns true if the stream is empty.
forEach	Terminal	Applies an action for each element in the stream.
reduce	Terminal	Applies a reduction operation to compute a single value from the stream.

Debugging a Stream Pipeline

You apply a sequence of operations on a stream. Each operation transforms the elements of the input stream, either producing another stream or a result. Sometimes you may need to look at the elements of the streams as they pass through the pipeline. You can do so by using the peek(Consumer<? super T> action) method of the Stream<T> interface that is meant only for debugging purposes. It produces a stream after applying an action on each input element. The IntStream, LongStream, and DoubleStream methods also contain a peek() method that takes a IntConsumer, a LongConsumer, and a DoubleConsumer as an argument. Typically, you use a lambda expression with the peek() method to log messages describing elements being processed. The following snippet of code uses the peek() method at three places to print the elements passing through the stream pipeline:

```
int sum = Stream.of(1, 2, 3, 4, 5)
                .peek(e -> System.out.println("Taking integer: " + e))
                .filter(n -> n % 2 == 1)
                .peek(e -> System.out.println("Filtered integer: " + e))
                .map(n -> n * n)
                .peek(e -> System.out.println("Mapped integer: " + e))
                .reduce(0, Integer::sum);

System.out.println("Sum = " + sum);
```

```
Taking integer: 1
Filtered integer: 1
Mapped integer: 1
Taking integer: 2
Taking integer: 3
Filtered integer: 3
Mapped integer: 9
Taking integer: 4
```

```
Taking integer: 5
Filtered integer: 5
Mapped integer: 25
Sum = 35
```

Notice that the output shows the even numbers being taken from the data source, but not passing the filter operation.

Applying the ForEach Operation

The `forEach` operation takes an action for each element of the stream. The action may simply print each element of the stream to the standard output or increase the income of every person in a stream by 10%. The `Stream<T>` interface contains two methods to perform the `forEach` operation:

- `void forEach(Consumer<? super T> action)`
- `void forEachOrdered(Consumer<? super T> action)`

`IntStream`, `LongStream`, and `DoubleStream` also contain the same methods, except that their parameter type is the specialized consumer types for primitives; for example, the parameter type for the `forEach()` method in the `IntStream` is `IntConsumer`.

Why do you have two methods to perform the `forEach` operation? Sometimes the order in which the action is applied for the elements in a stream is important, and sometimes it is not. The `forEach()` method does not guarantee the order in which the action for each element in the stream is applied. The `forEachOrdered()` method performs the action in the encounter order of elements defined by the stream. Use the `forEachOrdered()` method for a parallel stream only when necessary because it may slow down processing. The following snippet of code prints the details of females in the `person` list:

```
Person.persons()
      .stream()
      .filter(Person::isFemale)
      .forEach(System.out::println);
```

```
(3, Donna, FEMALE, 1962-07-29, 8700.00)
(5, Laynie, FEMALE, 2012-12-13, 0.00)
```

The program in Listing 13-7 shows how to use the `forEach()` method to increase the income of all females by 10%. The output shows that only Donna got an increase because another female named Laynie had 0.0 income before.

Listing 13-7. Applying the ForEach Operation on a List of Persons

```
// ForEachTest.java
package com.jdojo.streams;

import java.util.List;

public class ForEachTest {
    public static void main(String[] args) {
        // Get the list of persons
        List<Person> persons = Person.persons();
```

```
        // Print the list
        System.out.println("Before increasing the income: " + persons);

        // Increase the income of females by 10%
        persons.stream()
               .filter(Person::isFemale)
               .forEach(p -> p.setIncome(p.getIncome() * 1.10));

        // Print the list again
        System.out.println("After increasing the income: " + persons);
    }
}
```

```
Before increasing the income: [(1, Ken, MALE, 1970-05-04, 6000.00), (2, Jeff, MALE, 1970-
07-15, 7100.00), (3, Donna, FEMALE, 1962-07-29, 8700.00), (4, Chris, MALE, 1993-12-16,
1800.00), (5, Laynie, FEMALE, 2012-12-13, 0.00), (6, Li, MALE, 2001-05-09, 2400.00)]
After increasing the income: [(1, Ken, MALE, 1970-05-04, 6000.00), (2, Jeff, MALE, 1970-
07-15, 7100.00), (3, Donna, FEMALE, 1962-07-29, 9570.00), (4, Chris, MALE, 1993-12-16,
1800.00), (5, Laynie, FEMALE, 2012-12-13, 0.00), (6, Li, MALE, 2001-05-09, 2400.00)]
```

Applying thc Map Operation

A map operation (also known as mapping) applies a function to each element of the input stream to produce another stream (also called an output stream or a mapped stream). The number of elements in the input and output streams is the same. The operation does not modify the elements of the input stream—at least it is not supposed to.

Figure 13-7 depicts the application of the map operation on a stream. It shows element e1 from the input stream being mapped to element et1 in the mapped stream, element e2 mapped to et2, etc.

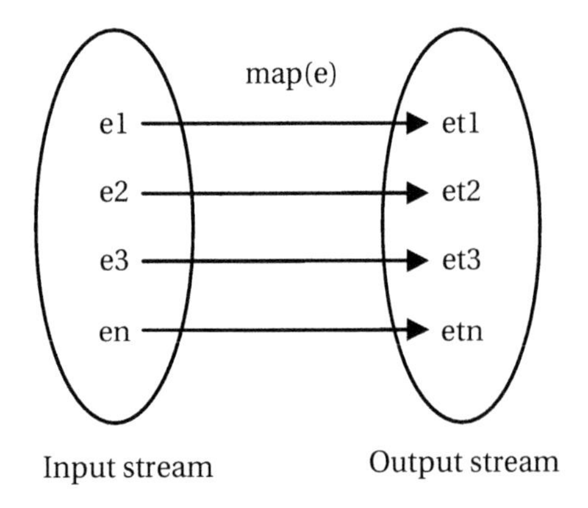

Figure 13-7. *A pictorial view of the map operation*

Mapping a stream to another stream is not limited to any specific type of elements. You can map a stream of T to a stream of type S, where T and S may be the same or different types. For example, you can map a stream of Person to a stream of int where each Person element in the input stream maps to the

Person's ID in the mapped stream. You can apply the map operation on a stream using one of the following methods of the Stream<T> interface:

- <R> Stream<R> map(Function<? super T,? extends R> mapper)
- DoubleStream mapToDouble(ToDoubleFunction<? super T> mapper)
- IntStream mapToInt(ToIntFunction<? super T> mapper)
- LongStream mapToLong(ToLongFunction<? super T> mapper)

The map operation takes a function as an argument. Each element from the input stream is passed to the function. The returned value from the function is the mapped element in the mapped stream. Use the map() method to perform the mapping to reference type elements. If the mapped stream is of a primitive type, use other methods; for example, use the mapToInt() method to map a stream of a reference type to a stream of int. The IntStream, LongStream, and DoubleStream interfaces contain similar methods to facilitate mapping of one type of stream to another. The methods supporting the map operation on an IntStream are as follows:

- IntStream map(IntUnaryOperator mapper)
- DoubleStream mapToDouble(IntToDoubleFunction mapper)
- LongStream mapToLong(IntToLongFunction mapper)
- <U> Stream<U> mapToObj(IntFunction<? extends U> mapper)

The following snippet of code creates an IntStream whose elements are integers from 1 to 5, maps the elements of the stream to their squares, and prints the mapped stream on the standard output. Note that the map() method used in the code is the map() method of the IntStream interface.

```
IntStream.rangeClosed(1, 5)
         .map(n -> n * n)
         .forEach(System.out::println);
```

```
1
4
9
16
25
```

The following snippet of code maps the elements of a stream of people to their names and prints the mapped stream. Note that the map() method used in the code is the map() method of the Stream interface.

```
Person.persons()
      .stream()
      .map(Person::getName)
      .forEach(System.out::println);
```

```
Ken
Jeff
Donna
Chris
Laynie
Li
```

Flattening Streams

In the previous section, you saw the map operation that facilitates a one-to-one mapping. Each element of the input stream is mapped to an element in the output stream. The Streams API also supports one-to-many mapping through the `flatMap` operation. It works as follows:

1. It takes an input stream and produces an output stream using a mapping function.

2. The mapping function takes an element from the input stream and maps the element to a stream. The type of input element and the elements in the mapped stream may be different. This step produces a stream of streams. Suppose the input stream is a `Stream<T>` and the mapped stream is `Stream<Stream<R>>` where `T` and `R` may be the same or different.

3. Finally, it flattens the output stream (that is, a stream of streams) to produce a stream. That is, the `Stream<Stream<R>>` is flattened to `Stream<R>`.

It takes some time to understand the flat map operation. Suppose that you have a stream of three numbers: 1, 2, and 3. You want to produce a stream that contains the numbers and the squares of the numbers. You want the output stream to contain 1, 1, 2, 4, 3, and 9. The following is the first, incorrect attempt to achieve this:

```
Stream.of(1, 2, 3)
      .map(n -> Stream.of(n, n * n))
      .forEach(System.out::println);
```

```
java.util.stream.ReferencePipeline$Head@372f7a8d
java.util.stream.ReferencePipeline$Head@2f92e0f4
java.util.stream.ReferencePipeline$Head@28a418fc
```

Are you surprised by the output? You do not see numbers in the output. The input stream to the `map()` method contains three integers: 1, 2, and 3. The `map()` method produces one element for each element in the input stream. In this case, the `map()` method produces a `Stream<Integer>` for each integer in the input stream. It produces three `Stream<Integer>`s. The first stream contains 1 and 1; the second one contains 2 and 4; the third one contains 3 and 9. The `forEach()` method receives the `Stream<Integer>` object as its argument and prints the string returned from the `toString()` method of each `Stream<Integer>`. You can call the `forEach()` on a stream, so let's nest its call to print the elements of the stream of streams, like so:

```
Stream.of(1, 2, 3)
      .map(n -> Stream.of(n, n * n))
      .forEach(e -> e.forEach(System.out::println));
```

```
1
1
2
4
3
9
```

You were able to print the numbers and their squares. But you have not achieved the goal of getting those numbers in a `Stream<Integer>`. They are still in the `Stream<Stream<Integer>>`. The solution is to use the `flatMap()` method instead of the `map()` method. The following snippet of code does this:

```
Stream.of(1, 2, 3)
      .flatMap(n -> Stream.of(n, n * n))
      .forEach(System.out::println);
```

```
1
1
2
4
3
9
```

Figure 13-8 shows the pictorial view of how the `flatMap()` method works in this example. If you still have doubts about the workings of the `flatMap` operation, you can think of its name in the reverse order. Read it as mapFlat, which means "map the elements of the input stream to streams, and then flatten the mapped streams."

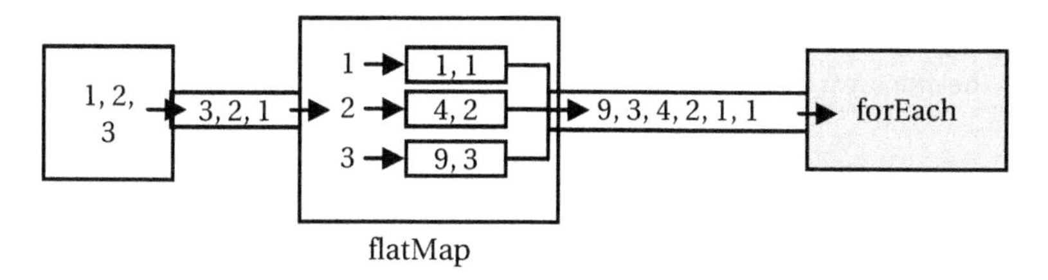

***Figure 13-8.** Flattening a stream using the flatMap() method*

Let's take another example of the flat map operation. Suppose you have a stream of strings. How will you count the number of the Es in the strings? The following snippet of code shows you how to do it:

```
long count = Stream.of("Ken", "Jeff", "Ellen")
                   .map(name -> name.chars())
                   .flatMap(intStream -> intStream.mapToObj(n -> (char)n))
                   .filter(ch -> ch == 'e' || ch == 'E')
                   .count();

System.out.println("Es count: " + count);
```

```
Es count: 4
```

The code maps the strings to `IntStream`. Note that the `chars()` method of the `String` class returns an `IntStream`, not a `Stream<Character>`. The output of the `map()` method is `Stream<IntStream>`. The `flatMap()` method maps the `Stream<IntStream>` to `Stream<Stream<Character>>` and finally, flattens it to produce a `Stream<Character>`. So, the output of the `flatMap()` method is `Stream<Character>`. The `filter()` method filters out any characters that are not an `E` or `e`. Finally, the `count()` method returns the number of elements in the stream. The main logic is to convert the Stream<String> to a Stream<Character>. You can achieve the same using the following code as well:

```
long count = Stream.of("Ken", "Jeff", "Ellen")
                   .flatMap(name -> IntStream.range(0, name.length())
                                             .mapToObj(name::charAt))
                   .filter(ch -> ch == 'e' || ch == 'E')
                   .count();
```

The IntStream.range() method creates an IntStream that contains the indexes of all characters in the input string. The mapToObj() method converts the IntStream into a Stream<Character> whose elements are the characters in the input string.

Applying the Filter Operation

The filter operation is applied on an input stream to produce another stream, which is known as the filtered stream. The filtered stream contains all elements of the input stream for which a predicate evaluates to true. A predicate is a function that accepts an element of the stream and returns a boolean value. Unlike a mapped stream, the filtered stream is of the same type as the input stream.

The filter operation produces a subset of the input stream. If the predicate evaluates to false for all elements of the input stream, the filtered stream is an empty stream. Figure 13-9 shows a pictorial view of applying a filter operation to a stream. The figure shows that two elements (e1 and en) from the input stream made it to the filtered stream and the other two elements (e2 and e3) were filtered out.

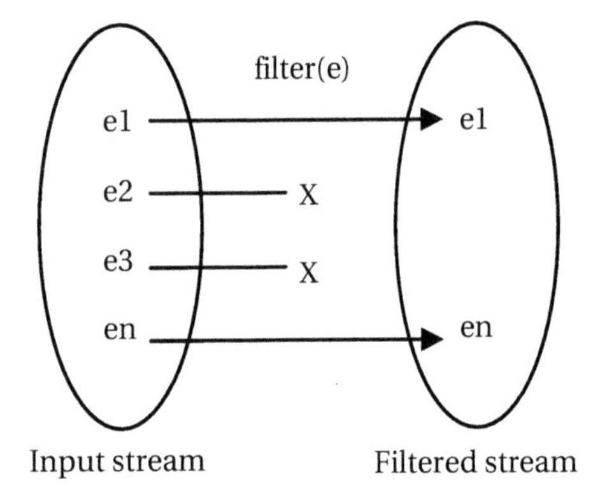

Figure 13-9. *A pictorial view of the filter operation*

You can apply a filter operation to a stream using the filter() method of the Stream, IntStream, LongStream, and DoubleStream interfaces. The method accepts a Predicate. The Streams API offers different flavors of the filter operations, which I discuss after a few examples of using the filter() method.

■ **Tip** In a map operation, the new stream contains the same number of elements with different values from the input stream. In a filter operation, the new stream contains a different number of elements with the same values from the input stream.

The following snippet of code uses a stream of people and filters in only females. It maps the females to their names and prints them to the standard output.

```
Person.persons()
      .stream()
      .filter(Person::isFemale)
      .map(Person::getName)
      .forEach(System.out::println);
```

```
Donna
Laynie
```

The following snippet of code applies two filter operations to print the names of all males having income more than 5000.0:

```
Person.persons()
      .stream()
      .filter(Person::isMale)
      .filter(p -> p.getIncome() > 5000.0)
      .map(Person::getName)
      .forEach(System.out::println);
```

```
Ken
Jeff
```

You could have accomplished the same using the following statement that uses only one filter operation that includes both predicates for filtering into one predicate:

```
Person.persons()
      .stream()
      .filter(p -> p.isMale() && p.getIncome() > 5000.0)
      .map(Person::getName)
      .forEach(System.out::println);
```

```
Ken
Jeff
```

The following methods can be used to apply filter operations to streams:

- `Stream<T> skip(long count)`
- `Stream<T> limit(long maxCount)`
- `default Stream<T> dropWhile(Predicate<? super T> predicate)`
- `default Stream<T> takeWhile(Predicate<? super T> predicate)`

The `skip()` method returns the elements of the stream after skipping the specified `count` elements from the beginning. The `limit()` method returns elements from the beginning of the stream that are equal to or less than the specified `maxCount`. One of these methods drop elements from the beginning and another takes elements from the beginning dropping the remaining. Both work based on the number of elements. The dropWhile() and takeWhile() are like skip() and limit() methods, respectively; however, they work on a Predicate rather than on the number of elements.

■ **Tip** The dropWhile() and takeWhile() methods were added to the Stream interface in Java 9. Java 9 also added these methods to the IntStream, LongStream, and DoubleStream interfaces.

You can think of the dropWhile() and takeWhile() methods similar to the filter() method with an exception. The filter() method evaluates the predicate on all elements, whereas the dropWhile() and takeWhile() methods evaluate the predicate on elements from the beginning on the stream until the predicate evaluates to false.

For an ordered stream, the dropWhile() method returns the elements of the stream discarding the elements from the beginning for which the specified predicate is true. Consider the following ordered stream of integers:

```
1, 2, 3, 4, 5, 6, 7
```

If you use a predicate in the dropWhile() method that returns true for an integer less than 5, the method will drop the first four elements and return the rest:

```
Stream.of(1, 2, 3, 4, 5, 6, 7)
             .dropWhile(e -> e < 5)
             .forEach(System.out::println);
```

```
5
6
7
```

For an unordered stream, the behavior of the dropWhile() method is non-deterministic. It may choose to drop any subset of elements matching the predicate. The current implementation drops the matching elements from the beginning until it finds a non-matching element. The following snippet of code uses the dropWhile() method on an unordered stream and only one of the elements matching the predicate is dropped:

```
Stream.of(1, 5, 6, 2, 3, 4, 7)
      .dropWhile(e -> e < 5)
      .forEach(System.out::println);
```

```
5
6
2
3
4
7
```

There are two extreme cases for the `dropWhile()` method. If the first element does not match the predicate, the method returns the original stream. If all elements match the predicate, the method returns an empty stream.

The `takeWhile()` method works the same way as the `dropWhile()` method, except that it returns the matching elements from the beginning of the stream and discards the rest.

■ **Caution** Use the `dropWhile()` and `takeWhile()` methods with ordered, parallel streams with great care because you may see a performance hit. In an ordered, parallel stream, elements must be ordered and returned from all threads before these methods can return. These methods perform best with sequential streams.

Applying the Reduce Operation

The reduce operation combines all elements of a stream to produce a single value by applying a combining function repeatedly. It is also called *reduction* operation or a *fold*. Computing the sum, maximum, average, count, etc. of elements of a stream of integers are examples of reduce operations. Collecting elements of a stream in a `List`, `Set`, or `Map` is also an example of the reduce operation.

The reduce operation takes two parameters called a *seed* (also called an *initial value*) and an *accumulator*. The accumulator is a function. If the stream is empty, the seed is the result. Otherwise, the seed represents a partial result. The partial result and an element are passed to the accumulator, which returns another partial result. This repeats until all elements are passed to the accumulator. The last value returned from the accumulator is the result of the reduce operation. Figure 13-10 shows a pictorial view of the reduce operation.

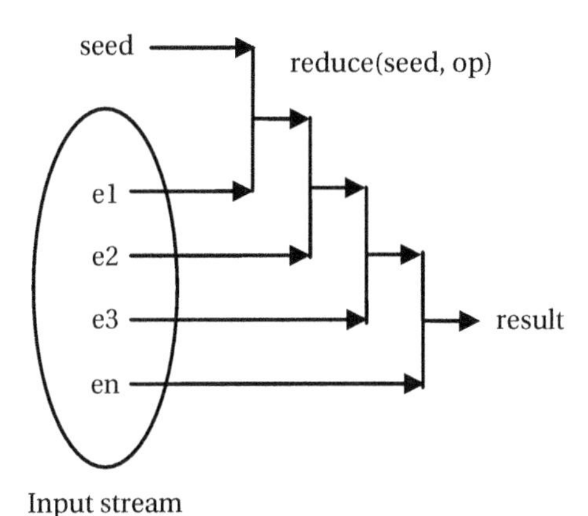

Figure 13-10. *A pictorial view of applying the reduce operation*

The stream-related interfaces contain two methods called `reduce()`and `collect()` to perform generic reduce operations. Methods such as `sum()`, `max()`, `min()`, `count()`, etc. are also available to perform specialized reduce operations. Note that the specialized methods are not available for all types of streams. For example, having a `sum()` method in the `Stream<T>` interface does not make sense because adding reference type elements, such as adding two people, is meaningless. So, you will find methods like `sum()` only in `IntStream`, `LongStream`, and `DoubleStream` interfaces. Counting the number of elements in a stream makes sense for all types of streams. So, the `count()` method is available for all types of streams. I discuss the `reduce()` method in this section. I discuss the `collect()` method in several subsequent sections.

Let's consider the following snippet of code, which performs the reduce operation in the imperative programming style. The code computes the sum of all integers in a list.

```
// Create the list of integers
List<Integer> numbers = List.of(1, 2, 3, 4, 5);

// Declare an accumulator called sum and initialize (or seed) it to zero
int sum = 0;

for(int num : numbers) {
    // Accumulate the partial result in sum
    sum = sum + num;
}

// Print the result
System.out.println(sum);
```

```
15
```

The code declares a variable named sum and initializes the variable to 0. If there is no element in the list, the initial value of sum becomes the result. The for-each loop traverses the list and keeps storing the partial results in the sum variable, using it as an accumulator. When the for-each loop finishes, the sum variable contains the result. As pointed out at the beginning of this chapter, such a for loop has no room for parallelization; the entire logic must be executed in a single thread.

Consider another example that computes the sum of incomes of persons in a list:

```
// Declare an accumulator called sum and initialize it to zero
double sum = 0.0;

for(Person person : Person.persons()) {
    // Map the Person to his income double
    double income = person.getIncome();

    // Accumulate the partial result in sum
    sum = sum + income;
}

System.out.println(sum);
```

This time, you had to perform an additional step to map the Person to his income before you could accumulate the partial results in the sum variable.

The Stream<T> interface contains a reduce() method to perform the reduce operation. The method has three overloaded versions:

- `T reduce(T identity, BinaryOperator<T> accumulator)`
- `<U> U reduce(U identity, BiFunction<U,? super T,U> accumulator, BinaryOperator<U> combiner)`
- `Optional<T> reduce(BinaryOperator<T> accumulator)`

The first version of the reduce() method takes an identity and an accumulator as arguments and reduces the stream to a single value of the same type. You can rewrite the example of computing the sum of integers in a list as follows:

```
List<Integer> numbers = List.of(1, 2, 3, 4, 5);
int sum = numbers.stream()
                .reduce(0, Integer::sum);
System.out.println(sum);
```

```
15
```

Let's attempt to do the same with the second example, which computes the sum of the incomes. The following code generates a compile-time error. Only the relevant part of the error message is shown.

```
double sum = Person.persons()
                   .stream()
                   .reduce(0.0, Double::sum);
```

```
error: no suitable method found for reduce(double,Double::sum)
                        .reduce(0.0, Double::sum);
                        ^
    method Stream.reduce(Person,BinaryOperator<Person>) is not applicable
      (argument mismatch; double cannot be converted to Person) ...
```

The stream() method in Person.persons().stream() returns a Stream<Person>, and therefore, the reduce() method is supposed to perform a reduction on the Person objects. However, the first argument to the method is 0.0, which implies that the method is attempting to operate on the Double type, not the Person type. This mismatch in the expected argument type Person and the actual argument type Double resulted in the error.

You wanted to compute the sum of the incomes of all people. You need to map the stream of people to a stream of their incomes using the map operation as follows:

```
double sum = Person.persons()
                   .stream()
                   .map(Person::getIncome)
                   .reduce(0.0, Double::sum);
System.out.println(sum);
```

```
26000.0
```

Performing a map-reduce operation is typical in functional programming. The second version of the reduce method, shown again for easy reference, lets you perform a map operation, followed by a reduce operation.

```
<U> U reduce(U identity, BiFunction<U,? super T,U> accumulator, BinaryOperator<U> combiner)
```

Note that the second argument, which is the accumulator, takes an argument whose type may be different from the type of the stream. This is used for the map operation as well as for the accumulating the partial results. The third argument is used for combining the partial results when the reduce operation is performed in parallel, which I elaborate on shortly. The following snippet of code prints the sum of the incomes of all people:

```
double sum = Person.persons()
    .stream()
    .reduce(0.0, (partialSum, person) -> partialSum + person.getIncome(), Double::sum);
System.out.println(sum);
```

```
26000.0
```

If you examine the code, the second argument to the `reduce()` method is sufficient to produce the desired result in this case. So, what is the purpose of the third argument, `Double::sum`, which is the combiner? In fact, the combiner was not used in the `reduce()` operation at all, even if you specified it. You can verify that the combiner was not used using the following code, which prints a message from the combiner:

```
double sum = Person.persons()
    .stream()
    .reduce(0.0, (partialSum, person) -> partialSum + person.getIncome(),
                (a, b) -> {
                    System.out.println("Combiner called: a = " + a + "b = " + b );
                    return a + b;
                });

System.out.println(sum);
```

```
26000.0
```

The output proves that the combiner was not called. Why do you need to provide the combiner when it is not used? It is used when the reduce operation is performed in parallel. In that case, each thread will accumulate the partial results using the accumulator. At the end, the combiner is used to combine the partial results from all threads to get the result. The following snippet of code shows how the sequential reduce operation works. The code prints a message at several steps along with the current thread name that is performing the operation.

```
double sum = Person.persons()
                   .stream()
                   .reduce(0.0,
                           (Double partialSum, Person p) -> {
                              double accumulated = partialSum + p.getIncome();
                              System.out.println(Thread.currentThread().getName() +
                                  " - Accumulator: partialSum = " +
                                  partialSum + ", person = " + p +
                                ", accumulated = " + accumulated);
                             return accumulated;
                           },
```

```
                        (a, b) -> {
                            double combined = a + b;
                            System.out.println(Thread.currentThread().getName() +
                            " - Combiner: a = " + a + ", b = " + b +
                            ", combined = " + combined);
                           return combined;
                        });

System.out.println(sum);
```

```
main - Accumulator: partialSum = 0.0, person = (1, Ken, MALE, 1970-05-04, 6000.00),
accumulated = 6000.0
main - Accumulator: partialSum = 6000.0, person = (2, Jeff, MALE, 1970-07-15, 7100.00),
accumulated = 13100.0
main - Accumulator: partialSum = 13100.0, person = (3, Donna, FEMALE, 1962-07-29, 8700.00),
accumulated = 21800.0
main - Accumulator: partialSum = 21800.0, person = (4, Chris, MALE, 1993-12-16, 1800.00),
accumulated = 23600.0
main - Accumulator: partialSum = 23600.0, person = (5, Laynie, FEMALE, 2012-12-13, 0.00),
accumulated = 23600.0
main - Accumulator: partialSum = 23600.0, person = (6, Li, MALE, 2001-05-09, 2400.00),
accumulated = 26000.0
26000.0
```

The output shows that the accumulator was sufficient to produce the result and the combiner was never called. Notice that there was only one thread named `main` that processed all people in the stream.

Let's turn the stream into a parallel stream, keeping all the debugging messages. The following code uses a parallel stream to get the sum of the incomes of all people. You may get different output containing a different message, but the sum value would be the same as 26000.0.

```
double sum = Person.persons()
                  .parallelStream()
                  .reduce(0.0,
                        (Double partialSum, Person p) -> {
                           double accumulated = partialSum + p.getIncome();
                           System.out.println(Thread.currentThread().getName() +
                               " - Accumulator: partialSum = " +
                               partialSum + ", person = " + p +
                             ", accumulated = " + accumulated);
                          return accumulated;
                        },
                        (a, b) -> {
                            double combined = a + b;
                            System.out.println(Thread.currentThread().getName() +
                            " - Combiner: a = " + a + ", b = " + b +
                            ", combined = " + combined);
                           return combined;
                        });

System.out.println(sum);
```

```
ForkJoinPool.commonPool-worker-4 - Accumulator: partialSum = 0.0, person = (5, Laynie,
FEMALE, 2012-12-13, 0.00), accumulated = 0.0
ForkJoinPool.commonPool-worker-2 - Accumulator: partialSum = 0.0, person = (6, Li, MALE,
2001-05-09, 2400.00), accumulated = 2400.0
ForkJoinPool.commonPool-worker-1 - Accumulator: partialSum = 0.0, person = (2, Jeff, MALE,
1970-07-15, 7100.00), accumulated = 7100.0
ForkJoinPool.commonPool-worker-2 - Combiner: a = 0.0, b = 2400.0, combined = 2400.0
ForkJoinPool.commonPool-worker-5 - Accumulator: partialSum = 0.0, person = (3, Donna,
FEMALE, 1962-07-29, 8700.00), accumulated = 8700.0
main - Accumulator: partialSum = 0.0, person = (4, Chris, MALE, 1993-12-16, 1800.00),
accumulated = 1800.0
ForkJoinPool.commonPool-worker-3 - Accumulator: partialSum = 0.0, person = (1, Ken, MALE,
1970-05-04, 6000.00), accumulated = 6000.0
main - Combiner: a = 1800.0, b = 2400.0, combined = 4200.0
ForkJoinPool.commonPool-worker-5 - Combiner: a = 7100.0, b = 8700.0, combined = 15800.0
ForkJoinPool.commonPool-worker-5 - Combiner: a = 6000.0, b = 15800.0, combined = 21800.0
ForkJoinPool.commonPool-worker-5 - Combiner: a = 21800.0, b = 4200.0, combined = 26000.0
26000.0
```

The output shows that six threads (five fork/join worker threads and one main thread) performed the parallel reduce operation. They all performed partial reduction using the accumulator to obtain partial results. Finally, the partial results were combined using the combiner to get the result.

Sometimes you cannot specify a default value for a reduce operation. Suppose you want to get maximum integer value from a stream of integers. If the stream is empty, you cannot default the maximum value to 0. In such a case, the result is not defined. The third version of the `reduce(BinaryOperator<T> accumulator)` method is used to perform such a reduction operation. The method returns an `Optional<T>` that wraps the result or the absence of a result. If the stream contains only one element, that element is the result. If the stream contains more than one element, the first two elements are passed to the accumulator, and subsequently, the partial result and the remaining elements are passed to the accumulator. The following snippet of code computes the maximum of integers in a stream:

```
Optional<Integer> max = Stream.of(1, 2, 3, 4, 5)
                              .reduce(Integer::max);
if (max.isPresent()) {
    System.out.println("max = " + max.get());
} else {
    System.out.println("max is not defined.");
}
```

```
max = 5
```

The following snippet of code tries to get the maximum of integers in an empty stream:

```
Optional<Integer> max = Stream.<Integer>empty()
                              .reduce(Integer::max);
if (max.isPresent()) {
    System.out.println("max = " + max.get());
```

```
} else {
    System.out.println("max is not defined.");
}
```

```
max is not defined.
```

The following snippet of code prints the details of the highest earner in the person's list:

```
Optional<Person> person = Person.persons()
                                .stream()
                                .reduce((p1, p2) -> p1.getIncome() > p2.getIncome() ? p1 :
p2);
if (person.isPresent()) {
    System.out.println("Highest earner: " + person.get());
} else {
    System.out.println("Could not get the highest earner.");
}
```

```
Highest earner: (3, Donna, FEMALE, 1962-07-29, 8700.00)
```

To compute the sum, max, min, average, etc. of a numeric stream, you do not need to use the `reduce()` method. You can map the non-numeric stream into one of the three numeric stream types (`IntStream`, `LongStream`, or `DoubleStream`) and use the specialized methods for these purposes. The following snippet of code prints the sum of the incomes of all people. Note the use of the `mapToDouble()` method that converts a `Stream<Person>` to a `DoubleStream`. The `sum()` method is called on the `DoubleStream`.

```
double totalIncome = Person.persons()
                           .stream()
                           .mapToDouble(Person::getIncome)
                           .sum();
System.out.println("Total Income: " + totalIncome);
```

```
Total Income : 26000.0
```

To get the minimum and maximum values of a stream, use the `min()` and `max()` methods of the specific stream. These methods in the `Stream<T>` interface take a `Comparator` as an argument and return an `Optional<T>`. They do not take any arguments in the `IntStream`, `LongStream`, and `DoubleStream` interfaces and return `OptionalInt`, `OptionalLong`, and `OptionalDouble`, respectively. The following snippet of code prints the details of the highest earner in a list of people:

```
Optional<Person> person = Person.persons()
                                .stream()
                                .max(Comparator.comparingDouble(Person::getIncome));

if (person.isPresent()) {
    System.out.println("Highest earner: " + person.get());
} else {
```

```
    System.out.println("Could not get the highest earner.");
}
```

```
Highest earner: (3, Donna, FEMALE, 1962-07-29, 8700.00)
```

The following snippet of code prints the highest income in the person list using the `max()` method of the `DoubleStream`:

```
OptionalDouble income = Person.persons()
                              .stream()
                              .mapToDouble(Person::getIncome)
                              .max();
if (income.isPresent()) {
    System.out.println("Highest income: " + income.getAsDouble());
} else {
    System.out.println("Could not get the highest income.");
}
```

```
Highest income: 8700.0
```

How will you get the highest earner among males and the highest among females in one stream pipeline? So far, you have learned how to compute a single value using the reduce operation. In this case, you need to group the people into two groups, males and females, and then compute the person with the highest income in each group. I show you how to perform grouping and collect multiple values when I discuss the `collect()` method in the next section.

Streams support a count operation through the `count()` method, which simply returns the number of elements in the stream as a `long`. The following snippet of code prints the number of elements in the stream of people:

```
long personCount = Person.persons()
                         .stream()
                         .count();
System.out.println("Person count: " + personCount);
```

```
Person count: 6
```

The count operation is a specialized reduce operation. Were you thinking of using the `map()` and `reduce()` methods to count the number of elements in a stream? The easier way is to map each element in the stream to 1 and compute the sum. This approach does not use the `reduce()` method. Here is how you do this:

```
long personCount = Person.persons()
                         .stream()
                         .mapToLong(p -> 1L)
                         .sum();
```

The following snippet of code uses the `map()` and `reduce()` methods to implement the count operation:

```
long personCount = Person.persons()
                         .stream()
                         .map(p -> 1L)
                         .reduce(0L, Long::sum);
```

The following snippet of code uses only the `reduce()` method to implement the count operation:

```
long personCount = Person.persons()
                         .stream()
                         .reduce(0L, (partialCount, person) -> partialCount + 1L,
                         Long::sum);
```

■ **Tip** This section showed you many ways to perform the same reduction operation on a stream. Some ways may perform better than others depending on the stream type and the parallelization used. Use primitive type streams whenever possible to avoid the overhead of unboxing; use parallel streams whenever possible to take advantage of the multicores available on the machine.

Collecting Data Using Collectors

So far, you have been applying reduction on a stream to produce a single value (a primitive value or a reference value) or `void`. For example, you used the `reduce()` method of the `Stream<Integer>` interface to compute a `long` value that is the sum of its elements. There are several cases in which you want to collect the results of executing a stream pipeline into a collection such as a `List`, a `Set`, a `Map`, etc. Sometimes you may want to apply complex logic to summarize the stream's data. For example, you may want to group people by their gender and compute the highest earner in every gender group. This is possible using the `collect()` method of the `Stream<T>` interface. The `collect()` method is overloaded with two versions:

- `<R> R collect(Supplier<R> supplier, BiConsumer<R,? super T> accumulator, BiConsumer<R,R> combiner)`
- `<R,A> R collect(Collector<? super T,A,R> collector)`

The method uses a mutable reduction operation. It uses a mutable container such as a mutable `Collection` to compute the results from the input stream. The first version of the `collect()` method takes three arguments:

- A *supplier* that supplies a mutable container to store (or collect) the results.
- An *accumulator* that accumulates the results into the mutable container.
- A *combiner* that combines the partial results when the reduction operation takes place in parallel.

■ **Tip** The container to collect the data using the `collect()` method need not be a `Collection`. It can be any mutable object that can accumulate results, such as a `StringBuilder`.

Suppose you have a stream of people and you want to collect the names of all of the people in an ArrayList<String>. Here are the steps to accomplish this.

First, you need to have a supplier that will return an ArrayList<String> to store the names. You can use either of the following statements to create the supplier:

```
// Using a lambda expression
Supplier<ArrayList<String>> supplier = () -> new ArrayList<>();

// Using a constructor reference
Supplier<ArrayList<String>> supplier = ArrayList::new;
```

Second, you need to create an accumulator that receives two arguments. The first argument is the container returned from the supplier, which is the ArrayList<String> in this case. The second argument is the element of the stream. Your accumulator should simply add the names to the list. You can use either of the following statements to create an accumulator:

```
// Using a lambda expression
BiConsumer<ArrayList<String>, String> accumulator = (list, name) -> list.add(name);

// Using a method reference
BiConsumer<ArrayList<String>, String> accumulator = ArrayList::add;
```

Finally, you need a combiner that will combine the results of two ArrayList<String>s into one ArrayList<String>. Note that the combiner is used only when you collect the results using a parallel stream. In a sequential stream, the accumulator is sufficient to collect all results. Your combiner will be simple; it will add all the elements of the second list to the first list using the addAll() method. You can use either of the following statements to create a combiner:

```
// Using a lambda expression
BiConsumer<ArrayList<String>, ArrayList<String>> combiner =
    (list1, list2) -> list1.addAll(list2);

// Using a method reference
BiConsumer<ArrayList<String>, ArrayList<String>> combiner = ArrayList::addAll;
```

Now you are ready to use the collect() method to collect the names of all people in a list using the following snippet of code:

```
List<String> names = Person.persons()
                           .stream()
                           .map(Person::getName)
                           .collect(ArrayList::new, ArrayList::add, ArrayList::addAll);
System.out.println(names);
```

```
[Ken, Jeff, Donna, Chris, Laynie, Li]
```

You can use a similar approach to collect data in a Set and a Map. It seems to be a lot of plumbing just to collect data in a simple collection like a list. Another version of the collect() method provides a simpler solution. It takes an instance of the Collector interface as an argument and collects the data for you. The

Collector interface is in the java.util.stream package and it is declared as follows. Only abstract methods are shown.

```
public interface Collector<T,A,R> {
    Supplier<A> supplier();
    BiConsumer<A,T> accumulator();
    BinaryOperator<A> combiner();
    Function<A,R> finisher();
    Set<Collector.Characteristics> characteristics();
}
```

The Collector interface takes three type parameters called T, A, and R, where T is the type of input elements, A is the type of the accumulator, and R is the type of the result. The first three methods look familiar; you just used them in the previous example. The finisher is used to transform the intermediate type A to result type R. The characteristics of a Collector describe the properties that are represented by the constants of the Collector.Characteristics enum.

The designers of the Streams API realized that rolling out your own collector is too much work. They provided a utility class called Collectors that provides out-of-box implementations for commonly used collectors. Three of the most commonly used methods of the Collectors class are toList(), toSet(), and toCollection(). The toList() method returns a Collector that collects the data in a List; the toSet() method returns a Collector that collects data in a Set; the toCollection()takes a Supplier that returns a Collection to be used to collect data. The following snippet of code collects all names of people in a List<String>:

```
List<String> names = Person.persons()
                           .stream()
                           .map(Person::getName)
                           .collect(Collectors.toList());
System.out.println(names);
```

```
[Ken, Jeff, Donna, Chris, Laynie, Li]
```

Notice that this time you achieved the same result in a much cleaner way.

The following snippet of code collects all names in a Set<String>. Note that a Set keeps only unique elements.

```
Set<String> uniqueNames = Person.persons()
                                .stream()
                                .map(Person::getName)
                                .collect(Collectors.toSet());
System.out.println(uniqueNames);
```

```
[Donna, Ken, Chris, Jeff, Laynie, Li]
```

The output is not in a particular order because a Set does not impose any ordering on its elements. You can collect names in a sorted set using the toCollection() method as follows:

```
SortedSet<String> uniqueSortedNames= Person.persons()
                                           .stream()
                                           .map(Person::getName)
                                           .collect(Collectors.toCollection(TreeSet::new));
System.out.println(uniqueSortedNames);
```

```
[Chris, Donna, Jeff, Ken, Laynie, Li]
```

Recall that the toCollection() method takes a Supplier as an argument that is used to collect the data. In this case, you have used the constructor reference TreeSet::new as the Supplier. This has an effect of using a TreeSet, which is a sorted set, to collect the data.

You can also sort the list of names using the sorted operation. The sorted() method of the Stream interface produces another stream containing the same elements in a sorted order. The following snippet of code shows how to collect sorted names in a list:

```
List<String> sortedName = Person.persons()
                                .stream()
                                .map(Person::getName)
                                .sorted()
                                .collect(Collectors.toList());
System.out.println(sortedName);
```

```
[Chris, Donna, Jeff, Ken, Laynie, Li]
```

Note that the code applies the sorting before it collects the names. The collector notices that it is collecting an ordered stream (sorted names) and preserves the ordering during the collection process.

You will find many static methods in the Collectors class that return a Collector meant to be used as a nested collector. One of these methods is the counting() method that returns the number of input elements. Here is an example of counting the number of people in the streams:

```
long count = Person.persons()
                   .stream()
                   .collect(Collectors.counting());
System.out.println("Person count: " + count);
```

```
Person count: 6
```

You may argue that you could have achieved the same result using the count() method of the Stream interface as follows:

```
long count = Person.persons()
                   .stream()
                   .count();
System.out.println("Persons count: " + count);
```

```
Persons count: 6
```

When do you use the `Collectors.counting()` method instead of the `Stream.count()` method to count the number of elements in a stream? As mentioned before, collectors can be nested. You will see examples of nested collectors shortly. These methods in the `Collectors` class are meant to be used as nested collectors, not in this case just to count the number of elements in the stream. Another difference between the two is their type: the `Stream.count()` method represents an operation on a stream, whereas the `Collectors.counting()` method returns a `Collector`. Listing 13-8 shows the complete program to collect sorted names in a list.

Listing 13-8. Collecting Results into a Collection

```
// CollectTest.java
package com.jdojo.streams;

import java.util.List;
import java.util.stream.Collectors;

public class CollectTest {
    public static void main(String[] args) {
        List<String> sortedNames = Person.persons()
                                        .stream()
                                        .map(Person::getName)
                                        .sorted()
                                        .collect(Collectors.toList());
        System.out.println(sortedNames);
    }
}
```

```
[Chris, Donna, Jeff, Ken, Laynie, Li]
```

Collecting Summary Statistics

In a data-centric application, you need to compute the summary statistics on a group of numeric data. For example, you may want to know the maximum, minimum, sum, average, and count of the incomes of all people. The `java.util` package contains three classes to collect statistics:

- `DoubleSummaryStatistics`
- `LongSummaryStatistics`
- `IntSummaryStatistics`

These classes do not necessarily need to be used with streams. You can use them to compute the summary statistics on any group of numeric data. Using these classes is simple: create an object of the class, keep adding numeric data using the `accept()` method, and finally, call the getter methods such as `getCount()`, `getSum()`, `getMin()`, `getAverage()`, and `getMax()` to get the statistics for the group of data. Listing 13-9 shows how to compute the statistics on a number of `double` values.

Listing 13-9. Computing Summary Statistics on a Group of Numeric Data

```
// SummaryStats.java
package com.jdojo.streams;

import java.util.DoubleSummaryStatistics;

public class SummaryStats {
    public static void main(String[] args) {
        DoubleSummaryStatistics stats = new DoubleSummaryStatistics();
        stats.accept(100.0);
        stats.accept(500.0);
        stats.accept(400.0);

        // Get stats
        long count = stats.getCount();
        double sum = stats.getSum();
        double min = stats.getMin();
        double avg = stats.getAverage();
        double max = stats.getMax();

        System.out.printf("count=%d, sum=%.2f, min=%.2f, max=%.2f, average=%.2f%n",
                count, sum, min, max, avg);
    }
}
```

```
count=3, sum=1000.00, min=100.00, max=500.00, average=333.33
```

The summary statistics classes were designed to be used with streams. They contain a `combine()` method that combines two summary statistics. Can you guess its use? Recall that you need to specify a combiner when you collect data from a stream and this method can act as a combiner for two summary statistics. The following snippet of code computes the summary statistics for incomes of all people:

```
DoubleSummaryStatistics incomeStats =
    Person.persons()
          .stream()
          .map(Person::getIncome)
          .collect(DoubleSummaryStatistics::new,
                   DoubleSummaryStatistics::accept,
                   DoubleSummaryStatistics::combine);

System.out.println(incomeStats);
```

```
DoubleSummaryStatistics{count=6, sum=26000.000000, min=0.000000, average=4333.333333,
max=8700.000000}
```

The `Collectors` class contains methods to obtain a collector to compute the summary statistics of the specific type of numeric data. The methods are named `summarizingDouble()`, `summarizingLong()`, and `summarizingInt()`. They take a function to be applied on the elements of the stream and return a

DoubleSummaryStatistics, a LongSummaryStatistics, and an IntSummaryStatistics, respectively. You can rewrite the code for the previous example as follows:

```
DoubleSummaryStatistics incomeStats =
    Person.persons()
          .stream()
          .collect(Collectors.summarizingDouble(Person::getIncome));

System.out.println(incomeStats);
```

```
DoubleSummaryStatistics{count=6, sum=26000.000000, min=0.000000, average=4333.333333,
max=8700.000000}
```

The Collectors class contains methods such as counting(), summingXxx(), averagingXxx(), minBy(), and maxBy() that return a collector to perform a specific type of summary computation on a group of numeric data that you get in one shot using the summarizingXxx() method. Here, Xxx can be Double, Long, and Int.

Collecting Data in Maps

You can collect data from a stream into a Map. The toMap() method of the Collectors class returns a collector to collect data in a Map. The method is overloaded and it has three versions:

- toMap(Function<? super T,? extends K> keyMapper, Function<? super T,? extends U> valueMapper)
- toMap(Function<? super T,? extends K> keyMapper, Function<? super T,? extends U> valueMapper, BinaryOperator<U> mergeFunction)
- toMap(Function<? super T,? extends K> keyMapper, Function<? super T,? extends U> valueMapper, BinaryOperator<U> mergeFunction, Supplier<M> mapSupplier)

The first version takes two arguments. Both arguments are Functions. The first argument maps the stream elements to keys in the map. The second argument maps stream elements to values in the map. If duplicate keys are found, an IllegalStateException is thrown. The following snippet of code collects a person's data in a Map<long,String> whose keys are the person's IDs and values are the person's names:

```
Map<Long,String> idToNameMap = Person.persons()
                                     .stream()
                                     .collect(Collectors.toMap(Person::getId,
Person::getName));
System.out.println(idToNameMap);
```

```
{1=Ken, 2=Jeff, 3=Donna, 4=Chris, 5=Laynie, 6=Li}
```

Suppose you want collect a person's name based on gender. The following is the first, incorrect attempt, which throws an IllegalStateException. Only partial output is shown.

```
Map<Person.Gender,String> genderToNamesMap = Person.persons()
        .stream()
        .collect(Collectors.toMap(Person::getGender, Person::getName));
```

```
Exception in thread "main" java.lang.IllegalStateException: Duplicate key Ken ...
```

The runtime is complaining about the duplicate keys because Person::getGender will return the gender of the person as the key and you have multiple males and females in the stream.

The solution is to use the second version of the toMap() method to obtain the collection. It lets you specify a merge function as a third argument. The merge function is passed the old and new values for the duplicate key. The function is supposed to merge the two values and return a new value that will be used for the key. In your case, you can concatenate the names of all males and females. The following snippet of code accomplishes this:

```
Map<Person.Gender,String> genderToNamesMap = Person.persons()
    .stream()
    .collect(Collectors.toMap(Person::getGender, Person::getName,
         (oldValue, newValue) -> String.join(", ", oldValue, newValue)));
System.out.println(genderToNamesMap);
```

```
{FEMALE=Donna, Laynie, MALE=Ken, Jeff, Chris, Li}
```

The first two versions of the toMap() method create the Map for you. The third version lets you pass a Supplier to provide a Map yourself. I do not cover an example of using this version of the toMap() method.

Armed with two examples of collecting the data in maps, can you think of the logic for collecting data in a map that summarizes the number of people by gender? Here is how you accomplish this:

```
Map<Person.Gender, Long> countByGender = Person.persons()
    .stream()
    .collect(Collectors.toMap(Person::getGender, p -> 1L,
                              (oldCount, newCount) -> oldCount + 1));

System.out.println(countByGender);
```

```
{MALE=4, FEMALE=2}
```

The key mapper function remains the same. The value mapper function is p -> 1L, which means when a person belonging to a gender is encountered the first time, its value is set to 1. In case of a duplicate key, the merge function is called that simply increments the old value by 1.

The last example in this category that collects the highest earner by gender in a Map is shown in Listing 13-10.

Listing 13-10. Collecting the Highest Earner by Gender in a Map

```
// CollectIntoMapTest.java
package com.jdojo.streams;

import java.util.Map;
import java.util.function.Function;
import java.util.stream.Collectors;

public class CollectIntoMapTest {
    public static void main(String[] args) {
        Map<Person.Gender, Person> highestEarnerByGender =
          Person.persons()
            .stream()
            .collect(Collectors.toMap(Person::getGender, Function.identity(),
                (oldPerson, newPerson) ->
            newPerson.getIncome() > oldPerson.getIncome()?newPerson:oldPerson));

        System.out.println(highestEarnerByGender);
    }
}
```

```
{FEMALE=(3, Donna, FEMALE, 1962-07-29, 8700.00), MALE=(2, Jeff, MALE, 1970-07-15,
7100.00)}
```

The program stores the `Person` object as the value in the map. Note the use of `Function.identity()` as the function to map values. This method returns an identity function that simply returns the value that was passed to it. You could have used a lambda expression of `person -> person` in its place. The merge function compares the income of the person already stored as the value for a key. If the new person has more income than the existing one, it returns the new person.

Collecting data into a map is a very powerful way of summarizing data. You will see maps again when I discuss grouping and partitioning of data shortly.

■ **Tip** The `toMap()` method returns a non-concurrent map that has performance overhead when streams are processed in parallel. It has a companion method called `toConcurrentMap()` that returns a concurrent collector that should be used when streams are processed in parallel.

Joining Strings Using Collectors

The `joining()` method of the `Collectors` class returns a collector that concatenates the elements of a stream of `CharSequence` and returns the result as a `String`. The concatenation occurs in the encounter order. The `joining()` method is overloaded and it has three versions:

- `joining()`
- `joining(CharSequence delimiter)`
- `joining(CharSequence delimiter, CharSequence prefix, CharSequence suffix)`

The version with no arguments simply concatenates all elements. The second version uses a delimiter between two elements. The third version uses a delimiter, a prefix, and a suffix. The prefix is added to the beginning of the result and the suffix is added to end of the result. Listing 13-11 shows how to use the `joining()` method.

Listing 13-11. Joining a Stream of CharSequence Using a Collector

```
// CollectJoiningTest.java
package com.jdojo.streams;

import java.util.List;
import java.util.stream.Collectors;

public class CollectJoiningTest {
    public static void main(String[] args) {
        List<Person> persons = Person.persons();
        String names = persons.stream()
                              .map(Person::getName)
                              .collect(Collectors.joining());

        String delimitedNames = persons.stream()
                                       .map(Person::getName)
                                       .collect(Collectors.joining(", "));

        String prefixedNames = persons.stream()
            .map(Person::getName)
            .collect(Collectors.joining(", ", "Hello ", ". Goodbye."));

        System.out.println("Joined names: " + names);
        System.out.println("Joined, delimited names: " + delimitedNames);
        System.out.println(prefixedNames);
    }
}
```

```
Joined names: KenJeffDonnaChrisLaynieLi
Joined, delimited names: Ken, Jeff, Donna, Chris, Laynie, Li
Hello Ken, Jeff, Donna, Chris, Laynie, Li. Goodbye.
```

Grouping Data

Grouping data for reporting purposes is common. For example, you may want to know the average income by gender, the youngest person by gender, etc. In previous sections, you used the `toMap()` method of the `Collectors` class to get collectors that can be used to group data in maps. The `groupingBy()` method of the `Collectors` class returns a collector that groups the data before collecting them in a `Map`. If you have worked with SQL statements, it is similar to using a "group by" clause. The `groupingBy()` method is overloaded and it has three versions:

- `groupingBy(Function<? super T,? extends K> classifier)`
- `groupingBy(Function<? super T,? extends K> classifier, Collector<? super T,A,D> downstream)`
- `groupingBy(Function<? super T,? extends K> classifier, Supplier<M> mapFactory, Collector<? super T,A,D> downstream)`

I discuss the first and second versions. The third version is the same as the second one, except that it lets you specify a `Supplier` that is used as the factory to get the `Map`. In the first two versions, the collector takes care of creating the `Map` for you.

■ **Tip** The `groupingBy()` method returns a non-concurrent map that has performance overhead when the stream is processed in parallel. It has a companion method called `groupingByConcurrent()` that returns a concurrent collector that should be used in parallel stream processing for better performance.

In the most generic version, the `groupingBy()` method takes two parameters:

- A *classifier* that is a function to generate the keys in the map.
- A *collector* that performs a reduction operation on the values associated with each key.

The first version of the `groupingBy()` method returns a collector that collects data into a `Map<K, List<T>>`, where `K` is the return type of the classifier function and `T` is the type of elements in the input stream. Note that the value of a grouped key in the map is a list of elements from the stream. The following snippet of code collects the list of people by gender:

```
Map<Person.Gender, List<Person>> personsByGender =
    Person.persons()
          .stream()
          .collect(Collectors.groupingBy(Person::getGender));

System.out.println(personsByGender);
```

```
{FEMALE=[(3, Donna, FEMALE, 1962-07-29, 8700.00), (5, Laynie, FEMALE, 2012-12-13, 0.00)],
MALE=[(1, Ken, MALE, 1970-05-04, 6000.00), (2, Jeff, MALE, 1970-07-15, 7100.00),
(4, Chris, MALE, 1993-12-16, 1800.00), (6, Li, MALE, 2001-05-09, 2400.00)]}
```

Suppose you want to get a list of names grouped by gender. You need to use the second version of the `groupingBy()` method that lets you perform a reduction operation on the values of each key. Notice that the type of the second argument is `Collector`. The `Collectors` class contains many methods that return a `Collector` that you will be using as the second argument.

Let's try a simple case where you want to group people by gender and count the number of people in each group. The `counting()` method of the `Collectors` class returns a `Collector` to count the number of elements in a stream. The following snippet of code accomplishes this:

```
Map<Person.Gender, Long> countByGender =
    Person.persons()
          .stream()
          .collect(Collectors.groupingBy(Person::getGender, Collectors.counting()));

System.out.println(countByGender);
```

```
{MALE=4, FEMALE=2}
```

Let's get back to the example of listing a person's name by gender. You need to use the `mapping()` method of the `Collectors` class to get a collector that will map the list of people in the value of a key to their names and join them. The signature of the `mapping()` method is as follows:

```
mapping(Function<? super T,? extends U> mapper, Collector<? super U,A,R> downstream)
```

Notice the type of the second argument of the `mapping()` method. It is another `Collector`. This is where dealing with grouping data gets complex. You need to nest collectors inside collectors. To simplify the grouping process, you break down the things you want to perform on the data. You have already grouped people by their gender. The value of the each key in the map was a `List<Person>`. Now you want to reduce the `List<Person>` to a `String` that contains a comma-separated list of the names of all the people. You need to think about this operation separately to avoid confusion. You can accomplish this reduction as follows:

1. Use a function to map each person to his/her name. This function could be as simple as a method reference like `Person::getName`. Think of the output of this step as a stream of person names in a group.
2. What do you want to do with the stream of names generated in the first step? You may want to collect them in a `String`, a `List`, a `Set`, or some other data structure. In this case, you want to join the names of people, so you use the collector returned from the `joining()` method of the `Collectors` class.

The following snippet of code shows how to group the names of people by gender:

```
Map<Person.Gender, String> namesByGender =
    Person.persons()
          .stream()
          .collect(Collectors.groupingBy(Person::getGender,
             Collectors.mapping(Person::getName, Collectors.joining(", "))));

System.out.println(namesByGender);
```

```
{MALE=Ken, Jeff, Chris, Li, FEMALE=Donna, Laynie}
```

The code collects the names for a group in a comma-separated `String`. Can you think of a way to collect the names in a `List`? It is easy to accomplish this. Use the collector returned by the `toList()` method of the `Collectors` class, like so:

```
Map<Person.Gender, List<String>> namesByGender =
    Person.persons()
          .stream()
          .collect(Collectors.groupingBy(Person::getGender,
              Collectors.mapping(Person::getName, Collectors.toList())));

System.out.println(namesByGender);
```

```
{FEMALE=[Donna, Laynie], MALE=[Ken, Jeff, Chris, Li]}
```

Groups can be nested. Let's create a report that groups people by gender. Within each gender group, it creates another group based on the month of their births and lists the names of the people born in this group. This is a very simple computation to perform. You already know how to group people by gender.

All you need to do is perform another grouping on the values of the keys, that is simply another collector obtained using the `groupingBy()` method again. In this case, the value for a key in the map representing the top-level grouping (by gender) is a `Map`. Listing 13-12 contains the complete code to accomplish this. Notice the use of the static imports to import the static methods from the `Collectors` class for better code readability. The program assumes that every person has a date of birth.

Listing 13-12. Using Nested Groupings

```
// NestedGroupings.java
package com.jdojo.streams;

import java.time.Month;
import java.util.Map;
import static java.util.stream.Collectors.groupingBy;
import static java.util.stream.Collectors.mapping;
import static java.util.stream.Collectors.joining;

public class NestedGroupings {
    public static void main(String[] args) {
        Map<Person.Gender, Map<Month, String>> personsByGenderAndDobMonth
            = Person.persons()
                    .stream()
                    .collect(groupingBy(Person::getGender,
                             groupingBy(p -> p.getDob().getMonth(),
                             mapping(Person::getName, joining(", ")))));

        System.out.println(personsByGenderAndDobMonth);
    }
}
```

```
{FEMALE={DECEMBER=Laynie, JULY=Donna}, MALE={DECEMBER=Chris, JULY=Jeff, MAY=Ken, Li}}
```

Notice that the output has two top-level groups based on gender: Male and Female. With each gender group, there are nested groups based on the month of the person's birth. For each month group, you have a list of those born in that month. For example, Ken and Li were born in the month of May and they are males, so they are listed in the output together.

As the final example in this section, let's summarize the income of people grouped by gender. The program in Listing 13-13 computes the summary statistics of income by gender. I used static imports to use the method names from the `Collectors` class to keep the code a bit cleaner. Looking at the output, you can tell the average income of females is 25 dollars more than that of males. You can keep nesting groups inside another group. There is no limit on levels of nesting for groups.

Listing 13-13. Summary Statistics of Income Grouped by Gender

```
// IncomeStatsByGender.java
package com.jdojo.streams;

import java.util.DoubleSummaryStatistics;
import java.util.Map;
import static java.util.stream.Collectors.groupingBy;
import static java.util.stream.Collectors.summarizingDouble;
```

```
public class IncomeStatsByGender {
    public static void main(String[] args) {
        Map<Person.Gender, DoubleSummaryStatistics> incomeStatsByGender =
            Person.persons()
                  .stream()
                  .collect(groupingBy(Person::getGender,
                                      summarizingDouble(Person::getIncome)));

        System.out.println(incomeStatsByGender);
    }
}
```

```
{MALE=DoubleSummaryStatistics{count=4, sum=17300.000000, min=1800.000000,
average=4325.000000, max=7100.000000}, FEMALE=DoubleSummaryStatistics{count=2,
sum=8700.000000, min=0.000000, average=4350.000000, max=8700.000000}}
```

Partitioning Data

Partitioning data is a special case of grouping data. Grouping data is based on the keys returned from a function. There are as many groups as the number of distinct keys returned from the function. Partitioning collects data into two groups: for one group a condition is true; for the other, the same condition is false. The partitioning condition is specified using a Predicate. By now, you might have guessed the name of the method in the Collectors class that returns a collector to perform the partitioning. The method is partitioningBy(). It is overloaded and it has two versions:

- partitioningBy(Predicate<? super T> predicate)
- partitioningBy(Predicate<? super T> predicate, Collector<? super T,A,D> downstream)

Like the groupingBy() method, the partitioningBy() method also collects data in a Map whose keys are always of the type Boolean. Note that the Map returned from the collector always contains two entries: one with the key value as true and another with the key value as false.

The first version of the partitionedBy() method returns a collector that performs the partitioning based on the specified predicate. The values for a key are stored in a List. If the predicate evaluates to true for an element, the element is added to the list for the key with a true value; otherwise, the value is added to the list of values for the key with a false value. The following snippet of code partitions people based on whether the person is a male:

```
Map<Boolean, List<Person>> partionedByMaleGender =
    Person.persons()
          .stream()
          .collect(Collectors.partitioningBy(Person::isMale));

System.out.println(partionedByMaleGender);
```

```
{false=[(3, Donna, FEMALE, 1962-07-29, 8700.00), (5, Laynie, FEMALE, 2012-12-13, 0.00)],
true=[(1, Ken, MALE, 1970-05-04, 6000.00), (2, Jeff, MALE, 1970-07-15, 7100.00), (4, Chris,
MALE, 1993-12-16, 1800.00), (6, Li, MALE, 2001-05-09, 2400.00)]}
```

The second version of the method lets you specify another collector that can perform a reduction operation on the values for each key. You have seen several examples of this kind in the previous section when you grouped data using the groupingBy() method. The following snippet of code partitions people into male and non-male and collects their names in a comma-separated string:

```
Map<Boolean,String> partionedByMaleGender =
    Person.persons()
          .stream()
          .collect(Collectors.partitioningBy(Person::isMale,
            Collectors.mapping(Person::getName, Collectors.joining(", "))));

System.out.println(partionedByMaleGender);
```

```
{false=Donna, Laynie, true=Ken, Jeff, Chris, Li}
```

Adapting the Collector Results

So far, you have seen collectors doing great work on their own: you specify what you want and the collector does all the work for you. There is one more type of collector that collects the data and lets you modify the result before and after collecting the data. You can adapt the result of the collector to a different type; you can filter the elements after they are grouped but before they are collected; you map elements as they are grouped, but before they are collected. The following static methods in the Collectors class return such collectors:

- `<T,A,R,RR> Collector<T,A,RR> collectingAndThen(Collector<T,A,R> downstream, Function<R,RR> finisher)`
- `<T,A,R> Collector<T,?,R> filtering(Predicate<? super T> predicate, Collector<? super T,A,R> downstream)`
- `<T,U,A,R> Collector<T,?,R> flatMapping(Function<? super T,? extends Stream<? extends U>> mapper, Collector<? super U,A,R> downstream)`

The filtering() and flatMapping() methods were added to the Collectors class in Java 9.

The collectingAndThen() method lets you modify the results of a collector after the collector has collected all elements. Its first argument is a collector that collects the data. The second argument is a finisher that is a function. The finisher is passed a result and it is free to modify the result, including its type. The return type of such a collector is the return type of the finisher. One of the common uses for the finisher is to return an unmodifiable view of the collected data. Here is an example that returns an unmodifiable list of person names:

```
List<String> names = Person.persons()
            .stream()
            .map(Person::getName)
            .collect(Collectors.collectingAndThen(Collectors.toList(),
                result -> Collections.unmodifiableList(result)));

System.out.println(names);
```

```
[Ken, Jeff, Donna, Chris, Laynie, Li]
```

The collector collects the names in a mutable list and the finisher wraps the mutable list in an unmodifiable list. Let's take another example of using the finisher. Suppose you want to print a calendar that contains the names of people by the month of their dates of birth. You have already collected the list of names grouped by months of their birth. You may have a month that doesn't contain any birthdays. However, you want to print the month's name anyway and just add "None". Here is the first attempt:

```
Map<Month,String> dobCalendar = Person.persons()
    .stream()
    .collect(groupingBy(p -> p.getDob().getMonth(),
             mapping(Person::getName, joining(", "))));

dobCalendar.entrySet().forEach(System.out::println);
```

```
MAY=Ken, Li
DECEMBER=Chris, Laynie
JULY=Jeff, Donna
```

This calendar has three issues:

- It is not sorted by month.
- It does not include all months.
- It is modifiable. The returned `Map` from the `collect()` method is modifiable.

You can fix all three issues by using the collector returned from the `collectingAndThen()` method and specifying a finisher. The finisher will add the missing months in the map, convert the map to a sorted map, and finally, wrap the map in an unmodifiable map. The `collect()` method returns the map returned from the finisher. Listing 13-14 contains the complete code.

Listing 13-14. Adapting the Collector Result

```
// DobCalendar.java
package com.jdojo.streams;

import java.time.Month;
import java.util.Collections;
import java.util.Map;
import java.util.TreeMap;
import static java.util.stream.Collectors.collectingAndThen;
import static java.util.stream.Collectors.groupingBy;
import static java.util.stream.Collectors.joining;
import static java.util.stream.Collectors.mapping;

public class DobCalendar {
    public static void main(String[] args) {
        Map<Month, String> dobCalendar = Person.persons()
            .stream().collect(collectingAndThen(
                groupingBy(p -> p.getDob().getMonth(),
                mapping(Person::getName, joining(", "))),
                result -> {
```

```
                // Add missing months
                for (Month m : Month.values()) {
                    result.putIfAbsent(m, "None");
                }

                // Return a sorted, unmodifiable map
                return Collections.unmodifiableMap(new TreeMap<>(result));
            }));

        dobCalendar.entrySet().forEach(System.out::println);
    }
}
```

```
JANUARY=None
FEBRUARY=None
MARCH=None
APRIL=None
MAY=Ken, Li
JUNE=None
JULY=Jeff, Donna
AUGUST=None
SEPTEMBER=None
OCTOBER=None
NOVEMBER=None
DECEMBER=Chris, Laynie
```

The `filtering()` method lets you group the elements, apply a filter in each group, and collect the filtered elements. The following snippet of code shows you how to group people by gender and collect only those people who make more than 8000.00:

```
Map<Person.Gender, List<Person>> makingOver8000 = Person.persons()
            .stream()
            .collect(groupingBy(Person::getGender,
                    filtering(p -> p.getIncome() > 8000.00, toList())));

System.out.println(makingOver8000);
```

```
{MALE=[], FEMALE=[(3, Donna, FEMALE, 1962-07-29, 8700.00)]}
```

Notice an empty list in the male group. In the collector, two group were collected: male and female. The `filtering( )` method filtered out all elements in the male group, so you got an empty list. If you had used the `filter()` method on the original stream to filter out people making 8000.00 or less, you would not have seen the male group in the output because the collector would have not seen the male group at all.

You have already seen the use of the collector returned by the `mapping()` function of the `Collectors` class in the "Grouping Data" section, which lets you apply a function to each element before accumulating the elements in a collector. The `flatMapping()` method lets you apply a flat mapping function on each element. Consider the list of people in Table 13-2. Suppose you want to summarize the table's data by grouping people by their gender and the list of unique languages spoken by people of each gender type.

Table 13-2. A List of People, Their Genders, and the List of Languages They Speak

Name	Gender	Language
Ken	Male	English, French
Jeff	Male	Spanish, Wu
Donna	Female	English, French
Chris	Male	Wu, Lao
Laynie	Female	English, German
Li	Male	English

For this example, I use a `Map.Entry<String,Set<String>>` instance to represent row in this table. I use only gender and spoken languages in each row of the table, ignoring the person's name. Listing 13-15 contains the complete code.

Listing 13-15. Applying a Flat Mapping Operation After Grouping

```
// FlatMappingTest.java
package com.jdojo.streams;

import java.util.List;
import java.util.Map;
import java.util.Map.Entry;
import static java.util.Map.entry;
import java.util.Set;
import static java.util.stream.Collectors.flatMapping;
import static java.util.stream.Collectors.groupingBy;
import static java.util.stream.Collectors.toSet;

public class FlatMappingTest {
    public static void main(String[] args) {
        // Represent the gender and the list of spoken languages
        List<Entry<String, Set<String>>> list = List.of(
                entry("Male", Set.of("English", "French")),
                entry("Male", Set.of("Spanish", "Wu")),
                entry("Female", Set.of("English", "French")),
                entry("Male", Set.of("Wu", "Lao")),
                entry("Female", Set.of("English", "German")),
                entry("Male", Set.of("English")));

        Map<String, Set<String>> langByGender = list.stream()
                .collect(groupingBy(Entry::getKey,
                        flatMapping(e -> e.getValue().stream(), toSet())));

        System.out.println(langByGender);
    }
}
```

```
{Female=[English, French, German], Male=[English, French, Spanish, Lao, Wu]}
```

The Entry::getKey method reference is used to group the elements of the list by gender. The first argument maps each entry in the list to a Stream<String>, which contains the languages spoken for that element. The flatMapping() method flattens the stream produced and collects the results, which are the names of the spoken languages in a Set<String>, giving you a unique list of spoken languages by gender.

Finding and Matching in Streams

The Streams API supports different types of find and match operations on stream elements. For example, you can check if any elements in the stream match a predicate, if all elements match a predicate, etc. The following methods in the Stream interface are used to perform find and match operations:

- boolean allMatch(Predicate<? super T> predicate)
- boolean anyMatch(Predicate<? super T> predicate)
- boolean noneMatch(Predicate<? super T> predicate)
- Optional<T> findAny()
- Optional<T> findFirst()

The primitive type streams such as IntStream, LongStream, and DoubleStream also contain the same methods that work with a predicate and an optional one for primitive types. For example, the allMatch() method in the IntStream takes an IntPredicate as an argument and the findAny() method returns an OptionalInt.

All find and match operations are terminal operations. They are also short-circuiting operations. A short-circuiting operation may not have to process the entire stream to return the result. For example, the allMatch() method checks if the specified predicate is true for all elements in the stream. It is sufficient for this method to return false if the predicate evaluates to false for one element. Once the predicate evaluates to false for one element, it stops further processing (short-circuits) of elements and returns the result as false. The same argument goes for all other methods. Note that the return type of the findAny() and findFirst() methods is Optional<T> because these methods may not have a result if the stream is empty.

The program in Listing 13-16 shows how to perform find and match operations on streams. The program uses sequential stream because the stream size is very small. Consider using a parallel stream if the match has to be performed on large streams. In that case, any thread can find a match or not find a match to end the matching operations.

Listing 13-16. Performing Find and Match Operations on Streams

```
// FindAndMatch.java
package com.jdojo.streams;

import java.util.List;
import java.util.Optional;

public class FindAndMatch {
public static void main(String[] args) {
        // Get the list of persons
        List<Person> persons = Person.persons();

        // Check if all persons are males
        boolean allMales = persons.stream()
                                  .allMatch(Person::isMale);
        System.out.println("All males: " + allMales);
```

```
        // Check if any person was born in 1970
        boolean anyoneBornIn1970 =  persons.stream()
                                           .anyMatch(p -> p.getDob().getYear() == 1970);
        System.out.println("Anyone born in 1970: " + anyoneBornIn1970);

        // Check if any person was born in 1955
        boolean anyoneBornIn1955 = persons.stream()
                                          .anyMatch(p -> p.getDob().getYear() == 1955);
        System.out.println("Anyone born in 1955: " + anyoneBornIn1955);

        // Find any male
        Optional<Person> anyMale = persons.stream()
                                          .filter(Person::isMale)
                                          .findAny();
        if (anyMale.isPresent()) {
            System.out.println("Any male: " + anyMale.get());
        } else {
            System.out.println("No male found.");
        }

        // Find the first male
        Optional<Person> firstMale = persons.stream()
                                            .filter(Person::isMale)
                                            .findFirst();
        if (firstMale.isPresent()) {
            System.out.println("First male: " + anyMale.get());
        } else {
            System.out.println("No male found.");
        }
    }
}
```

```
All males: false
Anyone born in 1970: true
Anyone born in 1955: false
Any male: (1, Ken, MALE, 1970-05-04, 6000.00)
First male: (1, Ken, MALE, 1970-05-04, 6000.00)
```

Parallel Streams

Streams can be sequential or parallel. Operations on a sequential stream are processed in serial using one thread. Operations on a parallel stream are processed in parallel using multiple threads. You do not need to take additional steps to process streams because they are sequential or parallel. All you need to do is call the appropriate method that produces a sequential or parallel stream. Everything else is taken care of by the Streams API. This is why I stated in the beginning of this chapter that you get parallelism in stream processing “almost” for free.

Most of the methods in the Streams API produce sequential streams by default. To produce a parallel stream from a collection, such as a `List` or a `Set`, you need to call the `parallelStream()` method of the `Collection` interface. Use the `parallel()` method on a stream to convert a sequential stream into a parallel stream. Conversely, use the `sequential()` method on a stream to convert a parallel stream into a sequential stream. The following snippet of code shows serial processing of the stream pipeline because the stream is sequential:

```
String names = Person.persons()              // The data source
                  .stream()                  // Produces a sequential stream
                  .filter(Person::isMale)    // Processed in serial
                  .map(Person::getName)      // Processed in serial
                  .collect(Collectors.joining(", ")); // Processed in serial
```

The following snippet of code shows parallel processing of the stream pipeline because the stream is parallel:

```
String names = Person.persons()            // The data source
                .parallelStream()          // Produces a parallel stream
                .filter(Person::isMale)    // Processed in parallel
                .map(Person::getName)      // Processed in parallel
                .collect(Collectors.joining(", ")); // Processed in parallel
```

The following snippet of code shows processing of the stream pipeline in mixed mode because the operations in the pipeline produce serial and parallel streams:

```
String names = Person.persons()            // The data source
               .stream()                   // Produces a sequential stream
               .filter(Person::isMale)     // Processed in serial
               .parallel()                 // Produces a parallel stream
               .map(Person::getName)       // Processed in parallel
               .collect(Collectors.joining(", ")); // Processed in parallel
```

The operations following a serial stream are performed serially and the operations following a parallel stream are performed in parallel. You get parallelism when processing streams for free. So when do you use parallelism in stream processing? Do you get the benefits of parallelism whenever you use it? The answer is no. There are some conditions that must be met before you should use parallel streams. Sometimes using parallel streams may result in worse performance.

The Streams API uses the Fork/Join framework to process parallel streams. The Fork/Join framework uses multiple threads. It divides the stream elements into chunks; each thread processes a chunk of elements to produce a partial result, and the partial results are combined to give you the result. Starting up multiple threads, dividing the data into chunks, and combining partial results takes up CPU time. This overhead is justified by the overall time to finish the task. For example, a stream of six people is going to take longer to process in parallel than in serial. The overhead of setting up the threads and coordinating them for such a small amount of work is not worth it.

You have seen the use of an `Iterator` for traversing elements of collections. The Streams API uses a `Spliterator` (a splittable iterator) to traverse elements of streams. `Spliterator` is a generalization of `Iterator`. An iterator provides sequential access to data elements. A `Spliterator` provides sequential access and decomposition of data elements. When you create a `Spliterator`, it knows the chunk of data it will process. You can split a `Spliterator` into two: each will get its own chunk of data to process. The `Spliterator` is an interface in the `java.util` package. It is used heavily for splitting stream elements into chunks to be processed by multiple threads. As the user of the Streams API, you will never have to work directly with a `Spliterator`. The data source of the streams provides a `Spliterator`. Parallel processing of a stream is faster if the `Spliterator` can know the size of the streams. Streams can be based on a data source that may have a fixed size or an unknown size. Splitting the stream elements into chunks is not possible if the size of the stream cannot be determined. In such cases, even though you can use a parallel stream, you may not get the benefits of parallelism.

Another consideration in parallel processing is the ordering of elements. If elements are ordered, threads need to keep the ordering at the end of the processing. If ordering is not important for you, you can convert an ordered stream into an unordered stream using the `unordered()` method.

`Spliterators` divide the data elements into chunks. It is important that the data source for the stream does not change during stream processing; otherwise the result is not defined. For example, if your stream uses a list/set as the data source, do not add or remove elements from the list/set when the stream is being processed.

Stream processing is based on functional programming that does not modify data elements during processing. It creates new data elements rather than modifying them. The same rule holds for stream processing, particularly when it is processed in parallel. The operations in a stream pipeline are specified as lambda expressions that should not modify the mutable states of the elements being processed.

Let's take an example of counting the prime numbers in a big range of natural numbers, say from 2 to 214748364. The number 214748364 is one tenth of `Integer.MAX_VALUE`. The following snippet of code performs the counting in serial:

```
// Process the stream in serial
long count = IntStream.rangeClosed(2, Integer.MAX_VALUE/10)
                      .filter(PrimeUtil::isPrime)
                      .count();
```

The code took 758 seconds to finish. Let's try converting the stream to a parallel stream as follows:

```
// Process the stream in parallel
long count = IntStream.rangeClosed(2, Integer.MAX_VALUE/10)
                      .parallel()
                      .filter(PrimeUtil::isPrime)
                      .count();
```

This time, the code took only 181 seconds, which is roughly 24% of the time it took when it was processed in serial. This is a significant gain. Both pieces of code were run on a machine with a processor that had eight cores. The code may take a different amount of time to complete on your machine.

Summary

A stream is a sequence of data elements supporting sequential and parallel aggregate operations. Collections in Java focus on data storage and access to the data, whereas streams focus on computations on data. Streams do not have storage. They get the data from a data source, which is most often a collection. However, a stream can get its data from other sources, such as file I/O channel, a function, etc. A stream can also be based on a data source that is capable of generating infinite data elements.

Streams are connected through operations forming a pipeline. Streams support two types of operations: intermediate and terminal operations. An intermediate operation on a stream produces another stream that can serve as an input stream for another intermediate operation. A terminal operation produces a result in the form of a single value. A stream cannot be reused after a terminal operation is invoked on it.

Some operations on streams are called short-circuiting operations. A short-circuiting operation does not necessarily have to process all data in the stream. For example, `findAny` is a short-circuiting operation that finds any element in the stream for which the specified predicate is true. Once an element is found, the operation discards the remaining elements in the stream.

Streams are inherently lazy. They process data on demand. Data is not processed when intermediate operations are invoked on a stream. Invocation of a terminal operation processes the stream data.

A stream pipeline can be executed in serial or in parallel. By default, streams are serial. You can convert a serial stream into a parallel stream by calling the stream's `parallel()` method. You can convert a parallel stream into a serial stream by calling the stream's `sequential()` method.

The Streams API supports most of the operations supported in the functional programming such as filter, map, `forEach`, reduce, `allMatch`, `anyMatch`, `findAny`, `findFirst`, etc. Streams contain a `peek()` method for debugging purposes that lets you take an action on every element passing through stream. The Streams API provides collectors that are used to collect data in collections, such as a map, a list, a set, etc. The `Collectors` class is a utility class that provides several implementations of collectors. Mapping, grouping, and partitioning of a stream's data can be easily performed using the `collect()` method of streams and using the collector provided.

Parallel streams take advantage of multicore processors. They use the Fork/Join framework to process the stream's element in parallel.

QUESTIONS AND EXERCISES

1. What are streams and aggregate operations on streams?
2. How do streams differ from collections?
3. Fill in the blanks:
    a. Collections have storage, whereas streams have ____ storage.
    b. Collections support external iteration, whereas streams support ________ iteration.
    c. Collections support imperative programming, whereas streams support ________ programming.
    d. Collections support a finite number of elements, whereas streams support ________ number of elements.
    e. Streams support sequential and ______ processing of its elements.
    f. A stream does not start pulling elements from its data source until a ____________ operation is called on the stream.
    g. Once a terminal operation is called on a stream, the stream ______ be reused.
4. Describe the difference between intermediate and terminal operations on streams.
5. Create a `Stream<Integer>` of all integers from 10 to 30 and compute the sum of all integers in the list.
6. Complete the following snippet of code, which computes the sum of characters in a list of names using a stream.

```
List<String> names = List.of("Mo", "Jeff", "Li", "Dola");
int sum = names.stream()
              ./* your code goes here */;
System.out.println("Total characters: " + sum);
```

The expected output is as follows:

```
Total characters: 12
```

7. Complete the following snippet of code, which creates two empty `Stream<String>`s. You are supposed to use different methods of the `Stream` interface to complete the code.

```
Stream<String> noNames1 = Stream./* Your code goes here */;
Stream<String> noNames2 = Stream./* Your code goes here */;
```

8. What method of the `Stream` interface is used to limit the number of elements in a stream to a specified size?

9. What method of the `Stream` interface is used to skip a specified number of elements in a stream?

10. Describe the characteristics of the stream produced by the following snippet of code:

```
Stream<Integer> stream = Stream.generate(() -> 1969);
```

11. What is the use of the instances of the `Optional<T>` class?

12. Complete the following snippet of code, which is supposed to print the names of people along with the number of characters in the names in the non-empty `Optional`s in the list:

```
List<Optional<String>> names = List.of(Optional.of("Ken"),
                                       Optional.empty(),
                                       Optional.of("Li"),
                                       Optional.empty(),
                                       Optional.of("Toto"));

names.stream()
     .flatMap(/* Your code goes here */)
     .forEach(/* Your code goes here */);
```

The expected output is as follows:

```
Ken: 3
Li: 2
Toto: 4
```

13. What is the use of the `peek()` method in the `Stream` interface?

14. What is the use of the `map()` and `flatMap()` methods in the `Stream` interface?

15. Compare the filter and map operations on a stream with respect to the type of elements and number of elements in the input and output streams of these operations.

16. What is a reduction operation on a stream? Name three commonly used reduction operations on streams.

17. Write the logic to compute the sum of all integers in the following array using a parallel stream and the `reduce()` method of the `Stream` interface.

```
int[] nums = {1, 2, 3, 4, 5, 6, 7, 8, 9, 10};
```

18. Complete the following snippet of code to print the unique non-null values in a map:

```
Map<Integer, String> map = new HashMap<>();
map.put(1, "One");
map.put(2, "One");
map.put(3, null);
map.put(4, "Two");

map.entrySet()
   .stream()
   .flatMap(/* Your code goes here */)
   ./* Your code goes here */
   .forEach(System.out::println);
```

The expected output is as follows:

```
One
Two
```

19. Complete the missing piece code in the following snippet of code, which is supposed to count the number of even and odd integers in a list of integers:

```
List<Integer> list = List.of(10, 19, 20, 40, 45, 50);
Map<String,Long> oddEvenCounts = list.stream()
        .map(/* Your code goes here */)
        .collect(/* Your code goes here */);

System.out.println(oddEvenCounts);
```

The expected output is as follows:

```
{Even=4, Odd=2}
```

20. The following snippet of code is supposed to print a sorted list of odd integers in the list, which are separated by colons. Complete the missing pieces of the code.

```
List<Integer> list = List.of(5, 1, 2, 7, 3, 4, 8);
String str = list.stream()
                 ./* Multiple method calls go here */;

System.out.println(str);
```

The expected output is as follows:

```
1:3:5:7
```

CHAPTER 14

Implementing Services

In this chapter, you will learn:

- What services, service interfaces, and service providers are
- How to implement a service in Java 9 and before Java 9
- How to use a Java interface as a service implementation in Java 9
- How to load service providers using the `ServiceLoader` class
- How to use the `uses` statement in a module declaration to specify the service interface that the current module discovers and loads using the `ServiceLoader` class
- How to use the `provides` statement to specify a service provider provided by the current module
- How to discover, filter, and select service providers based on their type without instantiating them
- How to package service providers before Java 9

What Is a Service?

A specific functionality provided by an application (or a library) is known as a *service*. For example, you can have different libraries providing a *prime number service,* which can check if a number is a prime and generate the next prime after a given number. Applications and libraries providing implementations for a service are known as *service providers*. Applications using the service are called *service consumers* or *clients*. How does a client use the service? Does a client know all service providers? Does a client get a service without knowing any service providers? I answer these questions in this chapter.

Java SE 6 provided a mechanism to allow for loose coupling between service providers and service consumers. That is, a service consumer can use a service provided by a service provider without knowing the service provider.

In Java, a *service* is defined by a set of interfaces and classes. The service contains an interface or an abstract class that defines the functionality provided by the service and it is known as the *service provider interface* or simply *service interface*. Note that the term "interface" in "service provider interface" and "service interface" does not refer to an interface construct in Java. A service interface can be a Java interface or an abstract class. It is possible, but not recommended, to use a concrete class as a service interface. Sometimes, a service interface is also called a *service type*—the type that is used to identify the service.

A specific implementation of a *service* is known as a *service provider*. There can be multiple service providers for a service interface. Typically, a service provider consists of several interfaces and classes to provide an implementation for the service interface.

K. Sharan, *Java Language Features*, https://doi.org/10.1007/978-1-4842-3348-1_14

The JDK contains a `java.util.ServiceLoader<S>` class whose sole purpose is to discover and load service providers at runtime for a service interface of type `S`. The `ServiceLoader` class allows decoupling of service providers from service consumers. A service consumer knows only the service interface; the `ServiceLoader` class makes the instances of the service providers that are implementing the service interface available to consumers. Figure 14-1 shows a pictorial view of the arrangement of a service, service providers, and a service consumer.

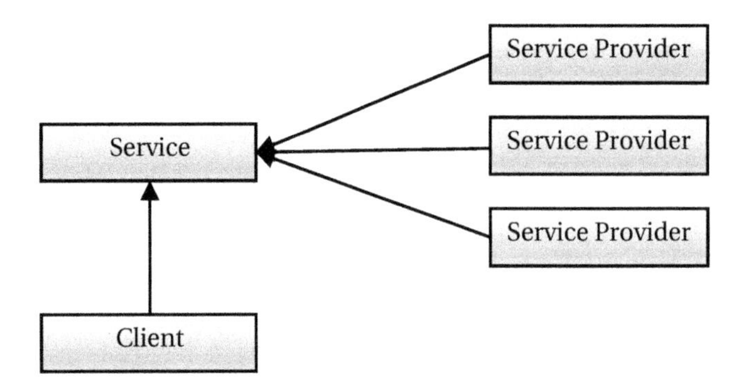

Figure 14-1. *The arrangement of a service, service providers, and a service consumer*

Typically, the service will use the `ServiceLoader` class to load all service providers and make them available to service consumers (or clients). This architecture allows for a plugin mechanism in which a service provider can be added or removed without affecting the service and service consumers. Service consumers know only about the service interface. They do not know about any specific implementations (service providers) of the service interface.

■ **Tip** I suggest reading the documentation for the `java.util.ServiceLoader` class for a complete understanding of the service-loading facility provided by JDK9.

In this chapter, I use a service and three service providers. Their modules, class/interface names, and brief descriptions are listed in Table 14-1.

Table 14-1. *Modules, Classes, and Interfaces Used in the Chapter Examples*

Module	Classes/Interfaces	Description
`jdojo.prime`	`PrimeChecker`	It acts as a service, a service interface, and a service provider. It provides a default implementation for the service interface.
`jdojo.prime.faster`	`FasterPrimeChecker`	A service provider.
`jdojo.prime.probable`	`ProbablePrimeChecker`	A service provider.
`jdojo.prime.client`	`Main`	A service consumer.

Figure 14-2 shows the classes/interfaces arranged as services, service providers, and service consumers, which can be compared with Figure 14-1.

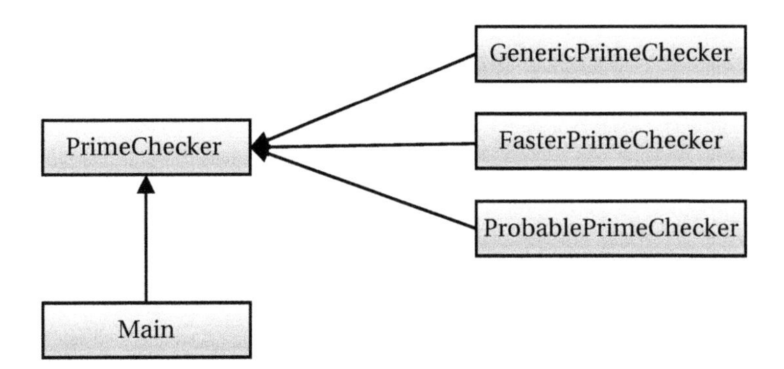

Figure 14-2. *The arrangement of a service, three service providers, and a service consumer used in the chapter's examples*

Discovering Services

In order for a service to be used, its providers need to be discovered and loaded. The `ServiceLoader` class does the work of discovering and loading the service providers. The module that discovers and loads service providers must contain a `uses` statement in its declaration, which has the following syntax:

```
uses <service-interface>;
```

Here, `<service-interface>` is the name of the service interface, which is a Java interface name, a class name, or an annotation type name. If a module uses the `ServiceLoader<S>` class to load the instances of service providers for a service interface named `S`, the module declaration must contain the following statement:

```
uses S;
```

In my opinion, the statement name, `uses`, seems to be a misnomer. At first glance, it seems that the current module will use the specified service. However, that is not the case. A service is used by the clients, not by the module defining the service. A more intuitive statement name would have been `discovers` or `loads`. You can understand its meaning correctly if you read its definition as: The module having the `uses` statement *uses* the `ServiceLoader` class to load the service providers for this service interface. You do not need to use the `uses` statement in client modules unless your client modules load the service providers for services. It is unusual for client modules to load services.

A module may discover and load more than one service. The following module declaration uses two `uses` statements indicating that it will discover and load services identified by the `com.jdojo.PrimeChecker` and `com.jdojo.CsvParser` interfaces:

```
module jdojo.loader {
    uses com.jdojo.PrimeChecker;
    uses com.jdojo.CsvParser:

    // Other module statements go here
}
```

A module declaration allows import statements. For better readability, you can rewrite this module declaration as follows:

```
// Import types from other packages
import com.jdojo.PrimeChecker;
import com.jdojo.CsvParser:

module jdojo.loader {
    uses PrimeChecker;
    uses CsvParser:

    // Other module statements go here
}
```

The service interface specified in a uses statement may be declared in the current module or in another module. If it is declared in another module, the service interface must be accessible to the code in the current module; otherwise, a compile-time error occurs. For example, the com.jdojo.CsvParser service interface used in the uses statement in the previous declaration may be declared in the jdojo.loader module or another module, say jdojo.csvUtil. In the latter case, the com.jdojo.CsvParser interface must be accessible to the jdojo.loader module.

Service provider discovery occurs at runtime. Modules that discover service providers typically do not (and need not) declare compile-time dependency on the service provider modules because it is not possible to know all provider modules in advance. Another reason for service discoverer modules not declaring dependency on service provider modules is to keep the service provider and service consumer decoupled.

Providing Service Implementations

A module that provides implementations for a service interface must contain a provides statement. If a module contains a service provider, but does not contain a provides statements in its declaration, this service provider will not be loaded through the ServiceLoader class. That is, a provides statement in a module declaration is a way to tell the ServiceLoader class, "Hey! I provide an implementation for a service. You can use me as a service provider whenever you need that service." The syntax for a provides statement is as follows:

```
provides <service-interface> with <service-implementation-name>;
```

Here, the provides clause specifies the name of the service interface and the with clause specifies the name of the class that implements the service provider interface. In JDK9, a service provider may specify an interface as an implementation for a service interface. This may sound incorrect, but it is true. I provide an example in this chapter where an interface serves as a service provider implementation type. The following module declaration contains two provides statements:

```
module com.jdojo.provider {
    provides com.jdojo.PrimeChecker with com.jdojo.impl.PrimeCheckerFactory;
    provides com.jdojo.CsvParser with com.jdojo.impl.CsvFastParser;

    // Other module statements go here
}
```

The first provides statement declares that com.jdojo.impl.PrimeCheckerFactory is one possible implementation for the service interface named com.jdojo.PrimeChecker. The second provides statement declares that com.jdojo.impl.CsvFastParser is one possible implementation for the service interface named com.jdojo.CsvParser. Before JDK9, PrimeCheckerFactory and CsvParser had to be classes. In JDK9, they can be classes or interfaces.

A module can contain any combination of uses and provides statements—the same module can provide implementation for a service and discover the same service; it can only provide implementation for one or more services, or it can provide implementation for one service and discover another type of service. The following module declaration discovers and provides the implementation for the same service:

```
module com.jdojo.parser {
    uses com.jdojo.XmlParser;

    provides com.jdojo.XmlParser with com.jdojo.xml.impl.XmlParserFactory;

    // Other module statements go here
}
```

■ **Tip** The service implementation class/interface specified in the with clause of the provides statement must be declared in the current module. Otherwise, a compile-time error occurs.

The ServiceLoader class creates instances of the service implementation. When the service implementation is an interface, it calls the interface's provider() static method to get an instance of the provider. The service implementation (a class or an interface) must follow these rules:

- If the service implementation implicitly or explicitly declares a public constructor with no formal parameters, that constructor is called the *provider constructor*.
- If the service implementation contains a public static method named provider with no formal parameters, this method is called the *provider method*.
- The return type of the provider method must be the service interface type or its subtype.
- If the service implementation does not contain the provider method, the type of the service implementation must be a class with a provider constructor and the class must be of the service interface type or its subtype.

When the ServiceLoader class is requested to discover and load a service provider, it checks whether the service implementation contains the provider method. If the provider method is found, the returned value of the method is the service returned by the ServiceLoader class. If the provider method is not found, it instantiates the service implementation using the provider constructor. If the service implementation contains neither the provider method nor the provider constructor, a compile-time error occurs.

With these rules, it is possible to use a Java interface as a service implementation. The interface should have a public static method named provider that returns an instance of the service interface type.

The following sections walk you through the steps to implement a service in JDK9. The last section explains how to make the same service work in a non-modular environment.

Defining the Service Interface

In this section, you develop a service called *prime checker*. I keep the service simple, so you can focus on working with the service provider mechanism in JDK9, rather than writing complex code to implement the service functionality. Requirements for this service are as follows:

- The service should provide an API to check if a number is a prime.
- Clients should be able to know the names of the available service providers. The name of a service provider will be the fully qualified name of the service provider class or interface.
- The service should provide a default implementation of the service interface.
- Clients should be able to retrieve a service instance without specifying the name of the service provider. In this case, the default service provider is returned.
- Clients should be able to retrieve a service instance by specifying a service provider fully qualified name. If a service provider with the specified name does not exist, `null` is returned.

Let's design the service. The functionality provided by the service will be represented by an interface named `PrimeChecker`. It contains one method:

```
public interface PrimeChecker {
    boolean isPrime(long n);
}
```

The `isPrime()` method returns `true` if the specified argument is a prime, and it returns `false` otherwise. All service providers will implement the `PrimeChecker` interface. The `PrimeChecker` interface is our service interface (or service type).

Obtaining Service Provider Instances

The service needs to provide APIs to the clients to retrieve instances of the service providers. The service needs to discover and load all service providers before it can give them to clients. Service providers are loaded using the `ServiceLoader` class. The class has no public constructor. You can use one of its `load()` methods to get its instances. You need to specify the class reference of the service interface to the `load()` method. The `ServiceLoader` class contains an `iterator()` method that returns an `Iterator` for all service providers of a specific service interface loaded by this `ServiceLoader`. The `ServiceLoader` class also implements the `Iterable` interface, so you can also iterate over all the service providers using a `for-each` statement. The following snippet of code shows you how to load and iterate through all service provider instances for `PrimeChecker`:

```
// Load the service providers for PrimeChecker
ServiceLoader<PrimeChecker> loader = ServiceLoader.load(PrimeChecker.class);

// Iterate through all service provider instances
Iterator<PrimeChecker> iterator = loader.iterator();
```

```
if (iterator.hasNext()) {
   PrimeChecker checker = iterator.next();

   // Use the prime checker here...
}
```

The following snippet of code shows you how to use a ServiceLoader instance in a for-each statement to iterate over all service provider instances:

```
ServiceLoader<PrimeChecker> loader = ServiceLoader.load(PrimeChecker.class);
for (PrimeChecker checker : loader) {
    // checker is your service provider instance
}
```

At times, you'll want to select providers based on their class names. For example, you may want to select only those prime service providers whose fully qualified class name starts with com.jdojo. Typical logic to achieve this would be to use the iterator returned by the iterator() method of the ServiceLoader class. However, this is costly. The iterator instantiates a provider before returning. JDK9 added a new stream() method to the ServiceLoader class:

```
public Stream<ServiceLoader.Provider<S>> stream()
```

The method returns a stream of instances of the ServiceProvider.Provider<S> interface, which is declared as a nested interface in the ServiceLoader class as follows:

```
public static interface Provider<S> extends Supplier<S> {
    // Returns a Class reference of the class of the service provider
    Class<? extends S> type();

    @Override
    S get();
}
```

An instance of the ServiceLoader.Provider interface represents a service provider. Its type() method returns the Class object of the service implementation. The get() method returns an instance of the service provider.

How does the ServiceLoader.Provider interface help? When you use the stream() method, each element in the stream is of the ServiceLoader.Provider type. You can filter the stream based on the class name or type of the provider, which will not instantiate the provider. You can use the type() method in your filters. When you find the desired provider, call the get() method to instantiate the provider. This way, you instantiate a provider when you know you need it, not when you are iterating through all providers. The following is an example of using the stream() method of the ServiceLoader class. It gives you a list of all prime service providers whose class name starts with com.jdojo.

```
static List<PrimeChecker> startsWith(String prefix) {
    return ServiceLoader.load(PrimeChecker.class)
                        .stream()
                        .filter((Provider p) -> p.type().getName().startsWith(prefix))
                        .map(Provider::get)
                        .collect(Collectors.toList());
}
```

Your prime checker service is supposed to let clients find a service provider using the service provider class or interface name. You can provide a `newInstance(String providerName)` method using the `stream()` method of the `ServiceLoader` class as follows:

```
static PrimeChecker newInstance(String providerName) {
    // Try to find the first service provider with the specified providerName
    Optional<Provider<PrimeChecker>> optional
            = ServiceLoader.load(PrimeChecker.class)
                    .stream()
                    .filter((Provider p) -> p.type().getName().equals(providerName))
                    .findFirst();

    PrimeChecker checker = null;

    // Instantiate the provider if we found one
    if (optional.isPresent()) {
        Provider<PrimeChecker> provider = optional.get();
        checker = provider.get();
    }

    return checker;
}
```

There is a big difference between using the `Iterator` and the `stream()` method of the `ServiceLoader` class to find a service provider. The `Iterator` supplies you with the instance of the service provider, which you can use to determine the details of the actual service provider implementation class. A service provider may use the provider constructor or the provider method to supply its instances. The `stream()` method does not create service provider instances. Rather, it looks at the provider constructors and provider methods to give you the type of the service provider implementation. If you use the provider constructor, the `stream()` method knows the actual class name of the service implementation. If you use the provider method, the `stream()` method does not (and cannot) peek inside the provider method to see the actual implementation class type. In this case, it simply looks at the return type of the provider method and its `type()` method returns the `Class` reference of that return type. Consider the following provider method implementation of the `PrimeChecker` service type.

```
// FasterPrimeChecker.java
package com.jdojo.prime.faster;

import com.jdojo.prime.PrimeChecker;

public class FasterPrimeChecker implements PrimeChecker {
    // No provider constructor
    private FasterPrimeChecker() {
        // No code
    }

    // Define a provider method
    public static PrimeChecker provider() {
        return new FasterPrimeChecker();
    }
```

```
    @Override
    public boolean isPrime(long n) {
        // More code goes here
    }
}
```

Suppose the `FasterPrimeChecker` class is available as a service provider. When you use the `stream()` method of the `ServiceLoader` class, you will get a `ServiceLoader.Provider` element for this service provider whose `type()` method will return the `Class` reference of the `com.jdojo.prime.PrimeChecker` interface, which is the return type of the `provider()` method. When you call the `get()` method of the `ServiceLoader.Provider` instance, it will call the `provider()` method and return the reference of an object of the `FasterPrimeChecker` class as it is returned from the `provider()` method. If you try to write the following code to find the `FasterPrimeChecker` provider, it will fail:

```
String providerName = "com.jdojo.prime.faster.FasterPrimeChecker";

Optional<Provider<PrimeChecker>> optional = ServiceLoader.load(PrimeChecker.class)
        .stream()
        .filter((Provider p) -> p.type().getName().equals(providerName))
        .findFirst();
```

If you want to find this service provider by its class name using the `stream()` method of the `ServiceLoader` class, you can change the return type of the `provider()` method as shown:

```
// FasterPrimeChecker.java
package com.jdojo.prime.faster;

import com.jdojo.prime.PrimeChecker;

public class FasterPrimeChecker implements PrimeChecker {
    // No provider constructor
    private FasterPrimeChecker() {
        // No code
    }

    // Define a provider method
    public static FasterPrimeChecker provider() {
        return new FasterPrimeChecker();
    }

    @Override
    public boolean isPrime(long n) {
        // More code goes here
    }
}
```

Defining the Service

Before JDK8, you had to create a class to provide the discovering, loading, and retrieving features for your service. From JDK8, you can add static methods to interfaces. Let's add two static methods to the service interface for these purposes:

```
public interface PrimeChecker {
    // Part of the service interface
    boolean isPrime(long n);

    // Part of the service
    static PrimeChecker newInstance() { /*...*/ };
    static PrimeChecker newInstance(String providerName) { /*...*/ };
    static List<PrimeChecker> providers() { /*...*/ };
    static List<String> providerNames(/*...*/);
}
```

The `newInstance()` method will return an instance of the `PrimeChecker` that is the default service provider. The `newInstance(String providerName)` method will return the instance of a service provider with the specified provider name. The `providers()` method will return all provider instances, whereas `providerNames()` method will return a list of all provider names.

Notice that your `PrimeChecker` interface is going to serve two purposes:

- It serves as a service interface with the `isPrime()` method as the only method in that service interface. Clients will use the `PrimeChecker` interface as the service type.
- It serves as a service with the two versions of the `newInstance()` method, the `providers()` method, and the `providerNames()` method.

At this point, you had a choice to have a separate service class, say `PrimeService` class, with `newInstance()`, `providers()`, and `providerNames()` methods in it- leaving only the `isPrime()` method in the `PrimeChecker` interface. If you decided to do so, clients would have used the `PrimeService` class to obtain a service provider.

Listing 14-1 contains the complete code for the `PrimeChecker` interface.

Listing 14-1. A Service Provider Interface Named PrimeChecker

```
// PrimeChecker.java
package com.jdojo.prime;

import java.util.ArrayList;
import java.util.List;
import java.util.Optional;
import java.util.ServiceLoader;
import java.util.ServiceLoader.Provider;
import java.util.stream.Collectors;

public interface PrimeChecker {
    boolean isPrime(long n);

    static PrimeChecker newInstance() {
        // Return the default service provider
        String defaultSP = "com.jdojo.prime.impl.GenericPrimeChecker";
```

```
        return newInstance(defaultSP);
    }

    static PrimeChecker newInstance(String providerName) {
        Optional<Provider<PrimeChecker>> optional
                = ServiceLoader.load(PrimeChecker.class)
                        .stream()
                        .filter((Provider p) -> p.type().getName().equals(providerName))
                        .findFirst();

        PrimeChecker checker = null;
        if (optional.isPresent()) {
            Provider<PrimeChecker> provider = optional.get();
            checker = provider.get();
        }

        return checker;
    }

    static List<PrimeChecker> providers() {
        List<PrimeChecker> providers = new ArrayList<>();
        ServiceLoader<PrimeChecker> loader = ServiceLoader.load(PrimeChecker.class);

        for (PrimeChecker checker : loader) {
            providers.add(checker);
        }
        return providers;
    }

    static List<String> providerNames() {
        List<String> providers
                = ServiceLoader.load(PrimeChecker.class)
                        .stream()
                        .map((Provider p) -> p.type().getName())
                        .collect(Collectors.toList());
        return providers;
    }
}
```

The declaration of the `jdojo.prime` module is shown in Listing 14-2. It exports the `com.jdojo.prime` package because other service provider modules need to use the `PrimeChecker` interface.

Listing 14-2. The Declaration of the jdojo.prime Module

```
// module-info.java
module jdojo.prime {
    exports com.jdojo.prime;

    uses com.jdojo.prime.PrimeChecker;
}
```

You need to use a uses statement with the fully qualified name of the PrimeChecker interface because the code in this module will use the ServiceLoader class to load the service providers for this interface. You are not done with the declaration of the jdojo.prime module yet. You will add a default service provider to this module in the next section.

Defining Service Providers

In the next sections, you will create three service providers for the PrimeChecker service interface. The first service provider will be your default prime checker service provider. You will package it with the jdojo.prime module. You will call the second service provider as a *faster prime checker provider*. You will call the third service provider as the *probable prime checker provider*. Later, you will create a client to test the service. You will have a choice to use one of these service providers or all of them.

These service providers will implement algorithms to check whether a given number is a prime. It will be helpful for you to understand the definition of a prime number. A positive integer that is not divisible without a remainder by 1 or itself is called a prime. 1 is not a prime. A few examples of primes are 2, 3, 5, 7, and 11.

Defining a Default Prime Service Provider

In this section, you will define a default service provider for the PrimeChecker service. Defining a service provider for a service is simply creating a class that implements the service interface or creating an interface with a provider method. In this case, you will be creating a class named GenericPrimeChecker that implements the PrimeChecker interface and will contain a provider constructor.

This service provider will be defined in the same module, jdojo.prime, which also contains your service interface. Listing 14-3 contains the complete code for a class named GenericPrimeChecker. It implements the PrimeChecker interface and hence, its instances can be used as a service provider. Notice that I have placed this class in the com.jdojo.prime.impl package, just to keep the public interface and private implementation separate. The isPrime() method of the class checks whether the specified parameter is a prime. The implementation of this method is not optimal. The next service provides a better implementation.

Listing 14-3. A Service Implementation Class for the PrimeChecker Service Interface

```
// GenericPrimeChecker.java
package com.jdojo.prime.impl;

import com.jdojo.prime.PrimeChecker;

public class GenericPrimeChecker implements PrimeChecker {
    @Override
    public boolean isPrime(long n) {
        if (n <= 1) {
            return false;
        }

        if (n == 2) {
            return true;
        }
```

```
        if (n % 2 == 0) {
            return false;
        }

        for (long i = 3; i < n; i += 2) {
            if (n % i == 0) {
                return false;
            }
        }

        return true;
    }
}
```

To make the GenericPrimeChecker class available to the ServiceLoader class as a service provider for the PrimeChecker service interface, you need to include a provides statement in the jdojo.prime module's declaration. Listing 14-4 contains the modified version of the jdojo.prime module's declaration.

Listing 14-4. The Modified Declaration of the jdojo.prime Module

```
// module-info.java
module jdojo.prime {
    exports com.jdojo.prime;

    uses com.jdojo.prime.PrimeChecker;

    provides com.jdojo.prime.PrimeChecker
        with com.jdojo.prime.impl.GenericPrimeChecker;

}
```

The provides statement specifies that this module provides an implementation for the PrimeChecker interface and its with clause specifies the name of the implementation class. The implementation class must fulfill the following conditions:

- It must be a public concrete class or a public interface. It can be a top-level or nested static class. It cannot be an inner class or an abstract class.
- It must provide either the provider constructor or the provider method. You have a pubic no-args constructor, which serves as the provider constructor. This constructor is used by the ServiceLoader class to instantiate the service provider using reflection.
- An instance of the implementation class must be assignment-compatible with the service provider interface.

If any of these conditions are not met, a compile-time error occurs. Note that you do not need to export the com.jdojo.prime.impl package that contains the service implementation class because no client is supposed to directly depend on a service implementation. Clients need to reference only the service interface, not any specific service implementation classes. The ServiceLoader class can access and instantiate the implementation class without the package containing the service implementation being exported by the module.

■ **Tip** If a module uses a `provides` statement, the specified service interface may be in the current module or another accessible module. The service implementation class/interface specified in the `with` clause must be defined in the current module.

That's all you have for this module. Compile and package this module as a modular JAR. At this point, there is nothing to test.

Defining a Faster Prime Service Provider

In this section, you will define another service provider for the `PrimeChecker` service interface. Let's call this a *faster* service provider because you will implement a faster algorithm to check for a prime. This service provider will be defined in a separate module named `jdojo.prime.faster` and the service implementation class is called `FasterPrimeChecker`.

Listing 14-5 contains the module declaration, which is similar to the one we had for the `jdojo.prime` module. This time, only the class name in the `with` clause has changed.

Listing 14-5. The Module Declaration for the com.jdojo.prime.faster Module

```
// module-info.java
module jdojo.prime.faster {
    requires jdojo.prime;

    provides com.jdojo.prime.PrimeChecker
        with com.jdojo.prime.faster.FasterPrimeChecker;
}
```

The `FasterPrimechecker` class will need to implement the `PrimeChecker` interface, which is in the `jdojo.prime` module. The `requires` statement is needed to read the `jdojo.prime` module.

Listing 14-6 contains the code for the `FasterPrimeChecker` class whose `isPrime()` method executes faster than the `isPrime()` method of the `GenericPrimeChecker` class. This time, the method loops through all the odd numbers starting at 3 and ending at the square root of the number being tested for a prime.

Listing 14-6. An Implementation for the PrimeChecker Service Interface

```
// FasterPrimeChecker.java
package com.jdojo.prime.faster;

import com.jdojo.prime.PrimeChecker;

public class FasterPrimeChecker implements PrimeChecker {
    // No provider constructor
    private FasterPrimeChecker() {
        // No code
    }

    // Define a provider method
    public static FasterPrimeChecker provider() {
        return new FasterPrimeChecker();
    }
```

```
    @Override
    public boolean isPrime(long n) {
        if (n <= 1) {
            return false;
        }

        if (n == 2) {
            return true;
        }

        if (n % 2 == 0) {
            return false;
        }

        long limit = (long) Math.sqrt(n);
        for (long i = 3; i <= limit; i += 2) {
            if (n % i == 0) {
                return false;
            }
        }

        return true;
    }
}
```

Note the difference between the GenericPrimeChecker and FasterPrimeChecker classes, as shown in Listing 14-3 and Listing 14-6. The GenericPrimeChecker class contains a default constructor that serves as the provider constructor. It does not contain the provider method. The FasterPrimeChecker class makes the no-args constructor private, which does not qualify the constructor to be the provider constructor. The FasterPrimeChecker class provides the provider method instead, which is declared as follows:

```
public static FasterPrimeChecker provider() { /*...*/ }
```

When the ServiceLoader class needs to instantiate the faster prime service, it will call this method. The method is very simple—it creates and returns an object of the FasterPrimeChecker class.

That's all you need for this module at this time. To compile this module, the jdojo.prime module needs to be in the module path. Compile and package this module as a modular JAR. At this point, there is nothing to test.

Defining a Probable Prime Service Provider

In this section, I show you how to use a Java interface as a service implementation. You will define another service provider for the PrimeChecker service interface. Let's call this a *probable* prime service provider because it tells you that a number is probably a prime. This service provider will be defined in a separate module named jdojo.prime.probable and the service implementation interface is called ProbablePrimeChecker.

The service is about checking for a prime number. The java.math.BigInteger class contains a method named isProbablePrime(int certainty). If the method returns true, the number may be a prime. If the method returns false, the number is certainly not a prime. The certainty parameter determines the degree to which the method makes sure the number is prime before returning true. The higher the value of the certainty parameter, the higher the cost this method incurs and the higher the probability that the number is a prime when the method returns true.

Listing 14-7 contains the module declaration, which is similar to the ones we had before for the jdojo.prime.faster module. This time, only the class/interface name in the with clause has changed. Listing 14-8 contains the code for the ProbablePrimeChecker class.

Listing 14-7. The Module Declaration for the com.jdojo.prime.probable Module

```
// module-info.java
module jdojo.prime.probable {
    requires jdojo.prime;

    provides com.jdojo.prime.PrimeChecker
        with com.jdojo.prime.probable.ProbablePrimeChecker;
}
```

Listing 14-8. An Implementation Interface for the PrimeChecker Service Interface

```
// ProbablePrimeChecker.java
package com.jdojo.prime.probable;

import com.jdojo.prime.PrimeChecker;
import java.math.BigInteger;

public interface ProbablePrimeChecker extends PrimeChecker {
    // A provider method
    public static ProbablePrimeChecker provider() {
        int certainty = 1000;
        ProbablePrimeChecker checker = n -> BigInteger.valueOf(n).isProbablePrime(certainty);
        return checker;
    }
}
```

The ProbablePrimeChecker interface extends the PrimeChecker interface and consists of only one method, which is the provider method:

```
public static ProbablePrimeChecker provider() {/*...*/}
```

When the ServiceLoader class needs to instantiate the probable prime service, it will call this method. The method is very simple—it creates and returns an instance of the ProbablePrimeChecker interface. It uses a lambda expression to create the provider. The isPrime() method uses the BigInteger class to check whether the number is a probable prime.

Listing 14-9 contains an alternative declaration of the ProbablePrimeChecker interface as a service provider.

Listing 14-9. An Alternative Declaration of the ProbablePrimechecker Interface

```
// ProbablePrimeChecker.java
package com.jdojo.prime.probable;

import com.jdojo.prime.PrimeChecker;
import java.math.BigInteger;
```

```
public interface ProbablePrimeChecker {
    // A provider method
    public static PrimeChecker provider() {
        int certainty = 1000;
        PrimeChecker checker = n -> BigInteger.valueOf(n).isProbablePrime(certainty);
        return checker;
    }
}
```

This time, the interface does not extend the `PrimeChecker` interface. To be a service implementation, its provider method must return an instance of the service interface (the `PrimeChecker` interface) or its subtype. By declaring the return type of the provider method as `PrimeChecker`, you have fulfilled this requirement. Declaring the `ProbablePrimeChecker` interface, as shown in Listing 14-9, has one drawback that you cannot find this service provider by its class name, `com.jdojo.probable.ProbablePrimeChecker`, using the `stream()` method of the `ServiceLoader` class without instantiating the service provider. The `type()` method of `ServiceLoader.Provider` will return the `Class` reference of the `com.jdojo.prime.PrimeChecker` interface, which is the return type of the `provider()` method. I use the declaration of this interface as shown in Listing 14-8.

That's all you have for this module. To compile this module, you need to add the `jdojo.prime` module to the module path. Compile and package this module as a modular JAR. At this point, there is nothing to test.

Testing the Prime Service

In this section, you test the service by creating a client application, which will be defined in a separate module named `jdojo.prime.client`. Listing 14-10 contains the module declaration.

Listing 14-10. The Declaration of the jdojo.prime.client Module

```
// module-info.java
module jdojo.prime.client {
    requires jdojo.prime;
}
```

The client module needs to know only about the service interface. In this case, the `jdojo.prime` module defines the service interface. Therefore, the client module reads the service interface module and nothing else. In a real world, the client module will be much more complex than this and it may read other modules as well. Figure 14-3 shows the module graph for the `jdojo.prime.client` module.

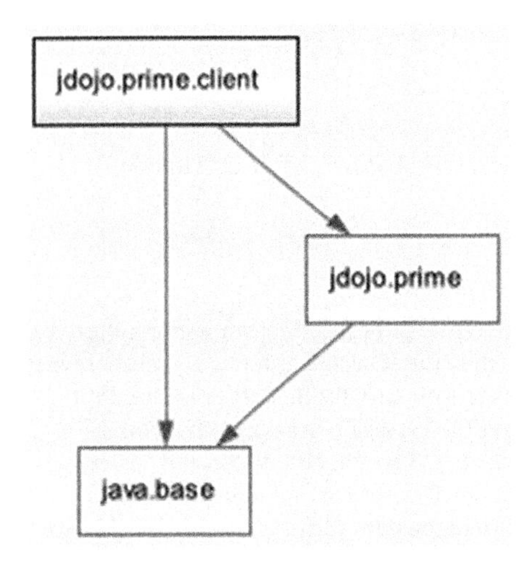

Figure 14-3. *The module graph for the com.jdojo.prime.client module*

■ **Note** A client module is not aware of the service provider modules and it need not directly read them as such. It is the responsibility of the service to discover all service providers and make their instances available to the client. In this case, the `jdojo.prime` module defines the `com.jdojo.prime.PrimeChecker` interface, which is a service interface and also acts as a service.

Listing 14-11 contains the code for the client that uses the `PrimeChecker` service.

Listing 14-11. A Main Class to Test the PrimeChecker Service

```
// Main.java
package com.jdojo.prime.client;

import com.jdojo.prime.PrimeChecker;

public class Main {
    public static void main(String[] args) {
        // Numbers to be checked for prime
        long[] numbers = {3, 4, 121, 977};

        // Use the default service provider
        PrimeChecker checker = PrimeChecker.newInstance();
        System.out.println("Using default service provider:");
        checkPrimes(checker, numbers);

        // Try faster prime service provider
        String fasterProviderName = "com.jdojo.prime.faster.FasterPrimeChecker";
        PrimeChecker fasterChecker = PrimeChecker.newInstance(fasterProviderName);
        if (fasterChecker == null) {
            System.out.println("\nFaster service provider is not available.");
        } else {
```

```
            System.out.println("\nUsing faster service provider:");
            checkPrimes(fasterChecker, numbers);
        }

        // Try probable prime service provider
        String probableProviderName = "com.jdojo.prime.probable.ProbablePrimeChecker";
        PrimeChecker probableChecker = PrimeChecker.newInstance(probableProviderName);
        if (probableChecker == null) {
            System.out.println("\nProbable service provider is not available.");
        } else {
            System.out.println("\nUsing probable service provider:");
            checkPrimes(probableChecker, numbers);
        }
    }

    public static void checkPrimes(PrimeChecker checker, long... numbers) {
        for (long n : numbers) {
            if (checker.isPrime(n)) {
                System.out.printf("%d is a prime.%n", n);
            } else {
                System.out.printf("%d is not a prime.%n", n);
            }
        }
    }
}
```

The checkPrimes() method takes a PrimeChecker instance and varargs long numbers. It uses the PrimeChecker to check whether numbers are prime and prints corresponding messages. The main() method retrieves the default PrimeChecker service provider instance and the instances of the faster and probable service providers. It uses all three service providers' instances to check the same set of numbers to be prime. Compile and package the module's code. Run the Main class with only two modules, jdojo.prime and jdojo.prime.client, in the module path, as follows:

```
C:\Java9LanguageFeatures>java --module-path dist\jdojo.prime.jar;dist\jdojo.prime.client.jar
--module jdojo.prime.client/com.jdojo.prime.client.Main
```

```
Using default service provider:
3 is a prime.
4 is not a prime.
121 is not a prime.
977 is a prime.

Faster service provider is not available.

Probable service provider is not available.
```

There was only one service provider in the module path, which was the default service provider packaged with the jdojo.prime module. Therefore, attempts to retrieve the faster and probable service providers failed. This is evident from the output.

▪ **Tip** When the module system encounters a `uses` statement in a module declaration in a resolved module, it scans the module path to find all modules that contain `provides` statements specifying implementations for the service interface specified in the `uses` statement. In this sense, a `uses` statement in a module indicates an indirect optional dependency on other modules, which is resolved automatically for you. Therefore, to use a service provider, just drop the service provider module on the module path; it will be discovered and loaded by the `ServiceLoader` class.

Let's run the same command by also including the `jdojo.prime.faster` module to the module path as follows:

```
C:\Java9LanguageFeatures>java
--module-path dist\jdojo.prime.jar;dist\jdojo.prime.client.jar;dist\jdojo.prime.faster.jar
--module jdojo.prime.client/com.jdojo.prime.client.Main
```

```
Using default service provider:
3 is a prime.
4 is not a prime.
121 is not a prime.
977 is a prime.

Using faster service provider:
3 is a prime.
4 is not a prime.
121 is not a prime.
977 is a prime.

Probable service provider is not available.
```

This time, you had two service providers on the module path and both were found by the runtime, which is evident from the output.

The following command includes the `jdojo.prime`, `jdojo.prime.faster`, and `jdojo.prime.probable` modules on the module path. All three service providers will be found, which is evident from the output:

```
c:\Java9LanguageFeatures>java --module-path dist\jdojo.prime.jar;dist\jdojo.prime.client.
jar;dist\jdojo.prime.faster.jar;dist\jdojo.prime.probable.jar
--module jdojo.prime.client/com.jdojo.prime.client.Main
```

```
Using default service provider:
3 is a prime.
4 is not a prime.
121 is not a prime.
977 is a prime.

Using faster service provider:
3 is a prime.
4 is not a prime.
```

```
121 is not a prime.
977 is a prime.

Using probable service provider:
3 is a prime.
4 is not a prime.
121 is not a prime.
977 is a prime.
```

This is how modules are resolved in this case:

- The main class is in the `jdojo.prime`.client module, so this module is the root module and it is resolved first.
- The `jdojo.prime.client` module reads the `jdojo.prime` module, so the `jdojo.prime` module is resolved.
- The `jdojo.prime` module contains a `uses` statement that specifies `com.jdojo.prime.PrimeChecker` as the service interface type. The runtime scans all modules in the module path to check if any of them contains a `provides` statement specifying the same service interface. It finds the `jdojo.prime`, `jdojo.prime.faster`, and `jdojo.prime.probable` modules containing such `provides` statements. The `jdojo.prime` module was already resolved in the previous step. The `jdojo.prime.faster` and `jdojo.probable` modules are resolved at this time.

You can see the modules resolution process using the `--show-module-resolution` command-line option as follows. Partial output is shown.

```
c:\Java9LanguageFeatures>java --module-path dist\jdojo.prime.jar;dist\jdojo.prime.client.
jar;dist\jdojo.prime.faster.jar;dist\jdojo.prime.probable.jar
--show-module-resolution
--module jdojo.prime.client/com.jdojo.prime.client.Main
```

```
root jdojo.prime.client ...
jdojo.prime.client requires jdojo.prime ...
jdojo.prime binds jdojo.prime.probable ...
jdojo.prime binds jdojo.prime.faster...
...
```

Testing Prime Service in Legacy Mode

Not all applications will be migrated to use modules. Your modular JARs for the prime service may be used along with other JARs on the class path. Suppose you placed all modular JARs for the prime service in the `C:\Java9LanguageFeatures\lib` directory. Run the `com.jdojo.prime.client.Main` class by placing the four modular JARs on the class path using the following command:

```
C:\Java9Revealed>java --class-path lib\com.jdojo.prime.jar;lib\com.jdojo.prime.client.
jar;lib\com.jdojo.prime.faster.jar;lib\com.jdojo.prime.generic.jar;lib\com.jdojo.prime.
probable.jar com.jdojo.prime.client.Main
```

```
C:\Java9LanguageFeatures>java --class-path lib\jdojo.prime.jar;lib\jdojo.prime.client.
jar;lib\jdojo.prime.faster.jar;lib\jdojo.prime.probable.jar com.jdojo.prime.client.Main
```

```
Using default service provider:
Exception in thread "main" java.lang.NullPointerException
        at com.jdojo.prime.client.Main.checkPrimes(Main.java:39)
        at com.jdojo.prime.client.Main.main(Main.java:14)
```

The output indicates that using the legacy mode—the pre-JDK9 mode by placing all modular JARs on the class path—did not find any of the service providers. In legacy mode, the service provider discovery mechanism is different. The `ServiceLoader` class scans all JARs on the class path looking for files in the `META-INF/services` directory. The file name is the fully qualified service interface name. The file path looks like this:

```
META-INF/services/<service-interface>
```

The contents of this file is the list of the fully qualified names of the service provider implementation classes/interfaces. Each class name needs to be on a separate line. You can use a single-line comment in the file. Text on a line starting from a # character is considered a comment.

The service interface name is `com.jdojo.prime.PrimeChecker`, so the modular JARs for the three service providers will have a file named `com.jdojo.prime.PrimeChecker` with the following path:

```
META-INF/services/com.jdojo.prime.PrimeChecker
```

You need to add the `META-INF/services` directory to the root of the source code directory. If you are using an IDE such as NetBeans, the IDE will take care of packaging the file for you. Listing 14-12, Listing 14-13, and Listing 14-14 contain the contents of this file for the modular JARs for the three prime service provider modules.

Listing 14-12. Contents of the META-INF/services/com.jdojo.prime.PrimeChecker File in the Modular JAR for the com.jdojo.prime Module

```
# The generic service provider implementation class name
com.jdojo.prime.impl.GenericPrimeChecker
```

Listing 14-13. Contents of the META-INF/services/com.jdojo.prime.PrimeChecker File in the Modular JAR for the com.jdojo.prime.faster Module

```
# The faster service provider implementation class name
com.jdojo.prime.faster.FasterPrimeChecker
```

Listing 14-14. Contents of the META-INF/services/com.jdojo.prime.PrimeChecker File in the Modular JAR for the com.jdojo.prime.probable Module

```
# The probable service provider implementation interface name
com.jdojo.prime.probable.ProbablePrimeChecker
```

Recompile and repackage the modular JARs for the generic and faster prime checker service providers. Run the following command:

```
C:\Java9LanguageFeatures>java --class-path lib\jdojo.prime.jar;lib\jdojo.prime.client.
jar;lib\jdojo.prime.faster.jar;lib\jdojo.prime.probable.jar com.jdojo.prime.client.Main
```

```
Using default service provider:
3 is a prime.
4 is not a prime.
121 is not a prime.
977 is a prime.
Exception in thread "main" java.util.ServiceConfigurationError: com.jdojo.prime.
PrimeChecker: com.jdojo.prime.faster.FasterPrimeChecker Unable to get public no-arg
constructor
...
  Caused by: java.lang.NoSuchMethodException: com.jdojo.prime.faster.
  FasterPrimeChecker.<init>()
...
```

Partial output is shown. The output indicates a runtime exception when the ServiceLoader class tries to instantiate the faster prime service provider. You will get the same error when an attempt is made to instantiate the probable prime service provider. Adding information about a service in the META-INF/services directory is the legacy way of implementing services. For backward compatibility, the service implementation must be a class with a public no-args constructor. Recall that you provided a provider constructor only for the GenericPrimeChecker class. Therefore, the default prime checker service provider works and the other two do not work in legacy mode. You can add a provider constructor to the FasterPrimeChecker class to make it work. However, it is not possible to add a provider constructor to an interface and the ProbablePrimeChecker will not work in the class path mode. You must load it from an explicit module to make it work.

Summary

A specific functionality provided by an application (or a library) is known as a *service*. Applications and libraries providing implementations of a service are known as service providers. Applications using the service provided by those service providers are called *service consumers* or *clients*.

In Java, a *service* is defined by a set of interfaces and classes. The service contains an interface or an abstract class that defines the functionality provided by the service and it is known as the *service provider interface, service interface,* or *service type*. A specific implementation of a service interface is known as a *service provider*. There can be multiple service providers for a single service interface. In JDK9, a service provider may be a class or an interface. Before JDK9, a service provider must be a class.

The JDK contains a java.util.ServiceLoader<S> class whose sole purpose is to discover and load service providers of type S at runtime for a specified service interface. If a JAR (modular or non-modular) containing a service provider is placed on the class path, the ServiceLoader class uses the META-INF/services directory to find the service providers. The name of the file in this directory should be the same as the fully qualified name of the service interface. The file contains the fully qualified name of the service provider implementation classes—one class name per line. The file can use a # character as the start of single-line comments. The ServiceLoader class scans all META-INF/services directories on the class path to discover service providers.

In JDK9, the service provider discovery mechanism has changed. A module that uses the `ServiceLoader` class to discover and load the service providers needs to specify the service interface using a `uses` statement. The service interface specified in a `uses` statement may be declared in the current module or any module accessible to the current module. You can use the `iterator()` method of the `ServiceLoader` class to iterate over all service providers. The `stream()` method provides a stream of elements that are instances of the `ServiceLoader.Provider` interface. You can use the stream to filter and select a specific type of providers based on the provider's class names without having to instantiate all providers.

A module that contains a service provider needs to specify the service interface and its implementation class using a `provides` statement. The implementation class must be declared in the current module.

QUESTIONS AND EXERCISES

1. What are services, service interfaces, and service providers in Java?
2. Write the declaration for a module named `M`, which loads service providers of a service interface whose fully qualified name is `p.S`.
3. Write the declaration for a module named `N`, which provides the implementation of a service interface `p.S`. The fully qualified name of the service implementation class is `q.C`.
4. How many types of services can a module load using the `ServiceLoader` class?
5. How many service implementations of a service type can a module provide?
6. When do you use the `java.util.ServiceLoader<S>` class?
7. When do you use the nested `java.util.ServiceLoader.Provider<S>` interface?
8. You can discover and load service providers of a specific type using the `iterator()` method or the `stream()` methods of the `ServiceLoader` class. Which method has better performance when you have to select a service provider based on the name of the service provider implementation class or interface?
9. What are the provider constructor and provider method? If both are available, which one is used when services are loaded from modular JARs?
10. What steps would you take while defining a service in JDK9 packaged in a modular JAR that should also work when placed in the class path?

CHAPTER 15

The Module API

In this chapter, you will learn:

- What the Module API is
- How to represent a module and a module descriptor in a program
- How to read a module descriptor in a program
- How to represent a module's version
- How to read a module's properties using the `Module` and `ModuleDescriptor` classes
- How to update a module's definition at runtime using the `Module` class
- How to access resources in a module
- How to create annotations that can be used on modules and how to read annotations used on modules
- What module layers and configurations are
- How to create custom module layers and load modules into them

What Is the Module API?

The Module API consists of classes and interfaces that give you programmatic access to modules. Using the API, you can programmatically:

- Read, modify, and build module descriptors
- Load modules
- Read modules' contents
- Search for loaded modules
- Create new layers of modules

The Module API is small. It consists of about 15 classes and interfaces spread across two packages:

- `java.lang`
- `java.lang.module`

K. Sharan, *Java Language Features*, https://doi.org/10.1007/978-1-4842-3348-1_15

The Module, ModuleLayer, and LayerInstantiationException classes are in the java.lang package and the rest are in the java.lang.module package. Table 15-1 contains the list of classes in the Module API with a brief description of each. The list is not sorted. I list Module and ModuleDescriptor first because application developers use them most frequently. All other classes are typically used by containers and libraries. The list does not contain exceptions classes in the Module API. I discuss these classes in detail in the subsequent sections.

Table 15-1. *Commonly Used Classes and Their Descriptions in the Module API*

Class	Description
Module	Represents a runtime module.
ModuleDescriptor	Represents an immutable module descriptor.
ModuleDescriptor.Builder	A nested builder class used to build module descriptors programmatically.
ModuleDescriptor.Exports	A nested class that represents an exports statement in a module declaration.
ModuleDescriptor.Opens	A nested class that represents an opens statement in a module declaration.
ModuleDescriptor.Provides	A nested class that represents a provides statement in a module declaration.
ModuleDescriptor.Requires	A nested class that represents a requires statement in a module declaration.
ModuleDescriptor.Version	A nested class that represents a module's version string. It contains a parse(String v) factory method that returns its instance from a version string.
ModuleDescriptor.Modifier	An enum whose constants represent modifiers used on a module declaration such as OPEN for an open module.
ModuleDescriptor.Exports.Modifier	An enum whose constants represent modifiers used on an exports statement in a module's declaration.
ModuleDescriptor.Opens.Modifier	An enum whose constants represent modifiers used on an opens statement in a module's declaration.
ModuleDescriptor.Requires.Modifier	An enum whose constants represent modifiers used on a requires statement in a module's declaration.
ModuleReference	A reference to a module's contents. It contains the module's descriptor and its location.
ResolvedModule	Represents a resolved module in a module graph. Contains the module's name, its dependencies, and a reference to its contents. It can be used to walk through all transitive dependencies of a module in a module graph.
ModuleFinder	An interface used to find modules on specified paths or system modules. Found modules are returned as instances of ModuleReference. It contains factory methods to get its instances.
ModuleReader	An interface used to read a module's contents. You can obtain a ModuleReader from a ModuleReference.
Configuration	Represents a module graph of resolved modules.
ModuleLayer	Contains a module graph (a Configuration) and a mapping between modules in the graph and class loaders.
ModuleLayer.Controller	A nested class used to control modules in a ModuleLayer. Methods in the ModuleLayer class return instances of this class.

Representing Modules

An instance of the `Module` class represents a runtime module. Every type loaded into the JVM belongs to a module. JDK9 added a method named `getModule()` to the `Class<T>` class that returns the reference of the module to which the type belongs. The following snippet of code shows how to get the module of a class named `BasicInfo`:

```
// Get the Class object for of the BasicInfo class
Class<BasicInfo> cls = BasicInfo.class;

// Get the module reference
Module module = cls.getModule();
```

A module can be named or unnamed. The `isNamed()` method of the `Module` class returns `true` for a named module and `false` for an unnamed module.

Every class loader contains an unnamed module that contains all types loaded by the class loader from the class path. If a class loader loads types from a module path, those types belong to named modules. The `getModule()` method of the `Class` class may return a named or unnamed module. JDK9 added a method named `getUnnamedModule()` to the `ClassLoader` class that returns the unnamed module of the class loader. In the following snippet of code, assuming that the `BasicInfo` class is loaded from the class path, `m1` and `m2` refer to the same `Module`:

```
Class<BasicInfo> cls = BasicInfo.class;
Module m1 = cls.getClassLoader().getUnnamedModule();
Module m2 = cls.getModule();
```

The `getName()` method of the `Module` class returns the name of the module. For unnamed modules, it returns `null`.

```
// Get the module name
String moduleName = module.getName();
```

The `getPackages()` method in the `Module` class returns a `Set<String>` containing all packages in the module. The `getClassLoader()` method returns the class loader for the module.

The `getLayer()` method returns the `ModuleLayer` that contains the module; if the module is not in a layer, it returns `null`. A module layer contains only named modules. So, this method always returns `null` for unnamed modules.

Describing Modules

An instance of the `ModuleDescriptor` class represents a module definition, which is created from a module declaration—typically from a `module-info.class` file. A module descriptor can also be created on the fly using the `ModuleDescriptor.Builder` class. A module declaration may be augmented using command-line options such as `--add-reads`, `--add-exports`, and `--add-opens`, and using methods in the `Module` class such as `addReads()`, `addOpens()`, and `addExports()`. A `ModuleDescriptor` represents a module descriptor added at the time of module declaration, not an augmented module descriptor. The `getDescriptor()` method of the `Module` class returns a `ModuleDescriptor`:

```
Class<BasicInfo> cls = BasicInfo.class;
Module module = cls.getModule();

// Get the module descriptor
ModuleDescriptor desc = module.getDescriptor();
```

Tip A `ModuleDescriptor` is immutable. An unnamed module does not have a module descriptor. The `getDescriptor()` method of the `Module` class returns `null` for an unnamed module.

You can also create a `ModuleDescriptor` object by reading the binary form of the module declaration from a `module-info.class` file using one of the static `read()` methods of the `ModuleDescriptor` class. The following snippet of code reads a `module-info.class` file from the current directory. Exception handling is excluded for clarity:

```
String moduleInfoPath = "module-info.class";
ModuleDescriptor desc = ModuleDescriptor.read(new FileInputStream(moduleInfoPath));
```

Representing Module Statements

The `ModuleDescriptor` class contains the following static nested classes whose instances represent a statement with the same name in a module declaration:

- `ModuleDescriptor.Exports`
- `ModuleDescriptor.Opens`
- `ModuleDescriptor.Provides`
- `ModuleDescriptor.Requires`

Notice that there is no `ModuleDescriptor.Uses` class to represent a `uses` statement. This is because a `uses` statement represents a service interface name that can be represented as a `String`.

Representing the exports Statement

An instance of the `ModuleDescriptor.Exports` class represents an `exports` statement in a module declaration. The following methods in the class return the components of the `exports` statement:

- `boolean isQualified()`
- `Set<ModuleDescriptor.Exports.Modifier> modifiers()`
- `String source()`
- `Set<String> targets()`

The `isQualified()` method returns `true` for a qualified export and `false` for a non-qualified export. The `source()` method returns the name of the exported package. For a qualified export, the `targets()` method returns an immutable set of module names to which the package is exported and, for a non-qualified export, it returns an empty set. The `modifiers()` method returns the set of modifiers for the `exports` statement that are constants of the nested `ModuleDescriptor.Exports.Modifier` enum. It contains the following two constants:

- `MANDATED`: The export was implicitly declared in the source module declaration.
- `SYNTHETIC`: The export was not explicitly or implicitly declared in the source of the module declaration.

Representing the opens Statement

An instance of the ModuleDescriptor.Opens class represents an opens statement in a module declaration. The following methods in the class return the components of the opens statement:

- boolean isQualified()
- Set<ModuleDescriptor.Opens.Modifier> modifiers()
- String source()
- Set<String> targets()

The isQualified() method returns true for a qualified opens and false for a non-qualified opens. The source() method returns the name of the open package. For a qualified opens, the targets() method returns an immutable set of module names to which the package is open and, for a non-qualified opens, it returns an empty set. The modifiers() method returns the set of modifiers for the opens statement that are constants of the nested ModuleDescriptor.Opens.Modifier enum, which contains the following two constants:

- MANDATED: The opens was implicitly declared in the source of the module declaration.
- SYNTHETIC: The opens was not explicitly or implicitly declared in the source of the module declaration.

Representing the provides Statement

An instance of the ModuleDescriptor.Provides class represents one or more provides statements for a specific service type in a module declaration. The following two provides statements specify two implementation classes for the same service type X.Y:

```
provides X.Y with A.B;
provides X.Y with Y.Z;
```

One instance of the ModuleDescriptor.Provides class will represent both of these statements. The following methods in the class return the components of the provides statement:

- List<String> providers()
- String service()

The providers() method returns the list of the fully qualified class names of the provider classes or provider factories. In the previous example, the returned list will contain A.B and Y.Z. The service() method returns the fully qualified name of the service type. In the previous example, it will return X.Y.

Representing the requires Statement

An instance of the ModuleDescriptor.Requires class represents a requires statement in a module declaration. The following methods in the class return the components of the requires statement:

- Optional<ModuleDescriptor.Version> compiledVersion()
- Optional<String> rawCompiledVersion()
- String name()
- Set<ModuleDescriptor.Requires.Modifier> modifiers()

Suppose a module named M having the following requires statement is compiled:

```
module M {
    requires N;
}
```

If the module version of N is available at the time of compilation, that version is recorded in the module descriptor of M. The compiledVersion() method returns that recorded version of N in an Optional. If no version for N was available, the method returns an empty Optional. The module version of the module specified in the requires statement is recorded in the module descriptor only for informative purposes. It is not used at any phase by the module system. However, it can be used by tools and frameworks for diagnostic purposes. For example, a tool may verify that all modules specified as dependence using the requires statement must be available with the same or higher version than the one recorded during compilation.

Continuing with the previous example, the rawCompiledVersion() method returns the version of module N in an Optional<String>. In most cases, the two methods, compiledVersion() and rawCompiledVersion(), will return the same module version, but in two different formats: one in an Optional<ModuleDescriptor.Version> object and another in an Optional<String> object. You can have a module with an invalid module version. Such a module may be created and compiled outside the Java module system. You can load such a module with an invalid module version as a Java module. In such a case, the compiledVersion() method returns an empty Optional<ModuleDescriptor.Version> because the module version cannot be parsed as a valid Java module version, whereas the rawCompiledVersion() returns an Optional<String> that contains the invalid module version.

■ **Tip** The rawCompiledVersion() method of the ModuleDescriptor.Requires class may return an unparseable version of the required module.

The name() method returns the name of the module specified in the requires statement. The modifiers() method returns the set of modifiers for the requires statement that are constants of the nested ModuleDescriptor.Requires.Modifier enum, which contain the following constants:

- MANDATED: The dependence was implicitly declared in the source of the module declaration.
- STATIC: The dependence is mandatory at compile time and optional at runtime.
- SYNTHETIC: The dependence was not explicitly or implicitly declared in the source of the module declaration.
- TRANSITIVE: The dependence causes any module that depends on the current module to have an implicitly declared dependence on the module named by this requires statement.

Representing a Module Version

An instance of the ModuleDescriptor.Version class represents a module's version. It contains a static factory method named parse(String version) that returns its instance representing a version from the specified version string. Recall that you do not specify a module's version in a module's declaration. You add a module version when you package module's code into a modular JAR, typically using the jar tool. The javac compiler also lets you specify a module version when you compile a module. A module version string contains three components:

- A mandatory version number
- An optional prerelease version
- An optional build version

A module version is of the following form:

```
vNumToken+ ('-' preToken+)? ('+' buildToken+)?
```

Each component is a sequence of tokens; each token is either a non-negative integer or a string. Tokens are separated by the punctuation characters ., -, or +, or by transition from a sequence of digits to a sequence of characters that are neither digits nor punctuation characters, or vice versa. A version string must start with a digit. The version number is a sequence of tokens separated by . characters, terminated by the first - or + character. The prerelease version is a sequence of tokens separated by . or - characters, terminated by the first + character. The build version is a sequence of tokens separated by ., -, or + characters.

The version() method of the ModuleDescriptor class returns an Optional<ModuleDescriptor.Version>.

Other Properties of Modules

There are other module properties that can be set in the module-info.class file while packaging the modular JAR, such as the main class name, OS name, etc. The ModuleDescriptor class contains a method to get each of these properties. The following methods in the ModuleDescriptor class are of interest:

- Set<ModuleDescriptor.Exports> exports()
- boolean isAutomatic()
- boolean isOpen()
- Optional<String> mainClass()
- String name()
- Set<ModuleDescriptor.Opens> opens()
- Set<String> packages()
- Set<ModuleDescriptor.Provides> provides()
- Optional<String> rawVersion()
- Set<ModuleDescriptor.Requires> requires()
- String toNameAndVersion()
- Set<String> uses()

The method names are intuitive to understand their purposes. I cover two methods that need a little explanation: packages() and provides().

The ModuleDescriptor class contains a method named packages() and the Module class contains a method named getPackages(). Both return a set of package names. Why do you have two methods for the same purpose? In fact, they serve different purposes. In the ModuleDescriptor, the method returns the set of packages defined in the module declaration whether they are exported or not. Recall that you cannot get a ModuleDescriptor for an unnamed module and, in that case, you can get the package names in the unnamed module using the getPackages() method in the Module class. Another difference is that the package names reported by a ModuleDescriptor are static; the package names reported by a Module are dynamic, which reports the packages loaded in the module at the time the getPackages() method is called. A Module reports all packages currently loaded in it at runtime.

The provides() method returns a Set<ModuleDescriptor.Provides>. Consider the following provides statements in a module declaration:

```
provides A.B with X.Y1;
provides A.B with X.Y2;
provides P.Q with S.T1;
```

In this case, the set will contain two elements—one for the service type A.B and one for the service type P.Q. The service() and providers() methods of one element will return A.B and a list of X.Y1 and X.Y2, respectively. These methods for another element will return P.Q and a list of one element containing S.T1.

Knowing Module Basic Info

In this section, I show you an example of how to read basic information about a module at runtime. Listing 15-1 contains the module declaration for a module named com.jdojo.module.api. It reads three modules and exports one package. Two of the read modules, com.jdojo.prime and com.jdojo.intro, are from previous chapters. You need to add these two modules to the module path to compile them and run the code in the com.jdojo.module.api module. The java.sql module is a JDK module.

Listing 15-1. The Declaration of a Module Named jdojo.module.api

```
// module-info.java
module jdojo.module.api {
    requires jdojo.prime;
    requires jdojo.intro;
    requires java.sql;
    exports com.jdojo.module.api;
}
```

Listing 15-2 contains the code for a class named ModuleBasicInfo that prints the module details of three modules using the Module and ModuleDescriptor classes.

Listing 15-2. A ModuleBasicInfo Class

```
// ModuleBasicInfo.java
package com.jdojo.module.api;

import com.jdojo.prime.PrimeChecker;
import java.lang.module.ModuleDescriptor;
import java.lang.module.ModuleDescriptor.Exports;
import java.lang.module.ModuleDescriptor.Provides;
import java.lang.module.ModuleDescriptor.Requires;
```

```
import java.sql.Driver;
import java.util.Set;

public class ModuleBasicInfo {
    public static void main(String[] args) {
        // Get the module of the current class
        Class<ModuleBasicInfo> cls = ModuleBasicInfo.class;
        Module module = cls.getModule();

        // Print module info
        printInfo(module);
        System.out.println("------------------");

        // Print module info
        printInfo(PrimeChecker.class.getModule());
        System.out.println("------------------");

        // Print module info
        printInfo(Driver.class.getModule());
    }

    public static void printInfo(Module m) {
        String moduleName = m.getName();
        boolean isNamed = m.isNamed();

        // Print module type and name
        System.out.printf("Module Name: %s%n", moduleName);
        System.out.printf("Named Module: %b%n", isNamed);

        // Get the module descriptor
        ModuleDescriptor desc = m.getDescriptor();

        // desc will be null for unnamed module
        if (desc == null) {
            Set<String> currentPackages = m.getPackages();
            System.out.printf("Packages: %s%n", currentPackages);
            return;
        }

        Set<Requires> requires = desc.requires();
        Set<Exports> exports = desc.exports();
        Set<String> uses = desc.uses();
        Set<Provides> provides = desc.provides();
        Set<String> packages = desc.packages();

        System.out.printf("Requires: %s%n", requires);
        System.out.printf("Exports: %s%n", exports);
        System.out.printf("Uses: %s%n", uses);
        System.out.printf("Provides: %s%n", provides);
        System.out.printf("Packages: %s%n", packages);
    }
}
```

Let's run the ModuleBasicInfo class in module mode and in legacy mode. The following command uses the module mode:

```
c:\Java9LanguageFeatures>java --module-path dist --module jdojo.module.api/com.jdojo.module.
api.ModuleBasicInfo
```

```
Module Name: jdojo.module.api
Named Module: true
Requires: [java.sql (@9), jdojo.prime, jdojo.intro, mandated java.base (@9)]
Exports: []
Uses: []
Provides: []
Packages: [com.jdojo.module.api]
------------------
Module Name: jdojo.prime
Named Module: true
Requires: [mandated java.base (@9)]
Exports: [com.jdojo.prime]
Uses: [com.jdojo.prime.PrimeChecker]
Provides: [com.jdojo.prime.PrimeChecker with [com.jdojo.prime.impl.GenericPrimeChecker]]
Packages: [com.jdojo.prime, com.jdojo.prime.impl]
------------------
Module Name: java.sql
Named Module: true
Requires: [transitive java.xml, mandated java.base, transitive java.logging]
Exports: [javax.transaction.xa, javax.sql, java.sql]
Uses: [java.sql.Driver]
Provides: []
Packages: [java.sql, javax.transaction.xa, javax.sql]
```

Now let's run the ModuleBasicInfo class in legacy mode by using the class path as follows:

```
c:\Java9LanguageFeatures>java -cp dist\jdojo.module.api.jar;dist\jdojo.module.api.jar;dist\
jdojo.prime.jar com.jdojo.module.api.ModuleBasicInfo
```

```
Module Name: null
Named Module: false
Packages: [com.jdojo.module.api]
------------------
Module Name: null
Named Module: false
Packages: [com.jdojo.module.api, com.jdojo.prime]
------------------
Module Name: java.sql
Named Module: true
Requires: [transitive java.xml, transitive java.logging, mandated java.base]
Exports: [java.sql, javax.transaction.xa, javax.sql]
Uses: [java.sql.Driver]
Provides: []
Packages: [javax.transaction.xa, javax.sql, java.sql]
```

The second time, the ModuleBasicInfo and PrimeChecker classes are loaded in an unnamed module of the application class loader, which is reflected in the isNamed() method returning false for both modules. Notice the dynamic nature of the getPackages() method of the Module class. When it is called the first time, it returns only one package name—com.jdojo.module.api. When it is called the second time, it returns two package names—com.jdojo.module.api and com.jdojo.prime. This is because packages in the unnamed module are added as types from the new packages are loaded into the unnamed module. The outputs for the java.sql module remain the same in both cases because platform types are always loaded into the same module irrespective of the mode the java launcher runs in.

Querying Modules

Typical queries that you may run against a module include:

- Can a module M read another module N?
- Can a module use a service of a specific type?
- Does a module export a specific package to all or some modules?
- Does a module open a specific package to all or some modules?
- Is this module named or unnamed?
- Is this an automatic module?
- Is this an open module?

You can augment a module descriptor using command-line options and programmatically using the Module API. You can put all queries for module's properties in two categories: queries whose results may change after the module is loaded and queries whose results do not change after the module is loaded. The Module class contains methods for queries in the first category and the ModuleDescriptor class contains methods for queries in the second category. The Module class provides the following methods for queries in the first category:

- boolean canRead(Module other)
- boolean canUse(Class<?> service)
- boolean isExported(String packageName)
- boolean isExported(String packageName, Module other)
- boolean isOpen(String packageName)
- boolean isOpen(String packageName, Module other)
- boolean isNamed()

Methods names are intuitive enough to tell you what they do. The isNamed() method returns true for a named module and false for an unnamed module. A module's type, named or unnamed, does not change after the module has been loaded. This method is provided in the Module class because you cannot get a ModuleDescriptor for an unnamed module.

The ModuleDescriptor contains three methods that tell you about the type of module and how the module descriptor was generated. The isOpen() method returns true if it is an open module and false otherwise. The isAutomatic() method returns true for an automatic module and false otherwise.

Listing 15-3 contains the code for a class named QueryModule, which is a member of the jdojo.module.api module. It shows you how to query a module.

Listing 15-3. A QueryModule Class That Demonstrates How to Query a Module at Runtime

```
// QueryModule.java
package com.jdojo.module.api;

import java.sql.Driver;

public class QueryModule {
    public static void main(String[] args) throws Exception {
        Class<QueryModule> cls = QueryModule.class;
        Module m = cls.getModule();

        // Check if this module can read the java.sql module
        Module javaSqlModule = Driver.class.getModule();
        boolean canReadJavaSql = m.canRead(javaSqlModule);

        // Check if this module exports the com.jdojo.module.api package to all modules
        boolean exportsModuleApiPkg = m.isExported("com.jdojo.module.api");

        // Check if this module exports the com.jdojo.module.api package to java.sql module
        boolean exportsModuleApiPkgToJavaSql
                = m.isExported("com.jdojo.module.api", javaSqlModule);

        // Check if this module opens the com.jdojo.module.api package to java.sql module
        boolean openModuleApiPkgToJavaSql = m.isOpen("com.jdojo.module.api", javaSqlModule);

        // Print module type and name
        System.out.printf("Named Module: %b%n", m.isNamed());
        System.out.printf("Module Name: %s%n", m.getName());
        System.out.printf("Can read java.sql? %b%n", canReadJavaSql);
        System.out.printf("Exports com.jdojo.module.api? %b%n", exportsModuleApiPkg);
        System.out.printf("Exports com.jdojo.module.api to java.sql? %b%n",
                exportsModuleApiPkgToJavaSql);
        System.out.printf("Opens com.jdojo.module.api to java.sql? %b%n",
                openModuleApiPkgToJavaSql);
    }
}
```

```
Named Module: true
Module Name: jdojo.module.api
Can read java.sql? true
Exports com.jdojo.module.api? true
Exports com.jdojo.module.api to java.sql? true
Opens com.jdojo.module.api to java.sql? false
```

Updating Modules

In the next chapter, I show you how to add exports, opens, and reads to a module using the `--add-exports`, `--add-opens`, and `--add-reads` command-line options. In this section, I show you how to achieve the same programmatically. The `Module` class contains the following methods that let you modify a module declaration at runtime:

- `Module addExports(String packageName, Module other)`
- `Module addOpens(String packageName, Module other)`
- `Module addReads(Module other)`
- `Module addUses(Class<?> serviceType)`

There is a significant difference between using command-line options and one of these methods to modify a module's declaration. Using command-line options, you can modify any module's declaration. However, these methods are caller-sensitive. The code that calls these methods must be in the module whose declaration is being modified—except for calling the `addOpens()` method. That is, if you do not have access to the source code of a module, you cannot use these methods to modify that module's declaration. These methods are typically meant to be used by frameworks, which can adapt to runtime needs to interact with other modules.

These methods throw an `IllegalCallerException` when dealing with a named module whereby the caller is not allowed to call these modules.

The `addExports()` method updates the module to export the specified package to the specified module. Calling this method has no effect if the specified package is already exported or open to the specified module or if the method is called on an unnamed or open module. An `IllegalArgumentException` is thrown if the specified package is `null` or does not exist in the module. Calling this method has the same effect as adding a qualified export to the module declaration:

```
exports <packageName> to <other>;
```

The `addOpens()` method works the same way as the `addExports()` method, except that it updates the module to open the specified package to the specified module. It is similar to adding the following statement in the module:

```
opens <packageName> to <other>;
```

The `addOpens()` method makes an exception to the rule about who can call this method. Other methods must be called from the code of the same module. However, the `addOpens()` method of a module can be called from the code of another module. Suppose module `M` opens package `P` to module `N` using the following declaration:

```
module M {
    opens P to N;
}
```

In this case, module N is allowed to call the addOpens("P", S) method on module M, which allowed module N to open package P to module S. This is done when the author of a module may open a package of a module to a known abstract framework module, which discovers and uses another implementation module at runtime. Both the dynamically known modules may need deep reflective access to the module being declared. In this case, the module's author has to know only about the module name of the abstract framework and open the package to it. At runtime, the abstract framework's module can open the same package to the dynamically discovered implementation module. Think about JPA as an abstract framework that defines a java.persistence module and discovers other JPA implementations such as Hibernate and EclipseLink at runtime. In this case, the module's author can open a package only to the java.persistence module, which can open the same package to the Hibernate or EclipseLink modules at runtime.

The addReads() method adds a readability edge from this module to the specified module. This method has no effect if the specified module is itself because every module can read itself or if it is called on an unnamed module because an unnamed module can read all other modules. Calling this method is the same as adding a requires statement to the module declaration:

```
requires <other>;
```

The addUses() method updates the module to add a service dependence, so it can use the ServiceLoader class to load the service of the specified service type. It has no effect when called on an unnamed or automatic module. Its effect is the same as adding the following uses statement in the module's declaration:

```
uses <serviceType>;
```

Listing 15-4 contains the code for an UpdateModule class. It is in the jdojo.module.api module as shown in Listing 15-1. Notice that the module declaration does not contain a uses statement. The class contains a findFirstService() method, which accepts a service type as an argument. It checks if the module can load the service type. Recall that a module must contain a uses statement with a specified service type to load that service type using the ServiceLoader class. The method uses the addUses() method of the Module class to add a uses statement for the service type if it was absent. In the end, the method loads and returns the first service provider loaded.

Listing 15-4. An UpdateModule Class Showing How to Add a uses Statement to a Module Declaration at Runtime

```
// UpdateModule.java
package com.jdojo.module.api;

import java.util.ServiceLoader;

public class UpdateModule {
    public static <T> T findFirstService(Class<T> service) {
        // Before loading the service providers, check if this module can use (or load)
        // the service. If not, update the module to use the service.
        Module m = UpdateModule.class.getModule();
        if (!m.canUse(service)) {
            m.addUses(service);
        }
```

```
        return ServiceLoader.load(service)
                .findFirst()
                .orElseThrow(
              () -> new RuntimeException("No service provider found for the service: "
                + service.getName()));
    }
}
```

Now we'll test the findFirstService() method of the UpdateModule class. Listing 15-5 contains the declaration for a module named jdojo.module.api.test.

Listing 15-5. The Declaration of a Module Named jdojo.module.api.test

```
// module-info.java
module jdojo.module.api.test {
    requires jdojo.prime;
    requires jdojo.module.api;
}
```

The jdojo.module.api.test module declares a dependence on the jdojo.prime module, so it can use the PrimeChecker service type interface. It declares a dependence on the jdojo.module.api module, so it can use the UpdateModule class to load the service. You need to add these two modules to the module path of the com.jdojo.module.api.test module in NetBeans. Listing 15-6 contains the code for a Main class in the com.jdojo.module.api.test module.

Listing 15-6. A Main Method in the com.jdojo.module.api.test Module

```
// Main.java
package com.jdojo.module.api.test;

import com.jdojo.module.api.UpdateModule;
import com.jdojo.prime.PrimeChecker;

public class Main {
    public static void main(String[] args) {
        long[] numbers = {3, 10};

        try {
            // Obtain a service provider for the com.jdojo.prime.PrimeChecker service type
            PrimeChecker pc = UpdateModule.findFirstService(PrimeChecker.class);

            // Check a few numbers for prime
            for (long n : numbers) {
                boolean isPrime = pc.isPrime(n);
                System.out.printf("%d is a prime: %b%n", n, isPrime);
            }
        } catch (RuntimeException e) {
            System.out.println(e.getMessage());
        }
    }
}
```

Try running the Main class as follows. Make sure to add the jdojo.intro module to the module path because the jdojo.module.api.test module reads the jdojo.module.api module, which reads the jdojo.intro module.

```
c:\Java9LanguageFeatures>java --module-path dist\jdojo.prime.jar;dist\jdojo.intro.jar;dist\
jdojo.module.api.jar;dist\jdojo.module.api.test.jar --module jdojo.module.api.test/com.
jdojo.module.api.test.Main
```

```
3 is a prime: true
10 is a prime: false
```

Accessing Module Resources

Resources are made up of data that your application uses, such as images, audios, videos, text files, etc. Accessing resources is an important task that every Java developer performs. Java provides APIs to access resources in location-independent way. Typically, class files and resources are packaged in the same JAR. With the introduction of the module system in JDK9, the rules to access resources have changed. In the next sections, I explain the APIs to access resources in the JDK9 and before JDK9.

Accessing Resources Before JDK9

In this section, I explain how resources were accessed before JDK9. If you already know how to access resources before JDK9, you can skip to the next section that describes how to access resources in JDK9.

In Java code, a resource is identified by a resource name, which is a sequence of strings separated by a slash (/). For resources stored in JARs, a resource name is simply the path of the file stored in the JAR. For example, before JDK9, the Object.class file in the java.lang package stored in a file named rt.jar is a resource and its resource name is java/lang/Object.class.

Before JDK9, you could use methods in the following two classes to access resources:

- java.lang.Class
- java.lang.ClassLoader

A resource is located by a ClassLoader. The resource-finding methods in the Class class delegate to its ClassLoader. Therefore, once you understand the resource loading process used by a ClassLoader, you won't have problems in using the methods of the Class class. The following two instance methods in both classes:

- URL getResource(String name)
- InputStream getResourceAsStream(String name)

Both methods find a resource the same way. They differ only in the return type. The first method returns an URL, whereas the second one returns an InputStream. The second method is equivalent to calling the first method and subsequently calling the openStream() on the returned URL object.

■ **Tip** All resource-finding methods return null if the specified resource is not found.

The ClassLoader class contains three additional static methods to find resources:

- static URL getSystemResource(String name)
- static InputStream getSystemResourceAsStream(String name)
- static Enumeration<URL> getSystemResources(String name)

These methods use the system class loader, which is also known as the application class loader, to find a resource. The first method returns the URL of the first resource found. The second method returns the InputStream for the first resource found. The third method returns an Enumeration of the URLs of all resources found with the specified resource name.

To find a resource, you have two types of methods to select from—getSystemResource* and getResource*. Before I explain which method to use, it is important to understand that there are two types of resources that you can access:

- System resources
- Non-system resources

You must understand the difference between them to understand the resource finding mechanism. A system resource is a resource found on the class path—bootstrap class paths, JARs in the extension directories, and application class paths. A non-system resource may be stored in locations other than class path such as in specific directories, on the network, or in a database. The getSystemResource() method finds a resource using the application class loader delegating to its parent, which is the extension class loader, which in turn delegates to its parent, the bootstrap class loader. If your application is a stand-alone application, and it uses only the three built-in JDK class loaders, you will be fine using the static methods named getSystemResource*. These methods will find all resources on the class path, including the resources in the runtime image such as in the rt.jar file. If your application is an applet running in a browser, or an enterprise application running in an application server or a web server, you should use the instance methods named getResource*, which let you find a resource using a specific class loader. If you call the getResource* methods on a Class object, the current class loader, the class loader that loads the Class object, is used to find the resource.

Resource names passed to all methods in the ClassLoader class are absolute and they do not start with a slash (/). For example, when calling the getSystemResource() method of the ClassLoader, you would use java/lang/Object.class as the resource name.

The resource-finding methods in the Class class let you specify absolute as well as relative resource names. An absolute resource name starts with a slash, whereas a relative resource name does not. When an absolute name is used, methods in the Class class remove the leading slash and delegate to the class loader that loaded the Class object to find the resource. The following call

```
Test.class.getResource("/resources/test.config");
```

is transformed into

```
Test.class.getClassLoader()
          .getResource("resources/test.config");
```

When a relative name is used, methods in the Class class prepend the package name, substituting dots in the package name with slashes followed with a slash, before delegating to the class loader that loaded the Class object to find the resource. Assuming that the Test class is in the com.jdojo.test package, the following call

```
Test.class.getResource("resources/test.config");
```

is transformed into

```
Test.class.getClassLoader()
          .getResource("com/jdojo/test/resources/test.config");
```

Let's look at an example of finding resources before JDK9. I run the example using JDK8. You can find its source code along with a NetBeans project in the downloadable source code for this book. The NetBeans project is named `jdojo.resource.preJDK9`. If you create your own project, make sure to change the Java platform and source for your project to JDK8. The classes and resources are arranged as follows:

- `wordtonumber.properties`
- `com/jdojo/resource/prejdk9/ResourceTest.class`
- `com/jdojo/resource/prejdk9/resources/numbertoword.properties`

The project contains two resource files: `wordtonumber.properties` at the root and `numbertoword.properties` in the `com/jdojo/resource/prejdk9/resources` directory. The contents of these property files are shown in Listing 15-7 and Listing 15-8.

Listing 15-7. Contents of the wordtonumber.properties File

```
One=1
Two=2
Three=3
Four=4
Five=5
```

Listing 15-8. Contents of the numbertoword.properties File

```
1=One
2=Two
3=Three
4=Four
5=Five
```

Listing 15-9 contains a complete program that shows how to find resources using different classes and their methods. The program demonstrates that you can use class files in your application as resources and you can find them using the same methods to find other types of resources. You may get different output, which depends on the location of your resources and JDK9 on your machine.

Listing 15-9. A Test Class to Demonstrate How to Find Resources in Pre-JDK9 Code

```
// ResourceTest.java
package com.jdojo.resource.prejdk9;

import java.io.IOException;
import java.net.URL;
import java.util.Properties;

public class ResourceTest {
    public static void main(String[] args) {
        System.out.println("Finding resources using the system class loader:");
```

```
        findSystemResource("java/lang/Object.class");
        findSystemResource("com/jdojo/resource/prejdk9/ResourceTest.class");
        findSystemResource("com/jdojo/prime/PrimeChecker.class");
        findSystemResource("sun/print/resources/duplex.png");

        System.out.println("\nFinding resources using the Class class:");

        // A relative resource name - Will not find Object.class
        findClassResource("java/lang/Object.class");

        // An absolute resource name - Will find Object.class
        findClassResource("/java/lang/Object.class");

        // A relative resource name - will find the class
        findClassResource("ResourceTest.class");

        // Load the wordtonumber.properties file
        loadProperties("/wordtonumber.properties");

        // Will not find the properties because we are using
        // an absolute resource name
        loadProperties("/resources/numbertoword.properties");

        // Will find the properties
        loadProperties("resources/numbertoword.properties");
    }

    public static void findSystemResource(String resource) {
        URL url = ClassLoader.getSystemResource(resource);
        System.out.println(url);
    }

    public static URL findClassResource(String resource) {
        URL url = ResourceTest.class.getResource(resource);
        System.out.println(url);
        return url;
    }

    public static Properties loadProperties(String resource) {
        Properties p1 = new Properties();
        URL url = ResourceTest.class.getResource(resource);
        if (url == null) {
            System.out.println("Properties not found: " + resource);
            return p1;
        }

        try {
            p1.load(url.openStream());
            System.out.println("Loaded properties from " + resource);
            System.out.println(p1);
        } catch (IOException e) {
```

```
            System.out.println(e.getMessage());
        }

        return p1;
    }
}
```

```
Finding resources using the system class loader:
jar:file:/C:/java8/jre/lib/rt.jar!/java/lang/Object.class
file:/C:/jdojo.resource.preJDK9/build/classes/com/jdojo/resource/prejdk9/ResourceTest.class
null
jar:file:/C:/java8/jre/lib/resources.jar!/sun/print/resources/duplex.png

Finding resources using the Class class:
null
jar:file:/C:/java8/jre/lib/rt.jar!/java/lang/Object.class
file:/C:/jdojo.resource.preJDK9/build/classes/com/jdojo/resource/prejdk9/ResourceTest.class
Loaded properties from /wordtonumber.properties
{One=1, Three=3, Four=4, Five=5, Two=2}
Properties not found: /resources/numbertoword.properties
Loaded properties from resources/numbertoword.properties
{5=Five, 4=Four, 3=Three, 2=Two, 1=One}
```

Accessing Resources in JDK9

Before JDK9, you were able to access resources from any JARs on the class path. In JDK9, classes and resources are encapsulated in modules. In the first attempt, JDK9 designers enforced the module encapsulation rules that resources in a module must be private to the module and, therefore, they should *only* be accessible to the code within that module. While this rule theoretically looked fine, it posed problems for frameworks that shared resources across modules and loaded class files as resources from other modules. A compromise was made to allow *limited* access to resources in modules and still enforce the module's encapsulation. JDK9 contains resource-finding methods in three classes:

- `java.lang.Class`
- `java.lang.ClassLoader`
- `java.lang.Module`

The `Class` and `ClassLoader` classes have not received any new methods in JDK9. The `Module` class contains a `getResourceAsStream(String name)` method that returns an `InputStream` if the resource is found; otherwise, it returns `null`.

Resource Naming Syntax

A resource is named using a sequence of strings separated by a slash, for example, `com/jdojo/states.png`, `/com/jdojo/words.png`, and `logo.png`. If a resource name starts with a slash, it is considered an absolute resource name. A package name is computed from the resource name using the following rules:

- If the resource name starts with a slash, remove the leading slash. For example, for the resource named `/com/jdojo/words.png`, this step results in `com/jdojo/words.png`.
- Remove all characters from the resource name starting from the last slash. In this example, `com/jdojo/words.png` results in `com/jdojo`.
- Replace every remaining slash in the name with a period (`.`). So, `com/jdojo` is converted to `com.jdojo`. The resulting string is the package name.

There are situations when using these steps will result in an unnamed package or an invalid package name. Remember that a package name, if present, must consist of valid Java identifiers. If there is no package name, it is called an unnamed package. Consider `META-INF/resource/logo.png` as a resource name. Applying the previous set of rules, its package name will be computed as `META-INF.resources`, which is not a valid package name, but it is a valid path for a resource.

Rules to Find Resources

Because of backward compatibility and the string encapsulation promised by the module system, new rules to find resources in JDK9 are complicated and based on several factors:

- The type of the module that contains the resource: named, open, unnamed, or automatic module.
- The module that is accessing the resource: Is it the same module or a different one?
- The package name of the resource being accessed: Is it a valid or invalid Java package? Is it an unnamed package?
- Encapsulation of the package that contains the resource: Is the package that contains the resource exported, opened, or encapsulated to the module accessing the resource?
- The file extension of the resource being accessed: Is the resource a `.class` file or some other type of file?
- Which class' method is being used to access the resource: `Class`, `ClassLoader`, or `Module`?

The following rules apply to a resource contained in a *named* module:

- If a resource name ends with `.class`, the resource can be accessed by code in any module. That is, any module can access class files in any named modules.
- If the package name computed from a resource name is not a valid Java package name, for example, `META-INF.resources`, the resource can be accessed by code in any module.
- If the package name computed from a resource name is an unnamed package, for example, for a resource name such as `words.png`, the resource can be accessed by code in any module.

- If the package containing the resource is opened to the module accessing the resource, the resource can be accessed by code in that module. A package can be opened to a module because the module defining the package is an open module, or the module opens the package to all other modules, or the module opens the package only to that specific module using a qualified `opens` statement. If a package is not opened in any of these ways, a resource in that package cannot be accessed by code outside that module.
- This rule is an offshoot of the previous rule. Every package in an unnamed, automatic, or open module is opened, so all resources in such modules can be accessed by code in all other modules.

■ **Tip** A package in a named module must be opened, not exported, to access its resources. Exporting a package of a module allows other modules to access public types (not resources) in that package.

Various resource-finding methods in the `Module`, `Class`, and `ClassLoader` classes behave differently while accessing resources in named modules:

- You can use the `getResourceAsStream()` method of the `Module` class to access a resource in a module. This method is caller-sensitive. If the caller module is different, this method applies all the resource accessibility rules as previously described.
- The `getResource*()` methods in the `Class` object for a class defined in a named module locate resources only in that named module. That is, you cannot use these methods to locate a resource outside the named module.
- The `getResource*()` methods in the `ClassLoader` class locate resources in named modules based on the list of rules described earlier. These methods are not caller-sensitive. A class loader delegates a resource search to its parent before trying to locate the resource itself. These methods have two exceptions: 1) They locate resources only in unconditionally open packages. If a package is open to specific modules using a qualified `opens` statement, these methods will not locate resources in those packages. 2) They search modules defined in the class loader.

The `Class` object will find resources only in the module it is part of. It also supports absolute resource names that start with a slash and relative resource names that do not start with a slash. Here are a few examples of using the `Class` object:

```
// Will find the resource
URL url1 = Test.class.getResource("Test.class");

// Will not find the resource because the Test and Object classes are in different modules
URL url2 = Test.class.getResource("/java/lang/Object.class");

// Will find the resource because the Object and Class classes are
// in the same module, java.base
URL url3 = Object.class.getResource("/java/lang/Class.class");

// Will not find the resource because the Object class is in the java.base module
// whereas the Driver class is in the java.sql module
URL url4 = Object.class.getResource("/java/sql/Driver.class");
```

Using the `Module` class to locate resources requires you to have the reference of the module. If you have access to a class in that module, using the `getModule()` method on that `Class` object gives you the module reference. This is the easiest way to get a module reference. Sometimes, you have the module name as a string, but not the reference of a class in that module. You can find the module reference from a module name. Modules are organized into layers that are represented by instances of the `ModuleLayer` class in the `java.lang` package. The JVM contains at least one layer called the boot layer. Modules in the boot layer are mapped to the built-in class loaders—bootstrap, platform, and application class loaders. You can get the reference of the boot layer using the `boot()` static method of the `ModuleLayer` class:

```
// Get the boot layer
ModuleLayer bootLayer = ModuleLayer.boot();
```

Once you get the reference of the boot layer, you can use its `findModule(String moduleName)` method to get the reference of a module:

```
// Find the module named com.jdojo.resource in the boot layer
Optional<Module> m = bootLayer.findModule("jdojo.resource");

// If the module was found, find a resource in the module
if (m.isPresent()) {
    Module testModule = m.get();
    String resource = "com/jdojo/resource/opened/opened.properties";
    InputStream input = module.getResourceAsStream(resource);
    if (input != null) {
        System.out.println(resource + " found.");
    } else {
        System.out.println(resource + " not found.”);
    }
} else {
    System.out.println("Module jdojo.resource does not exist");
}
```

Let's see the resource-finding rules in action. You will package resources in a module named `jdojo.resource` whose declaration is shown in Listing 15-10.

Listing 15-10. A Module Declaration for a Module Named jdojo.resource

```
// module-info.java
module jdojo.resource {
    exports com.jdojo.exported;

    opens com.jdojo.opened;
}
```

The module exports the `com.jdojo.exported` package and opens the `com.jdojo.opened` package. The following is a list of all the files in the `com.jdojo.resource` module:

- `module-info.class`
- `unnamed.properties`
- `META-INF\invalid_pkg.properties`

- com\jdojo\encapsulated\encapsulated.properties
- com\jdojo\encapsulated\EncapsulatedTest.class
- com\jdojo\exported\AppResource.class
- com\jdojo\exported\exported.properties
- com\jdojo\opened\opened.properties
- com\jdojo\opened\OpenedTest.class

There are four class files. Only the module-info.class file is significant in this example. Other class files define a class with the same name without any details. All files with a .properties extension are resource files whose contents are not important in this example. The source code supplied with this book contains the contents of these files. To save space, I do not show the contents of these files here.

The unnamed.properties file is in the unnamed package, so it can be located by code in any other module. The invalid_pkg.properties file is in the META-INF directory, which is not a valid Java package name, so this file can also be located by code in any other module. The com.jdojo.encapsulated package is not open, so the encapsulated.properties file cannot be located by code in other modules. The com.jdojo.exported package is not open, so the exported.properties file cannot be located by code in other modules. The com.jdojo.opened package is open, so the opened.properties file can be located by code in other modules. All class files in this module can be located by code in other modules.

Listing 15-11 contains the module declaration of a module named jdojo.resource.test. The code in this module accesses resources in the jdojo.resource module and the resources in this module itself. You need to add the jdojo.resource module to this module path to compile it.

Listing 15-11. A Module Declaration for a Module Named jdojo.resource.test

```
// module-info.java
module jdojo.resource.test {
    requires jdojo.resource;

    exports com.jdojo.resource.test;
}
```

The files in the jdojo.resource.test module are arranged as shown:

- module-info.class
- com\jdojo\resource\test\own.properties
- com\jdojo\resource\test\ResourceTest.class

The module contains a resource file named own.properties, which is in the com.jdojo.resource.test package. The own.properties file is empty. Listing 15-12 contains the code for the ResourceTest class. A detailed explanation of the code follows the output of this class.

Listing 15-12. A ResourceTest Class Demonstrating How to Access Resources in Named Modules

```
// ResourceTest
package com.jdojo.resource.test;

import com.jdojo.exported.AppResource;
import java.io.IOException;
import java.io.InputStream;
```

```
public class ResourceTest {
    public static void main(String[] args) {
        // A list of resources
        String[] resources = {
            "java/lang/Object.class",
            "com/jdojo/resource/test/own.properties",
            "com/jdojo/resource/test/ResourceTest.class",
            "unnamed.properties",
            "META-INF/invalid_pkg.properties",
            "com/jdojo/opened/opened.properties",
            "com/jdojo/exported/AppResource.class",
            "com/jdojo/resource/exported.properties",
            "com/jdojo/encapsulated/EncapsulatedTest.class",
            "com/jdojo/encapsulated/encapsulated.properties"
        };

        System.out.println("Using a Module:");
        Module otherModule = AppResource.class.getModule();
        for (String resource : resources) {
            lookupResource(otherModule, resource);
        }

        System.out.println("\nUsing a Class:");
        Class cls = ResourceTest.class;
        for (String resource : resources) {
            // Prepend a / to all resource names to make them absolute names
            lookupResource(cls, "/" + resource);
        }

        System.out.println("\nUsing the System ClassLoader:");
        ClassLoader clSystem = ClassLoader.getSystemClassLoader();
        for (String resource : resources) {
            lookupResource(clSystem, resource);
        }

        System.out.println("\nUsing the Platform ClassLoader:");
        ClassLoader clPlatform = ClassLoader.getPlatformClassLoader();
        for (String resource : resources) {
            lookupResource(clPlatform, resource);
        }
    }

    public static void lookupResource(Module m, String resource) {
        try {
            InputStream in = m.getResourceAsStream(resource);
            print(resource, in);
        } catch (IOException e) {
            System.out.println(e.getMessage());
        }
    }
```

```
    public static void lookupResource(Class cls, String resource) {
        InputStream in = cls.getResourceAsStream(resource);
        print(resource, in);
    }

    public static void lookupResource(ClassLoader cl, String resource) {
        InputStream in = cl.getResourceAsStream(resource);
        print(resource, in);
    }

    private static void print(String resource, InputStream in) {
        if (in != null) {
            System.out.println("Found: " + resource);
        } else {
            System.out.println("Not Found: " + resource);
        }
    }
}
```

```
Using a Module:
Not Found: java/lang/Object.class
Not Found: com/jdojo/resource/test/own.properties
Not Found: com/jdojo/resource/test/ResourceTest.class
Found: unnamed.properties
Found: META-INF/invalid_pkg.properties
Found: com/jdojo/opened/opened.properties
Found: com/jdojo/exported/AppResource.class
Not Found: com/jdojo/resource/exported.properties
Found: com/jdojo/encapsulated/EncapsulatedTest.class
Not Found: com/jdojo/encapsulated/encapsulated.properties

Using a Class:
Not Found: /java/lang/Object.class
Found: /com/jdojo/resource/test/own.properties
Found: /com/jdojo/resource/test/ResourceTest.class
Not Found: /unnamed.properties
Not Found: /META-INF/invalid_pkg.properties
Not Found: /com/jdojo/opened/opened.properties
Not Found: /com/jdojo/exported/AppResource.class
Not Found: /com/jdojo/resource/exported.properties
Not Found: /com/jdojo/encapsulated/EncapsulatedTest.class
Not Found: /com/jdojo/encapsulated/encapsulated.properties

Using the System ClassLoader:
Found: java/lang/Object.class
Not Found: com/jdojo/resource/test/own.properties
Found: com/jdojo/resource/test/ResourceTest.class
Found: unnamed.properties
Found: META-INF/invalid_pkg.properties
Found: com/jdojo/opened/opened.properties
```

```
Found: com/jdojo/exported/AppResource.class
Not Found: com/jdojo/resource/exported.properties
Found: com/jdojo/encapsulated/EncapsulatedTest.class
Not Found: com/jdojo/encapsulated/encapsulated.properties

Using the Platform ClassLoader:
Found: java/lang/Object.class
Not Found: com/jdojo/resource/test/own.properties
Not Found: com/jdojo/resource/test/ResourceTest.class
Not Found: unnamed.properties
Not Found: META-INF/invalid_pkg.properties
Not Found: com/jdojo/opened/opened.properties
Not Found: com/jdojo/exported/AppResource.class
Not Found: com/jdojo/resource/exported.properties
Not Found: com/jdojo/encapsulated/EncapsulatedTest.class
Not Found: com/jdojo/encapsulated/encapsulated.properties
```

The lookupResource() method is overloaded. They locate resources using the three classes: Module, Class, and ClassLoader. These methods pass the resource name and the resource reference to the print() method to print a message.

The main() method prepares a list of resources it wants to look up using different resource-finding methods. It stores the list in a String array:

```
// A list of resources
String[] resources = {/* List of resources */};
```

The main() method attempts to find all resources using the reference of the jdojo.resource module. Notice that the AppResource class is in the jdojo.resource module, so the AppResource.class.getModule() method returns the reference of the jdojo.resource module.

```
System.out.println("Using a Module:");
Module otherModule = AppResource.class.getModule();
for (String resource : resources) {
    lookupResource(otherModule, resource);
}
```

The code found all the class files and all resources in the unnamed, invalid, and open packages in the jdojo.resource module. Notice that java/lang/Object.class was not found because it is in the java.base module, not in the jdojo.resource module. Resources in the jdojo.resource.test module were not found for the same reason.

Now, the main() method locates the same resources using a Class object representing the ResourceTest class, which is in the jdojo.resource.test module.

```
Class cls = ResourceTest.class;
for (String resource : resources) {
    // Prepend a / to all resource names to make them absolute names
    lookupResource(cls, "/" + resource);
}
```

This Class object will locate resources only in the jdojo.resource.test module, which is obvious in the output. In the code, I prepended the resource name with a slash, because the resource-finding methods in the Class class will treat a resource name, which does not start with a slash as a relative resource name and prepends the package name of the class to it.

In the end, the main() method uses the system and platform class loaders to locate the same set of resources:

```
ClassLoader clSystem = ClassLoader.getSystemClassLoader();
for (String resource : resources) {
    lookupResource(clSystem, resource);
}

ClassLoader clPlatform = ClassLoader.getPlatformClassLoader();
for (String resource : resources) {
    lookupResource(clPlatform, resource);
}
```

A class loader will locate resources in all modules known to the class loader itself or to its ancestor class loaders. The system class loader loads the jdojo.resource and jdojo.resource.test modules, so it finds resources in these modules subject to the restrictions imposed by the resource-finding rules. Its parent's parent class loaders, which is the boot class loader, loads the Object class from the java.base module, so the system class loader can locate the java/lang/Object.class file.

The platform class loader does not load the jdojo.resource and jdojo.resource.test application modules. In the output, it is obvious that the platform class loader found only one resource, java/lang/Object.class, which was loaded by its parent, the boot class loader.

Accessing Resources in the Runtime Image

Let's walk through a few examples of accessing resources in the runtime image. Before JDK9, you could use the getSystemResource() static method of the ClassLoader class. Here is the code that looked up the Object.class file in JDK8. The output shows the returned URL using the jar scheme and pointing to the rt.jar file.

```
import java.net.URL;
...
String resource = "java/lang/Object.class";
URL url = ClassLoader.getSystemResource(resource);
System.out.println(url);
```

```
jar:file:/C:/java8/jre/lib/rt.jar!/java/lang/Object.class
```

JDK9 does not store a runtime image in JARs anymore. It is stored in an internal format that may be changed in the future. The JDK provides a way to access runtime resources in a format- and location-independent way using the jrt scheme. The previous code works in JDK9 by returning an URL using the jrt scheme, not the jar scheme as shown:

```
jrt:/java.base/java/lang/Object.class
```

Tip If your code accesses resources from the runtime image and expects an URL using the `jar` scheme, it needs to be changed in JDK9 because you will get an URL using the `jrt` scheme.

The syntax for using the `jrt` scheme is as follows:

```
jrt:/<module-name>/<path>
```

Here, `<module-name>` is the name of a module and `<path>` is the path to a specific class or resource file in the module. Both `<module-name>` and `<path>` are optional. The URL, `jrt:/`, refers to all class and resource files stored in the current runtime image. The `jrt:/<module-name>` refers to all class and resource files stored in the `<module-name>` module. The `jrt:/<module-name>/<path>` refers to a specific class or resource file named `<path>` in the `<module-name>` module. The following are examples of two URLs using the `jrt` scheme to refer to a class file and a resource file:

- `jrt:/java.sql/java/sql/Driver.class`
- `jrt:/java.desktop/sun/print/resources/duplex.png`

The first URL names the class file for the `java.sql.Driver` class in the `java.sql` module. The second URL names the image file `sun/print/resources/duplex.png` in the `java.desktop` module.

Tip You can access resources in the runtime image using the `jrt` scheme, which are rather inaccessible using the resource-fining methods in the `Module`, `Class`, and `ClassLoader` classes.

You can create an `URL` using the `jrt` scheme. The following snippet of code shows how to read an image file into an `Image` object and a class file into a `byte` array from the runtime image. Do not worry about the details such as modules and packages involved in this code:

```
// Load the duplex.png into an Image object
URL imageUrl = new URL("jrt:/java.desktop/sun/print/resources/duplex.png");
Image image = ImageIO.read(imageUrl);

// Use the image object here
System.out.println(image);

// Load the contents of the Object.class file
URL classUrl = new URL("jrt:/java.base/java/lang/Object.class");
InputStream input = classUrl.openStream();
byte[] bytes = input.readAllBytes();
System.out.println("Object.class file size: " + bytes.length);
```

```
BufferedImage@26a7b76d: type = 6 ColorModel: #pixelBits = 32 numComponents = 4 color
space = java.awt.color.ICC_ColorSpace@4cf4d528 transparency = 3 has alpha = true
isAlphaPre = false ByteInterleavedRaster: width = 41 height = 24 #numDataElements 4
dataOff[0] = 3

Object.class file size: 1932
```

When can you use the jrt scheme in other forms, in order to represent all files in the runtime image and all files in a module? You can use the jrt scheme to refer to a module to grant permissions in a Java policy file. The following entry in a Java policy file grants all permissions to the code in the java.activation module:

```
grant codeBase "jrt:/java.activation" {
    permission java.security.AllPermission;
}
```

Many tools and IDEs need to enumerate all modules, packages, and files in a runtime image. JDK9 ships with a read-only NIO FileSystem provider for the jrt URL scheme. You can use this provider to list all class and resource files in the runtime image. There are tools and IDEs that will run on JDK8, but will support the code development for JDK9. Those tools also need to get the list of class and resource files in the JDK9 runtime image. When you install JDK9, it contains a jrt-fs.jar file in the lib directory. You can add this JAR file to the class path of the tools running on JDK8 and use the jrt file system as follows.

The jrt file system contains a root directory represented by a slash (/), which contains two sub-directories named packages and modules:

```
/
/packages
/modules
```

The following snippet of code creates a NIO FileSystem for the jrt URL scheme:

```
// Create a jrt FileSystem
FileSystem fs = FileSystems.getFileSystem(URI.create("jrt:/"));
```

The following snippet of code reads an image file and the contents of the Object.class file:

```
// Load an image from a module
Path imagePath = fs.getPath("modules/java.desktop", "sun/print/resources/duplex.png");
Image image = ImageIO.read(Files.newInputStream(imagePath));

// Use the image object here
System.out.println(image);

// Read the Object.class file contents
Path objectClassPath = fs.getPath("modules/java.base", "java/lang/Object.class");
byte[] bytes = Files.readAllBytes(objectClassPath);
System.out.println("Object.class file size: " + bytes.length);
```

```
BufferedImage@371a67ec: type = 6 ColorModel: #pixelBits = 32 numComponents = 4 color
space = java.awt.color.ICC_ColorSpace@fe18270 transparency = 3 has alpha = true isAlphaPre
= false ByteInterleavedRaster: width = 41 height = 24 #numDataElements 4 dataOff[0] = 3

Object.class file size: 1932
```

The following snippet of code prints all entries—class and resource files—in all modules in the runtime image. Similarly, you can create a Path for packages to enumerate all packages in the runtime image.

```
// List all modules in the runtime image
Path modules = fs.getPath("modules");
Files.walk(modules)
     .forEach(System.out::println);
```

```
/modules
/modules/java.base
/modules/java.base/java
/modules/java.base/java/lang
/modules/java.base/java/lang/Object.class
...
```

Let's look at a complete program that accesses resources from the runtime image. Listing 15-13 contains the module declaration for a module named jdojo.resource.jrt. Listing 15-14 contains the source code for a class named JrtFileSystem, which is in the jdojo.resource.jrt module.

Listing 15-13. A Module Declaration for a Module Named jdojo.resource.jrt

```
// module-info.java
module jdojo.resource.jrt {
    requires java.desktop;
}
```

Listing 15-14. A JrtFileSystem Class That Demonstrates the Use of the jrt URL Scheme to Access Resources from a Runtime Image

```
// JrtFileSystem.java
package com.jdojo.resource.jrt;

import java.awt.Image;
import java.io.IOException;
import java.net.URI;
import java.nio.file.FileSystem;
import java.nio.file.FileSystems;
import java.nio.file.Files;
import java.nio.file.Path;
import javax.imageio.ImageIO;

public class JrtFileSystem {
    public static void main(String[] args) throws IOException {
        // Create a jrt FileSystem
        FileSystem fs = FileSystems.getFileSystem(URI.create("jrt:/"));

        // Load an image from a module
        Path imagePath = fs.getPath("modules/java.desktop", "sun/print/resources/duplex.png");
        Image image = ImageIO.read(Files.newInputStream(imagePath));
```

```
        // Use the image object here
        System.out.println(image);

        // Read the Object.class file contents
        Path objectClassPath = fs.getPath("modules/java.base", "java/lang/Object.class");
        byte[] bytes = Files.readAllBytes(objectClassPath);
        System.out.println("Object.class file size: " + bytes.length);

        // List 5 packages in the runtime image
        Path packages = fs.getPath("packages");
        Files.walk(packages)
             .limit(5)
             .forEach(System.out::println);

        // List 5 modules' entries in the runtime image
        Path modules = fs.getPath("modules");
        Files.walk(modules)
             .limit(5)
             .forEach(System.out::println);
    }
}
```

```
BufferedImage@371a67ec: type = 6 ColorModel: #pixelBits = 32 numComponents = 4 color
space = java.awt.color.ICC_ColorSpace@fe18270 transparency = 3 has alpha = true
isAlphaPre = false ByteInterleavedRaster: width = 41 height = 24 #numDataElements 4
dataOff[0] = 3
Object.class file size: 1932
packages
packages/com
packages/com/java.activation
packages/com/java.base
packages/com/java.corba
modules
modules/java.desktop
modules/java.desktop/sun
modules/java.desktop/sun/print
modules/java.desktop/sun/print/resources
```

Notice that the program prints only five entries from the packages and modules directories. Also notice that you were able to access `sun/print/resources/duplex.png`, which is in the `java.desktop` module. The `java.desktop` module does not open the `sun.print.resources` package. Using any of the resource-finding methods in the `Module`, `Class`, and `ClassLoader` classes to locate `sun/print/resources/duplex.png` fails.

Annotation on Modules

You can use annotations on module declarations. The `java.lang.annotation.ElementType` enum has a new value called `MODULE`. If you use `MODULE` as a target type on an annotation declaration, it allows the annotation to be used on modules. In Java 9, two annotations—`java.lang.Deprecated` and `java.lang.SuppressWarnings`—have been updated to be used on module declarations. They can be used as follows:

```
@Deprecated(since="1.2", forRemoval=true)
@SuppressWarnings("unchecked")
module com.jdojo.myModule {
    // Module statements go here
}
```

When a module is deprecated, the use of that module in `requires`, but not in `exports` or `opens` statements, causes a warning to be issued. This rule is based on the fact that if module `M` is deprecated, a `requires M` will be used by the module's users who need to get the deprecation warning. Other statements such as `exports` and `opens` are within the module that is being deprecated. A deprecated module does not cause warnings to be issued for uses of types within the module. Similarly, if a warning is suppressed in a module declaration, the suppression applies to elements within the module declaration, not to types contained in that module.

The `Module` class implements the `java.lang.reflect.AnnotatedElement` interface, so you can use a variety of annotation related methods to read them. An annotation type to be used on module declarations must include `ElementType.MODULE` as a target.

■ **Tip** You cannot annotate individual module statements. For example, you cannot annotate an `exports` statement with a `@Deprecated` annotation to indicate that the exported package will be removed in a future release. During the early design phase, it was considered and rejected on the ground that this feature will take a considerable amount of time that is not needed at this time. This could be added in the future, if needed. As a result, you will not find any annotation-related methods in the `ModuleDescriptor` class.

Now we'll create a new annotation type and use it on a module declaration. Listing 15-15 contains the module declaration for a module named `jdojo.module.api.annotation` that contains three annotations. The `Version` annotation type has been declared in the same module and its source code is shown in Listing 15-16. The retention policy of the new annotation type is `RUNTIME`.

Listing 15-15. A Module Declaration for a Module Named jdojo.module.api.annotation

```
// module-info.java
import com.jdojo.module.api.annotation.Version;

@Deprecated(since="1.2", forRemoval=false)
@SuppressWarnings("unchecked")
@Version(major=1, minor=2)
module jdojo.module.api.annotation {
    // No module statements
}
```

Listing 15-16. A Version Annotation Type That Can Be Used on Packages, Modules, and Types

```
// Version.java
package com.jdojo.module.api.annotation;

import static java.lang.annotation.ElementType.MODULE;
import static java.lang.annotation.ElementType.PACKAGE;
import static java.lang.annotation.ElementType.TYPE;
import java.lang.annotation.Retention;
import static java.lang.annotation.RetentionPolicy.RUNTIME;
import java.lang.annotation.Target;

@Retention(RUNTIME)
@Target({PACKAGE, MODULE, TYPE})
public @interface Version {
    int major();
    int minor();
}
```

Listing 15-17 contains the code for an `AnnotationTest` class. It reads the annotations on the `jdojo.module.api.annotation` module. The output does not contain the `@SuppressWarnings` annotation that is present on the module because this annotation uses a retention policy of `RetentionPolicy.SOURCE`, which means the annotation is not retained at runtime.

Listing 15-17. An AnnotationTest Class to Demonstrate How to Read Annotations on Modules

```
// AnnotationTest.java
package com.jdojo.module.api.annotation;

import java.lang.annotation.Annotation;

public class AnnotationTest {
    public static void main(String[] args) {
        // Get the module reference of the com.jdojo.module.api.annotation module
        Module m = AnnotationTest.class.getModule();

        // Print all annotations
        Annotation[] a = m.getAnnotations();
        for (Annotation ann : a) {
            System.out.println(ann);
        }

        // Read the Deprecated annotation
        Deprecated d = m.getAnnotation(Deprecated.class);
        if (d != null) {
            System.out.printf("Deprecated: since=%s, forRemoval=%b%n",
                    d.since(), d.forRemoval());
        }
```

```
        // Read the Version annotation
        Version v = m.getAnnotation(Version.class);
        if (v != null) {
            System.out.printf("Version: major=%d, minor=%d%n", v.major(), v.minor());
        }
    }
}
```

```
@java.lang.Deprecated(forRemoval=false, since="1.2")
@com.jdojo.module.api.annotation.Version(major=1, minor=2)
Deprecated: since=1.2, forRemoval=false
Version: major=1, minor=2
```

Working with Module Layers

Working with module layers is an advanced topic. Typically, a Java developer will not need to work with module layers directly. Existing applications will not use module layers. If you migrate your applications to JDK9 or develop new applications using JDK9, whether you want it or not, you are using at least one module layer, which is created by the JVM at startup. Typically, applications using plugin or container architecture will use module layers. In this section, I give a brief overview of module layers using a simple example. I use the terms, module layers and layers, interchangeably.

A layer is a set of resolved modules (a module graph) with a function that maps each module to a class loader, which is loads all types in that module. The set of resolved modules is called a configuration. You can visualize the relationship between modules, class loaders, configurations, and layers like so:

```
Configuration = A module graph
Module Layer = Configuration + (Module -> Class loader)
```

Modules are arranged into layers. Layers are arranged hierarchically. A layer has at least one parent layer, except the empty layer, which, as its name suggests, contains no modules and primarily exists to serve as the parent layer for the boot layer. The boot layer is created by the JVM at startup by resolving the application's initial modules (the root modules) against a set of observable modules. Loading types using class loaders has not changed in JDK9. Class loaders, typically, use the parent-first delegation model in which a request to load a type is delegated to the parent, which in turn delegates to its parent until the bootstrap class loader. If none of the parents loads the type, the class loader that initially received the request loads it. Figure 15-1 shows an example of the way modules, class loaders, and layers are arranged.

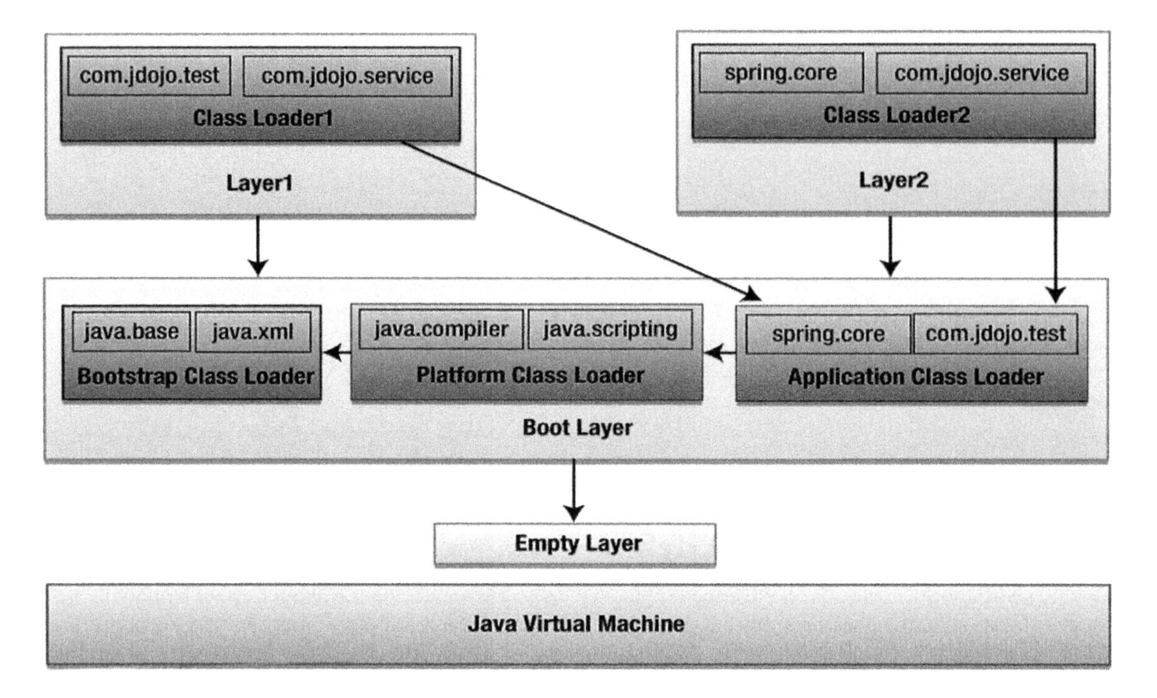

Figure 15-1. *An example of arranging modules into layers in an application*

In the figure, an arrow pointing from X to Y means that X is the parent of Y, where X and Y could be class loaders or layers. Layers are stacked—the empty layer and the boot layer are the lowest two layers. I ignore referring to the empty layer in our further discussion and treat the boot layer as the lowest layer in the stack of layers. In the figure, the boot layer is the parent layer of the two custom layers named `Layer1` and `Layer2`.

Modules in each layer in the stack can read modules in layers below it. That is, both `Layer1` and `Layer2` can read modules in the boot layer. However, `Layer1` cannot read modules in `Layer2` because they are siblings. Neither can the boot layer read modules in `Layer1` and `Layer2` because the boot layer is the parent layer for them. As shown in figure, the class loaders in both user-defined layers have the application class loader as their parent, which most often would be the case. Making the application class loader the parent of the custom class loader ensures that the latter will be able to read all types in modules in the boot layer. The readability property of modules is respected when modules in one layer read modules in layers below it.

Allowing modules to be arranged in layers works for two use-cases—override mechanism and extension mechanism—that are often encountered in advanced Java applications like Java EE application/web servers that act as containers for hosted applications. In the override mechanism, a hosted application needs to override the functionalities provided by the container such as using a different version of the same module. In the extension mechanism, a hosted application needs to supplement the functionalities that are already provided by the container such as providing additional service providers. In Figure 15-1, the `com.jdojo.test` module is in the boot layer as well as `Layer1`. This is a case of overriding modules. The module version in `Layer1` will be used by `Layer1`, whereas `Layer2` will use the version of this module from the boot layer.

It is often required that a container allows hosted applications to provide their own set of modules that may override the modules embedded in the container. This is made possible by loading modules of the hosted applications in a layer on top of the container layer. Modules loaded into the application-specific layers will override the modules in the server-level layers. This way, you can use multiple versions of the same module in the same JVM.

A hosted application may want to use a different service provider than the one provided by the container. This is possible by adding the application-specific service provider modules to a layer on top of the container layer. You can use the `load(ModuleLayer layer, Class<S> service)` method of the `ServiceLoader<S>` class to load service providers. The specified layer would be the hosted application specific layer. This method loads service providers from the specified layer and its parent layers.

■ **Tip** Layers are immutable. Once you create a layer, you cannot add modules to it or remove modules from it. If you need to add modules or substitute a module with another version of it, you must tear down the layer and recreate it.

Creating a layer is a multi-step process. You need to use the following steps to create a layer:

1. Create module finders.
2. Create a set of root modules.
3. Create a configuration object.
4. Create a layer.

Once you create a layer, you can use it to load types. I walk you through these steps in detail in the sections to follow. In the end, I show you how to use multiple versions of a module using layers.

Finding Modules

A module finder is an instance of the `ModuleFinder` interface. It is used to find modules during module resolution and service binding. A `ModuleFinder` returns the found modules as instances of the `ModuleReference` class. An instance of the `ModuleReference` class represents a reference to the contents of a module. The interface contains the two factory methods to create module finders:

- `static ModuleFinder of(Path... entries)`
- `static ModuleFinder ofSystem()`

The `of()` method locates modules by searching the specified sequence of paths, which can be paths to directories or packaged modules. The method finds the first occurrence of a module name searching the specified paths in order. The following snippet of code shows how to create a module finder that will search for modules in the `C:\Java9LanguageFeatures\lib` and `C:\Java9LanguageFeatures\customLib` directories:

```
// Create the module paths
Path mp1 = Paths.get("C:\\Java9LanguageFeatures\\lib");
Path mp2 = Paths.get("C:\\Java9LanguageFeatures\\customLib");

// Create a module finder using two module paths
ModuleFinder finder = ModuleFinder.of(mp1, mp2);
```

Sometimes, you need a reference to a `ModuleFinder`, for example, to pass to a method, but that module finder need not find any module. You can use the `ModuleFinder.of()` method without passing any paths as arguments to create such a module finder.

The ofSystem() method returns a module finder that finds system modules linked to the runtime. This method always finds the java.base module. Note that you can link a custom set of modules to a runtime image, which means that modules located using this method depend on the runtime image. A custom runtime image contains JDK modules as well as application modules. This method will find both types of modules.

You can also compose a module finder from a sequence of zero of more module finders using the static compose() method of the ModuleFinder interface:

```
ModuleFinder compose(ModuleFinder... finders)
```

This module finder will use each module finder in the order specified. The second module finder will find all modules not found by the first module finder, the third module finder will find all modules not found by the first and second module finders, and so on.

The ModuleFinder interface contains the following methods to find modules:

- `Optional<ModuleReference> find(String name)`
- `Set<ModuleReference> findAll()`

The find() method finds a module with the specified name. The findAll() method finds all modules that the finder can locate.

Listing 15-18 contains the code for a FindingModule class that shows you how to use a ModuleFinder. The code uses paths on Windows such as C:\Java9LanguageFeatures\dist, where modules are stored. You may need to change the module paths before you run the class. The class is a member of the com.jdojo.module.api module. You may get different output.

Listing 15-18. Using a ModuleFinder to Locate Modules

```
// FindingModule.java
package com.jdojo.module.api;

import java.lang.module.ModuleDescriptor;
import java.lang.module.ModuleFinder;
import java.lang.module.ModuleReference;
import java.net.URI;
import java.nio.file.Path;
import java.nio.file.Paths;
import java.util.Optional;
import java.util.Set;

public class FindingModule {
    public static void main(String[] args) {
        // Create module paths. Change these paths to point to the directories
        // where modules are stored on your computer
        Path mp1 = Paths.get("C:\\Java9LanguageFeatures\\dist");
        Path mp2 = Paths.get("C:\\Java9LanguageFeatures\\lib");

        // Create a module finder
        ModuleFinder finder = ModuleFinder.of(mp1, mp2);

        // Find all modules that this finder can locate
        Set<ModuleReference> moduleRefs = finder.findAll();
```

```
        // Print the details of the modules found
        moduleRefs.forEach(FindingModule::printInfo);
    }

    public static void printInfo(ModuleReference mr) {
        ModuleDescriptor md = mr.descriptor();
        Optional<URI> location = mr.location();
        URI uri = null;
        if (location.isPresent()) {
            uri = location.get();
        }

        System.out.printf("Module: %s, Location: %s%n", md.name(), uri);
    }
}
```

```
Module: jdojo.reflection.model, Location: file:///C:/Java9LanguageFeatures/dist/jdojo.
reflection.model.jar
Module: jdojo.prime.probable, Location: file:///C:/Java9LanguageFeatures/dist/jdojo.prime.
probable.jar
Module: jdojo.module.api, Location: file:///C:/Java9LanguageFeatures/dist/jdojo.module.api.jar
...
```

Reading Module Contents

In the previous section, you learned how to use a `ModuleFinder` to find module references, which are instances of the `ModuleReference` class. A `ModuleReference` encapsulates the `ModuleDescriptor` and the location of a module. You can use the `open()` method of the `ModuleReference` class to obtain an instance of the `ModuleReader` interface. A `ModuleReader` is used to list, find, and read the contents of a module. The following snippet of code shows how to obtain a `ModuleReader` for the `java.base` module:

```
// Create a system module finder
ModuleFinder finder = ModuleFinder.ofSystem();

// The java.base module is guaranteed to exist
Optional<ModuleReference> omr = finder.find("java.base");
ModuleReference moduleRef = omr.get();

// Get a module reader
ModuleReader reader = moduleRef.open();
```

The `open()` method of the `ModuleReference` class throws an `IOException`. I have omitted the exception handling in the previous snippet of code to keep the code simple.

The following methods in the `ModuleReader` are used to work with the contents of a module. The method names are intuitive enough to tell you what they do.

- `void close() throws IOException`
- `Optional<URI> find(String resourceName) throws IOException`

- `Stream<String> list() throws IOException`
- `default Optional<InputStream> open(String resourceName) throws IOException`
- `default Optional<ByteBuffer> read(String resourceName) throws IOException`
- `default void release(ByteBuffer bb)`

The resource name passed to these methods is a slash (/) separated path string. For example, the resource name for the java.lang.Object class in the java.base module is java/lang/Object.class.

Once you are done working with a ModuleReader, you need to close it using its close() method. If you try to read a module's contents using a closed ModuleReader, an IOException is thrown. The read() method returns an Optional<ByteBuffer>. You need to call the release(ByteBuffer bb) method to release the byte buffer after consuming it to avoid a resource leak.

Listing 15-19 contains a program that shows how to read contents of a module. It reads the contents of the Object class in a ByteBuffer and prints its size in bytes. It also prints the name of five resources in the java.base module. You may get different output.

Listing 15-19. Using a ModuleReader to Read a Module's Contents

```
// ReadingModuleContents.java
package com.jdojo.module.api;

import java.io.IOException;
import java.lang.module.ModuleFinder;
import java.lang.module.ModuleReader;
import java.lang.module.ModuleReference;
import java.nio.ByteBuffer;
import java.util.Optional;

public class ReadingModuleContents {
    public static void main(String[] args) {
        // Create a system module finder
        ModuleFinder finder = ModuleFinder.ofSystem();

        // The java.base module is guaranteed to exist
        Optional<ModuleReference> omr = finder.find("java.base");
        ModuleReference moduleRef = omr.get();

        // Get a module reader and use it
        try (ModuleReader reader = moduleRef.open()) {
            // Read the Object class and print its size
            Optional<ByteBuffer> bb = reader.read("java/lang/Object.class");

            bb.ifPresent(
                buffer -> {System.out.println("Object.class Size: " + buffer.limit());

                // Release the byte buffer
                reader.release(buffer);
            });
```

```
            System.out.println("\nFive resources in the java.base module:");
            reader.list()
                  .limit(5)
                  .forEach(System.out::println);
        } catch (IOException e) {
            e.printStackTrace();
        }
    }
}
```

```
Object.class Size: 1932

Five resources in the java.base module:
module-info.class
sun/util/BuddhistCalendar.class
sun/util/PreHashedMap$1$1.class
sun/util/PreHashedMap$1.class
sun/util/PreHashedMap$2$1$1.class
```

Creating Configurations

A configuration represents a set of resolved modules. A resolved module is a module whose dependences, specified using the requires statements, have been computed. The module resolution process uses two sets of modules: a set of root modules and a set of observable modules. Each module in the set of root modules is used as an initial module and its requires statements are resolved against the set of observable modules. A root module may require another module, which in turn may require another module, and so on. The resolution process computes the entire chain of dependencies for all root modules. The resulting graph of modules is called a dependency graph.

A dependency graph only takes into account the requires statements. If a module uses a requires transitive statement, modules depending on this module implicitly depend on the module specified in the requires transitive statement. The dependency graph is augmented with additional readability of modules caused by the requires transitive statements resulting in a module graph called a readability graph.

The uses and provides statements in modules also form a dependency. If a module M uses a service type S and another module N provides an implementation S with T, the module M depends on module N for using the service type S. The readability graph is augmented with modules computed for such service-use dependencies.

When the configuration for the boot layer is created, it contains modules by resolving the dependencies (requires statements), implied readability (requires transitive), and service-use dependencies (uses and provides statements). When you create a configuration for a user-defined layer, you have an option to include or exclude the service-use dependencies.

An instance of the Configuration class represents a configuration. A configuration has at least one parent, except an empty configuration.

An instance of the ResolvedModule class represents a resolved module in a configuration. The reads() method of the ResolvedModule class returns a Set<ResolvedModule> that a resolved module reads. Its configuration() method returns the Configuration that the resolved module is a member of. Its reference() method returns a ModuleReference that you can use to obtain a ModuleReader to read the module's contents.

The following methods in the Configuration class create a Configuration object:

- static Configuration empty()
- Configuration resolve(ModuleFinder before, ModuleFinder after, Collection<String> roots)
- Configuration resolveAndBind(ModuleFinder before, ModuleFinder after, Collection<String> roots)
- static Configuration resolve(ModuleFinder before, List<Configuration> parents, ModuleFinder after, Collection<String> roots)
- static Configuration resolveAndBind(ModuleFinder before, List<Configuration> parents, ModuleFinder after, Collection<String> roots)

The empty() method returns an empty Configuration. This primarily exists to serve as the parent configuration for the configuration of the boot layer.

There are two versions of the resolve() and resolveAndBind() methods: ones as instance methods and others as static methods. There is only one difference between them. The instance methods create a new configuration using the current configuration as the parent configuration, whereas the static methods let you pass a list of parent configurations for the new configuration.

The resolve() method creates a new Configuration object by resolving dependencies resulting from requires and requires transitive statements in the module declarations. Modules in the specified roots are used as root modules. During the resolution process, modules are searched using the specified before module finder first. If the module is not found, the parent configurations are searched. If the module is still not found, the specified after module finder is used to search for the module. If your configuration is supposed to override a module in the parent configurations, you will place that module in the before module finder path.

The resolveAndBind() method works the same as the resolve() method, except that it also resolves service-use dependencies. The following snippet of code shows how to create a configuration using the boot layer's configuration as its parent configuration:

```
// Define the module finders
String modulePath = "C:\\Java9LanguageFeatures\\dist";
Path path = Paths.get(modulePath);

ModuleFinder beforFinder = ModuleFinder.of(path);

// Our after module finder is empty
ModuleFinder afterFinder = ModuleFinder.of();

// Set up the root modules
Set<String> rootModules = Set.of("jdojo.layer");

// Create a configuration using the boot layer's configuration as its parent configuration
Configuration parentConfig = ModuleLayer.boot().configuration();
Configuration config = parentConfig.resolve(beforFinder, afterFinder, rootModules);
```

The following methods in the Configuration class are used to retrieve the details of resolved modules in a configuration:

- Optional<ResolvedModule> findModule(String name)
- Set<ResolvedModule> modules()
- List<Configuration> parents()

These methods' names and signatures are intuitive enough to understand their use. I do not discuss the Configuration class any further in this section. In the next section, I show how to use a Configuration to create a module layer.

Creating Module Layers

A module layer is a configuration and a function that maps each module to a class loader. To create a layer, you must first create a configuration and have one or more class loaders to map modules to them. The class loader for a module loads all types in that module. You can map all modules in a configuration to one class loader; you can map each module to a different class loader; or you can have a custom mapping strategy. Typically, class loaders use a delegation strategy that delegates class loading requests to their parent class loaders. You can use this strategy as well when you define class loaders for modules in layers.

An instance of the ModuleLayer class, which is in the java.lang package, represents a module layer. The class contains two methods, empty() and boot(), that return an empty layer with an empty configuration and the boot layer, respectively. The following methods in the class are used to create a custom layer:

- ModuleLayer defineModules(Configuration cf, Function<String, ClassLoader> clf)
- static ModuleLayer.Controller defineModules(Configuration cf, List<ModuleLayer> parentLayers, Function<String,ClassLoader> clf)
- ModuleLayer defineModulesWithManyLoaders(Configuration cf, ClassLoader parentClassLoader)
- static ModuleLayer.Controller defineModulesWithManyLoaders(Configuration cf, List<ModuleLayer> parentLayers, ClassLoader parentLoader)
- ModuleLayer defineModulesWithOneLoader(Configuration cf, ClassLoader parentClassLoader)
- static ModuleLayer.Controller defineModulesWithOneLoader(Configuration cf, List<ModuleLayer> parentLayers, ClassLoader parentLoader)

The defineModulesXxx() methods have two variants: one set contains instance methods and another set contains static methods. Instance methods use the layer on which they are called as the parent layer, whereas static methods let you specify a list of parent layers for the new layer. The static methods return a ModuleLayer.Controller object, which you can use to work with modules in the new layer. ModuleLayer.Controller is a nested class in the java.lang package with the following methods:

- ModuleLayer.Controller addExports(Module source, String packageName, Module target)
- ModuleLayer.Controller addOpens(Module source, String packageName, Module target)
- ModuleLayer.Controller addReads(Module source, Module target)
- ModuleLayer layer()

The addExports(), addOpens() and addReads() methods let you export a package in a module in this layer to another module, open a package in a module in this layer to another module, and add a read edge from a module in this layer to another module. The layer() method returns the ModuleLayer that this controller is managing.

The defineModules(Configuration cf, Function<String,ClassLoader> clf) method takes a configuration as its first argument. The second argument is a mapping function that takes a module name in the configuration and returns a class loader for that module. The method call may fail if:

- Multiple modules with the same package are mapped to the same class loader.
- A module is mapped to a class loader that already has a module of the same name defined in it.
- A module is mapped to a class loader that has already defined types in any of the packages in the module.

The defineModulesWithManyLoaders(Configuration cf, ClassLoader parentClassLoader) method creates a layer using the specified configuration. Each module in the configuration is mapped to a different class loader, which is created by this method. The specified parent class loader (the second argument) is set as the parent of the class loaders created by this method. Typically, you would use the application class loader as the parent class loader for all class loaders created by this method. You can use null as the second argument to use the bootstrap class loader as the parent for all the class loaders created by this method. This method will create a new class loader for each module in the configuration.

The defineModulesWithOneLoader(Configuration cf, ClassLoader parentClassLoader) method creates a layer using the specified configuration. It creates one class loader using the specified parent class loader as its parent. It maps all modules in the configuration to that one class loader. You can use null as the second argument to use the bootstrap class loader as the parent for all the class loaders created by this method.

The following snippet of code creates a layer with the boot layer as its parent layer. All modules in the layer will be loaded by one class loader whose parent is the system class loader.

```
Configuration config = /* create a configuration... */
ClassLoader sysClassLoader = ClassLoader.getSystemClassLoader();
ModuleLayer parentLayer = ModuleLayer.boot();
ModuleLayer layer = parentLayer.defineModulesWithOneLoader(config, sysClassLoader);
```

Once you create a layer, you need to load classes from modules in that layer. All types in a module are loaded by the class loader mapped to that module. Note that you may have the same module defined in more than one layer, but those modules will be mapped to different class loaders. The ModuleLayer class contains a findLoader(String moduleName) method that accepts a module name as an argument and returns the ClassLoader for that module. If the module in not defined in the layer, the parent layers are checked. If the module does not exist in this layer or its ancestor layers, an IllegalArgumentException is thrown. Once you get the ClassLoader for the module, you can call its loadClass(String className) method to load a class from that module. The following snippet of code, excluding the exception handling logic, shows how to load a class in a layer:

```
ModuleLayer layer = /* Create a layer... */

// Load a class using the layer
String moduleName = "jdojo.layer";
String className = "com.jdojo.layer.LayerInfo";
```

```
// Load the class
Class<?> cls = layer.findLoader(moduleName)
                    .loadClass(className);
```

Once you get the Class object, you can use it to instantiate its objects and call methods on that object. The following snippet of code creates an object of the loaded class and calls a method named printInfo on that object:

```
// A method name that prints the details of an object
String methodName = "printInfo";

// Instantiate the class using its no-args constructor
Object obj = cls.getConstructor().newInstance();

// Find the method
Method method = cls.getMethod(methodName);

// Call the method that will print the details
method.invoke(obj);
```

The following methods in the ModuleLayer class can be used to obtain information about the layer itself or the modules contained in the layer:

- Optional<Module> findModule(String moduleName)
- Set<Module> modules()
- List<ModuleLayer> parents()

The findModule() method finds a module with the specified name in the layer or its parent layers. The modules() method returns a set of modules in the layer, which may be an empty set if the layer does not contain any modules. The parent() method returns a list of parent layers for this layer, which will be empty for the empty layer.

Next, we walk through a complete example of how to create a custom layer and how to load the two versions of the same module in two layers in the same application.

The module name is jdojo.layer and it consists of one package named com.jdojo.layer that contains only one class named LayerInfo. You will have two versions of the same module, so everything will be repeated. I created two NetBeans projects in the source code with the names jdojo.layer.v1 and jdojo.layer.v2.

Listing 15-20 and Listing 15-21 contain version 1.0 of the module definition for the com.jdojo.layer module and the class declaration for the LayerInfo class, respectively.

Listing 15-20. Version 1.0 of the com.jdojo.layer Module

```
// module-info.com version 1.0
module jdojo.layer {
    exports com.jdojo.layer;
}
```

Listing 15-21. The LayerInfo Class in Version 1.0 of the com.jdojo.layer Module

```
// LayerInfo.java
package com.jdojo.layer;

public class LayerInfo {
    private final static String VERSION = "1.0";

    static {
        System.out.println("Loading LayerInfo version " + VERSION);
    }

    public void printInfo() {
        Class cls = this.getClass();
        ClassLoader loader = cls.getClassLoader();
        Module module = cls.getModule();
        String moduleName = module.getName();
        ModuleLayer layer = module.getLayer();

        System.out.println("Class Version: " + VERSION);
        System.out.println("Class Name: " + cls.getName());
        System.out.println("Class Loader: " + loader);
        System.out.println("Module Name: " + moduleName);
        System.out.println("Layer Name: " + layer);
    }
}
```

The `LayerInfo` class is very simple. It stores its version information in a static variable named `VERSION`. It prints a message in a static initializer that includes the version information. This message will help you understand which version of the `LayerInfo` class is loaded. The `printInfo()` method prints the details of the class: the version, class name, class loader, the module name, and the layer.

Listing 15-22 and Listing 15-23 contain version 2.0 of the module definition for the `com.jdojo.layer` module and the class declaration for the `LayerInfo` class, respectively. Only one thing has changed from version 1.0 to version 2.0 of this module—the value of the static variable `VERSION` changed from `1.0` to `2.0`.

Listing 15-22. Version 2.0 of the com.jdojo.layer Module

```
// module-info.com version 2.0
module com.jdojo.layer {
    exports com.jdojo.layer;
}
```

Listing 15-23. The LayerInfo Class in Version 2.0 of the com.jdojo.layer Module

```
// LayerInfo.java
package com.jdojo.layer;

public class LayerInfo {
    private final static String VERSION = "2.0";

    static {
        System.out.println("Loading LayerInfo version " + VERSION);
    }
```

```
    public void printInfo() {
        Class cls = this.getClass();
        ClassLoader loader = cls.getClassLoader();
        Module module = cls.getModule();
        String moduleName = module.getName();
        ModuleLayer layer = module.getLayer();

        System.out.println("Class Version: " + VERSION);
        System.out.println("Class Name: " + cls.getName());
        System.out.println("Class Loader: " + loader);
        System.out.println("Module Name: " + moduleName);
        System.out.println("Layer Name: " + layer);
    }
}
```

You are ready to test layers and load both versions of the `com.jdojo.layer` modules in two different layers in the same JVM. Create a modular JAR for version 2.0 of this module, name it `jdojo.layer.v2.jar` or give it any other name you want, and place the modular JAR into the `C:\jdojo.layer.v2\dist` directory. If you place your modular JAR in other directory, you need to change the path in the code in Listing 15-25.

The program to test layers is in a module named `jdojo.layer.test` whose declaration is shown in Listing 15-24.

Listing 15-24. A Module Declaration for a Module Named jdojo.layer.test

```
// module-info.java
module jdojo.layer.test {
    // This module reads version 1.0 of the jdojo.layer module
    requires jdojo.layer;
}
```

The `jdojo.layer.test` module declares a dependence on version 1.0 of the `jdojo.layer` module. How can you ensure that version 1.0 of the `jdojo.layer` module is used with the `jdojo.layer.test` module? All you have to do is place the code for version 1.0 of the `jdojo.layer` module on the module path when you run the `jdojo.layer.test` module. To achieve this in NetBeans, add the `jdojo.layer.v1` project to the module path of the `jdojo.layer.test` module.

Listing 15-25 contains code for a `LayerTest` class that contains the logic to create a custom layer and load modules into it. A detailed explanation of the logic used in this class follows the output of this class.

Listing 15-25. The LayerTest Class

```
// LayerTest.java
package com.jdojo.layer.test;

import java.lang.module.Configuration;
import java.lang.module.ModuleFinder;
import java.lang.reflect.InvocationTargetException;
import java.lang.reflect.Method;
import java.nio.file.Path;
import java.nio.file.Paths;
import java.util.Set;
```

```
public class LayerTest {
    /* Location for the custom module. You will need to change the path
       to point to a directory on your PC that contains the modular JAR for
       the jdojo.layer (version 2.0) module.
     */
    private static final String MODULE_LOCATION = "C:\\jdojo.layer.v2\\dist";

    // Module name
    private static final String MODULE_NAME = "jdojo.layer";

    public static void main(String[] args) {
        // Define the set of root modules to be resolved in the custom layer
        Set<String> rootModules = Set.of(MODULE_NAME);

        // Create a custom layer
        ModuleLayer customLayer = createLayer(MODULE_LOCATION, rootModules);

        // Test the class in the boot layer
        ModuleLayer bootLayer = ModuleLayer.boot();
        testLayer(bootLayer);
        System.out.println();

        // Test the class in the custom layer
        testLayer(customLayer);
    }

    public static ModuleLayer createLayer(String modulePath, Set<String> rootModules) {
        Path path = Paths.get(modulePath);

        // Define the module finders to be used in creating a
        // configuration for the custom layer
        ModuleFinder beforFinder = ModuleFinder.of(path);
        ModuleFinder afterFinder = ModuleFinder.of();

        // Create a configuration for the custom layer
        Configuration parentConfig = ModuleLayer.boot().configuration();
        Configuration config = parentConfig.resolve(beforFinder, afterFinder, rootModules);

        /* Create a custom layer with one class loader. The parent for
           the class loader is the system class loader. The boot layer is
           the parent layer of this custom layer.
         */
        ClassLoader sysClassLoader = ClassLoader.getSystemClassLoader();
        ModuleLayer parentLayer = ModuleLayer.boot();
        ModuleLayer layer = parentLayer.defineModulesWithOneLoader(config, sysClassLoader);

        // Check if we loaded the module in this layer
        if (layer.modules().isEmpty()) {
            System.out.println("\nCould not find the module " + rootModules
                    + " at " + modulePath + ". "
                    + "Please make sure that the com.jdojo.layer.v2.jar exists "
```

```
                + "at this location." + "\n");
        }

        return layer;
    }

    public static void testLayer(ModuleLayer layer) {
        final String className = "com.jdojo.layer.LayerInfo";
        final String methodName = "printInfo";

        try {
            // Load the class
            Class<?> cls = layer.findLoader(MODULE_NAME)
                    .loadClass(className);

            // Instantiate the class using its no-args constructor
            Object obj = cls.getConstructor().newInstance();

            // Find the method
            Method method = cls.getMethod(methodName);

            // Call the method that will print the details
            method.invoke(obj);
        } catch (ClassNotFoundException | IllegalAccessException
              | IllegalArgumentException | InstantiationException
              | NoSuchMethodException | SecurityException
              | InvocationTargetException e) {
            e.printStackTrace();
        }
    }
}
```

```
Loading LayerInfo version 1.0
Class Version: 1.0
Class Name: com.jdojo.layer.LayerInfo
Class Loader: jdk.internal.loader.ClassLoaders$AppClassLoader@63d4e2ba
Module Name: jdojo.layer
Layer Name: jdk.accessibility, jdk.unsupported, jdk.localedata, jdk.zipfs, java.security.
jgss, java.datatransfer, jdk.security.auth, java.scripting, java.desktop, jdk.scripting.
nashorn, java.prefs, jdk.jlink, jdk.management, jdk.security.jgss, jdk.dynalink, jdk.javadoc,
jdojo.layer, jdk.compiler, java.security.sasl, jdk.naming.rmi, jdk.jdeps, jdojo.layer.test,
java.xml.crypto, java.smartcardio, java.base, java.rmi, java.management.rmi, java.xml, jdk.
jartool, jdk.charsets, jdk.crypto.mscapi, jdk.crypto.ec, jdk.crypto.cryptoki, java.naming,
java.compiler, jdk.deploy, jdk.internal.opt, java.management, jdk.naming.dns, java.logging

Loading LayerInfo version 2.0
Class Version: 2.0
Class Name: com.jdojo.layer.LayerInfo
Class Loader: jdk.internal.loader.Loader@34b7bfc0
Module Name: jdojo.layer
Layer Name: jdojo.layer
```

You have declared a class variable named MODULE_LOCATION, which stores the location of version 2.0 of the jdojo.layer module. You must change the path to point to a directory on your computer that contains the compiled module code for version 2.0 of the jdojo.layer module.

```
private static final String MODULE_LOCATION = "C:\\jdojo.layer.v2\\dist";
```

You have declared a class variable named MODULE_NAME, which stores the name of the module:

```
private static final String MODULE_NAME = "jdojo.layer";
```

The main() method stores jdojo.layer as the sole root module for the custom layer's configuration:

```
Set<String> rootModules = Set.of(MODULE_NAME);
```

The createLayer() method is called to create a custom layer. The method uses logic to create a custom layer with version 2.0 of the jdojo.layer module from MODULE_LOCATION:

```
ModuleLayer customLayer = createLayer(MODULE_LOCATION, rootModules);
```

The main() method obtains the reference of the boot layer:

```
ModuleLayer bootLayer = ModuleLayer.boot();
```

Now, the testLayer() method is called—once for boot layer and once for the custom layer. The method finds the class loader for the jdojo.layer module in the layer and loads the com.jdojo.layer.LayerInfo class.

```
final String className = "com.jdojo.layer.LayerInfo";
final String methodName = "printInfo";
Class<?> cls = layer.findLoader(MODULE_NAME)
                    .loadClass(className);
```

An object of the LayerInfo class is created using its no-args constructor:

```
Object obj = cls.getConstructor().newInstance();
```

Finally, the reference of the printInfo() method of the LayerInfo class is obtained and the printInfo() method is invoked, which prints the details of the LayerInfo class:

```
Method method = cls.getMethod(methodName);
method.invoke(obj);
```

You can run the LayerTest class in NetBeans or use the following command. You may get different output. The layer name is the list of all the modules in that layer, which is returned by the toString() method of the ModuleLayer class.

```
C:\>java --module-path jdojo.layer.v1\dist;jdojo.layer.test\dist
--module jdojo.layer.test/com.jdojo.layer.test.LayerTest
```

The previous command uses relative paths in the module path such as jdojo.layer.v1. These paths will work if you have extracted the source code for this book in the C:\ directory on Windows. Replace the value for the module path if you have extracted the source code in a different directory.

Summary

The Module API consists of classes and interfaces that give you programmatic access to modules. Using the API, you can programmatically read/modify/build module descriptors, load modules, read module's contents, create layers, etc. The Module API is small, comprising about 15 classes and interfaces spread across two packages: `java.lang` and `java.lang.module`. The `Module`, `ModuleLayer`, and `LayerInstantiationException` classes are in the `java.lang` package and the rest are in the `java.lang.module` package.

An instance of the `Module` class represents a runtime module. Every type loaded into the JVM belongs to a module. JDK9 added a method named `getModule()` to the `Class` class; it returns the module to which the class belongs.

An instance of the `ModuleDescriptor` class represents a module definition, which is created from a module declaration—typically from a `module-info.class` file. A module descriptor can also be created on the fly using the `ModuleDescriptor.Builder` class. A module declaration may be augmented using command-line options such as `--add-reads`, `--add-exports`, and `--add-opens`, and using methods in the `Module` class such as `addReads()`, `addOpens()`, and `addExports()`. A `ModuleDescriptor` represents a module descriptor that exists at the time of module declaration, not as an augmented module descriptor. The `getDescriptor()` method of the `Module` class returns a `ModuleDescriptor`. A `ModuleDescriptor` is immutable. An unnamed module does not have a module descriptor. The `getDescriptor()` method of the `Module` class returns `null` for an unnamed module. The `ModuleDescriptor` class contains several nested classes, for example, the `ModuleDescriptor.Requires` nested class; each of them represents a module statement in programs.

You can augment a module descriptor using command-line options and programmatically using the Module API. You can put all queries for a module's properties in two categories: ones that may change after the module is loaded and ones that do not change after the module is loaded. The `Module` class contains methods for queries in the first category and the `ModuleDescriptor` class contains methods for queries in the second category.

You can update a module's definition at runtime using one of the methods in the `Module` class: `addExports()`, `addOpens()`, `addReads()`, and `addUses()`.

The rules to access resources in a module are a bit complicated. By default, resources in a named module are encapsulated, unless the package containing the resources is opened to the module accessing the resources. Resources in a named module contained in a directory whose name is not a valid Java package name are accessible to all other modules. The class files (`.class` files) in a module are always accessible to all other modules. The resource-finding methods in the `Class` class find resources only in the module in which the `Class` object is loaded. Use the `getResourceAsStream()` method in the `Module` class to access resources in other modules.

You can use annotations on module declarations. The `java.lang.annotation.ElementType` enum has a new value called `MODULE`. You can use `MODULE` as a target type on an annotation declaration, which allows the annotation type to be used on modules. In Java 9, two annotations—`java.lang.Deprecated` and `java.lang.SuppressWarnings`—have been updated to be used on module declarations. Using these annotations on a module affects only the module declaration, not the types contained in the module.

Modules are arranged into layers. A layer is a set of resolved modules with a function that maps each module to a class loader that is responsible for loading all types in that module. The set of resolved module is called a configuration. Layers are arranged hierarchically. A layer has at least one parent layer, except the empty layer, which, as its name suggests, contains no modules and primarily exists to serve as the parent layer for the boot layer. The boot layer is created by the JVM at startup by resolving the application's initial modules (the root modules) against a set of observable modules. You can create custom layers. Layers allow multiple versions of the same module to be loaded into different layers and used in the same JVM.

QUESTIONS AND EXERCISES

1. What is the fully qualified name of the class whose instances represent a module at runtime?
2. Write the code to get the reference of the module of a class named `Person`?
3. If you have a class named `Person`, how do you know whether this class is a member of a named module or unnamed module?
4. What does an instance of the `ModuleDescriptor` class represent? Is the instance of the `ModuleDescriptor` class immutable?
5. Can you directly obtain a `ModuleDescriptor` from a `module-info.class` file? If your answer is yes, explain how you do it.
6. Can you get a `ModuleDescriptor` for an unnamed module?
7. Name the classes whose instances represent `exports`, `opens`, `provides`, and `requires` statements in a module declaration.
8. What is the difference between the `ModuleDescriptor::packages()` and the `Module::getPackages()` methods? Both methods return a set of package names.
9. How do you check if a module exports a package to all other modules or to a specific module?
10. How do you know if a module is automatic?
11. Suppose there is a module named `M`, which contains a package named `P`, but does not export the package to any other module. Can the code in another module named `N` export the package `P` in module `M` to module `N` at runtime?
12. Suppose there is a module named `M`, which contains a package named `Q` and opens the package to module `N`. Can the code in module `N` open the package `Q` in module `M` to another module `T` at runtime?
13. If a module named `M` contains resources in a package named `P`. How can the module `M` make the resources available to all other modules?
14. If a module named `M` contains resources in a directory named `META-INF`, can other modules access those resources?
15. What is the name of the scheme you must use to access resources in Java runtime image in JDK9?
16. Write the URL that you need to use to access to the `Object.class` file from the runtime image in JDK9.
17. Can you use annotations on module declarations?

18. Is the following statement true or false?

    When a module is deprecated, the use of that module in `requires`, `exports`, and `opens` statements causes a warning to be issued.

19. Can you use annotation on `requires`, `exports`, and `opens` statements in a module declaration?

20. What is a module layer? How are the layers, configurations, and class loaders related?

21. What is the use of an instance of the `ModuleFinder` interface and an instance of the `ModuleReference` class?

22. Name the class whose instances represent a configuration in a module layer. Can a configuration have multiple parent configurations?

23. How many parent layers can exist for a given module layer? What is the parent layer of the boot layer?

24. Write a program that prints the names of all modules loaded into the boot layer.

CHAPTER 16

Breaking Module Encapsulation

In this chapter, you will learn:

- What breaking a module's encapsulation means
- How to export non-exported packages of a module using the `--add-exports` command-line option and using the `MANIFEST.MF` file of an executable JAR
- How to open non-open packages of a module using the `--add-opens` command-line option and using the `MANIFEST.MF` file of an executable JAR
- How to increase readability of a module using the `--add-reads` command-line option
- How to use the `--illegal-access` command-line option to access the JDK internal API using deep reflection

What Is Breaking Module Encapsulation?

One of the main goals of JDK9 is to encapsulate types and resources in modules and export only those packages whose public types are intended to be accessed by other modules. Sometimes, you may need to break the encapsulation specified by a module to enable white-box testing, use unsupported JDK internal APIs, or use third-party libraries. This is possible by using non-standard command-line options at compile time and runtime. Another reason for having these options is backward compatibility. Not all existing applications will be fully migrated to JDK9 and modularized. If those applications need to use the JDK APIs or APIs provided by libraries that used to be public, but have been encapsulated in JDK9, those applications have a way to keep working. A few of these options have corresponding attributes that can be added to the `MANIFEST.MF` file of the executable JARs to avoid using the command-line options.

Tip Every command-line option to break a module's encapsulation is also supported programmatically using the Module API, which is covered in detail in Chapter 15.

Although it may sound like that these options do the same things as before JDK9, there is a word of caution when accessing JDK internal APIs without any restriction. If a package in a module is not exported or open, it means the module's designer did not intend for these packages to be used outside the module. Such packages may be modified or even removed from the module without notice. If you still use these packages by exporting or opening them using command-line options, you do so at the risk of breaking your application in future!

K. Sharan, *Java Language Features*, https://doi.org/10.1007/978-1-4842-3348-1_16

Command-Line Options

Three module statements in a module declaration let a module encapsulate its types and resources and let other modules use the encapsulated types and resources from the first module. Those statements are `exports`, `opens`, and `requires`. There is a command-line option corresponding to each of these module statements. For the `exports` and `opens` statements, there are corresponding attributes that can be used in the manifest file of an *executable* JAR. Table 16-1 lists these statements and the corresponding command-line options and manifest attributes. The `--illegal-access` command-line option lets you work with illegal access to the JDK internal APIs. I describe these options in detail in the following sections.

Table 16-1. *Module Statements with the Corresponding Command-Line Options and Manifest Attributes*

Module Statement	Command-Line Option	Manifest Attribute
`exports`	`--add-exports`	`Add-Exports`
`opens`	`--add-opens`	`Add-Opens`
`requires`	`--add-reads`	(No attribute is available)
(No statement is available)	`--illegal-access`	(No attribute is available)

■ **Tip** You can use the `--add-exports`, `--add-opens`, and `--add-reads` command-line options more than once with the same command.

The --add-exports Option

The `exports` statement in a module declaration exports a package in the module to all or some other modules, so those modules can use the public APIs in the exported package. If a package is not exported by a module, you can export it using the `--add-exports` command-line option. Its syntax is as follows:

```
--add-exports <source-module>/<package>=<target-module-list>
```

Here, `<source-module>` is the module that exports `<package>` to `<target-module-list>`, which is a comma-separated list of target module names. It is equivalent to adding a qualified `exports` statement to the declaration of `<source-module>`:

```
module <source-module> {
    exports <package> to <target-module-list>;
}
```

■ **Tip** If the target module list is a special value, `ALL-UNNAMED`, for the `--add-exports` option, the module's package is exported to all unnamed modules. The `--add-exports` option is available with the `java` and `javac` commands.

The following option exports the sun.util.logging package in the java.base module to the jdojo.test and jdojo.prime modules:

```
--add-exports java.base/sun.util.logging=jdojo.test,jdojo.prime
```

The following option exports the sun.util.logging package in the java.base module to all unnamed modules:

```
--add-exports java.base/sun.util.logging=ALL-UNNAMED
```

The --add-opens Option

The opens statement in a module declaration opens a package in a module to all or some other modules, so those modules can use deep reflection to access all member types in the opened package at runtime. If a package of a module is not open, you can open it using the --add-opens command-line option. Its syntax is as follows:

```
--add-opens <source-module>/<package>=<target-module-list>
```

Here, <source-module> is the module that opens <package> to <target-module-list>, which is a comma-separated list of target module names. It is equivalent to adding a qualified opens statement to the declaration of <source-module>:

```
module <source-module> {
    opens <package> to <target-module-list>;
}
```

■ **Tip** If the target module list is a special value, ALL-UNNAMED for the --add-opens option, the module's package is open to all unnamed modules. The --add-opens option is available with the java command.

The following option opens the sun.util.logging package in the java.base module to the jdojo.test and jdojo.prime modules:

```
--add-opens java.base/sun.util.logging=jdojo.test,jdojo.prime
```

The following option opens the sun.util.logging package in the java.base module to all unnamed modules:

```
--add-opens java.base/sun.util.logging=ALL-UNNAMED
```

The --add-reads Option

The --add-reads option is not about breaking encapsulation. Rather, it is about increasing the readability of a module. During testing and debugging, it is sometimes necessary for a module to read another module even though the first module does not depend on the second module. The requires statement in a module declaration is used to declare dependence of the current module on another module. You can use the

--add-reads command-line option to add a readability edge from a module to another module. This has the same effect of adding a requires statement to the first module. Its syntax is as follows:

```
--add-reads <source-module>=<target-module-list>
```

Here, <source-module> is the module whose definition is updated to read the list of modules specified in the <target-module-list>, which is a comma-separated list of target module names. It is equivalent to adding a requires statement to the source module for each module in the target module list:

```
module <source-module> {
    requires <target-module1>;
    requires <target-module2>;
}
```

■ **Tip** If the target module list is a special value, ALL-UNNAMED for the --add-reads option, the source module reads all unnamed modules. This is the only way a named module can read unnamed modules. There is no equivalent module statement that you can use in a named module declaration to read an unnamed module. This option is available with the java and javac commands.

The following option adds a read edge to the jdojo.common module to make it read the jdk.accessibility module:

```
--add-reads jdojo.common=jdk.accessibility
```

The --illegal-access Option

Many applications written prior to JDK9 may not be modularized soon. To take advantage of the latest JDK, they may be migrated to JDK9 without modularizing them. Such applications will run from the class path. These applications were allowed to access non-public members of the JDK internal API using deep reflection. To ease migration of these applications, JDK9 allows deep reflection on the JDK9 modules by default, which breaks the JDK module's encapsulation. This is allowed to help the Java community adapt JDK9 sooner. Another reason behind allowing this was backward compatibility. Applications performing deep reflections on the JDK internals will continue to work in JDK9 because the Java community did not get advanced notice that deep reflection on JDK internals will stop working in JDK9.

JDK9 provides an --illegal-access option for the java command. As its name suggests, it is to work with illegal access by code in any *unnamed module* (code on the class path) to members of types in any named modules of the JDK using deep reflection. Its syntax is as follows:

```
java --illegal-access=<permit|deny|warn|debug> <other-arguments>
```

The option takes one of the four parameters: permit, deny, warn, and debug. The default is permit, which means that the absence of the --illegal-access option is the same as --illegal-access=permit. That is, by default, all packages in all explicit modules in the JDK are open to the code in all unnamed modules. The code performing illegal reflective access should be fixed sooner or later. To help identify such offending code, the JDK9 issues a warning to standard error on the first such illegal access. You cannot suppress this warning.

The deny parameter disables all illegal access to the members of the JDK internal types using deep reflection, except when it is allowed using other options such as `--add-opens`. In a future release, deny will become the default mode. That is, by default, illegal reflective access will be disabled in a future release and you will need to use `--illegal-access=permit` explicitly to enable illegal reflective access.

The `warn` parameter issues a warning for each illegal-reflective access. This is helpful in identifying all code in existing applications that uses illegal reflective access.

The debug parameter issues a warning and prints a stack trace for each illegal-reflective access. This is helpful in identifying all code in existing applications that uses illegal reflective access.

The `--illegal-access` option does not permit illegal access by code in a named module to the members of types in other named modules. To perform illegal reflective access in such cases, you can combine this option with the `--add-exports`, `--add-opens`, and `--add-reads` options.

■ **Tip** The `--illegal-access` option will be removed in a future release. First, its default mode will be changed from `permit` to `deny` and then the option itself will be removed. It is important to note that this option is only for allowing illegal access to the JDK internals by the code on the class path. This option does not allow illegal access to the members of the non-JDK modules; you must use the `--add-opens` option or open the module/package if illegal access is needed to the members of non-JDK modules.

I present an example of using all these options that allow breaking a module's encapsulation in the next section.

An Example

Let's walk through a few examples of breaking a module's encapsulation. I use trivial examples. However, they serve the purpose of demonstrating all concepts and command-line options that can be used to break a module's encapsulation.

You created the `jdojo.intro` module as your first module in the first volume of this series. It contains a `Welcome` class in the `com.jdojo.intro` package. The module does not export the package, so the `Welcome` class is encapsulated and cannot be accessed outside the module. Listing 16-1 and Listing 16-2 contain the declaration of the `jdojo.intro` module and its `Welcome` class, respectively.

Listing 16-1. The Declaration of a Module Named jdojo.intro

```
// module-info.java
module jdojo.intro {
}
```

Listing 16-2. A Welcome Class in the jdojo.intro Module

```
// Welcome.java
package com.jdojo.intro;

public class Welcome {
    public static void main(String[] args) {
        System.out.println("Welcome to Java 9!");
    }
}
```

In this example, you call the `main()` method of the `Welcome` class from another module named `jdojo.intruder`, whose declaration is shown in Listing 16-3. Listing 16-4 contains the code for the `TestNonExported` class in this module.

Listing 16-3. The Declaration of a Module Named jdojo.intruder

```
// module-info.java
module jdojo.intruder {
    // No module statements
}
```

Listing 16-4. A Class Named TestNonExported

```
// TestNonExported.java
package com.jdojo.intruder;

import com.jdojo.intro.Welcome;

public class TestNonExported {
    public static void main(String[] args) {
        Welcome.main(new String[]{});
    }
}
```

The `TestNonExported` class contains only one line of code. It calls the static `main()` method of the `Welcome` class passing an empty `String` array. If this class is compiled and run, it will print the following message:

```
Welcome to Java 9!
```

If you try compiling the code for the `jdojo.intruder` module, you will get an error:

```
c:\Java9LanguageFeatures>javac -d build\modules\jdojo.intruder
--module-path build\modules\jdojo.intro
src\jdojo.intruder\classes\module-info.java src\jdojo.intruder\classes\com\jdojo\intruder\
TestNonExported.java
```

```
src\jdojo.intruder\classes\com\jdojo\intruder\TestNonExported.java:4: error: package com.
jdojo.intro is not visible
import com.jdojo.intro.Welcome;
                 ^
  (package com.jdojo.intro is declared in module jdojo.intro, but module jdojo.intruder does
not read it)
1 error
```

The command uses the `--module-path` option to include the `jdojo.intro` module in the module path. The error is pointing to the `import` statement that imports the `com.jdojo.intro.Welcome` class. It states that the package `com.jdojo.intro` is not visible to the `jdojo.intruder` module. That is, the `jdojo.intro` module does not export the `com.jdojo.intro` package that contains the `Welcome` class. To fix this error, you need to export the com.jdojo.intro package of the jdojo.intro module to the jdojo.intruder module using the --add-exports command-line option as follows:

```
c:\Java9LanguageFeatures>javac -d build\modules\jdojo.intruder
--module-path build\modules\jdojo.intro
--add-exports jdojo.intro/com.jdojo.intro=jdojo.intruder
src\jdojo.intruder\classes\module-info.java
src\jdojo.intruder\classes\com\jdojo\intruder\TestNonExported.java
```

```
warning: [options] module name in --add-exports option not found: jdojo.intro
src\jdojo.intruder\classes\com\jdojo\intruder\TestNonExported.java:4: error: package com.
jdojo.intro is not visible
import com.jdojo.intro.Welcome;
                ^
  (package com.jdojo.intro is declared in module jdojo.intro, but module jdojo.intruder does
not read it)
1 error
1 warning
```

This time, you get a warning and an error. The error is the same as before. The warning message is stating that the compiler could not find the jdojo.intro module. Because there is no dependence on this module, this module is not resolved even if it is in the module path. To resolve the warning, you need to add the jdojo.intro module to the default set of root module using the --add-modules option:

```
c:\Java9LanguageFeatures>javac -d build\modules\jdojo.intruder
--module-path build\modules\jdojo.intro
--add-modules jdojo.intro
--add-exports jdojo.intro/com.jdojo.intro=jdojo.intruder
src\jdojo.intruder\classes\module-info.java
src\jdojo.intruder\classes\com\jdojo\intruder\TestNonExported.java
```

This time, the javac command succeeded even though the jdojo.intruder module does not read the jdojo.intro module. It seems to be a bug. If it is not a bug, there is no documentation that I could find to support this behavior. Later, you will see that the java command won't work for the same modules. If this command errors out with a message that the TestNonExported class cannot access the Welcome class, add the following option to it to fix it:

```
--add-reads jdojo.intruder=jdojo.intro
```

Let's try rerunning the TestNonExported class using the following command, which includes the com.jdojo.intruder module in the module path:

```
c:\Java9LanguageFeatures>java
--module-path build\modules\jdojo.intro;build\modules\jdojo.intruder
--add-modules jdojo.intro
--add-exports jdojo.intro/com.jdojo.intro=jdojo.intruder
--module jdojo.intruder/com.jdojo.intruder.TestNonExported
```

```
Exception in thread "main" java.lang.IllegalAccessError: class com.jdojo.intruder.
TestNonExported (in module jdojo.intruder) cannot access class com.jdojo.intro.Welcome
(in module jdojo.intro) because module jdojo.intruder does not read module jdojo.intro at
jdojo.intruder/com.jdojo.intruder.TestNonExported.main(TestNonExported.java:8)
```

The error message is loud and clear. It states that the `jdojo.intruder` module must read the `jdojo.intro` module in order for the former to use the latter's `Welcome` class. You can fix the error by using the `--add-reads` option, which will add a read edge (an equivalent of a `requires` statement) in the `jdojo.intruder` module to read the `jdojo.intro` module. The following command does this:

```
c:\Java9LanguageFeatures>java
--module-path build\modules\jdojo.intro;build\modules\jdojo.intruder
--add-modules jdojo.intro
--add-exports jdojo.intro/com.jdojo.intro=jdojo.intruder
--add-reads jdojo.intruder=jdojo.intro
--module jdojo.intruder/com.jdojo.intruder.TestNonExported
```

```
Welcome to Java 9!
```

This time, you receive the desired output. Figure 16-1 shows the module graph that is created when this command is run.

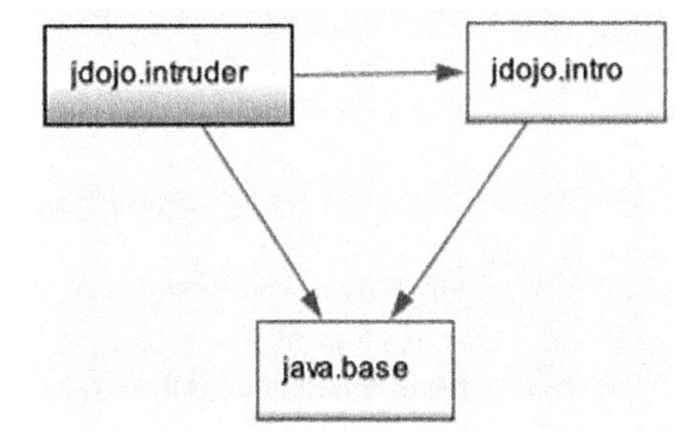

Figure 16-1. *The module graph after using the --add-modules and --add-reads options*

Both the `jdojo.intruder` and `jdojo.intro` modules are root modules. The `jdojo.intruder` module is added to the default set of root modules because the main class being run is in this module. The `jdojo.intro` module is added to the default set of root modules by the `--add-modules` option. A read edge is added from the `jdojo.intruder` module to the `jdojo.intro` module by the `--add-reads` option. Use the `--show-module-resolution` option with this command to see how the modules are resolved.

Let's walk through another example that will show how to open a package of a module to another module using the `--add-opens` command-line option. Listing 16-5 contains the declaration of a module named `jdojo.contact`. Listing 16-6 contains a class named `Phone`, which is in the `jdojo.contact` module. The `jdojo.contact` module exports the `com.jdojo.contact` package–making the public members of the `Phone` class accessible from the outside of the `jdojo.contact` module.

Listing 16-5. The Declaration of a Module Named jdojo.contact

```
// module-info.java
module jdojo.contact {
    exports com.jdojo.contact;
}
```

Listing 16-6. A Phone Class, Which Is a Member of the jdojo.contact Module

```
// Phone.java
package com.jdojo.contact;

public class Phone {
    private String phoneNumber = "9999999999";

    public Phone(String phoneNumber) {
        this.phoneNumber = phoneNumber;
    }

    public String getPhoneNumber() {
        return phoneNumber;
    }

    public void setPhoneNumber(String phoneNUmber) {
        this.phoneNumber = phoneNUmber;
    }
}
```

The `TestNonOpen` class, as shown in Listing 16-7, tries to load the `Phone` class, creates an instance of the class, and accesses its public and private members. The `TestNonOpen` class is a member of the `jdojo.intruder` module. The code in the `main()` method may throw several types of exceptions. I added only one exception in the `throws` clause to keep the logic simple.

Listing 16-7. A Class Named TestNonOpen

```
// TestNonOpen.java
package com.jdojo.intruder;

import java.lang.reflect.Constructor;
import java.lang.reflect.Field;
import java.lang.reflect.Method;

public class TestNonOpen {
    public static void main(String[] args) throws Exception {
        String className = "com.jdojo.contact.Phone";

        // Get the class reference
        Class<?> cls = Class.forName(className);

        // Get the no-args constructor
        Constructor constructor = cls.getConstructor(String.class);
```

```
        // Create an Object of the Phone class
        Object phone = constructor.newInstance("2222222222");

        // Call the getPhoneNumber() method to get the phone number value
        Method getPhoneNumberRef = cls.getMethod("getPhoneNumber");
        String phoneNumber = (String) getPhoneNumberRef.invoke(phone);
        System.out.println("Using method reference, Phone: " + phoneNumber);

        // Use the private phoneNumber instance variable to read its value
        Field phoneNumberField = cls.getDeclaredField("phoneNumber");
        phoneNumberField.setAccessible(true);
        String phoneNumber2 = (String)phoneNumberField.get(phone);
        System.out.println("Using private field reference, Phone: " + phoneNumber2);
    }
}
```

Try compiling the TestNonOpen class:

```
c:\Java9LanguageFeatures>javac -d build\modules\jdojo.intruder
src\jdojo.intruder\classes\com\jdojo\intruder\TestNonOpen.java
```

The TestNonOpen class compiles fine. Note that it accesses the Phone class using deep reflection and the compiler has no knowledge of the fact that this class is not allowed to read the Phone class and its private fields. Now try running the TestNonOpen class:

```
c:\Java9LanguageFeatures>java
--module-path build\modules\jdojo.contact;build\modules\jdojo.intruder
--add-modules jdojo.contact
--module jdojo.intruder/com.jdojo.intruder.TestNonOpen
```

```
Using method reference, Phone: 2222222222
Exception in thread "main" java.lang.reflect.InaccessibleObjectException: Unable to make
field private java.lang.String com.jdojo.contact.Phone.phoneNumber accessible: module jdojo.
contact does not "opens com.jdojo.contact" to module jdojo.intruder
        at java.base/java.lang.reflect.AccessibleObject.checkCanSetAccessible(AccessibleObj
        ect.java:337)
        at java.base/java.lang.reflect.AccessibleObject.checkCanSetAccessible(AccessibleObj
        ect.java:281)
        at java.base/java.lang.reflect.Field.checkCanSetAccessible(Field.java:176)
        at java.base/java.lang.reflect.Field.setAccessible(Field.java:170)
        at jdojo.intruder/com.jdojo.intruder.TestNonOpen.main(TestNonOpen.java:28)
```

I added the jdojo.contact module to the default set of root modules using the --add-modules option. You were able to instantiate the Phone class even if the jdojo.intruder module does not read the jdojo.contact module. There are two reasons for this:

- The jdojo.contact module exports the com.jdojo.contact package, which contains the Phone class. Therefore, the Phone class is accessible to other modules, provided other modules read the jdojo.contact module.

- The Java Reflection API assumes readability for all reflective operations. This rule assumes that the jdojo.intruder module reads the jdojo.contact module when reflection is used, even if in its module declaration the jdojo.intruder module does not read the jdojo.contact module. If you were to use types from the com.jdojo.contact package at compile time, for example, declaring a variable of the Phone class type, the jdojo.intruder module must read the jdojo.contact module either in its declaration or at the command line.

The output shows that the TestNonOpen class was able to call the public getPhoneNumber() method of the Phone class. However, it threw an exception when it tried to access the private phoneNumber field. Recall that if a type is exported by a module, other modules can use reflection to access the public members of that type. For other named modules to access the private members of the type, the package containing the type must be open. The com.jdojo.contact package is not open. Therefore, the jdojo.intruder module cannot access the private phoneNumber field of the Phone class. You can use the --add-opens option to open the com.jdojo.contact package to the jdojo.intruder module as follows:

```
c:\Java9LanguageFeatures>java
--module-path build\modules\jdojo.contact;build\modules\jdojo.intruder
--add-modules jdojo.contact
--add-opens jdojo.contact/com.jdojo.contact=jdojo.intruder
--module jdojo.intruder/com.jdojo.intruder.TestNonOpen
```

```
Using method reference, Phone: 2222222222
Using private field reference, Phone: 2222222222
```

It is time to see the --illegal-access option in action. You need to write code that will perform illegal access on a member of a JDK class. The java.lang.Long class contains a private instance field named value. Listing 16-8 contains the code for a TestIllegalAccess class that uses deep reflection to access the Long.value field. It accesses the private value field of a Long object three times.

Listing 16-8. A Class Named TestIllegalAccess

```
// TestIllegalAccess.java
package com.jdojo.intruder;

import java.lang.reflect.Field;

public class TestIllegalAccess {
    public static void main(String[] args) throws Exception {
        Long id = 1969L;
        Class<Long> cls = Long.class;
        Field valueField = cls.getDeclaredField("value");
        valueField.setAccessible(true);

        // Read the value in the Long variable using its private field value
        long idValue = (long) valueField.get(id);
        System.out.println("Long.value = " + idValue);

        // Read the value in the Long variable using its private field value
        valueField.set(id, 1968L);
```

```
        // Read the value in the Long variable using its private field value
        idValue = (long) valueField.get(id);
        System.out.println("Long.value = " + idValue);
    }
}
```

The TestIllegalAccess class must be run from the class path to see the effect of the --illegal-access option. Use the following command to compile the class.

```
c:\Java9LanguageFeatures>javac -d build\modules\jdojo.intruder
src\jdojo.intruder\classes\com\jdojo\intruder\TestIllegalAccess.java
```

Run the TestIllegalAccess class using the following command:

```
c:\Java9LanguageFeatures>java --class-path build\modules\jdojo.intruder com.jdojo.intruder.
TestIllegalAccess
```

```
WARNING: An illegal reflective access operation has occurred
WARNING: Illegal reflective access by com.jdojo.intruder.TestIllegalAccess (file:/C:/
Java9LanguageFeatures/build/modules/jdojo.intruder/) to field java.lang.Long.value
WARNING: Please consider reporting this to the maintainers of com.jdojo.intruder.
TestIllegalAccess
WARNING: Use --illegal-access=warn to enable warnings of further illegal reflective access
operations
WARNING: All illegal access operations will be denied in a future release
Long.value = 1969
Long.value = 1968
```

Notice the warnings in the output. The command prints warnings about the illegal access of the JDK internals and allows the access. The following commands run the TestIllegalAccess class using different modes of the --illegal-access option. In the deny mode, the illegal access throws a runtime exception. All other modes allow the access with warnings and other details about the illegal access. Note that using the --illegal-access=permit option has the same effect when you do not use the --illegal-access option.

```
c:\Java9LanguageFeatures>java --illegal-access=deny --class-path build\modules\jdojo.
intruder com.jdojo.intruder.TestIllegalAccess
```

```
Exception in thread "main" java.lang.reflect.InaccessibleObjectException: Unable to make
field private final long java.lang.Long.value accessible: module java.base does not "opens
java.lang" to unnamed module @2f410acf
        at java.base/java.lang.reflect.AccessibleObject.checkCanSetAccessible(AccessibleObj
        ect.java:337)
        at java.base/java.lang.reflect.AccessibleObject.checkCanSetAccessible(AccessibleObj
        ect.java:281)
        at java.base/java.lang.reflect.Field.checkCanSetAccessible(Field.java:176)
        at java.base/java.lang.reflect.Field.setAccessible(Field.java:170)
        at com.jdojo.intruder.TestIllegalAccess.main(TestIllegalAccess.java:11)
        at com.jdojo.intruder.TestIllegalAccess.main(TestIllegalAccess.java:10)
```

```
c:\Java9LanguageFeatures>java --illegal-access=warn --class-path build\modules\jdojo.
intruder com.jdojo.intruder.TestIllegalAccess
```

```
WARNING: Illegal reflective access by com.jdojo.intruder.TestIllegalAccess (file:/C:/
Java9LanguageFeatures/build/modules/jdojo.intruder/) to field java.lang.Long.value
Long.value = 1969
Long.value = 1968
```

```
c:\Java9LanguageFeatures>java --illegal-access=debug --class-path build\modules\jdojo.
intruder com.jdojo.intruder.TestIllegalAccess
```

```
WARNING: Illegal reflective access by com.jdojo.intruder.TestIllegalAccess (file:/C:/
Java9LanguageFeatures/build/modules/jdojo.intruder/) to field java.lang.Long.value
        at com.jdojo.intruder.TestIllegalAccess.main(TestIllegalAccess.java:11)
Long.value = 1969
Long.value = 1968
```

```
c:\Java9LanguageFeatures>java --illegal-access=permit --class-path build\modules\jdojo.
intruder com.jdojo.intruder.TestIllegalAccess
```

```
WARNING: An illegal reflective access operation has occurred
WARNING: Illegal reflective access by com.jdojo.intruder.TestIllegalAccess (file:/C:/
Java9LanguageFeatures/build/modules/jdojo.intruder/) to field java.lang.Long.value
WARNING: Please consider reporting this to the maintainers of com.jdojo.intruder.
TestIllegalAccess
WARNING: Use --illegal-access=warn to enable warnings of further illegal reflective access
operations
WARNING: All illegal access operations will be denied in a future release
Long.value = 1969
Long.value = 1968
```

Using Manifest Attributes of a JAR

An executable JAR is a JAR file that can be used to run a Java application using the `-jar` option:

```
java -jar myapp.jar
```

Here, `myapp.jar` is an executable JAR. An executable JAR in its `MANIFEST.MF` file contains an attribute named `Main-Class` whose value is the fully qualified name of the main class that the `java` command is supposed to run. Recall that there are other kinds of JARs such as modular JARs and multi-release JARs. It does not matter which kind of JAR a JAR is based on; an executable JAR is defined only in the context of the way it is used to launch an application using the `-jar` option.

Suppose an existing application bundled as an executable JAR uses deep reflection to access JDK internal APIs. It worked fine in JDK8. You want to run the executable JAR on JDK9. JDK internal APIs in JDK9 have been encapsulated. Now, you must use the `--add-exports` and `--add-opens` command-line options along with the -jar option to run the same executable JAR. Using new command-line options in JDK9 provides a solution. However, it is little inconvenient for the end users of the executable JAR to use these command-line options. To ease such migrations, two new attributes for the MANIFEST.MF file of executable JARs have been added to JDK9:

- Add-Exports
- Add-Opens

These attributes are added to the main section of the manifest file. They are counterparts of the two command-line options: --add-exports and --add-opens. There is one difference in using these attributes. These attributes export and open packages of modules to all unnamed modules. So, you specify a list of source modules and their packages without specifying target modules as values for these attributes. In other words, in a manifest file, you can export or open a package to all unnamed modules or none, but not to any named modules. Values of these attributes are space-separated lists of slash-separated module-name/package-name pairs. Here is an example:

```
Add-Exports: m1/p1 m2/p2 m3/p3 m1/p1
```

This entry will export the package p1 in module m1, package p2 in module m2, and package p3 in module m3 to unnamed modules at runtime. Rules for parsing manifest files are lenient and allow for duplicates. Notice the duplicate entry m1/p1 in the value.

The syntax for including an Add-Opens attribute in the manifest file is the same as that of the Add-Exports attribute. The following entry in the manifest file will open package p1 in module m1, package p2 in module m2, and package p3 in module m3 to unnamed modules at runtime.

```
Add-Opens: m1/p1 m2/p2 m3/p3
```

■ **Tip** It is important to note that the Add-Exports and Add-Opens manifest attributes are used by the runtime only when the application is run using an executable JAR, which you do by using the -jar option with the java command. In other cases, these attributes are ignored.

Let's create an example that will combine all three previous examples in this chapter. This time, you make the examples work using the Add-Exports and Add-Opens attributes in the manifest file. You create a class named BreakAll, as shown in Listing 16-9. The class simply calls the main() method of the TestNonExported, TestNonOpen, and TestIllegalAccess classes that you have already seen in action.

Listing 16-9. The BreakAll Class

```
// BreakAll.java
package com.jdojo.intruder;

public class BreakAll {
    public static void main(String[] args) {
        try {
            TestNonExported.main(new String[0]);
        } catch(Throwable e) {
            e.printStackTrace();
        }
```

```
        try {
            TestNonOpen.main(new String[0]);
        } catch(Throwable e) {
            e.printStackTrace();
        }

        try {
            TestIllegalAccess.main(new String[0]);
        } catch(Throwable e) {
            e.printStackTrace();
        }
    }
}
```

Listing 16-10 shows the contents of the MANIFEST.MF file. The file includes an Add-Exports entry that exports the com.jdojo.intro package in the jdojo.intro module to all unnamed modules. The file includes an Add-Opens entry that opens the com.jdojo.contact package in the jdojo.contact module and the java.lang package in the java.base module to all unnamed modules.

Listing 16-10. The Contents of the MANIFEST.MF File

```
Manifest-Version: 1.0
Main-Class: com.jdojo.intruder.BreakAll
Add-Exports: jdojo.intro/com.jdojo.intro
Add-Opens: jdojo.address/com.jdojo.address java.base/java.lang
```

The following command will compile all classes used in this example:

```
c:\Java9LanguageFeatures>javac -d build\classes\jdojo.intruder
--module-path build\modules\jdojo.intro
--add-modules jdojo.intro
--add-exports jdojo.intro/com.jdojo.intro=jdojo.intruder
src\jdojo.intruder\classes\module-info.java
src\jdojo.intruder\classes\com\jdojo\intruder\TestNonExported.java
src\jdojo.intruder\classes\com\jdojo\intruder\TestNonOpen.java
src\jdojo.intruder\classes\com\jdojo\intruder\TestIllegalAccess.java
src\jdojo.intruder\classes\com\jdojo\intruder\BreakAll.java
```

The following command creates an executable JAR with all classes for this example:

```
c:\Java9LanguageFeatures>jar --create
--file dist\jdojo.intruder.jar
--manifest=src\jdojo.intruder\classes\META_INF\MANIFEST.MF
-C build\modules\jdojo.intruder .
```

Now run the executable JAR using the following command:

```
c:\Java9LanguageFeatures>java
--module-path build\modules\jdojo.intro;build\modules\jdojo.contact
--add-modules jdojo.intro,jdojo.contact
-jar dist\jdojo.intruder.jar
```

```
Welcome to Java 9!
Using method reference, Phone: 2222222222
Using private field reference, Phone: 2222222222
Long.value = 1969
Long.value = 1968
```

The output indicates that you were able to break the encapsulation of the `jdojo.intro`, `jdojo.contact`, and `java.base` modules using the `Add-Exports` and `Add-Opens` manifest attributes in an executable JAR. Even though this example opened the `java.lang` package of the `java.base` module using the `Add-Opens` manifest attribute, it is not advisable to do so because you can run this example successfully without opening the `java.lang` package. The only difference in the output would be that you would get warnings for illegal access. Getting warnings for illegal access of the JDK internals is preferred because your code may not work in a future release. If you see the warnings, you need to take steps to fix your code.

Try running the `BreakAll` class from the class path, but not using an executable JAR with the `-jar` command:

```
c:\Java9LanguageFeatures>java --module-path build\modules\jdojo.intro;build\modules\jdojo.
contact --add-modules jdojo.intro,jdojo.contact --class-path dist\jdojo.intruder.jar com.
jdojo.intruder.BreakAll
```

```
java.lang.IllegalAccessError: class com.jdojo.intruder.TestNonExported (in unnamed module
@0x9f70c54) cannot access class com.jdojo.intro.Welcome (in module jdojo.intro) because
module jdojo.intro does not export com.jdojo.intro to unnamed module @0x9f70c54
        at com.jdojo.intruder.TestNonExported.main(TestNonExported.java:8)
        at com.jdojo.intruder.BreakAll.main(BreakAll.java:7)
Using method reference, Phone: 2222222222
java.lang.reflect.InaccessibleObjectException: Unable to make field private java.lang.String
com.jdojo.contact.Phone.phoneNumber accessible: module jdojo.contact does not "opens com.
jdojo.contact" to unnamed module @9f70c54
        at java.base/java.lang.reflect.AccessibleObject.checkCanSetAccessible(AccessibleObj
        ect.java:337)
        at java.base/java.lang.reflect.AccessibleObject.checkCanSetAccessible(AccessibleObj
        ect.java:281)
        at java.base/java.lang.reflect.Field.checkCanSetAccessible(Field.java:176)
        at java.base/java.lang.reflect.Field.setAccessible(Field.java:170)
        at com.jdojo.intruder.TestNonOpen.main(TestNonOpen.java:28)
        at com.jdojo.intruder.BreakAll.main(BreakAll.java:13)
WARNING: An illegal reflective access operation has occurred
WARNING: Illegal reflective access by com.jdojo.intruder.TestIllegalAccess (file:/C:/
Java9LanguageFeatures/dist/jdojo.intruder.jar) to field java.lang.Long.value
WARNING: Please consider reporting this to the maintainers of com.jdojo.intruder.
TestIllegalAccess
WARNING: Use --illegal-access=warn to enable warnings of further illegal reflective access
operations
WARNING: All illegal access operations will be denied in a future release
Long.value = 1969
Long.value = 1968
```

The output indicates that the Add-Exports and Add-Opens entries in the manifest were ignored. However, you were able to perform illegal access to the JDK internal with warnings. To fix the errors, you have to resort to the --add-exports and --add-opens command-line options to export and open needed packages to all unnamed modules as follows:

```
c:\Java9LanguageFeatures>java
--module-path build\modules\jdojo.intro;build\modules\jdojo.contact
--add-modules jdojo.intro,jdojo.contact
--add-exports jdojo.intro/com.jdojo.intro=ALL-UNNAMED
--add-opens jdojo.contact/com.jdojo.contact=ALL-UNNAMED
--class-path dist\jdojo.intruder.jar com.jdojo.intruder.BreakAll
```

```
Welcome to Java 9!
Using method reference, Phone: 2222222222
Using private field reference, Phone: 2222222222
WARNING: An illegal reflective access operation has occurred
WARNING: Illegal reflective access by com.jdojo.intruder.TestIllegalAccess (file:/C:/
Java9LanguageFeatures/dist/jdojo.intruder.jar) to field java.lang.Long.value
WARNING: Please consider reporting this to the maintainers of com.jdojo.intruder.
TestIllegalAccess
WARNING: Use --illegal-access=warn to enable warnings of further illegal reflective access
operations
WARNING: All illegal access operations will be denied in a future release
Long.value = 1969
Long.value = 1968
```

Summary

One of the main goals of JDK9 is to encapsulate types and resources in modules and export only those packages whose public types are intended to be accessed by other modules. Sometimes, you may need to break the encapsulation specified by a module to enable white-box testing or use unsupported JDK internal APIs or libraries. This is possible by using non-standard command-line options at compile time and runtime. Another reason for having these options is backward compatibility.

JDK9 provides two command-line options, --add-exports and --add-opens, that let you break encapsulation defined in a module declaration. The --add-exports option lets you export a non-exported package in a module to other modules at compile time and runtime. The --add-opens option lets you open a non-open package in a module to other modules for deep reflection at runtime. The value for these options is of the form <source-module>/<package>=<target-module-list>, where <source-module> is the module that exports or opens <package> to <target-module-list>, which is a comma-separated list of target module names. You can use ALL-UNNAMED as a special value for the list of target modules that exports or opens those packages to all unnamed modules.

There are two new attributes named Add-Exports and Add-Opens that can be used in the main section of the manifest file of an executable JAR. Effects of using these attributes is the same as using the similarly named command-line options, except that these attributes export or open the specified packages to all unnamed modules. The value for these attributes is a space-separated list of slash-separated module-name/package-name pairs. For example, an Add-Opens: java.base/java.lang entry in the main section of a manifest file of an executable JAR will open the java.lang package in the java.base module to all unnamed modules.

During testing and debugging, it is sometimes required that a module read another module where the first module does not use a `requires` statement in its declaration to read the second module. This can be achieved using the `--add-reads` command-line option whose value is specified in the form `<source-module>=<target-module-list>`. The `<source-module>` is the module whose definition is updated to read the list of modules specified in the `<target-module-list>`, which is a comma-separated list of target module names. A special value of `ALL-UNNAMED` for the target module list makes the source module read all unnamed modules.

By default, JDK9 allows illegal reflective access to JDK internals by the code on the class path. This is allowed for backward compatibility. That is, an application performing illegal reflective access on JDK internal that ran on JDK8 will continue to run on JDK9 from the class path. A warning is printed to the standard error on the first use of such an illegal reflective access. You can use the `--illegal-access` for the `java` command to print warnings and stack traces for all such accesses. The option takes one of the following four parameters: `permit`, `deny`, `warn`, and `debug`. The default is `permit`. In a future release, this default behavior will be changed to deny such illegal access and you will need to explicitly use `--illegal-access=permit` to allow such access. Further, in a future release, the `--illegal-access` option itself will be discontinued.

QUESTIONS AND EXERCISES

1. What is breaking module encapsulation?
2. Describe the effects of using the `--add-exports`, `--add-opens`, and `--add-reads` command-line options.
3. What is the difference between using the `--add-exports` and `--add-opens` command-line options and their counterparts, the `Add-Exports` and `Add-Opens` attributes, in the manifest file?
4. Suppose you have a module named `M`, which needs to use types in unnamed modules. Write the command-line option to achieve this.
5. Describe the `--illegal-access` command-line option with its default behaviors in JDK9 and its proposed behaviors in the future JDK.

CHAPTER 17

Reactive Streams

In this chapter, you will learn:

- What a stream is
- What the Reactive Streams initiative is and its specification
- The Reactive Streams API in JDK and how to use it
- How to create publishers, subscribers, and processors using the Java API for Reactive Streams in JDK9

All example programs in this chapter are in the `jdojo.reactive.stream` module, as declared in Listing 17-1.

Listing 17-1. The Declaration of a jdojo.reactive.stream Module

```
// module-info.java
module jdojo.reactive.stream {
    exports com.jdojo.reactive.stream;
}
```

What Is a Stream?

A stream is a sequence of items produced by a producer and consumed by one or more consumers. This producer-consumer model is also known as source/sink model or publisher-subscriber model. I refer to it as a publisher-subscriber model in this chapter. I use the terms *element, item, data item*, and *data* interchangeably to mean a piece of information that is published by a publisher and received by subscribers.

There are several stream-processing mechanisms, the pull model and the push model being the most common. In the push model, the publisher pushes items to the subscriber. In the pull model, the subscriber pulls items from the publisher. These models work great when both the publisher and the subscriber work at the same rate, which is an ideal situation. We consider a few situations when they do not work at the same rate, the issues involved in such situations, and the possible solutions.

When the publisher is faster than the subscriber, the latter must have an unbounded buffer to store fast incoming items or it must drop items it cannot handle. Another solution is to use a strategy called *backpressure* in which the subscriber tells the publisher to slow down and hold the items until the subscriber is ready to process more. Using backpressure ensures that a faster publisher doesn't overwhelm a slower subscriber. Using backpressure may require the publisher to have an unbounded buffer if it keeps producing and storing elements for slower subscribers. The publisher may implement a bounded buffer to store a limited number of elements and may choose to drop them if its buffer is full. Another strategy may be used in which the publisher retries publishing items to the subscriber, which could not accept the items when they were published.

K. Sharan, *Java Language Features*, https://doi.org/10.1007/978-1-4842-3348-1_17

What does the subscriber do when it requests items from the publisher and the items are not available? In a synchronous request, the subscriber must wait, possibly indefinitely, until items are available. If the publisher sends items to the subscriber synchronously and the subscriber processes them synchronously, the publisher must block until the data processing finishes. The solution is to have an asynchronous processing at both ends, where the subscriber may keep working on other tasks after requesting items from the publisher. When more items are ready, the publisher sends them to the subscriber asynchronously.

What Are Reactive Streams?

Reactive Streams started in 2013 as an initiative for providing a standard for *asynchronous* stream processing with *non-blocking backpressure*. It is aimed at solving the problems of processing a stream of items—how do you pass a stream of items from a publisher to a subscriber without requiring the publisher to block or the subscriber to have an unbounded buffer or drop.

The Reactive Streams model is very simple—the subscriber sends an asynchronous request to the publisher for `N` items. The publisher sends `N` or fewer items to the subscriber asynchronously.

■ **Tip** Reactive Streams dynamically switches between the pull model and the push model stream-processing mechanisms. It uses the pull model when the subscriber is slower and uses the push model when the subscriber is faster.

In 2015, a specification and a Java API for handling Reactive Streams were published. Refer to the web page at `http://www.reactive-streams.org/` for more information on Reactive Streams. The Java API for Reactive Streams consists of only four interfaces:

- `Publisher<T>`
- `Subscriber<T>`
- `Subscription`
- `Processor<T,R>`

A *publisher* is a producer of potentially an unbounded number of *sequenced* items. It publishes (or sends) items to its current subscribers based on the demands received from them.

A *subscriber* subscribes to a publisher to receive items. The publisher sends a subscription token to the subscriber. Using the subscription token, the subscriber requests `N` number of items from the publisher. When items are ready, the publisher sends `N` or fewer items to the subscriber. The subscriber can request more items. The publisher may have more than one pending request for items from a subscriber.

A *subscription* represents a token of a subscription of a subscriber to a publisher. The publisher passes this to the subscriber when a request to subscribe is successful. The subscriber uses the subscription to interact with the publisher, such as to request more items or to cancel the subscription.

Figure 17-1 shows a typical sequence of interactions between a publisher and a subscriber. The subscription is not shown in the diagram. The diagram does not show the error and cancellation events.

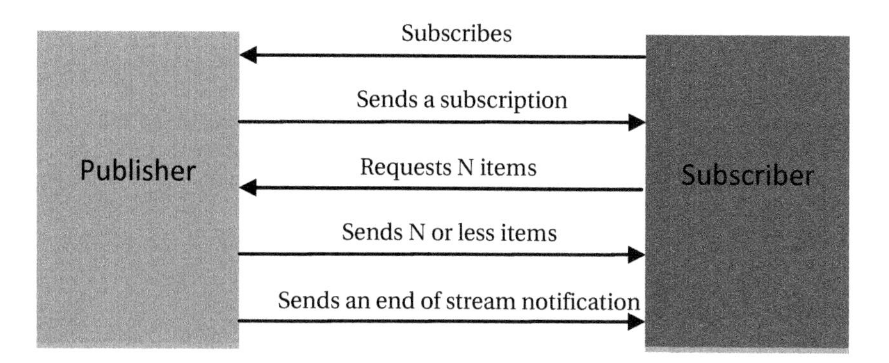

Figure 17-1. *A typical sequence of interactions between a publisher and a subscriber*

A *processor* represents a processing stage that acts as both a subscriber and a publisher. The `Processor` interface extends both the `Publisher` and the `Subscriber` interfaces. It is used to transform items in a publisher-subscriber pipeline. A `Processor<T,R>` subscribes for data elements of type `T`, receives and transforms the data to type `R`, and publishes the transformed data. Figure 17-2 shows the role of a processor as a transformer in a publisher-subscriber pipeline. You can have more than one processor in the pipeline.

Figure 17-2. *Using a processor as a transformer in a publisher-subscriber pipeline*

The Reactive Streams Java API, as provided by the Reactive Streams initiative, is shown in Listing 17-2. Notice that the return type of all methods is `void`. This is because these methods represent either an asynchronous request or an asynchronous event notification. I explain how this API has been incorporated in JDK9 and how to use it in the next section.

Listing 17-2. The Reactive Streams Java API

```
public interface Publisher<T> {
    public void subscribe(Subscriber<? super T> s);
}

public interface Subscriber<T> {
    public void onSubscribe(Subscription s);
    public void onNext(T t);
    public void onError(Throwable t);
    public void onComplete();
}

public interface Subscription {
    public void request(long n);
    public void cancel();
}

public interface Processor<T,R> extends Subscriber<T>, Publisher<R> {
}
```

The Java API for Reactive Streams seems very simple to understand. However, it is not simple to implement. The asynchronous nature of all interactions between publishers and subscribers and handling the backpressure make the implementation complex. As an application developer, you would find it complex to implement these interfaces. Libraries are supposed to provide implementations to support a broad range of use-cases. JDK9 provides a simple implementation of the `Publisher` interface that you can use for simple use-cases or can extend to suit your own needs. RxJava (`https://github.com/ReactiveX/RxJava`) is one of the Java implementations for Reactive Streams.

The Reactive Streams API in JDK9

JDK9 provides a Reactive Streams-compliant API in the `java.util.concurrent` package, which is in the `java.base` module. The API consists of two classes:

- `Flow`
- `SubmissionPublisher<T>`

The `Flow` class is final. It encapsulates the Reactive Streams Java API and a static method. The four interfaces specified by the Reactive Streams Java API are included in the `Flow` class as nested static interfaces:

- `Flow.Processor<T,R>`
- `Flow.Publisher<T>`
- `Flow.Subscriber<T>`
- `Flow.Subscription`

These four interfaces contain the same methods as shown in Listing 17-2. The `Flow` class contains a static method named `defaultBufferSize()` that returns the default size for buffers used by publishers and subscribers. Currently, it returns 256.

The `SubmissionPublisher<T>` class is an implementation class for the `Flow.Publisher<T>` interface. The class implements the `AutoCloseable` interface, so you can manage its instances using a `try-with-resources` block. JDK9 does not provide an implementation class for the `Flow.Subscriber<T>` interface; you will need to implement it yourself. However, the `SubmissionPublisher<T>` class contains a `consume(Consumer<? super T> consumer)` method that you can use to process all items published by this publisher. I explain it in more detail with examples later.

Publisher-Subscriber Interactions

Before you start using the JDK API, it is important to understand the sequence of events that occurs in a typical publisher-subscriber session using Reactive Streams. I include the methods that are used in each event. A publisher can have zero or more subscribers. For the purposes of this discussion, I use only one subscriber.

- You create a publisher and a subscriber and they are instances of the `Flow.Publisher` and `Flow.Subscriber` interfaces, respectively.
- The subscriber attempts to subscribe to the publisher by calling the `subscribe()` method of the publisher. If the subscription is successful, the publisher asynchronously calls the `onSubscribe()` method of the subscriber passing a `Flow.Subscription`. If the attempt to subscribe fails, the `onError()` method of the subscriber is called with an `IllegalStateException` and the publisher-subscriber interaction ends.

- The subscriber sends a request to the publisher for N items by calling the request(N) method of the Subscription. The subscriber can send multiple requests for more items to the publisher without waiting for its earlier requested to be fulfilled.
- The publisher calls the onNext(T item) method of the subscriber up to the number of items requested by the subscriber in all its previous requests—sending an item to the subscriber in each call. If the publisher has no more items to send to the subscriber, the publisher calls the onComplete() method of the subscriber to signal the end of stream, thus ending the publisher-subscriber interaction. If a subscriber requests Long.MAX_VALUE elements, it is effectively an unbounded request and the stream is effectively a push stream.
- If the publisher encounters an error at any time, it calls the onError() method of the subscriber.
- The subscriber can cancel its subscription by calling the cancel() method of its Flow.Subscription. Once a subscription is cancelled, the publisher-subscriber interaction ends. However, it is possible for the subscriber to receive items after canceling its subscription if there were pending requests before requesting the cancellation.

To summarize the previous steps for terminal conditions, once the onComplete() or onError() method is called on the subscriber, the subscriber does not receive any more notifications from the publisher.

After the subscribe() method of the publisher is called, the following sequence of method calls on the subscriber is guaranteed, assuming that the subscriber does not cancel its subscription:

```
onSubscribe onNext* (onError | onComplete)?
```

Here, the * and ? symbols are used as keywords in a regular expression—an * meaning zero or more occurrences and a ? meaning zero or one occurrence.

The first method call on the subscriber is the onSubscribe() method, which is a notification for a successful subscription to the publisher. The onNext() method of the subscriber may be called zero or more times, each call indicating publication of an item. One of the onComplete() and onError() methods may be called zero or one time to indicate a terminate state; one of these methods is called as long as the subscriber does not cancel its subscription.

Creating Publishers

Creating a publisher depends on the implementation class of the Flow.Publisher<T> interface. I cover the use of the SubmissionPublisher<T> class that implements this interface. The class contains the following constructors:

- SubmissionPublisher()
- SubmissionPublisher(Executor executor, int maxBufferCapacity)
- SubmissionPublisher(Executor executor, int maxBufferCapacity, BiConsumer<? super Flow.Subscriber<? super T>,? super Throwable> handler)

A SubmissionPublisher uses the supplied Executor to deliver items to its subscribers. If multiple threads are used to generate items to be published and the number of subscribers can be estimated, you use an Executor with a fixed thread pool, which can be obtained using the newFixedThreadPool(int nThread) static method of the Executors class. Otherwise, you use the default Executor, which is obtained using the commonPool() method of the ForkJoinPool class.

The SubmissionPublisher class uses an independent buffer for each subscriber. The buffer size is specified by the maxBufferCapacity argument in the constructor. The default buffer size is the value returned by the defaultBufferSize() static method of the Flow class, which is 256. If the number of published items exceeds the buffer size of a subscriber, the extra elements will be dropped. You can get the current buffer size of each subscriber using the getMaxBufferCapacity() method of the SubmissionPublisher class.

When a subscriber's method throws an exception, its subscription is cancelled. When the onNext() method of a subscriber throws an exception, the handler specified in the constructor is invoked, before its subscription is cancelled. By default, the handler is null.

The following snippet of code creates a SubmissionPublisher that publishes items of the type Long with all attributes set to their default values:

```
// Create a publisher that can publish Long values
SubmissionPublisher<Long> pub = new SubmissionPublisher<>();
```

The SubmissionPublisher class implements the AutoCloseable interface. Calling its close() method invokes the onComplete() method on its current subscribers. Attempting to publish elements after calling the close() method throws an IllegalStateException.

Publishing Items

The SubmissionPublisher<T> class contains the following methods for publishing elements:

- `int offer(T item, long timeout, TimeUnit unit, BiPredicate<Flow.Subscriber<? super T>,? super T> onDrop)`
- `int offer(T item, BiPredicate<Flow.Subscriber <? super T>,? super T> onDrop)`
- `int submit(T item)`

The submit() method blocks until resources for current subscribers are available to publish the item. Consider a case with the buffer capacity of 10 for each subscriber. A subscriber subscribes with the publisher and does not request any items. The publisher publishes 10 items and buffers them for all subscribers. Attempting to publish another item using the submit() method will block because the subscriber's buffer is full at the publisher's end.

The offer() method is non-blocking. The first version of the method lets you specify a timeout, after which the item is dropped. You can specify a drop handler, which is a BiPredicate. The test() method of the drop handler is called before dropping the item for a subscriber. If the test() method returns true, the item is retried one more time. If the test() method returns false, the item is dropped without a retry. A negative integer returned from the offer() method indicates the number of failed attempts to issue the item to a subscriber; a positive integer indicates an estimate of the maximum number of items submitted but not yet consumed among all current subscribers.

Which method should you use to publish an item: submit() or offer()? It depends on your requirement. If each published item must be issued to all subscribers, submit() method is the option. If you want to wait to publish an item for a specific amount of time with a retry, the offer() method is the option.

A Quick Example

Let's look at a quick example of using a SubmissionPublisher as a publisher. A SubmissionPublisher can publish an element using its submit(T item) method. The following snippet of code generates and publishes five integers (1, 2, 3, 4, and 5), assuming pub is a reference to a SubmissionPublisher object:

```
// Generate and publish 5 integers
LongStream.range(1L, 6L)
          .forEach(pub::submit);
```

You need a subscriber to consume items published by a publisher. The SubmissionPublisher class contains a consume(Consumer<? super T> consumer) method that lets you add a subscriber that wants to process all published items and is not interested in any other notifications such as on error and on completion notifications. The method returns a CompletableFuture<Void> that is completed when the publisher calls the onComplete() method of the subscriber. The following snippet of code adds a Consumer, which is internally added as a subscriber, to the publisher:

```
// Add a subscriber that prints the published items
CompletableFuture<Void> subTask = pub.consume(System.out::println);
```

Listing 17-3 contains the code for a NumberPrinter class, which shows how to use the SubmissionPublisher class to publish integers. A detailed explanation of the example code follows the output of the NumberPrinter class.

Listing 17-3. An Example of a Publisher-Subscriber in Which Five Integers Are Published and Printed

```
// NumberPrinter.java
package com.jdojo.reactive.stream;

import java.util.concurrent.CompletableFuture;
import java.util.concurrent.ExecutionException;
import java.util.concurrent.SubmissionPublisher;
import java.util.stream.LongStream;

public class NumberPrinter {
    public static void main(String[] args) {
        CompletableFuture<Void> subTask = null;

        // Create a publisher
        SubmissionPublisher<Long> pub = new SubmissionPublisher<>();

        // The publisher is closed when the try block exits
        try (pub) {
            // Print the buffer size used for each subscriber
            System.out.println("Subscriber Buffer Size: " + pub.getMaxBufferCapacity());

            // Add a subscriber to the publisher.
            // The subscriber prints the published elements
            subTask = pub.consume(System.out::println);
```

```
            // Generate and publish five integers
            LongStream.range(1L, 6L)
                      .forEach(pub::submit);
        }

        if (subTask != null) {
            try {
                // Wait until the subscriber is complete
                subTask.get();
            } catch (InterruptedException | ExecutionException e) {
                e.printStackTrace();
            }
        }
    }
}
```

```
Subscriber Buffer Size: 256
1
2
3
4
5
```

The main() method declares a variable named subTask to store the reference of the subscriber's task. The subTask.get() method will block until the subscriber is complete.

```
CompletableFuture<Void> subTask = null;
```

A publisher to publish items of the type Long is created and used in a try-with-resources block:

```
SubmissionPublisher<Long> pub = new SubmissionPublisher<>();
try (pub) {
  //...
}
```

The publisher is an instance of the SubmissionPublisher<Long> class. The publisher is closed automatically when the try-with-resources block exits.

The program prints the buffer size of each subscriber that will subscribe to the publisher.

```
// Print the buffer size used for each subscriber
System.out.println("Subscriber Buffer Size: " + pub.getMaxBufferCapacity());
```

A subscriber is added to the publisher using the consume() method. Note that the method lets you specify a Consumer, which is converted to a Subscriber internally. The subscriber will be signaled for each published item. The subscriber simply prints the item it receives.

```
// Add a subscriber to the publisher.
// The subscriber prints the published elements
subTask = pub.consume(System.out::println);
```

It is time to publish the integers. The program generates five integers, 1 to 5, and publishes them using the submit() method of the publisher.

```
// Generate and publish five integers
LongStream.range(1L, 6L)
        .forEach(pub::submit);
```

Published integers are signaled to the subscriber asynchronously. The publisher is closed when the try-with-resources block exits. To keep the program running until the subscriber is finished processing all published items, you must call subTask.get(). If you do not call this method, you may not see the five integers in the output.

Creating Subscribers

To have a subscriber, you need to create a class that implements the Flow.Subscriber<T> interface. How you implement the methods of the interface depends on your needs. In this section, you create a class named SimpleSubscriber that implements the Flow.Subscriber<Long> interface. Listing 17-4 contains the code for this class.

Listing 17-4. A SimpleSubscriber Class That Implements the Flow.Subscriber<Long> Interface

```
// SimpleSubscriber.java
package com.jdojo.reactive.stream;

import java.util.concurrent.Flow;

public class SimpleSubscriber implements Flow.Subscriber<Long> {
    private Flow.Subscription subscription;

    // Subscriber name
    private String name = "Unknown";

    // Maximum number of items to be processed by this subscriber
    private final long maxCount;

    // Keep track of the number of items processed
    private long counter;

    public SimpleSubscriber(String name, long maxCount) {
        this.name = name;
        this.maxCount = maxCount <= 0 ? 1 : maxCount;
    }

    public String getName() {
        return name;
    }

    @Override
    public void onSubscribe(Flow.Subscription subscription) {
        // Save the subscription for later use
        this.subscription = subscription;
```

```
        System.out.printf("%s subscribed with max count %d.%n", name, maxCount);

        // Request all items in one go
        subscription.request(maxCount);
    }

    @Override
    public void onNext(Long item) {
        counter++;

        System.out.printf("%s received %d.%n", name, item);

        if (counter >= maxCount) {
            System.out.printf("Cancelling %s. Processed item count: %d.%n", name, counter);

            // Cancel the subscription
            subscription.cancel();
        }
    }

    @Override
    public void onError(Throwable t) {
        System.out.printf("An error occurred in %s: %s.%n", name, t.getMessage());
    }

    @Override
    public void onComplete() {
        System.out.printf("%s is complete.%n", name);
    }
}
```

An instance of the `SimpleSubscriber` class represents a subscriber, which will have a name and the maximum number of items (`maxCount`) that it wants to process. You need to pass its name and `maxCount` to its constructor. If `maxCount` is less than 1, it is set to 1 in the constructor.

In the `onSubscribe()` method, it stores the subscription passed from the publisher in its instance variable named `subscription`. It prints a message about the subscription and requests all items it can process in one shot. This subscriber effectively uses a push model because, after this request, no more requests will be sent to the publisher for more items. The publisher will push `maxCount` or fewer number of items to this subscriber.

In the `onNext()` method, it increments the `counter` instance variable by 1. The `counter` instance variable keeps track of the number of items this subscriber has received. The method prints a message detailing the received item. If it has received the last item it can handle, it cancels the subscription. After cancelling the subscription, it will not receive any more items from the publisher.

In the `onError()` and `onComplete()` methods, it prints a message about its status.

The following snippet of code creates a `SimpleSubscriber` whose name is `S1` that can process maximum 10 items.

```
SimpleSubscriber sub1 = new SimpleSubscriber("S1", 10);
```

It is time to see the SimpleSubscriber in action. Listing 17-5 contains a complete program. It publishes items periodically. After publishing an item, it waits for 1 to 3 seconds. The duration of the wait is random. A detailed explanation follows the output of this program. The program uses asynchronous processing that may result in a different output.

Listing 17-5. A Publisher-Subscriber Example in Which a Publisher Publishes Items Periodically and Instances of the SimpleSubscriber Subscribe to Those Items

```
// PeriodicPublisher.java
package com.jdojo.reactive.stream;

import java.util.Random;
import java.util.concurrent.Flow.Subscriber;
import java.util.concurrent.SubmissionPublisher;
import java.util.concurrent.TimeUnit;

public class PeriodicPublisher {
    final static int MAX_SLEEP_DURATION = 3;

    // Used to generate sleep time
    final static Random sleepTimeGenerator = new Random();

    public static void main(String[] args) {
        SubmissionPublisher<Long> pub = new SubmissionPublisher<>();

        // Create four subscribers
        SimpleSubscriber sub1 = new SimpleSubscriber("S1", 2);
        SimpleSubscriber sub2 = new SimpleSubscriber("S2", 5);
        SimpleSubscriber sub3 = new SimpleSubscriber("S3", 6);
        SimpleSubscriber sub4 = new SimpleSubscriber("S4", 10);

        // Subscribe three subscribers to the publisher
        pub.subscribe(sub1);
        pub.subscribe(sub2);
        pub.subscribe(sub3);

        // Subscribe the fourth subscriber after 2 seconds
        subscribe(pub, sub4, 2);

        // Start publishing items
        Thread pubThread = publish(pub, 5);

        try {
            // Wait until the publisher is finished
            pubThread.join();
        } catch (InterruptedException e) {
            e.printStackTrace();
        }
    }
```

```
    public static Thread publish(SubmissionPublisher<Long> pub, long count) {
        Thread t = new Thread(() -> {
            for (long i = 1; i <= count; i++) {
                pub.submit(i);
                sleep(i);
            }

            // Close the publisher
            pub.close();
        });

        // Start the thread
        t.start();

        return t;
    }

    private static void sleep(Long item) {
        // Wait for 1 to 3 seconds
        int sleepTime = sleepTimeGenerator.nextInt(MAX_SLEEP_DURATION) + 1;

        try {
            System.out.printf("Published %d. Sleeping for %d sec.%n", item, sleepTime);
            TimeUnit.SECONDS.sleep(sleepTime);
        } catch (InterruptedException e) {
            e.printStackTrace();
        }
    }

    private static void subscribe(SubmissionPublisher<Long> pub, Subscriber<Long> sub,
            long delaySeconds) {

        new Thread(() -> {
            try {
                TimeUnit.SECONDS.sleep(delaySeconds);
                pub.subscribe(sub);
            } catch (InterruptedException e) {
                e.printStackTrace();
            }
        }).start();
    }
}
```

```
S1 subscribed with max count 2.
Published 1. Sleeping for 2 sec.
S3 subscribed with max count 6.
S2 subscribed with max count 5.
S3 received 1.
S1 received 1.
S2 received 1.
```

```
S4 subscribed with max count 10.
Published 2. Sleeping for 2 sec.
S3 received 2.
S1 received 2.
S2 received 2.
Cancelling S1. Processed item count: 2.
S4 received 2.
Published 3. Sleeping for 2 sec.
S4 received 3.
S3 received 3.
S2 received 3.
Published 4. Sleeping for 3 sec.
S4 received 4.
S2 received 4.
S3 received 4.
Published 5. Sleeping for 1 sec.
S4 received 5.
S3 received 5.
S2 received 5.
Cancelling S2. Processed item count: 5.
S3 is complete.
S4 is complete.
```

The PeriodicPublisher class uses two static variables. The MAX_SLEEP_DURATION static variable stores the maximum number of seconds the publisher should wait to publish the next item. It is set to 3. The sleepTimeGenerator static variable stores the reference of a Random object, which is used in the sleep() method to generate the next random duration to wait. The main() method performs the following actions:

- It creates a publisher that is an instance of the SubmissionPublisher<Long> class.
- It creates four subscribers named S1, S2, S3, and S4. Each subscriber can process a different number of items.
- Three subscribers are subscribed immediately.
- The subscriber named S4 subscribes in a separate thread after a minimum delay of two seconds. The subscribe() method of the PeriodicPublisher class takes care of this delayed subscription. Notice in the output that S4 subscribes after one item, 1, was already published and it will not receive that item.
- It calls the publish() method, which starts a new thread to publish five items, which starts the thread and returns the thread reference.
- The main() method calls the join() method of the thread publishing the items, so the program does not terminate before all items are published.
- The publish() method takes care of publishing the five items. It closes the publisher in the end. It calls the sleep() method that makes the current thread sleep for a randomly chosen duration between one and MAX_SLEEP_DURATION seconds.
- Notice in the output that a few subscribers cancel their subscriptions because they receive the specified number of items from the publisher.

Note that this program guarantees that all items will be published before it terminates, but does not guarantee that all subscribers will receive those items. In the output, you see that subscribers received all items published. This happened because the publisher waits for at least one second after publishing the last item, which gives the subscribers enough time, in this small program, to receive and process the last item.

This program did not demonstrate backpressure in action because all subscribers used the push model by requesting items in one shot. You can modify the `SimpleSubscriber` class as an assignment to see backpressure in action:

- Request for one item in the `onSubscribe()` method using the `subscription.request(1)` method.
- In the `onNext()` method, request more items after a delay. The delay should make the subscriber work at the slower rate at which the publisher publishes items.
- You will need to either publish more than 256 items, which is the default buffer used by the publisher for each subscriber, or use a smaller buffer size using another constructor of the `SubmissionPublisher` class. This will force the publisher to have more items published than the subscribers can handle.
- Subscribe the subscribers using a drop handler, so you can see when the publisher sees the backpressure.
- Use the `offer()` method of the `SubmissionPublisher` class to publish items, so the publisher does not wait indefinitely when the subscribers cannot handle more items.

Using Processors

A processor is a subscriber and a publisher at the same time. To use a processor, you need a class that implements the `Flow.Processor<T,R>` interface, where `T` is the subscribed item type and `R` is the published item type. In this section, I create a simple processor that filters items based on a `Predicate<T>`. The processor subscribes to a publisher that publishes six integers—1, 2, 3, 4, 5, and 6. A subscriber subscribes to the processor. The processor receives items from its publisher and republishes the same items if they pass the criterion specified by a `Predicate<T>`. Listing 17-6 contains the code for the `FilterProcessor<T>` class whose instances act as processors.

Listing 17-6. A Processor That Filters Items Based on a Predicate Before Republishing

```
// FilterProcessor.java
package com.jdojo.reactive.stream;

import java.util.concurrent.Flow;
import java.util.concurrent.Flow.Processor;
import java.util.concurrent.SubmissionPublisher;
import java.util.function.Predicate;

public class FilterProcessor<T> extends SubmissionPublisher<T> implements Processor<T, T> {
    private final Predicate<? super T> filter;

    public FilterProcessor(Predicate<? super T> filter) {
        this.filter = filter;
    }
```

```
    @Override
    public void onSubscribe(Flow.Subscription subscription) {
        // Request an unbounded number of items
        subscription.request(Long.MAX_VALUE);
    }

    @Override
    public void onNext(T item) {
        // If the item passes the filter publish it. Otherwise, no action is needed.
        System.out.println("Filter received: " + item);

        if (filter.test(item)) {
            this.submit(item);
        }
    }

    @Override
    public void onError(Throwable t) {
        // Pass the onError message to all subscribers asynchronously
        this.getExecutor().execute(() -> this.getSubscribers()
                                            .forEach(s -> s.onError(t)));
    }

    @Override
    public void onComplete() {
        System.out.println("Filter is complete.");

        // Close this publisher, so all its subscribers will receive a onComplete message
        this.close();
    }
}
```

The `FilterProcessor<T>` class inherits from the `SubmissionPublisher<T>` class and implements the `Flow.Processor<T,T>` interface. A processor has to be a publisher as well as a subscriber. I inherited the class from the `SubmissionPublisher<T>` class, so I don't have to write code to make it work as a publisher. The class implements all methods of the `Processor<T,T>` interface, so it will receive and publish the same type of items.

The constructor accepts a `Predicate<? super T>` and stores it in an instance variable name `filter`, which will be used in the `onNext()` method to filter items.

The `onNext()` method applies the filter. If the filter returns `true`, it republishes the item to its subscribers. The class inherits the `submit()` method, used for republishing items, from its superclass `SubmissionPublisher`.

The `onError()` method republishes the error to its subscribers asynchronously. It uses the `getExecutor()` and `getSubscribers()` methods of the `SubmissionPublisher` class, which return the `Executor` and a list of current subscribers. The `Executor` is used to publish messages to current subscribers asynchronously.

The `onComplete()` method closes the publisher part of the processor, which will send a `onComplete` message to all its subscribers.

Let's see this processor in action. Listing 17-7 contains the code for the `ProcessorTest` class. You may get a different output because several asynchronous steps are involved in this program. A detailed explanation of the program follows the program's output.

Listing 17-7. Using a Processor in a Publisher-Subscriber Chain

```
// ProcessorTest.java
package com.jdojo.reactive.stream;

import java.util.concurrent.CompletableFuture;
import java.util.concurrent.SubmissionPublisher;
import java.util.concurrent.TimeUnit;
import java.util.stream.LongStream;

public class ProcessorTest {
    public static void main(String[] args) {
        CompletableFuture<Void> subTask = null;

        // The publisher is closed when the try block exits
        try (SubmissionPublisher<Long> pub = new SubmissionPublisher<>()) {
            // Create a Subscriber
            SimpleSubscriber sub = new SimpleSubscriber("S1", 10);

            // Create a processor
            FilterProcessor<Long> filter = new FilterProcessor<>(n -> n % 2 == 0);

            // Subscribe the filter to the publisher and a subscriber to the filter
            pub.subscribe(filter);
            filter.subscribe(sub);

            // Generate and publish 6 integers
            LongStream.range(1L, 7L)
                      .forEach(pub::submit);
        }

        try {
            // Sleep for two seconds to let subscribers finish handling all items
            TimeUnit.SECONDS.sleep(2);
        } catch (InterruptedException e) {
            e.printStackTrace();
        }
    }
}
```

```
S1 subscribed with max count 10.
Filter received: 1
Filter received: 2
Filter received: 3
S1 received 2.
Filter received: 4
S1 received 4.
Filter received: 5
Filter received: 6
Filter is complete.
S1 received 6.
S1 is complete.
```

The main() method of the ProcessorTest class creates a publisher that will publish six integers—1, 2, 3, 4, 5, and 6. The method does a number of things:

- It creates a publisher and uses it in a try-with-resources block, so it will be closed automatically when the try block exits.
- It creates a subscriber that's an instance of the SimpleSubscriber class. The subscriber is named S1 and can handle a maximum of 10 items.
- It creates a processor that's an instance of the FilterProcessor<Long> class. A Predicate<Long> is passed that lets the processor republish even integers and discard odd ones.
- The processor is subscribed to the publisher and the simple subscriber is subscribed to the processor. This completes the publisher-subscriber pipeline—publisher-to-filter-to-subscriber.
- At the end of the first try block, the code generates the integers from 1 to 6 and publishes them using the publisher.
- At the end of the main() method, the program waits for two seconds to make sure that the filter and the subscriber get a chance to process their events. If you remove this logic, your program may not print anything. You had to include this logic because all events are processed asynchronously. The publisher will be done sending all notifications to the filter when the first try block exits. However, the filter and the subscriber need some time to receive and process those notifications.

Summary

A *stream* is a sequence of elements produced by a producer and consumed by one or more consumers. This producer-consumer model is also known as source/sink model or publisher-subscriber model.

There are several stream-processing mechanisms, the pull model and the push model being the most common. In the push model, the publisher pushes the stream of data to the subscriber. In the pull model, the subscriber pulls the data from the publisher. These models have problems when the two ends do not work at the same rate. The solution is to provide a stream that adapts to the speed of both the publisher and subscriber. A strategy known as *backpressure* is used in which the subscriber notifies the publisher as to how many items it can handle and the publisher sends only those many or fewer items to the subscriber.

Reactive Streams started in 2013 as an initiative for providing a standard for *asynchronous* stream processing with *non-blocking backpressure*. It is aimed at solving the problems with processing a stream of elements—how to pass a stream of elements from a publisher to a subscriber without requiring the publisher to block or the subscriber to have an unbounded buffer or drop. The Reactive Streams model dynamically switches between the pull model and the push model stream-processing mechanisms. It uses the pull model when the subscriber is slower and uses the push model when the subscriber is faster.

In 2015, a specification and Java API for handling Reactive Streams were published. The Java API for Reactive Streams consists of four interfaces: Publisher<T>, Subscriber<T>, Subscription, and Processor<T,R>.

A *publisher* publishes items to its subscribers based on the demands received from them. A *subscriber* subscribes to a publisher to receive items. The publisher sends a subscription token to the subscriber. Using the subscription token, the subscriber requests N number of items from the publisher. When the items are ready, the publisher sends N or fewer items to the subscriber. The subscriber can request more items.

JDK9 provides a Reactive Streams-compliant API in the java.util.concurrent package, which is in the java.base module. The API consists of two classes: Flow and SubmissionPublisher<T>.

The `Flow` class encapsulates the Reactive Streams Java API. The four interfaces specified by the Reactive Streams Java API are included in the `Flow` class as nested static interfaces: `Flow.Processor<T,R>`, `Flow.Publisher<T>`, `Flow.Subscriber<T>`, and `Flow.Subscription`.

EXERCISES

1. What are Reactive Streams? What are pull and push models in Reactive Streams?
2. Describe the four components—publisher, subscriber, subscription, and processor—of Reactive Streams.
3. List the fully qualified names of the four interfaces of the Reactive Streams API.
4. Is the following statement true or false?

   The Reactive Streams API supports asynchronous processing of stream of data.
5. Which method on the subscriber is called when the subscriber's subscription with a publisher succeeds?
6. Which method on the subscriber is called when the subscriber's subscription with a publisher fails?
7. How does a subscriber requests 200 items from a publisher?
8. Which method on the subscriber is called when it receives an item from its publisher?
9. How does a subscriber cancel its subscription with a publisher? Is it possible for a subscriber to receive more items from its publisher after it cancels its subscription?
10. What is the fully qualified name of the implementation class for the `java.util.concurrent.Flow.Publisher<T>` interface?

CHAPTER 18

Stack Walking

In this chapter, you will learn:

- What stacks and stack frames are
- How to traverse a thread's stack before JDK9
- How to traverse a thread's stack in JDK9 using the Stack-Walking API
- How to know about the class of a caller of a method in JDK9

All example programs in this chapter are a member of a `jdojo.stackwalker` module, as declared in Listing 18-1.

Listing 18-1. The Declaration of a jdojo.stackwalker Module

```
// module-info.java
module jdojo.stackwalker {
    exports com.jdojo.stackwalker;
}
```

What Is a Stack?

Each thread in a JVM has a *private* JVM stack that is created at the same time the thread is created. The stack is a Last-In-First-Out (LIFO) data structure. A stack stores frames. A new frame is created and pushed to the top of the stack each time a method is invoked. A frame is destroyed (popped out of stack) when the method invocation completes. Each frame on a stack contains its own array of local variables, its own operand stack, return value, and a reference to the runtime constant pool of the class of the current method. A specific implementation of the JVM may extend a frame to store more pieces of information.

A frame on a JVM stack represents a Java method invocation in a given thread. In a given thread, only one frame is active at any point. The active frame is known as the *current frame* and its method is known as the *current method*. The class that defines the current method is known as the *current class*. A frame is no longer the current frame when its method invokes another method—a new frame is pushed to the stack, the executing method becomes the current method, and the new frame becomes the current frame. When the method returns, the old frame becomes the current frame again. For more details on JVM stack and frames, refer to the Java Virtual Machine Specification at `https://docs.oracle.com/javase/specs/jvms/se9/html/index.html`.

K. Sharan, *Java Language Features*, https://doi.org/10.1007/978-1-4842-3348-1_18

■ **Tip** If a JVM supports native methods, a thread also contains a native method stack that contains a native method frame for each native method invocation.

Figure 18-1 shows two threads and their JVM stacks. The JVM stack for the first thread contains four frames and the stack of the second thread contains three frames. Frame 4 is the active frame in Thread-1 and Frame 3 is the active frame in Thread-2.

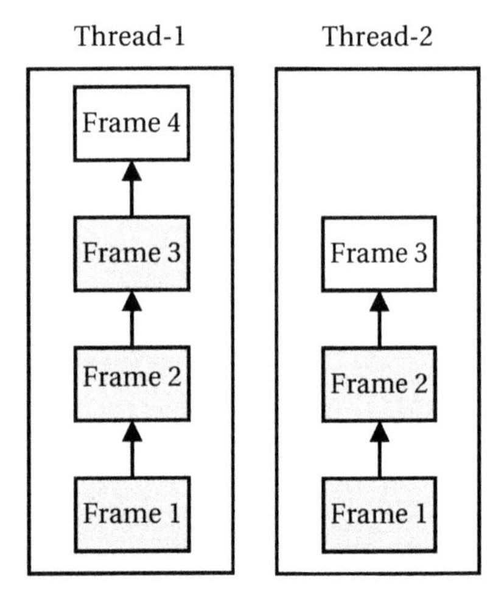

Figure 18-1. *Arrangements of threads and their private JVM stacks in a JVM*

What Is Stack Walking?

Stack walking (or stack traversal) is the process of traversing the stack frames of a thread and inspecting the frames' contents. Starting from Java 1.4, you can get a snapshot of the stack of a thread and get details about each frame, such as the class names and method names where the method invocation occurs, the source file name, the line number in the source file, etc. Classes and interfaces used for stack walking are part of the Stack-Walking API.

Stack Walking in JDK8

Before JDK9, it was possible to traverse all frames in a thread's stack using the following classes in the `java.lang` package:

- `Throwable`
- `Thread`
- `StackTraceElement`

An instance of the `StackTraceElement` class represents a stack frame. The `getStrackTrace()` method of the `Throwable` class returns a `StackTraceElement[]` that contains the frames of the current thread's stack. The `getStrackTrace()` method of the `Thread` class returns a `StackTraceElement[]` that contains the frames of the thread's stack. The first element of the array is the top frame in the stack, which represents the last method invocation in the sequence. Some implementations of JVM may omit some frames in the returned array. The `StackTraceElement` class contains the following methods that returns the details of the method invocation represented by the frame:

- `String getClassLoaderName()`
- `String getClassName()`
- `String getFileName()`
- `int getLineNumber()`
- `String getMethodName()`
- `String getModuleName()`
- `String getModuleVersion()`
- `boolean isNativeMethod()`

■ **Tip** The `getModuleName()`, `getModuleVersion()`, and `getClassLoaderName()` methods were added to this class in JDK9.

Most of the methods in the `StackTraceElement` class have intuitive names, for example, the `getMethodName()` method returns the name of the method whose invocation is represented by this frame. The `getFileName()` method returns the name of the source file that contains the method invocation code and the `getLineNumber()` returns the method invocation code's line number in the source file.

The following snippet of code shows how to inspect the stack of the current thread using the `Throwable` and `Thread` classes:

```
// Using the Throwable class
StackTraceElement[] frames = new Throwable().getStackTrace();

// Using the Thread class
StackTraceElement[] frames = Thread.currentThread()
                                   .getStackTrace();
// Process the frames here...
```

Listing 18-2 contains the code for a class named `LegacyStackWalk`. The output was generated when the class was run in JDK8.

Listing 18-2. Traversing a Thread's Stack Before JDK9

```
// LegacyStackWalk.java
package com.jdojo.stackwalker;

import java.lang.reflect.InvocationTargetException;

public class LegacyStackWalk {
    public static void main(String[] args) {
        m1();
    }
```

```
    public static void m1() {
        m2();
    }

    public static void m2() {
        // Call m3() directly
        System.out.println("\nWithout using reflection: ");
        m3();

        // Call m3() using reflection
        try {
            System.out.println("\nUsing reflection: ");
            LegacyStackWalk.class
                    .getMethod("m3")
                    .invoke(null);
        } catch (NoSuchMethodException
                | InvocationTargetException
                | IllegalAccessException
                | SecurityException e) {
            e.printStackTrace();
        }
    }

    public static void m3() {
        // Prints the call stack details
        StackTraceElement[] frames = Thread.currentThread()
                .getStackTrace();

        for (StackTraceElement frame : frames) {
            System.out.println(frame.toString());
        }
    }
}
```

```
Without using reflection:
java.lang.Thread.getStackTrace(Thread.java:1552)
com.jdojo.stackwalker.LegacyStackWalk.m3(LegacyStackWalk.java:37)
com.jdojo.stackwalker.LegacyStackWalk.m2(LegacyStackWalk.java:18)
com.jdojo.stackwalker.LegacyStackWalk.m1(LegacyStackWalk.java:12)
com.jdojo.stackwalker.LegacyStackWalk.main(LegacyStackWalk.java:8)

Using reflection:
java.lang.Thread.getStackTrace(Thread.java:1552)
com.jdojo.stackwalker.LegacyStackWalk.m3(LegacyStackWalk.java:37)
sun.reflect.NativeMethodAccessorImpl.invoke0(Native Method)
sun.reflect.NativeMethodAccessorImpl.invoke(NativeMethodAccessorImpl.java:62)
sun.reflect.DelegatingMethodAccessorImpl.invoke(DelegatingMethodAccessorImpl.java:43)
java.lang.reflect.Method.invoke(Method.java:498)
com.jdojo.stackwalker.LegacyStackWalk.m2(LegacyStackWalk.java:25)
com.jdojo.stackwalker.LegacyStackWalk.m1(LegacyStackWalk.java:12)
com.jdojo.stackwalker.LegacyStackWalk.main(LegacyStackWalk.java:8)
```

The main() method of the LegacyStackWalk class calls the m1() method, which calls the m2() method. The m2() method calls the m3() method twice—once directly and once using reflection. The m3() method gets a snapshot of the stack for the current thread using the getStrackTrace() method of the Throwable class and prints the frame details using the toString() method of the StackTraceElement class. You could have used methods of this class to get the same information for each frame. When you run the LegacyStackWalk class in JDK9, the output includes the module name and module version at the beginning of each line. The output using JDK9 is as follows:

```
Without using reflection:
java.base/java.lang.Thread.getStackTrace(Thread.java:1654)
com.jdojo.stackwalker/com.jdojo.stackwalker.LegacyStackWalk.m3(LegacyStackWalk.java:37)
com.jdojo.stackwalker/com.jdojo.stackwalker.LegacyStackWalk.m2(LegacyStackWalk.java:18)
com.jdojo.stackwalker/com.jdojo.stackwalker.LegacyStackWalk.m1(LegacyStackWalk.java:12)
com.jdojo.stackwalker/com.jdojo.stackwalker.LegacyStackWalk.main(LegacyStackWalk.java:8)

Using reflection:
java.base/java.lang.Thread.getStackTrace(Thread.java:1654)
com.jdojo.stackwalker/com.jdojo.stackwalker.LegacyStackWalk.m3(LegacyStackWalk.java:37)
java.base/jdk.internal.reflect.NativeMethodAccessorImpl.invoke0(Native Method)
java.base/jdk.internal.reflect.NativeMethodAccessorImpl.invoke(NativeMethodAccessorImpl.
java:62)
java.base/jdk.internal.reflect.DelegatingMethodAccessorImpl.invoke(DelegatingMethodAccessor
Impl.java:43)
java.base/java.lang.reflect.Method.invoke(Method.java:538)
com.jdojo.stackwalker/com.jdojo.stackwalker.LegacyStackWalk.m2(LegacyStackWalk.java:25)
com.jdojo.stackwalker/com.jdojo.stackwalker.LegacyStackWalk.m1(LegacyStackWalk.java:12)
com.jdojo.stackwalker/com.jdojo.stackwalker.LegacyStackWalk.main(LegacyStackWalk.java:8)
```

Drawbacks in Stack Walking

Prior to JDK9, the Stack-Walking API had several drawbacks:

- It was not efficient. The getStrackTrace() method of the Throwable class returned a snapshot of the entire stack. There was no way to get just a few top frames in the stack.
- The frames contained method names and class names, not the class reference.
- The JVM specification allowed a VM implementation to omit some frames in the stack for performance reasons. So, if you were interested in inspecting the entire stack, you could not do so if the VM hid some frames.
- Many APIs—in JDK and other libraries—are caller-sensitive. They function based on the caller's class. In the existing APIs, there was no easy and efficient way to get the caller's class reference. Such APIs depended on using the JDK internal API—the getCallerClass() static method of the sun.reflect.Reflection class.
- There was no easy way to filter out stack frames of specific implementation classes.

These drawbacks in the existing API led to a new Stack-Walking API in JDK9, which I explain in the next section.

Stack Walking in JDK9

JDK9 introduced a new Stack-Walking API, which consists of a single class named `StackWalker` in the `java.lang` package. The class provides easy and efficient stack walking. It provides a sequential stream of stack frames for the current thread. The stack frames are reported in order, from the top-most frame where the stack was generated to the bottom-most frame. The `StackWalker` class is very efficient because it evaluates the stack frames lazily. It also contains a convenience method to get the reference of the caller's class. The `StackWalker` class consists of the following members:

- The `StackWalker.Option` nested enum
- The `StackWalker.StackFrame` nested interface
- Methods to get an instance of the `StackWalker` class
- Methods to process stack frames
- A method to get the caller's class

I explain each component of the `StackWalker` class and their uses in subsequent sections in detail.

Specifying Stack-Walking Options

You can configure a `StackWalker` by specifying zero or more options. An option is one of the constants of the `StackWalker.Option` enum. The constants are:

- `RETAIN_CLASS_REFERENCE`
- `SHOW_HIDDEN_FRAMES`
- `SHOW_REFLECT_FRAMES`

If the `RETAIN_CLASS_REFERENCE` option is specified, the frames returned by the `StackWalker` will contain the reference of the `Class` object of the declaring class of the method represented by the frame. You also need to specify this option if you want to get the `Class` object's reference of the caller of a method. By default, this option is absent.

By default, implementation specific and reflection frames are not included in the stream of frames returned by the `StackWalker` class. Use the `SHOW_HIDDEN_FRAMES` option to include all hidden frames.

If the `SHOW_REFLECT_FRAMES` option is specified, the stream of frames returned by the `StackWalker` class includes the reflection frames. Using this option may still hide the implementation specific frames, which you can show using the `SHOW_HIDDEN_FRAMES` option.

I show how to use these options and their effects when I explain how to create instances of the `StackWalker` class in a subsequent section.

Representing a Stack Frame

Prior to JDK9, an instance of the `StackTraceElement` class was used to represent a stack frame. The Stack-Walking API in JDK9 uses an instance of the `StackWalker.StackFrame` interface to represent a stack frame.

■ **Tip** There are no concrete implementation class of the `StackWalker.StackFrame` interface for you to use directly. The Stack-Walking API in the JDK provides instances of the interface when you retrieve stack frames.

The StackWalker.StackFrame interface contains the following methods, most of which are the same as in the StackTraceElement class:

- int getByteCodeIndex()
- String getClassName()
- Class<?> getDeclaringClass()
- String getFileName()
- int getLineNumber()
- String getMethodName()
- boolean isNativeMethod()
- StackTraceElement toStackTraceElement()

In a class file, each method is described using a structure named method_info. The method_info structure contains an attribute table that holds a variable-length attribute named Code. The Code attribute contains an array named code, which holds the bytecode instructions of the method. The getByteCodeIndex() method returns the index to the code array in the Code attribute of the method containing the execution point represented by this frame. It returns -1 for native methods. For more information on the code array and Code attribute, refer to section 4.7.3 of the Java Virtual Specification at https://docs.oracle.com/javase/specs/jvms/se9/html/.

How do you work with the code array of a method? As an application developer, you will not use the bytecode index for an execution point in a method. The JDK does support reading a class file and all its attributes using internal APIs. You can see the bytecode index of each instruction in a method using the javap tool, which is located in JDK_HOME\bin directory. You will need to use the -c option with javap to print the code array of methods. The following command shows the code array for all methods in the LegacyStackWalk class:

```
C:\Java9LanguageFeatures>javap -c build\modules\jdojo.stackwalker\com\jdojo\stackwalker\
LegacyStackWalk.class
```

```
Compiled from "LegacyStackWalk.java"
public class com.jdojo.stackwalker.LegacyStackWalk {
  public com.jdojo.stackwalker.LegacyStackWalk();
    Code:
       0: aload_0
       1: invokespecial #1                  // Method java/lang/Object."<init>":()V
       4: return

  public static void main(java.lang.String[]);
    Code:
       0: invokestatic  #2                  // Method m1:()V
       3: return

  public static void m1();
    Code:
       0: invokestatic  #3                  // Method m2:()V
       3: return
```

```
  public static void m2();
    Code:
       0: getstatic     #4                  // Field java/lang/System.out:Ljava/io/
PrintStream;
       3: ldc           #5                  // String \nWithout using reflection:
       5: invokevirtual #6                  // Method java/io/PrintStream.println:(Ljava/
                                            lang/String;)V
       8: invokestatic  #7                  // Method m3:()V
...
      32: anewarray     #13                 // class java/lang/Object
      35: invokevirtual #14                 // Method java/lang/reflect/Method.
                                            invoke:(Ljava/lang/Object;[Ljava/lang/Object;)
                                            Ljava/lang/Object;
...
  public static void m3();
    Code:
       0: invokestatic  #20                 // Method java/lang/Thread.currentThread:()
                                            Ljava/lang/Thread;
       3: invokevirtual #21                 // Method java/lang/Thread.getStackTrace:()
                                            [Ljava/lang/StackTraceElement;
...
}
```

When you take a snapshot of the call stack in method m3(), the outputs in the boldface font represent the execution points in each method—main(), m1(), m2(), and m3(). Note that the m2() method calls m3() twice. For the first call, the bytecode index is 8 and, for the second call, it is 35.

The getDeclaringClass() method returns the reference of the Class object of the class declaring the method represented by the frame. It throws an UnsupportedOperationException if this StackWalker is not configured with the RETAIN_CLASS_REFERENCE option.

The toStackTraceElement() method returns an instance of the StackTraceElement class representing the same stack frame. This method is handy if you want to use the JDK9 API to obtain a StackWalker.StackFrame, but keep using your old code that uses the StackTraceElement class to analyze the frame.

Obtaining a StackWalker Class

The StackWalker class contains the following static factory methods that return a StackWalker instance:

- StackWalker getInstance()
- StackWalker getInstance (StackWalker.Option option)
- static StackWalker getInstance (Set<StackWalker.Option> options)
- static StackWalker getInstance (Set<StackWalker.Option> options, int estimateDepth)

You can configure a StackWalker differently using different versions of the getInstance() method. The default configuration is to exclude all hidden frames and not to retain class references. Versions that let you specify StackWalker.Option are configured using those options.

The estimateDepth argument is a hint that indicates the estimated number of stack frames this StackWalker is expected to traverse, so the size of an internal buffer may be optimized.

The following snippet of code creates four instances of the StackWalker class with different configurations:

```
import java.util.Set;
import static java.lang.StackWalker.Option.*;
...

// Get a StackWalker with the default configuration.
// It will exclude all hidden frames and retain no class references
StackWalker sw1 = StackWalker.getInstance();

// Get a StackWalker that shows reflection frames
StackWalker sw2 = StackWalker.getInstance(SHOW_REFLECT_FRAMES);

// Get a StackWalker that shows all hidden frames
StackWalker sw3 = StackWalker.getInstance(SHOW_HIDDEN_FRAMES);

// Get a StackWalker that shows reflection frames and retains class references
StackWalker sw4
        = StackWalker.getInstance(Set.of(SHOW_REFLECT_FRAMES, RETAIN_CLASS_REFERENCE));
```

■ **Tip** A StackWalker is thread-safe and reusable. Multiple threads can use the same instance to traverse their own stacks.

The next section explains how to use a StackWalker to walk through stack frames.

Walking the Stack

It is time to traverse stack frames of a thread. The StackWalker class contains two methods that let you traverse the stack of the *current thread*:

- void forEach(Consumer<? super StackWalker.StackFrame> action)
- <T> T walk(Function<? super Stream<StackWalker.StackFrame>,? extends T> function)

Use the forEach() method if you need to traverse the entire stack. The specified Consumer will be supplied with one frame at a time from the stack—starting with the top-most frame. The following snippet of code prints the details of each frame returned by a StackWalker:

```
// Prints the details of all stack frames of the current thread
StackWalker.getInstance()
           .forEach(System.out::println);
```

Use the walk() method if you want to customize the stack traversal such as by using filters and maps. The walk() method takes a Function, which accepts a Stream<StackWalker.StackFrame> as an argument and can return any type of object. The StackWalker will create the stream of stack frames and pass it to your function. When the function completes, the StackWalker will close the stream. The stream passed to the walk() method can be traversed only once. Attempting to traverse the stream second time throws an IllegalStateException. The following snippet of code uses the walk() method to traverse the entire stack, printing the details of each frame. This snippet of code does the same thing that the previous snippet of code did using the forEach() method.

```
// Prints the details of all stack frames of the current thread
StackWalker.getInstance()
           .walk(s -> {
               s.forEach(System.out::println);
               return null;
           });
```

■ **Tip** The forEach() method of the StackWalker is used to process stack frames one at a time, whereas the walk() method is used to process the entire stack as a stream of frames. You can use the walk() method to simulate the functionality of the forEach() method, but not vice versa.

You might wonder why the walk() method does not return a stream of stack frames instead of passing the stream to your function. Not returning a stream of stack frames from the method is intentional. The elements of the stream are evaluated lazily. Once the stream of stack frames is created, the JVM is free to reorganize the stack and there is no definite way to detect that the stack has changed while you are still holding the reference to its stream. This is the reason that creation and closing of the stream of stack frames are controlled by the StackWalker class.

As the Streams API is extensive, so is the use of the walk() method. I show a few of its sample uses before showing a complete example. The following snippet of code gets a snapshot of the stack frames of the current thread in a List.

```
import java.lang.StackWalker.StackFrame;
import java.util.List;
import static java.util.stream.Collectors.toList;
...
List<StackFrame> frames = StackWalker.getInstance()
                              .walk(s -> s.collect(toList()));
```

The following snippet of code collects the string form of all stack frames of the current thread in a List—excluding frames that represent methods whose names start with m2:

```
import java.util.List;
import static java.util.stream.Collectors.toList;
...
List<String> list = StackWalker.getInstance()
  .walk(s -> s.filter(f -> !f.getMethodName().startsWith("m2"))
              .map(f -> f.toString())
              .collect(toList())
       );
```

The following snippet of code collects the string form of all stack frames of the current thread in a List—excluding frames that represent methods whose declaring class name ends with Test:

```
import static java.lang.StackWalker.Option.RETAIN_CLASS_REFERENCE;
import java.util.List;
import static java.util.stream.Collectors.toList;
```

```
...
List<String> list = StackWalker
    .getInstance(RETAIN_CLASS_REFERENCE)
    .walk(s -> s.filter(f -> !f.getDeclaringClass()
                              .getName().endsWith("Test"))
                .map(f -> f.toString())
                .collect(toList())
          );
```

The following snippet of code collects the entire stack in a string—separating each frame with a platform specific line-separator:

```
import static java.util.stream.Collectors.joining;
...
String stackStr = StackWalker.getInstance()
 .walk(s -> s.map(f -> f.toString())
             .collect(joining(System.getProperty("line.separator")
       )));
```

Listing 18-3 contains a complete program to show the use of the `StackWalker` class and its `walk()` method. Its `main()` method calls the `m1()` method twice—each time passing a different set of options for the `StackWalker`. The `m2()` method uses reflection to call the `m3()` method, which prints the stack frame details. The first time, the reflection frames are hidden and the class references are not available.

Listing 18-3. Using a StackWalker to Traverse Stack Frames of the Current Thread

```
// StackWalking.java
package com.jdojo.stackwalker;

import java.lang.StackWalker.Option;
import static java.lang.StackWalker.Option.RETAIN_CLASS_REFERENCE;
import static java.lang.StackWalker.Option.SHOW_REFLECT_FRAMES;
import java.lang.StackWalker.StackFrame;
import java.lang.reflect.InvocationTargetException;
import java.util.Set;
import java.util.stream.Stream;

public class StackWalking {
    public static void main(String[] args) {
        m1(Set.of());

        System.out.println();

        // Retain class references and show reflection frames
        m1(Set.of(RETAIN_CLASS_REFERENCE, SHOW_REFLECT_FRAMES));
    }

    public static void m1(Set<Option> options) {
        m2(options);
    }
```

```
    public static void m2(Set<Option> options) {
        // Call m3() using reflection
        try {
            System.out.println("Using StackWalker Options: " + options);
            StackWalking.class
                    .getMethod("m3", Set.class)
                    .invoke(null, options);
        } catch (NoSuchMethodException | InvocationTargetException
                | IllegalAccessException | SecurityException e) {
            e.printStackTrace();
        }
    }

    public static void m3(Set<Option> options) {
        // Prints the call stack details
        StackWalker.getInstance(options)
                .walk(StackWalking::processStack);
    }

    public static Void processStack(Stream<StackFrame> stack) {
        stack.forEach(frame -> {
            int bci = frame.getByteCodeIndex();
            String className = frame.getClassName();
            Class<?> classRef = null;
            try {
                classRef = frame.getDeclaringClass();
            } catch (UnsupportedOperationException e) {
                // No action to take
            }

            String fileName = frame.getFileName();
            int lineNumber = frame.getLineNumber();
            String methodName = frame.getMethodName();
            boolean isNative = frame.isNativeMethod();

            StackTraceElement sfe = frame.toStackTraceElement();

            System.out.printf("Native Method=%b", isNative);
            System.out.printf(", Byte Code Index=%d", bci);
            System.out.printf(", Module Name=%s", sfe.getModuleName());
            System.out.printf(", Module Version=%s", sfe.getModuleVersion());
            System.out.printf(", Class Name=%s", className);
            System.out.printf(", Class Reference=%s", classRef);
            System.out.printf(", File Name=%s", fileName);
            System.out.printf(", Line Number=%d", lineNumber);
            System.out.printf(", Method Name=%s.%n", methodName);
        });

        return null;
    }
}
```

```
Using StackWalker Options: []
Native Method=false, Byte Code Index=9, Module Name=jdojo.stackwalker, Module Version=null,
Class Name=com.jdojo.stackwalker.StackWalking, Class Reference=null, File Name=StackWalking.
java, Line Number=42, Method Name=m3.
Native Method=false, Byte Code Index=37, Module Name=jdojo.stackwalker, Module Version=null,
Class Name=com.jdojo.stackwalker.StackWalking, Class Reference=null, File Name=StackWalking.
java, Line Number=32, Method Name=m2.
Native Method=false, Byte Code Index=1, Module Name=jdojo.stackwalker, Module Version=null,
Class Name=com.jdojo.stackwalker.StackWalking, Class Reference=null, File Name=StackWalking.
java, Line Number=23, Method Name=m1.
Native Method=false, Byte Code Index=3, Module Name=jdojo.stackwalker, Module Version=null,
Class Name=com.jdojo.stackwalker.StackWalking, Class Reference=null, File Name=StackWalking.
java, Line Number=14, Method Name=main.

Using StackWalker Options: [RETAIN_CLASS_REFERENCE, SHOW_REFLECT_FRAMES]
Native Method=false, Byte Code Index=9, Module Name=jdojo.stackwalker, Module Version=null,
Class Name=com.jdojo.stackwalker.StackWalking, Class Reference=class com.jdojo.stackwalker.
StackWalking, File Name=StackWalking.java, Line Number=42, Method Name=m3.
Native Method=true, Byte Code Index=-1, Module Name=java.base, Module Version=9.0.1, Class
Name=jdk.internal.reflect.NativeMethodAccessorImpl, Class Reference=class jdk.internal.
reflect.NativeMethodAccessorImpl, File Name=NativeMethodAccessorImpl.java, Line Number=-2,
Method Name=invoke0.
Native Method=false, Byte Code Index=100, Module Name=java.base, Module Version=9.0.1, Class
Name=jdk.internal.reflect.NativeMethodAccessorImpl, Class Reference=class jdk.internal.
reflect.NativeMethodAccessorImpl, File Name=NativeMethodAccessorImpl.java, Line Number=62,
Method Name=invoke.
Native Method=false, Byte Code Index=6, Module Name=java.base, Module Version=9.0.1, Class
Name=jdk.internal.reflect.DelegatingMethodAccessorImpl, Class Reference=class jdk.internal.
reflect.DelegatingMethodAccessorImpl, File Name=DelegatingMethodAccessorImpl.java, Line
Number=43, Method Name=invoke.
Native Method=false, Byte Code Index=59, Module Name=java.base, Module Version=9.0.1,
Class Name=java.lang.reflect.Method, Class Reference=class java.lang.reflect.Method, File
Name=Method.java, Line Number=564, Method Name=invoke.
Native Method=false, Byte Code Index=37, Module Name=jdojo.stackwalker, Module Version=null,
Class Name=com.jdojo.stackwalker.StackWalking, Class Reference=class com.jdojo.stackwalker.
StackWalking, File Name=StackWalking.java, Line Number=32, Method Name=m2.
Native Method=false, Byte Code Index=1, Module Name=jdojo.stackwalker, Module Version=null,
Class Name=com.jdojo.stackwalker.StackWalking, Class Reference=class com.jdojo.stackwalker.
StackWalking, File Name=StackWalking.java, Line Number=23, Method Name=m1.
Native Method=false, Byte Code Index=21, Module Name=jdojo.stackwalker, Module
Version=null, Class Name=com.jdojo.stackwalker.StackWalking, Class Reference=class com.
jdojo.stackwalker.StackWalking, File Name=StackWalking.java, Line Number=19, Method
Name=main.
```

Knowing the Caller's Class

Before JDK9, developers depended on the following methods to get the reference of the caller's class inside a method:

- The `getClassContext()` method of the `SecurityManager` class, which required sub-classing because the method is protected.
- The `getCallerClass()` method of the `sun.reflect.Reflection` class, which is a JDK-internal class.

JDK9 made getting the caller class reference easy by adding a method named `getCallerClass()` in the `StackWalker` class. The method's return type is `Class<?>`. Invoking this method throws `UnsupportedOperationException` if the `StackWalker` is not configured with the `RETAIN_CLASS_REFERENCE` option. Invoking this method throws an `IllegalStateException` if there is no caller frame in the stack, for example, running a class whose `main()` method invokes this method.

Which class is the caller class? You have two callable constructs in Java—methods and constructors. The following discussion uses the term *method*; however, it applies to both methods and constructors. Suppose you invoke the `getCallerClass()` method inside a method named `S`, which is called from a method named `T`. Further suppose that the method named `T` is in a class named `C`. In this case, class `C` is the caller class.

■ **Tip** The `getCallerClass()` method of the `StackWalker` class filters out all hidden and reflection frames while finding the caller class, irrespective of the options used to obtain the `StackWalker` instance.

Listing 18-4 contains a complete program to show how to get the caller's class. Its `main()` method calls the `m1()` method, which calls the `m2()` method, which calls the `m3()` method. The `m3()` method obtains an instance of the `StackWalker` class and gets the caller class. Note that the `m2()` method uses reflection to call the `m3()` method. In the end, the `main()` method attempts to get the caller class. When you run the `CallerClassTest` method, the `main()` method is called by the JVM and there will be no caller frame on the stack. This will throw an `IllegalStateException`.

Listing 18-4. Getting the Caller Class Reference Using the StackWalker Class

```
// CallerClassTest.java
package com.jdojo.stackwalker;

import java.lang.StackWalker.Option;
import static java.lang.StackWalker.Option.RETAIN_CLASS_REFERENCE;
import static java.lang.StackWalker.Option.SHOW_REFLECT_FRAMES;
import java.lang.reflect.InvocationTargetException;
import java.util.Set;

public class CallerClassTest {
    public static void main(String[] args) {
        // Will not be able to get caller class because the
        // RETAIN_CLASS_REFERENCE option is not set.
        m1(Set.of());

        // Will print the caller class
        m1(Set.of(RETAIN_CLASS_REFERENCE, SHOW_REFLECT_FRAMES));
```

```
        try {
            // The following statement will throw an IllegalStateException
            // if this class is run. If the main() method is called in code, no exception
            will be thrown.
            Class<?> cls = StackWalker
                    .getInstance(RETAIN_CLASS_REFERENCE)
                    .getCallerClass();

            System.out.println("In main method, Caller Class: " + cls.getName());
        } catch (IllegalCallerException e) {
            System.out.println("In main method, Exception: " + e.getMessage());
        }
    }

    public static void m1(Set<Option> options) {
        m2(options);
    }

    public static void m2(Set<Option> options) {
        // Call m3() using reflection
        try {
            CallerClassTest.class
                    .getMethod("m3", Set.class)
                    .invoke(null, options);
        } catch (NoSuchMethodException | InvocationTargetException
                | IllegalAccessException | SecurityException e) {
            e.printStackTrace();
        }
    }

    public static void m3(Set<Option> options) {
        try {
            // Print the caller class
            Class<?> cls = StackWalker.getInstance(options)
                    .getCallerClass();
            System.out.println("Caller Class: " + cls.getName());
        } catch (UnsupportedOperationException e) {
            System.out.println(e.getMessage());
        }
    }
}
```

```
This stack walker does not have RETAIN_CLASS_REFERENCE access
Caller Class: com.jdojo.stackwalker.CallerClassTest
In main method, Exception: no caller frame
```

In the previous example, the method collecting the stack frames was called from another method of the same class. Let's call this method from a method of another class to see a different result. Listing 18-5 contains the code for a class named CallerClassTest2.

Listing 18-5. Another Example of Getting the Caller Class Using the StackWalker Class

```
// CallerClassTest2.java
package com.jdojo.stackwalker;

import java.lang.StackWalker.Option;
import java.util.Set;
import static java.lang.StackWalker.Option.RETAIN_CLASS_REFERENCE;

public class CallerClassTest2 {
    public static void main(String[] args) {
        Set<Option> options = Set.of(RETAIN_CLASS_REFERENCE);
        CallerClassTest.m1(options);
        CallerClassTest.m2(options);
        CallerClassTest.m3(options);

        System.out.println("\nCalling the main() method:");
        CallerClassTest.main(null);

        System.out.println("\nUsing an anonymous class:");
        new Object() {
            {
                CallerClassTest.m3(options);
            }
        };

        System.out.println("\nUsing a lambda expression:");
        new Thread(() -> CallerClassTest.m3(options))
            .start();
    }
}
```

```
Caller Class: com.jdojo.stackwalker.CallerClassTest
Caller Class: com.jdojo.stackwalker.CallerClassTest
Caller Class: com.jdojo.stackwalker.CallerClassTest2

Calling the main() method:
This stack walker does not have RETAIN_CLASS_REFERENCE access
Caller Class: com.jdojo.stackwalker.CallerClassTest
In main method, Caller Class: com.jdojo.stackwalker.CallerClassTest2

Using an anonymous class:
Caller Class: com.jdojo.stackwalker.CallerClassTest2$1

Using a lambda expression:
Caller Class: com.jdojo.stackwalker.CallerClassTest2
```

The `main()` method of the `CallerClassTest2` class calls four methods of the `CallerClassTest` class. The caller class is `CallerClassTest2` when the `CallerClassTest.m3()` is called from the `CallerClassTest2` class directly. When you call the `CallerClassTest.main()` method from the `CallerClassTest2` class, there is a caller frame and the caller class is the `CallerClassTest2` class. Compare this with the output of the previous example when you ran the CallerClassTest class. At that time, the CallerClassTest.main() method was called from the JVM and you were not able to get a caller class inside the CallerClassTest.main() method because there was no caller frame. In the end, the CallerClassTest.m3() method is called from an anonymous class and a lambda expression. The anonymous class is reported as the caller class. In case of the lambda expression, its enclosing class is reported as the caller class.

Stack-Walking Permissions

When a Java security manager is present and you configure a StackWalker with the RETAIN_CLASS_REFERENCE option, a permission check is performed to make sure that the codebase is granted a java.lang.RuntimePermission with a value of getStackWalkerWithClassReference. A SecurityException is thrown if the permission is not granted. The permission check is performed at the time the StackWalker instance is created, not when the stack walking is performed.

Listing 18-6 contains the code for the StackWalkerPermissionCheck class. Its printStackFrames() method creates a StackWalker instance with the RETAIN_CLASS_REFERENCE option. The main() method calls this method, which prints the stack trace without any problems, assuming that no security manager is present. A security manager is installed and the printStackFrames() method is called again. This time, a SecurityException is thrown, which is indicated in the output.

Listing 18-6. Creating a StackWalker to Retain Class References when a Java Security Manager Is Present

```
// StackWalkerPermissionCheck.java
package com.jdojo.stackwalker;

import static java.lang.StackWalker.Option.RETAIN_CLASS_REFERENCE;

public class StackWalkerPermissionCheck {
    public static void main(String[] args) {
        System.out.println("Before installing security manager:");
        printStackFrames();

        SecurityManager sm = System.getSecurityManager();
        if (sm == null) {
            sm = new SecurityManager();
            System.setSecurityManager(sm);
        }

        System.out.println("\nAfter installing security manager:");
        printStackFrames();
    }

    public static void printStackFrames() {
        try {
            StackWalker.getInstance(RETAIN_CLASS_REFERENCE)
                    .forEach(System.out::println);
        } catch (SecurityException e) {
            System.out.println("Could not create a StackWalker. Error: " + e.getMessage());
        }
    }
}
```

```
Before installing security manager:
jdojo.stackwalker/com.jdojo.stackwalker.StackWalkerPermissionCheck.printStackFrames(StackWal
kerPermissionCheck.java:24)
jdojo.stackwalker/com.jdojo.stackwalker.StackWalkerPermissionCheck.
main(StackWalkerPermissionCheck.java:9)

After installing security manager:
Could not create a StackWalker. Error: access denied ("java.lang.RuntimePermission"
"getStackWalkerWithClassReference")
```

shows you how to grant the required permission to create a `StackWalker` with the `RETAIN_CLASS_REFERENCE` option. The permission is granted to the entire codebase. You need to add this permission block to the `java.policy` file located in the `JAVA_HOME\conf\security` directory on your machine.

Listing 18-7. Granting java.lang.RuntimePermission with a getStackWalkerWithClassReference Value

```
grant {
    permission java.lang.RuntimePermission "getStackWalkerWithClassReference";
};
```

When you run the class in Listing 18-6 with the permission granted in , you should receive the following output:

```
Before installing security manager:
jdojo.stackwalker/com.jdojo.stackwalker.StackWalkerPermissionCheck.printStackFrames(StackWal
kerPermissionCheck.java:24)
jdojo.stackwalker/com.jdojo.stackwalker.StackWalkerPermissionCheck.
main(StackWalkerPermissionCheck.java:9)

After installing security manager:
jdojo.stackwalker/com.jdojo.stackwalker.StackWalkerPermissionCheck.printStackFrames(StackWal
kerPermissionCheck.java:24)
jdojo.stackwalker/com.jdojo.stackwalker.StackWalkerPermissionCheck.
main(StackWalkerPermissionCheck.java:18)
```

Summary

Each thread in a JVM has a *private* JVM stack that is created at the same time the thread is created. A stack stores frames. A frame on a JVM stack represents a Java method invocation in a given thread. A new frame is created and pushed to the top of the stack each time a method is invoked. A frame is destroyed (popped out of stack) when the method invocation completes. In a given thread, only one frame is active at any point. The active frame is known as the *current frame* and its method is known as the *current method.* The class that defines the current method is known as the *current class.*

Before JDK9, it was possible to walk through all frames in a thread's stack using the following classes: `Throwable`, `Thread`, and `StackTraceElement`. An instance of the `StackTraceElement` class represents a stack frame. The `getStrackTrace()` method of the `Throwable` class returns a `StackTraceElement[]` that contains the frames of the current thread's stack. The `getStrackTrace()` method of the `Thread` class returns a `StackTraceElement[]` that contains the frames of the thread's stack. The first element of the array is the top frame in the stack, which represents the last method invocation in the sequence. Some implementation of JVM may omit some frames in the returned array.

JDK9 has made stack traversal easy. It introduced a new class named `StackWalker` in the `java.lang` package. You can get an instance of the `StackWalker` using one of its static factory methods named `getInstance()`. A `StackWalker` can be configured using options, which are represented by the constants defined in the enum named `StackWalker.Option`. An instance of the nested interface named `StackWalker.StackFrame` represents a stack frame. The `StackWalker` class works with `StackWalker.StackFrame` instance. The interface defined a method named `toStackTraceElement()` that can be used to get an instance of the `StackTraceElement` class from a `StackWalker.StackFrame`.

You can use the `forEach()` and `walk()` methods of the `StackWalker` instance to traverse stack frames of the current thread. The `getCallerClass()` method of the `StackWalker` instance returns the caller class reference. You must configure a `StackWalker` instance with the `RETAIN_CLASS_REFERENCE` if you want the reference of the class representing the stack frame and the reference of the caller's class. By default, all reflection frames and implementation specific frames are not reported by a `StackWalker`. Use the `SHOW_REFLECT_FRAMES` and `SHOW_HIDDEN_FRAMES` options to configure a `StackWalker` if you want those frames included in stack traversal. Using the `SHOW_HIDDEN_FRAMES` option also includes reflection frames.

When a Java security manager is present and you configure a `StackWalker` with the `RETAIN_CLASS_REFERENCE` option, a permission check is performed to make sure that the codebase is granted a `java.lang.RuntimePermission` with a value of `getStackWalkerWithClassReference`. A `SecurityException` is thrown if the permission is not granted. The permission check is performed at the time the `StackWalker` is created, not when the stack walking is performed.

QUESTIONS AND EXERCISES

1. Is the following statement true or false?

   Each thread in Java maintains its own stack in which each Java method invocation by the thread is represented as a frame on the stack.

2. What is stack walking?

3. What is the fully qualified name of the class that supports the Stack-Walking API in JDK9?

4. Name the class whose instances represents a frame on the stack of a thread.

5. JDK9 added an interface named `StackWalker.StackFrame`. What does an instance of this interface represent?

6. Explain the difference in behaviors of the `StackWalker` instance with respect to the following three options that you can use to configure it: `RETAIN_CLASS_REFERENCE`, `SHOW_HIDDEN_FRAMES`, and `SHOW_REFLECT_FRAMES`.

7. The following snippet of code obtains a `StackWalker` instance:

```
// Get a StackWalker with the default configuration
StackWalker sw1 = StackWalker.getInstance();
```

   Will this `StackWalker` include hidden frames and retain class references?

8. When the following `Test` class is run, it throws an `IllegalCallerException`. Explain the reason for this exception.

```
// Test.java
package com.jdojo.stackwalker.exercises;

import static java.lang.StackWalker.Option.RETAIN_CLASS_REFERENCE;

public class Test {
    public static void main(String[] args) {
        StackWalker stackWalker =
            StackWalker.getInstance(RETAIN_CLASS_REFERENCE);
        Class<?> callerCls = stackWalker.getCallerClass();
        System.out.println(callerCls);
    }
}
```

9. Is the following statement true or false?

   The getCallerClass() method of the StackWalker class filters out all hidden and reflection frames while finding the caller class, irrespective of the options used to obtain the StackWalker instance.

10. When a security manager is installed, what `RuntimePermission` must be granted to create a `StackWalker` with the `RETAIN_CLASS_REFERENCE` option?

11. What will be the output when the following class `Test2` is run?

```
// Test2.java
package com.jdojo.stackwalker.exercises;

public class Test2 {
    public static void main(String[] args) {
        StackWalker.getInstance()
            .forEach(f -> System.out.println(f.getClassName()));
    }
}
```

Index

A

add() method, 178, 593, 626, 688
Adler-32, 421
Advanced object serialization
    class evolution, 393
    stopping serialization, 394
    writing object mulitple times, 389–392
Aggregate operation methods, 592
allocateDirect() method, 451
allocate() method, 451
Annotation element
    array type, 16–17
    default value, 9–10
Annotations
    AccessAnnotation Test class, 44–45
    AnnotatedElement interface, 42
    element, 9–10
    Employee class, 1
    getAnnotationsByType() method, 46
    Manager class, 2
    modules, 41–42
    null reference, 17
    @Override annotation, 3
    package, 41
    processing
        AbstractProcessor class, 48
        getQualifiedName() method, 49
        printMessage() method, 50
        -proc option, 47
        process() method, 49
        process version annotations, 50
        SupportedAnnotationTypes annotation, 48
        test versionprocessor, 52
    setSalary() method, 2
    shorthand annotation syntax, 17
    standard annotations (*see* Standard annotation types)
    Test class, 43
    toString() method, 43
    types (*see* Annotations types)
    version annotation type, 43, 44
Annotations types, 16
    declaration, 4
    DefaultException class, 13
    enum type, 14–15
    evolving, 47
    instance, 10–11
    interface, 11
    marker annotation, 19
    meta-annotations (*see* Meta-annotations types)
    primitive types, 12
    restrictions, 7
    String type, 12–13
    TestCase annotation type, 13–14
Anonymous inner class, 65
Archive file
    byte array compressing
        deflate() method, 423
        Deflater and Inflater classes, 423, 425, 426
        end() method, 424
        finish() method, 423
    byte array decompressing
        end() method, 425
        finished() method, 424
        Inflater class, 424
    checksum
        Adler-32, 421
        CRC32, 421
        definition, 420
    data compression
        lossless, 420, 447
        lossy, 420, 447
        RLE, 420
        .tar archive, 420
        .tar.gz, 420
        ZLIB library, 420
    definition, 419
    GZIP file
        BufferedOutputStream, 434
        GZIPInputStream class, 434
        GZIPOutputStream class, 434
        InputStream, 435
        ObjectOutputStream, 434

K. Sharan, *Java Language Features*, https://doi.org/10.1007/978-1-4842-3348-1

Archive file (*cont.*)
- JAR file (*see* Java Archive (JAR) file)
- ZIP file
  - BufferedOutputStream, 428
  - closeEntry() method, 429
  - creation, 427–429
  - FileInputStream creation, 428
  - putNextEntry() method, 428
  - reading contents, 431
  - stream() method, 433
  - ZipOutputStream, 428

Array, Java, 589
array() method, 451
Array operation methods, 593
asList() method, 208
asReadOnlyBuffer() method, 461
Asynchronous file I/O
- AsynchronousFileChannel, 537
- completed()/failed(), 538
- CompletionHandler, 538
- CompletionHandler, asynchronous file read, 543–545
- CompletionHandler object, asynchronous file write, 539–542
- default/custom thread pool, 536
- Future Object, asynchronous file read, 545–546

Atomic variables
- arrays, 281
- CAS, 280
- compound variable, 282–283
- field updater, 282
- scalar, 281

B

Backpressure, 843
Behavior parameterization, 181
Blocking doubly ended queues, 619, 641
Blocking queues
- ArrayBlockingQueue, 631
- consumer class, 633
- definition, 618
- DelayQueue, 631
- fairness, 631
- features, 630
- LinkedBlockingQueue, 631
- PriorityBlockingQueue, 631
- producer class, 632
- producer/consumer program, 634
- remainingCapacity() method, 631
- SynchronousQueue, 631

Bounded queue, 619
Bound receiver, 200
BreakAll class, 838–840
Breaking module encapsulation, 825
- --add-exports command-line option, 831
- --add-modules option, 831
- command-line options, 826
- declaration
  - jdojo.contact module, 832
  - jdojo.intro module, 829
  - jdojo.intruder, 830
- jdojo.contact module, 834
- jdojo.intruder module, 830, 832
- module graph, 832
- TestIllegalAccess class, 835–836
- TestNonExported class, 830–831
- TestNonOpen class, 833–834

BufferedInputStream class, 369–370
Buffers
- clear() method, 459
- flip() method, 457–458
- hasRemaining() method, 458
- primitive values, 450
- properties, 451
- reading data, 453, 455
- read-only buffer, 460
- relative *vs.* absolute methods, 456
- reset() method, 460
- rewind() method, 460
- state, 454
- views, 461
- writing data, 454–455

Bulk operation methods, 592

C

CallableTaskTest class, 317
Callback mechanism, 90
capacity() method, 451
Cyclic Redundancy Check, 421
Character set
- CharsetDecoder class, 462, 463, 484
- CharsetEncoder class, 462, 463, 484
- CoderResult class, 464
- data source and sink, 465
- decoding, 462, 484
- encoding, 462, 484
- flush() method, 465
- getByteData () method, 465
- input characters, 463
- isOverflow() method, 464
- isUnderflow() method, 464
- JVM list, 470
- storeByteData () method, 465

Checked collections, 661
checkPrimes() method, 765
Checksum, 420, 447
Classes, 748

Class explosion, 338
Cleaner class, 581–582, 584, 585
Collection interface
- advantages, 590
- aggregate operation methods, 592
- array operation methods, 593
- basic operation methods, 591
- bulk operation methods, 592
- categories, 591
- class diagram, 591
- comparison operation method, 593
- definition, 591
- implementation classes, 590
- list, 593–594
- List interface, 590

Collections
- checked, 661
- create empty collections, 662
- create singleton collections, 662, 663
- definition, 587
- element, 587
- framework (*see* Collections framework)
- hash-based, 663
- jdojo.collections module, 587
- list (*see* List)
- maps (*see* Maps)
- money jar, 587
- queue (*see* Queues)
- read-only view, 659
- reversing list, 657
- rotating a list, 658
- search list, 656
- shuffling list, 657–658
- sort list, 655
- swapping list, 658
- synchronized view, 660
- WeakHashMap implementation class, 659

Collections framework
- arrays, 589
- collection of name-phone pairs, 588
- components, 590
- mathematical set (*see* Mathematical set)
- navigable set, 611
- pictorial view, 588
- sorted set (*see* Sorted set)
- traverse (*see* Traversing collections)

Collectors
- accumulator, 721
- argument, 735
- calendar example, 736
- collect(), 722
- collectingAndThen(), 736–737
- combiner, 721
- counting(), 724
- filtering(), 737
- flatMapping(), 737, 739
- grouping data, 730–731, 733
- joining(), 729–730
- map (*see* toMap() method)
- parameters, 723
- partitioning data (*see* Partitioning data)
- sorted(), 724
- summary statistics, 725–726
- supplier, 721
- toCollection(), 724

com.jdojo.CsvParser interfaces, 749
com.jdojo.PrimeChecker interfaces, 749
Command-line options
- --add-exports option, 826–827
- --add-opens option, 827
- --add-reads option, 827
- --illegal-access option, 828

Comparator interface, 184
Compare-and-swap (CAS), 280
comparing() method, 217
Comparison operation method, 593
Compress() and decompress() methods, 425
Concurrent maps, 653
Constructor references
- array constructors, 207
- ClassName, 206
- compile-time error, 208
- Item class, 206
- String object, 205

Container, *See* Collections
CRC32 class, 421
Critical section, 237

D

Data compression, 419
Decorator pattern
- abstract Component class, 357
- abstract superclass, 351
    - Drink class, 352
    - DrinkDecorator class, 354
    - Rum class, 353
    - Vodka class, 353
    - Whiskey class, 353
- class diagram, 351–352
- components arrangement, 356
- concrete decorator
    - Honey class, 354, 355
    - Spices class, 355
- input stream
    - abstract base component, 367
    - BufferedInputStream, 369–370
    - class design, 367
    - methods, 368
    - PushbackInputStream, 370

Decorator pattern (*cont.*)
    output stream
        BufferedOutputStream, 373
        ByteArrayOutputStream, 373
        class diagram, 371–372
        vs. drink application, 372
        methods, 372
        PrintStream class, 373–375
    testing drink application, 356
    wrapper pattern, 351
Deep reflection, 124, 140
    across modules, 129–133
    on JDK modules, 134, 136
    and unnamed modules, 134
    with module, 125–129
Default prime service provider, 758–760
DEFLATE algorithm, 420
Deflater class, 422
Delay queues, 618, 634
Denotable types, 159
Deque, *See* Double ended queues
Deque interface, 625
Dictionary, *See* Maps
Documented annotation type, 24–25
Double ended queues
    asLifoQueue() static method, 630
    categories, 626
    definition, 618
    FIFO queue, 626, 627
    for insertion, removal, and peek operations, 625
    LIFO queue, 626, 628, 630
    myMethod(), 630
    vs. queue interfaces, 626
    stacks, 626

E

EJB 3.0, 4
Empty collections, 662
Enterprise JavaBeans (EJB), 4
equals() method, 493
Exclusive file locking, 478
Executor
    advantages, 312
    completion service, 322–325
    disadvantages, 312
    methods, 313
    newCachedThreadPool(), 313
    newFixedThreadPool(int nThreads), 313
    newSingleThreadExecutor(), 313
    result-bearing tasks, 315–318
    RunnableTast, 311, 313–314
    scheduling task, 318–320
    uncaught exceptions, 321
    work queue, 313
ExecutorService.submit(), 317

F

Fairness, blocking queue, 631
FasterPrimeChecker class, 761
Faster prime service provider, 760–761
First In, First Out (FIFO), 588
File attributes
    AclFileAttributeView, 518
    ACL file permissions, 526–529
    BasicFileAttributeView, 517
    DosFileAttributeView, 517
    FileOwnerAttributeView, 518, 525
    Files.setOwner(), 525
    getUserPrincipalLookupService(), 524
    lookupPrincipalByGroupName(), 524
    PosixFileAttributeView, 518
    POSIX file permissions, 529–531
    reading and updating
        basic file attributes, 521–523
        Files.getOwner(), 520
        Files.isDirectory(), 520
        Files.setOwner(), 520
        getFileAttributeView(), 522
        readAttributes(), 520, 522
        setTimes(), 522
        static, 520
        view-name, 521
    UserDefinedFileAttributeView, 518
    view support, 518–519
flatMap, 708–709
for-each loop, 598–599
forEach() method, 193, 599–600, 705–706
Fork/join framework
    compute(), 327, 329
    creation, 327
    execution, 327, 329
    ForkJoinPool, 327
    RecursiveAction/RecursiveTask, 327
    types of tasks, 326
    work-stealing, 326
Formal type parameter, 146
forName() static method, 100
FunctionUtil class, 193–194

G

Garbage collection, 551
    accessing referent, 568
    BigObject Class, 566
    Cleaner class, 581–582, 584
    clear() method, 569
    clearing referent, 569
    dead object, 552
    finalization process, 553, 557
    finalize() method, 555
    FinalizeAsBackup class, 558

invoking, 553
java.lang.Runtime class, 553
Java object, 561
memory management
memory allocation, 551
memory reclamation, 550
object resurrection, 559
OutOfMemoryError, 555
PhantomReference Objects, 578, 579
post-finalization coordination, 580
reachable objects, 553
ReferenceQueue class, 573
SoftReference Class, 569
System.gc() method, 553
tracing algorithm, 552
WeakReference Class, 574
weak references
constructors, 563
memory state, 563
object's reachability, 564
PhantomReference, 563
referent instance, 563
SoftReference, 563
strong reference, 562, 564
Garbage collector, 551
Generic functional interface, 185
GenericPrimeChecker, 761
Generics
anonymous classes, 160
arrays class, 160
definition, 143
exception classes, 160
heap pollution, 162
lower bound wildcards
copy() method, 153
<? super T>, 153
WrapperUtil class, 154
methods and constructors, 155
object creation
ArrayList, 157
parameter type, 158
process() method, 159
type inference process, 158
printDeails()method
compile-time error, 149
nullpointerexception, 151
unknownWrapper variable, 150
Wrapper<Object> type, 149
Wrapper<String> type, 149
raw types, 148
RuntimeClassTest, 161–162
upper bound wildcards
<? extends Number>, 153
<? extends T>, 152
sum() method, 152
varargs method
compiler unchecked warning, 164
@java.lang.SuppressWarnings annotation, 164
process() method, 163
@SafeVarargs annotation, 164
wildcards
unbounded, 149–151
unknown type, 149
unknownWrapper.get(), 151
wildcard type, 149
Wrapper class, 143
compile-time error statement, 146
formal type parameter, 146
get() method, 146
MyClass, 145
parameter type, 145
printDetails() method, 149
set() method, 146
super/subtype rules, 147
ways, 144
WrapperUtil method, 149
Generic type, 147
getByteCodeIndex() method, 867
getCallerClass() method, 874
getClass() method, 100
getClassDescription() method, 111
getComponentType() method, 138
getConstructors() method, 118
getDeclaredConstructor() method, 118
getDeclaredField() method, 112
getDeclaredMethods() method, 116
getDeclaringClass() method, 868
getDefault() static method, 488
getExceptionTypes() method, 115
getFields() method, 112
getFileName(), 492
getFileStores(), 488
getInterfaces() method, 111
getLambdaPrinter() method, 209
getLength() method, 136
getMainAttributes() method, 442
get() method, 453
getMethods() method, 116
getModifiers() method, 111, 115
getName() method, 115
getNameCount(), 491
getParameters() method, 114
getParent(), 491
getPath() method, 491
getReturnType() method, 117
getRoot(), 491
getRootDirectories(), 488
getSimpleName() method, 111
getStrackTrace() method, 862

getSuperclass() method, 111, 113
getTypeParameters() method, 115
groupingBy()
  classifier, 731
  collector, 731
  mapping(), 732
  nested groups, 733
GZIP file format, 420, 434–435

H

hasArray() method, 451
Hash-based collections, 663
Heap pollution, 162

I

Infinite streams, 676
Inflater class, 422
Inherited annotation type, 24
Inner class
  accessing instance members, 73
  accessing local variables
    restrictions, 80–81
  advantages, 59
  anonymous class, 89
  callback mechanism, 89–90
  compiler magic
    decompile class files, 85
    decompiled code, 86–87
    instance variable, 87–88
    synthetic method, 89
  creating objects
    class declaration, 72
    instance, 71–73
    member inner class, 73
    titleIterator() method, 71
    TitleList class, 71
  declaration, 78
  enclosing class, 58
  generated class files, 84–85
  inheritance, 81
  ModifiedOuter2 class, 78, 79
  no static members, 83
  outer class, 58
  qualified keyword, 76–77
  same instance variable name, 75
  setValue() instance method, 76
  static context, 91
  static member class, 68
  testing, 74–75
  top-level class, 57–58
  types
    anonymous inner class, 65
    local inner class (*see* Local inner class)
    member inner class, 59
Input/output (I/O)
  advanced object serialization (*see* Advanced object serialization)
  class explosion, 338
  console, 410
  decorator pattern (*see* Decorator pattern)
  files
    absolute and canonical path, 340, 342
    attributes, 346
    checking existence, 340
    content copy, 404
    copying, 346
    creating, 342–346
    current working directory, 339
    deleting, 343–345
    directories, 347–349
    object creation, 338
    pathname, 338
    renaming, 343–345
    size, 346
  object serialization (*see* Object serialization)
  pipes (*see* Piped I/O)
  primitive data types, 378–379
  readers and writers
    append(), 398
    BufferedReader class, 397, 399
    BufferedWriter class, 397
    byte-based *vs.* character, 396
    character-based streams, 395
    classes, 395
    FilterReader class, 397
    InputStreamReader class, 397
    OutputStream class, 399
    OutputStreamWriter class, 397
    readLine(), 398
    writer object, 397
  Scanner class, 411–412
  StreamTokenizer, 414–415
  String object, 337
  StringTokenizer, 412
  transient fields serialization, 389
Input/output streams
  decorator pattern (*see* Decorator pattern)
  flow of data, 358
  input stream
    closing, 361
    creating, 360
    data source, 359
    luci1.txt file, 359
    reading, byte, 362
    reading data, 360
    Utility class, 361–362
  LowerCaseReader, 399, 401–402
  output stream
    closing, 365
    creating, 364

data sink, 363
decorator pattern (*see* Decorator pattern)
flushing, 365
writing bytes, 365–366
writing data, 364
random access files, 402–404
reading data, 358
standard error streams
BufferedReader, 409
DummyStandardOutput, 407
Java program interaction, 405
output redirection, 406
PrintStream, 405–406
public static, 405
reading from input device, 408
swallowing sent data, 408
writing data, 359
Instance method references
bound receiver, 200–201
length() method, 200
test() method, 205
unbound receiver, 201–202
Integrated development environment (IDE), 140
Interfaces, 748
isDirect() method, 451
isReadOnly() method, 461, 488
iterate() method, 689–693
Iterator
creates list of strings, 595
forEachRemaining() method, 596–597
hasNext() method, 595
next() method, 595
remove() method, 596
using print elements, 596

J

Java Archive (JAR) file
accessing resources, 446
API
getMainAttributes() method, 442
JAR file creation, 443–446
JarInputStream, 446
main() method, 443
Manifest object, 442
manifest file, 442–443
book/archives, 438
creation, 437
extracting, entry, 439
format, 435
indexing, 438
jar tool command-line options, 436–437
listing contents, 439
manifest file, 439–441
manifestMain-Class attribute, 440
MANIFEST.MF file, 838
META-INF directory, 435
sealed attribute, 441
sealing package, 441
test.jar file, 437
updation, 438
Java Hotspot VM, 552
Java Memory Model (JMM)
atomicity, 236
ordering, 236
visibility, 236
Java Virtual Machine (JVM), 862
jdojo.lambda module, 169

K

Key-value mappings, 641, 645

L

Lambda expression
anonymous class, 171
break and continue statements, 214–215
Comparator interface, 216
definition, 169
equivalent methods, 173–174
function abstraction, 169–170
functional interface
compare() and equals() methods, 184
default and static methods, 189
design APIs, 191
forEach() method, 195
@FunctionalInterface annotation, 184–185
function<T, R> interface, 188–189
FunctionUtil class, 193
Gender enum, 192
generic abstract method, 185
intersection type, 187
java.util package, 184
java.util.function package, 188
library users, 194–195
Mapper<T> interface, 186
Person class, 192–193
Predicate<T> Interface, 190–191
functional programming, 172
lexical scoping
anonymous class, 209–210
compile-time error, 210
getLambdaPrinter() method, 209
local/anonymous class, 209
printer functional interface, 209
local variables, 173
method references
constructor references (*see* Constructor references)
definition, 196

Lambda expression (*cont.*)
- generic method, 208
- instance method (*see* Instance method references)
- length() method, 196
- static method (*see* static method references)
- supertype instance, 203–205
- types, 197
- object-oriented programming, 172
- parameters
  - block statement, 176
  - modifiers, 175
  - no parameter declaration, 175
  - single parameter declaration, 175
  - types, 174
- recursive function, 215–216
- string parameter, 170
- StringToIntMapper interface, 170–172
- target type
  - Adder and Joiner interface, 177
  - add() method, 177–178
  - assignment context, 183
  - assignment statement, 177–178
  - cast context, 183
  - compile-time error, 182
  - functional interface, 178
  - join() method, 178
  - LambdaUtil class, 179–180
  - LambdaUtil2 class, 181–182
  - method invocation context, 183
  - parameters, 176
  - poly expression, 177
  - return context, 183
  - standalone expression, 176
- variable capture
  - compile-time error, 212
  - createLambda() method, 214
  - final declaration, 211
  - local and instance variables, 213
  - msg variable, 211
  - print() method, 214

LambdaUtil class
- functional interfaces, 179
- testAdder() method, 180
- testJoiner() method, 181

Last In, First Out (LIFO), 588
Lexical scoping, 209
Lightweight process, 226
limit() method, 452
List
- add(E element) method, 614
- ArrayList, 614, 616
- definition, 613
- features, 614
- forward and backward direction iterations, 617
- index, 613
- LinkedList, 614
- ListIterator interface, 617
- pictorial view, 613
- positional indexes, 614
- reversing, 657
- rotating, 658
- searching, 656
- shuffling, 657–658
- sorting, 655
- static of() method, 615
- to store names, 593–594
- swapping, 658

Local inner class
- addTitle() method, 62
- class declaration, 62
- RandomInteger class, 64
- removeTitle() method, 62
- someMethod() method, 63
- testing, 64

lock() methods, 283
- ReentrantLock, 285–287
- ReentrantReadWriteLock, 287–288
- synchronized keyword, 284–285

Lossless data compression algorithms, 420
Lossy data compression algorithms, 420
Lower-bounded wildcards, 153

M

Manifest file, 439
MANIFEST.MF file, 839
Maps
- basic operations, 642
- bulk operations, 642
- comparison operations, 643
- concurrent, 653
- concurrent navigable, 655
- entry, 645, 648
- HashMap, 643
- keys, values, and entries views, 646
- key-value mappings, 641
- LinkedHashMap, 643
- Map<K,V> interface, 641
- navigable maps, 652
- ofEntries() methods, 649
- of() method, 647–648
- sorted, 650–651
- usage, 643
- view operations, 642
- WeakHashMap class, 644

mapToInt() method, 186
Marker annotation types, 19
mark() method, 452

Mathematical set
- add elements, 601
- definition, 600
- difference/minus operations, 603
- HashSet class, 601
- implementation class, 601, 603
- intersection operation, 603
- LinkedHashSet class, 603
- of() method, 601
- Set interface, 604
- union operation, 603

Member inner class, 59

Memory
- allocation, 550
- leak, 550
- -mapped file I/O, 477
- reclamation, 550

Meta-annotations types
- Documented, 24–25
- Inherited, 24
- Repeatable, 25, 26
- Retention, 23
- Target, 20

Method references
- constructor references, 205–208
- generic method, 208
- instance
  - bound receiver, 200–201
  - unbound receiver, 201–202
- lambda expressions, 196
- length() method, 196
- static (*see* static method references)
- syntax, 196
- types, 197

Module API
- annotations, 803–804
- classes and interfaces, 771–772
- getModule(), 773
- JDK9
  - ClassLoader, 786–787
  - main(), 797–798
  - named module, 791–796
  - numbertoword.properties, 788
  - resource naming syntax, 791
  - runtime image, 798–802
  - Test class, 788–789
  - wordtonumber.properties, 788
- layers (*see* Module layers)
- ModuleDescriptor (*see* ModuleDescriptor class)

ModuleDescriptor class
- exports, 774
- getDescriptor(), 773
- ModuleBasicInfo, 778–780
- opens, 775
- packages(), 777
- provides, 775, 778
- requires, 775–776
- version(), 777

Module layers
- arranging modules, 805–806
- configurations, 811–813
- creation
  - defineModules, 814
  - defineModulesWithManyLoaders, 814
  - defineModulesWithOneLoader, 814
  - defineModulesXxx(), 813
  - empty() and boot(), 813
  - findModule(), 815
  - LayerInfo, 815–817
  - LayerTest, 817–820
- finder, 807, 809
- reading contents, 809–810

Money jar, 587

Multiple threads
- BalanceUpdate, 232–234
- execution, 231

Multiprocessing, 224

Multitasking, 224

Multi-threaded program, 226

N

Navigable map, 652–653

Navigable set, 611

New input/output (NIO)
- buffers
  - clear() method, 459
  - flip() method, 457–458
  - hasRemaining() method, 458
  - primitive values, 450
  - properties, 451
  - reading data, 453, 455
  - read-only buffer, 460
  - relative *vs.* absolute methods, 456
  - reset() method, 460
  - rewind() method, 460
  - state, 454
  - views, 461
  - writing data, 454–455
- byte order
  - big endian, 482
  - machine, 481
  - order() method, 482
  - setting, 483
- channel
  - close() method, 471
  - FileInputStream and FileOutputStream classes, 472
  - GatheringByteChannel() method, 471

New input/output (NIO) (*cont.*)
getChannel() method, 472
InterruptibleChannel, 472
isOpen() method, 471
ReadableByteChannel() method, 471
ScatteringByteChannel() method, 471
WritableByteChannel() method, 471
channel-based, 450
character set
CharsetDecoder class, 462–463, 484
CharsetEncoder class, 462–463, 484
CoderResult class, 464
data source and sink, 465
decoding, 462, 484
encoding, 462, 484
getByteData () method, 465
input characters, 463
isUnderflow() method, 464
JVM list, 470
flush() method, 465
isOverflow() method, 464
storeByteData() method, 465
definition, 449
file channel
copying contents, 480
reading data, 473
writing data, 475
file locking, 478
lock() method, 478
release() method, 479
try-catch-finally, 479
tryLock() method, 478
memory-mapped file I/O, 477
stream-based I/O, 450
New Input/Output 2 (NIO.2)
asynchronous file I/O (*see* Asynchronous file I/O)
features, 487
file attributes (*see* File attributes)
file system, 488–490
file tree traversing
directory tree deletion, 514–515
enum constants, 512
FileVisitor, 511–512
getFileVisitor(), 514
postVisitDirectory(), 512
preVisitDirectory(), 512, 514
SimpleFileVisitor, 511
subdirectories and directory files, 512–513
traversing steps, 511
visitFile(), 512, 514
walkFileTree(), 514–516
java.nio.file, 487
matches(Path path), 516–517
path
absolute, 490
comparing, 493–495
components, 490–493
copy(), 501–502
delete(), 500–501
deleteIfExists(), 500
exists(), 501
file attributes, 503
file contents reading, 504–506
Files.probeContentType(Path path) method, 504
getFileName(), 492
getNameCount(), 491
getParent(), 491
getRoot(), 491
isAbsolute(), 492
java.nio.file package, 490
move(), 502–503
new files creation, 499–500
normalize(), 495
notExists(), 501
Path interface, 490
Path object, 490–491
relative, 490
relativize(Path p), 496
resolve(Path p), 496
SeekableByteChannel, 508, 510
separator/delimiter, 490
toAbsolutePath(), 498
toRealPath(), 498
toUri(), 498
windows-based path, 492
write(), 507–508
symbolic link, 497
watch service
close(), 534–536
context(), 532
count(), 532
creation, 533
implementation, 532
kind(), 532
pollEvents(), 534
register(), 533
reset(), 534
StandardWatchEventKinds class, 532–533
WatchEvent, 532, 534
WatchKey, 534
Non-blocking backpressure, 844
Non-denotable types, 159
Non-reifiable type, 162

O

Object resurrection, 559–560
Object serialization
  deflating/marshalling, 380
  deserialization procedure, 383–385
  Externalizable interface, 380–381, 385–388
  ObjectOutputStream, 380
  Serializable interface, 380
  serialization procedure, 381–383
  storing sequence of bytes, 380
onSubscribe() method, 847
Operations interface, 185
Ordered streams, 680
Ordinary deprecation, 29
Override annotation type, 39, 40

P

Parallel streams, 740–742
Partitioning data, 734–735
Phantom reachable, 564
Phaser
  action, 300–301
  AdderTask, 301
  features, 295–296
  multiple AdderTask, 302–304
  StartTogetherTask, 297–300
Piped I/O
  creating and connecting ways, 376
  logical arrangement, 375–376
  producer-consumer pattern, 375
  usage procedure, 377–378
Poly expression, 177
position() method, 452
PrimeChecker interface, 752, 756
PrimeChecker Service Interface, 758, 760
Prime service testing
  jdojo.prime.client module, 767
    declaration, 763
    module graph, 764
  jdojo.prime.faster module, 766
  jdojo.prime module, 765
  legacy mode, 767–769
  Main class, PrimeChecker service, 764–765
  module path, 766
  --show-module-resolution command-line option, 767
Primitive data types
  DataInputStream, 378
  DataOutputStream, 378
  ReadingPrimitives, 379
  values and strings, 378
  WritingPrimitives, 379
PrintStream class, 373–375
Priority queues, 618, 622
Probable prime checker provider, 758
Probable prime service provider, 761–763
Process control block, 224
Producer/consumer synchronization, 250, 252–253
Program counter, 223
PushbackInputStream class, 370
put() method, 454

Q

QueryModule, 781–782
  updating, 783–785
Queues
  blocking (*see* Blocking queues)
  blocking doubly ended, 619, 641
  definition, 618
  delay, 618, 634
  double ended (*see* Double ended queues)
  head and tail, 618
  priority (*see* Priority queues)
  simple (*see* Simple queues)
  transfer, 619, 637

R

Race condition, 234
Random access files, 402–404
Reactive Streams
  Java API, 845–846
  JDK9
    Flow class, 846
    NumberPrinter class, 849–851
    processors, 856–859
    publishers, creating, 847–848
    publisher-subscriber interactions, 846–847
    publishing elements, 848
    SubmissionPublisher, 849
    subscibers, creating, 851–856
  processor, 845
  publisher, 844
  subscriber, 844
  subscription, 844
Read-only buffers, 460
Read-only view, 659
Recursive function, 215
Recursive lambda expressions, 215–216
Referent, 567
Reflection
  accessibility check
    AccessibleObject class, 125
    Djava.security.manager, 128
    Java security manager, 127

Reflection (*cont.*)
myjava.policy file, 128
setAccessible(true) method, 127
accessing fields, 122
arrays
arraycopy() static method, 138
array dimension, 138
ArrayList, 138
ExpandingArray, 139
getComponentType() method, 138
getLength() method, 136
isArray() method, 136
newInstance() static method, 136
behavioral intercession, 98
behavioral introspection, 98
class access modifiers, 108
class loaders
JDK8, 103–104
JDK9, 104–107
creating objects, 120
definition, 97
Executable class
constructors, 98, 118–119
getExceptionTypes() method, 115
getName() method, 115
getParameters() method, 114
getTypeParameters() method, 115
methods, 98, 116
utility class, 115
features, 99
getClassDescription() method, 111
getDeclaredField() method, 112
getFields() method, 112
getInterfaces() method, 111
getModifiers() method, 111, 115
getSimpleName() method, 111
getSuperclass() method, 111, 113
GUI tools, 140
intercession, 97–98
interface IConstants, 112
introspection, 97
invoke methods, 121
java.lang.Class class, 98
Bulb class, 101
byte code, 99
class literal, 99
class loader, 99
forName() static method, 100
getClass() method, 100
Testing class, 101–103
MyClass class, 111
person class, 107
reification, 98
structural intercession, 97
structural introspection, 97
Reifiable type, 162
Reification, 162
Removal warnings, 29
Repeatable annotation type, 25, 26
reset() method, 452
Retention annotation type, 23
Root directories, on machine, 347
Run Length Encoding (RLE), 420

S

Sequence, *See* List
Serializing transient fields, 389
serialPersistentFields, 392
Serial version unique ID (SUID), 393
Service consumer, 748
Service interface, 752
com.jdojo.impl.PrimeCheckerFactory, 751
com.jdojo.prime.PrimeChecker, 767–768
load() method, 752
PrimeChecker, 760
provides statement, 750
service providers, 747
uses statement, 750
ServiceLoader class, 748, 750–751
Service provider, 748
default prime service provider, 758–760
FasterPrimeChecker class, 755
faster prime service provider, 760–761
filters, 753
get() method, 755
interface, 747
iterator() method, 753, 754
jdojo.prime module, 758
PrimeChecker, 752, 754, 758
probable prime checker provider, 758
probable prime service provider, 761–763
provider() method, 755
provides statement, 759
ServiceLoader class, 753–754
ServiceProvider.Provider<S> interface, 753
stream() method, 754
type() method, 755
uses statement, 749
Services
definition, 747, 756
discovered and loaded, 749–750
implementations, 751
jdojo.prime module, 757
PrimeChecker interface, 756
ServiceLoader class, 749
service provider, 747
setAccessible(true) method, 127
setName() method, 121
Shared file locking, 478

Shorthand annotation syntax, 17
Simple queues
    bounded queue, 619
    definition, 618
    FIFO queue, 619–622
    head and tail, 619
    LIFO queue, 622
    operations, 619
    unbounded queue, 619
Singleton collections, 662–663
sleep() method, 255–256
Softly reachable, 564
Soft reference, 570–572
Sorted map, 650–651
Sorted set
    Comparator, 605, 607
    custom sorting, 608
    definition, 605
    natural ordering, 606
    null element, 610
    Person class, 606
    subsets, 609
    TreeSet class, 606
Spin-wait hints, 277–278
Stack, 861
StackTraceElement class, 866–867
StackWalkerPermissionCheck class, 877
Stack walking
    definition, 862
    drawbacks, 865
    JDK8
        LegacyStackWalk, 863–865
        StackTraceElement class, 863
        Throwable and Thread classes, 863
        toString() method, 865
    JDK9
        caller's class, 874
        forEach() method, 869–870
        options, 866
        StackWalker class, 866, 868
        StackWalker.StackFrame interface, 867–868
        stack-walking permissions, 877
        traverse stack frames, current thread, 871
        walk() method, 869–870
Standalone expression, 176
Standard annotation types
    deprecating APIs
        Box class, 31
        BoxTest class, 31–34
        @deprecated Javadoc tag, 27
        dynamic analysis, 38
        FileCopier utility class, 27, 28
        import statements, 38
        java.lang.Deprecated annotation type, 27
        JDK9, 28–30
        static analysis, 35–37
        suppressing deprication warnings, 30
        -Xlint, 34, 35
    @FunctionalInterface, 40
    @Override, 39, 40
    @SuppressWarnings, 38
startsWith() method, 494
static context, 91
static member class, 68
static method references
    Integer class, 197
    Integer::sum, 198
    Integer.valueOf(), 199
    Person class, 199
    toBinaryString() method, 197–198
static wrap() method, 451
Streams, 843–844
    API architecture, 680–681
    collect(), 721
    Collection, 682
    collectors, 675
    creation
        arrays, 694
        chars(), 697
        collection, 695
        empty stream, 689
        file I/O, 695–696
        generate(), 693
        iterate(), 689–693
        from values, 686–688
    definition, 675
    filter(), 682
    filter operation, 710–712
    finding and matching, 739
    flattening streams, 708–709
    forEach operation, 705–706
    IllegalStateException, 680
    imperative *vs.* functional programming, 678
    infinite streams, 676
    interface, 592
    intermediate/lazy operations, 678–680
    internal *vs.* external iteration, 676–677
    IntStream, 683
    map(), 682
    map operation, 706–707
    operations, 703–704
    optional value
        isPresent(), 698
        NullPointerException, 698
        OptionalDouble, 699
        OptionalInt, 699
        OptionalLong, 699
        program, 700–701
    ordered streams, 680
    parallel, 740–742

Streams (*cont.*)
Person class, 683–686
reduce operation
accumulator, 713–717
collect(), 713
compile-time error, 715
count(), 720
default value, 718
definition, 713
DoubleStream, 719–720
imperative programming style, 714
map-reduce operation, 715
mapToDouble(), 719
maximum integer value, 718
parallel stream, 717
pictorial view, 713
seed, 713
sum variable, 714
store elements, 676
stream pipeline debugging, 704
sum(), 683
terminal/eager operations, 678–680
StreamTokenizer, 412, 414–415
StringTokenizer, 412, 414
Strongly reachable, 564
Supertype instance method references
getPrice() method, 203
Item class, 203–204
test() method, 205
SuppressWarnings annotation type, 38
Synchronizers
barriers, 292–295
exchangers, 306–310
latches, 304–306
phaser (*see* Phaser)
semaphores, 289–291
Synthetic method, 89

T

Tarball, 420
Target annotation type, 20
Target type, 177
Tape Archive, 420
Terminal deprecation, 29
testAdder() method, 180
testJoiner() method, 181
test() method, 205
thenComparing() method, 217
Thread
atomic variables, 280–283
concurrency packages, 280
daemon, 264–265
definition, 225
execution, 254–255
executor framework (*see* Executor)
explicit locks (*see* lock() methods)
fork/join (*see* Fork/join framework)
interrupt, 266–268, 270
Java, 226–228
JMM (*see* Java Memory Model (JMM))
join(), 256–258
method reference, 230
multiple (*see* Multiple threads)
notify() or notifyAll() method, 247
object's monitor, 237–250
PrinterThread, 230
priority, 263
producer/consumer synchronization (*see* Producer/consumer synchronization)
program counter and stack, 225
Runnable interface, 229
sleep() (*see* sleep() method)
spin-wait hints, 277–278
stack size, 333
static yield(), 259
stop, suspend and resume, 273–277
synchronizers (*see* Synchronizers)
Thread class, 229
ThreadGroup, 270–271
ThreadLocal
CallTracker, 331–332
initialValue(), 332
methods, 330
withInitial(), 333
ThreadState class, 261–262
timed-waiting state, 260
uncaughtException(), 279
volatile variables, 271–273
Thread-local storage (TLS), 225
Thread synchronization
CriticalSection2 class, 239–240
monitorBalance(), 237, 249–250
MultiLocks class, 241
multiple threads, 243
objectRef, 246–248
synchronized instance method, 238
synchronized static method, 239
updateBalance(), 237, 249–250
wait(), 245–246
toBinaryString() method, 198
toMap() method, 727–729
toStackTraceElement() method, 868
Transfer queues, 619, 637

Traversing collections
    for-each loop, 598
    forEach() method, 599
    iterator, 595

U

Unbounded queue, 619
Unbounded wildcards,
        149–151
Unbound receiver, 201
uncaughtException() method, 279
Unmodifiable view, *See* Read-only view
Upper-bounded wildcards, 152

V

Varargs methods, 163
VersionTest class, 6, 7
Volatile variables, 271–273

W, X

walk() method, 870
WeakHashMap class, 576
Weakly reachable, 564
Wildcards
    lower-bounded, 153
    unbounded, 149–151
    upper-bounded, 152

Y

yield() method, 259

Z

ZipEntry class, 427
ZipFile class, 433
ZIP file format, 420, 427
ZipInputStream class, 427

Printed by Printforce, the Netherlands